COMBEE

COMBEE

HARRIET TUBMAN, THE COMBAHEE RIVER RAID, AND BLACK FREEDOM DURING THE CIVIL WAR

EDDA L. FIELDS-BLACK

OXFORD
UNIVERSITY PRESS

OXFORD
UNIVERSITY PRESS

Oxford University Press is a department of the University of Oxford. It furthers the University's objective of excellence in research, scholarship, and education by publishing worldwide. Oxford is a registered trade mark of Oxford University Press in the UK and certain other countries.

Published in the United States of America by Oxford University Press 198 Madison Avenue, New York, NY 10016, United States of America.

© Edda L. Fields-Black 2024

CIP data is on file at the Library of Congress
ISBN 978-0-19-755279-7

DOI: 10.1093/oso/9780197552797.001.0001

Printed by Sheridan Books, Inc., United States of America

Support for the book was provided by Furthermore grants in publishing, a program of the J.M. Kaplan Fund.

Dedicated to
Anna L. Richard Frasier (1900–2002)
Katie Richard Gilliard (1910–2016)
Jonas Fields (1929–2014)
who kept me linked to my ancestral home, shared with me what they
knew of our family's stories, and inspired me and generations to come

Contents

Timeline	ix
A Note on Names	xvii
Foreword	xix

PART ONE   "THE PRISON-HOUSE OF BONDAGE"

1. Last Captives	3
2. Old Heads	13
3. Stolen Children	53
4. Prime Hands	67
5. Freedom Seekers	91
6. Pikins	115
7. John Brown's "Men"	133

PART TWO   THE PROVING GROUND OF FREEDOM

8. "Gun Shoot at Bay Point"	155
9. Broken Promises	177
10. Beaufort's Boatmen	203
11. Two of Us	227
12. Forever Free	251

PART THREE   THE COMBAHEE RIVER RAID

13. "A Pleasure Excursion"   283

14. Day Clean   317

15. "Some Credit"   347

16. "Great Sufferers"   361

PART FOUR   "WE'S COMBEE!"

17. Reaping Dead Men   401

18. Charleston Siege   437

19. Closed His Eyes   475

Afterword   521
Acknowledgments   529
Appendixes   543
Notes   565
Index   717

Timeline

1632, June 30   Maryland Colony is established

1663, March 24   Carolina Colony is established

1672   Daniel Heyward emigrates to Carolina Colony from Derby, England

1678   Edward Middleton arrives in Carolina Colony from Barbados

1679   Arthur Middleton arrives in Carolina Colony from Barbados

1683   Benjamin Blake arrives in Carolina Colony from Bridgewater, England

1708   Enslaved people constitute the majority of Carolina Colony's population

1730s   Charles Lowndes arrives in Carolina Colony from St. Kitts

1750s   Moses Kirkland arrives in Carolina County from Berwickshire, Scotland

1773   *Peggy* is the last documented slave vessel to disembark West African captives in Maryland's ports

1775   Minus Hamilton is born

1784   Arthur Middleton bequeaths all of his lands on the south side of the Combahee River, including Newport Plantation, to his son Arthur Middleton

1785–1790   Ben Ross and Harriet "Rit" Green, the parents of Harriet Tubman, are born in Dorchester County, Maryland

1802   William Blake bequeaths Bonny Hall to his son Joseph Blake

1808   Act Prohibiting the Importation of Slaves takes effect in the United States

1808   Ben Ross and Harriet "Rit" Green marry

1820   Missouri Compromise

1822, March   Arminta "Minty" Ross (later Harriet Tubman) is born

1827   Dr. William L. Kirkland Sr. acquires Rose Hill Plantation from his father-in-law, Dr. Thomas E. Lynah

1831, January 1   William Lloyd Garrison launches *The Liberator*

1836, February 16   William C. Heyward purchases Cypress Plantation from his father for $100,000

1830s–1841   Arminta "Minty" Ross's sisters, Lina and Soph, and their children are sold away

1844   Arminta "Minty" Ross marries John Tubman and changes her name to Harriet Tubman

1845   Publication of Frederick Douglass's *Narrative of the Life of Frederick Douglass, an American Slave*

1848   Seneca Falls Convention

1849, fall   Harriet Tubman liberates herself and makes her way to Philadelphia, Pennsylvania

1850   Fugitive Slave Act goes into effect

1850   Harriet Tubman conducts her first rescue mission, bringing away her niece Kessiah and Kessiah's two children

1851   Harriet Tubman likely meets Frederick Douglass in St. Catharine's, Ontario

1851–1852   Harriet Tubman rescues her youngest brother, Moses, and two others; on a subsequent rescue mission, this time to Dorchester County; her husband, John Tubman, refuses to come with her, and she rescues another group of people and accepts God's calling her to help liberate her people

1852   Harriet Tubman settles in St. Catharine's, Ontario

1853, January 1   William L. Kirkland Jr. purchases 380 acres from Dr. Francis S. Parker and Sarah Parker, then combines it with other adjacent lands to assemble Longbrow Plantation

1854   Kansas-Nebraska Act becomes law

1854   Harriet Tubman rescues three more of her brothers, Ben, Harry, and Robert Ross, and Ben's fiancé,

Jane Kane, on Christmas Day, and takes them
to Philadelphia, then to safety in St. Catherine's,
Ontario

1855–1860 Harriet Tubman makes several additional rescue
missions to Maryland's Eastern Shore attempting
to rescue her sister, Rachel, and Rachel's children;
though she is unsuccessful at bringing away her
sister, nieces, and nephews, she does bring more than
sixty people safely to freedom and gave directions to
approximately seventy others

1856 Election of James Buchanan as president

1856, May John Brown is appointed captain of the Liberty
Guards of the First Brigade of Kansas Volunteers

1856, August 30 John Brown leads the Battle of Osawatomie

1857 Harriet Tubman rescues her elderly parents, Ben and
Harriet "Rit" Ross

1857 James Montgomery leads Free Soil fighters across
the border from Kansas into Missouri and defeats the
much larger and better armed force of pro-slavery
Missourians

1858 Harriet Tubman meets Franklin Sanborn in Concord,
Massachusetts

1859 Harriet Tubman meets Reverend Thomas Wentworth
Higginson in Boston

1859, October 16–18 John Brown raids the federal arsenal at Harpers Ferry,
Virginia, and attempts to start a slave rebellion

1859 Harriet Tubman purchases a seven-acre farm
in Auburn, New York, from William and
Frances Seward

1859, November *Wanderer* is the last documented slave vessel to
disembark West African captives in the Georgia and
South Carolina Lowcountry

1859, December 20 James L. Parker buys Palmetto Plantation from Arthur
M. Parker

1860, April Harriet Tubman plays a critical role in the escape of
Charles Nalle in Troy, New York

1860, November Abraham Lincoln is elected president

1860, December John Izard Middleton, Williams Middleton, Dr. Francis
                S. Parker, and Judge Thomas Jefferson Withers sign the
                Order of Seccession

1861, March The South secedes from the Union

1861 General resolution about property is passed by South
      Carolina General Assembly

1861, May 3 General Benjamin Butler designates enslaved people
             who liberate themselves and make their way to
             US-occupied territory at Fort Monroe, Virginia, as
             "contrabands" of war

1861, July 21 First Battle of Bull Run

1861, November 7 Battle of Port Royal, the "Great Skedaddle," and
                  "Gun Shoot at Bay Point"

1862, March Edward L. Pierce arrives in Port Royal with first
             group of northern teachers, missionaries, and
             superintendents to start the Port Royal Experiment

1862, March Five enslaved people escape the prison house of
             bondage on William L. Kirkland Jr.'s Rose Hill
             Plantation and find employment with the US Army
             quartermaster in Beaufort

1862, March USS McClellan arrives in Beaufort from Fort Pulaski
             and is unloaded by freedom seekers who liberated
             themselves from enslavement on lower Combahee
             rice plantations owned by William L. Kirkland Jr. and
             managed by Walter Blake

1862, May 9 General David Hunter declares martial law in
             coastal South Carolina and Georgia and emancipates
             enslaved people in these two areas

1862, May 25 Harriet Tubman begins her service for the US Army,
              Department of the South, as a spy, scout, nurse,
              and cook

1862, early June General David Hunter begins enlisting Black soldiers
                  in Hunter's Regiment

1862, June 26 and 27 US Navy raids Arthur Blake's South Santee Rice
                      Plantation

1862, early July US Navy sends USS Hale up the Combahee
                  River, gathering intelligence about it and the
                  Ashepoo River

1862, July 14 General Act of 1862 provides pensions for veterans
               disabled because of military service as well as for
               widows and dependents of soldiers killed in the line
               of duty

1863, January 1 Emancipation Proclamation celebration at
                 Camp Saxton

1863, January 31 1st South Carolina Volunteers Regiment is organized

1863, March 13 54th Massachusetts Regiment is organized

1863, April–May First siege of Charleston

1863, May 22 2nd South Carolina Volunteers Regiment is
              organized

1863, June 2 US Army raids rice plantations on the lower
              Combahee River (Combahee River Raid)

1863, June 3 Harriet Tubman gives a speech to the Combahee
              refugees at a church in downtown Beaufort

1863, June 3 One hundred fifty men who liberated themselves in
              the Combahee River Raid enlist in the 2nd South
              Carolina Volunteers Regiment

1863, June 3 Harriet Tubman testifies against Private John E.
              Webster, superintendent of contrabands and a white
              man, at his court-martial

1863, July 1 William C. Heyward applies for compensation from
              the Confederate government for losses at Cypress
              during the Combahee River Raid

1863, July 1–3 Battle of Gettysburg

1863, July 18 Battle of Battery Wagner

1863, August Second siege of Charleston

1863, August Harriet Tubman takes care of wounded Black
              soldiers and organizes relief support from the local
              Black community after the loss at the Battle of
              Fort Wagner

1863, September 7 Capture of Battery Wagner

1863, September 17 Joshua Nicholls applies for compensation from the
                    Confederate government for losses at Longbrow
                    during the Combahee River Raid

1863, November 15 William L. Kirkland Jr. applies for compensation
                   from the Confederate government for losses at Rose
                   Hill during the Combahee River Raid

1863, December	Major B. Ryder Corwin of the 2nd South Carolina Volunteers is court-martialed
1864, January 24	Charles T. Lowndes petitions the South Carolina State Senate and House of Representatives for exemption from his 1863 taxes because of his losses in the Combahee River Raid
1864, February 20	Battle of Olustee
1864, March 26	General Order No. 44 officially organizes the 2nd South Carolina Volunteers as the 34th Regiment of the US Colored Troops
1864, May 28	Battle of Haw's Shop
1864, June	Harriet Tubman leaves Beaufort, South Carolina, on furlough, intending to return after checking on her aged parents
1864, June 17	Wedding of multiple Black soldiers and their wives "under the flag" at Pigeon Point
1864, June 19	William L. Kirkland Jr. dies of injuries suffered at the Battle of Haw's Shop
1864, September 23	Resignation of Colonel James Montgomery as commander of the 2nd South Carolina Volunteers
1864, November 15–December 21	Sherman's March to the Sea
1865, January 1	General Sherman's Special Field Order No. 15 is delivered
1865, February 18	Charleston surrenders to 21st US Colored Troops Regiment (formerly the 3rd South Carolina Volunteers)
1865, April 9	General Robert E. Lee surrenders the Confederate Army of Northern Virginia to General Ulysses S. Grant at Appomattox Courthouse

1865, April 15 President Abraham Lincoln is assassinated

1865, April Harriet Tubman gives a speech to Black US Colored Troops veterans at Camp William Penn in Cheltenham, Pennsylvania

1866, February 6 Cypress Plantation is restored to William C. Heyward's heirs

1866, February 28 2nd South Carolina Volunteers muster out in Jacksonville, Florida

1865, July Harriet Tubman is appointed nurse or matron of the Colored Hospital at Fort Monroe, Virginia

1865, mid–October Harriet Tubman returns to Auburn, New York, concluding her military service for the US Army, Department of the South

1865, December 6 Thirteenth Amendment to the US Constitution is ratified

1866, April 28 Charles T. Lowndes sells Oakland Plantation to Rawlins Lowndes

1868 Harriet Tubman requests back pay from the federal government for her service during the Civil War

1868, July 9 Fourteenth Amendment to the Constitution is ratified

1868, November 9 Commissioner of Equity Benjamin Stokes sells William L. Kirkland Jr.'s Rose Hill Plantation to John D. Warren

1869 Sarah Bradford publishes her first biography of Harriet Tubman, *Scenes in the Life of Harriet Tubman*

1869 Harriet Tubman marries Nelson Davis in Auburn, New York

1869 Colonel Thomas Wentworth Higginson publishes *Army Life in a Black Regiment*

1870 Sarah Bradford publishes her second biography of Harriet Tubman, *Harriet Tubman: The Moses of Her People*

1870, February 3 Fifteenth Amendment to the Constitution is ratified

1872, December Sheriff John K. Terry sells Paul's Place to Lucien Bellinger

1874, March 2   Charles H. Simonton, referee of William Blake's estate,
                sells Bonny Hall to J. Bennett Bissell
1876, May   Laborers in the Combahee rice fields go on strike
1879, March 4   The Equity Court sold William C. Heyward's
                Cypress Plantation to Sarah H. Bissell
1887, August 7 Congress passes law to establish the pension system
1887, December 20 Langdon Cheves and other executors of Henry A.
                Middleton's estate sell Newport Plantation to Harriot
                Middleton, Anne Hunter, Isabella Cheves, and Allice
                Middleton
1888, October 14 Nelson Davis, Harriet Tubman's second husband, dies
1888, October   Harriet Tubman applies for a widow's pension for the
                Civil War service of her second husband, Nelson Davis
1890, June 29   Congress passes Dependent and Disability Pension Act
1895, October   Harriet Tubman's widow's pension claim is approved,
                granting her a monthly pension of $12
1895, October 31 William Drayton dies
1896   Harriet Tubman buys at auction a twenty-four-acre
                lot adjacent to her home in Auburn, New York, with
                the goal of establishing a home for sick and needy
                African Americans
1899, February 28 Harriet Tubman receives a pension increase to $20 per
                month for her service as a nurse during the Civil War
1913, March 10 Harriet Tubman dies
1914   Joshua Nicholls's heirs receive $33,450 for the loss of
                his life interest in Longbrow Plantation as a result of
                the Combahee River Raid
1923, September 27 Friday Hamilton dies in New York City
2021, June   Harriet Tubman is finally recognized for her service as
                a spy, scout, and leader of a group of spies, scouts, and
                pilots during the Civil War when she is inducted as a
                full member into the US Military Intelligence Hall of
                Fame

A Note on Names

In many ways this book is about naming, in that it uncovers the identities of people who were heretofore not identified. For many, this account represents their first appearance in the historical record.

The names given to or assumed by enslaved or formerly enslaved people reflect a wide variety of traditions and practices, making consistency in the historical record challenging for anyone trying to set the record straight. There are also multiple spellings of the names from a wide variety of sources. In recovering the historical actors' stories, I have done the very best I can to standardize the spellings, choosing one spelling (usually based on government-issue documents when available or attestations of their names from later in their lives—that is, after freedom). Variants still remain. In addition, I have tried to retain the original spellings in the primary source documents quoted in the text and cited in the endnotes.

Foreword

On June 20, 1863, less than two weeks before the Battle of Gettysburg, the *Wisconsin State Journal* reported with great excitement that earlier in the month Colonel James Montgomery of the US Army and his "gallant band of 300 Black soldiers" had "dashed" into what was widely considered a breadbasket of the Confederacy, the rice plantations along the Combahee River in South Carolina, destroyed millions of dollars of property and mansions along fifteen miles of the river, and struck fear into the heart of the rebellion. Moreover, it had done all this "under the guidance of a Black woman." It gave this Black woman and the Black soldiers "some credit for the exploit," which was now being called the Combahee River Raid.[1]

This woman was none other than Harriet Tubman, the fugitive slave known as "Moses." To Sarah Bradford, one of her biographers, Tubman recalled that she had "nebber see such a sight" as early on the morning of the Combahee raid: hundreds, if not thousands, of Blacks running for their lives—and their freedom—when they heard the whistles of the US Army gunboat *John Adams* and the armed transport steamer *Harriet A. Weed* coming up the river. First they peered out "like startled deer" from their hiding places in the rice fields and slave cabins. Then freedom seekers rushed to the boats with their children and belongings. They came loaded down with bags on their shoulders, baskets on their heads, young children struggling to keep up, pigs squealing, chickens squawking, and babies crying. Tubman told an interviewer decades after the war, "These here, puts me in the mind of the children of Israel, coming out of Egypt."[2]

Tubman remembered it as a chaotic scene. One mother carried a pail of rice on her head that was still smoking, as if just removed from the fire. Children trailed behind her, clinging to her dress. Another child was perched on her shoulders, gripping her forehead from behind and digging a hand in the smoking rice pot: breakfast in flight. On her back, the woman carried a bag with a pig in it. Another woman brought two pigs, one white and one black. Tubman remembered the white pig was named Beauregard

and the black pig Jeff Davis. She herself brought both Beauregard and
Jeff Davis onboard so that the woman, who was clearly weak from illness,
could carry her child onto the boat. Some women fled with twins hanging
around their necks. Tubman thought she had never seen so many sets of
twins in her life. They all came rushing to the Union gunboats, followed
close behind by enslaved drivers who lashed them with whips, trying to get
them to go back to the slave quarters and rice fields. Then the drivers, too,
got on the boats.[3]

The Union commanders, who were white, gave the orders for the Black
soldiers who had gone ashore—as well as others assisting in the raid, including Tubman—to "double-quick" back to the boats. Running, Tubman
tripped on her long dress and fell. In frustration she tore her garments so
that she could move freely. When she got back on the boat, her dress was
little more than shreds.[4]

By now hundreds of freedom seekers stood on the riverbanks, waiting
to board the small rowboats designated to transport them from the shore to
the gunboats. The rowboats filled up quickly. Another transport steamer, the
Sentinel, had earlier run aground on a sandbar and could not be dislodged;
it had been abandoned for the time being. Without that third vessel available to transport everyone who had rushed to the riverbank, most freedom
seekers were not able to bring on board any of the personal effects they had
laboriously toted to the riverbanks. In fact, they could not take anything
with them except the clothes on their backs. On the landing, they left an
assortment of clothes, pots, kettles, baskets, bolts of cloth, hats, and shoes,
everything they possessed in the world. Nevertheless, the loss of these possessions was a small price to pay for a way out of what Frederick Douglass
called the "prison-house of bondage."[5]

Those who hadn't yet boarded held on to the sides of the rowboats,
preventing the boats from taking off without them. They must have known
this would be their only opportunity to leave, and these boats the only way
out. Though the crews smacked their hands with the oars to get them to
let go, they were determined to hold on. The entire mission came close to
disaster.[6]

By this point the sun was coming up and Montgomery's mission would
be in full view of any Confederate forces that might have been in the
area. Any delay could have given the Confederate forces enough time to
regroup and attack, slaughtering everyone, soldiers and freedom seekers

alike. Confederate pickets could have shot them off like sitting ducks. Every second counted.[7]

Someone had to calm the desperate freedom seekers. Colonel Montgomery implored Tubman, or "Moses," as he called her, to "speak a word of consolation to your people." Decades later, Tubman told an interviewer that they were no more her people than they were Montgomery's—"only [they] was all Negroes." To Sarah Bradford she recalled that those she encountered in coastal South Carolina were foreign to her: "Why der language down dar in de far South is jus' as different from ours in Maryland as you can tink." In fact, Tubman and the Blacks in coastal South Carolina spoke different varieties of a Creole dialect that was evolving among enslaved and free Black people in the Atlantic basin. Tubman spoke a Chesapeake Creole that was influenced primarily by English and other European languages and thus likely revealed fewer African inflections. Freedom seekers in coastal South Carolina spoke a Lowcountry Creole that continued to incorporate elements of West African languages up until almost the Civil War. A similar creolization process created the two dialects, but different inputs put into different physical and social environments over time had resulted in different linguistic products. Thus, Tubman and the freedom seekers had difficulty understanding each other. As Tubman put it, "Dey laughed when dey heard me talk. An' I could not understand dem, no how."[8]

But why Tubman was in the South—in South Carolina, where the Civil War began—was unambiguous. She had known since the passage of the Fugitive Slave Act of 1850 that there was *"gwine to be war."* In 1862, she decided to do her part, risking her freedom, her safety, and her very life. She was ready to go to war for people she did not know and whose language and culture she could not even understand. However, she knew that they all had one thing in common: the pursuit of freedom.[9]

The centerpiece of Tubman's efforts was the Combahee River Raid. In the course of six hours, she, Montgomery, the 2nd South Carolina Volunteers, and one battery of the 3rd Rhode Island Heavy Artillery attacked no fewer than seven rice plantations. They destroyed $6 million in property, including homes, stables, storehouses, and other outbuildings, as well as millions of bushels of rice. They confiscated hundreds of heads of livestock, including eighty or ninety horses. Most of all, they set in motion the freedom of 756 enslaved people, Confederate planters' most valuable "possessions." The US forces did not lose a single life. One could argue that they executed the largest and most successful slave rebellion in US history.[10]

★★★★★★★★

Most know that Harriet Tubman escaped enslavement, led herself and more than sixty others out of bondage via the Underground Railroad—giving about seventy more people detailed instructions on how to get to freedom—and became a suffragist, fighting to expand voting and civil rights to those who had been excluded from them. Though some of Tubman's biographers, including Earl Conrad and Kate Larson, have written about Tubman's Civil War experiences, her work for the US Army's Department of the South during the Civil War remains the least-studied period of Tubman's otherwise well-studied life.

Tubman left Boston in 1862 and traveled to Port Royal, South Carolina, one year into the war, shortly after the port city had been liberated by Union forces. She embedded herself in the Beaufort Black refugee community, acting as a nurse, cook, spy, and scout for the US Army. There she recruited the men who piloted Colonel Montgomery, the 2nd South Carolina Volunteers, and the 3rd Rhode Island Heavy Artillery up the Combahee River and onto the plantations in the Combahee River Raid.

We know this because there are records of her service. Tubman's second husband, Nelson Davis, served in the 8th Regiment, Company C, of the US Colored Troops (USCT) from September 25, 1863, to November 10, 1865. After Davis's death on October 14, 1888, Tubman received a widow's pension of $8 per month for her husband's service. Her testimony is recorded in a report from the House Committee on Invalid Pensions submitted to the whole House of Representatives and requesting an increase to $25. Tubman's application for a widow's pension—similar to others in the massive collection of documents housed in the National Archives in Washington, DC—reveals that she worked as a "nurse and cook in hospitals and a commander of several men (eight or nine)." She therefore had a "double claim" on the US government—one for a widow's pension and the other for her own military service.[11]

The Combahee River Raid was Colonel Montgomery's most successful Civil War expedition. In fact, it was one of the most successful Union expeditions of the entire Civil War in terms of property damage and number of enslaved people freed. Yet aside from Jeff Grigg's study, *The*

Combahee River Raid: Harriet Tubman and Lowcountry Liberation, very little has been written about it. Why? The answer is that Tubman and the men and women she freed were all illiterate. Tubman never wrote her own account of the raid. She told parts of it to abolitionist friends—like Sarah Bradford, mentioned earlier—and supporters, who wrote it down for her. Taken together, all these accounts provide evidence of her Civil War activities in coastal South Carolina, where, despite language and cultural differences, she gathered from the Lowcountry Creoles the intelligence the US military commanders needed.

However, many of the critical elements of the Combahee story have been largely absent. Who were these people who gained their freedom? The majority of plantation records were destroyed when the plantations were burned (Colonel Montgomery's men spared only one on that stretch of the river). Incinerated were slave lists, plantation daybooks, diaries, ledgers, and business and personal correspondence. The Confederates had moved records for Beaufort and Colleton Counties to Columbia, South Carolina, during the war to protect them from the Union. Ironically, those burned in February 1865, when General William T. Sherman's army marched through the Carolinas (though Charleston County's archives survived). Thus, many documents filed in municipal archives located in the parishes where the raid took place are also lost forever.[12]

However, papers from other rice plantations in the area owned by the same planter families or their relatives help paint a picture of life on the lower Combahee. Moreover, planters whose property was burned during the raid applied for compensation from the Confederate government, cataloguing their losses. (One planter was a double-dipper, as I learned. He applied for compensation from both the Confederate and US governments.) In addition to buildings and equipment, bushels of rice, livestock, and personal possessions, the affidavits listed the names of the enslaved men, women, and children who seized their chance for their freedom on June 2, 1863. A number of planter families filed marriage settlements, wills, bills of sale for slaves, and court proceedings in Charleston or kept private collections that survived. Some planters scrawled back-of-the-envelope lists of the enslaved people they had lost in the raid or who had moved out of the area before and after June 2, and these, too, have survived. Finally, there are surviving letters in which planters, their family members, and neighbors lamented and commiserated about their losses. Still, while these help with names, family connections, and ages, they reveal too little about the lived experiences of enslaved people and their communities.

So telling the Combahee story presents challenges. What we have most of all, however, are the pension files, which allow us to reconstruct the story of Tubman's Civil War service, the Combahee River Raid, and the hundreds of husbands, wives, siblings, in-laws, cousins, childhood friends, neighbors, and sweethearts who all ran for their lives and their freedom when the steamboat whistle blew. They constitute the foundation of the story that follows.

★★★★★★★★

The United States Civil War Pension Files offer a fresh perspective on Harriet Tubman's Civil War service, putting this chapter of her life in the context of the Combahee River Raid, the freedom seekers who liberated themselves as a result of it, the Black regiments, and the evolution of a new Creole culture and language. They are an underutilized source. Like slave narratives (often dictated by formerly enslaved people to abolitionist amanuenses) and interviews collected among formerly enslaved people by the Federal Writers' Project from 1936 to 1938, the US Civil War Pension Files provide a window into the intimate lives of enslaved people, their families, and communities.[13]

Under the General Act of 1862, Congress created the US Pension Bureau to evaluate pension claims and administer pension benefits to white and Black US veterans disabled by military service and to the widows and dependents (children under sixteen at time of their father's death and adult dependents) of men killed in action. The Dependent and Disability Pension Act of 1890 greatly expanded the pension system, making disabled veterans eligible for pensions whether or not their disabilities were related to military service and their widows and dependents eligible for pensions whether or not the veteran's death was related to his military service. Successfully navigating the pension system was expensive, time-consuming, and frustrating. It presented untold challenges for African American Civil War veterans, the majority of whom were born enslaved and remained illiterate all of their lives. Roughly 83,000, slightly more than 42 percent, of African American veterans who applied for pensions were approved. Tens of thousands more veterans, widows, and dependents' applications were not approved and/or they did not live long enough to collect their benefits.[14]

USCT veterans and their widows applied for pensions for their Civil War service through local attorneys mostly located in Beaufort and Colleton Counties and attorneys in Washington, DC. Veterans and widows were required to produce many different kinds of documentation, including the soldier's discharge papers and a marriage certificate. The documents had to be notarized by a local notary in order for a successful pension application to be filed. The notaries also took affidavits from veterans, widows, comrades, "Old Heads" (the oldest people in the community, who knew everyone else's business), neighbors, church members, and others who had known the veteran, the widow, and their children for much of their lives. The Bureau of Pensions sent special examiners in to investigate when the process went awry, as it frequently did, because Black veterans' applications often lacked the necessary documentation (marriage certificates, birth certificates, even discharge papers) and required depositions from many more witnesses to verify the information. The testimonies were often contradictory. So special examiners took more affidavits from witnesses, attempted to assess whose testimony was most reliable, wrote a report back to the Bureau of Pensions, and made a recommendation whether the veteran, widow, or dependent should be granted a pension or the veteran an increase in pension benefits because of disability.[15]

Once the veteran or widow had secured pension benefits, they had to visit a notary every quarter to execute their pension vouchers and collect their monetary benefits. Four times yearly, many traveled from the towns of Dale and Sheldon to downtown Beaufort, from St. Helena Island to Frogmore (also in Beaufort County), or from Green Pond to Walterboro (in Colleton County) to pick up mail addressed to them and delivered to the general store, including their mail from the Bureau of Pensions. General stores were the one-stop shops of small southern towns in the post–Civil War era. Located in the center of town, they sold everything, including groceries, clothing, household goods, tools, and seed, to white and Black customers in the local area. In addition, the notary public's office was often located at the back of the store. This being Reconstruction, the general store had two doors and the office two rooms, and that segregation endured through the period of Jim Crow.[16]

White farmers browsed the wares at their leisure, catching up on the week's news with the store clerk and fellow white customers, and transacted business with the notary public in the main office. For them, the general store was a central social spot during the evening hours. Black customers, on the other hand, came in the back door and stated their business. If shopping, they requested items and had to purchase them without inspecting them or trying them on. If they came to transact business with the notary public, including pension business, they waited in a back room, often a storeroom, for the notary to finish attending to the needs of white customers. USCT veterans who had fought courageously and proudly for the Union, their freedom, and the freedom of others entered through the back door and sat in the back room waiting for the notary to have the time (or take the time) to notarize their pension vouchers and count out the payments due for their service.[17]

When called upon, the veterans and widows held up one hand, swore to tell the truth, signed—usually with a mark, as only a handful could sign their names—and had their signature or mark witnessed, usually by other veterans and/or widows sitting in the back room. If the pensioner needed to have a letter written or a form filled out to apply for a disability pension or an increase, the notary could perform all of these tasks in the same visit. Most veterans came alone and met their comrades at the general store; most widows did not come alone, instead accompanied by a male relative (brother, brother-in-law, son, grandson) or one of their husband's comrades. During these quarterly reunions, veterans and widows stayed abreast of one another's health, family, and financial circumstances, identified who among their community needed help, and pledged to keep in touch until they met again.

If a veteran or widow was applying for a pension, disability, or an increase, they often brought witnesses with them, in which case they all sat together in the back room and waited. If the witnesses did not come with the veteran or widow, they could come separately for the notary to take their affidavits. If the notary was attending to white customers, quite possibly the USCT veterans, widows, and witnesses would have to wait for a considerable amount of time, and if the notary did not have time that day, they would have to travel home or spend the night in town and come back another day, all at their own expense, to try their luck again. The costs associated with applying for a pension—particularly traveling to and from rural areas to attorneys, notary publics, and surgical boards, and paying notary publics to read, explain, and fill out forms, take depositions, and notarize documents—were prohibitive for many veterans and widows.[18]

In one trip, veterans and widows could execute and cash their pension vouchers, as well as spend their quarterly pension benefits on foodstuffs, clothing, shoes, and supplies for themselves, their families, and their households. Veterans and widows frequently left discharge papers and other important documents on file with the notary public with whom they executed their quarterly vouchers or at the general store where they did their shopping, so that the documents would not be destroyed by rats, fire, or water. Veterans and widows had to testify that they did not pledge their pension certificates to the storekeepers who kept their pension papers on file and/or where they collected their quarterly benefits, and storekeepers had to testify that they did not require veterans and widows to pledge their certificates in order to be granted store credit. However, it's highly likely that some of them were indeed leaving their pension papers at the stores as collateral, even though they told the pension officers they didn't and the practice was illegal under federal law. As the Federal Writers' Project interviews demonstrate, it is no surprise that poor Black people—especially ones dependent on government benefits—told federal interviewers what they thought the government officials wanted to hear, particularly about slavery.[19]

Formerly enslaved people told their stories to notary publics, pension attorneys, and officials from the Department of the Interior's Bureau of Pensions. Veterans who enlisted in the US Army after the Combahee River Raid told their story to apply for Civil War pensions; they told it to apply for increases in their pensions if they became disabled or had reached the age of seventy. When one of their comrades died, they told his story, and theirs in relationship to his, to be sure his widow and/or minor children received pension benefits. Widows, like Harriet Tubman Davis, applied for their husbands' pension benefits after their husbands died. After a comrade or widow died, their story was told to ensure that whoever nursed him or her in their last days and paid the burial expenses would receive accrued pension benefits to defray the costs. Moreover, the comrades, friends, and neighbors who knew the veteran, widow, and/or minor children during enslavement and after discharge told their stories as well.

When notary publics exercised best practices, they recorded witnesses' testimony given under oath. On a separate document, they rated the reliability of the witnesses; sometimes they asked postmasters to weigh in on the witnesses' standing in the community. Occasionally special examiners stepped out of their roles as neutral scribes and wrote their real feelings about a witness in a deposition or a special examiner's report. It is not surprising that when they let their guard down, special examiners admitted they thought Black people were ignorant. Many of special examiner James A. Bell's colleagues would have agreed with his judgments of the veterans, widows, and neighbors who lived on the isolated and unhealthful lands along the Combahee River. He pronounced that Sina Bolze Young Green had once "belonged to a rice planter" and that people who had been held in bondage by rice planters were among the "most ignorant and degraded." He continued by saying that those who had been enslaved on Lowcountry rice plantations and freedpeople in general had lost the morality they possessed in bondage by coming into contact with the world in freedom. Notary public N. G. Moore articulated how his colleagues likely felt when he wrote to his superiors to note that Moses Simmons's first wife's name was Christy, not Cushie as it had appeared previously in Moses's pension file, and opined that "these people talk very indistinct and it is very hard to write from pronunciation. They are all negroes and very ignorant. This explains the difference in the name as it appeared." Thus, most notary publics and special examiners filtered witnesses' testimony through their language, Standard English, obscuring the witnesses' Gullah Geechee dialect. The Gullah Geechee are the descendants of Blacks enslaved on Lowcountry rice, Sea Island cotton, and indigo plantations from the Cape Fear River in North Carolina to the St. John River in Florida and in the port cities of Charleston, Beaufort, Savannah, and Jacksonville.[20]

Inconsistencies in witnesses' stories may have contributed to special examiners' negative opinions about USCT veterans and their widows, though the rampant discrimination and racism among whites during Reconstruction and in the Jim Crow South were surely the root cause. When veterans, widows, and neighbors misrepresented information, such as their marital status or nature of their disability, the special examiners usually unearthed the truth, usually with help from the Old Heads. In 1911, Fannie Lee Green Simmons, widow of Moses Simmons, testified that "every old head on this plantation knows that I had no wife [sic] between Caesar [Green] and Moses [Simmons]." The Old Heads knew who was married before the war, who had remarried even though their first spouse was still living, who had never married even though they lived together as husband and wife, who told members of the community to say they were or were not married when the pension officer came around, and whose children were born out of wedlock. They did not hesitate to tell what they knew when the pension officers showed up. As the decades wore on, there were always Old Heads around who could tell the tale. The men who enlisted and the women they married all became Old Heads if they just kept living. It was the special examiners' job to find the Old Heads and ask the right question. Occasionally, witnesses told pension officers about the night when Colonel Montgomery and the "Yankee gunboats" came up the river and "took all of the colored people off" to freedom.[21]

★★★★★★★★

As noted, the US Civil War Pension Files hold a treasure trove of historical information about enslaved people's lives. Take, for example, the file—255 pages in all—of my great-great-great-uncle Jonas Fields, who enlisted in the United States Colored Troops, 128th Regiment, Company C, in April 1865, not long before the war ended. Medical examinations in Jonas Fields's pension file state that he was "height 5 feet 8 inches; complexion Dark; color of eyes Black; color of hair Black." For African American Civil War soldiers, that is the extent of what the pension files provide of their physical descriptions, except for their injuries and disabilities. It is enough for me to imagine that Jonas was taller than most, dark, and lean, like the men in my granddaddy's family. Like his namesake Jonas Fields, who was my grandfather's first cousin, my great-great-great-uncle likely had a back strong enough to work on the railroad (a line of work the Fields men followed south to Miami), arms strong enough to need only one to scoop his well-proportioned wife out of the baptismal pool and carry her up the stairs (as family and members of the Baptist Church in Ruffin, South Carolina, witnessed Cousin Jonas do), and hands big enough to grip the top of an errant child's head before we got away.[22]

My uncle Jonas testified in June 1902 that he had been born on Keans Neck in Beaufort, and that Dr. James Robert Verdier had held him in bondage. Jonas also revealed the names of his parents, Anson and Judy Fields (my great-great-great-great-grandparents), noting that "their owner was my owner." In his 1914 deposition, Emmanuel Gettes testified that Jonas had been a house slave; he had waited on Verdier and his son-in-law, a Mr. Sams, who was certainly Berners Bainbridge Sams. Jonas "used to travel about during slave times," even to the neighborhood of the Heyward Plantation, where he became acquainted with his future wife, Nellie Small. On that

same day in 1914, Phoebe Washington testified that she was Jonas's sister and
that they had a brother named Hector, my great-great-great-grandfather.
Verdier, she said, had enslaved both Hector and Jonas Fields; "Mrs. Sams,"
who was Sarah F. Verdier Sams (Verdier's daughter), held Phoebe in bondage.
During the Civil War the Verdiers evacuated the male and female house
slaves they held in bondage at their home in downtown Beaufort to different
locations, separating Jonas from his first wife, Margaret, whom the Verdiers
also held in bondage. Hector, a field hand on a rural plantation, had already
run away and joined the US Army. After the Civil War, Jonas testified that
he "went into the Heyward neighborhood to work in the rice fields" near
the small town of White Hall, and there married Nellie. White Hall is where
my father was born. I often visited cousins on my paternal grandfather's side
when I was a child, and many in my family still live there.[23]

When Jonas arrived in White Hall after the war, he worked as a coachman
for Barnwell Heyward, grandson of Nathaniel Heyward (the Heywards had
been one of the Combahee's most prominent rice families before the war),
and for Barnwell's great-uncle Colonel Alan Izzard, and he lived next door
to Nellie for a few years before they married. Nellie testified Nathaniel
Heyward had held her in bondage. Stephen Graham, who was younger
than Nellie, testified in his pension file that he had been enslaved on the
same Heyward plantation as Nellie and held in bondage by Blake Heyward,
another of Nathaniel Heyward's grandsons. Jonas and Nellie lived in White
Hall until January 17, 1891, when they moved to Lady's Island, where my
uncle died on September 22, 1911. On June 25, 1902, Jonas testified that his
brother Hector Fields lived on Lady's Island. Affiants testified that Verdier
had also held in bondage Margaret Fields, Jonas's wife during enslavement,
John Bryan, and Clara Gillison, and that the Heywards, Nathaniel and Blake,
had enslaved Moses Youngblood, Nellie Small's fiancé or possibly her first
husband, and a man named Stephen Graham. With one US Civil War pension file, I discovered ancestors in my Fields family line whose names were
previously unknown. This facilitated my reconstruction of the beginnings
of two enslaved communities.[24]

The 162 pension files of the men who escaped enslavement in the
Combahee River Raid and joined the USCT are like pieces of a jigsaw
puzzle. Each affidavit, letter, and special examiner's report plays a part in
constructing a greater picture. Yet that picture is partial. For example, these
pension files are not representative of all of the enslaved people who escaped

in the Combahee River Raid. Instead they reflect only the men who joined the Union Army immediately following the raid, the women who married them, and the neighbors and friends who knew them and testified on their behalf. The overwhelming majority of these people were illiterate, and very few left written accounts. Nonetheless, together with the planters' documents, I will use the pension files to reconstruct the enslaved communities and identify those who ran to the Combahee River and got on the US Army gunboats. Partial as it is, this picture reflects the experiences of the freedom seekers who escaped during the Combahee River Raid and the newly liberated men turned soldiers who freed them, allowing them all to tell the story of the raid in their own words.

★★★★★★★★★

I never intended to write a book about Harriet Tubman or about the Civil War, especially not one involving some of my ancestors. My scholarly focus has always been rice. I've studied peasant farmers who engineered mangrove rice farming technology in the Upper Guinea Coast (West Africa) during the precolonial period and enslaved Blacks forced to grow rice on coastal South Carolina's tidal rice plantations. However, Tubman and the Combahee River Raid *is* a rice story; indeed, it is one of the best rice stories I have ever come across. As much as possible, I will tell this rice story using sources by and about the Combahee planters impacted by the raid and their family members. After all, this raid didn't happen in Georgetown, on the Santee, or on the Savannah River; it happened on the Combahee, with its localized identity and tight-knit enslaved and planter communities. The pension files offer an invaluable window into the tidal rice plantations and enable me to envision African Americans' lives on these tidal rice plantations before, during, and after the Civil War. The journey to freedom begins by alternating scenes from Harriet Tubman's life (primarily from her biographies) with the lives of the Blacks enslaved on the lower Combahee rice plantations before the Civil War told through their testimony in the pension files and slave transactions. The intersection of their stories illuminates why Tubman and the formerly enslaved men turned soldiers risked their very lives that others might be free.

This story places Harriet Tubman and the Combahee River Raid in the context of the Civil War. It deals with big Civil War battles, such as the Battles of Port Royal and Fort Wagner, the sieges of Charleston, and Sherman's March to the Sea, the stories of which will also be told from the perspective of the Combahee freedom seekers, Combahee planters, and the soldiers and officers of the 2nd South Carolina. But the story I recount here is more than that.

Tubman is at the center of this drama. Her service in Beaufort and the surrounding Sea Islands during the war and in the Combahee River Raid in particular started the process by which enslaved people on the Combahee River took control of their lives. However, *Combee* is not intended to be another biography of Harriet Tubman. Biographers, particularly Kate Clifford Larson and Catherine Clinton, have covered her life artfully. But it does recount scenes from Tubman's life, showing what motivated her to risk her life by going to South Carolina during the Civil War and how her life intersected with the lives of the enslaved people she helped to liberate in the Combahee River Raid.

There are a number of challenges to writing about this period in the life of such an iconic figure. First, much of what we know about Tubman's Civil War service comes from her autobiographies, which do not provide a detailed chronology of her time in Beaufort and Port Royal. Second, according to the fragmentary documentary record, Tubman, the 2nd South Carolina Volunteers, and the Combahee refugees went in separate directions after the Combahee River Raid. Thus, while Tubman's Civil War experiences are directly tied to the Combahee freedom seekers' story, her Civil War experiences have less to do with the Gullah Geechee culture and language, for which the Civil War was an important catalyst and which ultimately crystallized in the early twentieth century.

The story is as local as it is national. Central as she was to the Combahee River Raid, in this book Harriet Tubman shares the spotlight with the men, women, and children who utilized the raid to seize their freedom and create a new community, one with roots in the South Carolina Lowcountry, with its indigo, rice, and Sea Island cotton plantations, urban areas, rivers, creeks, and those who spoke Creole dialects and practiced Creole cultures. Black freedom, the cause to which Tubman had already devoted so much of her life before the raid, was the cause for which she risked it yet again in the raid, though she could not have imagined what it would create. Even "Moses" did not envision all of the promised land.

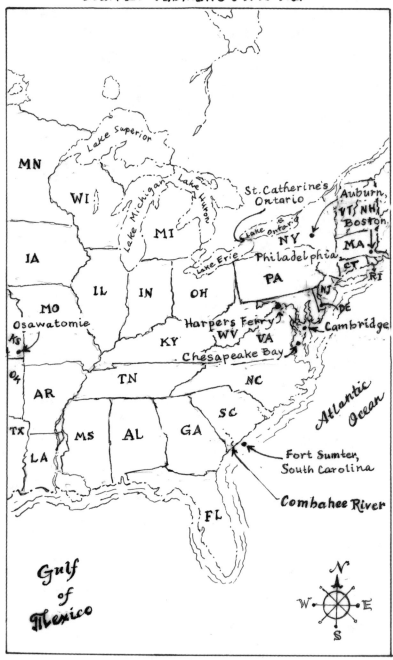

PART ONE

"The Prison-House of Bondage"

The cause of freedom is not the cause of a race or sect, a party or a class—it is the cause of human kind, the very birthright of humanity.
                              —Anna Julia Cooper, *A Voice from the South*, 1892

I

Last Captives

When Harriet Tubman told Sarah Bradford that she could not "understand" those who were enslaved in the South Carolina Lowcountry, she may have been referring to their speech, but there were larger differences between what she had experienced on Maryland's Eastern Shore and the systems of enslavement in the South Carolina Lowcountry, where some African Americans were freed months before the Emancipation Proclamation went into effect on January 1, 1863, as we will see. Enslavement was not the same across the South, and the Lowcountry's was distinct.[1]

But Tubman knew that all enslaved people yearned to be free and were ready to seize opportunities, to fight against white slaveholders, and to liberate themselves. Liberating themselves was not enough, though. They wanted their family members, friends, neighbors, and all enslaved people to be free. And, like Tubman, they were willing to risk it all—to put their own freedom and their very lives in jeopardy.

In the documented history of the New World, a very small number of Blacks who were born and reared in bondage and who escaped enslavement went back into slave territory. Tubman and the Black men who escaped in the Combahee River Raid—and who then enlisted in the 2nd South Carolina Volunteers—were anomalies among Black abolitionists. Even among those who were born enslaved, lectured about the evils of enslavement, and worked to end it for all, very few put their freedom on the line.[2]

The more than 186,000 Black men who enlisted in the United States Colored Troops made up approximately 18 percent of the African American population between the ages of fifteen and forty-nine in September 1862. Approximately three-quarters of the Black soldiers had been formerly enslaved when the Civil War broke out in 1861. Many more USCT soldiers were born to formerly enslaved parents. And they were exceptional, as they—like Tubman—were among the relatively few African Americans willing to venture back into slave societies.[3]

With the exception of Henry "Box" Brown and Sojourner Truth, who never learned to read and write, the majority of the well-known Black abolitionists—such as Prince Hall, Olaudah Equiano, Ottobah Cugoano, Henry Highland Garnet, and Frederick Douglass—became literate after their emancipation. They gave lectures and wrote or dictated their stories. Tubman and most of the men and women enslaved on Combahee River rice plantations, on the other hand, remained illiterate, though some of those individuals learned to sign their names. Tubman told her story in public lectures and dictated her life story to others, such as Sarah Bradford, but for most of those who never learned to read and write, we do not know their names, have not heard their voices, and do not know their stories.[4]

Nonetheless, the story of the Combahee River Raid is focused on two river ecosystems, the Blackwater River, on the eastern shore of the Chesapeake Bay in Maryland, and the Combahee River, located in the central coast of South Carolina, and the people who inhabited the watersheds of these rivers.

Tubman was born in Dorchester County, on the shores of the Blackwater River. The Blackwater River is part of the larger Chesapeake Bay ecosystem and is sandwiched between the Choptank River to the north and the Nanticoke River to the south on the Eastern Shore of Maryland. The tidal portion of the estuaries in this region of the Chesapeake are generally composed of broad tidal rivers with a tidal range of 1.6 to 2.5 feet. There is where Tubman's fight for freedom began.[5]

★★★★★★★★

From 1662 to 1775 the network of rivers emptying into Chesapeake Bay were the landing points for 116 slaving vessels, which transported a little over 21,000 captives from West Africa to Maryland's shores. That transatlantic transport began with 158 captives between 1662 and 1675. Between 1676 and 1700, 2,917 captives arrived after the terrible voyage, an increase of 1,746 percent. London slave traders dominated the transatlantic slave trade into Maryland in its early days; they were responsible for transporting more than 12,500 men and women into the colony. Bristol and Liverpool slave traders entered the trade in the early eighteenth century and played a distant second to London until the end of the legal trade: Bristol slave traders transported approximately 2,500 captives from western Africa to Maryland, and Liverpool slave traders brought more than 3,700.[6]

The Potomac and Patuxent Rivers on Maryland's Western Shore and the Choptank River on the Eastern Shore gave slave factors (brokers) ready access to planters in Maryland's interior. Planters purchased African captives between April and October so that they would be seasoned (that is, habituated to the disease environment) before the late fall, when temperatures began to dip.[7]

The earliest arrivals in Maryland, who were forced to grow tobacco on the region's plantations, encountered patchworks of dense mixed hardwood forests (largely oak and hickory) in the uplands, inhabited by bears, deer, wild turkeys, and passenger pigeons. Red maples, gums, white cedar, and bald cypress trees provided habitat for beavers, ducks, geese, waterfowl, and wading birds in the region's swampy southern lowlands. When storms and fire damaged the virgin forest, loblolly pines regenerated in the clearings. This landscape covered the tidewater region through the 1700s.[8]

The earliest enslaved Africans arriving on the Combahee River, farther south, would have observed a landscape similar to that around the Choptank River. Both estuaries were part of the American coastal plains. In both places, enslaved Blacks were forced to clear wetlands with rudimentary hand tools, having a profound and lasting impact on the environment and harming their health. There are differences, of course. The average temperature on Maryland's Eastern Shore is colder, with more frozen precipitation in the winter, and the level of salinity in the Chesapeake Bay is higher. Some plant and animal species would have been familiar to Tubman when she arrived in Beaufort, South Carolina. Others would have been foreign.

As I've noted, the examples of formerly enslaved people returning to places of bondage were rare. While Tubman was exceptional—in this and so many other ways—another who did so Ayuba Suleyman Diallo, though his story is quite different and his actions had an opposite effect to Tubman's.

Diallo, also known as Job ben Solomon, was the son of a wealthy and powerful Muslim Fulani family in Bundu, an Islamic kingdom located on either side of the middle valley of the Senegal River and stretching south to the Gambia River from the late fifteenth century. Diallo's grandfather founded the town of Bundu and became a religious leader, a position that Diallo's father inherited. The king of Futa Toro, another Muslim theocracy, sent his son to Diallo's father so he could be educated; thus, the future king of Futa Toro grew up in the same household as Diallo.[9]

In 1731, when Diallo was approximately thirty-one, he set out on a trade mission for his father, accompanied by two of his father's slaves, to sell two captives and purchase paper, essential to Islamic education. But his father warned him not to cross the Gambia River and leave the territory controlled by the Fulani; the Mandingo, who were the Fulani's enemies, lived on the other side of the Gambia. The enterprising young Diallo wanted a better price for his father's captives than Captain Stephen Pike, the English trader on the north side of the Gambia River, would pay. He therefore sent his father's slaves home and crossed the Gambia River. Mandingo soldiers seized the opportunity and captured Diallo and a translator who had joined him, Lamine Ndiaye. They shaved Diallo's and Ndiaye's hair and beards (an extraordinary disgrace for a noble Fulani such as Diallo) to disguise them as war captives, and offered them for sale to Pike.[10]

Through an interpreter, Diallo reminded Pike that he was the man who had negotiated with him to sell his father's captives a short time before on the other side of the Gambia. Pike allowed Diallo to send word to Bundu so that his father could redeem him and Ndiaye. Diallo's father sent more captives—whom he may have acquired in war or purchased from English traders—to exchange for his son's freedom. But the ransom arrived too late. Pike had already set sail with Diallo and Ndiaye on board, transporting them and more than 160 others to Maryland. There, an Annapolis slave factor named Vachell Denton sold Diallo to a Mr. Tolsey, who enslaved him on his tobacco plantation on Kent Island, north of Dorchester County (the county where Harriet Tubman was born and enslaved).[11]

Articulate and educated, Diallo continued to pray in secret, but a young white boy sometimes followed him and threw dirt on him as he prayed. Eighteen months into his captivity, Diallo ran away. He was caught and jailed in Kent County, Maryland, until Tolsey came to reclaim him. After he was released from jail and returned to the tobacco plantation, Diallo wrote a letter to his father asking to be redeemed. He sent his letter via the very same channels through which he had come: the transatlantic system through which Europeans extracted trade goods, including people in captivity, from West Africa and funneled them to markets in the New World. Diallo's letter and case came to the attention of James Oglethorpe, deputy governor of the Royal African Company, a former member of Parliament, and a philanthropist. Oglethorpe had Diallo brought to England and paid Denton a ransom of £45 upon his arrival.[12]

In England, Diallo dined with the Duke of Montagu and the queen, and received a gold watch, agricultural tools, reams of writing paper, and other gifts valued at £500, all packed carefully into wooden trunks. After touring England for fourteen months, Diallo wanted to go home. He traveled on the slave ship *William* in 1733 as it returned from London to the Gambia River. The Royal African Company gave specific instruction to the *William*'s captain that Diallo was to be treated with the utmost respect and civility and returned to his father. Diallo arrived at Fort James, Gambia, in August 1734, accompanied by Francis Moore, British factor for the Royal African Company. When they neared Bundu, messengers came to inform Diallo that his father had died sometime after receiving his son's letter containing the news that he had been redeemed. One of the younger Diallo's wives, thinking him dead, had remarried. And his country had been decimated by a long and bloody war with the Mandingo—a war that may well have been started by Diallo's abduction.[13]

Moore wrote in his memoir that Diallo was "the only man (except one) that was ever known to come back to this Country, after having been carried a Slave out of it by White Men." The inhabitants of Bundu, Moore wrote, "imagined, that all who were sold for Slaves, were generally either eaten or murdered, since none ever returned."[14]

Diallo also asked his English friend and biographer, Thomas Bluett, to redeem the interpreter with whom he had been captured in Mandingo territory. Bluett did indeed redeem Lamine Ndiaye and sent him back to Gambia in February 1738.[15]

Diallo had returned from one land of bondage, one where he had been enslaved, to another land of bondage, as Futa Toro was a place where people were captured and held or sold. He went not to liberate others but in the service of slave traders. As an ambassador and advisor for the British, who had redeemed him from his own bondage and then lavished gifts and large sums of money upon him, Diallo demystified and destigmatized European enslavement for the Fulani in Bundu. The Royal African Company hoped he could promote British trade interests along the Gambia River and help them challenge the French monopoly of West Africa's gum arabic trade. Here he stands in contrast to Tubman and the others—such as those in the 2nd South Carolina Volunteers—who chose to go back to the land of bondage to fight for the freedom of those still enslaved. Tubman remembered after her successful act of self-liberation, "Now I've been free, I know what a dreadful condition slavery is." She had seen hundreds of escaped slaves, but she "never saw one who was willing to go back and be a slave."[16]

Though born in bondage, Tubman must have imagined a time when her ancestors were free. In an interview published in 1907, six years before Tubman's death in 1913, a reporter wrote about her African ancestry: "The old mammies to whom she told [her] dreams were wont to nod knowingly and say, 'I recon youse one o' dem "Shantees," chile.'" They would have meant it as a compliment. Starting in the late seventeenth century, the Ashanti Empire was one of West Africa's most powerful kingdoms. And the Ashantis had a strong tradition of female political leadership: Yaa Asantewaa, queen mother of Ejisu, part of the Ashanti Empire, fought the so-called War of the Golden Stool against the British in 1900 and kept the British Empire, which controlled Gold Coast trade starting in the 1750s, from colonizing the interior. The British never conquered the Ashanti Empire; the interior state remained ascendant until present-day Ghana achieved independence from Great Britain in 1957. During the transatlantic slave trade, Ashanti warriors had fought the kingdom's enemies, who were their neighbors, to gain and maintain control over trade with Europeans on the coast. The Ashanti Empire sold people it captured in interstate warfare to European traders at one of eighteen ports along the Gold Coast. And its enemies certainly captured and sold people from the Ashanti Empire as well. Almost 2,000 captives from the Gold Coast were transported to Maryland's shores from the ports of Cape Coast or Anomabu between 1708 and 1720 and between 1752 and 1762.[17]

This relatively small number of captives was imported into a period of transitions for the economy in the mid-eighteenth-century Eastern Shore. Tobacco had been the dominant staple crop from earliest settlement. The growth in southern European demand for grains by the 1740s tempted planters like the Pattison family—a small but prosperous farming family with a long history on the Eastern Shore—to begin growing wheat and corn along with tobacco, eventually decreasing their tobacco production. Tobacco required less land per worker per year than wheat—two to three acres versus thirteen to eighteen acres, respectively. But it was much more land-intensive over time, a problem as land prices rose throughout the eighteenth century. Planters could sow tobacco for three years on the same plot of land but then had to let it lie fallow for twenty years. In contrast, they could sow wheat for two harvests, let the land lie fallow for one season, then sow wheat again. As long as planters owned adequate land to cultivate tobacco and grains and the labor to clear and farm that land, growing wheat in the winter did not interfere with producing tobacco or corn for the remainder of the year. By the 1760s, planters in Talbot County, just north of Tubman's Dorchester County, were thoroughly diversified, deriving equal shares of their income from tobacco and from grains (wheat and corn).[18]

Growing wheat did not require transforming the landscape in the way that growing rice in tidewater South Carolina did. However, wheat production did require felling large trees and removing stumps. Eastern Shore planters needed more enslaved labor to undertake these labor-intensive tasks. The region experienced a 400 percent increase in the importation of African captives between 1726 and 1750, from 2,000 to over 10,000 people.[19]

Tubman's first official biographer, Franklin Sanborn (an abolitionist and member of the so-called Secret Six, who supported John Brown's 1859 raid on the federal arsenal at Harpers Ferry, Virginia, as part of the attempt to start a slave rebellion), described her as "the grand-daughter of a slave imported from Africa." After reaching its height in 1750, the slave trade to Maryland's ports declined, ending altogether in 1773. The *Peggy* was the last recorded slaving vessel to disembark its human cargo in Maryland's ports in 1773, before the American Revolution. Its captain, Lionel Bradstreet, purchased people taken captive in the hinterlands of present-day Senegal at the port of Saint-Louis. In contrast to Maryland, more than 68,000 captives were brought to South Carolina and Georgia's ports after 1775. As late as 1858, fifty years after the legal importation of African captives ended and five years before the Combahee River Raid, 407 African captives were imported illegally into the Lowcountry.[20]

Harriet Tubman's grandmother Modesty is her earliest known ancestor. Modesty was born in West Africa likely around the mid-1760s and endured the Middle Passage. Modesty was almost certainly transported on one of the last slave ships to disembark captives in the Chesapeake region at a time when tobacco was no longer the staple crop. Atthow Pattison purchased her. Modesty was likely one of the five enslaved people in Pattison's household in 1776.[21]

Born between 1785 and 1789, Harriet "Rit" Green, Modesty's daughter and Tubman's mother, grew up in Pattison's household on the Eastern Shore. Pattison was owner of a modest 265-acre farm and a slaveholder. Like Rit, one-third to two-thirds of the people enslaved on Maryland's

Eastern Shore during the period after the American Revolution and through the end of the eighteenth century were forced to labor on relatively small farms, those with enslaved populations of twenty or fewer. The largest and wealthiest farmers in the tidewater region held more than a hundred African Americans in bondage; this would have been a medium-sized tidal rice plantation in coastal South Carolina and Georgia.[22]

In any case, by the end of the eighteenth century, fewer and fewer enslaved men and women on Eastern Shore plantations had been born in Africa. The diminishing numbers of African-born slaves were scattered throughout the sparsely settled region. More than likely, African-born enslaved people—of whom a little more than 40 percent originated in West Africa's Upper Guinea Coast, with slightly more than 30 percent originating in West-Central Africa—were intermingled with enslaved people born in Maryland. And even had they found themselves with other bonded African-born people, it was unlikely they would have spoken the same indigenous languages or engaged in the same cultural practices. The world Rit was born into was increasingly Creole, inflected by passage through the West Indies, Caribbean, and South America. Most African Americans on Maryland's Eastern Shore were born enslaved, never experienced the Middle Passage, and had already initiated the processes of creating new cultures and languages that fused West African and European elements.[23]

Whether African-born or Creole, enslaved Blacks on the Eastern Shore in the eighteenth century were surrounded by white people—farmers, indentured servants, and poor, landless whites. It would have been difficult, though not impossible, for enslaved people, regardless of their place of birth, to form communities based on Creole languages and cultures. Instead, Blacks on Maryland's Eastern Shore would be heavily influenced by the English language, English culture, and Christianity, more and more so over time. Little wonder that the language and culture of Blacks who had been enslaved in the South Carolina Lowcountry were unfamiliar to Tubman when she first encountered them, and that she could not "understand" them.[24]

Theatre of War, November 1861 - June 1863

Lower Combahee River

2

Old Heads

The Combahee River is a forty-mile-long tidally influenced black-water river in the central region of South Carolina's coastal zone, in what is now known as the ACE Basin. The term "blackwater river" comes from the color of the water, black from the tannic acid leached from trees lining the floodplains. The ACE Basin is composed of the lower portions of the Ashepoo, Combahee, and Edisto Rivers and drains the central coastal plain. Combahee waters range from tidal freshwater in its upper reaches to brackish waters in the middle regions to nearly full-strength seawater as it flows into St. Helena Sound, then out to the Atlantic Ocean. In contrast with the Blackwater River in Maryland's Eastern Shore, where the tidal range—the range between high and low tides—is 1.6 to 2.5 feet, the tidal range in the Combahee is on the order of 5 feet.[1]

In Tubman's time, the forested wetlands and swamps in the Blackwater River and the Combahee River were likely similar. The vegetation of both consisted of loblolly pine, tupelo, cypress, sweet gum trees, and many species of oaks. Cypress, tupelo, sable palmetto, and wax myrtle, however, likely were more abundant in the subtropical Combahee system than in the temperate Blackwater River system. The fauna of both rivers were similar: white-tailed deer; oysters and crabs; beavers, muskrats, possums, raccoons, and otters; sparrows, rails, wood ducks, and migrating waterfowl.[2]

Looking below the surface and comparing the two watersheds, however, is like comparing apples and oranges—both are fruit, but very different kinds. The tidal range on the Combahee is double that of the Blackwater River. The Blackwater River during Tubman's time likely was clear enough to see one's feet when walking in waist-deep water. Sea grasses would have been an important element of this ecosystem, providing ideal habitat for crabs and fish. Water in the Combahee likely would have been muddy, and sea grasses did not occur. Expansive tidal marshes including an abundant network of tidal creeks would have been a dominant element of the Combahee landscape. These marshes and meandering creeks provide important refuge and nursery habitat for shrimp, clams, and fish. William Elliott IV, an avid hunter and fisher who owned plantations on the nearby Chehaw and Ashepoo Rivers in the mid-nineteenth century, described in his memoir the "thick mass of grass that stretched upward six feet from the surface of the marsh" a few miles away from the lower Combahee River. By contrast, such expansive tidal marshes would not have been a dominant feature of the Blackwater River system, and the tidal rivers on Maryland's Eastern Shore would have been much broader than the tidal creeks of the Combahee. Crossing the open water would have been the challenge in Maryland. At low tide, water travel would have been limited on the tidal creeks of the Combahee River.[3]

Rice cultivation depended on the tides as well. In the Combahee River basin and other river basins in coastal South Carolina, enslaved laborers cleared cypress, tupelo, and black gum forests, creating a total of 240,206 acres of tidal and inland rice fields in the tidal freshwater regions of coastal rivers. The tidal freshwater region of the Combahee was an ideal environment for rice culture and supported an immensely productive and lucrative commercial rice industry. The amplitude of the flood tide (three to six feet) was high enough to channel in sufficient water to hold up the heads of the rice plants when the rice fields were flooded during the summer months, when the crop was maturing. During the ebb tide, excess water could be drawn off the rice fields to dry out the beds before the harvest in the fall months. On the Chesapeake, there was not enough tidal movement to manage rice, and the climate was not warm enough. On the other hand, the Chesapeake had prolific seafood and timber industries.[4]

In enslaved people's flight to freedom on the Combahee River, they would face the constant danger of snakes and alligators, particularly in June. To complicate matters, the muddy water made it impossible to see the bottom or guess its depth. The wetland vegetation made it easier to hide, but more difficult to see predators or slave catchers. And the quicksand-like "pluff" mud, the product of the oxidation of organic matter, made walking and running through the rice fields arduous. When Harriet Tubman came to coastal South Carolina to guide a group of freedom seekers who were scared, inexperienced, and desperate to secure their liberty, many aspects of the landscape were unfamiliar to her; her experience was on the Blackwater River, where the water was clearer, the danger from snakes and alligators was far smaller, and there were fewer mosquitoes and biting flies. Still, Tubman could draw on her considerable skills reading, surviving on, and leading groups of freedom seekers across the Eastern Shore landscape, and apply them to the South Carolina Lowcountry.

Because the rice economy that it supported proved so lucrative, the Combahee River became home to the winter country estates of some of South Carolina's most elite families. This story is about seven rice plantations on the lower Combahee. Located on the west side of the river were the Blake family's Bonny Hall Plantation and the Middleton family's Newport Plantation. The Heywards' Cypress Plantation was located on the east side of the river immediately across from Newport; south of Cypress were the Lowndeses' Oakland Plantation, the Kirklands' Rose Hill, the Nichollses' Longbrow, and the Pauls' Palmetto Plantation (more commonly called Paul's Place or Paul's Plantation). Decades after the Combahee River Raid, formerly enslaved men and women testified in their Civil War pension applications that the aforenamed planter families held them in bondage and exploited their labor on these plantations.

Planter families on the lower part of the Combahee were descendants of the first European settlers in Beaufort and Colleton Counties. Members of the Heyward and Middleton families had signed the Declaration of Independence. Decades later, in 1860, two Middleton descendants signed the South Carolina Ordinance of Secession. Members of the Blake, Middleton, Lowndes, and Heyward families all served as governors of South Carolina—several, in the cases of the Blakes and Middletons. Most of the families along the Combahee River were descended from wealthy and prominent families in England and the Caribbean; the Kirklands were an Upcountry family that had intermarried with prominent families in the South Carolina midlands.[5]

The Heyward family was the first to arrive in the Carolina Colony. Daniel Heyward immigrated to the Carolina Colony in 1672 from the county of Derby in England; he arrived less than ten years after King Charles II of England had given the land south of Virginia to eight lords proprietors. Heyward died in the Carolina Colony in 1684.[6]

The Middleton family was second to arrive. Henry Middleton was born in Twickenham, England, on the Thames River. His two sons, Arthur and

Edward Middleton, left England and emigrated first to Barbados, where they worked as merchants, then to the Carolina Colony, Edward arriving in 1678 and Arthur the following year. The Middletons became involved in the governance of the colony, serving as deputies of the lords proprietors and as members of the Lords Proprietors Council and the Grand Council. They also amassed large landholdings.[7]

Then came Benjamin Blake, founding ancestor of the Blake family. Blake was born in Bridgewater, England, and arrived in the Carolina Colony in 1683. He served as a captain in England's navy under his brother Admiral Robert Blake, commissioner of the navy and one of the most admired military commanders in England in the seventeenth century, when the English navy was becoming the largest and most powerful naval force in the world. In the Carolina Colony, Captain Blake served as deputy to the lords proprietors (though he was not a supporter of the Stuart dynasty in England) and a member of the Grand Council. He received large land grants, particularly in St. Bartholomew Parish on the north side of the Combahee River.[8]

The story of the Lowndes family is perhaps the most tragic of them all. Charles Lowndes was a member of the slaveholding and sugar-planting aristocracy of St. Christopher (St. Kitts), the largest of the Leeward Islands in the Caribbean, where he served in the Governor's Council before he immigrated to Carolina. In the mid-eighteenth century, Lowndes still had distant relatives in prominent political positions in England, including William Lowndes of Westminster and Thomas Lowndes of Overton, both of whom held seats in Parliament. Charles Lowndes left England sometime around 1713, at about twenty-three years of age; he arrived in St. Christopher at the moment when the British established rule over the island and opened up thousands of acres of the most fertile sugar-producing lands in the West Indies for settlement and investment. Lowndes married his cousin Ruth Rawlins, the daughter of a wealthy St. Christopher sugar planter. Both Lowndes and his father-in-law, Henry Rawlins, took advantage of emerging opportunities and settled lands formerly under French control, including an estate in St. Peter's Parish in Basseterre, which Henry Rawlins gave to his daughter before she married Charles in about 1717. Lowndes held political positions in St. Christopher commensurate with the rank of his and his in-laws' families, including representing St. Peter's Parish in the provincial council.[9]

Unfortunately for Lowndes, neither his political connections in England nor his prominence and land holdings in St. Christopher could save him from himself, or from ruin. His son Rawlins Lowndes, who was born in St. Christopher in 1720, told his children that his father "embarrassed his property by free living and unrestrained expenditure." Lowndes very well may have lived beyond his means, gambled to expand his sugar-planting enterprise, and tended toward ostentation in a futile attempt to keep up with the Rawlinses. He also may have been unable to compete in an industry in which sugar planters with small holdings were bought out and their estates consolidated into large sugar plantations, which tended to be owned by absentee investors living in England.[10]

As the 1720s progressed, Lowndes realized he needed greener pastures, a place where men with political connections and wealth had more opportunities for success. South Carolina seemed perfect. A full-fledged plantation society, Carolina must have felt to Lowndes like a British colony in the Caribbean. By 1708 it had become the only British North American colony in which the numbers of enslaved Blacks exceeded whites. The colony's enslaved labor force expanded exponentially after that: it rose 56 percent between 1710 and 1720 to 9,900; 102 percent to 20,000 in 1730; and more than 83 percent, to 36,700 in 1740. An important difference between the British Caribbean and Carolina colonies is that by the end of the seventeenth century, planters in the latter used enslaved labor to grow commercial crops, including rice, rather than sugar. In the 1720s, a decade before Lowndes arrived in the Carolina Colony, rice had become the colony's most successfully cultivated crop, both a staple food and an export crop. Demand for rice exploded in the 1730s, and exports rose from an annual average of 6,222,918 pounds in in the period 1728–1732 to 16,905,652 pounds in the years between 1738 and 1742. A decade after that exports had risen another 80 percent to 30,547,455 pounds. This exponential growth can in part be attributed to the British Parliament's relaxation of the Navigation Acts for rice in 1731, enabling South Carolina planters to export rice on British ships bound for southern Europe.[11]

Charles Lowndes arrived in the Carolina Colony at an opportune moment. Along with his wife, Ruth, and their sons, William, Charles, and Rawlins, he sailed to Charles Town (as Charleston was then called) in the 1730s, one of the gentlemen of great fortune whom the new colonial governor, Robert Johnson, reported came from the West Indies to see how they liked Carolina. Lowndes must have liked what he saw, because he decided to stay. Governor Johnson issued 500-acre units to Caribbean planters to encourage them to settle in the colony, and Lowndes purchased an additional two 500-acre tracts in Berkeley County on Goose Creek, a tributary of the Cooper River. This area had rich soil for growing rice in inland swamps and was popular among planters from the Caribbean. Lowndes soon took his place among wealthy planters such as Arthur Middleton and Robert Blake Jr., who also resided on rice plantations in Berkeley County, and he accepted a position as a major in the colonial militia.[12]

It appeared as if Lowndes had made a fresh start. But while he had left the West Indies, he had not left behind the spending habits that impelled him to leave his home in the first place. By February 1731, he was in debt: he owed James Crokatt, a Charleston merchant, £2,000 and did not have the cash to pay. Though he was able to secure a loan from local merchants and moneylenders Benjamin Godin and Benjamin de la Conseillere, the bills of exchange were drawn on a London merchant with whom Lowndes had previously done business, and they were payable to Godin in thirty days. Godin endorsed the bills to Crokatt, making himself liable for payment if the London merchant protested them—meaning the bills were presented and payment refused. To protect himself, Godin required Lowndes to take out a mortgage on his 1,000-acre Berkeley County plantation and to use it and ten members of his enslaved labor force as collateral. The London merchant did protest Lowndes's bills of exchange, and so Godin was entitled to foreclose on the mortgage on Lowndes's plantation within a year to pay Crokatt if Lowndes could not find another means to pay his debt. In order to buy himself more time to raise the funds and release himself from his financial obligation to Godin, Lowndes mortgaged his Goose Creek plantation, his rice and corn crops, twelve enslaved laborers, and household goods to his friend John Colleton. Mortgaging his rice crop greatly hindered Lowndes's prospects for raising the capital to pay his debts, for if Colleton foreclosed on the mortgage, Lowndes would lose everything.[13]

After receiving several renewals of the mortgage term from Colleton and making a number of unsuccessful attempts to secure a warrant for more land, Lowndes applied for a patent for a machine to process rice in preparation for export. The expansive rice industry had created a lot of competition. Lowndes was not the only entrepreneur to invent a labor-saving device for milling rice and to apply for an exclusive patent for it;

one of the earliest patented designs for a milling device consisted of two revolving wooden blocks with grooved channels to remove the outer husk of rice grains. Lowndes's design was probably neither the most effective nor the most efficient, and he did not receive a patent. He had gambled on a long shot and lost. Now he was running out of cards to play. Once again, Lowndes was unable to raise the capital to pay his debt when the mortgage came due in 1735. This time, however, Colleton chose not to renew. The colonial council rejected one of Lowndes's pending land claims, and he could not find a buyer for his Goose Creek plantation.[14]

It may have felt to Lowndes as if his world was collapsing. He prepared to carry out the unspeakable "Crime of Self Murder" but was interrupted by a visit from John Colleton. Lowndes's mental state did not improve. A few months later, in early 1736, he wrote Colleton, blaming officials for the "Violent Design of laying Hands on Himself" and declaring that he would clear his name or end his own life by shooting himself in the head or severing one of his arteries. Lowndes threatened to kill his own children as well, so that they might all be buried in one grave. Terrified, Ruth Lowndes left her husband and took their children with her.[15]

In May 1736, Lowndes arranged papers on a table, including an invitation to John Colleton to attend his funeral. He shaved, dressed, and then lay on the ground with his pistols pointed at both temples. This time there were no interruptions. But Charles Lowndes's tragic end did not prevent his descendants from achieving political prominence and business success in the thriving Carolina Colony.[16]

★★★★★★★★

The Heyward family represented perhaps the epitome of the Lowcountry rice aristocracy. They were among the earliest plantation owners, and their family tree branched far and wide over the centuries. Daniel Heyward's great-grandson, also named Daniel Heyward, was born on James Island in 1720. Sometime in the 1740s he settled into Old House Plantation, located on Hazzard's Creek, a tributary of the Broad River, which flows through Port Royal Sound and empties into the Atlantic Ocean. Daniel Heyward married three times—to Mary Miles in 1744, to Jane Elizabeth Gignilliat in 1763, and to Elizabeth Simons in 1771—and was widowed three times. He was the first member of the family to engage in tidal rice culture. In 1760 he began acquiring large tracts of rice lands in St. Bartholomew Parish along the upper portion of the Combahee River through grants, and established adjoining rice plantations, called Amsterdam and Rotterdam.[17]

By the time of his death in 1777, Daniel Heyward held 1,000 people in bondage—he brought some of his father's slaves from James Island but purchased many more African-born captives, using them to construct tidal rice fields along the Combahee. Daniel Heyward bequeathed the plantations—along with the skilled enslaved laborers who had constructed them—to his sons. The eldest, Thomas Heyward Jr., served as a member of the South Carolina Commons House of Assembly from 1772 to 1775 (along with his neighbor, Rawlins Lowndes, whom we've met, and who was elected Speaker in 1763). Thomas Heyward Jr. served as a delegate to the Continental Congress and, as noted earlier, was, along with Arthur Middleton, one of four South Carolinians to sign the Declaration of Independence. He was also a captain of South Carolina's colonial forces during the American Revolution. (Middleton's father had remained loyal to the Crown.) After the death of his father, Thomas Heyward Jr. inherited his father's best lands on the Combahee River. He made his home at White Hall Plantation, located near his father's Old House Plantation, facing the same creek and overlooking the same marsh. (George Washington, the new president, spent one night at White Hall Plantation in 1791.)[18]

Thomas's brother Nathaniel, a child of Daniel Heyward and his second wife, Jane Elizabeth Gignilliat, was born in 1766 in Charleston and spent much of his life on his father's Old House Plantation. He and his younger brother, Benjamin Heyward, inherited the smallest of their father's plantations. Nathaniel received an inland rice plantation near Old House and partially reclaimed tidal rice fields near the Combahee River.[19]

Nathaniel Heyward planted his inland rice fields for only one season before giving up after a storm damaged them. Inland swamp rice production was prone to natural disasters because it depended on natural irrigation. Planters and enslaved laborers learned to read the landscape and evaluate the vegetation and the soils in order to choose locations to construct the rice fields, taking advantage of water at higher elevations in the marsh and building embankments using the clay-like soil to trap freshwater in reservoirs. They then constructed quarter-drains for channeling the water downhill.[20]

Such fields were vulnerable to drought, when the reservoirs dried up. They were also vulnerable to hurricanes and other storms, when rainfall saturated the soils and produced sudden, violent torrents of water called freshets that breached these earthen embankments and washed away rice harvests. The expansion of land clearing and plowing in freshwater wetlands resulted in more frequent and severe flooding. By the end of the Revolutionary War, inland rice production in South Carolina and Georgia was less common than tidal rice production because of the difficulty of water control.[21]

According to a 1937 account written by Nathaniel's great-grandson Duncan Clinch Heyward (who was governor of South Carolina from 1903 to 1907), Nathaniel's first inland rice crop was almost ready to be harvested when a freshet destroyed the entire crop. Family lore had it that Nathaniel drove out to that field in his buggy the morning after the storm to survey the damage. He took one look at the water covering his fine rice crop, got back in the buggy, went home, and never planted the inland rice field again. Instead, Nathaniel drained the swamps on his partially reclaimed tidal rice fields (and on his brothers' larger tidal rice fields as well) and built his own empire.[22]

Nathaniel Heyward's wife, Henrietta Manigault, was the granddaughter of Gabriel Manigault, whose father, Pierre Manigault, was a French Huguenot refugee-turned-merchant believed to have amassed the largest fortune in South Carolina prior to the American Revolution (estimated to be in excess of $1 million, a colossal sum at the time). Gabriel Manigault continued his father's mercantile interests and expanded them to include export and import trade with the West Indies and northern colonies. By 1750 he had begun investing his fortune in rice lands and had acquired Silk Hope and Gowrie Plantations on Argyle Island, on the Savannah River in the Georgia Lowcountry.[23]

Nathaniel Heyward used a significant portion of his wife's dowry to acquire Lewisburg, Bluff, Rose Hill, and Pleasant Hill Plantations, along the upper reaches of the Combahee River. He used enslaved people on these plantations to reclaim the swamps and construct tidal rice fields. He also purchased his older brother Thomas's rice plantations and inherited his brother James's holdings. In the end, Nathaniel Hayward owned seventeen rice plantations on both sides of the Combahee River on which he planted

4,500 acres of rice. His descendants would dominate rice production in the entire American South.[24]

Tidal rice plantations are based on a simple principle of water control: they use the freshwater in river estuaries, where the water level rises and falls with the tides, to flood rice fields. Saltwater is denser than freshwater. Thus, freshwater floats atop saltwater, creating what is called the "wedge." The layering of freshwater at the surface of the estuary, on top of saltwater, makes it possible to tap the freshwater to flood the tidal rice field. Planters and enslaved laborers selected level land along rivers with tidal estuaries, accessing freshwater on either side, and constructed barriers and channels to direct freshwater into the fields at high tide and trap it there as the tide receded. This combination of freshwater and saltwater made for the only naturally irrigated soils in the colonies. By 1738, South Carolina rice planters were successfully producing rice along the Winyah Bay estuary and along the Waccamaw, Pee Dee, Santee, Cooper, Edisto, Ashepoo, and Combahee Rivers. Beginning in 1750, rice planters in Georgia, several of whom had migrated south from South Carolina, exploited Georgia's tidal rivers, the Savannah, Ogeechee, Altamaha, and Satilla, for rice production. These ideal conditions, where the fresh water layered atop the dense salt water, were located far enough upstream from the mouth of South Carolina and Georgia's tidal rivers, including the Combahee River, to reduce salinity.[25]

Reclamation of tidal swampland was, as Duncan Clinch Heyward wrote in his 1937 memoir, a "great undertaking." It required knowledge of the flora, fauna, and soils of the coastal wetlands that are spread along the coastal plains of South Carolina and Georgia alone, where cypress, tupelo, and sweet gum trees grow in tea-colored standing water and black, greasy soils with slow water permeability and higher water-holding capacity.[26]

It also required a large enslaved labor force of skilled and strong field hands, known as "Prime Hands," to uproot the broad, flaring trunks of bald cypresses (which could grow to up to twelve feet in diameter), along with the Spanish-moss-draped tupelo trees and sweet gum trees. They did this with hand tools, until they had made the ground, as historian Theodore Rosengarten describes it, "as level as a billiard table." Then they divided individual fields into quarter sections of ten to thirty acres each and constructed cross ditches and check banks with what Adam Hodgson, a Liverpool slave merchant turned abolitionist, termed "mathematical exactness" in his description of the rice fields on a plantation outside Charleston. The cross ditches and check banks served to trap incoming water at high tide and to maintain water levels within the fields as the rice matured. Lastly, they cut small channels across the fields to facilitate drainage. In the final stage of the "great undertaking," enslaved laborers planted rice on the floodplain.[27]

Reclaiming tidal swamps and constructing a hydraulic irrigation system required engineering and carpentry skills, as well as sheer brawn. Enslaved laborers built a temporary ditch and embankment around the entire field and then miles of networked permanent embankments—five to six feet tall (as tall as a man), approximately twelve to fifteen feet wide on top, and sixteen to twenty feet wide at the base—and inserted "plug trunks" deep into the embankments. According to David Doar, who was the last commercial planter to grow rice on the Santee River and who published a book about it in 1936, the "granddaddy" of these plug trunks was made of a hollowed-out cypress tree. A large plug was installed tightly to stop the water from flowing into it, acting, as Doar put it, like a "wooden spigot to a beer keg." As the technology became mechanized, these trunks resembled a wooden box with a wooden gate at each end of the box. On the river side, the gate slid up and down to let water in at high tide and out at low tide; the gate on the field side hinged open and closed as water flowed in and out. Enslaved laborers installed trunks with floodgates on the outer banks of the rice fields to channel water from the estuary into the fields. When it was time to flood the fields, the doors would swing open from the force of incoming water; they could also be kept closed to prevent water from entering or exiting. This allowed planters—via enslaved "trunkminders"—to control the flow of water into and out of tidal rice fields at critical moments in the rice production cycle. Even more enslaved labor was required to maintain the irrigation system, in particular to protect it against the threat of breaks in the embankments, which would allow water to rush in.[28]

★★★★★★★★

The Heyward, Middleton, Blake, and Lowndes families' founding ancestors voluntarily migrated from England, with the Middletons and Lowndeses trying their luck first in British colonies in the Caribbean before moving on to the Carolina Colony, where they sought new opportunities. Those enslaved people who worked for them had no such freedom of movement, of course. Sanko Van Dross and Manuel Bolze were two of those whose parents may have been born in western Africa and brought to a port in the Carolina Colony shackled in the hull of a slaving vessel.[29]

Between 1670 and 1866, an estimated 151,298 Africans were transported against their will to the South Carolina colony on 826 slaving voyages. These Africans had been captured and sold in the West African interior, marched to the coast, and imprisoned there, sometimes for months at a time, before being forced onto slave ships at ports from Senegambia and the offshore Atlantic islands to the Kingdom of Kongo. A smaller number— 850 human souls on four slaving vessels—were sold on the southeast coast of southern Africa and the Indian Ocean islands. Beginning in the 1750s, South Carolina's planters utilized enslaved labor to give birth to the region's commercial rice industry, which continued to expand exponentially.[30]

Rice cultivation grew in part because some of the enslaved laborers were already skilled rice farmers. On West Africa's Upper Guinea Coast, farmers had grown rice in the uplands, inland swamps, and mangrove swamps hundreds of years before the arrival of Europeans, the advent of transatlantic trade, and the subsequent emergence of the South Carolina and Georgia Lowcountry's commercial rice industry. They became coastal specialists and invented technology, including nurseries for rice seedlings and ways to harvest salt and reduce the salinity in coastal soils so that crops, such as rice, would grow. They constructed inland and mangrove rice fields, uprooting trees and expanding rice production farther away from their villages, and developed processing techniques to remove the husk, producing edible brown rice, and to remove the bran, to produce white rice suitable for the export market. In the mid-eighteenth century, at this critical moment in the evolution of the Lowcountry's most lucrative plantation economy, roughly 52 percent of the West African captives brought to South Carolina and Georgia had been sold at ports along West Africa's Upper Guinea Coast, in Senegambia and offshore Atlantic islands, Sierra Leone, and the Windward Coast.[31]

Sanko Van Dross's parents could have been among them, likely forcibly transported aboard a slaving vessel from a port in Sierra Leone. One such ship was the *Hare*, a sloop owned by brothers Samuel and William Vernon of Rhode Island. In 1754, its captain, Caleb Godfrey, embarked on the first of his two voyages as commander of the vessel. Godfrey and his crew purchased captives on the Upper Guinea Coast, specifically at Bance Island—a major slave-trading fort located at the farthest navigable point of the Sierra

Leone River. Though he purchased and embarked captives at Bance Island, Godfrey traveled as far north as the Rio Nuñez region in coastal Guinea to procure his complement of eighty-four captives.[32]

The Vernons wrote to Henry Laurens, a Charleston-based merchant, slave factor, and planter who became president of the Continental Congress, and his business partner, George Austin, requesting that their firm handle the sale of the *Hare*'s cargo in Charleston. Austin and Laurens was the largest slave-trading house in North America. It imported 8,000 African captives into Charleston's ports in the 1750s alone. In addition, Laurens was the leading Charleston factor serving Rhode Island slave traders. By 1756, when the *Hare* returned to Charleston with a cargo of captives for sale, Laurens had established a business relationship with Richard Oswald, the principal partner in the London trading firm that owned Bance Island. By the 1770s, trade in rice and captives from the Upper Guinea Coast had made Laurens one of the most successful slave factors in Charleston during the eighteenth century and one of the wealthiest planters in all of the British colonies.[33]

Approximately two months after its departure—and despite Laurens's warnings that Godfrey should take the human "cargo" to a more promising market in the Caribbean—the *Hare* disembarked its human cargo of sixty-three surviving captives in Charleston. They included twenty-two children, nine girls and thirteen boys. To announce the auction, Laurens placed an advertisement in the *South Carolina Gazette*. Though Laurens described the captives as "healthy" in the advertisement, he privately expressed his lack of confidence in Godfrey's ability to select "prime" Africans—only forty-two of his first complement sold on the day of the 1756 auction—or his ability to manage his crew, who deserted him shortly after the ship arrived in Charleston's harbor. Laurens described the remainder of the human cargo as "refuse slaves," too sick, infected with yaws (a contagious and at the time incurable skin disease), too small (three were very small children), or too old (six or eight were too old to perform heavy agricultural labor).[34]

According to Laurens, several planters were angry that they had traveled nearly a hundred miles to bid on such a cargo. Nonetheless, Laurens's brother-in-law Elias Ball seemed to have been a satisfied customer. Ball purchased six children, four boys and two girls, and noted their date of purchase, approximate ages, and newly given English first names in his plantation ledger. He named one girl of approximately ten years of age Priscilla, taking her—along with five other captives—back to his plantation on the

East Branch of South Carolina's Cooper River, on the South Carolina coast far north of the Combahee River.[35]

Another slave vessel, the *Black Joke* (sometimes spelled *Black-Joak*), also purchased its complement of captives on West Africa's Upper Guinea Coast along the Gambia River, another rice-growing subregion. It disembarked ninety captives in South Carolina in 1765, ending one of the most brutal slaving voyages in the region's recorded history. The chief mate who took over the ship after the captain died and who is identified only as Marshall flogged a baby to death with a cat-o'-nine-tails. According to Isaac Parker, one of the *Black Joke*'s crew members, this was because the baby "took sulk" and refused nourishment. The flogging took place in full view of the other captives, who watched helplessly through the "barricado," a wooden barrier intended to separate the crew from prisoners and defend against insurrections. To compound his sadism, Captain Marshall insisted that the baby's mother throw her own child's dead body overboard. Slave ship captains and crew members used violence and terror to subjugate those embarked on slaving vessels in western Africa. Between 1514 and 1866 these people numbered 10,643,598 on 34,448 voyages.[36]

Of the 151,298 African captives imported to South Carolina during the slave trade, a woman we know only as Priscilla is the sole example of a captive we have been able to trace from the slaving vessel on which she was transported through the Middle Passage to the plantation where she was enslaved (Comingtee Plantation). Unfortunately, Sanko Van Dross and Manuel Bolze's parents are not exceptions. We will never know where exactly they were born, or even the name of the slaving vessels in which they were brought to South Carolina.[37]

Likewise, little is known about the ancestors of the Blacks who were enslaved on the seven plantations on the lower Combahee River. In contrast to the Heyward, Middleton, Blake, Lowndes, and Kirkland families, the enslaved families' genealogies were neither recorded nor published. But veterans and widows who escaped in June 1863 kept the names of their parents and sometimes even their grandparents etched in their memories. Even decades after the raid Civil War, a handful of veterans and widows testified to US Bureau of Pensions officials that they had grown up with their fathers enslaved on the same plantations. They testified more infrequently about their mothers, because many were "titled" after their fathers. A "title" was a last name or a maiden name, and most people took their father's last name as their own (or, in the case of many women, until they married). It was not unusual for enslaved people to use surnames within the confines of enslaved communities to show familial relationships, maintain relationships with family members who had been sold away, or even to show that they belonged to a particular plantation community and slaveholder's family. To complicate things, enslaved people in the South Carolina Lowcountry did not always choose the name of the slaveholder who held them in bondage. Sometimes they chose the name of one who previously held them. This is likely because they wanted to enshrine their relatedness not to slaveholders but to family members from whom they had been separated. Often they chose a title that was completely unrelated to an enslaver. The titles Black people chose for themselves, however, were generally not recognized by white folks until after the end of the Civil War.

On the Middleton family's Newport Plantation, Wally Garrett testified, he was "titled" after his father and was never known or called by any name other than Wally Garrett. He testified that this was his "basket name," which, according to Lorenzo Dow Turner, the first linguist to study scientifically the Gullah Geechee language, was a pet name or a nickname by which family and close friends called an individual. It was different from the English name someone was known by in school or at work, for example, and was kept secret from those outside of the community. Until her first marriage, his sister Daphney Garrett Washington Wright was called Garrett after her father. Wally and Daphney's parents, Ofney and Lucinda Garrett, were enslaved with their children on Newport Plantation. Rachel Grant Washington (wife of Daphney Garrett Washington Wright's son Simon Washington) was titled after her father until her father died and her mother remarried. Afterward, people in the community called her by her stepfather's title, which was White.[38]

Across the Combahee from Bonny Hall and Newport on the Heyward family's Cypress Plantation, Sina Bolze Young Green and her younger brother, Cuffie Bolze, were enslaved with their father, Manuel Bolze; Neptune Nicholas with his father, Tobias Nicholas; William Hamilton with his father, who was also named William Hamilton; and Pool Sellers with his mother, Mollie. Robert Frazier was held in bondage on Cypress Plantation with his parents, Horris and Dolly Heyward. Robert's parents took the slaveholder's title; Robert chose his own surname.[39]

Parent-child relationships formed the foundation of multigenerational en-slaved families on the lower portion of the Combahee River. The majority of the aforementioned parents had the relatively good fortune to be together with their children, though some were separated from them. According to the pension files, many other veterans and widows seem to have forgotten their parents' names or at least didn't provide them—though it is possible that the pension officials never asked them. One reason more of these en-slaved families on the Combahee were not separated is they were held in bondage by the wealthiest and most politically powerful families in South Carolina, families whose wealth was derived from the growth of the com-mercial rice industry. Thus, these planter families typically retained rather than sold those whom they held in bondage. Unlike the declining tobacco industry in the Chesapeake region, Carolina Gold—the long-grain rice so called for the golden hue of its outer hull—made the rice planters all along the Combahee the wealthiest planters in British North America during the Revolutionary War, with the largest slave holdings in the South until 1850.

That is, until June 2, 1863.

★★★★★★★★

If the Lowndes family's earliest ancestor in South Carolina was a tragic figure, the founder of the Kirkland family was the most colorful. In contrast to the Heyward, Middleton, Blake, and Lowndes families, the Kirklands were not from England or English colonies in the Caribbean, and they were not among the oldest and wealthiest families to settle the South Carolina Lowcountry. Instead, the Kirklands had roots in Berwickshire, Scotland. They immigrated to the American colonies before the Revolutionary War and settled in Pennsylvania, Massachusetts, Virginia, and South Carolina. In the case of the last, they chose the Upcountry—Old Ninety-Six District, Craven County, and Edgefield District—in the 1750s.[40]

In the meantime, the commercial rice economy continued to grow. After a slight rise in production to 39,903,225 pounds annually between 1758 and 1762, South Carolina rice exports practically doubled, rising to 66,327,975 pound annually between 1768 and 1772. As South Carolina's commercial rice industry boomed, South Carolina planters migrated south to Georgia, reclaiming swamplands and jump-starting the commercial rice industry there, accounting for additional significant growth in rice exports. On the eve of the American Revolution, the Lowcountry was by far the wealthiest region in British North America.[41]

Like other migrants to the Lowcountry, the Kirklands went in search of gold, Carolina Gold. This variety of rice dominated South Carolina's commercial rice economy until the 1850s. Until the American Revolution, Moses Kirkland was known as a "backcountry settler," because he knew every inch of the Carolina Upcountry, every road, trail, and inhabitant. He was also a planter, owning more than 11,000 acres from South Carolina's Santee River to Alabama's Tombigbee River and holding approximately sixty enslaved laborers in bondage. Kirkland also operated a large saw-mill and gristmill, owned a ferry, and held a number of local offices in the Upcountry. Moses Kirkland made a respectable fortune before the Revolution from milling, speculating in land, and exploiting the labor of the people he held in bondage.[42]

A May 1776 issue of the *Pennsylvania Gazette* described Moses Kirkland as between fifty and sixty years of age, and having a "swarthy complexion" and wearing "his own gray hair tied behind." Prior to June 1775, Kirkland had served as a lieutenant colonel in the Provincial Militia of Rangers for the lower part of the Broad and Saluda Rivers. He betrayed his regiment when he sent a message to Colonel Thomas Fletchall, a Tory military commander, informing him that ammunition was being stored at the courthouse in the town of Ninety-Six. Kirkland promised that he would not offer any resist-ance if Fletchall's forces came and seized it. When Fletchall's two hundred horsemen arrived to do just that, Kirkland not only surrendered the ammu-nition but deserted to the Royalist side. He led his and Captain Ezekiel Polk's Rangers to join Fletchall's troops. Kirkland may have been motivated by his belief that Upcountry men like himself should not give up their allegiance to King George III in exchange for a risky new form of government.[43]

Kirkland became, as a result, one the most wanted men in South Carolina. He donned a disguise and traveled the backroads from Ninety-Six to Charleston, eluding both arrest and guards stationed to capture him. When he arrived in Charleston he was welcomed by the royal governor, Lord William Campbell, who offered Kirkland a commission and gave him correspondence to deliver to supporters in the Upcountry.[44]

Returning home, Kirkland went right to work and made plans to attack Fort Charlotte, in Old Ninety-Six District, but the Provincial Congress, which had been created in January 1775 to replace the royalist governing body, received intelligence of the impending attack and went to arrest him. Learning that his plan had been revealed and the Provincial Congress's forces were plotting to arrest him, Kirkland went into hiding. Legend has it that he disguised his twelve-year-old son in a girl's dress and a cap with curls sewed into the front. He mounted the child in the saddle in front of him and rode two hundred miles of backroads back to Charleston and Lord Campbell's mansion. Lord Campbell once again received Kirkland and revealed to him the Crown's plans to wage a three-pronged attack on Charleston, thereby putting an end to the rebellion. The first prong consisted of using Cherokee and other tribes as allies as well as men from the Upcountry; the second was a coastal invasion by the British fleet; and the third would involve deploying the British army from Boston at Charleston. As concerns the last prong, Governor Campbell asked Kirkland to be his emissary to General Thomas Gage, commander of the British army in Boston, and to inform Gage of the role his troops would play in the attack. Campbell entrusted Kirkland with a letter for Gage, attesting to Kirkland's "attachment to government" for which he had "sacrificed his all," and a letter of introduction for Colonel John Stuart, the king's superintendent of southern Indian affairs in Florida.[45]

Kirkland would never deliver these letters. He and his son traveled north along the coast toward Virginia, where they were scheduled to transfer to a ship that would take him to Boston. The vessel was waylaid by forces of the Provincial Congress, and Kirkland was imprisoned; the letters he carried were later made public as evidence of King George's plot to use Native Americans in the fight against the colonists.[46]

After the British were defeated, Kirkland had his estate confiscated for bearing "commissions, civil or military, under the British government, since the conquest of the Province," according to a March 1782 edition of the *Royal Gazette*. Legislative acts passed in South Carolina and Georgia in February and May 1782, respectively, banished Kirkland and his family from the state. Moses Kirkland Sr. died at sea traveling to London to present his claim for restoration. His son Moses Kirkland Jr. successfully petitioned the General Assembly of South Carolina in December 1799 to repeal the act of confiscation and restore to him his father's property.[47]

Other stories that run parallel to those of the Kirklands and Lowndeses are those of the enslaved people who were liberated in the Combahee River Raid, the same raid that destroyed those wealthy families' plantations. When he died, sometime around 1898, Sanko Van Dross, Mingo Van Dross's father, was one of the oldest members of the formerly enslaved communities in the cluster of Combahee River rice plantations. Mingo testified that his father died at age 125, and while Sanko Van Dross was certainly an Old Head, that has to have been an exaggeration; indeed, most born into slavery did not live even half that long. However, had it been true, it would have meant that Sanko Van Dross had been born in the mid-1770s, roughly around the time Moses Kirkland arrived in the South Carolina Upcountry.[48]

★★★★★★★★

Though the slave trade into South Carolina slowed after the American Revolution, it was still large compared to Maryland's. Between 1776 and 1800, 17,544 captives from 123 slaving voyages ended their terrible journey at South Carolina and Georgia's ports. Approximately 13 percent of those imported into South Carolina during this quarter century embarked on slaving vessels in ports in West-Central Africa. Though captives originating there made up a small slice of the supply relative to the Upper Guinea Coast's share, the proportions would shift dramatically after the turn of the nineteenth century.[49]

In the last quarter of the eighteenth century, roughly 42 percent of captives had been purchased on West Africa's Upper Guinea Coast; 25 percent, the next largest group, embarked on slaving vessels in West Africa's Gold Coast ports. Trade in Gold Coast captives spiked when the gold trade (for which the coast was named, of course) waned around 1700. By the end of the eighteenth century there had been an escalation in the transatlantic trade in slaves. The *General Huth* was one of the slave ships that arrived in Charleston in 1785 from the Gold Coast with 158 captives—44 men, 39 women, 35 boys, and 40 girls—on board.[50]

In the densely populated subregion of West-Central Africa—present-day Cameroon, Angola, and Democratic Republic of Congo—roughly four hundred years of succession disputes and internal conflicts, exacerbated by Portuguese missionaries, traders, and mercenaries, generated an elastic supply of war captives vulnerable to being exported to the New World. The slaving vessels that transported them were significantly larger than those that skipped through ports in the relatively sparsely populated Upper Guinea Coast. In 1784, the 700-ton *Comte du Nord*, a British slaver, embarked 701 captives at the West-Central African port of Malembo; the captain, James Penny, had been "laid in" for 1,000 captives, but French opposition on the coast drove up prices and prompted Penny to set sail before he had purchased his full complement. In the Middle Passage, mortality was high, despite the presence of four surgeons, medicines, wine, livestock, and a large hospital; 63 captives, or 9 percent, died as a result of a measles outbreak that infected as many as 300 captives at one time. One or both of Manuel Bolze's parents may have been among those on the *Comte du Nord* who made it to the New World alive; Manuel's given name may suggest that he or his parents could have been forced aboard a slaving vessel in West-Central Africa, where most people in the Kingdom of Kongo had converted to Catholicism by the mid- to late eighteenth century.[51]

By 1785, South Carolina's legislators had begun to debate the importation of captives and were under pressure to temporarily halt slave imports, an action that immediately affected the number of slaving vessels disembarking captives at Charleston's harbor. At approximately the same time, abolitionists in Britain were raising concerns about the brutality of the trade. Nationally, opposition to the traffic in human cargo manifested in a series of acts in the US Congress that would ultimately conclude by outlawing the transatlantic slave trade; the first of these was the Slave Trade Act of 1794. The passage of the 1794 act dramatically decreased the number of slaving vessels landing in American ports and resulted in vessels landing instead in ports, such as Havana, where slave trading was unrestricted. However, when prices for slaves rose, trafficking in human "cargo," usually to smaller ports in South Carolina and Georgia, became too attractive for slave traders and factors to resist.[52]

Records from the slave ship *Nancy* illuminate how the clandestine trade took place after 1794 and how slave trading operated in South Carolina and Georgia's smaller ports. They also foreshadow how African captives were brought into the Lowcountry decades after the passage of the Act Prohibiting the Importation of Slaves, which took effect on January 1, 1808.

A few weeks after the *Nancy* arrived in South Carolina in December 1801, the sixty-four captives it transported against their will were disembarked and left by the slave ship captain. Captain Charles Clark wrote to slave ship owner James DeWolf that the "cargo" had been left in a strange land to fend for themselves "on the beach to the northward of Charleston." "They had no clothes," he added, "and no shelter except for the sandhills and cedar trees." Clark was not the only slave trader risking seizure of his ship, goods, and furniture to defy the 1794 act in the hopes of making a profit. He reported to DeWolf that slaves "come in town 2 or 3 hundred some nights." Slave traders landed "them outside the harbor and march them in at night." The DeWolf family owned approximately twenty-five slaving vessels, all of which legally disembarked captives in South Carolina and Georgia ports, the overwhelming majority (2,235 captives between 1801 and 1807) in South Carolina. Their trafficking in human "cargo" continued beyond 1808 through members of their extended family, such as Charles Collins, collector of the customs house in Bristol, Rhode Island, and brother-in-law of James DeWolf (who acted as captain on four documented slaving voyages). In a report written in January 1802, Captain Clark predicted that more ships would embark captives on the African coast, sail to Havana, and then illegally sail to Charleston to sell their "cargo" there: "14 vessels belonging to the U. States, a great part of them for Charleston."[53]

After the South Carolina legislature approved a bill in November 1803 to reopen the legal trade in African captives, a trade that remained active until 1825, West-Central Africa continued to supply the overwhelming majority of captives—approximately 40 percent—taken to New World ports, including to South Carolina. When abolition went into effect in 1807 in Great Britain and its colonial possessions, a small number of slaving vessels defied the ban and continued to trade. In order to prevent competitors' slaving vessels from reaching their debarkation points, the Royal Navy's West Africa Squadron policed the Atlantic Ocean between West Africa and the New World. British naval vessels actively patrolled rivers and inlets up and down the Upper Guinea Coast, capturing a number of slaving vessels and confiscating those found aboard. The West Africa Squadron impeded some slaving voyages to American ports, such as Charleston, but many got through. Little wonder—after 1807, the West Africa Squadron rarely used more than six ships to patrol 3,000 miles of western Africa's coastline.[54]

Article I, Section 9 of the US Constitution specified that the transatlantic slave trade could not be banned, and it wasn't until January 1, 1808, when the United States followed the British in abolishing the legal trade in captives. However, this did little to stop the importation of African captives into the Lowcountry, which continued well into the 1850s. The mechanisms of capture, enslavement, and sale, and the conditions facilitating those— warfare, judicial processes, drought and famine, and kidnapping in western Africa—meant that the illegal trade continued to operate at a fever pitch. Legal slave trading may have waned in major ports such as Charleston and Savannah, but there were plenty of smaller ports in the Lowcountry where it persisted and made slavers a handsome profit. These smaller ports' lack of visibility made them impossible to monitor—if anyone was even trying. Enforcing the ban was nearly impossible. South Carolina and Georgia rice planters had threatened in 1787 not to ratify the new US Constitution if the international slave trade to the United States was abolished before 1808. There was little political will to enforce the Act Prohibiting the Importation of Slaves in the region, and demand remained high. Blacks enslaved on Lowcountry rice plantations died at twice the rates as those enslaved on cotton plantations elsewhere in the South, and so rice planters continued to hunt for fresh supplies of enslaved labor practically up until the Civil War.[55]

★★★★★★★★

Meanwhile, Daniel Heyward, the first in the Heyward family to reclaim tidal swamps and acquire tidal rice lands, had two sons with his first wife, Mary Miles. Both sons played important roles on the Combahee River. The elder, Thomas Heyward Jr.—who, as noted earlier, signed the Declaration of Independence—and his first wife, Elizabeth Matthews, had one surviving son, also named Daniel. Daniel married Ann Trezevant in 1795, then died a year later. The younger Daniel Heyward left a young daughter, Elizabeth Mathews Heyward. When Elizabeth was three years old, her mother married again, to Nicholas Cruger, who was from a family of merchants based in New York City, St. Croix, and Charleston. In 1802, the Crugers sued both Elizabeth's grandfather, Thomas Heyward Sr., who was still alive and trustee of the estate she inherited from her father, and her great-uncle Nathaniel Heyward. They accused Thomas Heyward Sr. of mismanaging Elizabeth's trust and Nathaniel Heyward of taking property actually bequeathed to Elizabeth for himself. The trust was likely designed to protect the property Elizabeth inherited from her father from being seized for debts. The Crugers won this case as well as the right to manage Elizabeth's trust. Four years later, the Crugers sued Thomas Heyward Sr. again for failing to turn over the deed to one of the properties bequeathed to Elizabeth.[56]

Though the Crugers lost the second suit, the harm done to family relations was irreparable. Seven-year-old Elizabeth was permanently alienated from the two most prominent members of her father's family. From the age of three, she was raised with her mother, stepfather, and five Cruger stepsiblings, including Sarah Cruger, in New York City and South Carolina. After her marriage to James Hamilton in South Carolina in 1813, Elizabeth continued to maintain ties to the family in which she was raised, taking all eleven of the children she bore to New York to spend the summers with her Cruger relatives. Despite the broken family ties, however, Elizabeth remained a Heyward, which is what mattered most in antebellum South Carolina aristocracy.[57]

Typically, unmarried women who owned slaves routinely signed marriage settlements or contracts with their intended husbands before (and sometimes after) their wedding to maintain control of property they owned, were bequeathed, or otherwise had acquired before and during their marriages, protect it from their husbands' control and seizure by their husbands' creditors, and pass it down to the next generation as they saw fit. James Hamilton may have been opposed to signing a marriage settlement, or perhaps Elizabeth was reluctant to assert her rights to make such an agreement with her husband before their marriage. It seems unlikely that the Heyward family would not have pressed the issue, because Elizabeth's inheritance from her father's estate made her one of the wealthiest women in coastal South Carolina—she brought into the marriage three plantations, two hundred enslaved people, and $50,000 in stock in the Charleston Bank of the United States. In any case, unhindered by a marriage settlement, Hamilton squandered much of his wife's wealth. Hamilton also played roles in politics. While serving as intendant mayor of Charleston, he deployed the militia to arrest suspects accused of what is called the Vesey Insurrection Plot, named after Denmark Vesey, a freed black pastor who was accused of fomenting a major insurrection in 1822. Hamilton supported the Court of Magistrates and Freeholders by ordering the executions of thirty-five enslaved and freed men found guilty of planning the insurrection, including Vesey, and the deportations of others. He subsequently served in the US House of Representatives (1822–1829) and then as governor of South Carolina (1830–1832).[58]

Daniel Heyward and Mary Miles Heyward's younger son, William Heyward, married Hannah Shubrick in 1778; William and Hannah's son William Heyward Jr. was born in 1779, probably at Old House Plantation in Granville. The elder William Heyward was the older half-brother of Nathaniel Heyward, who when he died in 1851 was both the richest man in the South and the largest slave owner. There were a lot of Heywards. William and Nathaniel's father, Daniel Heyward, was, as we've seen, married and widowed three times. William Heyward was Daniel Heyward's son by his first marriage and Nathaniel was his son by his second. In 1804,

William Heyward's son and Nathaniel Heyward's half-nephew, William Jr., married Sarah Cruger, Elizabeth Heyward Hamilton's stepsister with whom she grew up in New York City.[59]

★★★★★★★★

The overwhelming majority of enslaved people could not trace their family trees, nor did they leave written accounts. The only way to recover their names and to begin to tell their stories has been through the documents of enslavers, which generally list enslaved people by first names only, no titles. That's also the case with those who were enslaved on the Combahee River on June 2, 1863. However, the postwar pension file testimonies offer a guide; they allow us to see enslaved family groupings in the slavers' documents. Some of the earliest come from the Heyward family.

On January 10, 1817, Hannah Shubrick Heyward sold seventy-six enslaved people with the "issue and increase" of the female slaves to her son William Heyward Jr. (who was William C. Heyward's father and, as we have seen, Nathaniel Heyward's half-nephew), for the sum of $33,714.30. Thus any future children whom the female slaves would bear were sold before conception. The same day, William Heyward mortgaged the same seventy-six slaves back to his mother for $136,000, four times the original purchase price. Historian Walter Johnson has argued that the economy of the antebellum South was built on the monetary value intrinsic to the bodies of enslaved people and its translation to labor, both productive and reproductive. Planters routinely used enslaved people as collateral in credit transactions. The value existed whether or not a sale of the enslaved people actually took place. And unsold slaves were a much more valuable and reliable investment than land, stocks, or bonds, because they could be easily converted into cash. Credit arrangements like that between mother and son—a bill of sale combined with a mortgage—were fairly common in other parts of the South, such as cotton plantations in southern Louisiana, particularly during the cotton boom a decade or so before the Civil War. From their examples, we can be fairly certain that Heyward used this credit arrangement to take out a loan from his mother and secured it with slaves. It was unlikely that William Heyward would default on loan payments to his own mother, and it is even more unlikely that she would collect the debt if he did. It seems, instead, that the family was shifting its assets from one generation to the next. He would likely inherit the enslaved people eventually from his mother's estate.[60]

Both documents, the bill of sale and the mortgage, itemize many of the same enslaved people. By the terms of the agreement, if William Heyward defaulted on the loan and failed to make two payments of $68,000, his mother could take the slaves back into her custody and dispose of them as she saw fit. On both the bill of sale and mortgage, the names "Cuffie, Sina, Amelia, Martin, Catey, Manuel, Primus" are all written together on the same line. They refer to Cuffie and Sina, who were Manuel Bolze's parents; Manuel's wife, Amelia; and Manuel's brother Primus. (Manuel and Amelia were the parents of Sina Bolze Young Green and Cuffie Bolze, who were named after their grandparents. Primus was the father of Peggy Simmons Moultrie Brown. The younger Sina, the younger Cuffie, and Peggy were first cousins of Relia Middleton and Jack and Primus Barnwell.) In 1818, William Heyward Jr. purchased thirty-five enslaved people from Sarah Graves for $17,000, including two female slaves, listed as "Peggy, Daphne." They were likely Peggy Simmons Moultrie Brown and her mother. Without a larger family grouping, it is difficult to confirm whether it was in fact them. This is what we know about the grandparents of the Blacks enslaved on Combahee River rice plantations before the Civil War began.[61]

The enslaved communities held in bondage on the Combahee plantations were the antithesis of the planter aristocracy. They carried no material wealth, property, and political influence. Yet they had their own internal hierarchy, one largely built on age. Those considered Old Heads—born between 1780 and 1823 and married many years before the Civil War began—commanded respect from younger enslaved people, and sometimes less stringent work regimes from the planter family that held them in bondage. Younger members of the enslaved community "grew up under," as widow Elsey Jones Higgins said, the Old Heads. Isaac DeCauster, an Old Head himself who had been enslaved on Longbrow Plantation, testified in his pension file that he was "raised up under" Old Head Andrew Wyatt on Paul's Place. Only a handful of elderly enslaved Blacks remained on the Combahee River plantations in early June 1863.[62]

William Heyward Jr. continued to buy enslaved people whose labor he may have exploited in reclaiming swamps and expanding his plantation enterprise. For example, on March 22, 1822, John Huger Dawson sold eighty-one enslaved people for $39,500 to William Heyward Jr., who then the same day mortgaged the same eighty-one people back to Dawson for $79,000—more than twice the purchase price for them. It is not clear whether there was any familial relationship between Dawson and Heyward, so it may have been strictly a business transaction. Heyward had used eighty-one people as collateral to borrow $79,000 from Dawson and he kept his enslaved labor force. The bondspeople would remain in Heyward's possession if he repaid his debt. He must have made the payments.[63]

An enslaved family, "Hannah, Venus, Dinah, Priscilla, Frank, Bransom," the names all written on one line, is listed on the bill of sale. We don't know who Venus, Dinah, and Priscilla were. But Hannah was the mother of March Chisolm. Years later, Charles Nicholas and Moses Simmons would testify to the US Bureau of Pensions that they knew March Chisolm during his lifetime; they were all likely born and "raised on the same plantation," Cypress, and they "belonged" to (that is, were enslaved by) the same owner, William C. Heyward. Neptune Nicholas wrote a letter in his own handwriting stating that he knew March Chisolm "from a boy." Charles Nicholas added that he and March Chisolm "lived in the same house."[64]

The "Frank" listed on the bill of sale may be Frank Lyons. However, it is not possible to confirm that without knowing the names of Frank Lyons's parents or siblings, as we have no documentation such as a pension file or a Freedmen's Bank account application for him. Lucius Robinson and Edward Brown remembered that Frank married Venus Proctor Higgins on Cypress Plantation before the war. Venus is listed on the 1822 Heyward bill of sale/mortgage. But Venus Proctor Higgins, who after Frank Lyons's death married for the third time, to July Osborne (who was also enslaved at Cypress), did not include her own testimony in her application for a widow's pension under Osborne's name, and without knowledge of her approximate age and the names of her family members, we can't know whether she is the Venus sold with March, his family, and Frank in 1822. But we do know that in 1863, both March Chisolm and Frank Lyons were Old Heads on William C. Heyward's Cypress Plantation.[65]

William Heyward Jr. also engaged in slave trading on behalf of others. In 1823, he acted as a trustee, along with Charleston attorney Henry N. Cruger, in purchasing eighteen slaves for $5,630 from C. C. Keith, who was acting as the administrator of the estate of Dr. Matthew Irvine, a medical doctor in Charleston. The slaves were to be held in trust for Catherine De Nully Hassell (the bill of sale refers to a trust dated November 23, 1823, which could have been Hassell's marriage settlement, though the deed itself is not available; it may have been lost when General Sherman's forces burned the municipal archives in Beaufort and Colleton Counties). Henry N. Cruger was undoubtedly related to Heyward's wife, Sarah Cruger Heyward. And, according to the deed, James Hamilton—who, as we have seen, was Sarah Cruger Heyward's brother-in-law—paid "consideration money" to Heyward and Cruger as trustees to manage Hassell's property.[66]

Among the eighteen enslaved people itemized on the 1823 bill of sale, the names of two, Prince and Tyra, are written side by side, without even a comma separating them—exactly as they lived for decades. Tyra Polite later testified in her application for a widow's pension that she had been married to Prince Polite under the title Tyra Joiner or Tyra Brown (her memory of which title she had used during slavery times varied), and that none of her children had been "prayed for at infancy," indicating that they were not baptized as children. In their 1891 testimonies on Tyra Polite's behalf, Andrew Wyatt and Joan Legare stated that they had known Tyra Polite for "upwards of 50 years." Andrew Wyatt also offered that he lived on an "adjoining plantation," while Joan Legare maintained that she, Prince, and Tyra had been "slaves of the same owner and resided on the same plantation." Legare knew that one Tony Mintus had married the couple "under the slave custom," an expression referring to a ceremony without legal sanction. According to historian Tera Hunter, enslaved people were married "till death or buckra"— that is, white folks—did them part. Joan's husband, Tooman Legare, also came forward to state that he had known Tyra Polite since she "was a little girl"; they lived "on the same place." He remembered attending the Polites' wedding and knew they were "both very young when they got married." Joan and Tooman's daughter Phoebe Frazier told the pension official that she had known Tyra Polite as a "married woman" ever since she was a child.[67]

The testimony from Tooman Legare, Joan Legare, and Phoebe Frazier is as important as the 1833 bill of sale in which William Heyward Jr. acted as trustee, because Tooman and Joan Legare were Old Heads whom William Heyward Jr.'s son William C. Heyward purchased from his brother Dr. James Heyward in 1848. Tyra Polite's pension file provides one last clue of where she was held in bondage on June 2, 1863: she testified that she and Prince were married at Hickory Hill (where several people who had been held in bondage by William Lennox Kirkland Jr. lived after the war).[68]

Not every transaction listing people enslaved on the lower Combahee River has been salvaged. One missing set of documentation involves the enslaved people whom Thomas Rhett Smith and his wife, Anne Rebecca

Skirving Smith, sold to planters on the Combahee River. This was likely part of a sale from Anne Smith's separate estate, which she inherited from her father, in order to reduce the debts encumbering his estate. Moses Simmons testified in April 1901: "I was born on Cypress Plantation, Combahee River about 1833. . . . I was born a slave to William C. Heyward at Combahee River." Moses continued: "My father's name was Isaac Simmons; he belonged to Mrs. Smith. His father before him was called Simmons."[69]

Margaret Kelly Simmons, the widow of Joshua Simmons, Moses Simmons's eldest brother, testified that her husband "was born right here on Cypress Plantation on Mr. Heyward's Place." She too had been born and raised on Cypress and "knew him from the time she was a little girl." If the transaction in fact took place around 1823, before Joshua Simmons's birth, then Smith may have sold Isaac Simmons to William C. Heyward's father, William Heyward Jr. Thus the brothers Joshua, Moses, and Jim Simmons were all born on Cypress Plantation. Joshua Simmons and Margaret Kelly were married by Billy Higgins, and Moses Simmons and his first wife, Christie Anne, were also married on Cypress Plantation "in slave time," as Moses put it.[70]

Another piece of evidence suggesting that Anne Smith likely held Isaac Simmons in bondage and then gave him away or sold him is another slave transaction for which the documentation is missing: one between Thomas Rhett Smith and the Heywards. A man named Stephen Simmons testified in April 1901 that he "was born a slave to Tom Wright Smith, Plantation about three miles from here." His "father was July Simmons also a slave to Tom Wright Smith," who was almost certainly Thomas Rhett Smith. Stephen's "grandfather also was called Simmons." Unfortunately, there is no way to determine if Isaac Simmons (the father of Joshua, Moses, and James) and July Simmons (the father of Stephen) were related or, if not, why they chose the same title.[71]

William C. Heyward purchased Cypress Plantation, on which Cuffie and Sina and their children Manuel, Primus, and Sarah were all enslaved, from his father, William Heyward Jr., in 1836 for $100,000. Cuffie and Sina's grandchildren Sina Green, Cuffie Bolze, Peggy Brown, Relia Middleton, and Jack and Primus Barnwell were born in bondage on Cypress Plantation. Heyward combined this tract with a second 437-acre tract south of the causeway to Combahee Ferry, which he purchased from Nathaniel Heyward for $100,000. William C. Heyward was related to Nathaniel Heyward—as noted earlier, William C.'s father was Nathaniel's half-nephew—which shows the distant relationship between the Heyward family member who made a fortune on the upper Combahee and the lower Combahee planter affected by the raid.[72]

The ferry, incidentally, also demonstrates the linkages between the planter families along the Combahee. Combahee Ferry was chartered in 1715 by the South Carolina General Assembly, which authorized a ferry over the river in 1733. The following year, William Bull laid out a new town of 100 acres, 119 lots, a chapel, a free school, and 70 common acres, named Radnor and located at the Combahee Ferry landing on the road from Charleston to Port Royal. In 1741, the General Assembly approved the construction of a bridge over the Combahee River to Radnor, after which the ferry ceased to operate. At some point the bridge collapsed, and in 1766, a rope ferry replaced the bridge. Radnor was a market town and operated as a significant transportation center for unloading and loading ships sailing between Charleston and Port Royal. Subsequently Radnor was incorporated into the Middletons' Newport Plantation. Arthur Middleton Jr. (who, as noted earlier, signed the Declaration of Independence) was granted the ferry charter in 1831.[73]

★★★★★★★★

Though they too were plantation owners, the Kirklands lived in a world quite apart from that of the Heywards, Middletons, Blakes, and Lowndeses. As we've seen, the Kirklands were outsiders to the Combahee River rice aristocracy because they had moved to the Lowcountry from the Upcountry, and were originally from Scotland instead of England. They were not grandees and did not devote their lives to managing their plantations or to public service. Instead, many of the Kirklands pursued professions—medicine in particular.

Moses Kirkland Sr.'s grandnephew Dr. Joseph Kirkland, a medical doctor, married Marianne Kennan Guerard (widow of Governor Benjamin Guerard) of Charleston in 1795. When Joseph Kirkland died during a yellow fever epidemic in Charleston in 1817, his estate provided for his wife's nephew, William Lennox Moultrie, to be sent to medical school in Philadelphia and kept clothed while he pursued his professional education. And Joseph and Marianne's son William Lennox Kirkland Sr., a medical doctor like his father, married Mary Anna Lynah in 1824. Lynah's father,

Edward Lynah, had been born in Ireland and served as surgeon general of South Carolina after the American Revolution.[74]

Dr. William Lennox Kirkland Sr. established himself on the lower Combahee River. Three years later, after his father-in-law, Dr. Thomas E. Lynah, defaulted on a bond, William Lennox Kirkland received a judgment against him in the Charleston Court of Common Pleas. He purchased three tracts belonging to Edward Lynah's estate: 352 acres of Laurel Spring Plantation, including a rice mill; 1,670 acres of the Laurel Hill Plantation; and 1,300 acres of pineland. The three tracts were combined into one and renamed Laurel Hill. In 1828, William Lennox Kirkland Sr., like his father, died of fever, leaving Mary Anna a widow at the age of twenty-eight to raise their infant son alone.[75]

As the Kirklands' history demonstrates, the Combahee story is marked by disease. Malaria and the mosquitoes that carry the disease were byproducts of growing rice in standing water. The single-celled parasites that cause malaria, in the genus *Plasmodium*, were spread by female *Anopheles quadrimaculatus* mosquitoes, which bred in the freshwater swamps where Lowcountry planters produced rice. The mosquitoes bit hosts infected with the parasite and sucked their blood in order to nourish their eggs, and then with another bite transmitted the parasite to a second host. By the eighteenth century, medical science had already begun to make the connection between mosquitoes and infectious disease, and early Carolina settlers certainly recognized it. A British trader in the 1740s described mosquitoes as "long sharp Flies, whose Venom . . . is as Baleful as that of a Rattle Snake."[76]

Enslaved African laborers who had originated in western Africa and the Caribbean, where *Plasmodium falciparum* was endemic, could both be carriers of the disease and have built up some immunity to it. They introduced the disease to the Carolina colony and acted as the host population. As Carolina's plantation economy took hold in the last years of the seventeenth century, the enslaved population expanded rapidly, soon outnumbering the white population and further spreading *P. falciparum*. The mosquitoes were equal-opportunity vectors, but the effect of their bites depended on whom they bit. They bit enslaved Blacks who had inherited or acquired limited immunity to *P. falciparum*. They also bit whites who had no inherited immunity and little acquired immunity. The whites did have some immunity to *P. vivax*, another form of malaria endemic in England that caused mild illness for most. But *P. falciparum* was far deadlier, often causing cerebral malaria, a lethal complication that could lead to seizures, encephalopathy, and coma. *P. falciparum* produced high seasonal death rates among planter families in the summer and early fall months. Inland rice planters in particular were on the front lines of the struggle against *P. falciparum*. Those who built their homes on the edge of inland swamps, where it was moist and damp, endangered their own and their family's health until they learned—often the hard way—to build their plantation homes on higher ground.[77]

The transition from inland rice production to tidal rice production and swamp reclamation made *P. falciparum* a serious threat in coastal South Carolina and Georgia. Clearing hundreds of thousands of acres of cypress, tupelo, and sweet gum forests in the coastal wetlands and building embankments and floodgates for tidal rice production produced rotting vegetation and stagnant water. It also expanded the *Anopheles* mosquitoes' breeding grounds. The problem was that, unlike inland plantations, tidal rice plantations afforded no high ground. By the 1790s malaria transmission was well under way in the coastal regions.[78]

After her husband William Lennox Kirkland Sr. died, Mary Anna Lynah Kirkland and their son, William Lennox Kirkland Jr., continued to live at Laurel Hill. The elder Kirkland's will divided his estate between his mother, Marianne Guerard Kennan Kirkland, to whom he bequeathed one-half, and his wife, Mary Anna, and infant son, William Kirkland Jr., to whom he bequeathed one-quarter each. In November 1834, Marianne and Mary Anna decided to divide the bequest in half to simplify the young Kirkland's inheritance. Mary Anna took full possession of Laurel Hill Plantation, and Marianne took the Charleston townhouse at 37 Church Street. The rice plantation and the eighty-seven Blacks forced to labor on it were worth $15,000—more than the townhouse and the four enslaved Blacks whose labor was exploited there. To settle the difference, Mary Anna signed a $17,000 bond to her mother-in-law, payable in four years. When Marianne died in 1838, the bond had not yet been paid. Her will left the remainder of her estate, including the $17,000 bond, to her only surviving grandchild, William Lennox Kirkland Jr. This friendly agreement among enslavers would have profound effects on the Black people they held in bondage for decades to come.[79]

Among planter families on the lower Combahee, assets were transferred between generations by means other than inheritance as well. As we have already seen, a sale-and-mortgage arrangement shifted assets between Hannah Shubrick Heyward and her son William Heyward Jr. And in 1835,

Thomas Lowndes drew up a bill of sale in trust. First, it referred to a tripartite deed among himself, his wife, Sarah Bond I'on Lowndes, and John Bond Randall, an attorney who was his wife's trustee—a marriage settlement, which Thomas Lowndes and Sarah Bond I'on signed in March 1798, with John Bond Randall serving as trustee. Sarah's father, Jacob Bond I'on, had left her in his will a mulatto girl, £2,000, and one-third of his personal estate, consisting of enslaved people, cattle, furniture, and plantation tools. Sarah also inherited an interest in the estate of a woman named Sarah Lampriere. She brought these assets—and that is what enslaved people were to planter families: wealth, assets—into her marriage to Thomas Lowndes for her use and benefit. If she predeceased her husband, which she did, he would have use of the assets during his lifetime. Then they would pass to his heirs. The terms of this marriage settlement entitled Sarah to the enslaved people, their labor, and the issue and increase of the female slaves and any other real or personal property that might be bequeathed to her.[80]

The 1835 bill of sale stated that Thomas Lowndes had given away to his heirs some of the enslaved people to which his wife was entitled. To comply with the terms of the marriage settlement, he was required to replace them with enslaved people of equal or greater value from his own property. It also named Charles T. Lowndes, one of Thomas and Sarah's sons, as the substitute trustee since John Bond Randall had died. A slave schedule in the 1835 deed lists the names of bondspeople Thomas Lowndes had given to his heirs, Rawlins Lowndes and Charles T. Lowndes (two of the couple's sons), even though they had belonged to Sarah's trust. And it lists the names of ninety-eight slaves whom Thomas Lowndes sold to the trustee, Charles T. Lowndes, for $1 as replacements to his wife's trust. Among the ninety-eight were November Osborne, his mother, Phoebe (listed as "Phoebe November"), and his sister Flora; and Sarah Small (listed as "Sary") and her father, London Small.[81]

Sarah Small was born on Thomas Lowndes's Cat Island Plantation on the Santee River, where her father, London Small, had been held in bondage. Sarah testified in October 1901 that she was one hundred years old; she did not know her exact age, though she remembered she had been a "big girl" during the war in which Carolina colonists fought Native Americans, which may have been the so-called Cherokee War (1759–1761). She also remembered that she "belonged to one man . . . and his son until freedom." Sarah testified that she and November Osborne had grown up as "play children" together, and when they were old enough, Thomas Lowndes married them to each other. An itinerant white minister, Reverend Coleman, performed the ceremony in Lowndes's "mansion" house. It likely took place in the winter or early spring, when the Lowndes family resided on the Combahee River at Oakland Plantation. Sarah Small Osborne gave birth to ten or eleven children before the Civil War.[82]

★★★★★★★★

On February 11, 1761, Henry Middleton (1717–1784) acquired a half-interest in two tracts of land along the Combahee River, totaling 1,023.50 acres. Nine months later, he purchased the other half-interest in the original two tracts of land as well as a third tract of land, measuring 300 acres. At some point after 1763, Henry Middleton acquired a fourth parcel, this one also 300 acres, from William Bull, who still owned most of the plots in the town of Radnor at the time of his death. These four tracts, all acquired by the early 1800s, became Newport Plantation. Henry Middleton acquired land in Charleston on a bend of the Ashley River from his first wife, Mary Baker Williams, which he added to and named Middleton Place. It is situated on high ground with a commanding view of the wooded riverbanks below. Middleton Place was Henry and Mary's principal home and the birthplace of their son Arthur.[83]

In 1784, Henry Middleton bequeathed to his son Arthur "all my lands on S. side Combahee river" in his will. Arthur Middleton (1742–1787) was a signer of the Declaration of Independence. Arthur's son Henry (1770–1846), who served a term as governor of South Carolina, inherited his father's fortune, including Middleton Place and Newport Plantation. Governor Henry Middleton masterminded the layout of the elaborate grounds at Middleton Place, which required the labor of fifty gardeners over a period of ten years. Middleton Place remained the seat of the Middleton family until 1974. Arthur's widow, Mary Izard Middleton, bequeathed rice plantations from the Izard family, Hobonny and Old Combahee Plantations, to another son, John Izard Middleton, but he sold them to his brother Henry in exchange for a mortgage.[84]

In addition to serving as governor of South Carolina, the younger Henry Middleton also served in Congress between 1815 and 1819. Subsequently he served as the American minister to Russia between 1820 and 1830. Though diplomatic salaries were small, personal wealth from his rice plantations on the Combahee River enabled Middleton to enjoy the society of the Russian imperial court and diplomatic corps, and educate his children in England.[85]

In 1836, Governor Henry Middleton's son Williams Middleton mortgaged twenty-eight slaves to Martha Ann Matthews for $22,200. If he paid back the mortgage amount with interest, he would not have to surrender his property (if Mathews was not a family member). Middleton paid half of the purchase price, $11,100, at the time of signing. There is no evidence of when Middleton paid the mortgage off. However, he must have, because he maintained ownership of his enslaved labor force.[86]

Among this group of twenty-eight were Wally Garrett's whole family, including his parents, Ofney and Lucinda (listed as "Cinda"), who are named in his pension file, and his sisters Rose and Daphne. Wally also testified to pension examiners after the war that he was born "on the Ashley River, the slave of Williams Middleton," on a plantation located "18 miles north of Charleston." He was likely born at Middleton Place, which is unusual for bondspeople who were forced to live and labor on Newport Plantation.[87]

Williams Middleton may have inherited Wally and his family from his father, the former governor. However, Wally and his family are not listed in Governor Middleton's 1846 will. And there are no surviving records that suggest Governor Middleton gave his children slaves before he died (unlike Thomas Lowndes). It is possible that Wally and his family were part of an inheritance that Williams Middleton and his siblings received from their grandparents, Arthur and Mary Izard Middleton. This may be why Williams's older brother, John Izard Middleton, witnessed his signature on the document. Because no slave lists for Newport Plantation before the Civil War have survived, we don't know when Ofney, Lucinda, Rose, Daphney, and Wally were sent to Newport Plantation, where Wally worked against his will as a field hand.[88]

Wally Garrett testified that he had known the Old Head Balaam Burnett all his life and that Balaam had been married to his sister Rose before the war. Balaam Burnett, also a field hand, and James Sheppard (who grew up with Wally and another man named Jack Aiken) were held in bondage by Governor Middleton on Newport Plantation, where Balaam married his slave wife, Rose. Sally Sheppard, who married James Sheppard after the war, testified that she had known James, a cattle minder on Newport Plantation, "all her life." Previously James had been married to a fellow bondswoman named Betsey "under the slave way," meaning that they were committed to each other and had a ceremony that was not legally recognized but which bound them until either one died or the enslaver separated them. Sally also had a "slave husband," Tom Izzard. They all "belonged" to Henry Middleton.[89]

In 1837, Governor Middleton mortgaged Newport Plantation to his cousin Henry Augustus Middleton. With the price of rice falling, multiple annuities to pay to his siblings and children, and construction at Middleton Place and at the family's summer home in Newport, Rhode Island, the governor must have needed an infusion of cash. This kind of private transaction was definitely preferable to a public auction, which would have proclaimed poverty; in this case, the shortfall was seemingly temporary, until the price of rice rose again. Henry Middleton "of Combahee," as the deed describes him, signed three bonds to Henry Augustus Middleton for a total of $60,000 and agreed to pay him back with interest in annual increments of $10,000 on February 1, 1841, and February 1, 1842, then a final payment of $20,000 on February 1, 1843.[90]

In addition to the plantation, Henry Middleton also mortgaged 249 Blacks whom he held in bondage on Newport. They included the Prime Hand Edward Brown's mother, Chloe, and his siblings Honor, Caesar, and Bess (listed in a family group, "Chloe Honor, Caesar, Bess"); Selam White's parents, listed as "Dick, Lucy"; the Prime Hand Farbry Bowers and his parents, listed as "Sharper, Charlotte"; and the Prime Hand Frank Wright, his mother, Lucy, and his brothers Mauro and Dick (also listed as a family, "Lucy, Mauro, Dick"). Henry Middleton must have repaid the mortgage, because he reclaimed his enslaved property.[91]

Though some formerly enslaved people knew of and testified to transactions among enslavers that resulted in the sale, gift, bequest, or mortgaging of them or their family members, many did not. Prime Hand Captain Brown, for example, testified that Frank Hamilton was his brother and that both had been raised on William Kirkland's Rose Hill Plantation along with Friday Hamilton and Joe Morrison (Captain and Friday had known Joe Morrison "intimately" for forty and forty-five years, respectively), but their family was sold at least once along the way. Colonel James Cuthbert's 1837 estate inventory from his Bethel Plantation included 537 enslaved people among his worldly possessions. Among them were a family listed as "Pompey Pussy Hagar Frank Bina Silla" and valued at $2,400. This was

Frank Hamilton's family: Pompey and Pussy were his parents, and Cilla (listed as "Silla"), Bina (listed as "Mina"), and Hagar his siblings. On another of Cuthbert's plantations, Castle Hill, an enslaved family, listed as "Sam Sary Anna," was valued at $1,500. This was Jackson Grant's father, Sam, mother, Sarah (listed as "Sary"), and sister Anne (listed as "Anna"). Neither Captain Brown nor Jackson Grant is included in these lists. Likely they had not been born yet, but it was possible that they had been, for it was not uncommon for slaveholders not to list infants on slave lists and similar documents. Jackson Grant was sold and likely mortgaged multiple times also.[92]

Mary Anna Lynah Kirkland remarried in 1837 to Henry F. Faber, a lawyer and planter who renamed the Laurel Hill plantation Rose Hill. Faber died less than two years later, in 1839, leaving Mary Anna a widow for a second time. In his will (which survived because it had been registered in Charleston), Faber left his lot in Hampstead on the edge of Charleston, where there was an unfinished house and other improvements, to Mary Anna and her heirs. He instructed his brother Joseph W. Faber, with whom he had purchased the lot and begun construction on their respective houses, to complete the construction on the home for Mary Anna's comfort and safety according to their plans and to pay for the construction of both of their dwellings out of the proceeds of his plantation. In addition, Faber bequeathed back to Mary Anna all of the property he had acquired from her through marriage (suggesting that they had not signed a marriage settlement before their wedding): the carriages, horses, china, one-half of his wines and liquors at Rose Hill, and all of the furniture from Rose Hill Plantation and their house in Charleston. Lastly, Faber bequeathed his wife enslaved people, specifically all of the "Coachmen" and "House Servants" he owned at the time of his death. Though Faber does not list the names of any, one of the coachmen he bequeathed to Mary Anna was likely Aaron Ancrum. We know this because of information contained in the pension files, which fleshes out the incomplete information in Faber's will.[93]

In the pension files, Old Head Isaac DeCauster testified that he had known Aaron Ancrum "all his life." They had been "slaves under the same owner" and DeCauster had been "raised under" the older man's "hand." He remembered that Ancrum was the coachman who used to "drive the carriage for his owner and after his death for his widow." Another Old Head, Andrew Wyatt, remembered knowing Ancrum for a "long time before the war," when Ancrum was a "young lad driving for his owner, a Mr. Faber." Wyatt remembered that Faber had "married a Kirkland," Mary Anna Lynah Kirkland.[94]

Another case in which information from pension files needs to be combined with information from planters' documents is that of Old Head Mary Ann Lewis. Her husband, James, had died while in the army, and she said that she had applied for a widow's pension and "expected" that they "would give" her "something," but James Lewis does not have a pension file. So we have to glean genealogies from other sources. Mary Ann Lewis testified for her husband's fellow veterans, their widows, and even their dependent adult children. She told the pension official in testimony for Andrew Wyatt, for example, that William Kirkland was her "master before the War," that Kirkland's land "joined" the land of Wyatt's "master," and that she had known Wyatt "since childhood." She had also known Silvia DeCauster and her family "since childhood." Mary Ann Lewis and Silvia DeCauster's second husband, Isaac DeCauster, "belonged to one owner" and were "raised on the same plantation." Isaac DeCauster, too, had been married previously; he and his first wife, Katie, had married before the war. Silvia DeCauster was raised "on the next plantation." But Mary Ann Lewis had been taken to William Kirkland's plantation "as a little girl"; she wasn't born there.[95]

So, to find out where Mary Ann Lewis was born and to authenticate the testimony that she gave about her life, we have to go back through the slaveholders' records to an April 1839 "conveyance"—a document for the legal transfer of property—signed by Mary Clay of Bryan County, Georgia; Mary Nuttall of Apalachicola County, Florida; and Henry Middleton Parker and Eliza Parker in Beaufort County, along the Combahee River. The conveyance states that Clay and Nuttall were the heirs of the "undivided real estate of the late William Savage of Bryan County"; Clay was William Savage's sister, and Nuttall was his niece. They were represented by the prominent Savannah attorney, planter, and slave trader Robert Habersham in the sale of William Savage's Silk Hope Plantation. The property, containing 282 acres of tide swamp and 754 acres of highlands, was bounded by the Ogeechee River on its northeast side. In his 1833 will, Savage had instructed that his two plantations, Silk Hope and Genesis Point, and 500 acres of pineland were to be divided evenly, half of their value he bequeathed to his wife for the support of his children, and half was bequeathed to his nieces, Mary Nuttall and Eliza Parker. The will appointed Habersham as executor. The property was to be sold for cash, unless his nieces wished to retain it. In addition, Savage left $10,000 to his children, $1,000 and household furnishings to their mother, a watch to his son, and some china to his daughter. The will itself says nothing about slaves and provides no itemization of enslaved people on Silk Hope or Genesis. However, enslaved people are implied in the document; unless otherwise excluded, they were to be divided and sold with the livestock and tools on the plantations.[96]

William Savage's will may not explicitly mention the ownership of enslaved people, but the marriage settlement between his niece Mary W. Savage and William B. Nuttall does. And when Mary Savage later married for a second time, to George Noble Jones, that second marriage settlement also mentions enslaved people. Each of her marriage settlements states that Thomas and Mary Savage, her grandparents, bequeathed slaves, which belonged equally to both of them, to their granddaughters. Her second marriage settlement specifies also that she owned two sets of enslaved people. One set, the "William Savage negroes," came to her from the estate of her uncle. She acquired the second set, the "Thomas Savage Negroes," from her grandparents and shared them with her mother, also named Mary Savage, each receiving half. But the documents don't specify the names of the "William Savage Negroes."[97]

That information can be added from the pension file testimonies of Mary Ann Lewis's brother John A. Savage, who knew everyone's business. In March 1890, Savage testified on behalf of the pension claim by Andrew Harris that he had known Harris, who was about two years older, when Harris "was a boy." John A. Savage was born on December 15, 1823, in Bryan County, Georgia, on the same plantation as Andrew Harris. They were owned by the same man, William Savage. Then John A. Savage, in language commonly used among enslaved people on the western wedge of the Combahee River, specifically on William Kirkland's plantations, said that while neither he or Harris had ever been sold, on account of "deaths and change of property" Savage and Harris were "turned over to the same owners" until William Kirkland owned them both. At that point John A. Savage was about nineteen years old and Andrew Harris was about twenty-one. It wasn't the whole truth, but it was the truth John A. Savage knew. And it is enough truth to locate some of the "William Savage Negroes" on William Lennox Kirkland Jr.'s plantation. Old Head Jacob Jackson, uncle to Mary Ann Lewis and John A. Savage, was another of that group, known as the "Savage gang." Jackson testified for Prime Hand William Jones that he and Jones had been "owned by the same man," William Kirkland, and they were "raised together." Despite John A. Savage's insistence that he had never been sold, in fact some of those who had been enslaved by William Savage indeed were sold, including Prime Hands like himself and William Jones. They were not sold to the highest bidder at public auction on the steps of the courthouse in Bryan County, Georgia, as were other of the enslaved persons on William Savage's Silk Hope Plantation, but had been "previously disposed of by private sale," as the advertisement for the estate sale stated. Though the estate sale took place in Georgia, the advertisement ran in the *Charleston Daily Courier* twelve times between January 1 and February 1, 1839, to attract rice planters willing to make the trip. The enslaved families would be sold again after the liquidation of Silk Hope before they were brought to the Combahee in 1843.[98]

While the Lowndes family was not at the pinnacle of the aristocratic hierarchy, like the Middletons and the Haywards, their family records also are revealing of the enslaved community at the time the Combahee River Raid took place. Two months after the raid, Minus Hamilton described himself as a "very aged man" when he told his life story. "Ise eighty-eight year old," he proclaimed. He declared that he knew his age because his "ole Mas'r Lowndes"—presumably James Lowndes, who died in 1839, and not his nephew, who had the same name but died a year earlier at age thirty-two—kept the ages of all of the Blacks he held in bondage in a big book. After the enslaved youth came to the "age ob sense," they would mark their own ages down every year. Among the Gullah Geechee, the "age of sense" refers to a religious process known as "catching sense," through which an individual sought formal membership in the praise house or the African Methodist Episcopal church, where membership among worshippers created a sense of community.[99]

After the elder James Lowndes died in 1839, Minus Hamilton was listed on his estate inventory as "Minus Carptr 45 1500" (that is, he was forty-five years old and was valued at $1,500). If he was forty-five years old in 1839, that would have made him sixty-nine years old in 1863, the year of the raid, rather than the eighty-eight he said; either way, he would have been one of the oldest members of the enslaved community on the Combahee at the time of the raid.[100]

Minus Hamilton was by far the most valuable enslaved person listed on the estate inventory. The other enslaved men who worked trades, three carpenters, were younger, between twenty-two and twenty-nine years old, and were worth $1,000 each. In addition to training and supervising the young carpenters, Minus Hamilton may also have trained and supervised Lowndes's three coopers, who ranged in age from forty to seventy years old and in value from $400 to $900. After the carpenters, the coopers had the highest values among all of the enslaved people in Lowndes's estate record. The highest value of a male Prime Hand or field hand was $800.[101]

Minus Hamilton's wife, Hagar, was listed directly under Minus: "Hagar 22 500." She was one of the thirteen most highly valued women on the inventory, all worth $500. Women between the ages of fourteen and thirty-five were likely valued both for their productive labor as field hands and for their reproductive labor as mothers who gave birth to more bondspeople whose lifetime of labor would enrich the slaveholder's family for generations to come. Below Hagar is listed the couple's younger daughter, "Sibby 2 years 150," then their older daughter, "Binah 6 200."[102]

Even if they were not sold off when a slaveholder died, enslaved people were disposed of when the slaveholder's estate was divided. In this case, Edward Rutledge Lowndes inherited Minus, Hagar, Sibby, and Binah from his father.

★★★★★★★★

In this chapter we have followed some enslaved people through the slave transactions that brought many of them to the lower Combahee River rice plantations. In later chapters we will follow them all the way to their own land transactions as freedpeople after the end of the Civil War. However, the road from the one to the other is a long one.[103]

3

Stolen Children

Harriet Tubman, her parents, and all eight of her siblings were born enslaved. A farmer named Atthow Pattison held both Modesty, Harriet Tubman's maternal grandmother, and Rit (or Rittia) Green, Tubman's mother, in bondage. Pattison owned a 265-acre farm nestled along the Little Blackwater River, a tributary of the Blackwater River in western Dorchester County. From its mouth at Fishing Bay, the Blackwater winds twenty-five miles northwest; the Little Blackwater River meanders southeast for fifteen miles. The two serpentine rivers provided water access for area planters like Pattison to transport their goods to market in the Chesapeake and beyond.

Along with other small farmers on the Eastern Shore in the late eighteenth century, Pattison produced tobacco exclusively. When tobacco production declined and the economy waned on the Eastern Shore, many farmers began producing a diverse array of commodities, particularly timber, and sold them to European markets in exchange for goods. Pattison, on the other hand, stuck to what he knew best. Though a small farmer, he had become prosperous after he arrived in Dorchester as an indentured servant, completed his term of service, and paid off his indenture. Rit Green was born on Pattison's farm sometime between 1785 and 1790. She lived there with her mother, Modesty, until they were separated.

When Atthow Pattison died in 1797, he bequeathed Rit and her future increase to his granddaughter Mary Pattison. Rit was still a girl at the time of Pattison's death. Pattison had likely wanted Rit to train as a house slave, perhaps even a lady's maid for Mary. Then, once Mary married, she would take her well-trained house servants with her to continue to labor for her as she managed her husband's household. It was typical for wealthy white southern girls and women to inherit enslaved people who would take care of them, their children, and their homes, helping them maintain the proper station of a lady.

Pattison's will included an unusual provision limiting Rit Green's term of service. It specified that she would serve Mary Pattison and her heirs until she reached the age of forty-five. Though Pattison's will did not specifically state what would happen to Rit after she had completed her term of service, the implication was that she would be given her freedom. Rit's children would belong to Mary Pattison and serve her and her heirs until they too reached the age of forty-five; then they too would be freed. This unusual provision may be evidence that Pattison was Rit Green's biological father, though we can't be sure. The provision in Pattison's will decreased Rit and her children's value. Legally, Mary Pattison and her heirs could only sell Rit and her children for a limited term of service.[1]

By the late eighteenth century, the citizens of Maryland and other border states were beginning to debate the future of the institution of slavery. Legislators who represented counties on Maryland's Eastern and Western Shores, where small farms worked by small numbers of enslaved people predominated, sought to limit the importation of slaves from neighboring colonies, Europe, and the West Indies, and to implement the gradual manumission of Blacks enslaved within the state's borders. Legislators who represented counties where there were large plantations opposed this. Like rice planters in the South Carolina and Georgia Lowcountry, they wanted to expand slavery (some even favoring the importation of captives directly from western Africa) to expand rice cultivation, reclaim tidal swamps, and maintain tidal swamp fields. The debate played out on a national level in the early nineteenth century as the United States acquired territory north, south, and west of the original thirteen colonies and Congress debated whether to extend enslavement to these territories.

Farmers like Atthow Pattison took matters into their own hands. Pattison may have been motivated to limit Rit Green's servitude by the Act of 1790, by which the Maryland General Assembly allowed manumission of enslaved people under age fifty by deed or will. This was the first legislative step against enslavement passed in a southern state. In 1796, the age limit for manumission was lowered to forty-five. Representatives did not want to give slaveholders license to exploit the labor of enslaved people during their productive years and then manumit them when they were old and infirm to avoid being responsible for taking care of them. Such former slaves could become a burden on their communities and municipalities. Antislavery advocates felt the reduction made no difference. They deemed forty-five the age at which the majority of enslaved people became physically unable to work and support themselves.

Isabella Van Wagenen—who would later change her name to Sojourner Truth—was born in Ulster County, New York, located along the Hudson River. Until his death in 1745, Colonel Johannis Hardenbergh was the man who held Isabella, her parents, James and Elizabeth, and her brother Peter in bondage. His son Charles inherited Isabella's family and decided to free James so that Charles would not have to provide for him, because he was too old to work. He also freed Elizabeth so that she could take care of her husband. The couple was evicted from the cottage and the small plot of land on which they grew tobacco, corn, and flax to support their family and were relegated to the dank cellar in the younger Hardenbergh's home. Isabella and Peter were auctioned off to the highest bidder, as were Hardenbergh's livestock; the last of James and Elizabeth's ten or twelve children were to be taken from their parents and sold. After Elizabeth died, James lived alone in a cabin in the woods, where he eventually froze to death. Laws such as Maryland's 1796 act lowering the age at which slaves could be manumitted were supposedly designed to prevent cases such as this.[2]

★★★★★★★★

Though the value to enslavers of these "Old Heads," as USCT widow Fannie Lee Green Simmons referred to them, diminished, they played vital roles as heads of their households and families and as leaders within the Black community. In the South Carolina Lowcountry and on Maryland's Eastern Shore, the Old Heads lived, remembered, and recounted.[3]

After Atthow Pattison's death, Rit Green remained on Atthow Pattison's farm on Blackwater Creek until Mary Pattison married Joseph Brodess, a local farmer from Bucktown, in 1800. The Brodesses settled on a farm next door to where Mary's mother, Elizabeth Pattison, lived. Rit Green came of age there. Mary Brodess gave birth to a son, Edward, in June 1801. A few months later, Joseph Brodess was dead. His assets now belonged to their infant son, Edward.

In need of support for herself and her infant son, Mary Brodess made an advantageous match with a prosperous widower named Anthony Thompson, who had interests in several businesses, owned farmland and timberland on the Blackwater River, and possessed nine enslaved laborers. Thompson, in turn, needed a wife to raise his three young boys and keep his home tidy. In 1803, Mary Thompson and her son, Edward Brodess, moved to Mansion Farm, Thompson's plantation, situated on approximately 1,000 heavily forested acres in Peter's Neck, which is roughly six miles west of Pattison's farm. She took with her Rit Green and four enslaved men who were part of her deceased husband's estate. Rit likely had to leave behind her elderly mother, Modesty. Mary's marriage to Thompson had secured the future for herself and her young son, and it was the first in a series of transactions among white families that would determine whether Rit Green and her family could live together and be a family.

Ben Ross was one of the slaves on Mansion Farm, where he worked as a timber inspector and foreman. Thompson and other Eastern Shore planters were diversifying their economic pursuits, decreasing the amount of land and enslaved labor they devoted to planting tobacco and increasing both for agriculture and timber. When Rit Green joined Thompson's household, Ben was managing Thompson's timber enterprise. The historical record is silent on how and when Rit Green and Ben Ross fell in love and committed themselves to take care of each other. They likely "married"—that is, made a lifelong commitment to each other—in 1808, though the marriages of enslaved people were not legally binding. Their daughter Linah was born around 1808. By 1813 or 1814, their union had produced two more daughters, Mariah Ritty and Soph. But their marriage and their family were inherently insecure, because they were held in bondage by two different slaveholders, Anthony Thompson and Edward Brodess.[4]

Not all slaveholders would agree to permit an enslaved person to marry someone held in bondage by someone else. It split the wealth, so to speak, and did not offer any material benefits to the enslaver of the male partner. The enslaver of the female partner would hold in bondage any children born to the spousal union. That they were keeping all of the wealth in the family—Anthony Thompson managed Edward Brodess's property until he reached age twenty-one—may have encouraged Thompson to agree to the marriage. But once Edward claimed his inheritance, Ben, Rit, and their children would be forced to live separately and possibly some distance apart from each other in an "abroad marriage."

In parts of the slave South and North, "abroad marriages" were common on farms on which twenty or fewer Blacks were held in bondage. They were much less common on rice plantations in the Lowcountry, where the number of forced laborers often exceeded a hundred. On smaller farms, the smaller pool of potential partners made it more difficult for enslaved people to find spouses in the immediate vicinity. However, it is not clear that a lack of potential partners factored into Ben and Rit's choice of each other.[5]

Mary Pattison Brodess Thompson was dead by 1810. Her son, Edward, was still a minor. Her widowed husband, Anthony Thompson, became Edward's legal guardian and managed Edward's inheritance from his father until Edward reached the age of majority. Araminta Ross, whom we know today as Harriet Tubman, was born in March 1822 on Anthony Thompson's farm. Minty, as she was called by her family and community, was the fifth of Ben and Rit Ross's nine children. Edward Brodess reached the age of twenty-one just a few months later. Thus, though Minty Ross was born into a stable, two-parent, and loving home, it was inevitable that she and her family would be separated—"till death or buckra"—when Edward claimed his inheritance. The Rosses' nuclear family was inevitably going to be undone by the interests of the enslavers who held them in bondage.[6]

In 1813–1814, around the time when Tubman's parents met and married on Maryland's Eastern Shore, teenage Isabella Van Wagenen fell in love with a young man, Robert, who lived on a neighboring plantation in Ulster County, New York. Charles Catton, the man who held Robert in bondage, did not agree to their marriage. He already had picked out an enslaved woman for Robert to marry. After Robert defied Catton's orders to stop visiting Isabella, Catton and his son lay in wait for Robert along the path he walked down to reach Isabella's cabin. They seized Robert and beat him savagely with heavy canes until he was nearly unconscious. Catton never visited Isabella again; he married the woman Catton chose for him despite the fact that Isabella may have been pregnant with his child already. Isabella married someone else, too, a man named Tom who was enslaved on the same farm as she was.[7]

To return from Sojourner Truth to Tubman: Sometime around (possibly after) 1824, Edward Brodess moved to the 200 acres of farmland his father had left him in Bucktown and occupied the single-story, two-room house that his stepfather had built for him, along with a barn. He took with him the people whom he held in bondage (three surviving adult men he inherited from his mother, Rit Green, and six or seven of her children) to live with and work for him on his farm. Minty was a toddler when she was taken ten miles away from her father, Ben Ross, who stayed on Anthony Thompson's Mansion Farm.[8]

Tubman's earliest memory was of lying in a wooden cradle, which had likely been carved by her father and passed down to Tubman from her older siblings—and then would be passed down from Tubman to her younger siblings. Tubman called it a "gum," because the cradle was carved out of a hollow sweet gum tree, which were prevalent in the estuaries of Maryland's Eastern Shore. Tubman remembered being playfully tossed in the air by the young white ladies from the big house—Mansion Farm—when she was too young to walk. She also remembered taking care of her younger brother when she was about five years old and he was a baby. Minty could not wait for her mother to leave so she could hold her little brother by the hem of his dress and swing him around, which delighted him. When her brother got fussy, Minty would let him suck on a piece of fatback. He may have been teething, and gnawing on the leathery rind and rubbery fat soothed his inflamed gums. She was her baby brother's primary caretaker until he was too big for her to carry him anymore. Minty likely did not understand why her mother was forced to leave her younger children alone with no one to supervise them, because she had to cook in the big house and her older children were hired out. Tubman described her childhood as growing up "like a neglected weed,—ignorant of liberty, having no experience of it."[9]

Edward Brodess married Eliza Ann Keene in 1824, and the couple would soon start a family. They required Rit's expertise as a domestic slave to take care of their household; Rit, in turn, had to depend on Minty to take care of the Ross household. When she returned one day, probably exhausted from standing on her feet and cooking all day, and saw the baby asleep with a piece of fatback hanging out of his mouth, Rit thought the baby had choked to death. It must have terrified Rit to leave her baby alone with her five-year-old child, but she had no choice.[10]

Minty Ross's childhood ended abruptly once she turned six years old. By the end of the 1820s, Edward Brodess owned more enslaved people than he needed on his small farm. He hired some out to neighboring farmers for cash. It was not unusual for Eastern Shore planters to lease out men, women (including pregnant and nursing women), and children for wages.

It was typical for enslaved children to begin working as soon as they were old enough to earn their keep and perform useful labor, mainly helping adult laborers in the slaveholder's house or fields. Usually this was at about age eight—which was also the age when slaveholders often separated enslaved children from their parents and sent them away to live on other farms. When Aaron Cornish, an enslaved man whom Tubman later assisted in liberating, arrived at the Vigilance Committee in Philadelphia in the fall of 1857, he reported that the woman who held his wife in bondage had allowed her and their children to live together until the children were about eight. Then they were taken away or hired out. Edward Brodess hired Minty out when she was just six. He probably needed the money to support his own growing family. And he certainly benefitted from transferring the cost of housing, feeding, and clothing laborers, including Minty, to those who leased them.[11]

Brodess first hired Minty out to James Cook, a local farmer, to learn how to weave, clean, and take care of Cook's young children. It was the first time she had lived in a house with white people. She remembered feeling humiliated when she was forced to stand up in front of Cook's family wearing a petticoat that Brodess's wife had made for her and was the only dress she had. She later said that she was ashamed to eat standing in front of the white family; she refused Cook's wife's offerings of sweet milk, though she was as fond of it as any child would be. Cook may have hired Minty to weave cloth, diversifying his household's production and helping him weather the economic depressions prevalent on tobacco farms in the mid-eighteenth century. Minty, however, refused to learn how to weave, one of the few trades available to enslaved women. Learning it would have consigned her to life as a domestic slave, subjected to the cruelty of white people such as the Cooks. Minty may have been groomed to be a house slave because of the relatively privileged status of her parents—her mother as a cook and house slave, and her father as a highly valued timber inspector and foreman. In any case, she would have none of it. From an early age, Minty did not want to be forced to live and work in close proximity to white folks. Refusing to learn how to weave may have been Harriet Tubman's first act of rebellion.[12]

As an alternative, Cook set her to work checking his muskrat traps on the banks of streams and in the marshes where the animals built their burrows. The work kept Minty outside and gave her far more autonomy and mobility than most enslaved girls and even enslaved women had. It required her to wander alone through the marshy wetlands and wade through cold water during the winter trapping season. At one point Minty became dangerously ill with measles; she was eventually sent home to be nursed by her mother, then returned to the Cooks' farm when she recovered.[13]

Minty next was hired out to a young married woman known as Miss Susan, who drove up to the Brodesses' farm and inquired if they had an enslaved girl who could take care of her baby. In that job, Minty kept house during the day. Miss Susan kept a whip on the fireplace mantel and used it on Minty's head, face, and neck when she felt the young girl had not swept or dusted properly. Minty also took care of Miss Susan's baby during the day. She later told Sarah Bradford that the baby was always in her lap except when sleeping or nursing. Minty was so small that she had to sit on the floor to hold the baby. Taking care of Miss Susan's baby was not as fun as taking care of her brother had been. Young Minty was sometimes forced to sit up all night rocking Miss Susan's fussy, hungry, and sometimes sick baby after cleaning the house all day. If the baby's cries disturbed Miss Susan's sleep, she whipped Minty. Sarah Bradford's great-nieces and -nephews, who all remembered Tubman well, attested that she carried the physical and psychological scars of the abuse for the rest of her life.[14]

After Minty proved unwilling to learn a trade and unsuited for domestic work, Brodess rented her out as a field hand on the Bucktown farm of a man named Thomas Barnett. Now an adolescent, Minty worked with male field hands breaking flax. One day she encountered an angry overseer at the town's dry-goods store. He was in hot pursuit of another field hand who had left the plantation without permission. Minty got caught in the middle and tried to block the overseer, who grabbed a two-pound iron weight from a scale and hurled it at her, striking her squarely in the forehead and fracturing her skull. Minty was carried back to the farm but not given any medical attention. In fact, she was sent back to the field the very next day, still bleeding from the open wound in her head.[15]

According to Tubman biographer Kate Larson, Minty suffered from temporal lobe epilepsy as a result of the head injury and was permanently disabled. For the rest of her long life, Tubman experienced seizures and periods of semiconsciousness. She also had visions, which she interpreted as prophecies from God. Tubman would fall asleep by the side of the road; an elderly Tubman would sometimes drift off during social visits. Decades later,

Samuel Adams Hopkins (who was Sarah Bradford's grandnephew) remembered hearing as a child when Tubman visited his family: "There was forty thousand dollars in gold on that head." He and the other children always wanted to "see the dent that so much weight must surely have caused."[16]

Barnett, for his part, declared Minty "not worth a sixpence" and sent her home again to be cared for by her mother; Dr. Anthony C. Thompson, Edward Brodess's stepbrother, likely provided medical care for her. Minty's family feared she would never recover. Eventually, after a year or two, Minty did recover, well enough to work in the fields or in the house. Brodess attempted to sell Minty and had several potential buyers come to his farm to look at her. But Minty Ross was damaged goods, and Brodess could find no slaveholder who would purchase her.[17]

However, Minty's status as a "refuse slave" provided an opportunity. She would be her own boss. She offered to pay Brodess an annual wage for the privilege of hiring out her own labor. She would be responsible for her own housing, food, and clothing, thus determining where she would live. And she would choose her own master. Brodess accepted the arrangement, perhaps relieved to be done with her.[18]

In 1835 or 1836, at thirteen or fourteen years old, Minty hired herself out to John T. Stewart, a planter who lived on the north side of Tobacco Stick Bay, west of the township of Cambridge. Stewart operated his father's 225-acre farm, where he planted wheat and corn. He also owned a mill, a shipbuilding and lumber business, and the village store. Minty began her tenure with Stewart working as a domestic slave. But Minty Ross was still not made for housework. Although only five feet tall, she worked in Stewart's store and did men's work. She lifted heavy barrels of goods, hauling goods from the wharves to Stewart's store and grain from Stewart's mill to the store. She also worked in the fields, plowing, pulling carts of manure, and driving teams of oxen. Though hard work was not uncommon for enslaved female field hands in the Upper South, the physical feats Minty performed were a marvel to the male field hands with whom she labored and the man who held them all in bondage. By 1840, she was able to command wages made by male laborers, which were double or triple those paid to women and enough to pay Brodess $60 a year for the privilege of choosing who would control her labor.[19]

Before Anthony Thompson died in 1836, he added provisions into his will to manumit the Blacks he held in bondage in a phased manner, according to their ages and lengths of service. Thompson's will attested that Ben Ross was bound to serve for five more years. The will provided him with life-time use of ten acres of land in the vicinity of where his house stood and granted him the right to cut timber for his support. The will also immediately manumitted Jerry Manokey and his wife, Polly. It equally gave Jerry access to ten acres of land and rights to cut timber on the property for his support. Thompson's will further granted the Manokeys' children—John, Aaron, Moses, Eliza, and Matilda—phased manumission, with the number of years they would remain in bondage ranging from eighteen to thirty-three. Ben Ross and Jerry Manokey were the only two Blacks Thompson held in bondage to whom he left land and timber rights. He may have done this because of their long and faithful, albeit involuntary, service, providing skills that proved critical to the expansion of his timber business. He may also have given them land and material support because of their ages. As noted earlier, a 1796 state law had lowered the age at which Blacks enslaved in Maryland could be manumitted. Thus, Ben (born in 1783) was already an Old Head and well over forty-five years old at the time of his manumission.

After Thompson's death, around 1837 John T. Stewart acquired several tracts of Thompson's land and hired highly skilled members of the enslaved labor force from Thompson's estates in Harrisville and Peter's Neck, and from this constructed his timber and shipbuilding enterprise. Stewart became one of the wealthiest men in Dorchester from clearing vast tracts of timber and shipping it to market. In one year working for Stewart, Minty earned enough over and above the wages she was obligated to pay Edward Brodess to purchase a pair of steers worth $40. They helped her with plowing, pulling, and hauling, and thus with earning even higher wages than the average hired-out field hand. While she worked for Stewart, Minty lived with her father near Stewart's Tobacco Stick farm and also did some work for him as he cut and hauled timber for Baltimore shipyards. After manumission, Ben Ross hired himself out for a while as a free man to Stewart and others.[20]

Stewart was the driving force behind Stewart's Canal, which connected Blackwater Creek to Parson's Creek and facilitated the transportation of timber and timber byproducts from Dorchester County farms to Baltimore, from where they could be shipped to markets in Maryland, Virginia, and New England. Uprooting, clearing, bucking, and hauling thousands of acres of white oak and white and yellow pine, then dredging thousands of acres of waterlogged marsh soils, required the labor of hundreds of enslaved and free Black men skilled at many different trades; Ben Ross could have been one of the foremen working on Stewart's Canal. It was dangerous and arduous work, undertaken in the summer heat and freezing winter, hard on workers who were always poorly clad no matter the season. We do not know how many lost their lives building the seven-mile-long canal, whether from mosquito-borne illnesses proliferating in the swamps, respiratory ailments, infectious diseases, drowning, accidents, or sheer overwork.

During construction of the canal, the Black laborers lived in tents close to the construction site. A thriving community grew up among those enslaved by or formerly enslaved by Stewart and other planters in the Peter's Neck area. It was a hybrid community of families who worked in the timber trade, built churches (like Malone's Church), and opened schools. Its members were connected to other Black communities in the region's farms and work camps. Minty lived in Peter's Neck with both of her parents from the late 1830s into the early 1840s. It is where in 1844 she met and married John Tubman, changing her name from Araminta Ross to Harriet Tubman after they married.[21]

Historical records reveal little about John Tubman other than he was a dark-skinned, multiracial-looking free Black. He was born free to free parents in 1820 and was two years older than his wife, around twenty-four years old when they married. The sources do not reveal where he was born or his occupation. We do not know how they met. We do know they were both a part of the Peter's Neck community. John Tubman probably worked as a laborer on local farms or hauled goods along the canal in the White Marsh/Peter's Neck area. And we know that they planned to spend the rest of their lives together—as Minty's parents, Ben and Rit Ross, did for decades. The odds were decidedly against them, even though marriages between enslaved and free Blacks were not uncommon on Maryland's Eastern Shore or in Minty's family. Because Minty was enslaved, any child born to their union would be enslaved. First John and Minty would have to get Edward Brodess to agree that they could buy Minty's freedom and the freedom of each and every child she bore; then John, and Minty too, would have to earn the money. Free women outnumbered enslaved women in Maryland's Eastern Shore communities. Given the greater number of complications associated with marrying an enslaved woman as opposed to a free woman, John Tubman must have truly loved her to choose Minty Ross to be his wife.[22]

It is not clear what possessed Harriet Tubman—maybe her father's manumission, her marriage to a free man, or her own innate desire to be free—to use her surplus earnings to hire a lawyer to look into her own status and whether or not she should be free. For five dollars, the lawyer researched the will of Atthow Pattison, who originally had enslaved her mother, Rit Green. He found the provision in Pattison's will bequeathing Rit and her children to his granddaughter Mary; Rit and her children would serve Mary Pattison until Rit and then subsequently each of her children reached forty-five years of age. The lawyer's findings seem to confirm the lore passed down in the Ross family—that according to Atthow Pattison's will Rit was free.[23]

But five dollars could not buy Harriet Tubman justice. By the mid-1840s, Rit was over forty-five years old. Pattison's great-grandson Edward Brodess was illegally holding Rit in bondage, and so Tubman's siblings borne by Rit after she had reached the age of forty-five had legally been born free. The lawyer's findings confirmed what Tubman already felt in every fiber of her being. She told Sarah Bradford: "He [i.e., the Lord] set de Norf Star in de heavens; He gave me de strength in my limbs; He meant I should be free." This was the third and last time she attempted to ameliorate her condition as Edward Brodess's property. From here on out, she would take her freedom into her own hands and put her trust in God.[24]

By 1849, Brodess was in tough financial straits. His family had grown to eight children, six were still minors. His 225-acre farm could not support their growing brood. The enslaved people whom he had inherited from his grandmother and father along with their issue were his largest and most liquid asset. As early as the 1830s, he started to sell enslaved people as commodities into the domestic slave trade in the US Southwest, putting them "in his pocket," as historian Edward E. Baptist put it, and converting his liquid assets into cash, which he used to purchase fertile farmland.[25]

Brodess had already illegally sold several of Rit's children and grandchildren, disregarding the provisions in his great-grandfather's will. Pattison's will granted Rit and the other people he held in bondage their freedom at age forty-five. Rit should have been free in the 1830s; instead, she was given away to Pattison's granddaughter, who kept her in bondage. Brodess had sold Tubman's sister Mariah Ritty to Dempsey P. Kane, a slave trader from Mississippi, back in 1825 and her sisters Linah and Soph to a chain gang in the Deep South, separating them from their young children. Her brother Henry remembered that the sale made an orphan out of one of his sister's infants, two to three months old. As a child and after the sale of her sisters, Tubman was "afraid of being carried off," she told an interviewer. In 1849, Tubman was visited by visions of mothers, like her sisters Linah and Soph— and herself, should she and John Tubman have children together—having their children torn from them.[26]

The visions that disturbed Tubman's sleep may have resembled what Isabella Van Wagenen's parents endured before Isabella became Sojourner Truth. James and Elizabeth Wagenen mourned the loss of each and every one of their children who were torn from them. Half a century later, Sojourner Truth recounted the stories her parents passed down to her of the terrible day the enslaver Charles Hardenbergh abducted her sister Nancy, three years old, and brother Michael, who was five. Michael's initial excitement when Hardenbergh's big sleigh pulled up to their small cottage turned to terror when strange men entered their home, grabbed Michael, and put him in the sleigh. They took his sister away also and locked her in the sleigh box. Michael jumped off the sled, ran back into the house, and hid under the bed. The slave traders found him, put him back in the sleigh, and drove away with both children. Enslaved parents like James and Elizabeth had no legal parental rights. They could do nothing to protect their children or to guard the sanctity of their home the next time Hardenbergh determined to put one of their children "in [his] pocket." Eventually, after Charles Hardenbergh had died, even Isabella, who was the youngest, and her next-older brother, Peter, were sold away—nine-year-old Isabella for $100. We will never know if James and Elizabeth's bereavement was any less profound than Ben and Rit's. We do know that none of them would likely ever see their children again. James and Elizabeth grew old alone, with none of their children to care for them.[27]

Harriet Tubman knew this vision was God speaking to her, warning her of what was to come. She prayed day and night that God would change Brodess's heart so he would not sell her. And she prayed that if his heart could not be changed, God would instead strike him dead. Mainly, she remembered, she prayed that she would not be sold away from her loved ones. Then Edward Brodess died at age forty-nine.[28]

Once again, the Ross family's vulnerability to separation was exposed by Brodess family affairs, mirroring similar transactions in the South Carolina Lowcountry and on the Combahee River. Edward's death left his widow,

Eliza Ann Keene Brodess, deeply in debt. Eliza and the executor of Edward's will quickly sought to illegally convert her liquid assets—the enslaved people in her husband's and father's estates, which were left to her children—into cash to pay off Edward's debts. She decided to put Tubman and her brothers up for sale.

4

Prime Hands

The Prime Hands on the cluster of plantations on the lower part of the Combahee River were born between 1824 and 1844, meaning that they were between nineteen and thirty-nine when the Combahee Raid took place in 1863. Prime Hands were at the peak of their productive capacity. Unlike the Old Heads, most had not suffered injuries that would permanently reduce their productive and reproductive capacity to produce and reproduce; their bodies and constitutions were not yet broken down. The Prime Hands, for their part, grew up under the Old Heads, admiring and emulating them. Pool Sellers grew up under Elsey Higgins Jones on Cypress Plantation, and William Izzard "grew up under" Farbry Bowers on Newport Plantation.[1]

They had accumulated years of experience working at their crafts and completing full tasks. In the rice fields of Carolina Colony, the task system put enslaved laborers to work as individuals, as opposed to in gangs, to complete a daily allotment of work before the sun went down each day. When constructing a new rice field and reclaiming a tidal swamp, digging out 600 cubic feet of earth—which would include removing cypress tree roots—with a heavy spade and without a wheelbarrow was a full task. Duncan Clinch Heyward remembered that on his grandfather's plantations along the upper portion of the Combahee River, hoeing one-quarter of an acre to turn the topsoil before rice seeds were planted was equivalent to a full task. This increased to one-half of an acre to hoe after the rice had been planted and was maturing in the fields. One-half of an acre was also the task for cutting or harvesting rice. Children were typically put to work on a task adjoining the parent's, usually the mother's, at the age of twelve. The parent instructed the child in how to properly perform the forced labor. As the children grew, learned, and matured and their parents aged, the children could assist the parent in finishing the parent's task if the younger person finished first. A task was usually more than an average hand could complete in one day. But if they managed it, they were given the remainder of the day to grow food in provision grounds for themselves. The task system was unique to the Lowcountry (and used on Sea Island cotton plantations as well), where the disease environment limited the number of months in the year that planters and overseers spent on rice plantations. That meant that in addition to experiencing direct less white supervision of their labor, enslaved workers also received smaller rations.[2]

The overwhelming majority of those who were Prime Hands at the time of the raid had married in the 1840s and 1850s in "slave custom" and brought children into the world. They generally married spouses enslaved on the same plantations. Titus Burns (also known as Titus Brown), an enslaved class leader, performed the marriage ceremony for Prime Hands William Young and Sina Bolze in January 1858 in the church on Cypress Plantation. In praise houses and churches that followed the American Methodist tradition, including at Denmark Vesey's church, the class leader was a lay clergyperson who conducted nighttime prayer meetings that took place away from the gaze of the planter family and overseer. Though class leaders were not ministers, they married and buried enslaved people on the plantations before freedom, and did the same for freedpeople in churches after the Civil War. Sina Bolze and William Young stood up before the congregation with their hands joined. After Burns read from the Bible, Bolze and Young promised to remain man and wife through sickness and until death. Members of the enslaved community on Cypress—Venus Lyons, Elsey Higgins, and Lina Richard—attended. Others from adjoining plantations, particularly Newport Plantation, attended as well. Bina Mack testified in William Young's pension file that she grew up a bondsperson on an "adjoining" plantation, Paul's Place, and "knew they were married by going over on Sunday to meeting at Cypress Plantation where Sina and William lived"; she had known Sina since childhood. No white people were present. Titus Burns also married Prime Hands Peggy Simmons Moultrie and Edward Brown in June 1856; the Rev. William Higgins, an enslaved minister, performed the ceremony for Prime Hands Robert Frazier and Phoebe Burns at his house on Cypress around 1859. Either Burns or Higgins may have also married Prime Hands Moses Simmons and Christie Ann Kinloch. While white missionaries and pastors only married enslaved couples in the winter and early spring, when white planters lived on the Combahee (winter was the coolest and healthiest time of the year, relatively free of fevers and agues), enslaved preachers and class leaders performed weddings year-round, whether or not white planters resided on their rice plantations.[3]

The overwhelming majority of Prime Hands married other Prime Hands. On Rose Hill Plantation, Prime Hands Anthony Bartley and Moriah Heywood married when they were quite young. William L. Kirkland Jr. himself may have officiated at their wedding. He certainly officiated when Prime Hand Daphne Jackson married Tom Powell by slave ceremony. That which gave the slaveholder the power to join together also gave him the power to sunder; Tom Powell was sold and taken away from Daphne, who remarried to Prime Hand Ned Snipe long before the war. Wally Garrett and Elizabeth Fields, on Newport Plantation, across the Combahee River, were married long before the war. Next door to Newport, Prime Hands Charles Lucas and Bella Jones were "slave married" before the war at a church on Walter Blake's Bonny Hall by an enslaved preacher named Daniel.[4]

Old Heads sometimes also married Prime Hand women. Andrew Harris, for example, married Diana Days around 1848, when she was quite a young girl. They were married by Reverend Coburn, a white missionary who visited Rose Hill Plantation periodically on Sundays. Coburn also performed the ceremony for Prime Hand John A. Savage and his wife, Charlotte, several years later. Savage, who was a carpenter and deer hunter on Rose Hill Plantation, missed the Harrises' wedding. He testified that he had been off "hunting with [his] boss" on the Ashepoo River. When they returned, Andrew and Diana were man and wife. Quarko Chisolm, a "colored preacher," performed Old Head June Singleton's marriage to Prime Hand Eliza Ancrum in March 1853, and the marriage of Old Head Hardtime White to Prime Hand Flora Moultrie in November 1853 on Cypress Plantation. Reverend William Higgins married Old Head Joshua Simmons and Prime Hand Margaret Kelly.[5]

Prime Hands were the engines that generated millions of bushels of rice every year and made the Combahee planters so wealthy. On the lower Combahee River, 60 percent of the enslaved Prime Hands were skilled at trades or domestic labor. They were teamsters, like Charles Lucas on Bonny Hall and Edward Brown on Cypress, who hauled goods and handled draft animals. Or carpenters, such as Newport's Farbry Bowers and Cypress's William Hamilton and Moses Simmons (Simmons was also a blacksmith). Rose Hill's William Jones, along with Old Head Carolina Grant, fashioned the enormous cypress and sweet gum trees uprooted to create the rice fields into trunks for use in the hydraulic irrigation system, and into mortars and pestles for threshing rice. They built and repaired houses and fences, in addition to making shingles for the roof at Middleton Place. James Shields on Newport, Frank Hamilton on Rose Hill, Stepney Grant on Longbrow, and Old Head Andrew Harris were plowmen. Blacksmith Moses Simmons on Cypress and bricklayer Edward Brown on Newport were very skilled at their work. Jackson Grant was a coachman, like Aaron Ancrum, on Rose Hill; Elsey Higgins and James Simmons on Cypress, Nat Osborne on Oakland, and Stephen Simmons on The Bluff were all house servants. The overwhelming majority of enslaved people who had trades were men.[6]

After plowmen like James Shields, Frank Hamilton, Stepney Grant, and Andrew Harris turned and prepared the soil, female field hands, such as Diana Days Harris and countless other unnamed women and girls, planted the rice seeds in the cypress swamps. Working barefooted and barelegged—with ropes tied around their waists to raise the hems of their skirts up above their knees—they sank deeper with every footfall into the soft, gluey, viscous "pluff," which smelled of decayed matter and adhered to their feet, ankles, and legs. Progressing through it was not easy. Female field hands made shallow trenches four inches wide with their hoes, dropped rice seeds in the trenches eleven inches apart, and covered the seeds lightly with soil using their hoes (or their bare feet). Usually, field hands did the first and largest planting from the tenth of March to the tenth of April.[7]

No sowing took place mid-April through May, when bobolinks, beautiful little songbirds that migrated north across the Gulf of Mexico back to northern and western states in the United States and southeastern and southwestern provinces in Canada from their winter homes in South America, flew over the rice fields and pulled at the rice grains. If the seedlings were just breaking the ground, these "little enemies" of the rice planter, as Duncan Clinch Heyward called them, plucked the developing grain out of the earth for a satisfying snack. If necessary, a second planting occurred from the first to the tenth of June.[8]

Field hands constituted 40 percent of Prime Hands on the Combahee. We know many of their names: Richard Smith on Bonny Hall; Jack Aiken, Wally Garrett, and Jeffrey Gray on Newport; Edward Brown, Robert Frazier, William Middleton, Charles Nicholas, Neptune Nicholas, and William Young on Cypress; Captain Brown, Diana Days Harris, David

Jenkins, William Jones, Ned Snipe, and Tony Snipe on Rose Hill; Anthony Bartley, Friday Hamilton, and Mingo Van Dross on Longbrow; and Richard Smith Jr. on Paul's Place. Though women likely constituted the majority of the field hands, they had no reason to testify to pension officials or army officers about their occupations during enslavement.[9]

★★★★★★★★

Then there were the lives of the planters. Rice, which enslaved people were forced to grow, financed their lifestyles, as well as those of their children and grandchildren, across multiple households. During the ten years Governor Henry Middleton served as ambassador to Russia, Middleton Place had received little attention, and upon his return he and his wife, Mary Helen Middleton, found that the "old shackish mansion" needed extensive and expensive repairs. Profits from rice financed the repairs between 1840 and 1844, replacing the roof, covering the plantation house with Roman cement, and encasing the chimney tops with earthen pots to keep them from smoking. Mary wrote to her daughter in Philadelphia that "Carpenters from Combahee" were "preparing the timber for scaffolding" and making shingles, which would be used to repair the roof—for which the timber also came from the Combahee. They raised the upper ceiling by a foot and created a new wing with two bedrooms lit by dormer windows. They also repaired the stables. Farbry Bowers, listed as "February," was certainly one of these carpenters taken from Newport to repair the roof at Middleton Place.[10]

Middleton Place was the domain of the Middleton women, particularly Mary, who spent much of her time there. Visitors from Charleston would take a ferry across the Ashley River and ride ten miles up a sandy river road to the main gate. Soaring elms and live oaks, with enormous trunks and far-reaching branches, lined the long driveway. Four towering white camellias, for which Middleton Place became famous in the late nineteenth and early twentieth centuries, bloomed along the paths in the wintertime.[11]

The estate featured a three-story Tudor-style house. A semicircular portico faced the bend of the Ashley River. A pair of two-story, freestanding buildings flanked the house on either side, one housing the laundry on the first floor with guest bedrooms on the second and the other housing a conservatory on the ground floor with a library above. Middleton Place was filled with exquisite objects. Rare books crowded the library bookshelves.

Priceless works of art hung on the walls. A vast collection of miniatures and other treasures—by some counts numbering ten thousand—were displayed throughout the house. Many of them, such as a rare china set and full-length portrait of Tsar Nicholas I, which had been presented to Middleton at the end of his service as ambassador to the court of Russia, testified to the family's extensive overseas travels.[12]

When together at Middleton Place, the Middleton family promenaded along walks on which camellias and rhododendrons proliferated and rode horseback in the "pleasure gardens" where fragrant yellow jessamine, azalea, and honeysuckle bloomed in the spring. Ringed by weeping willow trees, the terraced gardens descended into the Ashley River. The family read a wide variety of books aloud to one another and played piquet. After dinner, the women played piano. The Middletons also hosted parties for family, friends, and neighbors, particularly at Christmastime.[13]

The Middleton women spent the winters at Middleton Place; the Middleton men traveled back and forth between it and the Combahee rice plantations. Henry and Mary Middleton and their eight children, like many other rice planter families, practiced a strict division of labor when it came to rice. Middleton and his sons supervised the overseers hired to manage their rice plantations. The drive between Middleton Place and the Combahee plantations took two days by horse and carriage, even longer on horse-back. The Middleton men stayed in a small house on Hobonny Plantation; there were not adequate accommodations for the whole family, particularly the women. By contrast, Middleton family cousins Walter and Daniel Blake, who owned Bonny Hall and Boardhouse Plantations, respectively half a mile and nine miles downstream along the Combahee River, spent the winter with their families on their rice plantations, hosting dinners and receptions.[14]

The Middleton men did not just oversee the production of rice. In the late fall, they hunted, waiting in deer stands in the woods while packs of hounds ran the deer. There were so many ducks feeding on rice stubble and shattered grains of rice that they hardly made good sport for the planters or the enslaved men who hunted for them. Flocks of wild turkeys were fa-vored prey for sportsmen in the early spring months.[15]

Spring in the Combahee was (and is) spectacular. In early spring, the evergreens were in bloom: *Illicium* shrubs produced flowers with vibrant red star-shaped petals; *Pilea* trees burst forth with clusters of small white and pink buds; *Lagerstoremia* trees and shrubs bloomed. And *Stewartia* trees and shrubs blossomed with large white rounded flower petals. The cacophony of vibrant colors and aromatic fragrances remains intoxicating.[16]

In March 1839, Governor Middleton's youngest child, Eliza, married Joshua Francis Fisher in the second-floor drawing room at Middleton Place. Fisher was a Philadelphian who stood to inherit a substantial fortune from his deceased father, a merchant in the East India trade, and from his maternal uncle. Middleton promised to give Eliza a lump sum of $30,000. Before marrying Eliza, Fisher also agreed to her spending two to three months with the Middletons, especially her mother, in Newport, Rhode Island, every summer. After their wedding, Eliza moved to Philadelphia to live with her husband.[17]

Two of Governor Middleton's sons chose wives outside of the close-knit planter circle. Eliza's eldest brother, Arthur, married Paolina (Paula) Bentivoglio in Rome in 1841. Though she was from an old Roman family, Paolina had no fortune to bring to the marriage. Alone among all the Middleton women at Middleton Place, Paolina disregarded Middleton family gender roles when she "undertook the journey to Combahee!"—as her sister-in-law Eliza wrote her mother in March 1852. Eliza speculated to her mother that the "hideous blackies" must have "alarmed" Paolina at first and that Paolina must have had a "dull time" when her husband went to the rice fields. Eliza hoped Paolina would spend her solitary moments writing to her about her "impressions of life on a Plantation." We don't know if Paolina was "alarmed" by the appearance of the Black people her in-laws held in bondage or if she recorded her feelings at all.[18]

Eliza's youngest brother, Edward, a lieutenant in the US Navy serving in the Mediterranean and South America, met Edwardina de Normann in Naples and married her in 1845. Edwardina (Edda) also possessed no money, and her lineage was questionable. Edward's parents and siblings tried in vain to discourage Edward from the marriage, fearing that as a result he would bind himself to the navy and to working for a living.[19]

Governor Middleton and his family led extravagant lives. Middleton Place with its extensive and ongoing repairs and multiple additions, entertainment during winter solitude at Middleton Place, summer retreats, and foreign wives with titles but no fortunes: all these things cost money. This plus the money Middleton contributed to his daughter Eliza's start in married life to ensure that she could maintain the lifestyle to which she was accustomed had to come from somewhere. It came, of course, from exploiting enslaved laborers working on the family's Combahee rice plantations. In 1839, Governor Middleton realized a gross income of $55,000 to $60,000; this was an immense fortune in the nineteenth century, when the average yearly wage for a farm laborer in the south Atlantic region was $7.16 with board.[20]

A depression in the 1840s had a negative impact on their standard of living. In 1842, with rice selling at half its previous price, Governor Middleton's income was also cut in half to $23,000, putting the family's plans for their annual summer retreat in Newport in jeopardy. He was unable for the first time to pay Eliza's annuity on schedule. The price of rice fell even further to one-third of the pre-1840 price in 1843.[21]

Meanwhile, Middleton's Combahee neighbors and cousins the Blakes typically spent the Christmas holidays on both the upper and lower parts of the river. William Blake's son Walter and his wife, Ann Izard Blake, used Bonny Hall in Beaufort County's Prince William Parish as their primary residence. Walter's brother Daniel and his wife, Emma Rutledge Blake, spent winters in nearby Colleton County's St. Bartholomew Parish on Boardhouse Plantation. The Blakes frequently invited their cousin Williams Middleton to dinner so that he would feel less lonely and isolated when he traveled to Combahee to manage his father's rice plantations, one of which was Newport.[22]

★★★★★★★★

By the nineteenth century, rice had bonded together the aristocracy of planters and the community of enslaved laborers on the lower Combahee. Political service, acquisition and management of rice plantations, and intermarriage within a tight circle of wealthy landed families—these all came to characterize the planter aristocracy. Tidal rice, as noted, had made Lowcountry planters the wealthiest in British North America by the American Revolution. In the early nineteenth century, rice would increasingly dictate how planters transacted business with one another in enslaved property. The outcome of these transactions tore apart enslaved families, continually shaping and reshaping the contours of enslaved communities along the Combahee River.

Even with fluctuations in the price of rice, the overall economy in the rice-growing Lowcountry South Carolina plantations was, as we've seen, more stable and prosperous than the former tobacco economy of

Chesapeake farms. Yet planters in the Lowcountry also bought, sold, and mortgaged the people they held in bondage whenever they saw fit. But during the 1840s, fluctuating rice prices and the deaths of planters increased uncertainty for Blacks enslaved along the Combahee River. As in the Chesapeake, the Christmas and the New Year holidays brought—in addition to weddings and a few days off from work—slave auctions.[23]

Rice planters on the lower Combahee River balanced their books at the end of the calendar year. And when the balance sheet did not add up, they often took out loans secured with slaves. On January 1, 1843, Henry Middleton Parker sold thirty enslaved people owned by his wife, Eliza Savage Heyward Parker, to Mary Anna Lynah Kirkland Faber for $9,800; then Faber mortgaged them back to Parker for $19,600, which included the original principal plus interest. The slaves came from the estate of Eliza's uncle, William Savage, and from Silk Hope Plantation on Georgia's Ogeechee River. Among those sold were Simon and Quasheba with their children, Daphne Jackson Snipe, Catharina, Jacob Jackson, and Anthony Bartley (listed together as "Simon, Quasheba, Daphne, Catharina, Jacob, Anthony"). And Kate was sold with her children Mary Ann Lewis, Maria Wineglass, and John A. Savage (also listed consecutively on the same line as "Kate, Mary Ann, Johnny, Maria"). Another of Kate's children, plowman Andrew Harris, was sold with them (listed on the line below as "Andrew"). The same configuration of names appears on the mortgage. Though all of the puzzle pieces have not been found to identify the relationship among Simon and Quasheba and Kate and Dick (the father of Kate's children, who is not listed on the documents), it is likely that there were siblings among these parents.[24]

This one transaction elucidates how the "Savage gang" (discussed in Chapter 2) got from William Savage's plantation on the Ogeechee to William Kirkland's Rose Hill Plantation on the Combahee and authenticates Mary Ann Lewis and John A. Savage's memories of their family told years after the war. For this transaction and the majority of other such transactions recorded on this section of the Combahee River in the early 1840s, there was no auction and no advertisement—as there had been, for example, with the 1759 sale of the West Africans imported aboard the slave ship *Hare*. Nor was there a slave factor, like Henry Laurens, who sold the *Hare* captives, or even Robert Habersham, who first divided William Savage's estate. Instead, two slave-owning women executed the transaction through their agents—Mary

Anna Faber through her attorney and Elizabeth Parker through her husband. The two women were neighbors and relations. The Ogeechee River was approximately seventy-five miles from the Combahee, but Parker's Place (as sisters Maria Phoenix and Silvia Jackson Gaylord DeCauster, who were held in bondage there, called it) or Palmetto Plantation (as the planter family called it) was adjacent to and just south of Mary Anna Lynah Kirkland Faber's Rose Hill Plantation. Throughout the antebellum South, direct financing from banks was rare. In subregions like southern Louisiana, planters borrowed investment capital primarily from factors like Robert Habersham. But on the lower portion of the Combahee, trade in enslaved people and the acquisition of investment capital were usually local business affairs, conducted among family, friends, and neighbors.[25]

While William Savage's death precipitated the division of his estate and sale of his slaves across state lines, Thomas Lowndes's death also created uncertainty for the people he held in bondage. November and Sarah Osborne, whom Thomas Lowndes had married and who had grown up together, were listed on his estate record. Lowndes appraisers identified his enslaved labor force by task, as well as by occupation and physical ability. The only November listed, as "November .1.," was a full hand. There are three female slaves named Sary: "Sary ½," who must have been a half hand; "Sary," who could have been a full hand or a woman past productive capacity; and "Sary .1.," who was likely a full hand. Without more information, it is difficult to determine which Sary was November's wife. By 1843, November and Sarah would have been parents to at least one living child, Nat. There are two Nats listed: "Natt___," which likely designated someone who was not yet a tasking hand, and "Natt .1." The family was on Lowndes's Combahee plantation among the 211 enslaved people, who were appraised at an approximate value of $300 each, with a total value of $63,300; there is a separate listing for the slaves and other assets on Lowndes's North Santee Plantation, which may be Cat Island, where November and Sarah were born. Thomas must have bequeathed them and his Oakland Plantation on the Combahee River to his son Charles T. Lowndes in his will. Unfortunately, Thomas Lowndes's will has not been found. In 1860, Charles T. Lowndes owned 370 enslaved people in St. Bartholomew's Parish, where their labor was exploited to produce 1.8 million bushels of rice on 11,000 acres of improved land and 3,500 acres of unimproved land.[26]

There is another transaction missing—actually, a set of them—involving the Smith/Elliott family selling enslaved humans to the Kirkland family. Mingo Van Dross testified that he was born a slave of "Tom Wright Smith" or "Tom Ricesmith" on The Bluff plantation on the "Chihaw," the Chehaw River. There was a history of the Smith and Kirkland families transacting in human property. In March 1827, William Elliott purchased fourteen enslaved people from his father-in-law, Thomas Rhett Smith, for $2,760; "Alto & Sancho for 440 instead of 550" were among those he bought. Sancho might have been Sancho Van Dross, Mingo's father. Unfortunately, there is not enough information about Sancho's family to identify the Alto with whom he was sold. Given the placement of her or his name before Sancho's, Alto was likely related to Sanko. Mingo Van Dross testified that before Sanko Van Dross died, he told Mingo the precise day Mingo was born: October 4, 1830. And he insisted that he remembered his and his father's birth years even though his birth, baptismal, and family records were "probably burned at the time the plantation dwelling was burned during the Civil War when the Union troops came in." His father, Sanko Van Dross—who, as we have seen, was one of the oldest Blacks enslaved on the lower Combahee—was also held in bondage by Thomas Rhett Smith. If a record of his birth existed, Mingo thought it probably also had been burned. Still, there is no trace of how William Kirkland acquired Sancho, Abigail, Mingo, and Hercules. Mingo remembered he was "first sold as a slave when he was 15 years old" by Thomas Rhett Smith Elliott to William L. Kirkland Jr., owner of Rose Hill Plantation; an 1851 bill of sale confirms the transaction in which Elliott sold Sancho and Mingo Van Dross, listed as "Big Sancho Little Sancho Mingo," to Kirkland. Little Sancho may have been Mingo's brother and Sancho's son, who was lost in the historical record. If Mingo's birthdate is correct, he would have been fifteen years old in 1845. The Smith/Elliott family and Kirkland families continued to socialize together and likely do business together over the decades. In addition to the aforementioned 1827 slave transaction, Thomas Rhett Smith sold William L. Kirkland Sr. nineteen enslaved people and their children from his father-in-law's estate on January 4, 1823. William Elliott, in particular, enjoyed recreation with William L. Kirkland Jr.; Elliott wrote to his wife in March 1849 that "Mr. Kirkland and Mr. Toomer" were "coming over to hunt with us tomorrow."[27]

When he died in 1846, Governor Middleton's original will provided annuities for certain family members: $4,000 per year to his wife, Mary Helen Hering Middleton; $1,200 a year each to daughters Eliza Fisher and Catharine Middleton; and $2,000 each per year each to sons Arthur, Henry, Oliver, John Izard, and Oliver Hering. To satisfy his debts, Governor Middleton authorized the trustees of his will to sell unproductive properties, except his home at Middleton Place and Hobonny and Newport

Plantations. He stipulated that these properties were not to be sold during his wife's lifetime without her consent. Once the debts were paid, Eliza would receive $30,000 (equivalent to $1,161,000 today) or an annual annuity of $1,200 until $30,000 had been paid. The remainder of Middleton's estate—land and enslaved people—was to be divided among his sons. The will bequeathed "my plantation Newport with all Negroes attached to the same" to Arthur and his heirs on the condition that Arthur pay his younger brother Henry one-half of Newport Plantation's value. It conveyed Old Combahee Plantation and all of the laborers held in bondage on it to sons John Izard and Oliver, and Hobonny Plantation, the adjoining tracts of land, and the enslaved people who labored there, as well as the residue and remainder of his estate, to Williams and his heirs.[28]

Governor Middleton's December 1846 estate record lists the 668 Blacks he held in bondage (worth $196,036—the equivalent of $7,117,036 in 2022) at Hobonny, Old Combahee, and Newport Plantations and at Middleton Place. His neighbors and cousins Walter Blake and Daniel Blake appraised the value of his estate. They identified the 224 people whom Governor Middleton held in bondage on Newport Plantation. The enslaved people were listed in family groups with each individual bondsperson's appraised value next to their first name. They included Francis Izard, his wife, Nancy, and their children, William Izzard, Sam, and Celia (listed as "Francis $600, Nancy $450, William $300, Sam $250, and Celia $50"), parents Josiah and Hetty with daughters Phoebe Cassell Gray and Celia Cassell Haywood (listed as "Josiah $700 Hetty $200 Phoebe $200 Celia $100"); parents Mary and York with sons Jack Aiken and William ("Mary $500 York $600 Jack $200 William $150)"; parents Smart and Mary Washington and son Solomon Washington ("Smart (Driver) 600 Mary 400 Solomon $100)"; and parents Chloe and Ned with children Honor, Caesar, Abram, Edward Brown, and Bess ("Chloe $500 Ned (Miller) 700 Honor $400 Caesar (Carpr) $450 Abram $200 Edward $200 Bess $100").[29]

Old Head Smart Washington was likely born on Newport Plantation in 1793. Before Henry Middleton's 1847 estate record, there are no records showing whether Middleton had inherited Smart or bought him. Smart was the driver and cooper on Newport Plantation. Coopers, of course, fabricated the specialized wooden barrels in which harvested rice was transported and stored. Their labor was essential to a plantation's efficient operation, because barrels were commonly used to transport bulk goods and commodities in the colonial and antebellum periods. Jonas Green knew Smart Washington long before the war. He gave a pension official an intimate portrait of Smart as a "young man in his prime" when Jonas himself "was a boy." According to their son Solomon Washington, Smart was "slave man and wife" with Mary. They were married at Newport many years before the Civil War.[30]

Drivers occupied one of the most important—and ambiguous—positions on Lowcountry rice plantations. On almost every plantation, the driver, who was himself a slave, and not the overseer ran the plantation's day-to-day operations. He was "second in authority only to the overseer," Frances (Fannie) Kemble wrote in her diary, and "second to none during the pestilential season, when the rice swamps cannot with impunity be inhabited by any white man." Kemble was a celebrated British Shakespearean actress, writer, and abolitionist who came to the United States for a year-long theatrical tour and met a wealthy and urbane American named Perce Mease Butler, who courted her relentlessly, following her from city to city throughout the tour. They were married in 1834. Butler was also a slave-holder who used overseers and enslaved drivers to manage his grandfather's estate, which included two rice and Sea Island cotton plantations outside Savannah, Georgia. In April 1836, Butler inherited (with his brother) the second-largest slave holdings in all of Georgia. Kemble kept a diary when she lived with Butler in coastal Georgia in the winter of 1838–1839. This diary provides one of the most trustworthy and intimate portraits of enslavement on rice plantations, and particularly the lives of enslaved women. The couple could not overcome their diametrically opposed views on slavery, and divorced in 1849; Butler was saved from bankruptcy by selling 436 enslaved people in March 1859, in the largest slave auction in American history. Kemble waited to publish her journal until 1863, the year of the Combahee River Raid.[31]

Kemble and others observed that on Lowcountry rice plantations the cultivation of the rice crop, the source of an enslaver's wealth and lifestyle, was under the control of enslaved men on a day-to-day basis. Some rice planters hired overseers to manage their plantations, but even when they did, overseers did not live on the rice plantations during the late spring to late fall months. Most rice planters gave enslaved men the responsibility of assigning daily tasks for the enslaved field laborers. Every morning before daybreak, drivers got the field hands into the rice fields; they organized the gangs, assigned the daily tasks, and, on some rice plantations, stood over the field hands, "whip in hand," while they performed their "daily task," according to Kemble. Such drivers would inflict a "dozen lashes" on those who did not finish their task and then give an accounting to the overseer, who had the authority to inflict an additional three dozen lashes upon the recalcitrant bondsperson (and often exceeded this limit).

Drivers needed to be intelligent, skilled, and strong, and able to command the obedience of the field hands. Those on the Combahee would likely have been Prime Hands. An Old Head could retain the position as long as he continued to meet the overseer's and/or planter's approval and his body did not break down.[32]

Decades after enslavement had ended, many freedpeople remembered that the drivers "control all the Buckra ting," as a Miss Georgie on Woodland Plantation in Georgetown, South Carolina, told Genevieve Wilcox Chandler, an interviewer from the Works Progress Administration in the 1930s. Drivers kept the keys to the storehouse, distributing rations (including meat), allowances of cloth, and tools to enslaved people, and safeguarding the planter family's provisions. Planters often entrusted them with firearms to protect the plantation and slaveholding family and to hunt deer and ducks for the planter family's table. On rice plantations without overseers, drivers who were literate (most of them were) traveled to or took letters to the city, pinelands, and seacoast, reporting plantation activity to the slaveholder. Under normal circumstances, the driver was first in command during the summers.[33]

As enslaved people, drivers were liable to have their family's rations reduced, to be demoted, and even to be sold "like a cart horse" if they fell out of favor with the slaveholder or overseer. In 1860, Gabriel Manigault's overseer on Gowrie Plantation dismissed an enslaved driver after he couldn't prevent another enslaved man from running into the river and drowning himself. Drivers' position did not always exempt their family members from deadly work in the rice swamps, nor protect their wives, daughters, and sisters from sexual predation by any white man on the plantation.[34]

Members of enslaved communities on Lowcountry rice plantations despised "de ole n[——] drivers" as "second devils." In addition to being authorized to whip fellow slaves at the time of an infraction, then report the wrongdoer to the overseer or slaveholder for additional lashes, some drivers were also hated for giving enslaved women tasks they could not complete, then sexually exploiting these women, who were desperate to spare themselves from the whip.[35]

Interestingly, the names of drivers are conspicuously absent from the pension files. Because the drivers had members of their own enslaved communities' blood on their hands, it is not surprising that Smart Washington (who was both carpenter and driver for Governor Henry Middleton) did not testify that he had been the driver on one of the Combahee rice plantations; none of their comrades, widows, or neighbors identified who the drivers were in slave times.[36]

Prime Hand Edward Brown was known as "one of the best working hands on the plantation," as Carolina Watson remembered him in her pension file. Watson, Farbry Bowers, and William Drayton all knew Brown "from his childhood . . . they lived on the same plantation"—Middleton's Newport Plantation—"all the time before Freedom." And they were both owned "by the same man as his slaves," according to Bowers. March Lawrence grew up on Newport. He testified for James Sheppard and Simon Washington that they were all held in bondage by Williams Middleton.[37]

Jack Aiken was known in the freed community on the western side of the lower Combahee River, primarily for his relations with women. How many and whom he married, and whether he married a particular woman at all or just "took up with" her, as his distant cousin Tom Washington put it, appears to have been a popular topic of conversation before and after the pension official visited. The youngest enslaved people—known as "Pikins," the Geechee Gullah word for children—like William Green, knew only Jack Aiken's last two wives, Nancy Washington and Rebecca. Some remembered that earlier Jack had married Chloe. Tom Washington, who appears to have had the most intimate relationship with Aiken, knew Jack had "five different women" during his lifetime. Jack married Priscilla during enslavement; she died during the war. Jack subsequently married Chloe, Janie (most people except those most intimate with Aiken forgot or did not know about Janie), and then Nancy and Rebecca during freedom. Prime Hands like Jonas Green, who was enslaved next door on Bonny Hall Plantation, and Charles Nicholas and William Hamilton, who were held in bondage across the Combahee River on Cypress Plantation, also testified that they knew Jack Aiken before the war.[38]

Phoebe Cassell testified that she was born on Newport Plantation; both her father, Josiah Cassell, and her mother, Hettie Cassell, were enslaved by Henry Middleton. Phoebe wasn't sure where her father got his title, but she was called Phoebe Cassell up until she married Jeffrey Gray "according to slave custom long before the war" on Newport Plantation. They had "four head of children when the war broke out," she told the pension official. William Izzard remembered attending the wedding at which his uncle Thomas Izzard married the couple. Farbry Bowers (who was one of the Newport carpenters sent to Middleton Place to repair the roof in 1846) testified that he was "born, raised, and grew up right here" on Newport Plantation. He had known Phoebe Gray all of her life and was acquainted with her husband also; "they were both raised up on the same plantation" with him. Simon Washington, Solomon Salter, Selam White, and Edward Brown testified that they knew Jeffrey Gray "from boyhood," as Solomon Salter put it.[39]

In the end, Governor Middleton's sons agreed among themselves to modify their father's will. Arthur still gained possession of Newport Plantation, but Williams received Old Combahee Plantation; John Izard and Oliver Hering shared the more valuable Hobonny Plantation. The impending war, the war itself, and the financial insolvency of the Confederacy devalued the properties. These external forces made it difficult, then impossible, to satisfy the debts and fully fund the annuities. Though Governor Middleton's will had been probated in June 1846, matters were not fully settled until the 1870s, years after the emancipation of those he enslaved. In 1860, John L. Middleton and five others owned 520 enslaved people who produced 3,200 bushels of rice on 600 acres of improved land and 600 acres of unimproved land on their Combahee River plantations in Prince William's Parish.[40]

William Heyward also died in 1846. But unlike Governor Middleton, whose will and estate record were both filed in Charleston, Heyward's will and estate record are missing. If found, they would likely include children Sina Bolze Young Green and Cuffie Bolze along with their parents, Manuel and Amelia; Peggy Simmons Moultrie Brown and her father, Primus; and their aunt and uncle Jack and Sarah Barnwell—if the older generation was still living. As noted in Chapter 2, Hannah Heyward sold them to her son William Heyward, then he mortgaged them back to her in 1817. Whether he paid his mortgage and retained his property and/or subsequently inherited the enslaved laborers from his mother, William Heyward's will would likely include March Chisolm and Frank Lyons, whom John Huger Dawson sold to Heyward and whom Heyward then mortgaged back to Dawson, both transactions occurring on March 1, 1822, as well as Tyra Joiner and her husband, Prince Polite, whom C. C. Keith sold to William Heyward and Henry N. Cruger, trustees for Catherine De Nully Hassell in 1833.

They must have been listed in Heyward's will, because Manuel and Amelia's children (and Cuffie and Sina's grandchildren), Sina Bolze Young Green and Cuffie Bolze, grew up in bondage together on Cypress Plantation. Peggy Simmons Moultrie was married to Edward Brown at Cypress in 1858 by Titus Burns, the same class leader who had married Peggy's first cousin Sina to her first husband, William Young (who, as noted, was also held in bondage by William C. Heyward on Cypress). Edward Brown's father, Siras Lee, was also held in bondage by Heyward. Edward titled himself "Brown" after his uncle. Neptune Nicholas had known both Edward and Peggy Brown all of his life, as they were all held in bondage on Cypress. Friday Hamilton and Mingo Van Dross grew up enslaved on Longbrow, the "next plantation." Mingo Van Dross testified that he was "raised three miles from William C. Heyward's Plantation and knew all his slaves." William Jones was enslaved a little farther away on William Kirkland's Rose Hill Plantation; nonetheless, he still knew Sina and William Young from their childhood and also knew when they were married. Jack and Sarah's children, Relia Barnwell Middleton, Primus, and Jack Barnwell, were born after 1848 and would not have been listed.[41]

In his will, William Heyward probably bequeathed these enslaved people to his sons, Dr. James Heyward and William C. Heyward. Lucy Lee Smith, one of Edward Brown's younger sisters, remembered being "born away from" Cypress Plantation "the slave of William C. Heyward, and he brought" her there "during slave time." The names Grahamville, Newhall, and even Sewhaw were all used by Combahee freedpeople to refer to Dr. Heyward's plantation.[42]

We know that a transaction must be missing because several of these bondspeople were among a group of forty-seven that Dr. James Heyward sold to his brother, William C. Heyward, two years after their father's death. He sold Old Heads Tooman and Joan Legare and two Prime Hands, Friday Barrington and Phoebe Burns, who were certainly the Legares' children. Their names are written in succession on the bill of sale—"Tooman, Joan, Phoebe, Friday"—as slaveholders sometimes recorded family groupings when they took the time to do so. When Joan Legare testified that she and Tyra Polite were "slaves of the same owner and resided on the same plantation," she could have been talking about Dr. James Heyward's plantation in Grahamville, South Carolina, as well as William C. Heyward's Cypress Plantation on the Combahee River. The couples Tooman and Joan Legare and Prince and Tyra Polite had been together for that long.[43]

Friday Barrington did not talk much about his origins in his pension file, and the comrades who testified for him weren't from the Combahee and didn't know him before the war. However, he did reveal that he had been enslaved by William C. Heyward on a 1902 circular from the Department of the Interior, which veterans were required to complete in order to prevent anyone from impersonating them or committing fraud in their names. Phoebe Burns married Robert Frazier on Cypress Plantation around June 1858. William Jones remembered knowing Robert since they were "little ones," and he knew Phoebe Burns Frazier ever "since she was a little girl," though he was enslaved on Rose Hill, a nearby plantation.[44]

John Parker was the last of the lower Combahee River rice planters to die in the late 1840s and pass his wealth, particularly the Black people he held in bondage, down to the next generation. When John Parker, Henry Middleton Parker's brother, made his original will in 1845, he instructed his executors to sell off a portion of his estate if necessary to pay his debts. He asked that if his 128 "negroes" could not be sold to one person that those "connected by birth and marriage not be separated." Of course, this was only a request; at the end of the day, his executors would do whatever they needed to do to satisfy his debts once he was dead and gone. John Parker also recommended to his sons and executors, Francis Simmons Parker and Arthur Middleton Parker, that they not sell the "Combahee place" he had worked "industriously and under very trying circumstances" to make prosper. John Parker had purchased 274 acres of highland and 406 acres of marsh from James Ladson and John Stock in 1832, changing its name from Eveleigh to Palmetto. That same year Parker sold a tract of Eveleigh Plantation to Dr. William L. Kirkland Sr., which became part of Kirkland's estate. Parker purchased additional tracts, Longbrow, and Plains, from Charles Lowndes in 1849. After putting $12,000 into Palmetto, Parker had refused an offer from a buyer willing to pay $20,000 for it. He counseled his sons that if they waited and managed it properly, in time the "Combahee place" would be worth $40,000. A few months after John Parker's death on December 17, 1849, his estate was appraised. Among the 128 people whom he held in bondage on the lower Combahee River, worth a total of $40,700, were Old Head Silvia Jackson Gaylord DeCauster and her first husband, Samson ("Samson 600" and "Silvy 400"), Silvia's brother-in-law Andrew Wyatt ("Andrew 650"), and her sister Maria ("Maria 550)." Andrew Wyatt and Sampson

Gaylord were two of the most highly valued—two of only three worth $600 or more each—listed and appraised on Parker's estate record for his Palmetto Plantation.[45]

Silvia DeCauster testified that she had known her second husband, Isaac DeCauster, when they "were quite young." They were "raised on adjoining plantations"; Isaac may have been born on Joshua and Mary Anna Nicholls's Longbrow Plantation, raised with Mary Ann Lewis and Anthony Bartley, while Silvia was literally next door on Parker's Palmetto Plantation. Andrew Wyatt ("Andrew 650"), whom Silvia DeCauster's sister Maria married after the war, was included in the estate record as well. Silvia DeCauster testified for her brother-in-law that she and Wyatt "grew up together," both slaves of John Parker, and were "about the same age."[46]

For enslaved people, the death of a slaveholder always involved a special kind of grief. Freedpeople surely remembered the trepidation of not knowing to whom they would "belong" after a slaveholder died and whether they would be sold and separated from their loved ones. Deaths in the planter aristocracy habitually fated enslaved family members to being taken from their families, from the enslaved communities to which they were integral parts, and from the ground in which their ancestors were buried. Division of the planter's estate among his or her heirs—such as the division of William Savage's estate after his death—regularly ensued after the planter's death. If the planter died in debt, his estate, or parts of it, would be liquidated and sold to pay off the debts. Throughout the Lowcountry, a good number of rice planters overextended themselves.

★★★★★★★★

Planter families on the Combahee tended to be wealthier, which somewhat insulated them from financial issues resulting from death, natural disaster, or market downturns; typically they would be the buyers, not the sellers, in estate liquidation sales. Nonetheless, they had their own problems.

Mary Anna Lynah Kirkland Faber had a problem as she prepared to marry Joshua Nicholls in 1848. Her second husband, Henry A. Faber, had hired Nicholls to tutor her son. Henry died in 1839, just two years after they married. According to family lore, Mary Anna and Joshua Nicholls married after a European tour during which he provided the son's education. He was nineteen years Mary Anna Faber's junior and nine years older than her only child, William Lennox Kirkland Jr.[47]

Now that Mary Anna Lynah Kirkland Faber was a woman of considerable means, she had to protect her assets and her son's inheritance. She
solved this problem by signing a marriage settlement with Joshua Nicholls
on November 20, 1848, before she and Nicholls married. Executed in
Warrenton, Georgia, the agreement put Mary Anna Lynah Kirkland Faber's
large personal estate in a trust, with her brother Edward T. Lynah as her
trustee, and reserved it for her sole and separate use and benefit. The trust
protected the estate from creditors suing Mary Anna's estate to pay off debts
her soon-to-be husband might incur. It included the undivided three-
fourths interest (owned in common by Mary Ann and William Jr.) in Rose
Hill Plantation's 1,425 acres, which consisted of 900 acres of uplands and
525 acres of tidal swamplands. Along with the furnishings in the main house
and outbuildings (paintings, furniture, china, glassware, utensils), carriages
and other vehicles, livestock, agricultural implements, and tools, the estate also included 102 people forced to labor against their will (an increase
from 1838, when Rose Hill and the eighty-seven laborers enslaved there
were valued at $15,000 in her mother-in-law's estate) and the unnamed
infants and future increase of the female bondspeople. One-fourth of Rose
Hill had been left to William L. Kirkland Jr. by his father's and paternal
grandmother's wills. The $17,000 bond that Mary Anna Lynah Kirkland
had signed to her mother-in-law in 1838 remained unpaid. And Mary Anna
alone would determine to whom she would bequeath her estate upon her
demise. The marriage agreement was not specific about who would inherit her estate; it left the door open for her to make an agreement with
her young adult son about the three-fourths of Rose Hill they owned
together and the $17,000 she owed his grandmother's estate. It also stated
that should she predecease her new husband, she would provide liberal
resources for him to maintain himself in the fashion to which he was becoming accustomed, though it offered no details. The year after the marriage settlement was signed, William Kirkland Jr. reached his majority and
began to help Joshua Nicholls to manage Rose Hill. In 1850, Mary Anna
Lynah Kirkland Faber Nicholls owned 107 slaves on Rose Hill Plantation
and eleven enslaved people at their Charleston home in St. Michael and St.
Phillip Parish. [48]

Of the enslaved people held in trust by Edward T. Lynah for his sister,
John Savage, Mary Ann Lewis, and Maria Wineglass and their mother,
Kate, and Simon Jackson and Quasheba with their children Anthony

Bartley, Jacob Jackson, and Daphne Jackson Powell Snipe, all had come from William Savage's plantation on the Ogeechee River, transported against their will by Henry Middleton Parker. Simon and Quasheba's daughter Catharina is not included in the family grouping; she may have died or been sold. The available sources don't reveal the origins of another family, Carolina Grant, his wife, Flora, and his son, Stepheny, nor the origins of Isaac DeCauster. But ownership of their bodies, labor, and increase was included also. The 1848 marriage settlement lists the enslaved men together (". . . Carolina, Stepney . . . Isaac . . . Johnny, Simon, Anthony, Jacob . . . Andrew . . .") and then the women together (". . . Daphney, Flora . . . Kate . . . Quasheba . . . Mary Ann . . . Maria . . ."), regardless of family grouping.[49]

Old Head Carolina Grant had been a carpenter on Joshua and Mary Anna Lynah Kirkland Faber Nicholls's Longbrow Plantation. According to Carolina's pension file testimony, he was born around 1784, making him one of the oldest Old Heads on the lower part of the Combahee River. A preacher named Coleman married Carolina and Flora long before the war, around 1836; Coleman was probably the very same itinerant white minister who married November Osborne and Sarah Small on Thomas Lowndes's Oakland Plantation, located right next door to Rose Hill Plantation on its northwest side.[50]

Carolina Grant's pension file also indicated that he had been physically disabled for some time. The typical labors of carpenters enslaved on Lowcountry rice plantations in the nineteenth century at least contributed to, if not caused, Carolina's disability. Enslaved carpenters built and repaired everything on the plantation made of wood, including small fleets of wooden flats and barges, which were the workhorses of tidal rice plantations, and dugout canoes that enslaved people used for transportation to other plantations and for fishing when they had finished their tasks. For years even before the war, Carolina could only do light work. According to Old Head Andrew Wyatt, the Kirkland/Nicholls family allowed him to work at his own slow pace, taking his time and doing what he could, because Carolina Grant was "crippled in the back." He had to be supported by his wife, Flora, and by their children. But Flora was also an Old Head, and their daughters were too young to provide for the family. Their oldest child and only son, Stepney Grant, took it upon himself to support his parents and siblings, providing them with whatever they needed. John A. Savage had worked with Carolina Grant as a carpenter since the war and testified that he knew Carolina's whole family. He knew that the old man could not do "as much work as a boy" since long before the Civil War.[51]

★★★★★★★★

While more weddings within enslaved communities on Lowcountry rice plantations took place in winter, that season was also one of the most intensive labor periods. The time when the planter families entertained themselves, celebrating their wealth, prosperity, and familial ties, was also the deadliest for enslaved men and women working in the rice fields. Beginning in the late fall and through the winter, the strongest enslaved men were forced to dig canals (through raw swamp when constructing rice fields) wide and deep enough to accommodate the passage of a rice flat, each enslaved laborer digging ten feet of length in one day's task. The flats—flat-bottomed, cross-planked, and wedge-ended boats, up to fourteen feet wide and forty feet long—plied main canals flowing from the river to the rice fields and carried harvested rice to the threshing house or rice mill, then transported threshed rice to market. Smaller work craft, three feet wide and thirty feet long, carried harvested rice along the quarter ditch canals, which sectioned off individual rice fields, to larger barges waiting in the main canal. Enslaved women, meanwhile, built banks with earth dug out by the men and raked vines out of the large ditches. When they worked outside, they often stood barefoot in the cold, wet, muddy swamps, lacking any winter clothing or even shoes to protect them from exposure to snow, ice, frost, freezing rains, and piercing winds. During the winter and early spring, tasks also included repairing the dikes, ditches, and floodgates, cleaning the ditches, digging canals, plowing the fields that had been kept under water since the harvest, and then hoeing in preparation for planting the rice crop. Winter work made enslaved field hands vulnerable to upper respiratory diseases and frostbite. It cost countless Prime Hands their lives.[52]

When the mercury sank to its lowest point, overseers would assign enslaved laborers to indoor tasks, such as threshing (also called milling or pounding) the rice. But indoor work during the winter was hardly easy. Before the 1780s, when steam-powered rice mills were first patented, enslaved women milled harvested rice by putting it into a mortar made from a hollowed-out cypress or pine tree trunk. They raised a pestle, a seven-to-ten-pound weight made from a portion of a cypress or pine tree approximately three to five feet long and six inches wide, and pounded the rice in the mortar by repeatedly and rhythmically rolling the pestle and striking the rice. These strenuous actions removed the hull from the rice grains, producing polished rice ready for market with as few broken grains as possible. This was primarily women's work, having its origins in West Africa's rice-growing region.[53]

The death rates among female Prime Hands from pounding rice were so high that enslaved men and children were taught to pound rice as soon as they were strong enough to lift a pestle and barely tall enough to see over the mortar. Most enslaved children who were made to pound rice did not survive until adulthood. Confined in cold, drafty, and poorly ventilated barns, enslaved people were vulnerable to contracting and spreading upper respiratory diseases, such as pneumonia, pleurisy, and peripneumonia, which killed them at alarming rates. Excessive slave mortality from pounding rice was a "great Damage," as a 1733 advertisement by Peter Villeponteaux, who patented the first animal-powered rice-pounding mill in the Lowcountry, termed it. Patents for mechanical threshing machines were commonplace by the time Charles Lowndes, the founder of the Lowndes family who committed suicide, submitted his patent application in the early 1730s. William Lowndes, Thomas Lowndes and James Lowndes's half-brother, wrote in his plantation book that the task for each enslaved man was to pound six bushels of rough rice and an enslaved woman four bushels if that was their only task for the entire day. However, if they were made to pound rice in addition to working another task, the enslaved men were to pound one and a half bushels and the women one bushel. It amounted to hours of extra backbreaking daily labor for enslaved laborers, accomplished in the early mornings before the rest of the day's work and in the evenings after performing their tasks in the rice fields. This was after they had been forced to exert themselves during the late summer rice harvest, another period of intense work. Even after steam-powered mills were patented, Nathaniel Heyward continued to enforce hand threshing on his seventeen upper Combahee River rice plantations. Otherwise, he said, the thousand people he held in bondage—his "darkies," as he put it—"would have no winter work." Mechanical threshing machines saved the lives of many women who otherwise might have died from indoor rice threshing, making them available to work outside in the damp, frosty winter weather cleaning the canals and ditches.[54]

★★★★★★★★

Fear of sale (particularly after the death of the enslaver), laboring in the rice fields against one's will, indoor and outdoor winter work and the sickness and death it wrought—these were all enough to impel some enslaved people on the lower Combahee River to try to escape to freedom. But where would they go? How would they get out of the Deep South? How could they make it almost seven hundred miles through slave territory to free states in the North——or to Maroon communities in Spanish Florida, which were closer (a little more than two hundred miles away)? Freedom was still out of reach for the overwhelming majority of Black people enslaved on the South Carolina Lowcountry's rice plantations.

5

Freedom Seekers

When Eliza Brodess decided to put Harriet Tubman and her brothers up for sale, she forced them to face a bleak prospect. Either they would be sold as slaves for life out of state, far away from family and friends, or they could run away, facing starvation, exposure, wild animals, and slave catchers, and very likely dying alone. If they were caught and returned to the plantation, they would be brutally punished and probably sold to slave traders in the Deep South.

On Maryland's Eastern Shore in the second quarter of the nineteenth century, countless enslaved men, women, and children faced the auction block and then life on a cotton plantation in the Deep South. The economy in the Eastern Shore had, as I've noted, shifted from tobacco to timber and grains, and then it slowed. Enslaved people faced being auctioned off and marched through town headed south on a slave coffle, bound by ropes around their necks and staples around their arms, and driven by the whip. Henry "Box" Brown's wife, Nancy, was pregnant with the couple's fourth child when she and their three children were sold and she was marched on a slave coffle to North Carolina, leaving her husband behind. Fast-growing and prosperous cotton plantations in the Deep South and the Southwest created a lucrative market for seasoned prime laborers. Slaveholders on the Eastern Shore were not the only ones tempted to put excess enslaved laborers "in their pocket."[1]

Thus in their uncertainty Tubman and her brothers had plenty of company. The threat of sale could be implicit. Nineteen-year-old Noah Ennells ran away constantly because he expected to be sold. He knew that Bill LeCompte, who held him in bondage in Cambridge, was in debt. Twenty-seven-year-old Joseph Grant, who was enslaved by Mary Gibson in St. Michael's on the Eastern Shore, also ran away, because he feared he would be sold along with Gibson's property to satisfy a mortgage. William Butcher, alias William Mitchell, ran away from his home in Georgetown, Kent County, after slaveholder William Boyd threatened to sell him. John Chase feared sale by John Campbell Henry of Cambridge, who held 140 Blacks in bondage and had already sold several.[2]

Slaveholders sometimes explicitly threatened those they held in bondage with sale to slave traders from the South. James Massey said that he ran away from slaveholder James Pittman because when he was drunk Pittman threatened to sell all of the laborers he held in bondage to Georgia. Pittman had already sold one of Massey's brothers, likely as a slave for life, though he had been entitled to his freedom at twenty-five. Also entitled to his freedom at twenty-five, Massey decided not to serve Pittman for five more years while waiting for it and took his freedom. Henry Predo, twenty-seven, ran away from enslavement in Bucktown, Maryland, and twenty-nine-year-old John Brown escaped enslavement in Fredericktown, because the men who held them in bondage threatened to sell them south. The constant threats, whether implicit or explicit, that they would be sold and separated forever from their families had been too much for these bondspeople to bear.[3]

For enslaved people, running away was always a heartbreaking decision. No matter if they ran away with other loved ones—husbands and wives, children, and siblings being the most likely candidates—they left behind family members, such as parents, cousins, aunts, and uncles. Those they had to leave behind would almost certainly be punished, tortured, and/or sold away, out of state, as slaves for life.[4]

George Rhoads ran away from enslaver John P. Dellum because Dellum had threatened to sell him. In the previous two to three years Dellum had sold an enslaved man and woman and told the people he still held in bondage that he would sell all of them to Georgia if one of them ran away. Rhoads ran anyway and took away with him as many of his family as he could, including his brother James. The odds were starkly against them ever seeing their family again. After Ann Johnson's brother fled to Canada, their enraged bondholder, Samuel Harrington of Cambridge, sold away two of her sisters in retaliation. Ann ran away shortly after she was sold to William Moore three years later. Whether they stayed or ran away, it was an inhuman choice.[5]

★★★★★★★★

In 1849, widow Eliza Brodess petitioned the court in Dorchester to sell Tubman's niece Kessiah Jolly Bowley and her children, James Alfred and

Araminta, the latter an infant still in her mother's arms. Kessiah was the daughter of Tubman's older sister Linah Ross Jolly, whom Edward Brodess had sold in the 1830s, separating her from her children. On the same fateful day—September 17, 1849—when the court decided whether another of Ben and Rit Ross's children and their grandchildren could be sold, Harriet and her brothers Ben Jr. and Henry ran away. The siblings had to leave behind their parents, their other brothers Robert and Moses, their sister Rachel, and a number of nieces and nephews. After the sale of their older sisters Linah, Soph, and Mariah, along with some of their children, Tubman and her brothers suspected they would be next, should the court give Brodess permission to sell Kessiah.[6]

By leaving their family members behind, Tubman and her brothers would leave them vulnerable. Tubman certainly could not imagine seeing her family again. It was unheard of for someone who crossed the Mason-Dixon Line to come back. It might as well have been the Atlantic Ocean.

But Harriet, Ben Jr., and Henry did not make their way to a free state, not this first time. Tubman told Sarah Bradford decades later that they had not ventured far before her brothers became "appalled" at the dangers that lay before them on the long dark road to freedom and the dangers that would overtake them if and when slave catchers caught and returned them to enslavement. Though younger than Tubman, her brothers may have asserted masculine authority and "dragged" her back to Anthony Thompson's plantation with them.[7]

Ben Jr. and Henry were deeply scared. Tubman may have been also. Still, untutored and unlettered though she was, she was a student of the natural environment, starting from the time James Cook had sent her out alone to the banks of streams and marshes to check his muskrat traps. During the winter trapping season, she had had to wade through cold streams, learning to feel their depth. Tubman learned directional navigation using the North Star from her father, and by identifying the way moss grew on tree bark. She always trusted in the Lord to guide her and keep her out of harm's way. And she had a God-given gift for reading the landscape better than any skilled hunter. Decades after the emancipation of enslaved people, Samuel Hopkins Adams remembered Tubman as a "pathfinder." He wrote that "she possessed a miraculous geographical instinct, never forgetting any detail of a route she had once traversed. Thus she was able to pilot unerringly her little, scared bands along unfrequented paths, lying up by day in swamp, cave, or abandoned shack, and dodging the patrols by night." Tubman herself maintained that she had no fear of bloodhounds; she knew how to rub red onions or spruce pine on the soles of her feet to throw them off her scent.[8]

She also knew the vegetation—the pine, red maple, sweet gum, and oak trees in the forest, the Atlantic white cedar trees and saltmeadow cordgrass and smooth cordgrass in the marshes. She could identify edible roots, berries, and flowers. She knew which small animals inhabited a particular micro-environment, and when they were secreting hormones whose smell might attract bloodhounds and slave catchers. From working with watermen on the Chesapeake Bay and its tributaries, Tubman had learned that the Eastern Shore's rivers ran north.[9]

Thus, by following the North Star and the rivers, Tubman could navigate her way toward Pennsylvania, the nearest free state to Maryland. She could survive until she found someone to help her. Most importantly, she was a natural leader who trusted her instincts and her knowledge, with faith that the Holy Ghost would guide and protect her. Her brothers lacked Tubman's confidence. They feared recapture—Ben Jr. knew that if he was recaptured, he would be sold to the Deep South, away from his wife and children—and did not possess their sister's conviction and confidence that, as Tubman said later, "there was one of two things I had a right to, liberty or death; if I could not have one, I would have the other."[10]

Though the siblings returned to Anthony Thompson's plantation in Caroline County, Tubman would remain only a few days, staying over Sunday. Then she ran away again, this time alone. Leaving everyone must have been an agonizing decision for Tubman. She had wanted to tell them she was leaving in case she never saw them again, but that was risky. She could not take the chance anyone might betray her plan, even unintentionally. Eliza Brodess would likely sell her as a slave for life to the Deep South, just as her deceased husband, Edward Brodess, had done with her sisters Linah, Mariah, and Soph many years earlier.[11]

Tubman sang as she walked down the lane on Thompson's plantation on which the slave cabins lined both sides; she encountered Dr. Thompson as she neared the gate, paused for a few minutes, and sang to him her farewell song. No one, not Dr. Thompson nor any other bondsmen lingering on the porch of their cabin, understood the message of her song until after she was long gone: "Goodbye, I'm going to leave you. Goodbye, I'll meet you in the kingdom." We know that Tubman sang Methodist hymns and occasionally sang songs when she gave lectures later in life. Samuel Hopkins Adams (Sarah Bradford's grandnephew) remembered an elderly Tubman expressing herself in her beautiful singing voice. Her departure song from Thompson's plantation is one of the earliest known examples of Tubman using her voice to deliver encoded messages about freedom.[12]

Leaving Thompson's farm, Tubman walked about a mile east of Thompson's plantation on Poplar Neck to the home of a Quaker woman, either Esther Kelley or Hannah Leverton (the latter an active abolitionist whose daughter married Dr. Anthony Thompson's son). Thompson's Poplar Neck farm was located in close proximity to Marshy Creek Friends of the Northwest Fork Meeting, a small Quaker settlement. Tubman confided in the woman, telling her her plans to secure her freedom; then she gave the Quaker woman a quilt she had made as a gift. Though she could have faced prosecution, a fine, and even jail time for aiding and abetting a fugitive slave, the woman allowed Tubman to wait there. When her husband returned home, he concealed Tubman in his covered wagon and took her to the home of the second contact, another stop on the Underground Railroad, which by 1849 was a well-established informal network of safe houses for freedom seekers. From here, she followed the North Star, traveling along the Choptank River, across the Delmarva Peninsula, then north–northeast into Pennsylvania.

Tubman may have gotten help in her self-liberation from Thomas Garrett or other Quakers or free Blacks living in the Wilmington area. Garrett was a blacksmith by trade and a Quaker abolitionist who had been assisting freedom seekers as early as 1813, when he rescued a free Black servant who worked for his family and who had been kidnapped by a slave catcher. Five years later, Garrett joined the Pennsylvania Society for the Abolition of Slavery. Garrett directed Tubman on to Philadelphia. In 1848, months before Tubman liberated herself from bondage, Garrett had been tried and sentenced for harboring a family of runaway slaves. Samuel Hawkins was a free man from Queen Anne's County, located approximately sixty miles north of Dorchester County. His wife, Emeline Hawkins, and their two sons, Chester and Samuel, were enslaved by a Mr. Glanding and subsequently bequeathed to his son, Charles Wesley Glanding. After Emeline was sold or given away, she and their four younger children were held in bondage by someone named Elizabeth N. Turner. In the winter of 1848, the Hawkins family ran away with the assistance of a man named Samuel

D. Burris, who took them to the home of John Hunn in Middletown, Delaware. They arrived in a wagon carrying Emeline Hawkins, who kept the infant at her breast warm with an old piece of carpet wrapped around the baby's back, and three small children. Samuel Hawkins and their two teenage sons walked alongside the wagon. All of the men (and the horse) suffered from exposure and fatigue and the young children were very sickly after they walked through the night and through a snowstorm.[13]

The constable came to Hunn's home to reenslave them. Samuel Hawkins produced papers proving his free status, but the constable denied that they were authentic. Hunn, for his part, would not turn over the Hawkins family without a warrant. The constable insisted that they be taken to the magistrate in Middletown. The constable offered Samuel a deal: Samuel, his wife, and their four younger children could go free, but their two older sons would be returned to the man who held them in bondage on the Eastern Shore. That the constable would collect a reward for recapturing the two older boys was an implicit part of the deal. Samuel felt he had no choice; he agreed to his older children being forced back into slavery so that his wife and younger children could be free.[14]

However, the Middletown magistrate declared the agreement not binding, because Samuel was free. The legal maneuvers bought Hunn enough time to call Thomas Garrett, who took the Hawkins family before the chief justice of Delaware—a man who happened to be sympathetic to the plight of enslaved people. The chief justice ruled that the constable's agreement was indeed null and void, and he released the Hawkins family, giving Garrett permission to hire a carriage and transport them to Wilmington. There they were reunited with Samuel D. Burris, who spirited them into hiding before the Middletown magistrate arrived with a new deal. As a result of that deal, the two older boys were indentured—according to a provision in Pennsylvania's 1780 Gradual Abolition Act—until they were twenty-one.[15]

By the time Tubman met him, Garrett had been summoned by the authorities and tried four times; each trial lasted for three days. Charles Glanding, who held the Hawkinses' two older sons in bondage, and Elizabeth Turner, who enslaved Emeline and their four young children, sued Garrett for $10,500 in damages. The judge instructed the jury that if they thought Garrett had harbored Blacks whom he suspected to be fugitive slaves, or had transported or arranged the transportation of Glanding's and Turner's property from New Castle to Wilmington, or had concealed them at his store to prevent them from being recovered and returned to bondage, they must find for the plaintiffs. The jury found Garrett guilty as charged and ordered him to pay the Maryland enslavers $5,400 in damages. Garrett ultimately paid a compromise settlement of $1,500, still a hefty sum, and one that came on top of significant business losses he had already sustained before the trial. Hunn was convicted as well and ordered to pay $1,500 in damages.[16]

Being "mulcted"—as it was called—by such a sizeable fine did not deter Thomas Garrett. Once court was adjourned, and after the marshal of the court had admonished Garrett to henceforth mind his business and not involve himself with runaway slaves, Garrett gave a self-incriminating speech. He stood before observers in the courtroom wearing one of the wide-brimmed hats and long waistcoats for which he was known. He condemned slavery, which by then was the cause of clashes in Congress as the nation expanded. Garrett predicted the dissolution of the Union in ten years' time (this being 1848, it was a fairly accurate prediction). He reproached himself for holding back on helping "God's poor," though he had helped more than two thousand over the course of forty years. Now that the court had fined him, it had given him a license to redouble his personal efforts. Garrett implored the audience to inform him if they knew of any slave in need, and to please send the slave to him. He promised to help the person secure freedom regardless of what it cost.[17]

Garrett and Hunn were two of a number of abolitionists, Black and white, who risked everything—homes, businesses, relationships with neighbors, friends, church members, and even families, and increasingly their own lives— because of their work with the Underground Railroad. Garrett was still working with it in 1849 when sometime in the late fall or early winter Tubman made it across the Mason-Dixon Line and into the Commonwealth of Pennsylvania. She was now a freedom seeker. She had successfully achieved what Atthow Pattison's will and the Dorchester County Court had not: she was finally free.[18]

Arriving in Philadelphia, Tubman sought assistance from the Pennsylvania Anti-Slavery Society's General Vigilance Committee and in particular William Still. The Pennsylvania Anti-Slavery Society (PASS) was a radical abolitionist organization that was aligned with William Lloyd Garrison's calls for immediate and uncompensated abolition and advocated African Americans' equality. Still had begun working in fall of 1847 as a clerk and assistant to James Miller McKim, an ordained Presbyterian minister who worked as lecturer, organizer, and correspondence secretary for PASS. In December 1852, Still would become president of a four-man Acting Committee within the Vigilance Committee. The 1850 Fugitive Slave Act meant that any Black person, no matter if they were legally free, could be kidnapped in a free state and sent south into bondage. Northern municipalities had to enforce and uphold southern slaveholders' property rights. In those perilous times, the Acting Committee's mission was to provide freedom seekers with food, clothes, shoes, housing, and transportation, and to assist them in finding employment in Philadelphia. Still linked the national network of abolitionists with the web of regional Underground Railroad conductors, such as Harriet Tubman and Thomas Garrett, and with the hungry, cold, scared, and often ill freedom seekers people who were desperate for their freedom.[19]

Still had been born free in Burlington County in southern New Jersey's pinelands east of and across Delaware Bay from Philadelphia. He was the youngest of his mother's eighteen children. His parents and several of his older siblings had been born enslaved in Caroline County on Maryland's Eastern Shore just north of Dorchester County, where Tubman was born. After the death of the enslaver who held both Levin and Sidney, Still's parents, in bondage, Levin and Sidney were bequeathed to separate family members, then sold and bequeathed again. Eventually, Still's father ended up the property of William Wood, a young Quaker, and was able to buy his freedom in November 1798 by hiring himself out to earn extra money and to pay Wood. His wife, Sidney, and the four children they had at that time remained in bondage to someone else who possessed the power and the right to sell them and separate the family forever. The longer it took for the family to buy Sidney's freedom, the more expensive it would be. Each child she bore inherited her unfree status. Levin most likely left Maryland for New Jersey to earn more money to free his family. But to do so, he had to leave them behind.[20]

In 1807, Sidney and their children escaped from bondage in Maryland, traversing more than forty-five miles, crossing Delaware Bay, and eventually arriving in southern New Jersey, where they were reunited with Levin. Unfortunately, the Stills' reunion ended violently when slave catchers kidnapped Sidney and the kids, dragging them back to the clutches of Alexander Griffith, the enslaver who held the five in bondage. After Griffith tortured her by locking her in a garret nightly for months as punishment, Sidney (who changed her name to Charity Still) decided to run away again. This time she faced the same horrific decision that Samuel Hawkins had—whether to attempt an escape with all four of her children or leave some of them behind. She made the heartrending choice to run away with their two younger daughters—likely to spare them from sexual abuse—and left their two older sons, Peter and Levin Jr., in God's hands. She and the girls made it safely back to Levin in New Jersey. Alexander Griffith sold Peter and Levin Jr. to Kentucky, and they were subsequently sold again multiple times. Levin Jr. died young, but Peter purchased his freedom and made his way to Philadelphia. Still's mother had doubtless thought she would never see her sons again.[21]

Motivated by his family's tragic history, William Still took a personal interest in the freedom seekers whom the Vigilance Committee aided, and boarded some at his home until permanent housing could be found. He also interviewed everyone seeking assistance, recording their names during enslavement and the new names they chose for themselves as free people, and asking them for their stories: who had held them in bondage, where they had been enslaved, what they had experienced, what had motivated them to run away, how they had fled, and what they had experienced in their flight. He further recorded the names of family members they had left behind, as well as his own observations about the freedom seekers' appearance and levels of education and industry. He preserved their stories to protect the Vigilance Committee and all of its volunteers from slave hunters, as well as to help families fleeing enslavement in the slave South find each other and begin their lives in freedom.[22]

In 1851, two years after Tubman's arrival in Philadelphia, a man by the name of Peter came before the Vigilance Committee requesting aid. He explained that he had been separated from his mother and two sisters when his mother ran away with her daughters and had had to leave her sons behind. Still discovered in recording Peter's story that he was none other than one of his own brothers, left behind, then sold multiple times and finally winding up in Alabama, where their older brother had died in bondage sixteen years earlier. Still's recorded stories helped to reunite him with his own lost family member. From 1852 to 1861, Still recorded the stories of 995 freedom seekers who received assistance from the Vigilance Committee.[23]

****

With its network of stations in Delaware, Pennsylvania, and New Jersey, the Pennsylvania Anti-Slavery Society's Vigilance Committee was efficient and well organized. Not all of the Underground Railroad's operations were. Historians have argued about its origins. Most agree that the expression was adopted by antislavery groups in border and northern states that were dedicated to assisting runaway slaves in the 1830s and 1840s, when railroads became common. They used the term "Underground Railroad" to protect themselves from prosecution. An informal network of free Blacks and white abolitionists, like Thomas Garrett, hid, sheltered, fed, clothed, and provided medical care for freedom seekers, transporting them from one safe house to another. These men and women became known as "station masters," and the freedom seekers as "passengers." The fact of the matter, though, is that enslaved people had sought their freedom well before the term "Underground Railroad" was coined. The overwhelming majority did not trust white folks and did not seek their help. Some, like Henry Highland Garnet's parents, found allies among individuals who were not part of a network.[24]

Given the dangers freedom seekers encountered and the physical stamina required, it is not surprising that young men constituted the overwhelming majority of those who made their way to William Still's Philadelphia office. The freedom seekers were also overwhelmingly Prime Hands, not Old Heads.

Harriet Tubman was one of a handful of women. Some wives ran away with their husbands and children, though husbands often had to leave behind their wives, enslaved or free. Daffney Cornish, whose children had been hired out at around ten years of age, terminated the enslaver's right to separate her from her children by running away with her husband, Aaron Cornish, and six children. Kit Anthony, his wife, Leah, and their three children joined the Cornish clan in fleeing enslavement from Cambridge. Lizzie Amby ran away from enslavement with her husband, Nat. John Muir, the man who held Nat—and forty or fifty other Blacks—in bondage had already sold two of Nat's sisters and one of his brothers. Muir's wife had made a deathbed pledge to Nat that he would not be sold; Nat even thought he might be freed. But Muir reneged on that promise. Caroline Stanly and her husband, Daniel Stanly, joined the Ambys in escaping from Cambridge County.[25]

Lear Green undertook a different sort of risk in an escape that remains one of the most celebrated in the history of slavery. She followed the example of Henry "Box" Brown. On March 29, 1849—in the same year

Harriet Tubman liberated herself from bondage—Brown had had himself shipped overland express from Richmond to Philadelphia in a wooden crate just over three feet long, two and a half feet deep, and two feet wide, with three gimlet holes bored in it for air. He was in the crate for twenty-seven hours and traveled 350 miles. Though it was marked "This Side Up," Brown's crate was turned upside down for extended periods before being delivered to the home of an abolitionist supporter on March 30. Eight years later, eighteen-year-old Green had fallen in love with a free Black man, a barber named William Adams. Slaveholder James Noble, who held her in bondage, had tried to break up the couple, but Green was determined to be free before she married. She wanted to prevent her children from being born enslaved and then sold away from her and her husband once they were old enough. She intended to start her family as a free woman in New York, where her fiancé's mother lived.[26]

Lear exchanged Henry "Box" Brown's custom-made dry-goods crate for a sailor's chest. She was packed inside with quilts, pillows, and a few articles of clothing; ropes were tied around the chest to keep it closed. The trunk was loaded on board a steamer. William Adams's mother traveled as a passenger on the same ship. From her station on deck, where Black passengers were required to sit, she kept an eye on the trunk, making sure Lear had enough air. Lear's daring and determination ultimately paid off. The passenger and her "freight" eventually arrived safely in Philadelphia.[27]

Like Lear Green, Harriet Shepard knew that her family faced a future of abuse, deprivation, and danger. She had already borne five children, increasing the wealth of the man who owned them all. She recruited five additional freedom seekers and together they seized four of the slaveholder's horses and two of his carriages. Shephard shuttled her children out of slavery in Chestertowne and safely to Thomas Garrett's farm in Wilmington. Since Blacks driving a carriage or riding horses without a white patron would have been conspicuous, Garrett separated the large party before sending them on to William Still.[28]

Freedom seekers knew that the odds were against their ever seeing their loved ones again. Still's journal is replete with letters from those who had settled in Canada, upstate New York, or Massachusetts, asking him to get word to those still in bondage. One escapee, Jefferson Pipkins, requested Still's assistance in liberating his children, who had been sold before he ran away. Sons Charles and Patrick were enslaved in Hartford County, North

Carolina; Emma, his daughter, was held in Gatesville, North Carolina; Susan, another daughter, was in Portsmouth, Virginia. It is remarkable that Pipkins had been able to keep abreast of his children's whereabouts. Unfortunately, Still knew it would be impossible to liberate them.[29]

Upon his safe arrival in Canada, James Massey wrote immediately to his wife, Henrietta, via William Still. Massey had run away from Queen Anne's County on the Eastern Shore after slaveholder James Pittman had threatened to sell him to a plantation in Georgia. Massey wanted to get word to his wife, who was still in bondage. Like many freedom seekers (including Harriet Tubman), Massey did not share his escape plans with those closest to him. Perhaps they feared their spouses would dissuade them from taking the risk. Escape frequently caused marital friction. If she and Massey had an "abroad marriage," his wife may not have known he was gone for good until he failed to arrive for his next scheduled visit, leaving her and his other family members behind. In the letter, Massey apologized for the pain this must have caused her and asked her to join him as soon as possible. He countered her fears about the dangerous journey to freedom and the harshness of the winters in Canada by promising to treat her as a lady for the rest of her life.[30]

We do not know if Jefferson Pipkins, James Massey, and countless other freedom seekers who wrote to Still and traveled the Underground Railroad, such as William Hogg and Samuel Miles, were ever reunited with their families. We do know that most enslaved people who liberated themselves from chattel slavery did so with a one-way ticket. Their letters asked, begged, for help to get those closest to them sent to them. Most did not try to go back for them. Had they been caught in the attempt, they would have been reenslaved and undoubtedly sold, severing their family ties forever.[31]

Henry Highland Garnet's parents devised a plan to escape bondage on Maryland's Eastern Shore by going with their family to a relative's funeral, then stealing away. Young Henry was only nine years old. Once they were settled in New York, the Garnets did not go back to Maryland to bring anyone else out. Lear Green did not climb back into the sailor's chest—not even to rescue her own mother. Even the idea that Henry "Box" Brown could have had himself packed back up in a crate and mailed back to Richmond to rescue his wife and children, who were still in bondage, was preposterous. Yet Harriet Tubman frequently went back into slave territory, risking her freedom for the freedom of others. When she took the train into southern states from the North. As she put it, no white person would suspect a Negro going south.[32]

Nonetheless, there are a few scattered references to enslaved people who liberated themselves and then returned to the slave South to liberate family members. Thomas Garrett described one case of a woman in New Jersey whose six children had been sold away from her many years before. When she heard the enslaver bargaining with a slave trader to sell her fifteen-year-old grandson, the last of her family, she risked everything to save him from sale and flee with him the very same night. Almost fifty, the Old Head and her grandchild made their way to Canada, where they settled in and worked for wages, which she saved to finance a rescue mission. Garrett reported that she traveled back south to the plantation to which some of her children had been sold, hid in the woods until she could gather her loved ones, and stole the freedom of her children and grandchildren. On their journey north, they stopped in Philadelphia—where Garrett met her—and received food and clothing, likely from the local abolitionist community, then continued on their way to Canada. Garrett did not have more information about this "noble woman," as he called her. There were probably others who went back into the "prison-house of bondage" to free those they had left behind, but their attempts are unrecorded.[33]

★★★★★★★★

After arriving in Philadelphia, Harriet Tubman relished her freedom—but she was also lonely, pining for her family, whom she had been forced to leave behind in slavery, "the next thing to hell." What good was freedom without anyone with whom to share it? It is not clear at this point whether she had determined to go back to Maryland to bring her family members out. Later, from Canada, she reflected that she knew hundreds of escaped enslaved people but did not know anyone willing to go back. The idea must have seemed inconceivable at the time. On the Eastern Shore, Tubman had been enmeshed in both enslaved Black and free Black communities. Her own family, as we've seen, was an example of how members could be both. Her husband, John Tubman, was free, and her brother Henry Ross was married to a free woman, Harriet Ann Parker Ross; her niece Kessiah Jolly Bowley was married to a free man, John Bowley. Thus Tubman had some idea of what it meant to be free. But it is unlikely that even she could conceive of anyone voluntarily returning to enslavement.[34]

We may never know what motivated Tubman to take her first trip back to Maryland. She loved her family dearly. And she risked reenslavement when they were in danger, when there was the likelihood that they would be either permanently exiled or physically harmed.

In December 1850, Tubman received a message that Eliza Brodess had advertised Kessiah and her two children for sale at auction. She would have been separated from her family and sold into a lifetime of bondage (in violation of Atthow Pattison's will, which had manumitted Rit Green at age forty-five and limited the service of her children). Tubman may have gotten the message regarding Kessiah's impending sale from the community of "Black Jacks" and other maritime networks plying the waterways along the Eastern Seaboard—the same men among whom she had worked when she had been hired out to Anthony Thompson. Upon receiving the news, Tubman made her way back to Baltimore. At the slave auction, Kessiah's husband placed the winning bid for his wife and children; afterward, he was discovered to be a free Black man, and he did not come forward to pay. Instead, he stole them away from the auction house and took them to the docks, then spirited them by boat up the Chesapeake Bay to Baltimore. Tubman, who was waiting for them, hid them there. This was incredibly dangerous. Baltimore was still a slave territory. According to William Still, it was one of the hardest places from which freedom seekers could escape. She kept her niece, her niece's husband, and their children there for a few months before taking them to Philadelphia. She made a second trip to Baltimore in 1851 to rescue her youngest brother, Moses (whom Rit had successfully prevented Edward Brodess from selling in 1844), and two other men.[35]

Though Tubman, her niece Kessiah, Kessiah's children, and now her younger brother Moses had liberated themselves from bondage, their freedom, as well as that of all Blacks who had stolen away to northern free states, became imperiled with the passage of the Fugitive Slave Act. Called "The Bloodhound Act" by abolitionists, the Fugitive Slave Act was part of the Compromise of 1850. It authorized southern slaveholders to reclaim their "property" on free territory in the North. It also required that all fugitive slaves be brought before federal commissioners, disallowing their testimony, trial by jury, and habeas corpus. Federal marshals and slave catchers could henceforth accuse any Black person in the North of being a runaway slave for whom an enslaver had advertised, apprehend them, remand them back to a southern enslaver, and collect the reward. Moreover, they could kidnap any Black person and sell them into slavery in the South. Under the act, federal commissioners received a $10 bonus for each guilty verdict against a fugitive slave and a $5 bonus for a verdict of innocent. They needed little or no evidence or positive identification.[36]

The Fugitive Slave Act also criminalized the work of anyone assisting freedom seekers, subjecting them to up to six years in jail and a $1,000 fine. It made antislavery activists like John Hunn, Thomas Garrett, Samuel D. Burris, William Still, Tubman herself, and hundreds of agents, Black and white, into lawbreakers for their work as conductors on the Underground Railroad. Rather than helping freedom seekers, the act mandated northern citizens to act as slave patrollers, assisting federal marshals to apprehend runaway slaves and return them to bondage. It terrorized northern Black communities, which were composed of intertwined families and communities of Blacks who had been born free and Blacks who had liberated themselves, legally or illegally. More than three hundred Blacks were captured as a result of the act; the majority were forcibly transported and sold in the South. Those who had been born free were thus enslaved for the first time in their lives; those who had liberated themselves were reenslaved. The growing demand for labor on cotton plantations in the Deep South and the Southwest drove the abduction of Black people in the North. Many northerners—even those who were not abolitionists before its passage—despised southern slaveholders for exploiting the federal government to turn them into slave catchers. The act contributed to growth of the abolitionist movement and catalyzed a radical reaction.[37]

Before passage of the Fugitive Slave Act, freedom had been a hundred miles away for Harriet Tubman. The act pushed it hundreds of miles north to the Canadian border, out of reach for those who did not have access to the Underground Railroad. By 1852, the population of Blacks in Canada had swelled to thirty thousand, the majority of them formerly enslaved people who had escaped from the United States. Tubman resettled her family in St. Catharine's, Ontario. Though she continued to pass through Philadelphia, visiting the Vigilance Committee and William Still's office, Tubman took and sent freedom seekers to Canada unless they were reuniting with family members still settled in the United States.[38]

After 1850, Tubman's actions would now subject her to imprisonment and fines as well as reenslavement. She easily could have stayed in St. Catharine's with her family and guarded her freedom. Though she did not publicly declare her intentions, as Thomas Garrett had done after sentencing in his trial, Tubman's actions spoke for her.[39]

Tubman continued to take freedom seekers out of Maryland, first to Delaware, then to Philadelphia, and ultimately to Canada. She rarely set foot on private property, and typically arranged to meet fugitives at a location eight to ten miles away from the place they were escaping from. She generally executed her rescue missions on Saturdays, since slaveholders usually allowed enslaved people to visit family and friends on Sundays and would not suspect they had run away until Monday afternoon. Thus slaveholders would not post runaway notices until Tuesday, giving her and her party several days' head start.[40]

Tubman worked as a cook and domestic at hotels and private homes in Philadelphia and resorts in Cape May, New Jersey, during the summer months in the early 1850s to help finance her early rescue missions, and received financial support from antislavery friends. Though she did conduct some missions in the warmer weather, Tubman preferred the winter. The Christmas holidays were, as we've seen, a time when enslavers often sold people they held in bondage in order to pay off debts before the end of the year; for this reason, enslaved people frequently called it the "weeping time." Long nights provided those escaping more time to travel under the cover of darkness, then conceal themselves in the woods and swamps when sleeping during the short days. If they ran out of food, Tubman would sometimes disguise herself as an old woman and go out foraging. Reptiles would have been hibernating. She carried a loaded pistol, less to shoot any wild bobcats, deer, muskrats, beavers and other rodents, skunks, racoons, foxes, or minks that she may have encountered than to protect herself and her group from slave catchers.[41]

Because of their exposure to the weather, Tubman and her group faced dangers from pneumonia and other respiratory diseases. In December 1854, they arrived at Thomas Garrett's home practically barefoot, having walked until they had worn the shoes off their feet. In addition to animals and bloodhounds, they faced starvation, drowning, turncoat operators, and slave hunters. To counter them all, Tubman relied on spiritual power. She told Sarah Bradford that she could feel the presence of the Holy Ghost guiding her every step; a fluttering in her heart was a sign danger when her heart would "go flutter, flutter," a sign that danger was near and she must alter her course.[42]

She often sang spirituals that contained secret messages and used fluctuating tempos to lift the spirits of, instruct, and prepare the freedom seekers along the way. When she arrived to gather a group or returned after a foraging expedition, she sang a song of peace to signal that everything was well. If the freedom seekers needed to hide, on the other hand, Tubman sang:

> Oh go down, Moses,
> Way down to Egypt's land.
> Tell ol' Pharaoh,
> Let my people go.[43]

Harriet Tubman made one of her trips for love. Her husband, John Tubman, had been a free man when he married her. Though slaveholders in Maryland routinely made life difficult for free Blacks like Tubman, there is no evidence that he was in immediate danger of arrest or expulsion. After two long lonely years of living as a free woman, however, Harriet wanted her husband's companionship. We do not know much about their relationship. Nor do we know whether she had communicated with John after she escaped to freedom and, if so, how he had responded. We are also left to speculate why she waited until 1851, two years—and two trips back to Maryland—before returning for him. She had spent the time finding housing and work in Philadelphia as a maid, furnishing her room, and making a suit of clothes for John to wear on the journey so that he would look like a free man from the North.[44]

Tubman took an enormous risk (particularly after the passage of the Fugitive Slave Act) going back to where her husband lived, which was outside of Cambridge in Dorchester County. She may even have gone back to the very neighborhood where she had grown up, conceivably as an act of contrition for having left him behind. Now she intended to ask him to come with her so that they could continue their lives together. When John Tubman received his wife's message, however, he refused even to see her. He had remarried and started his life over with a free woman, eliminating the power that an enslaver would have over an enslaved wife and future children and the expense of buying their freedom.[45]

Much has been made—both by Tubman herself and by her biographers—of John Tubman's disloyalty. She told antislavery audiences in New England (largely composed of white women) that she had a new suit of man's clothes and no husband; she had wanted to go to his house and make trouble, to fight the other woman for her man. But, she added, she realized that creating a scene would increase the chance of a slave catcher capturing her and returning her to Eliza Brodess.[46]

Tubman likely witnessed her share of heartrending separations. Henry "Box" Brown's wife, Nancy, and their three children were kidnapped from their home and sold to a Methodist preacher in North Carolina. Brown recalled watching the slave coffle move off. He had grasped Nancy's hand, holding it tightly and walking with her until he could go no farther. He and his wife exchanged looks that expressed what they could not say—that they hoped they would meet again in heaven.[47]

Sale of an enslaved partner was essentially equivalent to divorce if one's spouse was sold beyond a distance across which the husband could travel regularly or if the slaveholders would not allow the couple to continue their relationship. Though Harriet had not been sold, John Tubman could have considered them divorced when she willingly left him. Perhaps, like Ayuba Suleyman Diallo's wife, he assumed his spouse was dead. Diallo forgave his wife for marrying another man, as no one who had been captured at the coast and sold to English slave traders had ever returned to Bundu. We do not have evidence of anyone aside from Tubman and the formerly enslaved soldiers in the USCT escaping enslavement and then returning to liberate others.[48]

The profound disappointment of John Tubman's rejection and remarriage marked a crossroads for Harriet. Instead of her husband, she rescued a group of freedom seekers and brought them to Philadelphia. She had prayed for domesticity with her husband; God had not answered her prayers. But she had a higher calling, and henceforth she would risk her freedom so that others could be free. She started fulfilling her mission by going back to the Eastern Shore to bring out her family, friends, and neighbors and take them to the Promised Land. She would devote her life to doing God's work and to helping God's people.[49]

In 1852, following her attempt to bring out John Tubman, Harriet attempted to rescue her brothers Ben Jr., Robert, and Henry. However, they did not meet her at the designated place on time. She took a group of nine others instead. She returned to Dorchester County several times in 1854. Her brothers had previously made multiple escape attempts, and after their latest attempt, in 1854, Eliza Brodess threatened to sell them. They were able to postpone being put up on the auction block by getting themselves hired out. When Tubman returned for them in spring/summer 1854, they would not leave, because they did not want the man who hired them to lose his money. So she took Winnebar Johnson from Peter's Neck. She also gave detailed directions to Samuel Green Jr., son of Reverend Samuel Green, a free Black man and Methodist preacher who assisted freedom seekers over the years. Reverend Green and his wife, Kitty Green, were among the free Blacks on the Eastern Shore who harbored Tubman when she returned on rescue missions. Both Johnson and the younger Green made it safely to freedom, joining the growing communities of freedom seekers from the Eastern Shore in New Bedford, Massachusetts, and St. Catharine's, Ontario, respectively.[50]

Eliza Brodess indeed planned to sell Tubman's brothers during the Christmas holidays. But Tubman returned on Christmas Eve 1854 and spirited them away, along with Ben Jr.'s fiancée and an enslaved woman named Jane Kane, who disguised herself in men's clothing. Though their father, Ben Ross, wore a blindfold so that he would not have to lie when he told questioning authorities that he had not seen his sons before they ran away, it must have been a miracle for him to encounter his daughter for the first time in five years. He likely had assumed that he would never see her again.[51]

Robert Ross had to leave his wife, Mary Manokey Ross, shortly after she gave birth to their first daughter on Christmas Eve. The baby girl was named Harriet, after Harriet Tubman. Tubman's brother Henry also left behind his wife and sons, William Henry and John Isaac, who were all free. Running away without their families must have been broken the hearts of both Robert and Henry Ross (and, of course, there was of course always the chance that Eliza Brodess would sell those they left behind as retribution). Otherwise, though, they would have been sold off and never seen their loved ones again. Instead, under their sister's leadership, the Ross brothers, Jane Kane (who was Ben Jr.'s fiancée), and two other men who joined the party along the way made it safely to St. Catharine's.[52]

Early in 1855, Henry's wife, Harriet Ann Parker Ross, and their sons, three-year-old William and two-year-old Isaac, made their way to St. Catharine's with Tubman's assistance and reunited with Henry. Tubman returned yet again early in 1856 for her only remaining sister, Rachel, and her children, and her brother Robert's wife, Mary, and their three children, John Henry, Moses, and Harriet—the girl born the night Robert escaped. She was successful at bringing Mary and her children to freedom, but not Rachel. Liberating Rachel and her children became the focus of Tubman's efforts, and she tried three times in 1856, and then again in the fall of 1857, to bring them out of bondage. Eliza Brodess had hired out Rachel's children, Ben and Angerine, to other farms twelve miles away, keeping them apart and complicating Tubman's efforts. Moreover, Rachel refused to secure her own freedom without both of her children. Instead, in April 1856, Tubman rescued four men and then came back to bring away a young woman, Tilly, in October of the same year. She reunited Tilly with her fiancé and one of the men with his mother, both of whom she had rescued previously and sent to Canada. Once Tilly was safe in Canada, Tubman immediately returned to Dorchester County the following month and rescued three more men and one woman.[53]

In the spring of 1857, Tubman gave detailed directions to eight freedom seekers, Henry Predeaux, Thomas Elliott, Denard Hughes, the married couple James and Lavinia Woolford, the married couple Bill and Emily Kiah, and an eighth man who has not been identified. They all originated in Poplar's Neck in Dorchester County, the neighborhood where Tubman had been enslaved. Reverend Green and Tubman's father, Ben Ross, hid the men at their homes in their flight to freedom. Following Tubman's instructions, the group first traveled to Delaware to meet Thomas Otwell, a free Black man living outside of Dover who was an Underground Railroad stationmaster and who was to guide them to the next stop. They paid him £8 to pilot them thirty miles to the next station. Tubman, Thomas Garrett, William Still, and others had great confidence in Otwell. As it turned out, however, that confidence was misplaced. Otwell exposed a portion of Tubman's Underground Railroad network and put the lives of several freedom seekers and conductors in danger. He was in cahoots with a white man named James Hollis and betrayed the freedom seekers in order to collect the $3,000 reward. Otwell and Hollis conspired with the sheriff in Dover to hold the eight freedom seekers in jail overnight when they arrived in Dover. After Otwell led the freedom seekers to the jail and introduced them to Hollis, they became suspicious when they saw the iron bars on the window. The group refused to be locked in the jail cells. A confrontation with the sheriff ensued, and the sheriff pulled a revolver. Henry Predeaux, whom William Still described as "physically a giant," followed the sheriff to his private quarters where his family was sleeping and scattered burning embers around, which could have set the room, along with its contents and inhabitants, ablaze. Then Predeaux smashed a window with a heavy andiron and held the sheriff at bay while the other seven freedom seekers jumped out of the window into the mud twelve feet below, then ran. Predeaux was left with the sheriff, who tried to shoot him; thankfully, his revolver would not fire. Once outside of the jail, the others got over the wall and disappeared.[54]

The group had to split up and was concealed by the Underground Railroad network for a few weeks. Predeaux arrived safely at Thomas Garrett's home. Six more of the freedom seekers went back to Camden and confronted Thomas Otwell. Mercifully sparing his life, they compelled him to take them to the next stop on the Underground Railroad, the home of William Brinkley. Brinkley delivered them safely through miles of forested roads, which were heavily patrolled by slave catchers, through Dover and Smyrna to Garrett. Garrett brought Thomas Elliott and Denard Hughes to his home. He helped four more get across the Christiana River bridge to the next stop on the Underground Railroad. Despite the arrival of the enslavers who legally held three of the freedom seekers in bondage and posted advertisements offering a sizeable bounty on their heads, they were able, with Garrett's help, to navigate around Wilmington's heavily patrolled roads and bridges. Ultimately, five, including James Woolford, arrived safely in Philadelphia. Woolford's wife, Lavinia, who had been separated from him, arrived at Still's office some weeks later. William and Emily Kiah stayed behind, hoping to reunite with their daughter, Mary, whom they had had to leave behind. William Still sent the other freedom seekers safely on to Canada, where the Woolfords were eventually reunited.[55]

The escape of the eight Dorchester County freedom seekers, whom the newspapers dubbed the "Dover Eight," brought attention to the fact that a steady trickle of enslaved people had escaped from Dorchester and Caroline Counties in the 1850s and had not been recovered. The trickle grew to a stream when in the fall of 1857 Tubman's detailed directions led to the escape of more than forty people, including Nat and Lizzie Amby, as well as several large families, including twenty children and six more infants still in their mother's arms. The accumulated loss of property affected the region's slaveholding families and the regional economy. At this point, no one had been able to identify "Moses." Slaveholders on the Eastern Shore suspected that a white male abolitionist, like Thomas Garrett, was responsible. They never could have imagined that a Black woman was the mastermind.[56]

In the aftermath of the escape of the Dover Eight, Reverend Samuel Green's home was searched. He was arrested, tried, convicted for possessing a copy of Harriet Beecher Stowe's *Uncle Tom's Cabin*—a crime in the South—and sentenced to ten years' imprisonment. Tubman received word (likely through an active communication network of enslaved and free Blacks) that her father would soon also be arrested for aiding, abetting, and harboring the Dover Eight. He had purchased his wife's freedom in 1850, but Rit could not be liberated because she was already over forty-five years of age, and under state law enslaved people could not be manumitted after that age. In fact, when they undertook the journey to Canada, Ben and Rit were among the oldest freedom seekers whose stories William Still recorded in his journal.[57]

The Underground Railroad was an arduous journey; only a few Old Heads attempted it. Prime Hand Abram Harris escaped from Charles County on Maryland's Western Shore with Romulus Hall, alias George Weems. Both left their wives behind in bondage. Harris had to abandon Hall along the way, after they had walked for nine nights, been without food for three days, and endured extremely cold temperatures. If he was lucky enough to have them, Hall's boots may have frozen to his feet, as happened to one of the men traveling with Samuel Hawkins, his wife, and their children to John Hunn's house. When Hall arrived at Still's Philadelphia office, his legs and feet were badly frostbitten, leading to the removal of several of his toes. Hall was suffering from hunger and exhaustion too, and he died of his injuries a day or so after his liberation, never making it to Canada. Still took special note of Hall's case as the first death on the Underground Railroad and reported that before he died Hall had rejoiced that he had reached a free state and said that he never regretted seeking his freedom. Many others undoubtedly perished before and after Hall; their stories were not recorded.[58]

Tubman knew the journey would be dangerous for her septuagenarian parents. She found a set of old chaise wheels with a wooden board over one axle, on which they could sit, and another fastened to the other axle, on which they could rest their feet. Pulled by an old horse with a straw collar, the contraption also accommodated their treasured belongings—her mother's featherbed and her father's bow axe. Staying on the main roads and away from the woods and swamps, she managed to get her parents to Philadelphia, where they stopped in William Still's office. On their way to freedom in Canada, they passed through Rochester, New York, where they stayed for two weeks. It had been a close call—Ben and Rit Ross had gotten out of town shortly before white vigilante mobs started tarring and feathering free Black families whom they suspected of aiding and abetting freedom seekers. But Ben and Rit had had to leave behind their daughter Rachel, daughter-in-law Mary, and grandchildren in order for Ben to be safe.[59]

By 1855, the flight of hundreds of freedom seekers from the Eastern Shore had destabilized the economy and was threatening the social order. Chesapeake slaveholders held tight to their property, feeling as if their wealth was slipping out of their grasp. And it was.

★★★★★★★★

Down in the South Carolina Lowcountry, planters doubled down on slavery even as the commercial rice economy began to falter. For those enslaved there, freedom in the North or in Spanish Florida was a distant prospect. They had little or no exposure to free Black people or to free Black communities. Certainly no one had escaped to either the North or Florida and then returned to the plantation to lead others to freedom. Had they done so, we would know their story. Instead, those who were enslaved on South Carolina's coastal plains remained there, doomed to spend their relatively brief lifetimes laboring against their will in the rice swamps and enriching the planters who held them in bondage.

6

Pikins

If rice was what held the Lowcountry aristocracy together, rice simultaneously threatened to destroy it. On the one hand, trapping water using the embankments, trunks, and gates of the hydraulic irrigation system nourished the rice fields and generated a lucrative commercial industry, which, as we've seen, grew exponentially through the first half of the eighteenth century. On the other hand, that standing water produced ideal breeding places for mosquitoes carrying disease.

Trunkminders, typically male Old Heads with decades of experience, repaired and maintained the dikes and banks, manipulating the hydraulic irrigation system to flood the fields with river water. They lowered the inside doors of trunks on the river side and raised the outside doors of the trunks on the land side so that the next flood tide would cover the rice field completely. This accelerated the rice seeds' germination while simultaneously killing weeds, which could not survive underwater. Field hands had to wade into the water and muck to rake up old rice stubble and rice roots from the previous year's harvest, loosened when the field was flooded. In the first flooding, the "sprout-flow" formed what looked like a large lake in the rice fields. Trunkminders monitored the seeds' development underwater. Once the rice seeds began to open, or "pip," as Duncan Clinch Heyward described it, the field hands opened the inner doors of the trunk so that the next two ebb tides could drain the fields.[1]

Trunkminders flooded the rice fields a second time on the flood tide after long rows of light green blades of rice seedlings pushed above the earth. They flooded the fields up to the check banks, so that no land or rice was visible. Conventional wisdom was that the "stretch-flow" forced rice sprouts to stretch their necks up to reach the sunlight above the surface of the water. It also killed the weeds that could significantly decrease the crop's yield and the planter's profit. However, flooding the young seedlings at this critical stage of development could also kill the rice. Trunkminders carefully monitored the weather conditions and the rice as it grew under the water. They lowered the water on the ebb tide once rice planted on higher ground was taller than approximately three inches and kept the water at this level for a week to ten days. With the water slacked off, most of the rice stood above the water. A small portion grew on high ground in dry land. And another small portion grew horizontally, due to the pressure of the water, as if lying down to rest after stretching mightily to reach the sunlight.[2]

During the next period of "dry growth," the field hands were back in the wet and muddy fields, hoeing (for the second time) with their wooden-handled hoes, clearing away weeds that grew up between the rows of rice, and unpacking waterlogged, foul-smelling soils. The rice was typically hoed twice, the first time in early June (assuming the sowing had taken place between early March and early April).[3]

The rice was then kept dry for approximately forty days. For the "harvest flow"—beginning around sixty days before the actual harvest—the trunkminders opened the gates one last time to flood the rice fields and cover the rice plants, now around fifteen inches high. They raised the water every five to six days, changing it every ten days as the rice grew. Once trunkminders let off the water in the early fall, the rice was ripe and ready for harvest.[4]

Charles Ball was older than the oldest of the Old Heads on the Combahee River rice plantations. He had been born and originally enslaved in Calvert County, Maryland, on the opposite side of the Chesapeake Bay from Dorchester County, then around 1805 was sold to a South Carolina rice, indigo, and cotton plantation on the Congaree River. He observed in his memoir of slavery, published in New York in 1837, that no "stranger" could spend a week in a rice swamp during the summer months without falling ill, whether from malaria or another mosquito-borne illness, a waterborne disease, or diarrheal diseases. Three other field hands who were purchased and started work in the rice swamps at the same time as Charles Ball became ill in their first five days.[5]

Old Heads Andrew Wyatt, Silvia Jackson Gaylord DeCauster, and Mary Anne Lewis and Prime Hands Charlotte Savage, John A. Savage, and Diana Days Harris testified in their pension files that it was "sickly" down there on the Combahee. Wyatt and DeCauster agreed there was a "good deal of fever and malaria" and chills on Paul's Place, where Wyatt worked as plowman and field hand, and on the adjoining plantation, William Kirkland Jr.'s Rose Hill. Fever plagued enslaved laborers on all of the Combahee rice plantations; they all were occasionally "laid up with it," according to DeCauster. Malaria was rarely fatal to adults who had inherited or acquired some immunity against the disease. Wyatt observed that after being ill he "got hearty and strong again," likely after the rice harvest, to do even more forced labor in rice fields during the winter.[6]

Apologists for slavery used the fact that some Africans and people of African descent were immune to fevers and agues as a justification for enslaving them. However, American journalist and landscaper Frederick Law Olmsted (who conceived New York's Central Park), while visiting a Georgia rice plantation whose owner also purchased enslaved laborers from William Savage's estate in the 1850s, noted that enslaved Black infants were not immune to the "subtle poison of the miasma" in the rice swamps.[7]

These could have been Prime Hand Diana Days Harris's children. When she testified to a pension official in 1886 and again in 1889, Diana could not remember the exact years when her children were born, because it had been during slavery (the enslavers, the Kirkland family, likely would have recorded their birth dates). However, she remembered when she buried them. Diana and her husband, Old Head Andrew Harris, married before the Civil War. She recalled having five children before the war, all single births about fifteen months apart. Hannah was born the year after her marriage, twelve years before the war, and died as a baby. The second child, Rachel, only lived four months. The third one, Hagar, lived all of two years. Hercules only lived about one year. Her last son, Samuel, was born about four years before the Civil War. He died in Beaufort while his father was serving in the US Army.[8]

As a field hand, Diana could not avoid working in the pestilential rice fields, and she could not keep her children safe. The children likely died from malaria, feebleness at birth (what today might be called failure to thrive), respiratory diseases, or low birth weight caused by their mothers' chronic malaria and sheer overwork. Most mothers were "'most broke in two"—as an enslaved man on the rice plantation where Frances Kemble lived described his wife's condition—from labor in the rice fields, which they were forced to do even in late stages of pregnancy and too soon after childbirth, as long as and as soon as they could wield a hoe.[9]

Andrew and Diana Days Harris were not alone burying their children in "old time burial grounds" on low-lying lands sandwiched between the rice fields and creeks. It was virtually impossible to keep children born on rice plantations alive. Yet without slave lists and plantation journals it is almost impossible to know the percentage of children that died on the Combahee before the war. Typically, widows testified about children when their father, the veteran, died before the dependents reached sixteen. We do know that in the nineteenth century, two-thirds of enslaved children on rice plantations as a group (not specifically those on the Combahee) died before their fifteenth birthday, in contrast to 38 percent of enslaved children on large cotton and sugar plantations across the South. Child mortality rates were likely even higher during the eighteenth century, when enslaved laborers reclaimed cypress swamps, dug out thousands and thousands of acres of rice fields, and created vast pools of stagnant water across the coastal plains.[10]

Even without plantation records that were likely burned in the Combahee River Raid, the lack of children in the slave transactions is evidence enough that women enslaved on the Combahee rice plantations were not having successful pregnancies and/or giving birth to children who survived beyond the first few years of life. In all the years up to 1860, there were only two Pikins, as the Gullah Geechee called children, among those listed in the slave transactions. Both were born enslaved after 1848. One was Jack and Sarah Barnwell's son Jack (brother to Relia Barnwell Middleton and Primus Barnwell, and cousin to Sina Bolze Young Green and Cuffie Bolze), who was enslaved on Cypress Plantation; the other was Andrew and Diana Harris's son Samuel Harris, who was enslaved on Longbrow Plantation.

Andrew Harris, one of the Old Heads on Kirkland's Rose Hill Plantation, was, as he put it in his pension testimony, a "hearty man." Harris attended Kirkland's horses as a teamster and hostler. He was also Kirkland's head plowman and could follow the plow as well as anyone before the war. John A. Savage testified that Harris's skilled labor kept him off the plantation and out of the rice fields in the summer months; plowmen worked the rice fields in March before field hands planted rice in April. From late spring through early fall he traveled back and forth carrying provisions to the South Carolina Upcountry, where the Kirkland family spent the sickly season. Because of his work, Harris was less vulnerable to fall fevers than enslaved men who remained on the plantation year-round.[11]

The living and working conditions on Lowcountry South Carolina and Georgia rice plantations were significantly worse than elsewhere—certainly worse than on tobacco plantations on Maryland's Eastern Shore. Prime field hands and children enslaved on rice plantations died in record numbers from doing muck work in the icy cypress/tupelo swamps and pounding rice for hours in drafty, pestilential barns; conditions were even worse in the summer and early fall. There were few possibilities for enslaved children to grow up to be adults, no possibilities for enslaved people to steal their freedom, no manumission, and no Underground Railroad.

★★★★★★★★

Because of disease, Lowcountry rice planters took their wives and children to drier and healthier locales between late spring and the first hard frost. Planters on the lower Combahee River were no exception, effectively becoming absentee planters. Seasonal migration further limited whites' abilities to develop acquired immunity to the deadly disease.[12]

Most rice planters on the other lower Combahee plantations retreated to the pinelands—the Blakes went to Flat Rock, North Carolina, the Kirklands to Camden, South Carolina, and the Nichollses to Walterboro, South Carolina. Until the Civil War, William and Sarah Cruger Heyward's son William C. Heyward would spend his summers in New York, where his mother had grown up. In August 1845 William Elliott IV (the author of *Carolina Sports* and Thomas Rhett Smith's son-in-law) traveled with his older daughters to New York. Elliott wrote to his wife that he had seen William C. Heyward in New York and that Heyward was "anxious about his rice crop at Combahee." He asked her to inquire about it and inform him if she heard anything; he would let Heyward "know about it."[13]

Of all the planter families on the Combahee River, the Middleton family took seasonal migration to an entirely different level. They traveled north to Newport, Rhode Island, by steamboat or rail and then packet boat, stopping along the way in Charleston, Washington, DC, and Philadelphia to visit friends—and later family, once daughter Eliza had married and moved to Philadelphia—and to shop. By the 1750s, Newport had become the social capital of the Northeast, and it remained so for a century. Affectionately called "Carolina hospital" by seasonal visitors from the South, it gained the reputation of having a healthy seaside climate. Along with other Charlestonians, the Middletons found refuge in a locale where the sun was warm enough to ripen abundant fruits to perfection and the air was pure.[14]

Governor Henry Middleton purchased a home in Newport in 1835 and subsequently constructed two additions on the property, one in 1838 and another in 1845, in an attempt to provide enough space for his ever-expanding family—eight children, their spouses, his grandchildren, and the grandchildren's nurses. His wife, daughters, and daughters-in-law relished long walks and rides (particularly at night), family dinners, swimming and bathing in the ocean, and excursions to overlooks on Narragansett Bay. The men could hunt plover on the shore or go sailing and sport fishing in Newport Harbor. The Middletons' children delighted in musical parties, dances featuring new crazes like the polka, costume and fancy-dress balls, and band concerts.[15]

While planters from the lower section of the Combahee River entertained themselves in safe havens, those whom they held in bondage died in ghastly numbers growing their rice in the swamps. The planters continued to purchase enslaved people to offset the losses. We know this in part because of the combinations of pension file testimony.

The Nicholls/Kirkland family offers a good example. After Mary Anna Lynah Kirkland Faber Nicholls signed her marriage settlement with Joshua Nicholls, they and her son, William L. Kirkland Jr., went on a buying spree of enslaved people. They primarily purchased Prime Hands for Rose Hill Plantation. Though the documentation of the transaction is missing, Dr. James Heyward or his estate sold Moriah Haywood Bartley to Mary Anna Nicholls. Moriah Bartley testified in her pension file that her father's name was John Hayward. Her parents were enslaved on Cypress by William C. Heyward. Dr. James Heyward held her in bondage. She was born near Grahamville, which, she told the pension official, was located between Green Pond and Savannah. Moriah testified that she lived there "until Mr. Nickel [Joshua Nicholls] whose place was at Rose Hill . . . bought Moriah and brought her there." It happened when she was just a "little girl," long before the war. Nothing more is known about Moriah's parents, and independent evidence has not been found to document how Moriah became separated from them. However, she did have cousins on Cypress Plantation. William Hamilton testified that Moriah was his first cousin. Moses Simmons testified that he was her third or fourth cousin (as were his brothers Joshua and James Simmons). Jackson Grant testified that he had known Moriah since he "was a boy," had known her husband before the war, and lived in bondage with them on the same plantation. Grant knew that Moriah and

Anthony Bartley began living together as husband and wife and had two children together before the war began. Moriah met Anthony, the man who became her husband, when she "came to that country"—Rose Hill Plantation. Moriah did not know much about her husband's origins before she met him, though he did tell her he was born at "Ogeechee."[16]

The only way to identify the people the planters held in bondage—and their children—is by the planters' records. It is also the only way to complete their stories, even when the slave transactions themselves are incomplete. Though we do not have exact dates or sale amounts, we do know that sometime in the mid-1850s William L. Kirkland Jr. purchased three Prime Hands, Captain Brown, Jackson Grant, and Frank Hamilton, from Thomas Rhett Smith Elliott. On May 12, 1849, Thomas Rhett Smith Elliott signed two mortgages with James Cuthbert's estate. The enslaved people were listed in James Cuthbert's 1838 estate record. Given the pattern we have seen on the lower Combahee rice plantations of joint sale and mortgage transactions, it is highly likely that James Cuthbert's estate first sold the enslaved people to Thomas Rhett Smith Elliott, who subsequently mortgaged them back. Thus, Elliott essentially bought them on credit. The first transaction mortgaged forty-two enslaved people for $14,115 to James Cuthbert, including "Sam, Sarah, Ann, and Jack" (referring to Jackson Grant's parents, Sam and Sarah, his sister Anne, and Jackson). In the second transaction, Elliott mortgaged forty-four enslaved humans for $11,646.16. This transaction included "Pompey, Pussy, Binah, Sylla, Captain, Frank, Hamilton" (brothers Captain Brown and Frank Hamilton, their parents, Pompey and Pussy, and their sisters Hagar, Bina, and Sylla). William Elliott (Thomas Rhett Smith Elliott's father) also sold two more Prime Hands, a brother-sister duo, Tenah Jenkins Hamilton and Daniel Jenkins, to William Kirkland in 1850.[17]

Jackson Grant appeared to know everyone on the lower Combahee. And everyone knew Jackson Grant. A coachman, he likely traveled from plantation to plantation and interacted with a wider circle of people. It is more difficult to document his origins. Grant himself testified that he was born on James Island, held in bondage by Daniel Heyward, and raised in Beaufort County. His father, Samuel Grant, was enslaved by Daniel Heyward as well. He was titled after his grandfather, also named Jackson Grant. In a transaction for which the records have not yet been found, Jackson Grant (and possibly also his father, Samuel Grant) was sold by Daniel Heyward to James Cuthbert and ended up on the latter's 1838 estate inventory; then he passed from Cuthbert (or Cuthbert's heirs) to Elliott. He may have been sold or mortgaged again, and there may be another missing transaction. Grant testified for Richard Smith Jr. that he knew Smith before the war, as they "were both raised on William Paul's Plantation near" Rose Hill. The men his age at Cypress Plantation, including Lucius Robinson, Cuffie Bolze, Neptune Nicholas, Andrew Nicholas, and William Hamilton, along with Wally Garrett and Solomon Salter at Newport Plantation, all knew him before the war, as they testified in the pension files. They were "boys raised up together," as Neptune Nicholas characterized their relationship. Jackson was "short-legged and short winded," as Friday Hamilton described him, and a "puffy looking boy," according to Andrew Nicholas. He didn't or couldn't run very much or very far, which is likely why he was made a coachman. Ultimately in 1855, William Kirkland purchased him and brought him to Rose Hill Plantation.[18]

Male Prime Hands who married in the 1860s generally chose younger women. On Rose Hill Plantation in 1861, Jackson Grant married Dorcas Lee, who was born around 1845—hence he was in his forties, and she was around sixteen. Frank Hamilton and Tenah Jenkins, with about a nineteen-year age difference between them, lived together as man and wife on Rose Hill, though the date of their marriage has been lost. And several couples of Prime Hand men and even younger Pikin women were betrothed before the Civil War, like Prime Hand William Middleton and Pikin Relia Barnwell. Prime Hand Charles Nicholas courted Hagar (her surname has been lost) before the war. Combahee slaveholders did not allow enslaved couples who were engaged to live together before marriage. But the enslaved community recognized the young couples' commitment to each other.[19]

★★★★★★★★

In the early 1850s the up-and-coming planter families on the lower Combahee River continued to expand their plantation enterprises and attempted to pass their wealth down to their children, just as most had inherited substantial wealth from their parents. The timing was not particularly good. Coastal South Carolina's market share of rice production fell from roughly 64 percent in 1859 to almost 44 percent ten years later, and South Carolina never regained its ascendancy. Even before the Civil War, rice production was moving to the southwestern states and to Asia. But despite the decreasing market share of South Carolina's rice crop, the children of lower Combahee planters matured, inherited their parents' wealth, and continued to benefit from the exploitation of enslaved people's labor.[20]

After Mary Anna Lynah Kirkland Faber married Joshua Nicholls, the time came for her to settle with her now adult son, William Lennox Kirkland Jr., and provide for him a start in life. Serving as trustee for Mary Nicholls, Edward T. Lynah signed an agreement with William Kirkland Jr. partitioning Rose Hill Plantation. The December 1, 1853, agreement referenced Mary Anna and Joshua's 1848 marriage settlement, in which she promised that she would settle with her son on the $17,000 bond she had signed to her mother-in-law and which William Jr. inherited from his grandmother by dividing the three-fourths interest in Rose Hill that they owned in common. It set aside a quarter of Rose Hill's rice lands (bounded on the north and east by the remaining one-half of Rose Hill, on the west by the Combahee River, and on the south by lands that William Jr. already owned) and a quarter of Rose Hill's highlands (bounded on the north and east by Rose Hill and on the south and west by Dr. Francis S. Parker's lands).[21]

In addition, the partition gave William Jr. $4,000 and allocated nineteen enslaved people to him. The agreement does not specify the names of the enslaved people in his one-fourth share, but it valued them at $9,750 (an average value of $513 each). We do know some of the names of the fifty-eight enslaved people who stayed on what remained of the plantation: carpenter Carolina Grant, his wife, Flora, and their son, Stepney (listed as "Carolina Flora Stepney"); Friday Hamilton, his father, George, and his mother, Emily ("Amy George Friday," with Emily listed as "Amy"). Those fifty-eight enslaved people were valued at $9,250 (an average of $159 each), meaning it is certain that Nicholls had given her son Prime Hands with which to start his own enterprise.[22]

Like the Nicholls/Kirkland family, the Parkers, who lived just to the south of Rose Hill (Dr. Francis S. Parker had inherited Parker's Place with his brother, Arthur M. Parker, in their father's 1849 will), continued to expand, making capital investments in enslaved laborers from the estate of Edward Rutledge Lowndes (who was James Lowndes's son), which was liquidated in 1853. Notorious Charleston-based slave trader Alonzo J. White conducted the sale. White advertised the sale in the *Charleston Daily Courier* eight times between February 18 and March 8, 1853, and in the *Charleston Mercury* twice, on March 5 and March 10, 1853. The advertisement stated that the enslaved people offered for sale were "accustomed to the culture of rice on the Combahee River," though during the past five years they had been forced to grow Sea Island cotton on Lowndes's plantation. Ninety-six enslaved people were sold. Included were Minus Hamilton's family, who were sold to Arthur M. Parker; the bill of sale reads: "Minus (Carpt & Mill Wright) Hagar, Binah, Harry (cook) Frank Sibby 6 @ 680," referring to Minus, his wife, Hagar, their daughter Sibby, another daughter, Bina, and her husband, Harry Mack (Bina and Harry were married on or about November 1855 at Parker's Place by July Loundes, a "colored preacher"; Old Head Sanko Van Dross, who likely was a contemporary of Minus Hamilton, remembered attending her wedding). There is not enough information to know if or how Frank was related to Minus Hamilton or to Harry Mack.[23]

Just establishing himself, William Kirkland Jr. bought more enslaved people, also on credit. Though the bill of sale is missing, Thomas Rhett Smith Elliott must have sold at least two family groups to young Kirkland: one family included Frank Hamilton, his parents, Pompey and Pussy, Frank's sister Sylla, and his brother Captain Brown; another included Jackson Grant and his parents, Sam and Sarah (these were the enslaved people Elliott had purchased from Colonel James Cuthbert's estate in 1849). The Nicholls/Kirkland family continued to expand the land on which they planted rice, reclaiming tidal swamps and converting forested wetlands to rice fields right up to the outbreak of the Civil War. In 1857, Kirkland used the families as collateral and signed a bond to Thomas Rhett Smith Elliott for $9,572. Kirkland's mother, Mary Anna Nicholls, co-signed the bond. Kirkland must have repaid the bond with interest in three annual payments of $4,786, because he got his field hands and coachman back.[24]

In addition to slave trading among family, friends, and neighbors and by auction, the transatlantic slave trade continued into South Carolina and Georgia Lowcountry ports well beyond the implementation of the Act Prohibiting the Importation of Slaves on January 1, 1808. This illegal trade fed the commercial rice industry's insatiable need for enslaved labor. Unlike on Maryland's Eastern Shore, where the last slave ship disembarked African captives before the American Revolution, 1,678 enslaved people were disembarked in South Carolina and Georgia from eleven documented slaving vessels between 1808 and 1858. The majority of the captives aboard were purchased in West-Central Africa, particularly on the Congo River. The

Wanderer was the last slaving vessel to make the terrible voyage and dis-embark its human "cargo" in the Lowcountry. On the schooner turned slaving vessel, slavers purchased captives in the port of Ambriz (in present-day Angola), skirted both the Royal Navy and the West Africa Squadron by concealing itself along the Congo River, and subsequently disembarked 407 captives on Jekyll Island off the coast of Savannah in 1858.[25]

★★★★★★★★

Even as the illegal trade of African captives ceased, slaveholding families continued to trade in human beings within their families, as well as with ex-tended family members and neighbors. Enslaved people on the Combahee changed hands when the wealthiest families passed their wealth down to their children or upstart families liquidated their wealth to pay debts. The planters' intergenerational wealth was created by the labor of unfree Black people toiling in the pestilential rice swamps and losing their children in large numbers. Dr. James Heyward, who died in 1859, seems to have fallen into the first category. He must have bequeathed his intergenerational wealth to his only brother, Colonel William C. Heyward. If his will and es-tate record could be found, they would certainly list Old Heads Prince and Tyra Polite and Tooman and Joan Legare; Prime Hands Friday Barrington and Edward Brown; and Boys and Wives (enslaved people born between approximately 1845 and 1847, though many of the women in the age group married older Prime Hands, as we have seen) Phoebe Burns Frazier and Lucy Lee Smith. With the exception of the youngest, Lucy Lee Smith, Dr. James Heyward had purchased these very same enslaved people from the estate of his father, William Heyward, in 1848.

In 1859, William L. Kirkland Jr. married Mary Miller Withers. He, his mother, and his stepfather drew up another agreement, signed March 13, 1859, before his wedding. It stated that William Kirkland and his mother, in "effecting certain family arrangements"—which could have meant either Kirkland's impending nuptials, his mother's long-standing $17,000 debt to her mother-in-law's estate, or both—had decided to exchange plantations and slaves. Mary Anna gave William Kirkland Rose Hill, along with the Black people held in bondage on it. She took his Longbrow Plantation (which he had assembled from the pieces of Rose Hill he owned after the 1853 parti-tion, 14 acres of highland and 94 acres of swampland he had purchased from Dr. Francis S. Parker and his wife, Sarah S. Parker, on January 1, 1853, and an additional tract of 380 acres from the Parker family). Even after having been partitioned, Rose Hill was significantly larger and more productive than Longbrow. Rose Hill also had a house, which Longbrow did not. So Mary Anna gave her son a productive plantation and a house to get him off to a good start, allowing him and his bride-to-be to provide a comfortable life-style for their future children to provide his bride-to-be and future children with a comfortable lifestyle. Mary Anna had a relatively young husband who was up to the challenge of reclaiming Longbrow's tidal swamps, making them both productive and profitable, and building a house.[26]

To the enslavers, the enslaved labor force was, of course, merely property, like livestock, tools, or even household furnishings. So along with the land, main house, and outbuildings at Rose Hill, William L. Kirkland Jr. acquired seventy-five enslaved people. They were listed in groups of men, women, and children, but we children. We know that they included Andrew Harris, his wife, Diana Days Harris, and their son Samuel Harris (in the pension file documents, Diana Harris remembered she and her husband had been "slaves of Edward Means of Combahee" before Means sold them to William L. Kirkland Jr., though the records are lost). They also included two sets of siblings: Jacob Jackson, Anthony Bartley, and Daphne Jackson Snipe, and Mary Ann Lewis, John A. Savage, and Maria Wineglass (all of whom, as noted earlier, came from William Savage's estate on the Ogeechee River; Mary Anna Faber bought them from Henry Parker Middleton in 1843). Also sold were Anthony's wife, Moriah Haywood Bartley (whom Dr. James Heyward sold to Joshua and Mary Anna Nicholls when she was a little girl), and Daphne's second husband, Ned Snipe. Furthermore, the enslaved people included parents Sam and Sarah Grant, along with their son Jackson Grant (whom Thomas Rhett Smith Elliott must have sold to Kirkland in the 1850s, with Kirkland having mort-gaged them back to Elliott in 1857) and Jackson's wife, Dorcas; Carolina and Flora Grant, with their son Stepney Grant (ownership of whom Mary Anna Nicholls retained in the 1853 partition of Rose Hill); and Friday Hamilton's father, George, and mother, Emily (listed again as "Amy"), though Friday him-self is not listed. All were separated from their extended families and commu-nity on Rose Hill and sent to live next door at Longbrow.[27]

In exchange, young Kirkland gave to his mother and stepfather forty-five enslaved people. They included Sanko Van Dross (listed as Sancho) and his wife, Abigail, along with Sanko's son Mingo Van Dross (whom William L. Kirkland had purchased from Thomas Rhett Smith Elliott) and the cou-ple's younger son Hercules (Sanko likely started a new family on Rose Hill; neither Abigail nor Hercules is listed on the 1851 bill of sale); siblings

Daniel Jenkins and Tenah Jenkins Hamilton (listed as "Teneh"; Kirkland had purchased her from William Elliott in 1850); Pompey and Pussy (listed as "Pussey") and their children, Frank Hamilton, Captain Brown, and Sylla (listed as "Scylla"; William L. Kirkland had purchased them and then in 1857 mortgaged them back to Thomas Rhett Smith Elliott); and Isaac DeCauster (who was included in Mary Anna Lynah Kirkland Faber's 1848 marriage settlement). It is doubtful the people whom Mary Anna Nicholls and her son exchanged "for the purpose of effecting certain family arrangements," as the 1859 deed states, had any say in whether they lived and labored against their will on either Rose Hill or Longbrow.[28]

One week after he exchanged plantations and enslaved labor forces with his mother, William L. Kirkland Jr. married Mary Miller Withers. She was born to two prominent families in the South Carolina Upcountry, the daughter of Judge Thomas Jefferson Withers and Elizabeth Tunstall Boykin. Mary's mother was a member of the prominent Boykin family of Camden, South Carolina. The Boykins had emigrated from Ireland, settled first in Virginia in the 1680s, then arrived in the South Carolina Upcountry two decades before the American Revolution. Her first cousin Mary Boykin Chesnut, sixteen years older, was the wife of James Chesnut Jr., a US senator from South Carolina and a future brigadier general of the Confederate Army; her diary, which was published in the 1880s, offers a window into the life of an upper-class southern white woman and an upper-class southern white family during the Civil War years.

Because Mary Miller Withers's four older siblings died of scarlet fever, she was remembered as being a "terribly spoilt" child. Her father, Thomas Jefferson Withers, was elected common-law judge in 1846, signed the Order of Secession, and subsequently was chosen as one of six delegates to represent South Carolina at the Montgomery Convention in February 1861, when the South seceded from the United States, then elected one of two representatives to represent South Carolina in the Provincial Congress of the Confederacy. Shortly after the Montgomery Convention, Judge Withers resigned his seat in the Confederate States Congress and returned to his duties as judge.[29]

In the 1920s, when Mary Miller Withers Kirkland was in her eighties, she shared her memories with her grandson's wife, who recorded them; they were later turned into a book. Like her cousin Mary Chesnut, Mary Withers also kept a diary during the Civil War years, though it was never published. Mary Kirkland remembered meeting her husband-to-be, William Kirkland Jr., at the Mills House in Charleston one evening in the winter of 1856.

She was a young woman enjoying the social scene among the Charleston elite. Ten years her senior, he was a "rice planter of Combahee." Kirkland must have been immediately smitten with Mary because he gave her camellias and was flattered when she later wore the flowers to a ball hosted by Barnwell Heyward at Homestead, a plantation previously owned by William Kirkland Jr.'s mother's second husband. They were the perfect complement to her gown, with its silver crescent, and her light shoes, with silver fringe around the ankles and red heels. Mary remembered her whole family attending the ball. They also made sure she attracted the right suitors.[30]

At the height of her father's political career, Mary Miller Withers's family was touched by tragedy. In May 1858, her younger brother, Thomas Jefferson Withers Jr., eighteen, was killed by a fall from his horse. A week after Tom's funeral, Mary, her mother, and her other siblings left for the summer. As they traveled to Sullivan's Island, the family lodged for a few days at Mills House in Charleston, where Judge Withers always stayed when he traveled to the city. William L. Kirkland Jr. went to Mills House searching for Mary, but the Withers family had already departed. Upon learning where Mary would spend the rest of the summer, he headed there too.[31]

Mary and William L. Kirkland Jr. were married almost a year later, on April 6, in her father's home, Gander Hill, a colonial house with four rooms upstairs and down, a basement, and slave quarters in the yard where thirty enslaved people resided. The Withers family was still mourning Tom's death. Mary was married in a gray sport suit, a gray hat with black trim, and a black veil, which she brought home from a trip to Europe. Her cousin Mary Chesnut attended their wedding. After the lunch, the newlyweds were to go to Rose Hill, but flooding made the route impassable and delayed their trip until the following morning. After spending only a little more than a month there, they went back to Charleston on May 10 because they "could not be at 'Rose Hill' in the Summer." They wound up spending the month of June up in Camden with Mary's mother.[32]

An elderly Mary Miller Withers Kirkland remembered Rose Hill as "a beautiful old place with the avenue a quarter of a mile from the gate which entered into the house of wood." There was a Gothic-style church and a canopy of trees under which enslaved people worshipped. She remembered her mother-in-law was "very religious" and required the Black people she held in bondage to attend Sunday religious services. On the other side of the lawn stood the cattle minder's house and the pool where the cattle drank. The wooden plantation house featured eight rooms. The entrance opened into the dining room and led into the parlor. She also remembered a visit that her cousin Mary Boykin Chesnut paid her; during that visit, Mary Chesnut insisted that the tan linen slipcovers bound with a blue satin stripe, which matched the blue curtains, be removed from the parlor furniture so that she might "see what was under them."[33]

Rose Hill and Longbrow were never meant to be separated. The same mile-long canal was likely used on both plantations to flood and drain the rice fields farthest from the Combahee River. After the exchange, Joshua and Mary Nicholls's seventy-four enslaved people produced 54,000 bushels of rough rice in 1860 from Longbrow's 200 improved and 500 unimproved acres. That year William L. Kirkland Jr.'s ninety-six enslaved people produced 60,000 bushels of rice on Rose Hill, also from 200 improved and 500 unimproved acres. With a new wife and a new plantation, Mary Nicholls's son was all grown up and off to a good start.[34]

★★★★★★★★

It is fitting for Minus Hamilton to have been sold in the last documented slave transaction occurring among the Combahee families before the Civil War, because he, and Harriet Tubman, of course, are inarguably the stars of this story of the Combahee River Raid. Minus Hamilton was part of a transaction through which one family was striving to create wealth that they could pass down for generations to come. All of the planters extracted their wealth from the forced labor of enslaved Blacks growing Carolina Gold. This was to be the enslavers' legacy to their children.

As noted earlier, Arthur M. Parker had purchased a lot of six enslaved people from the estate of Edward Rutledge Lowndes in March 1853. On December 20, 1859, he included five of them among the sixteen enslaved people he sold to James L. Paul along with Palmetto Plantation, on the lower Combahee River. Those five were Minus Hamilton, his wife, two of his children, and a son-in-law (listed as "Minus 65, Hagar 50, Frank 19, Harry 25, Binah 22"). Daughter Sibby, who had been part of the 1853 transaction, was not sold with the family in 1859. However, Harry and Bina Mack's daughter Hagar, Minus and Hagar Hamilton's granddaughter, was sold with her family in 1859 (she is listed as "Hagar 2").[35]

On the same day, brothers Francis S. Parker and Arthur M. Parker sold an additional twenty-three enslaved humans to James L. Paul for $16,875.

Among them were Andrew Wyatt, his wife, Maria Phoenix Wyatt, and children Tanebar, Fatima, and Sambo (listed together on the same line: "Andrew 35, Maria 35 (Prolapsed Uterus), Tanebar 6, Fatima 3, Sambo 1"). In August 1889, Andrew Wyatt testified in his pension file: "I was owned by John Parker before I was owned by Mr. Paul . . . the same place where Parker lived that was the place I lived with Mr. Spaul [*sic*]." On the next line was listed Maria's sister Silvia Jackson Gaylord DeCauster along with her first husband, Sampson Gaylord, and Adam, Nester, and Molly, who may have been the couple's children ("Sampson 45, Silvia 37 (Prolapsed Uterus), Adam 19, Nester 5, Molly 1").[36]

The two references to "prolapsed uterus" deserve a brief comment. Prolapsed uterus (also called fallen womb) was a common condition of enslaved female field hands forced to work too far into or too soon after pregnancy. Three-fourths of the women over age thirty sold by Francis S. Parker suffered from this condition.[37]

★★★★★★★★

We have almost come to the end of our journey through the testimony of the freedom seekers and the records of the planters who held them in bondage. But not all of the people enslaved on the six lower Combahee rice plantations affected by the Combahee River Raid have yet been accounted for. A few more very important historical actors need to be introduced.

The only slave transaction found for planter Walter Blake's family occurred months before the war. On October 27, 1860, Joseph Blake signed a deed conveying his plantation, called True Blue, and two gangs of enslaved people to his son, Walter Blake, in order to make "immediate and future provisions for his son." Joseph Blake lived at the time and for much of his adult life in the town of Worthing, Sussex County, England (as noted earlier, Joseph Blake's father, William Blake, returned to England in 1774 and remained loyal to the British Crown). Walter Blake managed his father's plantations on the Combahee River. Joseph Blake owned True Blue, Dawson's (also called Cypress), and Elliott's Plantations (the last of these was part of Newberry Plantation, also owned by Joseph Blake) and approximately a hundred enslaved people who were "part of the Cypress and Newington Gangs," according to the conveyance. These two groups of bondspeople were located on the lands "purchased by William Blake Esquire the father of the said Joseph Blake from Thomas Middleton Esquire." That purchase included Bonny Hall Plantation. William Blake bequeathed Bonny Hall, Newington, and Cypress Plantations to Joseph Blake in his 1802 will.[38]

The 1860 deed does not list the names of the enslaved people whom Joseph Blake conveyed to his son along with True Blue. However, at one point, probably in the mid-1850s, Walter Blake made a list of the people his father held in bondage. Five plantations are included in the list and 313 enslaved people are named. There were 120 bondspeople on the slave list for Parker's Settlement (also owned by Blake, and located next door to his Bonny Hall). We can identify two enslaved people on the undated slave list written by Joseph Blake's son Walter. Jonas Green (listed as "Jonas F Newington") came from the Newington gang and was a full hand. And Wally Graham ("Wally F") was a full hand who may have been born on Parker's Place. Jonas Green was married to Dorcas before the Civil War. He and Wally Graham do not have pension files, nor were they Old Heads. But, like John A. Savage, they knew so much of the Combahee freedom seekers' and planters' business that one marvels at the extent of their knowledge, and cannot help wondering about its source. There was a family among the list of 103 people enslaved at New Ground (another of the Blake plantations): Paul, who also came from the Cypress Gang ("Paul (Cypress)") and was listed with the men; his wife, Dinah, a full hand ("Dinah F."); and their daughter Henny Middleton Morton, who were listed with the enslaved women. Neither Paul's nor Henny's capacity to labor was identified; Diana Middleton testified in July 1896 that her daughter was a "cripple gal; she could walk, but she limped." Paul's age and Henny's disability may have precluded them from task labor in the rice fields.[39]

In 1860, Walter Blake owned seventy-four enslaved people in Beaufort's St. Peter's Parish, and they produced 20,000 bushels of rice on 330 improved acres. He also held thirty-six Blacks in bondage at his summer home in Henderson, North Carolina. In addition, Blake was the agent for his father's 2,600 improved and 3,500 unimproved acres in Beaufort's Prince William's Parish, on which 545 enslaved people produced 48,000 bushels of rice.[40]

Around the time that South Carolina seceded from the Union (December 20, 1860), Edward Laight Wells, a New Yorker, traveled from New York and spent three weeks next door to William C. Heyward's Cypress Plantation with Charles T. Lowndes's family at their Oakland Plantation. Wells wrote to his mother that the Lowndeses had been "exceedingly kind" to him.

The pall of impending war must have hung over every conversation and every gathering of family and friends, and it was likely not a very festive season. He did, however, tell his mother that Christmastime among the enslaved community on the Lowndes plantation was a period of "great gaiety." One morning, enslaved Blacks performed by dancing on the piazza of the plantation house. Sabina Lowndes, Charles T. Lowndes's wife and Governor Henry Middleton's niece, "regaled" the participants with a "bucket of punch." Wells wrote that he was pleased to see everyone "enjoying themselves." It was likely the last season Sabina Lowndes and the other planters' wives and children spent on the Combahee.[41]

★★★★★★★★

The confluence of two streams of evidence—prewar planters' documents and postwar pension files—reveals how enslaved people were bought, sold, given away, mortgaged, and bequeathed. The pension files in particular are unprecedented in their wealth. Through them we can identify and members of their families and communities. Formerly enslaved African Americans named their parents, siblings, aunts, uncles, cousins, grandparents, great-aunts, great-uncles, neighbors, childhood friends, and sweethearts, and did so in their own words and in their own voices. They named the enslavers who held them in bondage. They recounted intimate details about their lives, loves, and labors, while in bondage and after. Most of all, the United States Civil War Pension files reveal how these people wound up against their wills on the lower Combahee River in early June 1863. All those with titles are present and accounted for, ready to tell the next part of our story in their own words.

7

John Brown's "Men"

In the run-up to the Civil War, Blacks enslaved on coastal South Carolina and Georgia's rice plantations died in appalling numbers. Sales and transactions also rose, as Upper South farmers sold enslaved people to plantations in the Deep South and Southwest. Blacks in places like Maryland's Eastern Shore intensified their efforts to liberate themselves by running away. This meant the efforts by kidnappers also intensified. Harriet Tubman continued to risk everything to help liberate enslaved people with help from free Blacks in Pennsylvania and elsewhere, expanding her role as an Underground Railroad conductor and liberator, and fundraising among abolitionists and abolitionist societies, especially in Massachusetts and upstate New York.

Letters from friends like William Still, who of course had worked closely with Tubman, served to introduce her work to abolitionists throughout the Northeast and indeed around the world. Thomas Garrett wrote to his abolitionist friends at the Edinburgh Ladies Emancipation Society in Scotland that he was "proud of her acquaintance" and that Tubman was the "greatest heroine of the age." Her name would have been "trumpeted over the land" were she white. In 1854, Garrett wrote to J. Miller McKim about his long-standing relationship with Tubman and her arrival at his home with her two brothers and four other freedom seekers. McKim was the corresponding secretary of the Pennsylvania Anti-Slavery Society and addressee of the large wooden crate in which Henry "Box" Brown had had himself shipped from Baltimore to Philadelphia.[1]

As they learned of Tubman's accomplishments and her needs, abolitionists like William H. Seward, former governor of New York and a US senator at the time, provided assistance. From Scotland, Mary Edmundson and her sister Eliza Wigham sent to Garrett a contribution of £5 for Tubman to support her mission to rescue her parents. Abolitionists' contributions supplemented Tubman's own earnings, which she saved for the same purpose. These abolitionists were part of an international network of local activists, men and women, dedicated to the abolition of slavery and the liberation of enslaved people, of which Underground Railroad operators were a small part. As we've seen, passage of the 1850 Fugitive Slave Act had energized the movement in the United States, though the leadership was largely white and overwhelmingly male.[2]

Most abolitionists who supported Tubman's work were "Garrisonians"— followers of William Lloyd Garrison, one of the first professional agitators, who gained a reputation for his bruising rhetoric, which threatened to destabilize the US political and social order and over time helped to shift the political center of northern public opinion. Garrison was infamous (in some circles) for his provocative acts, such as rewriting the Declaration of Independence to include African Americans and burning the US Constitution.[3]

Frederick Douglass, initially one of Garrison's most intimate protégés, eulogized Garrison after the latter's death in 1879 as "the chief apostle of the immediate and unconditional emancipation of all the slaves in America." Garrison was indeed ahead of his time, inspiring two generations of Black and white activists to build a movement that had roots in the natural-rights traditions of Britain, the French Revolution, the American Revolution, and Western Romanticism. Garrison agitated for the immediate emancipation of enslaved people in the United States, the cessation of enslavement in free states and territories, and equal rights for Blacks and women.[4]

In 1832, a year after Nat Turner's revolt, Garrison founded the New England Anti-Slavery Society (NEAS), the first organization of its kind. The NEAS advocated for the principle of immediate and uncompensated abolition of slavery and opposed colonization (a movement, spearheaded by the American Colonization Society, to send Blacks back to Africa—a stand that Abraham Lincoln endorsed for a time). As early as 1833, NEAS sent three full-time field agents out to establish a dozen local affiliates. This inspired the formation of nearly fifty abolition societies, from Bangor, Maine, to Paint Valley, Ohio, including J. Miller McKim and William Still's American Anti-Slavery Society (AAS), founded in 1833 in Philadelphia.[5]

Garrison also edited and published *The Liberator*, printed in Boston, which appeared weekly from 1830 until December 1865, when the Thirteenth Amendment was ratified, abolishing enslavement. *The Liberator* vociferously challenged antebellum southern slaveholders and their allies in the North and West for thirty-five years. Over this time Garrison perfected a form of stylized verbal combat that American man of letters Washington Irving called "slang-whanging." Garrison attacked southern slaveholders for the sinfulness of slavery and the stranglehold they had on Congress. *The Liberator's* readership and reach were global.[6]

Starting in the 1830s, abolitionists got "woke" from reading newspapers such as *The Liberator*, or essays and poems by Henry David Thoreau and John Greenleaf Whittier. They heard lectures by speakers like Garrison, and sermons by ministers like Henry Ward Beecher and Thomas Wentworth Higginson, as well as by Black abolitionists, such as Sojourner Truth and Henry "Box" Brown.[7]

Across the Atlantic, lectures and autobiographies by former slaves Ottobah Cugoano and Olaudah Equiano had fueled the British abolitionist movement. The lecture hall was equivalent to a college for liberal-minded whites in the nineteenth century, particularly for women, providing instruction on the most pressing social issues of the day—abolition, women's suffrage, and the dissolution of the Union—as well as entertainment. Most of all, it exposed middle- and upper-class white audiences to peoples and parts of the world otherwise foreign to them.[8]

Though there were Black radicals on the scene, including Benjamin Banneker, Richard Allen, James Forten, David Walker, and David Ruggles, the face of radical abolitionism was still predominantly white when Frederick Douglass electrified the abolitionist lecture circuit. In August 1841, while working as a stevedore and caulker in New Bedford, Massachusetts, Douglass attended the antislavery convention held at the Nantucket Atheneum. At the close of a session, Douglass, quaking at the unprecedented opportunity to speak as an equal to a white audience, rose and asked to be recognized. He told the audience of his status as a fugitive slave and the cruelty he had endured before he escaped. It was the first time many in the audience had heard a fugitive slave speak of his experiences for himself. Garrison hired Douglass as a full-time lecturer in 1842 and subsidized the printing costs of Douglass's first autobiography, *Narrative of the Life of Frederick Douglass, an American Slave*, which was published in 1845 with an introduction by Garrison.[9]

At six feet one inch tall, with smooth, walnut-brown skin, a lion's mane of tightly coiled hair and waves parted carefully on the left side, a prominent forehead, an aquiline nose, chiseled lips, a booming baritone voice, and a confidence that often overflowed into cockiness, Douglass took the abolition movement by storm. Garrison's writings and lectures made the physical, sexual, mental, and emotional cruelties inflicted by southern enslavers on those they held in bondage palpable to his audience of northern whites and free Blacks (some of whom, like James Forten, had never been enslaved). But Douglass embodied the quintessential fugitive slave and brought authenticity to the movement. White abolitionists could not speak to a "back covered with scars," words that characterized Douglass's own experiences and which were eloquently presented in a speech entitled "I Have Come to Tell You Something About Slavery," delivered in Lynn, Massachusetts in 1841. As Douglass continued, "Blood had sprung out as the lash embedded itself in [his] flesh," he made his audiences feel the wounds on his back and personally bear witness to the trauma of millions of Blacks. From the lectern and subsequently in his newspaper, the *North Star*, the self-taught Douglass wielded his erudition like a sword. He denounced the proslavery stance of Christian clergy and the government for hypocrisy, complicity, and the sanctioning of enslavement. Black abolitionists such as Douglass put a human face to the radical abolition movement.[10]

Douglass was uniquely poised to attack the 1850 Fugitive Slave Act, which contributed to an evolution in Douglass's own thinking and dovetailed with his break with the Garrisonian wing of the abolitionist movement. Garrison viewed the US Constitution as a proslavery instrument that protected southern slavery and slaveholders; Douglass was starting to see the Constitution as a document that could reach beyond the intent of the nation's founders, many of whom were slaveholders. Douglass read it as an abolitionist document, one built on antislavery principles that had been manipulated to serve proslavery practices; it would cease to protect slavery when it was no longer administered by slaveholders.[11]

The radical abolitionist movement was hardly monolithic; schisms developed even among and between well-meaning, reform-minded activists. A few of Garrison's tenets rubbed some abolitionists the wrong way. First, Garrison advocated nonresistance. He refused to hold public office, vote, join the US military, pay taxes, or obey any government requirements, and pledged to submit to the penalties of his disobedience. For him the Constitution had been irredeemably corrupted by compromises with slavery and therefore could not advance society to a just outcome. Garrison responded to South Carolina senator John C. Calhoun's calls for "disunion," threats that a southern state could nullify federal law and secede from the Union to protect its liberty and sovereignty, by saying that a Union without slaveholders was the highest and truest cause. Thomas Wentworth Higginson led a group within the abolitionist community to call for a disunion convention after the election of President James Buchanan in 1857 promised four more years of a proslavery national government. Higginson was a Unitarian minister from Worcester, Massachusetts, who had delivered fiery sermons against the 1854 Kansas-Nebraska Act (which repealed the 1820 Missouri Compromise and permitted self-determination on the question of slavery in newly created US territories). As we'll see, he became a Union officer during the Civil War. The Disunion Convention held in Wooster, Ohio, in January 1857 furthered Garrison's long-standing position that free states should separate from slave states. But even many abolitionist supporters thought that Garrison's disunionism and calls for equal rights for women were extraneous to the struggle for immediate emancipation of enslaved people, and that advocating equal rights for Blacks was heretical.[12]

Aside from Douglass, most Black abolitionists remained loyal to Garrison. His stance against colonization and for immediate emancipation and equal rights made Garrison a hero to Black readers. The free Black community was an important part of *The Liberator*'s audience. Five hundred free Blacks subscribed to the newspaper in its first year of publication. Providing a vehicle for biracial political coalition and serving as a voice for Black organizations and writers was part of *The Liberator*'s mission from its founding. Prominent members of the free Black community, such as James Forten, a wealthy sailmaker in Philadelphia and abolitionist, contributed early, providing ongoing financial backing to the newspaper.[13]

The Severance family of Boston had long been active in the abolitionist, temperance, and women's rights movements and was also part of the Boston-based abolitionist community that centered around Garrison. Caroline Seymour Severance found that the abolitionist movement welcomed women in leadership roles, which at the time the temperance movement prohibited. The 1837 Anti-Slavery Convention in New York was the first to have Black women serve as delegates (four out of seventy-one). Lydia Maria Child, a prominent antislavery feminist, journalist, and novelist, attended. In 1848, the year of the Seneca Falls women's convention, Severance joined forces with the new women's rights movements, and this became her life's work. She was elected to the first of several national offices at the 1853 National Woman's Rights Convention in Worcester, Massachusetts, where she also witnessed Sojourner Truth electrify the crowd with her famous "An't I a Woman?" speech. In the temperance and women's rights movements, Severance met and worked closely with supporters of temperance and women's rights, like Higginson and Garrison, who were also of course directly engaged in the abolitionist movement. She had been a close friend of Garrison and his wife years before the Severances relocated to Boston from Cleveland with their four children; the Garrisons were the Severances' neighbors in their new Boston home.[14]

Severance was one of the organizers of, and presided over, the second Women's Rights Meeting held at Boston's Melodeon Hall in June 1860. Harriet Tubman attended the meeting. When one of the scheduled speakers was too ill to take the platform, Ednah Cheney, who decades later would become another of Tubman's biographers, wanted Tubman to take the speaker's place. Someone else asked Higginson to be the substitute speaker. Higginson, though a staunch women's rights supporter, declined, saying he would not speak on a platform with so few women on it. When Tubman took the platform to speak, Higginson introduced her. He also took the opportunity to publicly berate Caroline Dall, who had invited him to speak, and corrected her statement about the number of rescue missions Tubman had made to the South (Dall had said that Tubman made thirteen rescue missions to the south, but Higginson insisted it was "only" eight); he then stormed out of the room. It was strange behavior for a fellow foot soldier in the abolition movement and a supporter of John Brown who would cross paths with Tubman in South Carolina.[15]

The Shaws were another Boston family with deep ties to the abolitionist movement and whose work also likely brought them to cross paths with Tubman. Francis Shaw and Sarah Blake Sturgis Shaw were part of Boston's elite. The Shaw and Blake families had become wealthy in the early 1850s through an import business to the West Indies and China. Francis and Sarah Shaw and their children moved to West Roxbury, Massachusetts, in 1841 to associate with the Brook Farm commune, a community of intellectuals and reformers. The Shaws were members of the American Anti-Slavery Society, as was Lydia Maria Child, one of their dear friends. It must have been difficult to find like-minded people willing to risk social ostracism for immediate abolition, even in Massachusetts, where slavery had been outlawed since 1783, and so it likely felt all the more refreshing to come upon equally passionate people. The abolitionist movement created close, personal relationships between families, as evidenced by the Severances' and Shaws' children playing and growing up together with William and Helen Garrison's children. As we'll see, multiple generations of abolitionists would continue their collaborative work and deep, abiding friendships in South Carolina.[16]

The Fugitive Slave Act had compelled radical abolitionists to take up arms. Though Garrison was unwavering in his nonviolent stance, he and many of his fellow abolitionists, Black and white, advocated self-defense for enslaved and free Blacks alike. In Frederick Douglass's speech "Resistance to Blood- Houndism," delivered in Syracuse in early 1851, he excoriated abolitionists allied with Garrison's nonresistance who sought to "frown slaveholders down" with moral suasion, trying to convince slaveholders that the Blacks they held in bondage were actually their fellow countrymen. Some radical abolitionists began calling for enslaved Blacks to rise up against slaveholders in insurrection. Douglass continued to implore his fellow abolitionists to take action, saying he "believed two or three dead slaveholders will make [the Fugitive Slave Act] a dead letter" and declaring that Blacks living in the North should be "resolved to die than to go back." Acting in self-defense would restore their humanity, and especially Black manhood. In response to the Fugitive Slave Act, many abolitionists, like Douglass, began to advocate for revolution.[17]

****

Four years after the Fugitive Slave Act, the 1854 Kansas-Nebraska Act, mentioned briefly earlier, undid the 1820 Missouri Compromise, which had prohibited slavery in any of the Louisiana Purchase lands north of 36' 30." The 1854 bill created two new territories, Kansas and Nebraska, and allowed territories to choose whether to allow or prohibit slavery, based on a popular vote. The result was the conflict now known as "Bleeding Kansas." "Border ruffians" from slaveholding Missouri rushed west into Kansas to tip the electoral balance in favor of slaveholding in the territory. The proslavery Kansas legislature passed some of the most draconian laws in the Union, punishing anyone speaking or writing against slavery with two years at hard labor, decreeing ten years at hard labor for anyone assisting a fugitive slave, and imposing the death penalty on anyone who instigated a slave insurrection. The conflict moved even more abolitionists away from Garrison's "spiritual weapons," as Garrison termed disunion, nonresistance, and paci-fism, and toward bloodshed.[18]

After border ruffians and southern-rights supporters attacked and burned to the ground the free-soil settlement in Lawrence, Kansas, in May 1856 and outmatched free-soil settlers, who could mount no resistance, John Brown was appointed captain of the Liberty Guards of the 1st Brigade of Kansas Volunteers. He, his teenage son Oliver, and his son-in-law Henry Thompson took justice into their own hands. In a surprise nighttime raid, they executed eight proslavery settlers at Pottawatomie, shooting them at point-blank range and hacking their bodies to pieces with broadswords. The brutal killings were retribution for proslavery militias' attacks on Lawrence and terrorized the proslavery community. They ultimately incited more violence.[19]

The fighting in Kansas and Missouri set the stage for Brown's Harpers Ferry raid. In 1857, Brown traveled to Boston, seeking money, weapons, and foot soldiers to wage guerrilla warfare. He somehow obtained a letter of introduction to Franklin Sanborn, a teacher in Concord and secretary of the Massachusetts State Kansas Committee, which raised money, collected provisions, clothes, boots, guns, ammunition, and other necessities, and sent free-soil settlers from New England to the territory. A year earlier, in 1856, Thomas Wentworth Higginson reported recruiting and sending two parties of emigrants and $2,000 from Worcester to Kansas, and writing to Kansas Committees in Boston and Chicago encouraging them to follow suit. Both Higginson and Sanborn traveled back and forth to the territories to aid the emigrants from New England. From working on local Kansas com-mittees, Sanborn's political career evolved into efforts to free Kansas from slavery and personal loyalty to John Brown. Like Tubman, he became one of John Brown's "men" and, alongside Higginson, would be one of the "Secret Six"—the group who secretly funded the Harpers Ferry action.[20]

As many as four hundred free-state men, including some from Massachusetts, poured into the Kansas territory. But Sanborn stayed over the border in Nebraska, then went back to Massachusetts to take charge of operating his school. In December 1856, he withdrew from his school to devote his time to the Kansas free-state efforts, serving as corresponding secretary of the state committee. From the time of their first meeting in January 1857, Brown was Sanborn's hero. Later Sanborn wrote to his friend Benjamin Lyman that with the Harpers Ferry raid Brown did the "most heroic thing ever done" and "struck the hardest blow at Slavery that it has ever felt."[21]

Later, after Harpers Ferry, Captain James Montgomery, who led a free-soil force, wrote to Sanborn from Mound City, Kansas, "Your views coincide, exactly, with mine." Neither Montgomery nor Sanborn supported invading slave states as long as their settlers stayed out of free states and their affairs. If they interfered with free states, however, Montgomery would consider "the war begun." Though the war had not in fact begun, fighting in Kansas and Missouri proved to be a precursor. When Brigadier General William S. Harney, commander of the US Army Department of the West in early 1861, threatened to institute martial law to stop the violence between border ruffians and Jayhawkers, Montgomery and the free-staters mounted a small force in defense. Montgomery crowed that the slave states' "large forces would have moved too slow, and small forces could not have taken us . . . with our knowledge of the country, and the favorable disposition of the inhabitants." Free-soilers in Kansas indeed supported Montgomery. Three months before the first shots were fired at Fort Sumter, Montgomery was revealing to Sanborn tactics he would later use in the Combahee River Raid, but asked that Sanborn not publish his letter; it would have sounded, he fretted, "immodest" in print.[22]

Sanborn gave Brown entree to prominent northern abolitionists, who provided financial backing for Brown and his soldiers. The Secret Six included Higginson, who later became commander of the 1st South Carolina Volunteers (as noted, the first regiment of Black soldiers composed of formerly enslaved men); Samuel Gridley Howe, a Philadelphia physician and husband of Julia Ward Howe, who authored the "Battle Hymn of the Republic" (and who, coincidentally, was one of Eliza Middleton Fisher's closest girlhood friends when the South Carolina Middleton family summered in Newport); Sanborn, who later wrote a biography of John Brown and the first piece about Harriet Tubman's involvement in the Combahee River Raid; Reverend Theodore Parker, a Transcendental Boston minister, abolitionist, and social reformer; Gerrit Smith, an abolitionist and wealthy philanthropist who in Peterboro, New York, operated a stop on the Underground Railroad, founded a manual labor school for Black boys, and divided 200,000 acres of his own land among poor and destitute people, including many formerly enslaved people; and George Luther Stearns, a prosperous manufacturer who also operated an Underground Railroad station in Medford, Massachusetts, and supplied John Brown with the pikes and rifles with which he and his men planned to take over the federal armory and lead a slave rebellion at Harpers Ferry. Sanborn further helped to arrange a speaking tour for Brown on which he lectured to antislavery audiences in the Northeast about free-soil settlers' struggles in Kansas and his role in making the territory "bleed."[23]

Back in Kansas in 1857, Brown led forty free-soil fighters across the border into Missouri and defeated a larger and better-armed force of Missourians. Along with James Montgomery's free-soil forces, Brown turned the Fugitive Slave Act on its head by kidnapping eleven enslaved Blacks, one of whom was going to be sold, and bringing them out of bondage. Brown's group took horses and hostages, then escorted the freedom seekers to Canada.[24]

It is not clear who among the Secret Six knew the full details of Brown's plans to take over the federal armory at Harpers Ferry, Virginia (located at the confluence of the Potomac and Shenandoah Rivers, just sixty-five miles from Washington, DC), steal the largest cache of munitions in the country stored there, liberate the Blacks enslaved on the private farms surrounding the armory, arm them to swell the ranks of Brown's army, incite them to rebel, and establish a Black self-governing state in the ridges and valleys of southwestern Pennsylvania's Allegheny Mountains. Brown intended to use the rugged terrain as a base from which to stage guerrilla warfare on southern slaveholders, raiding nearby plantations to liberate enslaved Blacks, who he believed were desperate for freedom and ready to fight for it. In addition to white abolitionists organizing for immediate abolition, Blacks enslaved on southern plantations had to be given—and take—an active part in their own liberation. According to John Brown, "Give a slave a pike and you make him a man," but depriving an enslaved man of the means of resistance would "keep him down." Brown was convinced his guerrilla actions with a small band of fighters and a large band of armed liberated slaves were part of God's plan. He would undermine the institution of enslavement in ways that the liberation of individual slaves did not.[25]

In his biography of John Brown, Tony Horwitz suggested that Brown's Secret Six group of supporters and financial stakeholders actually had eight members and included Frederick Douglass and Harriet Tubman. Brown first met and shared his nascent plans with Douglass in 1857. At that meeting, Brown impressed Douglass so much that Douglass wrote to readers in the *North Star* that Brown was "deeply interested in our cause, as though his own soul had been pierced with the iron of slavery." For years, Douglass had collected small contributions from the free Black community and transmitted them to Brown for his revolutionary activities. In 1858, Brown spent three weeks with Douglass and his family at their home in Rochester. He passed every waking hour writing a constitution for the revolutionary state he proposed to establish. Douglass wrote in his autobiography that Brown's obsession that he write and engage in dialogue about abolitionist revolution and the creation of a new government from "first thing in the morning" until "last thing at night" began to become something of a "bore" to him. Over the years, Brown and Douglass had nonetheless become close personal friends, bound by their burning desire to end enslavement, the aim of taking down slaveholders who were "guilty of a great wrong against God and humanity" (as Brown asserted when interrogated by Senator James Mason of Virginia while he was in custody awaiting trial), and their willingness to use violence to accomplish those ends.[26]

Douglass traveled in August 1859 to Chambersburg, Pennsylvania, less than twenty miles north of the Mason-Dixon Line, risking kidnapping by slave hunters to hear Brown's final plans to invade Harpers Ferry. At that point Douglass expressed his vehement objections to striking the first blow against the federal government. In *The Life and Times of Frederick Douglass* he described the federal armory at Harpers Ferry as a "perfect steel-trap" and thought that attacking it would set the entire country against the antislavery cause and incite an overwhelming military response from the federal government; slaves would fear for their lives and stay away from the rebellion. Douglass advocated that slaves defend themselves and commit acts of violence against slaveholders. However, he would not sign on to a plan that would essentially involve laying down his life for the cause of ending slavery rather than starting a genuine revolution. Brown, for his part, would not listen to strategic advice from Douglass or anyone else. He believed that he was God's avenger of slaveholders' sins.[27]

After drafting his constitution, Brown was introduced to Tubman in St. Catharine's, Ontario, by prominent members of the abolitionist community, including Douglass, Reverend Jermain W. Loguen, and philanthropist Gerrit Smith. Brown traveled to Canada on a mission in April 1858 to recruit foot soldiers from among free Black communities there. He wrote glowingly to his son John Brown Jr. about his meeting with Tubman, saying that "Harriet Tubman hooked on his whole team at once." Brown used a masculine pronoun to refer to Tubman: "He Hariet [sic] is the most of a man, naturally; that I ever met with." Tubman's biographer Kate Larson has hypothesized that Brown referred to Tubman as a man, and used masculine pronouns to describe her, in order to acknowledge her leadership status. He was aware that on her many trips on the Underground Railroad Tubman had developed highly valuable skills—familiarity with the terrain, an ability to disguise herself and her movements, the facility to conceal sometimes large groups of freedom seekers, and ways of tapping into Black communication networks on the border between eastern Maryland and Pennsylvania. He hoped she could use her experience to help mount the raid on Harpers Ferry and found an independent free Black colony in the Allegheny Mountains.[28]

Brown complained to Higginson that the other members of the Secret Six had gotten cold feet, insisting that he delay military action, because they "were not men of action." He had hired Hugh Forbes, a flamboyant British fencing teacher, drillmaster, and soldier of fortune who had fought with Italian revolutionary Giuseppe Garibaldi, to train and drill the men he recruited for his militia and to write a guerrilla warfare manual. When Brown could no longer pay him, Forbes blackmailed him, leaking details of his plan and naming some of his principal funders to members of the US Congress and the secretary of war.[29]

All of the other abolitionists Brown had met in New England pontificated against the Fugitive Slave Act and even theorized about slave insurrection. Tubman, in contrast, had taken matters into her own hands. Brown considered Tubman equal to a man because she was a "doer." She had freed herself, then risked her freedom by going back to liberate others. On April 7, 1858, Tubman assembled an audience of men she had brought to safety in Canada, including Thomas Elliott and Denard Hughes from the Dover Eight, Joe Bailey, Peter Pennington, and her brother Henry Ross (who had chosen the name William Stewart in freedom), as well as two friends who lived in Canada, Charles Hall and John Thompson. Brown addressed the men, read his constitution, and revealed his plans for insurrection. He and his men were destined to carry out God's wrath on sinful slaveholders. Brown's millennialist language must have been music to the ears of men who had recently prevailed over bondage. They all volunteered to serve in Brown's militia. He must have hoped they would serve under the leadership of "General Tubman," as Tubman remembered John Brown calling her.[30]

Hugh Forbes had warned Brown that the enslaved people on the nearby plantations would not rise up in revolt if they were not told in advance of the plot and Brown and his men simply showed up. Brown's planned slave insurrection would "meet no response or a feeble one" if the enslaved people were not forewarned. This may be why Brown beseeched Douglass, in a meeting in an abandoned stone quarry in Chambersburg, Pennsylvania, in August 1859, to join him and serve a "special purpose." Once Brown and his men struck the first blow "the bees [would] begin to swarm," and Brown wanted a former slave to "help hive them"—in other words, convince the liberated slaves to take up arms, fight for their freedom and the freedom of others, and join Brown's slave revolt. Indeed, "hiving off" enslaved people would be one of Tubman's central roles in the Combahee River Raid.[31]

Though he admired Brown, Douglass determined that he would not join him. In 1881, many years after the Harpers Ferry raid, he proclaimed in a speech he delivered at Harpers Ferry: "I could speak for the slave. John Brown could fight for the slave. I could live for the slave, John Brown could die for the slave."[32]

Tubman and the men she recruited lacked the funds to travel to meet up with Brown and drill with his militia. Instead, she traveled to Boston to raise money for the support of the St. Catharine's refugee community and her own household. As the Black community in St. Catharine's grew, Tubman expanded her role as a liberator and Underground Railroad conductor to provide funds, clothes, food, and other articles for their support.[33]

In June 1859, Tubman was in New England, meeting abolitionists and telling her story both before private audiences in supporters' homes and before larger audiences at public events. That month Higginson wrote a letter to his mother about her, saying that the humble fugitive slave called "Moses" was the "greatest heroine of the age." Higginson believed that Maryland slaveholders had put a $12,000 bounty on Tubman's head and would burn her alive if they caught her, though no evidence supports his claim. (He also assumed she would be caught because she was going back into Maryland on another rescue mission. But she never was.)[34]

Tubman mesmerized participants at the Massachusetts Anti-Slavery Society's Fourth of July picnic and rally in Framingham. Every year, a special train deposited hundreds of abolitionists from across the state there, where they gathered to consecrate the day to liberty, justice, and righteousness. Attendees felt the much-anticipated event offered a chance to get away from the "noise, dust, and turbulence of American patriotism" performed on Independence Day and hear the truth about America and the true duties of patriotism. At that gathering five years earlier, Garrison had set a match to the US Constitution.[35]

Preaching to this choir, at the 1859 event Higginson introduced Tubman as "Moses"—perhaps partly as a way of concealing her identity from any slave hunters who might have infiltrated their ranks. She told her story, regaling the audience with tales of her adventures, which were better than fiction. Her presentation was more soul-stirring than any abolitionist theory.[36]

July 4, 1859, came and went. John Brown's raid on Harper's Ferry was delayed again. Tubman remained in New England, meeting, speaking, and raising money to support the St. Catharine's refugee community and her own growing household in Auburn, New York. When she spoke to the New England Colored Citizen's Convention in Boston at the beginning of August, Tubman was introduced to the crowd, composed largely of Black abolitionists, as "Harriet Garrison." In addition to concealing her identity, this may also have been an attempt by Garrisonians to lay claim once again to a hero of the abolitionist movement. Prominent members of the movement, such as Douglass, Higginson, Sanborn, and other members of the Secret Six, had, as noted, become impatient with Garrison's pacifism. Indeed, by the end of the 1850s, even Garrison himself recognized that southern slaveholders in Congress were bent on expanding slavery into new territory and on using federal authority to protect their property. The ultimate test of the movement's ideals was a few short weeks away.[37]

★★★★★★★★

On October 16, 1859, Brown and his twenty-three men, including three of his sons, two of his son-in-law's brothers, and eight veterans from Kansas, attacked and took control of the federal armory and rifle works at Harpers Ferry. They took approximately thirty prominent townspeople hostage (including Lewis Washington, George Washington's great-grandnephew, whom they ultimately released unharmed), killed five people (including Fontaine Beckham, the mayor of Harpers Ferry), and wounded many others. After occupying the armory for roughly two days they were surrounded by federal forces and outgunned. In an attempt to surrender, ten of Brown's men were killed, including two of Brown's sons, Watson and Oliver. Bodies of fugitive slave insurgents were desecrated, left in the gutter to be picked over by rooting hogs, or donated to local medical colleges for students to dissect. Five of Brown's men escaped—the fugitive slaves among them utilizing the Underground Railroad to find safety in Canada. Brown and six other men were captured, jailed, tried, and sentenced to hang. Brown refused all attempts by his supporters and their legal counsel to declare him insane and save his life.[38]

In November 1860, before Brown was hanged, Tubman made a final attempt to rescue her sister Rachel and Rachel's two children. This was in the face of increasingly perilous conditions for free and enslaved Blacks on the Eastern Shore, conditions that had even jeopardized her reliable Underground Railroad networks in Maryland, Delaware, and Pennsylvania. She had told Thomas Garrett that if she could liberate her last sister, she would not undertake any more missions. It must have broken Tubman's heart and crushed her spirit to learn that her sister had died the year before. To compound her anguish, Tubman lacked the funds—she told Edna Cheney that it was thirty pieces of silver, which to one person was the price of an embroidered handkerchief or silk dress but to another was the price of freedom for two orphaned children—to bribe someone to get Rachel's children released from the plantations to which Eliza Brodess had hired them out.[39]

Tubman may have felt that she had failed her parents, who had pledged not to leave their homes until all of their children and grandchildren were freed. She may have felt as if she had failed her deceased sister by not succeeding in liberating her orphaned children. Once again, however, Tubman did not let her personal anguish get in the way of God's work. She could not bring her sister back to life or her niece and nephew out of bondage. However, she brought out a couple named Stephen and Marie Ennals and their three children (including one infant, to whom she gave laudanum to keep the baby from crying).[40]

By 1860, as we've seen, Harriet Tubman's rescue missions and detailed instructions had catalyzed the exodus of scores of freedom seekers from the Eastern Shore. But slaveholders in the region had not yet managed to capture the figure who had aided, abetted, and inspired others to liberate themselves. One reason was that she was not John Brown. She had neither engaged in violent actions nor incited a slave insurrection. Not yet.

In the end, Brown died a martyr in solidarity with the enslaved Blacks he fought to free. He proclaimed in a courtroom speech after he was found guilty of treason and conspiring with enslaved people to commit first-degree murder that he would "mingle [his] blood further with the blood of [his] children and with the blood of millions in this slave country, whose rights [were] disregarded by wicked, cruel and unjust enactments." On December 2, 1859, the state of Virginia hanged him, then kept his body dangling and on display for thirty-eight minutes for the crowd and newspapermen to see before cutting it down. The state then hanged six of his accomplices.[41]

Brown's death was the fulfillment of a recurring dream Tubman had had before they had met in St. Catharine's. She dreamed that she was in a wilderness strewn with rocks and bushes. From under the rocks, she saw a three-headed serpent raise its heads. One head had the face of an old white man with a long white beard. It gazed at her, as if wanting to speak to her. The serpent's other two heads bore the faces of younger white men. They also rose up, gazing at her as if they, too, had something to say. But a crowd of men rushed in and smote the heads of the two younger faces with rocks. Only the head of the old man's visage survived and continued to gaze at Tubman. She surmised that the faces of Brown's sons who had been killed during the raid were those on the second and third heads of the three-headed serpent. But Brown, the first head, survived the raid.[42]

After he was executed, Tubman said of John Brown: "It wasn't John Brown that died on that gallows. When I think how he gave up his life for our people, and how he never flinched, but was so brave to the end; its clar to me it wasn't mortal man, it was God in him."[43]

Brown's friends mobilized to support his widow and surviving children, and to free two of his men from jail. Higginson sent a message to Kansas to recruit Captain James Montgomery to lead the rescue mission, because he could not find anyone in New England to do it. In February 1860, Thomas Wentworth Higginson traveled to Kansas under the name Charles P. Carter, because rumor had it that spies were watching. Montgomery, some of his recruits, and Higginson had a meeting in which Higginson sketched out the many obstacles in the way of a successful rescue as well as a plan to overcome them. He was impressed that Montgomery was not deterred by either the obstacles or the odds. Montgomery first wanted to explore the terrain. Indeed, he took charge of the secret mission, sending a man named Silas Soule ahead to Virginia. After feigning intoxication, Soule got himself arrested. He was held in the same jail as John Brown's men and there was able to speak to them. They convinced Soule that a rescue attempt was hopeless, because of the inclement winter weather and the constant surveil-lance at the jail. Montgomery reluctantly abandoned this mission.[44]

Higginson, for his part, believed that Brown's collective actions opened "a new era in the history of Anti Slavery." In eulogizing Brown in December 1859, abolitionist Wendell Phillips proclaimed that "History will date Virginia Emancipation from Harper's Ferry. . . . So, when the tempest up-roots a pine on your hills, it looks green for months—a year or two. Still, it is timber, not a tree. John Brown has loosened the roots of the slave system; it only breathes—it does not live—hereafter." Brown certainly hastened the Civil War. Eighteen months after Brown's raid on Harpers Ferry, the South Carolina militia fired on Fort Sumter. Two years after Brown's raid, Union forces fought the Battle of Port Royal in Beaufort, South Carolina, shortly after which thousands of enslaved people liberated themselves. And a year following that, the United States began arming Black men formerly enslaved in and around Beaufort to fight for the freedom of others, particu-larly for the freedom of Blacks still enslaved on rice plantations along the Combahee River. It was a fulfillment of John Brown's plan—on a scale that only he probably could have imagined—and it would bring together in one place James Montgomery, Harriet Tubman, Thomas Wentworth Higginson, and Franklin Sanborn.[45]

In a speech he gave at the annual meeting of the Massachusetts Anti-Slavery Society in Boston on January 27, 1860 (and which was published in the February 17, 1860, edition of *The Liberator*), Garrison decreed that "in firing his gun" John Brown had signaled to abolitionists that it was "high noon, thank God!"—time for the long-anticipated showdown between North and South, free and slave states. It could lead to the dissolution of the Union, which Garrison had called for thirty years, and the immediate abolition of enslavement.[46]

★★★★★★★★

John Brown's raid also changed Harriet Tubman. Up to then she had risked her own freedom for the freedom of others. Now she decided to put it all on the line. In April 1860 she was in Troy, New York, approximately 180 miles east of her home in Auburn and home to a bustling free Black community, when she learned of the arrest of a young man named Charles Nalle. It was the first time in the ten years since the passage of the Fugitive Slave Act that slave catchers had breached Troy to kidnap a fugitive slave and forcibly transport that person back to the South. It threw the small city into turmoil.[47]

Nalle, twenty-eight, was tall, looked white, and bore a striking resemblance to Blucher W. Hansbrough, the white man who had held him, his mother, Lucy, and his siblings Harriet, Henry, and Maria in bondage in Culpepper County, Virginia, until October 1858. Hansbrough had inherited Nalle from Peter Hansbrough, who had fathered both young men. Blucher Hansbrough continued to exploit his half-brother's labor as a coachman, as his father had before him. Hansbrough then attempted to sell him, tearing him from his wife, Kitty, and their daughters Fanny, Anne, Lucy, and Agnes (all of whom had been manumitted after the death of the man who held them all in bondage and who were living in Washington, DC). Hansbrough was unsuccessful selling Nalle, however, because Nalle's skin was too white; he also refused to hire Nalle out (which would have enabled him to earn money to buy his freedom) and told him to remarry. Nalle was determined to keep his and Kitty's family together. While traveling on a pass to visit them in Washington, Nalle escaped and made his way to Philadelphia and eventually to Troy, New York. Illiterate, he had relied on an attorney named Horatio F. Averill to write letters for him. He confided in Averill that he was a fugitive slave, the legal property of Hansbrough in Virginia. Averill betrayed Nalle's trust. He wrote letters to Hansbrough, informing him of Nalle's whereabouts and offering his services as counsel (for a retainer) in Nalle's recapture. The enslaver hired an agent who traveled to Troy with an arrest warrant from a local commissioner in the Troy area.[48]

While Nalle was on an errand buying bread for his employer, he was arrested by a deputy marshal and taken into custody at the commissioner's office. William Henry, a Black man who lived at the same boardinghouse as Nalle, went looking for him after he did not return with the bread his employer had requested. Henry found Nalle at the commissioner's office in the Mutual Building, outside of which was gathered a crowd. Henry stirred the crowd's emotions by announcing that Nalle was being held inside; that he had committed no crime other than not owning himself; and that he would soon be brought down the stairs and out of the building. Henry asked the crowd—growing in number and excitement—if they were going to stand there watching as this man, who only wanted to be free, was forced to go back to the "prison-house of bondage" in the South, where he likely would be whipped to death.[49]

With throngs of Nalle's supporters present at the Mutual Building, Nalle's new attorney, Martin I. Townsend, arrived after the judicial proceedings had concluded and hurried to secure a writ of habeas corpus to stop the marshal from remanding Nalle. The *Troy Daily News* described another of Nalle's supporters as a seemingly harmless and "somewhat antiquated colored woman" in a sunbonnet. This was Tubman in one of her most effective disguises, making her appear much older than her thirty-seven years. She often stopped in Troy in her travels between Maryland and Auburn (two hundred miles from Troy) or St. Catharine's to visit her niece Kessiah Bowley and her husband, John, as well as abolitionist associates. Troy was also the place where on December 5, 1859, John Brown's body had made one of several stops on its way from Virginia to North Elba, New York, for burial, accompanied by his widow, Mary Brown, her youngest son, and Wendell Phillips.[50]

Tubman threaded her way through the angry throngs and past the armed police, entered the building, mounted the stairs, and blocked the entrance of the commissioner's office in which Nalle was held. She monitored the prisoner and his captors inside and the growing crowd below. As long as the antislavery supporters could see the top of her sunbonnet through an upstairs window, they knew that Nalle was still safe. She kept her head down and her arms folded, as if deep in prayer.[51]

The writ of habeas corpus was issued, and the marshal was required to bring Nalle before the judge. As the chief of police, marshal, and deputy sheriff brought Nalle down the stairway, Tubman gave the signal to Nalle's supporters. They sprang into action, taking on the Troy police force, which had been ordered to the scene. Two thousand angry Black and white supporters surrounded the officers and Nalle on the sidewalk. Fights broke out. Ultimately, an inner circle of Black men among Nalle's supporters managed to extricate him from the police officers. Meanwhile, the "antiquated colored woman" held Nalle's arm and refused to release her grip despite being pummeled by policemen with clubs. She led the crowd in chanting, "Give us liberty or give us death!" At this point, the crowd drew guns and chisels, and even Black women rushed into the fray. The *Troy Daily Times* called one Black woman "Moll Pitcher"—referring to the legendary Revolutionary War heroine—and said that she fought "like a demon."[52]

Nalle's supporters carried him to Dock Street, where he was spirited by ferry boat across the Hudson River to West Troy. His captors, however, overtook and detained him at the Corporation Hall, which was near the ferry dock. Nalle's supporters arrived ten minutes later and stormed the building. Tubman was among the throngs who surged into the room where Nalle was held; both she and Nalle were subsequently and violently ejected. In a hail of bullets fired by the officers from inside the room, the crowd managed to grab Nalle, put him in a wagon, and drive away. Nalle was concealed in the woods until his supporters appealed to his employer and other citizens of Troy to purchase Nalle's freedom for $650. Nalle returned to Troy a free man and was reunited with his wife and children a few weeks later.[53]

Years after Charles Nalle's rescue, Tubman remembered her role in it. She had not only instigated violence but engaged in it. She remembered rushing the police chief, marshal, and deputy when they brought Nalle down the stairs. A police officer had clubbed her; Tubman in turn had struck and choked him. She had fought to free Nalle, who was unconscious, then threw him over her shoulder like a bag of meal and carried him out of the building. She transported Nalle fourteen miles away to Schenectady, New York, in a wagon that she had taken from a white man in Troy.[54]

The question is why she risked everything—her identity, her freedom, even her life—for Nalle. We may never know whether Tubman had a personal relationship with him or his family. It may have been distress over the death of her sister and her inability to free the sister's children. Or it may have been John Brown's hanging and Brown's willingness to sacrifice his life for people whom he did not know.[55]

Whatever the case, Nalle's extraction was a turning point. Nearly all of the freedom seekers whom Tubman liberated from enslavement via the Underground Railroad were from Dorchester and Caroline Counties, Maryland. They were members of her immediate and extended family, as well as neighbors, friends, and members of her community. Now Tubman resolved to risk her life for people she did not know and whose language and culture she did not "understand."

PART TWO

The Proving Ground
of Freedom

The long, dark night of the Past, with all its sorrows and its fears, was forgotten; and for the Future,—the eyes of these freed children see no clouds in it. It is full of sunlight, they think, and they trust in it, perfectly.

—Charlotte Forten

8

"Gun Shoot at Bay Point"

On the morning of November 4, 1861, six months after the bombardment of Fort Sumter in Charleston, Confederate Army colonel William C. Heyward sent a dispatch to Brigadier General Thomas F. Drayton, commander of the Confederate Army's Third Military District. Heyward commanded the South Carolina Volunteers 9th Regiment, stationed at Camp Walker on Hilton Head, southwest of Fort Sumter. He reported that the Union Navy had been moving its armada into Port Royal Sound, which was located midway between Savannah, Georgia, and Charleston. The US Navy fleet entered the sound by the afternoon of the fourth, thirty-two warships, steamers, and transports—the largest fleet in US history up to that date, extending six miles when traveling from Fortress Monroe. Even more vessels were scheduled to arrive over the next two days. Colonel Heyward was clearly wondering whether Drayton knew what action the US Navy's fleet would take and how he could protect his fort and his three companies, which totaled 210 men. More than 400 men were already on the island near Fort Walker. By the time of the attack on November 7, another 1,150 had arrived on Hilton Head, and about 220 were in the fort.[1]

The night before and into the early morning hours of November 7, the US fleet had encountered a furious gale, which moderated by daylight. Driving rain had lashed the vessels and sent mammoth waves surging over the fore of the ships. The weather allowed the Confederate Navy time and opportunity to reinforce its forts. Though the attack was not a surprise—the US Navy expedition had been well publicized in both Confederate and Union newspapers—the size of the fleet was. And despite advance warning, the Confederate Navy was still not prepared. In fact, the Confederacy did not have much of a navy, just a handful of converted and armed tugs and small steamers, makeshift warships that could not challenge the US armada.[2]

On the morning of November 7, the sky was blue and crystal clear, the water as smooth as a mirror. US Navy captain Samuel Francis Du Pont mobilized an overwhelming force, consisting of seventeen warships, twenty-five coaling vessels, and thirty-three transport ships, and maneuvered them into the narrow channel, along with thirteen thousand soldiers and a battalion of Marines. The Confederacy had not imagined that the US Navy would marshal such an imposing force against Port Royal, and so up to that point had focused its energies on defending Charleston, predicting that port city would be the most likely target of a US attack (which, as we will see, it later was).[3]

Port Royal Sound is formed by the Broad and Beaufort Rivers and its entrance marks the easternmost point of Hilton Head and the southernmost tip of Bay Point, approximately two and a half miles apart. There was a Confederate battery, Fort Beauregard, at Bay Point on the southern end of Phillips Island, opposite the sound from Fort Walker on Hilton Head. Fort Walker was by far the more imposing of the two earthworks, flanked by twenty-three guns, including twelve 32-pounders, two 8-inch and two 10-inch columbiads, two 6-inch rifled guns, several heavy seacoast howitzers, and one English siege gun; collectively they were manned with 622 soldiers. With just thirteen mounted guns, Fort Beauregard was dwarfed by Fort Walker. But neither fort possessed sufficient firepower to defend itself against the Union's assault.[4]

Nonetheless, moving the Union Navy between the shoals at Gaskin's Bank on the west and those at Martin's Industry on the east side of the sound would take superior navigational skill. Piloting through the Port Royal Sound channel caused the US Navy considerable delay. The incoming flood tide lifted the height of the water enough to enable the heavier US warships and deep-draft transports to cross over the dangerous reef at Fishing Rip; the gunships and other vessels of lesser draft had crossed over the bar a few days earlier. General Drayton witnessed the "huge leviathan" *Wabash* cross the bar with one or two feet of water to spare. It was followed closely by the *Susquehanna*, the *Atlantic*, and the *Vanderbilt*.[5]

After the US gunboats had reconnoitered the shore and the enemy's fortifications, they fired a warning shot, putting the Confederate forces on notice. Commanded by Captain Christopher Raymond Perry Rogers, the US

Navy warship *Wabash* led thirteen men-of-war drawn up in two parallel lines to navigate the deeper channels; the gunboats followed on the right flank and exploited the river's upper channels. As General Drayton wrote in his official report, they together "vomit[ed] forth" their "iron hail" with "spiteful energy of long-suppressed rage and conscious strength." The formation of Union ships steamed up and around the eastern end of Fishing Rip, bearing down on Confederate captain Josiah Tattnall's fleet of four gunboats and delivering, General Drayton continued, a "terrific shower of shot and shell in flank and front."[6]

The *Wabash* guided the fleet midchannel, equidistant between Forts Beauregard and Walker, firing broadsides at both Fort Walker and Fort Beauregard. When it was built in 1855, the *Wabash,* with its forty-four guns, including two pivot guns and a Parrott rifled gun, was recognized as the finest warship in the world. It became the flagship of the US fleet under the command of Captain Du Pont. As soon as the fight began in earnest, the Confederates fired with great rapidity, but they were no match for the overpowering US firepower. The 4,800-ton *Wabash* and its thirteen consorts moved in a two-mile-long ellipse, turning in advance of Daws Island, then maneuvered along the shore and fired broadsides at the Hilton Head battery. Simultaneously, US gunboats concentrated their fire on Bay Point and on the Confederate vessels there. Once past the reef, the *Wabash* moved into position approximately 600 yards from the Hilton Head battery's guns and slowed its speed. The line of warships followed suit. The *Bienville* and the US gunboats on the right flank chased down the Confederate vessels, and the rebels retreated into Skull Creek. The Bienville moved aggressively, first targeting its 30-pounder at the Confederate vessels, then at the Bay Point battery holding Bay Point; then it turned its fire to pummel the Confederate Navy.[7]

The *Mohican* broke formation, steaming to the northwest of Fort Walker to fire without restriction down the full length of the battery; other warships followed. But the *Wabash, Susquehanna,* and *Bienville* stayed in the ellipse, coming around to engage the Hilton Head battery. Before they fired, a hail of Confederate shot and shell burst all around them. Then, an eyewitness remembered, came the deafening sound of the *Wabash* spraying the battery and the Confederate camp with forty shells at once, while also opening up its muzzle-loaded Dahlgren guns from the ships' gun decks, spar decks, and forecastles. Fire from the *Susquehanna* and the gunboats *Bienville* and *Pawnee* backed the *Wabash,* turning the clear air brown with sand and blue with smoke. By 11 a.m., the US warships had pivoted again to avoid a dangerous reef ten miles seaward and had begun firing their broadside cannons as they took up their positions opposite the Confederate Navy at Bay Point. Three Confederate steamers commanded by Commodore Josiah Tattnall opened fire on the US gunboats *Ottawa*, *Seneca*, *Pembina*, and *Penguin*. US gunboats also took crossfire from Fort Walker on Hilton Head and Fort Beauregard on Bay Point. The gunboats returned fire, forcing the Confederate steamers into a hasty retreat. Confederate gunboats joined then.[8]

Meanwhile, the *Wabash* and *Susquehanna* turned back toward the Hilton Head battery, taking Confederate fire. The pivot guns sent shells bursting into the battery, enveloping the air in dense clouds of white smoke and showers of sand and splinters. The Confederate forces inside the battery were crippled, with only two guns remaining, which they worked doggedly but ineffectively; as General Drayton wrote in his official report, the Confederate soldiers "fought gallantly at the batteries" to defend their homes, families, and livelihoods from enemy invasion. The Bay Point battery gave a last good rally at the *Wabash* as it moved back into its position. But the US gunboats fired a volley of shells on the Hilton Head battery, demolishing part of the fort and taking out one of the guns. The US gunboat *Pocahontas*, which towed in a transport steamer, played a decisive role in ending the drama. After the *Mercury* came up Port Royal Sound toward the Bay Point battery, opening fire with its 30-pound Parrott gun, not one Confederate boat remained on the Beaufort River; they all had fled behind Bay Point to embark and evacuate Confederate forces.[9]

Around 12:30 p.m., Brigadier General Thomas F. Drayton reported to the Third Military District that he was turning over command to Colonel William C. Heyward with instructions that his troops should "hold out as long as any effective fire could be returned," and then left the fort to prepare for the impending attack further upstream. By 2 p.m., all but three of Fort Walker's guns on the waterfront had been disabled, and only five hundred pounds of gunpowder remained in its magazine. General Drayton's command, including two companies of Colonel Heyward's infantry, was transferred to Bluffton. The Charleston Light Dragoons remained in observation at Pocotaligo and Port Royal ferries, maintaining a safe distance from the Union squadron. With rapidly diminishing ammunition and several disabled guns, Colonel Heyward and his forces evacuated Fort Walker. Captain Stephen Elliott followed suit, evacuating Fort Beauregard; he pulled down the Confederate Stars and Bars and took it with him. Soon the United

States flag would fly over South Carolina soil for the first time since the fall of Fort Sumter seven months earlier.[10]

The Battle of Port Royal, as it was called, was effectively over. The transport steamers launched nearly a hundred surfboats that disembarked seventy US Army soldiers and fifty US Marines. The *Wabash* fired one gun, then waited. There was no Confederate response. Subsequently the US Army landed twelve thousand soldiers on Hilton Head under the command of General Thomas W. Sherman, whose forces included the 8th Michigan, which was the only regiment from the West to take part in the battle. Union forces suffered eight soldiers killed and twenty-three wounded. The Confederates had fifty-nine soldiers killed and wounded, four soldiers missing, and three captured or sick. The US Navy did not lose any vessels in the battle.[11]

The Battle of Port Royal was the first major Union victory and it took place relatively early in the war. Confederate forces had been decisively overpowered by the Union naval fleet's leadership, navigation skills, precise, rapid, and unrelenting firepower. J. Smith DuShane, a soldier in the 100th Pennsylvania Regiment, proclaimed in a letter to his future wife (whom he affectionately called "Sister") that "Sumter was avenged."[12]

Jefferson Davis, president of the Confederate States of America, had appointed General Robert E. Lee commander of the Department of South Carolina, Georgia, and Florida a few days prior to the battle. Lee arrived in the area late in the day on November 4 and quickly realized that the Confederacy had neither enough manpower nor enough firepower to defend its entire coastline. In the aftermath of the battle, Lee withdrew the Confederate Army from the South Carolina Sea Islands and waterways, which they could not defend; he focused on protecting the port cities of Charleston, to the north, and Savannah, to the south. To defend Savannah, he rebuilt Fort Jackson, strengthened fortifications on Cumberland Sound, near Brunswick, Georgia, and reinforced Fort Pulaski.[13]

Lastly, Lee focused on defending the Charleston & Savannah Railroad, which the *Charleston Mercury* called the "military backbone" of the "tide water districts." Roughly a thousand miles of railroad had been constructed in South Carolina between 1830 and 1860 by enslaved people hired out by area slaveholders. They performed the arduous tasks of grading the road, cutting down cypress and yellow or pitch pine, making the crossties, and laying the iron rails. During the Civil War, the railroad became the second-most-important means of transportation—the first being water—for the

Confederacy, carrying provisions, artillery, and supplies. It became particularly important after the United States imposed the Southeast Atlantic
Blockade on the Confederacy (a plan known as Anaconda). Railroads were
therefore critical to the Confederacy's ability to move its troops into position to fight the war and get its goods to market to help finance it.[14]

Chartered in 1854, the 120-mile-long Charleston & Savannah Railroad
was located just inland of coastal waterways. It profited from commercial
activity in the two major port cities. When the line was completed in
November 1860, its primary purpose was to move commercial freight.
The shareholders expected that the railroad would enable Charleston,
in particular, to play an even larger role in the export of cotton. The
outbreak of the Civil War transformed the shareholders' original vision.
According to the Charleston & Savannah Railroad's 1863 annual report,
the enterprise earned roughly 90 percent of its revenue from transporting
private passengers and freight, as well as providing government passage. It
carried general freight, such as hides, bales ginned and unginned cotton,
casks of clean (milled) rice, and bushels of rough (unmilled) rice, meal,
and corn; government freight included bushels of corn, meal, clean and
rough rice, and bales of forage, with Charleston receiving almost ten
times as much general and government freight as Savannah. All of the
railroad's operations still depended on hired-out enslaved laborers. In
addition, using its twelve locomotive engines (including one named
"Combahee"), the railroad transported more than seventy-five thousand
Confederate troops a total distance of more than five and a half million
miles.[15]

The railroad fit into General Lee's overarching strategy to keep the fight
off the waterfront, far enough upstream and on land so that the guns of
the US naval fleet would be ineffective; Confederate troops had a better
chance of resisting if they were out of reach of US gunboats. He adopted
a three-pronged strategy: prepare for the US Navy bombardment of Fort
Pulaski, Charleston, and Savannah by shoring up fortifications around all
three; block the rivers, streams, and coastal waterways to prevent a naval
assault; and consolidate Confederate camps at Coosawhatchie, Pocotaligo,
Adams Run, and Green Pond, making them strong enough to resist an
initial assault at critical points of the railroad that were most vulnerable to
Union attack. Troops, artillery, ammunition, and supplies could be transported via the railroad from Charleston and Savannah to points where the

Confederacy most needed to resist assault. For the most part, Lee's strategy worked, even after his command was transferred from the Lowcountry region back to Richmond.[16]

Victory at the Battle of Port Royal meant the largest ships in the US fleet could enter its harbor and safely anchor, gaining the Union a foothold in enemy territory. Its location provided easy access to Charleston and Savannah, the two largest ports in the Southeast, giving the Union military a base from which to attack them. In addition, Union forces now controlled the inland waterways flowing between the South Carolina Sea Islands and the mainland, facilitating penetration miles into Confederate territory by means of creeks, streams, and rivers. This conferred a major advantage, in part because it disrupted both rice production and the production of the internationally sought-after Sea Island cotton.[17]

In order to successfully implement *Anaconda*, the strategy devised by Captain Du Pont in May 1861 to effectively blockade both the Atlantic and Gulf Coasts and thus prevent the Confederacy both from receiving supplies and from exporting its commodities, particularly cotton, the United States needed a friendly port within Confederate territory for coaling, supplying, and repairing its warships, as well as a suitable location to headquarter military staff. Port Royal Sound was the perfect location. Port Royal was also an ideal location for a base from which Union forces could occupy the inlets, waterways, and sea islands from South Carolina to Florida. In March 1862 it became the headquarters for the US Department of the South. General Orders 26, issued on March 15, 1862, transferred General Thomas Sherman's duties and forces to Major General David Hunter, commander of the Department of the South.[18]

A seasoned soldier of sixty-two when he arrived in Port Royal, Hunter had grown up in Washington, DC. His father had served as chaplain of the 3rd New Jersey Infantry during the Revolutionary War. Hunter graduated from West Point in 1822 and began his long military career as a second lieutenant in the 5th Infantry, stationed at Fort St. Anthony, Michigan. In 1860, he returned to Leavenworth, Kansas, where he was appointed commander of the Department of Kansas in November 1861. "Bleeding Kansas" and the atrocities committed by proslavery border ruffians from Missouri against the free-soilers from Kansas, including the Jayhawkers, may have instigated Major Hunter's conversion to abolitionism. (Colonel James Montgomery, who, as we'll see, commanded the 2nd South Carolina Volunteers in the

Combahee River Raid, had commanded a group of Jayhawkers, or mili-
tants associated with the free-state cause in Kansas, in 1860.)[19]

While in Kansas and Missouri, Hunter showed signs of the tendencies
that would lead to some of the controversial policies that he would implement in Port Royal. A week after assuming command of the Department
of Kansas, for example, he had written to Washington requesting authorization to muster in a brigade of Kansas Indians, which would allow the
Chickasaw, Creek, and Seminoles in the region to demonstrate their loyalty
to the federal government. By the end of 1861, a little more than six months
after South Carolina had seceded from the Union, Hunter was dissatis-
fied with the federal government's gradualist approach to emancipation and
compromises with the border states to keep them in the Union. He wrote
to Senator Lyman Trumbull of Illinois, "It is time slavery has its quietus."
He wanted to march his men into the border state of Kentucky and liberate
and arm enslaved people. He proclaimed that God had "determined this is
the only way in which this war is to be ended." According to Hunter, the
federal government had already wasted enough time; the sooner slavery was
done, he wrote, "the better."[20]

The Battle of Port Royal had shown that the Confederacy could not
match the US Navy, and the only remaining option was to attempt to defeat the US Army on the field. Within ten days of the battle, Lee positioned
twelve thousand to fourteen thousand Confederate troops, commanded
by General Drayton and Major Francis D. Lee, at Hardeeville, eighteen
miles west of Bluffton. Reinforcements were sent in daily to defend the
Charleston & Savannah Railroad.[21]

General Lee expected the Union Army to attempt to cut the Charleston
& Savannah Railroad at the head of the Broad River, a tidal channel that
flows between the mainland and Beaufort. This would sever communication and transportation between the two port cities and enable the Union
to unleash a combined naval and land assault on either or both cities.
By February 1862, the Confederacy understood that if the Union took
Charleston or Savannah (but especially Charleston), it would have a galvanizing effect on northern morale.[22]

In January 1862, the Confederacy's forts, which Lee termed "fixed batteries," did not have the firepower to match or beat the US Navy's gunboats, which he called "floating batteries" and which swept the riverbanks
with what he characterized as "irresistible force." Lee wrote to the adjutant

and inspector general in Richmond that he was positioning himself and his troops to protect the railroad "with all the means in [his] power" and vowed to "continue to the end." However, Lee had only seven thousand poorly trained and equipped troops between Charleston and Savannah. On the other hand, the Confederacy had better knowledge of the terrain and was better equipped to navigate it.[23]

With the capture of Forts Beauregard and Walker, the seizure of Port Royal Sound, and the occupation of the port city of Beaufort, Hilton Head, and its harbor, the Union had struck an economic as well as military blow against the Confederacy. The US Army capitalized on the military triumph by occupying Bay Point immediately and by February 1862 a number of more distant Sea Islands. On Port Royal Island, St. Helena, and Lady's Island in particular, the Union Army was confronted with large numbers of enslaved Blacks, whose labor, skill, and intelligence it had heretofore failed to use to its advantage. After the Battle of Port Royal, that began to change.[24]

★★★★★★★★

Even today, the Battle of Port Royal is remembered as "Gun Shoot at Bay Point" by the Gullah Geechee. Through the generations and into the twenty-first century, the Gullah Geechee have passed down stories of how in the days and hours leading up to the Union victory at Port Royal, many white plantation owners, slaveholders, and overseers precipitately fled Beaufort and the Sea Islands. While many of them traveled on steamers, others fled on the twelve-mile-long Seaside Road stretching up to Port Royal Ferry. This grand avenue, once famous for sporting competitions, was shaded by oak trees and fragrant flower vines. It became a site of disorder, confusion, and dismay in the "Great Skedaddle" as Beaufort's aristocracy ran with little more than the shirts on their backs, as Noah Brooks, a newspaper reporter who visited US troops stationed in the Sea Islands during the war, described it. This was after General Thomas Sherman had invited the loyal people of South Carolina to reoccupy and secure their property under the protection of the US Constitution, and the planters assumed that the Union would next attack Beaufort, which was located twelve miles up the Beaufort River. The river was both wide and deep enough for many US Navy ships to sail through. And attack Beaufort is exactly what the Union proceeded to do.[25]

It was indeed a "Great Skedaddle." Enslaved people and their descendants remembered slaveholding families leaving the silver on the table and
their dinners untasted. They packed a few clothes for their children and
abandoned their crops—fields billowing with Sea Island cotton ready to be
picked and exported for a handsome profit. They left behind their beautiful, ornate household furnishings, including Egyptian marble mantels, gilt
cornices, and centerpieces, mahogany wardrobes, bureaus, sideboards, and
libraries. The Gullah Geechee remember most vividly that the planters
had no choice but to abandon their most valuable property: their ancestors, whom the enslavers held in bondage. An enslaved population of seven
thousand to eight thousand in the occupied area had been abandoned by
fleeing planters and left on the plantations.[26]

An enslaved woman named Susannah, a seamstress on Dr. Daniel Pope's
plantation on St. Helena Island, maintained that Pope had been afraid the
Yankees were coming, and so he had kept the enslaved hands working
in the fields from morning until night, long past the completion of their
tasks, and whipped them every day, in the hope of getting his crop in
before the federal forces arrived. Pope and his wife had pleaded with
Susannah to come away with them into the interior, telling her that the
Yankees would kill her or sell her to Cuba. But Susannah had refused to
go. She could not be convinced that the Yankees would kill poor Blacks
who had done them no harm. However, she was momentarily conflicted
by Mrs. Pope's insistence that merely gazing upon a Yankee would drive a
person crazy. Susannah remembered the young plantation mistress insisting that the Union soldiers did not look like "natural folks." Other planters attempted to force enslaved people into the interior by destroying
crops and outbuildings, depriving them of food and shelter, but most were
not fooled.[27]

Though many enslaved people like Susannah refused to be driven into
the interior, not all were as openly defiant. Instead, they slipped into the
woods and hid until the firing ceased. Others, like Sam Mitchell, who had
been enslaved on Lady's Island, helped their counterparts to escape into the
wooded areas, and thus to freedom. On the morning of the Battle of Port
Royal, Sam saw a messenger approach the mansion riding on horseback
and overheard the plantation owner say that Union forces now occupied
Confederate forts on Hilton Head and Bay Point. The messenger told the
planter to gather his enslaved people together and be ready to evacuate

them. A war correspondent named Charles Carleton Coffin recorded that an enslaved man by the name of Sam ran to the slave quarters, going door-to-door and spreading the alarm:"To the woods! To the woods! De Yankees hah taken de forts—massa is going to de mainland, and is going to take us wid him." The enslaved people had deserted their cabins by the time the overseer came to gather them up and take them away. The slaveholder and his family were obliged to pack their own belongings and head for the mainland without their most valuable property.[28]

Some enslaved laborers, particularly house servants and Prime Hands, did leave the coastal plantations and move into the interior, whether by force or by choice (although a number who were driven into the interior escaped back to the Union-occupied areas). In the chaos, enslaved families were once again separated. Planters usually did not want to take the very young, the elderly, the infirm, or the disabled—those who could not work and would have to be fed—in their flight to the interior.[29]

While those who could ran into the woods, some were not able to go that far. A disabled woman named Aunt Bess and a child named Leah lived and worked, like Susannah, on Daniel Pope's St. Helena plantation. Because of her disability, Aunt Bess could not run—and certainly could not carry a young child. To make matters worse, little Leah suffered from a severe cough. They fled as far as the cornfield, with the older woman terrified that Leah's cough would reveal their hiding place among the cornstalks. To suppress Leah's coughing fits, Aunt Bess almost smothered the child and dosed her at night with tea made from ashes.[30]

Blacks who refused to leave the plantations with slaveholders and hid in the woods for days eventually returned to the coast, hundreds making their way to the Union lines. They came on foot. They came on boats, rafts, and makeshift watercraft. Many came with whatever possessions and food they could carry on their heads and whichever loved ones they could bring with them out of hiding, "toting" the sick, elderly, and infirm on their backs "to freedom." Even Confederate forces who still held the mainland and the slaveholders who retained their enslaved labor force on the plantations could not hold the enslaved for long once Union forces approached. Whenever word spread that the Yankee troops were near, enslaved people risked everything. They hoped that the victory at Port Royal was their "Jubilee," and that Union forces would be their protectors and friends. But since most enslaved people had never seen a Yankee, it was often difficult for runaways, once they got to Union lines, to distinguish which side was friend or foe.[31]

In the confusion following the Battle at Port Royal and before Union pickets were stationed to guard Beaufort and the Sea Islands, escaped slaves were exposed to new levels of danger and violence. Though Confederate forces had retreated, some plantation owners lurked in the area, making last-minute attempts to claim their legal property. Some slaveholders destroyed their cotton crop and plantation outbuildings; others murdered recalcitrant slaves in cold blood. For African Americans in Port Royal, Beaufort, and on the Sea Islands, these were truly perilous times indeed. Prime Hands were routinely executed when they refused to go with the planters. William Capers, from Pope's plantation, knew of thirty people shot down because they refused to go into the interior. After the US gunboats reached Beaufort, having taken Hilton Head, the former slaves were "wild with joy and revenge ... They have been shot down, they say, like dogs, because they would not go off with their masters," Du Pont wrote to the assistant secretary of the navy, Gustavus Fox.[32]

All enslaved people were vulnerable. House slaves, as noted, were targeted by slaveholders for forced relocation to the interior. After his family was evacuated, Dr. Pope returned to kidnap his family's washerwoman, Rina, and nanny, Bella, compelling an enslaved boy named Archie to assist him. Lurking behind Bella's quarters, Archie grabbed her as she ran away from Pope. Pope's son returned and ordered the enslaved laborers left on the plantation to burn the cotton. They refused to comply, knowing that the crop was valuable to them as well; selling the cotton would bring them money to buy shoes and salt. So, instead of destroying the cotton crop, they guarded it day and night and waited for the Union soldiers.[33]

Commodore Du Pont reported that when he sent gunboats to take possession of Beaufort, the Blacks were found to be "in a lawless condition." Downtown Beaufort saw extensive looting and destruction. Expensive furniture was despoiled, books and papers were torn and strewn about, pianos lay on the sidewalk, featherbeds were ripped open, and the parlors and bedchambers of gracious houses, in which only a week earlier planter families had lived in luxury, were used as latrines. Lieutenant Daniel Ammen, who had commanded the USS *Seneca* during the Battle at Port Royal, remembered that "crowds of Negroes" flooded the streets in Beaufort. They plundered houses and stores owned by slaveholders, putting everything humanly possible onto any scows or boats on which they could lay their hands. Ammen thought the freedom seekers "wild with joy" after the enslavers who held them in bondage fled; they "had, in their belief, wealth that should satiate desire in the planter property that had been left behind." Sea Island Blacks looted what was left of the stores and slaveholders' houses. Some Union officers accused the former slaves of seizing the opportunity to exact revenge against the planter class that had held them in bondage. Formerly enslaved people carried away furniture, knocking drawers out of bureaus to make fires for warmth. Some refugees moved into the mansions, putting on plantation mistresses' clothing and eating food from storerooms. A group at Coffin Point on St. Helena Island broke the gins used to process Sea Island cotton and hid the pieces. Charlotte Forten, a free Black woman who came from Philadelphia to teach freedom seekers on St. Helena Island after the Union occupation, believed that former slaves "had the best right" to slaveholders' wealth. Regardless of who did what, it must have seemed to one and all that for the Beaufort aristocracy the days of grandeur were forever over.[34]

★★★★★★★★

Though enslaved people had liberated themselves from slaveholders, their self-liberation raised the question of their legal status. Could they be reenslaved? In 1861 and 1862, the answer was complicated and somewhat variable, since "the contrabands," as they were called, "were slaves yesterday and may be again tomorrow," as Charles Francis Adams, son of former president John Quincy Adams, wrote to his son Henry Adams in April 1862. Secretary of the Treasury Salmon P. Chase thought that it would be inhumane of the US government to again reduce to slavery Blacks whom slaveholders had abandoned and whom the government had received into service. Instead, they should be prepared to become self-supporting citizens. This lofty ambition was easier evoked than accomplished.[35]

A precedent, however, had been set near Hampton, Virginia. Frank Baker, Shepard Mallory, and James Townsend, three enslaved field hands, had rowed across the James River slightly more than a month after the first shots were fired at Fort Sumter on May 23, 1861. They gave themselves up to the picket guards at the Union-controlled Fort Monroe, not knowing what their fate would be; they must have feared that they would have been severely beaten and/or sold from their families forever if the US Army sent them back.[36]

Major General Benjamin F. Butler, who had just taken up his position as commander of Fort Monroe the day before the three men arrived there, wrote to his superior, Lieutenant General Winfield Scott, on May 24 saying that he "gave personal attention to the matter," a gentleman's euphemism that suggests he had an audience with them. He "found satisfactory evidence"—the evidence coming from the three freedom seekers—that the men had fled because they were about to be sent even farther from their families, down to North Carolina. Two left their wives and children behind in bondage. The third fled for fear he would be forced to participate in Confederate Army activities. The Confederate military was forcing enslaved Blacks in the area to labor erecting batteries and other public works. The three men told Butler that those works were to be used for gun emplacements at Sewell's Point. The Sewell's Point batteries were within shooting distance of Fort Monroe.[37]

Butler debated what to do. Should the Confederates "be allowed the use of this property against the United States, and we not be allowed its use in aid of the United States?" He thought not—since the labor of enslaved laborers was essential to the Confederate war effort, it was critical that the Union deprive it of this resource. Initially, though, he was at a loss as to what to do with what he called this "species of property." Then Butler determined that the men could be useful, as his quartermaster's department needed labor. In that May 24 letter he told Scott that he planned to send a receipt to Charles Mallory, the slaveholder who was the three men's legal owner, stating that he had taken the men and that their labor would be used on behalf of the US Army. Mallory was a colonel in the Confederate Army, serving with the 115th Virginia Militia.[38]

The New Hampshire–born Butler may truly have thought that the surrender of three enslaved men would be an isolated event, one that did not involve the making of policy, but he had notified General Scott nonetheless. Three days later, he wrote again to Scott, saying that problem of slaves arriving at Fort Monroe was "becoming one of very serious magnitude," with more and more enslaved people arriving. Furthermore, the able-bodied men whom the Union could employ were bringing women, children, elderly, and disabled family members with them. Butler turned no one away, regardless of their capacity to work. He determined to employ the able-bodied, provide support for the entire family, and deduct the cost of support for the nonproducing family members from the wages paid to the workers.[39]

When Colonel Mallory's agent arrived at Fort Monroe under a flag of truce to reclaim the colonel's property, Butler refused to return the men. Mallory's agent reminded Butler that he was bound by a constitutional obligation to turn over the three enslaved men and restore the slaveholder's property under the 1850 Fugitive Slave Act. Butler replied that the Fugitive Slave Act did not apply to a foreign country, which "Virginia claimed to be." He meant to take Virginia "at her word" that it had seceded from the Union and joined the Confederacy. And since enslaved people were legally chattel property in states in rebellion to the Union, Butler would treat them as property as well. As an attorney and former member of the Massachusetts state legislature, Butler drew on his understanding of international law, in which enemy property may be seized when the enemy is using it for hostile purposes. He declared all bondspeople who came within federal lines in Hampton Roads to be "contrabands of war." But Butler did tell the agent that if Colonel Mallory himself would come to the fort and swear an oath of allegiance to the US Constitution, he would restore Mallory's property.[40]

By June 1861, the exodus of bondspeople spread to other Union-occupied territories in northern Virginia, on the Mississippi River, and in Florida, through what Edward L. Pierce called in a letter a "mysterious spiritual telegraph which ran through the slave population." Pierce was a private in the 3rd Massachusetts Infantry Regiment who was stationed in Fort Monroe under General Butler's command when Butler designated the first "contrabands of war." He was responsible for recording the freedom seekers' names and ages, as well as the names of the slaveholders who had held them in bondage. He supervised their labor and distributed tools and rations. Pierce would become the architect of what came to be called the "Port Royal Experiment," in which the refugees would serve the federal government as best as they could, primarily building fortifications, transporting goods, cooking, washing, serving, and even bearing arms against the rebellion. The First Confiscation Act, passed by the US Congress on December 2, 1861, gave legal standing to these acts of "self-emancipation," freeing all enslaved people who voluntarily came within the Union Army's lines in states that were in rebellion against the federal government. Frank Baker, Shepard Mallory, and James Townsend—the three men who had escaped slavery and sought Union protection—set a precedent in the evolving legal status of "contrabands" and the procurement of intelligence they could gather behind Confederate lines.[41]

After the Battle of Port Royal, Sea Island Blacks believed that President Lincoln and Union forces had secured their freedom when they occupied the Beaufort region. As one said, "Linkum make we free when the gun shoot at Bay Point." This was approximately thirteen months before the Emancipation Proclamation went into effect. Former bondspeople felt free in part because the Union soldiers had assured Blacks in Beaufort and on the Sea Islands that they were free and that no slaveholders could claim them again. Legally, however, they were still the property of those who held them in bondage—hence the legal designation of the enslaved laborers, cotton, and all other abandoned "property" of those in rebellion against the federal government as "contraband." They now "belonged" to the federal government.[42]

If planters in Fernandina, Florida, seventy miles away, heard the guns during the Battle of Port Royal, those on the lower Combahee River certainly heard them too. Likely they smelled the smoke that blew upriver in a northwesterly direction. Mary Boykin Chesnut, a cousin of William Kirkland Jr.'s wife, wrote in her diary that she ordered her carriage and rushed to Camden as soon as she heard the "terrible news" about US troops landing at Port Royal. She went directly to the home of Judge Thomas Jefferson Withers, William L. Kirkland Jr.'s father-in-law. She expected the Withers family to be "very unhappy" that Kirkland was in the "midst of it all."[43]

Mary Chesnut did not expect to find the Withers family having dinner and in "fine spirits" when she arrived. She was surprised that "no allusion whatever was made to Port Royal." Maybe it was because Kirkland was not on General Drayton's staff, as Chesnut had believed, but instead was on Brigadier General Roswell Ripley's staff, and so he hadn't been at Port Royal when the battle took place. Kirkland's mother-in-law, Betsey Boykin Withers, seemed to articulate the mood of everyone downstairs when she said she had learned to be as "cool and calm as an icicle" when the guns were first fired on Fort Sumter because there was no one there she cared for. Not everyone agreed with her. Chesnut, for one, was concerned about the young men who were risking their lives to defend the Confederacy. She considered the soldiers to be the "very flower of Southern life." She was so perturbed that she would not even sit down with her aunt and uncle even after her aunt said her continuing to "stand off there" made them all feel "uncomfortable."[44]

When she went upstairs, Chesnut wrote, she found that her cousin was "all fluffy and fluted," but also in a "terrible fret." Chesnut was incredulous that Mary Kirkland's "fret" was not about her husband's safety, though he served in the Charleston Light Dragoons; in fact, Port Royal was not mentioned at all between them. Rather, her cousin's fret was about "trimming" that someone had brought to Camden to finish her baby's "fine frock." The trimming must not have been fine enough, because it "did not suit her taste at all." So Mary Kirkland was in a "rage of disappointment" and refused to leave her bedroom or "show herself" downstairs.[45]

Chesnut left the Witherses' home in tears, sobbing as if her heart would break—not only over her own relatives' "inconceivable indifference" to the catastrophe that was the Battle of Port Royal, but also for the Confederate soldiers who were risking their lives so that the Witherses could remain indifferent. And, though her cousin seemed impervious to what was happening a few miles away, Mary Chesnut was worried about the security of Kirkland's Rose Hill Plantation and Joshua Nicholls's Longbrow Plantation, which the Kirkland children would inherit. She wrote, "Combahee is quite near and open also to the Gulf—body may be safe and mind easy, but estate is in danger. That's plain enough." At least it was to her.[46]

Combahee planters had every reason to worry both about the Union's next moves and about Blacks enslaved on Lowcountry rice plantations who could also hear the sound of freedom. Some brave individuals in Beaufort and the Sea Islands liberated themselves, but on the mainland rice plantations, "slaves were doubly watched and guarded," according to Elizabeth Hyde Botume, being "driven to and from the rice-fields like wild animals."[47]

Jack Flowers was a Prime Hand who had been enslaved on a mainland rice plantation in Beaufort, where he had endured brutal overseers and enslaved drivers as he was forced to work in the fields. After years of yearning to be free, Flowers seized his opportunity when the Union military occupied Hilton Head. Leaving his family behind, he hid in the rice swamps and crept along through the night until he reached the woods, where he evaded the bloodhounds sent after him. Then he crawled down to the banks of the creeks and marshes, stood in water up to his chin for a whole day, and sank deep in black mud to mask his scent. A boatman at heart if not by trade, Jack used an axe and knife to cut a mass of rushes and a tough oak tree for splints. It took him two days to weave what the *New York Tribune* later described as a "primitive boat" made of coarse grass that he first twisted into a rope one and a half inches thick, then bound with other grasses. Flowers had plaited the rope as one plaits a doormat, going around first to form the center, then continuing up to form the sides until it was more than five feet long, three feet wide, and eighteen inches deep. To make his basket-boat watertight, he caulked it with cotton picked in the fields smeared with pitch that he had made by cutting into a tree, catching the gum, and boiling it in a kettle; he nailed an old shutter, which he obtained from the home of a Dr. Fuller, on the bottom of the boat. Jack carried the basket-boat on his head for three miles. Then he paddled for two nights down the Coosaw River. He worked and traveled at night to avoid slave catchers, their dogs, and Confederate pickets. When he finally reached the Union lines at Port Royal, Jack identified himself to the Yankee picket as "coming ashore for freedom."[48]

If Jack Flowers knew that the smoke and tremors of the Battle of Port Royal meant Yankee occupation, and guessed that it was his opportunity to liberate himself, other Blacks still enslaved on Lowcountry rice plantations must have too. However, even with liberation a boat ride away, most of those enslaved on rice plantations along the lower stretch of the Combahee River could not and would not get to freedom. Not yet, at any rate.

★★★★★★★★

Harriet Tubman had certainly been following the news about the Battle of Port Royal and the thousands of enslaved people who liberated themselves in its aftermath.

She would have been aware that two months after "Gun Shoot at Bay Point," a portion of the hundreds, if not thousands, of Blacks who had inhabited the coastal lands and islands in the US Army's possession had made their way into camps. The able-bodied men were put to work for the Union war effort; their labor gave them access to government rations to support their families. But many had been left behind on plantations abandoned by planters who fled Beaufort and the Sea Islands. They subsisted on corn and potatoes left growing in the fields. When the supplies ran out, they would starve or be dependent on the US Commissary for their daily bread.[49]

Tubman must have heard General Thomas Sherman's call for "highly favored and philanthropic people" to take immediate action to help the "hordes of uneducated, ignorant, and improvident Blacks" of Beaufort and Port Royal in General Orders No. 9, which he issued on February 6, 1862.

According to Sherman, who commanded ground troops in the Battle of Port Royal, African Americans who flocked to Beaufort and Port Royal had been "abandoned" by their "constitutional guardians"—the slaveholders who held them in bondage. He declared that something had to be done, and quickly; some system of cultivation and instruction had to be put in place to provide for the Beaufort and Sea Islands Blacks' physical needs, prepare them for the responsibilities of freedom, and alleviate their impending burden on the federal government. According to Sherman, those released from enslavement were left in states of "abject ignorance" and "mental stolidity" and ill-prepared for self-governance or self-maintenance. He was concerned the burden on the federal government of the freedmen's care would soon become unsustainable. Philanthropic abolitionists from the North were needed to teach them the "rudiments of civilization and Christianity." Captain Rufus Saxton, who had served as chief quartermaster of the expeditionary force during the Battle of Port Royal, became chief quartermaster in Port Royal and subsequently of the Department of the South.[50]

Sherman's call led to the Port Royal Experiment, which the *Boston Advertiser* called "one of the noblest experiments which modern civilization has undertaken, by inaugurating a system of free labor combined with instruction for the freed slaves upon *their own native soil*." The South Carolina and Georgia Lowcountry became what historian Willie Lee Rose called a "'proving ground' for the freedmen," a harbinger of things to come in Reconstruction. This was no small enterprise. In Beaufort and the South Carolina Sea Islands, the capacity of four million Blacks to make new lives for themselves was tested and measured.[51]

Almost from the moment she had heard about "Gun Shoot at Bay Point," Tubman longed to go to South Carolina to assist the refugees. She asked only that her elderly parents be taken care of in her absence. In the first days of 1862 she addressed the congregation at Twelfth Baptist Church in Boston, according to *The Liberator*. The church had the reputation of having a number of fugitive slaves in its congregation and was known to be heavily involved with the Underground Railroad. A "donation festival" was held in the church's vestry after the program to raise money for Tubman. Though the amount raised was reportedly not large, it was a token of the free Black community's affection for Tubman and appreciation for her work. With the Civil War in full swing, the funds raised supported her family in upstate New York, as well as Tubman's travels and works. The money would help take her into South Carolina.[52]

Governor Andrew of Massachusetts supported the idea of her involvement wholeheartedly. Mutual abolitionist friends, likely William Lloyd Garrison or Wendell Phillips, had previously introduced Tubman and Andrew, who in addition to governor was president of the New England Freedmen's Aid Society (as well as its predecessor, the Boston Education Commission); early in the war Andrew had sent for Tubman and asked her to be prepared to go south at a moment's notice to "act as spy and scout for our armies, and be employed as a hospital nurse when needed, in short, to be ready to give any required service to the Union cause," according to Sarah Bradford, Tubman's biographer. Andrew had also secretly aided Thomas Higginson in trying to engage legal counsel for John Brown during his trial after the Harper's Ferry raid. And later Andrew would be sent Flowers's basket-boat, as a symbol of freedom and in acknowledgment of the work he and others did to aid the freedom seekers in Beaufort; Andrew in turn presented it to the Prince Hall Grand Lodge of Free Masons.[53]

Governor Andrew likely thought Tubman would be useful to the cause by gathering intelligence for the Union military and recruiting scouts from among the freedpeople, because he knew that for more than a decade Tubman had operated behind enemy lines in her role with the Underground Railroad; she had the ability to gather intelligence, navigate groups through a wilderness, and live off the land. Nonetheless, it is not clear that in late 1861 and early 1862 Union military officials had yet realized the extent to which formerly enslaved people could be a source of intelligence about the Confederacy, nor that in order for the refugees to be willing to provide that intelligence, military officials would first have to gain their trust.

Andrew sent Tubman to Colonel Frank Howe, a former member of the governor's staff who was at that point the Massachusetts state agent in New York. On January 10, 1862, Howe reported that Tubman had arrived safely in New York: "Colored woman arrived & is cared for." From New York, Tubman was going to go to Washington. However, on January 21, 1862, Howe reported that Tubman was not on the transport ship to which she had been assigned: "I have a letter from Washington informing me that the colored underground woman did not sail in the *Baltic*, but her luggage did—will send a pass for her—it's all I can do."[54]

The *Baltic* had been built by William H. Brown in New York and launched on February 1, 1849, along with its sister ship, the *Atlantic*. The *Atlantic* and *Baltic* had no rivals in speed, size, luxury of accommodations, or popularity among steamers crossing the Atlantic. Passengers favored their public salons, special smoking rooms, barber shops, double-bed staterooms, and ornate furnishings, which stood head and shoulders above those of any other ship. They were the first passenger steamships to use steam heat and to feature a bell system that kept stewards at passengers' beck and call. With the outbreak of the war, both vessels were chartered to bring reinforcements, passengers, and supplies from New York to South Carolina.[55]

Tubman remembered decades later that the reason she had declined to take passage on the *Baltic* was that after Governor Andrew asked her to go to Port Royal as a spy, scout, and nurse, "dey changed dey programme." They assigned an officer from New York to travel with her, because, according to Tubman, the federal government would not allow Black people to travel to the South unless accompanied by US military officers and in the capacity of servants. She went to meet the officer in the parlor of his hotel on Broadway. He told her she looked young enough—for what he did not specify—and instructed her to go to the US Army quartermaster and tell the quartermaster that he had sent her. Tubman decided then and there that she "didn't like dat man no how" and she would not go anywhere with him, especially not as a servant.[56]

So Tubman left without him. She went to Baltimore and saw General David Hunter, newly appointed commander of the Department of the South, who sent her to Beaufort. The vessel assigned to take her waited two days for her, while Hunter's orders were being processed through the appropriate channels. Hearing that Tubman was on her way, Franklin Sanborn, the teacher from Concord who, as noted in Chapter 7, had been part of the Secret Six, wrote to his friend and fellow abolitionist Benjamin Smith Lyman on February 6, 1862, that his "black heroine" had gone to "look after" the contrabands in Port Royal.[57]

★★★★★★★★

A few years earlier, on the day that six of John Brown's accomplices were hanged for their role in the Harpers Ferry raid, Tubman said to Ednah Dow Cheney, "When I think of all the groans and tears and prayers I've heard on the plantations, and remember that God is a prayer-hearing God, I feel that his time is drawing near." Now, as Tubman headed to South Carolina, "God's time" was here—and she was prepared to play her part in God's plan.[58]

9

Broken Promises

When Harriet Tubman arrived in Beaufort, she found a ruin. For a century or more before the war, Beaufort had been an elegant resort town, with stately homes embowered with southern foliage and groves of orange trees. The interlacing branches of majestic live oak trees, festooned with Spanish moss, shielded strollers below from the sun's rays. The population of Beaufort, located twelve miles north of Hilton Head and Bay Point, had hovered around two thousand during the prewar years, though it swelled during the sickly season with an influx of planters from the Sea Islands and rice plantations. Its location on a bluff made the city the perfect retreat for whites to escape the relentless heat, mosquitoes, and malaria. They lounged on broad verandahs and in piazzas, facing south toward the river and being cooled by sea breezes. Now, however, all Tubman saw were the effects of abandonment, vandalism, and violence.[1]

Getting to Beaufort meant first going via Port Royal, and that required a pilot who could navigate the shoals, knew the ins and outs of the narrow creeks and jagged shorelines, and was aware of how sandbars formed and reformed in the channels along South Carolina's coastline—just as the Union armada had had to do when putting its armada in range to fire on Forts Walker and Beauregard.

Everything in Port Royal and the Sea Islands depended on the tide. Frequently steamships ran aground in the mud during the ebb tide, and passengers might be delayed for hours and even days as their boats waited for the next flood tide. Once the pilot could navigate through the narrow passage to Hilton Head, the steamship dropped anchor in the magnificent harbor, amid scores of other steamers and transport ships. Now that Beaufort and Hilton Head were controlled by the US government, passengers had to wait for the quartermaster to approve permits for the ships to continue past the beaches and sandbanks and into Beaufort, where the provost marshal signed their passes—white people and refugees alike needed passes to travel back and forth among Hilton Head, Bay Point, and Beaufort—to allow them to land. Once the passes arrived, cargo could be transferred from the steamship to river steamers for the next part of the trip.[2]

The crooning of the African American boatmen who navigated through these narrow passages attracted the attention of many, including *London Times* correspondent William H. Russell, who described their singing in unison to the rhythm of their rowing as a "barbaric sort of madrigal." One singer began the melody; others followed in unison, repeating the refrain in chorus, and "full of quaint expression and melancholy." Charlotte Forten's transcriptions of the "sweetest, wildest hymns" sung by boatmen who transported her from Beaufort to St. Helena may have inspired her friend the poet John GreenleafWhittier to compose "Song of the Negro Boatmen" in 1862, written in a fictionalized version of Sea Island Blacks' dialect.[3]

As Tubman walked from Beaufort's port down Bay Street, the main thoroughfare in Beaufort's downtown, she would have passed dilapidated fences; tumbledown outbuildings, once well maintained; formerly manicured yards littered with dead branches fallen from untrimmed trees; and weedy walks that led to untended gardens once filled with rare flowers and plants. For months after the Battle of Port Royal, the planters' possessions had lain strewn around yards and streets. It was evident that enslavement was implicated in the town's "shiftlessness," wrote Austa Malinda Winchell French, the wife of Reverend Mansfield French, a minister who was a passionate abolitionist and advocate for women's rights and freedpeople's education. Since enslaved Blacks had freed themselves and found protection behind Union lines, there had been no one to clean it all up. By the time Tubman arrived, at least, the US military had completed the cleanup.[4]

In January 1863, a writer identified as "J" sent a letter to the editor of the *Free South* newspaper, a directory for northern visitors to Beaufort. This person may have been a US Army soldier, Treasury agent, superintendent, or teacher from a northern state who was part of the Port Royal Experiment. Having experienced confusion upon first arriving in Beaufort, the writer decided to provide a helpful guide for the northerners flowing into Beaufort. As "J" explained, the streets ran on a rectangular grid pattern originating at the waterfront: from east to west were Bay, Port Royal, Craven, North, King, Prince, Hancock, Lake, Washington, Greene, and

Congress Streets and Shell Road. Beginning at Sams Point or Fripp's Point and intersecting those streets at perpendicular angles were Finica (now Pinckney), Hamilton, East, New, Carteret, Scott, West, Charles, Newcastle, Church, Harrington, Wilmington, and Monson Streets.[5]

As she traversed this grid Tubman would have walked in ankle-deep sand as fine as ashes, along streets lined with orange gardens and shaded by live oak and sycamore trees. If there were street signs, Tubman would not have been able to read them. She asked a Black passerby for the "yard," as "J" recommended, to navigate her way. Northern soldiers and civilians who refused to invoke Confederate slaveholders' names after they had fled usually did not find theirs..[6]

When Tubman arrived, four thousand Union troops were occupying downtown Beaufort's mansions, which were used for military purposes. There were six military hospitals where white soldiers and officers were being treated. The offices of the governor's staff, adjutant, quartermaster, commissary, and provost marshal were in the former Fuller house, located at the corner of Bay and Carteret Streets. Tubman worked at the Contraband Hospital, which was located in the former B. B. Sams house, on the corner of Craven and New Streets, right in the center of town.[7]

Union Army general Rufus Saxton had established his residence in Lewis Reeve Sams's house on the northeast corner of Bay and New Streets, and the headquarters for the commander of Port Royal Island was in the Heyward house, facing the ferry at the other end of the bay from Heyward and overlooking a six-mile stretch of the Beaufort River. The post and brigade quartermasters were located in front of Pier Du Pont in the Cockroft and Porteous houses. The commissary set up on Bay Street in the former Fripp house.[8]

Wartime Beaufort was an occupied city. Fortifications and checkpoints prevented traffic from moving freely. The Union Army was unequivocally in charge. Regiments of northern soldiers pitched their camp tents in the public square. The town was under a nine o'clock curfew. Any person, Black or white, found on the streets after the curfew bell rang could be arrested if they did not know the countersign. Those taken into custody were detained in the guardhouse overnight until their purpose was identified by the proper authorities. Everyone, including newcomers, needed a pass to move around the city, as well as go in and out, though civilian travel from Hilton Head was easy with a government-issued pass.[9]

The Union Army surveilled Beaufort heavily because it was in constant danger of Confederate attack. Confederate pickets lurked on Port Royal, Lady's, and St. Helena Islands, across the Broad River on the southwest side and the Coosaw River on the northeast (along which Jack Flowers escaped enslavement in his handwoven basket-boat). The Combahee River was a short distance from the Coosaw, the next river north from Beaufort. Confederate enslavers were just a boat ride away.[10]

★★★★★★★★

When Tubman arrived in Beaufort, the influence of the Port Royal Experiment could be felt, though its main areas of operation were not in the city, where Tubman was headquartered, but in the rural areas. Still, she and those in the experiment would overlap considerably in the coming months.

Free labor was the essence of the Port Royal Experiment. In late November 1861, weeks after the Battle of Port Royal, Adjutant General Lorenzo Thomas seized the Sea Island cotton crop and the remainder of the Confederate planters' property for the benefit of the federal government. Some of the proceeds went into a "cotton fund" set aside for the Port Royal Experiment's expenses. William H. Reynolds, a rear admiral in the US Navy, was appointed supervisor of the cotton agents on the Sea Islands. These cotton agents, who were largely military men, were charged by the federal government with administering Black laborers' production of Sea Island cotton and then collecting the cotton and selling it in New York. Most were decidedly abolitionist and did not stick around after the crop was harvested. Sea Island Blacks working on the cotton plantations were employed as wage laborers for the federal government. Employing former slaves to pick and gin the valuable Sea Island cotton crop abandoned by fleeing plantation owners and selling the cotton had been the US government's first order of business after the "Great Skedaddle."[11]

The Port Royal Experiment had begun in January 1862, when General Thomas Sherman had written to the adjutant general of the US Army seeking a solution to the escalating refugee problem he had on his hands. Sherman's suggestion was to divide the US-occupied territory into four districts, each managed by a superintendent who would recruit, organize, and remunerate Black laborers to work on the plantations, take charge of all of the government's property found on the plantations, and handle administrative matters. It also called for teachers, one or more per district, to instruct former slaves, young and old, in the rudiments of "civilization," Christianity, federal laws, and proper social relationships. Two general agents, one supervising the plantation superintendents and the other supervising the teachers, would manage the entire enterprise. Sherman appealed to northern philanthropists to supply a quantity of "negro clothing" and other necessities to be sent to Beaufort and the Sea Islands immediately, particularly vestments for women and children. He anticipated the refugees would continue to need material assistance until the system he proposed was fully operational. Once expenses were paid, the federal government would reap the net profit from the Blacks' labor, using it to defray the costs of the war effort. Sherman sought not only to find a way to feed and clothe the contrabands but also to put in place a plan that would ensure the "future usefulness" of this most "unfortunate class" of people.[12]

The US War Department forwarded Sherman's request to the US Treasury Department. Secretary Salmon P. Chase had been put in control of the two hundred or so plantations abandoned by fleeing Confederate planters and an 1861 crop anticipated to be 2.5 million pounds of ginned Sea Island cotton. Chase was well known for holding abolitionist views. He was the one who had commissioned Edward Pierce as special agent to lead the Treasury Department's enterprise in Beaufort and the Sea Islands and to carry out his vision on the ground. Pierce was a Harvard-educated lawyer from Milton, Massachusetts, with whom Chase had a long working relationship, both in his Cincinnati law office and in the Treasury Department in Washington. He was an abolitionist in his own right who had demonstrated his commitment to emancipation. As a private in the 3rd Massachusetts, Pierce had supervised a detachment of refugees in Fort Monroe, Virginia.[13]

In January 1862, Chase dispatched Pierce to develop a plan for the collection and sale of the cotton crop and the care of the former slaves. Pierce visited coastal South Carolina and in February wrote a report to Chase about Blacks' agricultural production, need for food and clothing allowances, and capacity for labor, and he described current conditions on seventeen Sea Island plantations. He estimated that the federal government had had ten thousand to twelve thousand Blacks "thrown upon our hands," including those who had gone to Hilton Head and Beaufort from other places protected by the federal government and from Edisto Island (which federal forces occupied from February to June 1862). The government had to provide for their "present and future." Pierce argued persuasively that the first Blacks to seek Union protection came "by the invitation of no one." Because they were already there when the Union began its occupation, "they could not have been excluded." Based on Pierce's on-the-ground observations, he, Chase, and Sherman issued calls for northern philanthropists to assist Blacks in the Sea Islands in their transition to freedom.[14]

Pierce passed along a recommendation from Reverend Mansfield French. A native of Manchester, Vermont, and originally an Episcopalian, French had become an evangelical after a wave of religious revivals in Ohio in 1844, and he became a minister in the Methodist Episcopal Church. When Pierce arrived in Port Royal in January 1862, French was already there, assessing the condition and needs of the refugees for the American Missionary Association. Pierce wrote in his January 1862 report that Reverend French's mission was "authenticated and approved by the government." French believed that it was essential to the success of the social experiment that the federal government introduce "women of suitable ability" who could provide instruction to the refugee women, as he believed that women could best communicate with other women. French thought these "civilizing influences" would be welcome in Port Royal and that many "noble women" in the North would volunteer to take up this important task. Pierce duly wrote to the "benevolent" people of Boston to present the problem of the Port Royal refugees. Some of those he got in touch with had been part of the radical abolition movement for decades and had aided, sheltered, and befriended Tubman.[15]

In February 1862, Secretary Chase named Pierce superintendent general over the refugees at Port Royal, charged with securing the government-occupied plantations, supervising agricultural production, and promoting the welfare of Black laborers. Chase saw Port Royal as nothing less than an opportunity to answer what Charles Francis Adams, a first lieutenant in the 1st Massachusetts Cavalry who was stationed in Hilton Head, Beaufort, and James Island in 1862 and 1863, called "the N[——] Question": how would four million enslaved men, women, and children in the South cope with freedom? Northerners on both the pro- and antislavery sides of the argument debated in print and in public lectures about freed Blacks. Did they possess the capacities for self-support, self-improvement, and self-governance? Would they fight for their freedom? Pierce proclaimed in an essay in *The Atlantic* that an affirmative answer to the "Negro Question" was imperative. Neither full freedom nor full citizenship could or would be granted to a "race of paupers."[16]

In February and March 1862, organizations devoted to freedmen's relief in Port Royal were formed: the Educational Commission in Boston, the Freedmen's Relief Association in New York, and the Port Royal Relief Committee in Philadelphia. Secretary of War Stanton furnished transportation by sea from New York to Port Royal to all people with permits issued by the US Treasury Department who were traveling there under the federal government's authority to conduct the business of collecting, safeguarding, and disposing of Sea Island cotton and other property of individuals in insurrection against the United States. The permit was signed by the collector of customs in New York City and specified the kind of transportation to which the passenger was entitled, cabin or steerage; it also covered the passenger's baggage. Stanton charged the adjutant quartermaster general with providing food for the volunteers during their voyage. The Treasury Department did not have money to pay salaries for superintendents, teachers, or missionaries.[17]

So until July 1862 these three organizations paid superintendents' salaries—in addition to recruiting superintendents and teachers willing to leave on very short notice the comfort and security of their homes, taking leave of their professions and families and suspending most social ties, and devote themselves to helping refugees in Port Royal. After July 1862, the Treasury Department assumed payment of superintendents' salaries, drawing from the profits it reaped from the sale of the confiscated Sea Island cotton. It also paid for teachers' transportation, room, and board from its Cotton Fund. Northern abolitionist organizations and family members paid teachers and missionaries' salaries (between $25 and $50 per month) throughout the Port Royal Experiment.[18]

In the minds of the volunteers, Beaufort and Port Royal were the places to be. Formerly enslaved people who made their way into Union-occupied territory would have liberties beyond anything they had experienced. Do-gooding, "woke," and overwhelmingly white abolitionists could roll up their sleeves and put their beliefs to work. Pierce had implemented, according to the *Boston Advertiser*, "one of the noblest experiments which modern civilization has undertaken, by inaugurating a system of free labor combined with instruction for the freed slaves upon *their own native soil*." Rejecting the idea that plantations and Black laborers should be leased to a private organization to work the land, Pierce proposed appointing superintendents to enforce "paternal discipline" without coercion and to prepare Blacks in the Sea Islands for independence. Together with the teachers and donated money and supplies, they would assist Blacks in the Sea Island in their transition to freedom.[19]

★★★★★★★★

Despite all of the good intentions of the Port Royal Experiment—and those of the northerners who volunteered to execute it—the federal government essentially compelled the formerly enslaved to work for free. Many resented growing cotton for a new "master." The wages that they received, particularly for the 1861 cotton crop, were insufficient to support their families' needs. When Pierce found that, as mentioned earlier, refugees at Coffin Point on St. Helena island had broken the cotton gins and hidden the pieces, signaling their determination to break with enslavement, he promised to pay three cents per pound to anyone willing to gin, sort, clean, and pack the clean cotton for market. The refugees on Coffin Point found the pieces—two small rollers the size of spools of thread—and reassembled the gins. The men and women at Coffin Point set to work cleaning the fiber from the seed. On one knee, they pushed cotton with the seed still in it into the rollers. The rollers caught the cotton and pulled it through, separating it from the seed. When the workers tired of that kneeling position, they jumped up and changed legs to kneel on the other side. One of the superintendents thought refugees' movements when ginning cotton were so "elegant" that they "should be introduced into the ballet."[20]

From its inception, the Port Royal Experiment, with all of its high ideals, was hampered by poor planning and competing interests. Laura Towne, one of the northern volunteers, wrote in her diary that it had a "great want of system, and most incongruent elements." Edward Pierce discovered in March 1862 that some of the cotton agents, under the supervision of Admiral Reynolds, had subjected Sea Island freedom seekers to a "reign of terror," making them work without pay, charging exorbitant rates for staples like brown sugar in their stores, and using government property, such as horses, carriages, furniture, and provisions, for personal purposes. Moreover, when refugees refused to grow Sea Island cotton, some cotton agents attempted to enforce discipline by whipping, evoking a return to the old system of bondage. Laura Towne thought that the cotton agents had been a "great trouble" and promised "still to be." She and Susan Walker, a northern teacher, decried cotton agents' use of the lash and their economic exploitation of Blacks in the Sea Islands.[21]

Cotton agents also occasionally resorted to violence against the "Gideonites," as the northern volunteers were sometimes called, after the biblical figure sent by God to rescue the Israelites. One of Reynolds's agents was dismissed for physically assaulting Pierce. Reynolds himself was ultimately disgraced and dismissed for illegally trafficking in guns and Sea Island cotton with Confederate agents.[22]

Some of the cotton agents did better. A teacher on Parris Island praised the work of one who had gathered the cotton and set the Blacks to work; he had "already gained the respect and regard of the negroes on the island, and they cheerfully did whatever he required." Not all of the cotton agents were as trustworthy and caring in their dealings with Black laborers, however. On St. Helena Island Susan Walker reported that the cotton agent was "not a good man," because "he has done no good upon the plantation." She accused him of being more interested in personal profit and good living than in the welfare of the Blacks on his plantations, who looked "so neglected."[23]

Government wages were not enough for refugees to feed and clothe themselves and their families. Delays in paying wages didn't help. On Pope Plantation, cotton agents only paid the wages they had promised for the previous year in late April 1862. Many Sea Island Blacks had not received food and clothing allowances from slaveholders for months before the "Great Skedaddle." Now, the government agents paid them just one dollar in four of what they earned, giving the rest as credit in stores kept by cotton agents that sold foodstuffs and other goods. Those stores also charged refugees extortionate prices. For example, Susan Walker complained of one store where "for molasses they charged $1.00 per gallon when we could buy of commissary in Beaufort for 42cts." The cotton agents' unscrupulous greed diminished Blacks' trust in the government and established a climate of distrust that affected their interactions with the superintendents who followed.[24]

Pierce brought a group of fifty-three northern volunteers to Port Royal in March 1862. Before arrival, every member of this original delegation laid his or her right hand on the Bible and swore an oath of allegiance to the US government. They also had to swear not to give aid or information to the Confederate government. Only then were their passports stamped, as if they were traveling to a foreign nation. Tubman would have had to do the same.[25]

In the beginning, the plan was for the men—about forty in all—to serve as superintendents, to take charge of the abandoned plantations and the free labor of formerly enslaved people; the women were to open schools. In the course of the Port Royal Experiment, however, some women, such as Frances Gage and Nelly Winsor, served as superintendents, and some men, including William Channing Gannett and Edward Everett Hale, taught in the schools. They were a diverse group, though primarily schoolteachers and ministers rather than farmers or managers, and there was only one businessman among them. None of them had any experience growing cotton (or much else), but all wanted to do something to help the war effort and the cause of radical abolition, to which they had devoted their lives. They had the best of intentions, but—as Pierce feared—not the talent or skills required by the size and nature of the mission ahead. And the stakes were high: the participants were engaged in the largest social experiment to that point in the nation's history. If it was successful, the Sea Island freedpeople and northern volunteers would prove wrong proslavery advocates and northern capitalists who believed that cotton could not be grown with free labor and that Blacks would not work without the lash. The mission would be critical to the Union war effort, and even more so to the lives of refugees in coastal South Carolina and Georgia.[26]

Competing interests among different groups of northern volunteers complicated matters. Reynolds (who had experience in the cotton trade) and his cotton agents viewed the Gideonites dismissively and hampered their efforts by confiscating the furniture, tools, and farm animals they needed to do their work effectively. The superintendents (and, to a lesser extent, the teachers) controlled the refugees' labor, which the cotton agents needed to do their job effectively. There were also competing interests regarding how the freedom seekers' labor was to be managed. For example, the northern volunteers and the Sea Island Blacks were not in agreement about the best use of their labor. The superintendents were seeking to implement a free-labor ideology in which the freedom seekers would grow Sea Island cotton for the federal government. Freedom seekers wanted to be free from torture, sale, and separation from family members. They wanted to work to provide for their families and to be fairly compensated for their labors or able to sell the fruits of their labor for a fair price.[27]

Under Pierce's plan, the superintendents on Sea Island plantations were responsible for organizing and supervising the labor of Blacks who possessed years if not decades of experience producing Sea Island cotton and who had "not been learning cotton-raising, perforce, all these years for nothing," as one superintendent, Charles Pickard Ware, saw it. Each freed family received a small plot of land for growing cotton and provisions and could choose their own time and manner of working it. Self-emancipated Blacks strenuously objected to gang labor, a form of labor organization rarely if ever utilized on Lowcountry rice and Sea Island cotton plantations. Most superintendents steered clear of it.[28]

Each superintendent was given complete charge of between one and five plantations and two hundred to five hundred people. They protected cattle and government property, distributed clothes and tools, compiled census data, and paid Blacks for the cotton they raised and picked. Just as important as producing cotton was assisting refugees in becoming self-reliant, enforcing discipline, providing religious education, working in conjunction with teachers to provide rudimentary education, and generally helping refugees navigate their new status as former slaves but not yet freedpeople.[29]

One major problem was that growing cotton for the federal government required refugees to neglect growing the corn they needed to feed their families. Those on St. Helena Island did not receive rations from the federal government because there was corn left on the island. Planting of the 1862 Sea Island cotton crop was delayed two months, as Special Treasury Agents (another category of civilians who carried out the orders of the Treasury Department and the military and worked directly with the refugees) and then superintendents recruited and organized field hands, who were not inclined to grow cotton instead of subsistence crops. Refugees on Coffin Point paid more attention to their corn crops than to the cotton crop. On St. Helena Island, refugees begged Pierce to allow them to grow corn instead of Sea Island cotton (under enslavement, most plantations had allowed them to cultivate corn after they finished their tasks). Pierce tried to enforce the rule that refugees could not hoe their corn until they had planted the required amount of cotton. Actions such as these created even greater uncertainty and fear. And the Union Army had taken corn from Lady's

Island and other islands located closer to Beaufort, making food insecurity on these islands even more acute. Laura Towne reported in 1862 that freed people felt their own corn saved them from "starvation."[30]

Furthermore, the refugees did not see the value of growing cotton for the government. They had done it the year before, but when it was time to seed the following year's crop they had not yet received any wages for their labor. Most, understandably, did not fathom the concept of doing the work now and receiving wages later, and in any case they thought the amount the federal government promised to pay them for plowing, furrowing, planting, harvesting, and ginning was a pittance.[31]

Another stumbling block in the transition to a free-labor economy was whether the government should give rations to Sea Island Blacks. Everyone received some form of rations through August 1862, whether provided by the US government or through private northern philanthropy. On Lady's Island, where Union troops had seized corn for their own use, the government had to provide food rations for the island's inhabitants to keep them from overwhelming Union lines. And the federal government paid some of the wages in rations past 1862, though the practice was rejected by those superintendents who thought it would make Blacks dependent on the government. But freed people refused to work cotton when they had received "no clothes, no tobacco, no molasses, no bacon, no salt, no shoes, no medicine," and no wages, as the refugees on Coffin's Point grumbled.[32]

Some superintendents proved less effective than they might have been because of the attitudes they displayed toward the refugees. A number were "strongly prejudiced against," had "a contemptuous way of speaking of," and showed "a lack of sympathy" toward the very Blacks whom they had come to help. Charlotte Forten thought these superintendents probably "sh'ld not come here."[33]

In April 1862, shortly after it began, oversight of the Port Royal Experiment was transferred from the Treasury Department to the War Department and placed under Brigadier General Rufus Saxton, though the Treasury Department continued to control the sale of Sea Island cotton. Saxton, who had served as captain and chief quartermaster under General William Tecumseh Sherman, assumed control of the Sea Islands and its sixteen thousand to eighteen thousand quasi-free inhabitants. He oversaw the plantations abandoned by Confederate planters and production of cotton, supervised Black laborers, resettled refugees, and worked with teachers on individual plantations. Edward Pierce resigned his post in June 1862 to become a journalist. Despite these administrative changes, the Port Royal Experiment continued.[34]

★★★★★★★★

As we'll see, Harriet Tubman needed to find her own way in Beaufort after her arrival, learning where she might be most effective and finding her place, and she was not alone. Although the role of white women as instructors of refugee women was woven into the fabric of the Port Royal Experiment from the very beginning, the federal personnel on the ground were not prepared for women to travel to or live in wartime Beaufort or the occupied Sea Islands. When Boston volunteers traveled to Port Royal aboard the *Atlantic* in March 1862, half of the staterooms were in use to house troops and stow cargo. Though women and elderly men were given priority in the available accommodations, a number of women sat on the bare deck (when no chairs were provided for them) and sang Methodist hymns well into the night. A prominent male volunteer wrote and advised his wife to wait before joining him in Port Royal; he doubted the female volunteers would find sleeping accommodations on board the steamship. In April 1862, officers aboard the steamer *Oriental*, which was bearing volunteers from Philadelphia, avoided giving the passengers straight answers when they asked if the vessel's slight rolling spelled danger. Some told the ladies that the seas were the roughest they had ever experienced, and they did not know whether the vessel and passengers would survive through the night. They seemed to relish talking about Rebel attacks, yellow fever, and other unpleasant and alarming things, nodding and winking to each other as they did. The Philadelphia women were neither amused nor fooled.[35]

Laura Towne was one of the first women to arrive in Port Royal. Born in Pittsburgh in 1825, Towne as a young child moved with her family to Boston, where she became interested in the abolition movement while living in Boston. She deepened her own personal commitment to antislavery after moving to Philadelphia, where she attended the First Unitarian Church and soaked in Reverend William Henry Furness's soul-stirring sermons. Towne was a pioneer in the field of medicine, undertaking advanced coursework in homeopathy at the Female Medical College of Pennsylvania before the Civil War. She also trained with prominent

Philadelphia physician Dr. Constantine Hering, who later co-founded the first homeopathic school of medicine and served as the first president of the American Institute of Homeopathy. After the attack on Fort Sumter launched the Civil War, Towne performed one of the few socially accept-able roles for white women in the Union war effort: she sewed. She planned subsequently to contribute her medical skills by tending wounded soldiers in military hospitals. The Battle of Port Royal changed everything. Towne answered the pleas for northern volunteers to go south with the support of Philadelphia's Freedmen's Aid Society. Towne and twenty other northern volunteers departed from New York aboard the *Oriental* on April 9, 1862.[36]

The rural Sea Islands were Laura Towne's focus and base, while Tubman's was the town of Beaufort. From Beaufort, Towne traveled to the adjacent Lady's Island, then up the narrow strip of tidal river to St. Helena Island. St. Helena, thirteen miles long and six miles wide, is part of a cluster of Sea Islands that sit east of Port Royal, nestled along the Beaufort River between Parris and Lady's Islands in the northwest and Bay Point in the southeast, and right at the mouth of Port Royal Sound. Unlike Beaufort, much of St. Helena's terrain lies below sea level, and the heat and mosquitoes that bred in the summer and fall proved deadly to whites. Smallpox also claimed its share of victims, Black and white. When Towne arrived in April 1862, she found the new Sea Island cotton crop roughly three inches tall in the fields. Other fields left fallow after harvest of the previous crop appeared aban-doned or neglected, wild with weeds and thistles.[37]

There was also much less security in the Sea Islands than in Beaufort, which (as Tubman discovered) was heavily guarded by the Union Army. The islands were sandwiched between the Broad River and the narrow Coosaw River, beyond which, as noted earlier, Confederate scouting par-ties and pickets lay in wait. They were also a short distance from Port Royal Ferry, where Rebel forces faced off against Union pickets. Rumors circu-lated that Rebels were planning to land in force on the islands and snatch livestock and crops, as well as the people they had formerly held in bondage, in nighttime attacks. Northern volunteers were routinely awakened at night by the sounds of gunfire from pickets and gunboats and exploding shells; these noises terrified refugee children. It must have been hard to distinguish which side was firing.[38]

On at least one occasion, northern volunteers unknowingly dined with Rebel spies disguised as uniformed US officers. The spies inquired about the pickets, white soldiers, and armed Black men on St. Helena Island while making polite dinner conversation. Islands from Hilton Head in the south to Edisto in the north were within rifle range of Confederate outposts. Rebels raided Edisto Island as early as January 1862, Hutchinson Island in June 1862, and Morgan Island in May 1864, and carried off some Black refugees. Refugees lived in a constant state of fear that slaveholders would return to reenslave them or murder them. The Rebels were close enough and had ample opportunity to do so until US Army pickets and US Navy gunboats surrounded all sides of St. Helena Island in June 1862 and General Hunter evacuated the Blacks still living on Hutchinson, Morgan, and Edisto Islands.[39]

In any case, many of the US Army officers thought St. Helena Island was no place for white ladies, who, according to Towne, were "rejected as useless" for anything other than creating what superintendent William C. Gannett called a "paradise of mince-meat and family bread" and improving the bachelor-like existence of the superintendents. They were considered a burden, requiring extra protection from the ever-present threats of devilish Rebels, destitute Blacks, and deadly fevers.[40]

Towne nonetheless was indispensable to the Port Royal Experiment and wore many hats, as Tubman also would. She kept house and managed the house servants first for Edward Pierce, then for the superintendents and teachers on the plantation after Pierce had returned to the North. Towne was also administrator of northern relief efforts on St. Helena Island. She managed the store in the cotton house, selling clothes to most of the freedom seekers on St. Helena and giving items to destitute refugees, elderly residents, and those she called her "mudderless" children. In addition, Towne wrote scores of letters over the years requesting donations from the Philadelphia and Boston Port Royal relief committees, then received, processed, and managed these donations, distributing them to other plantations. Harriet Ware, a Massachusetts teacher at Coffin Point, thought keeping store was "busy, not to say nasty work" and physically very demanding. In some stores, volunteers had to go upstairs for sugar and dry goods and downstairs for flour, pork, and salt. Customers felt cheated if any of the measurements happened to come out short. They complained of the prices even though the stores kept by northern relief organizations offered prices significantly lower than those operated by cotton agents. Sometimes they accused the shopkeepers of making large profits at their expense.[41]

Towne provided medical care to Black men, women, and children, as well as to other northern volunteers. She went door-to-door treating ulcers, colic, injuries, respiratory ailments, measles, mumps, snakebite, diarrhea, malaria, and dysentery. She dealt with smallpox epidemics. She delivered babies and comforted grieving family members, especially mothers who lost a child. On any given day in addition to her other duties, Towne made house calls to one or two plantations, traveling by horse and carriage over terrible roads, often in inclement weather.[42]

Teaching brought her the most joy. It was also by far her hardest job. Towne was on call as a substitute for other teachers who operated schools on St. Helena Island. She helped to open the first school for Black students on the island with her companion, Ellen Murray, from Newport, Rhode Island, the lead teacher. Murray started teaching in June 1862 at the school at the Oaks Plantation, then, with Towne, opened a school at Brick Church with 80 pupils. That school moved to the town of Frogmore and into a schoolhouse donated by the Freedmen's Aid Society of Pennsylvania in early 1865. It was incorporated as Penn Normal School in 1901. Murray and Towne spent the remainder of their lives on St. Helena, educating thousands of students over the course of their forty-year careers.[43]

★★★★★★★★

Though, in theory at least, the Port Royal Experiment was designed to keep refugees living, supporting themselves, and producing Sea Island cotton and food on abandoned plantations, not all of the refugees could or would remain in the countryside. Elderly, sick, and disabled refugees, and women on their own or left alone with their children, needed the assistance of the federal government for food, clothing, and medical care. For them, the Union Army established refugee camps in Beaufort, Hilton Head, Otter Island, and Bay Point, and it was of course here that Tubman directed herself after her arrival. Those camps were there almost from the very beginning. Saxton reported that 150 "contrabands" had arrived in the two days after the Battle of Port Royal and that it would soon be necessary for the US Army to supply them with "coarse clothing." Bernard K. Lee, who was appointed general superintendent, established the refugee camp in Beaufort. Lee supervised Union Army soldiers and refugees as they hauled ropes, barrels of flour, and chests full of officers' personal belongings down gangplanks from the US vessels and into the formerly Confederate-owned buildings taken over by the federal government. The refugees did the work that white soldiers were unwilling to do, deeming it unfit.[44]

The Beaufort camp started with approximately sixty or seventy refugees but grew quickly. Lee reported that a few weeks later dozens more refugees were seeking the protection of the US government. As the refugee population continued to expand, so did the Union Army's responsibilities to care for, provide for, and protect them. In December 1861, roughly one month later, General Thomas W. Sherman reported, "Our labor here is enormous." Many of the refugees were suspicious of white folks, even northerners, and rendered little assistance to the US military in exchange for the rations and clothing they were given. They came and went from overcrowded, disorderly camps that teemed with epidemic diseases like smallpox, and their movements were not organized or accounted for. The provisions they were given were not accounted for either. Sherman feared that even larger families would come in from the surrounding plantations to seek assistance in the refugee camps and that provisions would run out. The US Army would then have even more mouths to feed. By mid-December, there were 320 refugees, sixty or so of whom were able-bodied men; the remainder were women, children, elderly, or disabled adults who needed support. The federal government had to decide, and decide quickly, what to do with them.[45]

According to Edward Pierce, "commodious barracks" were erected to house refugees in the Beaufort camp by June 1862. By the time that Charlotte Forten arrived in October 1862, the refugee camp encompassed "rows of small white-roofed houses" that had "lately been built for the freedmen." The camps also served as clearinghouses at which the government assessed the needs of the refugees, gave out work assignments every morning after roll call, and determined whether they would be paid wages or (if they could not work) would be given rations; the questions were how much and for how long. Several months earlier, in March, US Army captain Hazard Stevens (who was General Isaac I. Stevens's son), one of those in command in Beaufort after the battle, ordered the superintendent of contrabands to limit the Beaufort camp to only the number of refugees that the government needed to employ. Men from the rural plantations nonetheless continued to pour into Beaufort. The occupation and the introduction of wage labor had created competition for Black labor and brought new economic opportunities, particularly for young men and women. A number of them found employment outside the plantations controlled by the superintendents. Unskilled work, such as that done by cooks, body servants, and laundresses, and skilled work in mechanics, carpentry and other building trades, sewing, and soldiering, paid more than unkept promises from the federal government. The wages were higher and paid more regularly than the dollar per acre or thirty cents per day (instead of the three cents per pound that Pierce had initially promised to pay) that at first refugees were paid to plant, pick, and pack cotton on rural Sea Island plantations.[46]

Though it was a nearly impossible task, administrative personnel attempted to keep track of individuals and families, along with their needs, locations, and work assignments, as they came in and out of the refugee camps. One can imagine a lone US Army officer seated at a desk surrounded by masses of traumatized and destitute refugees who had just fled enslavement and terror on rural plantations. On a piece of parchment and using a quill pen, the adjutant general or quartermaster made lists of the refugees' first names (very few had titles), sex, age, physical description, occupation, where they came from, names of family members accompanying them, name of the slaveholder who had held them in bondage, and description of the slaveholders' character, as well as where and by whom they were now employed and whether or not they had been vaccinated against smallpox. The administrator may have tried to elicit the names of the planters who had held them in bondage in order to ascertain whether the planter was loyal to the Confederacy or to the Union. If the slaveholders were deemed loyal to the Confederacy, the refugees were officially "contrabands" and could be retained and employed by the federal government.

Most of the lists were lost or destroyed; a few survive. Though the information is fragmentary at best and much of the data is missing for most of the refugees, they give a snapshot for the month of March 1862, a few weeks before Tubman's arrival. They also provide a sense of who entered the Beaufort refugee camp, where they came from, and where and for whom they worked while there.

Of the 1,413 people recorded as being in the Beaufort refugee camps by the adjutant general and quartermaster in March 1862, the majority (consisting in this case of 234 men, 193 women, and 214 children) came from "the main" or "the mainland." Today, the coastal plains of Beaufort and Colleton Counties are considered the mainland. The true number is likely slightly larger because a number of refugees gave the names of particular localities within Beaufort, such Kean's Neck and the Chehaw River, as the locales from which they and their families had fled. The numbers of refugees from the Sea Islands, specifically Port Royal, Coosaw, St. Helena, Lady's, Johns, Hilton Head, Edisto, and Wadmalaw Islands, were far smaller—only 34 men, 40 women, and 23 children. While some adults traveled alone, most traveled with their spouses, and some were accompanied by their children; other women traveled alone or in groups with their children. One woman brought eight of her children with her—carrying most of them, somehow—when she fled. Refugees traveling on boats or makeshift watercraft from the Sea Islands understandably brought fewer kids.[47]

In the Beaufort refugee camp, the Union Army employed refugees as young as eleven years old. Assistant quartermaster C. E. Fuller employed the majority of refugees—335, to be exact. The number of individuals working for the Assistant Quartermaster's Department was almost evenly split between men and women, who performed similar work for the quartermaster—field work, digging (for trenches, graves, and latrines), construction of fortifications, and other menial labor.[48]

According to the quartermaster's records, 300 refugees in the Beaufort refugee camp were employed as fieldworkers and 254 were employed as servants on the plantations. Approximately one-quarter of the fieldworkers were women, and a similar proportion of the servants were men. After field worker and servant, cook, laundress, carpenter, and a job that involved unloading the steamer *McClellan* were the most common jobs performed by freedmen in the Beaufort refugee camps. Thirty-three did not work and received weekly rations. The majority of refugee women were employed as laundresses, one of Tubman's many jobs during her service in Beaufort. The laundresses were attached to Union Army regiments. The 8th Michigan Regiment alone employed ten laundresses, the 100th Pennsylvania Regiment employed six, the assistant quartermaster employed four, and the 50th Pennsylvania employed three.[49]

After the Black regiments had been organized, they employed Black laundresses as well, in addition to their mothers, wives, sisters, sisters-in-law, daughters, and granddaughters. Thomas Higginson (now a colonel) described one of the elderly laundresses for the 1st South Carolina Volunteers as having "self-imposed preeminence"; she walked at the head of the regiment and the company "never could quite overtake" her "vigorous stride." Higginson remembered the respectable elderly woman balancing an "enormous bundle" of laundry on her head and waving a tool of her trade, a "long-handled tin dipper," like a sword.[50]

Refugee women, including laundresses, frequently worked more than one job. Susie King Taylor, the sixteen-year-old wife of a Black sergeant in the 1st South Carolina Volunteers, enrolled as the company's laundress around October 1862. Though born enslaved, Taylor had learned to read and write as a child in Savannah and subsequently served as a teacher for the 1st South Carolina Volunteer soldiers, in addition to regimental laundress and nurse, for more than three years. In the Beaufort refugee camp, most laundresses were paid $6 per month, the same as male servants, hospital stewards, cooks, and surgeon's waiters. (By contrast, skilled male laborers earned $7 per month. The highest recorded wage paid to an individual in the camp was $15 a month; the mean wage was $7.22.) It was a good wage, especially for women who for most of their lives had been forced to work without compensation; that amount could enable a single mother or a married woman to support herself. The Black men who enlisted in the US Army were not paid for the first eighteen months of service, and when they were paid, the salary was sufficient to support only them. Even married refugee women had to work to support their families.[51]

Out of the 1,413 refugees in the Beaufort camp, we can document eight who had escaped enslavement on the Combahee rice plantations. Though small in number, this group can be identified because at registration they named the "notorious rebels" who held them in bondage. Seven named "W. Blake" as their enslaver. In 1862, there was only one planter in the Blake family with that first initial and last name, Walter Blake, so we can deduce it had to be him. Among those refugees was Sally Blake, who worked for the 50th Pennsylvania Regiment as a laundress and cook. The others who named W. Blake as their enslaver did not give their titles. One man, named Dick, had had an infant daughter, whom the quartermaster recorded as deceased. The others were named Joe, a second Joe, Sam, Titus, and Wally. All of these men worked unloading the *McClellan* steamer and earned "extra pay for extra work," according to the quartermaster's rolls. They received their last pay on April 6, 1862. The people from the Blake plantation likely came alone, having left their relations behind. There is no record of when they escaped, though it was certainly after the Battle of Port Royal.[52]

The pension records suggest that the full name of Wally was likely Wally Graham and that one of the Joes may have been Jonas Green. Neither enlisted in the Union Army, but they offered testimony on behalf of veterans and widows. (Jonas Green provided a very intimate portrait of Smart Washington, to whom he may have been apprenticed, though they were held in bondage on neighboring plantations by different slaveholders.) On December 14, 1876, Wally Graham testified to a pension official that he "and Jonas Green were formerly slaves of Walter Blake" and that they "came to Beaufort together"; he added that Jonas Green had had a wife at the time whose name was Dorcas, though he does not say whether Dorcas came with them. He also added that the woman with whom Jonas Green cohabitated during the Civil War came to Beaufort "sometimes afterwards."[53]

In 1862 Walter Blake, son of Joseph Blake, was still managing his father's Bonny Hall, Pleasant Hill, New Ground, Parker's, Blakefield, True Blue, Cypress, and Newington Plantations, while the elder Blake resided in England. Blake kept a written record of the people his father had held in bondage before the Combahee River Raid. He made a slave list, which he titled "List of Negroes Lost from the Estate of Jos. Blake," but did not date it. It appears as if he recorded it over a period of time—a running tally of how his father's assets were depleting rapidly after the Battle of Port Royal because the people his father had held in bondage had run away. Blake recorded that forty-year-old Ben, the driver, and fifteen-year-old Silas had fled from Bonny Hall; twenty-three-year-old cooper Jonas, thirty-one-year-old Wally, forty-five-year-old Dick, forty-year-old Binah, and sixteen-year-old Rose had all run away from Parker's Settlement; thirty-five-year-old Parris, a carpenter, had gone missing from Blakefield Plantation; forty-year-old London, thirty-year-old Sally, thirty-year-old Russell, thirty-four-year-old Tom, twenty-five-year-old Coomba, thirty-four-year-old cooper Charles, thirty-year-old house servant Dinah, forty-year-old carpenter Titus, and thirty-six-year-old Flora all made off from New Ground Plantation. Wally (Wally Graham), who worked for the US Army quartermaster in March 1862, was certainly the same Wally whom Walter Blake listed as escaped from Parker's Settlement with Jonas, who was surely Jonas Green. Walter Blake identified Jonas as coming from the Newington gang, which, as we've seen in Chapter 6, his father conveyed to him in 1860. Titus Barnwell was likely the carpenter whom Blake reported as having fled from New Ground Plantation. Parker's Ferry, Pleasant Hill, and New Ground Plantations were clustered together on the lower Combahee River with Bonny Hall Plantation, which was later destroyed in the Combahee River Raid; Parker's Ferry and Pleasant Hill were located next door to each other.[54]

Meanwhile, on the Beaufort camp list, the quartermaster crossed out Dick Kirkland's title and wrote "Conklin" in its place. It's possible the quartermaster misheard Dick's title or did not know how it was spelled. But when he wrote down the name of the planter who "owned" Dick, he wrote clearly "Kirkland." There was only one Kirkland family in the vicinity of the Beaufort refugee camp, and by 1862, decades after Dr. William L. Kirkland

Sr.'s death and his widow's remarriage two times over, it had one member, William L. Kirkland Jr. Dick Kirkland was a cook and stableman.[55]

William L. Kirkland Jr. later created a slave list he entitled "Negroes Run Off in March 62," and on it wrote the names of five enslaved men—"Tim, Tom, Billy, Janus, and Dick." While there are plenty of Toms and Billys on the quartermaster's list, only Dick Kirkland (Conklin) specified "Kirkland" as the man who held him in bondage. It is not clear where Tim, Tom, Billy, and Janus went after they escaped. In his affidavit, William L. Kirkland Jr. deposed that he "lost the services of 5 valuable negro slaves." They "absconded" from his plantation as a result of the federal government's occupation of coastal South Carolina. Kirkland had not heard any information about the people he formerly held in bondage. Nonetheless, he "believed that they were in the hands of the enemy."[56]

Like the seven enslaved people who liberated themselves from enslavement on Walter Blake's plantation, the five freedom seekers from William L. Kirkland's place must have seized the chance to free themselves after the Battle of Port Royal. It is clear that by March 1862, a small number of freedom seekers who had escaped enslavement from rice plantations on the lower Combahee were working in the Beaufort refugee camps.

★★★★★★★★

Union troops had difficulty winning the confidence of Black refugees and gaining information from them about the region and Confederate movements therein. Tubman, on the other hand, was able to gain the refugees' confidence through her very presence in the Beaufort refugee camps. According to Sarah Bradford, she offered the refugees "cheery words" and sang them "songs, and sacred hymns." Bradford contends that Tubman "obtained valuable information behind enemy lines"—that is, outside of the Beaufort town center and on surrounding plantations. Tubman embedded herself in the refugee community and erased all material differences between her and the refugees by refusing after twenty days to accept rations, which the government still did not provide to all of the refugees. Instead, she conducted her own independent economic activities, brewing root beer and baking gingerbread in the evenings after work—financed with her own money—and employing a refugee to sell them for her to Union soldiers and fellow refugees. Lastly, she used her earnings during the war to establish a washhouse to help refugee women earn independent incomes washing soldiers' clothes for hire.[57]

All of these activities made Tubman a vitally important member of the Beaufort refugee community, someone in the unique position to be

a go-between: to gather sensitive information for Union officers and to
bring the needs of refugees to the attention of the same. In February 1864,
Lieutenant George Garrison, quartermaster of the 55th Massachusetts
Regiment, visited Tubman at Folly Island and wrote home about the in-
valuable work she was doing for the Union Army. Lieutenant Garrison
was the firstborn son of William Lloyd Garrison, who had of course been
Tubman's close friend and partner in the abolitionist struggle, and his wife,
Helen Eliza Benson Garrison.[58]

Lieutenant Garrison had accompanied more of Tubman's Boston aboli-
tionist friends, Theodoric Severance (called "T.C.") and his wife, Caroline
Seymour Severance, on their visit to Tubman. On February 10, 1864,
Lieutenant Garrison wrote to his younger brother William that they found
Tubman ironing an officer's clothes. Unbeknownst to Lieutenant Garrison,
she had been on Folly Island, the same island where his regiment was stationed, for three months. She had been working at the quarters of Brigadier
General Alfred H. Terry, commander of the 7th Regiment of Connecticut
Volunteer Infantry and of Morris and Folly Islands, cooking and washing
clothes. She was not, however—as she made clear—General Terry's servant;
she was an entrepreneur who was working for herself, providing a service
that benefited officers in camp and earning money to send to her parents in
Auburn, New York, and to pay off her debts.[59]

Caroline Severance introduced George Garrison to Tubman, who took
one look at him and saw the family resemblance to her old and dear friend.
She threw her arms around him and gave him such a warm embrace that it
amused the others. Tubman told the younger Garrison that she wanted to
return north, likely to go home and see her aged parents, but that General
Quincy A. Gillmore wanted her to stay. If she did leave, Gillmore wanted to
be sure that she returned to his department. He thought her services were
"too valuable to loose [sic]" because, according to Garrison, "she has made it
a business to see all contrabands escaping from the rebels, and is enable [sic]
to get more intelligence from them than anyone else."[60]

Lieutenant Garrison's description of the work Tubman did among the
freedom seekers in coastal South Carolina—gathering "intelligence"—is
remarkable. As Susie King Taylor wrote in her memoir: "There are many
people who don't know what some colored women did during the war."
Washing, ironing, and cooking were clearly not Tubman's primary roles;
she was indispensable to the US Army Department of the South because
she was skilled at "debriefing" formerly enslaved people who had recently
fled bondage in territory still controlled by the Confederacy. They knew

firsthand the numbers, locations, and movements of the Confederate troops. They may even have been compelled to labor building Confederate fortifications. They brought all of this information into Union-occupied territory. The army needed someone to obtain information from the refugees while it was current and actionable. The freedom seekers trusted Tubman; so did the military commanders.[61]

I've characterized Garrison's description of Tubman's intelligence-gathering from other formerly enslaved people as remarkable because he saw her, recognized, and articulated her unique and invaluable contributions to the US war effort when the military record is silent. Furthermore, it should be noted that the Union Army had been gathering and using information from refugees for some time. An early example of freedom seekers providing the army with intelligence were Frank Baker, Shepard Mallory, and James Townsend, the three men who crossed the James River to seek protection at Fort Monroe and provided intelligence to General Butler about the fortifications they had been forced to build. As the trickle of enslaved people making their way to Union-occupied territories, not just in South Carolina but throughout the South, became a flood, so did the amount of information that they had gathered about what was going on behind Confederate lines. US Army officers and soldiers termed the intelligence gathered from freedom seekers "Black Dispatches."[62]

The freedom seekers of Beaufort, the Sea Islands, and the Combahee trusted Tubman, because she was their "people." Though she could not understand the dialect the Lowcountry Creoles spoke nor their cultural practices, she knew that they all understood freedom and the willingness to sacrifice to attain it. To reach Beaufort they had defied enslavers, hidden in the woods (sometimes for weeks), camouflaged their movements in the swamps, and sailed in makeshift rafts, basket-boats, and canoes. Like Tubman, they had stolen their freedom, snatching themselves and their families out of the jaws of death. To Harriet they "would tell anything." By questioning those who recently had come from behind Confederate lines about what they had observed and heard, Tubman gathered valuable intelligence for the Union Army. As George Garrison noted, she was able to get "more intelligence than anyone else." Furthermore, Tubman gathered information from men whom US Army commanders "took with them as guides." Thus it became important that Tubman "should accompany military expeditions up the rivers."[63]

Harriet Tubman's Beaufort

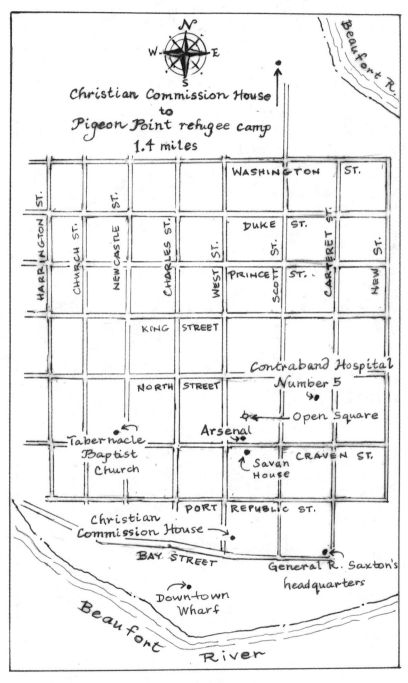

Port Royal Experiment

Coosaw River

Combahee River

Port Royal Island

Pigeon Point

Beaufort

Ladys Island

Coffin Point Plantation

Dr. Daniel Pope

Eustis Plantation

Penn School

St. Helena Island

Old Fort
J.J. Smith
Plantation
1st and 2nd
SC Volunteers'
Headquarters

Hilton Head Is.

General David Hunter's Headquarters

N W E S

10

Beaufort's Boatmen

By nearly all accounts, the Port Royal Experiment got off to a very rocky start. From the beginning, Blacks in Beaufort and on the Sea Islands were suspicious of whites, including Yankees, and their motives. Looting by Union soldiers who stole from refugees' meager belongings reinforced their fears. As we've seen, the cotton agents, superintendents, and Special Treasury Agents' requirement that refugees produce Sea Island cotton under their supervision for the federal government for deferred payment increased their suspicions.[1]

The refugees needed someone who looked like them, who understood the terror they had experienced, and who had a grasp of their liminal state between enslavement and freedom—someone whom they could trust to speak for them to the Union military, which had been charged with their protection. It is unlikely that the refugees ever articulated this need or formally made this request to the authorities. Northern abolitionists, however, were well informed about the refugees' condition through the relief committees. That was why her abolitionist friends in Boston determined Harriet Tubman was needed in Port Royal.

★★★★★★★★

On the same night in 1862 that Caroline Severance and Laura Towne arrived in Port Royal aboard the *Oriental*, the *McClellan*, a 1,003-ton sidewheel steamer, also arrived with 180 of the 380 Confederate prisoners the Union Navy had captured at Fort Pulaski. Originally built as the *Joseph Whitney* before it was purchased by the US Army and renamed, the *McClellan* (sometimes called the *General McClellan*) arrived from Fort Pulaski, located on an island in the Savannah River, at the entrance to the port of Savannah.[2]

Fort Pulaski, completed in 1847, had been seized by the state of Georgia after secession in 1860 and occupied by Confederate troops. Marshes and masonry casemates protected the fort. Beginning in December 1861, a month after the Battle of Port Royal, Acting Brigadier General Quincy Adams Gillmore engineered the fortification of Tybee Island, located across the Savannah River from Fort Pulaski, by building artillery batteries on mud flats. General Hunter steamed south on the *McClellan* and bombarded Fort Pulaski with mortars as well as rifled and smoothbore cannons after the Confederate commander refused his request for surrender.[3]

The capture of Fort Pulaski on April 11, 1862, was a second victory for the Union and solidified its control of the Atlantic Coast south of Charleston. It also effectively eliminated Savannah as a base for Confederate blockade runners. One Union soldier died and three Confederate soldiers were wounded in the battle. After the *McClellan* arrived in Port Royal, six Combahee freedom seekers—"Dick, Joe, Joe, Sam, Titus, and Wally"— earned extra pay for unloading the ship after the victory, as mentioned in Chapter 9.[4]

After the capture of Fort Pulaski, Hunter became commanding officer of the US Army Department of the South. Two days later, on April 13, he issued General Orders No. 7, declaring that all formerly enslaved Blacks in Fort Pulaski and on the nearby Cockspur Islands were "confiscated and declared free" and would thereafter "receive the fruits of their labor." Although the planters who held them in bondage had fled, and despite Hunter's order, the "contrabands" were still left to wonder whether or not they were free, as the relationship between refugees and Union forces and personnel remained ambiguous.[5]

On May 1, 1862, James Seymour Severance (known as Seymour) wrote in his diary that while he and Edward Pierce were waiting a long time for the ferry on Lady's Island—perhaps the ferry from there back to Port Royal—the two men had had a conversation at the cotton house on Eustis Plantation.[6]

Seymour Severance's parents, T.C. and Caroline Severance, were, as we've seen, dedicated activists in the tight-knit Boston abolitionist community. As a teenager, Seymour boarded with the Alcott family in Concord. His friend Louisa May Alcott described him as a "grand person" who was "sensible, kind & interested in the thing," meaning Port Royal. In February 1862, the Port Royal Relief Committee in Concord had begun recruiting volunteers, and T.C. asked his old friend Salmon Chase, the Treasury secretary, to assist him in securing the position of collector of customs for the Treasury in Port

Royal. The elder Severance also asked Chase and the Port Royal Relief Committee about a position in Port Royal for Seymour, then nineteen and a freshman at Harvard College. Seymour wrote to Frank Sanborn, a teacher turned journalist with the committee in Concord, and requested a recommendation. T.C. and his son traveled to Concord to meet with Sanborn in person. Sanborn gave his approval, and the day after their meeting Seymour received a commission from the committee as the fiftieth volunteer from Boston sent to Port Royal by the Port Royal Relief Committee.[7]

Young Seymour took leave from Harvard and headed to New York with his parents, where he boarded the *Oriental* and made the five-day journey to Port Royal, arriving in March 1862. There he took a position as a Special Treasury Agent. His father joined him by May. (His younger brother Mark Sibley Severance would round out the trio of Severance volunteers by coming down to work for the federal government at Port Royal and Savannah in January 1865.) Seymour spent his first weeks working in the commissary on Eustis Plantation. Like Laura Towne, he distributed clothes and food, handled livestock, and paid wages to the refugees. Keeping store was not likely to be the job he had envisioned he would be doing when he signed on. Then again, he also did not properly introduce himself to Pierce and the Treasury agents on the ground in Port Royal, which his parents had expected him to do. Though he recorded humorous episodes in his diary—such as catching, tying, and penning forty mules and ten horses at a seminary in Beaufort—he must also have written to his parents to complain about the work. Caroline threatened to write Pierce and Eustis to ask if they were going to keep her son working in that "miserable position." She also blamed Seymour for not presenting his letters of introduction to Treasury officials in Port Royal and instead keeping them "in [his] pocket!"[8]

In Severance's conversation with Pierce in the Eustis Plantation cotton house, the latter expressed his extreme frustration about the Port Royal Experiment. The federal government had broken the promises it had made to the refugees, and this had put the superintendents and teachers who were in its employ in a difficult position. According to Severance, Pierce also referred to "Moses," saying that after he had "made a pressing appeal [to Frank Sanborn] for a capable man to aid him," he was later "notified that she"—Harriet Tubman—"was to be sent to him."[9]

Multiple members of the Boston abolitionists must have been recommending that Tubman be sent to Port Royal. According to Severance's recollection of his conversation with Pierce, William Lloyd Garrison had already asked Pierce whether he "couldn't do something about" Tubman "being brought to Port Royal." Pierce had apparently asked Garrison whether Tubman could teach; the answer was no. He rephrased the question: "Can't she do anything of that sort?" Again Garrison's reply was no. Pierce replied, "I don't see what can be done for her." Severance wrote in his diary that Pierce thought it would take someone with "considerable tact and education" to carry out the Port Royal Experiment properly.[10]

For starters, there was the question of discipline. In his February 1862 report to Chase, Pierce wrote that "compulsory labor, enforced by physical pain," in the short run would not equal voluntary labor—though the refugees were not volunteers. Pierce should perhaps have written "wage labor" rather than "compulsory labor," though the federal government had repeatedly broken its promises to pay the refugees regular wages. In the very same report, Pierce noted that southern slaveholders had told northerners that enslaved people were "lazy, and would not work unless whipped to it," although Pierce added that he did not believe the slaveholders. He wrote that he had told the refugees that "Mr. Lincoln" had sent the northern volunteers down there to see if it was so, and that everyone in the North was free, Black and white, and no one sold anyone's children. Nonetheless, he told them, free people had to work or they would lose privileges, and that the northern volunteers would report directly to Lincoln how the refugees carried out the experiment in free labor. Pierce invoked Lincoln when he addressed the refugees because he thought they were more likely to be impressed by a man—a white man—taking care of them than by the "abstract idea of government."[11]

This paternalistic rhetoric was a far cry from what Pierce expressed to young Severance at Eustis Plantation on Lady's Island on May 1 when he noted that it might be "necessary at this stage that discipline be used." According to Severance, there was talk that the "old system of punishment must be retained, perhaps a different form, milder," among refugees who refused to grow cotton. Pierce did not specify that Treasury agents and superintendents should whip the contrabands, and we do not have firm evidence that any did. Seymour thought that if superintendents resorted to using the lash it would cause the Port Royal Experiment to lose its moral center. But two superintendents, David Thorpe and William Park, who supervised labor on thirteen plantations on St. Helena Island, did quell an uprising that was brewing among the field hands and compelled refugees to work cotton even when they were unpaid. The freedom seekers had lost confidence in and respect for the superintendents due to the federal government's broken promises, and labor relations on these plantations in particular would deteriorate to the point where Thorpe and Park resorted to following the refugees to the field and staying there until they completed their tasks. Thorpe and Park were in essence acting like overseers and enslaved drivers.[12]

Because of this state of affairs, Pierce thought—again, according to Severance's recollection—that it was doubtful that "Moses would at all be the person to operate" the plantations. Severance wrote that Pierce asked him a clearly rhetorical question: "What can they have thought of sending her out here for[?]" Severance's idealism may have gotten the best of him, for he "ventured to hint" that Tubman's coming to the Sea Islands "might ultimately be of use." She could not teach the refugees letters or numbers, which she did not know herself, but she could "ultimately be of good use in teaching them to make good use of liberty." Severance went a step further and told Pierce that Tubman could teach the refugees about liberty "as had been carried out so well by her in Maryland."[13]

What Tubman had carried out in Maryland, of course, were intelligence-gathering and rescue missions. Severance may have been suggesting that Tubman could lead the freedom seekers to demand their freedom at a moment when the federal government was forcing them to work without pay and compelling them when they resisted. Pierce, not taking kindly to Severance's sentiments, retorted that that "was all very well," but what Tubman did in Maryland "could not be done here" in Union Army–occupied Beaufort. All of the northern volunteers—and Tubman would be one of them—were, according to Pierce, "under government here." Thus, Pierce said, they all had to be "cautious of their actions," even though he and Severance might personally feel that they should "like to see the refugees free by any means." Pierce, for his part, did not think it would help the refugees for him and other northern volunteers to "urge this matter." As representatives of the federal government, they could not push harder or faster than President Lincoln and Congress were willing to move. Lincoln was engaged in a delicate balancing act to keep the border states, including Tubman's own Maryland, from leaving the Union and joining the Confederacy. So the volunteers should be "grateful," Pierce concluded, for what freedom they could manage to provide for the refugees.[14]

★★★★★★★★

In late March 1862, Hunter had ordered 50,000 muskets, sets of weaponry, and red pantaloons, plus 10 million rounds of ammunition, and also requested that Secretary of War Edwin Stanton authorize him to arm and outfit the loyal men he could find. The only loyal male civilians in the area who were not part of the Port Royal Experiment were Black men, whom he had attempted to free with his General Orders No. 7. Hunter believed that they should and would fight for their freedom. But recruitment proceeded slowly, not yielding enough to fill even one regiment. This is perhaps not surprising, given that the federal government had, in effect if not formally, rescinded the Lowcountry freedom seekers' emancipation with their policies about labor, pay, and discipline.[15]

Few volunteered for "Hunter's Regiment," as it came to be called. When a subordinate whom Hunter had tasked with raising a regiment, Sergeant Trowbridge of the New York Volunteer Engineers, could not come up with adequate numbers of men, Hunter took drastic steps. On May 9, he issued General Orders Number 11, which declared martial law in the Department of the South—the states of South Carolina, Georgia, and Florida—and proclaimed that all persons who had formerly been held in slavery in these states would thenceforth be "forever free." Hunter then went a step further and required the men who were freed under martial law to fight for the Union, though he pledged that he would not take men against their will, and that if they did enlist they would receive papers certifying their free status. He may have been motivated by his earlier attempts to muster in a brigade of Kansas Indians and to march his regiment into Kentucky to liberate and arm enslaved men. Or he may have been motivated by what he perceived to be troop shortages. Whatever the case, the repercussions, as we will see, were enormous.[16]

Hunter ordered the superintendents to provide lists of all men between the ages of eighteen and forty-five on Saint Helena, Lady's, and Coosaw Islands who were capable of bearing arms, and subsequently sent squads of soldiers to the plantations to forcibly enlist them. At first, however, he did not inform the superintendents what would happen to the men, so they were unable to tell the refugees why they were being taken away from their families and for how long. This was from fear of the men "taking to the woods," as Laura Towne and other northern volunteers described it, when they found out. Nor did he inform the superintendents how and why his emancipation decree was linked to Sea Island freedmen fighting for their freedom.[17]

There was less discontent on plantations where the teachers and superintendents explained the situation (the best that they knew of it) to the refugees in ways they could understand. On plantations where this care had not been taken, on the other hand, trouble ensued. On Pope's Plantation on St. Helena Island, refugees became suspicious when they saw soldiers marching through the island under the cover of darkness. Fearing the Rebels had invaded to retake their plantations and reenslave the people, they stood guard to protect their families.[18]

The night before Susan Walker had to turn the able-bodied men over to General Hunter, she, Laura Towne, and Austa Malinda Winchell French went to the praise house to "weep and pray with the people," as Towne put it. She described writing the names of the men who would report to Hunter "almost as signing their death warrants." In the morning, soldiers seized the men from the fields, rounded them up in groups, and marched them off at gunpoint. They gave only a few the opportunity to go back and say goodbye to their wives and children or even get their jackets. Wives received no explanation about their husbands' fate. Many clung to their husbands and sons, wailing, shrieking, and throwing themselves to the ground in despair.[19]

On Jenkins Plantation on St. Helena, all of the refugees ran away and hid in the woods. The soldiers searched for them and brought in all but two. One woman told the superintendent there that under slavery she had already lost all of her children and friends; now that her husband had been taken from her, she had no one to care for her and thought she would die alone.[20]

Schoolchildren in St. Helena who witnessed the soldiers marching their fathers and brothers away sobbed uncontrollably. Nelly Winsor, a teacher, dismissed school after her pupils became inconsolable. In her diary, Laura Towne labeled May 12, 1862, when the superintendents had to implement orders to separate Black families and communities so recently liberated, as "the black day." In one day, a total of five hundred men were seized from St. Helena and Lady's Island. Though they yielded to the Union Army's authority, the superintendents felt their months of working with refugee families had been undone in a few days' time.[21]

Fears of sale to Cuba and kidnapping, forced removal to the mainland, and reenslavement by Confederate guerrillas and former slaveholders—all these still haunted the refugees. During the forced enlistments of the spring of 1862, an elder on St. Helena Island told Laura Towne, "Dey used to catch we up like fowls and sell we when dey wanted a little money for spend." The departure of the planters since the "Great Skedaddle" had given Black families hope that they would not be arbitrarily separated and could "gather close to their parents"—that is, their relatives. The forced enlistments undercut all of this.[22]

The involuntary recruits to what became known as Hunter's Regiment were taken first to Old Fort Plantation on the Beaufort River, then to Hilton Head, where Hunter's Department of the South had its headquarters. Towne wrote that Sea Island Blacks remembered "Hilty-Head" as the disembarkation point where slaves who had been sold to places like Cuba boarded vessels.[23]

Forced enlistment sowed seeds of distrust among Sea Island Blacks against military service and confirmed racist assumptions among a number of northern observers that freed Black men would not fight. In addition, Black soldiers in Hunter's Regiment were abused by racist white officers and soldiers hostile to their enlistment in the first place. Some white soldiers told the Blacks that they would be sold to Cuba, or put on the front lines in battle. Many refugee men deserted the regiment by fleeing to the woods and swamps—the very same places where they had hidden to steal their freedom from Sea Island slaveholders. A number even fled back to the mainland—where the whites who had held them in bondage had taken refuge. These events forced many refugees to wonder whether the "old fetters" under which generations of their families had been torn apart had been any worse than this new liberty, which seemed just as determined to destroy families. Though he had intended to advance their cause by making Blacks whom he had proclaimed free enlist to fight for freedom, General Hunter undercut the fragile progress of the largest social experiment to date.[24]

However, it soon became clear that Hunter had issued his General Orders No. 11 without having the authority to make such a sweeping grant of freedom himself, nor had he requested authorization from President

Lincoln. Furthermore, he had not consulted with those protecting the refugees, whether military or civilian. Upon learning what Hunter had done, Pierce protested to Secretary Chase that Hunter's military recruitment order was in direct conflict with the Treasury Department's charge to superintendents to supervise Black laborers on Sea Island cotton plantations.[25]

By this point the Treasury Department had invested heavily in planting roughly 1,000 to 3,000 acres of corn and vegetables and 5,000 acres of Sea Island cotton, spending $5,000 for tools and seeds, $15,000 for ninety mules and ten horses, and $3,200 for other costs. An additional $4,000 had been budgeted to pay Black laborers after the harvest. To pay for these, the Treasury Department was planning to use the so-called war tax, which Congress had imposed on South Carolina and all of the other states in rebellion. And, of course, proceeds from the sale of the Sea Island cotton crop were projected to defray the cost of the US war effort. Now, with the able-bodied men away for military service, Hunter's orders left women, children, and sickly men to bring in the precious Sea Island cotton crop. It would be virtually impossible to harvest anything of value, potentially making the Treasury Department's investment a total loss.[26]

Hunter's illegitimate decree forced the president's hand, and on May 19, Lincoln declared General Orders No. 11 null and void. Consequently, Blacks who had made their way to US-occupied territory wound up in a state of limbo—one perpetuated by General Hunter, who was continuing to offer recruits their freedom.[27]

In August 1862, after four months, Hunter disbanded the regiment on President Lincoln's orders, sending the men back to the plantations to gather a crop overgrown with weeds. Furthermore, the men of Hunter's Regiment never received any payment for their service—though Hunter requested that they be paid and be given "free papers." His request was denied by the War Department, though his initiative may have had the tacit approval of the Secretary of War all along.[28]

Despite it all, the 150 to 200 men from St. Simon's Island in Georgia who had voluntarily joined Sergeant Trowbridge's unit (when it was assigned garrison duty on the island in August 1862) showed their bravery when they joined with armed Black civilians from St. Simon's to hunt down a group of Rebel guerillas. It was likely the first time that freedmen had confronted former slaveholders in battle. Their courage proved that freedmen would fight against the whites who had held them in bondage. Trowbridge's unit remained together even after the rest of Hunter's Regiment had been disbanded. Technically, it was the first and the longest-serving US regiment of Black soldiers during the Civil War.[29]

One northern volunteer observing these events, Edward Philbrick, an engineer from Brookline, Massachusetts, wrote in June 1862, "I suppose we shall lose General Hunter." But Hunter remained in his post as head of the Department of the South until July 1863. In the larger view, Hunter's over-stepping had more of an impact on politics in northern states than it did on the lives of freedom seekers in coastal South Carolina.[30]

In July 1862, weeks after Lincoln's nullification of Hunter's General Orders No. 11, Congress passed the Second Confiscation Act and the Militia Act, which declared that all slaves whose slaveholders had re-belled against the U.S. government and who resided within territory oc-cupied by the United States "shall forever thereafter be free." (Passed on August 6, 1861, the First Confiscation Act had authorized the US military to seize Confederate slaveholders' property and liberated Blacks who had been forced to work or fight for the Confederacy.) These acts secured the freedom of Sea Island Blacks (as well as those in other parts of US-occupied South Carolina and in Georgia and Florida) six months before Lincoln's Emancipation Proclamation went into effect on January 1, 1863. In add-ition, the legislation reaffirmed the president's authority to marshal the labor of formerly enslaved individuals in whatever capacities were benefi-cial to the war effort.[31]

In retrospect, we can see that although Hunter's actions were un-orthodox, controversial, and potentially damaging to the fragile Port Royal Experiment, his declarations of freedom and efforts to enlist Black troops nudged President Lincoln toward later declaring the Emancipation Proclamation, and with it the formal enlistment of Black troops.

★★★★★★★★

The Battle of Port Royal taught Union Navy commanders that they needed to learn to navigate the labyrinth of narrow, shallow coastal waterways, with their numerous obstacles. In December 1861, Samuel F. Du Pont, hero of the battle, wrote to Gideon Welles, secretary of the navy, decrying the navy's lack of pilots with enough local knowledge to make nautical charts for the coastal waterways. In theory, the Union had a technological advantage, but its larger and more powerful fleet consisted mainly of deep-water vessels, which were unsuitable for shallow water. Without firsthand knowledge of coastal waterways, the US Navy was at a disadvantage compared to the Confederates. Union vessels frequently ran aground, got stuck in the mud, and came dangerously close to damaging shoals, all of which could leave the powerful warships vulnerable to Confederate fire. The Union Navy and Army needed people who knew the rivers.[32]

During the course of the Civil War, Black boatmen transported more than Sea Island cotton and rice. For example, March Haynes, a "daring commando and spy," according to the chaplain of the 3rd Rhode Island Artillery, was strong and experienced. Born in Pocotaligo, South Carolina, in March 1825 and enslaved in the Savannah area, he hired himself out as a stevedore and a pilot. After the outbreak of war, Haynes continued hiring himself out, now as a carpenter to the Confederate Army at Fort Pulaski. He was granted his freedom under Hunter's emancipation edict after the capture of Fort Pulaski by Union forces.[33]

As a free man, Haynes worked for the Union, specifically for Brigadier General Quincy Adams Gillmore, who furnished him with a staunch, swift boat, painted a drab color to camouflage his movements in the Savannah River. The chaplain mentioned above wrote in his memoir about Haynes's "countless deeds" that remained "unsung." He thought Haynes's name was "worthy of honorable mention" for undertaking many "perilous missions." For two years, Haynes kept the boat secreted in a creek among the marshes below the Savannah River. He made nighttime reconnaissance missions along the creeks and brought "boat-loads of negroes," freedom seekers, to safety behind Union lines, employing others to assist him as he saw fit. He also gathered information about Confederate forts, batteries, and camps by landing in the marshes below the Savannah River, entering the city at night, and lodging with the Black refugee community. Haynes did not enlist in the US military until August 1864. Fearing detection by Confederate forces, he eventually brought himself and his wife behind Union lines. According to the chaplain, Haynes was one of a "few daring spirits" and nonmilitary personnel "who volunteered to brave the hazards of secret service" in support of Union military operations.[34]

★★★★★★★★

While General Hunter's enforced enlistment orders were being carried out— arguably the low point of the Port Royal Experiment—the experiment simultaneously experienced one of its greatest achievements. Sometime early in the predawn hours of May 13, 1862, a man named Robert Smalls, the pilot of the CSS *Planter*, stole the vessel from the Confederate Navy and surrendered it to Union forces, liberating his wife and children plus his crew and their families, a total of eight men, five women, and three children.[35]

Born enslaved in 1839 in Beaufort, Smalls hired himself out on Charleston's waterfront and spent around a decade working as a stevedore, rigger, sailor, wheelsman, and master boatsman. He had mastered the channels, bars, currents, and tides and worked independently for three years but was still unable to purchase his, his wife's, or his children's freedom. After the war broke out, the *Planter* was leased to the Confederacy. Smalls and his crew hired out to Brigadier General Roswell S. Ripley, commander of the Second Military District of South Carolina, who was responsible for all military vessels, including the *Planter*. Ripley used the *Planter*, his dispatch boat and flagship, to lay torpedoes (what today in the naval context are often referred to as mines) and to transport guns and ammunition to Confederate troops.[36]

On the day of his escape, Smalls ordered forty cords of wood to be stacked in both boilers and cast off the hawser, unmooring the *Planter* from the wharf directly in front of General Ripley's residence. The sentinel on guard thought nothing was amiss, assuming that the civilian captain, C. J. Relyea, and the engineer were in charge and had decided to get an early start. In reality, Captain Relyea and other white officers had gone ashore the night before to spend the night with their families. Smalls had disguised himself as Captain Relyea by donning a jacket and pulling the floppy straw hat Relyea typically wore down over his face.[37]

He guided the *Planter* to a neighboring wharf, where the Confederate ship *Etowah* was docked, and dispatched a rowboat to pick up nine passengers, including his and his crew members' families. Then the *Planter*, flying the Confederate Stars and Bars and the palmetto flag of South Carolina, steamed down the bay, passing Castle Pinckney, Fort Ripley, and Fort Johnson, and finally came to Fort Sumter at 4:15 a.m. At Fort Sumter, Smalls pulled the whistle, giving the signal required to pass, then leaned out of the window of the pilot house with his arms folded across his breast, doing his best impersonation of Relyea. The fort answered with an acknowledging signal as the sentinel watched, musket in hand, then turned his back, suspecting nothing.[38]

The *Planter* was a 313-ton wooden, wood-burning, light-draft sidewheel steamer that could navigate the coastline's shallow inland waters, drawing less than 3 feet 9 inches of water despite being 147 feet long and 30 feet wide. According to Seymour Severance's later conversation with the *Planter's* crew, she could "turn on her centre without advancing a rod." Its red cedar planking on its live-oak frame housed two oscillating steam engines, which flanked a paddle wheel on each side. Early in the war, light-draft steamers and sailing vessels like the *Planter* became indispensable to the US Navy because they could access the shallow sounds of the Atlantic coast and go up coastal rivers.[39]

The *Planter* was armed with two cannons, a 32-pound pivot gun and a 24-pound howitzer. In addition, the day before Small took command of it, it had been loaded with 100 pounds of ammunition, five large loose cannons, a "banded rifle 42," an eight-inch columbiad, an eight-inch sea-coast howitzer, a 32-pounder, and a columbiad carriage. The same morning Smalls took it over, the ship had been scheduled to transport the columbiad carriage to Fort Sumter and three of the loose cannons to the Middle Ground Battery, a new fort under construction.[40]

Once past Fort Sumter, the engineer put on more steam and Smalls guided the boat beyond the limits of Confederate-controlled waters, beyond the range of the Confederate fleet's guns, and toward the Union fleet. By the time the sentries at Fort Sumter realized that the vessel was not taking the route a Confederate vessel normally would, it was too late to stop the *Planter*.[41]

Approaching the Union blockade squadron, Smalls and his crew hauled down the Confederate and South Carolina flags and hoisted up a large white bedsheet, which Smalls's wife had smuggled aboard—a flag of surrender. Just before sunrise, the *Planter* steered straight for the USS *Onward*. Acting Volunteer Lieutenant J. F. Nickels, commander of the *Onward*, turned the vessel so that its port guns faced the *Planter*. He readied his vessel to fire—he thought the Confederate vessel was planning to fire on them—until he saw the white flag of surrender flapping from the foremast. Nickels ordered the *Planter* to pull up alongside the *Onward* so that he could board the vessel. After discovering the true nature of Smalls's heroic act, Nickels hauled down the sheet and hoisted up the Stars and Stripes. (The *Planter's* two secessionist flags were eventually sent as a trophy to the secretary of war.)[42]

Nickels sent Smalls and the *Planter* to Commander E. G. Parrott of the USS *Augusta*, putting the steamer and its crew at his disposition. Parrott in turn led the new acquisition through St. Helena Sound and down an inland passage through the Beaufort River to Port Royal, station of the USS *Wabash* and the flag officer of the US fleet, Captain Du Pont. Four days earlier, Du Pont had reiterated his ongoing complaint that his fleet was inadequate for blockading the thirty miles of coastal waterways between Stono Inlet and Bull's Bay. Though eight of the blockade squadron's eleven vessels guarded the thirteen-mile arc off the coast of Charleston, Charleston Harbor, in particular, presented the biggest challenge, and now Smalls had delivered exactly the kind of vessel the Union needed.[43]

Smalls, for his part, told Du Pont everything he knew about the Confederate Navy's operations. Du Pont later described Smalls to Secretary Welles as "superior to any [contrabands] who have come into our lines—intelligent as many of them have been." (More than 160 years later, the US Navy would rename a warship after Smalls—a warship that previously had been named after a Confederate sailor.)[44]

Perhaps the most critical information that Robert Smalls provided Du Pont was that the Rebel forces had abandoned Cole's and Battery Islands in Stono Inlet, leaving the mouth of the Stono River vulnerable. A few days previously, freedom seekers had provided the Union Navy with intelligence that the Confederates had laid down torpedoes. Du Pont found Small's intelligence to be of the "utmost importance" and subsequently sent a senior officer, Captain John B. Marchand, from Charleston to investigate its accuracy. Finding Small's intelligence about Confederate troop strengths to be reliable, Du Pont acted quickly on it, driving the US gunboats *Unadilla*, *Pembina*, and *Ottawa* up the Stono, shelling both sides as they went upriver, firing on the barracks as Confederate infantry withdrew, and capturing six Confederate prisoners. Two other gunboats, the *Huron* and *Pawnee,* followed over the next few days. In large part based on Smalls's intelligence, the Union Navy successfully secured the Stono River, which allowed Union forces to access James Island, giving them a base of operations from which they potentially could take advantage of the many water routes leading into the city of Charleston. In practice, however, neither the US Navy nor the US Army would capitalize on this advantage; it would be almost another year before Du Pont attempted to take Charleston.[45]

Du Pont recognized Smalls's mastery of the inland waterways and employed him as pilot of the USS *Planter*. He requested that the navy appraise the *Planter* and award prize money for its seizure to Smalls and his crew. The final appraisal of $9,000 for the *Planter* and $168 for the five large loose guns was thousands of dollars below the true value, and Smalls was awarded $1,500 of that (splitting half of the vessel's appraised value with his crew and two of the women who had been onboard), the first time such an honor was bestowed on a Black man. Robert Smalls was inarguably the first African American hero of the Civil War.[46]

The southern press was furious once they learned that Smalls had stolen the *Planter* from the Confederacy right under its nose. Lieutenant F. G. Ravenel declared in his report to Brigadier General Roswell S. Ripley that two white men and a white woman had boarded the vessel the night before Smalls made off with it and had never left, implying that the white people were responsible for delivering the *Planter* into Union hands. It was simply inconceivable to them that a crew of Black men could have pulled this off. Moreover, Ripley wrote his superiors, the *Planter's* officers had repeatedly defied the order that all Confederate light-draft vessels must be prepared to move at short notice and so their crew and officers were required to remain onboard the vessels day and night. General Lee himself capped off the chorus of voices calling for those who had failed to prevent the seizure of the *Planter* to be charged with negligence.[47]

Robert Smalls was actually not the only enslaved boatman to bring out a Confederate naval vessel and surrender it to the US Navy. A couple of weeks earlier, on April 28, 1862, a crew of fifteen men, led by Gabriel Pinckney, had made their way to the USS *Bienville* in a boat they had commandeered in Charleston Harbor from the quartermaster of the Confederate Navy. Pinckney gave US commander J. R. M. Mullany intelligence about the Confederate Navy. He provided information about Forts Moultrie, Sumter, and Johnson and batteries at Castle Pinckney, up Wappo Creek. He told the Union officers about a new fort, not yet armed, being built at the fortifications protecting Charleston and the harbor. Confederate naval capacity was limited, Pinckney assured them; in Charleston Harbor the Rebel navy had no ironclad vessels and two gunboats that lacked steam power and had to be towed.[48]

Further, Pinckney revealed that a surprisingly limited number of Confederate troops was stationed in and around Charleston to protect the port city and harbor. A week earlier, three railroad cars of Confederate soldiers had been transported out of Charleston but were captured by Union forces, leaving so few troops that the Confederate command was forced to draw daily from the forts for sentinel duty. A Confederate brig and steamer, Pinckney said, were stationed at the batteries, awaiting an opportunity to run the US blockade. Given the Union Navy's military advantage, it seemed that Confederate forces were likely to abandon Charleston, just as they had abandoned Beaufort after the Battle of Port Royal.[49]

★★★★★★★★

Harriet Tubman arrived in Hilton Head roughly two weeks after Small's heroism. She recalled later in life that she arrived in May 1862 aboard the *Atlantic*, the sister ship of the *Baltic*, on which she had been scheduled to travel in January 1862. Charles P. Wood, a banker from Auburn, New York, who later wrote a history of Tubman's pension claim, stated that she "was sent to Hilton Head . . . in May 1862 at the suggestion of Gov. Andrew, with the idea that she would be a valuable person to operate within enemy lines in procuring information & scouts." Surviving records indicate that *Atlantic* arrived in Port Royal on April 27, 1862, then left for New York on May 14, 1862. It is not clear when the *Atlantic* departed again for Port Royal. But on May 30, 1862, the *Charleston Mercury* reported that "two large Yankee steamers came up the river to within a couple of miles . . . of our batteries, and remained there all day." The unnamed steamers, which were "of the largest class," may have come from Hilton Head, and Tubman may have been aboard one of them. On January 31, 1865, when Tubman submitted a request for $766 as payment for "services as a scout in the Military Department of South Carolina," the request identified May 25, 1862, as the first day of Tubman's service. It may also have been the day she arrived. Once in Beaufort, she was attached to the headquarters of Brigadier General Isaac Ingalls Stevens (who would lead a division at the Battle of Secessionville in June 1862).[50]

There was a ready pool of men in the Lowcountry's urban areas and surrounding rural plantations from which Tubman could recruit her ring of spies, scouts, and pilots. They included enslaved and formerly enslaved boatmen, like London Blake and Ben Green, on the South Santee River; Robert Smalls; Isaac Hayward, in Beaufort; Peter Blake, who worked on the wharves in Hilton Head; and March Haynes, along the Savannah River. They knew and could navigate the region's serpentine rivers and shallow waterways, with their shoals, canals, and tides. And they knew how to take

boats laden with Sea Island cotton, rice, and people through the straight-
line cuts, dug by enslaved men, that facilitated efficient transportation by
bypassing the rivers' tight curls and wide bends.[51]

Those whom Harriet Tubman recruited to work with General Rufus
Saxton and Colonel James Montgomery possessed valuable intelligence
about the plantations on which Blacks were still enslaved. Through Tubman
they gained direct access to the most senior military commanders, as well
as Black regiments, bigger boats, and greater firepower. Only one of them
formally enlisted in the Union forces.

★★★★★★★★

The June 1863 incursion into the lower Combahee River did not represent
the first time that the US military went after a group of "notorious rebels."
Perhaps the most significant attack prior to the Combahee River Raid took
place approximately 140 miles northeast of Port Royal, starting in the port
city of Georgetown. Georgetown is situated at a nexus of rivers—Winyah
Bay in the south, the Sampit River in the west, and the Great Pee Dee and
Waccamaw Rivers on the east. After the Union Navy took it over in June
1862, Georgetown promised to facilitate the Union Navy's potential to
penetrate hundreds of miles into Confederate territory. Fair Bluff, located
inland, was a central artery of the railroad, the location of the mile-long
Northeastern Railroad Bridge and trestlework that connected rail transportation and communication between Charleston and Richmond. If they
could destroy the bridge, Union forces would force the Confederates to
make a time-consuming and costly 130-mile detour through Columbia.[52]

When George A. Prentiss, commander of the USS *Albatross,* arrived in
the Georgetown area in June, Confederate forces there withdrew ten miles
north to the Black River, where they built a small fort. Confederate planters attempted to drive the Blacks they held in bondage into the pine woods
and the interior. As in the Battle of Port Royal, a number of contrabands
in the vicinity of Georgetown hid in the woods, and then formed a small
colony of refugees under the protection of Union forces.[53]

Prentiss reported to Du Pont that he had acquired the names of all the
prominent planters and enslavers around Winyah Bay and the Santee River,
where *Albatross* was stationed. Not surprisingly, all of the planters supported the Confederacy. Prentiss asked what course of action he should
pursue against the "known rebels" and their property. Was it the federal
government's policy to deprive Confederates of their slaves? As the freedom

seekers continued to seek refuge with Union forces, Prentiss wondered whether he should let them stay in the Georgetown area or send them on to Port Royal. Should he capture or destroy the rice mills so that they could not be used to support the Confederacy's war effort? Four to five million bushels of rice were stored along the banks of the Santee, Pee Dee, Waccamaw, and Black Rivers. The Confederate military used it to provision its troops in Charleston and Savannah.[54]

Prentiss requested light-draft vessels to blockade the Santee River and transport these immense quantities of rice for use by the Union. He warned that he would have to seize the rice mills as well; otherwise the Confederates would burn both the mills and the rice stored there, just as Daniel Pope and other Sea Islands planters had attempted to burn Sea Island cotton before the Battle of Port Royal. Du Pont replied that it would be a "very handsome thing" if Prentiss could destroy the Northeastern Railroad Bridge. He also authorized Prentiss to capture rebel property—cotton, rice, and enslaved people—and send the contrabands to Port Royal. However, Du Pont did not authorize Prentiss to destroy private houses or buildings unless they were being used for military purposes.[55]

On June 20, 1862, Commander Prentiss sent two steamers, one sloop, and one tugboat approximately fourteen miles up the Santee River. The group, led by the USS *Ben De Ford* under the command of Acting Master Theodore B. DuBois, captured the CSS *Louisa*, which was carrying no papers and flying no flag. It was a blockade runner bound for Nassau in the Bahamas to sell goods, including cotton and rice, for hard currency.[56]

The following day, the Union steamers *Hale* and *Andrew* entered the South Santee. On June 24, the *Hale*, *Western World*, and *Andrew* successfully passed over the bar. The vessels faced westerly winds, low tides (they had missed the higher spring tide by a couple of days), intricate channels, and bad steerage, all of which hampered their attempt to reach the passage to the North Santee River. Eventually, on June 25, the steamers entered the North Santee River in water deep enough for the deep-draft vessels. But the turns in the serpentine channels were too constricting; only the *Hale* could navigate all the way through the channel. All three vessels had to turn back.[57]

Traveling again on the South Santee, the Union fleet passed Arthur Blake's plantation. Confederate forces there fired on the ships. The shots passed over the USS *Andrew*, which in turn fired shells until the Rebels retreated into the woods. Marines then landed on Blake's property and burned his house and rice mill, as well as other buildings, and 100,000 bushels of rice. Contrary to Du Pont's explicit orders, some of the officers and men plundered Blake's house and carried their booty back aboard the Union vessels. Du Pont later ordered that all of Blake's belongings be found, packed, and sent to General Saxton in Port Royal via the USS *Western World*. One of the primary perpetrators, an acting assistant paymaster named Seymour F. Frizelle, refused to surrender all of the stolen goods in his possession. He was detached, sent back north, and dismissed from the US Navy.[58]

The Marines pursued the Rebels into the woods, then retreated under Confederate fire to allow the steamers' guns to finish the fight. One Marine was wounded. Several Confederate soldiers were badly wounded or killed. The people whom Arthur Blake had enslaved on his South Santee River plantation ran to the protection of the Union Navy. Following the advice of a contraband pilot, whom we know from the records only as Prince, and after consulting members of the Santee refugee community—among whom there were certainly Lowcountry watermen—Prentiss abandoned the Santee expedition entirely on July 3. The water had fallen to five feet. Only the *Hale* could navigate the shallow water and sharp bends in the river. However, the *Hale*'s stern had been shelled and it was likely incapable of completing the mission without reinforcements.[59]

Some of the story of the Santee River Raid we get from pension files. We also get the names of those enslaved by Arthur Blake. Penda Blake and others whom Arthur Blake held in bondage remembered him as a bachelor and an "English gentleman who owned hundreds of slaves." Blake was the first cousin of Walter Blake, owner of Bonny Hall Plantation, located on the lower portion of the Combahee River. He had indeed been born in England, and grew up there and at his father's Boardhouse Plantation, which was located across the Combahee from Bonny Hall Plantation. He was a confirmed bachelor. Legend has it that Blake visited England every other year and brought back with him a new housekeeper each time. Blake owned 1,400 unimproved acres and 7,700 improved acres in St. James Parish. He held 439 people in bondage; their labor had produced 2.7 million pounds of rice in 1860. Blake returned to England the week after the fall of Fort Sumter, leaving his plantations in the care of an overseer, and died there in 1881. The Englishman may not qualify as a "notorious rebel"—a phrase used by the *Chicago Tribune* in an article about the Combahee River

Raid—though Confederate troops were stationed on his plantation when the Union Navy raided it. But his cousin Walter Blake, whose bondspeople ran away to Beaufort and identified him in the US Army quartermaster's register, certainly did.[60]

Mary Fields White testified that she had known Peter and Penda Blake since childhood; they were all held in bondage by the Blake family. Mary Fields was married to Parris White by David Blake (also known as Davy or Daniel Blake), who was the class leader (as noted in Chapter 4, a class leader was an enslaved person who led nighttime prayer meetings in the praise house) on Walter Blake's plantation, about three years before the Civil War began. Mary White specified that the Blakes appointed two ministers among the enslaved population: "one minister to marry his cold. [colored] people and another to bury them." David Blake may have also been the same Davey who was identified as the "keeper of the keys" on the undated slave list that Walter Blake made after 1855 and before he enumerated the enslaved people who had run away during the Civil War. David Blake officiated at the marriages of Wamey Simmons and Sarah in August 1847, Benjamin Pryor and Cornelia in 1855, Balaam Burnett and Diana Simmons shortly after the end of the war, and Charles Lucas and Bella Jones in April 1866, all on Bonny Hall Plantation.[61]

According to Mary White, "the war was just begun" when she and Parris "went away from" Blake Plantation to Hilton Head. They "came away from Combahee with the first crowd of cold. [colored] people, with General Stevens." She remembered that Walter Blake had gone to another of his plantations in Savannah. In his absence, the people he held in bondage "stole off and went to the Yankees." William McNeil (who was also known as William McBride, which he later called his "Army name" in the pension interview) had been enslaved on Bonny Hall and testified that he stayed behind when Parris and Mary "went to the Yankees." He wasn't sure if it was in 1861 or 1862, let alone the month, but was fairly certain that "they came away on a boat, and maybe they left at night as some of them did go away at night." Jonas Green (who, as we have seen, escaped enslavement on Bonny Hall Plantation with Wally Graham, who worked for the US Army quartermaster in March 1862) told the pension officer that he and the Whites were "fellow servants," all held in bondage by Walter Blake. Green's testimony for Mary White's pension file begs the question of whether he and Wally Graham were in the same group as Parris and Mary White when they stole away from Bonny Hall Plantation.[62]

To return to the Santee raid, Penda told the pension officer the tragic story of when the "rebels" came up to Arthur Blake's plantation before the US Navy raided it and "poisoned the drinking water and the colored people died like fowls." It is a mystery why the Confederates would have done this. They may have sought to kill off enslaved populations, or to keep them from running to the protection of US troops and aiding the Union war effort. Whatever the case, on Arthur Blake's Santee plantation the strategy worked. Penda and Peter had seven children living when the Confederates came to Arthur Blake's plantation. All seven of their children died; Penda was close to death herself. Peter was spared, his wife speculated, because he worked in Blake's house. Little wonder that they left as soon as they could. When the Union Navy steamed up the South Santee River, it boarded "402 of Arthur Blake's slaves valued at $600 each" and transported them to Hilton Head. His losses of people he held in bondage totaled $241,200 and included Penda Singleton Blake, her husband, Peter Blake, her brother Sam Singleton, Joe Singleton, Mary White, Nannie Campbell, Catherine Young, Joseph Blake, Dick Howard, London Brown, Patty Kelton, and Robin Jackson. Joe Singleton and his family settled in Beaufort. Renty Greaves (also known as Renty Cruel), who later became one of the few Black pension attorneys in Beaufort and Colleton Counties, testified that Peter Blake had worked for the US Army quartermaster on the government wharves for several months before he enlisted in the 21st USCT Regiment, Company D, with Stephen Polite and Parris White, Mary White's husband. Joe Singleton and Pompey Blake enlisted in the 21st Regiment, Company C.[63]

Mary and Parris White were reunited with Penda and Peter Blake at Mitchelville in Hilton Head "after the Yankees brought the colored people there," according to Mary White. Her husband and Peter Blake went into the US Army on the same day, enlisting in the same regiment. The pension files don't provide all of the details. For example, freedom seekers did not remember the full name of General Stevens; it could have been Brigadier General Isaac Ingalls Stevens, who commanded the 2nd Brigade of Expeditionary Forces, which occupied Beaufort after the Battle of Port Royal, and to whose staff Tubman was attached upon her arrival in Beaufort. Stevens commanded an expedition on May 29, 1862, that destroyed an

important bridge over the Pocotaligo River and gathered importance reconnaissance about the railroad between the Coosawatchie and Combahee
Rivers; during this expedition he could have brought freedom seekers from
the lower Combahee down to Beaufort.[64]

Nonetheless, the pension files suggest that by June 1862, roughly one
year before the Combahee River Raid, there was a small community of
freedom seekers in Beaufort and Hilton Head's US-occupied territory
who had liberated themselves from enslavement on Blake plantations on
the Combahee and Santee Rivers. Mary White said it best when she
told the pension officer that her husband was on the plantation "until
he went to the war when we went to Hilton Head." Before Congress
and President Lincoln acted to allow Blacks to enlist in the US military,
working for the military was how freedom seekers "went to war." It could
have meant working for the US Army quartermaster or, like Peter Blake,
on the federal government's wharves. Parris White became what Scipio
Murry, one of his apprentices, called a "boss carpenter," and Jonas Green
likely worked as a cooper. Parris White was surely the same carpenter
whom Walter Blake listed as having been lost to his father's estate during
the Civil War. Scipio Murry had been enslaved by Arthur Blake (whom
the enslaved people called Otto Blake), Walter Blake's first cousin. Murry
testified that he went to Beaufort "with General Steven's command" to
learn the carpentry trade. In Hilton Head, he apprenticed with Parris
White and received rations while he was in the federal government's employ. Mary White cooked and washed for the unmarried young man until
he enlisted in the US Navy.[65]

Motte Blake, freed in the Santee raid, is an example showing that enslaved
people in the Lowcountry chose their titles for reasons all their own and did
not always take the last name of the family that enslaved them. Blake had
been born on Woodville Plantation along the South Santee River, where
he was held in bondage by James Shoolbred and his son, Dr. John Gibbes
Shoolbred. James Shoolbred came to South Carolina sometime around
1790 as the British consul to Charleston. He married Thomas Middleton's
daughter Mary in 1793. Mary Middleton Shoolbred's marriage settlement
included property in England, on Kiawah Island, South Carolina, and in
Georgia, along with a house in downtown Charleston and plantations on
the North and South Santee Rivers, including Woodville Plantation. James
Shoolbred built a house on Woodville. In his 1847 will he left the property

to his son, Dr. John Gibbes Shoolbred, who according to the records produced 540,000 pounds of rice in 1860. James Shoolbred's 1848 estate record lists Motte Blake and his parents, Bungy and Clarenda Blake, among the 142 people he held in bondage. Motte Blake and his parents were listed again twelve years later in John G. Shoolbred's estate inventory.[66]

As a seasoned deer hunter, Motte Blake would have known every inch of the cypress swamps on Shoolbred's Woodville Plantation and been able to navigate the forested wetlands with their poisonous snakes and alligators. Along with the people Arthur Blake held in bondage on nearby Washo Plantation, Motte Blake escaped in the Santee raid, boarded a US steamer, and was taken to Beaufort. He would contribute his knowledge of the rice fields and forested wetlands to the US war effort. He would also later work as one of Harriet Tubman's spies and scouts.[67]

Prentiss's June 1862 Santee Raid was therefore hardly the failure he apparently felt it to be. He captured multiple prizes for the federal government, including the schooner *Louisa*, which was sent to Boston, the steam tug *North Santee*, and two lighters (flat-bottomed barges) full of rough rice, which were sent to New York. In addition, Prentiss destroyed Arthur Blake's plantation, which was being used as the headquarters of a regiment that protected Confederate vessels running the Union Navy's blockade at the South Santee River and Alligator Creek. And more than six hundred Blacks had liberated themselves, with their numbers continuing to swell even after Prentiss called off the mission. General Hunter sent a steamer to transport a total of seven hundred refugees, including women and children, to Port Royal.[68]

The Santee raid also created the blueprint for the Combahee River Raid, which the US Army would stage less than one year later. On the Combahee River, however, the Union would leave hardly anything or anyone standing, including the rice.

II

Two of Us

Most of the northern women who volunteered to come down to Port Royal and the Sea Islands from the North served as teachers. Among the exceptions were Laura Towne and Esther Hill Hawks, both doctors (homeopathic and allopathic doctors, respectively), and Frances Gage and Nelly Winsor, who served as superintendents. Virtually all of the northern women were white; Harriet Tubman would be the only Black northern volunteer to participate in the Port Royal Experiment until Charlotte Forten arrived in October 1862.

Tubman and Forten could not have been more different. Tubman was a forty-year-old married woman when she arrived in Beaufort. Given that the majority of enslaved women began bearing children a few years after menarche—often by force—Tubman was almost old enough to have been Charlotte Forten's mother. Forten may have thought of Tubman as she would a favorite aunt.[1]

Charlotte L. Forten (later Grimké)—a "pretty little Quadroon," Thomas Higginson described her in a letter to his wife—was born in Philadelphia in 1837. Her obituary remembered her as a "woman of great refinement" without the "slightest trace of coarseness about her in any shape or form." She was the fourth generation in her family to be born free; the Fortens had been free since the days of William Penn, founder of the colony of Pennsylvania. Charlotte's paternal grandfather, James Forten, was an "opulent man of color," according to Joseph Sturge, the English Quaker abolitionist who visited him in 1841, and had served as a powder boy aboard a privateer during the Revolutionary War. Forten traveled to England, where he met prominent abolitionists, including Granville Sharpe. He became actively involved in the abolitionist movement when he returned home to Philadelphia. Apprenticed to one of the most successful sailmakers in

Philadelphia, Forten became foreman of the sailmaker's crew. When his employer died, Forten purchased the company. His sail loft was described as the "best representative business establishment of colored men in the United States." James Forten's business generated a fortune and was the foundation for the Forten family's wealth.[2]

Charlotte Forten's grandfather would therefore have been about as rich as the rice planters on the Combahee River. They certainly had many more material comforts than other free Blacks, including a stately and spacious home at 92 Lombard Street in Philadelphia's Head House Square neighborhood. They could afford travel abroad, private education, and patronage of the arts, and enjoyed interaction with progressive whites as virtual equals. For generations, the Forten family was one of the most elite free Black families in Philadelphia.[3]

They could have played it safe and focused on living in "handsome style," as Ray Allen Billington, editor of Forten's journal, described it. But they were willing to sacrifice everything to fight for equality. From James Forten's time onward, the family risked their wealth and social status to further the causes of radical abolition and equality. In 1800, James Forten and a group of Philadelphia free Blacks petitioned Congress for modification of the 1793 Fugitive Slave Act, abolishment of the transatlantic slave trade, and immediate emancipation of enslaved people. In 1813, Forten published a pamphlet so influential that it made him almost singlehandedly responsible for galvanizing opposition to the colonization movement. Like Tubman, James Forten was a Garrisonian. He was one of William Lloyd Garrison's largest financial backers in the establishment of *The Liberator*.[4]

In addition to providing him money, Forten introduced Garrison to his friends and supplied him with information, particularly about colonization and Liberian immigrants. He wrote fiery treatises that Garrison routinely published in *The Liberator*, sharing with readers the hopes and dreams of free people of color as he knew them. Forten also personally sold subscriptions to the newspaper among members of Philadelphia's free Black community and the American Anti-Slavery Society before the first issue was even printed. By the time of Charlotte's birth in 1837, her family was the closest thing to anti-slavery celebrities. Garrison was one of many prominent abolitionists who rarely traveled to Philadelphia without enjoying the Forten family's hospitality and making their Lombard Street home a headquarters. It was a mecca for abolitionists. Only the New York merchants and brothers Arthur and Lewis Tappan contributed more to the abolitionist cause than James Forten. The Fortens' commitment to the antislavery cause maintained their prominence in abolitionist circles even as the family's fortune dwindled.[5]

In contrast to Tubman, who could not read or write, Charlotte Forten was highly educated in literature, poetry, languages, Latin, French, and German, music, and sewing. After receiving instruction from tutors at home, in 1853 she was enrolled in the Salem Normal School, in Massachusetts, to begin training as a teacher. She was the first Black person offered a permanent teaching position at Epes Grammar School, also in Salem. But a series of health crises caused by an unspecified respiratory disease—called "lung fever" at the time—rendered her unable to work, and Charlotte was forced to resign her teaching position in the spring of 1860. She remained passionate about education and racial uplift and continued to pursue her education, reading literature, writing poetry, studying French and German, attending lectures, supporting the arts, and playing the piano for the rest of her life. Her translation of the French novel *Madame Thérèse* was published in 1889.[6]

John Greenleaf Whittier, poet, stalwart of Massachusetts's abolition movement, and longtime close friend of the Forten family, suggested that Charlotte go to Port Royal. He wrote her a letter of introduction to the Boston Educational Committee in August 1862, asking that she be sent as a teacher to Port Royal. He thought that she could accomplish more by teaching newly liberated children on the South Carolina Sea Islands than by teaching white children in Massachusetts. However, the Boston committee was too slow to take action. So Charlotte went home to Philadelphia, where the Philadelphia Port Royal Relief Association welcomed her into its ranks. Forten sailed to Port Royal in October 1862, almost a year after "Gun Shoot at Bay Point." She lived with Laura Towne at The Oaks Plantation, taught school with Ellen Murray at Brick Baptist Church, which was situated on St. Helena Island in a grove of large live oak trees, their branches heavily draped with Spanish moss, giving them a funereal look. Forten also taught adults at night after their work was done.[7]

Despite her distinguished heritage, Forten had faced discrimination in northern states from both white and Black people. She and her parents were barred from many restaurants and stores. Her classmates in Salem's integrated schools were afraid to greet her when she encountered them on the street. While she was boarding with an antislavery woman in Boston after attending the annual Fourth of July celebration in Framingham, a US Navy officer refused to sit at the dining table with Forten, because her skin was "not colored like his own," as Forten noted in her diary. She maintained that she had not noticed this and was instead thinking about the inspiring antislavery lecture she had just attended.[8]

Both Tubman and Forten faced bigotry in the North when they stepped outside of free Black communities and abolitionist circles. They also some-times experienced it within abolitionist circles among whites who, while committed to the abolition of enslavement, were not committed to equality for Blacks under the law. In Beaufort and the Sea Islands, she noted, white officers often used racial epithets to talk about the Blacks they were charged with protecting. She implored in her diary, "When, oh! when will this cease . . . How long oh? How long must we continue to suffer—to endure?"[9]

Nonetheless, as a highly educated woman of multiracial ancestry who was born free, Forten experienced a different kind of discrimination than Tubman did. For one thing, there were the slights from Blacks who did not think her Black enough. When she first arrived in South Carolina, freedom seekers on St. Helena also did not recognize her as one of their own kind. Her com-plexion was light; her features were European; she taught school and had never worked as a field hand or a house servant. Forten even lived with the white folks in the mansions formerly owned and occupied by the planters, not in the slave cabins on the slave street. In short, the refugees on St. Helena were suspicious of Forten. Higginson wrote in a letter to his wife that the freedom seekers on St. Helena had a "decided prejudice against Lottie Forten," whom they called "dat brown gal," when she first arrived. Laura Towne even had to insist that one of the house servants clean Forten's room. In time, St. Helena Blacks grew to love Forten, once they learned what a devoted teacher she was and how talented she was at sewing and playing the piano.[10]

In coming to the slave South, Forten risked having the freedom her family had enjoyed for four generations taken away. If captured by Confederates, she could have been tortured, sexually violated, enslaved, and even sold. When Forten was consumed by her loneliness, she reminded herself via her diary not to be "selfish." She must let "the work" to which she had "sol-emnly pledged" herself fill up her "own existence to the exclusion of all vain longings," especially for home.[11]

★★★★★★★

Education was perhaps the most successful aspect of the Port Royal Experiment. The establishment of schools in the Sea Islands had nonetheless been a slow process, delayed in the first several months of the experiment's existence by extreme heat and personnel shortages. In addition to their students learning the alphabet, reading from primers, writing, singing hymns, and doing arithmetic, northern teachers also noted improvements in their hygiene, manners, and self-confidence. One teacher described a student as having initially "look[ed] like a whipped dog" but noted that after a year of attending school he could look whites "full in the face and [speak] out as if he were not ashamed of himself."[12]

By December 1862, more than seventeen hundred students were attending school on St. Helena, Lady's, and Port Royal Islands, with another five hundred on Hilton Head and Parris Islands. Edward Pierce reported in the *Atlantic Monthly* that by March 1863—a year after the experiment had started—more than forty teachers from Boston, Philadelphia, and New York were teaching two thousand children (three thousand were actually enrolled) between the ages of eight and twelve in thirty Sea Island schools.[13]

Pierce enjoined readers of the *Atlantic Monthly* to understand that giving freedpeople in South Carolina access to literacy "transcend[ed] in moral grandeur anything that has ever come from mortal hands." For Charlotte Forten, educating freedom seekers gave her an active role in securing something that she and her family had possessed since before the American Revolution. She wrote that she hoped the "long dark night of the Past, with all its sorrows and its fears, was forgotten; and for the Future—the eyes of these freed children see no clouds in it. It is full of sunlight, they think, and they trust in it perfectly."[14]

Teaching slaves to read had been illegal before the Civil War, and most freedpeople were now eager to learn how to read the Bible, write their names, and more. Those who could not devote more time to attending class took their school wherever they went—to the fields, even to the encampments when they enlisted in the army. Forten marveled that a "people who have been so long crushed to the earth, so imbruted as these have been,—and they are said to be among the most degraded negroes of the South,—can have so great a desire for knowledge, and such a capacity for attaining it."[15]

When teachers from the North arrived in early 1862, they found a handful of formerly enslaved people who already knew their letters; a few could read. Those who could read had already established schools. In St. Helena, Will Capers ran a "secret night-school" for enslaved men on The Oaks, Laura Towne wrote in her diary. In Beaufort, two men, one of whom was named John Milton, had established a school "for just a few weeks" after "Gun Shoot at Bay Point," under the direction of Reverend Solomon Peck. Newly arrived teachers hired freedom seekers who could read to assist them. By April 2, 1862, Reverend Peck was supervising a school in which the northern teacher was assisted by four Lowcountry Creole assistants, Peter, Paul, Thomas, and Ephraim. On Edisto Island, a woman named Hettie had been taught by the daughter of the planter who held her in bondage. She was put in charge of the children's day school when the northern teacher opened an evening school in March 1862. Pierce wrote in the *Atlantic Monthly* that when the Union Army evacuated Edisto Island and brought the inhabitants to St. Helena, Hettie continued to teach her students the alphabet and to read one-syllable words, then brought them to school at the Baptist Church in St. Helena village, because she "could carry them no further." Sea Island Blacks who could read and write found ways to teach others. Parents who could afford to do so made a weekly contribution of five cents, paying freed teachers' salaries. Teachers accepted students' contributions as their entire salary.[16]

The first teachers to arrive in the Sea Islands held classes in repurposed churches, cotton barns, sheds, old kitchens, and praise houses, as well as outside under trees in good weather on makeshift furniture. One schoolroom consisted of a tent provided by the federal government. The students put down pine sprays for flooring and surrounded them with rough pine branches. Lacking adequate desks, they knelt on the ground in front of wooden benches on which they placed their slates, books, and papers in order to write. Teachers found that their school buildings had no blackboards, desks, or slates for the students; the wooden boxes and benches were too high for the younger children's feet to reach the ground. Eventually relief associations donated desks for teachers and students, as well slates and pencils.[17]

In these makeshift facilities, students were initiated into the mysteries of literacy. They learned how to use a pencil, not hold it like a hoe or dig into their slates, sometimes leaving furrows deep enough to plant sesame or

Sea Island cotton seeds. Typically, two or three classes occupied a one-room schoolhouse, with no partitions to separate the classes. Teachers had to strain their vocal cords to be heard over each other, while classes of a hundred or more children recited their letters and sang at the same time. And, in addition to teaching, they had to keep order over the noise and distractions of babies crying or exhausted children sleeping or talking out of turn.[18]

Despite the hardships and the makeshift facilities (which may have provided better shelter than most houses), freed children on the Sea Islands did not want to miss school. "'Us wants book-larning, too, bad," one student told a teacher from Boston. They rarely missed school even in the most difficult of circumstances, arriving barefoot and bare-headed in cold and stormy weather, as one teacher remembered. Their schoolbooks were among their most prized possessions; they "exalted" in the new books the way white children did in "playthings," a Philadelphia teacher wrote back to the Port Royal Relief Committee. When there was not a school on the plantation on which they lived, such as on parts of St. Helena, children walked for miles to find schools that were open.[19]

Out of necessity, the school day and school year were organized around agricultural and household labors. Children too young to work in the fields attended school in the morning. Older children began in the afternoon. As Charlotte Forten described to readers of the *Atlantic Monthly*, they came to school after their "hard toil in the hot sun," as anxious to learn as ever. When the older boys and girls went to school instead of working in the fields, one superintendent accused the teachers of interfering with his cotton picking and corn breaking. Student attendance declined once the season for tilling began in February. Superintendents praised parents for keeping their older children in the fields and only sending them to school for part of the day, taking that as a sign that freedpeople were developing industrious habits and beginning to feel the "responsibilities of free men," as one teacher reported in a letter to the Education Commission for Freedmen in Boston.[20]

In addition to fieldwork, parents kept children at home from school to perform household chores, such as laundry. Those who had to mind younger siblings while adults worked could not leave them behind. So they brought the babies and toddlers to school, often carrying with them a tin can of hominy to feed the children when they were hungry. Girls took turns minding their little charges; one girl came in the morning and got a lesson, then ran home to mind the child, after which the other girl who had stayed at home to mind the child came to school for her lesson. Unwilling to miss out on the excitement of the classroom, the little nurses sometimes brought the babies to school and handed them off as best they could. Though the babies slept on the piazza, their presence did cause confusion at school. Teachers at Old Fort Plantation established a "primitive nursery" at which the girls dropped off their young charges on their way to school.[21]

Parents who were themselves illiterate insisted that their children, a Boston teacher recalled in her memoir, "*mus'* go to school sure." "Us wants to larn, fur we've been in darkness too long, an' now we're in light." A grandfather who wanted to be sure his grandson learned something implored the teacher if necessary to "take [her] leetle paddle" to him, meaning her ruler, "so him shall bring home something in his head." One mother offered to "work her girl's task" if she might be allowed to come to school. Families on the Sea Islands made tremendous sacrifices for their children to take advantage of the educational opportunities offered by the Port Royal Experiment.[22]

When they could steal away from their responsibilities at home and in the fields, adults also sometimes took advantage of the presence of northern teachers to learn to read and write. One woman quite literally crawled to the teacher's house, because she only wanted to "larn one t'ing to take wid me w'en I go to de Big Massa," the teacher from Boston wrote in her memoir. That woman could not walk as the result of permanent injuries caused by the heavy shackles that the enslaver put on her feet to prevent her from running off during "Gun Shoot at Bay Point." It was harder for married women—with their childcare and household responsibilities—than it was for men to get away from household duties to "catch a lesson." Even adults who could not attend school regularly proudly came to keep their names in the roll, to "get themselves ticketed."[23]

A few intrepid souls attended day schools with younger students, often their own children. The kids relished their mastery over something like the alphabet, which was harder for their parents to grasp. When one husband and wife stood together to read their lesson aloud in front of the class, their three children ran to their side to tease them mercilessly. One son named Dick taunted his father, "Boy! Daddy, boy! Him don't know nothing." Dick's father seemed to take it in stride, responding, "Shut you mouf, boy! I only want to catch dat word, sure." He was pleased with his son's progress and struggling to make his own. Dick's mother also showed pride in her children having accessed a world of literacy into which she could only glimpse: "Dem chillen too smart. I ain't know what to do wid' dem."[24]

It was of course harder for adults to make time for and progress on their lessons than it was for children. Unlike most adults, one formerly enslaved woman named Becky, who was disabled, was able to come to school regularly. She learned to write well with her left hand; her right arm had been cut off in a rice mill when a slaveholder had become distracted in his attempt to beat another slave. Her friends described her as "mad fur larn," the Boston teacher wrote. Most adults who wanted to learn to read and write took lessons individually at night. Adults, particularly soldiers, saw the value in reading and writing in order to write letters to keep in touch with spouses, lovers, potential lovers, parents, and children serving in the military and living on other plantations. "Writing-larning's a powerful thing," as the Sea Islanders described it to the Boston teacher, one that they used to connect their scattered families.[25]

It was also a revolutionary act. Charlotte Forten was pleased to hear the children in the St. Helena Island school sing "John Brown's Body," likely to the melody of Julia Ward Howe's "Battle Hymn of the Republic" which Laura Towne had taught them. It was for them that John Brown died, and Towne taught the children all about him. Forten felt the significance of being a woman of color singing about the radical abolitionist and slave insurrectionist in the "prison-house of bondage." She also taught the children about "the noble" Toussaint Louverture, the general and leader of the Haitian Revolution who had ended enslavement in and French colonial rule of Haiti in 1804. Always a champion of racial uplift, Forten wanted the children in her class to know what "one of their own color c'ld do for his own race."[26]

Though the educational aspects of the Port Royal Experiment were successful, the labor aspects continued to receive mixed reviews. Cotton production never returned to prewar levels. Treasury agents had estimated they would gather, as noted earlier, 2.5 million pounds in 1861, when in reality they gathered and ginned significantly less. The 1862 crop produced approximately 70,000 pounds of ginned Sea Island cotton—"a trifle in itself," as Edward S. Philbrick, who acted as superintendent of Coffin's Point Plantation on St. Helena Island, put it—when the same inputs by enslaved laborers would have produced 500,000 pounds before the war, as Edward Philbrick observed when he reported to the Boston Educational Commission for Freedmen.[27]

A combination of natural and human factors had resulted in the disappointing cotton crop. Superintendents and Black workers started at a disadvantage, because the crop confiscated after the "Great Skedaddle" was ginned in New York, leaving a shortage of cotton seeds on the Sea Islands for the following year. The Confederate Army and the US Army quartermaster had stripped the plantations of draft animals, thereby slowing the pace at which Sea Island Blacks plowed, listed, and planted the fields, and depriving the plantations of manure. On top of all that, late planting made the immature pods vulnerable to natural factors—rainfall, insect infestations, and frost—as the cotton matured.[28]

Moreover, while Black workers understood that the pay they received was only a very small fraction of the proceeds from the sale of the cotton, it was difficult for them to understand the risk that the federal government assumed. Most, as we've seen, preferred to own their own small piece of land and plant for themselves. Superintendent Reuben Tomlinson, for one, remained convinced the experiment was working: "We have not laid ourselves out for the purpose of raising cotton, but to make the people self-supporting and independent. In this I have no doubt that we have succeeded; and we shall have raised enough cotton to pay all our expenses besides."[29]

★★★★★★★★

After the fits and starts of agricultural production and advances in education, the weight of the Port Royal Experiment and the "'n[——]' question," as Charles Francis Adams Jr. described it in a March 1862 letter to his father, came to rest on the enlistment of Black soldiers. Between September 1862, when President Lincoln issued the Emancipation Proclamation and January 1, when it went into effect, the nation waited to see whether or not formerly enslaved men would fight for their freedom. If so, the army would recruit them as soldiers once the Emancipation Proclamation went into effect.

Among New England abolitionists, some, like Garrison and most Quakers, opposed the war as inconsistent with their values. Their sons, however, enlisted after the Proclamation went into effect and the dream of abolishing slavery seemed within reach, even if violence was necessary to see it through. As we've seen, Garrison's son George Garrison enlisted—over his parents' objections—and served as a commissioned officer in the 55th Massachusetts Regiment.[30]

Some abolitionists working among freedom seekers in coastal South Carolina supported the war but not the enlistment of Black soldiers—even after freedmen on St. Helena, for example, armed themselves and guarded remote locations, such as Eddings Point. There were those who considered themselves abolitionists and working actively as superintendents or teachers in the Port Royal Experiment who doubted whether Black men would fight. Edward S. Philbrick wrote in a letter to his business partner, with whom he purchased eleven Sea Island plantations, including Coffin's Point, where he had been superintendent, that the freedmen were not a "military race." He doubted whether they had "sufficient intelligence to act in concert in any way where firmness of purpose is required." Edward Pierce, the architect of the Port Royal Experiment, agreed and characterized Sea Island Blacks as showing a "general disinclination to military service," though he did acknowledge that a "more manly feeling was only latent" among freedmen and ready to be aroused under the right circumstances and leadership.[31]

Susan Walker reluctantly turned over names of the able-bodied men on the plantation she managed for enlistment in General Hunter's unauthorized regiment. She believed former slaves' "spirit has been so crushed down" by enslavement that there was "nothing left to rise up in defence of their just rights or to secure freedom." A chorus of superintendents and U.S. army officers, including superintendant Charles Pickard Ware, agreed. They thought freedmen "timid and cautious" and lacking the "pluck" to fight against whites, particularly against the planters and slaveholders who had held them and their families in bondage, even in their own defense.[32]

Edward Philbrick, for one, thought the will of the freedom seekers he came to help was so debased that he pronounced even Robert Smalls's heroic exploit with the CSS *Planter* as really only about self-interest: "The secret of such exploits as the crew of the *Planter* have lately performed lies in the fact that the men were forcibly taken from this region last November and wanted to get back home again." Had Charleston been their "old home," he thought, they never would have risked their lives to steal their freedom.[33]

As we saw in Chapter 10, General David Hunter disbanded his regiment, but Sergeant Trowbridge did not disband his company and continued to drill. In late August, General Rufus Saxton made a request to raise a Black regiment and received authorization to enlist and organize five thousand troops in the 1st South Carolina Volunteers. The War Department authorized Saxton to enlist freedmen to protect the plantations and their inhabitants from capture by the enemy. Thus the initial scope of their service—"to guard the plantations, and protect the inhabitants from captivity and murder"—was more narrowly defined than what Hunter had attempted to implement. Black men would not actually fight the enemy until after the Emancipation Proclamation went into effect.[34]

Nonetheless, among freedmen, the negative experiences associated with Hunter's regiment made the prospect of signing on with Saxton unappealing. Clergy and superintendents joined the effort to recruit volunteers but had little success. Men even took to the woods again; when Sea Island Blacks suspected that recruitment might begin again, "hardly a man on the plantation under sixty years of age . . . slept in his bed," Charles Pickard Ware wrote in a letter. They became so suspicious that any "strange white face [drove] them from the field into the woods like so many quails." Men of eligible age would not even go to church for fear of being rounded up there and hauled off. Sea Island freedmen feared falling into a trap similar to Hunter's Regiment.[35]

Freedpeople's fears were confirmed when voluntary enlistment turned to forced recruitments again, despite General Saxton's assurances. The second time around, the draft was carried out, as Boston teacher William Gannett wrote in a letter, with "excessive severity, not to say horrible cruelty." Armed Black soldiers carried out orders to hunt down, seize, and even shoot able-bodied men who refused to enlist, as well as deserters. On Coffin's Point plantation, two white captains came with approximately fifty Black soldiers to seize men who had not enlisted. They caught a man named Primus, who should not have been taken because he was a foreman on the plantation. And they chased two young men, Sancho and Josh, shooting and wounding Josh and capturing Sancho after he shot at them. The soldiers did not catch more men, though they hung around for two weeks.[36]

Trowbridge's men formed the nucleus of the new regiment, Company A, even as General Saxton searched for the right man to serve as its commander. On November 8, 1862, Charles Pickard Ware reported in a letter that he had just seen the "first full company of the new regiment" march through the streets of downtown Beaufort with "regularity" and "steadiness." They made a "fine appearance" and were a "fine body of men." Northerners involved with the Port Royal Experiment were "encouraged" with how quickly the regiment was filling up and how comparatively smoothly enlistment went—accomplished by word of mouth among the men. Not everything went smoothly, however. The general serving as acting commander of the Department of the South denied General Saxton's request for tents for the new recruits—though thousands were available in the warehouse—forcing the men to sleep outside. The general likely thought the tents should go to white soldiers instead.[37]

General Saxton ultimately chose Thomas Wentworth Higginson to command the 1st South Carolina Volunteers. Higginson was not among those abolitionists who believed Black men would not or should not fight for their freedom. He had already raised and was training a regiment of white soldiers, the 51st Massachusetts Infantry Regiment. He assumed command of the 1st South Carolina on November 24, 1862. Though Higginson claims in his memoir (entitled *Army Life in a Black Regiment*) that the 1st South Carolina was the first regiment of Black soldiers to be formed in service of the US military, three regiments of the Louisiana Native Guards and the 1st Kansas Colored had mustered in before the South Carolina unit. The Native Guards had previously been in Confederate service; after being reorganized by the Union, the 1st Regiment of the Louisiana Native Guards mustered in on September 27, 1862, and was constituted by free men of color. Formerly enslaved men filled the ranks of the 2nd and 3rd Regiments, mustered in on October 12, 1862. All of them were organized before General Benjamin Butler (who had been appointed military governor of New Orleans) received passive authorization from the federal government on November 6. The 1st South Carolina Volunteers mustered in on November 15, 1862. Despite the disastrous Hunter experiment and the blunders in recruiting the second time around, the 1st South Carolina continued to grow, numbering approximately seven hundred men by January 1863.[38]

In the months after sending Harriet Tubman to Beaufort in early 1862, Governor Andrew of Massachusetts had lobbied President Lincoln to enlist Black men in the US armed forces. On February 5, 1863, he wrote to Captain Higginson in Port Royal to ask for "any suggestions which your experience may afford" concerning organizing a "colored infantry regiment" in his home state. Andrew was preparing to raise the 54th Volunteers, which would become the first regiment of Black soldiers to be organized in the North. Most of the soldiers, including Frederick Douglass's sons Charles and Lewis Douglass and Sojourner Truth's grandson James

Caldwell were already free when they enlisted. Prominent free Black men, such as Frederick Douglass and Charles Lenox Remond, in whose household Charlotte Forten lived in Salem, Massachusetts, recruited hundreds of men to the regiment. Douglass heralded the rallying cry "TO ARMS! TO ARMS! NOW OR NEVER. This is our golden moment."[39]

The 54th Massachusetts Regiment was commissioned several months after the 1st South Carolina. It was a national regiment, composed primarily of freedmen from northern, border, and Confederate states, as well as men from Canada and the West Indies who had been born free. Less than one-half of 1 percent of the 54th Massachusetts soldiers were former slaves. In contrast, the 1st South Carolina was a regional regiment, composed almost exclusively of men who had been enslaved on Sea Islands and coastal mainland South Carolina, Georgia, and Florida plantations. Once again, the divided nation watched coastal South Carolina and Georgia Blacks on the "proving ground" for freedom.[40]

By the war's end, more than 186,000 Black men—18 percent of the Black male population ages eighteen to forty-nine—had enlisted in the Union Army. Formerly enslaved soldiers constituted a full three-fourths of those who enlisted. More than half were recruited in Confederate states, including South Carolina. Charles Adams, a first lieutenant in the 1st Massachusetts Cavalry, surmised in a letter to his son from London in August 1862 that it would be "years before they can be made to stand before their old masters, unless (and the exception means a great deal) some leader of their own, some Toussaint rises, who is one of them and inspires them with confidence." In fact, it would not take years for Black men turned soldiers to confront enslavers and tear down the institution of enslavement. It would take a few months, or even just weeks.[41]

Because the 1st South Carolina Volunteers regiment was composed of men who had seized their freedom after "Gun Shoot at Bay Point," Higginson wrote in his memoir, they had "voluntarily met more dangers in their escape from slavery than any of [his] young captains had incurred in all their lives." The soldiers of the 1st South Carolina would fight to protect "home and household and freedom . . . besides the abstraction of 'the U.S.,'" Higginson continued. A December 1862 Confederate order mandated that formerly enslaved men who fought for the Union and were captured would be turned over to the Confederate states and subjected to the laws of the Confederacy—that is, they would be reenslaved or executed. A May 1863 resolution reinforced the order, specifying that all Blacks captured while fighting for the Union would be turned over to the Confederate states in which they had been held in bondage or in which they lived as free people. Black soldiers were well aware that quite literally, as Higginson pronounced it, they "fought with ropes round their necks."[42]

★★★★★★★★

As we've seen, there were still African-born people living in the Lowcountry region when the Civil War commenced. The *Wanderer*, the last slaving vessel to make the Terrible Voyage, had disembarked its human cargo in Jekyll Island, Georgia, on November 28, 1858. The Lowcountry was more African than, say, the Chesapeake.[43]

The presence in the Sea Islands and coastal mainland of people who were born in Africa and liberated themselves after the Battle of Port Royal intrigued northern volunteers. The overwhelming majority were elderly. As a child, a woman named Daphne had been captured and sold along with her parents to traffickers. She was said to be over a hundred years old, have fifty grandchildren, sixty-five great-grandchildren, and three great-great-grandchildren. Blind Maum Katie, who was also said to be over a hundred years old, possessed the mental clarity of someone far younger. She told northern volunteers that she remembered worshipping her own gods in West Africa as a child before she was taken away. Both Daphne and Maum Katie lived on St. Helena. Laura Towne wrote in her diary that she feared that Cupid, "one of her old Africans," had died. But Monday still brought his "tattooed forehead and whip-scar-marked breast" to get his rations. Cesar was said to be another centenarian living on Port Royal. He had been taken from his children, family, and homeland as an adult. The parents of a freedwoman named Harriet had been brought against their will from Africa to Darien, Georgia.[44]

The northerners took note that languages spoken by African-born former slaves and their children were also different—a "very foreign tongue," as Charlotte Forten described it in her diary—compared to the dialect spoken by Lowcountry Creoles. Even the religion practiced by some of the African-born former slaves was different from that of freedpeople who were born in the Lowcountry. Maum Katie, for example, was a great "spiritual mother," Laura Towne wrote in her journal, "a fortune-teller, or rather prophetess, and a woman of tremendous influence over her spiritual children."[45]

Nothing attracted more interest and attention among northern observers than Sea Island Blacks' religious practices. Typically, praise meetings were held several nights during the week, multiple times on Sundays, and whenever the community came together or an individual church member or church family needed collective prayer, including but not limited to sickness and death. Sea Island Blacks sang, prayed, preached, and "[shook] hands all round," according to Harriet Ware. Such meetings were conducted by a lay church member who was a member of the Lowcountry Creole community, as opposed to a church service officiated by a white pastor or clergy member. In the first systematic attempt to record, preserve, and catalogue the spirituals sung by freedpeople in the Lowcountry, teacher William Allen, superintendent Charles Pickard Ware (Harriet Ware's brother), and Lucy McKim Garrison (who served as secretary to her father, Reverend James Miller McKim) described praise meetings as an occasion when church members listened to the "vociferous exhortation" or prayers by the presiding elder from a hymnbook, singing two lines at a time with "wailing cadences" that were "indescribably melancholy." But these hymnbook hymns had been taught to them by whites. Even during enslavement, praise houses were the "special property of the people," as Charlotte Forten described them, places where slaveholders permitted the enslaved community to meet, read the Bible, sing, and, of course, pray. Praise houses were often located in the cabin of the oldest enslaved person living in the slave quarters.[46]

In the aftermath of "Gun Shoot at Bay Point," self-emancipated freedom seekers in the Sea Islands had plenty to pray about, and turned to the praise house to combat the uncertainty, dislocation, violence, and chaos of war. On plantations, the ceremonies were held on a variety of occasions, including the examination of new church members, funerals of church members, Christmas, and New Year's Eve. They occurred at the beginning of forced recruitment, during the auction of plantations on which they had once lived and worked, and at times of celebration, such as January 1, 1863, when the Emancipation Proclamation went into effect.[47]

During the Port Royal Experiment, Sea Island Blacks and northern whites prayed together during praise meetings. Northern volunteers introduced themselves and their services to the communities, addressed those gathered about affairs on the plantations, and were occasionally invited to lead prayers and give eulogies for church members. Laura Towne, Susan Walker, and Austa Malinda Winchell French attended a praise meeting the night before able-bodied men were forcibly recruited into Hunter's Regiment. Whites could lead prayer and singing of Methodist hymns in praise meetings.[48]

After praise meetings were over, freedom seekers pushed the benches in the praise house back to the wall and began to shout. The shout was an ecstatic form of religious expression and spirit possession practiced by Lowcountry freedom seekers. According to historian Sterling Stuckey, this ancestors' ritual served as the foundational way that enslaved people and their descendants forged a sense of community. Though shouts typically took place in the praise houses, they were distinct from praise meetings. The shouts began with the singing of "quaint, monotonous, endless negro . . . chants, with obscure syllables recurring constantly, and slight variations interwoven," Higginson remembered in his memoir. It began over a campfire as the singers "deaconed" out the hymns, wailing a line or two repetitively with a mournful and melancholy cadence.[49]

The best singers and tired shouters formed a band, standing at the side of the room and articulating syncopated rhythms that complemented the movements and music. The lead singer who started each verse was "based" by more singers, who sang the refrain of the hymn and/or joined the solo. The "basers" improvised, as Harriet Ware described in a letter, starting the hymn an octave above or below. They hit some other notes and chords. The effect was a miraculous complication and variety in perfect time and with little discord. Shout-goers used their bodies as percussive instruments, accompanying the singing by drumming their feet and clapping their hands, making sounds like castanets and creating fervent polyrhythms. On some islands, musicians playing barrel-headed drums, jawbones, and keys accompanied the singers.[50]

As the excitement built, a circle would form in the middle of the floor. Church members began first walking and then shuffling around, one after the other, in a ring. In the slow, counterclockwise shuffling motions, shouters barely raised their feet from the floor. The tempo and intensity of the singing grew, and spiritual energy rose to a fevered pitch until the shouters moved in jerking, hitching motions, causing them to perspire profusely.[51]

Church members, particularly elders, adamantly distinguished the shout from dancing, which would involve crossing one's feet and would be considered blasphemous. "Dancing in the usual way is regarded with great horror by the people of Port Royal, but they entered with infinite zest into the movements of the 'shout,'" noted Allen, Ware, and Garrison. As the shout progressed, the tempo of the music and movements got faster and more furious. The rhythmic foot-stomping, shuffling, and hand-clapping made the wooden floor vibrate and the walls sway. Attending a shout in a wooden praise house must have felt and sounded like standing inside a drum being struck repeatedly. Shouts started late at night and lasted for hours, sometimes until the first light of morning. During a shout, the praise houses were lit only by fires in the hearth, which shouters kept replenished with wood. Shouts may have attracted observers' attention because the monotonous stamping of feet prevented anyone within a half mile of the praise house from sleeping.[52]

Shouts were completely the purview of Sea Island Blacks. Northern volunteers sometimes attended as spectators but were not allowed to participate. They remained a "little white crowd" at the door of the praise house, observing the "wild firelight scene," Towne wrote in her journal. In any case, the teachers and superintendents may have been reluctant to join in a ceremony they viewed as "half pow-wow, half prayer-meeting . . . half bacchanalian, half devout" and a "rhythmical barbaric dance," as Higginson described it. They assumed in particular that shouts were foreign in origin and not Christian at all, the "remains of some old idol worship," Towne wrote, rather than a sacred religious ceremony. Generations of folklorists, anthropologists, and historians have agreed with observers who began speculating during the Civil War about the African origins of the ring shout and various other aspects of Gullah Geechee language, culture, and religious practices.[53]

Charlotte Forten also assumed the shout was an African relic, the "barbarous expression of religion, handed down to them from their African ancestors," as she wrote in the *Atlantic Monthly*. She thought it was "destined to pass away under the influence of Christian teachings." Still, Forten confided in her diary that she once amused herself by "practicing a little" with Lizzie Hunn, the young white teacher with whom Forten had traveled from New York, and whose father operated a store in one corner of a praise house.[54]

Night burial was another ritual that fascinated outsiders. Harriet Tubman attended a night burial, which she described to Sarah Bradford. They were, she said, a custom that Lowcountry Blacks had developed during enslavement, because enslavers did not allow them to stop working during the day to bury their dead. The British actress Fannie Kemble had witnessed one as well, years earlier. Kemble recorded in her diary that members of the enslaved community had appealed to her for some cotton fabric to make a "winding-sheet" to wrap the corpse of a man whose name has come down to us only as Shadrach. The cooper on Butler's rice plantation, whom we only know as London, built the coffin, which rested atop trestles in front of London's cabin. The mourners gathered around Shadrach's coffin, many holding pine-wood torches. In unison, they began to sing a hymn in high wailing tones. While London prayed, the mourners, including Kemble, knelt before the coffin. Then the enslaved people carried it to the burial ground, where London read the funeral service from the prayer book and the mourners knelt in the sand again, lit by a ring of pine-wood torches. The cooper-turned-preacher ended the torchlight funeral with a short sermon on the biblical story of Lazarus, who rose from the dead after four days. He ended by admonishing those in attendance not to lie, steal, or shirk their duties to the man who held them all in bondage.[55]

Visiting journalist and landscape architect Frederick Law Olmsted attended a "very quaint and picturesque" nighttime slave funeral, of which he left an account. Olmsted observed that the enslaved people processed by the light of wood torches. They sang hymns, "sad, wailing, chanting," in their travels from the cabin where the deceased person had lived to the slave burial ground tucked in a dense evergreen grove. Evanescent wooden posts marked where the dead lay entombed. Olmsted witnessed a simple iron hoe used to dig a fresh grave around the protruding tree stumps and cypress knees; this was all that remained of the cypress swamps reclaimed for tidal rice fields.[56]

Kemble had characterized London's speech as plain and rustic, the "peculiar sort of jargon which is the habitual negro speech." Tubman's account of the slave funeral on the Sea Islands is peppered with words from what is today called Gullah Geechee, such as "shum," meaning "see him," and "buckra," which denoted white folks. The unfamiliar scene and sounds must have made a strong impression on Tubman for her to remember the vocabulary so many years after the end of the Civil War.[57]

The Sea Island funeral Tubman attended ended after the whole congregation moved around in a sort of solemn dance, which Tubman called a "spiritual shuffle." Members of the Beaufort refugee community would have called it a shout. As Tubman described it, the whole congregation went around shaking hands, calling each other by name, and improvising a spiritual song:

> My sis'r Mary's boun' to go;
> My sis'r Nanny's boun' to go;
> My brudder Tony's boun' to go;
> My brudder July's boun' to go.

Unlike Charlotte Forten, who reported never participating in a shout nor being invited to participate in one, Tubman joined in. The refugees recognized that Tubman was a "stranger" but nonetheless included her in the circle dance and song, singing when they came to her: "Eberybody's boun' to go!"[58]

Tubman was immersed in a new and unfamiliar world in the South Carolina Lowcountry. Blacks in Maryland and Blacks in South Carolina and Georgia were descended from different western African peoples, who spoke different indigenous languages. Throughout the colonial and antebellum periods, they had been exposed to varieties of English by European and American slave traders, slaveholders, and overseers. By the Civil War, English-based Creole languages still thrived on the rice plantations, on the Sea Island cotton plantations, and in the urban centers of coastal South Carolina and Georgia. Lowcountry Creoles in these areas started to share common religious and spiritual beliefs, such as the ring shout. Nonetheless, the transformation of Lowcountry Creole languages and cultures into what is today called Gullah Geechee wasn't complete until the early twentieth century. Creole languages had previously existed in Maryland's Chesapeake region and other areas of the US South but had all but died out in the eighteenth century. In any case, Tubman spoke the English language very differently from the Lowcountry refugees she lived and worked among: "Dey laughed when dey heard me talk; an' I could not understand dem, no how."

★★★★★★★★

One morning in early January 1863, when the sounds of the birds in the evergreens far exceeded what one heard during a winter in Philadelphia or Boston, Charlotte Forten and another teacher named Lizzie Hunn went to Beaufort to buy bread. They spent almost the entire day with Tubman at her home in downtown Beaufort: Savan House, across from the arsenal. Despite their differences—or maybe because of them—Forten admired Tubman unabashedly. In her diary, she called Tubman "Moses" and described her as a "wonderful woman—a real heroine."[59]

Tubman knew Lizzie Hunn's father, John Hunn, an elderly Quaker from Middletown, Delaware, who had for decades been an Underground Railroad conductor. Fifteen years before, John Hunn had brought freedom seekers Samuel Hawkins and his family to Thomas Garrett in Wilmington, Delaware, en route to freedom in Pennsylvania; as noted in Chapter 5, Hunn and Garrett were charged, convicted, and fined for that assistance. And, of course, Garrett had assisted Tubman in approximately eight Underground Railroad rescues, including when she liberated herself and her parents. Historian Charles Blockson attested that Tubman also knew John Hunn well from their work on the Underground Railroad: "Harriet Tubman was well acquainted with this family ... for their homes were the first known railroad stops on her route to freedom." After the Battle of Port Royal, Forten sailed from New York with John Hunn and Lizzie Hunn. John Hunn came down to St. Helena and opened a store in a praise house, selling foodstuffs and used clothing to freedom seekers. The two young, single women roomed together beginning on their trip aboard the steamer and throughout their time on St. Helena. They taught school and occasionally tended John Hunn's store together.[60]

Forten reveled in the stories Tubman told her and Lizzie Hunn about how she freed enslaved people on the Underground Railroad after liberating herself, including how she hid freedom seekers in the woods during daylight while she went out and foraged for food. Tubman told them the story of an enslaved man named Joe, one of a group she was leading to freedom, whose description was posted by slave hunters, advertising a $1,500 reward for his capture and return under the Fugitive Slave Law. When Tubman told Forten and Hunn that when she let Joe know that they had reached Canada and was safe, he became possessed in a "perfect delirium of joy," springing to his feet, shouting, and clapping his hands "as if he were crazy." Forten was entranced. She had never experienced the horrors of enslavement, because of her privileged background. But she felt empathy for Tubman and everything she had been through, and she venerated Tubman for risking her freedom to liberate other enslaved people. Charlotte recalled that her eyes filled with tears as she took in the enormousness of the sacrifices made by "this heroic woman."[61]

Tubman told Forten and Hunn that enslavers in Maryland had put a $10,000 price on her head. This may indeed be what her friends and supporters had told Tubman in order to get her to move to Canada after the passage of the Fugitive Slave Act, but no evidence of such a reward has been found. In any case, Tubman's move out of US territory had been temporary. She took up again what Forten called her "good brave work" of helping freedom seekers, and that was why she was in Beaufort. In February 1863, General Hunter gave her free government transport around the Beaufort area and permission to purchase provisions from the commissary, which otherwise was granted only to US Army officers. Her pass read:

> Pass the bearer, Harriet Tubman, to Beaufort, and back to this place, and wherever she wishes to go, and give her free passage at all times on all Government transports. Harriet was sent to me from Boston, by Gov. Andrew, of Mass., and is a valuable woman. She has permission, as a servant of the Government, to purchase such provisions from the Commissary as she may need.

We know that Tubman used her pass and traveled to the government's commissary, where she purchased brown sugar from a private named John E. Webster on two occasions. Though she could not remember the amount she purchased on a later occasion, it was something like forty or fifty pounds. Tubman later told a biographer that she "made about fifty pies, a large quantity of ginger-bread, and two casks of root beer" at night and "would hire some contraband to sell for her through the camps" during the days after she refused to accept federal government rations, as noted in Chapter 9. Forten wrote in her diary that Tubman ran an "eating house"—an early form of the American restaurant—in downtown Beaufort. Tubman likely served prepared food and also cooked food that patrons brought in, providing a valuable service to Beaufort's refugee and abolitionist communities.[62]

At Tubman's home, Forten and Hunn encountered a Port Royal superintendent who was from Boston. He in turn took them to visit Esther Hawks, wife of Dr. John Hawks, surgeon of the 1st South Carolina. But Hawks had gone with her husband to the 1st South Carolina Volunteers' camp at Old Fort Plantation and so was not at home. Forten wrote in her diary that she had been sorry to miss seeing Hawks, but "very glad" that she had had the opportunity to see Tubman.[63]

By the time Charlotte Forten met her, Tubman was using her access to both Beaufort's refugee community and enslaved communities on neighboring islands to gather intelligence for the Union Army about the

locations of Confederate troops; information on resources, including enslaved laborers who could serve in and work for the military; and word
on the location of torpedoes in the rivers. The Union military was also
employing her to find men who knew how to navigate coastal Lowcountry
waterways. Her description of the shout at the torchlight funeral service,
earlier in this chapter, is evidence that Tubman's movements and networks
were not confined to the Beaufort refugee camps.

12

Forever Free

Charlotte Forten thought January 1, 1863, "the most glorious day this nation [had] yet seen." She rose early and took a carriage to the ferry, which she took from St. Helena Island to Beaufort. There she caught the *Flora*, which was crowded with passengers. Another steamship, the *Boston*, also brought people from Hilton Head. Some were Forten's friends and fellow northern abolitionists. Many of the passengers, however, were freed-women. They wore gaily colored handkerchiefs tied on their heads and gilt necklaces to adorn their Sunday or holiday best. Harriet Tubman may have been among them.[1]

They traveled four miles downriver from Beaufort. Upon arrival, the tide was too low for the *Flora* to dock at the landing, so Union soldiers transported Forten and the other passengers to the landing and to Camp Saxton on small boats, flats, and other makeshift watercraft. Located on Old Fort Plantation, Camp Saxton was the home of the 1st South Carolina Volunteers, the first regiment of Black soldiers mustered into the US Army. Camp Saxton was also the headquarters of its commander, Colonel Thomas Higginson. Throngs of people marched to the music the 8th Maine Volunteers band played as they wended their way into a grove of stately live oaks near the plantation's mansion (where, as we'll see, refugees from the Combahee River Raid were later housed).[2]

At Camp Saxton, soldiers from the 1st South Carolina greeted the in-coming guests. They were dressed in the same blue coats as their white counterparts, but the Black soldiers' trousers were bright scarlet. The soldiers disliked those trousers intensely, because they made it easy for the Confederates to spot them, as one of the 1st South Carolina Volunteers complained to Susie King Taylor: "The Rebels see us, miles away." The soldiers escorted guests from the landing to a grove adjoining the camp of some of the largest live oak trees Forten had ever seen, their gnarled branches and trunk draped with Spanish moss.[3]

Forten sat under the trees on a raised wooden platform facing the crowd. The soldiers marched in and stopped at the foot of the platform. It must have been an abolitionist's dream to see free Black soldiers in their uniforms. Looking out from the platform, Forten would have observed a sea of freedom seekers. Double-file lines of the 1st South Carolina, mounted on horseback, encircled the visitors. The placid Broad River loomed in the distance. The audience's excitement was palpable and contagious. For everyone present, the dream was only just beginning.[4]

After prayers and speeches given by various friends of the abolition movement, Colonel Higginson took the platform and introduced the Rev. Dr. W. H. Brisbane, a former slaveholder who had emancipated the people he held in bondage on Lawtonville Plantation in Beaufort. Brisbane's journey from slaveholder to slave emancipator had been a long one, with many twists and turns. Like most elite South Carolinians, he had been born into a class that believed people of African descent were created by God to labor as slaves. But he became proslavery forcers' worst nightmare—a former slaveholder who knew the master class and their arguments intimately and could counter them. In 1833, Brisbane, then twenty-seven and the pastor of Beech Branch Baptist Church, read an abolitionist pamphlet and began to question whether or not it was sinful for white men to hold Black people in bondage. He did not initially want to sacrifice his livelihood for his evolving convictions. Indeed, he wrote an essay published in the *Charleston Mercury* purporting to prove that the Bible sanctioned the enslavement of Africans and people of African descent. In 1835, Brisbane began editing the *Southern Baptist and General Intelligencer*, in which he published articles defending enslavement.[5]

But abolitionists' arguments gnawed at Brisbane. In 1835, he emancipated the people whom he held in bondage, permitting them to continue to work on his plantation. He fired the overseer, allowed the freedpeople to manage the plantation, provided for their needs, and promised to divide its proceeds with them. Brisbane's friends, neighbors, and peers subjected him, and the former bondspeople in his care, to abuse and even violence, claiming he was an abolitionist. Brisbane sold all but three of the people whom he had held in bondage to his brother-in-law and fled with his family and three of their former slaves for Ohio, where he became pastor of the First Baptist Church in Cincinnati in 1838. There he determined he had been wrong to sell his slaves. He spent more than half of his personal wealth to buy back all of the people—all but one man, who could not be found—he had formerly held in bondage, and move them to Ohio three years later.[6]

Brisbane and his family returned to Beaufort in 1849, then fled again, narrowly escaping a lynch mob. Afterward, he continued his campaign from exile in the Midwest. Brisbane would not return to South Carolina until after the Battle of Port Royal. In late 1861, he enlisted in the US Army as chaplain in the regiment in which his two sons were serving, the 2nd Wisconsin Cavalry, then became a tax commissioner in Beaufort in 1862. The Union Army relied on his reputation as a liberator who had risked everything. In an effort to rebuild lost trust among refugees seeking their protection, soldiers and officers invoked his name.[7]

On January 1, 1863, Brisbane, "a South Carolinian addressing South Carolinians," as Colonel Thomas Wentworth Higginson described Brisbane in his memoir, took his antislavery message directly to the freedom seekers gathered at Camp Saxton. From the speaker's stand, he read the Emancipation Proclamation issued by President Lincoln. Everyone cheered loudly at the declaration that the formerly enslaved were "forever free"; they may have been cheering at the promise of freedom for their family and friends who were still enslaved on plantations just beyond the bounds of Union occupation. On hand at the ceremony was the lone enslaved man whom Brisbane had not been able to buy back and free twenty-seven years earlier. This man had made his way back to freedom, and now Brisbane could speak directly to him.[8]

After Brisbane's speech, Reverend Mansfield French, the Methodist Episcopal minister who ran the US Army Department of the South commissary, presented Colonel Higginson with two flags for the 1st South Carolina Volunteers. The first, a silk flag with the unit's name and the message "The Year of Jubilee" embroidered on it, had been sent by Reverend Dr. George B. Cheever's congregation in New York. The second flag, a gift from a northern abolitionist, carried the words "1st Reg. S.C. Volrs. God gives Liberty to all," and in the middle a large silver hand bore the inscription "Presented to the 1st S.C. Volunteers by a Daughter of Connecticut." As Higginson received the colors and waved the flag, an elderly Black man broke out in song, his cracked and slightly hoarse voice blending with two female voices. Together, they sang "My country 'tis of thee, sweet land of liberty, for thee I sing." Higginson shushed white people on the platform to discourage them from joining in. This most affecting and inspiring tribute became the keynote of the entire celebration. Those witnessing the spontaneous tribute were moved to tears.[9]

Higginson made a few remarks and then handed the flags to the unit's color bearers, Corporal Robert Sutton and Sergeant Prince Rivers, who had been held in bondage by P. G. T. Beauregard, the Confederate officer of Creole descent who led the attack on Fort Sumter in April 1861. After receiving the colors of the regiment, Sutton and Rivers addressed the audience. Still, not even the sight of Black officers with gold chevrons on their sleeves, shiny gold buttons and stripes on their chests, gleaming swords at their sides, and sashes across their torsos could surpass in effect the sound of freedpeople singing for their country and their flag for the very first time. The program ended with the 1st South Carolina Volunteers soldiers and officers singing "John Brown's Body."[10]

After the program, there was a grand feast for the gathered people, who numbered between one thousand and two thousand. Ten oxen had been roasted for three hours, suspended over deep pits of burning oak wood. There was hard bread with molasses for dessert, then tobacco. Each company quenched its thirst with a barrel of water mixed with three gallons of molasses, half a pound of ginger, and a quart of vinegar. Soldiers and guests sat at crudely constructed wooden tables and ate with tin ware, their meals served by the unit's officers. The feast was for Black members of the audience—the soldiers, their families, and other freedpeople in attendance. By that point most of the northern volunteers had left, to return home by boat, carriage, and horse, but Charlotte Forten and several other volunteers dined at Colonel Higginson's table, along with Higginson's men.[11]

As Forten wrote, the "glorious day" ended with a dress parade of the 1st South Carolina Volunteers to music played by the 8th Maine Volunteers. Spectators would have reveled in the "long line of men," formerly enslaved men, "in their brilliant uniform, with bayonets gleaming in the sunlight." It was a "grand triumph" for the northerners who had left their homes and families to assist Blacks in Beaufort and on the Sea Islands in the Port Royal Experiment. Decades of abolitionist struggle had helped bring about this "first dawn of freedom," the *New York Times* reported the following day. In Forten's eyes, freedom would likely not break out everywhere all at once. But she now thought it might happen sooner than any of them had dared to imagine. The band played on as the boats taking the crowd back to Beaufort departed under the soft moonlight.[12]

Not everyone in Beaufort and on the Sea Islands participated in the festivities. Some freedom seekers absented themselves, including some who hid in the woods, as some of the white soldiers who held proslavery views told them that the celebration was an ambush. General Saxton, they said, planned to gather them all in one place and betray them to the planters who had held them in bondage. Memories of General Hunter's forced enlistments also engendered fear that once gathered, the men would be taken from their families and forced to serve in the US Army. One house servant remembered that when he was asked about the meaning of President Lincoln's Emancipation Proclamation, he picked up a broom, stood as if he was shouldering arms, and shook his head knowingly. He feared that the federal government wanted to put a musket in his hands and enlist him into the 1st South Carolina Volunteers, and that the violent seizures of young, able-bodied Black men carried out by Hunter in 1862 would be repeated. He was certainly not alone in having such concerns. Furthermore, proslavery attitudes persisted among some of the very federal government and military officials who were supposed to protect the freedom seekers. Lincoln had finally made their free status official, but now it was essential to bolster trust.[13]

★★★★★★★★

Within weeks after the Emancipation Proclamation went into effect, the US-occupied territory in South Carolina could boast two Black regiments. The US Army Department of the South authorized James Montgomery to raise a regiment of Black troops under General Saxton's direction two days after the Emancipation Proclamation celebration. Montgomery swore in an affidavit in his own postwar pension file that he was a resident of Mound City, Kansas, the seat of Linn County, and had been an early settler of the county. He had received a commission from the War Department on January 13, 1863, as a colonel; he then reported to General David Hunter for duty, and started efforts to raise a second regiment of the South Carolina Volunteer Infantry under Hunter's direction.[14]

Once Hunter left his post and Saxton was appointed as military governor of the Department of the South, some confusion arose about the commissioning of officers in the 2nd South Carolina Volunteers. According to

Montgomery, the War Department conferred on him the rank of colonel and instructed him to report to Major General David Hunter. Based on these orders, Montgomery raised the 2nd South Carolina and appointed officers to the regiment. Saxton, on the other hand, insisted that his August 25, 1862, instructions from the War Department gave him the authority to appoint officers to the 2nd South Carolina Volunteers, and Colonel Montgomery reported to him. Montgomery, the "mustering officer of this department," dissented in a letter to Brigadier General L. Thomas.[15]

Nonetheless, Saxton, Montgomery, and Secretary of War Edwin Stanton all agreed on one of Saxton's first appointments—that of Reverend Homer H. Moore as the unit's chaplain. Moore, an ordained Methodist Episcopal minister, was mustered in on January 31, 1863. He came highly recommended by multiple trusted sources, including the venerable Reverend French and three local ministers from Beaufort. Reverend Moore had been appointed chaplain at Jamestown, New York, and mustered into the service of the Union "by special authority from the Sec'y of War in endorsement on application to Brig. Gen. L. Thomas, Adj. Gen. from Beaufort, S.C." In a letter to General Thomas, Montgomery noted that Chaplain Moore's services were of "primary value to the regiment" and "second to those of no other officer in the regiment." Indeed, Moore's ministry was seen as vital to the five hundred Black men who had enlisted by the end of January 1863. As Colonel Montgomery wrote, the "religious element" that Reverend Moore provided was the "only foundation on which we can build in making soldiers of these freedmen." Chaplain's Moore's "policy" was to make the "regiment . . . a school," one in which the soldiers were taught "all the privileges & duties of social and civic life," not just military duty. General Saxton added his endorsement that Moore's services were "absolutely essential" to the soldiers of the 2nd South Carolina Volunteers and that "his influence had been all-powerful for good for these ignorant, simple-hearted people."[16]

While recruitment for the 2nd South Carolina was under way, the 1st South Carolina set off on its first expedition. Toward the end of January 1863, Higginson and four hundred men went forty miles up the St. Mary's River, located between Georgia and Florida, traveling in three steamers— the *John Adams, Planter,* and *Ben De Ford.* The steamers' time of departure from Beaufort was staggered. They rendezvoused at. St. Simon's Island.[17]

The *John Adams*, which would play a pivotal role on this mission, was actually an "old East Boston ferry boat" that had been built in Boston for the People's Ferry Company in 1854. It weighed 470 tons and was 145 feet in length and 65 feet in width. The Union Army quartermaster purchased the *John Adams* on November 24, 1862, for $36,000 and outfitted it with armaments that included a 30-pound Parrott gun, two 10-pound Parrott guns, and an 8-inch howitzer, creating its "own armed gunboat," though those guns were small relative to the 32-pound and 64-pound guns utilized by the navy. The vessel's fairly shallow draft (only seven feet) made it ideal for navigating narrow channels and sandbars. The double-ended ferryboat skillfully navigated the river's sharp angles as it cut through the obstructions thrown in its path. Higginson marveled that the "powerful paddles, built to break the Northern ice, could crush the Southern pine as well."[18]

Whereas the *Planter* and its worn-out machinery proved useless on this expedition, Higginson heralded the *John Adams* for fighting its way up and down the St. Mary's River. It was one of the most dangerous rivers in the Department of the South because of its forceful current and torturous channels, which easily could have been choked by felled trees and branches. The "narrow and rapid stream," as Colonel Higginson described it in his memoir, was bordered on each side by steep wooded bluffs. The *John Adams* also protected the troops from the "sharp shots" spilling down on them from the Confederates perched on the high bluffs. Many more 1st South Carolina soldiers would have been killed had they not been kept below-decks; the *John Adams* transported 250 soldiers in its "very scanty quarters," and inside the vessel's hull the soldiers jostled each other for positions in front of portholes through which they could continue to fire. Nevertheless, by the end of the mission the vessel's "very conspicuous" twin "pilot houses" were riddled with bullets.[19]

As the *John Adams* progressed, the troops carried the regimental flag and the Emancipation Proclamation, which they read to the enslaved people they came upon. The expedition was considered a success. Colonel Higginson and his men had skirmished with Confederate cavalry units three times, killing twelve Confederate soldiers and wounding an unknown number. Moreover, they plundered railroad iron from St. Simon's and Jekyll Islands, and lumber from the St. Mary's River; they gathered sixty-seven Confederate prisoners and a number of new Black recruits, a Confederate flag, and cannon. They also collected other items that were useful to the

Union cause, like bricks, rice, resin, cordage, oars, and a flock of sheep. Higginson had been adamant about only taking Confederate property for the US Army's use, and he prohibited any wanton destruction. He did not allow individual soldiers or officers to appropriate anything for their own use. Higginson would have been willing to make one exception: a piano from one of the storehouses located along the river. Crated and ready to go, it would have been a perfect gift for Charlotte Forten's school on St. Helena Island. As it turned out, however, there was not enough space for it in the gunboats and steam transports' holds, and they had to leave it behind.[20]

Higginson noted in his official report on the St. Mary's expedition that despite the rules against seizing property he did allow "instruments of torture" and the keys to the slave jail, a "villainous edifice," to be removed from Alberti's Mill. Corporal Robert Sutton—one of the commissioned officers who had addressed the audience and received the regiment's flag at General Saxton's Emancipation Proclamation Celebration—had been held in bondage by the Alberti family on the Florida side of the St. Mary's River. He personally led the troops there and confronted his former enslaver. Seeing African American men in the uniform of the Union Army was what Higginson called the "last crowning humiliation" for the Confederates. The 1st South Carolina soldiers also confiscated chains and shackles as relics of the "infernal barbarism" of the institution of enslavement, which the Union was fighting against.[21]

Higginson reported to his wife that the 1st South Carolina had made "one of the most daring expeditions of the war" and that his men "behaved splendidly," displaying the utmost respect and restraint, when they were faced with Confederate civilians. Unit surgeon Seth Rogers wrote to his wife that Confederate civilians—"the secesh," as the freedom seekers called them—expressed "horror and dread" at seeing former slaves, and sometimes the very individuals they had held in bondage, now in positions of power over them. One 1st South Carolina soldier reported to Charlotte Forten that some Confederate women had called the Black troops "baboons in soldiers' clothes" and told them they should be working in their enslaver's rice fields or lashed to death, rather than harassing white women and children. The troops just laughed. Forten, for one, rejoiced that the 1st South Carolina had come back heroes "with laurels." She wrote in her diary on the night the regiment returned to Camp Saxton: "My heart is filled with an exceeding great joy to-night!"[22]

The weight of the entire experiment of enlisting Black men rested on the shoulders of the 1st South Carolina Volunteers, and they bore it well. Colonel Higginson wrote in an official report that he firmly believed that the key to winning the war was the "unlimited employment of black troops" who knew the country and had the "peculiarities of temperament, position, and motive which belongs to them alone." They were fighting for their homes and families. Now that the men had had a taste of active duty, they wanted to be "constantly employed." Rogers wrote to his wife: "Give us a good gunboat and plenty of ammunition" to get the troops into the interior, where more Blacks were still held in bondage, and they could "trust God and our determination for the result."[23]

The Union Army now knew that these soldiers could and would fight, and could be trusted not to retaliate against the planters who had held them and their kin in bondage. The question was how to recruit more of them.

★★★★★★★★

As the 1st South Carolina finished up its initial expedition, Colonel Montgomery was in the early stages of filling the 2nd South Carolina Volunteers. Some who had escaped enslavement in Beaufort after the Battle of Port Royal joined even before the regiment was formally organized. Edward Bennett was one of Montgomery's earliest recruits. Bennett had been born free in Charleston around 1831. His status may have followed from the "yellow" skin he had inherited from one of his parents. At approximately twelve years of age, he was taken to Beaufort by a German man, Henry Hauseman (who could have been his father), and worked for Hauseman until he was an adult. In Beaufort, he was also taught carpentry.[24]

After war broke out, Bennett went to work (probably as a carpenter) on the *Pawnee*, one of the Union warships involved in the Battle of Port Royal. After a short time, he was put to work on the *Wabash*, the Union Navy's flagship. Bennett subsequently enlisted in the 2nd South Carolina Volunteers, Company D. He testified in his pension file after that war that he was "with the 2nd South Carolina for several months before we were mustered into service" and that he had served "three years and nine months" by the time he mustered out on February 28, 1866. If his memory was correct (his affidavit is dated 1871, so only five years later), his service with the military service would have begun in February 1862, though Bennett's pension file states that he enlisted March 24, 1863.[25]

We know from the pension files that three other men joined Bennett before the 2nd South Carolina Volunteers was mustered into service. Jacob Campbell had been born around 1822 and raised in Walterboro, South Carolina, twenty or so miles inland and due north of Beaufort. He had made his way to Charleston early in the war, then—according to his file—"took a small boat to Beaufort." He served in Company D with Edward Bennett before the regiment was mustered in; he was then transferred to Company H, where he served out his enlistment. Henry Smith was born in Charleston around 1835. He escaped enslavement and went to Beaufort, where he joined Colonel Montgomery's regiment in 1862. Alfred Fripp, the third man, enlisted in 1862 under Captain Levi H. Markley. At fifty, he was the oldest of the three.[26]

There were few willing recruits to be found in South Carolina after Montgomery's initial arrival at the end of February 1863. According to Captain (later Lieutenant Colonel) William Lee Apthorp of the 90th New York Regiment—a graduate of Amherst College born in Georgia to a mother from New England Puritan stock and a father who was the first Congregational minister in Iowa—Montgomery's operations "began with one hundred and thirty colored men recruited in Key West." Montgomery's Key West recruits included David Taylor. The interviewer from the WPA who recorded the life history of Taylor's son in the 1930s described his speech as "a queer mixture of geechy, sea terms, and broad 'a's' acquired by long association with Nassau conchs." The younger Taylor remembered that Montgomery had gone down to Key West and "took advantage" of the slave owners there by sowing "discord" among the enslaved populations. Many enslavers from elsewhere in the South had fled with their enslaved property and livestock and taken a chance on a fresh start in the Florida wilderness still inhabited by Native Americans, where they figured they could hold people in bondage whether or not the South lost the war. Pierre Pinckney, the man who enslaved Taylor, as well as Taylor's parents and nine siblings, was a prime example. Taylor remembered that Pinckney had forced them to flee Virginia; he angled to get his family and property on a boat to St. Augustine, but ended up in Key West.[27]

On February 7, 1863, the assistant adjutant general of the 10th Army Corps, under the command of General Hunter, wrote to Colonel Joseph S. Morgan of the 90th New York (the same regiment Apthorp was in) in Key West, where the 90th was on garrison duty and Morgan was in command.

He instructed Morgan to send to Colonel Montgomery at his headquarters, via the steamer *Cosmopolitan*, "every adult negro man between the ages of 15 and 50" within his command who was "capable of bearing arms." A few days later, Morgan issued Special Orders No. 6 of the US Army Department of the South, requiring all men of African descent between the ages of fifteen and fifty who had not already enlisted in the Union Army to report to the courthouse in Key West. The men were to undergo a medical examination in preparation for their embarkation to Hilton Head aboard the *Cosmopolitan*. Those determined capable of bearing arms would be enlisted in Montgomery's regiment and sail to Hilton Head. David or Daniel Taylor, the younger David Taylor's father, "jined de Yankees," one of Montgomery's first recruits in Key West. He enlisted in Company E of the 2nd South Carolina Volunteers in February 1863, one week before Colonel Morgan issued Special Orders No. 6.[28]

William Riley also answered the call and enlisted on February 13, 1863, in Company B. He was born around 1829 and held in bondage by Sarah Cuthbert on her farm about twenty-one miles from Beaufort. Cuthbert had also enslaved Riley's father, Billy Riley, and his mother, Nannie. Sometime after the Battle of Port Royal, Riley ran away to Beaufort and worked as a cook for a white "Yankee Rgt." This was the 90th New York under Morgan. Riley went with the regiment when it was sent to Key West and stayed with it there for six or seven weeks. On June 28, 1902—nearly half a century after the events in question—William Riley testified in his pension file: "I joined with Col. Montgomery. I joined Co. B" of the 2nd South Carolina Volunteers. Montgomery made up the remainder of Company B, as well as Companies C through F, with men from Beaufort and the Sea Islands.[29]

★★★★★★★★

Back in Beaufort, the commanders of the 2nd South Carolina Volunteers began to take the measure of their men. On February 24, 1863, seven weeks after the Emancipation Proclamation celebration at Fort Saxton, surgeon Seth Rogers wrote to his wife that Montgomery's arrival from Key West with the "nucleus of the Second S.C. Volunteers is an event of importance to our life here and also to the history of the war." Rogers recounted that he had heard Colonel Higginson declare that simply on his own Montgomery was "equal to one regiment." He confided to his wife that he had never before heard Higginson "express deeper confidence in anyone."[30]

Part of Montgomery's mystique was likely his appearance. The colonel was tall and slender, with distinct features, dark brown curly hair, and a penetrating gaze. His wife, Clarinda, wrote in an affidavit for her widow's pension in October 1889 that her husband stood over six feet tall and was broad in the shoulders. John Francis, who knew Montgomery as an older man, after his retirement from military service, remembered him as generous, kind, very social, and pleasant. He thought Montgomery had an "effeminate"-sounding voice, "soft, smooth, and gentle." When he met Montgomery, Rogers probed his background; he was rewarded, he said, with a "wonderful autobiography" of a "born pioneer." Some of this story we've seen earlier. Montgomery had been born on the "frontier" in the free state of Ohio, in the northeastern town of Ashtabula, located on Lake Erie. He identified two antislavery congressmen from Ohio—Joshua R. Giddings, a member of the House of Representatives who also lived in Ashtabula, and Benjamin F. Wade, a senator—as two of his earliest influences. Both Giddings and Wade were champions of abolition and free-state legislation. Both began their careers as lawyers, partners in a thriving practice in Jefferson, Ohio, the county seat. Theirs was the largest legal practice in what was called the Western Reserve in the late 1820s through the mid-1830s, with clients in Ashtabula, Trumbull, and Geauga Counties.[31]

Giddings, the senior partner in Giddings & Wade, began his career as a Whig, then became a Free-Soiler, and ultimately a Republican. He served one term as an Ohio state senator and then served in the US House of Representatives from 1838 until 1859. What Giddings described in his diary as the "barbarous spectacle" of sixty-five men, women, and children chained together in a slave coffle on a downtown street in the nation's capital, a slave driver cracking a whip over their heads, may have impelled the former colonizationist to take a much more radical and sectional stance against slavery. Giddings resigned his seat after the House censured him for upholding the freedom of the captives who in 1841 revolted aboard the slave ship *Creole* and liberated themselves, but his constituents voted him back into office in a special election. In 1854, Giddings made an impassioned speech urging his colleagues to act by describing in graphic detail the institution of enslavement, extension of which the Kansas-Nebraska Act proposed. He predicted that allowing popular sovereignty in Kansas and Nebraska would only be the beginning of the institution's advancement; it would not be long before the country witnessed bloodshed over the issue of slavery.[32]

By then, Senator Wade had endorsed an appeal written by Representative Giddings and Ohio's senior US senator, Salmon P. Chase, protesting that the Kansas-Nebraska Act's extension of slavery involved the "repeal of ancient law, and the violation of solemn compact." Once the Kansas-Nebraska Act passed, Giddings surmised that only successful slave insurrections under the "bloody apostle of abolition," as he called John Brown, would resolve the slavery issue.[33]

Wade, the junior partner for the duration of his partnership with Giddings, had been a radical from the beginning of his career. Growing up in rural poverty had impelled him to fight for enslaved and freed-people's rights, not only abolition but full citizenship for Blacks; he also supported women's suffrage. Wade began his career as a Whig while promoting Free Soil principles. He gained a reputation as one of Ohio's most outspoken proponents for the rights of Black people, first in the Ohio Senate and then in the US Senate. Despite the fact that Wade lost his seat in the Ohio Senate in large part because of his determined and vocal stance on the "Negro question," according to the Ashtabula *Sentinel*, he never backed down. He helped win repeal of Ohio's 1839 Fugitive Slave Law. He tried to amend the Black Codes almost simultaneously, using his impassioned speeches and parliamentary maneuvers. During the Kansas-Nebraska debates, Wade gave a speech on the US Senate floor reprinted in newspapers around the country. He called his southern colleagues out for their hypocrisy in refusing to stand behind the solemn compact of the Missouri Compromise. Wade's attacks marked him as one of the Kansas-Nebraska Act's chief opponents and one of the Senate's best debaters.[34]

These, then, were the men the young James Montgomery looked up to. Abolitionists like William Lloyd Garrison were theorists of radical abolition. In contrast, Giddings and Wade took action in Congress, chipping away at the expansion of slavery into the Western territories. Montgomery himself was also the opposite of a theorist. In Kansas, he and his Jayhawkers took up arms on the front lines, preventing the Border Ruffians from bringing their slaves into the territory. He organized free-state fighters to go into Missouri and retaliate in self-defense, becoming a "Kansas hero." Colonel Higginson, for one, was certain that whatever Montgomery did would be found to be "right when; it is understood." But it might take a long time for his actions to be understood, and history would be the judge. Higginson had written to his wife on March 16, 1863, that in 1860 Kansas Montgomery had been "a noble person." Three months later, Higginson would first laud Montgomery again for one series of actions in South Carolina, then condemn him for a subsequent choice.[35]

Abolitionist circles in New England had been "watching Kansas hopefully and lovingly," as Lydia Maria Child wrote in an impassioned letter to Montgomery in December 1861, addressing him as "dear honored friend," though she had never met him. She knew of his service in Kansas and his staunch support of John Brown. She wrote that she had no desire to work for the Union Army so long as soldiers were returning contrabands to the Confederate citizens who held them in bondage. Child wondered if any US Army regiments, except those in Kansas, could be trusted to protect the "poor hunted slave." She knitted socks and mittens and sewed suspenders for Montgomery's regiment, putting her heart into every stitch.[36]

For his part, Dr. Rogers also concluded shortly after meeting him in early 1863 that Montgomery was "one of the John Brown men of destiny." From their conversations he came away convinced that James—the two tentmates were on a first-name basis after just a few hours of conversing together—was an "inborn gentleman." The organizing work done by radical abolitionists in New England paled in comparison to Montgomery's "lusty life on the frontier," which had prepared him, even propelled him, to be a fierce warrior in the fight against slavery and its expansion. Rogers was convinced that Montgomery was a natural-born leader who had "fought many battles, but never surrendered." Montgomery was not the "slow, calculating sort" of man like Edward L. Pierce, who had told young Seymour Severance that the northern volunteers had to act cautiously, within the limits of the federal government's incremental steps related to the freedom seekers. Rogers admired Colonel Montgomery for trusting "his intuition more than his calculations." In the letter to his wife Higginson continued by praising Montgomery's "military experience," which he thought would be of "unspeakable value" to him.[37]

Montgomery's assumption of command of the 2nd South Carolina Volunteers would change the course of the war for the formerly enslaved.

★★★★★★★★

The ranks of the 2nd South Carolina were slowly but surely growing. Montgomery wrote in an affidavit in his pension file that he began

recruiting around February 21, 1863, to fill his regiment with soldiers so
that it could muster in. Two days later, Higginson speculated that the 1st
and 2nd South Carolina Volunteers would go out together on expeditions,
and that he would again be in command. It didn't take much longer to fill
out the 2nd's ranks: according to Montgomery's pension file affidavit, he
officially started his active command on February 26.[38]

In his February 23 letter Higginson had described Montgomery's sol-
diers as "all Key West men," though actually Montgomery had recruited
his first soldiers in Beaufort before any additional recruits arrived from Key
West. Montgomery also had already recruited officers in Beaufort. In his
account of his service in the Second South Carolina Volunteers, Captain
Apthorp wrote that he had been appointed captain of Company B on
March 3, 1863, having previously served in Company D of the 90th New
York Infantry, in which he had enrolled as a private on October 4, 1861.[39]

On the same day as Apthorp's appointment to Company B, Augustus
Alonzo Hoit, 38, was appointed captain of Company A. Hoit had enlisted
on September 5, 1861, in Augusta, Maine, with the 8th Maine Volunteer
Infantry, which had formed part of General Thomas Sherman's forces during the Battle of Port Royal. General Saxton characterized Hoit's company,
Company G, as "one of the best companies" of the 8th Maine. So he convinced Hoit to resign from it, detailed him to assist with recruiting Black
men to the regiment, and commissioned him in the 2nd as a senior captain
with the promise of another promotion when there was a vacancy in the
regiment.[40]

Operations were already being discussed. In the aftermath of the St.
Mary's expedition, Higginson and General Saxton planned a second exped-
ition, this time on the St. Johns River in Florida. The 2nd South Carolina
Volunteers were ready for duty, though Apthorp wrote in his journal that
Colonel Montgomery's Key West recruits were "just clothed and not yet
armed." Nonetheless, Montgomery and the 2nd South Carolina accom-
panied the 1st South Carolina Volunteers, with both regiments under
Higginson's command, on an expedition to Florida.[41]

Jacksonville was an attractive target. A port city located on the St. Johns
River, it could provide an entry point to strike into what Rogers called the
"heart of Florida." The US Navy had gained control of the St. Johns River
early in 1862 and had begun running patrols up as far as Palatka, but the
US Army had not gained a foothold on land in the fifteen months since

then. With a successful attack on Jacksonville, Higginson's men could access those enslaved in the interior and make war on slavery. North Florida also supplied the Confederate Army with food and provender, so seizing Jacksonville would interrupt that source of supply.[42]

It seemed like a logical operation. Several of Colonel Higginson's men knew the river well from being held in bondage on plantations along the St. Johns (according to their commander, two of the 1st South Carolina soldiers who had escaped enslavement on the St. Johns River would point out where they had "seen their brothers hanged by Lynch law"). In addition, the commanders had intelligence that Confederate military presence in the area was light. General Saxton sent the troops to entrench the US Army in the city and surrounding countryside and to establish a post of Black troops, from which to communicate with the people still in bondage on nearby plantations and to liberate, enlist, and arm the men who would flood into US-occupied territory.[43] (Ash 2008, 73–74, 76–77, 144)

In the first few days of March 1863, approximately 900 Black soldiers—775 from Higginson's 1st South Carolina Volunteers and the remainder from the first two companies of Colonel Montgomery's 2nd South Carolina Volunteers—embarked on the St. Johns expedition. Union ships on blockade duty escorted three steamers—including, again, the *John Adams*—over the difficult sandbar in the river; they also looked out for torpedoes. Later Susie King Taylor would travel frequently aboard the *John Adams* with the 1st South Carolina officers and soldiers when it went between Jacksonville and Cole Island and Folly Island in South Carolina. She remembered that the gunboat had a skilled gunner who was "always ready to send a shell at the enemy."[44]

In addition to his regiment, Higginson also commanded five companies from the 8th Maine and four companies of the 6th Connecticut that reinforced them. The arrival of the white troops put four regiments under his command, half of which were white and half Black. Thus, the 1st and 2nd South Carolina were the first Black regiments in US Army to fight alongside white soldiers. At first the soldiers were suspicious of each other. Some white soldiers resented having to fight alongside Black soldiers, doubting that they would fight. Officers reminded the white soldiers that the men of the 1st South Carolina had already fought in the St. Mary's expedition, and fought more bravely than any white soldiers ever had, first for themselves and their families to be free and then for the Union cause.[45]

They landed at Jacksonville, meeting little Confederate resistance besides a few skirmishes. Once there, though Higginson commanded the troops, Montgomery acted unilaterally and in ways that Higginson thought "splendid, but impulsive and changeable." He chided Montgomery for not planning ahead and going off on a "tangent" when he moved out in advance of Higginson and the remainder of the troops. Higginson had planned to go upriver and occupy a point up the St. Johns River. Montgomery and his men were to have followed the 1st South Carolina's advance. Instead, Montgomery boarded a steamer and took 120 of his soldiers seventy-five miles upriver to Palatka, to strike directly at the place where a critical mass of men were fleeing bondage and attempting to get to the Union-occupied territory downriver. He may have wanted his men to get their feet "blistered"—that is, toughened up—since many of those who had enlisted in Key West had likely never walked more than eight miles at a time around the island. Or he may not have wanted his men to take up Higginson's rear. Whatever his reasoning, Montgomery and his men landed at a place called Federal Point and proceeded to the town of Orange Mills. When they arrived at a plantation, they proclaimed the enslaved people free, according to the terms of the Emancipation Proclamation, and confiscated all of the human property they could. Saxton wrote to Secretary of War Stanton on March 6, 1863, reporting that he had sent the 1st and 2nd South Carolina Volunteers up the St. Johns River: "I have reliable information that there are large numbers of able-bodied negroes in that vicinity who are watching for an opportunity to join us." Montgomery was eager to seize the opportunity to get to the freedom seekers in the interior and bring them to freedom.[46]

Montgomery and his men took Confederate fire a few days later near Palatka; Higginson wrote in his journal that Montgomery had "landed incautiously" and was subsequently fired upon. Montgomery resisted the desire to burn the town; historian Stephen Ash surmised that it was because he planned to seek retribution elsewhere. On a plantation owned by a Confederate officer named Dupont, Montgomery encountered the officer's wife and the people she held in bondage. He took fourteen Confederate soldiers prisoner, along with all their arms—they had been sleeping on picket duty—freed more enslaved people, and took several thousand dollars' worth of cotton, horses, rifles, and other property. Though Montgomery had struck out on his own without orders from his commander, Higginson wrote in his notebook that Montgomery elevated the "up-river raids" to the "dignity of a fine art."[47]

By March 10, Higginson's men had captured the city of Jacksonville. General Saxton wrote to Secretary Stanton that the Black soldiers had conducted themselves with "utmost bravery." But Saxton's dream of maintaining control of Jacksonville and using it as a foothold to establish a chain of posts upriver along the St. Johns River to Palatka and out to Fernandina ended abruptly. On the same day that Montgomery returned from his expedition upriver to Palatka, Higginson received orders to evacuate his troops from Jacksonville. The US Army had already evacuated Jacksonville twice before, in March and October 1862. Now the commanders were concerned that without a Union gunboat, Higginson's nine hundred men could not hold the town. General Hunter also needed the 8th Maine and 6th Connecticut soldiers and the gunboats to fight in the planned siege of Charleston; he promised to send the 1st and 2nd South Carolina back to Jacksonville after the Union captured the South Carolina port. In the meantime, the *John Adams* would be used to transport coal for the US Navy.[48]

The soldiers and commanders of the 1st and 2nd South Carolina Volunteers were sorely disappointed and dejected. Worse still, they had to betray enslaved people who were coming in from all quarters, risking their lives to make it to freedom. By evacuating, they were abandoning them to the mercy of Confederate enslavers and the Confederate Army, which would certainly return them to bondage. Dr. Rogers wrote to his wife that the day the soldiers evacuated Jacksonville was "one of the sad days" in his life, the "burial of so many hopes," hopes he had "cherished for the oppressed."[49] (Ash 2008, 141, 177)

Before they left, however, the 8th Maine and 6th Connecticut soldiers ignored the US Army commanders' orders not to burn or pillage Jacksonville. As the 1st and 2nd South Carolina withdrew, following General Hunter's orders, soldiers from those other units did just that. Higginson was adamant that white soldiers, not his men, were responsible for the blaze set in the part of town where they were quartered. The fire destroyed approximately twenty-five buildings.[50]

The St. Johns raid, following on the St. Mary's expedition, shifted public opinion on the enlistment of Black troops. After the 1st South Carolina's successes, abolitionist friends and foes alike who had doubted whether the men from the Sea Islands had the requisite "pluck" to fight for their freedom and for the freedom of their race now admitted that their "latent manhood" had been "recovered its rightful sway." "It was their demeanor under arms," wrote Higginson in his memoir, "that shamed the nation into recognizing them as men." General Saxton was overjoyed at the 1st South Carolina's success. They hadn't flinched or panicked or resorted to cruelty when they met danger. Saxton thought they "seemed like men who were fighting to vindicate their manhood." And they did.[51]

President Lincoln—who had, as we've seen, rescinded General Hunter's original order to declare martial law and enlist Black men, needing to take things more slowly in order not to antagonize the border states—wrote to Hunter after the St. Johns expedition, telling him that he was pleased to read of the Black soldiers' success. He wrote to General Hunter acknowledging that it was important to the Confederacy "that such a force not take shape and grow and thrive in the South," but also that it was equally important to the Union "that it *shall*." So while the Confederates would make every effort to destroy the Black soldiers and their white commanders, in contrast the Union "should do the same to preserve and increase them."[52]

★★★★★★★★

So who were the Beaufort men in the 2nd South Carolina? We need to put names and faces to the story. Hector Fields, my great-great-great-grandfather, was one of the Beaufort men who joined Colonel Montgomery. Hector was born around 1836, possibly on Dr. James R. Verdier's plantation in Keans Necks in Beaufort, the oldest of at least three children. We don't know the location of Verdier's plantation, where Hector was held in bondage. Maybe it was in Keans Neck, where his brother Jonas testified he was born; maybe it was in Garden's Corner, where several people testified that Verdier owned a plantation and sold it before the Civil War; or maybe it was on Lady's Island, where Hector lived with his parents, Anson and Judy Fields, after the end of the war. As noted, Hector's younger brother Jonas Fields and their younger sister Phoebe Fields Washington were enslaved by Verdier. At some point Verdier gave or sold Phoebe to his daughter Sarah F. Verdier Sams, separating her from her brother Jonas (and possibly from their parents, whom Verdier also held in bondage, though it is not known if they were held in captivity with any of their children).[53]

Hector may have been separated from his parents and siblings or left them behind. If he was in bondage on Lady's Island, he would have been in US-occupied territory after "Gun Shoot at Bay Point" and the "Great

Skedaddle." If he was still in Confederate-controlled territory after the Battle of Port Royal, the sound of the guns, the whiffs of smoke, and the shock waves of the battle must have made it too tempting for him not to risk his life to get to freedom. In any case, he enlisted in the 2nd South Carolina Volunteers, Company C, on March 20, 1863. His military service record lists him as "height 5 ft. 7 inch, complex. Eyes & hair black."[54]

A few days later, William Fields (no known relationship to Hector, Jonas, Phoebe, and me) enlisted in Company D. Known as Billy during enslavement, he had been born on Parris Island and enslaved by Dr. Thomas Fuller. William's father, Hector Fuller, and his mother, Mintee, were also held in bondage by Fuller. William Fields testified in his pension file that he did not enlist in the Union Army of his "own free will." He "had just been married" to Emma Polite on October 26, 1862, when he was "forced to go by some soldiers and an officer, who came to Parris Island, SC," and took him and "10 others from our homes to Beaufort, S.C." He enlisted at Port Royal on March 24, 1863.[55]

John Green enlisted in Company D on the same day as William Fields. But he enlisted at Pigeon Point, a "mile out of Beaufort." Twenty-one years old and six feet tall, he had born and raised enslaved on Hugh Wilson's place on Wadmalaw Island.[56]

Samuel Gillard may have been among the ten men Union soldiers took from Thomas Fuller's Parris Island plantation along with William Fields. Gillard and his parents, Dan and Beck, were all held in bondage on Fuller's Farm. He was already a father of three and a skilled carpenter when the soldiers came. He enlisted as a corporal in Company E on April 10, 1863, two and a half weeks after William Fields, at Pigeon Point. Ten days later, also at Pigeon Point, Sharper Rivers enlisted in Company F under Captain John M. Adams as a recruiting officer. Rivers had been born on St. Helena Island, the legal property of Edgar Fripp. Though over six feet tall, at eighteen he was "only a boy."[57]

Friday Barrington, whom Edward Bennett described as a "small man," was likely born on the lower Chomabee River, probably on William C. Heyward's Cypress Plantation, around 1835. As noted in Chapter 4, on January 25, 1848, Dr. James Heyward sold thirteen-year-old Friday, his four-year-old sister Phoebe, and their parents, Tooman and Joan, to his brother William C. Heyward. The two brothers, James and William Heyward, may have transacted in slaves more than once between 1835 and 1848. After the

war, when Friday was working in the city stables in Charleston, he testified for his comrade Edward Bennett. In the pension file affidavit dated
February 8, 1901, Friday affirmed: "I was born and raised on the Combahee
and ran away early in the war." Friday testified in his pension file that he
"went to Beaufort with Col. Montgomery before the regiment was made
up." And he testified for Edward Bennett that he "served in Co. D with Sgt.
Bennett before we were organized," then likely enlisted along with Bennett
on March 24, 1863, though Barrington told the pension officer that he
could not remember the exact day in "spring 1863." Jacob Campbell corroborated Friday's testimony: "Friday Barrington was one of the men who
was with us before the Reg. was mustered into the US service & prior to
the time he & I served in Co D with Sgt. Bennett but when the Reg. was
mustered into service he & I were put in Co. H." We can deduce from the
files that Friday Barrington had escaped enslavement on Cypress Plantation
by the spring of 1863.[58]

★★★★★★★★

A few months after the end of the war, Colonel William Watts Davis
published his remembrance of the regiment he had served in, the 104th
Pennsylvania. That unit arrived in Beaufort on April 11, 1863. Davis described a "village green," with abundant potable water and trees offering
shade from the South Carolina sun, located just a few hundred yards from
the banks of the Beaufort River. Mockingbirds and other songbirds in cages
suspended throughout the area provided music and companionship.[59]

At that time, Beaufort was still the headquarters of the Department of
the South's humanitarian efforts, and the so-called Gideonites were still
supervising the labor of the freedpeople as they planted, harvested, and
processed Sea Island cotton, and still operating schools to teach literacy
and Christian values. In Davis's opinion, General Rufus Saxton was "nom-
inally at the head" of the Department of the South; Reverend Mansfield
French, he thought, was its "moving spirit." Like Seymour Severance almost
a year earlier, Davis was not hopeful about the progress of the Port Royal
Experiment. He thought that only a few of the northern volunteers had
unselfish motivations about helping freedpeople; most had come to coastal
South Carolina to serve "their own selfish ends."[60]

Two of the officers from the 104th Pennsylvania left that unit and received commissions in the 2nd South Carolina Volunteers a few weeks after

arriving in Beaufort. First Lieutenant James M. Carver was promoted to captain and Lieutenant Levi H. Markley was appointed as first lieutenant of the 2nd South Carolina on April 15 and 30, 1863, respectively. Both may have been persuaded to muster into the new Black regiments by the promise of promotion.[61]

From the Sea Islands to the rice fields, from coastal South Carolina to the St. Johns River in Florida, military recruitment brought together formerly enslaved men seeking to liberate others with white commanders seeking both to make war on slavery and to accelerate the advancement of their careers. It put guns in the formerly enslaved men's hands. Sea Island freedmen fought for the freedom of Blacks on coastal plain rice plantations who were still enslaved after the Emancipation Proclamation had gone into effect. Together, their courageous and honorable service in battle helped the nation to envision the future for four million newly freed people.

★★★★★★★★

On April 7, 1863, the long-awaited joint US Navy and US Army attack on Charleston began. The War Department's goals were to blockade the port and capture the city. Charleston, of course, possessed both strategic and symbolic value for the Union. It was the dominant shipping port in the South and, indeed, in the entire Confederacy. Its deep, expansive harbor accommodated most oceangoing vessels, including blockade-running vessels from the Confederacy's European trading partners, particularly Great Britain. Its location also made for easy connections to the railroads on which the Confederacy depended. In short, this essential transportation hub was critical to the Confederacy, maintaining its access to arms, munitions, and supplies and thus essential to sustaining its war effort. Furthermore, it was the birthplace of secession. From the moment the Stars and Stripes had been pulled down from Fort Sumter, the North's populace had wanted its military to take back Charleston.[62]

Ironclad vessels were to be involved in the fight to take Charleston. With their bulk nearly submerged under the waterline, they featured heavily armored turrets from which they fired at the enemy. They were uniquely effective but also uniquely vulnerable—an explosion underwater could cause the top-heavy ships to either flood or capsize, either way quickly becoming death traps for the crew. The Confederates' ironclad, the *Virginia* (formerly the CSS *Merrimack*), sank two wooden Union vessels at the Battle of Hampton Roads in early March 1862. With slanting sides on its 24-inch-thick casement, which was covered with four inches of armor and featured ten gun ports, the 4,000-ton vessel suffered only minor damage from the operation and prepared to finish off the federal fleet the following day. But the US Navy brought in the 987-ton *Monitor*, with one or two feet of free-board, a single iron revolving turret, and two XI-inch Dahlgren guns. In a two-hour bout—with a thirty-minute intermission—the two ironclads dueled at close range to a draw. This was the first-ever battle of ironclads in naval history.[63]

Two months after Hampton Roads, Assistant Secretary of War Gustavus Fox began pushing for the use of ironclads in a siege against Charleston. When planning began in earnest at the end of January 1863, Navy secretary Welles added the Union's first seagoing ironclad frigate, *New Ironsides,* and four other ironclad vessels—the *Passaic, Montauk, Patapsco,* and *Weehawken*—to Du Pont's command (Du Pont had been promoted to rear admiral by this time). The *New Ironsides* had been used in the Southeast coastal blockade, pursuing blockade-runners in the Atlantic near the West Indies. Once again, the Union Navy had assembled an impressive fleet—the siege of Charleston marked the first deployment of a fleet composed entirely of ironclads. In theory, the technologically advanced Union fleet could outgun the under-funded, poorly equipped, and significantly smaller Confederate Navy.[64]

The US Navy Department tried to light a fire under General Hunter—who had resumed command of the Department of the South after his re-placement, General Ormsby MacKnight Mitchel, died of yellow fever—by sending him and ten thousand soldiers to Port Royal, putting them into position to follow Du Pont's direction. Hunter dismissed the plan of one of his subordinates for a joint Union Navy and Army operation in which the army would capture Morris Island and Battery Wagner outside Charleston and construct batteries fortified with rifled guns on Cummings Island to counter the Confederacy's firepower. The navy's ironclads would have to take Charleston on their own, without the US Army's assist (though the army would take a supportive role). Secretary Welles later wrote to Du Pont emphatically that the capture of Charleston would rest "solely upon the success of the naval force." He "committed" the operation to Du Pont's "hands to execute."[65]

Charleston was not Port Royal. The US Navy would not catch the enemy unawares this time. The Confederate Army had been preparing for an attack by an ironclad US fleet at least since September 1862, a few months after the Union took control of the Stono River. Moreover, it had prepared for the defense of Charleston, including constructing rams, which could be built quickly and cheaply and which General P. G. T. Beauregard had argued would be more effective at countering the Union's ironclads. One young Union officer wrote to his mother and sisters in November 1862 that the Confederacy considered both Charleston and Savannah "impregnable." The Confederacy had begun reinforcing Charleston's principal defenses—Fort Sumter and Fort Moultrie—even before the first shots of the war were fired in April 1861, and they had ramped up their efforts after the Battle of Port Royal. To defend Charleston, the Confederates had lined the entrance of the channel from Fort Sumter to Fort Moultrie with obstructions, including ropes, logs, and kegs, leaving an opening only large enough for blockade-runners to pass safely through. An officer with the Confederate 5th South Carolina Cavalry commented that he did not think the Union would attempt an operation between the Ashepoo and Combahee Rivers, where his regiment was stationed.[66]

The War Department was not acquainted with the conditions on the ground—or in the water, in the case of the torpedoes planted by the Confederates. Thus the decision to go ahead with the plan was dependent on Du Pont—and on the reconnaissance of his spies, scouts, and pilots—as well as on Charles O. Boutelle, who commanded the US Coast Survey steamer *Bibb* (the US Coast Survey mapped the South Carolina coast and other essential areas along the southern coastline in support of the US Navy's implementation of the Southeast Atlantic Blockade). Secretary Welles wrote to Du Pont that he should move ahead with the siege if he thought torpedoes would not block the entrance of the fleet into Charleston. The War Department presumed that if the obstructions could not prevent the Union Navy from entering the harbor, Confederate firepower and manpower would not be strong enough to prevent it from achieving its goal.[67]

Du Pont wrote in his official report that he moved the *New Ironsides*, along with eight *Passaic*-class ironclads with seven single-turret monitor guns, across the bar and into Charleston's harbor. The *Weehawken* led the fleet and the *Keokuk*, a 677-ton experimental double-turreted ironclad with two XI-inch guns mounted in stationary drums, brought up the rear. Du Pont positioned *New Ironsides* in the middle of the fleet, to facilitate communication via signals to vessels on both of its flanks; the ironclads did not fly large flags, likely so that they wouldn't provide the Confederacy with a bull's-eye. According to the battle plan, the fleet was to sail down the channel past Morris Island without firing until they came within six hundred to eight hundred yards of Fort Sumter. Then they would turn and attack on the northwest side. After Fort Sumter was reduced, they would take on Morris Island. Once they had gained control of Charleston Harbor, the Union's ironclad fleet, as well as the US Army, would force Confederate forces to withdraw from the city.[68]

The warships sailed in line, three hundred yards between them. Each ship moved forward in turn, fired from its turrets, then moved back so as not to present a stationary target for the forts. There was trouble almost immediately. Fort Moultrie fired first on the Union fleet. Then Fort Sumter fired from its fifty-foot-high brick walls—walls that were designed to withstand a naval attack. The Confederacy's most powerful cannons lined its top tier, trained on the enemy vessels. If the Union ships made it past Fort Sumter, they would be forced to thread their way through a constricted channel with fire coming at them from all sides. Confronting yet more strong fortifications, shot, and shell would be the reward for making it safely through the strait.[69]

The *Weehawken* had an anti-torpedo raft, called the "devil" by the Confederates, that sat atop its prow and was designed to identify and explode torpedoes. But it had not been tested for efficacy, and it malfunctioned, causing delay. When the vessels resumed their movement up into the harbor, sailors observed buoys splayed out in different directions, indicating that there may have been underwater torpedoes in the area. In laying the torpedoes, the Confederates intended to slow down the Union vessels entering the channel, so that the powerful guns atop Fort Sumter's high walls had time enough to pound them. Both the US War Department and the Navy underestimated the Confederate's capacity in this regard, though a Confederate commander reported afterward that torpedoes and obstructions had played a very small role in the battle. However, a number of the exploding canisters hit their mark and did their share of damage. One of the torpedoes exploded close to the *Weehawken*, though no sailors were seriously injured.[70]

Had the Union fleet tried to move any farther into the narrow, constricted channel lined with torpedoes and obstructions, it would have made an easy target for the Confederate batteries lining the mouth of Charleston's harbor. Already the Confederate Army had opened "fierce" and "obstinate" fire from Fort Sumter and Fort Moultrie. Batteries at Cummings Point, Mount Pleasant, the Redan, and Fort Beauregard opened fire as well too. The US fleet was forced to turn around to retrace its path back through the narrow channel. But it was difficult to maneuver the enormous vessels—in which the pilot houses were the only lookout—and keep them from colliding into each other. Thick, acrid smoke further reduced visibility. Du Pont's crew lost control of the *New Ironsides* in the narrow channel due to the swift ocean current, disordering the ironclad formation. An onslaught of Confederate fire also prevented the *New Ironsides* from coming within a thousand feet of its target, Fort Sumter. It fell behind, then was forced to anchor to keep from running aground. The other ironclads got as close as they could, but not within striking distance, and finally fired at Fort Sumter's masonry walls. The Confederate Army's "tremendous concentrated fire" had kept them at bay.[71]

Du Pont decided to retire and renew the attack the following day. Five of the eight Union ironclads had been disabled in only forty minutes of battle. The *Nahant* was the most seriously damaged. Its turret was jammed and bolts on the turret and pilot house had broken off, preventing the turret from turning and firing effectively. Fire from Fort Moultrie and Fort Sumter had disabled the guns on the *Passaic*, *Patapsco*, and *Nantucket*. As a result, on that first day the Union fleet had been outgunned by more than fifteen to one. In addition, Du Pont reported, the Confederates spewed an "incessant storm of round shot and shell, rifled projectiles, and red hot shot" at their vessels from the top of Fort Sumter's walls. At one point, the *Keokuk* (which Robert Smalls piloted) came from behind and got within around nine hundred yards of the fort. All three of its batteries fired ten-inch shot and seven-inch rifle bolts, hitting the fort almost ninety times. The chaplain of the 3rd Rhode Island Heavy Artillery wrote to his brother after the siege that the 3rd Rhode Island had "let daylight through" Fort Sumter and "marred" Fort Moultrie. Yet the *Keokuk* was riddled by Confederate shot and shell, primarily at or below the waterline, and it had to retire to keep from sinking; subsequently, it sank anyway off the south end of Morris Island the following day, leaving only the smokestack and turrets visible at low tide. *Keokuk's* two Dahlgren guns, flags, pennants, and signal book (useful for intercepting federal code) became prized trophies for the Confederacy.[72]

Given the impassibility of the torpedoes, especially under fire, Du Pont determined that taking further action the next day would "convert a failure into a disaster." It might even enable the enemy to capture some of the ironclads, making it more difficult for the Union to blockade the southeast coast. After the Union did not renew its attack, one of the Confederate commanders said in a letter home to his mother and sisters: "We may have given them their fill."[73]

Du Pont wrote to General Hunter that "he had tried to take the bull by the horns, but he was too much for us." His official report maintained that the Union Army had given him "no cooperation." In fact, had the US Navy been able to reduce Fort Sumter, that would have set the stage for the army to get into the fight and add its fire. General Hunter had his men positioned on Folly Island, ready to enter Charleston Harbor through Morris Island if and only if the navy succeeded in taking the harbor. But the navy had not been able to do its part. Hunter proclaimed he was a "mere spectator" to the rain of "concentric fire" by the Confederate Navy, which was unparalleled in the "history of warfare." He could not do anything but pray for Rear Admiral Du Pont, which, he assured the admiral, he "did most heartily."[74]

Six weeks after the siege attempt on Charleston, General Hunter continued to hold Folly, Cole's, and Seabrook Islands, waiting for repair of the ironclads and Du Pont's next move. Hunter described the Confederate Army as "thoroughly aroused." They had fortified defenses on the island forts surrounding Charleston, making them ready to counter the Union Army's every move. The Confederate Army had sustained a larger number of casualties than Union forces. However, had the Union Army gotten into the fight or had the Union Navy renewed the attack, they could have faced significantly more loss of life.[75]

Du Pont closed his official report with an admission of the failure that overshadowed his spectacular victory at Port Royal and marked the end of an otherwise stellar career. He reiterated the misgivings he had articulated before the siege: "Charleston can not be taken by a purely naval attack." The navy had not given up on taking Charleston, but it needed a different strategy to do so. Furthermore, Du Pont presumed that the moment to besiege Charleston had also passed, because the sickly season was approaching; it was, after all, early April. For the time being, the navy's focus would shift back to blockading Charleston, keeping the Rebels off balance and anxious that a renewed attack might be coming at any time. But Welles's analysis was that for the siege of Charleston the US Navy had "made the most expensive and formidable preparations ever undertaken," and that Du Pont had abandoned the siege after only brief effort.[76]

After six weeks of inaction, while Du Pont waited for the ironclads to be repaired, Hunter begged leave from orders that the US Army Department of the South collaborate with the Union Navy on the siege of Charleston. He proposed his next move: marching ten thousand of the best-trained soldiers into the heart of Georgia to destroy railroad communications, then laying waste to all of the available resources in the countryside. Hunter believed that by avoiding the strongholds where the Confederate Army was well prepared to defend its territory, his men would meet little opposition. Thus he would force the Confederacy to break up its large armies and scatter to protect every assailable point in response to his attacks. Clearly, Hunter was still raring to move forward.[77]

But it was not meant to be. In the end, David Hunter seems once again to have been too far ahead of his time, as he had been earlier with the emancipation of slaves and the enlistment of Black men went. He was temporarily removed from command of the Department of the South on June 3, 1863. The change in leadership became permanent a few days later when Brigadier General Quincy Adams Gillmore replaced him as interim commander of the department. Gillmore was the engineer who had fortified the artillery batteries on Tybee Island and made the April 1862 bombardment of Fort Pulaski both feasible and successful.[78]

Rear Admiral Du Pont had faithfully served the US Navy for forty-seven years, but a successful siege of Charleston would require new leadership. He had been publicly critical of the ironclads—in which the US Navy had invested heavily—and was reluctant to take subsequent action against Charleston. Welles removed Du Pont as commander of the South Atlantic Blockading Squadron and replaced him with John A. Dahlgren, a career naval officer best known for developing the Dahlgren guns, heavy cast-iron smoothbore cannon that had become standard US Navy armaments by the early 1850s. Ultimately, the Union Army, not the Union Navy, would bring down Charleston.[79]

Until then, other places would provide the "proving ground of freedom." And one of the plans would involve Harriet Tubman.

PART THREE

The Combahee River Raid

"I was gwine to de boat,"

—Minus Hamilton, in Thomas Higginson,
Army Life in a Black Regiment, 1900

Combahee River Raid Route

Combahee River Raid Union

N W S

BONNY HALL

NEWPORT ⓙ

CYPRESS ⓘ

Combahee Ferry ⓗ

ⓚ

OAKLAND ⓖ

ROSE HILL

LONGBROW ⓕ

Stocks Road

PAUL'S ⓔ

EARTHWORKS

TAR BLUFF ⓓ

FIELDS POINT ⓒ

ⓑ

Mouth of Combahee River

Coosaw River

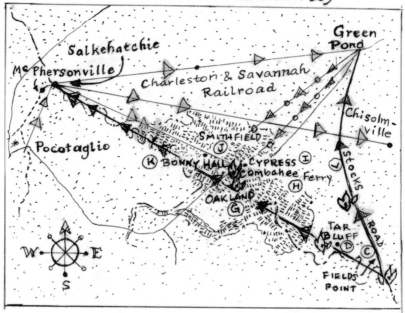

Combahee River Raid Confederacy

13

"A Pleasure Excursion"

In November 1861, six months after the start of the war, Confederate brigadier general R. S. Ripley wrote to Captain T. A. Washington, the assistant adjutant general, that "messrs. Walter Blake, Rawlins Lowndes, and Paul"—planters who all served as volunteer aides-de-camp—were endeavoring "to block" the Combahee, Ashepoo, and Pon Rivers "at some point below the railroad bridges." The planters had initiated this action after the Battle of Port Royal twelve days earlier. They may even have heard the Union Navy's bombardment as they sat on the porticos of their rice plantations on the Combahee. Likely, they had communicated by courier with their neighbor Colonel William C. Heyward, who had commanded the forces at Fort Walker during the battle. Heyward, after all, lived right next door to Rawlins Lowndes's brother Charles T. Lowndes. The plantations owned by William L. Kirkland Jr., who served in the Charleston Light Dragoons, and Joshua Nicholls separated Lowndes's Oakland Plantation from James L. Paul's plantation. Walter Blake's Bonny Hall Plantation was located on the other side of the Combahee. These local planters provided material assistance to Confederate Army units, and particularly to their commanding generals.[1]

One of them was Alexander Robert Chisolm, the owner of Chisolm Plantation on Chisolm Island (also known as Coosaw Island). Several years earlier, in 1855, when Alexander and his sister Sarah Constance Chisolm were co-owners of the plantation, among the 208 enslaved people listed in Sarah's marriage settlement were listed together, one after another, on two lines: Isaac Heyward's mother, Sibby; his brother Adam; Isaac himself; his brothers Joe, Kit, Buncombe, Oliver, and Gadsden; and his sister Matilda. The family grouping is listed again in an 1856 mortgage in which Samuel Prioleau Ravenel (acting as Sarah Constance Chisolm Thurston's trustee) sold 109 enslaved people to Alexander Chisolm and Alexander Chisolm mortgaged them back to his sister's trustee. After Sarah's death in 1858, Alexander became sole owner of the plantation and the enslaved people on it. In early 1861, at the request of the governor of South Carolina, he brought some of the men he held in bondage to Charleston to work on building fortifications at Morris Island. He offered to bring his own boatmen and oarsmen, and personally supervised the enslaved men's labors for the Confederate military. In return, Chisolm received a commission in March 1861. Nine months later, he was listed as first lieutenant and aide-de-camp on the personal staff of General P. G. T. Beauregard, the commander of the headquarters of the Department of South Carolina, Georgia, and Florida, and served Beauregard through the end of the war. But his plantation had already been attacked by Union forces: in a joint Union Navy and Army operation up the Coosaw River in December 1861, flatboats manned by Black boatmen and organized by an officer of the 50th Pennsylvania landed three thousand soldiers from the 47th, 48th, and 79th New York, 50th and 100th Pennsylvania, 8th Michigan, 5th Connecticut, and 15th Massachusetts Regiments and raided Chisolm Island. Freedom seekers whom they picked up on shore guided the soldiers inland.[2]

To protect their properties, Heyward, Chisolm, and the others used enslaved men to construct barricades (which may have resembled similar barricades used elsewhere, such as the "strong wooden piles across" the South Edisto River). Their ultimate goal was likely to block the rivers so that they could keep enslaved people from seeking protection under the US flag and stop the Union from ascending the rivers. The country surrounding those three rivers was so valuable because it was effectively one of the Confederacy's breadbasket. Plantations along South Carolina's tidal rivers produced two-thirds of the state's rice crop; the Confederate Army relied on such crops to support both the civilian population and the military, and all were produced by enslaved labor. In November 1861, the plantation owners went to General Drayton's makeshift camp, where Heyward's 9th South Carolina Volunteers were stationed, and offered use of their materials and their enslaved labor in defense of the area. It was a win-win proposition, as this would protect both their personal interests and the Confederate military's interests.[3]

Around that time, the Confederate Army's concern about the security of the Charleston and Savannah Railroad was mounting as well. Ripley had made it a priority to have troops protecting all of the railroad bridges going south toward Savannah. He also wanted the troops to be ready at a moment's notice to move north to protect Charleston or south to protect Savannah. General Robert E. Lee wrote to General R. S. Ripley on December 7, 1861,

that defense of the Ashepoo, Combahee, and Pon was of the "greatest importance" for "protection of the railroad." Lee recommended that Ripley's forces
prevent the Union from advancing toward the Charleston and Savannah
Railroad from the north by obstructing their path near the Stono River and
from the south by doing so at the Edisto River. However, he cautioned it was
unlikely that the batteries could be made strong enough, or that the troop
levels Ripley requested to secure the area could be made available.[4]

Earlier, on November 7, 1861, after the Confederacy's defeat at Port
Royal, General Ripley had ordered the Charleston Light Dragoons out
to Pocotaligo to defend the railroad. Founded in 1792 and incorporated in
1835, the Charleston Light Dragoons was one of Charleston's most prominent militia organizations. As an autonomous volunteer militia governed
by bylaws and funded by assessed dues, its members could select and recruit
new members, ensuring that it remained homogenous, consisting exclusively
of the Lowcountry's social and political elite—the oldest, wealthiest, and
most powerful families. Members had to supply their own horses, mounts,
and uniforms, making the cost of joining prohibitive to men of lower social
status. Although the blockade, the "Great Skedaddle," and Union raids had
diminished their net worth from prewar levels, the majority of the militia's
membership were still the region's largest rice planters and slaveholders,
along with their sons, nephews, and cousins, as well as factors and merchants
who sold their slaves and crops, as well as managed their profits. The Light
Dragoons enjoyed the privileges of serving with men who were their social
equals, and doing so close to their plantations, so they could oversee their
crops while in camp and draw on their plantations' produce to supplement
their government rations. Among the Charleston Light Dragoons were
Combahee rice planters William L. Kirkland Jr., Joseph Blake's son Walter
Blake, and Oliver Hering Middleton Sr.'s son Oliver Hering Middleton Jr.
Charles Tidyman Lowndes's only son, Rawlins Lowndes, was a member
until Colonel Wade Hampton appointed Lowndes to his staff.[5]

These planters, and the factors and merchants who catered to them,
had of course the most to gain—or lose—when South Carolina seceded
from the Union. From their founding, the Charleston Light Dragoons
displayed their skills in musters and acted as slave patrols to protect the
state's white residents from insurrections (or at least diminish their fears
of them). Neither function set them apart from other South Carolina volunteer militia, although they occupied highly visible and privileged positions in ceremonial events. When war broke out, they mobilized to protect

their wealth (in land and slaves), values, privilege, and way of life. However, even while serving the Confederacy, the Charleston Light Dragoons did not mix with militias whose members, in their view, did not match their social status. In May 1862, when the Charleston Dragoons were ordered by Colonel William S. Walker, commander of the Third Military District, to McPhersonville from Pocotaligo, they had to borrow several wagons to haul the large collection of furniture, boxes, trunks, iron bedsteads, tables, and chairs that the regiment had amassed and which the soldiers needed to maintain their lifestyle.[6]

While stationed in McPhersonville, the Charleston Light Dragoons were on picket duty between Combahee Ferry and Mackey's Point. To relieve the boredom and monotony of camp life, they played cards, raced their purebred horses against those of other cavalry companies, gambled, dueled (in a couple of instances, fatally), and enjoyed the hospitality—fine wine, generous banquets, and parties—provided by their own estates and those of family members and wealthy planters in the area, particularly on the Middletons' Hobonny Plantation and the Heywards' Bluff Plantation. In addition, they engaged in their favorite pastimes. William L. Kirkland participated in a hunt organized at William Heyward's deer enclosure. It was all, at least initially, a great adventure. Confederate commanders shielded the Charleston Light Dragoons, to whom they were inextricably bound by ties of blood and marriage, from fighting on the front lines and therefore experiencing the horrors of combat. As the war wore on, however, they could not shield the Dragoons anymore.[7]

From early in the war the Combahee seemed likely to become a front line. After General Lee had written to General Pemberton in December 1861 about placing obstructions in the river and reiterated his concern that the Union Army could reach the Charleston and Savannah Railroad by land. He recommended building more obstructions near the mouth of the river below Tar Bluff, where the Combahee was two hundred yards wide and at least forty feet deep. Blocking it would provide "more stability to the battery" and perhaps prevent the Union from ascending the river. Pemberton replied that this would require tremendous labor. Lee replied that he understood, but that "the planters interested in the project are willing to furnish labor and material." He meant, of course, enslaved labor.[8]

By early 1862, the Confederate Army had succeeded in constructing obstructions in the Combahee and in mounting two 12-pound cannons at

Tar's Bluff. However, the placement of the obstructions and the artillery did not solve the problem. Even with both in place, the Union Navy could still get within a little more than thirty miles of the Charleston and Savannah Railroad—entirely too close. It could also land at Field's Point, one and a half miles away from Tar Bluff, and potentially capture it. This was near enough for Union forces to reach the railroad by land. Lee recommended placing more obstructions. Walter Blake, Rawlins Lowndes, and James L. Paul must have known their vulnerabilities. They were willing to supply their own enslaved manpower and materials to undertake the "great labor," according to General Lee, of protecting their rice crops, whether they were ready to be harvested or had already been harvested and were stored in the rice barns awaiting processing and sale. Lee left the decision to General Pemberton's discretion.[9]

However, being a breadbasket of the Confederacy was not enough to keep the Combahee River at the top of the Confederate military's list of priorities. By mid-February 1862, protecting the region's rice plantations was secondary to defending the railroad. The Confederacy focused its energies on defending the Santee and Georgetown districts, two important rice-growing areas, in order to secure the army's subsistence. General Ripley assumed no more rice would be coming from the plantations along the Pon Pon, Ashepoo, and Combahee. He wrote to Captain W. H. Taylor, assistant adjutant general, that the region was already "well-nigh exhausted" of the resources that made it relevant to begin with, given that the rice crop had been harvested three or four months before and likely had already been fully requisitioned by Confederate forces. At this point, the Combahee River was important to the Confederacy mainly because it and the Ashepoo were the "weak point on the Charleston and Savannah road." If the Union Army made a "dash," they would have "comparatively no distance to march to cut the rail." And it was close to Charleston, which did not have enough boots on the ground to defend it. If Charleston or Savannah fell, the Confederacy would be consigned to the interior and forced to give up the coast, breadbasket and all.[10]

Ripley also assumed that the Confederacy could not hold the railroad around Coosawhatchie, Pocotaligo, Salkehatchie, or Ashepoo Ferry for "more than six or seven weeks longer"—nor could the Union if it managed to seize it. He must have been anticipating the onset of the sickly season. The Confederate military planned to send its troops to Adam's

Run, the Charleston area, and north to Grahamville, both "healthy regions." But Ripley's assumption was a costly miscalculation on several fronts. The sickly season began in late May, not the end of March. Rather than avoiding the rice plantations during the sickly season, the Union Army would seize the opportunity to take a shot at one of the Confederacy's weak spots.[11]

In late February 1862, Captain Ralph Ely's 8th Regiment of the Michigan Volunteers stumbled onto Combahee Ferry. Ely and twenty-two men left Lady's Island at Brickyard Point in three rowboats to conduct reconnaissance on the Bull River and Confederate forces in the area. After traveling nine miles down the Coosaw to the mouth of the Bull, they proceeded up Schooner's Channel to William's Island, where the regiment landed. Ely left the bulk of his troops hidden in a wooded area, then pressed on with a small contingent of his men. They followed the North Wimbee River until they were around twelve miles from the mouth of the Bull. Here Ely left his small contingent and sailed his own boat a mile up a branch of the North Wimbee with three men, landing on Robert Barnwell's boat landing. The proprietor may have been the same Robert Barnwell who had served as a delegate at the Confederate States of America's Provisional Congress in Montgomery, Alabama, in 1861, which undoubtedly qualified him as a "notorious rebel leader." His vote had helped elect Jefferson Davis as the first (and, as it would turn out, only) president of the Confederacy. Barnwell also signed the Confederate Constitution and was serving in the Confederate Senate when Captain Ely scoped out his plantation.[12]

In the vicinity of Barnwell's plantation, Ely encountered two freedom seekers, an elderly man who had come from Pocotaligo through Garden's Corner to Barnwell's plantation and a younger man who had come down to the coast with a "loaded team," presumably horses or mules hauling cargo, from Walterboro, approximately thirty miles inland and due north of the Combahee. Ely learned a great deal from the two men, who had likely very recently liberated themselves: fewer than a hundred Confederate troops were stationed at Garden's Corner; most of the troops there were recent arrivals; and only two Confederate soldiers were guarding as many as a hundred rowboats and flats at the bridge near Garden's Corner. The younger man provided intelligence about the nearest pickets: six were located a mile and a half away at a fork in the road connecting Garden's Corner and Combahee Ferry.[13]

With three soldiers and the younger freedom seeker as a guide, Ely probed further—to Combahee Ferry. Keeping to the woods, they passed the pickets at the fork in the road undetected. But the dense woods interspersed with streams and marshes proved too challenging. After traveling a mile beyond the fork, they turned around. Ely did collect additional intelligence, learning that approximately three hundred Confederate soldiers were stationed at Combahee Church, two miles from Combahee Ferry on the road to Garden's Corner, and that Confederate forces had mounted "two pieces of artillery, placed behind an earthwork and covered with pine brush." In the early morning, Ely, his freedom seeker guide, and his small contingent of men rejoined the others. Their boats retraced the path to the Coosaw River, and at Field's Point Ely spotted Confederate forces repairing the fort. On the left bank of the Combahee River, Ely saw "extensive rice fields on fire." Enslaved laborers may still have been burning the yellow straw-like stubble from the rice fields in preparation for planting the next crop in March or April, though this labor was typically done late in the fall or early in the winter, after the first frost. In the evening, the fires were "visible at a long distance."[14]

Captain Ely reported to General Isaac Ingalls Stevens, who complimented Ely on the valuable information he had gathered—that Confederate forces in the vicinity had recently been transferred and thus the remaining numbers were small, and that "the Combahee Ferry is made passable by flats, so the teams pass over as on a [pontoon] bridge"—and instructed him to explore the Ashepoo River. Stevens likely subsequently explored the Combahee River himself. He may have been the same General Stevens with whom Mary White testified in her pension file she and her husband, Parris White, "came away from Combahee with the first crowd of cold. [colored] people." He was certainly the same General Stevens in whose Beaufort headquarters Harriet Tubman worked. Mary White did not tell the pension officer after the war exactly when she had escaped enslavement on Bonny Hall Plantation, and neither did Jonas Green, Wally Graham, or any of the other people who liberated themselves from Walter Blake's plantations and went to Beaufort or Hilton Head. However, it was likely after February 1862, when Captain Ely made the first reconnaissance trip up the Combahee River.[15]

It would be another five months before Union forces visited Combahee Ferry, the Combahee River, or Field's Point again. However, Blacks enslaved on the lower portion of the Combahee River must have seen or heard word

of the Yankee soldiers. In addition to those who liberated themselves from
Walter Blake's plantations, this may have inspired Tim, Tom, Billy, Janus, and
Dick, the five men whom William Lennox Kirkland identified as escaping
from his Rose Hill Plantation in March 1862.

★★★★★★★★

On April 10, 1862, the Confederate Army issued orders to abandon
Chapman's Fort, constructed on a bend of the Ashepoo River and located
on Chapman's Plantation, for the sickly season. They dismantled the fortification, dismounted the guns, and took them to Green Pond, the headquarters of the 4th Squadron of South Carolina Cavalry, Company E, which
Major William P. Emanuel had commanded since October 1862. Logs were
left in position and in place of the guns to act as decoys to deter the Union's
approach. An artillery unit which had occupied the fort was moved to
another location. The only troops left on the Ashepoo to prevent the US
Army from advancing up the river were a small picket force.[16]

   While no orders have been found for the Combahee River, the Ashepoo
orders appear to have been replicated on the larger river. According to
a letter written in November 1863 by Nathaniel Barnwell Heyward
(Nathaniel Heyward's grandson and Colonel William C. Heyward's distant
cousin), who lived on the river north of Combahee Ferry, the Confederate
Army followed these directives in the spring, weeks before the raid. Thus,
by the spring of 1863 the lands along both rivers were left virtually un-
protected, with the batteries dismantled and the troops withdrawn and relocated to camps near the railroad. From late spring until after the first hard
frost they would be protected only by a small guard unit. A little more than
two weeks after the Combahee River Raid, Joshua Nicholls complained in
a letter written to a friend (and later published in a newspaper as a letter to
the editor), because the cannons which had been mounted at Combahee
Ferry could have done serious damage to the Union effort had they not
been removed to Green Pond. Heyward wrote General Beauregard on behalf of himself and his neighboring planters, requesting the return of artillery and the strategic placement of one or two rifled 24-pounders to
command the entrances of the Ashepoo, Combahee, and Chehaw Rivers
and the points where the rivers unite. In the planters' "unmilitary eyes,"
guns at these locations would be able to stop a US assault on the Charleston
and Savannah Railroad and ultimately on Charleston.[17]

   A few months after the abandonment of Chapman's Fort and roughly
one year before the raid, Confederate major Robert J. Jeffords of the 6th

Battalion South Carolina Cavalry conducted a mission on Hutchinson Island on the Ashepoo River. There were an estimated 125 freedom seekers living on Hutchinson Island at the time, left there after the Battle of Port Royal by the families that had held them in bondage. When in July 1862 the Union Army had withdrawn from some of the most distant Sea Islands to concentrate its forces in proximity to Charleston along the Stono River, some freedom seekers elected to stay on those islands, which included Hutchinson Island, where they had been born and lived their lives before the war. On Hutchinson, the freedom seekers had planted 250 acres of corn, 25 acres of potatoes, and 10 acres of peanuts, and had planted Sea Island cotton on higher ground (under the direction of a white person, Jeffords assumed). But the inhabitants of those islands were subjected to constant and frequent Rebel attacks, primarily for provisions.[18]

On the night of June 12, 1862, Jeffords went down the river in three boats with 105 men (the Union Army reported it was 300) to the north side of the island. A formerly enslaved man who had worked for the Union Navy informed the Confederate Army that Union troops were absent; he directed the Confederate forces to a plantation on the island. Jeffords reported to his superiors that he was certain the Union Army was on the island. An enslaved watchman who was posted as a guard on the island saw the Confederate soldiers approaching what Captain A. B. Mulligan of the 5th Regiment Cavalry, South Carolina Volunteers, Company B called the "negro colony"; the watchman gave a signal, and enslaved men attempted to run away from the soldiers, refusing to halt when ordered to. In the middle of the night Jeffords surrounded a house and chapel. As the terrified people ran out of the house, Jeffords ordered his men to open fire, murdering in cold blood everyone in sight. Jeffords reported that he could not initially tell they were slaves because of the high brush and darkness and that he had ordered his men to cease firing once he was able to determine whether or not they were Union soldiers. He reported killing ten to fifteen people and wounding the same number. The US Army commander did not give a specific number of deaths, but he stated that a large numbers of Blacks were ambushed when Jeffords and his men started shooting. Jeffords ordered his men to apply the torch to the settlement and its fields, then stole their chickens. He burned everything on the island, leaving those who had survived his attack exposed to the elements and likely to starve.[19]

Jeffords's forces retired as three Union gunboats, including the USS *Dale*, moved up the Ashepoo River between Chapman's Fort and Hutchinson

Island and fired shells. The *E. B. Hale*, under the command of Lieutenant W. T. Truxtun, responded to the large fire on the island at four in the morning. As he was unable to provide provisions for the large number of freedom seekers remaining on the island, Truxtun evacuated approximately seventy of them, several badly wounded, to Hilton Head; five of the wounded later died. Subsequently, in his official report after the massacre, Truxtun noted that the dead freedom seekers had been riddled with bullets and buckshot or clubbed to death with muskets. And he pointed out that the freedom seekers had depended on the Union Navy's gunboats to defend them and their homes. He urged that light-draft Union gunboats, like the *Planter* or the *Ellen*, be released to travel up the Ashepoo and visit Hutchinson Island for a few days, in order to deter more Rebel attacks.[20]

Du Pont submitted Truxtun's official report along with a letter earnestly requesting more steamers and more troops to guard this part of the South Carolina coast. Du Pont's manpower was stretched precariously thin enforcing the Southeast Atlantic Blockade, since a good portion of his ships had been redirected to assist the army on the Stono River. Du Pont nonetheless contended the US military had a duty to protect the freedom seekers under its care.[21]

Unfortunately, neither Du Pont's nor Truxtun's request was granted. While the Union military had conducted strategic reconnaissance of the Combahee and Ashepoo Rivers in early 1862, its attention waned thereafter. Both the Union and the Confederates were keeping their eyes on the Charleston and Savannah Railroad. General O. M. Mitchel wrote on October 15, 1862, to Commodore S. W. Godon of the South Atlantic Blockading Squadron and informed him that the Union Army planned an attempt to cut the railroad. By October 1862, the Union Army possessed its own fleet of small light-draft boats, ideal for plying the Lowcountry's coastal waterways. What it lacked was a steamer, a tugboat, and an adequate number of gunboats to execute the mission. Mitchel asked the Union Navy to "unite" with the army in its own best interests and furnish vessels from the Blockading Squadron for the important mission. He also proposed discussing with Godon an expedition on Georgia's Ogeechee River that the Union Navy planned to undertake.[22]

A month later, in early July 1862, Major Jeffords was back at Chapman's Fort. He led a Confederate scouting expedition with 130 soldiers, going first to Fenwick Island. A smaller force continued in rowboats to the Pon Pon

River, where it stopped to survey the environs. While doing reconnaissance, Jeffords spotted two Union warships, one sloop and one gunboat, patrolling the mouth of the Ashepoo River. He waited to see if the Confederate vessel on the Edisto would fire on them. When it did not, he returned to his boat and maneuvered his vessel to make a show of force. The Confederate row-boats came in sight of Truxtun's gunboat, but it was low tide, and the large Union warship could not move without getting stuck on a sandbar. Jeffords reported that he thought it safe "baiting the Yankees." Then Jeffords rowed his boats furiously until they were twenty-five miles up the Ashepoo, out of the Union warships' range.[23]

Truxtun wrote to his superiors that the "rebel marauding parties" were becoming bolder—Jeffords baiting the US Navy from a rowboat certainly was bold—and showing increased confidence. They were trespassing in Union-occupied territory and stealing chickens, hogs, and crops from the freedom seekers living there. Truxtun made his own show of force up the Ashepoo in the vicinity of Chapman's Fort twice after Jeffords's latest visit, but he complained that he was dependent on the tides to get up to Chapman's Fort and back before nightfall to prevent exposing his men to malaria. It was, after all, the middle of the sickly season, and the Ashepoo River lay at the heart of the "fever district," as contemporaries called it. Truxtun respectfully requested that the steamer that had come to provision his ship be made available to drive up the Ashepoo. He was certain that a brief show of force, even if the steamer was unarmed, would be enough to deter the Confederates. Another option Truxtun mentioned was having a small steamer like the *Planter* be put at his disposal for a short time to accomplish the same objective. Admiral Du Pont heard his lieutenant's appeals and was able to detail the *E. B. Hale* to go approximately six miles up the Ashepoo to the fort to "scour the waters." The *E. B. Hale* did not stop there. Truxtun sketched the forts along the Ashepoo and Combahee Rivers, as well as Chapman's Fort and Field's Point, respectively, adding instructions that the forts be approached head-on because the rivers were narrow.[24]

Squat and very sturdy, the *E. B. Hale*, which had been commissioned in September 1861 to transport troops, had been originally built to carry stones in New York's Adirondack Mountains. At 117 feet long, 28 feet wide at the beam, and 7½ feet deep, the wooden-screw steamer was smaller than the *Planter*. It was also lighter, weighing 220 tons. As the *E. B. Hale* sailed up the Ashepoo and came within sight of Chapman's Fort, the mounted

Confederate picket on duty fled. Freedom seekers had provided intelligence to the Union Navy that the Confederates had attempted to barricade the river by driving piles across it slightly south of the Fort Chapman earthworks. The *E. B. Hale* was the ideal warship for crossing the barricade of piles safely. It proceeded with caution at four knots. Drafting 7 1/2 feet, almost twice as much as the *Planter*, it glanced the piles but made its way over them. The Union Navy had learned the benefits of navigating the Lowcountry's coastal waterways on the flood tide.[25]

After the *E. B. Hale* anchored near the earthworks at Fort Chapman, the sailors found nothing at which it was worth aiming the gunboat's four 32-pounders. The earthworks proved not to be too imposing—a low protective wall about 300 yards in length and flanked on both sides by projections. The sailors were more concerned about the tide going out before they could pass back over the barricades. So they shot a few shells into the woods behind the earthworks and left the fort intact. They succeeded in crossing back over the piles.[26]

The following day, July 20, 1862, the *E. B. Hale* proceeded northward three miles up the Combahee River. Truxtun wrote in his official report that the Combahee "heretofore has never been visited" by Union forces prior to this reconnaissance mission. Thirteen miles up the Combahee, the sailors encountered Field's Point and found a well-built battery with a rifle pit. It was deserted aside from a single Confederate picket. He must have found the sight of a Union warship coming up the Combahee terrifying, as he jumped up from his hammock and fled. The Union sailors confiscated his personal effects and searched the magazine of the fort, finding little. The magazine was filled with earth and the gun platforms burned out. On the *E. B. Hale* went, moving four miles further up the Combahee before it ran aground at the height of the flood tide. Once dislodged, it retraced its path south along the Combahee and Ashepoo. Truxtun instructed that it make its way to Beaufort to deposit several freedom seekers who had been taken up on the river expeditions, then return to Port Royal.[27]

Du Pont found the reconnaissance mission to have been "most satisfactory." He intended to let Truxtun employ the *E. B. Hale* (or a steamer of similar draft) occasionally to keep the Confederates "in check," as Truxtun had envisioned. However, he also had seven broken-down vessels in the South Atlantic Blockading Squadron that needed to be sent north for extensive repairs. The subsequent eleven months of inaction may have lulled the Combahee planters into believing that the Union was not coming for them or their rice crops after all.[28]

★★★★★★★★

On March 27, 1863, the Third Military District issued a circular, a directive from Confederate captain and assistant adjutant general John F. O'Brien, calling for planters and other slaveholders to evacuate their enslaved property as far into the interior as possible. It was similar to a circular that Colonel A. M. M. Manigault, commander of the First Military District, had issued on December 6, 1861, a month after the Battle of Port Royal, instructing rice planters in the Georgetown area to remove their enslaved laborers to the interior, as far as two hundred miles from the coast—beyond the reach of the Union's gunboats and other vessels—and to do so with as much haste as possible. The March 1863 circular was posted at Green Pond, the nearest railroad station to the Combahee, two weeks before Combahee planters typically planted their rice crops. Many planters must not have seen the circular; those who did simply chose not to comply. Having been able to plant, harvest, and profit from their rice crops unmolested for two seasons after the Battle of Port Royal, they were confident that they could do so again.[29]

Before the Battle of Port Royal, Brigadier General William S. Walker (who had been promoted from colonel in October 1862) predicted that the Union would attack the Charleston and Savannah Railroad, then attempt to capture Charleston. Walker commanded approximately three thousand Confederate troops in the Third Military District. To protect the railroad, he ordered Major Emanuel's forces, as well as the Rutledge Mounted Riflemen, to report to Green Pond three or four weeks before the Combahee River Raid.[30]

Emanuel's military career to this point had not been particularly distinguished. In October 1862, General Beauregard reorganized the 4th South Carolina's cavalry regiments into two regiments, consolidating Emanuel's battalion of ordinary enlisted men from the Georgetown area with the Charleston Light Dragoons. For the first time in its seventy-year history, the Charleston Light Dragoons lost its autonomy, becoming one of ten companies in the 4th South Carolina Cavalry. Its members were obliged to commingle with men who were—in the minds of the Dragoons—beneath their social class. With the reorganization, Emanuel found himself reporting to a new commander, Captain Rutledge of the Charleston Light Dragoons, who previously had held a rank junior to his.[31]

This was clearly a rebuke. Emanuel had not gained the confidence of the wealthy planters in the Georgetown district, where he and the 4th South Carolina had been stationed since mid-January 1862 before being transferred to Green Pond in May 1863. He had several strikes against him, being middle-class (his holdings were modest and he owned only ten enslaved people, 86 percent fewer slaves than the smallest planter impacted by the Combahee River Raid), Jewish, and from Marlborough District, located in the northeasternmost corner of the state. The Georgetown planters thought he had been ineffective in preventing Union Navy raids of the Black, Waccamaw, and Pee Dee Rivers and protecting their interests. He was just not one of them.[32]

While stationed at Georgetown, Emanuel wrote to General Thomas Jordan on January 31, 1863, requesting leave to return home. His overseer's enlistment had left his plantation without protection. He was granted a twelve-day leave but must not have been able to retain an overseer, as he wrote Jordan again on August 7, requesting leave that month to attend to his plantation, which he had had to leave in the hands of the people he held in bondage.[33]

With Confederate forces recently transferred to the Combahee, rumors circulated that the Union was looking to strike. In a circular of May 29, 1863, the acting assistant adjutant general, Captain James Lowndes, quotes a *New York Tribune* article stating that "Negro troops at Hilton Head, S.C., will soon start upon an expedition, under the command of Colonel Montgomery, different in many respects from any heretofore projected." In hindsight, slaveholders thought Blacks enslaved in St. Bartholomew's Parish must have known the Yankees were coming. But at the time, Confederate forces were not prepared for what would happen next.[34]

In a report dated June 1, 1863, Francis Izard told the Union provost marshal that he escaped from Combahee Ferry on "Saturday week," as he put it—Saturday, May 23. As a civilian, Izard came in contact with the military police while passing through a military zone, though the report does not identify where the encounter took place. Izard told the US military police that he lived at the "floating" (pontoon) bridge at Governor Henry Middleton's plantation and that the plantation was located ten to twelve miles from Tar Bluff, twenty miles by water, fourteen or fifteen miles downriver from the Salkehatchie railroad bridge. As we've seen, Francis Izard was listed in Henry Middleton's 1846 estate inventory with his wife, Nancy, and their children, William Izzard, Sam, and Celia. In bondage, Francis made shoes for people as a "shoe maker" and horses as a "farrier" on the Middletons' Newport Plantation.[35]

Though he did not say how he knew what he knew, Izard gave the US provost marshal valuable military intelligence about the Combahee River. Fourteen or fifteen miles farther up the river was the Salkehatchie Bridge, the Charleston and Savannah Railroad crossing. He described the obstructions in the river: "Cypress spruce logs [were] fallen across the river." He remarked that piles had been driven in the channel up near Mackey's landing, near the Salkehatchie Bridge. He revealed that the Confederates had had a four-gun battery at Combahee Ferry but had "taken the guns away so now have a picket only there." And they had two torpedoes at Combahee Ferry in "tin or iron cans"—here he must have gestured at something—"about as big as this stove (26 × 1 × 10 in)" as in a pot belly stove. Then he described what the pontoon bridge at Combahee Ferry was made of, "flat boats," and how it was used ("for teams" to traverse the river). He informed the US Army that the Confederates were building a pontoon bridge across the Ashepoo River; they had six pickets from the "Rutledge squadron," the Rutledge Mounted Riflemen, at Cotton Hope Plantation (the rest of this unit was at Green Pond) and six pickets at Field's Point, and these pickets were relieved every Saturday. There was another regiment at McPhersonville. There were no batteries at the Salkehatchie Bridge, but General William S. Walker's troops were stationed at Pocotaligo and Colonel Rutledge's troops were stationed at Cavalry. There were three or four batteries at Pocotaligo, but he didn't say anything about the guns there.[36]

This detailed intelligence had likely facilitated Izard's planning and execution of his successful act of self-liberation a week earlier. He had come down the river in a "small boat" to Coosaw Isd" (meaning Coosaw Island). He traveled for five days and arrived on Wednesday, which would have been May 27. And he confirmed what the US Army must have known from its year-and-a-half-occupation of Beaufort, the South Carolina Sea Islands, and coastal Georgia, as well as its expeditions in northern Florida: "The colored people all want to get away." They "don't get enough to eat." He added that the Confederate "soldiers don't get enough to eat or coffee" to drink. They—and he doesn't differentiate here between the Blacks enslaved on the lower Combahee River and the low-ranking Confederate soldiers—"are very bad off." Even the horses and cattle were "in bad condition." He had heard many people say they would "run off if they could get a chance."[37]

One day after this report was written, the US Army would act on Izard's intelligence and the Black people still held in bondage on the lower Combahee River would get the opportunity to "get away." All of the enslaved people who could take advantage of this opportunity seized it.

★★★★★★★★

On June 19, 1863, the Charleston paper *The Mercury*, which had advocated for secession as early as three decades before the Battle of Fort Sumter, printed a letter from St. Bartholomew's Parish planter Joshua Nicholls. Nicholls, whom the editor of the paper called an "intelligent planter," offered a "simple, succinct account of what he saw and suffered" on his own plantation on the morning of June 2, in the "late raid on the Combahee River." The editor of the *Mercury* urged citizens of the state of South Carolina, the governor, and military authorities to give it their serious and careful attention.[38]

At five o'clock in the morning on June 2, Nicholls's driver "rushed precipitately" into Nicholls's bedroom without so much as knocking, awakening him from a sound sleep. That an enslaved man would barge unannounced into a white man's bedchamber was exceptional enough. Equally exceptional was that any planter would be spending the night on the rice plantation during the sickly season. But after the Battle of Port Royal, circumstances on the lower Combahee were no longer normal. In addition to Joshua Nicholls, Walter Blake and William C. Heyward also slept on their Combahee rice plantations on June 1, 1863.[39]

As described previously, Nicholls was the third husband of William L. Kirkland Jr.'s mother, Mary Anna Lynah Kirkland Faber. His ancestry traced back to Sir Richard Nicolls, who had commanded the royal cavalry during the English Civil War. In 1664, Sir Richard led the English expedition against New Amsterdam, forcing the Dutch to surrender, and becoming the governor of what is today New York. Sir Richard and his brother Simon received a grant of several thousand acres of land in Maryland, called Moores Plains. One descendent married Martha Smith (Joshua Nicholls's grandmother), who was the great-granddaughter of Sir William Smith, nephew to Captain John Smith, leader of the British colony established at Jamestown.[40]

Joshua Nicholls was born in the District of Columbia in 1821. Studious and intelligent, he attended university, graduated at age nineteen, and became a linguist. His erudition—his knowledge of Greek and Latin, his fluency in French, Italian, and German, and his grasp of philosophy—were likely the reasons Henry Faber hired Nicholls to tutor his stepson, William L. Kirkland Jr. When, after Faber's death, Nicholls and Mary Anna married, he was twenty-seven and she was forty-six.[41]

Prior to his marriage to Mary Anna Faber, Nicholls did not own land in South Carolina. Mary Anna Faber's marriage settlement and her will gave Nicholls a life interest in Longbrow, guaranteeing him a "competent and liberal resource of maintenance" among South Carolina's landed gentry for the remainder of his life. But by June 1863, Joshua Nicholls was alone—Mary Anna had died in late 1862—and was living what he described as a "quiet student's life" on the Combahee rice plantation. He may not have had anywhere else to go, no retreat where he could spend the sickly months, such as a townhouse in Charleston or a sprawling mansion in Newport, Rhode Island.[42]

The driver who awoke Nicholls told him two US steamers were "in full sight." Though moving slowly up the Combahee, the enemy steamers would soon be "opposite to" "his boat landing." Nicholls jumped out of bed and dressed quickly. He went out on his portico, from which he had an "extensive view of the river and all the neighboring plantations."[43]

From the portico, "sure enough," Nicholls saw the two Union steamers— "one quite small and the other very large"—approaching his property. The "very large" one was the *John Adams*. The "quite small" vessel Nicholls saw was the 290-ton *Harriet A. Weed*, a sidewheel steam transport that was often employed in carrying lumber and people and towing vessels. It was named after Harriet Weed, daughter of Thurlow Weed, a newspaper publisher, Republican politician, and close advisor to Secretary of State William H. Seward. Harriet was her father's personal secretary, housekeeper, and hostess after her mother died. She entertained important and influential people, including Seward (who, as described previously, was also an abolitionist and close friend and supporter of Harriet Tubman).[44]

The light-draft boats in Colonel Montgomery's "motley fleet" (as General Ambrose Burnside had described the Union's variety of retrofitted light-draft boats in 1862) were fast enough and their small guns big enough to deter the Confederates from attempting to stop them. The *Harriet A.*

Weed steamed up the Combahee River, then turned into a creek—actually a canal used to flood rice fields—between Longbrow and Rose Hill.[45]

These canals were a critical means of transportation. On his plantation (confusingly, also called Rose Hill, like William L. Kirkland's, but located up-river on the Combahee River from Longbrow), Charles Heyward (Nathaniel Heyward's son and Colonel William C. Heyward's distant cousin) exploited the labor of enslaved children too young to work their own tasks in the rice fields by forcing them to load rough rice into rice schooners. Under the supervision of an elderly woman, the children scooped rice out of the rice house in baskets and carried the full baskets on their heads. Keeping their heads and necks erect, they walked from the rice house, situated on high ground, to the wharf where the schooner waited. They dumped the contents of their baskets onto the large pile of rough rice mounting in the schooner's hatches until the rice reached the top of the vessel's interior (3,500 bushels or so). The schooner transported it to Charleston for sale. The Kirkland and Nicholls families likely used a rice schooner, their own or hired, to transport their rice up and down the same canal. Now the same canal was bringing in US Army vessels.[46]

Nicholls watched from his portico as the Union vessels drove practically up to his front door. He might have wondered how the boats could have navigated the tight curls of the Combahee River with its marshy banks and treacherous sandbars. How could whoever was commanding them have known that the narrow creek was deep and wide enough to get a boat from the river through the rice fields? The Combahee was forty miles long; why had they chosen this creek of all the creeks?[47]

The answer to these questions is that some of the South Carolina Volunteers aboard the US Army vessels had traversed this stretch of the Combahee when they were held in bondage. It was a stretch of rice fields in which they had worked, against their wills, for much of their lives.[48]

★★★★★★★

Joshua Nicholls wrote that he could see the steamers crowded with "armed men in dark uniform"—dark blue Union Army uniforms. He recalled seeing "women seated in chairs upon the upper deck" of the *Harriet A. Weed*. These women seemed to be "surveying with curiosity" the "beautiful and peaceful" view of the Combahee before them. It is unlikely that Harriet

Tubman was among the women Joshua Nicholls saw—or imagined he saw—sitting atop the *Harriet A. Weed*.[49]

Nicholls thought the boats must have been on a "pleasure excursion." It was a "very pleasant morning." The sky was blue and crystal clear, so clear that parts of Longbrow's country estate—the stables where Nicholls kept his horses and livestock, the storage barns where he kept his rice and corn, and the threshing mills—"loomed out." Nicholls described his rice crop as "growing luxuriantly" in Longbrow's rice fields. The slave quarters looked to him like a "succession of tranquil villages" on the high ground above Longbrow's rice fields.[50]

Tubman would have had no time for leisure. As Tubman later recalled, General Hunter had requested that she accompany the US gunboats up the Combahee River in order to help remove torpedoes placed by the Confederates along the river (including the ones Francis Izard had described) and then destroy railroad bridges and supply lines, cutting Rebel troops off from the rural plantations. Tubman agreed and asked if one of "John Brown's men," Colonel James Montgomery, "was to be appointed commander of the expedition." She knew Colonel Montgomery and thought him a fellow "General" in the army fighting a guerilla war against slavery. Colonel Montgomery was appointed.[51]

This is Tubman's side of the story. Montgomery never told his version, except in a brief paragraph; thus, we do not know from his own words how he came to command the Combahee River Raid, or what he thought the goals and objectives of the raid were, or why he had Tubman accompany the expedition and the role he envisioned her playing. In a letter to General Quincy A. Gilmore, commanding the Department of the South, written from St. Helena a month after the raid, Montgomery stated simply, "I wish to commend to your attention, Mrs. Harriet Tubman, a most remarkable woman, and invaluable as a scout. I have been acquainted with her character and actions for several years."[52]

Tubman testified in her US Civil War pension file that she was "commander of several men (eight or nine)." Like most intelligence professionals whose success and survival depended on secrecy, she never divulged how she recruited her team. Allan Pinkerton, who ran the Chicago Detective Agency (and later his eponymous security and investigation force), developed a network of operatives whom he instructed to identify freedom seekers who appeared exceptional at observing and recalling military details and had some degree of formal education. Pinkerton groomed these men to be part of his intelligence network, then sent them behind Confederate lines. Tubman may have used similar strategies to identify candidates among the sea of refugees flowing in and out of Beaufort's camp. They had to be knowledgeable about the rivers, creeks, sandbars, plantations, enslaved populations, and geography behind Confederate lines in areas of interest to the Union Army commanders. Their mission was to learn the strength of the Confederate forces, the design of their fortifications, and the locations of their guns and encampments, and then communicate the information to Tubman. She in turn communicated it to the Union military. By the spring of 1863, the intelligence Tubman had gathered helped shape the US Army Department of the South's military strategy for its Black regiments.[53]

So who were these men? When Tubman applied for her pension in 1890, General Rufus Saxton wrote a letter in support of her application, stating that she had recruited "scouts who are residents of Beaufort and well-acquainted with the mainland: Peter Burns, Mott Blake, Sandy Salters, Solomon Gregory, Isaac Hayward, Gabriel Cohen, and George Chrisholm." Tubman had also recruited "pilots who know the channels in this vicinity, and who acted as such for Col. Montgomery up the Combahee River: Samuel Heyward and Charles Simmons."[54]

Of Tubman's ring of scouts, spies, and pilots, only two enlisted in the US Army. The first was Walter Plowden, who was described in his pension affidavits as having a "mulatto" complexion, "sandy" hair, and black eyes. Multiple versions of his life story are found in various records. In one version, Plowden's father was enslaved and his mother was a "free Indian woman," which would have made her children free; the family subsequently moved to Pennsylvania after his father was freed, and that was where Plowden was born. Others who met Plowden after he was freed, including Annie Simms Plowden, his legal widow, testified that he had been born in New York. They may have gotten this impression from Plowden himself and not questioned him about it. According to Annie Plowden, Walter was the kind of man who did not believe wives "should know much about their husband's business." Despite what he told people and why, when the census taker came in both 1870 and 1880, Plowden reported that he had been born enslaved in Washington County, Maryland, located in the upper northwest corner of the state. We will see after the war that Plowden did not always tell the truth, even about his Civil War service. Whatever the truth, he became free and made his way to New York in 1861 and joined up with the 47th New York Volunteers (commanded by Colonel Henry Moore), serving as a steward for the regimental surgeon, Major White. He came to South Carolina with the 47th New York.[55]

After Major White mustered out, Plowden went to work for General Hunter in the Department of the South as a scout and spy. The military records show him enlisting in the 13th USCT on April 23, 1861, and being honorably discharged on August 16. According to his widow, he was "cooking for General Gillmore" when she married him. Cooking for General Quincy A. Gillmore, who was assigned to the staff of General Thomas W. Sherman before Sherman was promoted to brigadier general himself and took charge of the siege of Fort Pulaski, was likely a subterfuge. Several of Annie Plowden's witnesses confirmed that her husband served as a spy under Generals Mitchel, Hunter, and Gillmore. Plowden himself testified that he was "continuously employed as a scout and spy" for the Department of the South under Generals "Michael Benham, Hunter, Saxton and Gillmore from September 1862 to January 2, 1864."[56]

According to the bill for Plowden's relief that was presented to the US House of Representatives on February 1, 1896, Plowden was a "guide in various expeditions from the coast into the interior of the State." The bill provides specific details about five expeditions in which Plowden was engaged, including these: "In the spring of 1863 he was sent by night on a secret expedition, with a row-boat and eight colored men, up the Combahee River 131 miles to the crossing of the Charleston and Savannah railroad [the Salkehatchie Bridge] in the vicinity of Pocotaligo." They returned five days later and reported on the "bridges and trestle-work, and the strength of the military guard of the enemy at the crossing." "Immediately following" this expedition in spring 1863, Plowden "accompanied the well-known expedition of Colonel Montgomery, 34th United States colored troops, against Pocotaligo, as a guide."[57]

Not all of the details about the Combahee River Raid in the 1896 bill were accurate. The 1896 bill reports that the Combahee River Raid was "successful in the destruction of the railroad bridge, and the release from slavery . . . [of] 800 colored men, and a large amount of property, which were used by the United States government." It states that Plowden acted as a spy and scout in a third expedition on the Coosawhatchie with five Black men to cut the telegraph on the Charleston and Savannah Railroad at Garden's Corner. Lastly, the following June, Plowden reportedly was sent up the Ashepoo with a boatload of eight Black men. They were successful at burning the Charleston and Savannah bridge. Then, in July 1863, Plowden was sent up the Broad River with four men who were likely also spies and scouts.[58]

While the author of the bill did not get all of the details right, he makes it clear that the US Army had admitted Plowden was engaged in two expeditions up the Combahee River, one prior to the June 2, 1863, raid. It establishes that the US Army was conducting reconnaissance on the lower Combahee River on at least four separate occasions before June 2, 1863, collecting intelligence about the ferry itself and the Salkehatchie Bridge, where the Charleston and Savannah Railroad crossed the Combahee. The first was when Captain Ralph Ely and his men went up the Ashepoo and then up the Combahee in rowboats in February 1862. The second occurred during the expedition from Port Royal Ferry to Pocotaligo that had been authorized by General Stevens (mentioned in Chapter 10), which could have brought down freedom seekers from Walter Blake's Bonny Hall, William L. Kirkland's Rose Hill, and likely William C. Heyward's Cypress Plantation. The third was when the *E. B. Hale* sailed up the Combahee in July 1862. Finally, there was the expedition by Plowden and several other Black men in the spring of 1863. Plowden's 1890 application for a disability pension claimed that he suffered from overexertion in the inclement weather, fatigue, and severe chest and head colds during the spring 1863 expedition. In addition, the bill for Walter Plowden's relief demonstrates how dependent the US Army commanders were on freedom seekers gathering vital information about what was happening behind enemy lines. A number of details are still missing, such as the identities of the other Black men with Plowden in the rowboat. Who was in command? Who had ordered the expeditions? Lastly, was Harriet Tubman involved in any way? We simply don't know.[59]

Through the end of 1863, Plowden was sent on several subsequent expeditions: up the Ashepoo, up the Broad River inland from Hilton Head into Bluffton, and up the Stono River. Plowden was captured by the Confederates while aboard the *J. C. Smith* in June 1864 and imprisoned in Charleston for fifteen months. Isaac Hawkins, a sergeant in the 54th Massachusetts Volunteers, testified that Plowden gathered intelligence from behind Confederate lines, information that "saved thousands of dollars' worth of supplies and thousands of lives of our fellow soldiers." Hawkins added that he would not have "incurred the risk of being captured and hung as a spy, not for $20,000." Plowden never received $20,000 from the federal government, but he would be buried at Arlington National Cemetery upon his death on June 9, 1893.[60]

Tubman and Plowden may have known each other in Maryland, though they would have been born in two opposite corners of the state. Their paths possibly crossed in New York after they had liberated themselves from bondage and pursued the path of helping others. In any case, they were unquestionably a team in South Carolina in the business of gathering espionage, and possibly of making money also. They had some dealings with Private John Webster, superintendent of contrabands, who in June 1863 was court-martialed on seven charges, including embezzling and misapplying military stores; illegally selling rations that the government had issued to "contrabands" (including selling brown sugar to Harriet Tubman and Walter Plowden); and withholding rations from contrabands. Webster pled not guilty on all charges; his defense was that regiments such as the 47th Pennsylvania entrusted their excess provisions with him before they departed and asked him to sell them. He did so, then sent on the money, keeping the agreed-upon portion for himself as compensation for his trouble.[61]

Tubman testified during the court-martial that "we," meaning she and Plowden, had bought sugar twice from Private Webster. The first time was for forty or fifty pounds of brown sugar, the same amount she had previously purchased at the commissary in Hilton Head. Tubman could not tell whether the brown sugar she purchased was the same as what was issued to the contrabands. She likely used it to make the gingerbread she baked and sold in the Beaufort camps, or resold it. Based on her testimony and the testimony of refugees from the camps, Tubman and Plowden were in business together. They also worked in unison to use their influence with the commanders of the Department of the South to advocate for the refugees— such as by reporting Webster's underhanded dealings to General Saxton. Their complaint was what had led to his court-martial.[62]

Mott Blake was the second of Tubman's spies and scouts who enlisted in the US Army; he enlisted in the 21st Regiment, Company I, on October 24, 1864. Blake, as noted in Chapter 10, was a deer hunter who had escaped in the June 1862 attack on Arthur Blake's plantation on the South Santee River. He was taken to Beaufort by a gunboat, and this is likely where he met up with Tubman. Blake appears in the 1870 census in the household of his father, Bungy, along with his mother, Clarinda, and his wife, Nancy. In the 1880 census Mott was listed as head of household, living with his mother, wife, and children Mary, Fibbie, Nitsey, Sheppard, and Sarah Blake. Blake does not appear in the 1890 census. His mother must have died before the

1900 census, in which Blake appears with his wife and children Mary, James, and Elias Blake. There is only one Mott Blake in the census from 1870 to 1910 in South James Township. There's no question this is the same man.[63]

Tubman likely became aware of both Plowden and Blake through the networks of Beaufort watermen, and may have recruited them after Robert Small's daring exploit as well as Blake's escape during the 1862 Santee raid. Isaac Hayward, another scout, was trained as a boatman and knew the rivers off St. Helena Sound. When he applied to open a Freedmen's Bank Account in March 1870, Hayward testified that he had been born on Coosaw Island and brought up at Beaufort. Whoever filled out Heyward's application described him as thirty-seven and with a light complexion. Heyward named his family in the application: his wife, Lucy; their children Celia, Henrietta, Mary, Sibby, Rosa, Emma, and Adeline; his mother, Sibby; his brothers Adam, Joe, Kit, Tom, January, and Overt; and his sisters Matilda and Cinda. His family must have still been enslaved until the end of the war; they only had first names. And he named his father as "Cap. Wm. C. Heyward, with "/dead/" and "White" written after his name. There are many men in the Heyward family with the first name William, but only one with the middle initial C: William C. Heyward, mentioned earlier in this story (he was not reelected colonel of the 11th South Carolina regiment in the May 2, 1862, reorganization of the Confederate Army).[64]

Wally Graham later testified that William C. Heyward "was not a married man." Instead of bringing his mistresses from England like Arthur Blake, Heyward "used to have a colored woman," who could have been Isaac Hayward's mother, though Graham did not know what had become of her. It is a mystery how Wally Graham knew so much about Heyward's personal life; Graham had been held in bondage by Walter Blake on Bonny Hall Plantation, located on the other side of the Combahee. One possible explanation is that they likely learned it the Beaufort refugee camp, where the personal business of Colonel Heyward—and other "notorious rebels"'—may have been the talk of the town.[65]

Isaac Hayward also listed his current occupation (steward of the *Planter*) and his employer (a "Capt. Foster"). He claimed to have been born in bondage on Coosaw or Chisolm Island, where Alexander Robert Chisolm's plantation was located (and, as we saw earlier in this chapter, Isaac Hayward, his mother, Sibby, and eight siblings were among the enslaved people listed in Alexander's sister Sarah's marriage settlement and mortgage). Hayward may have come to Beaufort as a result of the joint Union Navy and Army operation up the Coosaw River in December 1861. Or Hayward could have been one of the enslaved men Chisolm sent to Charleston in early 1862 to build fortifications for the Confederacy and escaped at that time. After the war, Isaac Hayward appears in the 1870 census (listed as Isaac Heyward) with his wife, Lucy, their children Isaac, Lucy, Cecelia, Harriet, Mary, Cipper, and Jane, and a female relative, Jane Heyward.[66]

Yet another of Tubman's scouts was Peter Burns, who told his story to Dr. Seth Rogers of the 1st South Carolina Volunteers. Rogers described Burns as a dark-skinned multiracial-looking man with a "face and form resembling John Brown." This "extraordinary colored man" had "for a long time, been employed by Gen. Hunter and by Gen. Saxton for a scout." A month and a half before he participated in the Combahee Raid, Burns "brought off one hundred and thirty-two persons with him from the mainland."[67]

Peter Burns apparently never enlisted in the US Army, but his son, Jack Burns, did. Jack Burns was born in bondage around 1838 on Stuart's Place, in Beaufort on the mainland, and raised on Port Royal Island. Sometime after the Battle of Port Royal, he escaped enslavement and joined the 1st South Carolina Volunteers, Company F. He stated on his Freedmen's Bank Account application that his parents were named Peter Burns and Lizzie (who was already dead), and his siblings Moses, Maurice, Thomas, Paul, Lizzie, and Martha. On his own Freedmen's Bank Account application, Peter Burns claimed that he had been born enslaved in Pocotaligo and raised in Beaufort. His wife's name was Susan and his parents were Jack Jenkins and Miriam. The elder Burns would have been born around 1818, if not earlier, thus making him too old to enlist in the 1st South Carolina Volunteers.[68]

The other members of Tubman's ring of spies, scouts, and pilots who were named in General Saxton's 1890 letter in Tubman's pension file—Sandy Selters, Solomon Gregory, Gabriel Cohen, and George Chrisholm—likely worked with the US Department of the South, though there is no record of their enlistment in the military. Searches of the pension files, censuses from 1870 to 1920, and Freedmen's Bank applications yielded four men named George Chisolm in the 1870 census (one each in St. Helena, Beaufort, Orangeburg, and Johns Island) and one Solomon Gregory on St. Paul's. No corroborating details appear in the pension files, Freedmen's Bank accounts, or life histories (like Peter Burns's, which was recorded by northerners during the Port Royal Experiment) about the names of their family members and the planters who held them in bondage, nor their places of residence after the war. Thus it is impossible to determine whether any of these men were the ones who served with Tubman. Searches for the remaining men have yielded nothing. There are many possible reasons why no records mentioning them have been found. For example, they may have died before the 1870 census was taken, or they may have migrated out of South Carolina. Like Peter Burns, they may have been too old to enlist in active service, though alternatives to active service for older men were common. One seventy-six-year-old man who served as a nurse for the 1st South Carolina Volunteers testified, "I know I can't double-quick but I can do something, and I'se bound to." Or they may have been civilians employed by the US Army quartermaster, like Captain Turner alias Blake, who served as a pilot on the *John Adams* from January 19, 1863, to May 1, 1864. And, of course, they may simply have not trusted the Union Army enough to enlist. Years after the raid, Tubman told her biographer that the freedom seekers had been as afraid of the Union Army as they were of the people who held them in bondage. She remembered African Americans in the Lowcountry calling them the "Yankee Buckra." This lack of trust made it difficult for the Union soldiers to win their confidence. Without it, it was impossible for them to secure critical information from the freedom seekers. However, the freedom seekers trusted Tubman. They saw in her someone like themselves. They would tell her anything.[69]

★★★★★★★★

Watching from his portico on the morning of June 2, 1863, Joshua Nicholls eventually began to fathom that the men in dark uniform were Black soldiers. In fact, they were Companies A–F of the 2nd South Carolina Volunteers, total-ing three hundred men. The enslaved people around him would have started to realize the same thing. Duncan Clinch Heyward later suggested that the people his grandfather Charles Heyward had held in bondage first heard the distant sound of gunfire in Charleston Harbor while they were planting rice in the fields in April 1861, when Fort Sumter fell. Seven months later, they must have heard the big guns in the Battle of Port Royal, smelled the smoke, and felt the vibrations of war. Some enslaved people decided to risk it all and try to get themselves to Union-occupied territory. Now some of those who had done so were returning. A little over a year after he had escaped enslavement on the Combahee, Friday Barrington came back to Cypress Plantation with the 2nd South Carolina Volunteers, Company D, in the raid. He may have helped the Union Army target Colonel William C. Heyward, as well as liberate his mother, father, and sister, whom Heyward still held in bondage.[70]

On July 4, 1863, *Harper's Weekly* published an article, "A Raid Among the Rice Plantations," and an engraving entitled "Raid of South Carolina Volunteers (Col. Montgomery) Among the Rice Plantations on the Combahee, SC." The image shows the *John Adams,* followed by the *Harriet A. Weed.* Both sidewheel steamers are flying the US flag as they proceed up the Combahee. Off to the left, the image depicts the *John Adams* with two small pilot houses on the steamboat's highest deck and cannons on the fore side. Colonel Montgomery would later remark that he had been on the *John Adams* during the raid and that the ship "was in advance." While Montgomery did not mention Tubman, she and her associates were on the *John Adams* as well. From one of the pilot houses on the *John Adams,* Montgomery and Tubman had a commanding view for miles up and down the Combahee as the pilots navigated the boats through the bends and away from the shifting sandbars.[71]

One cannon on the *Harriet A. Weed,* in contrast, is depicted aft, pointed at musket-carrying enslaved drivers who are trying to prevent people from fleeing the rice fields and getting on the boats. The fleeing men and women are shown outside a wooden slave cabin, carrying bundles on their heads, and running into the tall grasses along the riverbank. Both boats are shown moving through the water, leaving distraught Combahee freedom seekers behind. Some are pictured jumping into the water in an effort to swim after the *Harriet A. Weed.*[72]

The author of the *Harper's* article was likely William T. Robinson, an officer and assistant surgeon from Montgomery, Pennsylvania, who had enlisted in the 104th Pennsylvania Infantry. Robinson wrote the account in the first person: "we" destroyed a vast amount; "we" broke the sluicegates or floodgates and flooded the rice fields; "we" carried out the president's Emancipation Proclamation; "we" skirmished all day with the Confederates; "we" are now commencing operations on the Georgia coast. But it seems likely that Robinson was not himself at the scene of the raid. Had he been there, he would have known that the engraving was not accurate in some of its details. In the illustration, the angular and geometrically manicured rice fields dwarf the Combahee River, which also appears to flow in a linear fashion, without its characteristic tight curls. The slave quarters are depicted as pressed up against the rice fields and a stone's throw from the river, when in actuality they were located up to two miles from the river and on higher ground. Some of Robinson's comrades, such as James E. Carver and Levi H. Markley, former lieutenants of the 104th Pennsylvania, were there (as noted in Chapter 12, they had accepted commissions as captains in the 2nd South Carolina Volunteers). Robinson may have communicated with them in Beaufort, where the 104th Pennsylvania remained stationed until July 1863, to procure the information used to provide the only image of the Combahee River Raid.[73]

Other participants were twenty-two-year-old Captain Charles Brayton, who had written a letter to his father on May 21 reporting excitedly that he had "volunteered" to go on an expedition with Colonel Montgomery. Harassing the enemy was the object of the expedition, wrote Brayton. They would take approximately five hundred muskets and one section of the 3rd Rhode Island Heavy Artillery. Brayton anticipated "much fun" under the command of Montgomery, whom he described as of "Kansas notoriety" and a "noted Bush-whacker" as well as a "shrewd and brave man." Brayton thought he was going with Montgomery to Georgia and Florida to destroy saltworks, railroads, and sawmills, and to "do all the damage" they could possibly do. Instead, he would command the artillery unit on a raid up the sleepy, serpentine Combahee.[74]

What is known about the raid comes primarily from newspaper articles written days afterward, from a firsthand account written by Captain William Lee Apthorp in June 1864, from regimental histories of the 104th Pennsylvania and the 3rd Rhode Island Heavy Artillery, and from official Union and Confederate military records. Montgomery himself wrote very little about the raid. The Confederate reports describing it are conflicting. They obscure much about the Confederate troops' movements and the Confederate commanders' orders. Tubman, the overwhelming majority of the Black troops who conducted the raid, and the freedom seekers who escaped enslavement during it were all illiterate and thus did not leave written accounts, but we have their testimony in the pension files and in the life story of the esteemed Old Head Minus Hamilton.

Still, we can piece together the facts. Colonel Montgomery, the 2nd South Carolina Volunteers, and Company C of the 3rd Rhode Island Heavy Artillery, commanded by Captain Brayton, left the downtown Beaufort wharf at approximately 9 p.m. on Monday, June 1, 1863, after the sun had finally set. They traveled under the light from the full moon. The pilots of the three boats, the *John Adams*, *Harriet A. Weed*, and *Sentinel*, could read the glistening water, spotting sandbars and debris in the water and avoiding them. In contrast, the marsh on one side and the cypress swamps on the other side would have appeared to be undifferentiated dark, static masses.[75]

Having studied the tides and recognizing their importance to navigating coastal waters, the army conducted the raid on the spring tide, which accompanies the full moon. Spring tides occur twice in a lunar cycle—during the new moon and full moon phases—when the tidal forces of the sun and the moon reinforce each other. This produces higher high tides and lower low tides than average. The highest tide of the twenty-eight-day lunar cycle would have opened up the narrow channel of the Combahee and helped the warships avoid sandbars, particularly at the river's mouth.[76]

The *Sentinel* transported the Black soldiers and white officers in the 2nd South Carolina Volunteers, as well as Company C of the 3rd Rhode Island Heavy Artillery. Originally called the *Mayo*, it was a 350-ton screw steamer, outfitted with one 30-pound Parrott gun and two rifled 12-pound field pieces.[77]

The *John Adams* and *Harriet A. Weed*—both armed, of course—and the *Sentinel* crept along at around six or seven miles per hour at the ebb tide, which would have hit Brickyard Point at the mouth of the Coosaw River at 2:30 a.m. or so. Going via the Coosaw River saved precious time; had they taken longer, they could have been detected by the Confederates and shot out of the water. But it was also risky because of the sandbars, which would have been even more treacherous at low tide. These sandbars would have been difficult to see even under the light of the full moon. A boatman who knew the Coosaw River, like Isaac Hayward, was likely influential in the decision to get to the Combahee by going upriver and northeast through the Coosaw River, rather than downriver and southeast around Port Royal and Parris Island, approaching the Combahee through St. Helena Sound, which was the original plan that the chaplain of the 3rd Rhode Island described in his memoir. If the plan was changed, then who changed it, when, and why? Decades after the end of the war, Harriet Tubman told Emma Telford: "We found where the torpedoes was and saw that we could find another channel." The Coosaw River may have been the other channel up to the Combahee River. And Isaac Hayward may have played a critical role in finding it.[78]

All was going well until the *Sentinel* ran aground on a sandbar passing through the mouth of the Coosaw. Some sandbars rose gradually and the water's depth decreased gradually around them. Others rose precipitously, making the water sharply and unexpectedly shallow. Whichever kind this was, the ship could not be dislodged off it, nor could the US Army wait three hours for the next high tide to dislodge it. The soldiers aboard the *Sentinel* disembarked and boarded the *Harriet A. Weed*. Then the two remaining vessels proceeded along their way.[79]

Early Tuesday morning, the steamers reached the mouth of the Combahee. They glided twenty miles upstream and met no opposition. Colonel Montgomery landed his small fleet at Field's Point, where Confederate pickets had first constructed a battery. Field's Point commanded the main road to Ashepoo, where the Confederate Army had a picket. Ashepoo, about fifteen miles away, was also the nearest point of the Charleston and Savannah Railroad. Days after the raid, the *New South* newspaper reported that the Confederate pickets fled so quickly at the sight of the Black soldiers armed with loaded muskets that they left their blankets behind.[80]

Montgomery left Captain Thomas N. Thompson and his Company D in charge at Field's Point, where they occupied the deserted breastworks. The remainder of his forces proceeded upriver on the *John Adams* and the *Harriet A. Weed*. The pilots successfully avoided running aground again by navigating the outer edges of the river's wide bends and avoiding the inner edges, where sand collected and sandbars were more common. They pushed two miles ahead to Tar Bluff, where sandy bluffs rising twenty feet in height commanded the Combahee River. Unlike the sandbars at high tide, the white sandy bluffs would have reflected the full moon's light, as if the coastline was wrapped in a wide white horizontal ribbon. To the pilots, the loblolly, slash, and longleaf pine forest grown up on the bluffs and surrounding wetlands would have been a dark blur.[81]

Tar Bluff also commanded the second principal road leading to Ashepoo village. Captain James M. Carver's Company E was left behind to occupy the deserted rifle pits at Tar Bluff and protect the line of communication. Later in the day, Captain Carver covered a second road leading from Tar Bluff to Ashepoo village by means of the *John Adams*'s firepower. A Confederate battery opened fire and threatened to overwhelm Carver's small force, which remained unsupported. But Carver's men went to work and poured volley after volley into the Confederate battery, killing and wounding several, and leading the Confederates to believe there were more reinforcements ready to join the battle. Captain Augustus Alonzo Hoit and the *Harriet A. Weed*'s well-directed cannon fire then scattered what was left of the Confederate artillery in a hasty retreat.[82]

Early on the morning of June 2, Major William P. Emanuel was stationed in Green Pond at the headquarters of the Confederate Third Military District. Under Emanuel's command, Lance Corporal H. H. Newton of Company E and his six men were stationed at Field's Point. Newton was chief of the pickets at Field's Point. In the Confederates' official report on the raid, Captain John F. Lay, inspector of cavalry, reported what he learned from Corporal Newton: the "night was bright," certainly because of the full moon, and "he could see a long distance." What he saw was the *John Adams* and *Harriet A. Weed* moving up the Combahee two miles below Field's Point. Newton and his men mounted their horses and fell back a few hundred yards, dismounted and secured their horses, then returned to Field's Point on foot. Newton watched a number of 2nd South Carolina Volunteer soldiers proceeding up the bank of the Combahee and then heard their gunboats moving farther up the river. Newton immediately sent first one and then a second courier to Lieutenant William E. Hewitt of the 4th South Carolina Cavalry, Company F, commander of the outpost ten miles away at Chisolmville, informing him of the enemy's presence in the river near Field's Point. Newton could not determine how many Union soldiers occupied Field's Point. He assumed the force was larger than it was, and that more soldiers and artillery were on the way. He was also mistaken about the strength of Captain Thompson's forces. Neither Union reinforcements nor artillery came to Field's Point or Tar Bluff. Yet both Thompson's small force at Field's Point and Carver's at Tar Bluff held off Confederate skirmishers.[83]

On the sandy bluffs of Tar Bluff, Colonel Montgomery's men went to work. They had only six hours—"six mortal hours"—to destroy the Combahee planters' property before the lowest ebb tide (effectively the same amount of time teams of enslaved men would have had to build or repair an embankment in a tidal rice field before the flood tide washed away the product of their toil). The soldiers burned Baker's home and outbuildings to the ground. In addition, they burned several large steam-powered rice mills, three cotton gins, and a sawmill, including Oliver Hering Middleton's rice mill at his Launch Plantation. The destruction at Tar Bluff offered a sample of what was to come.[84]

After passing Tar Bluff, the Union vessels had a clear passage up the Combahee to the rice plantations, meeting with practically no Confederate resistance. Even at this early hour—it was now close to 4 a.m.—Captain Apthorp saw that the rice fields on James L. Paul's plantation were "well sprinkled with wooley heads hard at work." The sight of a Union warship coming up the Combahee would not have been completely foreign to those working in the rice fields. Some had been there in late November 1861 after the Union Navy's armada pushed through St. Helena Sound in the Battle of Port Royal. Others likely had spotted the USS *E. B. Hale* coming from the Ashepoo River up the Combahee in July 1862. Before they saw the *John Adams* and the *Harriet Weed* approaching, they would have made out the rhythmic cadence of the boiler's high-pressure engine. The sound was deafening inside the ship and audible from miles away, and the coal-burning engine spewed thick black clouds of acrid smoke. They would have seen the Stars and Stripes waving from both and likely would have known by this point that the flags meant freedom.[85]

Overseers were in the rice fields as well, supervising the labor. At the sight of the Union boats, they quickly mounted their horses and rode off. Once the overseers left and they were unsupervised, the laborers left the rice fields and ran down to the river. The *Harriet A. Weed* (which Colonel Montgomery testified that Major B. Ryder Corwin "had charge of"), carrying troops under the command of Captains William Lee Apthorp and John M. Adams, landed Companies B and F of the 2nd South Carolina Volunteers at Joshua Nicholls's Longbrow plantation. They set up a picket, then went about their work of destruction.[86]

When the *Harriet A. Weed* landed at the Longbrow boat landing, a landing party commanded by Major B. Ryder Corwin burned the threshed rice, the stacked rice, the steam-powered rice mill, and the rice barns. The soldiers had to move quickly. Thick clouds of smoke blew northward, in the direction of Colleton. Apthorp also saw smoke rising in the rear of his position on the lower Combahee. It was coming from Tar Bluff and Field's Point, where Montgomery had left Captain Carver and Captain Thompson and their men.[87]

When Joshua Nicholls witnessed the *Harriet A. Weed* moving up the canal to his boat landing, he ordered the enslaved driver to bring the field hands to him. They did not exhibit the slightest degree of alarm. Nicholls later maintained that they professed their "utmost attachment" to him. Thus Nicholls was surprised that the field hands did not obey him by coming back to the main house. Instead, many walked through the forest behind Nicholls's plantation home, "skirting" the tidal rice fields, and headed back to their slave quarters. Nicholls later found the field hands "all about their houses."[88]

Seeing that the Union had landed "twenty negroes under the leadership of two white men" on his property, Nicholls ordered the field hands to follow him and "take to the woods" that separated Nicholls's plantation home from that of his stepson, William L. Kirkland Jr. The field hands professed their "willingness" to follow Nicholls to the woods, but "not one made a sign of moving." Nicholls later testified that he was unarmed and had nothing with which to force them to obey him, nor to protect himself from the soldiers. So he ran into the woods "for protection." From there he observed what was happening on his plantation as well as those of his neighbors.[89]

14

Day Clean

Unlike Joshua Nicholls, Minus Hamilton could not write a letter to a friend, let alone have it subsequently published in the newspaper as a letter to the editor. Nor could he write an official military report, like Colonel William C. Heyward. What the "very aged man" could do was recollect what he saw with his own eyes and experienced on the plantation where he was held in bondage when the Union Army drove its two retrofitted gunboats up the Combahee River. Like Harriet Tubman, the overwhelming majority of soldiers in the 1st and 2nd South Carolina Volunteers, and those people enslaved on the Combahee rice plantations, Hamilton was illiterate.[1]

However, Hamilton did tell his story to Colonel Thomas Wentworth Higginson, whom Higginson identified as "MINUS HAMILTON AGED 88(?) one of those who came down on Montgomery's Combakee [sic] Raid." He recorded Hamilton's life story in his war journal while Hamilton was standing at the door of his tent a little more than a month after the Combahee River Raid and after the 1st South Carolina Volunteers returned to camp after an expedition up the Edisto River. Higginson took pains not only to record the man's story but also to capture his dialect because, as he later wrote in his memoir, he wanted to paint the scene of freedom seekers' "birthdays of freedom" from the "point of view from the slaves themselves." Higginson understood what a rare privilege it was to view the raid through the eyes of an enslaved person who secured liberation from bondage as a result of it. At eighty-eight, Minus Hamilton was likely the oldest of the bondspeople on record as having escaped the "prison-house of bondage" in the raid. I will let Mr. Hamilton tell his story:

> De people was all a-hoein', mas'r. . . . Dey was a-hoein' in the rice-field when de gunboats come. Den ebry man drap dem hoe, and leff de rice. De mas'r he stand and call, "Run to de wood for hide! Yankee come, sell you to Cuba! run for hide!" Ebry man he run, and, my God! Run all toder way!

Mas'r stand in de wood, peep, peep, 'faid for truss. . . . He say, "Run to de wood!" and ebry man run by him straight to de boat.

An hour or two before "day clean," as dawn is called, Hamilton was among the enslaved people laboring in the tidal rice fields on James L. Paul's Combahee rice plantation where, as we've seen, he and his family were sold in December 1859. Paul's Place was the first rice plantation that Montgomery and his men encountered on the east side as they steamed up the river into Colleton. Minus Hamilton could have been one of the "wooley heads hard at work" in the rice fields that Apthorp observed. Every person forced to labor in the rice fields dropped their long-handled hoe with the angled blade and left the rice in the fields. The overseer, whom Hamilton called "mas'r"—the formerly enslaved appear to have called every white man "mas'r," including Higginson—did much what Joshua Nicholl did. He stood in the rice field and called to the enslaved field hands working there to run and hide in the woods. The Yankees had finally come and would sell them all to Cuba.[2]

Hamilton and his fellow bondsmen were not fooled. They did not feign attachment to the enslaver nor obedience to the overseer, despite Joshua Nicholls's later insistence. They also did the opposite of what they were or-dered to do. The overseer, like Joshua Nicholls, ran into the woods. From his forested hiding place, he looked back at the enslaved people, then looked again. He told the enslaved people one last time to run and hide in the woods. They ignored him utterly. They ran for their lives to freedom, straight to the boat.[3]

★★★★★★★★

Getting to the rice fields in the darkness of the early morning was perilous. Snakes, for example, were a constant threat. Enslaved people walking from the slave cabins through the hardwood or longleaf pine forests in the predawn hours would have frequently encountered copperheads skulking in the dark-ness or dark brown or black cottonmouths hiding in a pile of wood or leaves. The younger copperheads' pixilated drab olive or yellow-tan pattern, with narrow bands at the top and wider ones toward the bottom, would have been indistinguishable from the leaves. The patterns fade as the snake's skin ages, so an older snake would be completely camouflaged in the grass or dirt. Whereas a rattlesnake's rattle warned anyone not to come closer to it, one likely would not see a cottonmouth until it aggressively stood its ground on land or in the water. Enslaved laborers may have been able to discern the white inner band around the snake's mouth—which is how cottonmouths get their name—as it bared its fangs to defend its territory. But at four or five o'clock in the morning on June 2, it was too dark even for enslaved laborers to see their hands in front of their faces or their long-handled hoes in their hands.[4]

In addition to cottonmouths, American alligators made their nests in the rice fields. In early June, the female alligators prepared their nests after fertilization took place in late May. At that time of the morning, enslaved laborers working in the rice fields would not have been able to see the upturned nostrils or bony spines of the nocturnal animals as they swam through the water. They would not have been able to see the alligators as they high-walked on all four legs into the lower dikes in the rice fields, lifting their tails out of the warm water as the sun came up. Enslaved children working half tasks adjacent to their parents were much less experienced at avoiding or hunting alligators, which *Carolina Sportsman* author William Elliott described as "ravenous," and so they could more easily become what racist stereotypical caricatures of the late nineteenth and early twentieth centuries called "alligator bait." Even though the prime laborers escaped the hottest part of the day by starting work before daybreak, they were vulnerable to ticks and deerflies. Sunup and sundown are also the times of the day when mosquitoes carrying falciparum malaria are most likely to transmit the disease.[5]

Enslaved laborers learned to distinguish the rice shoots from weeds and algae even in the predawn darkness. The threat of the driver's whip would have taught them. Fear compelled them to complete their half-acre task and to help half-hand family and friends in adjoining fields to complete theirs. All enslaved field hands in the rice fields used their hoes to stir the waterlogged earth.[6]

By early June 1863, Joshua Nicholls wrote in his letter to the editor, his rice crop was growing "luxuriantly" in the rice fields. The rice's dry growth produced a collage of various shades of green from forest to lime, as the plants were "putting forth their leaves." The people Nicholls held in bondage stood, their feet and ankles sunk deep in muck and water, between the rows of Joshua Nicholls's rice. Water from the "stretch-flow" had been drained off before they were sent in to hoe. But it was impossible to evacuate all of the water, and small amounts remained in the fields. Being underwater for four to six weeks left the ground swampy and quicksand-like. Soft stems of algae growing up between the rows of rice would have felt prickly under their feet and

added to the collage of shades of green. With each step, enslaved laborers put first their toes and the balls of their feet down on the ground,
then their heels, and their heels sank deeper into the swampy muck
with each step they took. The faster they walked, the more they sank
down—and the more they slipped on the steamed-spinach-like algae
floating in the water. The mélange of muck and slippery algae would
have hindered them from running through and climbing quickly out of
the rice fields and onto the dikes around the fields. However, once they
were able to extricate themselves and others from the morass, running
along the grand dike holding the Combahee back from the rice fields
was the quickest path to the source of the sound coming up the river—
"Lincoln's gunboats." "Lincoln's gunboats" became the names that the
bondspeople used to describe the vessels liberating them from enslavement, according to Tubman.[7]

There are so many things about enslaved people and their experiences
that we do not know and likely will never know. For example, who among
the bondspeople in the rice fields up and down the Combahee, from just
above James L. Paul's plantation to just below Combahee Ferry six miles
upriver, saw the two black smokestacks before the steamboats came around
the bend? We'll never know who heard the walking beam turning the *John
Adams's* paddlewheels—like a huge iron seesaw shimmying up and down
above the upper deck—and understood that it spelled freedom. We will
never who called it first, but some man, woman, or child who was standing
up to their ankles in muck that dark morning would have yelled "Yankee
gunboat!" Minus Hamilton told Colonel Higginson what he and his family
experienced when he saw the gunboat; the overseer saw it too.[8]

Hamilton likely never had thought he would see such a day in his life,
and it was a long life. He had been sold with his wife, Hagar, and their
daughter, Bina, in 1853 from Edward Rutledge Lowndes's estate to John
Parker. On Parker's Place, Bina married Harry Mack—both of them were
Prime Hands—and gave birth to Minus's granddaughter, also named Hagar.
John Parker's heir, Arthur Middleton Parker, went bankrupt and ultimately
sold his plantation and the people he held in bondage to James L. Paul in
December 1859. Little Hagar was four or five when the "Lincoln gunboats"
came up the Combahee.

De brack sojer so presumptious, dey come right ashore, hold up dere head. Fus'
tin I know, dere was a barn, ten thousand bushel rough rice, all in a blaze, den

mas'r great house, all cracklin' up de roof. Did n't keer for see 'em blaze? Lor, mas'r, did n't care notin' at all, *I was gwine to de boat.*

Hamilton likely considered himself blessed to have lived long enough to see Black soldiers so "presumptious," as he called them. (His consonant alternation of the "l" and "r" is characteristic of the speech of early speakers of English-based Creole, particularly African-born slaves, for whom Creole was their second language, or first-generation bondspeople, for whom Creole was their first language.) An enslaved person could not look a white person in the eye without inviting insult or, worse, injury. In contrast, the Black soldiers who came right ashore wearing the Union blue coats and pantaloons and carrying loaded muskets stood with their backs straight and held their heads up.[9]

Hamilton told Higginson what he saw after the 2nd South Carolina Volunteers left Lincoln's gunboats. They went to the slaveholder's barn, where he stored the rice his enslaved labor force had grown and harvested the previous year, ten thousand bushels of rough rice, and set it all on fire. The "presumptious" Black soldiers did not stop there. The next thing Minus Hamilton saw was the country estate of the man who held him and his family in bondage engulfed in flames up to the roof.[10]

Hamilton's gesticulations became even more animated, Higginson recalled. Higginson may have asked Hamilton how he felt watching the property of the man who legally owned him and his family go up in flames; Hamilton didn't care at all. But he made it clear to Higginson that what he did care about was seizing the opportunity to liberate himself and his family: *"I was gwine to de boat."*[11]

★★★★★★★★

At around five-thirty in the morning on June 2, roughly thirty minutes after Joshua Nicholls's enslaved driver had barged unceremoniously into his bedroom, and approximately one hour after Minus Hamilton and his fellow bondspeople had reached the rice fields to begin hoeing, CSA lieutenant W. E. Hewitt, who was stationed at Chisolmville, received the message from the first courier sent by Corporal H. H. Newton that two US Army gunboats had arrived at Field's Point. Almost simultaneously, he received Newton's second courier with the message that the enemy had anchored 100 yards from the picket's guard house. By the time the second courier arrived, Hewitt had already sent his own dispatch by courier north to Major Emanuel at

Green Pond. Hewitt called back his own courier, who was still in sight. He left the courier in charge of the guard house at Chisolmville, mounted his horse, and galloped south to Field's Point so he could see for himself the strength and position of the Union forces. When he arrived at Oliver Hering Middleton Sr.'s plantation, four miles from Field's Point, Hewitt found that Newton and the pickets had fallen back to Middleton's property. Newton must have reported to Lieutenant Hewitt that the Union soldiers were occupying Middleton's rice mill. Hewitt stated in his official report to Major Emanuel that he had reported everything he knew as soon as he knew it.[12]

Hewitt reported that the enemy had landed about an hour after Corporal Newton first spotted the Union boats. From the outset, the Confederate forces lost valuable time and advantage in stopping the 2nd South Carolina Volunteers from gaining a foothold at Field's Point and Tar Bluff. By the time Hewitt figured out what was going on, Union forces had landed the *Harriet A. Weed* at Nicholls's boat landing, put soldiers on the ground, and continued their advance up the Combahee.[13]

While Confederate pickets were stationed in the southeast part of the lower Combahee River at Field's Point and in the northwest portion at Combahee Ferry, the Third Military District's main forces were stationed in the northeast point of the triangle at Green Pond, with a smaller contingent at Chisolmville. Yet the 2nd South Carolina Volunteers' gunboats were unopposed as they penetrated a roughly twenty-mile stretch of the Combahee, virtually under the Confederates' noses. The Confederate pickets were seemingly paralyzed by their commanders' indecision.

Meanwhile, the 2nd South Carolina Volunteers continued their work. Amid billowing columns of smoke, hundreds if not thousands of enslaved people ran for their lives. Tubman remembered, years after the Civil War ended, that when "Lincoln's gunboats come to set them free," displaying their flags and blowing what the *New South* and Frederick Douglass's *Douglass' Monthly* described as the "uninterrupted pipe of the steam whistle," that somewhere around eight hundred freedom seekers ran for their lives and boarded the vessels. It was as if there was a "mysterious telegraphic communication existing among these simple people," Tubman told Sarah Bradford, bringing people not just from Joshua Nicholls's plantation, where the *Harriet A. Weed* landed, but from James L. Paul's plantation in the southeast direction and plantations as far away as Combahee Ferry, several miles to the northwest.[14]

Minus and Hagar Hamilton were among those who fled down to the *Harriet A. Weed*. Most freedom seekers toted their worldly possessions in large bundles on their heads. Captain Apthorp wrote in his journal that many of their bundles were so large they "completely overshadowed" the freedom seekers themselves.

> Ole woman and I go down to de boat; dem dey say behind us, "Rebels comin'! Rebels comin'!" I hab notin' on but my shirt and pantaloons; ole woman one single frock he hab on, and one handkerchief on he head; I leff all-two my blanket and run for de Rebel come, den dey did n't come, did n't truss for come.

The elderly couple left the rice fields with the clothes they had on their backs. Minus wore only his shirt and pantaloons; Hagar, the "old ... woman" (whom Minus Hamilton referred to with the masculine pronoun "he," which is a morphological feature of the Gullah dialect), wore a one-piece shift and a head-tie covering her hair. Hamilton may have regretted leaving his only possessions—two blankets—behind in the slave quarters when he ran before the Rebels came. But he did not regret escaping the land of bondage.[15]

The Hamiltons almost did not make it onto the *Harriet A. Weed*, because they were among the oldest of the Old Heads on the lower Combahee could not run to the boat like the Prime Hands, Boys and Wives, or Pikins. When Minus and Hagar Hamilton got down to the steamboat, freedom seekers running behind them told the couple that the Confederates were in pursuit. Hamilton remembered Hagar retorting that the Confederates could bring it on if they wanted to; let them challenge the Yankee gunboat head-on. Surprisingly, the Confederates did not challenge Lincoln's gunboats or the "presumptious" Black soldiers. Hamilton surmised that this was because they did not think they could win the fight.

> Ise eighty-eight year old, mas'r. My ole Mas'r Lowndes keep all de ages in a big book, and when we come to age ob sense we mark em down ebry year, so I know. Too ole for come? Mas'r joking. Neber too ole for leave de land of bondage. I old, but great good for chil'en, gib thousand tank ebry day. Young people can go through, *force* . . . , mas'r but de ole folk mus' go slow.

Colonel Higginson had asked Minus Hamilton if he had thought was too old to run to the US Army gunboats. It was an odd question for a determined abolitionist to ask; perhaps he simply wanted to draw the story out of the old man. Hamilton was grateful for the young people; he said a thousand thank-yous every day. He was grateful for the young Black people who were ready to fight for their freedom, because young people could go forcefully. The old people, like him and Hagar, had to go slowly.[16]

Joshua Nicholls later wrote in his letter to the editor that he assumed that the freedom seekers had recognized among the Black soldiers a number of formerly enslaved men who had already liberated themselves. Though Nicholls was likely too far away in the forest to positively identify the soldiers' faces or voices, he was correct. Friday Barrington was a member of Company D, which came ashore at Colonel Heyward's Cypress Plantation, which, as we have seen, was where he, his parents, and his sister were held in bondage. Barrington may not have been the only Combahee freedom seeker to return during the raid.[17]

At any rate, while Nicholls ran off to the woods, the 2nd South Carolina Volunteers came ashore from his boat landing and onto his plantation. From his hiding place he saw them come up to his country estate and set it ablaze. Nicholls also saw smoke rising from the direction of his stepson's property next door and knew the soldiers had torched Rose Hill Plantation. The soldiers moved swiftly, their movements on different plantations seeming almost synchronized. Before Nicholls knew it, thick billows of smoke rose simultaneously from the north and west, coming from the steam-powered rice mill, overseer's house, and stables at Oakland and Cypress Plantations.[18]

What Nicholls described was a chaotic scene of destruction and mayhem: The "roaring of flames" and "towering column of smoke from every quarter" as fire engulfed his and his neighbors' property. The "barbarous howls of the negroes" as they reunited family members, retrieved belongings, and decided what they would do next. The "blowing of horns, the harsh steam whistle" signaling the enslaved population to hurry to the river and steal their freedom. Nicholls witnessed Blacks "carrying bags of rice upon their heads" from his own barn and running toward the steamboat. He thought the raid a "repetition of San Domingo," when free people of color and Africans held in bondage on sugar plantations in Saint-Domingue (what is now Haiti) overthrew the planters and the colonial government, abolished enslavement, and created the first Black republic in the Western Hemisphere.[19]

When the freedom seekers rushed to the safety of the *Harriet Weed*, they stopped to greet the soldiers before climbing aboard. They overwhelmed

Captain Apthorp. He remembered them saying, "Lord bless you Massa," "Good Morning massa Oh bless the good Lord," and other utterances, all expressed with intense earnestness. Tears of joy ran down their faces as they scrambled to touch freedom with their own hands, clinging to the soldiers and officers' hands, knees, clothing, weapons—anything they could grasp. Apthorp was touched by their inability to find words to express their relief, joy, and gratitude. Nicholls, on the other hand, was horrified. He wrote that the people he formerly had held in bondage "seemed utterly transformed, drunk with excitement, and capable of the wildest excesses."[20]

Yet not everyone was *"gwine to de boat."* Some were left behind and separated from their family and friends. John A. Savage, for example, did not get on the Yankee gunboat, because his enslaver, William L. Kirkland Jr., had taken him with him to the Charleston Light Dragoons camp, where Savage was forced to labor against his will. It was not the first time Kirkland had taken Savage away from the plantation with him. Savage had known Andrew Harris, who was a couple of years older, since he was a boy, and both had been born enslaved by William Savage on the Ogeechee River in Georgia. After they both became Kirkland's legal property, Kirkland had exploited Savage's labor as a "deer hunter," and he had been off hunting with Kirkland on the Ashepoo River when Andrew married Diana Days. Nor was Savage there, he testified in Diana Harris's pension file, when "General Montgomery came up on the Combahee and took them away." In June 1863, the Charleston Light Dragoons had been camped at McPhersonville for a little less than a month. The soldiers' camp was approximately eighteen miles from Rose Hill. Once a week, every week, Savage walked approximately nine hours, including stops for rest and water breaks, in the spring, summer, and fall heat, and then took the ferry across the Combahee to visit his family—his wife, Charlotte, and children Primus, Sandy, Cathy, John, and Nelly. The week before the raid, Savage had visited his family at Rose Hill. The next time he went, he found that his family and the remainder of the people William Kirkland had held in bondage were gone.[21]

Kirkland had also taken Tomson, described as a "boy," with him to camp with the Charleston Light Dragoons. Tomson died in bondage sixteen miles from home in McPhersonville. There is no record whether Tomson left family on Rose Hill or Longbrow, and if so, whether the family he was forced to leave behind liberated themselves in the Combahee River Raid.[22]

Margaret Moody did not get on the gunboat either. She had been born on Rose Hill, where she had known Diana Days Harris all her life. She testified that she lived at Rose Hill "until June 1863 when I was hired out upcountry. In June of that year, Gen. Montgomery come up and took all of the colored folks that were left there away."[23]

As Moody noted, most who were on the plantations when the Yankees arrived went down to the boats. William Jones testified, "I was up on the William Kirkland Place on the Combahee when General Montgomery came up there with the boats in June 1863 and took up about 60 head of us." Andrew Harris, his wife, Diana Harris, and their son Samuel, who was their sole surviving child when the war began, "were of the party that came down with Montgomery." Martha Singleton was a girl of seven at the time of the raid. Born on Rose Hill, she testified that she had "lived there until Gen. Montgomery come up there . . . and took all of the colored people off." Among others who "went off on the gunboat together" and were subsequently taken to Beaufort were Jack Wineglass, who had been sold to Rose Hill as a small boy; Ned Snipe, who had been sold to William Kirkland twelve years before the war; and Jackson Grant, who was sold to William Kirkland in 1856 at age nineteen. And Old Head November Osborne and his wife, Sarah Small Osborne, fled bondage on Oakland Plantation. They had grown up as "play children together," were married to each other when they were old enough by the man who held them both in bondage, were bequeathed together from Thomas Lowndes's estate to his son Charles T. Lowndes, and were sent to Oakland after Thomas Lowndes's death in 1843.[24]

Captain Apthorp remembered that the "duskey tide" of freedom seekers grew over the hours as the Black soldiers continued to devote themselves to the work of destroying the Combahee rice plantations. Apthorp and his Company B broke down the floodgates holding the saltwater of the Combahee River back from the rice fields until the "ricefields were a lake." The flood of brackish river water ruined the growing rice crop. They burned the rice mills, the barns full of rice ready for sale, and the mansion homes. In the process they ruined two or three years' worth of the lucrative harvest of Combahee planters' Carolina Gold.[25]

When it was time for the *Harriet A. Weed* to depart, crowds of freedom seekers flocked to the shore to board. They poured in not only from the immediate Combahee region but also from several miles around. Apthorp recalled that the crowds stretched in every direction as far as the eye could see. The freedom seekers toting bundles of their meager belongings on their heads looked like an "army of black ants . . . lugging a huge white egg larger than itself." By this point, however, the *Harriet A. Weed* was loaded to its carrying capacity, as was the *John Adams*, which had "very scanty quarters" and a "narrow hold" and so could transport fewer. The loss of the *Sentinel* had, of course, reduced the number of freedom seekers they could take with them. Apthorp remembered that he was heartbroken that they had to leave anyone behind, especially knowing they would surely be brutally tortured by the planters and overseers for trying to escape to freedom. Nonetheless, they could not safely take anyone else. As the *Harriet A. Weed* swung away from Joshua Nicholls's boat landing and into the Combahee, one can only imagine what the 2nd South Carolina Volunteer soldiers, men who had liberated themselves from bondage only a few months or weeks before they fought in the raid, felt about leaving others behind.[26]

The *John Adams* continued further up the Combahee and into Colleton, heading across Combahee Ferry to the pontoon bridge. Manning the ship's guns were members of Captain Charles Brayton's 3rd Rhode Island Heavy Artillery, which, according to its chaplain, acted as "infantry, engineers, light and heavy artillery on shore, and both light and heavy artillery on gunboats" as well. Its companies were often broken up and detailed to different operations, from South Carolina to Florida.[27]

The *John Adams* kept its guns and two howitzers trained on the road and water approaches to the bridge. Montgomery's forces had opened up the mouth of the Combahee and covered all three approaches to the Ashepoo River and the Charleston and Savannah Railroad—by road via Field's Point and Tar Bluff and by water via Combahee Ferry.[28]

The Confederates constructed floating pontoon bridges in order to be able to take the enemy by surprise. Though temporary, such bridges had to be able to support the weight of heavy equipment and survive the current, which had the capacity to tear away the moorings. No description of the particular pontoon bridge across the Combahee River has been found. However, a caption on the back of Timothy O'Sullivan's photograph of US troops building one across the Port Royal River describes it being constructed with timber and light-draft flatboats, and it is reasonable to assume that Confederate pontoon bridges were built in much the same way. The flatboats used in these bridges were the kind of boat that "every rice planter had . . . for transporting rice," as Alexander Chisolm once replied when asked if there were any on the Savannah River with which to build a pontoon bridge. Wagons carried the boats to the water's edge, and here they were unloaded and placed into the water. Engineers then anchored to them a row of wooden beams and supports covered with planks. Each of the boats was positioned parallel to the current to resist its action. The planks were fastened together on top of the boats, creating the bridge.[29]

Pontoon bridges were strong enough to get large numbers of infantry and even cavalry across bodies of water and coastal wetlands. Confederate guards at Savannah later used them to escape General William Tecumseh Sherman's army as it marched from Atlanta to the sea. Pontoon bridges were also dismantled relatively easily, making them flexible and able to respond to the army's needs. They could be opened for the passage of steamers by dismantling the floor timbers from the moorings underneath and letting the current sweep aside the boats. Once the steamers had passed, engineers refastened the boats and timbers to the moorings, restoring the bridge. Alternatively, the pontoon bridges could be completely dismantled. Shortly after the *John Adams* reached the pontoon bridge at Combahee Ferry, a Union Army force landed and "immediately commenced cutting" away and setting it on fire. At one point a detachment of Confederate cavalry came across the pontoon bridge; Brayton moved them along by firing a few shells from the *John Adams*. The chaplain of the 3rd Rhode Island would later describe how Captain Brayton "mowed his swath broad and smooth" with his guns.[30]

A long, narrow causeway, with rice fields on both sides, led from the pontoon bridge to Cypress Plantation. It predated the war and appears on plats as early as 1795. (Today, the causeway extends beneath US Highway 17.) The Union and the Confederate soldiers had to cross this slender passageway to get from the pontoon bridge to the plantation; it was the only way in or out. Captain Hoit's Company A of the 2nd South Carolina Volunteers marched over the elevated causeway on the east side of the Combahee. His men skirmished with Confederate forces, scattering them with artillery, and pushed through until they reached Cypress Plantation.[31]

★★★★★★★★

Like Joshua Nicholls, Colonel William C. Heyward was sleeping on the morning of June 2, 1863, when he was awakened by a loud rap on the door at 6:15 a.m. Heyward wrote in his report that his enslaved driver was supervising the labor of the enslaved field hands at work in the "lower fields" at Cypress Plantation and had sent a message about the approach of the Union vessels up to him by messenger. Heyward dressed hurriedly and rushed out to get a view of the river.[32]

Given the risks Heyward had faced as commander of Fort Walker during the Battle of Port Royal, which he had witnessed firsthand as part of General Thomas F. Drayton's observational force stationed at Bluffton, it seems surprising that he had devised no plan to protect the property of the lower Combahee rice planters—other than, like Joshua Nicholls, hiding himself in the woods and urging those he had enslaved to do the same. Heyward later wrote in his official military report that he had sent word to have the enslaved laborers working in the lower rice fields brought up and taken "back into the woods" to hide. Heyward walked a few hundred yards, looked out with his spyglass, and saw what he described as a "large ferry boat" "very slowly" making its way to his property. The *John Adams* was flying the US flag, and its upper deck was crowded with people.[33]

As Heyward watched incredulously, a small group of soldiers took a small rowboat ashore on the plantation. Once landed, they "walked to and from the causeway blowing a horn and waving a small flag." The freedom seekers made their way to them. At that point his enslaved driver found Heyward and presented the field hands whom he had brought up from the lower rice fields. Heyward ordered the driver to "take the [field] hands back into the woods" to hide. He also asked the driver whether he had seen any Confederate pickets passing on the causeway. The driver replied that he had not. Heyward looked through his spyglass at the picket station at Combahee Ferry. Everything seemed quiet and calm; even the horses were hitched. It appeared no alarm had been given about the Union boats that sailed "within 1¼ miles" of where the pickets were stationed.[34]

While Heyward, the driver, and the field hands stood together, one of the field hands spotted four Confederate soldiers coming down the causeway; one of them was on horseback, his horse spurred to a run. The *John Adams* fired at them. One of the pickets reported to Heyward, "Yankee boats in river." Heyward must have wondered where they had been. It was their duty to protect his and his neighbors' property. Had the soldier been sleeping on duty when he should have sounded an alarm? The Confederate pickets could have and should have reported before then.[35]

Major Emanuel was, as noted, in charge of the Confederate picket forces at Field's Point. Corporal Wesley D. Wall of the 4th Carolina Cavalry, Company F, commanded the pickets at Combahee Ferry. The Combahee Ferry picket later justified his negligence in reporting the presence of US boats on the Combahee by referring to Captain James Lowndes's orders, issued on May 26, 1863, after Confederate pickets stationed on the Combahee River had issued a false alarm. Lowndes had ordered the pickets to confirm whether or not the US boat had landed and, if so, how many men were aboard. If there were two Confederate pickets on duty and five or six Union soldiers, the Confederate pickets were to engage them in a firefight. If more than five or six Union soldiers were aboard the boat, the Confederate pickets were to fire a warning shot to inform troops stationed nearby of the presence of the enemy and monitor the enemy's movements. The picket likely did not report the boats' appearance sooner because he had been warned that the next false alarm would result in a court-martial.[36]

In any case, the pickets stationed at Combahee Ferry did not report anything until they were certain of the facts. After all, they rationalized, the boats might have belonged to the Confederacy, and they were under orders to be certain. And the picket confirmed to Colonel Heyward that he was the first to give any information about the impending attack; no Confederate couriers had been sent to Pocotaligo, due west of Combahee Ferry along the lower Combahee River, where General William Stephen Walker, the commanding officer of the Third Military District, was stationed. Heyward sent a courier on horseback to Green Pond for reinforcements.[37]

While Colonel Heyward waited for reinforcements, the *John Adams* continued up the Combahee. The tide was coming in. Colonel Heyward reported that "the river was at three-fourths flood."[38]

Around 7 a.m., Major Emanuel received the news from both ends of his command—Field's Point and Combahee Ferry—almost simultaneously. The courier whom Lieutenant William E. Hewitt had dispatched from Field's Point to Emanuel an hour and a half earlier finally arrived (after taking what must have been the longest possible route to Green Pond) with the message that two US gunboats had arrived at Field's Point and were landing troops. A second courier brought the message sent by Corporal Wall, chief of the pickets at Combahee Ferry, that a Union boat was headed up the Combahee and was about a half mile from the pontoon bridge.[39]

Unlike Newton, Corporal Wall did not fall back when confronted by the enemy, even by the fire coming from the *John Adams*. He and his men on horseback stepped to the enemy and moved past fires set by Montgomery's soldiers. As the Confederates crossed the long causeway connecting Cypress Plantation to the pontoon bridge, Captain Brayton and his men fired at them twice. Then the gunboat proceeded further upriver to the pontoon bridge and landed more soldiers. At that point Corporal Wall sent another courier to Emanuel, stating that the Union had landed on the pontoon bridge. Wall remembered that twenty-five to thirty Union soldiers marched up and down the riverbank waving the Stars and Stripes.[40]

Wall sent one of his men to Lowndes's Oakland Plantation to see if the Union had boots on the ground there, and left another soldier at the head of the causeway connecting to Cypress Plantation and the pontoon bridge. Corporal Wall rode to Cypress Plantation to see if he could assist Heyward in moving his enslaved labor force to a safe location—that is, the woods. Heyward himself rode to Green Pond to telegraph General William S. Walker.[41]

Heyward saw twenty Union soldiers come marching two abreast along the long, narrow causeway to Heyward's plantation. Though Heyward later reported that he had not noticed whether the soldiers were Black, they were. These men had escaped enslavement only weeks or months before joining the 2nd South Carolina Volunteers and were fighting with "ropes around their necks." Yet they marched courageously, not knowing if Confederate forces were hiding in the rice fields or marsh on either side of the causeway, ready to pick them off. Though the Confederates fired on the freedom seekers, they were outgunned by the *John Adams*, which beat the rebels off.[42]

Wall, on horseback on his way back from Cypress, came within a few hundred feet of a few dozen Black soldiers and their white officers marching along the causeway. He fell back to the breastworks that commanded the causeway and fired on them. Then Wall heard firing coming from the direction of Oakland Plantation, and so he retreated. The 2nd South Carolina Volunteers came up to the breastworks and pushed on until they entered Heyward's gate. Following them, Wall watched as the soldiers began to burn the property.[43]

The author of the 104th Pennsylvania regimental history reported that Colonel Montgomery had told the freedom seekers that "the country would belong to them after the war"; they should burn the planters' mansions, because they would have no use for them, but should leave the slave quarters unmolested, which they did. After torching all the other buildings on Cypress, a group marched toward the slave quarters, turned, and fired at Corporal Wall for the first time. He returned fire, then retreated back onto the road as Lieutenant Peter Lindsay Breeden approached. Breeden was the first lieutenant of Major Emanuel's Company E, 4th Regiment of the South Carolina Cavalry. He was not a planter, but he owned a horse, which he used in his service to the Confederate military.[44]

By this time, the gunboats were within a mile and a half of the pontoon bridge. Emanuel recounted in his official report that he ordered Captain H. Godbold of Company F of the 4th South Carolina Cavalry to send Lieutenant Archer E. Gilchrist and twenty men from the Company E of the same regiment as an advance guard down Stock's Creek Road, the direct road to Field's Point, to "harass" the enemy. The Confederate pickets told Lieutenant Gilchrist that Union forces were on the main road leading from the Third Military District's headquarters in Green Pond to Field's Point. They could not stop the Union advance.[45]

Emanuel ordered Captain Godbold and the remainder of his forces to remain at Stock's Causeway, where two pieces of Captain Thomas Haynes Bomar's artillery were positioned. Bomar was captain of the Chestatee Light Artillery, Georgia Volunteers, Wright Legion. Two additional pieces of his artillery were ordered to Heyward's plantation at Combahee Ferry as well, but they never arrived.[46]

At that point Emanuel received secondhand information from one of his subordinates, Lieutenant Hendricks, that the gunboats had passed the pontoon bridge and now were headed to the Charleston and Savannah Railroad bridge. The intelligence was inaccurate, sort of. The *John Adams* did go beyond the pontoon bridge, until it encountered the piles positioned by the lower Combahee rice planters to block the river and protect their property. But the *John Adams* was not headed to destroy the railroad crossing. Anyway, it turned around before it got entangled in the obstructions. Taking the report at face value, however, Emanuel ordered Captain Bomar's artillery, which might have been able to stop the Union's ascent further up the Combahee River, to take a position that would prevent the Union forces from reaching the railroad.[47]

Then Emanuel left his position and headed to reinforce the Third Military District's headquarters. Colonel Heyward met Major Emanuel on the road, and when Emanuel asked for directions to the road to Salkehatchie,

Heyward asked why, given that it was fourteen or fifteen miles away and General Walker and his forces were stationed at Pocotaligo, five or six miles from there. Why did Emanuel need to reinforce the Third Military District's headquarters when Heyward's and his neighbors' properties on the Combahee River were burning? Nevertheless, Emanuel proceeded to Salkehatchie; he was just following orders.[48]

★★★★★★★★

Decades after the war, when she applied for a widow's pension, Peggy Moultrie Brown offered her recollection of what happened on Cypress Plantation on the morning of June 2, 1863: "The government boat came right up to the plantation landing on the Combahee River. We all, were then 100 of William C. Heyward's slaves went onboard and were carried to Beaufort, South Carolina." Margaret Kelly Simmons testified that her husband, Joshua Simmons, had stayed on Cypress Plantation during the war "until Colonel Montgomery, a Yankee, came through that country, and took all the people around there to Beaufort." Sina Bolze Young testified that she and her husband had been "brought to Port Royal by Capt. Montgomery in June." By that time, their daughter Flora had "cleared her 2nd year and was in her 3rd one." Lucius Robinson testified he "went on the boat together" with Cuffie Bolze, William Middleton, Charles Nicholas and his wife, Hagar, Jack Barnwell, Neptune Nicholas, and Betsey Singleton Simmons Nicholas. They all were with the "crowd" that Montgomery and his men took to Beaufort.[49]

Elsey Higgins Jones testified in the pension files that Pool Sellers, whom she knew on Cypress Plantation and who called her "Coz," left Colonel Heyward's plantation. "All the young and old left the place," Elsey said, aside from her, because she was "in no condition to go." Elsey may have stayed behind because she was in a "delicate state," as another Combahee woman put it, the most likely meaning of which is that she had recently given birth and her month of confinement after childbirth had not yet elapsed. If in fact she was in confinement, one must wonder who would have attended her. The other female Prime Hands, her agemates Sina Young, Venus Lyons, Lina Richard, and Bina Mack, had all gotten "on board the boat that carried off Sina and William Young together with the balance of the colored people from Cypress plantation."[50]

Cypress Plantation was located on the east bank of the Combahee and Newport Plantation on the west, where the Combahee makes such a tight curve that it resembles an open oval with the two extremities of the oval coming within yards of meeting. The rice fields on the two plantations faced each other across the narrow stretch of river. Captain T. J. Allen, leader of a "company of State troops" who called themselves "the Combahee Rangers," remembered advancing his troops to Newport Plantation. Approximately five minutes after Heyward first saw the *John Adams* land at Combahee Ferry, a Confederate lieutenant named Brunson reported from Middleton's stables that he spotted a gunboat. Captain Allen and his men could see it also. While Lieutenant Brunson's forces did not fall back, neither were they able to stop the advance of Montgomery's men. The chaplain of the 3rd Rhode Island Heavy Artillery wrote that the Confederate soldiers instead moved with "hot haste" to warn Combahee planters and overseers, and to offer to help them move their enslaved labor forces off their plantations, because the "Abolition army" was coming.[51]

Freedom seekers from the upper reaches and the east and west banks of the Combahee remembered boarding the *John Adams* together and recalled the Black soldiers who took them off to freedom. Decades after the raid took place, Sally Middleton Green White testified that she was raised on Newport Plantation and that she knew Pool Sellers, his mother, and his sister, who all were held in bondage by Heyward and "lived right over the river" from her. Sally recalled that on the morning of June 2, "when the Yankee boat went up there after the colored people the Heyward people and our people came down on the same boat." Sally and Pool both got on the *John Adams*: "The boat brought us all down here to Beaufort and Pool and others went into the Army."[52]

William Jones testified he had never met James Sheppard "til the Yankee gunboat went up Combahee River and brought us down here and put us in the same company." Jones had been enslaved on William L. Kirkland's Rose Hill Plantation, located south of Cypress on the east bank of the Combahee River. Sheppard had been held in bondage across the Combahee River with Sally Middleton Green White on Newport Plantation. Monday Lighthouse testified he was "very small" when the raid took place, but remembered "when the soldiers were here" at Newport Plantation, where he was born and grew up in bondage.[53]

Due west of Newport Plantation and on the same side of the river is Bonny Hall Plantation. Here, as on Longbrow, enslaved laborers had dug a canal that facilitated the transportation of goods and people to the river. The 3rd Rhode Island soldiers likely used the canal to bring Blacks held in bondage on Bonny Hall out to the river and to freedom in rowboats, or freedom seekers came down the canal themselves on rowboats, barges, or makeshift watercraft.

Jonas Green, Wally Graham, Parris White, Mary White, and likely others whose stories are not documented had escaped from Blake's Bonny Hall Plantation before the Combahee River Raid, but they did not specify in their pension file affidavits exactly when. Like enslaved people on Cypress Plantation and Rose Hill Plantation, freedom seekers on Bonny Hall likely had advance warning of what was coming by means of that "mysterious telegraphic communication," which must have encompassed people like Jonas Green and Wally Graham, Tim, Tom, Billy, Janus, and Dick, and Friday Barrington, all of whom were born and grew up enslaved on the lower Combahee rice plantations, but liberated themselves and made their way to Beaufort before the raid.

★★★★★★★★

We don't know exactly where Harriet Tubman was during the Combahee River Raid. She told Emma Telford decades after the war that she "was in de forwar' boat whar de Colonel and Captain an de colored man dat was to tell us whar de torpedoes was." *The John Adams* proceeded up the Combahee past Longbrow Plantation, where the *Harriet A. Weed* landed at Joshua Nicholls's boat landing, to Combahee Ferry. But if Tubman disembarked from the *John Adams*, did she go up the east bank with Captain Hoit's Company A of the 2nd South Carolina? Did she go up the west bank of the Combahee with Captain Brayton's 3rd Rhode Island? We still don't know. But we know that she was there. Harriet Tubman's nephew Harkless Bowley wrote in a letter to Earl Conrad on August 8, 1939, that Tubman "found the men who had helped place torpedoes in Combahee River to keep the Union boats from ascending." How would Bowley have known these details about the Combahee River Raid if Tubman had not told them to him?[54]

A teacher from Massachusetts wrote in a letter to her parents on June 11, 1863, that "a colored woman by the name of Harriet Tubbs went with" Colonel Montgomery's regiment. She, of course, was writing about Tubman. According to Tubman, the freedom seekers had been told by the planters that the Yankees had horns and tails like the devil. And Tubman told Emma Telford decades after the war that "the Colonel blowed the whistle and stopped the boat and a company of soldiers went ashore. Colonel Montgomery blew the whistle again . . . you could look over the rice fields, and see them coming from every direction." We also know that Tubman did not stay on the *John Adams*. Harkless Bowley wrote to Earl Conrad that Tubman "made her way to the cabins of the slaves, talked with them, . . . brought them to the spot where she was landed and many women and children." The Massachusetts teacher reported that when Tubman "got over to the main a few days ago she went to burning buildings and she helped bring away contrabands." As described in the foreword, Tubman helped a poor, sick woman carry two pigs "in a bag for roasters, one for Gen. Hunter and the other for Gen. Saxton." Tubman also remembered that when the officer gave the order to "double-quick," "I started to run, stepped on my dress, it being rather long, and fell and tore it almost completely off." When she got back aboard the boat, "there was hardly any thing left of it but shreds."[55]

Meanwhile, rather than rely on their small detachment of reinforcements in Ashepoo to pursue the US Army and prevent them from going up the Combahee, the Confederates confined themselves to the task of notifying overseers and enslaved drivers of the approach of the Black troops. Confederate soldiers stayed on Walter's Bonny Hall Plantation for three or four hours. maintaining a position between the freedom seekers and the US boats to keep them from escaping. Their efforts were partially successful, but they could still see Union soldiers and freedom seekers trying to get to the boat (Tubman could have been among them, of course). They rode down to Newport and found the US soldiers had left after burning all of the buildings on Newport and taking the enslaved labor force to the *John Adams*, which was still landed at the pontoon bridge.[56]

Freedom seekers from Bonny Hall were still trying to get to Combahee Ferry. Three Confederate soldiers, John D. Sanders, Lieutenant Brunson, and a private named Leightley, rode back to the plantation and sicced "negro dogs" on the freedom seekers to cut off their freedom pursuit. Bloodhounds long had been used by enslavers to maintain a culture of violence on southern plantations, hunt runaway slaves, and generally use terror to keep Black people in their place. During the Civil War, they became the weapon of choice for fighting against Black soldiers. Seeing and hearing the dogs, some of the Bonny Hall freedom seekers did turn back.[57]

Though they were on different vessels and disembarked at different plantations, Tubman and Captain Apthorp both recollected that droves of freedom seekers, sparked by the display of flags and the steam whistle, headed down to the river, toting their meager earthly possessions on their heads. Colonel Montgomery sent small rowboats out from the *John Adams*, and it is possible that freedom seekers also came down to the river in row-boats. Tubman recalled that masses of freedom seekers continued to try to board rowboats even after the boats were full. They held on to the sides of the small boats to prevent the vessels from taking off without them. The boatmen struck at their hands with their oars, but the freedom seekers held on for dear life. They were afraid, Tubman recalled, that the gunboats that came to set them free would leave them behind, and they wanted to make sure they were aboard "one of these arks of refuge." The 3rd Rhode Island's chaplain described "so many souls within sight of freedom, and yet unable to attain it" as "the saddest sight of the whole expedition."[58]

It was at this moment that Montgomery shouted down to Tubman from the upper deck of the *John Adams*, his voice rising above the clamor. Addressing her as "Moses," Montgomery asked her to sing to the freedom seekers to bring calm. Tubman lifted her beautiful voice to sing "Uncle Sam's Farm," an abolitionist song composed by Edward Pearce Christy and Jesse Hutchinson Jr.; it had been popularized by the Hutchinson Singers, which Hugh Higginson, the founder and patron of the Boston Symphony, characterized as "a band of Puritan Bohemians." Tubman likely had heard the song at an antislavery meeting in the North. She sang it spontaneously—to encourage the freedom seekers to trust the federal government and to reassure them that life would be better for them in freedom than it ever was in the "prison-house of bondage":

> Of all the whole creation in the East or in the West,
> The glorious Yankee nation is the greatest and the best.
> Come along! Come along! don't be alarmed,
> Uncle Sam is rich enough to give you all a farm.

Tubman invoked the image of a benevolent "Uncle Sam" as someone who would take care of the Combahee refugees—not just set them free but give them land on which they could live safely and produce enough food to feed their families. She recalled her intervention working. After she sang each verse, those who were on the shore holding on to the sides of the rowboats released them, lifted their hands in prayer, and shouted "Glory!" The rowboats pushed off, carrying the freedom seekers aboard to safety on the *John Adams* and liberation, leaving those still standing on the shore or in the water behind in bondage. As noted earlier in this chapter, one of the Union vessels had been grounded, and the remaining two gunboats could take only a fraction of those who ran to the river for freedom.[59]

★★★★★★★★

As noted earlier, it is somewhat surprising that, despite his experience with the US Navy and Army from his service in the Confederate Army, William C. Heyward took no precautions to protect Cypress Plantation against a possible incursion by the Yankees, and because he did not, many of the enslaved people there escaped to the Union gunboats. But other planters had taken such precautions.

A nearby plantation, Myrtle Grove, was owned by one of William C. Heyward's cousins and Nathaniel Heyward's sons, Charles Heyward; its main dike tied off of the main dike of Cypress Plantation going west. For years those enslaved on Cypress and Myrtle Grove Plantations must have passed each other every morning as both groups reported to the rice fields. However, when the enslaved labor force on Cypress went to the fields to hoe rice early on the morning of June 2, the people held in bondage on Myrtle Grove were not there. They never got the message to run to the river because they had been moved inland.

Charles Heyward kept a plantation journal that he had started before the war, for his Amsterdam, Lewisburg, Rose Hill, Pleasant Hill, and Myrtle Grove Plantations on the Upper Combahee. In it, he recorded the names of bondspeople to whom he gave blue and white cloth (specifying how many yards for each), caps, kerchiefs, and blankets every December for the winter and April or May for the summer. All of the plantations except Myrtle Grove were located north of the Combahee Ferry and the pontoon bridge. A few weeks after the Battle of Port Royal, Heyward wrote about Myrtle Grove: "In December 1861 and January 1862 moved all the Negroes up to Wateree, except the following Jacob, William, Eve, Davy, Sary, Molly, Sylvia, Dolly, Nelly, Mathew, James, child." Charles Heyward acted, unlike most of his neighbors and relations south of Combahee Ferry and the pontoon bridge. One of the few others who did was Walter Blake, who evacuated some of the people his father held in bondage, though it is unclear if he did so before or after the raid. One of them, Simon (Chisolm) Blake, testified he was born on the Combahee around 1837 and taken by Walter Blake in the summer of 1863 upcountry to Henderson, North Carolina, where he "refugeed." Simon liberated himself, fell in with Union soldiers, and went with them to Tennessee, where he enlisted in the 40th US Colored Troops, Company K, in Greenville, Tennessee, on April 29, 1865.[60]

Unlike Hector Fields, my great-great-great-grandfather on my paternal grandfather's side of the family—who, as described previously, liberated himself from bondage, joined the 2nd South Carolina Volunteers, and fought in the raid—my paternal grandmother's family was enslaved on Myrtle Grove and other Heyward plantations a few miles away on the upper Combahee River, according to family oral traditions and burial places. Some of them may well have been among those evacuated by Charles Heyward. Either way, they remained enslaved until the end of the Civil War. They did not join the US Army or have pension files. Thus, it has to date been impossible to document their exact locations before the 1870 census. It is safe to say, though, that we got left behind.

★★★★★★★★

As we've seen, Lieutenant Breeden's men arrived at Cypress Plantation within the hour after the Confederate pickets had reported the enemy gunboats approaching the pontoon bridge and encountered volumes of smoke. Six days after the raid, the *New South* reported about Cypress: "Colonel Haywood's [*sic*] plantation, at Green Pond," where he lived in "magnificent style," "was visited by a company" of Union soldiers. It described his country estate as "a mansion that equaled any on the main" land in downtown Charleston or Beaufort. The Confederates arrived at Cypress as well—but too late, of course. They witnessed the magnificent country estate, rice mill, and storage bin filled with rice being torched. Lowndes's neighboring plantation was engulfed in flames as well. Breeden divided his cavalry forces and sent part out as skirmishers, then proceeded down the main road with the rest and took a position at the breastworks on the edge of the causeway.[61]

From a position three hundred yards away from Breeden, the 2nd South Carolina Volunteers and 3rd Rhode Island retired to the *John Adams,* which was still landed near the pontoon bridge and was being followed by freedom seekers escaping bondage on Heyward's plantation. Among the items the soldiers had taken from the plantations were Heyward's prize white stallion, which was still saddled and bridled and carried his saber and pistols, and several of his carriages with additional horses. Breeden's cavalry and sharpshooters pursued the Union soldiers as they marched across the causeway.

Captain Hoit and his Company A had not been idle since they left the *John Adams*, advancing down the road to Combahee Ferry and upriver to the pontoon bridge. The Union officer and his men took a stand across the road. The *New South* reported that while Breeden's men fought with "spirit and determination," Captain Hoit's forces and the "negroes" "maintained their ground stoutly," keeping up a "sharp effective fire" for thirty minutes until the *John Adams* returned and dispersed the Confederates; during this time, Confederate fire killed one of Colonel Heyward's horses. Then the 2nd South Carolina Volunteer soldiers and Cypress freedom seekers took cover, running to the boat. Breeden did not pursue them for fear of the *John Adams*'s howitzers, which Captain Brayton still had trained on them.[62]

In military strategy, there is a marked difference between the circumstances under which soldiers retreat and those under which they retire. On the one hand, soldiers retreat from a position of weakness, such as when the Confederate corporal H. H. Newton first saw the 2nd South Carolina Volunteers at Field's Point, ascertained that their numbers and artillery were superior to his, and retreated. On the other hand, soldiers retire from a position of strength. The 2nd South Carolina Volunteers maintained a position of strength throughout the raid in large part because of the firepower of the *John Adams*. As Breeden and his men fired on the soldiers and freedom seekers at Cypress Plantation, the *John Adams* was still docked near the pontoon bridge, commanding the causeway. Once the soldiers were safely aboard, the 3rd Rhode Island's gunners on the *John Adams* bore down on Breeden's men and forced them to retreat to the woods, which must have been already quite crowded with fleeing planters and retreating Confederate troops.[63]

Major Emanuel arrived shortly after the *John Adams* had cleared out Breeden's forces. He was told there was a second Union gunboat farther downriver at Longbrow Plantation and that a few dozen soldiers had disembarked from the gunboat. Mr. Pipkin, Charles T. Lowndes's overseer, requested aid from Emanuel to prevent the people Lowndes held in bondage from escaping to freedom. Emanuel dispatched a small force of Breeden's men; three accompanied Pipkin back to Lowndes's plantation, arriving within 150 yards of the barn at Oakland Plantation. Montgomery's men and a portion of the Lowndes bondspeople were making their way to the boat. Lowndes's overseer wanted to get closer and stop the freedom seekers from boarding. Breeden's men told him the guns on the *John Adams* would kill him if he did.[64]

Pipkin saw an enslaved girl going toward the boat. He ran within twenty-five yards of Lowndes's boat landing and within ninety yards of the girl.

Pipkin shot the girl in cold blood when she refused to stop her advance to the gunboat and to freedom. She was the only freedom seeker to die in the raid. We don't know her name. The newspaper coverage a few days later nevertheless reported that enslaved drivers brandished pistols and "decreed death" to any freedom seeker who refused to follow them to the woods. If they behaved this way, these enslaved men must have done so before they too got on the boats. Lowndes's overseer and a small Confederate force succeeded in apprehending two dozen freedom seekers before they got on the boat, taking them back to the slave street on Oakland Plantation, even as the *John Adams* fired on them with its small guns. The remainder of Breeden's men remained at the causeway and kept watch over the *John Adams*, which returned to dock at the pontoon bridge.[65]

After the Confederate cavalry came across the pontoon bridge, the *John Adams* steamed upriver, but obstructions in the Combahee prohibited it from ascending much farther. These are the same obstructions that Francis Izard had described to the US provost marshal. The raid therefore never got past Cypress Plantation to Heyward's and Blake's plantations north of the pontoon bridge. The *John Adams* went back down to the bridge, moving up and down the short stretch of the river from the pontoon bridge to below Oakland Plantation. Then it anchored half a mile southeast of Oakland Plantation, ready to defend its position as Breeden's forces advanced to Oakland. John D. Sanders, Lieutenant Brunson, and Privates Lumpkin and Leightley of Captain T. A. Allen's Combahee Rangers stayed on Bonny Hall for three or four hours, then moved back to Combahee Ferry, where they found the *John Adams* gone.[66]

Meanwhile, at Oakland, Major Emanuel received a message that more of Montgomery's men were marching toward Stock's Causeway, which ran up the peninsula from Field's Point to Green Pond. Once again, the Union Army was several steps ahead, mainly because the Confederate forces stationed in Green Pond were unfamiliar with the area. And they were ignorant of the US Army's position at Field's Point.[67]

Casting off again, the *John Adams* proceeded downriver and joined the *Harriet A. Weed*. It picked up a few additional freedom seekers who initially had been unable to get on the boat. Then both US gunboats headed downriver, with the *John Adams* taking the lead.[68]

Emanuel had left Lieutenant Breeden to surveil the enemy's movements on the Combahee. He took Mr. Pipkin as a guide to show him the way to Stock's Causeway. As the 2nd South Carolina's troops came up Stock's

Causeway, Emanuel and his guide pursued them. Captain H. Godbold and Captain Thomas H. Bomar were also in pursuit. Godbold reported that the 2nd South Carolina Volunteers were marching north toward the Confederate camp and railroad station at Green Pond. But Green Pond was many miles away, at the north end of Stock's Creek Road. He remained on Stock's Creek Road until one or two o'clock in the afternoon, then received intelligence that the Union Army was destroying Confederate citizens' property. He proceeded north along Stock's Creek Road toward Oliver Middleton's rice mill at Tar Bluff to reinforce Lieutenant Gilchrist. Gilchrist, in turn, impressed Oliver Middleton's enslaved driver to act as a pilot and steer him along the same road from Green Pond to Field's Point. Gilchrist came within two hundred yards of Middleton's rice mill. There he found Captain Carver and his forces entrenched. Carver's forces were significantly superior in number and arms to Breeden's forces. Breeden knew he could not win the fight, so he retreated to the dense woods and posted pickets on three sides of Middleton's house. By the time reinforcements came, neither Captain Godbold, Lieutenant Gilchrist, Major Emanuel, nor Captain Bomar could reach the enemy, Montgomery's men had already set Middleton's rice mill ablaze.[69]

The *John Adams* returned to Tar Bluff to pick up Captain Carver and Company E of the 2nd South Carolina Volunteers, whom it had left there before daybreak. Carver could be seen standing at the edge of the bluff, waving his hat, which Captain Apthorp remembered to be the signal that everything was fine. Confederate troops had arrived at Tar Bluff in the morning, then fallen back. Captain Carver and his troops had skirmished with Major Emanuel's forces for most of the day after the remainder of Colonel Montgomery's men moved upriver. Carver held it down until they returned.[70]

The *Harriet A. Weed* continued down the Combahee River to Field's Point, where Captain Thompson and his troops had been left when the US gunboats first came up the river from Beaufort through the Coosaw River. Thompson and his men had been skirmishing with Lieutenant Gilchrist and Captain Godbold (who was sent to reinforce him) for most of the day and their ammunition was almost exhausted. The Confederates had just set ablaze the earthworks where Thompson's men were concealed when the *Harriet A. Weed* arrived, in the nick of time.[71]

A firefight had erupted along the road leading to Field's Point. Emanuel had moved the second piece of Captain Bomar's artillery to the gate of Oliver Middleton's Launch Plantation on Tar Bluff, two miles from Field's Point. He then reported that he and his troops advanced to Field's Point, because he thought he heard gunfire and assumed it came from Confederate forces. It was actually the 2nd South Carolina Volunteers' shells exploding in the vicinity. Emanuel found Lieutenant Hewitt and a Private Fripp watching the *Harriet A. Weed*, which was 150 yards away, from a small earthwork on the edge of the bluffs. Emanuel ordered the artillery piece he had left at Tar Bluff be brought down. Emanuel and his small party of soldiers rolled the single artillery piece along the back road to Field's Point to attempt an attack on the gunboat.[72]

Captain Thompson successfully held off Confederate skirmishes by mounting half of his forces on horses they had captured from surrounding plantations and sending those men out as pickets and scouts. These Union pickets and scouts must have spotted Emanuel and Lieutenant Hewitt as they rode up Stock's Causeway. By two o'clock in the afternoon, three infantry regiments, a hundred cavalry, and one full battery of artillery had arrived in Green Pond. The Confederate cavalry marched down the main road leading from Ashepoo to Field's Point. The Black soldiers commanded by one white man stood on the edge of the swamp and ambushed them, firing their guns at Emanuel, Captain Bomar, and Lieutenant Hewitt and their men. Emanuel returned fire—he got in four shots—into the dense woods, then ordered the artillery to retreat. The Confederate private by the name of Fripp was wounded in the firefight and later died of his wounds.[73]

Pitching shells over and among the Confederates, the *John Adams* prevented their reinforcements from shaking Captain Thompson's grasp. Before the Confederates could cut off the gunboat anchored at the edge of the bluffs at Tar Bluff, it pushed off downriver toward Field's Point. Captain Godbold ordered his men back to Field's Point. His forces came within range of the *John Adams*'s guns, which fired furiously at them; Union pickets shot at his pickets. Godbold was ordered to move his men back to Tar Bluff. The gunboats ceased firing and moved on downriver.[74]

Emanuel met Lieutenant Breeden at Tar Bluff and ordered Lieutenant Allen Edens to go down toward Field's Point with Breeden's forces and scour the woods. Breeden took the main road down to Field's Point with his remaining forces, arriving at roughly nine in the evening. After coming down the river with the incoming tide, the *John Adams* and *Harriet A. Weed* were well on their way back through the Coosaw River to Beaufort passing through the mouth of the Coosaw River before the ebb tide. They arrived in advance of the highest tides of the June lunar cycle. Neither Lieutenant Edens nor Breeden found any trace of the Union Army. Harriet Tubman, along with her crew, Colonel Montgomery, the 2nd South Carolina

Volunteers, the 3rd Rhode Island Heavy Artillery, their white commanders, and the freedom seekers were all back on the *John Adams* and *Harriet A. Weed* and were already on their way to Beaufort. As they left Field's Point, loud thunderclaps from an impending thunderstorm competed with the sounds of their cannons firing, both to bid goodbye to the Combahee River and to discourage Confederate troops from counterattacking.[75]

Captain Apthorp fully expected that the Confederate forces would indeed counterattack. He assumed the Confederate cavalry and artillery outnumbered Colonel Montgomery's small force, and that additional reinforcements could be mobilized from the Confederate Third Military District headquarters. But the Confederates had been outsmarted. Every Union move—coming up the Combahee River, occupying Field's Point and Tar Bluff, closing off the two main arteries to Confederate Army headquarters in Ashepoo down which Confederate artillery and cavalry and their reinforcements would have likely come, then proceeding up the river to burn the pontoon bridge—reflected sound military strategy. Ironically, the Confederate forces feared they were outnumbered; they weren't.[76]

Apthorp, for one, determined that the "suddenness and audacity with which" Montgomery's men had occupied the countryside was the reason the Confederate forces did not counterattack. Montgomery's highly skilled and strongly motivated commanders and men had duped the Confederate commanders into believing that the entire US Department of the South was upon them. The Confederates were completely "bewildered" and absolutely "stupefied." Taken by surprise by the sudden attack, they never mounted decisive action. By the time they did, the "mischief was done" and the US gunboats were "out of their reach."[77]

★★★★★★★★

According to Confederate brigadier general W. S. Walker's official military report on the Combahee River Raid, several "intelligent negroes" had escaped to the enemy shortly before the raid. He reported that the freedom seekers included a "pilot reported to be thoroughly familiar with the river." Any of the pilots on the list of those with Harriet Tubman (especially Isaac Hayward and even Robert Smalls) could have conceivably been the pilot in question. At least Walker gave the "intelligent negroes" credit for leading the US Army up the Combahee River. Walker may also have been attempting to cover up his own ineptitude. It seemed a mystery how the Union Army could have gotten from Beaufort to Field's Point and then up the Combahee to the pontoon bridge at Combahee Ferry before his troops could reach them from Green Pond.[78]

At 11 p.m., twelve hours after Walker had requested them, the reinforcements arrived, in the form of Colonel Lawrence M. Keitt's 20th Regiment South Carolina Infantry. Captain W. L. Trenholm of the Rutledge Mounted Riflemen and Horse Artillery, Company A, subsequently sent official word via telegram that all of the Union troops had left the area—hours after they had. Colonel Keitt later wrote in his official report: "Damage done yesterday very great. Messrs. Lowndes, W. C. Heyward, W. H. Heyward, Kirkland, and Paul lost nearly all their negroes, about 700; houses mostly destroyed. Mr. Nichols and overseer supposed to be taken."[79]

★★★★★★★★

"De brack sojers so presumptious!" Colonel Higginson remembered in his memoirs that after Minus Hamilton had told his story, he repeated that phrase three times and shook his head as he savored what that meant. Higginson reflected on the old man's deep pride at the sight of armed Black men in US Army uniforms, a sight that must have astounded those like Hamilton, who were still held in bondage, as a "butter-fly just from the chrysalis might astound his fellow-grubs." Higginson vowed inwardly, as the commander of the 1st South Carolina Volunteers, that Black troops would be "as 'presumptious' as [he] could make them."[80]

15

"Some Credit"

S everal days after the Combahee River Raid, the *New South* newspaper reported that a tremendous reception of well-wishers had awaited the "strange spectacle" that would take place when the expedition arrived in Beaufort. They were not disappointed, as several hundred "genuine contrabands" paraded down Bay Street "early on the morning" of June 3. They wore the clothes in which they had escaped: the men, pantaloons and shirts like Minus Hamilton; and the women, single frocks and handkerchiefs covering their heads like Hagar Hamilton. Many were in their "field suits of dirty gray," which they had donned to report to the tidal rice fields before "day clean." In spite of all they had been through, their faces beamed, according to the *New South*, with "that intelligence, which is inseparable" from formerly enslaved people fresh off the plantation enjoying their newfound and hard-won liberty, notwithstanding the "filth and tatters of slavery." The Combahee freedom seekers did not have much, but, finally, they had their freedom.[1]

Beaufort was, of course, the command center of the federal government's Port Royal Experiment and the clearinghouse for freedom seekers who had been able to make their way on foot or by water to Union lines since the Battle of Port Royal in November 1861. Yet six months after the Emancipation Proclamation went into effect, enslavers still held people a few miles west of Beaufort, up the rivers and tidal creeks. The morning of June 3, 1863, however, "all the darkies in town were in the streets," the *New South* reported, gazing with "unaffected surprise and admiration" at the freedom seekers whom Colonel Montgomery, Harriet Tubman, the 2nd South Carolina Volunteers, the 3rd Rhode Island, and Tubman's ring of spies, scouts, and pilots had released from the "prison-house of bondage."[2]

The sight of genuine contrabands would have been strange to Black folks in Beaufort who had already adjusted to freedom after the Battle of Port Royal in November 1861. Freed people who had been enslaved on remote Sea Islands, which the Union Army could not defend, and re-settled in Beaufort were on hand also. And there were freedpeople who had hired themselves out in Beaufort, including watermen like Robert Smalls and March Haynes. They too would have turned out to witness the parade. All freedom seekers in Beaufort who were freed before and by the Emancipation Proclamation and those who had stolen their own freedom since then gazed on with unaffected surprise and admiration. This is an-other example of how during the Civil War, Lowcountry Creoles who had been enslaved on rural Sea Island cotton and rice plantations and in urban centers of the South Carolina, Georgia, North Carolina, and Florida Lowcountry like Charleston, Beaufort, Savannah, and Jacksonville were brought into sustained contact with one another for the first time.[3]

Northern abolitionists were also on hand to witness the parade of Combahee refugees down Bay Street. The *Wisconsin State Journal* corres-pondent, James Yerrington, embedded with the Department of the South, wrote that he had the "satisfaction of witnessing the return of the gal-lant Col. Montgomery" from a successful raid into the Confederate ene-my's country with the "trophies of war," including 780 freedom seekers and thousands of dollars' worth of rice and other Confederate property. Members of the 104th Pennsylvania Regiment also witnessed the parade. The author of a postwar history of that regiment lauded Montgomery. While he declared the expedition successful, achieving its goal of getting recruits, he also thought that the refugees looked like "walking rag-bags." He pronounced the roughly 800 "darkies" of both sexes and all ages, shapes, sizes, and conditions to be much better suited to "hoe cotton than carry a musket." And, the author proclaimed, some would not see the difference between "stealing negroes from their home on the Congo, in Africa, to hoe cotton and cane and stealing them from the Cumbahee in South Carolina." There was more than a little Copperhead (the term used for northern apologists for slavery) in his sentiments—indeed, there always was a touch of Copperhead in the entire Port Royal Experiment.[4]

Clara Barton was in Beaufort when Colonel Montgomery and his men returned. She wrote a letter to her cousin on July 3, 1863, describing the "singular sight." Barton had served as a nurse and relief worker in battlefield hospitals throughout the Civil War, particularly at the Battle of Antietam. She arrived at Hilton Head with her brother Captain David Barton of the Quartermaster Bureau in April 1863. Like Tubman and Laura Towne, Barton was not paid for her services; she was an independent nurse supported by northern women's auxiliaries and her own funds, and under the authority of the US Sanitary Commission. Barton wrote in her diary that on June 3 a carriage drawn by four horses and driven by a Union Army officer picked her up along with Lieutenant Colonel John J. Elwell, chief quartermaster of the US Army, Department of the South, and took them to the home of a friend of General Hunter's in Beaufort for a dinner party. Colonel Higginson, other US Army officers, and a *New York Tribune* correspondent were among the guests.[5]

Even on the Sea Islands, the "gallant raid" conducted by Colonel Montgomery and the 2nd South Carolina Volunteers was the "great theme of the day" among northern volunteers. With the US military reorganizing at the top—both General Hunter and Admiral Du Pont had been dismissed—everyone was talking about how Montgomery's raid had brought a small measure of "vigor and activity" to the Department of the South. Barton wrote to her cousin, "Our military operations have been as cool as the weather."[6]

After dinner, Barton and Elwell took a carriage ride to the old Smith Plantation in Port Royal. There Barton saw the beautiful live oak trees with Spanish moss hanging from their branches, "like the drapery of death." Barton and Elwell rejoined the other dinner guests after sunset on the verandah, where they were serenaded by a regimental band and continued the discussion of Montgomery's raid. Later, Barton wrote in her diary that the Combahee freedom seekers were "worthless in any country" except as "subjects for missionary labors, and candidates for eternity," certainly not like military recruits at all. In essence, her assessment mirrored the 104th Pennsylvania officer's assessment. She presumed that the condition of the Combahee freedom seekers was so poor because "active" working enslaved laborers would not have been left on the plantations and that with no slaves of value to protect, the Confederates left few soldiers in the area. This was of course untrue.[7]

Despite a few inaccuracies—she wrote that the *Sentinel* had made it upriver rather than running aground—we can trust Barton's account that the Combahee refugees were all "delighted, to meet relatives already here."

"Here" was Port Royal Island and Beaufort. "Here" was freedom. Freedom seekers like Jonas Green and Wally Graham, who had previously escaped bondage, were already "here" when their family and friends among the Combahee freedom seekers arrived at Old Fort Plantation. Barton also noted that 2nd South Carolina Volunteer soldiers who had escaped enslavement on Combahee plantations and then executed the Combahee River Raid, like Friday Barrington, were "anxious" to go out on another expedition and waiting to "find opportunity."[8]

★★★★★★★★

Northerners and southerners agreed that Colonel Montgomery, the 2nd South Carolina, and the 3rd Rhode Island Heavy Artillery did extensive damage to private property, but they differed on the number of enslaved people liberated and the estimated dollar amount in property damage.

Major Emanuel wrote in his official report to Captain James Lowndes that five hundred to six hundred enslaved people had escaped in the raid. Clara Barton wrote in her diary after her visit to Old Fort Plantation that Montgomery had taken "seven hundred Negroes." Her estimates the day after the raid are in line with those of Colonel Keitt, who reported to his superiors at the Confederate Third Military District that the Union had taken seven hundred contrabands. In a letter accompanying his report to Secretary of War Stanton, General Hunter reported that Colonel Montgomery had "penetrated the country of the enemy 25 miles, destroyed a pontoon bridge across the Combahee River, together with a vast amount of cotton, rice, and other property, and brought away with him 725 slaves and some 5 horses." The raid was, Hunter wrote, the "initial experiment of a system of incursions which will penetrate up all the inlets, creeks, and rivers of this department."[9]

Two media outlets reported Hunter's figure, 725. *Douglass' Monthly* and the *New South* echoed Montgomery's count. Tubman told Frank Sanborn a few weeks after the raid that she and Montgomery's men had taken 756 "head of their most valuable livestock known up in your region as 'contrabands.'" That Tubman's accounting is higher than Montgomery's by twenty-nine people raises the question of which people counted. Tubman couldn't read or write, but she could likely count. As an enslaved woman, she had hired herself out and purchased steers with her earnings; as a free woman, she worked for wages and ran an eating house in Beaufort. She may have considered freedom seekers who were of no use to the Union

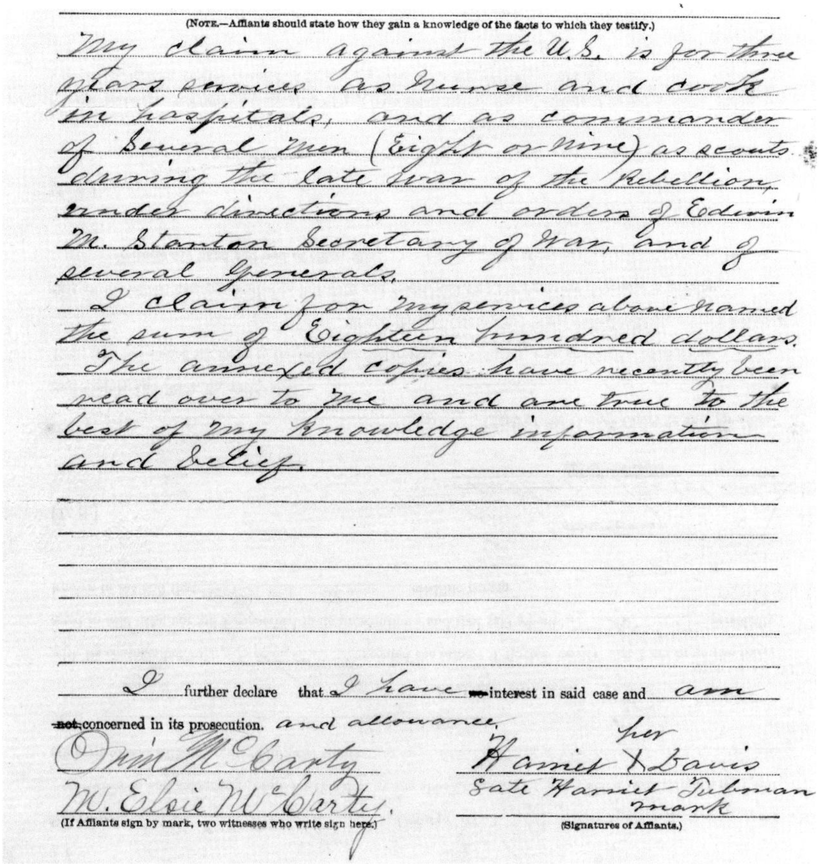
(NOTE.—Affiants should state how they gain a knowledge of the facts to which they testify.)

My claim against the U.S. is for three years service as Nurse and cook in hospitals, and as commander of several men (Eight or Nine) as scouts during the late War of the Rebellion, under directions and orders of Edwin M. Stanton Secretary of War, and of several Generals.

I claim for my services above named the sum of Eighteen hundred dollars. The annexed copies have recently been read over to me and are true to the best of my knowledge information and belief.

I further declare that I have ~~no~~ interest in said case and am ~~not~~ concerned in its prosecution. and allowance.

Orin McCarty
M. Elsie McCarty
(If Affiants sign by mark, two witnesses who write sign here.)

her
Harriet X Davis
Late Harriet Tubman
mark
(Signatures of Affiants.)

Plate 1 On January 19, 1899, Harriet Tubman in her general affidavit attested to her work during the Civil War as a spy, scout, and nurse. She was never compensated for her service as a spy or scout during the Civil War.
Courtesy National Archives and Records Administration

Plate 2 Located at Sams Point on Lady's Island, this is one of seven stores owned by the Keyserling brothers where USCT veterans, including men from the 2nd South Carolina Volunteers, executed their pensions four times every year, circa 1935.
Special Collections, College of Charleston Libraries

Plate 3 Born in the Bundu region of Senegal, Ayuba Suleyman Diallo, also known as Job Ben Solomon, was the son of a Fulani nobleman. He became one of a very small number of people who were captured in Africa and endured the Middle Passage to return home. *(1733), Lusail Museum*

Plate 4 Nathaniel Heyward (1766–1851) was the wealthiest man and the largest slaveholder in the US South when he died in 1851, owning seventeen rice plantations on the upper Combahee River where he held more than 2,500 people in bondage. He was William C. Heyward's distant cousin.
Portrait by Charles Fraser (1829), Gibbes Museum of Art, Gift of Mr. and Mrs. William H. Grimball

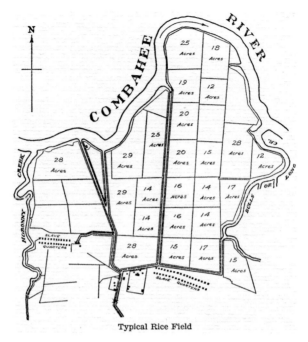

Typical Rice Field

Plate 5 This map of a section of Hobonny Plantation shows rice fields on the south side of the upper Combahee River, which had been reclaimed from swampland.
Courtesy Charleston Museum

Plate 6 Enslaved laborers cleared forested wetlands, uprooting cypress trees, and making the landscape as flat as a billiard table in order to create 274,000 acres of tidal rice fields. This aerial view of the Combahee River wetlands shot from the west shows the marsh in the foreground and the rice fields in the background.
Photo by J Henry Fair, 2022; flight thanks to Southwings

Plate 7 Enslaved laborers removed broad-bottomed cypress trees as large as twelve feet in diameter when they cleared the landscape and reclaimed cypress swamps to construct the Lowcountry's tidal rice fields.
Photo by J Henry Fair, 2016

Plate 8 Poisonous snakes, like copperheads and cottonmouths *(Agkistrodon piscivorus)*, made their homes in the Lowcountry's forested wetlands and tidal rice fields. They surely threatened enslaved laborers as they walked to and from and worked against their will in the rice fields.
Photo by J Henry Fair, 2016

Plate 9 The American alligator also made its home and nests in the Lowcountry's forested wetlands and tidal rice fields, living in fresh and brackish water.
Photo by J Henry Fair, 2022

Plate 10 Originally, plug trunks were made from hollowed-out cypress trees and buried in the earthen embankments along the perimeters of the rice fields. Here, the plug is put snugly in the top of the trunk.
Photo by J Henry Fair, 2022, private collection

Plate 11 The gate on this Combahee-style trunk can be ratcheted up as the tide comes in to allow the river water to flow into the rice field. Or, as the tide goes out, the river water forces the gates open as it flows out of the rice fields.
Photo by J Henry Fair, 2022, Nemours Wildlife Foundation

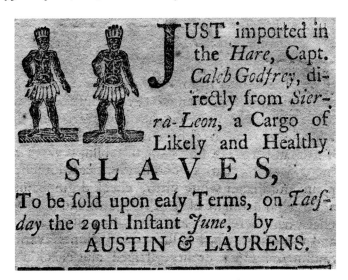

JUST imported in the *Hare*, Capt. *Caleb Godfrey*, directly from *Sierra-Leon*, a Cargo of Likely and Healthy SLAVES, To be fold upon eafy Terms, on *Taefday* the 29th Inftant *June*, by AUSTIN & LAURENS.

Plate 12 In 1756 the *Hare* transported sixty-three West African captives against their will from Bance Island in Sierra Leone to Charleston, where they were sold by Henry Laurens, one of Charleston's most notorious slave factors.
Courtesy Charleston Library Society

Plate 13 Dr. William Lennox Kirkland Sr. (1797–1828) was a medical doctor and rice planter on the Combahee River. His son, William Lennox Kirkland Jr., owned Rose Hill Plantation.
Gibbes Museum of Art, Gift of Randolph and Mary Louise Kirkland

Plate 14 Williams Middleton (1809–1883) was the son of Henry Middleton and Mary Helen Hering Middleton. He signed the South Carolina order of secession and inherited Newport Plantation from his father.
Courtesy of Middleton Place Foundation

Plate 15 Henry Middleton (1770–1846), Williams Middleton's father, served as governor of South Carolina from 1810 to 1812. When he died, Governor Middleton owned 662 enslaved people, including 217 on Newport Plantation. *Middleton Place Foundation*

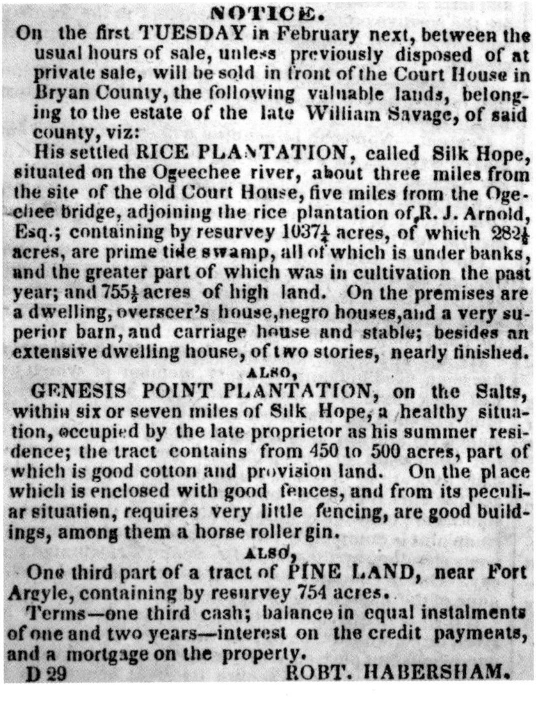

NOTICE.

On the first TUESDAY in February next, between the usual hours of sale, unless previously disposed of at private sale, will be sold in front of the Court House in Bryan County, the following valuable lands, belonging to the estate of the late William Savage, of said county, viz:

His settled RICE PLANTATION, called Silk Hope, situated on the Ogeechee river, about three miles from the site of the old Court House, five miles from the Ogechee bridge, adjoining the rice plantation of R. J. Arnold, Esq.; containing by resurvey 1037½ acres, of which 282½ acres, are prime tide swamp, all of which is under banks, and the greater part of which was in cultivation the past year; and 755½ acres of high land. On the premises are a dwelling, overseer's house, negro houses, and a very superior barn, and carriage house and stable; besides an extensive dwelling house, of two stories, nearly finished.

ALSO,

GENESIS POINT PLANTATION, on the Salts, within six or seven miles of Silk Hope, a healthy situation, occupied by the late proprietor as his summer residence; the tract contains from 450 to 500 acres, part of which is good cotton and provision land. On the place which is enclosed with good fences, and from its peculiar situation, requires very little fencing, are good buildings, among them a horse roller gin.

ALSO,

One third part of a tract of PINE LAND, near Fort Argyle, containing by resurvey 754 acres.

Terms—one third cash; balance in equal instalments of one and two years—interest on the credit payments, and a mortgage on the property.

D 29   ROBT. HABERSHAM.

Plate 16 The January 1839 auction of William Savage's two rice plantations, Silk Hope and Genesis Point, was advertised in the *Charleston Daily Courier*. William L. Kirkland Jr. purchased people who had been enslaved on William Savage's estate. *Courtesy Charleston Library Society*

Plate 17 The Blackwater River is located in Dorchester County, Maryland, where Harriet Tubman was born. The twenty-eight-mile-long river drains into a watershed similar in size to the ACE Basin, into which the Combahee River drains. The flora and fauna along both rivers are similar as well. This, however, is where the similarities end.
Photo by J Henry Fair, 2021; flight thanks to Southwings

Plate 18 "Blackwater National Wildlife Refuge" by J Henry Fair] An aerial view to the north of Blackwater National Wildlife Refuge. In these forested wetlands, salinity is lower; tides are significantly shorter; tidal marshes play a more limited role; and, the water is clearer than on the Combahee River.
Photo by J Henry Fair, 2021; flight thanks to Southwings

Plate 19 Sojourner Truth (c. 1797–1883) was born Isabella Baumfree and enslaved in Swaterkill, New York. Her older siblings were sold away from the family when they were children; her father was manumitted and turned out; Baumfree was violently separated from the father of her first child to prevent them from forming an abroad marriage.
1864, National Portrait Gallery, Smithsonian Institution

Plate 20 Harriet Tubman (born Araminta Ross) was born at Anthony Thompson's home, which was built circa 1800–1810. It was located on Mansion Farm, Anthony Thompson's plantation, which was situated on approximately 1,000 heavily forested acres in Peter's Neck, Dorchester County, Maryland. *Brooks Family*

Plate 21 As a child, Harriet Tubman stood up to the institution of slavery by refusing to assist an overseer in the capture of an enslaved boy at the Bucktown Village Store. The overseer hurled an iron weight at the enslaved boy, but it struck young Tubman in the forehead. *Lorie Shaull, 2018*

Plate 22 African Americans enslaved on the lower Combahee River lived in slave cabins that may have resembled these remnants on Newport Plantation. On all except one of the plantations impacted by the Combahee River Raid, the slave cabins were the only structures left standing. *Photo by J Henry Fair, 2022, Nemours Wildlife Foundation*

Plate 23 Charles T. Lowndes (1808–1884) was a South Carolina rice planter and a businessman, owner of an insurance agency that is one of Charleston's oldest family-owned businesses. He inherited Oakland Plantation on the lower end of the Combahee River from his father, Thomas Lowndes.
Henry Lowndes

Plate 24 Harvested rice was pounded in mortars made of hollowed-out cypress or pine trees, removing the hull from rice grains. This process was subsequently mechanized with the patenting of steam-powered mills designed to reduce the extremely high death rates that enslaved laborers suffered as a result of polishing rice grains for a commercial market.

Collection of the Smithsonian National Museum of African American History and Culture (Gift of Oprah Winfrey)

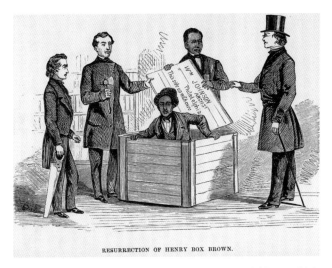

RESURRECTION OF HENRY BOX BROWN.

Plate 25 In March 1849, Henry "Box" Brown (1815–1897) liberated himself by hiding in a wooden crate and shipping himself to Philadelphia. William Still and other members of the Philadelphia Vigilance Committee received the package. *Courtesy Library of Congress*

Plate 26 Thomas Garrett (1789–1871) was a Quaker abolitionist who assisted freedom seekers on the Underground Railroad for more than four decades. He assisted Harriet Tubman on approximately eight rescue missions, including when she liberated herself and her aged parents. *Boston Public Library*

Plate 27 William Still (1821–1902) was an abolitionist and president of the Acting Committee of the Pennsylvania Vigilance Committee. He assisted approximately eight hundred freedom seekers between 1847 and 1865. During the intake process, he documented freedom seekers' stories. *Charles L. Blockson Afro-American Collection, Temple University Libraries*

Plate 28 Harriet Tubman's younger brother William Henry Stewart (1830–1912) was born Henry Ross and enslaved in Dorchester County, Maryland. Tubman returned to Caroline County on Christmas night in 1854 to lead Stewart and nine other freedom seekers to freedom.
Stewart Family Collection

TWENTY-EIGHT FUGITIVES ESCAPING FROM THE EASTERN SHORE OF MARYLAND.

Plate 29 By the fall of 1857, Harriet Tubman was helping the trickle of enslaved people seeking their freedom from bondage to become a flood.
1872; courtesy Schomburg Center for Research in Black Culture, Manuscripts, Archives and Rare Books Division, The New York Public Library

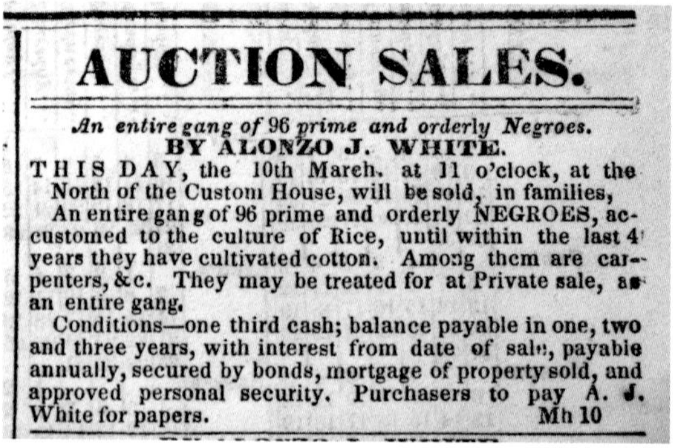

AUCTION SALES.

An entire gang of 96 prime and orderly Negroes.
BY ALONZO J. WHITE.
THIS DAY, the 10th March, at 11 o'clock, at the North of the Custom House, will be sold, in families,
An entire gang of 96 prime and orderly NEGROES, accustomed to the culture of Rice, until within the last 4 years they have cultivated cotton. Among them are carpenters, &c. They may be treated for at Private sale, as an entire gang.
Conditions—one third cash; balance payable in one, two and three years, with interest from date of sale, payable annually, secured by bonds, mortgage of property sold, and approved personal security. Purchasers to pay A. J. White for papers.   Mh 10

Plate 30 Arthur M. Parker purchased six enslaved people in March 1853 at the auction of Edward Rutledge Lowndes's estate, which was advertised in the *Charleston Daily Courier* and the *Charleston Mercury*, and brought them to his plantation on the Combahee River.
Charleston Library Society

Judge T. J. Withers

Plate 31 Thomas Jefferson Withers (1804–1865) was a South Carolina politician, one of the signers of the order of secession for South Carolina, and a delegate to the South Carolina Secession Convention.
South Caroliniana

Plate 32 William Lloyd Garrison (1805–1879) was a prominent radical abolitionist, suffragist, social reformer, and founder of *The Liberator*, a widely read antislavery newspaper. Harriet Tubman and most of the fellow abolitionists who supported her considered themselves "Garrisonians," adherents of Garrison's philosophy of Christian nonresistance.
Library of Congress

Plate 33 Frederick Douglass (1818–1895) was born enslaved in Talbot County, Maryland, learned to read and write, and liberated himself from slavery. In freedom, he became an abolitionist, social reformer, and dynamic orator who electrified the abolitionist lecture circuit with his lectures about his firsthand experience with the horrors of slavery. He was also founder of *The North Star* and author of three autobiographies.
Samuel J. Miller (1845), The Art Institute of Chicago/Art Resource, NY

Plate 34 Colonel Thomas Wentworth Higginson (1839–1911) was a Unitarian minister and militant abolitionist from Worcester, Massachusetts. During the Civil War, Higginson served as a colonel in the 1st South Carolina Volunteers. *University of California Santa Barbara Library, Department of Special Research Collections, Wyles Mss 30*

Plate 36 Franklin Sanborn (1831–1917) was a journalist, author, abolitionist, reformer, and member of John Brown's "Secret Six." Sanborn wrote an early biography about Harriet Tubman and her participation in the Combahee River Raid. *West Virginia Archives*

Plate 35 John Brown (1800–1859) was a militant abolitionist who as captain of the 1st Brigade of Kansas Volunteers led a nighttime massacre, killing eight proslavery settlers in Pottawatomie, Kansas, in 1856. He was the mastermind and commander of the 1859 raid on the federal arsenal at Harpers Ferry. *The National Portrait Gallery*

GEORGE L. STEARNS

GERRIT SMITH

FRANK B. SANBORN

T. W. HIGGINSON

THEODORE PARKER

SAMUEL G. HOWE

JOHN BROWN'S NORTHERN SUPPORTERS

Plate 37 The "Secret Six" was a group of prominent, wealthy, white male northern abolitionists who supported John Brown behind the scenes and provided financial support to Brown and his soldiers. Reverend Thomas Wentworth Higginson considered Harriet Tubman to be the seventh member of the "Secret Six." *West Virginia Archives*

Plate 38 Xanthus Smith's iconic painting depicts the US fleet of warships as it sailed through Port Royal Sound between Fort Beauregard and Fort Walker in the Battle of Port Royal. Enslaved people as far away as the lower Combahee River must have heard, smelled, and sensed that these leviathans spelled freedom if only they could reach Beaufort.
Xanthus Smith (1889), Ships of the Sea Maritime Museum

Plate 39 General David Hunter (1802–1886) was commander of the US Army Department of the South. In 1862 he issued an order declaring slavery illegal in Georgia, South Carolina, and Florida and enlisted Black men (sometimes forcibly) into the unauthorized Hunter's Regiment.
Library of Congress

Plate 40 Taken five years after the Combahee River Raid, this photograph depicts a much younger Tubman, her wavy hair pulled back from her face, wearing a fashionable plaid cage crinoline gown and looking unflinchingly into the camera lens, projecting unparalleled strength, power, poise, and grace. *Smithsonian National Museum of African History and Culture/Library of Congress*

Plate 41 After the Battle of Port Royal, the federal government seized the Sea Island cotton crop left in Beaufort and the Sea Islands by fleeing planters. In the Port Royal Experiment, superintendents supervised the labor of formerly enslaved people cultivating and processing Sea Island cotton.
Memphis Brooks Museum of Art

Plate 42 Rufus Saxton (1824–1908) was the quartermaster (as captain) who initiated the US Army's employment of "contrabands" after the Battle of Port Royal. In May 1862, Saxton was promoted to brigadier general and named military governor of the US Army's Department of the South. General Saxton was authorized to recruit five thousand Black soldiers, which became the 1st and 2nd South Carolina Volunteers.
Library of Congress

Laura M. Towne

Plate 43 Laura Towne (1825–1901) was one of the first northern women to come to Union-occupied Beaufort during the Port Royal Experiment. At Penn School, Towne served as a homeopathic doctor, administrator, and teacher until her death.
The Penn School Collection at the UNC–Chapel Hill Wilson Library; Penn Center, Inc., St. Helena Island, South Carolina

Plate 44 Susie King Taylor (1848–1912) was born enslaved in Liberty County, Georgia. After learning to read and write in Savannah, she escaped during the Battle of Fort Pulaski. Susie was the first African American nurse, also worked as a teacher and laundress during the Civil War, and became one of the first Black women to self-publish her memoirs.
Courtesy Library of Congress

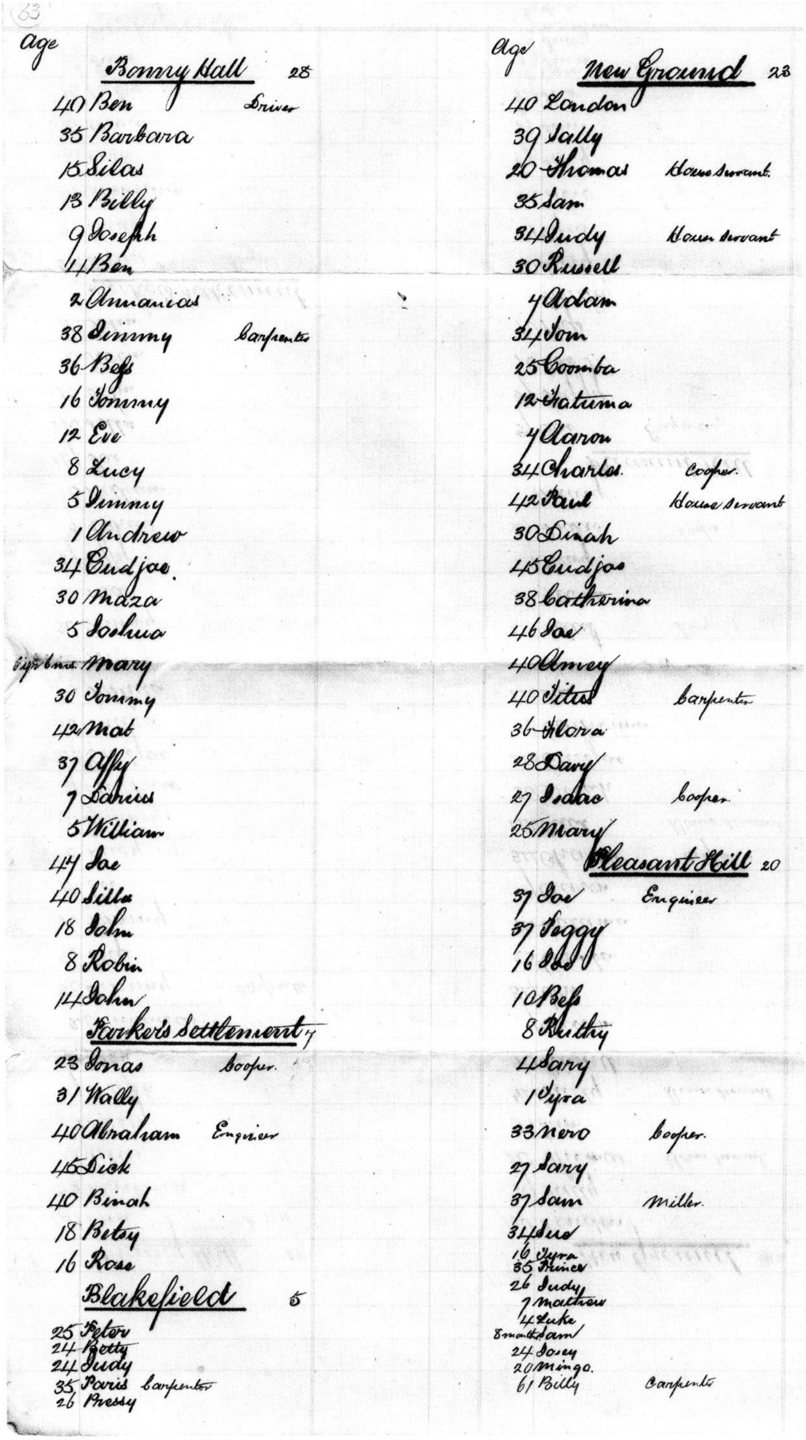

age			age
Bonny Hall 28			**New Ground** 23
40 Ben	Driver		40 London
35 Barbara			39 Sally
15 Silas			20 Thomas	House servant
13 Billy			35 Sam
9 Joseph			34 Judy	House servant
4 Ben			30 Russell
2 Annanias			4 Adam
38 Jimmy	Carpenter		34 Tom
36 Bess			25 Coomba
16 Tommy			12 Katuma
12 Eve			4 Aaron
8 Lucy			34 Charles	Cooper
5 Jimmy			42 Paul	House servant
1 Andrew			30 Dinah
34 Cudjoe			45 Cudjoe
30 Maza			38 Catherina
5 Joshua			46 Joe
Mary			40 Amey
30 Tommy			40 Titus	Carpenter
42 Mab			36 Flora
37 Affy			28 Davy
7 Darius			27 Isdao	Cooper
5 William			26 Mary
44 Joe			**Pleasant Hill** 20
40 Silla			37 Joe	Engineer
18 John			37 Peggy
8 Robin			16 Ned
44 John			10 Bess
Parkers Settlement 7			8 Betty
23 Jonas	Cooper		4 Sary
31 Wally			1 Cyra
40 Abraham	Engineer		33 Nero	Cooper
45 Dick			27 Sary
40 Binah			37 Sam	Miller
18 Betsy			34 Sue
16 Rose			16 Cyra
Blakefield 5			35 Prince
25 Peter			26 Judy
24 Betty			7 Matthew
24 Judy			4 Luke
35 Paris	Carpenter		8 Mark Sam
26 Pressy			24 Sary
		20 Mingo
		61 Billy	Carpenter

Plate 45 Walter Blake documented the eighty-three enslaved people who liberated themselves during the Civil War and before the Combahee River Raid from the plantations of his father, Joseph Blake. The list was written before March 1862, at which time some of the freedom seekers on it are recorded as working for the US Army quartermaster in Beaufort.

Pringle Family Papers, 1745–1897, South Carolina Historical Society

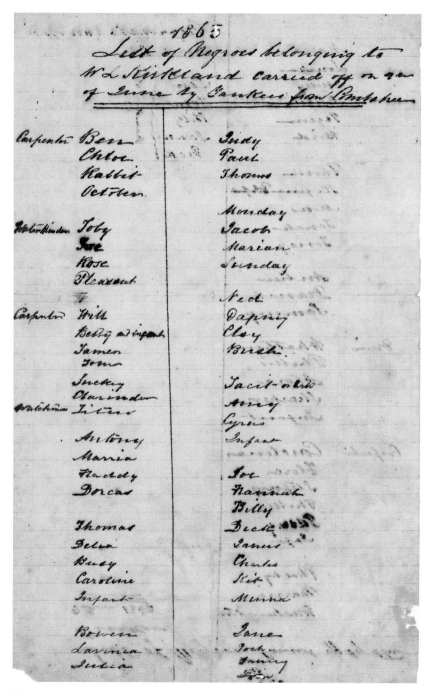

Plate 46 "Negroes Run off in March 62"] William Lennox Kirkland Jr. documented the five of the men whom he held in bondage on Rose Hill Plantation who liberated themselves and went to Union-occupied Beaufort months before the Combahee River Raid. *South Caroliniana Library, Papers of Kirkland Withers Snowden and Trotter Families, 1790-1959*

Plate 47 George Thompson Garrison (1836–1904) was the son of William
Lloyd Garrison and Helen Benson Garrison. A captain in the 55th Massachusetts
Infantry Regiment, he was stationed in February 1864 on Folly Island, where
Harriet Tubman was working for General Alfred H. Terry.
A. H. Locke (ca. 1864–1866); Massachusetts Historical Society, From the Association of
Officers of the 55th Massachusetts Infantry Regiment Carte de Visite Album, Photo 59.27

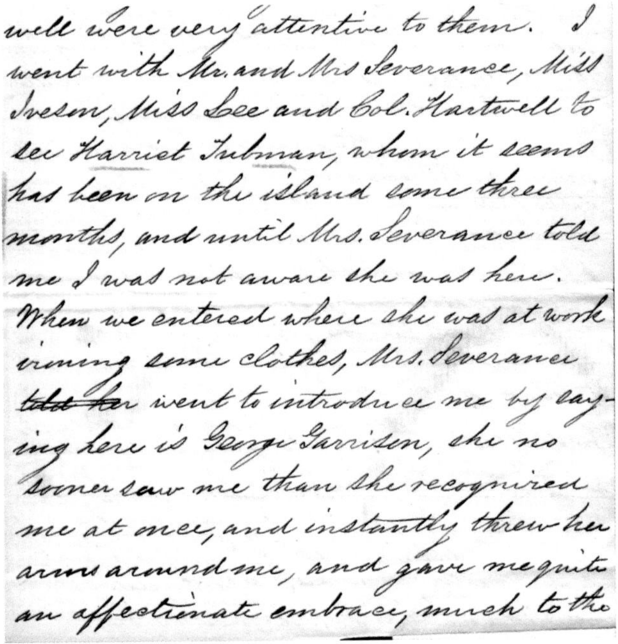

> well were very attentive to them. I
> went with Mr. and Mrs Severance, Miss
> Iveson, Miss Lee and Col. Hartwell to
> see Harriet Tubman, whom it seems
> has been on the island some three
> months, and until Mrs. Severance told
> me I was not aware she was here.
> When we entered where she was at work
> ironing some clothes, Mrs. Severance
> ~~told her~~ went to introduce me by say-
> ing here is George Garrison, she no
> sooner saw me than she recognized
> me at once, and instantly threw her
> arms around me, and gave me quite
> an affectionate embrace, much to the

Plate 48 On February 10, 1864, Lieutenant George T. Garrison wrote to his
younger brother, William Lloyd Garrison Jr., about his visit to General Terry's
camp, where he encountered Harriet Tubman. He observed that Tubman was more
successful at intelligence-gathering among the Beaufort refugees than anyone else.
Courtesy of Smith College Special Collections

Plate 49 James Seymour Severance (1842–1936) was the oldest son in a Massachusetts abolitionist family and volunteered in the Port Royal Experiment. He wrote in his diary on May 1, 1862, that Harriet Tubman, "Moses," would soon arrive, and he described how architects of the social experiment felt about her being sent. *Severance Family Papers, Collection of Michael S. Emett*

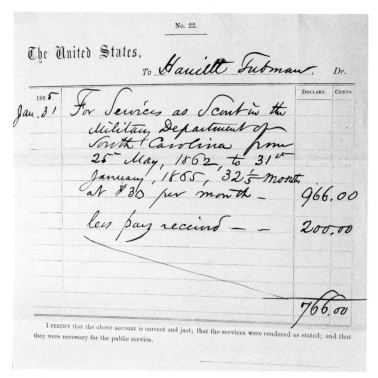

Plate 50 Harriet Tubman requested payment for her service to the US Army as a scout. The document lists May 25, 1862, as the day her service began, confirming both that she arrived aboard the *Atlantic* on that day and that she came to Beaufort to gather intelligence for the US Army behind enemy lines. *Courtesy The Harriet Tubman Home*

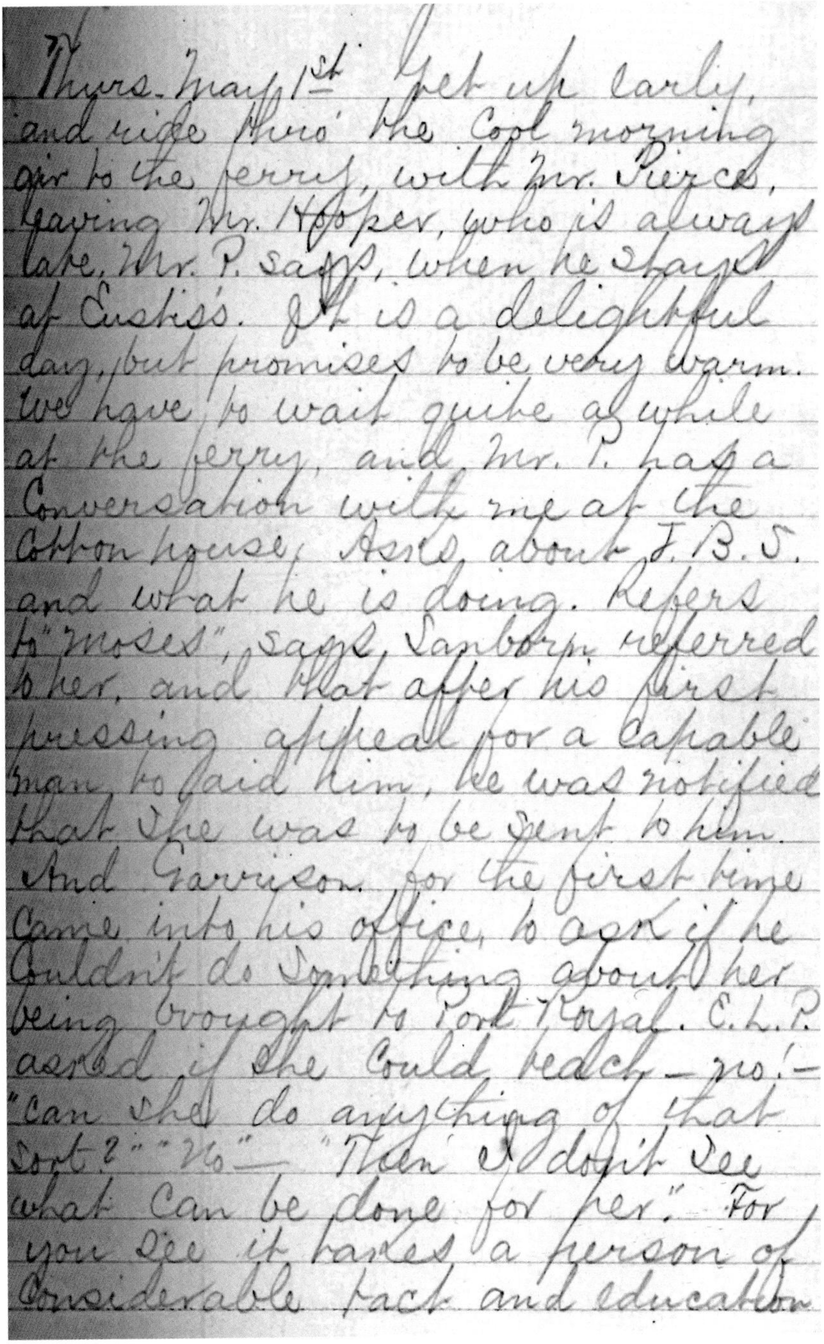

Thurs. May 1st Get up early, and ride thro' the cool morning air to the ferry, with Mr. Pierce, leaving Mr. Hooper, who is always late. Mr. P. says, when he stays at Eustis's. It is a delightful day, but promises to be very warm. We have to wait quite a while at the ferry, and, Mr. P. has a conversation with me at the Cotton house; Asks about J. B. S. and what he is doing. Refers to "moses", says, Sanborn referred to her, and that after his first pressing appeal for a capable man to aid him, he was notified that she was to be sent to him. And Garrison, for the first time came into his office, to ask if he couldn't do something about her being brought to Port Royal. E. L. P. asked if she could teach — no! — "can she do anything of that sort?" "No" — "Then I don't see what can be done for her." For you see it takes a person of considerable tact and education

Plate 51 In his diary on May 1, 1862, young James Seymour Severance recounted that Edward Pierce had disclosed to him his misgiving about Harriet Tubman coming to Beaufort. He thought Tubman too radical and preferred to back President Abraham Lincoln's gradualist approach.
Courtesy of Michael S. Emmett Sr.

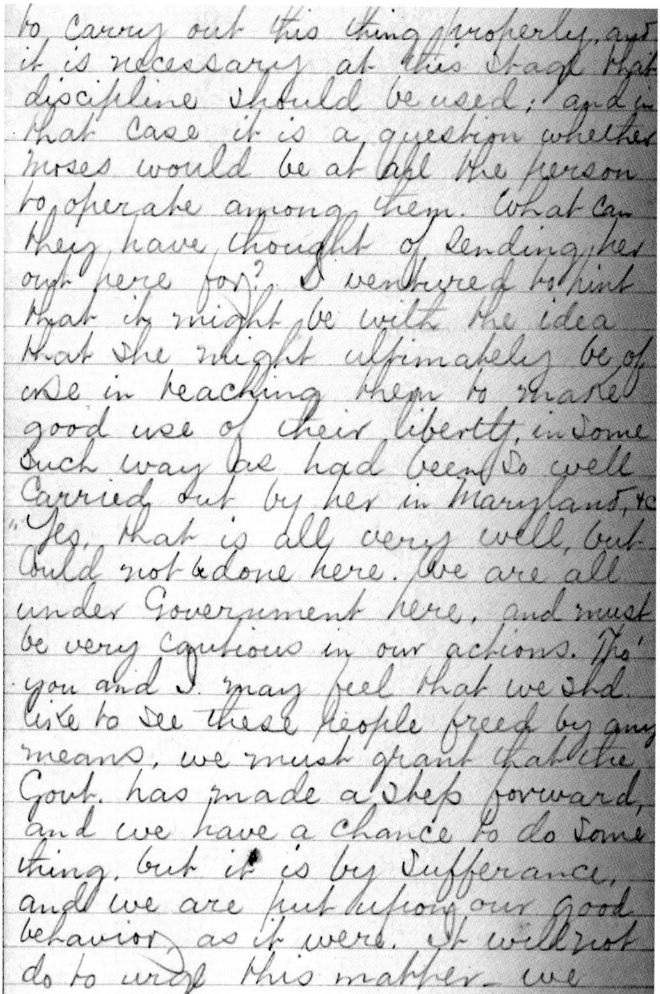

to carry out this thing properly, and
it is necessary at this stage that
discipline should be used; and in
that case it is a question whether
Moses would be at all the person
to operate among them. What can
they have thought of sending her
out here for? I venture to hint
that it might be with the idea
that she might ultimately be of
use in teaching them to make
good use of their liberty, in some
such way as had been so well
carried out by her in Maryland, &c
"Yes, that is all very well, but
could not be done here. We are all
under Government here, and must
be very cautious in our actions. Tho'
you and I may feel that we shd.
like to see these people freed by any
means, we must grant that the
Govt. has made a step forward,
and we have a chance to do some
thing, but it is by sufferance,
and we are put upon our good
behavior, as it were. It will not
do to urge this matter — we

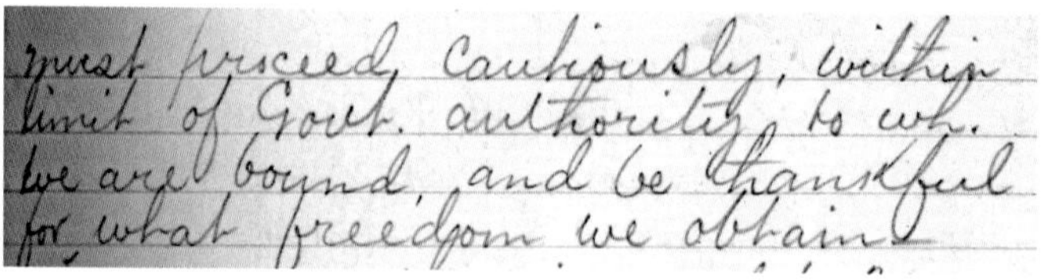

must proceed cautiously, within
limit of Govt. authority to wh.
we are bound, and be thankful
for what freedom we obtain

Plate 52 James Seymour Severance diary (continued)

Plate 53 Robert Smalls (1839–1915) was born enslaved in Beaufort, South Carolina, and hired himself out as a stevedore, rigger, sailor, wheelsman, and master boatman on Charleston's waterfront, then worked on the CSS *Planter* in the first year of the war. Smalls became the first African American hero of the Civil War when he piloted the *Planter* out of Charleston Harbor and surrendered it to the US Navy.
Hagley Digital Archives

HE GUN-BOAT "PLANTER," RUN OUT OF CHARLESTON, S. C., BY ROBERT SMALLS, MAY, 1862.

Plate 54 Robert Smalls piloted this wooden light-draft tug steamer, the CSS *Planter*, and surrendered it to the US Navy on May 13, 1862. It served as part of the South Atlantic Blockading Squadron until the summer of 1862.
Courtesy U.S. Naval Historical Center

Plate 55 Charlotte Forten Grimké (1837–1914) was born into a wealthy and prominent free Black Philadelphia family. She taught freedmen on St. Helena Island. Grimké's diary and poetry, published after the war, give an unparalleled firsthand account of a free African American women's experiences in the Civil War South. *Presbyterian Historical Society*

Plate 56 The 1st South Carolina Volunteers was the first regiment of African American troops authorized by President Lincoln. By order of Confederate president Jefferson Davis, Black soldiers would be enslaved or reenslaved and their white commanders hung if captured. *Library of Congress*

Plate 57 "Doing the Ring Shout in Georgia" (circa 1930s) depicts members of the Gullah community expressing their spirituality through the sacred circle dance known as the ring shout during a service at a local praise house. Dr. Lorenzo Dow Turner captured the iconic image, recordings of Gullah pronunciation, vocabulary, grammar, basket names, and texts during the course of his fieldwork, beginning in June 1932. *Anacostia Community Museum, Smithsonian Institution, Lorenzo Dow Turner Papers*

Plate 58 The Beaufort Arsenal is located on Craven Street in downtown Beaufort. Harriet Tubman described the Savan House, where she was living when Charlotte Forten and Lizzie Hunn visited her in January, as across the street from the arsenal.
Library of Congress

Plate 59 "Emancipation Day in South Carolina—The Color Sergeant of the First South Carolina (Colored) Volunteers Addressing the Regiment, After Having Been Presented with the Stars and Stripes, at Smith's Plantation, Port Royal Island, January—From a Sketch by Our Special Artist." Published in *Frank Leslie's Weekly* on January 24, 1863, the illustration depicts the grand celebration hosted by General Rufus Saxton at Camp Saxton in Port Royal, South Carolina, to commemorate the Emancipation Proclamation going into effect.
Library of Congress

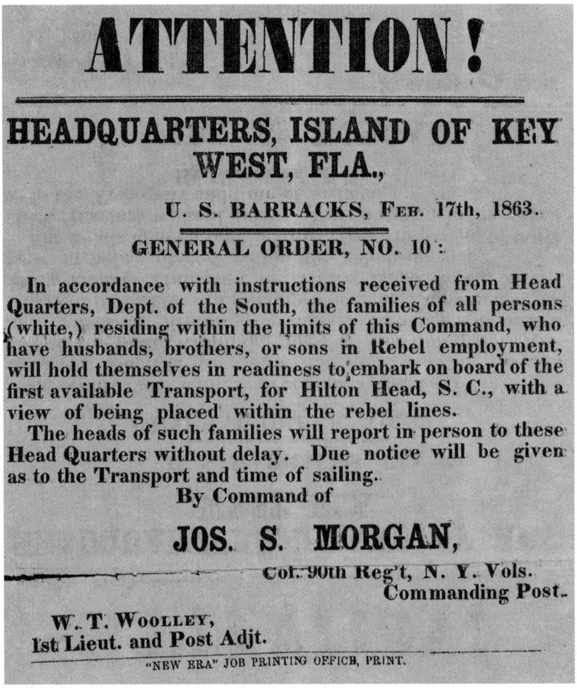

ATTENTION!

HEADQUARTERS, ISLAND OF KEY WEST, FLA.,

U. S. BARRACKS, Feb. 17th, 1863.

GENERAL ORDER, NO. 10:

In accordance with instructions received from Head Quarters, Dept. of the South, the families of all persons (white,) residing within the limits of this Command, who have husbands, brothers, or sons in Rebel employment, will hold themselves in readiness to embark on board of the first available Transport, for Hilton Head, S. C., with a view of being placed within the rebel lines.

The heads of such families will report in person to these Head Quarters without delay. Due notice will be given as to the Transport and time of sailing.

By Command of

JOS. S. MORGAN,

Col. 90th Reg't, N. Y. Vols.
Commanding Post.

W. T. WOOLLEY,
1st Lieut. and Post Adjt.

"NEW ERA" JOB PRINTING OFFICE, PRINT.

Plate 60 A month after the Emancipation Proclamation, Colonel Joseph S. Morgan ordered all men of African descent between ages fifteen and fifty to report to the Key West courthouse to undergo a medical examination in preparation for enlistment in the US Army, in Colonel James Montgomery's 2nd South Carolina Volunteers. *Southern Historical Collection, Weedon and Whitehurst Family Papers #4057-z*

Plate 61 Colonel James Montgomery (1814–1871) was a militant abolitionist, Jayhawker, and captain of the 3rd Kansas Infantry in Bleeding Kansas. On June 2, 1863, Colonel Montgomery commanded the 2nd South Carolina Volunteers and one battery of the 3rd Rhode Island Heavy Artillery in the Combahee River Raid. *Bennington Museum*

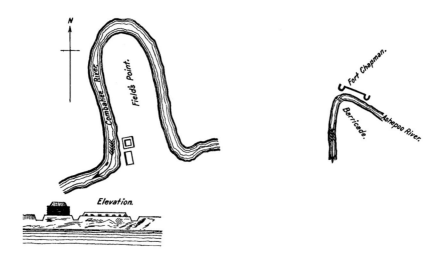

Plate 62 Lieutenant W. T. Truxten drew this sketch of the Combahee and Ashepoo Rivers, indicating the location of Confederate fortifications, in 1862, after the USS *E. B. Hale* successfully conducted reconnaissance on the Combahee River. Official Records of the Union and Confederate Navies in the War of the Rebellion, *ser. 1, vol. 13 (Washington, DC: Government Printing Office, 1900), 201*

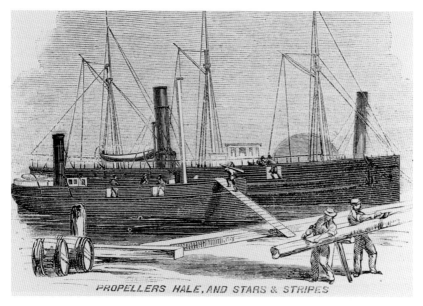

Plate 63 "Propellers Hale and Stars & Stripes," *Harper's Weekly*, July–December 1861. The *E. B. Hale* was a wooden screw steamer originally built to carry stones in New York's Adirondack Mountains before it was commissioned by the US Navy in September 1861 to transport troops. In July 1862, Lieutenant W. T. Truxten sailed the *E. B. Hale* up the Ashepoo River and proceeded to the Combahee River.
Naval History and Heritage Command Photograph

Plate 64 The *Oneota* (shown here at St. Helena, South Carolina, November 16, 1864) was a double-ended steam-powered ferry, the same design and similar age and size as the *John Adams*, the Boston ferryboat and retrofitted gunboat that the US Army used in the Combahee River Raid. Both vessels would have had a vertical walking-beam steam engine exposed in between pilot houses at each end. *Records of the War Department General Staff, Record Group 165, National Archives and Records Administration*

Plate 65 The 309-ton USS *Rose Standish* was a side-wheel steam transport comparable in age and size to the *Harriet A. Weed*. *Small Print Collection, Steamship Historical Society of America*

Declaration for an Original Invalid Pension.

NOTE.—To be executed before a Court of Record or some officer thereof having custody of its seal, a Notary Public or Justice of the Peace whose official signature shall be verified by his official seal, and in case he has none, his signature and official character shall be certified by a Clerk of a Court of Record or a City or County Clerk.

State of *Washington* City, County of *Columbia*, SS:

ON THIS *1* day of *November* A. D. one thousand eight hundred and ninety personally appeared before me, a *Justice of the Peace* within and for the County and State aforesaid *Walter D. Plowden* aged *73* years, who, being duly sworn according to law, declares that he is the identical *Walter D. Plowden*, who was ENROLLED as a *Surgeon's Steward* on the *23* day of *October* 186*1*, in Company *"I"* of the *47* Regiment of the *N. Y. Vols.* commanded by *Col. Henry Moor* and was honorably DISCHARGED at *Brooklyn, N.Y.* from the *13* on the *96* day of *August*, 186*1*; That his personal description is as follows: Age *73* years; height *5* feet *8* inches; complexion *Mullato* hair *Black sandy*; eyes *black* That while a member of the organization aforesaid, in the service and in the line of duty at .... in the State of .... on or about the .... day of *Spring of* 186*3*, he *I was sent by* (Here state the name or nature of disease, or the location of wound or injury. If disabled by disease, state fully its cause; if by wound or injury, the precise manner in which received.) *night on a secret expedition in a Rowboat up the Combahee River (131) one hundred & thirty one miles, I contracted from over exertions & inclemencies of the weather & of long & continued fatigue, a severe cold settling on chest & in head & otherwise affecting me resulting in deafness disease of chest & respiratory organs & in impaired vision I was sound at enlistment & free from disability. My disabilities were augmented by prison confinement at Charleston from Jan 29 1864 until 15 months afterward, a part of which time I was at Columbia S.C. for which I ask pension* That he was treated in hospitals as follows: (Here state the names or numbers, and the localities of all hospitals in which treated, and the dates of treatment.) *I was treated in Columbia S.C. Hospital & was discharged from prison but did not receive an honorable discharge or pay. The war was nearly over. I remained in Charleston N.C. &c* That he has .... been employed in the military or naval service otherwise than as stated above (Here state what the service was, whether prior or subsequent to that stated above and the dates at which it began and ended.)

That he has not been in the military or naval service of the United States since the *28* day of *Feb*, 18*65* That since leaving the service this applicant has resided in the *City* of *Washington Dist.* in the State of *Columbia*, and that his occupation has been that of a *laborer & watchman* That prior to his entry into the service above-named he was a man of good, sound, physical health, being when enrolled a .... That he is now *totally* disabled from obtaining his subsistence by manual labor by reason of his injuries, above described, received in the service of the United States; and he therefore makes this declaration for the purpose of being placed on the invalid pension roll of the United States. He hereby appoints, with full power of substitution and revocation, *Wm. M. Goodlow* of *Washington, D.C.* his true and lawful attorney to prosecute his claim. That he has *not* received *but has* applied for a pension; that his residence is No. *1850 Ledroit Court*, street *Bet 6" & 7. St. S. City* and that his post office address is *(new Law June 27 1790 2984 Nd 4 Clause)*

Walter D. Plowden
(Signature of Claimant.)

2 Wm. W. Gowans
J B Hanaher
(Two witnesses who can write sign here.)

Plate 66 Walter Plowden was born enslaved on Maryland's Western Shore, liberated himself, and joined the US Army in New York. He served as a spy for the US Army Department of the South and was part of Harriet Tubman's ring of spies, scouts, and pilots. On November 1, 1890, Plowden testified in his pension file that he was sent on a secret expedition up the Combahee River in a rowboat in the spring of 1863.
Record Group 15, National Archives and Records Administration

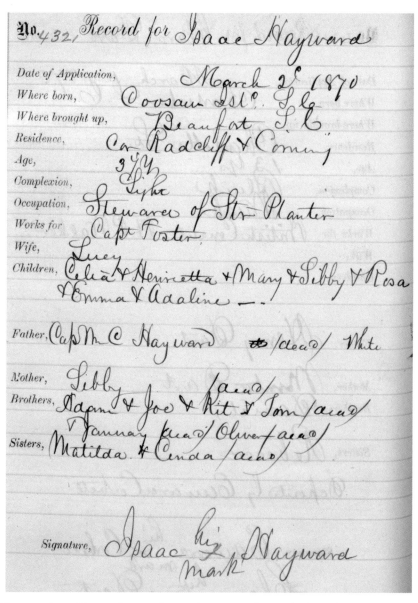

No. 432/ Record for Isaac Hayward

Date of Application, March 2? 1870
Where born, Coosaw Isl? S.C.
Where brought up, Beaufort S.C.
Residence, Cor Radcliff & Coming
Age, 3?
Complexion, Light
Occupation, Steward of Str Planter
Works for Capt Foster,
Wife, Lucy
Children, Celia & Henrietta & Mary & Sibby & Rosa & Emma & Adaline —.
Father, Capt M C Hayward /dead/ White
Mother, Sibby /dead/
Brothers, Adam & Joe & Kit & Tom /dead/ January /dead/ Oliver /dead/
Sisters, Matilda & Cinda /dead/

Signature, Isaac his X mark Hayward

Plate 67 Isaac Heyward, one of many boatmen who worked on the rivers in Beaufort, was one of Harriet Tubman's spies, scouts, and pilots who executed the Combahee River Raid. When he opened his Freedmen's Bank Account on March 2, 1870, Heyward identified Coosaw Island as his birthplace and Captain William C. Heyward as his deceased white father.

Records of the Office of the Comptroller of the Currency, Record Group 101, National Archives and Records Administration

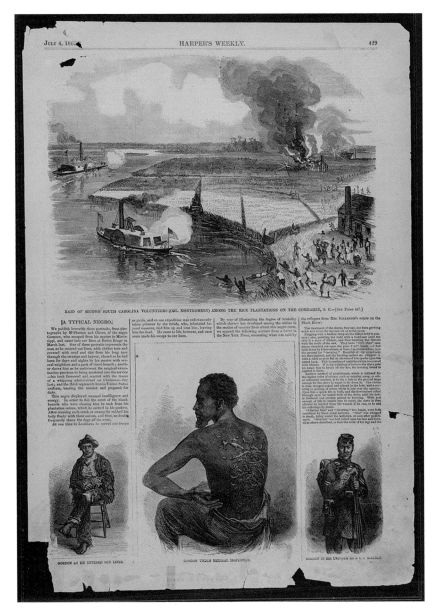

RAID OF SECOND SOUTH CAROLINA VOLUNTEERS (COL. MONTGOMERY) AMONG THE RICE PLANTATIONS ON THE COMBAHEE, S. C.—[SEE PAGE 427.]

[A TYPICAL NEGRO.]

GORDON AS HE ENTERED OUR LINES   GORDON UNDER MEDICAL INSPECTION   GORDON IN HIS UNIFORM AS A U. S. SOLDIER

Plate 68 *Harper's Weekly* published this full-page spread, "Raid of South Carolina Volunteers (Col. Montgomery) among the Rice Plantations on the Combahee, S.C.," on July 4, 1863. The angular appearance of the rice fields and canals, the location of the rice gates, and the proximity of the slave quarters to both the rice fields and the river suggest that the sketch artist was not an eyewitness. But the depiction of distraught freedom seekers standing on the riverbank toting their belongings as the *John Adams* sailed away, jumping in the river, and attempting to swim after it was likely accurate. *Library of Congress*

"A Typical Negro," *Harper's Weekly*, July 4, 1863, shows three views of a man identified as Gordon. In the first view, a disheveled Gordon appears as he did when he successfully made his way to US-occupied territory. In the second, a medical examination reveals his badly scarred back. The final sketch depicts Gordon dressed in a US Army uniform. The formerly enslaved African American men who joined Black regiments were all "Gordon." *Library of Congress*

FEEDING THE NEGRO CHILDREN UNDER CHARGE OF THE MILITARY AUTHORITIES AT HILTON HEAD, SOUTH CAROLINA.—[SEE NEXT PAGE.]

Plate 69 "Feeding the Negro Children under Charge of the Military Authorities at Hilton Head"] This cartoon was printed below sketches of Robert Smalls and the *Planter* and an article celebrating Small's heroic act in *Harper's Weekly* in June 1862. It highlights the destitute conditions of refugee women and children in the US Army's care in Hilton Head. *American Antiquarian Society*.

Plate 70 William Lee Apthrop began his
military service as captain of the 2nd South
Carolina, moving up the ranks to the rank
of lieutenant colonel before the regiment
merged into the 34th Colored Troops, and
serving from 1863 to 1866.
Apthorp Family Papers.
HistoryMiami Museum

Plate 71 Oliver Hering Middleton
(1798–1892) was owner of Launch
Plantation at Tar Bluff on the lower
Combahee River. The 2nd South
Carolina Volunteers burned Middleton's
rice mill in the Combahee River Raid.
Middleton Place Foundation

Plate 72 The *John Adams, Harriet A. Weed*, and *Sentinel* departed from this wharf
in downtown Beaufort on June 1, 1863, around nine o'clock at night, under a
full moon.
Sam. A. Cooley, 1862–1863, Library of Congress

Plate 73 A modern view of the bustling downtown Beaufort wharf from which Harriet Tubman, her ring of spies, scouts, and pilots piloted Colonel James Montgomery, the Second South Carolina Volunteers, and Third Rhode Island Artillery up the Combahee River. They returned to the same wharf the following morning with 756 Combahee freedom seekers.
Photo by J Henry Fair, 2016

Plate 74 An aerial view from the southeast of how the Combahee River would have looked the night of the raid, when the *John Adams* and *Harriet A. Weed* went upriver under a full moon.
Photo by J Henry Fair, 2022; flight thanks to Southwings

Plate 75 An aerial view to the south toward the ocean of the Coosaw River leading to the mouth of the Combahee River. It shows the tight curls of the Combahee River nestled between the marsh in the foreground and the historic rice fields in the background.
Photo by J Henry Fair, 2016

Plate 76 A drone view of where the 2nd South Carolina Volunteers landed on the sandy bluffs that give Tar Bluff its name. These majestic bluffs stood above the low-lying marsh and rice fields farther upriver, beginning at James L. Paul's plantation. Though the photo was not taken under the full moon, the moonlight would have illuminated the sandy bluffs.
Photo by J Henry Fair, 2022

Plate 77 The tight curls of the Combahee River in all of their glory in this aerial view to the northeast, south to Beaufort. The two extremities of the river come to a point, and the land separating them, Field's Point, is where the 2nd South Carolina Volunteers, Company D, landed. One can imagine the amount of time it took the relatively slow-moving gunboat and transport to get around the bends in the river, time during which they could have been exposed to Confederate fire.
Photo by J Henry Fair, 2015

Plate 78 Confederate officers Major Emanuel, Captain Godbold, Captain Bomar (with his artillery pieces), and Lieutenant Hewitt pursued the 2nd South Carolina Volunteers down this wooded country road running from Green Pond to Field's Point. Confederate called Stock's Creek Road. The 2nd South Carolina, however, waited for them in ambush and drove them back into the dense woods.
Photo by J Henry Fair, 2023

Plate 79 This drone photograph from the west shows Joshua Nicholls's view from his portico when he saw the US Army winding its way up the Combahee River to Nicholls's boat landing. The canal that the *Harriet A. Weed* drove up—a canal that was constructed to bring water from the river to the rice fields (on the left)—is prominent toward the middle of the photograph.
Photo by J Henry Fair, 2022

Plate 80 An aerial view from the east-northeast of Jack's Creek on Charles T. Lowndes's Oakland Plantation. At the slave quarters near Jack's Creek, Lowndes's overseer shot and killed an enslaved girl as she was running to the river in an attempt to liberate herself.
Photo by J Henry Fair, 2022; flight thanks to Southwings

Plate 81 An aerial view from the south toward the ocean shows the rice fields at Newport Plantation in the foreground, and the sharp bend in the Combahee River around which Colonel William C. Heyward saw with his spyglass the *John Adams* coming upriver. His Cypress Plantation is also in the background on the left side, directly across the river from Newport.
Photo by J Henry Fair, 2015

Plate 82 A modern aerial view looking due west at the causeway down which the 2nd South Carolina Volunteers marched to Cypress Plantation, skirmished with Confederate forces, then marched back across with the freedom seekers, delivering them safely to liberty on the *John Adams*. Today the causeway is Highway 17, a four-lane, 221-mile thoroughfare from Myrtle Beach to Savannah, which on the lower Combahee still separates the historic rice fields on the left side from the Combahee River on the right.
Photo by J Henry Fair, 2022

Plate 83 A modern aerial view from the north of the Harriet Tubman Bridge, where the Cypress causeway ended. During the Civil War, it was the pontoon bridge where the *John Adams* landed after finding the river obstructed as it attempted to move farther upriver. The US Army also destroyed the pontoon bridge during the Combahee River Raid. Today the bridge goes across the Combahee River and straddles the Beaufort/Colleton County line.
Photo by J Henry Fair, 2022; flight thanks to Southwings

Plate 84 A modern aerial view from the north (with Brickyard Creek and the Coosaw River behind) of the bustling downtown Beaufort wharf from which Harriet Tubman and her ring of spies, scouts, and pilots piloted Colonel James Montgomery, the 2nd South Carolina Volunteers, and a battery of the 3rd Rhode Island Heavy Artillery up the Combahee River. They returned to the same wharf the following morning with 756 Combahee freedom seekers.
Photo by J Henry Fair, 2022

Plate 85 After the raid, women, children, the elderly, and disabled men among the Combahee freedom seekers were resettled in a refugee camp at Old Fort Plantation on the Beaufort River.
Photo by J Henry Fair, 2022

Plate 86 Aerial photograph of Mitchelville from the southwest (with Hilton Head airport in the background). Mitchelville, Saxtonville, and Higginsonville were three areas where Combahee freedom seekers settled after the end of the Civil War.
Photo by J Henry Fair, 2022; flight thanks to Southwings

Plate 87 "Building a Pontoon Bridge at Beaufort, S.C." (March 1862). Timothy O'Sullivan may have been embedded with the Topographical Engineers when he captured the construction of a pontoon bridge by what looks like US Army engineers. The Combahee River Raid stopped at the Combahee Ferry pontoon bridge over the Combahee River. The US Army burned the bridge, halting the Confederacy's pursuit.
Library of Congress

Plate 88 This is how the downtown Beaufort street the Combahee freedom seekers marched down the morning after the raid would have looked. One can imagine African Americans who had been free since the Battle of Port Royal lining the street to pay their respects to this relic of enslavement finally free. *Sam. A. Cooley, 1862–1864, Library of Congress*

Plate 89 Sergeant Major Lewis Henry Douglass (1840–1908) was the oldest son of radical abolitionist Frederick Douglass and his first wife, Anna Murray Douglass. During the Civil War, Douglass enlisted on March 25, 1863, in the 54th Massachusetts Volunteer Infantry, the second African American regiment organized in the northern states, and earned the rank of sergeant major, the highest rank for African Americans at the time. *Moorland-Spingarn Research Center, Howard University Archives, Howard University*

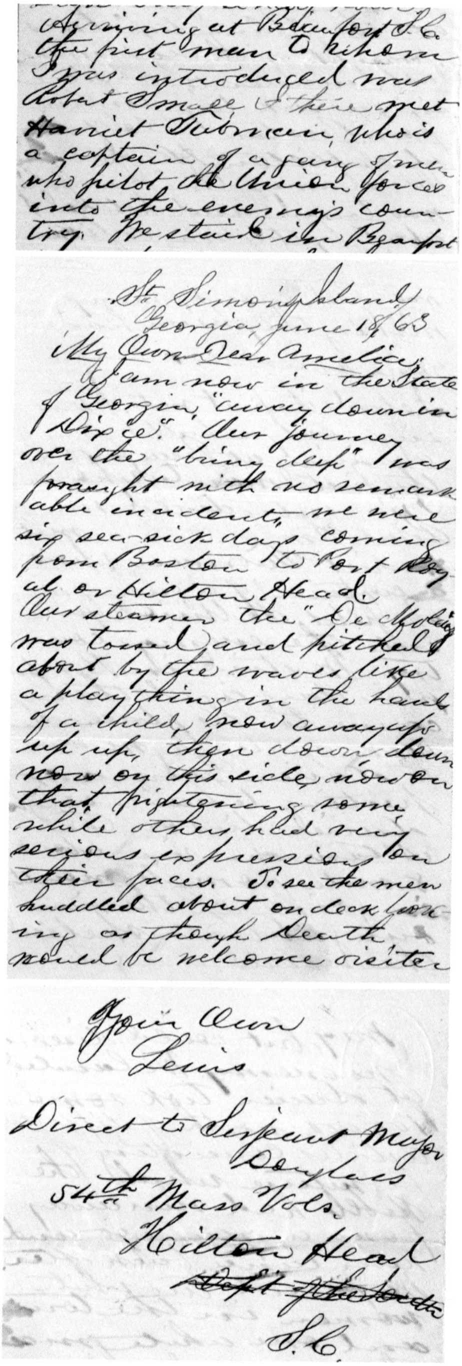

Arriving at Beaufort S.C. the first man to whom I was introduced was Robert Smalls & there met Harriet Tubman, who is a captain of a gang of men who pilot the Union forces into the enemy's country. We staid in Beaufort

St. Simonspland
Georgia, June 1863

My Own Dear Amelia,
I am now in the State of Georgia, away down in Dixie. Our journey over the "briny deep" was fraught with no remarkable incidents, we were six sea-sick days coming from Boston to Port Royal or Hilton Head. Our steamer the "De Molay" was tossed and pitched about by the waves like a plaything in the hand of a child, now away up up, then down down now on this side now on that, frightening some while others had very serious expression on their faces. To see the men huddled about on deck looking as though Death would be welcome visiter

Your Own
Lewis

Direct to Sergeant Major
Douglass
54th Mass Vols.
Hilton Head
S.C.

Plate 90 Sergeant Major Lewis Henry Douglass wrote more than twenty letters to his fiancée, Helen Amelia Loguen (whom he married in 1869), that document his service in the 54th Massachusetts. The 54th Massachusetts was stationed in Beaufort in mid-June 1863, a little more than two weeks after the Combahee River Raid. There Douglass met Robert Smalls and Harriet Tubman.
Walter O. Evans Collection of Frederick Douglass and Douglass Family Papers, James Weldon Johnson Collection, Yale Collection of American Literature, Beinecke Rare Book and Manuscript Library

Rose Hill Plantation on Combahee.

BY I. S. K. BENNETT.

At Private Sale—

"ROSE HILL," a first class Rice and Provision Plantation, of about 800 acres, situated in St. Bartholomew's Parish, near the Combahee River, and about two miles from the Ferry. It has 300 acres of tide swamp under cultivation, 200 of which is now planted. These acres, for richness of soil, cannot be surpassed in the State. Being located on a creek adds materially also to their value, since they are as fully secured from salts as lands four miles above on the river, and at the same time rendering river banks of little use.

The provision lands are from 80 to 90 acres, and are very fine—500 acres are in woods.

The fencing is all good, Corn House new and very large, all outbuildings and Dwelling are in good order. Also, the settlement for 100 negros.

For further particulars, apply as above, at

June 11   thstu4   No. 40 BROAD STREET.

Plate 91 "Rose Hill Plantation on Combahee by I. S. K. Bennett," *Charleston Mercury.* Nine days after the Combahee River Raid, William Lennox Kirkland Jr. was the first of the lower Combahee River rice planters whose plantations were demolished by the raid to offer their plantations for public sale. Unfortunately for Kirkland, there were no buyers in June 1863.
Charleston Library Society

Plate 92 William Mason Smith (1843–1864).

Plate 93 Eliza Smith (1824–1919) owned Smithfield Plantation, which neighbored William C. Heyward's Cypress Plantation on its northwest side. On land, the Combahee River Raid stopped before the soldiers reached Smithfield.
George Smith Cook; South Caroliniana Library, University of South Carolina

Plate 94 Charles Heyward (1802–1866) was Nathaniel Heyward's son and William C. Heyward's distant cousin. Charles Heyward's son Edward Barnwell Heyward had the foresight to evacuate most of the people his father held in bondage on the Combahee River, taking them to Goodwill Plantation, outside Columbia, after the Battle of Port Royal. Unfortunately for Heyward, they were in General William Tecumseh Sherman's path.
Gibbes Museum, Gift of Ms. Leslie Townsend Jervey in Memory of C. H. Jervey, Jr.

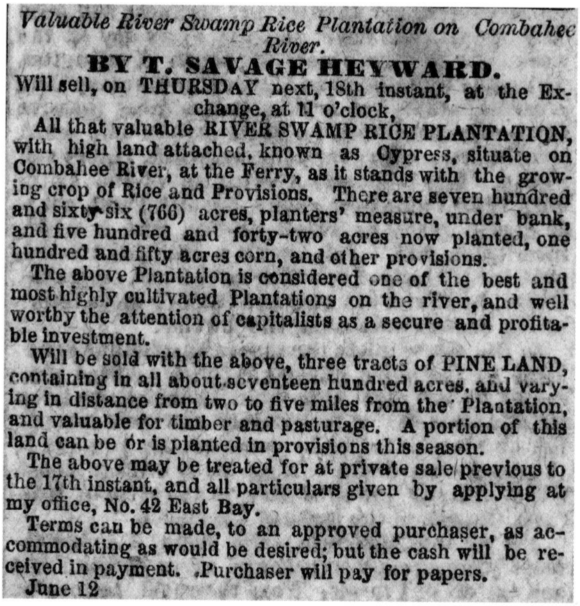

Valuable River Swamp Rice Plantation on Combahee River.

BY T. SAVAGE HEYWARD.

Will sell, on THURSDAY next, 18th instant, at the Exchange, at 11 o'clock,

All that valuable RIVER SWAMP RICE PLANTATION, with high land attached, known as Cypress, situate on Combahee River, at the Ferry, as it stands with the growing crop of Rice and Provisions. There are seven hundred and sixty-six (766) acres, planters' measure, under bank, and five hundred and forty-two acres now planted, one hundred and fifty acres corn, and other provisions.

The above Plantation is considered one of the best and most highly cultivated Plantations on the river, and well worthy the attention of capitalists as a secure and profitable investment.

Will be sold with the above, three tracts of PINE LAND, containing in all about seventeen hundred acres, and varying in distance from two to five miles from the Plantation, and valuable for timber and pasturage. A portion of this land can be or is planted in provisions this season.

The above may be treated for at private sale previous to the 17th instant, and all particulars given by applying at my office, No. 42 East Bay.

Terms can be made, to an approved purchaser, as accommodating as would be desired; but the cash will be received in payment. Purchaser will pay for papers.

June 12

Plate 95 "Valuable Rice Lands on Combahee River by T. Savage Heyward," *Charleston Mercury*, June 18, 1863. A week after William Lennox Kirkland Jr. put Rose Hill Plantation up for public sale, William C. Heyward had to do the same for Cypress Plantation. The result was the same, however; no buyers came forward to purchase Cypress Plantation either.
Charleston Library Society

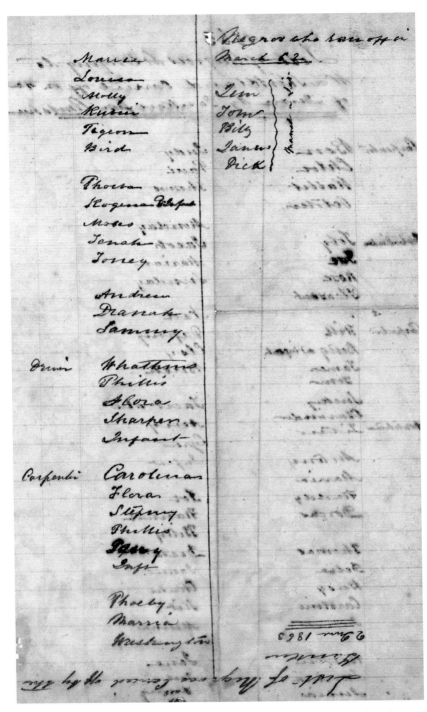

Plate 96 William Lennox Kirkland Jr. kept a list of the enslaved people who escaped enslavement on Rose Hill Plantation during the Civil War. On two sides of one sheet of paper, Kirkland recorded the names of enslaved people who liberated themselves in March 1862 and on June 2, 1863. The June 1863 list was likely written shortly after the Combahee River Raid, when the painful details were fresh in his mind.

Papers of the Kirkland, Withers, Snowden, and Trotter Families, 1790–1959, South Caroliniana Library, University of South Carolina, Columbia

Plate 97 Image of the Freedman's School in Beaufort. After the Combahee freedom seekers arrived in downtown Beaufort on the morning after the raid, they were taken to a church. At the church, Colonel James Montgomery addressed them, followed by Harriet Tubman. Then the refugees' needs were assessed, the men were examined for military service, and the women and children were given rations and clothing. The church may have been Tabernacle Baptist Church, the oldest continuously operating Black church in Beaufort. *Sam. A. Cooley, 1862–1864, Library of Congress*

Plate 98 Located on Craven Street in downtown Beaufort, Tabernacle Baptist Church is the current home of the Robert Smalls monument and future home of the Harriet Tubman Memorial. *Photo by J Henry Fair, 2023*

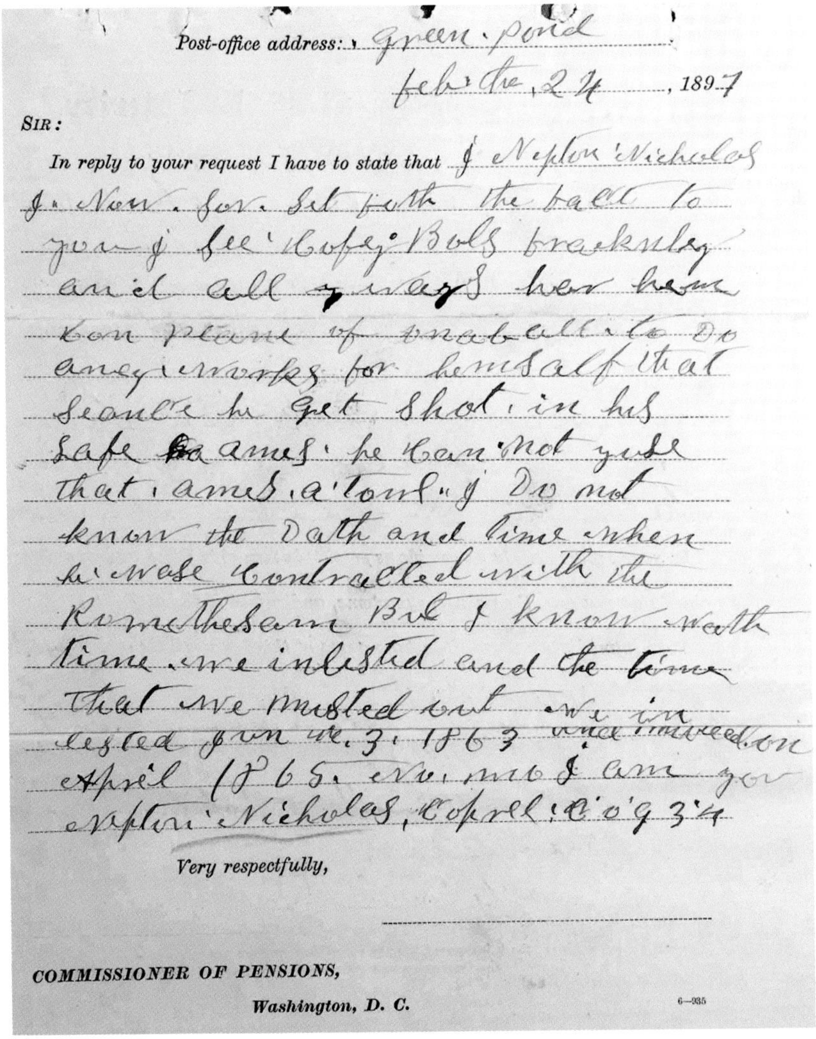

Post-office address: _Green pond_

feb the 24 , 189_7_

SIR :

In reply to your request I have to state that _I Neptor Nicholas_
J. Now for set forth the ball to
you I see Cofey Bols brackuly
and all ways her hem
can plane of unaballite Do
aney works for hemsalf that
Seance he get shot in his
Safe ba ames he can not yuse
that ames a toul. I Do not
know the Dath and time when
he wase contracted with the
Romethesam But I know woth
time we inlisted and the time
that we musted out we in
lested jun the 3. 1863 and muved on
April 1865 eve me I am you
explor Nicholas coprel co 93'4

Very respectfully,

COMMISSIONER OF PENSIONS,

Washington, D. C.

6—935

Plate 99 Neptune Nicholas was one of the few Combahee freedom seekers in the USCT who could write. In this handwritten affidavit dated February 24, 1897, Nicholas testified for his comrade Cuffee Bolze that they enlisted on June 3, 1863, the morning after the raid.
Pension file for Cuffee (Sophia) Bolze, Record Group 15, National Archives and Records Administration

Plate 100 In May 1863, Harriet Tubman was nursing "contrabands" at Contraband Hospital No. 5, which was also called Barnwell Castle. Here she was on the front lines of self-liberation, providing basic medical care for freedom seekers who had escaped from enemy territory and found refuge in US-occupied territory, helping them find housing and employment, and gathering intelligence from them. *Sam. A. Cooley, 1862–1864, Library of Congress*

Plate 101 The Swamp Angel was one of the most unusual military innovations of the Civil War, an immense cannon embedded in the salt marsh between James Island and Morris Island and aimed at Charleston. The US Army used it to its advantage to overtake Morris Island.

Haas & Peale, July or August 1863; Library of Congress

Plate 102 Private William Lennox Kirkland Jr., owner of Rose Hill Plantation at the time of the raid, served in the Charleston Light Dragoons. Kirkland was mortally wounded in the Battle of Haw's Shop in Hanover County, Virginia, in May 1864.
South Caroliniana Library, University of South Carolina, Columbia

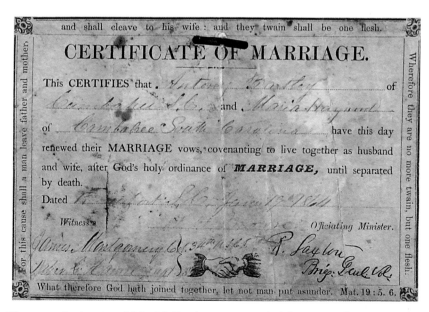

Plate 103 Anthony and Moriah Bartley were married for a second time at Pigeon Point, along with several other couples, by Reverend Homer H. Moore. Their marriage certificate is dated June 19, 1864. Both Colonel James Montgomery and Brigadier General Rufus Saxton signed the document.
Pension file for Anthony (Moriah) Bartley, Record Group 15, National Archives and Records Administration

Plate 104 J. J. Smith's plantation, also known as Old Fort Plantation, was abandoned by its owners after the Battle of Port Royal. It was the location of the refugee camp where groups of freedom seekers were housed, including those who liberated themselves in the Combahee River Raid.
E. W. Sinclair for Sam. A. Cooley, 1862–1864, Library of Congress

Plate 105 Little is known about Elizabeth Hyde Botume before she took charge of the school for freedpeople at Old Fort Plantation in October 1864. She is pictured here in black hat and cape with another teacher at Old Fort Plantation. The structure in the background on the right may be the schoolhouse where Botume taught freedpeople.

Hubbard & Mix, 1863–June 1866, Library of Congress

Plate 106 Senator William Henry Seward and his wife, Frances Seward, sold this farmhouse in Auburn, New York, to Harriet Tubman in 1859 for $1,200 on a no-interest mortgage with no money down. The home became a sanctuary for Tubman, her second husband, Nelson Charles, extended family, and freed people in Auburn whom she took in.
The Harriet Tubman Home Inc.

85

Recorded this 29 January 1886 —

Red Dark

South Carolina ⎰ Lot No.7 containing thirty one
Colleton County ⎱ and one half acres high in
black and two and four tenths acres Rice
land in red nick. the property of Brutus
Rutledge. It is a part of the Gough tract
on ashepoo. January 6 — 1886 —
Recorded 29 th Jan 1886 ⎰ Campbell and Lemacks
⎱ Surveyors

Neptune Nichols ⎱
   et al. ⎰ Conveyance.
   To
April Singleton

The State of South Carolina. Colleton County.
Know All Men by these Presents, That We, Neptune
Nichols & others, whose names are subscribed as
Grantors hereto, in the State aforesaid, Farmers, in
consideration of the sum of five dollars, to us in
hand paid, at and before the sealing of these
presents, by April Singleton in the State aforesaid
Farmer (the receipt whereof is hereby acknowledged)
have granted, bargained, sold and released, and
by these Presents do grant bargain, sell and release
unto the said April Singleton (which we own as ten-
ants in Common) All those three tracts of land situate
in the County, and State, aforesaid, known as portions
of the Gough (or Fripp) lands, designated on a Plat made
by H. W. Fishbourne Surveyor, of date January 18th 1859. As part
A No.4. B No.3, & C No.2" containing in the whole nine hundred and sixty six (966) acres more or less and bounded on the North by tract No.1 of the Gough lands belonging to Anthony Fraser, and others, South by lands
formerly of Northrop, East by lands of Estate of A. A
Fraser, and West by lands of Estates of McDonald, and
Wm C. Heyward As will fully appear by aforesaid Plat.
(The Plat attached represents the reservation of April
Singleton, he having sold off the balance.) Together
with all & singular the Rights, members, Hereditta-
ments & Appurtenances to said Premises belonging
or in any wise incident or appertaining. To Have
& To Hold, all & singular the said Premises before
mentioned, unto the said April Singleton his
Heirs & Assigns forever. (Die Jenkins & Sally Whitford
being Heirs at law of Cuffee Kinsly, Monstrie Rice, at
bar of Cyrus Smalls: Molly Brown Heir at law

86

of John Graham; and Phebe Smalls pins at law
of Jno Smalls.) And We do hereby bind, our Heirs
Executors and Administrators, to warrant and
forever defend all and singular the said premises unto the said April Singleton, his Heirs and
Assigns against myself and my Heirs, and all
others lawfully claiming, or to claim the same, or
any part thereof. Witness my Hand and Seal
this second day of January in the year of our
Lord one thousand eight hundred and eighty
six and in the one hundreth and tenth year
of the Sovereignty & Independence of the United
State of America   Neptune Nichols (L S)
Signed, Sealed & Delivered (Robbin X Mitchell (L S) Sarah X Butler (L S)
in the presence of   Charles X Nichols L S Die X Jenkins (L S)
Richard Mitchell   Solly X Whitford (L S) Sampson X McNeill (L S)
Archie McGraw   Jenny X Meyers (L S) Cymly X Moultrie (L S)
Molly McGraham (L S) Briny X McNeill (L S) Edward X Brown (L S)
Charlie X LeSeure (L S) Peter X James (L S) Solomon X Glover (L S)
Moses X Simons (L S) Phebe X Smalls (L S) Horace X Robinson (L S)
Brutus X Rulledge (L S) Dick X Brocton (L S) Sue X Freignan (L S)
R. Wm X Huggins (L S) John X Pinckney (L S) Joshua X Polite (L S)
Juno X Grandison (L S) Dick X Ferguson (L S) Sampson X Hamilton (L S)
July X Osborn (L S) Joshua X Simons (L S)   The State of
South Carolina, Colleton County } Personally ap-
peared before me Richard Mitchell and made
oath that he saw the within named Parties whose
signatures are written, as Grantors hereto sign, seal
and as their act & deed, deliver the within written
Deed; and that he with Archie McGraw witnessed
the execution thereof.   Richard Mitchell
Sworn to before me this second
day of January A.D. 1886 } Recorded 29th January 1886.
(Seal) C. G. Henderson
        Not. Pub. (L S)

South Carolina) Lot No 4 containing Thirty one and one half
Colleton County) acres high in Black, and two and four
tenths acres Rice land in red ink, the property of
April Singleton. It is a part of the Gough tract out. Lithe June
January 6. 1886.
                Campbell & Sigwacks
                    Surveyors

The above Plat represents the reservation of April Singleton he
having sold off the balance. Henderson & Kehie
Jan 6. 1886   Recorded 29 Jan 1886

Plate 108 Toward the end of his long life, Friday Hamilton migrated to New York City, where two of his children already lived. He died in there the care of his daughter and daughter-in-law. Here he is pictured in New York wearing the latest fashion, a three-piece suit with wide lapels, after liberating himself from enslavement and Jim Crow.
Claire Hamilton; photo by J Henry Fair, 2022

Plate 109 Molly Graham escaped enslavement on William C. Heyward's Cypress Plantation along with her son-in-law April Singleton. The Molly Graham Memorial Bridge (which goes over the railroad tracks) on Highway 17 in Green Pond, South Carolina, was dedicated to Molly Graham on July 4, 2019.

Photo by J Henry Fair, 2022

Plate 110 William Drayton was the youngest man to liberate himself in the Combahee River Raid and enlist in the 2nd South Carolina Volunteers. He enlisted as a drummer at age fourteen. Drayton died in October 1895 and was buried in Beaufort National Cemetery among nineteen thousand veterans. *Photo by J Henry Fair, 2023*

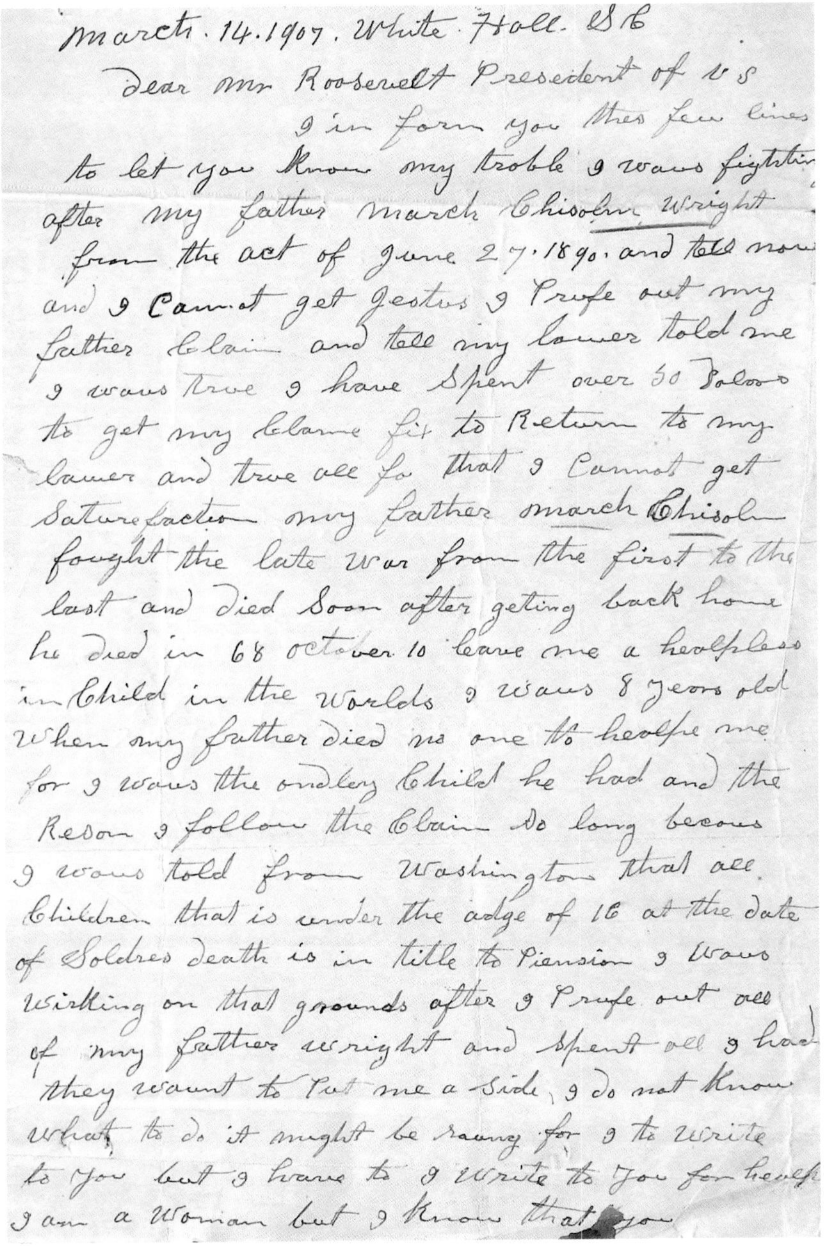

March. 14. 1907. White. Hall. SC

Dear Mr Roosevelt President of US

I in form you thes few lines to let you know my troble I waus fightin after my father march Chisolm Wright from the act of June 27. 1890. and tell now and I Cannot get Jestus I Prufe out my father Claim and tell my lawer told me I waus True I have Spent over 50 Doloors to get my Claime fix to Return to my lawer and true all fo that I Cannot get Satusfaction my father march Chisolm fought the late war from the first to the last and died Soon after geting back home he died in 68 october 10 leave me a heolpless in Child in the worlds I waus 8 years old when my father died no one to heolpe me for I waus the ondley Child he had and the Redon I follow the Claim So long becous I waus told from Washington that all Children that is under the adge of 16 at the date of Soldres death is in title to Piension I waus wirking on that grounds after I Prufe out all of my father wright and Spent all I had they waunt to Put me a Side, I do not know what to do it mught be raung for I to write to you but I have to I write to you for heolp I am a Woman but I know that you

Plate 111 Molcy Chisolm's father, March Chisolm, died in 1868, leaving her orphaned. In 1907, she wrote a letter to President Roosevelt stating that she could not get justice on her pension application even after paying her lawyer $50 and waiting several years.

Pension file for March (Molcy) Chisolm, Record Group 15, National Archives and Records Administration

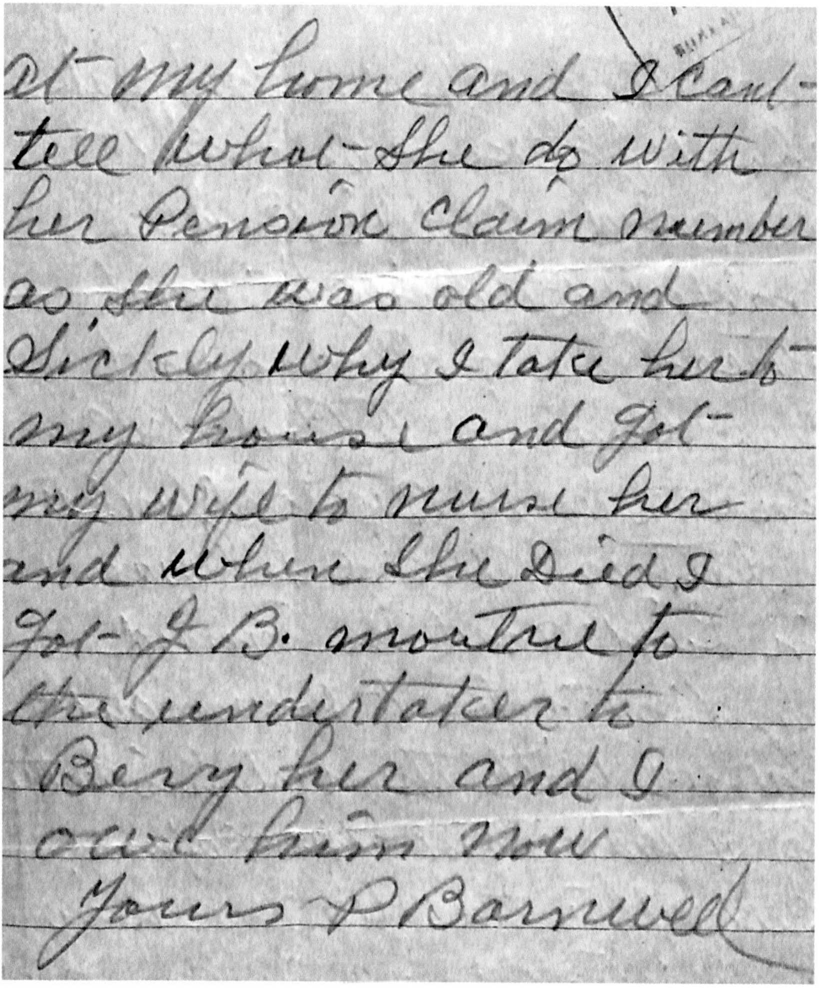

at my home and I can't tell what She do with her Pension claim number as She was old and Sickly why I take her to my house and got my wife to nurse her and when She died I got J. B. mouture to the undertaker to Bery her and I owe him now

Yours P Barnwell

Plate 112 A young child when his family liberated themselves from bondage on Cypress Plantation, Primus Barnwell applied for his sister's accrued widow's pension after she died, more than forty years after the raid, to cover the expenses of her last illness and burial. In this handwritten letter, Barnwell described what he could remember of his brother-in-law's military service.
Pension file for William (Relia) Middleton, Record Group 15, National Archives and Records Administration

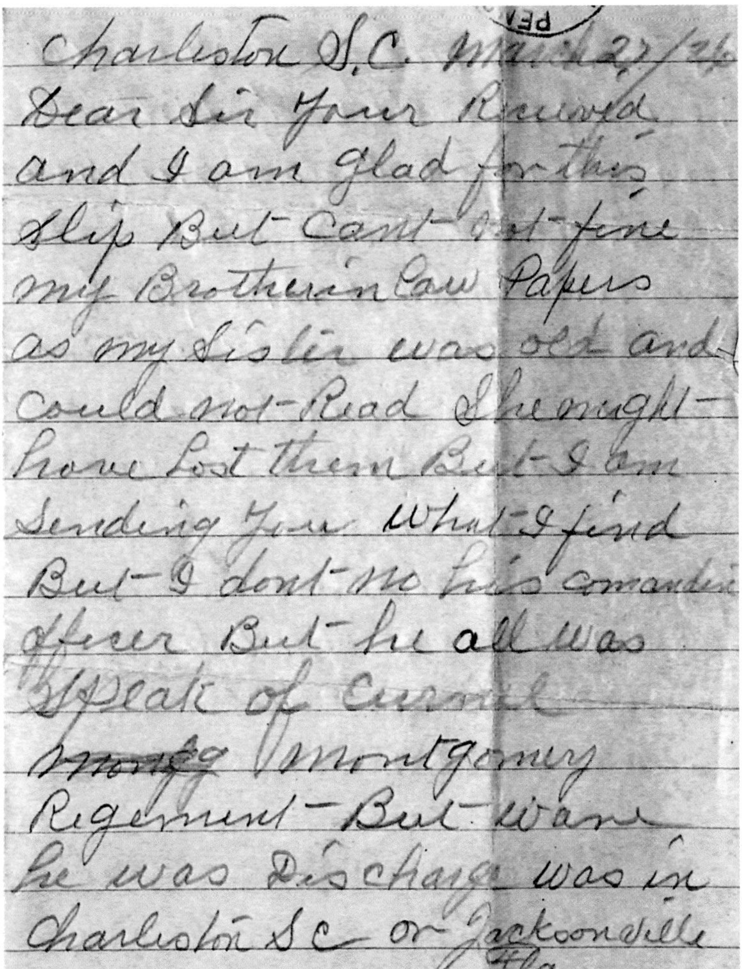

charleston S. C. March 27/26

Dear Sir Your Received
and I am glad for this
slip But cant not find
my Brother in law Papers
as my Sister was old and
could not Read She might
have Lost them But I am
Sending You what I find
But I dont no his comandie
officer But he all was
speak of Cur~~~
~~money~~ montgomery
Regiment But ware
he was Dis Charge was in
charleston S C or Jacksonville
                              Fla

Plate 112 Continued

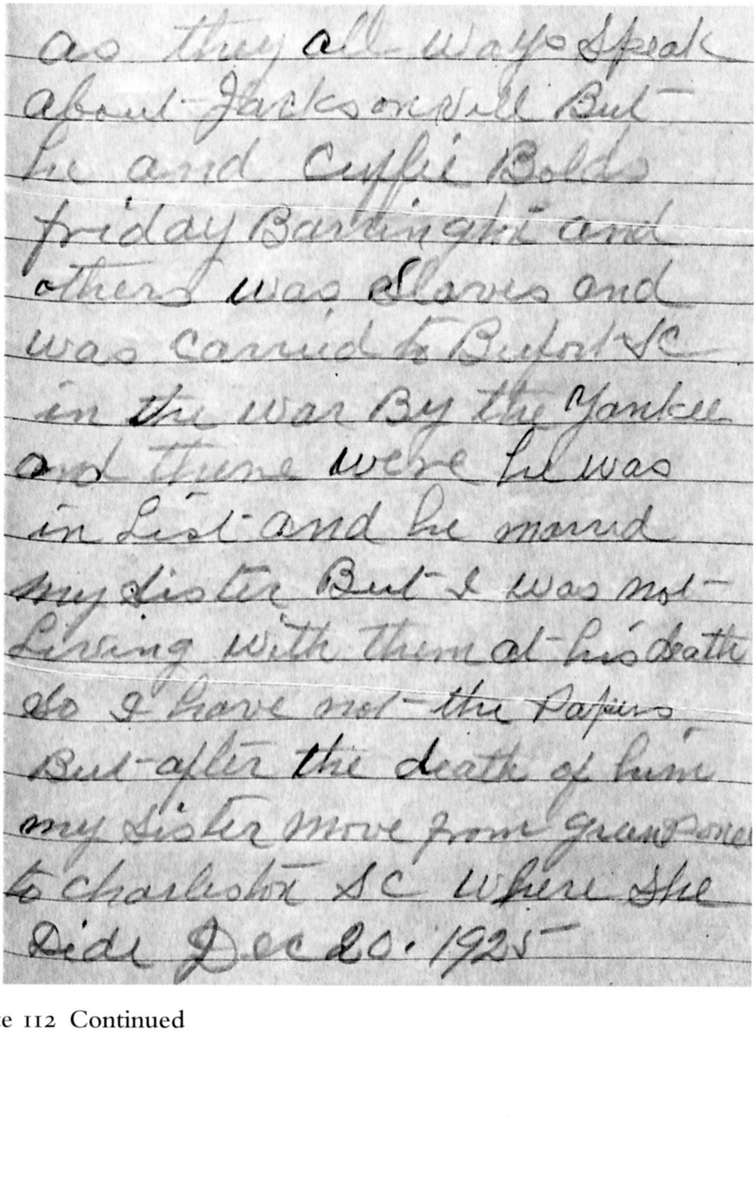

as they all ways speak
about Jacksonvill But
he and cuffie Bolds
friday Bartingtn and
others was slaves and
was carried to Bufort SC
in the war By the Yankee
and thune were he was
in List and he marrid
my sister But I was not
Living with them at his death
so I have not the papers
But after the death of him
my sister move from grunsone
to charlston SC where she
Dide Dec 20. 1925

Plate 112 Continued

CIRCULAR.]   HEADQUARTERS THIRD MIL. DIST.,
                        Pocotaligo, March 27, 1863.
   The attention of planters and other slave-holders in this military district is called to the following communication from department headquarters :

Plate 113 "Circular" Headquarters Third Military District, 3/23/1863] The War of the Rebellion: *A Compilation of the Official Records of the Union and Confederate Armies.* Washington: Government Printing Office. 1880-1901, Series 1, Volume 14, 292-293

HDQRS. DEPARTMENT SOUTH CAROLINA, GEORGIA, AND FLORIDA,
Charleston, S. C., March 23, 1863.

GENERAL: It is the wish of the commanding general that you advise all planters and owners of negroes in your military district to remove their negroes as far as practicable into the interior of the State, as otherwise they are liable to be lost at any moment.

Very respectfully, your obedient servant,

JNO. F. O'BRIEN,
Captain and Assistant Adjutant-General.

By order of Brigadier-General Walker:

JAMES LOWNDES,
Captain and Acting Assistant Adjutant-General.

Plate 114 "Names of Harriet Tubman's Spies, Scouts, and Pilots"

SPECIAL ORDERS, } HDQRS. THIRD MILITARY DISTRICT,
No. 112. } *McPhersonville, May 26, 1863.*

* * * * * * *

XV. The recent false alarm of the pickets stationed on Combahee River was not justified by circumstances. Before giving such an alarm the pickets should have ascertained positively whether a boat had landed or not and how many men were in it. If only 5 or 6, it is the duty of the pickets, if only 2 should be on post, to engage them. If a large number, it is the duty of the pickets to fire a signal for their comrades and closely watch the enemy's movements. As these troops have but recently arrived in this district, and may be ignorant of existing orders, they are warned that if another groundless alarm is given the pickets will be court-martialed. If sufficient courage is not shown in watching the enemy pickets will be subject to the charge of cowardice and to be tried by court-martial.

By order of Brigadier-General Walker:

JAMES LOWNDES,
Captain and Acting Assistant Adjutant-General.

[Inclosure No. 3.]

Plate 115 "Special Orders, No. 112 Hdqrs. Third Military District, McPhersonville, May 26, 1863"] *The War of the Rebellion: A Compilation of the Official Records of the Union and Confederate Armies.* Washington: Government Printing Office. 1880-1901, Series 1, Volume 14, 292

Combahee May 3rd 1863

My Dear Mother

The Yankees came up to Combahee Ferry yesterday morning with two gunboats & broke up the ponton bridge, burning all of the houses up to that point + carrying off all the negroes + I am sorry to say that about 25 or 30 of ours ran away + went to them, all of them men and boys with one only exception Saucys brothers John + Peter + Fields brother Charley went also Saucys son Prince + Aprils brother Charles + a lot more whose names I do not know. They carried away all the negroes from Newport + from William C Hey= wards + burnt the dwelling Houses + Mills + did the same to all the other plantations lower down. I believe none of Blakes or Cousin Daniels negroes went they were too far off to get down easily. I had

Plate 116 Walter Blake's Letter to Maria Hough Blake, 5/3/1863] South Caroliniana Library, Walter Blake Papers

just got up from picket when I heard
of it + came down here immediately
but two late to be of any service for
the Yankees had gone, before any
of the troops could get down here.
I went out this morning with some
of Captain Alleus men to try and
find them with dogs but we could
not find one.
April has just come up from Bonin
he is quite well + still on Johns
Island.
Papa has gone to headquarters to see
General Walker + I have to go back
to camp this evening.
This was a regular nigger raid of
the Yankees they found out that
this country was undefended + came
to destroy the crops + carry off the
negroes, I suppose they must have
got nearly 500. Write soon I remain
Your affect Son
Walter Blake

Plate 116 Continued

military—because of age and/or disability—worthy of being counted; Colonel Montgomery may not.[10]

Some estimates were higher than Tubman's, particularly those published weeks after the raid. The *Wisconsin State Journal* reported that Colonel Montgomery had returned with 780 freedom seekers and that his men destroyed thousands of dollars' worth of rice and millions of dollars' worth of provisions, cotton, and "lordly dwellings." Captain John F. Lay, adjutant assistant adjutant general and inspector of cavalry, weighed in with the highest Confederate estimate, "700 to 800 slaves of every age and sex," nearing the *Chicago Tribune*'s estimate of nearly 800 valuable slaves and $2 million in property damage. Even officers who commanded during the raid (or were close to other officers who did) reported inflated numbers. In *Harper's Weekly*, a surgeon (who may have been William T. Robinson) reported 800 contrabands and total losses for the Confederate planters as amounting to several millions of dollars. The 104th Pennsylvania regimental history reported some 800 "darkies." Captain Apthorp, who along with Montgomery and Tubman was closest to the situation, reported more than "800 Negroes." One hundred and fifty of them volunteered to join the 2nd South Carolina Volunteers.[11]

Determining whose numbers are correct remains hard. Tubman's is a relative mean point among the officers' figures. Montgomery's number was likely based on an account of the freedom seekers before they were sent to Old Fort Plantation. If a written log exists, it has been lost to time. The US commanders and Tubman were counting different things. To the military, they were contrabands; to Harriet, they were people. Nonetheless, Colonel Montgomery's official report (picked up in independent publications, but not part of the official military record) possesses a kind of inherent authority. On June 8, he wrote to General Hunter:

> General: I have the honor to report that, in obedience to your orders, I proceeded up the Combahee River, on the steamers *John Adams* and *Harriet A. Weed*, with a detachment of three hundred (300) men of the Second South Carolina volunteer regiment, and a section of the Third Rhode Island battery, commanded by Captain Brayton. We ascended the river some twenty-five (25) miles, destroyed a pontoon bridge, together with a vast amount of cotton, rice, and other property, and brought away seven hundred and twenty-seven slaves, and some fine horses. We had some sharp skirmishes, in all of which, the men behaved splendidly.

Though the written record is typically privileged over oral memory, I will use Tubman's count of 756 enslaved people freed, though it is higher than Montgomery's count, as her number reflects people over "contrabands."[12]

As for the damage assessment, Barton estimated that Montgomery's men inflicted several hundred thousand dollars in property damage, specifically in terms of the cotton and rice fields. These numbers were the lowest among the figures circulated. The abolitionist weekly *Commonwealth Boston* reported more than $1 million in property damage, and the *Philadelphia North American and United States Gazette* reported $1 million.[13]

Property damage is even harder to determine than the numbers of enslaved people liberated, and for the same reason—because the stories have been lost, particularly among the planter families who were most likely to know. The *Chicago Tribune*'s estimate of $2 million is based on the destruction of a total of thirty-four private dwellings (with their contents, including furniture and rare works of art) belonging to "notorious rebels" during the raid, a figure the 104th Pennsylvania regimental history also cites.[14]

The Combahee freedom seekers who testified in pension applications had escaped enslavement on seven plantations along the river, a fraction of the thirty-four located there. The planters who owned the remaining twenty-six plantations may have followed the Confederate Army's mandate and evacuated the people they held in bondage before the raid took place. If the *Chicago Tribune*'s estimate is accurate, the Combahee River Raid damaged nearly $2 million in Confederate property (the equivalent of $23.5 million in 2022). This figure is based on the loss of physical property, including the value of chattel property, people who were enslaved on seven rice plantations who ran for their freedom and off the enslavers' balance sheets. If enslaved people had inhabited the other twenty-six plantations on June 2, 1863, and their value was included, the amount of total damage would be even higher.[15]

Colonel Montgomery took full responsibility for burning private residences and all of the other acts of destruction committed under his command. He defended it as the correct policy for conducting "war against rebels." Though he left no official documentation of this strategy of guerilla warfare, his officers may have inferred Montgomery's philosophy from his actions. Raids such as that on the Combahee were likely also the "great theme of the day" among US Army officials, much as they were among northern volunteers in Beaufort and on the Sea Islands. According to an officer of the 3rd Rhode Island, Montgomery was persuaded that South Carolina was built on principles that were morally wrong. He might have extended these views to the entire Confederacy, or he may have reserved his spite for South Carolina, the first state to secede from the Union. He thought that such an immoral foundation demanded complete destruction and that he had a role to play in clearing the "ground by fire and sword." An officer of the 54th Massachusetts reported to the *Commonwealth Boston* that Montgomery believed in "making the enemy pay the way." His goal was to damage the Confederacy by inflicting damage on its private citizens.[16]

Captain Apthorp, who wrote in his journal about three expeditions in which he served under Montgomery, including the Combahee River Raid, was his most ardent supporter. In his reflections on his service with the 2nd South Carolina Volunteers, Apthorp called out the "patriotic" northerners who wanted a speedy and triumphant end to the war but were shocked by Montgomery's "shameful raids" and "wanton destruction of private property." These "patriotic" northerners wanted a fair fight; they thought Montgomery should have confined his attacks to the battlefield and fought the Confederacy where its army was best prepared to defend itself. According to Apthorp, they failed to comprehend that "every dollar's worth" in resources that was taken and "every negro, and every foot of inhabited land" that was "captured, taken from the enemy, or surrendered, laid waste" injured the Confederate government and took support from its military, thus undermining the Confederacy itself. Assaulting the resources of private citizens inflicted a "deeper and more lasting injury" on the Confederate cause than defeating its army on the battlefield.[17]

Apthorp characterized southerners as "warlike people" who would continue to support the military with their sons and their material resources as long as they perceived a benefit from doing so. If the Union wiped out the wealthy planters' capital and occupied the Atlantic coast, driving them inland from their country estates and townhomes along the coast, they would begin to feel the true impact of secession and eventually withdraw their support for a military and government that could not protect them. Apthorp predicted southerners would be confronted with two choices, "capitulation or starvation." Moreover, Montgomery's military tactics, though unorthodox, would shorten the struggle and ultimately cost the Union fewer lives. Apthorp ended by reminding the "patriotic" northerners who wanted a quick end to the war that this was not a "friendly boxing match" fought so as to injure neither side. This was a struggle between life and death, and the "quickest and surest" victory was the best.[18]

Not all of the Union Army officers in Beaufort, even those closest to Montgomery, agreed. The officer who wrote the 104th Pennsylvania's regimental history registered disgust, his own and possibly that of other officers in his regiment. While he agreed that Montgomery had inflicted considerable damage on the Confederacy, he also thought that "wanton pillage" "marred" the "good effects" of the raid. There was no excuse for burning thirty-four private dwellings, making the planters' families, particularly women and children, homeless. In fact, the regimental historian stated in his official after-action report that it was fortunate the Combahee rice planters had removed their families from the Combahee River before the raid so that they were not subjected to the outrage and insult. It was extraordinary for three planters in the "fever district" to remain on their rice plantations during the sickly season. It would have been unprecedented for white women and children to do so also.[19]

The 104th Pennsylvania officer considered the Combahee River Raid a "disgrace" to the US military. He may have implicitly been criticizing General Hunter, who had approved the raid and appointed Montgomery to execute it. He was appalled that the officers had not been censured for failing to observe the rules of war. Colonel Higginson, who was closest in terms of his abolitionist activism and military rank to Montgomery, wrote in a letter to his mother after the raid that it was "a brilliant success" and that Montgomery had captured "nearly 800 contraband." But Higginson also did not "believe in burning private houses." The chorus of Union Army commanders criticizing Montgomery for "making the enemy pay the way" grew in the weeks after June 2.[20]

★★★★★★★★

This means they wouldn't have approved of Harriet Tubman or her part in the raid. On June 20, 1863, the *Wisconsin State Journal* reported that Colonel Montgomery and his "gallant" band of three hundred Black soldiers had struck a "bold and effective blow" and struck fear into the heart of the Confederacy "under the guidance of a black woman." As noted earlier, the article introduced "this black heroine—this fugitive slave" called "Moses" for her many daring feats on behalf of enslaved people. The article recounted

Tubman's illustrious accomplishments: liberating herself a decade before the war on Maryland's Eastern Shore, returning on approximately nine trips to rescue family and friends, deliver them to freedom, and establish a safe haven for them in Canada. Tubman had since then devoted herself to liberating Blacks who were still enslaved with unparalleled "energy and sagacity." Though Tubman was not named, the *Wisconsin State Journal* article was the first time her central role in Union expeditions was spoken of publicly outside of the highest echelons of the US Army and War Department.[21]

Frank Sanborn, who reprinted the *Wisconsin Journal*'s dispatch in the July 10, 1863, issue of *The Commonwealth,* promised his readers more about the "black heroine" in the next issue. (During "Bleeding Kansas," Sanborn had been a supporter of the Kansas free-state movement, and he became the editor of the anti-slavery weekly *The Commonwealth* in February 1863. Sanborn published his first biography of Tubman in July 1863, years before the one he did of John Brown.)[22]

Sanborn begins the two-part feature article by paying tribute to the "desperation or the magnanimity" of Harriet Tubman. She was a poor Black woman with the power to shake a nation that too long had been "deaf to her cries" and whose story—the fugitive slave's story—was the "true romance" of America. He then recounts Tubman's fugitive slave and abolitionist credentials: granddaughter of a captive imported from Africa; daughter of enslaved parents who were married and faithful to each other; born enslaved, but freed herself and then risked her safety and freedom to liberate her parents and three of her siblings. He notes that, as we have seen, Tubman had gone back to liberate a fourth just before the war broke out, but was too late. Tubman's story is laid out to readers. How at six she was hired out to cruel slaveholders who neglected and abused her; how she sustained a life-threatening and life-altering brain injury; how she had hired herself out, working part of the time for her father in the shipyards of Maryland's Eastern Shore; how she had married a free Black man, escaped to freedom alone, went back for her husband years later, and was devastated to learn he had married someone else; how she continued to bring enslaved people to Canada after passage of the Fugitive Slave Act in 1850; how she found friends and supporters in the abolitionist communities in Philadelphia and New York; how she became one of John Brown's confidants, promised to secure recruits and contributions for him from freedom seekers, foresaw his death, and kept his memory alive after he was hanged;

how she made her last rescue mission to Maryland in 1860 but was hurried back to safety in Canada by her abolitionist supporters when war broke out; and how she went to Port Royal in 1862 to help the freedmen.[23]

The first part of Sanborn's biography plays like a medley of Tubman's greatest hits. Anyone who had heard her speak in person would have heard this song before. Sanborn likely heard it himself for the first time in 1858, when he first became acquainted with Tubman in Concord, when she spoke at a meeting there. He met her again when she returned to Massachusetts a year later. But in July 1863, most of the Boston abolitionists who had been central to Tubman's going to Beaufort had not heard Tubman tell her story since she went south, so Sanborn sang it again.[24]

Tubman did eventually tell her own story to the readers of *The Commonwealth* in an interview with Sanborn. Hers did not involve the trials and tribulations of growing up in bondage. Nor did it involve an account of her self-liberation and bringing scores of people to freedom via the Underground Railroad. She did not boast of her triumphs. Her interview with Sanborn was nonetheless different in tone from later interviews. She may have felt comfortable with one of "John Brown's men"; she may have been exceptionally proud of her role, or more likely that of the Black soldiers, in executing the raid. The story Tubman wanted to tell abolitionists in Boston and beyond was about the 2nd South Carolina Volunteers and why they deserved credit for the Combahee River Raid. She was determined that the stories of the heretofore nameless, faceless Black soldiers be told:

> Don't you think we colored people are entitled to some credit for the exploit under the lead of the brave Colonel Montgomery? We weakened the rebels somewhat on the Combahee river, by taking away and bringing away *seven hundred and fifty-six* head of their most valuable live stock, known up in your region as "contrabands," and this, too without the loss of a single life on our part, though we have good reason to believe that a number of rebels bit the dust. Of these seven hundred and fifty-six contraband nearly or quite all the able-bodied men have joined the colored regiments here.

In addition to giving herself and the 2nd South Carolina Volunteer soldiers credit, Tubman made clear that the raid was executed "under the lead of the brave Colonel Montgomery." The official Union and Confederate military records also gave Montgomery credit for planning and executing the Union Army's military expeditions in South Carolina and Florida in the summer of 1863; these raids were the Department of the South's primary activity during an otherwise dormant period. But they obscured Harriet Tubman's role.[25]

Earl Conrad, who published his biography of Tubman in 1943, begin to shift the focus. He wrote that the leadership of the Combahee River Raid, though Montgomery's "most celebrated raid," has "been attributed undisputedly to Harriet." The pilots she enlisted in her service possessed the knowledge to navigate safely up the winding coastal rivers in the dark. And her spies and scouts knew how to lead the troops safely overland into Confederate territory and onto the plantations. The men whom Tubman recruited, trained, and led had made Montgomery's raids not only possible but successful. According to Conrad, Montgomery's leadership was secondary, an "auxiliary command." He also claimed Montgomery executed the raid based on a "complete preliminary survey made by Harriet Tubman's espionage troops."[26]

Precious little primary source evidence exists about Tubman's service with the US Army Department of the South, except for what we find in her autobiography, interviews, and pension application. A letter dated January 7, 1863, instructed the bearer to pass Tubman $100 "secret service Money." However, Union Army commanders, at least those who were closest to the raid—not Saxton, Hunter, Montgomery, or Apthorp, nor the authors of the 104th Pennsylvania and 3rd Rhode Island regimental histories—mention Tubman playing an important role.[27]

Beginning with the first enslaved people fleeing to Fort Monroe in July 1861, all of the Union commanders relied heavily on intelligence provided by freed and free Black people, yet there is little documentation of this. Very rarely are these guides, scouts, spies, and pilots named in the official military records. George Scott (a scout employed by General Butler), Robert Smalls (one of the pilots whose intelligence was acted on by Admiral Du Pont), and March Haynes (the pilot employed by General Gillmore) are exceptions to this rule. Rather than deny her credit, the Union commanders were perhaps trying to protect Tubman, given that she was risking her life going into Confederate territory. As a fugitive slave and a spy, Tubman, along with the formerly enslaved men who enlisted as soldiers, risked their lives for the freedom of others; all had "ropes around their neck," for they would be hanged if captured.[28]

Nonetheless, there are hints. A month after the raid, Montgomery described Tubman as "a remarkable woman, and invaluable as a scout."

He endorsed Tubman's character, adding that he had known her for several years. To General Gillmore Montgomery also recommended Walter D. Plowden, a member of Tubman's ring (as mentioned in Chapter 13), as a "man of tried courage and can be made highly useful." General Saxton scribbled an endorsement on the back of Colonel Montgomery's letter, "I approve of Col. Montgomery's estimate of the value of Harriet Tubman's services," and wrote his own testimonial for Tubman in March 1868 (which Sarah Bradford included in her autobiography), stating that Tubman "was employed in the Hospitals and as a Spy" and that Tubman gathered espionage behind Confederate lines and "made many a raid behind enemy's lines displaying remarkable courage, zeal, and fidelity." Three years after the war ended, Saxton recalled that Tubman had been employed by several Union generals, including Hunter, Stevens, and Thomas W. Sherman.[29]

According to Charles P. Wood, Tubman misplaced documents from US Army officers about her war service, because she could not read them and was unaware of their value. Wood was a banker from Auburn, New York, who wrote a manuscript about Tubman's Civil War service. The manuscript was to have been published in Sarah Bradford's autobiography. Bradford's slim volume, however, first appeared in print in 1869 without it. Subsequently, Wood's manuscript was the chief evidence presented by Secretary of War Seward to Congress when Seward petitioned for Tubman to receive a pension. It included Tubman's 1865 request that the US Army pay $766 for her "services as a Scout in the Military Department of South Carolina" from May 1862 to June 1865 (at $30 per month, deducting $200 paid to Tubman during her tenure with the US Army). In an affidavit accompanying her pension application, Tubman herself attested:

> My claim against the U.S. is for three years' service as nurse and cook in hospitals, and as a commander of several men (eight or nine) as scouts during the War of the Rebellion, under direction of the orders of Edwin M. Stanton, Secretary of War, and of several Generals

Even Tubman did not reveal all of her military intelligence activities during the Civil War. Though hanging was likely no longer a threat, the southern senators who deliberated over her petition for a widow's pension and her claim for an increased pension based on her own military service could not have fathomed a Black woman serving as a Union spy.[30]

Tubman did tell Bradford that she was employed to procure "Black Dispatches," the very valuable category of intelligence provided to the military by those who escaped bondage in Confederate territories. Tubman remembered being sent into enemy territory to collect intelligence from freedom seekers whom the Union had taken on as guides, like the two enslaved men Captain Ely used when he and his small contingent of soldiers from the 8th Michigan landed on Robert Barnwell's plantation and then headed up to Combahee Ferry in February 1862. As described previously, many of the freed Blacks in Beaufort, most of whom had escaped enslavement on Lowcountry plantations as recently as the Battle of Port Royal, were "as much afraid of 'de Yankee Buckra' as of their own masters." And they would not readily talk to white people, Union or Confederate. They would, however, talk to Tubman. Decades after the war, Tubman recalled to an interviewer and to her nephew that she had gathered intelligence in the Beaufort refugee community to identify the freedom seekers who laid the torpedoes for the Confederates in the Combahee River, and then she took Colonel Montgomery and his forces to the torpedoes' location so that they could defuse the explosives and enable Union vessels to ascend the Combahee River. Tubman's memories of her Civil War efforts echoed Lieutenant George Garrison's words: "She has made it a business to see all contrabands escaping from the rebels, and is able to get more intelligence than anyone else."[31]

Frederick Douglass's eldest son, Lewis Henry Douglass, enlisted in the 54th Massachusetts in March 1863. Colonel Robert Gould Shaw appointed him sergeant major, the highest rank a Black soldier could achieve at the time. Sergeant Major Douglass wrote in a letter to his fiancée, Helen Amelia Lougen, dated June 18, 1863, that the first man he was introduced to after his arrival in Beaufort was Robert Smalls. Then he met Harriet Tubman, and he described her in the letter as "a captain of a gang of men who pilot the union forces into the enemy's country." Douglass did not hesitate to reveal Tubman's identity or greatest military accomplishment. Neither Lieutenant George Garrison, William Lloyd Garrison's son, nor Sergeant Major Lewis Henry Douglass were in positions of real authority, nor did they have direct involvement in the 2nd South Carolina Volunteers or the Combahee River Raid. Yet they were all part of a tight network of northern abolitionists who gave Tubman the credit for the raid.[32]

The Confederacy itself inadvertently gave Tubman credit for gathering the intelligence on which the Combahee River Raid was based. In his investigation about the raid, Confederate captain John F. Lay found that Colonel Montgomery's men had been "well posted"—that is, they were knowledgeable about the locations, numbers, and capabilities of Confederate troops and knew there was a "small chance" of encountering opposition. It seemed that the Union had been "acquainted" with the Combahee River and its rice plantations by "persons thoroughly acquainted with the river and the country."[33]

The Combahee River Raid aligned closely with the Union's playbook of expeditions executed before early June 1863 along Georgia, Florida, and South Carolina's coastal rivers to plunder the resources of "notorious rebels," albeit on a grander scale. The basis of it was inside knowledge of the Lowcountry waterways, plantation, and transportation network—knowing that goods and people moved up and down coastal rivers by boat and that the Confederacy moved its troops and artillery across coastal rivers like the Combahee via pontoon bridges (and, less often, by railroad). Destroying the Combahee's pontoon bridge was one of the raid's primary goals.[34]

While destroying the railroads was a Union priority, Montgomery's men did not come within miles of the Salkehatchie railroad bridge and did not disrupt the railroad's operations in any way. According to the Charleston and Savannah Railroad's 1863 annual report, it earned net income of $393,199 in 1863, roughly the same as 1862. The president told stockholders that 1863's gross receipts would have outpaced 1862's had it not been for the siege of Charleston. While he did not name the Combahee River Raid explicitly, the president did inform stockholders that the Union's military activity on land and sea along the coast had caused "apprehension" that the Charleston and Savannah's operations could have been "wholly interrupted or seriously damaged by successful raids." On the morning of June 2, the Charleston and Savannah Railroad crossed the Green Pond and Salkehatchie Bridges unmolested.[35]

16

"Great Sufferers"

The fallout from the Combahee River Raid was profound. A letter by Joshua Nicholls published in *The Mercury* in June 1863 said that the raid on the Combahee River had threatened the "whole grainery of the State." The interior barely produced enough for its own subsistence. But the coast, particularly the coastal rice plantations, produced surplus crop that fed the Confederate soldiers and fodder that fed the cavalry horses. Were the region ever abandoned, the entire state of South Carolina would be "pinched for mere subsistence." The railroad would not remedy the dire situation. The rice crop needed protection.[1]

According to Nicholls's letter, Colonel Montgomery and other officers of the 2nd South Carolina Volunteers and 3rd Rhode Island Heavy Artillery were "foreign officers" who violated "international law" governing the conduct of one sovereign nation, the United States of America, toward another, the Confederate States of America. Montgomery's making war on private citizens was "subversive" of the rules and customs of war that dated back to the Crusades. The white commanders and Black soldiers had all broken the state laws of South Carolina, forfeiting their lives. They would be executed as insurrectionists and traitors to the state if caught now or in the future; no prisoners would be taken. This debt had to be paid regardless of whether or not the formerly enslaved men turned soldiers were the property of any white man.[2]

There was some soul-searching and lots of scapegoating. The editors asked where the Confederate forces had been when two Union gunboats came up the Combahee River in broad daylight and anchored at plantations along the river and small bands of Black soldiers with their white commanders plundered and burned plantation homes. Why had the Confederacy failed to kill the "insurrectionist" and "traitor" invaders or save the private property of its citizens? The Confederacy was undoubtedly capable of defending itself. The whole state of affairs was disgraceful.[3]

Joshua Nicholls admitted that he was no military expert; he was, after all, a linguist, not a soldier. But he gave *The Mercury*'s readers his armchair opinion anyway. Nicholls was convinced that Major Robert J. Jeffords's troops could have stopped the enemy had they still been stationed on the Combahee River. By March 1863, Jeffords's squadron had been posted on the Combahee for eighteen months and knew "every foot and by-path of the country, all the plantations," according to Nicholls. It is not clear, though, which iteration of Major Jeffords Nicholls wished had been stationed in the Combahee: the Major Jeffords of Chehaw near Pocotaligo, who shared and would protect the interests of planters; the Major Jeffords of Hutchinson Island, who treated Black people with extreme barbarity and never would have let 756 enslaved people escape alive; or the Major Jeffords of Joshua Nicholls's imagination, who would have put a few soldiers on each plantation and stopped the enemy's ascent up the Combahee with his horse artillery and two manned rifled guns. Which version of the Confederate military commander was Nicholls referring to? Possibly all three. [4]

Lieutenant Colonel Robert J. Jeffords and Captain Thomas Haynes Bomar had protested in March about their soldiers being stationed in the unhealthy environment during the sickly season. Jeffords knew firsthand the deadly impact the sickly season could have on white folks. He was a son of the soil. Captain Bomar, on the other hand, had enlisted at Camp Kirkpatrick (near Atlanta) in October 1861. His Company H of the Chestatee Artillery, Wright's Legion of the Georgia Volunteers, was stationed at the "head of Cheehaw Road" near Green Pond as of April 1863, according to his official military record. Nonetheless, he too complained about the "large amount of sickness" in his command the previous summer in his letter requesting that his men be transferred or exchanged with "some artillery company in Gen'l Bragg's Department" and sent to a "colder climate." Captain Bomar wrote to Samuel Cooper, adjutant and inspector general, stationed at Richmond, that most of his men were from the "mountainous" regions of Georgia, as he described it, and "unable to stand the enervating effect of the coast climate." Brigadier General Walker proposed an infantry command three and a half miles east of Field's Point, but the regimental surgeon overruled the plan, also because of the prevalence of mosquito-borne disease. Jeffords's troops were moved out to Green Pond. Major William P. Emanuel's troops were moved in.[5]

By early June, Major Emanuel's troops had been stationed at Field's Point and Combahee Ferry for only three weeks. Nicholls assumed them "entirely ignorant" of the area, willing to assist but unable to do so effectively because of their lack of familiarity, though General Walker noted in his official report that Major Emanuel had been sent an "excellent map of the country." Three or four weeks before the raid, Major Emanuel was apprised of the article in a New York newspaper stating that the Union Army's forces at Hilton Head were planning military action previously unseen in the state. He was told to be on high alert. Emmanuel had Captain Bomar's light artillery and a small number of pickets at Field's Point and Combahee, both of which sent couriers to inform him when the action commenced, as he had ordered. However, as he admitted in his official report, his ignorance of the country and his lack of knowledge of the Union's position at Field's Point were the biggest hindrances to stopping the Union advance at Field's Point.[6]

The officers of the 4th South Carolina Cavalry under Major Emanuel's command—Captain Godbold, Lieutenant Breeden, Lieutenant Gilchrist, and Lieutenant Hewitt—all reported that they were following Emanuel's orders during the raid. He received inaccurate intelligence from one of his lieutenants (Lieutenant Hendrix) that the US Army was advancing beyond the pontoon bridge to destroy the Charleston and Savannah Railroad bridge. The intelligence was inaccurate in two ways. First, though the *John Adams* did advance beyond the pontoon bridge, as we've seen, it encountered obstructions in the river and returned to the bridge. Second, Colonel Montgomery and his men were not advancing toward the Salkehatchie railroad bridge, which was sixteen miles away. This Confederate stronghold was located only five miles from the Third District headquarters in McPhersonville, where General Walker was stationed. Had Montgomery's two hundred men advanced to the railroad, Walker's troops could have gotten in the enemy's rear, separated them from their gunboats, and given them a fair fight. And with the reinforcements that Brigadier General Walker sent on his "special train" from Salkehatchie to Green Pond under the command of Captain Trenholm, Montgomery and his forces would have been vastly outnumbered.[7]

Captain Lay's report on the Combahee River Raid found Major Emanuel to have committed the "serious error" of sending reinforcements to Salkehatchie. Not only was the enemy not there or headed there, but he "materially [weakened] his small force to guard a point," the Salkehatchie railroad bridge, "well protected by troops much nearer," five miles away at Third Military District headquarters in McPhersonville. Previously, in a February 1863 inspection, Lay had found that Emanuel's men were not "prosper[ing]" or improving under his command, and he had recommended a regular and systematic program of drills. But either these drills were never carried out or they were but the men did not improve, because Lay found again that Emanuel's men were poorly drilled. Lay's report also determined that Emanuel acted with indecision and temerity; he never took a position but instead roamed around with an escort because he did not know the country. His pickets had allowed the enemy to get too close to Field's Point and Combahee Ferry, then fled without any resistance; they were "neither watchful nor brave."[8]

Even non-expert Joshua Nicholls knew that one or two cannons on the twenty-foot bluffs at Tar Bluff and at Combahee Ferry could have stopped the steamboats' progress up the Combahee. Captain Trenholm wrote in his official report that he would have attacked the Union at Field's Point. Had their attack been successful, he could have posted a field artillery piece at Tar Bluff to stop the enemy. And if the pickets posted at Combahee Ferry had fired down from the breastworks at the head of the causeway to Cypress Plantation, they should have been able to stop the 2nd South Carolina Volunteers from landing on Cypress Plantation and driven them back to the *John Adams*. But the cannon had been removed from Combahee Ferry (likely replaced with a log) and taken to Green Pond because of the sickly season.[9]

According to Captain Lay's official report, the gravest sin was in allowing the Confederate Army to be mortified and humiliated by a "parcel of negro wretches, calling themselves soldiers," and "degraded whites." Major Emanuel had to take the fall for his commanders' failings. The Confederate Army brought charges against him, his lieutenants Hewitt and Breeden, and the head of the picket at Combahee Ferry, Corporal Wall. Major Emanuel was arrested by General Beauregard on June 21, 1863, on "charges of neglect in the conduct of command, when a raid was made by the enemy on the 2 June last." He was deprived of his command and put on trial.

His military service record does not specify when Emanuel's trial began, but it was halted by the July 10, 1863, attack on Charleston. He wrote to Brigadier General Thomas Jordan on August 31 that he had been deprived of his command, though the trial had not resumed. Lieutenant Breeden and Lieutenant Hewitt were also arrested by General Beauregard. After brief imprisonments, both were returned to duty. Hewitt was detached on a recruiting tour for the 4th South Carolina Cavalry, Company F, then promoted to captain. Breeden was detached and ordered to inspect troops at Hardeeville, then also promoted to captain in early 1864. Both lieutenants were summoned to Charleston on January 15, 1864, to appear as witnesses in Major Emanuel's trial.[10]

The Confederate Army's military strategy, on the other hand, was never put on trial. The Confederate leaders never rethought their strategic position and did not pivot to keep troops and artillery in place in the "fever district" during the sickly season. The Confederacy persisted in the practice of reassigning Confederate soldiers stationed at posts in the South Carolina Lowcountry to healthier climes in advance of the sickly season even after the Union Army had begun enlisting Black troops. Many of the Black troops likely would have had some degree of inherited immunity to *P. falciparum* malaria, particularly those men who had been enslaved in the Lowcountry region. Thus, the gunboats, the "Black Dispatches," and the Black soldiers who were deployed to fight year-round in the Lowcountry gave the Union a military advantage.

General Lee's concentration on the railroad since just after the Battle of Port Royal was never questioned. Lay incorrectly identified Major Emanuel as having been responsible for sending troops to the Salkehatchie bridge, when in fact it was Brigadier General Walker who ordered one company of cavalry and one section of the battery to Salkehatchie to reinforce the Charleston and Savannah Railroad bridge and to the pontoon bridge at Combahee Ferry on the morning of the raid. These errors should have taught the Confederate leadership a lesson or two about the critical role pontoon bridges played in the Lowcountry, particularly on the Ashepoo, Combahee, and Edisto Rivers, but it did not.[11]

In recounting what he saw and experienced on Longbrow Plantation in his letter to the editor, Joshua Nicholls equated his plight with that of Aeneas, the Trojan prince in Virgil's *Aeneid*, who in the poem is often characterized as "pius Aeneas" or "dutiful Aeneas." Aeneas had fulfilled his duty by carrying his father and his ancestral gods out of burning Troy. Nicholls felt it was his duty to tell the world what the Yankees had done to him and his neighbors. Nicholls wanted the world to know that he thought Colonel Montgomery and his men despaired of winning a fair fight against the Confederacy. So the Union took to destroying private property. In Nicholls's view, it was Montgomery (though of course the raid depended on Harriet Tubman, her ring of spies, scouts, and pilots, the 2nd South Carolina Volunteers, and the 3rd Rhode Island Heavy Artillery) who had irrevocably breached the security of southern homes and the integrity of southern honor and attempted to uproot the South's entire social system. Not mentioned in the letter, of course, was the fact that that system was built on the exploitation of the bodies, minds, and labors of enslaved Black people. Instead, Nicholls quoted Aeneas's sorrowful response when Queen Dido asked him to recount the fall of Troy at the hands of the Greeks: recalling "the piteous sights that he himself saw and in which he played a large part" brought renewed grief to both Joshua Nicholls and his co-sufferer Aeneas. But Nicholls hoped his brave countrymen would repay the Union's deeds in full and with interest.[12]

★★★★★★★★

Walter Blake's letter to his mother, Maria Hough Blake, is a rare example of how the planters whose plantation homes and enterprises were destroyed in the raid reacted immediately after. (He must have been in a hurried and/ or confused state, because he dated his letter "May 3, 1863," instead of June 3, 1863.) Blake delivered the shocking news that the Yankees had come up to Combahee Ferry with two gunboats, broken up the pontoon bridge, burned "all" of the houses up to that point, and carried off "all" the enslaved people.[13]

We know that Blake was disoriented, because he wrote to his mother that he was sorry to have to tell her that about "25 or 30 of ours" ran away to the Union Army, including one woman, Saucey. Those who escaped enslavement from Bonny Hall were mainly men and boys: brothers John and Peter, Willis's brother Charley, Saucey's son Prince, and April's brother Charles. Blake regretted that he could not remember the names of all the people whom he had held in bondage and lost the night before. He also reported that the Yankees had taken all of the enslaved people from Williams Middleton's Newport Plantation and William C. Heyward's

Cypress Plantation and burned their plantation houses and rice mills as well as those on plantations further down the river. However, his cousin Daniel Blake's Board House Plantation had not suffered attack. (Board House was located too far away from the Combahee for the US Army to reach.)[14]

Blake had been on picket duty, serving in the 4th South Carolina Cavalry (which the Charleston Light Dragoons were part of after the October 1862 reorganization), Company K, with William L. Kirkland Jr., when he received the shocking news. Though he came down to the Combahee immediately, he arrived too late. The morning after he arrived at Bonny Hall, Blake went out with Captain T. J. Allen's men, looking for enslaved people who might have been hiding in the woods or otherwise gotten left behind. They tried "to find them with dogs" but could not find any. He had to go back to camp the same evening. Blake pronounced the Combahee River Raid a "regular n***** [intentionally deleted] n—— raid of the Yankees" and proclaimed that they came to destroy crops and carry out enslaved people from the area, which they knew was "undefended." He reckoned that the US Army had carried off five hundred people, a low estimate indeed.[15]

William Lennox Kirkland Jr. was serving in the Charleston Light Dragoons when the Combahee River Raid took place. In letters to his family he recounted what happened on Rose Hill Plantation, how he felt about the devastation, and what steps he was taking. Some letters written to him also survive. His commanding officer, Captain Louis D. DeSaussure, wrote to him two days after the raid that he had heard "with great pain" of the loss of Kirkland's enslaved population and "most sincerely sympathize[d]" with him at this "trying time," which required "great nerves to meet." DeSaussure hoped Kirkland would ultimately recover many of the people he held in bondage. He granted Kirkland a fifteen-day furlough; he had wanted to grant Kirkland a thirty-day furlough, but the adjutant general thought thirty days was too long. DeSaussure promised to extend the furlough should Kirkland need more time.[16]

Five days later, Kirkland began to sell off what assets he had left on Rose Hill Plantation. Thomas Taylor, who enlisted in the Charleston Light Dragoons in late April 1863, wrote to Kirkland saying that he was inclined to accept Kirkland's offer to sell Taylor his mules. Taylor also "deeply sympathize[d]" with Kirkland about the "heavy loss" he had sustained. He "could not realize the suddenness . . . to have all taken in a night." He hoped the Confederate Army would make examples of some of its officers, those who could have stopped the raid but did not for a "want in management and promptness."[17]

On June 11, Captain DeSaussure responded to another letter from Kirkland. Kirkland may have written his letter to his commanding officer in a hurried and unsettled state, as he forgot to date the letter. Regardless, as soon as DeSaussure received Kirkland's missive, he sent an order to Captain T. J. Allen to "send a detachment of his men with their dogs to [Kirkland] at Combahee." Allen was the same officer who had prevented some freedom seekers on Blake's Bonny Hall Plantation from reaching the *John Adams*. According to Lay, they were not armed, "only accompanied by some of their Track Dogs for the benefit of whose service to the Planters," as Captain Thomas Pinckney of the 4th South Carolina Cavalry described Allen's unit. The bloodhounds were used to search for freedom seekers who had not been able to board the gunboats and who might still be hiding in the woods. Captain Allen wrote back to DeSaussure that "Mr. Walter Blake has been and still using the dogs" and would be "for two days" longer. After Captain Allen's men and their dogs left Blake's Bonny Hall, they would be sent to Rose Hill Plantation. In any case, Kirkland would have to provide for Captain Allen's men, horses, and dogs, because Allen did not possess the means to transport them across the Combahee or from one plantation to another. DeSaussure ended his letter by assuring Kirkland that he continued to feel deeply for him in his losses. He was to know the extent of Kirkland's property losses and "sincerely hoped" that Kirkland "had saved some of his Negroes." An enslaved boy known only as "Dago" was the only bondsperson from Rose Hill or Longbrow that his stepfather, Joshua Nicholls, "saved"—meaning prevented the enslaved boy from running to freedom in the raid.[18]

Though before the raid Kirkland had hired out some of the people he held in bondage (meaning they had not been on the Combahee during the raid and so remained his property), including Margaret Moody, he did not retain enough chattel property to save his fortune. On June 11, 1863, one I. S. K. Bennett advertised the private sale of Rose Hill's three hundred acres of cultivated tide swamp, two hundred of which were planted. The ad, which appeared in the *Charleston Mercury,* extolled the richness of Rose Hill's soils, which it claimed could not be surpassed anywhere else in South Carolina, and touted its location on a creek, which protected the tidal swamp acreage from saltwater. It does not mention that this was the very creek separating Rose Hill from Longbrow, at whose boat landing the *Harriet A. Weed* landed.[19]

Two days after the raid, Susan Matilda Chisolm Middleton in Columbia, South Carolina, wrote to her second or third cousin Harriott Middleton in Flat Rock, North Carolina, that all of the bad news she received that morning almost made her "too dull" to write. She reported that when the news reached the Middleton family in Columbia, they thought Launch Plantation at Tar Bluff, which belonged to her father, Oliver Hering Middleton Sr., had been destroyed. The buildings on Tar Bluff, "Pap's place on the river low down," were "worth but little," except the steam-powered rice mill (which Captain Carver and Company E of the 2nd South Carolina Volunteers had set ablaze). According to Susan Middleton, the family's chief concern was the twenty enslaved people, "nearly all old or infirm," who had been left at Tar Bluff. (That they were elderly at the time of the raid could explain why they do not appear in the pension files.) The family feared they had been left without provisions when the Union burned the buildings to the ground. The Middletons had evacuated the remainder of Tar Bluff's enslaved population before the raid.[20]

The Middleton family in Columbia initially had been "pitying" the Lowndes, Heyward, and Kirkland families, who "had so much more to lose and lost it." Then the members of the Middleton family sequestered in Flat Rock, North Carolina, realized just how bad was their fortune on the lower Combahee when they received a letter from Oliver Hering Middleton Jr., who was serving in the Charleston Light Dragoons and stationed at McPhersonville with William L. Kirkland Jr. in early June 1863. He wrote to his mother in Flat Rock that the Combahee raid was "most distressing." He had met with and talked to his uncles Williams Middleton and John Izard Middleton on South Bay Street in downtown Charleston, he told her, but neither he nor they made any "allusion" to the subject of the raid or their losses. Then Oliver had visited his cousin Sabina Elliott Huger Lowndes, who was married to Charles T. Lowndes, and her "troubles"— that is, the losses at Oakland Plantation—were "freely discussed." Although he felt "very sorry" for her, Oliver wrote, he was "disgusted" by his cousin's "absurdly affected & dictatorial manner" (which stood in contrast to the manner of her namesake daughter, "little meek Sabina"). Though the Lowndes family's losses were catastrophic, Oliver reported, they had fared better than some of their neighbors. Thanks to their overseer, Mr. Pipkin, and Lieutenant Breeden's men, who brought scores of freedom seekers back to the plantation at gunpoint, they were able to keep eighty enslaved people in bondage and did not have to sell their townhouse in downtown Charleston or their carriage.[21]

Oliver Jr. also delivered the bad news to his mother that every enslaved person, nearly 180, had been driven off Newport. They had to pity their own family, "those nearer home." Newport, the "Estates place at the Ferry," was still part of Governor Henry Middleton's estate—the "unlucky estate," according to Susan Middleton (actually, his entire estate was still in the "executor's hands," because the will, as noted earlier, had not yet been settled by June 1863, though Governor Middleton had died in 1846). The losses at Newport Plantation were devastating; after the raid, nothing was left for Governor Middleton's heirs to divide.[22]

Still, Oliver Jr. reported in a letter to his mother that has not been found that one of the freedom seekers returned from the Union Army, providing no specifics about how this was possible. In writing to Harriott Middleton about Oliver's letter, Susan Middleton did not specify if the freedom seeker who supposedly returned to bondage had been enslaved on Launch or Newport Plantation. When he evacuated all of the chattel property from the Combahee River after Newport was destroyed, Williams Middleton moved two enslaved men, named Zahler and George, from Newport and thirty-eight enslaved laborers from Hobonny and Old Combahee, the other two plantations owned by his late father's estate, and took them all to Middleton Place, the family seat, located on the Ashley River outside of Charleston. Williams Middleton wrote to his brother three days after the raid took place that one of their overseers had remained on Hobonny with thirty-five or forty white men prepared to defend it. As we know, the Union gunboats did not round the bend in the Combahee after reaching Cypress Plantation. Thus, both Hobonny and Old Combahee were spared.[23]

In the immediate aftermath of the raid, the Combahee River rice planter families—a close-knit group, as described previously—reacted with shock and horror at the gall of Union forces and the ineptitude of Confederate forces, as well as to the devastation of their plantations and the carrying off of more than seven hundred people they held in bondage. William Mason Smith II wrote his mother that the raid had been "perfectly terrible" and that the "desolation was terrible." Everyone was "worn out with anxiety." Smith was one of many who watched their relatives try to pick up the pieces after the raid. His uncle Charles T. Lowndes had lost about three hundred enslaved people, his provisions, and his mills, except the pounding mill on his Oakland Plantation (on the east side of Cypress). Smith also reported that Mr. Kirkland and Mr. Paul had lost everything, as had Mrs. Nicholls, aside from two enslaved people, a little boy and a dying woman, and that Mr. Heyward had lost two hundred enslaved people, his plantation home and outbuildings, and two slave quarters.[24]

Unlike Walter Blake, Smith had the good fortune to report to his mother that the Smith family "had cause to thank God for his infinite mercy." Smith's youngest brother, Daniel Elliott Smith, had received a letter from Cleland Kinloch Huger Jr. reporting on the "Yankee raid on the Combahee" (which Huger thought was "shamefully managed" by the Confederate Army) and saying that while the Smith brothers' uncle Mr. Lowndes had "met with serious loss," by all accounts "Smithfield was not injured." William Mason Smith's younger brother Robert Tilghman Smith also wrote to their younger sister, Isabella Johannes Middleton Smith, on June 7 that he had been "so anxious about Smithfield & Oakland . . . Smithfield is safe, thank God, but Oakland has suffered very severely." Robert reported that at Oakland the US Army had "burnt all the mills except the pounder and run off all the Negroes except fifty."[25]

By all accounts, Smithfield was indeed spared in the Combahee River Raid. Not one of the enslaved people on Smithfield escaped to the Union Army. On the adjacent Cypress Plantation, the Black soldiers came within a hundred yards of Smithfield's rice barn and rice mill; at that point Smith's overseer, William Lowry, had gathered all of the enslaved people in his yard, prepared to take them to the woods to hide. But the soldiers on Cypress ultimately turned back without breaching Smithfield's borders when men held in bondage on Smithfield fired upon them and they were "rendered uneasy." Smith specified that the "marauders" were all "Negroes," led by white officers, "white chiefs." He lamented that there were still too few Confederate troops stationed on the coast, "hardly enough to keep off Negro raids."[26]

Why would people held in bondage turn away Black soldiers, the very people who came to set them free? As noted, the Union gunboats turned around after proceeding only a short distance above the pontoon bridge, because of the obstructions in the Combahee. The *John Adams* therefore never reached Smithfield. The enslaved people on Smithfield may have smelled the acrid smoke and heard the low rumble of the coal-burning steam engine. They likely heard the steam whistle. But they may not have seen the Union flags flying. If they did, they may not have known they spelled freedom; no Union Army or Navy boats had ventured that far up the Combahee River and into enemy territory by June 1863. These people had likely seen Confederate pickets and officers. Did they know the difference between white men in Confederate uniforms and Black and white men in Union uniforms? When they encountered Black soldiers trying to get across the property line, did they know who they were or why they had come? Was it even true that they had driven the soldiers away, or was that just what they had told the young slaveholder who managed his widowed mother's plantation? Because they feared being removed from their homes and separated from their families, as their neighbors had been when evacuated from the lower Combahee, the people whom Smith's mother held and forced to labor against their will likely did not tell Smith the truth.

Smith requested that his mother give him permission to evacuate all of the enslaved people from Smithfield. The enslaved people should be removed immediately for two reasons, Smith said. First, the "demoralization" of the raid was "awful." Though they had not escaped on June 2, the enslaved people at Smithfield may have been encouraged by the raid to free themselves should the opportunity present itself again. The other reason Smith asked his mother for permission to evacuate the slaves was that they were the "only people left on Combahee this side of the river." That meant Smithfield was extremely vulnerable should the Union return and attempt another raid.[27]

Smith wrote that "God only [knew]" if the Union would take another shot at the Combahee, or when. However, he knew for certain that the Confederate Army could not protect his property. His uncle Lowndes had advised the "confounded" and "distressed" twenty-year-old William to remove his slaves immediately. It was "painful" for Smith to watch how his uncle had "suffered" such losses from the raid and simultaneously struggled to "bear it cheerfully." Given that Smithfield was Smith's mother's property, he would wait in a state of "great anxiety" for her reply, and hoped for her consent.[28]

Smith's mother must have consented. Over the next two weeks, he wrote to update his mother as he executed his evacuation plan. His overseer transported ten bondspeople at a time to the Refuge, Smith's land on the

Salkehatchie River, while the labor of those who remained on Smithfield was exploited in growing the rice crop. He had to accelerate the evacuation in late July 1863 when Billy, the enslaved head plowman, escaped from Smithfield. On August 10, 1863, Smith reported to his mother that he had moved "Nat's family 5 in number" from Smithfield to the Refuge. Nat was the brother of Ansel Gilliard, who testified for March Chisolm's daughter, Molcy Chisolm, that they "knew the soldier since boyhood." Ansel Gilliard never joined the 2nd South Carolina Volunteers. He and his family were enslaved on Smithfield and remained held in bondage until the end of the war. William Mason Smith's 1852 estate record lists "Nat 7 Bella 8 2 @ 600 120," referring to Polly Smith's brother Nat and his wife, Bella, as well as "Andrew 30 Phoebe 31 Emanuel 32 Polly 33 4 @ 300 $1200," referring to Polly Smith's father, Andrew, and brother Emanuel. On the line below are found "Nelly 36 Harry 37 Anson 38 Isiah 39 4 @ $450 1.800," which includes Ansel Gilliard and his mother, Nelly. The five people in Nat's family whom William Mason Smith removed from Smithfield Plantation were likely Nat, Bella, Andrew, Polly, and Emanuel. Sometime around 1860, Ansel Gilliard married Polly Smith on Smithfield Plantation. Their grandson, Richmond Gilliard, married my father's maternal grandmother's first cousin Katie Richard on November 3, 1927.[29]

On the same day that Smith wrote to his mother, Catherine Maria Clinch Heyward, better known as "Tattie," wrote to her stepmother and sister, Sophia Gibbs Couper Clinch and Mary Lamont Clinch, recounting the raid. Tattie Heyward was writing to her relatives, who were in Georgia, from the relative safety of Wateree, South Carolina, which was well into the interior of the state—about thirty miles southeast of the capital, Columbia, and a hundred miles north of the Combahee. She had married Edward Barnwell Heyward four months before the raid. In March 1862, a full year before the Confederate Army's Third Military District issued the circular instructing planters to evacuate their slaves, fifteen of the people whom Edward Barnwell Heyward's father, Charles Heyward (who, as mentioned, was the son of Nathaniel Heyward), held in bondage escaped. Heyward had planted his rice crop in spring 1862 but chose to abandon it when the Confederate government required planters within a twenty-five-mile radius of Beaufort to evacuate their slaves to the interior of South Carolina, where their labor would be exploited to produce the agricultural crops on which the Confederate civilians and military depended. In June 1862,

Edward Barnwell Heyward moved his elderly father and 150 of his father's bondspeople from Charles Heyward's Rose Hill plantation, which was on the upper Combahee River, to his Goodwill Plantation in Wateree.

Decades after the war, Sally Ladsden Frasier Dash Burnett testified in her application to obtain a widow's pension based on her husband Balaam Burnett's service that she had been born enslaved by Charles Heyward and married to her second husband, Louis Dash, by Heyward before the war. She could not remember her age, but she remembered bearing seven children. Sally Ladsden Frasier Dash and Louis Dash were two of the enslaved people whom Charles Heyward took off Rose Hill to Wateree, where they were exploited to grow inland rice. The Heywards left the Old Heads who were beyond their ability to produce—and, for the women, to reproduce—on Charles Heyward's Rose Hill and separated them from their families.[30]

Herein lies the likely reason people enslaved on Smithfield either drove the Black soldiers away with gunfire or at least told William Mason Smith that they had done so. All of the planters who owned plantations northwest of Smithfield and on the east side of the Combahee River had already evacuated the people they held in bondage, in some cases separating families. It is highly likely that the enslaved people on Smithfield knew this and even suffered this separation. Enslaved people who labored in the house may have heard the planter families discussing plans and weighing options. They all would have known they were vulnerable to being removed from their homes and possibly separated from their families and friends.

In her letter to her stepmother and sister, Tattie Heyward remarked that the news of the raid on the Combahee had been "rather startling" to the Heywards in Wateree, and she estimated the damage among those planters who were directly affected by the raid. Her husband's third cousin William C. Heyward (whose mother, Sarah Cruger Heyward, she described as "the old lady in New York") was supposedly ruined. She identified Charles T. Lowndes and Walter Blake to be the "next great sufferers." William L. Kirkland and his stepfather, Joshua Nicholls, also had suffered very much. Tattie Heyward reminded her stepmother and sister that Heyward, Lowndes, and Blake had "boasted" that they were planting full crops of rice on their Combahee plantations. The planters on the lower Combahee had been smug about their decision to stay and keep planting rice, and they "rather *smiled* at Mr. Heyward," her husband, for evacuating his father's enslaved people and protecting the family's investment.[31]

Tattie Heyward wrote to her relations that her father-in-law's overseer, who had remained on his Rose Hill Plantation, had sent the news about the raid. He had seen the burning buildings further down the Combahee below the pontoon bridge and expected the Union gunboats to get up the river to him any minute. Tattie Heyward noted that her father-in-law's overseer had reported to them that "five of Mr. W. C. Heyward's negroes, went down 5, or 6 days ago, and told them, that a good many soldiers had been removed and brought them up to their master's place." The overseer was implying that the bondspeople gave the Union intelligence that helped Colonel Montgomery and his men execute the raid. That may well have been the case, though the historical record has not revealed their identities. And the enslaved people on Walter Blake's plantation "left their work in gangs" and went to the Union Army as soon as they heard the soldiers had come. Blake's overseer surmised that the bondspeople were "evidently expecting them."[32]

Though the overseer's claims mentioned in Tattie Heyward's letter are unsubstantiated, one can imagine her asking her relations who was laughing last when the smoke from the raid settled. Charles Heyward's Rose Hill, one of the seventeen Heyward plantations formerly owned by Nathaniel Heyward, was located beyond the pontoon bridge and had remained safe from the raid. Tattie Heyward's letter dripped with the veiled sarcasm she had learned as part of her upbringing as a wealthy white southern woman. Her father-in-law's enslaved laborers were safe at Wateree; the slaves of William C. Heyward (who, as noted, had laughed at her husband) were gone.

This was not the end for the Heyward family. Charles Heyward could not bear to give up his Rose Hill Plantation, even though his son had finally convinced "the old gentleman," as Tattie Heyward called her father-in-law, to get out and move to Wateree. He sent the enslaved people from Rose Hill who had been evacuated to Wateree back down to Combahee and threatened to visit Rose Hill himself a few days before the raid. Tattie Heyward hoped the rather startling news would now put an end to his plans and the obstinacy of people like him. She thought her cousin-in-law Charles T. Lowndes and Walter Blake actually "did the country harm" by exploiting the labor of enslaved people in place after the Confederate Army required planters to remove them to the interior; that had made all of their plantations vulnerable to Union attack.[33]

June 6, the day after Tattie Clinch Heyward wrote to her relatives, William C. Heyward advertised his Cypress Plantation, with 766 "Acres Rice Land under bank, 542 Acres now planted with a good crop on it," for private sale in the *Charleston Mercury*. Heyward's agent and second cousin, Thomas Savage Heyward, described Cypress's rice fields as having been "well worked up to this time." He made no mention of how a Union raid had destroyed the rice crop by opening the dikes and flooding the fields with saltwater. The advertisement ran again twelve days later. No buyer was found.[34]

Four months after the raid, Heyward's wealth continued to hemorrhage from the destruction of his plantation. His overseer, Stephen Boineau, was "questioned too closely to evade" when he attempted to pay Heyward's taxes with sheaf rice that "was in a damaged condition." Boineau proposed that officials thresh the rice before assigning value to it. If Heyward had still owned enslaved people, the overseer would have made them thresh it. A few days after his proposal was rejected, Boineau sold four of Heyward's five beef cattle and used the $1,000 in proceeds to pay Heyward's taxes. Nicholls and Kirkland were all relatively small planters on the Combahee River and in the Lowcountry region. Nonetheless, even the largest planters and slaveholders in the US South had a lot to lose, and they lost a significant portion of it in one night.[35]

★★★★★★★★

In response to inquiries on "the proof and payment of private claims for losses sustained from the war," the state's auditor published an article, "Losses from the War," in the June 18, 1863, edition of the *Charleston Mercury*. It informed residents that the South Carolina General Assembly had passed a resolution in 1861 that provided for compensation and gave instructions for those whose property had been seized and/or destroyed by the US government or the Confederate military, or those who had destroyed their own property to prevent it from falling into Union hands. The governor was authorized to appoint a five-member commission to review the claims and report to the state legislature. The commission was charged with estimating the character and value of the Confederate property destroyed or seized.[36]

Published sixteen days after the raid, the *Charleston Mercury* article informed readers how property owners could file claims for compensation with the Confederate government. Property owners or their legal representatives were required to prepare affidavits and swear to their accuracy before an officer authorized to administer oaths. The affidavits had to specify "with PARTICULARITY AND ACCURACY" who owned the property, provide a description and value of the lost property, and describe the time, place, and circumstances of their property's seizure, destruction, or loss. The 1861 resolution required at least one disinterested witness to swear under oath to the ownership of the property, its destruction, and its value as outlined in the property owner's affidavit.[37]

In theory, the claims would be paid from a fund established with the proceeds of the 1861 Sequestration Act, in which the Confederate government authorized the confiscation of the property of disloyal citizens. It must have sounded very good in those early days of the war when loyal Confederate citizens had full confidence that their government would indemnify them against losses caused by the United States or the Confederacy. Three Combahee rice planters whose plantations were destroyed by the US Army on June 2, 1863, filed for compensation from the Confederate government for their losses. One of them double-dipped and applied to the federal government as well.[38]

Their affidavits provide evidence of the scale of destruction meted out to Combahee River rice planters during the raid, including the size of the exodus of the enslaved. In many cases, the affidavits can be used to itemize the losses of the Combahee planters and positively identify which enslaved families seized their freedom on June 2, 1863.

One month after the Combahee River Raid, William C. Heyward submitted his affidavit to the South Carolina state auditor, requesting compensation from the Confederate government with a "List of Negroes Carried Off by the Yankees from Cypress Plantation June 2nd 1863" and also a "statement of valuation of buildings and other property destroyed by fire." Heyward assigned an age to each of the enslaved people he included in his affidavit. He grouped the sixty-eight men together, and did the same with the sixty-four women, thirty-five boys, and thirty-two girls; he included the enslaved mothers' names after the enslaved children's names. Though he does not give individual values, these enslaved people were by far his most valuable assets.[39]

The literature on the Combahee Raid has speculated about the identities of the enslaved people who escaped from Cypress Plantation before June 2, 1863. Colonel Heyward did not report these escapes in the statement that he provided to the Confederate Army. Nor have his papers and letters been found. What we have is Tattie Clinch Heyward's letter. It is questionable how reliable this thirdhand information is. Samuel Hayward, one of Harriet Tubman's crew, has been the main contender to be one of those who escaped before the raid, in large part because his title, Hayward, appears to be derived from William C. Heyward's surname.

The pension files shed more light, providing evidence that Friday Barrington was born enslaved on and was raised in bondage on Cypress Plantation with his sister, Phoebe Burns. Barrington testified he ran away from Cypress Plantation "early in the war," joined Colonel Montgomery before the 2nd South Carolina Volunteers were organized, and enlisted in Company D around the time—mid-March 1863—when Edward Bennett enlisted. Not only did Barrington's Company D drive the *John Adams* up the Combahee River and walk across the causeway to Heyward's Cypress Plantation in full sight and range of Lieutenant Breeden's forces, but twenty-six-year-old Phoebe Burns Frazier got on board the *John Adams* with her husband, Robert, whom Heyward listed as "Bob 36." Friday Barrington and Phoebe Burns Frazier reunited with their parents, Tooman and Joan Legare, who escaped in the raid also. Friday and Phoebe's parents were enslaved on Rose Hill Plantation, which was, as noted, next door to where the *Harriet A. Weed* landed.[40]

Colonel Heyward did not list any pilots or boatmen on his affidavit. William Hamilton's brother Samuel is the only Samuel among the losses for which Heyward applied for compensation. He escaped in the raid and not before. Thus Samuel Heyward's title alone is not evidence that he liberated himself from bondage on Cypress Plantation before June 2, 1863, when he piloted Tubman, Montgomery, and Union troops up the Combahee.[41]

Sina Bolze Young, twenty-two, escaped in the raid with her first husband, whom she married during the winter around the Christmas holidays before the war, possibly as early as 1858, at Cypress Plantation. Will Young, whom Heyward listed as "William 36," his wife, who was likely listed as "Binah 18," and their daughter, three-year-old Flora, whom Heyward listed as "Flora 3 Binah," escaped, along with Sina's younger brother, sixteen-year-old Cuffie Bolze, "Cuffy 16." Will and Sina went off to freedom with fellow bondspeople who had known them all their lives, including thirty-year-old Peter James, thirty-eight-year-old Elizabeth Small, and forty-year-old Venus Proctor Higgins Lyons (listed as "Venus 40"). They all had witnessed Will and Sina promise to be faithful through sickness and death, kiss, and then be pronounced man and wife by the enslaved man who served as class leader. Elizabeth Small testified in Sina Bolze Young's pension application that they had been at work in a field close by at the time Sina was "confined" and Flora was subsequently born. Peter James saw Flora the same day she was born. Both Peter James and Elizabeth Small got on the *John Adams* at Cypress with Will, Sina, and Flora Young. Both Venus's second husband, Frank Lyons, and her third husband, whom she would marry after the war, forty-year-old July Osborne, got on the gunboat at Cypress also.[42]

Bina Hamilton Mack had been a guest at Will and Sina Young's wedding as well. However, she traveled to their wedding at Cypress from the adjoining Paul and Dalton Plantation; she was already in the habit of going "over on Sunday to meeting at Cypress Plantation." Bina Hamilton Mack got on the *Harriet A. Weed* at Longbrow with her parents, Minus and Hagar Hamilton, her husband, Harry Mack, and their young daughter, Hagar Mack. She came to "Port Royal in the same gang of colored people" as the Young family. Annie Cassell McNeal Lawrence Holmes testified that she too had been a guest at Will and Sina Young's wedding. She, her first husband, Scipio McNeal, and her second husband, March Lawrence, whom she married after the war, were all enslaved directly across from Cypress on Williams Middleton's Newport Plantation. Both Scipio McNeal and March Lawrence got on the *John Adams* with the enslaved people from Cypress; Annie was likely with them. The man with whom Sina would cohabitate during the war, Jonas Green, had escaped from Walter Blake's Newington Plantation by March 1862 and was already in Beaufort at the time of the raid. He and Wally Graham had gone to Beaufort together. Wally Graham testified that "sometimes afterwards, Sina Young was brought here by Mr. French," meaning Reverend Mansfield French. Actually, Colonel Montgomery "carried off" William and Sina Young together with the "balance of the colored people on Cypress Plantation," as Bina Mack, Venus Lyons, and Lina Richard testified.[43]

When he freed himself from bondage on Bonny Hall Plantation, Jonas Green left behind Jack Aiken and Smart Washington, both of whom he had known since boyhood. Smart Washington was Green's fellow enslaved cooper, someone whom he had known intimately since Washington was in the prime of his life and Green was a small child. Jack Aiken and Smart Washington did not stay behind when the Union Army came up the river in June 1863. They and Washington's son Solomon Washington got on the *John Adams* via rowboat at Newport Plantation.[44]

The Bolze siblings boarded the gunboat with their aunt Sarah Barnwell and their cousins (Sarah's children), sixteen-year-old Relia, listed as "Aurelia 16," eleven-year-old Jack, thirteen-year-old William, six-year-old Moses, three-year-old Joseph, and one-year-old Primus Barnwell, who was listed as "Primus 1 Sarah." Relia Barnwell married William Middleton during the war. He got on the gunboat too, along with his elderly mother, Affy, who was listed as "Affy 60 (old)." She was one of the oldest people held in bondage on Cypress Plantation in 1863. Middleton and his two sisters, Liddy, thirty-five, and Juno, nineteen, got on the boat. Also getting on the boat with them was Sina and Cuffie's first cousin, twenty-year-old Peggy Simmons Moultrie Brown, who was listed as "Peggy 20," and Peggy's husband, twenty-four-year-old Edward Brown, who appears as "Edward 24"; Peggy and Edward had married the year before the raid. In addition, Edward Brown's sisters, thirty-year-old Jane Lee Barnwell and twenty-three-year-old Lucy Lee, listed as "Lucy 23," got on the boat with them. Richard Smith, the man whom Lucy Lee married after the war, got on the boat from William Paul's plantation; they may have been courting before the raid. Though too young to remember the raid himself, Primus Barnwell grew up hearing his sister Relia Barnwell Middleton's husband, William Middleton, talk about it and Colonel Montgomery.[45]

Andrew, Neptune (listed as "Neptune 23"), and Charles Nicholas (who appears as "Charles 20"), all brothers and all in their twenties, escaped with their mother, forty-six-year-old Rose, and their half siblings, thirty-year-old Margaret Kelly Simmons (who appears as "Margaret 30"), eleven-year-old Jacob, and nine-year-old Chance Ogee. Charles Nicholas's fiancée, fourteen-year-old Hagar, Hagar's mother, thirty-five-year-old Louisa, and Bella Gaillard, the seventeen-year-old mother of Neptune's child, plus her infant son (whom Heyward listed as "one not named ½ Bella"), all got on the *John Adams* together. Margaret's husband, thirty-five-year-old Joshua Simmons (who is listed as "Joshua 35"), whom she married long before the war broke out, also escaped with his brothers, thirty-year-old Jim and twenty-seven-year-old carpenter Moses (whom Heyward listed "Moses

Carpt 27"), Moses's wife, twenty-two-year-old Lucretia Kinlaw Simmons, Moses's one-year-old son, Beauregard, and Lucretia's three-year-old son, Daniel. Lucretia was a first cousin of Edward Brown, Jane Lee Barnwell, and Lucy Lee. And Bella Gaillard, Neptune Nicholas's baby's mother, was a cousin of Jim, Joshua, and Moses Simmons. Andrew, Charles and Neptune Nicholas's thirty-year-old cousin Amy, her husband, twenty-eight-year-old carpenter William Hamilton, and their children, four-year-old Florence and one-year-old Will, joined the exodus.[46]

In all, William C. Heyward claimed more than $53,000 in property damage. He requested compensation for his second-most-valuable assets: 10,000 bushels of rough rice, worth $22,000, and his rice threshing mill, valued at $7,500. According to Heyward's affidavit, each of these two assets was individually more valuable than his plantation home and furniture, which together were worth $7,000. The remainder of his assets combined were not worth more than the 10,000 bushels of rough rice: two barns, worth $3,000; an overseer's house, kitchen, and storeroom, a coach house and stables, and a slave hospital and five slave quarters, each valued at $2,000; two corn houses and 500 bushels of corn, which Heyward assessed as worth $1,500 each; two lofts full of grass, valued at $1,200; an unspecified number of grist mills, worth $1,000; $700 in mule stables; four flatboats and a flat house, with a value of $500; two wagon sheds, worth $300; and a cattle shed, with an estimated value of $200.[47]

On September 17, 1863, three months after the raid and two months after Heyward had submitted his affidavit, Joshua Nicholls appeared before a notary public in Charleston District. Nicholls swore that he was making a true and accurate statement of the amount of "property captured and destroyed by United States forces" during the Yankee raid on his Longbrow Plantation. On the same day, Thomas Leger Hutchinson, who served as the mayor of Charleston from 1846 to 1850 and then from 1853 to 1855, and Dr. Richard L. North testified that Nicholls "duly sustained" the losses he was claiming and that his valuation of his property was accurate. The notary public certified that Nicholls's witnesses, Hutchinson and North, and the magistrate were "perfectly reliable gentlemen," an appellation that notary publics and special examiners rarely if ever bestowed on the Black veterans who fought for the Union during the war, or their widows and neighbors who testified for them in the pension claims.[48]

According to Nicholls's affidavit, the seventy-three enslaved people he lost had been appraised at a value of $65,400. He did not list ages or skilled occupations. However, he did list the enslaved people in family groupings. Thus he left a record of the enslaved people who escaped from Longbrow Plantation during the Combahee River Raid, which the pension files confirm.[49]

As a result of the 1859 agreement that Mary Anne Lynah Kirkland Faber Nicholls made with her son, William L. Kirkland Jr., when she gave him Rose Hill Plantation to support him as he started his family (keeping Longbrow for herself and her new husband, Joshua Nicholls), most of the people enslaved on Longbrow Plantation in 1863 were older. However, their age did not stop them from being able to "double-quick" and get themselves and their loved ones on the boat when the whistle blew. Old Head Sancho Van Dross got on the *Harriet A. Weed* with his wife, Abigail, and their sons Mingo, Robert, and Hercules when Company B of the 2nd South Carolina Volunteers arrived at Joshua Nicholls's boat landing.[50]

Isaac De Causter, Isaac's first wife, Kate, and their children, Pompey, Cornelia, and May, got on the *Harriet A. Weed* with Sancho Van Dross at Longbrow. His second wife, Silvia Jackson Gaylord, whom Isaac would marry after the war, may have gotten on the same boat with her first husband, Samson Gaylord, at James L. Paul's plantation with Minus Hamilton and his family. It is not certain, though, because Charles T. Lowndes did not file an application for compensation for his losses in the raid and Sampson Gaylord does not have a pension file. Isaac De Causter was "raised up under" Andrew Wyatt from "boyhood." They became brothers-in-law when after the war Isaac married Silvia, who was the sister of Wyatt's wife, Maria Phoenix Wyatt. The two men "came free" together on June 2, 1863, Isaac De Causter from enslavement on Longbrow and Andrew Wyatt from Paul's Plantation; Maria Phoenix Wyatt may have gotten on the boat with her husband and sister. November Osborne and Isaac were "boys" together before the war, and November attended Isaac and Silvia's wedding after the war. Both November and his son Nat Osborne got on the gunboat at Charles T. Lowndes's Oakland Plantation. William Drayton, who had known Nat Osborne since boyhood, took a rowboat to the *John Adams* from Newport Plantation, across the way.[51]

Childhood friends boarded the boat together. Jackson Grant testified for Captain Brown's pension application that at one time Frank Hamilton had lived with him on Rose Hill. Frank escaped enslavement from Longbrow with his parents, Pompey and Pussy, his siblings Captain, Cilla, and Binah, his wife, Tenah Jenkins Hamilton, and Tenah's brother Daniel Jenkins. Captain's wife, Jane, and their children, Emma and an unnamed infant, made the family complete. Friday Hamilton grew up with Frank Hamilton. Friday got on the gunboat with his childhood friend, bringing his parents, George and Emily, along to freedom.[52]

George had been the driver and Pompey the gardener on Longbrow. Nicholls wrote in his letter published in the Charleston *Mercury* that "Old Janus" would miss tending his garden and his favorite vegetables. He also thought Old Janus would miss captivating an admiring audience by misquoting the Bible. And "Old Driver George" would find his job— supervising the labor of the enslaved, distributing rations, and torturing the enslaved laborers to ensure they completed their daily tasks—gone in freedom. There would be no one to curry his favor. Nicholls was convinced that the enslaved people who left Longbrow would be a "wiser and sadder people" in freedom when they learned that liberty did not include "clothes, comfortable houses, kind treatment, and medical attention." Indeed, Nicholls predicted instead freedom would bring to the Blacks he once held in bondage "misery, privation, hunger and a cheerless death."[53]

Maybe it would, maybe it wouldn't. The Longbrow bondspeople were willing to take the risk. When they and their families ran for their lives and their freedom, Pompey was likely not thinking about the garden nor about the vegetables in it; Janus was certainly not thinking about impressing anyone with his biblical knowledge; and even George was surely not thinking about the power he once wielded over his fellow bondspeople. And it is highly probable that none of these bondspeople were studying Joshua Nicholls when, in the words of Minus Hamilton, they were "gwine to the boat."

Though most of the freedom seekers had to leave their belongings behind, George must have grabbed his family Bible and taken it with him aboard the *Harriet A. Weed*. In it, George had himself recorded the names and birthdates of his children, including Friday. Friday Hamilton later testified that the "record of his birth was taken from the plantation record of his former owner by his father." Upon George's death, the Bible came to Friday as his "family record." It would not have been unusual for an enslaved driver like George to be literate or to have some access to plantation records, particularly in the summer and fall sickly season, when the planters and overseers moved to higher and healthier ground. In 1904, C. M. Grace certified the publication of the Hamilton family Bible by the American Bible Society of New York in 1850 and assessed the script in it, based on its appearance, as having been the publication of the script in it as written many years before. Hamilton would use his father's inscriptions for decades to prove his age in his applications for pension increases due to being disabled or over seventy-five years of age.[54]

In addition to his "property" that ran away, Joshua Nicholls filed for compensation for the loss of his property destroyed by the US Army. He claimed that 7,000 bushels of rough rice valued at $21,000 had been burned. As with William C. Heyward, Nicholls's rice harvest from the previous year was his most valuable asset. In contrast, 300 bushels of corn were valued at $600. He did not estimate the loss of the rice growing in the fields. In his letter in *The Mercury*, Nicholls—a scholar and teacher—lamented the burning of his 3,500-volume library, containing the "shelved thoughts of the richest minds of ancient and modern times," which he said had taken him twenty years to collect (a substantial portion of the titles had actually belonged to his deceased wife's first husband). He claimed that the library plus a number of engravings were worth $15,000. Essentially, they were priceless, because Nicholls "treasured" his books as a "consolation for the present, and as a refuge against disease and old age." Now that refuge was gone, as was the livelihood pilfered from the exploitation of enslaved people's labor that enabled him to live the life of a perpetual student.[55]

The "pleasant and comfortable" plantation house with all of its furnishings and china, "every memorial" Nicholls possessed of his "past life," "every material object" to which his "heart still clung"—all had just "vanished, perished in the flames," as well as his barn, corn house, and steam threshing mill, valued at $10,000 each. His wash kitchen, kitchen, and storeroom (worth $1,000), three slave quarters, including Old Driver George's house, and the mule stable (also worth $1,000) were in ashes. The US Army had carried off three of Nicholls's good mules, which he valued at $600. He estimated that $60,200 worth of his personal property had been destroyed in the raid. Adding in the people whom Nicholls had held in bondage and who ran away in the raid, he reported losses totaling $125,600.[56]

On November 5, 1863, five months after the raid, William Lennox Kirkland Jr. filed a request for compensation to the state of South Carolina's comptroller. Kirkland claimed his plantation house and furniture—both burned in the raid—were worth a total of $14,000. He had renovated the wooden house for his bride before their wedding; they spent their honeymoon at Rose Hill during the month of April 1859, before the sickly season began. Though not specified, his losses must have included the family's silver, two sugar bowls and a creamer, a wine stand made of raffia, crystal, a wine stand of blue cut glass, gilt-edged wineglasses, and four decanters. In addition, at Rose Hill there were items that had been gifts to Mary Miller Withers Kirkland, including silver forks with a shell pattern, her rosewood bedroom suite, given to her by her father, and a large silver water pitcher with the initials WLK, from her husband (and which William Lennox Kirkland Jr. intended for their grandson who would bear his name and his initials— though he and his wife had just gotten married and did not have any children yet. Only memories were left after the US Army drove up the Combahee River and set Rose Hill ablaze. Kirkland included in his affidavit a list of eighty enslaved people, valued at $64,000. Kirkland's slave list documents the people who escaped bondage from Rose Hill in the raid, though it does not include ages, occupations, or family groupings.[57]

This was not the first time Kirkland put pen to paper to make a list of enslaved people who ran away in the Combahee River Raid. Another list was found among his in-laws' papers. (It was not listed in the description of the archival collection. This is the kind of document that a historian finds only by searching for the collections of a planter family's extended family members, in-laws, neighbors, friends, and business partners, then turning over and skimming each and every piece of paper in every folder in every box in every collection identified.) Kirkland titled the other list "1863 List of Negroes Carried Off on 2nd June by Yankees from Combahee." In two columns on one and a half pages, he listed eighty-five enslaved people he lost in the raid in family groupings and identifies the occupations of some bondspeople who practiced a trade. "[2 June 1863]" is written in pencil in the top right-hand corner of the first page, but he did not date it; this date was likely written by the archivist who processed the collection decades later (the handwriting does not match Kirkland's). Kirkland drew a line down the center of the page and in the second column of the second page, after the list of those who escaped in June 1863, he wrote a list of the enslaved people who had escaped in March 1862—and for whose loss he swore an affidavit for compensation on March 6, 1863. Though it is unknown when Kirkland wrote the list found in his in-laws' papers, one can hypothesize that he wrote it closer to the time of the actual raid, so likely before Kirkland swore to the November 5, 1863, affidavit. He may have written it while encamped at McPhersonville with the Charleston Light Dragoons, soon after he received the news that his property had been captured and destroyed. This would explain how the other list survived in his wife's family's papers when the Kirkland family's papers were destroyed in the raid and why Kirkland remembered five more enslaved people and recollected more details about them than he did approximately five months later.[58]

Kirkland's mother did not take all of the Old Heads to Longbrow in the 1848 slave exchange. William L. Kirkland Jr. kept carpenter Carolina Grant, his wife, Flora, and their children, son Stephany and daughter Phillis. Kirkland listed the family group on both his undated and November 5, 1863, slave lists. Carolina Grant had become "crippled in the back" many years before the war began, but he still found the strength and likely had the necessary assistance to get down to the river and board the gunboat to freedom with his wife and children.[59]

Kirkland's losses also included Prime Hands Moriah Haywood Bartley (listed as "Maria"), her husband, Anthony (listed as "Antony"), and their unnamed infant, who must have been Tecumseh Bartley, their only child born before the war to survive. Their older children all died before what Moriah remembered to be the start of the war. Both Anthony and Moriah Bartley were field hands, but Kirkland and his neighbors did not list field hands' occupations. Moriah Haywood Bartley testified in her own pension claim that she and Anthony Bartley lived as husband and wife before the war on Longbrow, but their family appears on William L. Kirkland's undated and November 5, 1863, slave lists. They were another casualty of Mary Anne Lynah Kirkland Faber Nicholls's slave exchange.[60]

Phoebe Burns Frazier, Friday Barrington's sister, testified she was "well acquainted" with Tyra Brown Polite, the woman who was sold by Dr. James Heyward, Colonel William C. Heyward's brother, from his plantation in New Hall, South Carolina, near Grahamville, to William L. Kirkland in 1848, with her mother, Joan Legare; Phoebe had known them from her "earliest recollection." The women must have had a special bond for Phoebe to speak so intimately of Tyra Polite so many years after the raid. We have no word for such a bond at present; if they had endured the terrible voyage of the Middle Passage together, we could have called them "shipmates" (or, in the Dutch Caribbean, *sibbi* or *sippi*; in Brazil, *malungo*; in Haiti, *mati*), but they didn't. Rather, new language is required to describe the kinship bonds enslaved people and their descendants forged with one another after they were torn from their families and homes by sale. Moriah Haywood Bartley, Prince Polite, siblings Daniel Jenkins and Tenah Jenkins Hamilton, and William Hamilton (Moriah's first cousin, whom Dr. James Heyward sold to William C. Heyward) all got on the Union gunboats together. Once on the boat, Tyra Brown Polite and Moriah Haywood Bartley, who both had been held in bondage on Rose Hill, reunited with Tyra's daughter, Phoebe Burns Frazier, and Moriah's third or fourth cousins James, Joshua, and Moses Simmons, all enslaved on Cypress Plantation, and together they sailed off to freedom in Beaufort.[61]

Though Kirkland only listed one enslaved man named Jack on the list dated November 5, and none on the undated list, two Jacks got on the gunboat at Rose Hill: Jack Wineglass and Jackson Grant. Jack Wineglass's wife, Maria Savage Wineglass, got aboard also, but her brother, John A. Savage, did not escape enslavement in the raid; as we've seen, he was encamped with William L. Kirkland Jr. at McPhersonville. Jackson Grant testified that "I left my wife and children behind"; it's not clear whether Dorcus Lee Grant stayed behind on Rose Hill, like Elsey Higgins stayed behind on Cypress, or fled with Jackson but afterward remained in Beaufort, like Sarah Small Osborne. But Maria and John A. Savage's older sister, Mary Ann Savage Lewis, and John A. Savage's wife, Charlotte Savage, did make it safely to freedom.[62]

We learn from the pension files that Phyllis Wineglass Pinckney, Jack and Maria Wineglass's daughter, was the niece of Daphne Jackson Powell Snipe (and Anthony Bartley was her great-uncle). Daphne and her second husband, Ned Snipe, escaped enslavement in the raid and both were on Kirkland's November 5 list. Richard A. Smith—with whom, as noted, Jackson Grant testified he grew up with on James Paul's plantation—was one of a handful of bondspeople from Paul's Plantation, downriver from Rose Hill, to get on the boat.[63]

Andrew Wyatt also boarded the Union gunboat at Paul's Plantation; Charlotte Savage testified later that while he was "no kin to me," "he lived with mother during slavery times." Andrew Wyatt's second cousin Diana Deas Harris (their grandfathers were brothers), her husband, Andrew Harris, and their last surviving child, Sammy (Diana and Andrew's four older children died enslaved on Rose Hill Plantation), were able to get on the boat together. Kirkland included the names of Andrew, his wife, and their son—Andrew had been his head plowman, hostler, and teamster and his wife a field hand—on both his undated and November 5 lists. William Jones, who had attended the Harrises' wedding on Rose Hill more than a decade before the war, Martha Singleton, who knew Diana Deas Harris all of her life, and Diana Harris's niece Pleasant Rutledge got on the gunboat also (Kirkland listed William Jones, a carpenter, on both affidavits). William Jones's future brother-in-law William Hamilton got on the *John Adams* from Cypress Plantation.[64]

What Tubman described years after the end of the war as the "mysterious communication system" that had spread the news of the arrival of the Union ships was, in fact, not at all mysterious once we take into account the perspectives of the 2nd South Carolina Volunteers veterans and their relatives and neighbors, revealed in the pension files. It boiled down to kinship among enslaved people on seven plantations along the lower Combahee River. They grew up together and were interrelated by blood, marriage, and even fictive kinship. They did their very best not to leave their kinfolk behind. However, those who had been enslaved farther up the river, some literally next door to the affected plantations, did not have the chance to get on the boats. My paternal grandmother's ancestors did not get on the boats in time. They would remain enslaved on Combahee rice plantations until the end of the war.

When the steam whistle blasted, men, women, and children who had grown up together, multigenerational families who had lived as neighbors, agemates who attended praise meeting and each other's weddings and then greeted each other's babies shortly after they came into the world, people who had been separated years or even decades before by being sold, bequeathed, and even given away, liberated themselves. They were reunited with their parents, husbands, wives, children, aunties, uncles, cousins, praise house members, sweethearts, ex-sweethearts, and baby mamas, and sailed off to Beaufort, where they would all be free together. The "mysterious communication system" proved the enduring power of family in outright defiance of the very peculiar institution that was designed and wielded to tear them apart.

★★★★★★★★

After parading down Beaufort's Bay Street still in their dingy gray field suits, the Combahee freedom seekers were taken to a church in downtown Beaufort. James Yerrington wrote in the *Wisconsin State Journal* that he doubted the church had ever before been "appropriated to so good a purpose" as finally welcoming to freedom enslaved people who had stolen their liberty while hoeing in the rice fields six months after the Emancipation Proclamation went into effect, or that "so true a gospel had ever been preached" within the church's walls as the gospel of freedom.[65]

Before November 1861, African Americans worshipped at two churches in downtown Beaufort, Tabernacle Baptist Church and Beaufort Baptist Church. Beaufort Baptist had been organized in 1800, and before the war both white and Black congregants worshipped there. There were consistently more Black than white members at the Beaufort Baptist Church throughout the antebellum period, and they were required to sit in a segregated section in the balcony. Tabernacle Baptist Church was founded in 1804 with eighteen white members and a larger number of Black members, all previously worshipped at the Beaufort Baptist Church on Charles Street. The congregation split in 1807: one faction left Beaufort Baptist and founded Tabernacle Baptist Church on Craven Street. The two congregations reunited in 1811, with the Tabernacle congregation returning to the Charles Street church; both congregations continued to use the Craven Street church for special services and as a lecture hall.[66]

Tabernacle's Black congregation had been worshipping in the edifice on Craven Street since July 1862. On January 1, 1863, Tabernacle's congregation issued a resolution thanking President Abraham Lincoln for the Emancipation Proclamation. They wrote that they had "gathered together two or three times a week for the last five months" to pray that God would help Lincoln and the Union soldiers, bless them, and crown them with glory. The Reverend Solomon Peck, an abolitionist from Providence, Rhode Island, and an ordained minister, ministered to the Black congregation at the Beaufort Baptist at the same time as he was assisting Dr. Richard Fuller, a wealthy Beaufort slaveholder who had moved to Baltimore, to maintain his family's land and slaveholdings in US-occupied territory. Tabernacle dates its official founding to September 1, 1863, when Reverend Peck became pastor and organized this church with 5,500 members. Freedpeople and abolitionists likely gathered at Tabernacle to bear witness to Colonel

Montgomery's return from the raid on the Combahee River. Tabernacle Baptist Church is the future home of the Harriet Tubman Monument.

In his June 20, 1863, piece in the *Wisconsin State Journal*, Yerrington wrote he had never felt such a "swelling of emotions of gratitude" to God as he did at that moment. Colonel Montgomery, the "gallant deliverer," addressed the crowd in "strains of thrilling eloquence." The Combahee refugees and other freedom seekers at the church intoned a song so "heartfelt and cordial," "There Is a White Robe for Thee." It may have reminded those in the audience of freedom seekers' spontaneous rendition of "My Country 'tis of Thee" at General Saxton's Emancipation Proclamation celebration six months earlier, on January 1, 1863. As "unbridled tears" fell, there was not a dry eye in the house.[67]

According to Yerrington, a speech by "the black woman" followed Colonel Montgomery's address. The speaker was not just any Black woman, though there were certainly hundreds in the room—women who had liberated themselves from bondage in the raid, women who had liberated themselves from bondage in Beaufort and the surrounding Sea Islands as early as the Battle of Port Royal. Since the other two Black women who took part in the Port Royal Experiment, Charlotte Forten and Susie King Taylor, were not on the scene, it could only have been one Black woman who addressed the crowd at the church in downtown Beaufort the day after the raid—Harriet Tubman, "the black woman who led the raid, and under whose inspiration it was originated and conducted."[68]

Tubman gave the Combahee refugees a lecture full of "soundness" and "real native eloquence," which "would do honor to any man." Without a transcript, we are left to wonder which words Tubman chose to deliver to the crowd. She certainly told her story of growing up in and escaping bondage. She probably spoke of liberating freedom seekers in rescue missions for over a decade and giving instructions to others. She likely spoke to the throngs of freedom seekers in the Beaufort church that day about the responsibilities of freedom. Nor is there a record of whether she raised her melodious voice in song, as she often did when speaking about her experiences as a bondsperson, self-liberator, and conductor on the Underground Railroad. If she sang to the assembled crowd—all of whom would surely have preferred death to a return to bondage—, she might have chosen:

> O, freedom, O, freedom
> O, freedom oba me

An befo A be a slabe
A be bury een me grabe
An gone home ta me Lawd an be free
O, freedom![69]

Because she, her ring of spies, scouts, and pilots, and the 2nd South Carolina Volunteers had risked their freedom, the Combahee freedom seekers were free and safe in Union-occupied territory. But this was no time to rest. The Combahee freedom seekers would have to fight to defend their freedom and fight for the freedom of others—as Tubman and the 2nd South Carolina Volunteers had fought for their freedom.

Six days after the raid, the *New York Herald* reported that "Negroes were quartered at a church and all able-bodied men were drafted into Col. Montgomery's"—the 2nd South Carolina Volunteers, the same regiment of Black soldiers that had executed the Combahee River Raid and liberated them. Decades after the end of the war, veterans and widows were unanimous in their understanding of what would happen when they got on the gunboats and went to Beaufort: the men were going to join the army and they were going to war. Combahee men ages fourteen to sixty, as well as one man who claimed to be (and likely was) seventy, enlisted in the army. They may have been inspired to enlist by Moses's speech. The veterans also were unanimous in remembering that Colonel Montgomery personally recruited them. He backdated most of their enlistment papers, putting June 1, 1863, as their enlistment date. Still, June 3, 1863, is written in some of the files, even by veterans themselves—veterans like Neptune Nicholas, who learned to write and sign their names after the war—leaving no doubt that the Combahee men who were liberated in the raid filled the 2nd South Carolina Volunteers Companies G and H on June 3, 1863, the same day the companies were organized.[70]

All recruits, Black and white, underwent a medical examination before they were enlisted. Colonel Montgomery's examination of the Combahee men was unusual, because it did not take place in the field, at a military camp, or at a recruitment office. Instead, the men were "stripped and examined at a church in Beaufort," according to Moses Simmons. The medical examinations would have begun with the recruits removing the clothes they had worn to labor in the rice fields early the previous morning. It was typical for soldiers to have to disrobe. Colonel Thomas Jefferson Morgan, who organized the 14th US Colored Troops regiment in November 1863, conducted medical examinations of his recruits "*a la Eden, sans* the fig leaves," doing so himself with the assistance of an aide. Simon Washington could not forget that "there was a crowd examined at the same time" that he was. Men who had escaped enslavement on seven adjoining plantations—some of whom had known each other before the raid, but many of them who had never met—were "all in the same room, stripped." Wally Garrett testified in April 1902 that he had been examined by a doctor, and in October 1902 he remembered that two doctors had examined him. Garrett may have gotten one of the most thorough physical exams of all his comrades. The doctors measured him, "felt of" him (probably checking his groin for evidence of inguinal hernia, his teeth for rot, or both), and made him run. Jackson Grant reported having been examined by four doctors. Solomon Salter was stripped naked and made to "jump about the room." James Sheppard was weighed. Neither programmatic nor thorough, the perfunctory medical exams were designed to enlist as many men as possible as quickly as possible.[71]

Veterans' memories of their medical examinations at enlistment are likely affected by the disability claims they submitted after they were mustered out and in which they needed to prove that they had passed a physical examination before enlistment and that a medical doctor had pronounced their health and physical condition to be "sound." Solomon Cunningham, also of Company G, remembered four doctors being present; he had to take his shoes off and "run and jump around and kick up," with the doctors thoroughly examining him, "feet and all." Decades after the war, Cunningham claimed disability for frostbite to his feet and toes as a result of military service.[72]

Andrew Wyatt insisted he was examined by a "good doctor" before enlistment and was "stripped off naked." The results of the examination were that he was deemed "worthy" and taken into the military. Wyatt protested decades later that he did not know why the doctor had enlisted him even though he was fifty-two or fifty-three years old at the time. Men who were found not to be "worthy" were rejected. Given the average age of men in Company G and Company H, Colonel Montgomery, his officers, and his medical staff certainly did not reject nearly as many of the Combahee recruits as they probably should have. In contrast, the 54th Massachusetts surgeon rejected one-third of that regiment's initial recruits in February 1863.[73]

The men who enlisted in Company G and Company H could not remember the names of the doctors who "carefully examined" them; James Sheppard remembered "two white men and one colored man" examining him. It is possible that one of the doctors examining the Combahee recruits was Dr. John Milton Hawks. Stephen Gatson, who enlisted in the 2nd South Carolina Volunteers, Company E, in April 1863, remembered that he and another recruit, Sandy Haywood, were "stripped and examined by Dr. Hawk." Hawks was appointed acting assistant surgeon of Colonel Higginson's 1st South Carolina Volunteers in October 1862 and later became assistant surgeon. His duties included conducting medical exams of Higginson's officers' recruits. He could have performed the same duties for Colonel Montgomery's 2nd South Carolina Volunteers when the two regiments were stationed together in Beaufort.[74]

Arthur W. Greenleaf may have been another of the doctors. At age twenty-five he joined the 2nd South Carolina Volunteers on May 9, 1863, on St. Helena Island as assistant surgeon. The Field and Staff Muster Roll states he was detailed to the General Hospital M.C. in Beaufort in May and June 1863 and thus was not in the field with the regiment at the time of the Combahee River Road. A June 28, 1863, letter from Colonel Montgomery to Brigadier General Quincy A. Gillmore requests that Greenleaf "be ordered to report for duty in his Regiment" because the 2nd South Carolina Volunteers had "no Surgeon with the Regiment" and felt "the need of one very much." To fill the void, particularly at a time when most white doctors would not treat Black patients, Montgomery promoted a free "mulatto" recruit, George Garvin, to the post of hospital steward of the 2nd South Carolina on June 10, 1863, by Regimental Special Order No. 5 while the regiment was stationed in Key West. Six feet tall and light-complexioned, with black eyes and hair, Garvin was born in St. Augustine, Florida. The former carpenter, then forty-five years old, had enlisted as a first sergeant in Company A four months earlier, but at the time of the raid had not yet taken on the medical role. Thus Montgomery, like Colonel Morgan of the 14th USCT, may have personally performed the medical examinations of the Combahee men with the assistance of some of his officers, white doctors from one of the Beaufort hospitals (such as Arthur W. Greenleaf), or one of the surgeons or assistant surgeons of the 1st South Carolina Volunteers (like Hawks).[75]

On Independence Day 1863, *Harper's Weekly* printed an article entitled "A Typical Negro," accompanied by three engravings of a Black man as he entered Union lines, underwent a military medical examination, and dressed as an enlisted man. This article ran on the same page as Surgeon Robinson's engraving of the *John Adams* and *Harriet A. Weed* in the Combahee River. The juxtaposition of these iconic images of the Combahee River Raid and the Black man was not accidental. Six months after it went into effect, the Emancipation Proclamation remained unpopular among a large segment of the northern population. The Union Army was far from winning. Union defeats at the Battles of Fredericksburg and Chancellorsville confirmed that the war, which was well into its second year, would slog on. Public support for the war effort among northerners was sinking.[76]

The article identifies the man portrayed in the engravings as "Gordon." In the first image, a barefoot Gordon is seated on a chair facing forward with his legs crossed at the knee. This is how he appeared after escaping enslavement in Mississippi and finding safety behind Union lines in Baton Rouge in March 1863, according to the article. He is dressed in a filthy and tattered pair of pants, shirt, jacket, and hat. The middle engraving, significantly larger than the first, depicts a seated Gordon facing away from the reader but looking over his left shoulder with his left hand on his hip, the palm turned up. His shirt is stripped off and bunched up on one side around the waist of his pants. Gordon boldly presents his horribly mutilated bare back to the reader. The article states that the lacerations attested to Gordon being subjected to torture on Christmas Day the previous year, and the caption intimates that Gordon's wounds were discovered by US Army medical staff during his medical examination. In the third and final image, the confident-looking, clean-shaven Gordon is dressed in the uniform of a Union Army Black regiment corporal with two chevrons on his sleeve, a canteen over one arm, a pack on his back, and a military-issue musket in his hand. He was transformed.[77]

The three engravings printed in *Harper's Weekly* were not based on the images and stories of just one man. Writing under the pseudonym "Bostonian," someone responded to Copperheads' denunciations of the images as fakes in the December 3, 1863, issue of the *New York Daily Tribune* with the claim that the first two engravings printed in *Harper's Weekly* were made faithfully from two original photographs that he had brought from Louisiana six months previously. The writer identified the man depicted in the first photograph as a young black man named Gordon who had arrived at US lines in Baton Rouge weak from hunger, and the man in the second photograph as someone named Peter, who likely was enslaved by Captain John Lyon, a cotton planter near Washington, Louisiana, near the Atchafalaya River. The third image, of the US Army corporal, was likely of Furney Bryant, who was an enslaved driver born in Kingston, North Carolina. At twenty-eight he escaped enslavement and enlisted in the 1st Regiment North Carolina Colored Infantry, Company D, on May 21, 1863, in New Bern, North Carolina.[78]

Montgomery's raid on the Combahee rice planters had been a small military success, but it proved to be a big recruitment success amid a sea of Union defeat and disappointment. It laid bare the barbarous realities of enslavement and put forth the redemptive narrative of freed slaves turning into soldiers—a narrative that abolitionists needed northerners to buy into if the Union was to win the war. "Gordon" could have been any formerly enslaved man who had escaped enslavement, eluded slave catchers and bloodhounds, and made it safely to US-occupied territory in the South.[79]

Most of the Prime Hands liberated from the Combahee River enlisted in Company G. Two exceptions were Andrew Harris of Rose Hill Plantation, who was born between 1818 and 1821, definitely making him an Old Head, and Joshua Simmons from Cypress Plantation, whose 1823 birthdate made him one of the youngest of the Old Heads. They may have been placed in the same company as younger men because of their appearance of sound health, vigor, and vitality compared to the rest of their agemates. Of the Combahee men born between 1824 and 1845, Ned Snipe, Jackson Grant, William Jones, and Daniel Jenkins (who escaped enslavement on Rose Hill), Mingo Van Dross, Anthony Bartley, and Friday Hamilton (who escaped from Longbrow), Moses Simmons, Andrew Nicholas, Robert Frazier, Will Young, Neptune Nicholas, William Hamilton, Edward Brown, William Middleton, and Charles Nicholas (who liberated themselves from enslavement on Cypress), and Richard Smith (who was enslaved on Paul's Plantation) enlisted together in Company G. Decades after the war, they remembered growing up as boys, getting on the gunboats, and enlisting in the US Army on the same day together.[80]

Neither Williams Middleton, who owned Newport Plantation, nor Walter Blake, who managed his father's Bonny Hall Plantation, applied for compensation from the Confederate or federal government. Nor have back-of-the-envelope slave lists that they may have recorded ever been found. However, pension applications filed decades after the war confirm that Company G included a number of men who had liberated themselves from bondage on one of those two plantations. Enslaved on Newport Plantation had been Old Heads Solomon Salter, Balaam Burnett (whose first wife, whom he married during enslavement, was Rose Middleton Burnett, one of Wally Garrett's sisters), and James Sheppard, along with Prime Hands Salem White, Farbry Bowers, Wally Garrett, March Lawrence, and Jack Aiken. Enslaved on Bonny Hall had been Prime Hands John Jones and Charles Lucas. Charles Lucas was the first husband of Bella Jones Lucas Garrett, whom she married while held in bondage, and Wally Garrett was her second husband, whom she married after freedom.[81]

Jack Wineglass, who escaped from Rose Hill Plantation, Simon Washington and Mexico Washington, who escaped from Newport Plantation, and Cuffie Bolze, who escaped from Cypress Plantation, all enlisted together in Company G. Simon Washington, Daphne Garrett Washington Wright's son, served in the same company as his uncle Wally Garrett and his distant cousin Jack Aiken, and the same regiment as his future stepfather, Frank Wright. On June 13, 1895, Mexico Washington testified in his pension file that he was so "small" when he had mustered in that he could not remember the date. It was June 3, 1863. Cuffie Bolze was listed as "about 20" years old when he enlisted, though later he testified that he in fact had been older—certainly so that he could qualify for disability benefits sooner. William C. Heyward listed Bolze as sixteen on his affidavit for compensation from the Confederate government.[82]

The overwhelming majority of the Combahee Old Heads enlisted in Company H. Stephen Simmons was younger, enlisting at thirty. In addition, Nat Osborne from Oakland, James Shields, Solomon Washington, and Edward Brown from Newport, and Stephany Grant from Longbrow enlisted together in Company H. Nat Osborne and Solomon Washington may have enlisted in Company H instead of G, because their fathers, November Osborne and Smart Washington, were also in the regiment. From Newport Plantation, Mexico Washington and William Drayton rounded out Company H. Drayton was the youngest Combahee freedom seeker to enlist in the 2nd South Carolina Volunteers after the raid. At fourteen years old, he enlisted as the "drummer." Reuben Rutledge, a boy of about nine years old, was too young to enlist when he escaped from Longbrow. He served as "officer boy" for Company G.[83]

From the nine-year-old to the seventy-year-old, each and every one of the 150 men who escaped in the Combahee River Raid and enlisted in the 2nd South Carolina Volunteers could be said to be "Gordon"—"Gordon as He Entered Our Lines," "Gordon Under Medical Inspection," and "Gordon in His Uniform as a US Soldier." However, many of their scars and disabilities were not discovered until after enlistment. Time would tell what the initial medical examinations did not reveal.

After Colonel Montgomery swore them in, the men from the Combahee were "carried right into camp at Pigeon Point," Neptune Nicholas remembered, where they mustered in. According to Moses Simmons, the Combahee men exchanged their field suits for "army clothes at Pigeon Point." Colonel Montgomery, the 2nd South Carolina Volunteers, two batteries of the 3rd Rhode Island Heavy Artillery, Harriet Tubman, and her ring of spies, scouts, and pilots had taken the men out of the rice fields. Then they had taken the hoes out of their hands and put muskets in them. Until the end of the Civil War, Montgomery's men in Companies G and H would risk their lives—as Tubman, her ring of spies, scouts, and pilots, and all the Black soldiers and sailors had risked theirs—to fight for the freedom of others still enslaved months after the Emancipation Proclamation went into effect.[84]

PART FOUR

"We's Combee!"

However far the stream flows, it never forgets its source.

—Ibo proverb

17

Reaping Dead Men

In a letter published in the *Boston Commonwealth* on July 17, 1863, six weeks or so after the Combahee River Raid, journalist Frank Sanborn made it clear that Harriet Tubman needed contributions to continue her work in South Carolina. He assured his reading public that "none has better deserved it." The letter included text that Tubman dictated to Sanborn (who wrote, as previously noted, the first biographical sketch of Tubman) in which she stated her case. In the fall of 1862, when people in Beaufort were on alert for an enemy invasion, her clothes were packed up, sent to Hilton Head, and subsequently lost. She was sick at the time and could not transport them herself. Tubman lamented that she had been unable to find any of them after she recovered. She asked for the replacement of her wardrobe, though Sanborn speculated that she would share the items with the first needy freedom seeker she met. In addition, Tubman requested that "the ladies" among her abolitionist Boston friends send her a *"bloomer dress made of coarse, strong material, to wear on expeditions."* Having had to shred her dress during the raid, Tubman had told Sanborn afterward that she had "made up" her mind and "would never wear a long dress on another expedition of the kind."[1]

Named for women's rights activist Amelia Jenks Bloomer, the "bloomer dress," also called "Turkish trousers" or "reform dress," was an alternative to the heavy and constricting garments—with layers of heavy and cumbersome underskirts, some weighing as much as ten to thirteen pounds, supported only on the hips—that upper-class women wore in the mid-nineteenth century. Bloomer wrote that a woman's "slavery to clothes" made her a "corseted, crippled, dragged-down creature"; she wanted women to be "free." The bloomer featured a shorter skirt, covering the knees but stopping short of the ankle. Elastic gathered the full Turkish trousers or pantalettes at the ankle underneath the skirt. Elizabeth Smith Miller, daughter of Gerrit Smith of John Brown's Secret Six, is credited with developing the dress and wearing it. After Miller wore a bloomer dress at the 1848 Women's Convention in Seneca Falls, New York, the wife of future secretary of war Edwin Stanton adopted it as well. Amelia Bloomer advocated that women wear it, first writing about it in the February 1851 edition of her newspaper, *The Lilly*, the first newspaper to be edited by and for women. The *New York Daily Tribune* proclaimed a "bloomer craze."[2]

William Lloyd Garrison's *The Liberator* published several articles in the early 1850s extolling the virtues of bloomer costume for reform-minded women, including women's rights activists and abolitionists. Reverend Thomas Higginson supported a "Bloomer Delegation" of women at the World's Temperance Convention in May 1853. Higginson had made a resolution to seat female delegates at the convention, including Amelia Bloomer and Susan B. Anthony, and insisted that his name be stricken from the list of delegates when his resolution was opposed. Caroline Seymour Severance joined a "bloomer" group in Dansville, New York, where she and her younger son, Mark Sibley Severance, took the water cure, a treatment combining water therapy with a strict diet and exercise. The water cure movement advocated women's engagement in physical labor and exercise, contradicting nineteenth-century notions of white women's femininity, which required them to be ladylike, delicate, and weak.[3]

This was Tubman's tribe, though it does not appear that other free or freed Black women were wearing bloomers in the 1850s and 1860s. She asked the ladies of Boston to send her a "bloomer" as soon as possible, because she expected to have use for it "very soon, probably before they could get it to [her]." In an interview later in her life, Tubman expressed pride in wearing "pants" and carrying a musket, haversack, and canteen on expeditions. Tubman's niece Alice Brickler wrote to Earl Conrad that when she was a child, she wandered off into the tall grass behind her aunt's home to pick wildflowers, then sensed "something moving toward" her "thru the grass." It was her aunt, who frightened her, "so smooth did" the elderly Tubman "glide" through the grass "and with so little noise." Once Brickler and her mother had helped Tubman get resettled in her chair, Tubman told them "that was the way she had gone by many a sentinel during the war." Certainly, a bloomer dress would have facilitated such clandestine movements.[4]

At the time she dictated the letter published in *The Commonwealth*, dated June 30, 1863, Tubman was working at the Contraband Hospital No. 5 in downtown Beaufort. Dr. Henry K. Durant, acting assistant surgeon in charge of the contraband hospital, wrote in May 1864: "I certify that I have been acquainted with Harriet Tubman for nearly two years and my position as Medical Officer in charge of 'contrabands' in this town, and in hospital, has given me frequent and ample opportunity to observe her general deportment particularly her kindness and attention for the sick and suffering of her own race." "I take much pleasure," he added, "in testifying here to the esteem in which she is generally held." General Saxton endorsed Dr. Durant's recommendation.[5]

Contraband Hospital No. 5, also called Barnwell Castle, was a refuge for freedom seekers in Union-occupied Beaufort. It was a soldiers' hospital, for white soldiers from August 1862 to June 1864, then for Black soldiers from June 1864 until July 1865. In her work at the hospital, Tubman met those who had just left enslavement. She was in the ideal position to make "it a business to see all contrabands escaping from the rebels" and be successful at getting "more intelligence than anyone else," as Lieutenant George Garrison had argued. According to Tubman, they were "very destitute" when they arrived, "almost naked." In addition to providing basic medical care, she helped find work for those who could work, shelter, food, and clothing for the remainder. Her goal was to help the refugees to get back on their feet, both to lessen the "burden" of their care on the federal government and to foster self-respect and a strong work ethic.[6]

The Combahee River Raid was neither the first nor the last raid for Harriet Tubman, though her presence on others not at all documented. Despite the raid's success, Tubman was not detailed again to work with Colonel Montgomery and the 2nd South Carolina Volunteers. However, during their tenures in Beaufort and Port Royal, Tubman, Montgomery, and the 2nd South Carolina continued to work on the US Army Department of the South's immediate goal: capturing Charleston.

★★★★★★★★

A week after the Combahee men had enlisted in the 2nd South Carolina Volunteers, 150 in all, the soldiers took the *John Adams* down to Darien and Brunswick, Georgia, where the 2nd South Carolina fought along with the 54th Massachusetts. Montgomery and Colonel Robert Gould Shaw commanded the regiments of Black soldiers on the expedition. Cuffie Bolze testified in his pension file affidavit in 1901 that his "first battle was in Darien."[7]

Robert Gould Shaw was born in 1837 in Boston to Francis Shaw and Sarah Blake Sturgis Shaw, wealthy and ardent social reformers who were devoted to the cause of antislavery. The Shaws were part of the tight circle of Boston-based abolitionists who supported the work of Garrison and Tubman. Shaw did not always share his parents' dedication to the antislavery movement. Like most young people, he had to find his own way. He favored parties and balls, traveled to Europe, spent his parents' money, flirted with debutantes, attended Harvard College, and avoided the antislavery issue altogether in his youthful pursuits, even after passage of the Fugitive Slave Act and the Kansas-Nebraska Act. However, in 1861 he enlisted in the 7th New York National Guard after the first shots were fired at Fort Sumter and was promoted to captain after fighting at Cedar Mountain and Antietam. When Governor Andrew decided to raise the 54th Massachusetts, the first regiment of Black troops from the North, he offered twenty-five-year-old Shaw the colonelcy of the regiment.[8]

After the 54th Massachusetts mustered in, General David Hunter requested Governor Andrew send the regiment to the Department of the South, where the free and freed Black men from the North would serve with white soldiers and with formerly enslaved men from the South. Hunter promised to give the 54th Massachusetts the opportunity to go into battle, not just dig trenches. When the regiment arrived in Hilton Head on June 3, 1863—a day after the Combahee raid—they reported to Hunter. A twelve-mile steamer ride up the Beaufort River to Beaufort brought the 54th Massachusetts face-to-face with Colonel Montgomery and the 2nd South Carolina Volunteers as they returned from the raid. Colonel Shaw wrote to his mother about Montgomery's return "from an expedition with 725 blacks from plantations."[9]

Two days later, Montgomery prepared to take the 2nd South Carolina Volunteers out on another expedition in Georgia. Colonel Shaw requested permission for the 54th Massachusetts to go with him. Shaw wrote his father that he thought the best thing for the regiment was to "get my men at work as soon as possible." He also described Montgomery as a "good man to begin under" as brigade commander. He seemed to admire Montgomery's quiet, unruffled, gentlemanly demeanor and discipline, and enforced this among his soldiers and officers—no swearing, drinking, or smoking permitted. Shaw was impressed with Montgomery always holding religious services with his soldiers and officers before an expedition. Shaw thought Montgomery the "only active man" in the Department of the South, a sharp contrast to General Hunter. However, he also called Montgomery a "guerrilla-man by profession" and disapproved of bushwhacking and destroying private property. Shaw did not approve of Montgomery's penchant for "hanging people & throat-cutting" when he deemed it warranted. Montgomery's actions and rhetoric as a bringer of God's wrath upon southern civilians bordered on fanaticism. In time, Shaw would choose not to be associated with either.[10]

On June 11, 1863, under the command of Montgomery, the 3rd Rhode Island Heavy Artillery shelled the woods along the Altamaha River as the US Army steamers and gunboats wound their way through the creeks eight miles up to Darien. The shells drove away Confederate guerillas, whom the Union soldiers "could plainly see break from their hiding places," as Captain Apthorp of the 2nd South Carolina Volunteers, Company C, wrote in his account. The Confederate guerillas had been "skulking" behind the trunks of a stand of butternut trees until a few "well aimed shells" from the US Army gunboats forced them to clear out. Shaw wrote to his wife that he thought Montgomery's military tactics were "brutal," because he did not know whether or not Confederate civilians, particularly women and children, lived on the plantations behind the woods in Darien (which Shaw described as a "beautiful little town"). In the end the 3rd Rhode Island shelled Darien. Shaw and Apthorp agreed that the Confederate inhabitants had deserted it, and Apthorp himself insisted that Darien was a "rendezvous for guerillas," which "belonged entirely to full blooded rebels all in arms against" the federal government.[11]

Montgomery's five companies of the 2nd South Carolina Volunteers, the 54th Massachusetts, and one section of the 3rd Rhode Island landed fifteen miles north of Darien and marched down two roads. Private Jack Wineglass testified that the regiment "had to do very hard drilling at Darien," which resulted in Old Head Andrew Harris becoming disabled—Harris's feet swelled after the 2nd South Carolina returned from Darien and remained swollen until after the regiment was deployed to Morris Island. Montgomery had the soldiers remove all of the furniture and moveable property from the elegant mansions they came upon and transfer it to the US Army's boats.[12]

Colonel Montgomery was in favor of putting Darien to the torch, employing highly combustible lucifer matches. According to Apthorp, what was left of Darien after the slaveholders abandoned it was already thoroughly "disembowelled." One day after Montgomery's men struck the city, a "citizen" wrote from Dunwoody Plantation to the *Charleston Mercury* describing how the soldiers had leveled it to "one plain of ashes and black-ened chimneys." The "Yankee-negro vandals," as the writer described them, had laid Darien low, just as they had done to the Combahee River's rice plantations eight days earlier. By the end of the military expedition, only three small houses remained standing. The writer accused the "villains"— that is, Black soldiers—of breaking open all the houses and stores, looting their contents, pouring "spirits over turpentine on the floors," and applying "the torch."[13]

All churches but one, the market house, the courthouse, the jail, and the clerk's office were burned to the ground. Livestock and domesticated ani-mals were not spared either. The soldiers took some aboard the transport steamers, but shot the milk cows and calves and left them dying in the street.[14]

Furthermore, the "vandals" also liberated "every negro in the place," ex-cept for one. An elderly, African-born woman named Nancy refused to go. Nancy remembered the horrors of the Middle Passage from western Africa to the New World. She told the Black soldiers that "she would not go again on the big water." The overwhelming majority of those who came to liberate Nancy had been born enslaved and liberated themselves in the Combahee River Raid just days before. Unlike Minus Hamilton, who was "gwine to the boat" no matter what, Nancy rejected her "birthday of freedom."[15]

Shaw told his commander that he did not want any responsibility for what he described as this "dirty piece of business," because Confederate guerillas were not hiding out in Darien, the enemy had not fired upon the US Army's troops or gunboats, and those on horseback in the distance may or may not have been soldiers. Shaw complained that his men had participated in the destruction because he had to follow Montgomery's orders. Montgomery's reasoning for burning a town was that the enemy had to feel the effects of a "real war" and they would be "swept away" by

God's hand. Moreover, the Black troops and their officers were "outlawed" by the Confederacy, whose policy was to execute white officers of Black troops and to enslave (or reenslave) Black men in Union military uniforms if they were captured, and so Montgomery reasoned that he was not bound by the "rules of regular warfare." Frederick Douglass, for one, agreed with Montgomery's position that rules of civilized warfare did not apply. Some would argue that in Darien Montgomery was making "the enemy pay the way," as he had done so successfully on the Combahee River, and giving the Black soldiers "a relish" for the work they were to do along the south-eastern coast.[16]

Colonel Higginson also detested and condemned Colonel Montgomery's "brigand practices." He thought Montgomery should restrain his soldiers and wrote to his wife that Black soldiers enlisted in the 1st South Carolina would adhere to Montgomery's orders. Higginson also later referred to the 2nd South Carolina as "Montgomery's guerillas."[17]

Young Colonel Shaw was concerned that Montgomery's "barbarous sort of warfare" would harm the reputations of Black soldiers, their commanders, and maybe even political officials, like Governor Andrew, who raised the regiments. He distinguished the men in his regiment who were free before the war and commanded by northern abolitionists from men in the 2nd South Carolina Volunteers who had recently escaped enslavement. Shaw wanted his men to fight battles against Confederate soldiers—to occupy, hold, and destroy Confederate territory—but not to punish the enemy by looting and burning. Given that the enemy did not fire on the troops, Montgomery's actions were not justified, according to Shaw. Furthermore, he did not think the Department of the South gained anything by looting, other than supplying furniture and other items to make camp life more comfortable; now the soldiers and officers could "sit on chairs" and sofas "instead of camp-stools," eat at tables with china, tinware, and earthenware, play pianos, sleep on beds with bedsteads, use carpenter's and cooper's tools, and read a seemingly unlimited supply of books.[18]

When Shaw inquired whether Montgomery had burned Darien by order of General Hunter—who, as Shaw wrote, did "not impress" him as "being a man of power"—he was surprised to learn that Montgomery was indeed carrying out orders from Hunter. However, President Lincoln had temporarily removed Hunter as commander of the Department of the South on June 3 and replaced him with Major General Quincy A.

Gillmore; Darien burned eight days later. Hunter's scorched-earth policies would take a backseat to Gillmore's campaign against Charleston until May 1864, when Major General John G. Foster replaced Gillmore and William Tecumseh Sherman swept through Georgia and South Carolina on his legendary "march to the sea."[19]

There were no deaths among the 2nd South Carolina at Darien, according to Cuffie Bolze's pension file testimony. However, there were injuries. Edward Brown testified that the "premature discharge of a gun" had injured his leg, and Jackson Grant testified that one of the cannons bruised Tony Snipe's feet. Colonel Montgomery and Captain Apthorp had made another successful raid, depending on how one defined success and warfare.[20]

By early July 1863, a month after the Combahee raid, the change of command was complete in the Department of the South. Hunter was out and Gillmore, a former instructor of practical military engineering at West Point, was in. Gillmore's victory at Fort Pulaski had placed him in the top ranks of Union engineers and artillerists. After Pulaski, he supervised the construction of Fort Clay in Lexington, Kentucky, and commanded a division in the Army of Kentucky. Then he added a different skill to his arsenal, commanding a cavalry unit that was successful in battle, which demonstrated the diversity of his military and leadership capabilities. Gillmore put his engineering and artillery genius to the task of reducing the fortifications protecting Charleston Harbor and seizing Fort Sumter. His leadership revivified the Department of the South's siege of Charleston.[21]

As noted earlier, Hunter had acted without authority by instituting his own emancipation proclamation after the Battle of Fort Pulaski and enlisting Black troops, some by force, into Hunter's Regiment. Lincoln had of course condemned and rescinded both orders, then subsequently moved closer to Hunter's abolitionist position in implementing the Emancipation Proclamation and the conscription of Black men into the US military forces. But Hunter's order to burn Darien was the last straw in this string of overreaches.[22]

Despite the forced enlistments of Hunter's Regiment and his other missteps, Hunter believed that Black people should be both free and equal to whites. Hunter not only talked the talk but he walked the walk. Union captain Francis Jackson Meriam wrote to Governor John Andrew ten days after the Combahee River Raid about a scene he had witnessed a scene that exemplified Hunter's values. He saw Hunter "fetch a pitcher of water and stand waiting with it in his hand while a Black woman drank, as if he had been one of his own servants—that woman was Harriet Tubman." Jackson didn't think Hunter would even remember this extraordinary gesture afterward. He determined made missteps because he was pushing to get the federal government and the president to realize African Americans' freedom and equality.

Though Hunter was ousted, not everyone in the Department of the South wanted to throw out all of his initiatives. And Hunter had been instrumental in bringing Harriet Tubman to the Department of the South. Gillmore endorsed a pass Hunter had written for Harriet Tubman in February 1863 so that she could travel freely and safely throughout the department and purchase provisions at the commissary:

FROM GEN. HUNTER
HEADQ'RS DEP'T OF THE SOUTH
Hilton Head, Port Royal, S. C.
Feb. 19, 1863

Pass the bearer, Harriet Tubman, to Beaufort, and back to this place, and wherever she wishes to go, and give her free passage at all times on all Government transports. Harriet was sent to me from Boston, by Gov. Andrew, of Mass., and is a valuable woman. She has permission, as a servant of the Government, to purchase such provisions from the Commissary as she may need.

D. HUNTER,
Maj. Gen. Com'g.
H. Q. DEP'T OF THE SOUTH
July 1, 1863
Continued in force.
Q. A. Gilmore
Brig. Gen'l Com'g.

The commanding officers who remained after Hunter's departure, Colonel Montgomery and General Saxton, wanted to ensure Tubman's role in the department was secure. So Montgomery wrote to Brigadier General Gillmore to introduce Tubman as a "most remarkable woman." Tubman wore many hats in the Department of the South. Montgomery did not write to Gillmore about Tubman's work as a cook, nurse, or laundress. Rather, he commended her intelligence-gathering skills—he described her as "valuable as a scout"—as critical to the ongoing work of the Department of the South:

> HdQrs Col Brigade St. Helena Island July 6, 1863
> Brig. Genl. Gilmore Comd'g. Dept. of the South General:
>
> I wish to commend to your attention Mrs. Harriet Tubman, a most remarkable woman, and valuable as a scout. I have been acquainted with her character and actions for several years. Walter D. Plowden is a man of tried courage and can be made highly useful.
>
> I am General
> your most obt. servt.
> Signed James Montgomery
> Col Com'd'g Beaufort

On the back of Colonel Montgomery's note, Brigadier General Saxton endorsed his recommendation of the value of Tubman's skills to the Department of the South:

> I approve of Col. Montgomery's evaluation of the value of Harriet Tubman's services.
>
> Signed R. Saxton
> Brig. Genl.[23]

With Hunter gone, however, Colonel Higginson was free to express his views of Montgomery. He wrote to his wife that Montgomery had been a "sore disappointment" to him. Until Darien he had been one of Montgomery's biggest supporters. But now Montgomery was at "sword's point" with General Saxton. Higginson wrote that he had not wanted Montgomery in his brigade, because Montgomery would "chafe" at being under Higginson's command again. Higginson must have been thinking of the St. Johns River expedition, when Montgomery had acted independently, going upriver to Palatka on what Higginson thought was a risky mission. Colonel Shaw, another admirer turned critic after the burning of Darien, would express similar sentiments about not wanting to be brigaded with Colonel Montgomery. Higginson thought that convincing the bushwhacker of his notions of "civilized warfare" would be too hard. He also reported that Montgomery had recently had one of his own enlisted men shot for desertion and would have shot two more had Dr. Seth Rogers, surgeon of the 1st South Carolina Volunteers, not interceded. Time had brought about a change: by mid-1863, Higginson thought Montgomery a "mixture of fanaticism, vanity, and genius."[24]

What Gillmore thought of Montgomery, however, was what really counted. He was likely more focused on his subordinate's genius than on his fanaticism or vanity when in early July 1863 he promoted him to commander of the 3rd Brigade (as part of General Alfred H. Terry's 1st Division). Then in late August 1863, Montgomery was appointed to command the 4th Brigade, also under General Terry. The 1st Division included the 2nd and 3rd South Carolina Volunteers, as well as the 54th Massachusetts for part of Montgomery's tenure. They engaged in battles, not just raids. After attending a dress parade of the 54th Massachusetts and having tea with Gillmore and Colonel Shaw, Charlotte Forten wrote in her diary that Shaw and his men were "eager to be called into active service."[25]

★★★★★★★★

The 2nd South Carolina was stationed at St. Helena Island on July 8, 1863, when they received orders to prepare for an expedition and take nothing but their haversacks, canteens, and gum blankets. Four monitors were positioned off the bar in Charleston Harbor. And Brigadier General Alfred H. Terry's 3,800-man brigade moved up the Stono River, heading toward Stevens Landing on James Island and supported by the gunboat *Pawnee* and two transports. Their mission was to distract the enemy's attention from Morris Island by causing the Confederacy to send reinforcements to James Island instead. General Terry's diversion was successful. The Confederates diverted a large portion of their scarce defenses to James Island, where there was no threat, leaving an insufficient garrison of four hundred men to defend Morris Island.[26]

A few days later, on July 10, 1863, after hours of furious firing from both sides, the US Army brought barges full of reinforcements up the Little Folly River and landed them on Oyster Point. They advanced quickly, repulsing the small Confederate infantry force. This battle by joint US Army and US Navy forces gained them control of the southern half of Morris Island and helped them capture a significant amount of Confederate artillery—three 8-inch naval guns, two 8-inch seacoast howitzers, one rifled 24-pounder, one 30-pound Parrott, one 12-pound Whitworth, and three 10-inch seacoast mortars—and two hundred prisoners. The July 10 assault at Oyster Point may be where Private Robert Frazier of the 2nd South Carolina Volunteers sustained a gunshot wound in the right hip, which would leave him permanently disabled for the remainder of his relatively short life.[27]

General Gillmore was criticized for not finishing the job and not making an immediate assault on Battery Wagner, which was insufficiently defended by demoralized troops. After the quick initial victory, he chose instead to rest his own battle-weary and heat-stricken troops. The twenty-four-hour delay gave General Beauregard's forces a chance to regroup and garner reinforcements of men and ammunition.[28]

Gillmore and Admiral John A. Dahlgren worked to reduce the battery, which appeared to be a succession of low sand hills. In reality, it was an eight-hundred-foot-long sand earthwork, stretching across the narrow (eighty-foot) neck of the island from the harbor to the sea, with eleven heavy guns and several mobile artillery pieces to defend it. Captain Charles R. Brayton (who had manned the guns on the *John Adams* and "mowed his swath broad and smooth," firing shells that destroyed the pontoon bridge, halted the Confederate defense, and protected the soldiers and freedom seekers during the raid) would be promoted to assistant chief of artillery shortly after taking up his position on Morris Island. With a foothold on Morris Island, US forces constructed batteries against Fort Sumter and Battery Wagner. The 3rd Rhode Island and 7th Connecticut Volunteers mounted and manned the guns. By day the US Army's brigades fired the guns and the monitors' cannons fired on Battery Wagner's east flank. But none of it had much impact. Gillmore's dawn assault, under terrific Confederate fire, was also unsuccessful. Forty-nine soldiers were killed, 123 wounded, and 167 captured as the Union army pushed its battery construction forward.[29]

Major B. Ryder Corwin was sick in his hammock all day, complaining of diarrhea. (During the Combahee River Raid, Corwin had had charge of the *Harriet A. Weed*, which landed at Joshua Nicholls's boat landing) He performed picket duty that night with his regiment but could not carry out any other duty for five days. For this he would be court-martialed. Captain Oliver B. Holden later testified in Major Corwin's defense at the court-martial, saying that he had advised Corwin not to go with the regiment when it moved. The siege of Charleston advanced despite Major Corwin's troubles.[30]

Overall the general feeling was that eventually the Union would succeed. Colonel Shaw wrote to his wife: "General Gillmore will get Charleston at last." On July 10, the 2nd South Carolina arrived at James Island. The Union attack resumed at daybreak on July 11 with the 7th Connecticut leading the infantry charge. When the Confederates fired on the US brigade as they came through the narrow neck at Battery Wagner, the 7th

Connecticut broke out and charged the earthworks. Under murderous fire from musketry and shells from big guns, they passed through the moat and up the sandbag parapet only to be cut down by Confederate sharpshooters. They fought and held on until reinforcements came, but the reinforcements themselves had taken a powerful pounding and been driven back. So the Union force retreated down the parapet and back through the moat strewn with bodies in blue uniforms amid a hurricane of grape, canister, and musket fire. The 7th Connecticut lost forty-three soldiers killed or mortally wounded, with fifty-seven men wounded or missing. [31]

Less than a week later, it would be the turn of the 54th Massachusetts. Captain Brayton wrote to his father on July 16 and informed him that at midnight he was going into position for "another Artillery duel." Initially seizing the element of surprise, the Confederates unleashed a superior force of infantry, artillery, and cavalry, raining musketry and artillery on both Union flanks. But they lost the advantage when General Terry's 7th Connecticut took to its guns and the 54th Massachusetts stood its ground and stopped cold the Confederacy's advance on the right flank. Terry set up two battle lines of infantry three hundred yards apart and positioned his four rifled cannon to command the road. The *John Adams* was one of the armed transports that came up a creek in the Stono River and opened up on the Confederate right flank. The *Pawnee* secured Terry's left. The Confederates retreated. [32]

The goal of the mission was, by any means necessary, to reduce Battery Wagner. Brayton confessed that he was no longer as "sanguine" about the mission's success as he had been a few days before. However, his feelings would "make no difference in his fighting"; he would give it all he had. He also intimated to his father that he might not survive. In case he did not, Brayton gave him an accounting of his savings and debts and instructions that his servant Tom would handle his personal effects. The 2nd South Carolina marched to Cole's Island, arriving a day later. On the evening of July 17, they marched to Pawnee Landing on Folly Island. [33]

In the seven days between the July 11 and the July 18 assaults on Battery Warner, General Gillmore built land batteries, set up artillery, and coordinated an attack plan with Admiral Dahlgren's naval forces. After a heavy rain on the evening of the seventeenth had flooded the works, Gillmore's land forces and a fleet of five monitors, six mortar boats, and two other ships began a joint land-and-sea bombardment of Battery Wagner at noon on July 18, with little effect. Gillmore was confident—tragically, overconfident—that his guns had reduced the battery's walls to rubble before the infantry assault, as the artillery had done victoriously at Fort Pulaski. However, the earthen walls of Battery Wagner could withstand more pounding than the brick masonry walls of Fort Pulaski. Nevertheless, the ground assault began at dusk. Captain Brayton of the 3rd Rhode Island manned three field rifles.[34]

Colonel Shaw seized the opportunity for his 54th Massachusetts Infantry to be placed in front and lead the charge with two brigades of white soldiers behind to storm Battery Wagner. Shaw wanted his Black regiment to fight alongside white soldiers, who could then attest to their capabilities to engage in battle against the enemy, not just take part in guerilla warfare. He hoped the fighting would displace memories of the burning of Darien in the public imagination. Shaw feared he would not survive this fight, but he did not allow his fears to interfere with preparing his regiment for their biggest—and only—battle yet. After the battle, Harriet Tubman told Hildegard Hoyt Swift, author of *The Railroad to Freedom*, that she had been present with Shaw before the battle, and much later Swift wrote Earl Conrad that Tubman "always stoutly maintained that she fed Col. Shaw his last meal."[35]

On July 18, Colonel Shaw led the men of the 54th to the front, six hundred yards from the fort, where they formed two battle lines, two men abreast, fixed their bayonets, and lay facedown in the sand. He walked up and down between the lines, sat with the soldiers, chatted with them, and encouraged them. He may have known that he had brought them all the way from Readville, today part of the city of Boston and where the 54th Massachusetts was organized, to pay the ultimate price. He told them that they were making history and reminded them that the world was watching. They were to "take the fort or die there." They replied that they would.[36]

As the men of the 54th Massachusetts arose, marched across the beach, and waded through seawater, their commander leading the charge, it soon became clear that the joint Union bombardment had not weakened Battery Wagner. When they got within two hundred yards of the battery, Wagner and Fort Sumter and a garrison of Confederate soldiers unleashed a thick hail of grapeshot, canister, and rifle shot. At Shaw's "double quick" order, the men jogged across the beach in a veritable whiteout created by the sand flying from the shot and shell hurled at them. As men fell, those behind them jumped over their fallen comrades to take their place. Colonel Shaw urged his men onward. They scrambled over the sand hills as shot and shell continue to fly, then hunkered down in the sand, sheltering from Confederate fire. After nightfall they crossed the moat and abatis, the latter a defensive obstacle made of felled trees with sharpened branches facing the enemy, and scaled Battery Wagner's slanted walls. Once they pulled themselves up over the walls and inside the battery, they engaged in hand-to-hand combat with the Confederate garrison. All they had were their bayonets. As Shaw and a small group of his men clawed their way to the top of the parapet, Confederate bullets cut Shaw down. His body plummeted into the battery. Half of the 54th Massachusetts held a portion of Battery Wagner for more than an hour, but then had to abandon it due to exhaustion and lack of reinforcements, according to Brayton. The guns on Fort Sumter, James Island, and Sullivan's Island joined in to drive the Union from its position. The loss of two other commanders, General Truman Seymour, who was wounded early, and General George C. Strong, who was wounded later on in the battle (and subsequently died of his wounds), contributed to the disastrous outcome.[37]

The 2nd South Carolina Volunteers were part of the rear guard. They received orders late in the day on July 18 to get ready for the assault on Battery Wagner and marched from Light House Inlet across the south end of Morris Island. They were ordered to "fall in with arms" and then "march to the beach." They proceeded up the beach, marching in "column of Company," to Beacon House. The columns were deployed between the beach and the marsh, where they remained in position while two other brigades made the charge. After dark, they were ordered to "advance" in the battle line to reinforce the second brigade that had charged and was supposed to have seized Battery Wagner. The 2nd South Carolina moved forward a few steps, then was ordered to halt. Another regiment filled the 2nd's recently vacated position. According to Colonel Montgomery, approximately four hundred soldiers from the 2nd South Carolina went "behind the sand hills" shortly after the battle ended, and the "shattered regiments," including what was left of the 54th Massachusetts—having lost 40 percent of its men and more than 60 percent of its officers—passed by. The 2nd was to do guard duty, in case Confederate forces made any moves. Approximately a hundred men from the 2nd South Carolina performed fatigue duty, making a rifle pit. Surgeon Daniel D. Hanson (who was appointed unit surgeon on July 3, 1863) later testified he had been with the regiment at Beacon House during the battle, then received permission to tend to the wounded after the battle.[38]

The news of the battle took several days to reach northern volunteers on the Sea Islands. When Charlotte Forten learned of the outcome at Battery Wagner two days after the assault, she wrote in her diary that the news was "so Sad, so heart sickening" and "too terrible, too terrible to write." The northern volunteers—many of whom had come to South Carolina from Massachusetts—could only wait and hope that by some miracle Colonel Shaw was alive and the 54th Massachusetts, which Forten described as a "splendid looking reg[iment]—honour to the race," had not been "cut to pieces." The sad, terrible news was all true, however. This was likely the scene Harriet Tubman described to historian Albert Bushnell Hall, a scene that Earl Conrad identified as the Battle of Fort Wagner:

> And then we saw the lightning, and that was the guns; and then we heard the thunder, and that was the big guns; and then we heard the rain falling, and that was drops of blood falling; and when we came to git in the cr[o]ps, it was dead men that we reaped.

All hands were on deck when the wounded men from the 54th Massachusetts were brought into Beaufort. The northern volunteers mobilized to care for the wounded and collect relief supplies for the soldiers and their families. According to Esther Hawks, who cared for the 54th Massachusetts in field hospitals, "torn-and mangled bodies" arrived by the hundreds. Edward Pierce summoned Laura Towne to Beaufort to care for the officers. Charlotte Forten went also to provide comfort for both the Black soldiers at the contraband hospital and the white officers at the military hospital after hearing nurses were "sadly needed." Forten wrote in her diary that Mrs. Jean Landers, who was head of the nurses in Beaufort, was sure Forten would be unable to "endure the fatigues of hospital life" even for a few days. Forten sewed, mending bullet holes and bayonet cuts in their jackets, and wrote letters for the men. She talked with the patients and helped the nurses to distribute medicines. She returned to St. Helena three days later.[39]

Even before the wounded of the 54th arrived, Tubman recalled going to the hospital early in the morning, getting a big chunk of ice, and putting it in a basin with water and a sponge. She started with the first man, brushing away the flies that swarmed around his wounds "like bees roun' a hive." Then she washed his wound with the sponge wet with cold water. By the time she had bathed three or four men, the ice had melted from the heat of the day or the heat of the fire. The water would be warm and as "red as clar blood." She would empty the basin and get more ice. By the time she started again, flies had swarmed around the wounds of men she had already washed, as "black an' thick as eber."[40]

Even the 2nd South Carolina rear guard was in danger. In August 1901, Private Edward Brown testified for Andrew Wyatt that the 2nd South Carolina had been "under Genl. Gillmore on Folly and Morris Islands." Their goal had been to "take Fort Wagner." They had "hard work," constructing fortifications and breastworks while on fatigue duty. Black soldiers carried out slightly more than half of this work. And they had a "pretty hard time of it," because the Rebels shelled all night long while they worked. Although there were bombproof shelters, they could not always get into them in time and so were always vulnerable. They "had to work hard," but they "finally did take the fort."[41]

And their families felt the impact of their vulnerability. Moses Simmons later testified in his pension file that Private Neptune Nicholas had taken his girlfriend, Bella, with him to Beaufort when "we went there during the war." Though he is not explicit, Private Simmons was referring to the Combahee River Raid, when all the Blacks enslaved on Cypress Plantation—including himself, Nicholas, and Bella—had run to the river, gotten on the US gunboats, and escaped enslavement. Bella was his cousin. She and Nicholas had already had one child together when they got on the gunboat, and they stayed in Beaufort until the 2nd South Carolina Volunteers were sent off to Morris Island. At that point Nicholas sent Bella back to Hilton Head, according to Simmons. He "deserted" Bella and never lived with her again after he mustered out and the war ended. [42]

After the failure to take Battery Wagner, General Gillmore strengthened the Union's position by digging zigzag trenches protected by batteries. He planned to continue the siege and shell Fort Sumter into surrender. The danger of fatigue duty at Battery Wagner took its toll on the 2nd South Carolina even though they were not directly involved in the assault. Sergeant Edward Bennett suffered a gunshot wound in his left side. Private Friday Hamilton suffered a bayonet wound in his left arm. Private Andrew Wyatt injured his right arm and strained the small of his back while sheltering under a big gun, which overturned on him when hit by a Confederate shell. Subjection to severe weather while performing fatigue duty caused or exacerbated illness and disability. Private Wyatt, the former plowman on James L. Paul's plantation, contracted severe colds and experienced rheumatic pains all over his body, especially in his loins and shoulders, and a "rupture" or hernia from building small forts and sleeping on damp ground at Morris Island in the summer of 1863. Private Samuel Grimball did picket duty under heavy rain, then dislocated his shoulder while discharging his rain-soaked gun. According to a comrade, Private Daniel Simmons, Private John Proctor got sunstroke while in charge of a "squad" and "digging intrenchment on Morris Island" for the Union breastworks. A shell also struck Proctor's head above his temple, cutting all the way down to the bone.[43]

One soldier from the 2nd South Carolina Volunteers died in action in the first month at Morris Island. Private James Shields, who had been a guest at Scipio and Annie McNeal's wedding on Newport Plantation at Christmastime in or around 1859, testified for Annie Cassell McNeal Holmes that Private McNeal "got struck by a piece of shell" fired from a Confederate battery while he was on fatigue duty, and was killed instantly.[44]

The Union lost 1,515 men in battle and the Confederates 174 men at Battery Wagner. By charging into a thick hail of bullets and fighting and dying alongside white men, the fallen heroes of the 54th Massachusetts, 272 in all, proved that Black men would and could fight for their freedom and the freedom of people still in bondage.[45]

★★★★★★★★

Major Corwin of the 2nd South Carolina Volunteers had once again not been part of it. He had left Morris Island on the morning of July 20 and gone to Beaufort. He was reported absent without leave and a deserter eight days later, when his name was dropped from the rolls. One of the 2nd South Carolina's second lieutenants testified at Corwin's court-martial that Corwin had asked the lieutenant to accompany him to find shelter from the driving rain, as he was sick and could not stand it anymore. The lieutenant took Corwin to the nearby camp of the 48th New York Volunteers, the white regiment in which he had been an officer before he was commissioned to the 2nd South Carolina Volunteers. The morning afterward, at Beaufort, Corwin obtained a surgeon's certificate of disability and was granted a leave of absence by Department of the South headquarters to travel home to New York for twenty days. His commanding officer had no information about Corwin's whereabouts until headquarters granted his leave. The board of inquiry court-martialed Major Corwin in September 1863, charging him with disobedience of orders. Corwin declined to plead on this charge, insisting that if he had committed an offense, it would be being absent without leave, not disobedience of orders.[46]

In the aftermath of the July 18 assault, General Gillmore changed his strategy. Two failed assaults on Battery Wagner had proved to him that he could not take it with infantry. So he went back to artillery, the kind of warfare that he knew best and which had brought him victory at Fort Pulaski. With superior artillery and the cooperation of Admiral Dahlgren's ironclads and other warships, Gillmore intended to bombard Battery Wagner into surrender. He appointed General Terry to command of Morris Island and supervised the construction of land batteries, digging miles of parallel trenches reaching right up to the battery.[47]

On July 24, the US Navy's five monitors, two gunboats, and two mortar vessels, along with the US Army's land batteries, hammered at Battery Wagner. Union shells disabled a recently repaired 10-inch columbiad, tore off the roof of the magazine, and dug into Battery Wagner's walls. On the same day, Joshua Nicholls wrote a letter to his stepson, Private William L. Kirkland Jr., who was stationed in McPhersonville in service with the Confederate Charleston Light Dragoons. Nicholls had returned to Charleston a week before. He reported that he had left Warrenton, Georgia, "as soon as" he heard that Charleston "was in danger." He knew that his presence alone could not change the city's fate but thought he should "be at [his] post." Now that Longbrow had been destroyed in the Combahee River Raid and Charleston was in peril, Nicholls had enlisted in the 11th South Carolina Infantry (the 9th South Carolina Volunteer Infantry was reorganized and reissued on May 3, 1862) as acting quartermaster sergeant. Colonel William C. Heyward had commanded the unit as one of the company's sergeants until the reorganization of May 1862. Nicholls had just completed his second stint of guard duty, patrolling the wharves in Charleston's Harbor, across from where the US Army and Navy assaulted Battery Wagner. The bombardment had been heavy on that night, not ceasing until midnight.[48]

Nicholls wrote that while on guard duty in Charleston he had witnessed a prisoner exchange. Moreover, he saw Confederate soldiers with legs and arms missing, "wounded in every possible way," and rushed away in ambulances. It was a sight he wished never to witness again. It made his "blood run cold." Despite the carnage at Battery Wagner and the US bombardment, Nicholls did not think Charleston would fall, because the Confederacy had built new breastworks on Morris Island after the first siege of Charleston in April and May 1863. Nicholls reassured Kirkland, telling him to "have no fear about the safety of Charleston." The Union could continue its bombardment of the forts and batteries in Charleston Harbor "at the present rate," but they would not gain access, he thought. Nicholls had no idea when he penned his letter that the Union Army was implementing a plan to modernize its artillery and construction technology and augment its forces to take Battery Wagner, Fort Sumter, and ultimately the city of Charleston. Nicholls also had no idea that the Kirkland family was about to experience the "horror of this war" firsthand. [49]

Meanwhile, on the other side, Captain Brayton wrote his father that he was alive and well. His unit had been hard at work "constructing Batteries and mounting heavy guns" designed to "tell on" the Confederacy's fortifications. Battery Wagner remained the "only Obstacle" to the Union taking Fort Sumter. Brayton thought it "only a question of time" until they were successful. He reported proudly that he had escaped the "Rebel shells," which had killed and wounded men at his side, and that the Confederate sharpshooters were unrelenting if thankfully not very accurate. One explosion had occurred just four feet away from where Brayton had been sitting. Still, he reassured his father that he had become accustomed to shells flying and could tell where they would land as soon as he could spot them, so as to protect himself from injury. The "terrible Artillery fight" was yet to come. He did not know who would survive when it did. That fight would make Fort Pulaski look like "boy's play." [50]

When that fateful day would come was not clear. Both the Union Army with its land batteries and the Union Navy with the USS *New Ironsides*, six monitors, eight gunboats, three mortar hulks, and fourteen other vessels inside the bar were relatively quiet on August 15; they fired only occasionally on Battery Wagner and later in the day turned their firepower on Battery Gregg. The Confederates, meanwhile, continued to repair Fort Sumter's gorge wall with sandbags as quickly as they could transport the materials. Union sergeant major Lewis Douglass wrote that he had not been in a fight since the July 18 assault on Battery Wagner. The 54th Massachusetts, like the 2nd South Carolina Volunteers, was still stationed on Morris Island. Three days earlier they had been ordered out early in the morning. A Confederate attack was anticipated; nothing materialized, and they returned to camp. On August 15, Douglass wrote to his fiancée, Amelia Lougen, giving her instructions, which she must have requested, on how to send relief supplies to the regiment's sick and wounded who were still hospitalized in Beaufort.

He told Lougen that she could address her packages to "Sick and Wounded Hospital No 6." Douglass added that the "colored women of Beaufort" had shown their "appreciation of the cause" by nursing the wounded and sick soldiers "under the irrepressible Harriet Tubman." Tubman not only was serving as a nurse at the Beaufort contraband hospital but also had organized Black women in the local community to nurse the Black soldiers; nurses were in short supply, and it was unusual for white women to nurse Black men. What better way to both lessen the federal government's burden for their care and foster self-respect, a strong work ethic, and a sense of collective responsibility among freedom seekers who were still understanding what it meant to be free?[51]

Captain Brayton wrote to his father that he could not disclose the preparations the US forces were taking for the bombardment of Fort Sumter or when the bombardment would begin, as the military's orders were properly "stringent." Instead, as he wrote in his diary, both the Union and Confederate forces continued firing on each other. Confederate forces had built batteries on Fort Johnson from which to fire on the Union's batteries. The range was too long to cause significant damage on either side, however. Fort Sumter and Battery Wagner fired at night, when the US Army constructed its batteries. Captain Brayton did not think the guns of Fort Sumter could hold out much longer, though it retained thirty-eight guns and two mortars. The Confederates had withdrawn at least twenty guns since the US Army landed on Morris Island. Brigadier General Roswell S. Ripley had received orders to transfer all guns from Fort Sumter not necessary for the fortification's defense to other points along Charleston Harbor.[52]

Brayton wrote to his father that what the US Army was doing on Morris Island was "entirely new." They were bringing "heavier" artillery and guns with "longer range than ever before used." The artillery expert commented that they "[knew] nothing of" these new guns, "except experimentally." As they tested them in the field, the artillerists were to keep records about how they worked. In his diary, Brayton wrote that the US Army was firing five 200-pound Parrott guns, nine 100-pound Parrott guns, and one 300-pound Parrott gun from its batteries and the US Navy was firing two 200 par Parrott guns and two 80-pound Whitworth guns. No military had placed a "greater calibre" in a similar position. But the Confederates were not giving up the fight. They piled sandbags behind Fort Sumter to protect their magazines and mounted a large-caliber columbiad between Battery Gregg and Fort Sumter, which reached and caused damage to some of the Union batteries. Confederate sharpshooters stationed atop the bombproof shelters on Battery Wagner struck the roof of Beacon House, but few other targets.[53]

At daylight on August 17, the combined Union forces opened fire on Fort Sumter, Battery Wagner, and Battery Gregg. The US Army and Navy unleashed everything they had on the two Confederate batteries. This was the largest display of artillery power to date in the Civil War, with the artillery teams firing at 78 percent accuracy; hurricane-force winds diminished the accuracy of the Union floating batteries. The shells ripped large holes in Fort Sumter, to the point where Brayton described the fort as "honeycombed" after an onslaught of several hours. Debris fell from the gorge wall onto the wharf and into the water. The Union kept up its fire to prevent the Confederate forces from placing sandbags to reinforce its gorge wall. By the end of the first day, the Union bombardment had exposed the fort's magazines and disabled many of its cannons, particularly the guns on the gorge wall.[54]

Fort Sumter's gorge wall began to collapse. Two of the navy's monitors engaged Battery Wagner, but the Union held off on launching an incursion. A second breakthrough occurred when two soldiers from the 1st Regular Army of the Confederacy deserted from their positions at Battery Gregg, bringing with them intelligence. They reported that one of the guns at Battery Wagner had been disabled and that several remaining guns from Fort Sumter had been moved to James Island. Finally, Fort Sumter's scarp wall fell, allowing the US forces to view the arches of four casements filled with tightly compacted sandbags, making them impassable.[55]

Additional technological advances facilitated the fall of Fort Sumter. But it came at a cost. his pension testimony in June 1867, Sergeant Aaron Ancrum remembered that he became sick from exposure in late August 1863, when he had been in charge of a "squad" of soldiers that was detailed to build a battery on Morris Island where the "Swamp Angel" was to be mounted. The Swamp Angel was one of the most unique military innovations of the Civil War. Embedded in the salt marsh between James Island and Morris Island, the battery consisted of a 16,300-pound, eight-inch Parrott gun mounted on a parapet and designed to fire on Charleston. To construct the parapet, Union soldiers worked at night to drive sheet pilings into the marsh, then bolted a three-sided log grillage two layers thick. The soldiers placed thirteen thousand sandbags on the grillage. The gun and carriage sat on a platform inside the rectangular area of the grillage. Thus, the parapet was not connected to the platform and the gun deck floated independently on the marsh. To distract the Confederate forces, the US Army built a decoy battery just south of the real one.[56]

Sergeant Wyatt and his men from the 2nd South Carolina worked on the Swamp Angel in mud up to the waist for seven weeks, lifting heavy logs and moving them into place (which was how Sergeant Ancrum strained his back and caught a severe cold, which he testified settled in this part of his body). The men were exposed to the night air when they slept in the trenches, which resulted in rheumatism in Ancrum's spine and limbs and caused great fatigue; Ancrum would be hospitalized at Morris Island for several months. Private Jacob Campbell strained his back while detailed to build the Swamp Angel. He developed hemorrhoids and lung disease from pulling heavy guns from Folly to Morris Island. In fact, the arduous labor required to construct the battery for the Swamp Angel and put it into place disabled a good number of soldiers in the 2nd South Carolina, some of them for the rest of their lives. Living in trenches for weeks on end with little fresh water for drinking and washing their hands and no access to separate toilet facilities could be deadly. Edward Brown testified in his pension file in April 1890 that he had contracted chronic diarrhea and bowel disease during the Darien expedition, and it continued to ail him in the summer of 1863 on Morris Island. He thought "bad water" was the cause.[57]

Private Stepney Grant died of typhoid fever in the hospital at Morris Island on August 23, 1863, the same day that General Gillmore ended the bombardment of Fort Sumter. Grant had taken care of his mother, sisters, and permanently disabled father on Rose Hill Plantation. His mother, Flora Grant, testified in August 1874 that her son had contracted chronic diarrhea at Morris Island from drinking what the soldiers and veterans called "bad water" while on picket duty.[58]

The Swamp Angel began to shell Charleston, bringing the war to the residents who remained, including Williams Middleton, who would have inherited Newport Plantation, which had been destroyed in the Combahee raid. Middleton wrote to his wife that his neighbor woke him up late at night on August 23 to inform him that the "Yanks were shelling the city." He was not concerned about the bombardment moving to the city. He wrote that the Confederates' robust response would soon make it too "hot" for the Union to continue its "deviling."[59]

In the course of seven days, from August 17 to 23, the Union pumped 5,643 shots into Fort Sumter, totaling 385 tons. The majority hit their mark. The bombardment left the remaining guns in Fort Sumter unserviceable and the gorge wall and northwest face severely damaged. The powerful US artillery could do little additional damage to what was left of this fort. Moreover, several additional batteries protecting Charleston Harbor remained. In the face of Confederate shelling and sharpshooters during the bombardment, the US soldiers had pushed their trenches closer and closer to the front of Battery Wagner. At long last, taking Battery Wagner once and for all was within reach.[60]

★★★★★★★★

The US occupation of the southern end of Morris Island wore on, with both sides shelling the other. Sometime in August 1863, a Minié ball smashed through Private Bacchies Robinson's right shoulder on a Saturday night attack on Morris Island. The bullet shattered the bone near his shoulder socket. He was sent to the Contraband Hospital No. 5 in Beaufort so doctors could try to repair the damage.[61]

As shells flew, danger was all around. Colonel Montgomery wrote to his wife that their son James Montgomery had arrived safely in South Carolina and was commanding a unit in the 2nd South Carolina Volunteers. He took his son to the front immediately and gave him some practice dodging cannonballs, a skill that would prove lifesaving for officers and soldiers alike during the second siege of Charleston. Montgomery reported that their heavy artillery opened fire on Fort Sumter on August 17. On this ninth day of the bombardment, US forces attempted an assault on a sand hill, with little success. The Confederates continued shelling, doing little damage. Union forces had by now driven their trenches closer and closer to Battery Wagner. Behind it on the north side of Morris Island lay Battery Gregg.[62]

And accidents happened too. Private Moses Simmons later testified in his pension file that 2nd South Carolina Companies G and H (formed of men who liberated themselves in the Combahee River Raid and who mustered in the day after the raid, having "got army clothes at Pigeon Point and arms at Morris Island") participated in assaults on Battery Wagner after the July 18 battle and during the subsequent sixty days of Union bombardment of Battery Wagner and Fort Sumter. On one of the assaults, when they were "charging to take the fort," Private Simmons fell in a pit, a "sink," in front of the fort. In the fall, he injured his leg and suffered a cut down to the bone over his eye, according to his comrades Privates Cuffie Bolze and Charles Nicholas. The three men had grown up together on Cypress Plantation, gotten on the US gunboat together in the Combahee River Raid, and enlisted in Company G of the 2nd South Carolina Volunteers together—in fact, as mentioned previously, on the day after the raid. The surgeon stitched the cut up, but Private Simmons's eyesight never recovered, as he testified. Like many other soldiers in his regiment, Simmons suffered from exposure, which resulted in rheumatism in his knees, back, and hips for the remainder of his life.[63]

Colonel Montgomery declared the Union bombardment on Fort Sumter and Battery Wagner to be the "greatest siege the world ever saw" in terms of the number and strength of fortifications built by the Confederacy and the manpower and firepower brought to bear on them by the Union. With one fortification encircling Charleston Harbor reduced, the Union Army commenced shelling Charleston with a 200-pounder, launching incendiary shells filled with combustible liquid. The Union was throwing everything it had into Charleston. The Confederates responded in kind to protect Charleston, even lobbing a compound shell—a shell within a shell, a device invented by the Union that exploded multiple times—back at Union forces. Unlike the initial siege of Charleston, the US Navy did not play a significant role in the August 1863 bombardment. Colonel Montgomery wrote to his wife that the ironclads got into the fight once, "with considerable spirit." They subsequently retired after two US Navy officers were killed in the advance. General Gillmore was disgusted that the US Navy was unwilling to enter the harbor and use the ironclads to clear an opening through the obstructions, which, according to military intelligence, were interlaced with torpedoes. They made clear that they would not advance until the US Army controlled Fort Sumter, not just silenced it.[64]

Acting as general field officer, Montgomery and his forces stormed the Confederate forces' rifle pits facing Battery Wagner, finally gaining the position from which to take Battery Wagner. He placed the 54th Massachusetts and 3rd New Hampshire (a white regiment) in the "advanced trenches." Montgomery explained to his wife that he commanded white troops because the three brigade commanders served rotating twenty-four-hour periods as commander at the front in battle, during which they were second in rank only to the commanding general. He was one of the three

brigade commanders under General Alfred Terry. Brigade commander was
a rank Colonel Higginson, who, as noted earlier, became disenchanted with
Montgomery, never achieved before his retirement in October 1864 because of disability and Colonel Shaw, another of Montgomery's critics, did
not live long enough to get. One day later, Sergeant Major Lewis Douglass
wrote to his fiancé that the 54th Massachusetts had once "again been placed
in Colonel Montgomery's brigade."[65]

Though a mortar battery kept the Confederate soldiers under cover by
shelling the rifle pits, the 54th Massachusetts charged and took sixty-six
Confederate pickets as prisoners. (Later, after the battery was taken, the
Union would use those same mortars to cover Union troops while they
entrenched themselves, and to prevent Confederate forces from attempting
to recapture the battery.) Montgomery told his wife that Major General
Gillmore had complimented his work highly. The previous general field
officer had failed to accomplish the task. Now the Union charged the sand
hill again. This time they met with some success, capturing one Confederate
lieutenant and twenty-four soldiers. And they completely dismantled the
howitzer disabled a few days earlier by the Union bombardment of Battery
Wagner.[66]

Sergeant Major Douglass saw reason for hope. Though he admitted to
Amelia that "Charleston is not yet ours," progress had been made. All of the
Union efforts, costly though many had been, had effectively weakened the
Confederacy and strengthened the Union positions. According to Douglass,
it had made the fall of Charleston a "certainty." He dreamed about the
day Charleston would fall, and the way northerners would rejoice at the
"downfall" of the city that was home to so much of the "treason and disloyalty which has overturned our nation."[67]

The bombardment continued at all hours of the day and night after Fort
Sumter was silenced. Colonel Montgomery acknowledged that it was an incredibly dangerous business. Union forces hurled "monster bolts and shells"
against Fort Sumter's walls "incessantly" for seven days and nights consecutively. The Confederate Army had reinforced the fortification after Admiral
Du Pont's ironclads fired on it in May 1863. The Union troops, inclusive
of the 2nd South Carolina Volunteers, were in trenches, protected only by
earth-and-wood shelters known as "splinter proofs." They were surrounded
by mortars and cannons "booming" and shells "bursting." When they saw
the shells approaching in their direction, the men in the trenches had to
dodge and take cover. Montgomery's brigade of the 2nd and 3rd South

Carolina Volunteers and 54th Massachusetts was losing an average of ten to twelve men each day. He described to his wife some of the "sad, sickening sights" he witnessed.[68]

Nonetheless, the Union soldiers moved ever closer to the walls of Battery Wagner under the full moon. There were many "narrow escapes" under "terrific fire" from rifles mounted atop Battery Wagner's parapet and from canisters at Batteries Wagner and Gregg and Fort Johnston, according to Colonel Montgomery. Twenty-four men were killed or wounded in the trenches around his son. The explosion of a shell bursting over his head had knocked the younger Montgomery down and a rifle shot grazed his head. As Colonel Montgomery prepared for his next rotation as general field officer, he was not sure when the commanding general would order the storming of Battery Wagner. He very much hoped that his reputation as a Kansas bushwhacker and his command of the three brigades in the field at Morris Island would convince General Gillmore that he had the "courage necessary for desperate undertakings" and just might be the man for the job. In preparation, Montgomery sent his wife money and enumerated the debts he wanted her to pay with it should he not live to see another day. As the assault wore on, he wrote more frequently about dying, promised to send his wife more money to manage his affairs, and assured her that she would be able to pay all of his debts and live comfortably on a widow's pension if in fact he died in battle.[69]

On August 31, Captain Brayton wrote to his father that the second "'Siege'" of Charleston was "progressing well" and Fort Sumter was "*defenseless.*" The US Army had silenced every gun without any cooperation from the US Navy. He apologized for not being able to tell his father more about the bombardment; orders forbade it. However, he made sure to give the US Army the credit for demolishing Fort Sumter, describing the navy as the "biggest pack of cowards." He complained that the ironclads did not cooperate with the army at all, forcing it to rely on its own resources. By the time the US Army took control of Fort Sumter, the 2nd South Carolina had seen "more service than either of the others" in his brigade, according to Colonel Montgomery. One soldier had died in battle; three men had been wounded, one seriously.[70]

The US Navy continued to disappoint General Gillmore, Colonel Montgomery, and all the other US Army commanders. The ironclads did not act as "bravely" as the job demanded. In the joint US Army and US Navy mission, Gillmore's job had been to silence Fort Sumter; the US

Navy's fleet was to then finish the job and open Charleston Harbor. Even after Gillmore did his job and Fort Sumter was a "perfect ruin" that had been silenced for more than one week, the ironclads hung back, avoiding the fight. Gillmore decided to act and not wait for Admiral Dahlgren. He would capture Battery Wagner and use the battery on Cummings Point to provide cover for the navy.[71]

Meanwhile, a council of Confederate officers deliberated over how much longer their forces could continue to hold Batteries Wagner and Gregg and the north end of Morris Island. As noted, the US Army had advanced its trenches almost up to the moat of Battery Wagner, and it was just a matter of time before they bombarded it again, this time successfully. The council decided it was most important for them to hold on to Morris Island, and they opted not to move the five heavy guns still there. They would destroy their own guns rather than let them fall into the hands of the enemy before they evacuated—if evacuation became necessary. Then, when the trenches finally reached the moat two days later, Confederate forces began to evacuate.[72]

In the meantime, soldiers continued to die—and not always from wounds. Private Tony Snipe died on September 4 in the regimental hospital of fever, which he contracted while on duty at Morris Island from drinking "bad water," according to his widow, Betsey or Beck Brown Snipe. Until Private Snipe's death, Tony and Beck Snipe had been together since they married about fifteen years before the raid.[73]

On or about September 6, General Terry led the final Union assault against Battery Wagner. He was determined not to replicate the July 18 slaughter. Because Tubman had debriefed freedom seekers coming from behind enemy lines, he learned that a number of Confederates had already fled Battery Wagner, and partly based on their information he had sketches made of the fortification for his officers before the assault. Colonel Montgomery's brigade, which of course included the 2nd South Carolina Volunteers, was once again in reserve, detailed by General Terry to occupy a trench south of Beacon House before daybreak.[74]

Captain Brayton wrote to his father on September 9 that the bombardment of Fort Sumter and Batteries Wagner and Gregg was finally complete. The Union Army had finished it off by bombarding Battery Wagner—it was the strongest earthwork Captain Brayton had ever seen, stronger than Fort Sumter even—for two consecutive days. According to an official

military report by General Beauregard, their twenty-four-hour "extraordinary fire" made Battery Wagner so hot the Confederate forces could not
stay there. Confederate forces evacuated Batteries Wagner and Gregg, leaving behind twenty heavy guns and a large quantity of ammunition after
realizing the guns could not be effectually spiked nor the magazines deton-
ated. The Confederacy lost 641 men between July 10 and September 7; the
United States had lost 2,318, with the heaviest losses on July 10 and 18. After
fifty-eight days of "hard labor" and tremendous "loss of life," the US Army
controlled all of Morris Island.[75]

As we learn from the pension files, the 2nd South Carolina Volunteers
made many sacrifices in the taking of Battery Wagner. Private Nicholas
sustained a wound on the inside of his left leg while on detail constructing
barricades shortly after the Union occupied Battery Wagner, which resulted in chronic rheumatism in his back and hips. Private Farbry Bowers,
who had grown up with Private Jeff Gray on Newport Plantation, testified
that Gray partially lost his hearing when they skirmished together against
the enemy and a shell exploded over Private Gray's forehead, a fragment
striking him on the left side of his forehead. Private James Shields testified
for Private Jack Morton that the day after the Union captured Battery
Wagner, about a hundred men of the 2nd South Carolina Volunteers
and soldiers from the 54th Massachusetts were detailed to move a three-
hundred-pound cannon, some pushing it, others pulling it "with ropes
on timber wheels." Privates Shields and Morton had grown up together
on adjoining plantations, Shields on Newport Plantation and Morton on
Bonny Hall Plantation, enlisted in the army together, and were detailed together. Captain James Carver was commanding the soldiers as they pulled
the cannon when the lookout called for them to cover from Confederate
shells shot from Fort Johnson. Private Abraham Grant later testified that
"to cover" meant to "lay down." Private Morton and Private Grant sheltered under the gun from the blast. But the butt of the gun went up and
the muzzle came down, crushing Private Morton's head and torso underneath; both Private Morton's upper and lower jaws were broken and his
entire body was bruised, including internal bleeding, and as a result his eyes
permanently protruded from their sockets. The big gun crushed Private
Grant's ankle and left side when it fell. Both soldiers were treated at the
regimental hospital.[76]

Private Harry Mack died on September 26, 1863. Privates John Proctor and Friday Hamilton testified that Private Mack became ill from drinking "bad water" in August 1863, the period when the 2nd South Carolina Volunteers was on fatigue duty constructing entrenchments, fortifications, and breastworks, and sleeping in the trenches on Morris Island. The disease worsened and he died, leaving behind his wife, Bina Hamilton Mack, whom he had married in 1855 on Parker's Place, their five-year-old daughter, Hagar Mack, and his elderly in-laws, Minus and Hagar Hamilton.[77]

****

Although the Union still did not yet occupy Fort Sumter, it was within striking distance of Fort Moultrie and the other Confederate fortifications on Sullivan's Island and, now, closer than ever to Charleston. Brayton thought they would soon control what was left of Fort Sumter, a "mere mass of masonry" after Union shells reduced its tall vertical walls to rubble. The Union assessed it as being "defenseless, battered, and played out" and judged that it could never be repaired or rearmed. All the Confederate Army could do was to arm it with a small force. Confederate forces did just that, refashioning the rubble of Fort Sumter into a new, smaller fort, manned by a garrison. Captain Brayton wrote the Union would likely have taken possession of Fort Sumter by the time his father received his letter. He was very proud of what the Union Army had already achieved.[78]

The US Navy, which Brayton had described as the "biggest pack of cowardly skunks" he knew, continued to be the object of his ire. He wrote to his father that the Union would already control Charleston had the US Navy a "tenth part" the "pluck and perseverance" of the army. Many blamed Admiral Dahlgren for being overly cautious and avoiding his charge to seize Charleston after the destruction of Fort Sumter. The navy could have saved "many brave lives" of US Army soldiers had they given the army cover from Confederate shells and struck the final blow. Brayton believed that the navy was in "mortal terror" of advancing and fighting when it had been fired at by rifled guns. The Confederates therefore maintained control of Charleston. He trusted General Gillmore to push forward to take the city as fast as was possible.[79]

With his exhausted and depleted forces around Charleston reduced, Gillmore did not have the capacity to mount an overland assault on Charleston. Forts Moultrie and Sumter, as well as Charleston, the bastion of secession, remained in Confederate control. More delays by and infighting among US military leadership gave the Confederates time to build new fortifications on James Island (across from US-occupied Morris Island), remount guns from Fort Sumter on Sullivan's Island, and interlace the obstructions protecting Charleston Harbor with torpedoes. US forces moved from Port Royal closer to Morris Island and Folly Island, where General Terry's headquarters were located, then into Florida. Union forces would not finish the job of taking Charleston until February 1865, a year and a half later.[80]

Major Corwin, meanwhile, returned to his regiment, the 2nd South Carolina Volunteers, after being absent sixty-four days, forty-four of them without leave and twenty with leave. Upon his return, he reported to his commanding officer, saying that he had already reported to the commanding general, who had ordered him back to his regiment for duty. The adjutant general struck from the rolls the notation that Corwin was a deserter. Corwin's case was submitted to a board of inquiry, giving him the opportunity to explain why he left his regiment, went to Beaufort, and remained absent from his regiment for forty-four days without authority. Colonel Montgomery did not arrest or even reprimand Major Corwin at the time when he allegedly deserted his guns in Palatka, nor did he report him to Colonel Higginson, who was in command of the St. Johns expedition. Montgomery did not even censure him when he returned to the regiment after allegedly deserting on Morris Island. Moreover, he did not bring charges against Corwin for seven months after the first infraction at Palatka occurred. This leniency was a far cry from what Corporal William B. Howard of the 48th New York State Volunteers, Company F, wrote in his diary on June 28, 1863: "A soldier of the 2nd South Carolina Vol shot for desertion." A second soldier who deserted the 2nd South Carolina in March or April 1864, Hardtime White, was hanged in October.[81]

Privates Jack Wineglass, Andrew Wyatt, and July Osborne were honorably discharged from the US Army on the same day, September 30, 1863, at Morris Island. Privates Osborne and Wyatt were both Old Heads when they enlisted. Dr. Daniel D. Hanson, the surgeon of the 2nd South Carolina Volunteers, wrote on Osborne's discharge certificate that he was "doubtless between 50 and 60 years of age." The former field hand suffered from "lameness" and an "enfeebled constitution" resulting from old age and "previous hard usage" before enlistment, during enslavement. Private Wyatt suffered from similar ailments. Captain L. H. Markley, who commanded Private Wyatt's company, noted that he was over sixty and "doubtless broken down" before he enlisted. Then, Dr. Hanson added, he quickly became "unfit for duty" for sixty days before he was discharged. His comrade Private Edward Brown was also in sick call when he heard Private Wyatt complain to the regiment's doctor about pains in his back and side. Private Wyatt's discharge certificate stated that he took sick on July 9 with severe pain in his back and limbs, which was made worse by extreme fatigue.[82]

In contrast, Private Wineglass was still a teenager. He contracted rheumatism from hard marching and "camp exposure," sleeping on the damp ground, according to testimony given by his comrade Private Jackson Grant. Privates Grant and Wineglass had grown up together on Rose Hill, liberated themselves, and enlisted in the regiment together. Private Grant testified that Wineglass's dysentery, rheumatism, and asthma got worse during their duty on Morris Island. Second Lieutenant Andrew Hessel and Surgeon Hanson, both of the 2nd South Carolina, disagreed with Private Grant's assessment; Private Wineglass was discharged, according to his certificate of discharge, because he had a "defected articulation" of his knee joint, caused by an injury he had sustained seven years prior, when he was held in bondage. It made him appear as if he had "knock-knee." Dr. Hanson added that Private Wineglass's performance on drill and parade was "ludicrous and demoralizing to the command." His knee joint was so weak that he had to be carried in a "baggage wagon" on long marches. Thus, Private Jack Wineglass was "unfit for duty" when he enlisted and remained so for sixty days before he too was discharged.[83]

In early October 1863, Private James Sheppard was covering from a shell fired from Fort Johnson at Battery Wagner and attempting to get inside the bombproof shelter when he gashed his leg on a disabled cannon; he subsequently suffered from rheumatism. He stayed in the tent used as a hospital on the beach at Morris Island. After he was released, the captain removed Private Sheppard, whom Neptune Nicholas described as a "puny man," from active duty and assigned him to cook and wash for the regiment.[84]

Sina Bolze Young testified in June 1873 that she learned at the end of October 1863 from her uncle, Harry Robinson, that her husband, Private William Young, had been killed in action. Company G sergeant William Jones testified in September 1887 that he had known William and Sina Young "almost from their childhood," though they had grown up enslaved on Cypress Plantation and he on Rose Hill. He and Private Young were on fatigue duty when Young died from the explosion of a shell cutting off his leg. According to Private Jackson Grant, Young was "killed by explosion of one of our own shells." Privates Jack Aiken and Selam White were also present when Private Young was killed by friendly fire. Even though they had been enslaved across the Combahee River on Newport Plantation, they testified that they "knew all about him and his family even before the war." As best as Sina Young could remember, she and William Young had been married at Christmastime two or three years before she had learned that the war had broken out; people from adjoining plantations, like Newport and Rose Hill, attended. They had two children together, a girl named Flora, and a boy who died before his father was killed. Flora was three years old when her father died and left his young family behind. Sergeant William Jones helped to bury Young and sent word of Private Young's death to his wife.[85]

According to Corporal Friday Barrington, "bleak winds" off the ocean and drenching rains made the winter of 1863 through the early part of 1864 at Morris Island severe for the 2nd South Carolina Volunteers. Private William Hamilton described the weather as "extreme cold, frosty, and windy winter weather." Corporal Barrington was the Combahee veteran who had escaped enslavement before the raid, joined Colonel Montgomery before the 2nd South Carolina Volunteers was organized, and during the raid returned to Cypress Plantation to liberate his parents, his siblings, and the bondspeople who had been sold along with his parents decades before. He testified that his comrade Sergeant Edward Bennett, in Company D, suffered from exposure and contracted rheumatism from doing guard and picket duty and other duties "incidental to army service."[86]

The list goes on. Private Jim Simmons injured his foot while on picket duty one night in November 1863 when he could not see where he was walking and his left ankle hit a snag or stump. Private Jacob Campbell contracted lung disease and rheumatism, according to his comrade Private William Hamilton. In addition to the lacerations he suffered on his leg from running into a busted cannon in October 1863, Private James Sheppard contracted rheumatism from sleeping on the damp ground and exposure. Sergeant William Jones was "crippled up with rheumatism" by the winter of 1863–1864, according to Private Charles Nicholas, who grew up on adjoining Cypress Plantation. Sergeant Jones had been detailed to work as a carpenter at Morris Island. In addition, he served several months of picket duty after the Union took Battery Wagner. He developed rheumatism in his hands, arms, and legs, making it difficult for him to walk; when he was able, he walked with a limp. Private Frank Hamilton took sick with a "hacking cough," according to his comrade and childhood friend Private Jackson Grant. He was hospitalized in Beaufort in early 1864 but was never able to do "hard duty after he took that cold and cough."[87]

Private Andrew Harris was discharged from the US Army on December 2, 1863. His feet had been swollen since the regiment did hard marching in Darien in June 1863. In addition, he contracted a severe cold from exposure while on duty in the fall of 1863 and rheumatism set in. The cold caused his entire body to swell. When he was discharged, Old Head Private Harris had been "unfit for duty" for three months. Private Harris testified he could "do nothing, but sit" and "lie about." He could not march or do any duty because of the swelling in his feet and legs. Surgeon Daniel Hanson wrote that Private Harris was nearly fifty years old, well over the age of enlistment, and was disabled by "rheumatic lameness" and "edema" in his legs. Sergeant William Jones testified that he, Private Andrew Harris, Andrew's wife, Diana Deas Harris, and the Harrises' only surviving child had all been in bondage on Rose Hill Plantation when Colonel Montgomery steamed up there with the US gunboats. Sergeant Jones had known Diana Harris since she was a little girl; he had attended their wedding. They all came down the Combahee River with Colonel Montgomery together; he and Andrew Harris joined the army at the same time. But Private Harris "wasn't with the company very long," according to Sergeant Jones. He was sent to the hospital, then mustered out and sent back to Beaufort, where he and his wife lived.[88]

On January 29, 1864, the *John Adams* took the 2nd South Carolina back to Beaufort. Mingo White was the fireman aboard the steamer. After he recognized the familiar face of Private John Jones—White later testified that he had known Jones as a boy; both had grown up on Bonny Hall Plantation—he struck up a conversation with him. Jones must have told White that he was suffering from cold, cough, and pleurisy. Like several of the 2nd South Carolina Volunteers' soldiers, the illnesses they contracted on Morris Island would follow them for their entire lives. But they were proud of their service. Private Mingo Van Dross, who also contracted rheumatism from exposure and was hospitalized in March 1864, boasted many years later in his pension testimony that the 2nd South Carolina Volunteers had "won at Morris Island." Private Stephen Simmons celebrated the victory at Morris Island as well, though he complained that Colonel Montgomery had not allowed the Volunteers to "charge" because they were "green hands."[89]

★★★★★★★★

As the 2nd South Carolina fought for the freedom of others still enslaved, now more than a year after the Emancipation Proclamation had gone into effect, planters on the lower Combahee continued to seek compensation from the Confederate government for their losses. As noted, Charles T. Lowndes did not file for compensation from the state auditor. His neighbors William C. Heyward, Joshua Nicholls, and William L. Kirkland did. However, Lowndes did petition the South Carolina state Senate and House of Representatives on January 14, 1864, stating that he was the owner of a "valuable rice plantation on Combahee River in Colleton District and of a large gang of negro slaves were employed in the cultivation thereof." He had reported these assets to the local tax collector of St. Bartholomew's Parish for his 1862 taxes. Then, between the time he filed his 1862 tax return and when the taxes were due to be collected, a "raid was made by the public enemy"—that is, the US military—upon his property in June 1863. "Two hundred and thirty six of his negro slaves were taken possession of." They were "carried off by the public enemy" and never returned to his ownership. Lowndes claimed that he was "obliged to abandon" Oakland Plantation, its rice crop, and the enslaved laborers left there. Unlike his neighbors, he does not list the names of the 236 people who liberated themselves.[90]

Because his plantation was destroyed and the people he held in bondage "abducted," Lowndes thought he should be exempt from paying taxes. While he awaited a decision from the comptroller general, a tax execution was issued against him for $551.55. The comptroller general ordered the sheriff of Colleton County to stay the tax execution after Lowndes made a payment of $254.19. Lowndes appealed to the state Senate and House of Representatives, providing a receipt for the payment along with a letter from the sheriff. He thought himself entitled to get his money back and he wanted the remainder of his tax execution cancelled, all because of the loss of his plantation and his slaves in the raid. Though there is no evidence that Lowndes's request was granted, he evidently felt that it was worth a try.[91]

18

Charleston Siege

In late January 1864, following the campaigns against Morris Island, Fort Sumter, and Battery Wagner, General Gillmore moved on to St. Augustine. Colonel Montgomery's brigade, which of course included the 2nd South Carolina Volunteers and 54th Massachusetts, was transferred to Hilton Head under Brigadier General Alfred H. Terry's command. While Montgomery and the 2nd South Carolina left Charleston, Harriet Tubman stayed on Folly Island, where she had been since the end of the Morris Island campaign. She worked out of the quarters of General Terry, commander of the 7th Regiment of Connecticut Volunteer Infantry and of Morris and Folly Islands. General Terry's headquarters was transferred from Morris Island to Folly Island in January 1864 because of what Terry's biographer describes as "tidal conditions and sinking sand." Lieutenant George Garrison of the 55th Massachusetts and T. C. and Caroline Severance encountered Tubman on February 10, 1864. As mentioned, Garrison wrote home to his brother about Tubman's value to the US Army and her skill in gathering intelligence, adding that she had been on Folly Island for "some three months." Garrison had been unaware Tubman was on Folly Island until Caroline Severance told him so.[1]

Had Tubman been on Folly Island for three months, she would have arrived after the US Army took control of Battery Wagner and reduced Fort Sumter to rubble, and at the moment when Admiral Dahlgren was vacillating about using his warships to open up Charleston Harbor. Terry's intelligence showed that the Confederates had planted torpedoes across the mouth of the harbor for protection. By this point the US Army commanders saw Tubman as an indispensable spy and scout, and it's tempting to consider that General Gillmore or General Terry had sent Harriet Tubman to Folly Island to gather information about the location of the torpedoes, as she remembered locating the man who had planted them in the Combahee River before the raid. If so, Tubman also would have been involved in the US Army's strategy to seize Charleston. We can't be sure. Garrison's letter is the only evidence to date when she was at Folly Island—Tubman did not tell this part of the story of her war service in South Carolina to her biographers.

At the beginning of February, Colonel Montgomery and the 2nd South Carolina Volunteers may have separated briefly. Tubman may have remained on Folly Island, though we really don't know where she was after George Garrison met her on Folly Island in February 1864. The theater of war for the Department of the South had shifted to Florida, where General Gillmore had multiple goals: bring Florida under US control, revive trade along the Saint Johns River, recruit Black and white soldiers to the US Army, organize a regiment of white soldiers, and sever supply lines coming from east and south Florida to Confederate armies. Beginning on February 6, 5,500 Union soldiers commanded by Brigadier General Truman Seymour landed and began to advance into the Florida interior. Montgomery's brigade of Black regiments, the 1st North Carolina, the 8th Pennsylvania, and the 54th Massachusetts, were all part of the division. They moved southwest until February 20, toward the Florida, Atlantic, and Gulf Railroad, with the aim of destroying the railroad communication between east and west Florida. The 2nd South Carolina Volunteers were sent to Doctor's Lake and Green Cove, located on the west bank of the St. Johns River, to capture rebel pickets posted in the vicinity; the 54th Massachusetts went to Baldwin with two days' rations; two companies were ordered stationed in Jacksonville.[2]

After marching fifteen miles, General Seymour's troops met stiff Confederate resistance on February 20. The engagement that ensued, the Battle of Olustee, was part of the largest Civil War campaign in Florida and one of the deadliest for Black troops. Colonel Montgomery's brigade was part of the rear guard. Confederate infantry pickets fell back into their position in the pine woods three miles east of Olustee, which is located forty-five or fifty miles west of Jacksonville. At the start of the battle, the 7th Connecticut, under Colonel J. R. Hawley, were advanced as skirmishers. The Confederates allowed them to advance, and then drove them back a short distance, enabling the 7th Connecticut to form a semicircle around the Confederate lines. Running low on ammunition, the Confederates were exposed to concentric fire and had to retreat.[3]

The 7th New Hampshire and 8th US Colored Troops—the latter a Black regiment that had mustered in at Camp William Penn two months before but had not finished its training—came through the 7th Connecticut's middle. There they encountered four thousand Confederates, who flanked the Union troops. Despite their lack of preparedness, the 8th USCT double-quick marched a half mile in the direction of the battle sounds, loaded their guns, and went into battle. Many of the men were initially stunned by the firepower from Confederate units, which came from three sides and overlapped their lines; some initially curled up on the ground to shield themselves. In a short time, though, they recovered, stood their ground, and fired the guns they had not been trained yet how to use. They chose to die fighting the enslavers rather than to fall into the Confederacy's hands and certainly be reenslaved or killed.[4]

Meanwhile, the 7th New Hampshire fell back in chaos and confusion. The enemy closed in behind the retreating troops and engaged in a fierce close-range battle for three hours. Both the 8th USCT and the 7th New Hampshire were shattered by the unrelenting Confederate musketry. One-third of General Seymour's division fell, in large part because the 7th New Hampshire regiment was supposed to have the rear and the 8th USCT was not yet fully trained. The 7th New Hampshire's disorderly retreat left the 8th USCT without cover against enemy fire as it followed orders to retreat. Facing a storm of Confederate artillery, the inexperienced soldiers fell back behind Colonel Montgomery's brigade, which had pushed ahead from a distance of six miles. In the 8th USCT was Nelson Davis, who served under the name of Nelson Charles and married Harriet Tubman after the war. Tubman testified that she first became acquainted with Davis when he boarded at her "house in the town of Fleming Cayuga County, NY," but her testimony does not reveal whether or not she was present at the Battle of Olustee.[5]

From here, the battle devolved for the Union, which could not escape its dangerous position with its lines overlapping its flanks, exposed to concentric fire pressing on its middle. The 7th New Hampshire, 54th Massachusetts, and 1st North Carolina had managed to push the enemy back, but the US forces were exhausted, poorly conditioned, and outnumbered by five thousand Confederate troops that were advancing and threatening the Union's flanks and rear. Only when the Confederates ran low on ammunition could the 7th Connecticut regroup, giving General Seymour a chance to withdraw his men; they retreated with defiant and lusty cheers, though they were decisively beaten. Colonel Montgomery's brigade, the 54th Massachusetts, and the 1st North Carolina then went to work, halting the Confederates' surge and preventing the enemy from attacking a Union field hospital and devastating the Union flank. The 2nd South Carolina remained in the rear, guarding the main roads and fords to prevent the Confederates from flanking the federal troops.[6]

At the end of the fight, the Confederates had captured five pieces of US artillery and large numbers of small arms and chests of ammunition. General Seymour's forces were forced to leave large numbers of wounded Black soldiers on the battlefield. Lieutenant A. H. McCormick of the 2nd Florida Cavalry had announced to his unit that he wouldn't take any Black soldiers prisoner in this fight. Overall, the Union lost 1,861 men killed, wounded, or missing. Of the three Black regiments, the 8th USCT sustained the largest losses—49 soldiers killed, 188 wounded, and 73 missing. The expulsion of US forces in the Battle of Olustee put a pause on the US Army's efforts to control Florida. By the end of April 1864, General Terry was transferred to Gloucester Point, Virginia, to command the 1st Division of General Gillmore's Tenth Army Corps in the Army of the James. General Seymour praised Colonel Montgomery for commanding his brigade with "great personal intelligence and valor." On March 26, 1864, General Orders No. 44 officially organized the 2nd South Carolina Volunteers as the 34th Regiment of the United States Colored Troops.[7]

There were more losses in Florida. The *Harriet A. Weed* was destroyed on May 6, 1864. It had teamed up with a gunboat, the *Ottawa*, just as it had in the Combahee River Raid, to protect a stretch of the St. Johns River near Orange Mills, Florida. Two Confederate plunger-pattern torpedoes exploded under it as it passed over a sandbar in the river. At the time, the *Weed* had been towing a schooner and transporting three officers and twenty soldiers from the 3rd South Carolina Volunteers. It was "blown to atoms" and sank to the bottom of the river. Five US Army soldiers were killed instantly, five quartermaster crew members drowned, and two were badly wounded in the blast.[8]

★★★★★★★★

Back on Morris Island, the board of inquiry ruled on Major Corwin's court-martial on May 24, 1864. The only commissioned officer to testify for Corwin, Colonel Higginson, took the white officers' and Black 2nd South Carolina soldiers' side against Colonel Montgomery. (In contrast, at Private John E.

Webster's court-martial on June 5, 1863, three days after the Combahee River Raid, Tubman, Walter Plowden, and one additional freedom seeker testified for the prosecution against Webster, the former superintendent of contrabands who, as described previously, was accused of embezzling and eventually found guilty on three counts. In Beaufort and in the US-occupied Sea Islands, Black people, including Black women like Harriet Tubman, could testify in court against a white man and win.) In closing arguments, Major Corwin's counsel juxtaposed the "countenances" of five enlisted Black men, which included Sergeant Fulton McGuire, one of 2nd South Carolina's, and evidence of their "truth and intelligence" against Colonel Montgomery's "opinion." Corwin's counsel argued that the Black soldiers' "straight forward statements" were as much a contrast to Colonel Montgomery's "story" as the "contrast in the color of their skin and his."[9]

Major Corwin's counsel accused Montgomery of malice against his client and wondered at the boldness of court-martialing him months after the St. Johns expedition and the fight for Battery Wagner. Moreover, he pointed out, Montgomery had given Corwin positions of responsibility, such as command of the *Harriet A. Weed* during the Combahee River Raid, at Darien, and at Battery Wagner; now he was claiming that Corwin had deserted his guns. In his summation, Corwin's counsel went after Montgomery. Though his "boldness" and "dash" and that of his regiment were written about in all the northern papers, none of Montgomery's raids upon the southern coast, which showed his true "qualities," had been "shown to the world to their full extent." Corwin's counsel noted sarcastically that the burning of towns like Darien "[fell] in splendor before" the "courage" Montgomery displayed in court-martialing Major Corwin for deserting his guns aboard the steamer *General Meigs*, then testifying against him.[10]

Corwin's counsel presented a convincing case but lost. In January 1864 the judge advocate and president of the court found Corwin guilty on all four charges; he was dismissed from the military of the United States and forfeited his salary and pension. But two months later, on March 24, the verdict was annulled by the judge advocate general on technical grounds. Major Corwin went back to duty in the 2nd South Carolina, his salary and pension restored.[11]

★★★★★★★★

On May 4, 1864, the Charleston Light Dragoons were ordered to move out to Virginia. By then, the Dragoons were one company in a brigade

comprising the 4th, 5th, and 6th South Carolina Cavalry regiments commanded by Major General J. E. B. Stuart. Colonel Robert R. Jeffords, who
had brutally slaughtered Black refugees on Hutchinson Island and who
was the man Combahee planters wished had been there to protect their
plantations during the Combahee raid, commanded the 5th South Carolina
Cavalry. Mary Miller Withers Kirkland recorded in her notes, which may
have served as a diary, that her husband, "Mr. K.," and her brother Randolph
Withers, whom she referred to affectionately as "Tanny," left for Virginia
on May 6, 1864. Withers had joined the Charleston Light Dragoons in
November 1863. In the same month, Charlotte Forten ended her tenure as
a teacher on St. Helena Island; grief over her father's death made her unable
to work. [12]

After days of hard marching on very meager rations, the Charleston Light
Dragoons rode down Atlee's Station Road toward Haw's Shop and into
battle on May 28, 1864. Haw's Shop was an inconspicuous and nondescript
settlement strategically positioned at the intersection of five roads. John
Haw's farm, called Oak Grove, and shop, which ceased operations during
the war, were located within the settlement. One of the feeder roads led
seven miles east to Atlee's Station, home of the Virginia Central Railroad,
and then to Richmond, capital of the Confederacy. The Battle of Haw's
Shop was a small part of General Ulysses S. Grant's Overland or Wilderness
Campaign against Robert E. Lee's Army of Northern Virginia. It had devastating consequences for the 4th South Carolina Cavalry. [13]

Lee moved south to Atlee's Station to protect the railroad by putting his
troops between Grant's troops and the rail line, crossing the Pamunkey River
at Hanovertown. Union brigadier general Henry E. Davies Jr. and his brigade moved into Haw's Shop from Brockenborough and conducted reconnaissance west of Atlee's Station. Simultaneously, Confederate major general
Wade Hampton and his forces, which included the 5th South Carolina
Cavalry under the command of Colonel Robert J. Jeffords and the 4th
South Carolina Cavalry under the command of Colonel Benjamin Huger
Rutledge, followed. Upon arriving at Haw's Shop, US forces posted pickets
west on Atlee's Station Road. One cavalry unit continued west on Atlee's
Station Road and met General Hampton's forces. A "sharp fight" ensued, as
the commanding officer described it in the general report about the battle;
it lasted seven hours, amplified as each side sent in more troops to reinforce
their respective flanks. The Union drove the Confederates as far west as

possible until they reached a fork in the road, where the Confederates had taken a stand and would not be budged. Though Hampton had originally held Rutledge's men in reserve, the 5th South Carolina and 4th South Carolina were sent in to reinforce the 1st and 7th Virginia on the north side of Atlee's Station Road and the 2nd Virginia and 3rd Virginia straddling Atlee's Station Road and occupying a position to its south.[14]

The long ride to Virginia on poor-quality saddles—the horses were accustomed to being mounted with sporting saddles—left a large number of the 4th South Carolina's horses out of commission and reduced the number of men. This did not dampen the cavalry's enthusiasm. First, CSA captain Thomas Pinckney positioned them in the woods at the bottom of a hill in front of a ditch. While this shielded them from the full impact of the Union cavalry's artillery. On the other, it exposed their right flank. They dismounted their horses, took their stand, and fought on foot, pausing to reload their long Enfield rifles like mounted infantry soldiers. They held their own, bravely standing up to the Union cavalry, which also fought dismounted until its reinforcements turned the tide.[15]

The absence of one Confederate commander, Brigadier General Matthew C. Butler—he did not arrive in time for the battle—and the fact that Colonel Rutledge remained back with the horse handlers ruptured the chain of command and caused confusion when it mattered most. After the Virginia cavalry regiments withdrew, the South Carolina cavalry should have retreated also, but it never received orders to do so. Without clear command, the inexperienced soldiers of the 4th South Carolina were flanked on their right and left, almost surrounded. The Charleston Light Dragoons, stuck on the other side of the ditch, "stood still, to be shot down in their tracks," Mary Boykin Chesnut, William L. Kirkland Jr.'s wife's cousin, wrote in her diary. They gallantly, or imprudently, maintained their positions on the battlefield too long, until Colonel Hampton himself brought them out.[16]

The orderly retreat became a rout, because the Union cavalry had flanked the 4th South Carolina Cavalry almost to the extent of encircling them. In the stampede to get out of the ditch through US fire, some riders were thrown from their horses; others were shot down at close range. One man, Sergeant Benjamin F. Huger, was wounded and left behind until his men, the Charleston Light Dragoons, rode back into the thick of the fight and brought him out. Their withdrawal left the 5th South Carolina's flank exposed, leading the unit to retreat also, during which Colonel Jeffords was wounded. Demoralized after witnessing their commander being carried from the field, the 5th South Carolina joined the 4th in rushing to the rear. General Hampton was only able to rally his troops once they arrived at Cold Harbor. The 4th South Carolina lost 127 out of its 300 men. The Charleston Light Dragoons, in particular, had the highest losses, and had finally proved their mettle. It was no longer accurate to refer to them, as Edward Laight Wells did, as the "kid-gloved company."[17]

The Virginia cavalry described the South Carolinians as "new issue" and "new recruits," because they were new to the theater of war. This was the Charleston Light Dragoons' first time under fire. Mary Kirkland spent three weeks of "dark and anxious days, hours, and nights" agonizing over the safety of those she held most dear. She described this as the "most heart-felt misery" she had experienced in her "*whole life*" and prayed fervently that God would spare her the "greatest calamity that could befall" her and bring her beloved husband back safely. The South Carolina Cavalry's lack of battle-readiness and battle experience contributed to what one Union soldier described as a "perfect slaughterhouse." The 5th South Carolina and a portion of the 4th South Carolina, which was still straddling Atlee's Station Road, should have retreated, but they stood their ground, and despite their lack of battle-readiness held it until Union reinforcements overwhelmed them. Major General Hampton rode out and finally ordered their retreat, which turned into a rout. The scattering of their "queer bundles of clothes" through the pines on the battlefield—they had not followed the directive to dispense with their immense baggage before the march to Virginia—was one symptom of the 4th South Carolina's inexperience in battle. When the dust settled, they had suffered significant losses. The 5th South Carolina Cavalry had one soldier killed, twenty-seven wounded, and six captured. Union major general Phillip Henry Sheridan praised the 4th and 5th South Carolina Cavalry: "These Carolinians fought very gallantly in their first fight."[18]

One of the Confederate captains wrote about the Virginia campaign: "We who are just from North and South Carolina have just begun to realize the war." The Kirkland/Withers family would experience war in a very tragic and personal way. Randolph Withers wrote to his father the morning after the Battle at Haw's Shop that his regiment of the Charleston Light Dragoons had met and engaged the enemy. His brother-in-law William L. Kirkland Jr. had been one of the couriers riding into US fire to tell the Dragoons'

2nd Regiment to retreat when he was shot by a Minié ball through his left knee, and his leg had to be amputated above the knee. Randolph Withers saw Kirkland at the hospital and found him in considerable pain but grateful to be alive. Rawlins Lowndes also visited Kirkland in the hospital. Rawlins Lowndes's father, Charles Tidyman Lowndes, was William Kirkland's neighbor on the Combahee River; both Kirkland's Rose Hill Plantation and Lowndes's Oakland Plantation had of course been destroyed in the Combahee River Raid. Withers and Kirkland's unit went into battle with thirty-nine men; just under half were killed, captured, or wounded. Withers thanked God that he was not one of them. But he felt deeply for his brother-in-law and sister. Turner MacFarland wrote in a letter to her childhood friend Kate Withers (Mary Miller Withers Kirkland's sister): "All around—what suffering! Wounded and dying on every side," now even at the gates of the South's wealthiest families. Starvation also stared them in the face. Turner MacFarland prayed: "God have mercy on us."[19]

When the Witherses received the news that William Lennox Kirkland Jr. had been wounded in action, they telegrammed dear friends in Virginia, the MacFarland family. Bad news traveled quickly: the MacFarland family knew even before Turner MacFarland received Kate Withers's telegram that Kate's brother-in-law was in Seabrooks Hospital in Richmond. The MacFarlands sent word to authorities, begging for permission for Kirkland to come to their home in Richmond so they could nurse him and stand in for his loved ones, who were so far away. The day after the amputation of his left leg, Kirkland was removed from the military hospital and taken to the MacFarlands' home. Back in Camden, South Carolina, Judge Withers continued to take care of his son-in-law's family and handle his affairs. Kirkland's rice—34½ barrels of whole rice and 3 barrels of middling rice from Rose Hill—sold for $6,481.37.[20]

The outlook for his recovery initially seemed promising, and Kirkland sent word he did not want his wife to come to Virginia to be with him. Instead, Mary Kirkland sent her husband a pair of her beautiful gloves as a keepsake. He also enjoyed hearing Turner McFarland, who had known Mary in childhood, play music and read newspapers sent to him from his family and friends in South Carolina.[21]

Two days later, Kirkland's condition began to deteriorate despite his receiving the best medical care and the loving attention of the MacFarland family and of his brother-in-law, Randolph Withers. During the Civil War, the cure was often as damaging as the injury. Captain Carlos Tracy wrote to Mary's father, Kirkland's father-in-law, that Kirkland's "case was utterly hopeless." Kirkland fought off gangrene, but then pyemia—blood poisoning caused by bacteria released into Kirkland's bloodstream from his wound and amputation—set in. He had been "sinking for some time."[22]

Kirkland's stepfather, Joshua Nicholls, was clearly not in close touch. After receiving the news of Kirkland's injury, Nicholls wrote to Judge Withers that he had heard Kirkland was doing well. He went on to describe his current situation, with his wife dead since 1862 and his plantation destroyed. After the Combahee River Raid, Nicholls was living in a small house, which he described as a "cooter shell"; he was plagued by the mosquitoes, heat, and fever that the sickly season wrought, and had gone back to teaching at a school for "unruly boys." Nicholls asked Judge Withers to write to him if Kirkland improved. He wrote next to Mary Kirkland telling her that he wanted to go to Richmond to nurse his stepson. He was certain Kirkland would want his stepfather at his bedside at this time. Nicholls asked Mary Kirkland if her father, Judge Withers, could use his connections to secure a pass for Nicholls to travel to Virginia. Judge Withers had already sent Monroe, his trusted slave, to nurse his son-in-law.[23]

One day after Nicholls had penned his letter to Judge Withers, Randolph Withers wrote to his sister Mary that William L. Kirkland Jr. had died on June 19, 1864, at age thirty-six. Kirkland's last words were for his wife, according to Tanny, saying that he loved her more than a woman could be loved and he longed to marry her again in heaven. He was laid to rest at the MacFarlands' enclosure. Mary Kirkland wrote in her notes that she feared God had laid his hand "so heavily upon" her that she was "too crushed ever to rise." She prayed for the strength to do her duty for her children's sake and for God's healing balm to make her whole again.[24]

Other Combahee planters had their tragedies as well. The Middleton family lost Oliver Hering Middleton Jr., who had enlisted in the Charleston Light Dragoons in January 1863 at seventeen years of age, making him one of the youngest men in the company. And, as noted earlier, his father's Launch Plantation at Tar Bluff was destroyed by the Union Army during the Combahee River Raid.[25]

Less than one month after Kirkland's death, Eliza C. Middleton Huger Smith wrote to Mary Kirkland. Though Eliza and Mary Kirkland did not know each other, the Smiths and the Kirklands had been neighbors on the east bank of the lower Combahee River for decades. As we've seen, Cypress and Oakland Plantations separated Smithfield from Rose Hill. And the enslaved people on Smithfield supposedly turned the Black soldiers away on the day of the raid. Eliza Smith wrote that God in his infinite wisdom had chosen to "divide her life." Eliza "knew how to sympathize" with her; she herself had been left with four small children in 1851, at age twenty-seven, when her husband died. She reminded Mary that her children were now her "sacred duties." And "every unselfish effort" she made for them would be a sacred "offering" to her beloved husband's memory.[26]

In his pension file, Jackson Grant testified in October 1896 that William L. Kirkland Jr. had been "killed in the Confederate Army." Grant may have tried to contact the planter family who formerly held him, his family, and his first wife, Dorcus, in bondage, possibly to testify to his age in his pension application. He seemed to have kept up with the Kirkland family's whereabouts after the war, testifying that Kirkland's "widow and son and daughter" had still been living in Camden, South Carolina, nine years earlier. If he did, he would have learned that the bereaved Mary Kirkland took to her bedroom after receiving the tragic news of her husband's death and only reemerged once in the rest of her long life.[27]

★★★★★★★★

Though battle tore apart the Kirkland and Middleton families, Black soldiers in the 34th Regiment were reunited with their wives. William Hamilton, Mariah Bartley's first cousin, testified in his pension file that Mariah "came to" her husband, Anthony Bartley, when the 34th returned to Beaufort. While the regiment was stationed in Beaufort in June 1864, couples who had been married in "slave fashion" while in bondage on the Combahee rice plantations were lawfully joined. Saxton had issued General Orders No. 7 in August 1862, requiring all Black men in the Department of the South's territory to support only the wives to whom they were lawfully married. Men with multiple wives were to lawfully marry the woman with whom they had children in a ceremony performed by a minister of the Gospel. Moreover, Colonel Montgomery had issued an order that all men living with their wives had to be married to them. He mandated that the couples must be married under US law and not just in slave fashion.[28]

No marriage of an enslaved couple was legally binding before the Civil War. In addition, with this order, Montgomery may have been forcing men living with other men's wives, or men whose wives were living with other women's men, to get married. Not all of the freedom seekers who were married before the Combahee River Raid got on the boat with their husband or wife. When Cuffie Bolze testified for his comrade Neptune Nicholas's widow, Betsy, he remembered (as noted earlier) that Neptune Nicholas had not been married before he married Betsy Singleton Simmons. But he had had a child with a woman named Bella before the war and never lived with her after it was over. Betsy herself had been married before, to Shiloh Simmons, whom she married in Beaufort after freedom, in 1865 or 1866. However, Shiloh had been married before, sort of. According to Cuffie, Shiloh Simmons "got" a woman named Martha "out of the window one night and took her to Beaufort," then lived with Martha for a while. To complicate matters, Martha was already married to another soldier in the 2nd South Carolina Volunteers, William Hamilton. Martha may have gone back to Hamilton; she died in Beaufort. Betsy must have been nonplussed about Martha and Shiloh; she testified that he was "much older than I, so I just left him and came back here" to Green Pond at the end of the war, and there she met Neptune Nicholas; they married in 1869. Freedom seekers had a host of new options presenting themselves—choices that had not existed in bondage and now did not require sanction by anyone except the willing parties. Some, like Betsy and Shiloh, chose to exercise them.[29]

Anthony Bartley remembered that prior to Colonel Montgomery's order, some of the 2nd South Carolina Volunteer's soldiers lived with their wives just as they had during enslavement—without being "officially married" to them. Everyone who was cohabitating was supposed to come before Brigadier General Saxton and be married by clergy in order to make their unions "valid." Reverend Homer H. Moore, chaplain of the 34th Regiment USCT, married Anthony and Mariah Bartley, who had already been married "long before the war" on Rose Hill Plantation. Anthony Bartley's comrades Jackson Grant, Friday Hamilton, and Moses Simmons were all present when the Bartleys were joined "under the flag." Moses Simmons testified that he was "right there" at their wedding and the "flag waved over [him]."[30]

According to their marriage certificate, on June 17, 1864, Anthony Bartley and Mariah Haywood had renewed their marriage vows, "covenanting to live together as husband and wife after God's holy ordinance of Marriage" until separated by death. Colonel James Montgomery and Brigadier General Rufus Saxton signed the marriage certificate along with Moore. Mariah Bartley sent the certificate to Washington after Anthony

Bartley's death to prove she was Anthony's legal widow and had the right to claim a widow's pension. After the Pension Bureau sent the marriage certificate back, Mariah Bartley deposited it at Captain Shaffer's store in Walterboro so that the rats would not eat it.[31]

Lucy Lee Smith claimed that Reverend Moore had also married her and Richard Smith "under the flag" after Colonel Montgomery issued his order. A fire at her mother's home had destroyed her marriage certificate, Lucy Smith later told the special examiner, and she therefore did not possess the indisputable written proof required for approval of her widow's pension claim. Cuffie Bolze, Mingo Van Dross, and Andrew Nicholas testified that they had been present at the ceremony. Lucy Smith testified that several of her husband's comrades in Company G, Neptune Nicholas, Jackson Grant, Charles Nicholas, and Moses Simmons, had been present as well. Her brother Edward Brown testified that "Capt. Moore" had married them, though he did not get the date right. Unfortunately for Lucy Smith, none of this would be enough for the Pension Bureau.[32]

Richard Smith and Lucy Lee may have been married on the same day, possibly even in the same ceremony, as Anthony and Mariah Bartley's remarriage. Reverend Moore must have conducted a mass wedding of multiple soldiers and their brides—some witnesses testified that as many as thirty-five couples were married—on June 17, 1864, at Pigeon Point. According to Jackson Grant, he and his wife, Dorcus, were "among the numbers" and were given a marriage certificate, which Grant duly presented to the pension official after the war. Also married that day were Ned and Daphne Snipe; Frank and Tenah Hamilton, who first married by slave ceremony on Rose Hill before the war; Moses and Christie Ann Simmons; and Harry and Flora Robinson, who married before the war on Cypress Plantation. Anthony Bartley remembered that he and his wife, Mariah, were "officially married at the same time" as the Snipes. The US government's recognition of their unions meant to Black men serving in the military that the federal government would protect their wives and children. According to historian Tera Hunter, "marriage under the flag" was one of the "first 'rites' of freedom" exercised by "newly freed" Blacks. The formerly enslaved couples no longer had to vow to stay together "'til buckra do us part."[33]

Death did part Balaam Burnett and his first wife, Rose Middleton Burnett (who, as noted previously, was also Wally Garrett's sister). Rose died in Beaufort while Balaam was serving in the military.[34]

★★★★★★★★

Harriet Tubman may have arrived in Florida around the same time the 2nd South Carolina Volunteers was sent there in early February 1864. Either General Gillmore, whose headquarters moved to Fernandina, or Dr. Henry O. Marcy, the Department of the South's medical director, may have sent for Tubman and brought her to Fernandina to treat Black soldiers during a dysentery epidemic. Tubman told her biographer Emma Telford that "dey was dyin' off like sheep" when she arrived; she cured them with roots growing near the water that had made the men sick.[35]

Dr. Esther Hawks, whose husband was the surgeon for the 35th Regiment, 3rd South Carolina Volunteers, saw Tubman in Florida. Hawks wrote in her diary on May 29 about meeting "Moses" or "'Aunt Harriet' as we call her here." Marcy came to Dr. Hawks asking for help with a "pretty *white* colored girl" named Priscilla. The young woman had at one point been taken to New York, where she continued to be held in bondage. Once she arrived in Fernandina, Tubman was called, found Priscilla, learned her story, then told Dr. Marcy about her. He promised to find a safe home for the young woman among his friends in the North. And he asked Dr. Hawks to allow the girl to live with her until he went back north, when he would take her with him to his northern friends. We don't know what happened to Priscilla, nor do we know how long Tubman stayed in Fernandina. Marcy also became known for treating soldiers with dysentery in Charleston and Florida.[36]

In the meantime, we also don't know what happened to Hector Fields, my great-great-great-grandfather. According to his military service record, Hector deserted his regiment, 34th Regiment, Company C, on August 1, 1864. Though it was recorded on this date, Hector may have deserted a short while before the 34th Regiment was ordered back to Florida. He did not go with them.[37]

When the 34th Regiment returned to Jacksonville at the end of July 1864, Colonel Montgomery allowed the soldiers to bring their wives. Cuffie Bolze testified that his comrade Charles Nicholas had been "courting" his fiancée, Hagar, since they were all held in bondage on Cypress Plantation, before he and Nicholas enlisted in the army. After Nicholas wrote a letter to Hagar, she came to him in Jacksonville and lived with him in camp until the 34th Regiment mustered out. Lucy Lee Smith testified that she "followed the Army" with her fiancé, Richard Smith

Jr., to Hilton Head, South Carolina, and to Fernandina and Jacksonville, Florida.[38]

Like Lucy Smith, Daphne Jackson Powell Snipe followed her husband, Ned Snipe, and Company G to Hilton Head and Jacksonville. Peggy Moultrie Simmons Brown testified that the regiment was a "long time in Florida." She went down to Jacksonville to be with her husband, Edward Brown, and stayed with him for five months. Relia Barnwell Middleton went with her husband, William Middleton, when the "Yankees" took him to Beaufort, then to Fernandina and Palatka, Florida (even though the 2nd South Carolina was only in Palatka in February–March 1863), finally to Jacksonville. She testified that she was with Middleton when "Cunnel Montgomery came to camp." Montgomery had greeted and talked with her. While she knew his name, she explained to the pension official that she could not tell him all the names of her husband's other officers because she could not read. But Relia offered the pension officer the opportunity to ask her whatever he wanted. She would tell him and give him "white folk proof."[39]

Tubman had used her own money—some of the $200 that the federal government paid her for "Services as Scout in the Military Department of South Carolina" during the war—to establish a washhouse in Beaufort for women like Mariah Bartley, Relia Middleton, Daphne Snipe, Lucy Smith, and Hagar Nicholas, who lived in camp with their husbands. There they earned money to help support their families so that they would not be a burden on the government. But while Tubman was in Florida, a regiment of Union soldiers took over the washhouse and used it as shelter. She was never compensated for the money she used to build it.[40]

★★★★★★★★

Colonel James Montgomery resigned his commission in the 34th US Colored Troops on September 23, 1864, because of chronic asthma. A little more than a month later, on October 25, 1864, a Boston teacher named Elizabeth Botume was commissioned by the New England Freedmen's Aid Society to join "Gideon's Band." General Rufus Saxton sent Botume's papers directly to her; she traveled from Boston to New York, where she boarded the steamer *Arago* to Charleston—now of course in Union possession. From Charleston she traveled first to Hilton Head and then to Beaufort with Catherine Porter Noyes, another female teacher, who was from Philadelphia. Noyes wrote to her sister Nelly that they had a "miserable" trip. First, the *Arago* left New York during a terrible storm and had to pause its travel for several hours because of very thick fog. The sea was extremely rough their first night, causing the steamer to dip and pitch so much that Noyes felt as if they were being dragged through the water. Almost all of the women and many of the men aboard suffered from seasickness.[41]

Though this was the two teachers' first tour of duty with the Port Royal Experiment, there were others on the trip who had previously served in the military or worked among the freedom seekers as teachers and superintendents. They had returned north for a rest and now were heading back down to South Carolina to resume their service. Among them were Major Willard Saxton (who served as aide-de-camp to his older brother, Brigadier General Rufus Saxton), along with his wife and their baby, and Dr. Henry K. Durant, acting assistant surgeon of the US Army, who had been in charge of the Contraband Hospital in Beaufort, and his wife. Because they were traveling with the military governor, Major Saxton, and his family, Botume and Noyes may have received better treatment than most women. Botume would have agreed with Laura Towne that women traveling alone and without a military companion received very little favor from the steamer's purser or steward. After arriving in Hilton Head, Botume, Noyes, Major Saxton and his family, and a number of troops transferred to a smaller riverboat to continue the journey to Beaufort. Botume taught school at Old Fort Plantation on Port Royal. Old Fort was, of course, where the federal government had resettled freedom seekers who liberated themselves in the Combahee River Raid more than a year earlier.[42]

A few years after she had left Port Royal, Botume wrote in her memoir that she had seen nothing but "Negroes, negroes, negroes" when she arrived; they "hovered" around her "like bees in a swarm." The freedom seekers sat, stood, and laid down on their backs with their faces turned up to the sun, occupying every doorstep, box, and barrel as far as the eye could see. They remained destitute, dressed in cast-off clothing, such as soldiers' coats. For garments they were still making do with what little they had or could find, such as fastening crocus bagging together, stitching together pieces of old carpeting, cutting armholes in blankets, tying pants with pieces of rope, and using sailcloth for head ties. To Botume, their appearance was "grotesque."[43]

Yet she chose to minister to the Combahee refugees, because Dr. Marvin Manville Marsh of the US Sanitary Committee considered them the "most degraded" of all the freedpeople. He told Botume he thought they were "the connecting link between 'human being' and the 'brute' creation." His attitude shows that even some of the abolitionists who had left their families and given up their comfortable lives to live and work among freedpeople in Beaufort, Port Royal, and the Sea Islands could not hide their prejudiced attitudes toward Black people. This included female teachers who themselves broke conventions. In time, Botume realized that she had come to teach the freedom seekers, and she committed herself to doing so. Their eagerness to learn made them less "grotesque" than Botume initially judged. Abiding need existed despite almost two years of northern philanthropy and federal government rations. Northern philanthropists could not fathom the depths of it unless they saw it for themselves.[44]

By the time Botume arrived at Old Fort, only a seawall with trees remained of Fort Frederick, which had been built by the British in 1733. (That fort also represented the first use of tabby—concrete made from oyster shells—as a building material.) For her first trip out to Old Fort, Botume rode in an ambulance. Along the way she passed a settlement of Combahee refugees that the freedom seekers called "Mon'gomery Hill." Located just outside of Beaufort, it consisted of a "collection of low buildings" on level ground, without the "slightest perceptible elevation," according to Botume. The Combahee refugees who lived at Montgomery Hill came out to greet Botume, asking how she was, bowing to her, and inquiring about her family. Then she proceeded to the Old Fort Plantation house, which was to be her future home. The Smith family had fled Old Fort Plantation during the "Great Skedaddle." The formerly enslaved had removed every stick of furniture from the main house. Subsequently, the US Army had used it as a barracks. A confluence of abandonment, neglect, and abuse resulted in the low, two-story mansion looking like a "perfect old rathole"; it was "well ventilated in every direction," likely by missing windowpanes and shutters. This is how Catherine Noyes Porter described it in a letter she wrote to her sister when she and Botume returned in November 1869 to Old Fort from a furlough.[45]

The old plantation was nonetheless "perfectly situated," according to Porter. A bend in the Broad River stretched half a mile in front of the plantation house, providing a picturesque view of Union gunboats afloat in the broad arm of the sea. An avenue of magnolias bordered by Spanish bayonets, which got their name from the sharp pointed leaves topped with six-part bell-shaped flowers drooping downward, led from the Broad River to the main house. A croquet pitch separated the Old Fort Plantation house from the river. The plantation was nestled on sixty acres of live oaks and water oaks, their boughs, as always, draped with Spanish moss that hung dank and heavy after rain. The quarters for the house slaves had been in outbuildings located near the kitchen and laundry; the small row of slave quarters where the field slaves had lived stretched out diagonally a short distance from the main house. Blacks who worked for the teachers and superintendents now lived in the house slaves' quarters, and those who had remained on Old Fort after "Gun Shoot at Bay Point" inhabited the field slaves' quarters. Colonel Higginson's headquarters, and the 1st South Carolina Volunteers' camp, was located at Old Fort between November 1862 and February 1863. General Saxton had, as described earlier, hosted a huge gathering of Black soldiers, their commanders and families, and northern volunteers at his Emancipation Day Celebration in Old Fort's live oak grove on January 1, 1863.[46]

The Old Fort school lay beyond the Sea Island cotton fields and live oak grove. Botume remembered catching a glimpse of the freedom children crowding the school's open piazza. They infused the primitive wooden building, perched on palmetto posts two or three feet off the ground, with life. From a distance they looked to Botume like a "flock of jays and blackbirds" quarreling, but they scattered as soon as they saw her. She found that her one-room schoolhouse had no partitions and that the walls were either unplastered or made of planks. However, the glazed windows made the schoolhouse an upgrade compared to the makeshift schoolrooms on the Sea Island plantations at the beginning of the Port Royal Experiment. It also had heavy wooden shutters and was furnished with wooden benches for the students, a tall pine desk for the teacher, a blackboard, and a large wood-burning stove to take the chill off on cold mornings. It may have been the first school built specifically for Blacks in the state of South Carolina, erected with funds sent to General Saxton by the Ladies' Freedmen's Aid Society in England.[47]

After the war, Tubman said about the freedom seekers with whom she had spent time in Beaufort: "Why der language down dar in de far South is jus' as different from ours in Maryland as you can tink." Tubman, as noted, could not understand Blacks in Beaufort and the Sea Islands when they spoke. And they could not understand her: "Dey laughed when dey heard me talk. An' I could not understand dem, no how."

Tubman was not alone in her views. Just about all of the northern volunteers who came in contact with freedom seekers in Port Royal, the Sea

Islands, and Combahee pronounced their language to be unlike anything they had heard before. Many admitted they could not understand their Black neighbors, students, and workers in the South Carolina Sea Islands. Botume possessed firsthand knowledge of the interactions between refugees from the Combahee River and the freed people already settled in Beaufort. During her time at Old Fort, she also witnessed the arrival of refugee populations from the mainland of coastal South Carolina, Edisto Island, and Savannah, and the reaction to them by freed Blacks who had previously reconstituted their communities in Port Royal after "Gun Shoot at Bay Point." She admitted her "head grew dizzy trying to understand the dialect of these people." It took years for the language of her students at Old Fort School to become "more intelligible" to Botume.[48]

Another northern volunteer declared, "We are not used to these people— it is even very difficult to understand what they say. They have been born and brought up just here, in the most isolated way, for generations, with no chance of improvement." During the war, northern volunteers began to pinpoint exactly what was so different about Beaufort and Sea Island Blacks' speech—which some northern abolitionists characterized as "plantation" dialect and culture and considered to be products of "debasement," as one of the northern teachers characterized Lowcountry Creole language and culture.[49]

In 1932, Lorenzo Dow Turner encountered African American students speaking a peculiar language and answering to unusual nicknames. Turner was teaching summer school at South Carolina State College in Orangeburg, South Carolina, sixty miles northwest of Charleston. The 1930s and 1940s were a time when few scholars had formal linguistic training; those who did have such training did not focus their research on languages spoken by Black people. A former slaveholder named Ambrose Elliott Gonzales had fictionalized the speech of formerly enslaved people and published sketches beginning in 1922 based on stories he heard as a child from Black people whom his family held in bondage and who lived and worked on his family's plantations after freedom. Gonzales also styled himself an amateur linguist. His theory was that Gullah Geechee, the name by which it had become known, was "slovenly and careless speech," as he put it, the result of enslaved Blacks seizing the language of English settlers and indentured servants, "wrapp[ing] their clumsy tongues about it," enriching it with African words, and issuing it "through their flat noses and thick lips."[50]

Gonzales was a grandson of William Elliott IV, owner of The Bluff Plantation. Elliott had purchased Sancho Van Dross from his indebted father-in-law, Thomas Rhett Smith. His son Thomas Rhett Smith Elliott sold Sancho and his son Mingo Van Dross to William L. Kirkland Jr. in 1851. Thus, some of the enslaved laborers who may have told Gonzales folktales, and whose dialect he fictionalized, could have had children on the lower Combahee River.[51]

Turner became the first African American scholar trained in linguistics. He spent ten years conducting the first systematic study of the Gullah Geechee language, interviewing Blacks on the South Carolina and Georgia Sea Islands, recording words, personal names, folktales, prayers, and songs, and then analyzing the language's vocabulary and grammar. Turner's research showed their speech to be deserving of study. His findings—Gullah Geechee was a creolized form of English in which vestiges of West African languages spoken by enslaved people had survived—were nothing sort of groundbreaking.[52]

Decades before Turner's pioneering study, northern volunteers had recorded the Creole language spoken by Blacks in Lowcountry South Carolina. Botume was one teacher who took note of Sea Island Blacks' "basket names." In the 1930s Turner found Gullah-speakers using one name in public and more personal names among close relatives and friends. These basket names protected the bearer from harm by negative spiritual energy. During the Port Royal Experiment, northern teachers took note that their students often had a number of names, because "nem'says [namesakes] gives folks different names." This complicated teachers' efforts to take roll at school, pass out books and supplies, and account for each student in attendance. Many basket names reflected the months of the year, days of the week, and prevailing circumstances when a child was born. The name Rode puzzled one teacher until she was told by a freed woman that the child had been born in the road on the way from the field the day of "Gun Shoot at Bay Point." Northern teachers also had to contend with the schoolchildren's titles, which they sometimes gave as the surname of the family that had held them in bondage during enslavement. But siblings in the same family could each take different titles. Often they answered roll call with one combination of names—alternating between basket names (such as Squash, Pumpkin, or Cornhouse for the boys, and Baby, Missy, or Tay for the girls) and their given names, plus a title, such Rhett, Barnwell, Elliott,

Middleton, or Stuart—but when asked to repeat their name, they would give the teacher an entirely different combination.[53]

Aspects of Sea Island Blacks' grammar perplexed northern teachers as well. They found Sea Island Blacks' use of pronouns—as noted in Chapter 14, eighty-eight-year-old Minus Hamilton had referred to his wife with the masculine pronoun "he" when he described how they went to the gunboat during the Combahee River Raid—very confusing. One teacher observed that "these people do not use any feminine adjective[s]" in their dialects. Botume observed that she never knew whether her students and neighbors were referring to boys or girls, men or women; "they spoke of all as 'him.'" Students greeted their teachers with squeals of "Dar, da him!" when the ladies approached the schoolhouse in the mornings; they identified their primers by saying "Him's mine"; and sometimes they answered roll call with only their given name, saying of their title, "I lef' him . . . on the main," meaning that they had left the slaveholders' title on the mainland when they liberated themselves from bondage. A grieving mother whose only child, a daughter, died was resigned to her fate, because "the Big Massa [the Lord] want him." A husband said of his wife, "Ef the ole hen run away, I shall cotch him sure." The children condemned a hen that killed its chicks as "de old mudder, him kill all but t'ree of him chickens."[54]

Another pronoun in the Lowcountry Creole dialect confounded northern teachers as well. Blacks on the Sea Islands used "oonah" for the plural form of "you." Thomas Higginson searched for the origins of "oonah" and eventually concluded that it was an "Indian formation of the second person plural" pronoun.[55]

By the fall of 1863, refugees liberated by the Combahee River Raid had joined a makeshift community previously formed by overlapping waves of refugees. Their predecessors included freedom seekers who had liberated themselves after the Battle of Port Royal, as well as those who had seized their freedom after the US Army drove the *John Adams* up the Ashepoo River in the winter of 1862, evacuating Blacks from the more remote Sea Islands, such as Hutchinson's Island. As we've seen, some of the islands were still inhabited by slaveholders and overseers who told the enslaved people the same old lie—that the Yankees would sell them away from their family members to Cuba or some other far-off place where life was even more brutal and cruel than on the Ashepoo. Blacks enslaved on the Ashepoo, did not buy this. They hid, waiting for the white folks to evacuate to the mainland. When the US Navy gunboats came up the river, anyone who could make it to the riverbanks got on the gunboat and sailed to Beaufort. By the time the Combahee River Raid occurred, that falsehood was a familiar story.[56]

One teacher remembered that so many refugees were brought to Beaufort by the federal government and quartered in every nook and cranny of churches, storehouses, and even jails and arsenals that the town was overflowing. Once the US Treasury Department's superintendents were in control of the plantations, some freedom seekers even returned to the plantations on which they had been enslaved. There they occupied the same slave quarters in which they had lived before the Battle of Port Royal, often bringing with them family members with whom they had reunited in Beaufort. Thus the slave quarters on the rural plantations were overcrowded as well. A homeless population emerged; they were housed in tents outside of town, then in newly constructed barracks. One of these communities was called Montgomery District, the settlement Botume had noticed on her first trip out to the school.[57]

The Combahee refugee camp at Montgomery District was located approximately a half mile from the Old Fort School. It consisted of a row of approximately a dozen wooden barracks. Each box-shaped building was divided into four one-room dwellings. Families of between five and fifteen people lived in each of those dwellings; the settlement housed an estimated 360 women, children, disabled adults, and men who could not enlist in the 2nd South Carolina Volunteers. Botume guessed that she had half of the families of both the 33rd and 34th Regiments living at Old Fort Plantation. Able-bodied men who did not enlist in the army hid from Botume, who, with a notebook in her hands, may have looked like a government inspector; indeed, they hid from anyone they suspected of being an official. The prospect of the government seizing and drafting men against their will likely did not feel sufficiently different from the constant fear of separation the freedom seekers had felt when held in bondage.[58]

Each dwelling had its own fireplace for heating and cooking, and a large opening covered by a wooden shutter for cooling and ventilation. The furnishings were sparse: low wooden benches, bunks hung from the wall, rude shelves, pine tables. The dwellings also contained utensils like long-handled dippers called "piggins," pans, and large iron spoons, as well as threadbare clothing patched with coarse thread. Beer-barrel washtubs leaned against the exteriors until Friday, which was washday. Most of the inhabitants kept their dwellings tidy; they swept the floors clean free of debris, scoured them until they were smooth, and then sprinkled white sand from the bluff in front of the threshold and on the floor. The barracks alternated between being too hot and too cold, depending on the season, and were routinely overcrowded, depending on the size of each family and the time of day. Malnutrition and outright starvation killed many of the most vulnerable. When the barracks were first constructed, twice as many refuges needed housing as these structures could accommodate. Many freedom seekers died of pneumonia from cold, exposure, and malnutrition, living through the winter in tents with no fireplaces or floors, erected by the federal government to shelter the homeless. Smallpox killed even more. However, the inhabitants could call the little they possessed in freedom their own. It was so much more than they had possessed in bondage.[59]

When Botume visited the refugee camp, both to inspect the dwellings and check on her pupils, many of the women told her their husbands were serving with Colonel Montgomery's regiment. In October 1864, the 2nd South Carolina Volunteers were, as noted earlier, in Florida. The women who stayed behind at the camp were likely slightly older, had been married longer, and had several children to look after. Many of the younger women who either did not have a house full of children or were not married yet, like Hagar (who was engaged to Charles Nicholas), went with their husbands, fiancés, and lovers.[60]

A few years after she had left Old Fort, Botume wrote that the Combahee refugee women, unlike the Blacks who had been enslaved on the Sea Islands, "knew how to do many things." They spun cotton thread on wooden spindles and long wooden pins, sewed and knitted with homespun cotton thread, made "shapely gloves and stout stockings" out of the coarse yarn, and knitted "on reeds, cut in the swamp." They proudly sent the gloves and socks to their husbands, sons, and lovers in the military. Botume observed a Combahee woman named Old Leah stitching up a soldier's coat with thread she had spun herself. When Botume praised her work, Old Leah replied, "Us all larn to do little tings for wesels. . . . We's *Combee*." Old Leah said this, Botume added, "as if to be 'Combee' implied everything." It did. The Combahee refugees identified themselves as "Combee" because they "came from the Combahee River."[61]

To the Combahee refugees, being "Combee" implied differences from others. As former bondspeople on rice plantations on the coastal plains, they labored in rice swamps, learned specialized skills (for example, as blacksmiths and coopers), and worked in swamps (and had transformed the coastal wetlands into productive rice fields generations before). Though Old Leah told Botume she had "been cook for white folks steady," Blacks enslaved on Lowcountry rice plantations, including on the Combahee, spent the majority of the year with little direct white supervision or inter-ference, particularly during the sickly months. In contrast, Blacks who had been held in bondage and forced to labor on Sea Island cotton plantations, while they also worked under the task system, labored in a healthier climate, one that attracted white folks to exercise supervision and interference year-round. Now that the refugees from "Gun Shoot at Bay Point" and those from the raids on various Sea Islands, the Ashepoo, and Combahee Rivers were thrown together and living side by side in camps, differences in their syntax, grammar, and religious practices became evident. The Combahee refugees still identified themselves as "Combee" almost a year and a half after they had boarded the gunboats and sailed off to freedom.[62]

Once Botume had enrolled her pupils and the field hands finished their fieldwork for the season—picking the Sea Island cotton, gathering the pea-nuts, and banking the sweet potatoes—Old Fort Plantation in Port Royal provided the first practical training in the Sea Islands. Girls attended this training after the half-day session of regular instruction. Botume had a gen-erous supply of needles, thimbles, and thread from northern supporters (General Saxton added several yards of coarse dark hickory-colored twilled cotton). Her pupils "learned readily, and soon developed much skill and ingenuity." They were "delighted beyond expression" to have "free use of sewing materials" and to take home their finished dresses and wear them to Sunday school after many weeks of hard work. Boys complained that they were not allowed to attend sewing school and that "dem gals has all de t'ings." When she had ample supplies, Botume opened a class for boys, some of whom, she reported, "did most creditable work."[63]

The Old Fort sewing school was so popular that freedom children who attended another school begged to attend. This was a small school in a praise house located in the live oak grove on Old Fort but assigned to a different district. Nonetheless, according to Botume, the pupils had ridi-culed the Combee refugees "with a degree of scorn," calling them "'dem rice n[——]' [intentionally deleted]." When the children from the praise house school wanted to attend Botume's sewing school, however, they were "ready to fraternize" with the Combee refugees. "Combee" was not only how the Combahee refugees saw themselves but also how freedom seekers from Beaufort and the Sea Islands saw them. At first, Botume had to refuse admission to the students from the other district, because her supplies were limited (mainly due to Sherman's March, which was passing through the South Carolina Lowcountry). In time, however, she had enough supplies for all of the students and united the two districts.[64]

One of the households Botume visited on her rounds was that of November and Sarah Osborne. After fleeing Oakland Plantation during the Combahee River Raid, November had enlisted in the 2nd South Carolina Volunteers (along with another Old Head, Frank Wright), leaving Sarah behind in Beaufort; it may have been the first time the elderly couple was separated. According to his discharge papers, November Osborne claimed to be fifty-three. He was hospitalized for rheumatism in his knees, an ailment "existing prior to his enlistment" and caused by being enslaved for most of his life. Unsurprisingly, his preexisting condition worsened due to "exposures incident to the army service." He never served any active duty, was hospitalized as early as July 25, 1863, and then was sent to Contraband Hospital No. 6 in Beaufort at the end of August without having shown any improvement. Ultimately, the US Army discharged Osborne from military service on March 28, 1864.[65]

The Osbornes' oldest son, Nat Osborne, was "wid Mon'gomery's boys in de regiment," as the Combee refugees put it. Nat Osborne served in the 2nd South Carolina Volunteers until the regiment mustered out on February 28, 1866. Their two younger children, William and Rebecca Osborne, lived with Sarah and then November in the Old Fort refugee camp. When Botume visited the Osbornes' dwelling, November and Sarah told her their children "mus' go to school." The Osbornes wanted their children and themselves to "larn something, for sure." Frank and Daphney Wright may have resided at Old Fort also. Private Wright was discharged on February 22, 1864, after being unfit for duty for sixty days due to impaired vision, disability to his right leg, and a knee injury that, like Jack Wineglass's, he had sustained before enlistment.[66]

Isaac De Causter was another Combee Old Head who came back early from war. By his own admission, De Causter was fifty-six years old when he was discharged on May 4, 1864. Like November Osborne, he had been admitted to the Hospital No. 6 in Beaufort by August 27, 1863, but did not show permanent improvement. He suffered from general debility and chronic arthritis in his ankles, the results of old age and a lifetime of servitude before enlisting in the military. The assistant surgeon specified in De Causter's discharge that military service had not caused his infirmities. Because the surgeon deemed theses disabilities to be preexisting conditions resulting from enslavement, these soldiers, their wives, and dependents were not initially eligible for pensions. De Causter could well have met Botume as she made her rounds through the Old Fort refugee camps, where they formed a friendship that would last for the rest of Isaac De Causter's life.[67]

The Barnwells were a family of Combee refugees recalled in the memoirs Botume wrote after she left Port Royal. Sarah Barnwell was likely the woman who came to Botume's school every day with a baby in her arms and two small boys by her side. The baby may have been little Rhina. The Barnwells' older daughter, Relia Barnwell, married a 2nd South Carolina Volunteers private, William Middleton, in December 1865. Botume identified one of the mother's small boys as Primus. He was surely Primus Barnwell, Relia Barnwell Middleton's younger brother, who was born on Cypress Plantation approximately two years before he, his mother, siblings Jack, Relia, Rhina, Moses, and Joseph Barnwell, and cousins Sina Bolze Young, Cuffie Bolze, and Peggy Moultrie Simmons Brown liberated themselves from enslavement by William C. Heyward in the Combahee River Raid.[68]

Primus Barnwell learned to read with his mother and siblings at Old Fort Plantation's school. He became a teacher, a preacher, and a "wise man" of his neighborhood, according to Botume. He would always be his mother's "A No. 1 scholar."[69]

★★★★★★★★

The capture of Atlanta in November 1864 opened a portal for General William Tecumseh Sherman's army—more than sixty thousand soldiers in an array forty miles wide—to head southeastward, all the way to the coast. On December 22, 1864, a little more than five weeks later, Sherman wrote in his official report that his army had entered the city of Savannah and captured about eight hundred Confederates and a string of forts from Savannah to Fort McAllister. When the Confederate Army evacuated the city, it left behind heavy-caliber guns, shells, shot, and other kinds of ammunition, as well as 12,000 bales of cotton, large amounts of rice, 190 cars,

13 locomotives, and 3 steamboats. Sherman's army marched methodically, roughly ten miles per day, in four columns, each one fifteen or twenty miles apart. Major General Oliver Otis Howard drove the right wing, consisting of his Army of Tennessee and the cavalry commanded by Brigadier General Judson Kilpatrick. They were on the southeast edge of the march. Major General Henry Warner Slocum, commanding his Army of Georgia, brought up the left wing, along the northeast edge of the march. They moved with wagon trains loaded with ammunition and provisions—twenty days' worth of bread and forty days' worth of sugar, coffee, salt, and beef, but only three days' worth of grain. Thus the soldiers were ordered to uphold a "judicious system of foraging," by which they were to live "chiefly, if not solely, upon the country, which I knew to abound in corn, sweet potatoes, and meats," as General Sherman wrote in his official report. By November 22, Sherman had realized his first objective—lodging the Union Army in the heart of Georgia between Macon and Augusta. This strategy forced the Confederacy to divide its scarce resources to defend multiple points— Macon, Augusta, Savannah, and Charleston—simultaneously.[70]

The army kept moving eastward. Engineers and the so-called Pioneers— Black laborers who worked day and night with axes and spades—led the way, tearing up the railroad General Lee had so judiciously protected since the Battle of Port Royal, salvaging if possible pontoon bridges that had been burned by departing Confederate units, clearing obstructions, and building new pontoon bridges where needed.[71]

Sherman had ordered his commanders not to "risk battle" with the enemy unless they were at "great advantage" in numbers and artillery, which they almost always were on the march eastward. The Confederacy mustered surprisingly little resistance to the Union Army's movements through its territory. When they attempted to defend Macon, the Rebel soldiers were "so roughly handled" that they "never repeated the experiment," according to Sherman. Macon was one of the very few places where Sherman's army met any Confederate resistance on its March to the Sea; they also encountered (and squelched) more Confederate resistance at Sandersville. Union cavalry attacked and drove out a Confederate cavalry unit near Waynesboro. The Confederate Army marshaled environmental forces to block the Union path, opening trunk gates and allowing water from the Savannah River to flood the rice fields and beyond. As the Union forces came within fifteen miles of Savannah, they found flooded terrain, roads obstructed with felled trees, and burned pontoon bridges, making swamps and streams impassable. This and the heavy artillery covering the flooded rice fields and the five approaches to Savannah represented the stiffest resistance to Sherman's advance, but even they barely slowed the juggernaut.[72]

When they reached Savannah, Sherman decided to wait for heavy artillery, including multiple 30-pounder Parrott guns arriving from Port Royal, before countering the Confederacy's heavy artillery protecting the city and the ironclad gunboats protecting the Savannah River. While most of the army camped on the outskirts, along with several thousand freedom seekers, Howard's right wing and a force under Major General John G. Foster broke up the railroad, prohibiting reinforcements, provisions, and supplies from reaching the city (Foster also closed off any possibility of the Confederate Army evacuating via the Broad River). It seemed as if Sherman intended to starve the citizens out. The siege lasted from November 30, 1864, until January 1865. The 2nd South Carolina Volunteer soldiers were involved, though men of Companies G and H do not talk about this in their pension files. After successfully assaulting Fort McAllister, General Sherman opened communication with Admiral Dahlgren and the US Navy fleet on Tybee, Wassaw, and Ossabaw Sounds. Flanked by the US Army coming from the west and the US Navy positioned on the coast, the Confederates found themselves jammed between "the upper and nether millstones of war; and the grinding made them groan loudly," as the chaplain of the 3rd Rhode Island mused.[73]

In the end, no assault by either the US Army or the US Navy was necessary. Without bloodshed, Sherman's army entered Savannah, took the valuable harbor, river, and forts, and destroyed the Central of Georgia Railroad, which had served to facilitate east-west communications in the heart of Georgia. The Confederate Army and Navy evacuated under the cover of darkness the night before Sherman's army entered the city. The Confederates blew up the ironclad *Savannah*, a ram, three transports, and small steamers in its own Savannah Squadron. Sherman estimated that his army had foraged through a sixty-mile-wide swath of country as it proceeded southeast from Atlanta to Savannah, consuming crops and livestock and emboldening an untold number of enslaved Blacks to liberate themselves. He also estimated that the march had resulted in a staggering $100 million in damage. There was more to come. Obstructions and torpedoes remained in the Savannah River. Once cleared by Admiral Dahlgren's fleet, the way would be clear to open the river and secure the waters so the army could "smash South Carolina all to pieces," heading due north "[breaking] up roads" as far as the Seaboard and Roanoke Railroad in Roanoke Rapids, North Carolina, as Sherman boasted. It would put his army within eighty-five miles of Richmond, the capital of the Confederacy.[74]

Some ten thousand refugees, mostly women, children, the aged, and the infirm, followed the columns of Sherman's forces on their path toward the coast. A number found their way to Port Royal. It being the middle of winter, these refugees arrived there "shivering, hungry, so lean and bony and sickly that one wonders to what race they belong," according to William Channing Gannett, one of the northern teachers.[75]

On January 1, 150 refugees from Georgia arrived at Port Royal and were housed in tents at the wharf. Most had been marching for days with little if any food and wore only threadbare clothing, bits of blanket, old carpet, and coarse sacks closed up with sticks and thorns to protect themselves from the freezing temperatures.[76]

These overlapping waves of population movement throughout the Lowcountry—and, as we'll see, access to land ownership—would begin to transform highly localized identities in the aftermath of the war. The influx of refugees into Beaufort and the Sea Islands accelerated toward the end of the war. As refugees previously settled on St. Helena were taken back to Edisto Island, those who followed Sherman's army were moved into their former homes on St. Helena. The Edisto freedpeople who had come to St. Helena as refugees approximately two years before considered the incoming refugees "only Georgia n[——]s . . . low down country n[——]s [intentionally deleted]," different from themselves and those freed from the South Carolina Sea Islands as early as 1861. However, Laura Towne wrote in her diary that the departing Edisto refugees received the new recently arrived refugees "to their 'chimbly,'" a privileged place in Sea Island freedpeople's homes, which they considered to be "a man's castle."[77]

Despite the kindness of the Edisto freedpeople, the Georgia refugees considered St. Helena an "uncomfortable and strange place." To Sea Island Blacks who had lived on St. Helena plantations before the war broke out, Georgia refugees were unfamiliar and unwelcome. Superintendent Edward Philbrick described freedpeople previously settled on St. Helena as "rather inclined to be jealous of the new-comers," who made "the labor-market rather easier than before" for superintendents looking for cheap, reliable labor. The work ethic of the Georgia refugees, who gathered and sold moss, marsh grass, and hay to teachers and superintendents to feed livestock, gave the impression that "if the old residents don't work, *somebody else will.*" The arrival of destitute Georgia refugees, who were willing to work in more adverse conditions and for lower wages than the St. Helena freedpeople, brought unwanted competition to old residents, who had developed expectations about the value of their labor as a result of the Port Royal Experiment's use of labor. Elizabeth Botume had, as noted, observed differences in the dialects spoken by freedpeople from different corners of the Sea Islands and coastal mainland. The dialect of the Georgia refugees who followed Sherman's army was very different; "they spoke clearly and distinctly."[78]

Identity in coastal South Carolina, south to the St. Johns River in Florida, would remain highly localized into the twentieth century. However, with its massive population resettlement within the Lowcountry, the Civil War period ushered in a widening of Lowcountry Creoles' culture, language, and identity—the next step in the making of the Gullah Geechee. The broadening of multiple localized identities into a common coastal identity, however, was just beginning. At the end of the war, Lowcountry Creoles were not one people and, most importantly, did not see themselves as such, but they were on the way. Blacks in multiple areas of the Lowcountry already had had similar experiences at various points during the war, fleeing their homes, hiding in the woods and swamps, seeking or following the US Army, and ultimately securing their freedom. Over time, Blacks from the coastal South Carolina, Georgia, and Florida region would continue to have similar experiences dealing with white military and government officials, including but not limited to gaining and maintaining access to land, and their identity would widen even more.

★★★★★★★★

After evacuating Savannah, the Confederate Army established a defensive line on the eastern side of the Combahee/Salkehatchie river system, all the way from the coast to Barnwell, South Carolina, to defend the Charleston and Savannah Railroad. They had two separate commands to contend with. The US Army Department of the South marched on Charleston, which was already so beleaguered that General Sherman and his armies bypassed it. Both parts of the Union Army worked to flush out the Confederate forces and attempted to destroy the railroad. After Sherman had captured Savannah, his right wing swept from Pocotaligo toward Charleston. Once again, the environment became a factor when heavy rains from a freshet caused the rivers to swell and the whole area to flood with water more than a mile wide and twenty feet deep. The 3rd Rhode Island crossed "swollen rivers, and detestable marshes, and dense rice swamps," as the chaplain of the unit remembered in his memoir.[79]

On January 25, 1865, before moving inland, Sherman's army and the Confederates skirmished at Combahee Ferry and on the railroad bridge across the Salkehatchie. According to Sherman, the demonstration was designed to "amuse the enemy," which now had adopted the bridge over the Salkehatchie River as its defensive line. It would distract the Confederates from Sherman's true objective, Columbia.[80]

In early February 1865, units from the US Army Department of the South reached the Combahee River and made multiple crossings in its march from the Coosawhatchie River to Charleston (though the Confederate Army struck back by sinking the USS *Dai Ching* when it ran aground). Blacks who had been left behind in the Combahee River Raid were "wild with delight" at the approach of Union soldiers, which allowed them to liberate themselves. They greeted the soldiers by "clapping their hands and dancing all sorts of antics." Private Andrew O. Keach of the 3rd Rhode Island, Company A, remembered that one elderly woman wanted to see General Sherman in person. She probably wanted to thank him for bringing the US Army back through the neighborhood where she had been held in bondage so that she could seize her freedom while still living. One of the 3rd Rhode Island soldiers attempted to impersonate General Sherman, but the old woman refused to be fooled. She announced that he couldn't possibly be General Sherman, because his beardless "face [was] too smooth." Fannie Lee came to the lower Combahee from Newburne, North Carolina, where she was born, raised, and held in bondage by John Wise. Cuffie Bolze testified he "found Fannie on the same place where I was born," Cypress Plantation, after the war. Bolze and several of Fannie's neighbors thought that she "came through with Sherman."[81]

By the end of February 1865, Sherman's army had swept inland toward Columbia, cutting a swath forty miles wide. Meanwhile, General Gillmore (who had returned as commanding officer of the Department of the South on February 9, 1865) and Admiral Dahlgren were again "brothers in battle," the chaplain of the 3rd Rhode Island wrote in his memoir, this time in the final capture of Charleston. The mayor, Charles Macbeth, surrendered the city to a small force of the 21st USCT Regiment, a Black regiment (formerly the 3rd South Carolina Volunteers). Among them were Parris White, who had escaped enslavement on Bonny Hall Plantation during a US Army reconnaissance mission up the Combahee River in the spring of 1862, and Peter Blake, who had escaped in the US Navy's raid on Arthur Blake's North Santee River plantation in June 1862. They had enlisted together in the 3rd South Carolina at Hilton Head in April 1863 (Parris White would be discharged later in 1865 because of disability). Arriving in Charleston after the 21st USCT was the 3rd Rhode Island, which had marched through the soaking rain and ubiquitous mud across nine of South Carolina's rivers from the Salkehatchie to the Ashley River.[82]

For the formerly enslaved in the South Carolina Lowcountry, another day of Jubilee had come. Their expressions of joy, shouts of amazement, and prayers of thanksgiving "knew no bounds," again according to the 3rd Rhode Island's chaplain. Simon Washington and his wife, Rachel, may have been somewhere in the teeming masses of humanity lining Charleston's streets. The couple had grown up in bondage on Middleton Place on the Ashley River, where Simon's uncle, Wally Garrett, was also born. Simon's parents, Thomas Washington and Daphne Garrett Washington, along with Sunday Briscoe (Rachel Washington's cousin) and Wally Garrett, had all liberated themselves from enslavement on Newport Plantation twenty months prior, in the Combahee River Raid. In advance of the final, successful siege of Charleston, the 34th Regiment (which had been ordered to march back to Beaufort after another expedition on the Combahee) was sent to the Pocotaligo Bridge to relieve the 25th Ohio Regiment. That's where they were when Middleton Place (where Wally Garrett's father, Thomas Washington, also received medical treatment) burned. Thomas Washington, though a "sickly old man" who "could not carry a gun," as Corporal Neptune Nicholas testified in his pension file, fought for his country until his death in November 1865. The three younger men went on together to fight for the freedom of others through the end of the war.[83]

The soldiers of the 21st USCT and the 55th Massachusetts (Sergeant Major Lewis Douglass's regiment) sang "John Brown's Body" as they entered the streets of Charleston, which had been deserted by most white residents and were lit up from fires burning ammunition, cotton, and valuables to keep them out of the hands of the enemy. The significance of the sight—Black soldiers who risked their freedom and very lives fighting for the freedom of those still enslaved in the birthplace of secession—was not lost on any spectator. They paraded and sang with a "zest" the chaplain could not forget.[84]

Meanwhile, the Charleston Light Dragoons had been performing picket duty in Bellefield, Virginia, when General Sherman's army engulfed Savannah and began its ascent into South Carolina. Major General Wade Hampton secured permission for the regiment to return and defend their state. They headed south in January 1865, reaching Columbia just in time to watch the city go up in flames on February 17.[85]

★★★★★★★★

Harriet Tubman had left the Lowcountry in June 1864, when she went on furlough and traveled home to Auburn to visit her parents. Illness caused her to overstay her leave. By the time she was able to travel to New York, where she planned to board government transport, she was refused passage back to Hilton Head. Tubman went back to Washington, DC, where she explained her situation to officials at the War Department, which was still under the leadership of her longtime ally, Edwin Stanton. She was given a new pass: "Pass Mrs. Harriet Tubman (colored) to Hilton Head and Charleston, S.C."[86]

While doing relief work for the National Home for the Relief of Destitute Colored Women and Children in the Washington, DC, area, Tubman encountered Julia Wilbur, a Quaker abolitionist and suffragist from Rochester, New York. Wilbur was working in Alexandria, Virginia, for the New Freedmen's Relief Association, which was founded in April 1862 to respond to the rapidly changing needs of formerly enslaved people streaming into the nation's capital by providing clothing and medical care. She worked providing relief supplies alongside Harriet Jacobs, author of *Incidents in the Life of a Slave Girl*, who endured sexual harassment and hid in a garret for seven years before she was able to liberate herself in 1842. Wilbur recorded in her diary on January 12, 1865 (when she spent nearly all day mending, ironing, and distributing clothes and reported on the suffering among the freedom seekers who couldn't work and thus were not entitled to rations): "Harriet Tubman here." Wilbur and Tubman's paths crossed on March 5, 1865, when both attended a speech about President Lincoln's second inauguration given by Frederick Douglass at Reverend Henry Highland Garnett's Fifth Street Presbyterian Church. The occasion was the passage of the Thirteenth Amendment, which finally ended the institution of slavery and involuntary servitude, except for punishment of crimes. Wilbur wrote that Senator Samuel Pomeroy (who was elected by the Kansas legislature in April 1861 to be one of Kansas's first federal senators and fervent advocate of colonization), "Harriet & other notables" were present.[87]

As Tubman continued her relief work among the formerly enslaved people in Washington, DC, the New England Freedmen's Aid Society sponsored her return to Hilton Head as a teacher of domestic arts for the refugees. Of course, Tubman was illiterate and could not teach the refugees to read or write. She had, however, a wealth of knowledge to offer. Tubman needed the support the Aid Society offered, $10 per month, as the federal government still had not compensated her for her service for the US Army of the South (though, as noted earlier, they had paid her $200 for her service to the US Army), and her elderly parents depended on her for their support.[88]

On her way back to South Carolina in April 1865, Harriet Tubman gave a speech to USCT soldiers at Camp William Penn, located on the northern outskirts of Philadelphia in Cheltenham, Pennsylvania, where approximately eleven thousand Black troops in eleven infantry regiments were trained. The camp—with wooden barracks for soldiers, officers, and administration buildings--was unique in that it was designed and designated exclusively for the organization and training of Black troops. It became the most significant training site for African American soldiers in the states of Pennsylvania, New Jersey, and Delaware. The *Christian Recorder* reported that soldiers at the camp enjoyed a "very interesting homespun lecture, from a colored woman." Tubman seemed already to be "very well known by the community . . . as the great Underground Rail Road woman" who had "done a good part to many of her fellow creatures" toward securing their freedom. William Wells Brown, an abolitionist who had liberated himself from enslavement in Kentucky, described how much Tubman loved Black soldiers: "When the negro put on 'the blue,' Moses was in her glory." And, according to Brown, the Black soldiers loved Tubman back: "These Black men would have died for this woman." These were her people.[89]

To the soldiers at Camp William Penn, Tubman lectured "in her own language," which the northern soldiers understood, and gave a "thrilling account of her trials in the South, during the past three years, among the contrabands and the colored soldiers." She told her audience about how she had "administered to thousands" of contrabands and African American soldiers and "cared for their numerous necessities." Her lecture included "several gems of music," continued the article, which she sang in her beautiful voice. We are left to wonder if Tubman spoke about the expeditions in which she had been integral, particularly piloting Colonel James Montgomery's troops up the Combahee River in the June 2, 1863, raid. Whether she did or not, Tubman's speech was greeted with thundering and passionate applause from the soldiers.[90]

Nine days later, Robert E. Lee surrendered to Ulysses S. Grant at Appomattox Courthouse in Virginia. The war was over.

★★★★★★★★

Despite the cessation of hostilities, the soldiers of the 34th Regiment continued to serve their country. And the older men continued to get discharged. Privates Benjamin Prior and Pool Sellers were discharged on May 21, 1865. They were both over the maximum age and had been unfit for duty for sixty days, like Andrew Harris, July Osborne, November Osborne, Frank Wright, Andrew Wyatt, and Smart Washington. Prior complained of hip pain caused by a tree falling on him before enlistment. Private Sellers became exhausted from light marching and complained of lower back pain, which he told his commander, Captain L. H. Markley, was caused by being thrown from a horse before enlistment. Pain prevented both soldiers from carrying their rucksacks.[91]

Smart Washington was the oldest of the Old Heads to enlist in the 34th Regiment the day after the Combahee River Raid, and he served in the US Army the longest—he was honorably discharged on June 2, 1865, after serving his country for two years. Captain Markley described Washington as "very decrepit and unable to perform the ordinary duties of a soldier," no longer the young man in his prime that Jonas Green had remembered from his boyhood. Private Washington had done no military duty for one year before discharge; Surgeon Paul P. Hanson added that Washington had been "completely worthless as a soldier." Washington was significantly "over age," and his military file says that he was at least sixty-five years old. However, Washington had actually been seventy when he enlisted. On Smart Washington's discharge form, Captain Markley listed his occupation as a cooper, though Governor Henry Middleton identified Smart as a driver in his 1846 estate inventory. As noted, in no pension application, either his own or someone else's, did a veteran testify that he had been a driver while in bondage. And no one in the Combahee freed community who offered testimony for the pension files identified anyone as having been a driver. After discharge Washington came home to Old Fort and served as a leader in his community. Smart and his first wife, Mary, became Elizabeth Botume's "staunch allies" at the Old Fort School and beyond, Botume's veritable "chief of staff," whom she described as helping her in every possible way.[92]

Tubman continued to serve her country as well. On the way to New York, from which she was to board government transport to Beaufort, she encountered members of the Sanitary Commission in Philadelphia. They convinced her there was a "pressing need," as Charles P. Wood put it, for her skills nursing soldiers in Fort Monroe's hospital on James Island, Virginia, and Tubman went where she thought she was needed most. She could not have known that not returning to the Department of the South would greatly complicate her claim for a pension many years later. She remained in Virginia, serving the US Army and nursing the soldiers, until July 1865.[93]

As she had done successfully among abolitionist military commanders in the Department of the South, Tubman leveraged her relationships with members of President Lincoln's cabinet—who stayed on after his assassination in April—to try to improve conditions for freedpeople. She went back to Washington, DC, to report to the federal government about the unacceptable conditions among the hospitals at Fort Monroe.[94]

Once in the city, Tubman met with her old friend Secretary of State Seward. She needed money and had not received any payment from the federal government for her wartime service other than the $200 for "secret service," much of which she had used to build the washhouse for refugee women and families. Seward wrote a letter to General Hunter (who after being relieved of military duty in March 1865 served as head of the military commission investigating Lincoln's assassination) requesting that he assist Tubman in settling her compensation claims for wartime service to the federal government in South Carolina:

Washington, July 25, 1865
Major Gen'l Hunter—My Dear Sir:
    Harriet Tubman, a colored woman, has been nursing our soldiers during nearly all the war. She believes she has a claim for faithful services to the

command in South Carolina with which you are connected, and she thinks that you would be disposed to see her claim justly settled.

I have known her long, and a nobler, higher spirit, or a truer, seldom dwells in the human form. I commend her, therefore, to your kind and best attention.

Faithfully your friend, Wɪɪɪ. H. Seward

Surgeon General Joseph K. Barnes appointed her nurse or matron of the Colored Hospital at Fort Monroe. However, it is not clear that Tubman ever filled this position or that she stayed much longer in Virginia. What is clear is that her financial needs were not met—her compensation claim would not be settled for decades. Military commanders at the time, however, recognized that Tubman "made many a raid inside the enemy's lines, displaying remarkable courage, zeal, and fidelity."[95]

Tubman returned to Auburn in mid-October by train using a ticket for employees of the federal government. Not only had she been denied the respect due to someone who had faithfully and selflessly served her country, at risk to her own freedom and life for three and a half years, but she was assaulted by a racist train conductor and racist passengers. They threw her off the train, breaking her ribs and injuring her shoulder. Not enough had changed since Frederick Douglass was accosted and thrown off the Eastern Railroad in 1841 or Sojourner Truth was thrown off a Washington streetcar earlier in 1865. It did not matter how well known they were nor that the North had fought to preserve the Union; during Reconstruction, racism pervaded the lives of African Americans in the North as well. Despite these obstacles, Tubman was finally reunited with her parents and other family members, whose needs surpassed, for Tubman, even those of the nation.[96]

★★★★★★★★

Before the 34th Regiment mustered out on February 28, 1866, at Jacksonville, Florida, Chaplain Moore performed one last mass wedding ceremony. As described earlier, freedom had allowed the formerly enslaved to choose their partners. Whereas "abroad marriages"—marriages between people enslaved by different plantation owners—had been very uncommon on the lower Combahee during the antebellum period, several soldiers chose wives who had not been bondspeople on the same plantation. Sergeant Edward Brown, who liberated himself from enslavement on Newport Plantation, met Mary Belton in Florida. She had been held in bondage in Camden, South Carolina, then taken against her will Gainesville, Florida, during the war and left there. She remembered that Edward "wore his soldier's clothes" for the ceremony. The couples, including the newlyweds, were separated after their nuptials. The wives were sent ahead; the soldiers followed several weeks later.[97]

Phoebe Frazier may have been allowed to stay with her husband, Robert, when the other wives were sent ahead, because she was in a very advanced stage of pregnancy. When the child was born the Fraziers named her Lauretta. Her basket name was Sea-Bird, because she was born on the steamboat as her parents were returning home to Beaufort from Jacksonville. William Izzard's father, Francis Izard, had, as noted earlier, liberated himself from Middleton's Newport Plantation and gave critical intelligence about Confederate positions, movements, obstructions, and torpedoes on the lower Combahee to the US provost marshal a week before the raid. Young Izzard was among the boys who watched the grown men, their older brothers, cousins, friends, and neighbors, go off to fight, because they themselves were too young to serve during the war. He remembered many years after the war that he met Jack Aiken at the wharf when Jack came home from the war blind in one eye from contracting smallpox in the service. The Pikins did not know all of the details of the older men's lives, such as the names of all of women, but they would remember—into the twentieth century—the Combahee River Raid and the sacrifices its veterans had made for freedom.[98]

19

Closed His Eyes

There was a wide chasm between the federal government's promises when it came to land redistribution and freedpeople's "extravagant expectations," as Edward Barnwell Heyward, Charles Heyward's son and Nathaniel Heyward's grandson, described them to the *Savannah Republican*. Land ownership was the last phase of the Port Royal Experiment, one unanticipated by northern teachers and superintendents, though many associated it with the height of "manliness" and "civilization." It was the phase that freedom seekers themselves attempted to control. It began with the promises of the November 1863 preemption land sales (in which freedom seekers could acquire the land on which they had been held in bondage by petitioning the tax commission, making a down payment, and thereby stopping the land from being purchased by northern speculators). And it crescendoed with General Sherman's Special Field Orders No. 15, issued on January 1, 1865, which set aside 400,000 acres of confiscated land on the Sea Islands, the rice fields along the rivers, and uplands, stretching thirty miles into the interior from Charleston in the north to the St. Johns River in the south, for the settlement of formerly enslaved people. Thus began a well-known saga continuing to this day, with twists and turns exacerbated by development and climate change.[1]

Sherman's order severed—or, at least, was intended to sever—General Sherman from the tens of thousands of freedom seekers following his army seeking safety, refuge, and provisions. And it was designed to provide a solution to the rapidly growing refugee problem in US-occupied territory by setting aside forty-acre homesteads for tens of thousands of landless freedom seekers to settle under the protection of the federal government without giving them permanent titles to the land. It appointed Brevet Major General Rufus Saxton, formerly military governor of the Department of the South, as inspector of settlements and plantations.[2]

By the beginning of April 1865, General Saxton had resettled 20,000 people on 100,000 acres of confiscated lands. Freedom seekers from the islands and the mainland flocked to the all-Black colonies created by Sherman's order. Except for US military personnel, no whites were allowed to live in the area. In theory, freedpeople had use of the land for three years and then had the option either to leave or to purchase the land and secure title to it. But after Lincoln's assassination, President Andrew Johnson pardoned former Confederate planters and restored their property. Special Orders No. 15 was reversed less than nine months after it had been enacted; the federal government allowed African American settlers in the Sherman colony to remain only until they had harvested their crops, then began evicting them.[3]

The land encompassed by Sherman's order included rice plantations along the Combahee River, and the Combahee planters were on high alert after the end of the war to see whether the order would be enforced on their plantations. Allen S. Izard tried to reassure Eliza C. Middleton Huger Smith, owner of Smithfield Plantation on the lower Combahee River, in his September 15, 1865, letter to her that President Johnson and his administration were doing everything "reasonable & possible for the planters." The widow was managing her own property after her oldest son, William Mason Smith Jr., had been mortally wounded in the Battle of Cold Harbor in Virginia. Izard counseled Eliza Smith to "work; take hold & persevere; get labour of some kind; get possessions of some places; stick to it; oust the negroes and their ideas of proprietorship." The planters needed protection on their "exposed" Combahee River lands, on both the upper and lower portions of the river. Izard managed the plantations of his brother-in-law Edward Barnwell Heyward on the upper Combahee after Heyward's death (he died at age forty-four a few years after evacuating his father's slaves from Rose Hill Plantation on the upper Combahee) until Heyward's sons reached their majority. More than anything else, Izard conveyed the message that the Combahee planters needed to stick together and "present a united front" so they could all "make as much rice" as they could and sell it for "$2 to 2-1/2 a bushel."[4]

Izard wrote to Eliza Smith again a week later, reporting he had had a personal audience with General Saxton in August. Smith used the opportunity to present his own application for the restoration of his rice plantation on the Savannah River and make Saxton generally aware of the needs of rice planters on the coast. According to Izard, Saxton had 17,000 freedmen for whom to implement the government's resettlement promises. Eliza Smith's brother William Elliott Huger wrote that their family would spend the winter in Charleston, rather than on the Combahee, as they had before the war started. Combahee still wasn't safe for the planters' families.[5]

The time was not yet ripe for the old Combahee planters to return to their plantations, but it soon came. Williams Middleton had what was left of Newport Plantation, destroyed in the raid, restored to him at the end of September 1865. Cypress Plantation was restored to William C. Heyward's heirs on February 6, 1866. And the Freedmen's Bureau restored Smithfield Plantation to Eliza Smith on December 18, 1865. She signed labor contracts with the freedpeople on Smithfield. They were the same former bondspeople who had been left behind when their neighbors next door on Cypress Plantation liberated themselves in the raid. The contracts allowed them to remain on the plantation and plant 46 acres of rice land and 50 acres of provision grounds. They were subject to Eliza Smith's right to search any building on the premises, and required to render to her or her agent any service requested. Yet it prohibited them from doing plenty of other things, such as cut wood for sale, live on or plant any lands without authorization, disturb the gardens, lawns, or pastures on the premises, or conduct themselves in a disorderly manner. If they violated any of these stipulations, they would be dismissed from the property.[6]

Eliza Smith signed the labor contract with the freedpeople on Smithfield on March 2, 1866, just in time to plant the next crop of rice. Getting the rice crop planted—and eventually sold for a price that would enable them to resume their prewar lifestyles—was the planters' goal in sticking together while negotiating labor contracts with the freedpeople, presenting a united front to the politicians and the military, and putting pressure on the Johnson administration to protect their interests. Once again, they were willing to make significant investments so that they could grow rice again on fields that had been little cultivated since June 1863, in the hope that it would be profitable again. A contractor wrote to Charles T. Lowndes in January 1870, providing an estimate to relocate a threshing mill from the rice plantation of a Mr. Lucas in Christ Church Parish to Lowndes's Oakland Plantation. He would build a boiler, construct a 20-by-40-foot brick engine house and a 20-by-30-foot carrier house, and install a 15-horsepower engine secured in solid brickwork. The price tag was $5,400.[7]

Most of the Combahee freedpeople lacked the means to purchase land in either Beaufort or Colleton Counties. Those who did not went back to work in the tidal rice fields and signed labor contracts with Eliza Smith, Joshua Nicholls, John D. Warren, and other planters on the lower portion of the Combahee River, which locked them into labor conditions so exploitative that they resembled the period of enslavement. On March 26, 1866, Williams Middleton signed a labor contract with the freedpeople on Newport Plantation, many of whom (including Frank Wright, Tom and Daphne Washington, Wally and Elizabeth Garrett, Simon Washington, Farbry and Mary Bowers, and Jack Aiken) also escaped enslavement on Newport in the raid. Though testimony in the pension files does not mention it, they resisted the exploitation of the labor contracts in every way possible and fought for the right to control the labor of their family members.[8]

Penda Blake alias Washington (who liberated herself from enslavement on Arthur Blake's plantation in the March 1862 raid) went further afield. After her husband, Peter Blake, died from diarrhea (which was likely dysentery) in March 1867, she stayed in Hilton Head for three months. Then, she testified, "a whole crowd" of freedpeople left Hilton Head with her and went to the southwestern part of South Carolina along the Savannah River near Savannah, where she "worked in the rice fields for William C. Hayward, Mr. Stribben, and Mr. Taylor." Penda Blake likely worked for Daniel Heyward—not William C. Heyward, who was of course deceased— on Fife Plantation. Among the group was Stephen Polite, another former bondsman who had liberated himself from enslavement in the March 1862 raid and enlisted in the 21st USCT, Company C, the same day as Penda's husband. Polite testified that after the war he worked as an "overlooker" in the Savannah River rice fields for approximately six years; Penda Blake worked under him and stayed in the rice fields for about twenty years before returning to Beaufort. While she was on the Savannah River, Penda Blake changed her title to Washington, which, she later testified, had been her husband's title before the war.[9]

Years after the war was over, Colonel Higginson recollected seeing one of the wives of the men in his regiment hoeing in the fields near the regiment's old camp while wearing conspicuous red stockings. It was during a visit to Florida in 1878—his first trip back south since the end of the war, fourteen years after the 1st South Carolina was ordered to return from Florida. Slavery was over; the veteran and his wife had purchased the land formerly owned by the planter who had held their family members in bondage. Higginson was impressed that during his trip to the Lowcountry he "rarely met an ex-soldier who did not own his house and ground"; the homesteads ranged from five to two hundred acres. He thought there was no "finer example of self-respecting peasant life." Yet not all veterans became landowners within the first few decades after the end of the war.[10]

A number of the veterans and widows who liberated themselves from bondage on Bonny Hall Plantation returned to it after it was purchased. Mexico Washington testified that Charles Lucas was a "rice day worker" after the end of the war and their military service in the 34th Regiment USCT, Companies G and H, respectively. Lucas was a "hearty man" before he contracted fever. After an illness that Susan Blake, who testified that she "grew up under" Charles Lucas's wife, Bella Jones Lucas Garrett, in bondage on Bonny Hall Plantation, described as a "short spell," he died in 1868 at Bonny Hall, from which both he and Bella had liberated themselves. On June 18 in the same year, the heirs of William Blake (who had been heir to his father, Joseph Blake; before the Civil War, William's brother Walter managed their father's plantations) filed a suit in the Charleston Court of Equity seeking to settle Blake's estate and sell all of his property in Charleston and Beaufort Counties. Referee Charles H. Swinton sold Bonny Hall Plantation to one John Bennett Bissell on December 17, 1872, for $15,400. Bonny Hall would remain in the Bissell family for more than thirty years. Dr. Henry E. Bissell (who earned a medical degree at the Medical College of South Carolina in 1860, served in the Confederate Palmetto Guards during the Civil War, then practiced as a surgeon in Charleston) served as the superintendent and general agent on Bonny Hall for his brother. Jack Morton, who had grown up enslaved on the same plantation before liberating himself and joining the army, worked for Dr. Bissell as a field hand and water minder.[11]

Jeffrey Gray and his wife, Phoebe, returned next door to Newport Plantation after Jeffrey mustered out of service in the 34th Regiment USCT, Company G, after the war. Farbry Bowers (who grew up with Jeffrey and Phoebe, served with Jeffrey, and returned to Newport as well) testified that Jeffrey had worked in the rice fields. He was made "watchman" or trunk minder eight or nine years before his death. Simon Washington worked as assistant fireman at Newport as well.[12]

On the lower Combahee River, the story of Black land ownership began when the soldiers, spies, scouts, and pilots who had executed the Combahee River Raid and the enslaved people who liberated themselves in it purchased land from the US direct tax commissioners of South Carolina under the June

7, 1862, Act for the Collection of Direct Taxes in Insurrectionary Districts Within the United States and for Other Purposes, and its amendments of February 6, 1863, and March 3, 1865. The legislation gave the federal government the authority to foreclose on and then sell the land of landowners who had failed to pay direct taxes for their properties or to redeem their properties by paying back taxes and penalties. The land that went through foreclosure then fell into one of three categories: it could be sold in small parcels (with a maximum of 320 acres to one person at one time), set aside for members of the US military, or set aside for educational purposes. Lastly, the US government sold some of this land to freedom seekers and their heirs, executors, and assigns. Most paid $15 for ten acres of land on abandoned plantations and were issued a "Head of Household Certificate." Brigadier General Saxton fought so that the land would not be alienated from Black heads of families until at least six years later, in order to keep it from speculators. Unfortunately, he lost this and several other battles. The deeds did not protect against land speculators with deep coffers who would outbid freedom seekers and consign them to being landless laborers.[13]

Reverend William Henry Brisbane, Judge Abram D. Smith, and Judge William E. Wording were the three federal tax commissioners who signed all of these Head of Household Certificates. Brisbane was the Beaufort District native turned abolitionist who read the Emancipation Proclamation at Brigadier-General Saxton's celebration on January 1, 1863. The three had been appointed to these positions in October 1862, charged by the US Treasury Department with executing and enforcing in South Carolina the direct tax act mentioned above. The federal government held district tax sales in a total of five states: Virginia, Florida, Arkansas, Tennessee, and South Carolina. And the government acquired most of the land in all of the other states except for South Carolina. Of course, during the war, Confederate property owners who had fled coastal South Carolina in the "Great Skedaddle" did not recognize the authority of the US government and would not pay taxes to it. The planters also had been confident they would return to their property after the Confederacy won the war.[14]

All of the Civil War land sales posed problems for freedom seekers. As tax commissioner, Brisbane had opposed the preemption land sales on the Sea Islands, arguing that sale of land for $1.25 per acre, far below market value, would not prepare freedom seekers for the responsibilities of freedom. He thought the government should focus on Sea Island Blacks as productive wage laborers at this stage of the Port Royal Experiment, not as landowners.[15]

Together, preemption land sales, land sales carried out by US direct tax commissioners, and Sherman's Special Field Order No. 15 made Lowcountry Creoles the first freed Blacks to have access to landowner-ship in the American South. Some of the purchasers had been enslaved on the Sea Islands before "Gun Shoot at Bay Point"; some had come to to Beaufort and the Sea Islands as refugees from raids on the St. Mary's, St. Johns, and Combahee Rivers, or Darien; some had come their own to seek protection under US occupation.

But freedpeople's land ownership would prove tenuous and often tem-porary, even for military veterans and widows. Lowcountry Creoles would have to fight hard to hold on to their land during Reconstruction and through the decades that followed. This fight to acquire, maintain, and regain ownership of coastal lands would galvanize diverse antebellum Lowcountry Creole identities into the Gullah Geechee identity by the early twentieth century.

★★★★★★★★

Harriet Tubman had of course owned land since 1859, when she accepted an offer from William Henry Seward, then a senator for New York, and his wife, Frances, to sell her a seven-acre farm in Auburn, which Frances Seward had inherited from her father, Elijah Miller. Senator Seward sold the farm to Tubman for $1,200, gave her a no-interest mortgage, and re-quired no money down. That Seward was a powerful upstate New York Republican (he would be a presidential candidate in the 1860 election) likely helped to safeguard the transaction, for what he did was unprece-dented; at the time it was illegal in New York, and all other states, for fu-gitive slaves to own property. Nonetheless, Tubman made the house, barn, outbuildings, and arable land a homestead for her parents and other family members. She also took on the responsibility for paying her mortgage, sup-porting her parents in Auburn, and providing relief for the refugee commu-nity in St. Catharine's, Ontario, in addition to liberating family, friends, and neighbors still in bondage on the Eastern Shore.[16]

Generally, the men who escaped enslavement and enlisted in the US Army first (after the Battle of Port Royal) also purchased land first. Peter Burns, one of Harriet's spies and scouts, and his son, Jack Burns, were early landowners. Jonas Green, who escaped enslavement on Bonny Hall and went to Beaufort in March 1862, spent $30 for twenty acres in two separate purchases in the same month. They all purchased land in Port Royal.[17]

Jonas Green had an additional source of income, which likely facilitated his purchasing land. By the time the 2nd South Carolina Volunteers mustered out, he was living with Sina Bolze Young, a widow whose husband, Will Young, had been killed in action in 1864 at Morris Island. She was eligible for a widow's pension under the General Act of 1862. Sina Young testified that she had been "in bed in childbirth with her first child by Jonas Green when Sherman's Army passed through," though the couple was not married. It must have been through his cohabitation with Sina in Beaufort that Green and his friend Wally Graham, as described previously, learned that Colonel William C. Heyward had a "colored mistress," since Sina Young had escaped bondage from Heyward's Cypress Plantation. Though enslaved people who had been held in bondage on different plantations had always interacted regularly on the lower Combahee River, they only began intermarrying once they liberated themselves and were relocated to Beaufort.[18]

William Fields, Parris Dawson, Samuel Gillard, and William Green, all 34th Regiment veterans who fought in the Combahee River Raid, each bought ten acres on Parris Island for $15 in October 1866. July Green spent $30 to acquire twenty acres there nine months later. Parris Island was where Parris, Samuel, William, and July had been held in bondage by Dr. Thomas Fuller before freedom.[19]

Also in October 1866, the first veterans to have liberated themselves in the Combahee River Raid became landowners. Though they had been enslaved on the Combahee and escaped bondage from its rice plantations, they made their land purchases on the Sea Islands. This time the Old Heads did not lead the way; rather, the Prime Hands were the primary buyers. Prime Hand Dembo Frazier was the first to purchase ten acres on Port Royal Island. Less than three weeks later, Jackson Grant (who escaped bondage on Rose Hill Plantation) purchased the same amount on Lady's Island. In December, Old Head Aaron Ancrum (who was enslaved on Longbrow Plantation) and Prime Hand William Jones (who liberated himself from bondage on Rose Hill) followed, also buying ten acres each. Ancrum bought twenty acres on Port Royal Island, outside of Old Fort Plantation. Jones bought land in very small increments, one-fifth of an acre at a time. First, he paid $5 each for two 1/5-acre pieces of land in Higginsonville (a refugee camp in northwest Beaufort named after Colonel Higginson) in December 1866 and January 1867. The following year, he paid $3 for another one-fifth of an acre in Port Royal.[20]

Sons also led their fathers. On December 10, 1866, Nat Osborne paid $30 for twenty acres of land on Lady's Island. About a week later, his father, November Osborne (who, like Nat, had escaped bondage on Oakland Plantation), followed Nat's lead and settled on twenty acres of land on Lady's Island, for which he also paid $30. At the end of the month, Solomon Washington joined the ranks when he paid $15 for ten acres on Port Royal. His father, Smart Washington (who, like his son, liberated himself from bondage on Newport Plantation), followed Solomon's lead two months later, buying land in two installments, first ten acres and then eight acres, both in February 1867.[21]

Elizabeth Botume described Smart and Mary Washington as the "most notable people" at Old Fort's refugee camp. After the end of the war, the state of South Carolina passed an order mandating that all "slave man and wife" must be married by ceremony and issued a legal marriage certificate. Solomon Washington testified in his father's widow's pension file that his father and mother were "slave man and wife and lived together up until the death of [his] mother." They were joined under slavery's code by the man who held them both in bondage, and they had stayed together, living as husband and wife for forty years. The Washingtons led their neighbors at Old Fort Plantation in getting remarried. Their ceremony complete, they beamed as they walked hand in hand for the first time as legal husband and wife. Botume wrote in her memoir that Smart Washington joked that Mary was his wife for certain now, and if she ran away, he would "cotch him sure."[22]

After receiving a new Bible from the teachers at Old Fort School, Smart Washington took it to Botume so that she could write his family record in it. Smart told Botume that he was the proud father of nineteen sons, though he worried that he could not remember all of his sons' names—they had been given so many basket names by different people that Smart could not recall their given names. When he finally named them, Botume thought that he substituted Christian names like Moses and Benjamin for the basket names by which Washington's sons had been known, such as January, Hasty, Primus, Rooster, and Mealbag, names given to reflect the time, place, and circumstance of their births or special characteristics that they exhibited as youngsters. Except for Solomon, Washington's "army of boys" had all died in bondage. The proud father remembered his only living son's name and described him as a "big man, so tall" his father "could eat off his head."

Solomon Washington continued to serve in "Montgomery Regiment" until the regiment mustered out on February 28, 1866.[23]

Botume thought Smart and Mary "two of the most intelligent and thrifty people around us." After buying land, they built a little house and grew a large crop of cotton and corn. General Saxton had advised the freedom seekers and then the freedpeople not to continue living in the old slave quarters, where most had lived all of their lives, but to build small houses for themselves. Botume recalled Saxton's sentiments: "They would never be entirely free until they had abiding-places they could . . . call their own." On Old Fort Plantation, those who couldn't build houses constructed mud huts for shelter. A hut consisted of four posts four to six feet tall, plank sides, and a roof made of boughs from pine trees coated with mud from the swamps. Lacking a floor, it provided no protection from flooding after a heavy rainstorm; lacking a chimney, it provided no protection from frost. Those who had saved enough money built small two-story houses with chimneys, piazzas, and glazed windows.[24]

Smart and Mary Washington opened their home to fellow bondspeople who had also been enslaved on Newport Plantation. One year, the Washingtons' house caught on fire along with their corn crop after they had harvested and stored it. They lost everything. Botume and Fanny Langford, who taught together at Old Fort, wrote to abolitionist friends in the North, who sent money for the Washingtons to rebuild their house. Once resettled, they resumed opening their home to family and fellow bondspeople who were not as fortunate as they were.[25]

★★★★★★★★

Not all of the Combahee planters could pick up where they had left off before the war. In December 1867 Benjamin Stokes, commissioner in the Equity Court, sold Rose Hill, which had belonged to William L. Kirkland Jr. Joshua Nicholls acted as the executor of Kirkland's will after his death in June 1864. John D. Warren filed suit against Nicholls as executor of the will of his wife, Mary Anna Lynah Kirkland Faber Nicholls, in the Court of Equity in Walterboro. It referred to Faber's 1848 marriage settlement in which, as noted earlier, she conveyed her interest in Rose Hill to her brother Edward Lynah or in trust to his heirs. Eleven years later, in 1859, Joshua and Mary Anna Nicholls and William Kirkland executed a bond for $15,000 from John D. Warren. Mary Anna Nicholls died in August 1862, before the debt was satisfied. Edward Lynah also died in 1861; his wife, who was his heir, was dead by 1867, leaving their daughter, Ellen Rose Lynah Nicholls, as her heir. Joshua Nicholls married Ellen, his deceased wife's niece, maintaining his access to her wealth, while starting a family of his own. Ellen Nicholls inherited her father's share of Rose Hill. The land at Rose Hill and all of the improvements the Nicholls and Kirkland family had made to the property in the 1850s, when they took out multiple bonds and mortgages, were "still there." However, the enslaved labor force they had gone into debt to purchase was not. They had liberated themselves in the raid. The court sold Rose Hill to John D. Warren for $5,000 in satisfaction of the 1859 debt. Nicholls and his new wife walked away from the judgment with the proceeds of the sale minus the debt, a tidy sum to invest in planting rice next door on Longbrow.[26]

★★★★★★★★

It feels miraculous to be able to trace the Combahee freedom seekers through multiple sets of transactions: the slave transactions in which they were bought, sold, mortgaged, used as collateral, bequeathed, and given away as slaves; the Confederate compensation affidavits that prove they did in fact liberate themselves and take themselves off the enslavers' balance sheets; and the transactions in which they purchased land as freedpeople.

As we've seen, the Combahee freedom seekers first achieved land ownership in the Beaufort area, which remained a center for Blacks in the Lowcountry after the war. It became the location of a Freedmen's Bureau office, which took over the responsibilities of the US Army Department of the South in protecting freedpeople and helping them find their families, return home, and make a living. Some of the men of the 34th USCT Companies G and H and their wives, like Isaac and Silvia De Causter, Jonas and Sina Green, William and Elsie Jones, and Pool Sellers, remained in and around Beaufort for a few years after they were discharged from the military on February 28, 1866. They settled there and continued to put roots down where they had found refuge immediately following the raid.

Wally Graham and Jonas Green (this was Jonas' third land purchase) both purchased land in 1868. For $8, then $3, Graham bought two-tenths of an acre in both Higginsonville and Port Royal. Jonas Green also purchased a small plot in Higginsonville for $2. Green's plots were small, suggesting they might have been added on to existing holdings. It was not the last land purchase for his family. As noted earlier, William Jones made a second land purchase and bought another fifth of an acre in Port Royal, diversifying his Higginsonville holdings. Land in Port Royal may have been hard to come by, or the prices may have been too inflated. Many lost their land as a result of the federal government's issuing an order that back tax for 1866 and penalties totaling $4.85—an exorbitant amount for poor freedpeople—must be paid after they had already sold what little they owned to pay 1867 taxes. Elizabeth Botume reported that by the fall of 1869, speculators had managed to gain ownership of much of the land around Old Fort Plantation.[27]

Mary Ann Lewis (a widow who escaped enslavement on Longbrow Plantation) made the largest purchase, paying $120 for two lots in Beaufort in July 1871. In 1876, Margaret Moody (who William Kirkland hired out upcountry before the raid) chose to settle in Beaufort rather than return to Rose Hill. And Bina Mack purchased five acres of property in downtown Beaufort, bordering Beaufort National Cemetery, for $50 in January 1872. There is no record of Bina Mack's father, Minus Hamilton's death. He must have died before 1870 because he is not listed in the 1870 or subsequent censuses. He would have been ninety-five had he lived until 1870, assuming that he was in actuality eighty-eight when he liberated himself in the Combahee River Raid. He lived to see African-American men serving in the US Army, "de brack sojer so presumptious," and relish freedom, but not to witness his daughter buy her first piece of land.[28]

Bina Mack likely also used either bounty (money to which soldiers were entitled for enlisting and which they or their heirs often had to go through a protracted bureaucratic process to get) or pension money from her husband's service in the 2nd South Carolina Volunteers. Harry Mack was killed in action at Morris Island in August 1863. In May 1868, Old Head Sancho Van Dross, who was one of Bina Mack's father's contemporaries, testified for Minus Hamilton's daughter and granddaughter so that they could receive their pensions. Sancho Van Dross told the notary public he attended Harry Mack and Bina Hamilton's wedding in November 1855, and was also present when their daughter Hagar Mack was born on February 1, 1858, though they were enslaved and married on Parker's Place and he was held in bondage on Rose Hill Plantation.[29]

The first wave of Combahee landowners did not go back to the rice plantations where they had grown up in bondage. Instead they purchased land on the Sea Islands in US-occupied territory. They settled among fellow US Colored Troops comrades and their comrades' wives, widows, and children. And they settled among fellow freedom seekers—those who liberated themselves and went to the urban areas before the war, or after "Gun Shoot at Bay Point," or as a result of the Emancipation Proclamation, or after the multiple raids the US Army and Navy conducted from coastal South Carolina to northern Florida, including the Combahee River Raid. They settled among freedom seekers from the mainland and the coast who followed General Sherman's army as it made its way through the interior to and along the coast.

For the first time, Lowcountry Creoles from all of these different directions were brought together by their desire to own land and their ability to own it earlier than in other parts of the South. Their common experiences during the war—dislocation, liberation, military service, and land ownership—would galvanize this diverse group of people into one in the postwar period.

★★★★★★★★

For Black folks, the Combahee River was enemy territory for a long time after the Civil War had ended. It became even more so after the US government restored to former landowners and enslavers the lands it had confiscated for non-payment of taxes. Freedpeople who had occupied and cultivated the lands without title to them were evicted. And yet, despite the uncertainty and danger, most Combahee freedom seekers, like Aaron Ancrum, Cuffie Bolze, Edward Brown, Jackson Grant, Andrew and Diana Harris, Charles and Neptune Nicholas, Joshua and Moses Simmons, Stephen Simmons, Mingo Van Dross, and Simon Washington, including those who stopped in Beaufort for a few years after the war, eventually went back to the plantations from which they escaped bondage on June 2, 1863. They worked in the rice fields where they had been forced to labor against their will and lived on the land where multiple generations of their families were buried. As the Gullah Geechee elders say: "However far the stream flows, it never forgets its source."

Whether the planters were new to the Combahee, such as John D. Warren and John Bennett Bissell, or former slaveholders, like Joshua Nicholls, the Combahee freedom seekers saw them as "Secesh," as Blacks in US-occupied territory had called supporters of the Confederacy during and after war. These whites still supported the Confederacy even though to reclaim their land they had taken an oath of allegiance to the United States of America.

Within ten years after the Combahee River Raid, those who fought and escaped in it banded together and started going back to Colleton County en masse. By 1870, Hector Fields, my great-great-great-grandfather, did not return to Beaufort immediately after the war ended. Hector owned six acres of improved land in Colleton County, one horse, and two pigs; he produced 25 bushels of Indian corn and 2,200 pounds of rice. The total value of his farm produce and stock was $86 and the value of his farm was $160. He and his wife, Peggy Fields, then purchased twenty-four acres for $72, the second lot from the Younghall Tract, one of three plantations formerly owned by William Henry Heyward (another one of Nathaniel Heyward's grandsons and William C. Heyward's cousins) in Colleton County, in February 1879. The land was in the "Heyward neighborhood" in White Hall where Hector and his brother, Jonas, had gone to work in the rice fields after the war. But they were still unhealthy places for Black and white people alike. A two-year-old child, also named Hector Fields, who I surmise would have been Hector Fields's son was reported dead of bilious fever in 1880. Hector left Colleton County after his son's death and never returned to live.[30]

Combee people pooled their resources and talents to achieve land ownership. First, they acted through white intermediaries, former planters and slaveholders who may have been their employers. On February 2, 1876, William Manigault purchased 278¼ acres of Woodlawn Plantation from a bankruptcy sale of the estate of Dr. Charles Witsell (the physician who had attended the enslaved population on Longbrow Plantation and who continued to practice medicine in Walterboro after the war; Witsell testified that Aaron Ancrum had been "taken from his plantation by Montgomery of the US forces in 1863"). Manigault was acting as trustee for Cuffie Bolze and twenty-four other freedpeople. The deed stated that "each contributed an equal share in payment of fee and bond." They paid $5 in the bankruptcy sale.[31]

Widow Flora Robinson was able to pay off the land that her husband, veteran Harry Robinson, had earlier purchased on a mortgage. After Harry died in January 1877, Flora agreed to pay $3 per acre for it until she had paid it off. Flora "managed by hard labor" to pay off her poor barren pineland. Then she built a one-story, two-room clapboard house on it.[32] It didn't take long, however, for the Combee freedpeople to take the responsibility on themselves. On January 2, 1880, Neptune Nicholas and Charles Nicholas, acting as trustees for seven others who are not named, sold 966 acres to

April Singleton for $5. On January 26, 1880, April Singleton and Neptune Nicholas purchased 334 acres from Albert Wichman, a German immigrant who owned the largest store in downtown Walterboro. Three days later, the sheriff of Colleton County, Robert Black, sold April Singleton and Neptune Nicholas (acting as trustees for twenty-nine others) 334 acres of the Fripp plantation at auction for $950—not a small sum for people only ten years out of bondage. The tract, one of three tracts of 334 acres each, could have been part of the estate of Charles E. Fripp, who died in 1884. The January 29 deed conveying the 334 acres from the Colleton County sheriff to Nicholas and Singleton described the duo as "planters of Colleton County."[33]

By 1886, twenty-five-year-old Singleton had acted as trustee for members of his community in no fewer than three land transactions, purchasing at least 1,634 acres of land in Colleton County. Nicholas and Singleton acted as trustees for Singleton's mother-in-law, Molly Graham, and Nicholas's 2nd South Carolina Volunteers comrades and their relatives, including Edward Brown, Moses Simmons, Charles Nicholas, Joshua Simmons, July Osborne, Neptune Nicholas, Nicholas's comrade Harry Robinson's widow Flora Robinson, and Cuffie Bowles's cousin Jack Barnwell. They had all escaped bondage on Cypress Plantation. Examining the deed for the 1880 transaction, it becomes evident why Nicholas and Singleton served as trustees and why Old Heads (who were Prime Hands during the Civil War) would entrust their business affairs to a young man among the Boys and Wives: literacy. Nicholas, Singleton, and the witnesses signed their names. The twenty-nine others, including Charles Nicholas, Edward Brown, Flora Robinson, and Joshua Simmons, signed by mark. Neptune Nicholas testified in 1902 that he "never signed by mark since freedom." He knew he "must sign if he could write." (He also wrote an affidavit for his comrade Cuffie Bolze's pension application, and he wrote on behalf of other comrades too.) Freedpeople who could read and write were slightly less likely to be taken advantage of by land speculators. But even those who were literate could not understand the legalese of the deeds, titles, mortgages, and bonds.[34]

Neptune Nicholas and April Singleton leased some of the land they held in trust to local white farmers. They acted as trustees to lease a portion of lands they had purchased from the Gough place, bordering the Charleston and Savannah Railroad and William C. Heyward's estate (which may have belonged to Marianna Barnwell Gough Smith, who was Nathaniel Barnwell Heyward's mother- in- law and who died in 1837) to R. B. Grant for $6 annual rent . Then they sold Elizabeth M. Grant a parcel for $300; it bordered the Charleston and Savannah Railroad and the estate of William C. Heyward, which John Bennett Bissell had purchased by the end of December 1885.[35]

On January 6, 1886, the freedmen and freedwomen for whom Neptune Nicholas and April Singleton had acted as trustees purchased their shares of land from Singleton. Most bought roughly 33 acres acres and paid $100 each, except for July Osborne, who paid $29.62, and Jack Barnwell, who acquired 67 9/10 acres for $200. Second South Carolina Volunteer veterans July Osborne, Neptune Nicholas, Neptune's brother, Charles Nicholas, Moses Simmons, Lucius Robinson, Edward Brown, Moses's brother, Joshua Simmons and men who were too young to serve in the US Colored Troops, like Jack Barnwell, all bought their land on the same day. As described previously, they had all been held in bondage on Cypress Plantation before the raid. Now they were back as close to the land on which they were raised in bondage as most of them would get. The share that Charles Nicholas purchased that day from Singleton he later sold to Wichman in January 1893 for $130.90, a tidy profit from the $100 purchase price.[36]

Among the Combahee veterans, the Old Heads either did not live long enough to get their pensions or did not live long after getting them. Like Harriet Tubman Davis, their widows applied for their pensions. On May 29, 1890, Elizabeth Botume testified for Silvia De Causter that she had "known Isaac DeCosta since 1864." She knew Isaac's whole family from living near the De Causters and visiting them frequently. Isaac's first wife, Kathy, had died twenty years earlier, and their only son, Pompey, was killed in battle. About seven years after Kathy's death, Isaac brought a woman, Silvia, to Botume and introduced her as his wife. Botume testified she was at the De Causters' house in Beaufort soon after Isaac died on April 15, 1890; she helped provide suitable burial clothes for him. Isaac's body was taken home to Rose Hill Plantation on the Combahee for burial. November Osborne died on May 24, 1893, on Lady's Island, where he and his wife, Sarah Osborne, had first purchased land in December 1866. They did not return to Oakland Plantation or the lower Combahee before November's death.[37]

Several remained in Beaufort and purchased land there. A 2nd South Carolina Volunteers widow named Pleasant Rutledge bought a lot in 1889 for $25, and in 1891 Sina Green bought one for $75. Sina Green may have been adding to the twenty acres Jonas Green purchased in Port Royal in 1866 and the lot in Higginsonville he purchased in 1868, thereby augmenting and diversifying the Green family's holdings. Catherine Noyles, another Massachusetts teacher who taught with Elizabeth Botume, wrote to her sister that when she departed Port Royal in November 1869 "she left a great many of the men owning nice little homesteads of their own." However, construction of additional portions of the Charleston and Savannah Railroad spurred land speculators to buy up the land from freedpeople.[38]

Old Head Andrew Wyatt, who escaped bondage on James L. Paul's plantation, remained in Beaufort and purchased one acre for $30 in the town in 1892. His sister-in-law Silvia De Causter testified in the pension file that Wyatt had a mortgage on a piece of land on Lady's Island but had been "compel[led] to leave it" because he had been "burnt out" in a house fire and lost "every thing he had in the world"—that is, Wyatt lost the land on Lady's Island because he was not able to pay the taxes on it. From January 1893 until December 1897, Julia Proctor, James Sheppard, Jack Aiken, and James Shields purchased land. Julia Proctor bought the smallest piece of land, for $5. Jack Aiken bought the largest, forty acres, for $76.75. James Shields's ten acres in Beaufort for $100 was certainly the most expensive investment. Proctor, Sheppard, Aiken, and Shields had all escaped bondage on Newport Plantation.[39]

Margaret Simmons, Joshua Simmons's widow, testified in her pension file that she owned thirty-two acres of land, valued at $2 per acre (though her 1894 tax return showed that the county valued the parcel at $100). She could not live on her land because it was in a "sickly place," according to Simmons. However, she was still able to use it to raise vegetables, which she sold to make her living. After James Sheppard died around Christmastime in 1898, his widow, Sally Sheppard, testified that the five acres of land that her husband had bought in Sheldon, cut from the Fuller family's tract, were valued at $50. Unfortunately, the land did not have a house on it and was "no good for cultivation," she said. She still owned it in 1901, though she derived no income from it nor did she live on it.[40]

Sina Green testified in 1901 that she still owned her house and lot in the town of Beaufort on Harrington Street, valued at $175, and five acres of land in Port Royal near the oak grove, valued at $75. After the death of her second husband, Jonas Green, in February 1901, she was entitled to her widow's dower (a surviving widow inherited a life estate of one-third of any real property her husband had owned during their marriage; upon her death, the property passed to the husbands' heirs or creditors), three more acres in Beaufort town that were valued at $75. She had likely used money from her first husband's pension to amass one of the largest landholdings among Blacks freed in the Combahee River Raid.[41]

Moses Simmons sold to his wife, Fannie Simmons, ten acres bordering Jack Barnwell's land for $20 in March 1904. There is no record of whether or not Fannie was able to pay the taxes on it and keep it until the end of her life. Fulton McGuire (who was one of the gunners on the St. Johns expedition, had participated in the Combahee River Raid, and testified against Colonel Montgomery in Major Corwin's court-martial) left his wife a small dwelling and lot in Punta Gorda, Florida, that in 1907 were valued at $100. It wasn't much, but it belonged to Eliza Gabriel Basquiat Lewis McGuire and her children after Fulton's death in May 1907. And James Shields's wife, Jone Colonel Shields, owned ten acres in Sheldon Township valued at $100 in January 1905. She used it for her "planting purposes," she testified, cultivating cotton, corn, and peas.[42]

★★★★★★★★

The dawn of the twentieth century brought the death of the remaining veterans—Neptune Nicholas on November 1, 1903, Moses Simmons on October 5, 1905, and Jackson Grant on October 3, 1909. In addition, African Americans on the Combahee continued to experience the same hardships with maintaining landownership as did those in other parts of the Lowcountry, from Georgetown south to the St. Johns River, from the coast to thirty miles into the interior.[43]

Even Combahee freedpeople who had been fortunate in earlier decades fell on hard times. Edward Brown had purchased land in March 1873 and January 1886, with his comrade and childhood friend Neptune Nicholas acting as trustee along with April Singleton, then purchased his share, 33 9/10 acres, from April Singleton in January 1886. He subsequently mortgaged it to Albert Wichman for $47.17, then deeded it over to Wichman in April 1900 because he could not pay the mortgage. When Edward died a few months later, in January 1901, his wife, Peggy Brown, "thought the land belonged to her and her husband." She was told she thought wrong by Albert Wichman, who owned her land. Wichman informed Peggy she would have to pay $100 if she wanted to own the land on which she lived. Peggy and her grandson went to Captain Shaffer's store in Walterboro (likely owned by Alexander Castner Shaffer, who came to Walterboro after the war to work for the Freedmen's Bureau and operated Terry and Shaffer downtown in Walterboro), where they met up with her husband's comrades Cuffie Bolze and Neptune Nicholas, who were there conducting pension-related business. Peggy told her old friends her story. Bolze and Nicholas took Peggy and her grandson to another general store owned by a Mr. Henderson (likely the store owned by Edward P. Henderson, though the Pension Bureau charged C. G. Henderson, the notary public, with forgery in Peggy Brown's case), where Edward Brown had processed his quarterly pension benefits. They asked if Henderson could "arrange for her to get some money on his Grand Pa's pension papers," according to Peggy's grandson, Ned Brown. Henderson must not have loaned Peggy the money she needed, for she testified that a man named Mr. Sanders bought her land and she had to pay him rent in order to continue living there.[44]

The family of Neptune Nicholas—the man who tried to help Peggy Brown and had once led his community, acting as a trustee in land purchases—had similar problems. Neptune's wife, Betsy Singleton Simmons Nicholas, testified that she and Neptune had been trying to buy the place where they lived, but she "had to give it up" after he died in November 1903. She subsequently paid rent on a house and a little piece of land. In October 1908, his heirs lost thirty-four acres of his land for nonpayment of taxes. The tract they lost bordered land owned by April Singleton and Margaret Simmons, his comrade Joshua Simmons's widow. Neptune's heirs owed $5.85 in taxes and $2.00 in penalties. Colleton County sold his land for $18.50. Mingo Van Dross (listed in the record as Mingo Vanderhorst) bought two acres for $10 in March 1909, and Friday Hamilton bought even less for $1 in October 1909. Annie Barnwell, who was a cousin of Cuffie Bolze and Sina Green, made one of the last large land purchases, thirty acres for $50 in 1932. But none of the three was able to keep the land they purchased.[45]

Charles Nicholas, also one of the people who escaped enslavement on Cypress Plantation, executed multiple transactions. As we've seen, on January 2, 1880, he served as a trustee (along with his brother Neptune and April Singleton) for seven others in a land sale. In 1929, after his widow, Ella McGrath Nicholas, had died, Ella's brother I. S. McGrath wrote to E. W. Morgan, the acting commissioner of pensions, on April 4, 1929, regarding a ten- acre parcel in Colleton County, saying that a good portion of that low-lying land was "grow up" and had not been planted for fifteen or twenty years. Cuffie Bolze had testified for Ella more than two decades earlier that the land would be worth $1 per acre annually in income if rented. It did not have a house on it, and on the 1928 tax receipt it was valued at $30, though Charles had paid $100 for it. A few years later, in 1934, McGrath wrote a letter to President Franklin Roosevelt regarding the ten acres of land in Colleton County. He claimed that Charles's daughter by his first wife, Hagar, had sold the land after Ella's death (Ella herself didn't have any children). The $49 she gave McGrath after the sale was not sufficient to cover the expenses of his sister's final illness and burial.[46]

One of the youngest veterans to enlist after the raid, Cuffie Bolze, died on June 21, 1920 or 1922. After Cuffie's death, his estate lost thirty-four acres (which may have been part of the 278¼ acres in Colleton County he purchased in February 1876) in March 1926 for nonpayment of $25.93 in taxes and fees. Annie Barnwell lost thirty-three acres (which may have included the thirty acres in Colleton she purchased in August 1916) in March 1932 for not paying $18.84 in taxes and penalties.[47]

Some veterans, widows, and neighbors would never return to Combahee, preferring to migrate to Walterboro (as did Friday Hamilton), Charleston (Friday Barrington and Relia Barnwell Middleton), Lady's Island (November, Sarah, and Nat Osborne), Savannah and other parts of Georgia (Richard A. Smith and Solomon Washington), and Jacksonville and Fernandina, Florida (Jim Simmons). Wherever they settled, veterans and widows of the 33rd, 34th, and the 21st USCT regiments led the way in land ownership, investing their military bounties and pensions to buy land beginning after the 1863 tax sale.

Friday Hamilton went first to Walterboro, South Carolina, where he lived and worked as a cook until sometime after 1910. This was not his last stop. He was one of the only Combahee freedom seekers who enlisted in the 2nd South Carolina Volunteers to migrate to the North, and one of the longest-lived as well. He died in his late eighties in New York City on September 22, 1923. It is likely he wound up there because his son Frederick Ulysses Hamilton and his wife, Arizona, were already living there (the 1890 census shows Frederick and Arizona living there and that their son Harold had been born the year before), and perhaps they sent for him when his health began to fail. And Friday's daughter-in-law, Arizona Hamilton, and granddaughter, Irene Hamilton, took care of him until the end of his life.[48]

★★★★★★★★

One of the most enduring legacies of the Combahee River Raid is the window it opens into the process by which Lowcountry Creoles became those whom today we call the Gullah Geechee. As this long and detailed epic has chronicled, Lowcountry Creoles were held in bondage on Sea Island indigo and cotton plantations, on coastal rice plantations, and in urban areas. In the South Carolina, Georgia, and Florida Lowcountry, the Civil War was simultaneously a destructive act, wiping out the planters' and enslavers' social and economic order, and a creative act, creating a new community. And while freedom seekers from the Combahee River saw themselves as distinct, they had experiences similar to those of other African Americans who liberated themselves and found refuge in US-occupied territory in coastal South Carolina, Georgia, and Florida. The Battle of Port Royal, the Port Royal Experiment, the US Army's multiple raids, displacement, military enlistment, land ownership, and migration to US-occupied territory in the Sea Islands and urban areas sowed the seeds of this linguistic, cultural, and social transformation.

Freedom was the catalyst for Lowcountry Creoles to make marriages and families, to build churches, and to establish communities with those who may have had different experiences in bondage but similar experiences in freedom—and in fighting for the freedom of others during the Civil War. In the aftermath of the war Lowcountry Creoles transformed themselves. And as Friday Hamilton's family reveals, by the early twentieth century the generation born to the USCT veterans and their children had forged a full-force Gullah Geechee diaspora.

★★★★★★★★

In the foreword to this book I noted how critical the US Civil War pension files and their testimonies are to piecing together the stories of its main historical actors, and I said a little bit about the process of drawing a pension. It bears repeating that this process was confusing and convoluted, particularly for the overwhelmingly illiterate veterans and widows whose lives were little documented in the kind of paperwork that the federal government's bureaucracy would recognize—"white folk proof," as Relia Barnwell Middleton called it. addition, veterans and widows sometimes offered conflicting testimony, complicating their pension applications. When they did not tell the truth, did not tell the whole truth, or recanted their testimony, it was usually for reasons having to do with their marital relations. But eventually witnesses stepped forward and spilled the proverbial beans, enabling the special examiners to get to the bottom of things.

On April 24, 1875, Sina Bolze Young testified that she had never remarried after the death of her husband, William Young. She told the special examiner she had been cohabitating with Jonas Green, occupying the same bed with him at night for several years, and living like married folk—they even had two children together. Yet, she insisted, she was not married to him. The examination of her pension claim had started two years prior to Sina's testimony. Many in the Cypress community testified in support of her application, including her girlfriends Venus Lyons, Elsey Jones, and Lina Richard. They told the pension official that they had lived before the war at Cypress Plantation, where they had been enslaved by William C. Heyward, and had returned there in freedom after the war; they also said they had known Sina Young since she was a child, had known her deceased husband, William Young, for many years, and had attended Sina and Will's wedding. We've seen that people from Cypress were on the *John Adams* with Will and Sina when they all left the plantation, and that they were present when Will Young enlisted in the US Army with Frank Lyons, Venus Lyons's first husband, and William Jones, whom Reverend Peter White married to Elsey Jones in Higginsonville in 1868.[49]

People in the community called her Sina Green, but Sina insisted she had maintained her status as William Young's legal widow. Jonas Green declared that he was not Sina's husband and had never acknowledged her as his wife. He did not deny that they lived together as married people, but asserted that he considered her to be William Young's widow. When the pastor of their church inquired why they were living together as if married yet were not married, Sina told him she had made a pension claim that her remarriage would jeopardize; as soon as her claim was settled, she and Jonas would comply with the church's requirement and get married.

Neighbors who had known Jonas and Sina during enslavement supported the couple's account that they were not married. Eventually a neighbor in Beaufort who had not known them during enslavement testified that two years previously, Jonas and Sina had begun telling their neighbors—who all thought they were married—that were actually not married. This was around the same time a pension agent had showed up asking questions and taking depositions. Sina Bolze Young Green was dropped from the pension rolls in December 1876.[50]

The pension files help illuminate the ends of lives, particularly because death certificates don't exist before the mid-1910s for African Americans in rural Beaufort County and the 1920s in Colleton County. In addition to those like William Young and Harry Mack who were killed in action, the regiment lost several former Prime Hands in the 1880s. Frank Hamilton, who contracted a hacking cough in the army during the winter of 1864, died of what we know now was tuberculosis on February 10, 1884, on Rose Hill Plantation, where he and his wife lived after the war. Frank's wife, Tenah Jenkins Hamilton—they married on Rose Hill—died four months before him. Frank's comrade Jackson Grant wrote the dates of the Hamiltons' deaths in his Bible, which served as the church's record. Grant preached at both Tenah's and Frank's funerals. As noted, Frank's and Jackson's parents had been sold together from Castle Hill Plantation in 1837; they subsequently liberated themselves from bondage on Rose Hill. Frank was buried at Rose Hill by his brother, Captain Brown, who also had supported Frank (he was unable to work because of his disease) and nursed him, then subsequently buried Frank's son. Frank Jr. contracted tuberculosis three years before his death on December 24, 1896; his brother Pompey died around the same time. Captain Brown applied for $100 of Frank's accrued pension to cover the expenses he paid during the illnesses and for the burials of his loved ones.[51]

Joshua Simmons was a member of Jackson Grant's church (which is unnamed in the pension files). Simmons died on March 6, in either 1889 or 1890, on Oakland Plantation, next door to Cypress Plantation, from which he had liberated himself. His brother Moses Simmons and comrades Jackson Grant and Friday Hamilton attended him day and night during his last illness, then "laid him out"—dressed his body in the clothes in which he was buried, and assisted in their brother and comrade's burial. Grant also assisted in laying out his comrade Anthony Bartley when Bartley died in

February 1898. The pension official described him as "Rev. Grant" when Grant testified for Anthony's wife, Moriah Bartley, and swore to having attended her second wedding (as mentioned in Chapter 18, Reverend Moore married the Bartleys and several other couples in June 1864).[52]

There were many things witnesses neglected or refused to tell pension officials. They did not always divulge their family relationships, for example, particularly if those ties were not material to the case they were trying to prove. Phoebe Burns Frazier applied for a widow's pension after her husband, Robert Frazier, died in December 1872. Robert Frazier had been wounded in the left hip on July 1864 on Johnson's Island. His injury was so severe that he could hardly walk and experienced extreme pain, especially in rainy, damp weather. Daphney Drayton—who according to William Jones had known Robert since they were all "little ones"—described Phoebe's husband as able to do no "more work than a 10 year old boy." Phoebe's brother Friday Barrington eventually helped his brother-in-law get a job in Charleston at a gunsmith owned by a Mr. McLush, though according to Edward Elliott, who also worked for the gunsmith, Robert could not do much work other than "job about the yard." Then Mr. McLush's wife became ill, and Robert Frazier's employer reassigned Robert as his wife's care giver until she died in October 1872. When Robert became ill shortly afterward, Mr. McLush sent him to the smallpox hospital, where he died around Christmas of the same year.[53]

When she applied for a widow's pension, Phoebe, who may have been given only part of the story by Robert's employer, testified the wound in his leg was the cause of his death. She also likely thought her pension depended on it (and it did, at least before the Dependent and Disability Pension Act of June 27, 1890, made all veterans who had served for at least ninety days, as well as their widows and dependents, eligible for pension benefits once they became disabled or died, regardless of whether their disability or death had resulted from their military service). But Friday Barrington, who had said to the special examiner he had known Phoebe "all of his life; she was his sister," and whom the examiner had noted as "brother to claimant," had also told the special examiner Robert "waited on" Mrs. McLush until she died. Afterward, in December 1893, Phoebe Frazier testified she did not have a brother living in Charleston; when the special examiner asked her directly who Friday Barrington was, she did not reply he was her brother, instead saying only, "He was dead a long time ago." Her fear that her brother's testimony might lead to a judgment that her husband had died of smallpox and not from injuries related to his military service, thus disqualifying her for a pension, was likely why Phoebe lied to the special examiner.[54]

The pension system worked slowly, and these complexities usually took years or even decades to sort out. Harriet Tubman's fight to secure a pension was not quick, easy, or inexpensive. In 1868, as we've seen, she first applied for back pay for her service as a spy and scout. By Tubman's calculations, the government owed her $766 for "32½ Months" of service —$966.00 "For Services as Scout in the Military Department of South Carolina" from her arrival in Beaufort on "25 May, 1862" to the time she went on furlough, "31st January, 1865," "less pay received," the $200 she was paid and which she used to establish the washhouse for the Beaufort refugee women. Charles P. Wood, a prominent banker in Auburn, was one of the people who helped her request the funds; the request was denied by Congress.[55]

The federal government's denial of her request for back pay left Tubman in need of money to pay her mortgage and support the many needy people who depended on her. The Auburn community persuaded one of its local authors, Sarah Bradford, to write a biography of Tubman. Bradford was a published author of sentimental novels and short stories, the kind that appealed to a middle- and upper-class white female readership, and the sister of Samuel M. Hopkins Jr., the pastor of Auburn's Central Presbyterian Church, where Tubman married her second husband, Nelson Davis, in 1869. His children, like William Lloyd Garrison's and Frederick Douglass's children, could see what Tubman risked and contributed to the US military effort by gathering intelligence, leading a ring of spies, scouts, and pilots, and piloting Colonel Montgomery and his regiment up the Combahee River. And they provided the only contemporary record of both feats (in letters from George Garrison and Lewis Douglass) as well as an account many years after the war (in the case of Hopkins's *Grandfather Stories*). Tubman used the proceeds from book sales to pay her mortgage and household expenses, as well as provide clothes and books to two schools for freed people in the South for which she continued to fundraise after she returned to Auburn.[56]

As Bradford was writing the biography over a few months during the summer of 1868, she contacted several of Tubman's associates to provide their testimonials and reminiscences of Tubman's life. Though Bradford interviewed Tubman, she only used interviews that she could corroborate with testimony from other people. She included letters from people who knew and supported Tubman when she was the most famous conductor on the Underground Railroad, such as Gerrit Smith, Wendell Phillips, and Frederick Douglass, and while she served with the US Army Department of the South during the Civil War, such as General Rufus Saxton, William H. Seward, and Colonel James Montgomery. With the testimonials, she included letters written by US Army officials, like Montgomery, Seward, and Dr. Henry K. Durant, written to prominent Auburn banker Charles P. Wood as part of Tubman's unsuccessful request for back pay from the federal government.[57]

This strategy was likely Bradford's way of backing up Tubman's memories of her own extraordinary life, which, according to Bradford, seemed "too strange for belief, and . . . were invested with the charm of romance." Certainly the testimonials from well-known figures in the abolitionist movement, the overwhelming majority of whom were white and male, would make Tubman's stories more palatable and believable to her readers. After all, Tubman's stories, though dramatic, were not fiction, as was Harriet Beecher Stowe's *Uncle Tom's Cabin* (most in Bradford's readership would have read this second-best-selling novel of the nineteenth century), and Bradford's biography was not intended to be a work of fiction. Bradford declared that Tubman "deserved to be handed down to posterity side by side with the names of Joan of Arc, Grace Darling, and Florence Nightingale." None of these women had "shown more courage and power of endurance" in risking their own lives and facing death to "relieve human suffering" than Tubman in "her heroic and successful endeavors" to save members of her "oppressed and suffering race" and "pilot them from the land of Bondage to the promised land of Liberty." She was appealing to her readership to help Tubman by purchasing the book.[58]

The oil painting *Harriet Tubman, ca. 1945,* which graces the cover of this volume, is American painter William H. Johnson's take on the iconic and "spirited woodcut likeness of Tubman, in her costume as a scout." The original woodcut was featured as the frontispiece of *Scenes in the Life of Harriet Tubman*, Sarah Bradford's 1869 biography, but not Bradford's *Harriet Tubman, the Moses of Her People*, published in 1886. Written after Reconstruction, the 1886 edition was shorn of violent, dehumanizing images of enslavement in Tubman's life. Both images depict Tubman wearing a Union blue greatcoat over a striped ankle-length coat, likely in an effort to make Tubman's life story more palatable to a northern public forging reconciliation with southerners. A haversack is draped over her right shoulder and across her body. She is wearing a patterned head scarf and carrying a specially made sharpshooter's rifle. Both the woodcut and the painting are fitting tributes to Tubman's career as a US Army scout.[59]

As noted earlier, Bradford had written to several of Tubman's associates seeking their perspective on Tubman's life. She printed Frederick Douglass's poignant letter, written on August 29, 1868, and addressed to Harriet Tubman, in the introduction of the original 1869 edition of Tubman's biography. In it, Douglass said that in asking for a "word of commendation," Tubman (actually, it was Bradford's request) had asked for what Tubman did not need. He declared that he needed words of commendation from her much more than she needed them from him, particularly because he knew intimately her "devotion to the cause of the lately enslaved of our land."[60]

But the nation, beyond a small and dwindling circle of northern abolitionists, still did not know Harriet Tubman. Douglass acknowledged that "the difference between" them was "very marked." Most of the antislavery work he had done for decades was public and "wrought in the day," lecturing, writing in abolitionist newspapers (particularly his own *North Star*), advocating for Black men to be allowed to serve in the military, recruiting Black soldiers to serve in Black regiments, and lobbying for the equality of Black people with government officials as high up as President Abraham Lincoln. Douglass attested that he had "received much encouragement every step of the way."[61]

In contrast, Tubman had labored in the night "in a private way," when only the "midnight sky and the silent stars have been the witnesses" to Tubman's "devotion to freedom" and her "heroism." Her courage, selflessness, and sacrifice were only "witnessed by a few trembling, scarred, and foot-sore bondsmen and women" whom she "led out of the house of bondage." The only rewards she received were the benedictions of their "heartfelt '*God Bless you*.'" Except for John Brown, who died for the cause of freedom, Douglass knew of no other person who had "willingly encountered more perils and hardships to serve our enslaved people" than Tubman did.[62]

Yet the US government refused to recognize her service during the Civil War. A second attempt in 1888 was also unsuccessful.

Then her second husband, Nelson Davis, died of consumption on October 14, 1888. In July 1890 she filed for a widow's pension under the Dependent and Disability Pension Act of June 27, 1890. She could not have received a widow's pension before 1890 because, as in the case of Phoebe Burns Frazier, her husband's death was not related to his military service. But with the passage of that act she could apply, and for her application to be successful she had first to prove his identity. She and her witnesses had to establish that Nelson Davis was the same Nelson Charles who had been born in bondage in Elizabeth City, North Carolina, where he worked against his will as a bricklayer and laborer, and that he had enlisted in the 8th Regiment, Company G, on September 25, 1863, as the Nelson Charles Davis who married her in Auburn in March 1869. In her affidavits, Tubman emphasized that both she and her husband were not enslaved at the time they married and that her husband had not been in bondage when he enlisted; they had been "freed from slavery by the Proclamation of President Lincoln." She and her witnesses had to prove that she and Nelson Davis were legally married, that he had never been married before he married her, and that her first husband, John Tubman, was dead. One witness testified that John Tubman had died in an "altercation" on the county road between Airey's and Cambridge, Maryland, in September 1867. She and Nelson Davis married after John Tubman's death, after Nelson Davis had traveled to Auburn after mustering out and boarded at Tubman's home.[63]

More than 42 percent of the African American Civil War veterans who applied for pensions had their applications approved. That means, of course, that 58 percent of those who applied were denied. It is harder to quantify how many didn't apply or didn't complete their applications because they could not produce the necessary paperwork or witnesses, could not pay the notaries' and/or attorneys' fees, could not prove that they served in the USCT and had been honorably discharged, or died before they completed the application process.

My great-great-great-grandfather falls into the third category. On October 1, 1890, poor Hector went to E. A. Crofut, a local attorney in Beaufort, to get help filing for a pension. Crofut wrote in his ledger that Hector served as "Priv Co C 34th March '63 to August '65"—but, as noted earlier, Hector's military service record states that he deserted in August 1864. He must have told Crofut in August 1865, because Crofut wrote that date instead of August 1864 as the date Hector's service ended. The entry continues: "Went home on furlough when he got back Co had gone and could not find them so went home." Crofut scribbled in the margins that Hector "was not prevented from completing his term by phys. Disability contracted in line of duty." We have no way of knowing how many times Hector engaged the attorney or how much it cost him. Ten years later, on August 11, 1900, Hector filed a declaration for an invalid pension. His application was rejected on February 6, 1901.[64]

Working in the rice fields after the war brought a host of illnesses that were hardly new to African Americans who had toiled in the Lowcountry rice swamps against their will for centuries. Because of the veterans' pension applications, these illnesses came to the attention of the federal government. Andrew Wyatt, who was once described as being able to "follow the plow as well as any man," told the pension official in August 1891 that his body was "'ruptured' with disease." Wyatt testified that there was a "good deal of fever and malaria around the neighborhood" of William Paul's Combahee rice plantation before he enlisted in the army. Many of Wyatt's family, friends, and neighbors, including Wyatt's sister-in-law Silvia De Causter as well as Charlotte Savage, John A. Savage, Diana Days Harris, and Mary Ann Lewis, agreed that "it was sickly down at Combahee," as Charlotte Savage put it. Some admitted Wyatt had chronic malaria; they had had it as well before the war, but they recovered and kept working. The US Army discharged Wyatt, as noted, because he had pains all over his body, especially in his shoulders and loins. His condition deteriorated rapidly once he returned home. According to De Causter, he was "all crippled up" with rheumatism, from which, many testified, Wyatt had never suffered before the war. He could no longer follow the plow or do any work for himself or his family. He died on July 2, 1894.[65]

Death came to Ned Snipe on February 17, 1894. Ned's brother-in-law and comrade Anthony Bartley testified for his sister, Daphne Jackson Powell Snipe, that he "saw Ned dead" and assisted in his funeral and burial the following day. Another comrade, Andrew Nicholas, assisted also. We've seen that Anthony Bartley and his wife, Moriah, and Ned and Daphne Snipe were all remarried together by Reverend Moore at Pigeon Point in June 1864.[66]

Smart Washington remarried twice after the death of his first wife, Mary. He and his third wife, Lucretia Davis Washington, settled in Fernandina Beach, Florida. Dr. W. E. Frasier, a physician in Fernandina who examined

Washington for his disability claim, wrote, "This is the case of a very old man who served his country when far past his time of exemption." In November 1890, the physician described him as "nearly 104 years of age as taken from the records from his old master." Washington had "served his country faithfully" for two and a half years and had been honorably discharged. All Washington asked for was whatever the Pension Bureau "may see fit to allow." Dr. Frasier thought Washington's case was "well worthy of government aid" and that it "would be wrong to let go unrewarded." Smart Washington died a few weeks after Ned Snipe, on March 6, 1894, in Fernandina, Florida. In the absence of a death certificate, a copy of the burial permit certified his death date for the Pension Bureau.[67]

As the files show. rheumatism and chronic malaria were not the only ailments plaguing day laborers on Combahee rice plantations after their military service. After the war Richard Smith returned next door to Bonny Hall Plantation and worked as water minder for George A. Bissell. In June 1895, Bissell testified that though Smith's eyes watered, he did not think Smith's eyesight rated him for disability, because a water minder needed good eyesight to manage the water levels in the tidal rice fields properly. Bissell declared—in a bit of twisted logic—that neither the direct glare of the sun nor the glare of the sun reflecting off steel hoes affected the laborers' eyes; what was more concerning was the glare of the sun off the water and the rays of the sun on their heads and necks. Richard Smith, however, was too old to perform "half a man's task," according to Bissell. The special examiner found Smith's claims of "moon blindness," which Smith described as "pains in the balls of my eyes," to be unfounded, though he allowed that the job of water minder was "one of the most responsible and trying position in a rice plantation to the eyes." He wrote in his report to the commissioner of pensions that even if Smith's eye ailments had developed after he entered the service, they were caused by "his former labor in rice fields."[68]

Dr. Bissell (who, as mentioned, served as the superintendent and general agent on Bonny Hall for his brother John Bennett Bissell) testified on October 29, 1896, he treated Jackson Grant for rheumatism and what he called "malarial fever" beginning around 1867. Wally Garrett and others of Grant's comrades told the pension official that Jackson lived on a rice plantation. Bissell testified that he "resided on the Combahee river bottoms for years after the war" and began treating the freedpeople who lived there also in 1861, but he "kept no account" of his "treatment of the colored people what ever." This lack of documentation must have made it difficult for Dr. Bissell to remember the people for whom he was asked to testify and the details of their conditions and medical care thirty years later. Yet he confidently confirmed that "residence and exposure in rice fields would be as conducive to rheumatism as army service." He also affirmed that "malaria and the hot sun in the rice fields" could induce vertigo, from which Jackson claimed he suffered as well. Some, like Friday Hamilton, testified that Jackson complained of rheumatism in his legs, just as he had in the army. In Dr. Bissell's opinion, "work in rice fields after service told on" Jackson Grant because he had worked as a house slave (coachman) and a servant in the US Army. He wasn't accustomed to such exposure. Still, the Pension Bureau approved Jackson Grant's application for a pension increase. Under the 1890 act, veterans were entitled to disability benefits or an increase thereof whether it was military service or muck work in the rice fields that had caused their disabilities.[69]

John A. Savage must have died toward the end of the 1890s, though the exact date is unknown. Savage didn't serve in the military and thus does not have a pension file. Yet, he provided a lot of testimony for his family members and neighbors who had all liberated themselves from enslavement on Rose Hill Plantation. Savage, as noted previously, was left behind because he was encamped with the "boss," William L. Kirkland, and the Charleston Light Dragoons in McPhersonville at the time of the raid. His last testimony was for Isaac De Causter on February 15, 1892, when Savage signed his name to his affidavit. On May 22, 1897, the special examiner in Captain Brown's application for his brother Frank Hamilton's accrued pension, wrote "Savage is dead" in the margins of his letter to the Commissioner of Pensions. Savage was one of the original witnesses in Brown's application, but he could not be reinterviewed to verify details of his testimony, because he died sometime between his 1892 testimony and the examiner's 1897 letter. I've noted that death certificates for African Americans in this rural part of South Carolina don't exist before as late as the 1920s. Pension files are one of the few reliable sources of death dates before this period for those who had such files; they tell us all we can know without a death certificate or church record. We can't always have closure.[70]

For the most part, the pension files are the only source with which to chronicle the final illnesses and deaths of the Prime Hands, who had been the strongest laborers on the rice plantations where they were held in bondage. They served their country and, despite injuries, were not discharged early. Yet their bodies were broken down both by military service and by labor in the rice fields.[71]

★★★★★★★★

Not until October 1895, five years after the original application—and after a petition by the local community in Auburn, New York, and indeed an act of Congress—was Tubman's widow's pension claim approved. In addition to an $8-per-month widow's pension, she received a lump-sum back payment retroactive to the date of her first pension application in 1890. It amounted to approximately $500 and allowed her to pay off some bills and fund the construction of her church, Thompson Memorial AME Zion Church, in Auburn. By this time her old horse was dead. Her house and seven acres of lowland farmland were worth $900. But, according to the Cayuga County Clerk, a second mortgage had been taken out on the house and land on April 21, 1892, to Edwin French for $500 at 6 percent interest—a substantial increase from the original mortgage of $200. Tubman also had incurred debt for necessities for her large household, including groceries, coal, and the purchase of a cow for $27. And she needed to pay $130 in medical bills, likely for her husband's final illness.[72]

On October 31, 1895, William Drayton, who enlisted as a drummer at age fourteen—the youngest of the Combahee freedom seekers to enlist in the 2nd South Carolina Volunteers the morning after the raid—died. He was buried at Beaufort National Cemetery. The burying ground was designated by President Abraham Lincoln in 1863 as a national cemetery for soldiers who died in service of their country. Drayton is one of 7,500 Union and Confederate soldiers buried in a semicircular arrangement, with US Colored Troops soldiers interred by regiment.[73]

Tubman's fight for just compensation for her Civil War service continued even after she was granted a widow's pension, for she had not been compensated for her own service. On January 19, 1899, Congressman Sereno Payne introduced a bill, H.R. 4982, that would authorize the secretary of the interior to place Tubman on the pension rolls and pay her a monthly pension of $25. For what the bill claimed was "her faithful service as an Army nurse," it was "none too much." The bill, which was referred to the House Committee on Invalid Pensions, reprinted Secretary Seward's letter written to General David Hunter fourteen years before and described Tubman as by then about seventy-five years old, "physically broken down and poor."[74]

In the end, Tubman never got that monthly $25 pension. An amended bill passed both houses of Congress on February 28, 1899, authorizing the secretary of the interior to provide her with a total pension of $20 per month—so an additional $12 per month for her service as a nurse for the US Army Department of the South in addition to her $8-per-month widow's pension. She was never compensated for her service as a spy and scout for the US Army.[75]

★★★★★★★★

The Combahee veterans had fought for their pension benefits after the war. By the turn of the century, their widows, children, and caretakers had to fight for their benefits, too. Veteran Jackson Grant testified that his daughter Rebecca Grant Wineglass was the legal widow of Jack Wineglass, his comrade in the 34th Regiment, Company G (who though younger than he was discharged first because of his weak knee joints). Wineglass had given birth to four children—only one of whom was born before her husband's death in February 1891—and admitted her husband was not the father of any of her children. However, she claimed she was still Jack Wineglass's widow and was entitled to his pension. Rebecca was Jack Wineglass's third wife. They had been married in March 1888 by Reverend J. H. Connelly at the Methodist Episcopal Church at Rose Hill Plantation. Jackson Grant testified that Jack died from a "severe cold taken while threshing rice. Had an attack of pneumonia and never recovered." Serving as a minister of the Gospel, Grant preached his comrade and son-in-law's funeral and buried him.[76]

Phyllis Wineglass Pinckney, who was the oldest of Jack Wineglass's children with his first wife, Maria Savage Wineglass, who died in May 1881, claimed Rebecca Wineglass had taken up with "old man Andrew Nicholas," one of their father's comrades from Company G, and "lived with him before" Jack Wineglass died; furthermore, she continued to do so up until the time of her pension application. The special examiner found that Rebecca was no longer Jack Wineglass's legal widow, because she had violated the Act of August 7, 1882 (under which adulterous cohabitation terminated a widow's pension benefits). Phyllis was appointed guardian of Jack's surviving son (and her full brother), Hercules Wineglass. Hercules—who witnesses called Harkless—was around sixteen in 1897, when the special examination took place, and was "not particularly delicate," according to J. M. Johnson, the special examiner. After all, he worked in the rice and corn fields. However, Hercules would still be entitled to pension benefits as an adult, because he was mentally disabled and unable to take care of himself.[77]

Rebecca Wineglass denied cohabitating with or having a sexual relationship with Andrew Nicholas. Margaret Simmons (widow of Company G veteran Joshua Simmons) testified that the man with whom Rebecca was accused of committing adultery was a "eunuch, and known to be such by everyone." Rebecca's father testified that Andrew Nicholas (who didn't have a pension file, and thus his death date is unknown) worked for him on land he rented and that Rebecca washed Nicholas's clothes for him. However, she could not deny having four illegitimate children. One way or another the truth usually came out about widows' sexual indiscretions, while the veterans' extramarital activities were never questioned.[78]

Pension officials, especially special examiners, routinely reserved their sharpest criticism and harshest scrutiny for Black women who they deemed neither respectable nor worthy. Yet these desperately poor widows were doing what they had to do to ensure their and their children's survival—demanding their full citizenship rights from the federal government and pressing their claims to respectable widowhood.[79]

Case in point: Diana Simmons Burnett's husband of almost twenty years left her and their five children in Beaufort County and moved over to Colleton County, where he married Sally Ladsden Fraser Dash and then subsequently died. According to Diana, she was "12 years old when Freedom came," which begs the question of which "Freedom" she was referring to: June 2, 1863, when she liberated herself from bondage on Bonny Hall Plantation, or April 1865, when the war ended. Either way, she was a teenager when she and Balaam Burnett were first married while Balaam was in the service and when they were married again, this time by ceremony, in April 1867 at the Baptist Church on Bonny Hall by David Blake, a class leader. Prior to her marriage to Balaam, she had lived with and likely cared for his first wife, Rose Middleton Burnett, in Beaufort after Rose contracted smallpox (Balaam and Rose didn't have any children) and until Rose died in June 1864, a few months after the Battle of Olustee. Balaam married her a few months later. Rose's brother Wally Garrett and several of Balaam and Wally's comrades who escaped enslavement on Newport Plantation confirmed Diana's story.[80]

Sally Ladsden had been enslaved on one of Charles Heyward's plantations, and Heyward married her first to Sam Fraser. She was married to

Sam until Charles Heyward sold her husband. Then Heyward married Sally off to Lewis Dash, who died, according to witness Ben Johnson, "at the time of the big strike." That would be 1876, when day laborers in the Combahee rice fields (including on John Bennett Bissell's Bonny Hall and Cypress Plantations) went on strike, refusing to work for "scrip," checks redeemable only at the plantation store.[81]

Diana testified that Sally had come to her and asked her "if she [Sally] could have Balaam for her husband." If it actually occurred, Sally's request may have been a relic of slave marriage during the antebellum period, one that persisted even after freedpeople were able to legalize their marriages. Diana told her yes, then lived with another man, Peter Ferguson, for ten years and had three children with him. Their pastor, Reverend Sam Chisolm, who described himself as "minister of the gospel" and lived near Salkehatchie, refused to marry Diana and Peter because Diana's husband, Balaam, was still alive. Peter told his minister that he needed a woman to keep house for him, so the church didn't bother the couple anymore. For her part, Sally testified that she knew Balaam had had a relationship with Diana, but she thought it was "meretricious, not matrimonial," according to Acting Commissioner L. M. Kelley. In essence, Sally thought that Balaam and Diana were not legally married, that Rose had been Balaam's only wife, and that Rose had died much later than she really did (at least that must have been what Balaam told her). A new pastor, Reverend John P. Randolph, came to Sally and Balaam's church and insisted that all the couples who had taken up with each other get married or leave the church. He gave them a marriage certificate after their wedding, which Sally presented to Colonel E. P. Henderson, the notary public who filed her pension application. Since Balaam came from a different, albeit neighboring, county, Reverend Randolph surely did not know that Balaam's wife, Diana, was still very much alive. In fact, Sally's family and friends in Colleton County thought, as Ben Johnson put it, that "Diana quit Balaam," but of course they had no direct knowledge. Balaam never told Sally that he and Diana had been legally married for decades, since Rose's death.[82]

After Balaam Burnett's death on March 24, 1901, both Diana and Sally applied for pension benefits, claiming to be his legal widow. The case was closed after Diana told the special examiner in December 1901, in front of witnesses, that she would have intercourse with any man she liked. She would not accept money for sex from the men, but they would help her with her garden and cut wood. Acting Commissioner L. M. Kelley ruled that Diana had forfeited pensionable status because she was guilty of open and illicit adulterous cohabitation. However, Sally's marriage to Balaam was null and void, because Diana, Balaam's legal wife, was still alive. In short, neither woman got widow's pension benefits; Diana got nothing for Jeremiah, her ninth child, whom she testified she and Balaam had conceived on one of her many "visits" to him after he left her; Sally got nothing for taking care of Balaam in his final illness or burying him.[83]

In April 1901, Moriah Haywood Bartley testified that she had not remarried since the death of her husband, Anthony Bartley, in February 1898. However, she had had illicit sexual intercourse with her husband's comrade Mingo Van Dross at least six or seven times out in the woods since becoming a widow. According to the special examiner, Read Hanna, Moriah "confessed" to it. Her neighbors, her daughter-in-law, and Anthony and Mingo's comrades testified that their relationship was "open and notorious." Mingo Van Dross testified that he had had sex with Moriah Bartley beginning one year after his comrade's death. Mingo embellished the "neighborhood talk," as neighbor Maria Norwell called it, adding that he and Moriah had carried on right at her house. He thought she was also sleeping with a neighbor, Tom Baker.[84]

Moriah swore to an affidavit on August 19, 1901, written by an attorney in Walterboro named Charles H. Farmer. In it, she called the charges that she had been living in "open and notorious adulterous cohabitation" with another man since the death of her husband "unfounded, frivolous, and untrue." Moriah declared she was "old and the charge ridiculous to say the least." Moreover, Mingo Van Dross was an "enemy" of hers. She requested that if her statement was insufficient that a special examiner be appointed to conduct a full investigation of her case. She also forwarded affidavits by her neighbors contradicting the allegations of adultery to which she had confessed and which other neighbors had made. Moriah and several other witnesses recanted their testimony as false. Some also thought Mingo was too old to be carrying on with his comrade's widow; on July 30, 1910, William Elliott (whose father, Thomas Smith Elliott, had sold Van Dross and his family to William L. Kirkland around 1845) certified "Mingo Vanderhorst," as he called him, was seventy-four years old. Witnesses like Jackson Grant, Anthony and Mingo's comrade who had also grown up in bondage with them, testified he had never heard anything negative about Moriah's chastity. Grant confirmed Moriah was a member of the church in good standing (the reverend's credibility should have been questioned given that he also upheld his daughter Rebecca Grant Wineglass's chastity even though she had four children fathered by a man other than her husband). Some witnesses confirmed that Moriah and Mingo were not on good terms and testified they had heard him saying he would get back at her by keeping her from getting her pension money. Lastly, Moriah's son Cumsey Bartley thought Mingo had started rumors about his mother because they had had difficulty over land.[85]

Moriah accused Read Hanna of having "bull-dozed" her into confessing that she had a sexual relationship with Mingo and having "everything in his own hands." They alleged that Hanna threatened to put both Moriah, if she did not confess, and Cumsey, if he interfered with the interrogation, in jail. Cumsey, who testified that he lived within two hundred feet of his mother's house—and thus would have seen men coming in and going out or seen her sneaking out to the woods with a man—came to his mother's rescue when he heard her crying because the special examiner tried to force her to lie and say she had cheated on her dead husband.[86]

Despite Moriah's and her family's protests, the Pension Bureau believed Mingo Van Dross and found Moriah in violation of the Act of August 7, 1882. She lost her widow's pension of $8 per month.[87]

Sometimes bigamists were called out, though not punished. Eliza Gabriel Basquire Lewis McGuire married three USCT soldiers and collected pensions from two, including Fulton McGuire, of the 34th Regiment. When she applied for widow's benefits after McGuire's death in 1907, Eliza testified that she had been married twice. First she had married Noah Lewis, who was also in the 34th Regiment, in Key West in May 1868, according to their marriage certificate. They had three children together. After his death in September 1872, she was married to Fulton McGuire in Key West by a Black preacher named Thomas Darling. Eliza and Fulton had five children together. McGuire had been married before. Like Balaam and Diana Burnett, Fulton's first wife died of smallpox; Eliza had helped care for her during her last illness.[88]

However, Eliza either forgot or neglected to tell the pension official she had been married before she married Noah Lewis. Frank Shavers, a soldier from the 34th Regiment, Company A, who had known Eliza since their childhood and who had served in the same regiment, mustered out, and come home with her second husband, testified she had been married to a soldier from Louisiana named Rudolph Beckwith, and was known as Eliza Beckwith. A number of witnesses, including Winnie Gabriel, Eliza's sister-in-law, confirmed the marriage, which Eliza eventually acknowledged. However, Eliza testified she didn't know if she and Rudolph were legally married, because they had been married "under martial law." Eliza had gone with her husband's regiment to Tallahassee; after Beckwith's regiment returned to Louisiana, her brothers—she had seven brothers in the 34th Regiment—brought her back to Key West. She was likely pregnant with their son, Adolphus Beckwith, who would never see his father. Several witnesses and Eliza herself testified that they believed Beckwith never came back for his wife and baby because he had died during the war.[89]

The pension examiner conducted a search of USCT pension files in Louisiana and identified one Sergeant Major Rudolph Basquire of the 99th Regiment, Company B—a pretty impressive feat in decades before electronic records—and confirmed that he had married Eliza Gabriel while his regiment was stationed in Key West, Florida. He had deserted her and their infant son when the regiment returned to Louisiana, married approximately four other women, and committed bigamy with at least two of them; subsequent to a Mary Basquire being pensioned as his widow, a competing claim came in from another woman also claiming to be his legal widow. But since Rudolph Basquire had died in August 1905, Eliza was deemed to be McGuire's legal wife at the time of his death in 1907, and she was entitled to accrued pension benefits.[90]

Soldiers' dependents also struggled to claim the benefits from their father's service to which they were, or thought they were, entitled. Molcy Chisolm wrote a letter to President Theodore Roosevelt (whom she addressed as her "Great king" who ruled over all of the United States) on March 14, 1907, pleading for help claiming her pension benefits. Her father, March Chisolm, had fought in the Civil War "from the first to the last." She claimed that he had suffered from exposure in the line of duty and was not able to do any manual labor between mustering out with his regiment on February 28, 1866, and his death on October 10, 1868. Moses Simmons, his comrade with whom he grew up enslaved and liberated himself from bondage on Cypress Plantation, was with March in his final hours and closed his eyes in death. At the time of his death, Molcy, his only child on earth, was just eight years old, and he left her a "healpless child . . . in the worlds." She knew that under the Dependent and Disability Pension Act of June 27, 1890, she was entitled to a dependent's pension, and she had already spent $50 on attorneys over a period of four years trying to secure it. Molcy wrote that she would be satisfied if she could just get back what she had expended chasing her father's pension claim. She left her case with the "king of the United State" and the "Lord" and prayed that both would say "blesset" were those who consider the poor, like her.[91]

In November 1909, Lucy Lee Smith testified that she and Corporal Richard Smith Jr. were one of the couples (perhaps as many as thirty-five) whom Reverend Homer H. Moore had married "under the flag" in 1864 at Pigeon Point, after Colonel Montgomery issued the order that all soldiers had to be married to the women with whom they were cohabitating. Jackson Grant and Anthony Bartley both testified that Reverend Moore had married them to their wives in the same ceremony as Richard Smith and Lucy Lee. The couple had three children together, all of whom died in infancy. After the regiment mustered out, Richard and Lucy lived with his mother on Cypress Plantation. They planted one crop. One day during the summer of 1866, after he mustered out, he supposedly went to the train station in Green Pond "after his trunk," according to Lucy, which he said was on the Savannah steamer from Charleston. He was never heard from again. Lucy finally admitted that after Richard left her, she took up with Caesar Green and had a child with him. Subsequently, Caesar married a woman named Fannie Lee (who settled at Cypress Plantation after General Sherman swept through the upper Combahee River). Richard Smith's comrade Cuffie Bolze confirmed that Lucy and Richard had married in 1864. Fannie Lee, however, initially testified that Lucy Smith had been married by ceremony to Caesar Green but that he had left Lucy after he found out that she was already married and that her husband was still alive. He then married Fannie Lee and lived with her until he died. Fannie Green later recanted and corroborated Lucy's claim that Lucy and Caesar were never married.[92]

Richard Smith probably never had a trunk. If he did have one, it was likely stored at Fannie Pitts's house in Clinton, Georgia, about 175 miles from Savannah. And if he had indeed gone to the Green Pond station, he went to meet Fannie Pitts and "left the state in the company of another woman," according to T. A. Cuddy, the chief of the Law Division in the Pension Bureau. The Reverend George Simmons had married Richard Smith to Fannie Pitts in July 1869. By the time the special examination to determine legal widowhood was conducted in 1909, Fannie Pitts Smith had been dead for eleven years. Nellie Ann Brown, Richard and Fannie Smith's daughter, testified that her father had died eight years before her mother. She did not know exactly where her father had been born, whether in North or South Carolina. Her father had talked about being a soldier and being married before he married her mother. She thought she remembered the names of his mother, Nelli, and siblings, Isaac and Sarah, and that they lived in "Rice Pond, North Carolina." But she wasn't really sure. It had been eighteen years since she'd thought about it. There is no way to verify what Nellie Brown remembered. Unfortunately, this state of affairs was common for soldiers and widows who migrated outside of Beaufort and Colleton Counties and the communities where veterans lived after the war. The people who met, married, and took care of them did not know anything about their origins, family, or military service.[93]

The special examiner found that Richard and Lucy Smith's civil marriage was not binding, since it had been repudiated in 1866. Plus, both Richard and Lucy Smith had later formed matrimonial relations with other people. Furthermore, Lucy Smith did not have a marriage certificate for her marriage to Corporal Smith—she claimed it had burned up in a house fire. The Law Division chief called this a "badge of fraud" and did not believe Lucy Smith's assertion that she and Richard Smith were ever married. Nor did he believe her witnesses, Anthony Bartley or Mingo Van Dross, because Moriah Bartley, Anthony's widow, had been dropped from the pension rolls for adulterous relations with Van Dross. The commissioner of the Pension Bureau thus rejected Lucy Smith's claim for a pension. Fannie Smith's claim was also rejected; she was dead and none of her children had been under sixteen when her husband died and therefore had no standing to pursue a claim. Richard Smith Jr., like many other bigamists, got off. Ultimately, it was impossible to sanction a dead man.[94]

Whether the government took care of them or not, the Combahee veterans took care of each other and their comrades' widows. When Wally Garrett died on November 6, 1911, his comrade Jack Aiken was present. Jack dressed Wally's body before he was buried. As noted, the two had been enslaved together on Newport Plantation. The former Newport bondspeople and Wally's comrades rallied around his widow, Bella Jones Lucas Garrett, after his death. Wally's comrade Mexico Washington, for example, testified that Bella "didn't seem quite right . . . she talked but did not know what she was saying." He was one of several witnesses to recommend that Bella be assigned a guardian to attend to her business and handle her money so that she would not be cheated. Before Jack Aiken died on January 30, 1914, he left his only minor child, Jack Jr., with Ellen Harris and appointed her the child's guardian. Her death certificate (according to which she died September 3, 1931, in Beaufort) confirms that Harris was Jonas and Sina Green's daughter, born and raised in Beaufort. Harris testified on September 1, 1915, that "Jack Sr. was a friend of her family even before [she] was born. This is the way he came to give her Jack [Jr.]." She enrolled Jack Jr. in the "Martha School . . . for colored students and had white teachers," which may have been Schofield Normal School in Aiken, South Carolina.[95]

Cheating is in the eye of the beholder. The fact of the matter is that Harriet Tubman and many USCT veterans, widows, and dependents all spent their meager resources over the years trying, like Molcy Chisolm, to get pensions. Granted, these pensions made a significant difference in the lives of most recipients, enabling many to feed and house their families, seek medical care, and in some cases purchase land, pay the taxes on it, and (hopefully) pass it down to their heirs. But after making them jump through hoops to obtain their benefits, the federal government gave them crumbs, comparatively speaking.

Walter Plowden made two unsuccessful attempts in 1868 and 1869 to acquire compensation for his Civil War service. He tried again to get compensation for his work as a spy in April 1874 and February 1875. Finally, in March 1875, Congress passed an amendment to "pay the claim of Walter D. Plowden, for services to the Government during the war, as scout and spy, under Generals Hunter and Saxton, in South Carolina, in 1863, 1864, 1865, $4,000." Though no letters of commendation accompanied Plowden's claims, Plowden got paid $4,000 for his work as a spy and scout for the Department of the South; by contrast, Tubman's petition was accompanied by multiple such letters, yet she did not get paid. After this payment, he continued to petition Congress; H.R. 1148 was introduced on Plowden's behalf in January 1876. Plowden kept up his claim for another fifteen years. Finally, another bill, S. 4796, was sent to the House Committee on Foreign Relations to pay Plowden's additional claim. Even without letters from generals as proof of his service, Plowden got paid $1,000 by the federal government for his services as a scout. Then he requested an additional payment of $4,000. Plowden was charged with larceny (for stealing three cows and one colt) and receiving illegal pension fees from a disabled veteran. The charge for defrauding the veteran was dismissed.[96]

One non-pension-related case in which a USCT veteran did manage to get some compensation from the government was that of William Drayton, who requested $170 for a mule that had belonged to his father and which William purchased from his mother after his father's death. Drayton testified about his self-liberation from enslavement on Williams Middleton's Newport Plantation in the Combahee River Raid: "I came through the lines with my mule on a dark night . . . and enlisted in the Union Army," 2nd South Carolina Volunteers, Company H. He wasn't able to keep his mule, according to his claim. William Dickey, one of the US Army quartermasters, seized it and used it for military purposes for two years without compensating Drayton. Drayton was one of 578 loyal South Carolinians to be compensated by the federal Southern Claims Commission by December 1877, receiving $130. It was something, but a far cry from what Joshua Nicholls's heirs would receive.[97]

On June 6, 1914, a subcommittee of the House of Representatives met to consider S. 2180, A Bill for the Relief of the Heirs of Joshua Nicholls. The heirs in question were Elizabeth and Joanna Nicholls, the two surviving daughters of Joshua Nicholls and his second wife, Ellen R. Lynah. In the original petition to the Senate and House of Representatives, dated December 2, 1878, Nicholls claimed he was "throughout said war a loyal citizen of United States of America." This petition was a way for Nicholls to try, try again after his claim to the Confederate government for compensation for his losses during the Civil War bore no fruit. According to Nicholls, after the death of his first wife, Mary Ann Kirkland Faber Nicholls, he was living the life of a student on Longbrow Plantation when US troops destroyed the plantation, burned two years' worth of rice crops, and drove away the enslaved labor force. Nicholls was therefore deprived of his life interest in the estate his first wife had provided for him in their marriage agreement and her will. Now, after his death, his daughters asked the US government to restore the value of Nicholls's personal property.[98]

Several US Army generals, including General Ethan Allen Hitchcock, Nicholls's brother-in-law, wrote letters on Nicholls's behalf, attesting to the Nicholls family's settlement in Maryland and Washington, DC, to Joshua's academic accomplishments as a scholar of Greek and Latin and a fluent speaker of French, German, and Italian, and to his loyalty to the United States during the Civil War. They therefore supported the request for compensation.[99]

Harriet Tubman and the Black veterans had to fight and wait—Tubman for over a decade—for a few dollars per month. Some never received anything for their military service; some died before they ever could. In contrast, fifty-one years after the Combahee River Raid, Joshua Nicholls's heirs got paid $33,450.[100]

The struggle for widows' pensions continued until the first third of the twentieth century, as some of the veterans, including Charles Nicholas and Jackson Grant, had married again to much younger women. Others sought accrued pensions to pay the expenses of the veterans' and widows' final illnesses and burials. Primus Barnwell wrote in his own handwriting to the Pension Bureau on March 27, 1926, saying he could not find his brother-in-law William Middleton's papers. He speculated that his sister Relia Barnwell Middleton might have lost them or thrown them away, as Relia was older than he was and illiterate.[101]

Primus didn't know the name of his brother-in-law's commanding officer or whether he had been discharged in Charleston or Jacksonville. But he knew William always spoke of "Cunnel . . . Montgomery Regiment" and Jacksonville. And he knew that his brother-in-law, "Cuffie Bolds Friday Barrington," and others had been enslaved and were "carried to Beaufort SC in the war By the Yankees" in the Combahee River Raid. In Beaufort, William "in List" in the 2nd South Carolina volunteers and married his sister.[102]

Primus Barnwell (who had been his mother's "A No. 1 Scholar" on Old Fort Plantation) cherished the memory of his brother-in-law's military service. William Izard had been too young to serve in the military, so he went to the wharf to meet his hero, Jack Aiken, when Jack arrived home after mustering out. April Singleton put the community on his back by serving as trustee for scores in numerous land transactions over many decades. Ellen Harris took in the orphaned child of a family friend who had been enslaved on a plantation near where her mother had been enslaved. Frederick Ulysses Hamilton, Arizona Hamilton, and Irene Hamilton devotedly cared for Frederick's aged father (Irene's grandfather) he was too old and frail to care for himself. These young people carried the spirit of the Combahee River Raid and Black freedom well into the twentieth century, honoring Harriet Tubman and the 2nd South Carolina Volunteers, who had risked their freedom and their very lives fighting for America's democratic principles when the nation's fundamental values were imperiled.

As described earlier, Tubman was never adequately compensated for her military service as a spy and scout. The $20 monthly pension that she was finally granted, for her work as a nurse and her widowhood, was hardly enough to pay her household's expenses. Aside from a little credit for her intelligence-gathering and piloting the Combahee River Raid that she received during the Civil War from Lewis Douglass, Franklin Sanborn, and George Garrison, she never got her due.

Yet it was all about the value of the intelligence. Biographer Earl Conrad claims that Tubman was in charge of the "Intelligence Service" of the Department of the South. But Tubman did not get the credit she deserved for her work during the Civil War until 2020, when, thanks to the tireless efforts of Tubman's great-niece Ernestine Wyatt and Tubman's biographer Kate Larson, Tubman was inducted as a full member of the Military Intelligence Corps Hall of Fame (she had already been inducted as an honorary member in June 2019). FBI special agent Rusty Capps, General John W. Nichols, Brigadier General Charles H. Cleveland, and Major General Robert P. Walters Jr. all wrote letters applauding Tubman for defying the gender and racial conventions of her time and exhibiting the utmost courage and valor in risking her life for her country and for enslaved people in South Carolina.[103]

The honor was hard-won. Harriet Tubman first taught herself the tradecraft of intelligence by liberating herself, then making multiple trips back into a slave state to free scores of family, friends, and community members from bondage on Maryland's Eastern Shore. She debriefed freedom seekers, collected intelligence from her networks, and relayed these Black Dispatches to US Army commanders in the Department of the South. By June 1863, the US military had realized the Black Dispatches were a critical part of their tactical military strategy. Even General Robert E. Lee had to admit less than a month before the raid that "the chief source of information to the enemy is through our Negroes." According to retired senior FBI special agent Rusty Capps, Tubman's "experiences, common sense, creativity, and courage allowed" her "to conduct operations that are the envy of every modern intelligence professional." It took more than 150 years, but Tubman's extraordinary military service during the Civil War has finally been seen and appreciated for what it gave to the nation and to those seeking freedom.[104]

★★★★★★★★

In the documented history of the New World, a very small number of Black people who were born and reared in bondage and then escaped enslavement later went back into slave territory. Today, we'd call it a *very* exclusive club. Tubman and the Black men who escaped in the Combahee River Raid—and who then enlisted in the 2nd South Carolina Volunteers—were anomalies even among Black abolitionists who lectured about the evils of enslavement and worked to end it for all. Most Black abolitionists were born enslaved. However, they did not go back into the land of bondage to bring enslaved people out—not Henry Highland Garnet, Sojourner Truth, Frederick Douglass, or Henry "Box" Brown, for example. Tubman and the Black men enslaved on the Combahee were part of the small number among the four million people enslaved in the United States when the Civil War broke out in 1861 who were willing to go back into slave societies after they had liberated themselves. The potential consequences of failure were catastrophic: recapture, physical torture, and sale to the Deep South, forever severed from family, friends, and community.

In the long history of Black freedom, the Combahee River Raid belongs on the same spectrum as the Stono Rebellion, Tacky's Revolt in Jamaica, Denmark Vesey's conspiracy, and Nat Turner's Rebellion. Because of her revolutionary activities, Tubman was more akin to the Stono leader Jemmy, Tacky, Denmark Vesey, Nat Turner, and her hero, John Brown, than she was to abolitionists like Frederick Douglass. To Tubman, as to the men of the 2nd South Carolina and the 1st South Carolina, and to all of the other more than 180,000 Black men who went to war and whose military service had a significant impact on the Union war effort, Black freedom meant that they had to be willing to put it all on the line, risking their freedom and maybe even their very lives for the freedom of others. Put it all on the line Tubman did when she effectively led the largest and most successful slave revolt in US history, second only to the Haitian Revolution in the entire New World. Tacky, Vesey, Turner, and Brown, along with most of the people who plotted and fought with them, were martyred. Tubman helped to bring 756 enslaved people out of bondage without the US forces losing a single life.

The Combahee River Raid overturned the social order and destroyed slavery on the lower Combahee River and among Black people who—despite the issuance of the Emancipation Proclamation six months earlier—were still held in bondage there. This act of war and destruction was simultaneously an act of creation, giving birth to freedpeople, giving birth to soldiers, and giving birth to more freedom fighters. It was a new birth of freedom.

Ultimately, from Maryland's Eastern Shore to Georgetown, Beaufort, Combahee, coastal Georgia, and Florida, the men and women who liberated themselves from bondage, and the soldiers, spies, scouts, and pilots who risked themselves that others might be free, were all Tubman's people. They all spoke the same language—the language of Black freedom.

Afterword

"Say Their Names"

The story in this book has taken us from the forested wetlands of Maryland's Eastern Shore to forested wetlands of the lower Combahee River, from tobacco farms to tidal rice fields, and from the "prison-house of bondage" to the delirium of freedom. A story of triumph, it is also one of broken promises and fractured pasts, one I have tried to tell not just in terms of its greater events, as part of the momentous upheaval of the Civil War, but also in the details of human life—in the slave transactions through which enslavers bought, sold, bequeathed, and gifted their property, separating husbands from wives and parents from children, and in the land transactions through which after the war freed people in coastal South Carolina bought land, tried to hold on to it and pass it down, and often lost it.[1]

In the end it is a story about transformation: African Americans who had been held in bondage on lower Combahee rice plantations identified themselves in freedom as "Combee" through the end of the nineteenth century. Over time, they became part of a broader community and forged common institutions, which flowered and caught the attention of outsiders who called it Gullah in popular media in the 1920s and 1930s.

Lastly, this story ties in with and chronicles the least-known chapter of the life of one of America's best-known patriots, Harriet Tubman, while simultaneously featuring the stories of heretofore nameless and faceless enslaved people who joined her in fighting for freedom.

I began my research on the Combahee River Raid as an extension of two projects: an artistic collaboration, *Unburied, Unmourned, Unmarked: Requiem for Rice*, and an academic book on the history of the Gullah Geechee and creolization. The Combahee River Raid was a section in the libretto of *Unburied, Unmourned, Unmarked* and a planned chapter in the Gullah

Geechee book. But each project was expansive in its own way, and both were expanding in different directions. There came a point when I needed to bring the two projects into much closer alignment with each other. The Combahee River Raid was a point of intersection between the two.

I was not sure there was anything new to say about Harriet Tubman's life. Her biographers, among them Earl Conrad, Kate Clifford Larson, and Catherine Clinton, had done such an exhaustive job. So I took some time to explore the primary sources and determine if I could find a new angle on what I assumed was an old story. At the time, Toni Carrier, director of the Center for Family History at the International African American Museum in Charleston, South Carolina (which was still in the planning stages), and I were contemplating an online exhibit on Hector Fields, my great-great-great-grandfather. Toni suspected that Hector fought in the raid, but we couldn't prove it at the time. During the summer of 2016, I took brief trips to the Heritage Library in Hilton Head and acquired all of the pension files they held for 34th Regiment USCT soldiers who were born on the Combahee. Then, a few weeks later, I went to the National Archives and requested several pension files with a dual purpose: to see whether I could find any leads shedding light on Hector Fields, and to test whether or not there was anything new in them that could potentially enable me to contribute something new about the Combahee River Raid and Harriet Tubman's military service during the Civil War.

The first goal was a bust. I didn't find anything on Hector Fields.

However, I hit the jackpot on my second objective. To my surprise, on the first trip I acquired more than one pension file of the men who enlisted in the 2nd South Carolina Volunteers (later 34th USCT), Companies G and H, the day after the raid in which Combahee veterans, widows, and neighbors testified about the raid. The testimony was in the files of Cuffie Bolze, Edward Brown, and Neptune Nicholas. It was months after my trip before I had the time to look carefully at the files. When I did, I could not believe what I was reading. The soldiers and widows testified about growing up together on Cypress Plantation until they all got on the gunboat. I remember taking a picture with my cellphone camera of the word "gunboat" as it was written in an affidavit, texting it to Toni Carrier, and asking if she agreed that I was seeing what I thought I saw. Nonetheless, I had no way of knowing how pervasive testimony about the Combahee River Raid was in the pension files. It would be many months and many files before I found more testimony about it. I had not imagined that the testimony existed, and soon I realized the pension files would provide a unique perspective; I had something new to say about the Combahee River Raid.

So I needed more files. I used a network approach to decide which files to request next by making note of all of the other soldiers who had testified in each file, researching whether they had pension files, and requesting their files next if they did (and I kept a database of the pension files I requested). I used this approach until I had transcribed and put into a database all of the available files for the 34th Regiment USCT Companies G and H, as well as a sampling of other companies in the 34th Regiment and the 21st, 33rd, and 128th Regiments.

As I made my way through the pension files, my thinking was that if I had to read files that were between thirty-five and three hundred pages of cursive handwriting, I was going to do it once, and only once. In addition, I needed to be able to access everything I read with a keyword search. So I decided to make full-text transcriptions of each and every page of each and every pension file. It was extremely time-consuming and tedious. In the early days, I did the transcriptions myself until I had funding to hire research assistants.

And I created a database starting with the very first pension files. In the database columns I put the primary questions I saw developing from the files, such as where a veteran, widow, or neighbor was born, where they were enslaved, whom the veteran married, which minister married the couple, the battles in which the veteran fought, his disabilities, and when, where, and how he died. This is just a small sampling; the database has thirty-seven columns. In the rows I put the names of the veterans in Companies G and H, which I entered from rosters published in Janet Hewett's *The Roster of Union Soldiers, 1861–1865* and posted on the online National Park Service Soldiers and Sailors Database. I would also add rows for 34th Regiment soldiers in different companies and a separate database (with the same columns) for soldiers in other South Carolina Black regiments. Once a pension file was transcribed, I cut and pasted excerpts from the transcriptions into the appropriate columns. I read and added to the database all of the pension files, whether or not I or one of my research assistants transcribed them. I included in the database a total of 209 files, 162 from Companies G and H of the 34th Regiment alone. Entering the files into my database emblazoned them on my memory to this day, in some cases seven years later. It also enabled me to cross-reference them. A keyword search of the database called up the pension file in which I could find whatever detail I sought. And a keyword search of the file produced the detail.

Two things kept me going through this painstaking process. First and foremost was the drama of it all. The files revealed who had left their spouse (and under what pretext), taken up with someone else, and had children. Better than any prime-time drama, the pension files kept me thoroughly entertained.

Second, I wanted to figure out where everyone who testified in the file had been enslaved and to which family they were related. This, of course, was not always possible. I could read or even transcribe a three-hundred-page pension file and come away lacking the necessary information to solve the puzzle. When this happened, it was a disappointing end to several days' worth of tedious work. Still, I added the file to my database with hopes of solving that particular puzzle one day. I just had to keep reading. Sometimes I would include in the database a file in which the enslaver was not revealed but the names of people enslaved on the same plantation were (without specifying the plantation), sometimes along with the name of the minister who married a couple before the war. By searching my database for one of these two details, I was able to solve several otherwise cold cases. Lastly, I pulled out every person from the first database of veterans for whom I could identify the person who held them in bondage and an approximate birth year. These folks (veterans, widows, and neighbors included) became rows in a separate database, in which I layered in slave transactions, Freedmen's Bank account records, life stories (recorded by people who were in Beaufort or the Sea Islands as part of the Port Royal Experiment, such as Dr. Seth Rogers, Colonel Thomas Wentworth Higginson, and Elizabeth Botume, for example), censuses, and land transactions (these are just a sampling of the primary sources collected in this database). The folks for which I could find the most primary source materials, illuminating their lives before, during, and after the Combahee River Raid, became the main historical actors in this story.

One of my proudest moments was finding Minus Hamilton's family. Hamilton was the star of the show ever since I became acquainted with his life story in Higginson's 1870 memoir, *Army Life in a Black Regiment,* early on in my research. The only clue Hamilton left was that he was enslaved by "Ol' Mas'r Lowndes." He provided no more specific details about "old master Lowndes's" identity. I assumed he was on Charles T. Lowndes's plantation and that "old master Lowndes" was Charles T. Lowndes' father or maybe even his grandfather, because of Minus's advanced age. I hypothesized that Hamilton would be among the Old Heads, like November Osborne and Sarah Smalls Osborne. Maybe he had been enslaved by Thomas Lowndes as well and came from his Cat Island plantation on the Santee River.

Months of work with my genealogist research assistant on the Lowndes slave transactions went by. Minus Hamilton simply wasn't there, and I decided it was almost time to move on to another set of research questions. We went back through all of the Freedmen's Bank accounts, and Bina Mack emerged. Her Freedmen's Bank application stated she was born in Combahee; her father's name was Minus (he was dead by the date of her application, December 28, 1872), and her mother's name was Hagar. But she did not provide the name of the plantation where she had been enslaved nor the name of the enslaver. I remembered Bina's name immediately because she had testified for Sina Bolze Young Green, first with James Green (whom I could not identify) and then with Hagar Hamilton (who was later identified as her mother), that she had been enslaved on an adjoining plantation. Bina Mack testified that she had attended William Young and Sina Bolze's wedding before the war. And I could not forget the affidavit revealing that Bina was one of the Combee women—one of several women whose husbands died in action—who showed up in force to testify that Sina had not remarried after William Young's death, to help her continue getting her widow's pension benefits.

Charles T. Lowndes's Oakland adjoined Cypress Plantation, where Sina Bolze Young was held in bondage. But Bina Mack was not named among the enslaved individuals listed on Sarah Bond I'on's marriage settlement, nor on the bill of sale by which Charles T. Lowndes purchased enslaved people from his mother, nor on Thomas Lowndes's estate record. However, locating Bina Mack's family grouping, documenting the Lowndes family's genealogy, and searching in the Lowndes family's slave transactions more widely led to identifying Minus and Hagar Hamilton and Harry, Bina, and Hagar Mack in Arthur M. Parker and James L. Paul's slave transactions. It was a joyous day when at last Minus Hamilton and his family were located in the archival record and I knew from where he and his wife, daughter, son-in-law, and granddaughter had liberated themselves by getting on the boat to freedom.

My goal from the beginning of the project was to find independent evidence to document what the Combahee freedom seekers testified in

the pension applications about their families and their experiences during enslavement with other primary sources. Because many plantation records were burned in the raid, one way to do this was by identifying every
single transaction—every will, marriage settlement, estate record, bill of
sale, and mortgage—that documented in spite of themselves the identities
of the Combahee freedom seekers, their family members, and the enslavers
who held them all in bondage. Minus Hamilton's story is just one of many
examples of how this came together. It was an incredibly tedious and time-
consuming but immensely rewarding process. The incredible research finds
were the exception; moments of frustration were more typical.

Toward the end of my research and writing process, I had to go back to
the cemetery on the rice plantation on Cuckold's Creek where relatives
from both sides of my dad's family are buried and which first impelled me
to write the libretto for *Unburied, Unmourned, Unmarked: Requiem for Rice*.
Most African American cemeteries in the South Carolina Lowcountry, it
is built on higher ground (though it is still below sea level) overlooking a
creek. Over almost a decade, I have spoken publicly about the shock, horror,
and grief I felt after I visited the cemetery and encountered the open grave
of one of my ancestors. A tree limb must have fallen and cracked open the
concrete slab covering my ancestor's final resting place, and pieces of the slab
and the wooden vault fell into the shaft. The open shaft was full of water,
and his remains floated at the top. Soon after my first visit in 2013, our family
repaired the open grave and reinterred our ancestor's remains. Nonetheless,
the experience fundamentally changed me as a person and as a historian.

I have spoken less frequently of the fact that I actually went to the cemetery looking for the unmarked graves of Hector Fields's descendants. Their
unmarked graves—most just depressions in the ground, slight concavities
where the earth on top of the wooden coffins has sunk over time—still
haunt me. They are rendered invisible when the vegetation is "grow'd up"
after the end of hunting season. No matter where I am (even sitting at my
desk in my offices in Pittsburgh), I can call up the cemetery in my imagination when I need to recollect why the work I am doing is important, why
I am doing it in the first place, and why it is mine to do. My ancestors' unmarked graves induced me to undertake the painstaking task of recovery
and prompted me not to give up.

The global pandemic only complicated matters. I made a strategic decision early on to focus the book on the pension files, planter papers, and

other written sources to document the history of the Combahee freedom seekers on the Combahee rice plantations before, during, and after the raid. It was a difficult but practical choice. I started writing the book in earnest in February 2020; a few weeks later the country went into lockdown because of COVID-19. In light of this, I surmised that it would be difficult for me to build the relationships necessary to conduct widespread interviews with descendants of the Combahee freedom seekers. Travel restrictions precluded in-person meetings, which I thought essential to building these relationships. And African American families, including my own, were suffering during the global pandemic. It did not feel respectful to impose on descendant families at what was a very difficult and uncertain time. Simultaneously, as a transnational scholar, I am always aware of the turf I can credibly cover and cognizant of the danger of overstepping my fields of expertise and getting too far away from the questions about with I am passionate. Rice plantations, enslavement, and the antebellum period are what I am passionate about on the US side of the Atlantic; the twentieth century really isn't. This leaves plenty of work to be done on the descendants of the Combahee River Raid—formerly enslaved and enslaver—and on the twentieth-century transformation of historic rice fields along the Combahee River.

Moreover, I didn't want this book to be about stories passed down and told about the raid over time. Nor did I want to write another book about what we don't and can't know about enslaved people, because of the gaps, silences, and violence of the archival record. Though this work is vital (I have done some of it myself, particularly on the precolonial West African side of the Atlantic). I wanted to extend what can be said and known about the lives of enslaved people and tell the story of the enslaved people who liberated themselves in the Combahee River Raid. Because of the pension files, I knew it was possible to unearth the voices of formerly enslaved people, let them tell their own stories, and compel the planters' records to speak to our enslaved ancestors—my enslaved ancestors. I knew I could contribute to the restoration of the humanity—which the institution of enslavement was designed to deny and strip away—from the first reference I found to "gunboats"—and then from the names of siblings, parents, grandparents, cousins, aunties, and uncles going back four generations, and references to weddings, childbirth, funerals, and burial practices—in the pension files, and to family groupings in a planter's documents. And speak to me they did.

The Combahee freedom seekers' acts of liberation and self-liberation erased their own traces in the planters' historical records and destroyed those records. Simultaneously, when the social order turned upside down and the enslaved people liberated themselves, becoming free people, soldiers, and liberators, it created a small fissure in what had seemed an impenetrable edifice. With this crack, Black soldiers could support themselves and their families because of the bounties and pensions due them for their military service in the Civil War. And, because of their pension files, they, along with their widows, children, and neighbors, could tell their stories of enslavement and freedom in their own words. The world turned upside down on June 2, 1863, and the Combahee River Raid teaches us much more about the intimate lives, loves, families, and labors of enslaved and formerly enslaved people, finally from their own words, than we ever knew before. With approximately 83,000 African American veterans approved for pensions, there may be tens of thousands more stories their pension files could tell and thousands of enslaved communities their files could be used to reconstruct.

In commemoration of the 150th anniversary of the Combahee River Raid on June 2, 2023, we have a lot to celebrate. We can say we know who risked their freedom and their lives to execute one of the greatest slave rebellions in New World history, and we know who got on the boat, liberated themselves, and reunited their families in the raid. Our enslaved ancestors don't have to be nameless, faceless, and storyless any longer. In addition to freedom, this is one of the greatest and most enduring legacies of the Combahee River Raid, and of Harriet Tubman's Civil War service.

We are finally able to "say their names." And saying our ancestors' names and telling our stories is a pillar of Black freedom in the twenty-first century.

Acknowledgments

An endeavor such as this is impossible to undertake alone. I am blessed to have had many people to assist me in its undertaking and thus, have many people to thank.

The testimony of Combahee freedom seekers in the US Civil War Pension Files is the heart and soul of *Combee*. I am indebted to the International African-American Museum (IAAM's) Center for Family History's US Colored Troops (USCT) Pension File Project (and their partner Twisted Twigs on Gnarled Branches Genealogy) to obtain access to the more than 160 pension files I analyzed for this book. I hope my work will help to fulfill the center's mission to help individuals and families advance their understanding of their family's history and the role our ancestors have played in shaping American history. And, I am indebted to Toni Carrier, Director (retired) of IAAM's Center for Family History who encouraged me to find the Combahee freedom seekers. Toni is also a dear friend who opened her home to me when I traveled to Charleston for archival research. We had such fun before the COVID pandemic!

The rice fields are the bones of the book. I spent as much time as possible in the lower Combahee rice fields thanks to Nemours Wildlife Foundation. In the summer of 2016, as I contemplated whether or not I could make a unique contribution about Harriet Tubman and the Combahee River Raid, I attended the National Park Service's Underground Railroad Conference in St. Helena, I was invited to Nemours Wildlife Foundation to visit the rice fields and have lunch. I returned in July 2021, in the midst of the COVID global pandemic. Sincere thanks to Mike McShane (President, Board of Directors) and Gigi McShane, Dr. Ernie Wiggers (President and CEO, retired), and Dr. Andrew Bridges (President and CEO) of Nemours Plantation Wildlife Foundation, for inviting me to live at Nemours for 10-day stretches every month from July 2021 to March 2022, then periodically thereafter, and giving me ongoing access to the Nemours grounds, including Newport Plantation. As the scientists and students studied alligators and waterfowl, they routinely discovered things in the rice fields that they thought I should see, everything from eagles' nests to old rice mills. And, in the course of writing and figuring out how to tell the story, I developed many questions, which I had the good fortune to be able to ask the scientists around the kitchen counter or breakfast room table. We'd jump in the truck and check it out. Then, I would head to my little office upstairs and enhance my draft.

Current plantation owners on the lower and upper Combahee River played a critical role in telling this story. In December 2019, I met Dr. Ann Kulze through a chance encounter. Ann took me on my first trip to the lower Combahee River rice plantations and introduced me to the owners of Longbrow, Rose Hill, and Oakland plantations. We toured the cemeteries, rice fields, and river front of the three plantations and James L. Paul's Palmetto Plantation. The owners arranged for me to meet African-Americans who had worked on the properties and for their families for decades. It was my first time seeing the Combahee River. And, I was fortunate on my first trip to see the Combahee from where Joshua Nicholls would have stood when he saw the US Army vessels approaching his boat landing.

During the height of COVID, I was having difficulty with completing Part Two. My editor advised me to abandon it for a while, go to South Carolina, and write Part Three. In June 2021 as soon as CMU allowed faculty to travel by air, I headed to the Combahee and reconnected with the landowners whom I met in December 2019. While I enjoyed hospitality at Longbrow Plantation, I adopted the practice of walking the rice fields and the Combahee River.

I recorded the sounds of birds, fish, and alligators in the rice fields. I went outside at four and five in the morning to observe what I could see under the light of the full moon so that I could imagine what it was like for enslaved people walking through the grass to the river. I couldn't see my hand in front of my face, not to mention a copperhead or water moccasin striking at my feet. I stopped myself from going out to the rice fields, reminding myself that I, after all, had a choice. It was too dangerous by myself in the darkness, even driving the Kubota. Having experienced the plethora of alligators in the rice fields during daylight hours, I could only imagine the rice fields teemed with the nocturnal animals in darkness. Alligators were always of particular interest to me. I got used to them; and, they stayed on their side of the dikes and in the rice fields. During my trip in June 2021, Ann Kulze and her husband, John, took me out in their boat to explore the creek and canal leading up to Longbrow's boat landing. The manager also took me out to observe the creek at Longbrow and pilings of old boat landing from many angles several times during my stay.

In the middle of the global pandemic, getting to know the Combahee Raid plantations and walking the Combahee rice fields kept me going and inspired me. My head was filled with the primary source accounts of the Raid, newspaper accounts, pension files, life stories of the Combahee freedom seekers, and the official military record. I returned countless times to these properties to map the historical accounts on the landscape, try to see the Raid from the perspectives of the enslaved people who were working in the rice fields, test many theories about and measure the distance of how the enslaved people would have gotten from the rice fields, slave quarters, and main house sites to the Combahee River, and measure the distances the enslaved people and US Army soldiers had to travel. It was different on every plantation. During my hikes, I observed the entire historic rice field ecosystem, the flora and fauna, especially the alligators, snakes, and birds. I saw the tidal rice field ecosystem in every season and at every stage of the lunar/tidal cycle from June 2021 to November 2022. Special thank you to Daniel

Beach, Darryl Hickman, Forrest Morgan, Durwin Carter (project leader, South Carolina Lowcountry National Wildlife Reserve Complex, US Fish and Wildlife Service), Brett Craig (Wildlife Refuge Specialist, Ernest F. Hollings ACE Basin National Wildlife Refuge), and Mark Purcell (refuge manager, Ernest F. Hollings ACE Basin National Wildlife Refuge, retired) who endured my endless questions and supported my measuring, and Arthur Williams (who shared with me his family's oral history about the Combahee River Raid and his oldest known ancestor, of whom he shared a photograph). And, thank you to the current owners of Field's Point, Tar Bluff, Paul's Plantation, Longbrow, Rose Hill, Oakland, Newport, and Bonny Hall Plantations Mike McShane (past president), Charles Lane (president) of the ACE Basin Task Force and all the members, as well as for welcoming me on their properties whenever I requested access. And, thank you to my cousins in Green Pond and Charleston (Lloyd and Willa Fields and the Fields family, Cleveland and Valarie Frasier and the Frasier and Richards families) who always made time for me when I was in town.

Without a doubt, the Combahee River is the backbone of this story. My friend and colleague, Dr. Travis Folk, biologist (Folk Land Management, Inc.), helped me get to know the Combahee and the rice fields in the A. C. E. Basin. Travis grew up in Green Pond living next door to and deer hunting with the patriarch of my family, my grandfather's cousin, Jonas Fields. In 2013, I began hanging out with Travis in the rice fields; every time I came to town, he had some new feature to show me the historic rice fields, which he uncovered. His company, Folk Land Management Inc. while restoring rice fields throughout the region.

Towards the end of 2017, I also joined a team of scientists, Dr. Travis Folk, Dr. Ernie Wiggers, Dr. Rob Baldwin The Margaret H. Lloyd and SmartState Professor, Clemson University, Forestry and Environmental Conservation Department), and Dr. Daniel Hanks (Aquatic Ecologist, Environmental Research South Division, Weyerhaeuser Company, who were engaged in using LiDar to map all of South Carolina's rice fields, then using algorithms to measure the cubic earth moved by enslaved laborers moved to construct South Carolina's rice fields. The project has recently completed mapping and measuring Georgia's rice fields. Dr. Andrew Agha (Teaching Affiliate, Coastal Carolina University, Department of Anthropology/ Geography and Research Affiliate, University of South Carolina, Department of Anthropology) and Dr. Dan Richter subsequently joined us. I have benefitted immeasurably over the years from our work on historic rice fields, their scientific knowledge, and our conversations about rice fields on both sides of the Atlantic, the coastal wetlands ecosystem, and enslaved and peasant labor.

Three-time Emmy™ Award winner, John Wineglass and I visited rice fields in South Carolina (twice with Travis and Ernie in 2018), then Guinea Bissau and Senegal in 2019 as John was writing the score for *Unburied, Unmourned, Unmarked: Requiem for Rice* to record the sounds of the rice fields. In hindsight, participant observation with Travis and our team of scientists and recording sounds with John Wineglass ignited my senses to the reptiles, birds, insects, and vegetation in the rice fields. These experiences also began to embolden me to want to put my readers in the rice fields with the freedom seekers as they were forced to work in every season, hoed rice at four o'clock on the morning of the Raid, and ran through the rice fields to Lincoln's gunboats and freedom.

Reenacting the trip up the Combahee River provided my most impactful lessons on imagining the raid. The Dr. Travis Folk organized the first expedition. We tried to recreate the Combahee River Raid as closely as we could. We departed at 9pm from Field's Point, did not use GPS, spotlights, nor depth meters, navigated by the light of the full moon only, crept upriver about three to five miles per hour, and traveled 35.5 miles roundtrip to the Harriet Tubman Bridge. I experienced first-hand what the pilots would have been able to see under the full moon. The moon glistened off the water; the rice fields and marsh (on opposite sides of the water) were dark shapeless masses. And, I learned to navigate the boat under these conditions by driving us back downriver. I had never driven a boat before, certainly not at night and on a serpentine river like the Combahee. So, I did what Travis and Josh told me to do: steer around the tight curls of the Combahee River that night, staying in the middle where the water shimmered, and avoiding the edges which were shrouded in darkness. Coming back to Field's Point, I am proud to say that I "dead headed" the boat at the landing as instructed. Not bad for a first time! Sincere thanks to Dr. Travis Folk, Josh Bell, David Ray, and Christine Magnarella Ray for our nighttime expedition up the Combahee River and back.

After a few hours of sleep after our night-time reenactment of the trip up the Combahee, the following morning I took up a daytime trip up the Combahee River organized by Virginia Beach. This time, we used all of the gadgets, including the boat's motor and depth meters, and maps and traveled at a must faster speed. We departed from the Pigeon Point boat landing in the morning, went up the Beaufort River to the Coosaw River, downstream to St. Helena Sound through the intracoastal waterway to the mouth of the Combahee. We had the challenge of finding the mouth of the Combahee River. Once we got to Field's Point, I could actually see the obstructions in the water, trees fallen from the bluffs due to soil erosion, which Josh Bell instructed me in navigating away from the night before. We proceeded upriver to the Harriet Tubman Bridge, then returned. On the way back, we ran aground halfway down the Beaufort River at low tide. Dana and John pushed the boat off of the sandbars and back into deep water. Subsequently, the captains fought five foot waves, which caused Virginia and I to repeatedly fly out of our seats. The nighttime and daytime trips on the Combahee were complimentary and indispensable in helping me to know the river. Special thanks to Dana and Virginia Beach and John Beach for our adventure.

I also wanted to re-enact freedom seekers getting from the rice fields to the boats. Travis recommended this could best be accomplished by me walking barefoot through the rice fields. This was easier said than done, because I really can't tolerate getting my feet dirty since I was a child. But, I wanted to re-enact how freedom seekers got from the rice fields onto the US Army vessels and put the readers into the rice fields with the freedom seekers. In late September 2022, Travis, Dr. Daniel Hanks, and I walked the rice fields with no shoes, insect repellent, or other protective gear, including pants in my case (I wore a long dress). Feeling the rice plants and algae under my feet was revelatory! During this re-enactment, I also had my closest encounter with an alligator. A group of baby gators swam into the second tidal-influenced field we walked through, pretty close to where Travis, Daniel, and I were standing. I figured the mother alligator was not far behind and would be protective of her babies. I left Travis and Daniel in the rice fields telling jokes and got up out of there as quickly as I could. I managed to get over to the main dike and Ernie Wiggers (who was driving the get-away Kubota) pulled me up out of the rice fields. It all happened pretty fast. But, I was sitting in the Kubota when we heard the mother gator belly-flop into the rice fields. This is how I learned it was unlikely with the quicksand-like pluff mud, slippery algae, and prickly rice plants that the freedom seekers ran through the rice fields to get to the gunboats. Even stepping up from the field onto the main dike might have been difficult for older enslaved people, like Minus Hamilton and Sanko Van Dross, or enslaved people with limited mobility, like Carolina Grant, Henny Middleton Martin, or Jack Wineglass. They likely stepped up from the rice field bed to the internal dike, from the internal dike to the perimeter dike holding the Combahee River back from the rice fields and ran along the perimeter dike to freedom. Thank you to Dr. Travis Folk and Dr. R. Daniel Hanks, who

In addition to Travis and I spending countless hours together in the historic rice fields, Travis enduring my endless questions about the Combahee rice fields, the lower Combahee region, and its inhabitants, his company, New World Cartography LLC, hand drew the maps for this book, applying his encyclopedic knowledge of the lower Combahee landscape and his collection of historic maps along with the McCrady Plat Collections at the Charleston County Register of Deeds and the South Carolina Department of Archives and History.

Environmental photographer, climate change activist, and upper Combahee River native, J Henry Fair's, friendship and expertise were also indispensable in picturing the Combahee River and the rice plantations destroyed in the Raid for the reader. I estimate that 80 percent of the land where the Combahee River Raid took place is today private property. So the public would not get to see where the largest slave rebellion in US history took place. Our mutual friend, Dr. Ann Kulze, introduced me J Henry Fair and I.

From our first meeting in July 2021, Henry suggested (ok, if you know Henry, you know he insisted) that I use his images in my book to help put my readers on the ground on the rice plantations, in the rice fields, and on the Combahee. Henry had been shooting the Combahee for decades and had a corpus of amazing photographs which invited me to use. He also offered to create more aerial photographs (by hanging out of airplanes) and drone photographs to get the specific shots I wanted of sites important to the story. Henry also shot my author photo at his NYC studio in December 2022. The photo shoot was a lot of fun; and, I think the results are amazing. This book would not have been the same without the friendship and generosity of Henry Fair. Southwings (https://www.southwings.org) provided all of Henry's flights over Blackwater National Forest and up the Combahee River.

Last, but not least, I could not have written *Combee* without the commitment and investment of Carnegie Mellon University. I must thank the following people for believing in me and investing in this project: Dr. Nico Slate (Department of History, Head), Dr. Richard Scheines (Dietrich College of the Humanities and Social Sciences, Dean), Dr. Jim Garrett (Provost), Dr. Wanda Heading-Grant (Vice Provost for Diversity, Equity and Inclusion and Chief Diversity Officer), and Dr. Joe Trotter (Giant Eagle Professor of History and Social Justice, Director of the Center for African-American Urban Studies in the Economy). Carnegie Mellon's support contributed to my travel for research and writing, purchase of pension files, hiring of a dedicated team of research assistants: graduate students (Wyatt Erchak and Kari Thomas), post-graduate research assistants (Mallory Page), undergraduate research assistants (Tobi Aina, Stan Becton, Samantha Carney, Omasan Richardson, Sohrab Saljooki, and Brittany Tirado), independent contractors (Darius Brown, a very talented genealogist and research associate at the International African American Museum's Center for Family History who led the extensive genealogical research; DaNia Childress, a very talented curator who handled the image research and permissions; and, Dr. Michael Gallen, a very talented editorial specialist who verified and formatted my citations on always tight, yet shifting deadlines). I want to encourage this next generation of very talented professionals in their chosen fields. The following fellowships sponsored research and early writing stages of *Combee*: Smithsonian Institution Fellowship in Spring semester 2013 (advisor, Fath Ruffins, Curator of African American History and Culture in the Division of Cultural and Community Life, Smithsonian National Museum of American History); Andrew W. Mellon New Directions Fellowship academic year 2014-2015 (advisor, Dr. Shelome Gooden, Professor, University of Pittsburgh, Department of Linguistics; Dr. Don Winford, Professor, Ohio State University, Department of Linguistics; Dr. Salikoko S. Mufwene, Edward Carson Waller Distinguished Service Professor, University of Chicago, Department of Linguistics); Ford Foundation Senior Fellowship Spring 2018 to Fall 2018 (administered by National Academies of Sciences).

The COVID global pandemic closed libraries and archives for months at a time. Thank you to CMU Hunt Librarians: Sue Collins ordered books I needed and had them shipped directly to my home; Charlotte Kiger Price and Ashley Werlinich helped me find digitally available primary sources. The COVID pandemic made it impossible for me to travel to archival repositories for at least a year while I was writing *Combee*. Sincere thanks to the following repositories which both digitized, emailed, or mailed documents and accelerated their digitization projects: American Antiquarian Society, Cayuga County Community College Library, Charleston Library Society (Lisa Hayes),

College of Charleston Special Collections (Mary Jo Fairchild, Harlan Green, and Dale Rosengarten), Connecticut Historical Society and Research Center, Duke University Rubenstein Library, East Carolina University Joyner Library Special Collections, Emory University Stuart A. Rose Manuscript, Archives, and Rare Book Library, The Gilder Lehrman Collection, Harvard University Houghton Library and Schlesinger Library, Historical Society of Pennsylvania (thank you to Jessica Loring and Tracy Todd for assisting me with Middleton family documents), Kansas Historical Society, Library of Congress, Mariner's Museum and Park, Massachusetts Historical Society, National Archives and Record Administration (Paul Harrison), New York Historical Society, New York Public Library, Onondaga Historical Society, Rhode Island Historical Society, Schomburg Library, Seymour Library, Smith College Special Collections, South Carolina Department of Archives and History (Wade Dorsey), South Carolina Historical Society (Molly Silliman), South Caroliniana (Edward Blessings and Wade Duncan who transcribed illegible pages of archival documents for me), Southern Historical Collection, University of California at Santa Barbara Special Research Collections, University of Michigan Bentley Historical Library and William L. Clements Library, University of Pennsylvania Kislak Center for Special Collections, Rare Books and Manuscripts, Yale University Beinecke Rare Book and Manuscript Library. The Severance Family Collection is a hidden gem. I was determined to consult it for myself in its entirety. And, once CMU lifted its ban on faculty travel, I flew out to Billings, Montana in July 2021. Michael S. Emett Sr. preserved the collection, made it available to me, and shared his knowledge of the Severance family with me, including Mark Sibley Severance's arrival in Beaufort/Port Royal (in September 2022). Ashley Trujillo at HistoryMiami accommodated my in-person visit in August 2021 when the repository was still closed.

In addition to relying on their published works, I benefitted from correspondence with Dr. Kate Larson, Dr. Larry Rowland, Dr. Stephen Wise, and Jeff Grigg and am eternally grateful to for their generosity and expertise. Over a period of many months, Dr. Kate Larson shared with me her insights, her contacts, and many documents from years of researching, interpreting, and writing about Harriet Tubman's life. I had Dr. Larry Rowland at "pension file." During our first meeting (and, we had lunch together most times when I was in town from July 2022), Larry told me he had long been curious about what the pension files could tell us about African American history. He was pleased that someone was excavating them and eager to see my findings. Dr. Stephen Wise and Jeff Grigg were skeptical about Harriet Tubman's role in the Raid. I embraced their skepticism (anticipating it was a taste of what I would encounter from the Civil War audience if I overshot my sources and/or didn't get the details right) and encyclopedic the Civil War in the Lowcountry. Despite their initial skepticism, Stephen and Jeff embraced me and helped me shape the project. From 2019, Jeff Grigg helped me learn the lay of the land by taking me out multiple times to tour Confederate embankments in Green

Pond and plantation sites related to the Combahee River Raid. Their expertise helped me to get the Civil War details right and their skepticism kept me close to my sources; I think they appreciated my uncovering of many new sources.

I had a variety of conversations over a period of years while researching and writing *Combee* which were important to me telling this story. In the Foreword, my cousin, Cleveland Frasier, told me the story of Jonas Fields scooping his wife out of the baptismal pool with one arm and carrying her down the stairs in January 2023 and many times before.

For Part One, during Fall Semester 2023, I taught a graduate seminar on "Topics in the African Diaspora." Graduate students in this class read chapters two, six, and fourteen of *Combee* and made very astute observations. In particular, seminar discussion with Trista Powers (a graduate student in CMU's English Department) about slave narratives which were written by formerly enslaved people, as opposed to dictated to amanuenses, helped me to think about the pension files in relation to both kinds of slave autobiographies. A series of discussions from September 2022 to July 2023 with Dr. Jim Anderson (director of the James C. Kennedy Waterfowl & Wetlands Conservation Center, Clemson University), Dr. Walter Boynton (professor emeritus of the University of Maryland Center for Environmental Science), David Burden Jr., Dr. Travis Folk, and Dr. Fred Holland (retired director of the National Oceanic and Atmospheric Administration's Hollings Marine Laboratory and former director of the South Carolina Department of Natural Resources Marine Resources Research Institute at Fort Johnson) helped me to understand the Chesapeake and ACE Basin water sheds and ecosystems, their similarities and differences. Dr. Shelome Gooden and I have maintained an ongoing conversation about Creole languages since she served as my primary advisor for the Andrew W. Mellon New Directions Fellowship in 2014-2015. Shelome's thoughts in January 2023 particularly on the existence of a Creole language spoken by Blacks in the Maryland Eastern Shore and the Creole language spoken by Blacks in the South Carolina, Georgia, and Florida Lowcountry, from which Gullah Geechee evolved informed my interpretation of Harriet Tubman telling her biographer that she could not understand the Lowcountry Creole's speech and they could not understand her either. In January 2023, Dr. Walter Johnson (Winthrop Professor of History and African American Studies, Harvard University, Department of History) generously discussed with me the bill of sales/mortgages and other credit instruments, which Lower Combahee rice planters used in their slave transactions and the similarities and differences among the slave transactions of planters on lower Combahee rice plantations and other parts of the antebellum US South. In August and September 2022, Henry Lowndes confirmed the Lowndes family genealogy and allowed me to view the Lowndes family scroll as I unraveled the Lowndes' family's slave transactions and worked to identify which Lowndes ancestor held Minus Hamilton in bondage. In December 2022, Dr. Kate Larson encouraged me to be as careful naming Harriet Tubman's family and community members whom she led to freedom on the Underground Railroad as I had been in recovering the names of the Combahee freedom seekers. And, my husband, Samuel W Black (Senator John Heinz History Center, Director of African American Programs) and I have had an ongoing conversation related to his "From Slavery to Freedom" exhibit and garden (at Frick Environmental Center) about what foods freedom seekers hunted and gathered as they lived off the land in their flight on the Underground Railroad in pursuit of freedom.

For Part Two, a meeting in February 2021 with Chris Barr, Interpretive Supervisor and Public Information Officer, Reconstruction Park in Beaufort, gave me a great start on thinking about downtown Beaufort after the Battle of Port Royal and Beaufort through Tubman's eyes. I am grateful to Toni Carrier for bringing the Captain's Letters in "Letters Received by the Secretary of the Navy from Commanding Officers of Squadrons, 1841-1886" to my attention in September 2020. January and September 2023, dialogue with Dr. Stephen Wise helped me to confirm the "General Stevens" who freedom seekers testified brought freedom seekers down to Beaufort from the Combahee before the Combahee River Raid was most likely General Isaac Ingalls Stevens. And, Benjamin Guterman in March 2022 helped me think through conflicting accounts of Tubman's arrival in Beaufort.

Part Three, in November 2023, Dr. Stephen Wise and I discussed Francis Izard's testimony to the US Provost Marshal. Because there had been skepticism about whether or not the Confederacy had planted torpedoes along the Combahee River before the raid, I wanted Stephen's take on the document. He helped me refine my transcription of the original, identifying that Izard was comparing the size of the torpedoes to a pot belly stove. My editor had emphasized getting the boats and guns right would be critical to garnering an audience among Civil War buffs. In October and November 2021, Dr. Robert Gudmestad, professor and chair, Colorado State University, Department of History, got me off to a good start imagining what the US gunboats might have looked, sounded, smelled, and felt like to enslaved people working, walking, and running along the Combahee River. Also in October 2021, Michael Galloway and Ashley Intemann, educational specialists at the National US Navy Museum, Washington DC helped me confirm details about the *John Adams* and *E. B. Hale*. Michael recommended that I find a steamship society in New England to help me find more information. So, I turned to the Steamship Society of America. From August 2022 to June 2023, I worked with Heather Kisilywicz (Archives Assistant) and Astrid Drew (Archivist) first to identify the *John Adams, Harriet A. Weed, and Sentinel* and to find details of their history and specifications. Ultimately, I also hoped for images of all three vessels. We could not find images of the three specific ships which the US Army used in the raid. so, Heather found images of steamers of the comparable age and size. Secondarily, I wanted to find out whether Tubman arrived on the *Atlantic* or the *Baltic*, when she arrived, and specification details for the ship on which she sailed. Once again, Heather uncovered fascinating details about the *Atlantic* and *Baltic*. We couldn't find Tubman's actual arrival date, but came very close.

Equally important to the boats and the guns for Civil War readers, the tides are essential to the history and culture of the Lowcountry. Michael Galloway recommended that I contact the National Oceanic and Atmospheric Administration (NOAA) for help with the tides. In February 2022, Todd Ehret, Oceanographer in NOAA's Center for Operational Oceanographic Products and Services, Stakeholder Services shared with me NOAA'S Tide Predictions and a map of the Tide Prediction Stations along the Combahee River. The Tide Predictions are generated for past, present, and future dates and calculated from expected tidal conditions, based on the gravity and relative motion of the Moon, Sun, and Earth. They are available on NOAA's website: tidesandcurrents.noaa.gov. Armed with the NOAA website, I called on Dr. Travis Folk to help me map the tide predictions onto the primary sources about the raid, particularly when the sources specified the time and/or tidal conditions. From February 2022 to November 2023, discussions with Travis helped me to understand the timing of the raid around the spring tide and the flood tides, including important story details such as the *Sentinel* ran aground at the mouth of the Coosaw River because of sandbars and tidal conditions. J Henry Fair helped as well with my database which correlated the Tide Prediction Stations, historic Tide Predictions from June 1-3, 1863, and narrative points of the US Army boats moving up and down the river. And a conversation with Mike and Gigi McShane at the Nemours Wildlife Foundation 25th Anniversary/ Fall Event in October 2021 for helping me envision the connection between the six hour window between high and low tides, the work of enslaved laborers building and repairing the hydraulic irrigation system in Lowcountry rice fields, and the amount of time the 2nd South Carolina Volunteers and 3rd Rhode Island Artillery's spent on the ground on the lower Combahee rice plantations during the raid.

In June 2019, I had a conversation with Dr. Edward E. Baptist, Professor, Cornell University, Department of History, about his depiction of the mechanics of cotton-picking in his award-winning book, *'The Half Has Never Been Told': Slavery and the Making of American Capitalism*. This conversation was a catalyst in my decision to put the readers in the rice field, particularly hoeing rice at the time of the raid, with the Combahee freedom seekers. Conversations with Dr. Shelome Gooden about Creole linguistics informed my thinking about Minus Hamilton's speech and contributed to my hypothesis that Hamilton may have been African-born or first generation Creole-born. In addition to alligators, I had a lot to learn about snakes. Dr. Anne Kulze and I encountered a cotton mouth standing its ground on a walk in the upper Combahee area in June 2021. My cousin, Lloyd Fields who is a skilled deer hunter—Cousin Jonas was and all of his sons are skilled deer hunters—and outdoorsman, shared his vast experiences with the behaviors of reptiles in the Green Pond area during the summer in November 2021. In June 2022, Dr. W. Eric Emerson, Agency Director, State Historic Preservation Officer, and State Archivist, South Carolina Department of Archives and History, and I discussed why Colonel William C. Heyward was no longer colonel in the Confederate Army by June 1863 and Joshua Nicholls enlistment in the 11th South Carolina Infantry/

9th South Carolina Infantry after the raid. Eric also helped me to imagine John A. Savage's journey from McPhersonville back and forth to Rose Hill Plantation to visit his family. On more than occasion while we toured Confederate earthworks, particularly in July 2021, Jeff Grigg emphasized the lack of experience and simultaneous extraordinary courage of the 2nd South Carolina Volunteers as they walked across the causeway not knowing if they would encounter Confederate fire. My cousin, Cleveland Frasier, told to me over the years family oral histories about Myrtle Grove Plantation and old members of St. Mary's AME Church (now merged with White Hall AME) praying on the mourners' bench about labor relations there. My cousin, Mother Katie Richards Gilliard, talked to me over the years about her deceased husband's family on Smithfield Plantation before she died in 2016. My former professor, Dr. Peter Bing, Professor Emeritus, Emory University's Department of Classics, provided me with the translation of Virgil's *Aeneid* and discussed it with me in the context of Joshua Nicholls' letter published as a letter to the editor. A number of conversations with Chris Barr, Tricia Bush and Judy Copeland (Historians, The Baptist Church of Beaufort), Reverend Kenneth Hodges (Pastor, Tabernacle Baptist Church), and Reverend Alexander McBride (Pastor, First African Baptist Church) from July 2021 to November 2023 shaped my thinking about the morning after the raid, where the Combahee freedom seekers were taken, and where Harriet Tubman made her only speech in Beaufort, SC for which documentation has to date been found. Lastly, Victoria Small (Executive Director, Gullah Geechee Cultural Heritage Corridor's) remarks at the National Park Service's wreath laying event on June 2, 2023 in commemoration of the 160th Anniversary of the Combahee River Raid at the Harriet Tubman Bridge contributed to my imagination that the Beaufort and Sea Islands' freedomseekers who liberated themselves after the Battle of Port Royal, including the Black soldiers who risked their lives so that Black people still enslaved on the St. Mary's, St. John's, and Combahee Rivers could be free and the Combahee freedomseekers could have sung "O Freedom" in the church as they assembled the morning after the raid.

In Part Four, my editor and I had decided to open each part of the book with an epigraph. I hadn't found just the right epigraph to open Part Four and frame the end of the Combahee freedom seekers' story until I heard Victoria Smalls' opening remarks at the NPS 160th Anniversary wreath-laying. The Ibo proverb was often quoted by Dr. Herman Blake, Founding Executive Director, Gullah Geechee Cultural Heritage Corridor, on whose shoulders we all stand. In October 2023, Dr. Dottie Stone, Research/ Development Associate at Middleton Place helped me confirm Middleton family genealogy among two Middleton cousins who wrote letters to each other after the raid. In September 2020, November 2021, and January 2023, Dr. Kate Larson and I also discussed Harriet Tubman wearing a Union blue coat and carrying a sharpshooter's rifle in the Civil Special woodcut, as well as the handing down of Tubman's guns un her family. Way back in April 2017, Toni Carrier brought the document from the Waterhouse-Croft Collection at the South Carolina Historical Society which records Hector Fields' (and other Black soldiers') protest of his pension denial to my attention and to Mary Jo Fairchild for helping me identify Hector Fields therein. As I was writing the Afterword at Middleton Place, I included my theory that the Combahee River Raid was the largest slave rebellion in US history in my lecture at the Middleton Family Reunion. Then, Dr. Peter Wood, (Professor Emeritus, Duke University, Department of History) discussed this theory afterwards, which got me thinking of the implications of a slave rebellion during the Civil War. Lastly, I had the honor with J Henry Fair and Dirk Vandenberk of interviewing Claire Hamilton in White Plains, New York in December 2022. She shared with us what she knew about her great-great grandfather and his iconic photograph. We knew she was ill, but had no idea how near her end was. Claire Hamilton passed away a few months after our interview. May her soul rest in peace.

When I step out or get pushed out on a limb or two, I need good people to have my back, to tell me to get up and fly, even if I fall a few times. I am eternally grateful to the following people, without whom I could not have realized my dream of writing this book: Dr. Tera Hunter (Chair of African-American Studies and Edwards Professor of History, Princeton University), my home girl, friend, and mentor, has advised every stage of my career from 1997 until tomorrow. Dr. Markus Rediker (Distinguished Professor, University of Pittsburgh, Department of History) was instrumental in me meeting my literary agent, Elise Capron of Sandra Dijkstra Literary Agency. Working with Elise has been an absolute joyful and ongoing revelation. My editor, Tim Bent, Executive Editor, Oxford University Press Trade Division, shared my vision of Combee from our first conversation (before OUP even signed the book); he refused to cut any of the "slavery material" (I did trim it some) or otherwise disrupt the narrative arc to make this "Brick House" of a book fit a more cookie cutter style. Tim taught me how to tell a story, one of my most deeply held aspirations since first visiting the Lowcountry cemetery where my paternal ancestors are buried. My entire OUP team was stellar: Paloma Escovedo and Zara Cannon-Mohammed (project editors), Amy Whitmer (production editor), and Amy Packard Ferro (publicist), as well as Sue Warga (copy editor). Only Elise has read more versions of my book proposal and advised me on pitching more than my dear friend from graduate school days, William Jelani Cobb (Staff Writer, The New Yorker, Dean, Graduate School of Journalism, and Henry R. Luce Professor of Journalism, Columbia University, School of Journalism). Bernadette Adams Davis, my dear friend from college, (founder of Bernadette Davis Communications) and Alesa Gerald have supported me with social media and publicity. Charles Tolbert, Esq. takes care of all of my IP and has been a wonderful advocate for "Unburied, Unmourned, Unmarked: Requiem for Rice" and Combee.

Since my first visit to the "grow'd up" cemetery in the woods and first sight of my ancestor's uninterred remains and unmarked graves, I have devoted myself to telling our ancestors' stories. I am profoundly humbled to have been chosen as the vehicle to tell this story of the Combahee River Raid. And, I am deeply grateful to the many people who have helped me to tell it. Any errors in the telling are mine and mine alone. And, I pray that the ancestors will forgive me for my shortcomings.

I would refuse to give Cancer the last word, but one is obliged to testify after going through the fire and making it through to the other side in every African and African-descended spiritual system I know of. My diagnosis at the end of December 2016 of aggressive breast cancer (stage three in my breast and metastatic in my lymph nodes) is the missing piece in my decision to write *Combee*. And, spots on my liver and abdomen could have been metastatic disease. I decided that interrupting chemotherapy, immunotherapy, and now hormone therapy to was a risk I was not willing to take at the time. I resolved to do everything in my power to stay around raise my children who were ages thirteen and seven when I was diagnosed. So, I pursued my passion project, *Combee*, that gave me something to focus on when I couldn't control my body. It also enabled me to continue to move forward with my career and make an impact on the other side of the Atlantic as I priortized defeating cancer. Then, after treatment, I submitted to what my breast surgeon called "an aggressive surveillance program," seeing as many as seven doctors (several quarterly at first) and hormone therapy to prevent a recurrence and undergoing CT scans (also quarterly at first) to monitor for metastatic disease. I have been in remission since July 2017, completed immunotherapy in January 2018, and finally graduated to no more CT Scans in November 2022 after my oncologist determined that the spots on my lungs and abdomen are scar tissue, not metastic disease.

Thank you to Dr. Carey Andrew-Jaja and Dr. Jeannette South-Paul (both retired from University of Pittsburgh Medical Center), as well as my cousin, Dr. Corbin R. Johnson (radiation oncologist, Vanderbilt University Medical Center) and my high school best friend, Mary Joe Fernandez Godsick, who worked tirelessly to be sure that I was properly and promptly diagnosed, got into treatment in a few weeks' time, and got a second opinion on my treatment options. Dr. Adam Brufsky (oncologist who still calls the shots as he continues to closely monitor my hormone therapy), Dr. Ron Johnson (breast surgeon who performed both my and my mother's surgeries), Dr. Marsha Haley, and Dr. Sushil Beriwol (both radiation oncologists), all of the UPMC Magee Women's Hospital Women's Cancer Center and Dr. Vu T. Nguyen of the UPMC Aesthetic Plastic Surgery Center provided state of the art treatment. Dean Richard Scheines (CMU Dietrich College), Dr. Donna Harsch (Head at the time of CMU's History Department), Leslie Levine (CMU Dietrich College Research Office now retired), and Ray Gamble (National Academies of Sciences, Engineering, and Medicine also retired), made sure that I did not have to spend my inaugural Senior Ford Fellowship year in cancer treatment. And, Dr. Antonio D. Tillis, who was then Dean of College of Charleston, invited me to be in residence at the College of Charleston once I resumed traveling domestically in Fall 2017. The Senior Ford Fellowship gave me the opportunity to pivot my work while I continue hormone therapy, find satisfaction working in South Carolina Lowcountry rice fields, and conduct archival research for *Combee*. Thank you

542 ACKNOWLEDGMENTS

to Pink Steel/Steel City Dragons for teaching me how to cross the finish line, Paddles and Pearls/Dragonboat Charleston, Cancer Bridges, and CMU'S Camp Kesem for nurturing my and my family's socio-emotional health and acupuncturists, Francie Desmone and Tricia Smith, for helping me manage side effects of cancer treatment and hormone therapy.

After cancer treatment, the global pandemic exploded. Our family lost so many people we loved with no end in sight (we dearly miss Cousin Judge Leo Adderly, Mom-in-Love Edna Earle McNeil Black, Cousin-in-Law Melvin Black, Uncle James Fields, Cousin Larry Fields, Aunt "Mama" Kadiatou Conte Forte, Uncle Robert Goode, Cousin Rosalyn Johnson, Brother-in-Law Monty Standifer, and dear friend and partner in crime Dr. James Wilson). During the COVID pandemic, I became caretaker for several family members, including Mama Kadiatou Conte Forte. Thank you to Mama K's family and Baba Anthony Forte for trusting me to take care of Mama K and her estate. I have eternal gratitude for those who helped me during this delicate time when I balanced Mama K's care, *Combee* writing and revisions, and my own health and family: Imam Walter Shahid, Mother Sarah Jameelah Martin, Mary Martin, the Pittsburgh Muslim Women's Association, Fode and Makhissa Camara, Hajah Tantie Saran Doumbouya Berete, Maimouna Sylla, Franklin Robinson, Esq., Kimberly Tarshis (CMU Care.com), staff at AHN Hospital and AHN Hospice, Jay Arnone (Coldwell Banker), and Balafon West African Dance Ensemble, Inc. (and Balafon International). And, special thanks to Djembe who we know Mama K sent to amuse us, be our company, and keep our spirits up even through our tears.

My family made too many sacrifices to count so that I could write this book. I owe my deepest gratitude to my parents, Eddie Fields and Dr. Dorothy Jenkins Fields, my sister and brother-in-law, Marcus and Katherine Marsh, my husband, Samuel W Black, for his steady love and support, and our children, Akhu and Meri. Watching them blossom into their own loving, increasingly responsible, and constantly hilarious people has been my greatest gift.

Appendixes

Appendix 6.A.1. Walter Blake, List of Negroes Lost from ... Estate of Jos. Blake

Pringle Family Papers, 1745–1897, South Carolina
Historical Society, Charleston, SC

Bonny Hall (28)

Age	Name	Occupation (if specified)
40	Ben	Driver
35	Barbara	
15	Silas	
13	Billy	
9	Joseph	
4	Ben	
2	Annanias	
38	Jimmy	Carpenter
38	Bess	
16	Tommy	
12	Eve	
8	Lucy	
5	Jimmy	
1	Andrew	

Age	Name	Occupation (if specified)
34	Cudjoe	
30	Maza	
5	Joshua	
1 yr 6 months	Mary	
30	Tommy	
42	Mat	
37	Affy	
7	Darius	
5	William	
47	Joe	
40	Silla	
18	John	
8	Robin	
14	John	

Parker's Settlement (7)

Age	Name	Occupation (if specified)
23	Jonas	Cooper
31	Wally	
40	Abraham	Engineer
45	Dick	
40	Binah	
18	Betsy	
16	Rosa	

Blakefield (5)

Age	Name	Occupation (if specified)
25	Peter	
24	Betty	
24	Judy	
35	Paris	Carpenter
26	Pressy	

New Ground (23)

Age	Name	Occupation (if specified)
40	London	
39	Sally	
20	Thomas	House Servant
35	Sam	
34	Judy	House Servant
30	Russell	
4	Adam	
34	Tom	
25	Coomba	
12	Fatuma	
4	Aaron	
34	Charles	Cooper
42	Paul	House Servant
30	Dinah	
45	Cudjoe	
38	Catherina	
46	Joe	
40	Amey	
40	Titus	Carpenter
36	Flora	
28	Davy	
27	Isaac	Cooper
25	Mary	

<u>Pleasant Hill</u> (20)

Age	Name	Occupation (if specified)
37	Joe	Engineer
37	Peggy	
16	Joe	
10	Bess	
8	Ruthy	
4	Sary	
1	Tyra	
33	Nero	Cooper
27	Sary	
37	Sam	Miller
34	Sue	
16	Tyra	
35	Prince	
26	Judy	
7	Mathew	
4	Luke	
8 months	Sam	
24	Josey	
20	Mingo	
61	Billy	Carpenter

Appendix 10.A.1. James Seymour Severance's Diary, May 1, 1862

Collection of Michael Emett Sr., Billings, Montana

Thurs, May 1st. Get up early and ride thro' the cool morning air to the ferry with Mr. Pierce leaving Mr. Hooper, who is always late. Mr P says, when he stays at Eustis. It is a delightful day, but promises to be very warm.

We have to wait quite a while at the ferry, and Mr. P has a Conversation with me at the Cotton house. Asks about J.B.S. and what he is doing. Refers to "Moses," says Sanborn referred to her, and that after his first pressing appeal for a capable man to aid him, he was notified that she was to be sent to him. And Garrison for the first time came into his office, to ask if he couldn't do something about her being brought to Port Royal. E.L.P asked if she could teach _ no!_ "can she do anything of that sort?" "No" _ "Then I don't see what can be done for her." For you see it takes a person of considerable tact and education to carry out this thing properly, and it is necessary at this stage that discipline should be used; and in that case it is a question whether Moses would be at all the person to operate among them. What can they have thought of sending her out here for? I ventured to hint that it might be with the idea that she might ultimately be of use in teaching them to make good use of their liberty, in some such way as had been so well carried out by her in Maryland, & c. Yes, that is all very well, but could not be done here. We are all under Government here, and must be very cautious in our actions. Tho' you and I may feel that we shd like to see these people freed by any means, we must grant that the Govt. has made a step forward, and we have a chance to do some thing, but it is by sufferance, and we are put upon our good behavior, as it were. It will not do to urge this matter__ we must proceed cautiously, within limit of Govt. authority to wh. we are bound, and be thankful for what freedom we obtain

We go over the river, and to Mr. Forbes's with some blackberries, and meet Mr. F. on the way, on horseback. Mr. P. introduces me, and we go on to his house, where I meet Mrs. Forbes, and have a short talk with her, about Concord, & c. A very fine lady, I should say, from first look, and I was reminded at once of her daughter Mary. I think there is a great resemblance. Mr. P. asks me about Concord, the Ripleys, Fay, Keyes, with whom he went to the Chicago Convention, & c. About 10, while sitting in Dr. Peck's office, we see the Azalia sailing by for Hilton Head, with Mr. & Mrs. Forbes on board. one of the neatest yachts I ever saw; light and trim. Soon after a severe storm comes up wh. lasts until 20'c. So I do not return then, as I had expected. Hooper came over at . . .

Appendix 13.A.1. Circular, Headquarters Third Military District, March 23, 1863

The War of the Rebellion: A Compilation of the Official Records of the Union and Confederate Armies, ser. 1, vol. XIV (Washington, DC: GPO. 1880–1901), 292–293

[Inclosure No. 3]

CIRCULAR.]   HEADQUARTERS THIRD MIL. DIST.,

Pocotaligo, March 27, 1863.

The attention of planters and other slave-holders in this military district is called to the following communication from department head quarters:

HDQRS. DEPARTMENT SOUTH CAROLINA, GEORGIA, AND FLORIDA,

Charleston, S.C. March 23, 1863.

GENERAL: It is the wish of the commanding general that you advise all planters and owners of negroes in your military district to remove their negroes as far as practicable into the interior of the State, as otherwise they are liable to be lost at any moment.

Very respectfully, your obedient servant,

JNO. F. O'BRIEN,

Captain and Acting Assistant Adjutant-General

Appendix 13.A.2. Statement of Francis Izard, Contraband, June 1, 1863

US Provost Marshal Papers, 1861–1867, Record Group 109, National Archives and Records Administration, Washington, DC

1 June 1863

Francis Izard—Colored

Left Combahee ferry on Saturday week—Lived at floating bridge at Henry Middleton's plantation, about 10 or 20 miles from Tar Bluff 20 m by water—14 or 15 m further up the river is Saltketcher Bridge—Cypress & pine logs are fallen across the river—Piles are driven up near Hickory landing, near Saltketchers Bridge—They had a battery at Combahee ferry with 4 guns.—They have taken the guns away & now have a picket only there. They have two torpedoes there—They are in tin or iron cans, about as big as the store (26 x 1 x 10 in)—The Combahee floating bridge is of flat boats & is used for teams & C. They are building such a bridge across the Ashepoo—6 pickets are at Cotton Hope & 6 at Fields point—They release pickets every Saturday—They belong to Rutley's Squadron & the main body are at Green Pond—The other Regt is at McPhersonville—I came down the river in a small boat to Coosaw lsd, got there on Wednesday

There are no batteries at Saltketchers Bridge—There is a guard of 3 or 4.

There are troops at Pocotaligo—Genl Walker is there—Col Rutley of Cavalry. They have 3 or 4 batteries at Pocotaligo I don't know what they are.

The colored people all want to get away—Don't get enough to eat. The soldiers don't got enough to Eat or coffee,—They are very bad off—I have heard a great many say they would run off if they could get a chance— Most of the white people want to get back into the Union—The horses & cattle are in bad condition—Corn $3.50 per bushel—Coffee 3.50 pd. Bacon $1 = pd.—Flour $50 to $60 = bbl.

I am a shoe maker & also a farrier.

By order of Brigadier-General Walker

Captain JAMES LOWNDES
Captain & Acting Adjutant-General.

Appendix 13.A.3. Names of Harriet Tubman's Spies, Scouts, and Pilots

Charles P. Wood, "A History Concerning the Pension Claim of Harriet Tubman," Record Group 233, National Archives and Records Administration, Washington, DC

"Isaac Hayward" "Mott Blake"
"Gabriel Cahern" "Sandy Sellers"
"Geo Chisolm" "Solomon Gregory,"
"Peter Burns,"

"Pilots who ^ know the channels of the Rivers
"in this vicinity, and who acted as
"such for Col. Montgomery up the
"Combahee river

"Cha Simmons"
"Saml Hayward"

Appendix 14.A.1. Special Orders No. 112, Headquarters Third Military District, McPhersonville, May 26, 1863

The War of the Rebellion: A Compilation of the Official Records of the Union and Confederate Armies, ser. 1, vol. XIV (Washington, DC: Government Printing Office, 1880–1901), 292

[Inclosure No. 2]

SPECIAL ORDERS,   HDQRS. THIRD MILITARY DISTRICT,
No. 112.   McPhersonville, May 26, 1863.

★ ★ ★ ★ ★ ★ ★

XV. The recent false alarm of the pickets stationed on Combahee River was not justified by circumstances. Before giving such an alarm the pickets should have ascertained positively whether a boat had landed or not and how many men were in it. If only 5 or 6, it is the duty of the pickets, if only 2 should be on post, to engage them. If a large number, it is the duty of the pickets to fire a signal for their comrades and closely watch the enemy's movements. As these troops have but recently arrived in this district, and may be ignorant of existing orders, they are warned that if another groundless alarm is given the pickets will be court-martialed. If sufficient courage is not shown in watching the enemy pickets will be subject to the charge of cowardice and to be tried by court-martial.

By order of Brigadier-General Walker:

JAMES LOWNDES,
Captain and Acting Assistant Adjutant-General

Appendix 16.A.1. Walter Blake to Maria Hough Blake, May 3, 1863

Walter Blake Papers, 1821–1874, South Caroliniana Library, University of South Carolina, Columbia

Combahee May 3rd 1863

My Dear Mother

The Yankees came up to Combahee Ferry yesterday morning with two gunboats & broke up the pontoon bridge, burning all of the houses up to that point & carrying off all the negroes & I am sorry to say that about _25 or 30_ of ours ran away & went to them, all of them men and boys with only one woman. Saucey's brothers John & Peter & Will's brother Charley went also Saucey's son Prince & April's brother Charles & a lot more whose names I do not know. They carried away all the negroes from Newport & from William C. Heyward's & burnt the dwelling houses & mills & did the same to all the other plantations lower down.

I believe none of the Blakes or Cousin Daniel's negroes went they were too far off to get down easily. I had just got up from picket when I heard of it & came down here immediately but two late to be of any service for the Yankees had gone before any of the troops could get down here. I went out this morning with some of Captain Allen's men to try and find them with dogs but we could not find one.

April has just come up from Bonny he is quite well & still on Johns Island.

Papa has gone to headquarters to see General Walker & I have to go back to camp this evening.

This was a regular nigger raid of the Yankees they found out that this country was undefended & came to destroy the crops & carry off the negroes. I suppose they must have got nearly 500. Write soon I remain your affect Son

Walter Blake

Appendix 16.A.2. Claim by William C. Heyward, June 27, 1863

Claims of Property Loss, 1862–1864, South Carolina Department of Archives and History, Columbia

List of the Negroes carried off by the Yankees from Cypress Plantation on the Combahee River June 2nd 1863 belonging to W. C. Heyward also a statement and valuation of buildings and other property destroyed by fire.

	Age		Age		Age		Age
1. Frank	50	18. Joe	30	35. William	36	52. Andrew	24
2. Prince	45	19. Edward	24	36. Ben	35	53. Friday	24
3. Tecumseh	35	20. Jimmy	35	37. Tom	36	54. Primus	27
4. Isaac Carpt.	48	21. July	35	38. Daniel	32	55. Mike	22
5. Joe Engineer	30	22. Quash	44	39. Alfred	35	56. Neptune	23
6. Moses Carpt	27	23. June	40	40. Joshua	35	57. Stephen	22
7. Will Carpt.	28	24. Sampson	40	41. Hard Times	35	58. Samuel	20
8. Will Carpt.	27	25. Billy	40	42. Adam	35	59. Charles	20
9. Lucius	35	26. Will	45	43. Dembo	28	60. Captain	17
10. July	40	27. Daniel	35	44. Ned	30	61. Cuffy	16
11. Bob	36	28. March	35	45. Will	30	62. Sampson	17
12. Wance	45	29. John	30	46. Jim	30	63. Edward	16
13. Cuffy	45	30. June	32	47. Richard	29	64. Abram	16
14. Ben	26	31. Terry	35	48. Monday	28	65. Joe House	39
15. Bobben	30	32. Winget	40	49. Joe	28	66. Jim	55
16. Peter	30	33. Limus	36	50. Pool	27	67. Mingo (old)	56
17. Ansel	53	34. Harry	40	51. Toby	27	68. Boatswain (old)	69

In all 68 men.

	Age		Women		Age		Age
1. Rose	46	13. Mary	30	25. Lucy	23	37. Peggy	20
2. Bransome	47	14. Mary	30	26. Lucretia	22	38. Caty	19
3. Tomah	35	15. Mary	25	27. Liddy	35	39. Juno	19
4. Rose	40	16. Amy	30	28. June	20	40. Sarah	14

5. Sarah	42	17. Dinah	35	29. Bella	17	41. Binah	18
6. Eliza	38	18. Peggy	35	30. Harriet	32	42. Binar	
7. Louisa	35	19. Tyra	46	31. Eve	30	43. Sibby	36
8. Pindar	35	20. Joan	45	32. Margaret	30	44. Daphne	48
9. Clarinda	35	21. Patience	46	33. Mary	45	45. Aurelia	16
10. Lizzy	37	22. Phoebe	26	34. Sinah	22	46. Amelia	16
11. Nanny	37	23. Venus	40	35. Venus	21	47. Lindy (old)	60
12. Flora	34	24. Sarah	46	36. Suckey	21	48. Rose (old)	60
49. Hannah ½	58	53. Delia sickly	30	37. Poly (old)	60	61. Affy (old)	60
50. Mary ½	58	54. Molly old	60	58. Doll "	65	62. Jane	30
51. Dinah (old)	56	55. Molly "	65	59. Sally "	60	63. Mary	52
52. Daphne "	56	56. Molly "	65	60. Affy "	65	64. Sinah	28

In all 64 Women.

Boys.

Names	Age	Mother's Name	Names	Age	Mother's Name
1. Quaco	14	Mary	19. Christmas	4	Sally
2. Thomas	14	Elsy	20. Glasgow	4	Euhaw Elsy
3. William	13	Sarah	21. Joseph	3	Sarah
4. Ben	12	Lucy	22. Daniel	3	Lucretia
5. Jacob	11	Rose	23. Toby	2	June
6. Jackson	11	Tamar	24. Paul	2	Tamar
7. Josey	11	Elsy	25. Bacchus	2	Mary Ann
8. Jack	11	Sarah	26. Mark	1	Pindar
9. Primus	11	Patty	27. Adam	1	Mary
10. Dick	10	Louisa	28. Beauregard	1	Cretia
11. Isaac	10	Lizzy	29. Primus	1	Sarah
12. April	9	Eliza	30. Lucius	1	Sinah
13. Chance	9	Rose	31. Solomon	1	Suckey
14. Bob	8	Tamar	32. Will	1	Amy
15. Henry	8	Jane	33. Tim	1	Nanny
16. Elijah	7	Elsy	34. Mingo	6	Sarah
17. Moses	6	Sarah	35. one not named ½		Bella
18. Benjamin	6	Clarinda			

all

In all 35 Boys.

Girls.

Names	Age	Mother's Name	Names	Age	Mother's Name
1. Rachal	15	Pindar	7. Nelly	8	Mary
2. Hagar	14	Louisa	8. Kate	8	Louisa
3. Siddy	14	Binar	9. Sally	8	Nanny
4. Hetty	10	Peggy	10. Miley	7	Lucy
5. Maria	10	Lizzy	11. Silvy	7	Patty
6. Delia	10	Patience	12. Betty	7	Phoebe
13. Emily	6	Eliza	23. Violet	2	Eve
14. Binar	6	Patience	24. Tenah	2	Rose
15. Cale	6	Louisa	25. Nora	2	Venus
16. Cale	6	Jane	26. Tamima	2	Patience
17. Ann	5	Lizzy	27. Molly	2	Clarinda
18. Dolly	5	Peggy	28. Sarah	2	Elsy
19. Nancy	4	Nanny	29. Cale	1	Peggy
20. Florence	4	Amy	30. Sibby	1	Louisa
21. Phebe	3	Harriet	31. Daphne	1	Peggy
22. Flora	3	Binah	32. Lucy	1	Venus.

In all 32 Girls

Recapitulation Men 68

Women 64

Boys 35

Girls 32 Total 149

Buildings &c burnt with their value

Threshing mill	$ 7500.00
Two Barns	3000.00
4 Flats & Flat House	1500.00
Dwelling House & Furniture	7000.00
Overseer's House	2000.00 Kitchen & Store Room
Two Corn Houses	1500.00
Grist Mill	1000.00
Coach House & Stables	2000.00
Mule Stable	700.00
Two Wagon Sheds	300.00
Cattle Shed	200.00
Hospital & 5 Negro Houses	2000.00
10,000 Bushels Rough Rice	22,200.00
800 Bushels Corn	1200.00
2 Lofts full of Blades	1200.00

$53,100.00

Claim of Wm C. Heyward

Losses from War

Class 3

Filed in Book no3 pg 2-28-72-156

July 1863

State of South Carolina, Charleston District

Personally appeared W. C. Heyward, who being duly sworn, deposes, that the written statement contains a true and correct account of the losses sustained by him from the hands of the enemy. The said loss being estimated at fifty three thousand one hundred dollars exclusive of one hundred & ninety nine slaves_

Sworn to 27th June 1863

G. M. Dingle Mag.

Wm. C. Heyward

Personally appeared F. Hughes, who deposes that he is well acquainted with W. C. Heyward above-named__that he is cognizant personally of the loss sustained by said Heyward, and that said Heyward was the owner of the property within specified and that the estimate of his loss is fair and correct to the best of deponents knowledge and belief__

T. Hughes

Sworn to 27 June 1863 G. W. Drirgle Mag.

Appendix 16.A.3. Claim by Joshua Nicholls, September 17, 1863

Claims of Property Loss, 1862–1864, South Carolina Department of Archives and History, Columbia

State of South Carolina Charleston District

Personally appeared before me J. Nicholls Planter this day of our Lord 17th September 1863, and swore the following is a true and correct statement of the amt of property captured and destroyed by the United States forces on the 2nd of June 1863, on Longbrow Plantation, situated on Combahee River St. Bartholomews Parish S.C.

Sworn to before me

Thos. P. Lockwood   J. Nicholls

Mag & Not. Pub.

Burnt house—furniture and plate $10,000
Library and engravings 3500 vols $15,000
Wash Kitchen-Kitchen and store room $ 1,000
Three negro houses $ 1,000
One mule stable $ 1,000
Barn_Corn house, and steam threshing mill $10,000
Seven thousand bushels of rice $21,000
Three hundred bushels of corn 600
Carried off three prime mules 600
$60,200

The negroes captured, have the following names and were appraised at the value of $65,400 a record of which is in the ordinary office at Walterboro· Colleton District S.C.

Pussey_ Pompey_ Sylla_ Peter_ Simon_
Sally_ Stephen_ Josey_ Fred, Jimy
Charlotte,_Sandy_ Huckey, Marianne_
Caesar, Dorcas, Amy_
Solomon_ Mary_ Hercules infant
Betsy_ Lewis, Affee_ Sharper_ Hagar
George_ Amy_ Friday_ Lenny
Kate_ Isaac_ Pompey_ Cornelia_ May
Tom_ Rachel_ Aaron_ Jane
Frank_ Tenet_ Binah
Captain_ Jane_ Emma infant
Ellen_ Molly_ Susannah_ James, Daniel_ Jemy infant
Sam_ Sarah & Jack
Nelly_ Ben_ Ben child
Janus & Liddy
Dorcas_ London & Beck
Juno_ Linda infant
Phillis_ Jim & Jack
Sancho_ Abigai_, Mingo_ Hercules and Robert
Louisa & Reuben

State of South Carolina
Charleston District

Personally appeared Hon. T. Legare Hutchinson and Dr. Richard L. North who being duly sworn, declare an oath, that they are well acquainted with Mr. Joshua Nicholes that to the best of their knowledge and belief the losses enumerated by Mr. Nicholls were duly substantiated by him and finally that the valuation affixed by him is a just and true appraisment thereof.

Sworn to before me
this 17th Sept 1863
Thos. P. Lockwood
Mag & Not Pub
Rich L. North
T. Leger Hutchinson
South Carolina
Charleston District
South Carolina
Colleton Dist   I, I. K. Linder, Clerk for said District Colleton Do hereby certify that T. Leger Hutchinson and R. L. North whose signatures appear to the above affidavit are perfectly reliable gentlemen. And that Thos. P. Lockwood whose signature appears as Notary Public is such and Notary Public for Charleston District and that all his acts as such are entitled to full faith and credit.

Given under my hand and seal
   of officer at Walterboro
   November 9th A.D. 1863
   I. K. Linder

Appendix 16.A.4. Claim by William L. Kirkland, November 5, 1863

Claims of Property Loss, 1862–1864, South Carolina
Department of Archives and History, Columbia

Colleton District
State of South Carolina

Personally appeared William L. Kirkland Planter of the District and state aforesaid, who being duly sworn, deposes that the following is a true and correct statement of the property and value thereof captured and destroyed by the United States forces on the second day of June 1863 on Rosehill plantation situate on Combahee River St. Bartholemews parish

Sworn to before me   W. L. Kirkland

this 5th day of November 1863
Ch. Richardson Miles
Not Pub & Ex; off; Mag.

> Dwelling house & furniture $14,000
> Threshing mill $ 7,000
> Twelve hundred bushles of rice $ 3,600
> Stable & Carriage house $ 400
> Mule stable $ 500
> Fodder & Winnowing house $ 500
> One servt house $ 1,200
> $27,200
> Names of Negroes captured
> Ben_ Chloe_ Rabbit_ October, Toby_ Rose, Joe, Pleasant,
> Paul, Margaret, Bush, Amy, Minna, Will, Betty_
> James, Clarinda, Huckey, Antony, Maria, infant, 1. Thomas,
> 2. Thomas, Daphne, Elsy_ infant, Billy, Delia, child, Caroline_
> infant, Kit, Bonen, Lavinia, Julia, Judy, Rhody, Ned,
> Tacit, Charles, Dick, Janus, Lilus, Jack, Louisa, Martha,
> Virginia, Moses, Andrew, Watkins, Charlton, Carolina,
> Phillis, Pussy, Maria, Hannah, Lane, Fanny, Molly,
> Bud, infant, Tenah, Dianah, Flora, child, Flora, Sarah,
> Phoebe, Tom_ Joe, Jim, Maria, infant, Phoebe, Laney,
> Samy_ Dorcas, Ellen, Stephny, infant_John.
> The value of the above named negroes $64,000

Appendix 16.A.5. Claim by William L. Kirkland, March 6, 1863

Claims of Property Loss, 1862–1864, South Carolina Department of Archives and History, Columbia

State of South Carolina
Colleton District

  Personally appeared William L. Kirkland Planter of the District and State aforesaid who being duly sworn deposeth that in consequence of the occupation of the Coast of the State aforesaid by the Enemy he has lost the services of five (5) valuable Negro slaves who absconded from his Plantation on or about the[ ]day of March Anne Domini One Thousand Eight hundred and Sixty-Two, and have not since been heard of, he being informed and believing that they are in the hands of the Enemy__And that the said William L. Kirkland was at the aforesaid an officer in the Confederate Army, and absent from and unable to attend to the interests of his Plantation__

Sworn to before me this   W. L. Kirkland

sixth (6th) day of March AD 1863

Arthur P. Linning L.S. C.S.
Mag Ex Off
and Capt. & A.C.S. Rutledge Cavalry

Appendix 17.A.1. Petition with Attached Sheriff's Letter, Order, and Copy of the Tax Execution, Asking to Be Refunded Part of His Taxes Collected Under Execution for Property and Slaves Abandoned or Seized by the Enemy in Colleton District

Petitions to the General Assembly, South Carolina
Department of Archives and History, Columbia, SC

To the Honble the Senate and House of Representatives
The memorial of Charles T. Lowndes
    Sheweth
That your memorialist at the time of the passage by your Honble Bodies of an Act to raise supplies for the year commencing in October one thousand eight hundred and sixty two, was the owner and possessed of a valuable rice plantation on Combahee River in Colleton District and of a large gang of negro slaves employed in the cultivation thereof: that he returned the same for taxation to the Tax Collector of St Bartholomew Parish, and that in the interval between such return and the collection of taxes, a raid was made by the public enemy upon his plantation and on[ ]June 1863 Two hundred and thirty six of his negro slaves were taken possession of and carried off by the public enemy and have never since returned into the possession of your memorialist, and in consequence he was obliged to abandon his said

plantation with its growing crop and remove such negro slaves as were left him. That believing himself in regard to the said plantation and abducted negro slaves to come under the exemption of the said Act, he had the matter referred to the Comptroller General, but in the meantime a Tax Execution issued against him: That the Comptroller General deeming the case to come under the spirit of the Act, instructed the Sheriff of Colleton District to stay the Execution upon payment by your Memorialist of the tax on the plantation amounting to Two hundred and fifty four Dollars 19 cents, which payment was promptly made and the evidence thereof is herewith submitted.

Wherefore your memorial prays that in consideration of the circumstances of the loss of his slaves and the abandonment of his plantation, the said sum of Two hundred and fifty four Dollars 19 cents may be refunded to him, that the instructions of the Comptroller General for a stay of Execution be confirmed, and that the Comptroller General may be directed to have satisfaction entered upon the said Execution.

And your Memorialist will ever pay and so forth

C T Lowndes

Appendix 19.A.1. Neptune Nicholas to April Singleton (In Trust for Others), Deed for Sale, January 2, 1880

Neptune Nicholas et al. to April Singleton, Jan. 2, 1880, Deed Book 4, 85, Colleton County Register of Deeds

The State of South Carolina Colleton County Know all men by these presents that Mr. Neptune Nichols & others, whose names, are subscribed as Grantors hereto, in the state aforesaid, Farmers in consideration, of the sum of five dollars, to us in hand paid, at and before the sealing of these presents, by April Singleton in the State, aforesaid Farmer (the receipt whereof is hereby acknowledged have granted, bargained, sold and released, and by these Presents, do grant bargain, sell, and release unto the said, April Singleton (which we own as tenants in common) All those three tracts of land, situated in the county, and state, aforesaid, known as portions of the Gough or Fripp lands, designated on a Plat made by H W Fishburne Surveyor of date January 18th 1859. As tract "A No 4 _ " "B No 3," & "C No 2." containing in the whole nine hundred and sixty six (966) acres more or less and bounded on the north by tract No 1 of the Gough lands belonging to Anthony Fraser, and others South by lands formerly of Northrop, East by lands of Estate of Dr A Fraser and West by lands of Estates of Mr Donald and Wm C. Heyward As will fully appear by aforesaid Plat (The Plat attached represents the renunciation of April Singleton, he having sold off the balance) Together with all & singular the rights, hereditaments & appertenances to said Premises belonging or in any miss incident or appertaining. To Have & Hold, all & singular the said Premises before mentioned, unto the said April Singleton his Heirs & Assigns forever. (Die Jenkins & Dolly Whitford being heirs at law of Cuffee; Cyndy Moultrie heirs at law of Lyman Smalls; Molly Graham heirs at law of John Graham, and Phebe Smalls Heir at law of Jno Smalls.) And we do hereby bind, our Heirs Executors and Administrators, to warrant and forever defend all and singular the said premises unto the said April Singleton, his Heirs and Assigns against myself and my Heirs and all others lawfully claiming, or to claim the same, or any part thereof. Witness my Hand and Seal this second day of January in the year of our Lord one thousand eight hundred and eighty six and in the one hundred and tenth year of the Sovereignty & Independence of the United States of America Signed, Sealed & Delivered in the presence of Richard Mitchell, Archie McGraw. Neptune Nicholas {LS} | Robbin X his mark Mitchell {LS}, Sarah X her mark Britter {LS}, Charles X his mark Nichols {LS}, Die X her mark Jenkins{LS}, Dolly X her mark Whitford {LS}, Sampson X his mark McNeill {LS}, Jerry X his mark Meyers {LS}, Cyndy X her mark Moultrie {LS}, Molly X her mark Graham {LS}, Prince X his mark McNeill {LS}, Edward X his mark Brown {LS}, Charlie X his mark Lesesne {LS}, Peter X his mark James {LS}, Solomon X his mark Glover {LS}, Moses X his mark Simmons {LS}, Phebe X her mark Smalls {LS}, Flora X her mark Robinson {LS}, Brutus X his mark Rutledge {LS}, Dick X his mark Proctor {LS}, Sue X her mark Ferguson {LS}, R. W. X his mark Higgins {LS}, John X his mark Pinckney {LS}, Joshua X his mark Polite {LS}, Lewis X his mark Grandison {LS}, Dick X his mark Ferguson {LS}, Cumpsee X his mark Hamilton {LS}, July X his mark Osborn {LS}, Joshua X his mark Simmons {LS}. The State of South Carolina, Colleton County | Personally appeared before me Richard Mitchell, and made oath that he saw the within named parties whose signatures, are written as grantors hereto sign seal and as their act & deed, deliver the within written deed: and that he with Archie McGraw witnessed the execution therof.

Richard Mitchell Sworn to before me this second day of January A. D. 1886

Recorded 29th January 1886}

C. G. Henderson
SEAL Not. Pub. {LS}

Appendix 19.A.2. Molcy Chisolm's Letter, 1907

Pension File for March (Molcy) Chisolm, Record Group 15, National Archives and Records Administration, Washington, DC

March.14.1907. White Hall.SC
dear mr Roosevelt Presedent of U S

I in form you THE few lines to let you know my troble I was fighting after my father March Chisholm Wright from the act of June.27.1890 and tell now and I cannot get jestus I Prufe out my Father Claim and tell my lawer told me I was true I have spent over 50 dolors to get my balance fix to Return to my lawer and true all fo that I cannot get saturefaction my father March Chisholm fought the late war from the first to the last and died soon after getting back home he died in 68 october 10 leave me a healpless in child in the worlds I waus 8 years old when my father died no one to healpe me for I was the ondley Child he had and the Reason I follow the Claim so long becous i waus told from Washington that all Children that is under the adge of 16 at the date of Solders death is in title to Piension I Waus wirking on that grounds after I Pprofe out all of my father wright and spent all I had they waunt to put me a side, I do not know what to do it might be raung for I to write to you but I have to I write to you for healpe I am a woman but I know that you Rools all of these uninted State

and I know that you can healpe my father done the wirk and died from it and I things – I am the ondley Child on Eirth I should reseive the benefit of his Labor and if they did not in tend to

Pay me they should not folow me for 4 years Straight and make Spent all I Could get and tell I borow money to wirk that Claim so I lodge you my Great King to looke in to my distress and healpe me if I Could get What I Spent after my father Claim I Would be Saturefie I worried So much and going from one Place to the other and tell it make me sick from my father claim and no one to healpe me my father did not leave Eney things for me for he fought for his Country and died from Exposure Whilse on line of dutey after getting home the last of 1866 he waus not able to do Eney Manuel Labor he died in 1868 october 10 I leave my Case with the King of the Unintied State and the Lord wish he Say Blesset or those that Consider the Poor from Molcey Chisholm minor Daughter of March Chisolm Co G 34 u SC White Hall SC

Appendix 19.A.3. Primus Barnwell's Letter

Pension File for William (Relia) Middleton,
Record Group 15, National Archives and Records
Administration, Washington, DC

Charleston S.C. March 27/26

Dear Sir Your Received and I am Glad for this Slip But Cant jest fine my Brotherin law Papers as my Sister was old and Could not Read She might-have Lost them But I am Sending You What I find But I dont no his com-mandin officer But he all was Speak of Curnel montgomery Regement But ware he was Discharge was in Charleston SC or Jacksonville Fla as they all ways Speak about Jacksonvill But he and Cuffie Bolds friday Barrignton and others was Slaves and was carried to Bufort SC in the war By the Yankees and thene were he was in List and he marrid my Sister But I was not Living with them at his death So I have not the Papers But after the death of him my Sister move from greenpond to Charleston SC Where She Dide Dec 20 1925 at my home and I Cant tell what She do with her Pension Claim number as She was old and Sickley why I take her to my house and Got my wife to nurse her and when she Died I Got J B moultrie to the undertaker to Bery her and I owe him now

Yours P. Barnwell

Notes

FOREWORD

1. "Col. Montgomery's Raid—the Rescued Black Chattel—a Black 'She' Moses—Her Wonderful Sagacity—the Black Regiments—Col. Higginson's Mistakes—Arrival of the 54th Massachusetts, & c., & c.," *Wisconsin State Journal*, Jun. 20, 1863; Frank Sanborn, "Harriet Tubman," *The Commonwealth* Boston, Jul. 17, 1863.

2. "The Expedition up the Combahee," *The New South*, Jun. 6, 1863; "Col. Montgomery's Raid—the Rescued Black Chattel"; Sanborn, "Harriet Tubman"; "Miscellaneous Items," *Douglass' Monthly*, Aug. 1863; Sarah Bradford, *Scenes in the Life of Harriet Tubman* (1869; repr., North Statford, NH: Ayer, 2004); William Lee Apthorp, "Montgomery's Raids in Florida, Georgia, and South Carolina," 16, Apthorp Family Papers, 1741–1964, HistoryMiami Museum, Miami, FL; Sarah Bradford, *Harriet Tubman: The Moses of Her People* (1886; repr., New York: J. J. Little, 1901), 100–101; Anne Fitzhugh Miller, "Harriet Tubman," *American Review*, Aug. 1912, 422.

3. Bradford, *Scenes in the Life of Harriet Tubman*, 40–41; Bradford, *Harriet Tubman*, 100–101; Telford, "Harriet"; Miller, "Harriet Tubman," 422.

4. Sanborn, "Harriet Tubman"; Bradford, *Scenes in the Life of Harriet Tubman*, 86.

5. Frederick Douglass, *Narrative of the Life of Frederick Douglass an American Slave* (Boston: Anti-Slavery Office, 1849), iii; "The Expedition up the Combahee"; "From South Carolina—the New Federal Commander—Col. Montgomery's Late Raid," *Chicago Tribune*, Jun. 20, 1863; Apthorp, "Montgomery's Raids in Florida, Georgia, and South Carolina," 17.

6. Bradford, *Scenes in the Life of Harriet Tubman*, 41; Bradford, *Harriet Tubman*, 101.

7. Bradford, *Scenes in the Life of Harriet Tubman*, 41; Bradford, *Harriet Tubman*, 101.

8. Bradford, *Scenes in the Life of Harriet Tubman*, 41–42; Bradford, *Harriet Tubman*, 102–104; Telford, "Harriet," 18.

9. Sanborn, "Harriet Tubman."

10. "The Enemy's Raid on the Banks of the Combahee," *The Mercury*, Jun. 4, 1863; "The Expedition up the Combahee"; "The Combahee Expedition," *Philadelphia North American and United States Gazette*, Jun. 8, 1863; "Our Hilton Head Correspondence," *New York Herald*, Jun. 9, 1863; "The Raid on Combahee," *The Mercury*, Jun. 19, 1863; "From South Carolina—the New Federal Commander—Col. Montgomery's Late Raid"; "Col. Montgomery's Raid—the Rescued Black Chattel"; "A Raid Among the Rice Plantations,"

Harper's Weekly, Jul. 4, 1863; Sanborn, "Harriet Tubman"; "The Port Royal (S.C.)," *Douglass' Monthly*, Aug. 1863; Charles P. Wood, "A History Concerning the Pension Claim of Harriet Tubman," 1868, Record Group (henceforth "RG") 233, National Archives and Records Administration (henceforth "NARA"), 17; Cpl. James Henry Gooding, "A First Class Regiment: South Carolina and Georgia, June 1863," in *On the Altar of Freedom: A Black Soldier's Civil War Letters from the Front*, ed. Virginia Matzke Adams (Amherst: University of Massachussets Press, 1991), 28.

11. Harriet Tubman, general affidavit, in "Accompanying Papers of the 55th Congress," RG 233, NARA; Earl Conrad to W. C. Black, Aug. 14, 1939, US Civil War Pension File (henceforth "pension file") for Nelson (Harriet) Davis, RG 15, NARA.

12. Bryan F. McKown and Michael E. Stauffer, "Destroyed County Records in South Carolina, 1785–1872," *South Carolina Historical Magazine* 97, no. 2 (1996): 156–157; Robert H. Woody, "The Public Records of South Carolina," *American Archivist*, Oct. 1939, 253–255.

13. It is important to note the slave narratives written by formerly enslaved people themselves, for example: Harriet A. Jacobs, *Incidents in the Life of a Slave Girl: Written by Herself*, edited by Koritha Mitchell (Peterborough, ON: Broadview Editions, 2023); Olaudah Equiano, *The Interesting Narrative of the Life of Olaudah Equiano, Written by Himself* (Auckland: Floating Press, 2009).

14. Elizabeth Ann Regosin and Donald Robert Shaffer, *Voices of Emancipation: Understanding Slavery, the Civil War, and Reconstruction Through the U.S. Pension Bureau Files* (New York: New York University Press, 2008), 2; Donald Robert Shaffer, *After the Glory: The Struggles of Black Civil War Veterans* (Lawrence: University Press of Kansas, 2004), 45, 121–123, 33.

15. Regosin and Shaffer, *Voices of Emancipation*, 3–4; Shaffer, *After the Glory*, 9, 128–130.

16. Deposition by James Houston, Feb. 28, 1901, pension file for Edward (Catherine) Bennett, RG 15, NARA; William Chauncy Langdon, *Everyday Things in American Life, 1776–1876* (New York: Charles Scribner's Sons, 1941), 2:139–144.

17. Deposition B by Ned Brown, deposition by Cuffy Bowles, and deposition H by Stephen Burlesque, Feb. 11, 1902, pension file for Edward (Peggy) Brown, RG 15, NARA.

18. Deposition B by Ned Brown, deposition by Cuffy Bowles, and deposition H by Stephen Burlesque, Feb. 11, 1902, pension file for Edward (Peggy); Shaffer, *After the Glory*, 123.

19. Regosin and Shaffer, *Voices of Emancipation*, 4; Shaffer, *After the Glory*, 135–36; Langdon, *Everyday Things in American Life*, 2:144–146.

20. N. G. Norvall to J. L. Davenport, Jan. 30, 1911, pension file for Moses (Fannie) Simmons, RG 15, NARA; D. Bell to Department of the Interior Pension Office, Feb. 19, 1873, pension file for William (Sina) Young, RG 15, NARA; Melissa L. Cooper, *Making Gullah: A History of Sapelo Islanders, Race, and the American Imagination* (Chapel Hill: University of North Carolina Press, 2017), 23–25; Regosin and Shaffer, *Voices of Emancipation*, 5; *Low Country*

Gullah Culture: Special Resource Study and Final Environmental Impact Statement (Atlanta: National Park Service, Southeast Regional Office, 2005), 9, 13–21.

21. Depositions by Margaret Moody, Mar. 14, 1890, and Edward Snipe, Mar. 20, 1890, pension file for Andrew (Diana) Harris, RG 15, NARA; deposition by Fannie Simmons, Apr. 14, 1911, pension file for Moses (Fannie) Simmons; Regosin and Shaffer, *Voices of Emancipation*, 3; Shaffer, *After the Glory*, 129.

22. Personal communications with Cleveland Frasier, Jan. 22, 2023, and earlier; "Act of February 6, 1907, Declaration for Pension," Jun. 4, 1910, surgeon's certificates, May 3, 1891, Jun. 14, 1893, Oct. 18, 1894, Mar. 9, 1898, Jun. 5, 1901, Sep. 3, 1902, Sep. 5, 1906, pension file for Jonas (Nellie) Fields, RG 15, NARA.

23. Jonas Field, "Declaration for the Increase of an Invalid Pension," Oct. 29, 1906, deposition B by Stephen Graham, Jul. 3, 1914, deposition by Jonas Fields, Jun. 25, 1902, deposition E by Emmanuel Gettes, Jul. 29, 1914, deposition H by Phoebe Washington, Jul. 29, 1914, deposition J by John Bryan, Aug. 6, 1914, deposition K by Clara Gillison, Aug. 8, 1914, deposition A by Nellie Fields, Aug. 2, 1914, C. M. Lane to Department of the Interior, Bureau of Pensions, Aug. 23, 1914, general affidavit by Jonas Fields, Oct. 22, 1904, pension file for Jonas (Nellie) Fields, RG 15, NARA; Lula Sams Bond and Laura Sams Sanders, "The Sams Family of South Carolina (Continued)," *South Carolina Historical Magazine* 64, no. 2 (1963): 109.

24. Hector Fields file, Sep. 6, 1900, Compiled Military Service Records of Volunteer Union Soldiers Who Served with the United States Colored Troops, RG 94, NARA; No. 972974, Oct. 12, 1911, deposition B by Stephen Graham, Jul. 3, 1914, deposition by Phoebe Washington, Jul. 29, 1914, deposition by Clara Gillison, Aug. 8, 1914, deposition by Jonas Fields, Jun. 25, 1902, deposition J by John Bryan, Aug. 6, 1914, deposition A by Nellie Fields, Jul. 2, 1914, Department of the Interior, Bureau of Pensions, circular, Apr. 18, 1899, William Fletcher & Co. to Superintendent of Beaufort National Cemetery, Mar. 30, 1912, general affidavit by Emanuel Gettes, Dec. 14, 1911, general affidavit by Laura Scott, Aug. 18, 1913, pension file for Jonas (Nellie) Fields.

CHAPTER 1

1. There is a richly researched literature on Harriet Tubman's life. Throughout my book, I have relied on Kate Clifford Larson, *Harriet Tubman Underground National Monument: Historic Resource Study* (Washington, DC: National Park Service/US Department of the Interior, 2019); Kate Clifford Larson, *Bound for the Promised Land: Harriet Tubman: Portrait of an American Hero* (New York: One World/Ballantine, 2009); Milton C. Sernett, *Harriet Tubman: Myth, Memory, and History* (Durham, NC: Duke University Press, 2008); Catherine Clinton, *Harriet Tubman: The Road to Freedom* (Boston: Little, Brown, 2004);

Jean McMahon Humez, *Harriet Tubman: The Life and the Life Stories* (Madison: University of Wisconsin Press, 2003); Earl Conrad, *General Harriet Tubman* (1943; Baltimore: Black Classic Press, 2019); Charles P. Wood, "A History Concerning the Pension Claim of Harriet Tubman" (1868), RG 233, NARA.. I have also relied on the rich history of Beaufort County, Stephen R. Wise, Lawrence Sanders Rowland, Gerhard Spieler, and Alexander Moore, *The History of Beaufort County, South Carolina, Volume 2: Rebellion, Reconstruction, and Redemption, 1861–1893* (Columbia: University of South Carolina Press, 2015)..

2. David W. Blight, *Frederick Douglass: Prophet of Freedom* (New York: Simon & Schuster, 2018), 1, 9–86; Solomon Northup, *Twelve Years a Slave: Narrative of Solomon Northup, a Citizen of New York, Kidnapped in Washington City in 1841, and Rescued in 1853, from a Cotton Plantation near the Red River in Louisiana* (Vancouver, BC: Sapling Books, 2014), 5, 78; Ottobah Cugoano, *Thoughts and Sentiments on the Evil and Wicked Traffic of the Slavery and Commerce of the Human Species: Humbly Submitted to the Inhabitants of Great Britain* (Cambridge: Cambridge University Press, 2013), 5–9; Olaudah Equiano, *The Interesting Narrative of the Life of Olaudah Equiano, Written by Himself* (Auckland: Floating Press, 2009), 26–44; Henry Box Brown, *Narrative of the Life of Henry Box Brown, Written by Himself* (Chapel Hill: University of North Carolina Press, 2008), 7, 51, 147, 85; Nell Irvin Painter, *Sojourner Truth: A Life, a Symbol* (New York: Norton, 1996), 3, 5, 7, 11–14, 18–20, 252, 73; Carleton Mabee and Susan Mabee Newhouse, *Sojourner Truth—Slave, Prophet, Legend* (New York: New York University Press, 1993), 1–21, 50, 142, 160, 202, 215; Lorenzo J. Greene, "Prince Hall: Massachusetts Leader in Crisis," *Freedomways* 1, no. 3 (1970): 238–239, 245–246, 250, 252, 254; Henry Highland Garnet and James McCune Smith, *A Memorial Discourse: By Henry Highland Garnet Delivered in the Hall of the House of Representatives, Washington City, D.C., on Sabbath, February 12, 1865* (Philadelphia: Joseph M. Wilson, 1865), 17; Frederick Douglass, *Narrative of the Life of Frederick Douglass, American Slave* (Boston: Anti-Slavery Office, 1849), iii, iv, viii.

3. Dora Costa and Matthew Kahn found that 186,017 African Americans served in the US Colored Troops during the Civil War. See Dora L. Costa and Matthew E. Kahn, *Heroes and Cowards: The Social Face of War* (Princeton, NJ: Princeton University Press, 2008), 63–64, 66, 69, 71–72; Irvin D. S. Winsboro, "Give Them Their Due: A Reassessment of African Americans and Union Military Service in Florida During the Civil War," *Journal of African American History* 92, no. 3 (2007): 327–346; John David Smith, ed., *Black Soldiers in Blue: African American Troops in the Civil War Era* (Chapel Hill: University of North Carolina Press, 2002), 8; Jacob Metzer, "The Records of the U.S. Colored Troops as a Historical Source: An Exploratory Examination," *Historical Methods* 14, no. 3 (1981): 123–132; Kelly D. Mezurek, *For Their Own Cause: The 27th United States Colored Troops* (Kent, OH: Kent State University Press, 2016), 56–57.

4. Sarah H. Bradford, *Scenes in the Life of Harriet Tubman* (1869; repr., North Stratford, NH: Ayer, 1971); Sarah Bradford, *Harriet Tubman: The Moses of Her People* (1886; repr., New York: J. J. Little, 1901); Brown, *Narrative of the Life of Henry Box Brown*, 181; Equiano, *The Interesting Narrative of the Life of Olaudah Equiano*, 37–38, 40, 44, 85–87, 89–90; Cugoano, *Thoughts and Sentiments*, 12.

5. Philip D. Curtin, Grace S. Brush, and George W. Fisher, *Discovering the Chesapeake: The History of an Ecosystem* (Baltimore: Johns Hopkins University Press, 2001), xviii, 62.

6. "Trans-Atlantic Slave Trade Database," www.slavevoyages.org (David Eltis and Martin Halbert, original principal investigators); Lorena S. Walsh, "The Chesapeake Slave Trade: Regional Patterns, African Origins, and Some Implications," *William and Mary Quarterly* 58, no. 1 (2001): 148, 151; Darold D. Wax, "Black Immigrants: The Slave Trade in Colonial Maryland," *Maryland Historical Magazine* 73, no. 1 (1978): 40.

7. "Trans-Atlantic Slave Trade Database"; Walsh, "The Chesapeake Slave Trade," 148–151; Allan Kulikoff, "The Origins of Afro-American Society in Tidewater Maryland and Virginia, 1700 to 1790," *William and Mary Quarterly* 35, no. 2 (1978): 236; Wax, "Black Immigrants," 38, 40.

8. Helen C. Rountree, Wayne E. Clark, Kent Mountford, and Michael B. Barber, *John Smith's Chesapeake Voyages, 1607–1609* (Charlottesville: University of Virginia Press, 2007), 24–26; Curtin, Brush, and Fisher, *Discovering the Chesapeake*, 151–153, 159, 172, 319, 333, 336; N. L. Christensen, "Vegetation of the Southeastern Coastal Plain," in *North American Terrestrial Vegetation*, ed. Michael G. Barbour and William Dwight Billings (Cambridge: Cambridge University Press, 1988), 320–326; Ann Sutton and Myron Sutton, *Eastern Forests* (New York: Alfred A. Knopf, 1985), 32; John L. Vankat, *The Natural Vegetation of North America: An Introduction* (New York: Wiley, 1979), 142–147.

9. Thomas Bluett, *Some Memoirs of the Life of Job, the Son of Solomon the High Priest of Boonda in Africa: Who Was a Slave About Two Years in Maryland, and Afterwards Being Brought to England, Was Set Free, and Sent to His Native Land in the Year 1734* (London: Richard Ford, 1734), 9, 12–13, 15; Francis Moore, *Travels into the Inland Parts of Africa: Containing a Description of the Several Nations for the Space of Six Hundred Miles up the River Gambia . . .* (London: E. Cave, 1738), i, 69, 202–203, 414, 418, 420; Sylviane A. Diouf, *Servants of Allah: African Muslims Enslaved in the Americas* (New York: New York University Press, 2013), 72.

10. Bluett, *Some Memoirs of the Life of Job*, 12, 15, 16–18; Moore, *Travels into the Inland Parts of Africa*, 69, 202, 206; Elizabeth Donnan, ed., *Documents Illustrative of the History of the Slave Trade to America, Volume II: The Eighteenth Century* (Washington, DC: Carnegie Institution of Washington, 1931), 400–421; Diouf, *Servants of Allah*, 58, 192; Weaver, "The Red Atlantic," 418.

11. "Trans-Atlantic Slave Trade Database"; Bluett, *Some Memoirs of the Life of Job*, i, 2, 18–23; Moore, *Travels into the Inland Parts of Africa*, 202–203, 224; Donnan, *Documents Illustrative of the History of the Slave Trade to America*, 414–415, 421–423; Diouf, *Servants of Allah*, 72, 86–87, 192; Kulikoff, "The Origins of Afro-American Society," 236.

12. "Trans-Atlantic Slave Trade Database"; Bluett, *Some Memoirs of the Life of Job*, i, 2, 18–23; Moore, *Travels into the Inland Parts of Africa*, 202–203, 224; Donnan, *Documents Illustrative of the History of the Slave Trade to America*, 414–415, 421–423; Diouf, *Servants of Allah*, 72, 86–87, 192; Kulikoff, "The Origins of Afro-American Society," 236.

13. Bluett, *Some Memoirs of the Life of Job*, i, 19, 31; Moore, *Travels into the Inland Parts of Africa*, 202–207; Donnan, *Documents Illustrative of the History of the Slave Trade to America*, 416, 421, 425–426; Weaver, "The Red Atlantic," 419.

14. Moore, *Travels into the Inland Parts of Africa*, 207.

15. Moore, *Travels into the Inland Parts of Africa*, 204, 208, 224–225; Diouf, *Servants of Allah*, 233–234; Donnan, *Documents Illustrative of the History of the Slave Trade to America*, 416–417.

16. "Trans-Atlantic Slave Trade Database"; Bluett, *Some Memoirs of the Life of Job*, i, 1–13, 15–18, 37–38; Moore, *Travels into the Inland Parts of Africa*, 69, 247–256, 264, 266, 270–272, 279–280; Donnan, *Documents Illustrative of the History of the Slave Trade to America*, 399, 414, 420–427; Diouf, *Servants of Allah*, 58, 63, 72, 86–87, 172, 191–193, 233–234; Wax, "Black Immigrants," 46; Benjamin Drew et al., *A North-Side View of Slavery: The Refugee, or, the Narratives of Fugitive Slaves in Canada: Related by Themselves, with an Account of the History and Condition of the Colored Population of Upper Canada* (Boston: John P. Jewett, 1856), 30.

17. "Trans-Atlantic Slave Trade Database"; Frank C. Drake, "The Moses of Her People. Amazing Life Work of Harriet Tubman," *New York Herald*, Sep. 22, 1907; Kwabena Adu-Boahen, "The Impact of European Presence on Slavery in the Sixteenth to Eighteenth-Century Gold Coast," *Transactions of the Historical Society of Ghana* 14 (2012): 175.

18. Allan Kulikoff, *Tobacco and Slaves: The Development of Southern Cultures in the Chesapeake, 1680–1800* (Chapel Hill: University of North Carolina Press, 1986), 78–79, 81, 93–94, 99–100, 116.

19. "Trans-Atlantic Slave Trade Database"; Curtin, Brush, and Fisher, *Discovering the Chesapeake*, 155, 173, 235, 238, 241–242, 332; Paul G. E. Clemens, *The Atlantic Economy and Colonial Maryland's Eastern Shore: From Tobacco to Grain* (Ithaca, NY: Cornell University Press, 1980), 165–205.

20. "Trans-Atlantic Slave Trade Database"; Frank Sanborn, "Harriet Tubman," *The Commonwealth Boston*, Jul. 17, 1863.

21. "Trans-Atlantic Slave Trade Database"; Ednah Dow Cheney, "Moses," *Freedmen's Record*, Mar. 1865, 34; Clemens, *The Atlantic Economy*, 183; Kulikoff, "The Origins of Afro-American Society," 249; John W. Blassingame, *Slave Testimony: Two Centuries of Letters, Speeches, Interviews and Autobiographies* (Baton Rouge: Louisiana State University Press, 1977), 457; Kulikoff, "The Origins of Afro-American Society," 249; Clemens, *The Atlantic Economy*, 183.

22. Kulikoff, "The Origins of Afro-American Society," 253.

23. "Trans-Atlantic Slave Trade Database"; Kulikoff, "The Origins of Afro-American Society," 243–249.

24. Kulikoff, "The Origins of Afro-American Society," 256, 258.

CHAPTER 2

1. William H. Conner, Thomas W. Doyle, and Ken W. Krauss, *Ecology of Tidal Freshwater Forested Wetlands of the Southeastern United States* (Dordrecht: Springer, 2007), 113, 224; James H. Tuten, "Salkehatchie/Combahee Rivers," University of South Carolina, Institute for Southern Studies, https://www.scencyclopedia.org/sce/entries/salkehatchiecombahee-rivers/; F. Holland and D. Sanger, *Tidal Creek Habitats: Sentinels of Coastal Health* (Charleston, SC: Sea Grant Consortium, 2008), 4; "Blackwater River Education Guide," South Carolina Department of Natural Resources, 2008; J. D. Lewis, "South Carolina Watersheds—Salkehatchie River Basin," http://www.carolana.com/SC/Transportation/sc_salkehatchie_river_basin.html; Loren M. Smith, Roger L. Pederson, et al., eds., *Habitat Management for Migrating and Wintering Waterfowl in North America* (Lubbock: Texas Tech University, 1989), 27, 58.

2. Smith, Pederson, et al., *Habitat Management*, 27–28, 38, 60, 62; Grace S. Brush, Cecilia Lenk, and Joanne Smith, "The Natural Forests of Maryland: An Explanation of the Vegetation Map of Maryland," *Ecological Monographs* 50, no. 1 (1980): 79.

3. William Elliott, *Carolina Sports, by Land and Water: Including Incidents of Devil-Fishing, Wild-Cat, Deer and Bear Hunting, Etc. 1846* (New York: Derby & Jackson, 1859), 176; James Hungerford, *The Old Plantation, and What I Gathered There in an Autumn Month* (New York: Harper & Brothers, 1859), 54; Philip D. Curtin, Grace S. Brush, and George W. Fisher, *Discovering the Chesapeake: The History of an Ecosystem* (Baltimore: Johns Hopkins University Press, 2001), 41; Smith, Pederson, et al., *Habitat Management*, 27, 28, 38, 60, 62.

4. R. Daniel Hanks et al., "Mapping Antebellum Rice Fields as a Basis for Understanding Human and Ecological Consequences of the Era of Slavery," *Land* 10, no. 8 (2021): 841; Smith, Pederson, et al., *Habitat Management*, 28, 60, 65; Conner, Doyle, and Krauss, *Ecology of Tidal Freshwater Forested Wetlands*, 231; Smith, Pederson, et al., *Habitat Management*, 35, 64; Duncan Clinch Heyward, *Seed from Madagascar* (1937; Columbia: University of South Carolina Press, 1993), 38.

5. Eliza Cope Harrison, ed., *Best Companions: Letters of Eliza Middleton Fisher and Her Mother, Mary Hering Middleton, from Charleston, Philadelphia, and Newport, 1839–1846* (Columbia: University of South Carolina Press, 2001), 66, 152; Jessica Stevens Loring, *Auldbrass: The Plantation Complex Designed by Frank Lloyd Wright, a Documented History of Its South Carolina Lands* (Greenville, SC: Southern Historical Press, 1992), 109; James B. Heyward, "The Heyward Family of South Carolina (Continued)," *South Carolina Historical Magazine* 59,

no. 4 (1958): 206–223; Langdon Cheves, "Middleton of South Carolina," *South Carolina Historical and Genealogical Magazine* 1, no. 228 (1900): 228–230.

6. James B. Heyward, "The Heyward Family of South Carolina," *South Carolina Historical Magazine* 59, no. 3 (1958): 143–145.

7. Harrison, *Best Companions*, 66, 152; Loring, *Auldbrass*, 109; Henry A. M. Smith, "The Ashley River: Its Seats and Settlements (Continued)," *South Carolina Historical and Genealogical Magazine* 20, no. 2 (1919): 162; Cheves, "Middleton of South Carolina," 228–230.

8. Smith, "The Ashley River: Its Seats and Settlements (Continued)," 162; Langdon Cheves, "Blake of South Carolina," *South Carolina Historical and Genealogical Magazine* 1, no. 2 (1900): 153–155, 158–166; George B. Chase, *Lowndes of South Carolina: An Historical and Genealogical Memoir* (Boston: A. Williams, 1876), 12–23; personal communication with Dr. Larry Rowland and Dr. Stephen Wise.

9. Henry Schulze Holmes, "Odds and Ends of Family History Collected by Henry S. Holmes," Henry S. Holmes Papers, 1894–1919, South Carolina Historical Society, Charleston; Carl J. Vipperman, "The Brief and Tragic Career of Charles Lowndes," *South Carolina Historical Magazine* 70, no. 4 (1969): 213–215.

10. Tom Robinson, "How to Be Charleston's Oldest Family-Owned Business," Lowndes Family History and Genealogy Research Files (30–4), 1, 11, South Carolina Historical Society; Carl J. Vipperman, *William Lowndes and the Transition of Southern Politics, 1782–1822* (Chapel Hill: University of North Carolina Press, 2017), 211–25; Chase, *Lowndes of South Carolina*, 2, 8–9, 12–23, 41, 44, 52.

11. Ras Michael Brown, *African-American Cultures in the South Carolina Lowcountry* (New York: Cambridge University Press, 2012), 45; Peter A. Coclanis, *The Shadow of a Dream: Economic Life and Death in the South Carolina Low Country, 1670–1920* (New York: Oxford University Press, 1989), 78–83; Russell R. Menard, "The Africanization of the Lowcountry Labor Force, 1670–1730," in *Race and Family in the Colonial South*, ed. Winthrop Jordan and S. L. Skemp (Jackson: University Presses of Mississippi, 1987), 104; Peter H. Wood, *Black Majority: Negroes in Colonial South Carolina from 1670 Through the Stono Rebellion* (New York: Knopf 1974); Vipperman, "The Brief and Tragic Career of Charles Lowndes," 217.

12. James M. Clifton, ed., *Life and Labor on Argyle Island: Letters and Documents of a Savannah River Rice Plantation, 1833–1867* (Savannah, GA: Beehive Press, 1978), xi–xii; Hayden R. Smith, *Carolina's Golden Fields: Inland Rice Cultivation in the South Carolina Lowcountry, 1670–1860* (Cambridge: Cambridge University Press, 2019), 84, 92, 94, 96, 178, 183; Vipperman, *William Lowndes and the Transition of Southern Politics*, 3–4; Hayden R. Smith, "Reserving Water: Environmental and Technological Relationships with Colonial South Carolina Inland Rice Plantations," in *Rice: Global Networks and New Histories*, ed. Francesca Bray, Peter A. Coclanis, Edda L. Fields-Black, and Dagmar Schaffer (Cambridge: Cambridge University Press, 2015), 191–200; S. Max Edelson, *Plantation Enterprise in Colonial South Carolina* (Cambridge, MA: Harvard University

Press, 2006), 73, 75, 103–105; Vipperman, "The Brief and Tragic Career of Charles Lowndes," 212–213, 217–218, 218n25; Duncan Clinch Heyward, *Seed from Madagascar* (1937; Columbia: University of South Carolina Press, 1993), xii–xiii, 11–14; Chase, *Lowndes of South Carolina*, 2, 8, 12, 42.

13. Vipperman, "The Brief and Tragic Career of Charles Lowndes," 218; Chase, *Lowndes of South Carolina*, 12–23.

14. For a full discussion of the evolution of rice milling technology, see Richard Dwight Porcher and William Robert Judd, *The Market Preparation of Carolina Rice: An Illustrated History of Innovations in the Lowcountry Rice Kingdom* (Columbia: University of South Carolina Press, 2014), 153–275; Judith A. Carney, "Rice Milling, Gender and Slave Labour in Colonial South Carolina," *Past and Present*, no. 153 (1996): 119n38; Vipperman, "The Brief and Tragic Career of Charles Lowndes," 221–222; Chase, *Lowndes of South Carolina*, 15.

15. "Charlestowne, May 29," *South Carolina Gazette*, May 29, 1736; Vipperman, "The Brief and Tragic Career of Charles Lowndes," 222–223.

16. Holmes, "Odds and Ends of Family History"; Robinson, "How to Be Charleston's Oldest Family-Owned Business," 1, 11; Holmes, "Odds and Ends"; Vipperman, *William Lowndes and the Transition of Southern Politics*, 3; Vipperman, "The Brief and Tragic Career of Charles Lowndes," 224; Chase, *Lowndes of South Carolina*, 2, 8–9, 12–23, 41, 44, 52.

17. Heyward, "The Heyward Family of South Carolina," 148–150.

18. Heyward, "The Heyward Family of South Carolina," 148–150, 153; Heyward, *Seed from Madagascar*, 51–52; Chase, *Lowndes of South Carolina*, 2.

19. William Dusinberre, *Them Dark Days: Slavery in the American Rice Swamps* (Oxford: Oxford University Press, 1996), 31; Heyward, "The Heyward Family of South Carolina," 148–149; Heyward, *Seed from Madagascar*, 65.

20. Smith, *Carolina's Golden Fields*, 30, 37–38, 40, 43, 79–80, 96–97, 113, 120, 122–123; Smith, "Reserving Water," 192–197; Edelson, *Plantation Enterprise in Colonial South Carolina*, 75; Judith A. Carney, "Landscapes of Technology Transfer: Rice Cultivation and African Continuities," *Technology and Culture* 37, no. 1 (1996): 23–25; Sam B. Hilliard, "Antebellum Tidewater Rice Culture in South Carolina and Georgia," in *European Settlement and Development in North America*, ed. James R. Gibson (Toronto: University of Toronto Press, 1978), 96, 97, 98, 104; Sam Hilliard, "The Tidewater Rice Plantation: An Ingenious Adaptation to Nature," *Geoscience and Man* 12 (1975): 57–58; Heyward, *Seed from Madagascar*, 65.

21. Clifton, *Life and Labor on Argyle Island*, xi–xii; Smith, *Carolina's Golden Fields*, 84, 92, 94, 96, 178, 183; Smith, "Reserving Water," 191–200; Edelson, *Plantation Enterprise in Colonial South Carolina*, 73, 75, 103–5; Heyward, *Seed from Madagascar*, xii–xiii, 11–14.

22. Dusinberre, *Them Dark Days*, 32; Heyward, *Seed from Madagascar*, 14.

23. Clifton, *Life and Labor on Argyle Island*, vii, xvii–xviii.

24. Dusinberre, *Them Dark Days*, 31; Heyward, *Seed from Madagascar*, 66, 67.

25. Carney, "Landscapes of Technology Transfer," 17, 27; Hilliard, "Antebellum Tidewater Rice Culture in South Carolina and Georgia," 103–4; Hilliard, "The Tidewater Rice Plantation," 64.

26. Heyward, *Seed from Madagascar*, 13.

27. Adam Hodgson, *Remarks During a Journey Through North America in the Years 1819, 1820, and 1821: In a Series of Letters, with an Appendix Containing an Account of Several of the Indian Tribes and the Principal Missionary Stations, &c.; Also, a Letter to M. Jean Baptiste Say, on the Comparative Expense of Free and Slave Labour* (New York: Samuel Whiting, 1823); Scott Huler, *A Delicious Country: Rediscovering the Carolinas Along the Route of John Lawson's 1700 Expedition* (Chapel Hill: University of North Carolina Press, 2019), 28, 35, 37, 39, 69, 183; Ralph W. Tiner, *Tidal Wetlands Primer: An Introduction to Their Ecology, Natural History, Status, and Conservation* (Amherst: University of Massachusetts Press, 2013), 246, 249, 252, 254, 266, 282, 284; Tom Downey, "Riparian Rights and Manufacturing in Antebellum South Carolina: William Gregg and the Origins of the 'Industrial Mind,'" *Journal of Southern History* 65, no. 1 (1999): 88; Theodore Rosengarten, "In the Master's Garden," in *Art and Landscape in Charleston and the Lowcountry: A Project of the Spoleto Festival USA*, ed. John Beardsley (Washington, DC: Spacemaker Press, 1998), 40.

28. Judith A. Carney, *Black Rice: The African Origins of Rice Cultivation in the Americas* (Cambridge, MA: Harvard University Press, 2001), 93; David Doar, *Rice and Rice Planting in the South Carolina Low Country* (Charleston, SC: Charleston Museum, 1970), 12; Leland G. Ferguson, *Uncommon Ground: Archaeology and Early African America 1650–1800* (Washington, DC: Smithsonian Institution Press, 1992), xxiv–xxv, 147.

29. Cuffie Bolze, Oct. 10, 1868, and Sina Young, Apr. 11, 1874, "Freedman's Bank Records, 1865–1874," NARA, microfilm publication M816 (henceforth "Freedman's Bank Records"); deposition A by Cuffie Bolze, Apr. 8, 1901, pension file for Cuffee (Sophia) Bolze, RG 15, NARA; deposition A by Mingo Van Dross, Apr. 9, 1901, pension file for Mingo (Emma) Van Dross, RG 15, NARA. Sancho Van Dross told the census taker that he was born in South Carolina. No information is available about his parents. See Colleton County, United States Census, 1870. Cuffie Bolze and Sina Bolze Young Green both told the census taker that their mother and father were born in South Carolina. No more information is available about their grandparents besides the names of their paternal grandparents, Cuffie and Sina. See Cuffie Bowls in South Carolina, US Census Records 1910; Boles in South Carolina, US Census Records 1920; Siva Green in Port Royal, US Census Records 1900.

30. "Trans-Atlantic Slave Trade Database," www.slavevoyages.org (David Eltis and Martin Halbert, original principal investigators); Coclanis, *The Shadow of a Dream*, 79–86.

31. "Trans-Atlantic Slave Trade Database"; "Transatlantic Slave Trade Database." In a national climate in which politicians assert that Black people who were held in bondage learned skills as a result of enslavement that benefited them and their families (nullifying decades of scholarship on slavery), it is important to reiterate that enslaved laborers on Lowcountry South Carolina and Georgia's rice plantations did have skills; some of these skills were critical to the development of a Creole agricultural technology, which laid the foundation for the

Lowcountry's commercial rice industry. See Edda L. Fields-Black, "Rice on the Upper Guinea Coast: A Regional Perspective Based on Interdisciplinary Sources and Methods," in *Rice: Global Networks and New Histories*, ed. Francesca Bray, Peter A. Coclanis, Edda L. Fields-Black, and Dagmar Schaffer (Cambridge: Cambridge University Press, 2015); Walter Hawthorne, "From 'Black Rice' to 'Brown': Rethinking the History of Risiculture in the Seventeenth- and Eighteenth-Century Atlantic," *American Historical Review* 115, no. 1 (2010); Edda L. Fields-Black, *Deep Roots: Rice Farmers in West Africa and the African Diaspora* (Bloomington: Indiana University Press, 2008); Walter Hawthorne, "Planting Rice and Harvesting Slaves: Transformations Along the Guinea-Bissau Coast, 1400–1900," (Portsmouth, NH: Heinemann, 2003); Carney, *Black Rice*.

32. "122. Samuel and William Vernon to Thomlinson, Trecothick, and Company, 1754," William Vernon Letter-Book, Slavery Collection, Patricia D. Klingenstein Library, New-York Historical Society.

33. Henry Laurens, *The Papers of Henry Laurens, Volume II, 1755–1788*, ed. Philip M. Hamer (Columbia: University of South Carolina Press, 1968), 217–219, 208–210; David Hancock, *Citizens of the World: London Merchants and the Integration of the British Atlantic Community, 1735–1785* (New York: Cambridge University Press, 1997), 21.

34. "Advertisement," *South Carolina Gazette*, Jun. 17, 1756; Laurens, *Papers*, 238; Sowandé M. Mustakeem, *Slavery at Sea: Terror, Sex, and Sickness in the Middle Passage* (Urbana: University of Illinois Press, 2016), 12, 46, 51, 162, 164.

35. Ball Family Account Book, Ball Family Documents Series, 1631–1858, South Carolina Historical Society; Laurens, *Papers*, 238.

36. Sheila Lambert, ed., *House of Commons Sessional Papers of the Eighteenth Century: Minutes of Evidence on the Slave Trade: 1788 and 1789: George III* (Wilmington, DE: Scholarly Resources, 1975), 68:121–123; "Trans-Atlantic Slave Trade Database"; Marcus Rediker, *The Slave Ship: A Human History* (New York: Penguin, 2007), 69–70, 97, 165, 282.

37. Leslie Goffe, "Priscilla: The Story of an African Slave," BBC, Nov. 23, 2005.

38. Simon Washington, Aug. 10, 1869, Freedman's Bank Records; depositions by Wally Garrett, Apr. 5 and Oct. 18, 1902, pension file for Wally (Bella) Garrett, RG 15, NARA; deposition by Solomon Salter, Apr. 6, 1902, pension file for Solomon Salter, RG 15, NARA; deposition by Daphne Wright, Apr. 8, 1902, pension file for Frank (Daphne) Wright, RG 15, NARA; deposition by Annette Lewis, April 14, 1902, pension file for Simon (Christiana now Wilson and Minors of Simon Brown) Brown, RG 15, NARA; Commissioner to Auditor for the War Department, Nov. 14, 1901, deposition A by Rachel Washington, deposition D by Jonas Gadsden, deposition E by Sunday Briscoe, Oct. 5, 1901, depositions by Rachel Washington and Diana Green, Oct. 5, 1902, general affidavits by Jack Aiken and Phoebe Gray, May 17, 1910, and by Wally Garrett, Apr. 27, 1910, E. D. Gallien to Hon. William Lochren, Jun. 27, 1895, "Widow's Application for Accrued Pension" by Rachel Washington, Jan. 31, 1910, "Board of Review, Department of the Interior," May 12, 1910, "Act of April 19, 1908, Widow's

Pension," May 10, 1910, "Declaration for Widow's Pension, Act Approved April 19, 1910," "Department of the Interior, Bureau of Pensions," Nov. 29, 1897, pension file for Simon (Rachel) Washington, RG 15, NARA; Lorenzo Dow Turner, Michael Montgomery, and Katherine Wyly Millie, *Africanisms in the Gullah Dialect* (Columbia: University of South Carolina, 2002), 40–42.

39. Sina Green, Apr. 11, 1874, Freedman's Bank Records; deposition by Sina Young, Jun. 26, 1873, pension file for William (Sina) Young, RG 15, NARA; general affidavit by Elsey Jones, Jan. 6, 1891, pension file for Robert (Phoebe) Frazier, RG 15, NARA; deposition by Elsie Jones, Apr. 30, 1895, pension file for Pool (Julia) Sellers, RG 15, NARA; depositions B and C of Neptune Nicholas, Oct. 20, 1896, pension file for Jackson (Jane) Grant, RG 15, NARA; deposition by Cuffie Bolze, Apr. 8, 1901, pension file for Cuffie (Sophia) Bolze; deposition A by Neptune Nicholas, Apr. 8, 1901, and deposition by Charles Nicholas, Apr. 11, 1905, pension file for Neptune (Betsey) Nicholas, RG 15, NARA; deposition by William Hamilton, Apr. 12, 1901, pension file for William (Harriet, Nancy) Hamilton, RG 15, NARA; deposition B by Neptune Nicholas, Nov. 15, 1901, and deposition E by Neptune Nicholas, Feb. 12, 1902, pension file for Edward (Peggy) Brown, RG 15, NARA.

40. Clifton, *Life and Labor on Argyle Island*, xxi, 439. Jean R. Leonard, Mrs. Robert L. Green, Wilma C. Kirkland, and Elizabeth Kirkland Schladensky, *Kirkland Source Book of Records* (Greenwood, SC: privately printed, 1977–1988), 2:439–440.

41. Clifton, *Life and Labor on Argyle Island*, xxi; Wood, *Black Majority*, 75, 83; Daniel Elliott Huger Smith, Arney Robinson Childs, and Alice Ravenel Huger Smith, eds., *Mason Smith Family Letters, 1860–1868* (Columbia: University of South Carolina Press, 1950), 34, 219; Carney, "Landscapes of Technology Transfer," 3; Coclanis, *The Shadow of a Dream*, 82; Jill Dubisch, "Low Country Fevers: Cultural Adaptations to Malaria in Antebellum South Carolina," *Social Science and Medicine* 21, no. 6 (1985): 641–645; H. Roy Merrens and George D. Terry, "Dying in Paradise: Malaria, Mortality, and the Perceptual Environment in Colonial South Carolina," *Journal of Southern History* 50, no. 4 (1984): 541–542; Rosengarten, "In the Master's Garden," 17, 27; St. Julien Ravenel Childs, "Malaria and Colonization in the Carolina Low Country, 1526–1696," *Johns Hopkins University Studies in Historical and Political Science* 58, no. 1 (1940): 204, 208; Heyward, *Seed from Madagascar*, xi, xiv, xviii; Arthur H. Cole, "The American Rice-Growing Industry: A Study of Comparative Advantage," *Quarterly Journal of Economics* 41, no. 4 (1927): 625.

42. Leonard et al., *Kirkland Source Book of Records*, 1:43–45, 47–54, 57–58, 71, 79, 87; Mary-Elizabeth Lynah, "Tory Played Hide & Seek with Carolina Safety Council," *News & Courier*, Mar. 18, 1934, in Kirkland Family History and Genealogy Research Files, South Carolina Historical Society, Charleston; Cole, "The American Rice-Growing Industry," 625; Randall M. Miller and Moses Kirkland, "A Backcountry Loyalist Plan to Retake Georgia and the Carolinas, 1778," *South Carolina Historical Magazine* 75, no. 4 (1974): 207. For estimates of the wealth Moses Kirkland accumulated before the Revolution, see Richard Maxwell Brown, *The South Carolina Regulators* (Cambridge, MA: Belknap Press of Harvard University Press, 1963), 15–16, 40, 116, 118–119, 128–129.

43. "Historic Camden"; Lynah, "Tory Played Hide and Seek"; Leonard et al., *Kirkland Source Book of Records*, vol. 2; Brown, The South Carolina Regulators, 129.

44. "Kirkland Family" (pages in document 32–33), Papers of the Kirkland, Withers, Snowden, and Trotter Families, South Caroliniana Library, University of South Carolina, Columbia, SC, 99–100; Mary Miller Withers Kirkland to Kate Withers, Oct. 14, 1862, Kirkland Family History and Genealogy Research Files, South Carolina Historical Society; Mary-Elizabeth Lynah, "Tory Played Hide and Seek with Carolina Safety Council," *News and Courier*, Mar. 18, 1934; Leonard et al., *Kirkland Source Book of Records*, 1:74, 86.

45. Leonard et al., *Kirkland Source Book of Records*, 1:74, 86; "Kirkland Family" (pages in document 32), Papers of the Kirkland, Withers, Snowden, and Trotter Families, 99; Lynah, "Tory Played Hide & Seek."

46. Leonard et al., *Kirkland Source Book of Records*, 1:86; Lynah, "Tory Played Hide and Seek."

47. "Kirkland Family" (pages in document 32–33), 99–100. This is what we know abut the Kirkland line of descent according to available sources: Richard Kirkland (d. 1743) likely had two sons, Richard Snowden Kirkland and William Kirkland. Richard Snowden Kirkland had two sons, Isaac Kirkland and Moses Kirkland, the latter the notorious backcountry Loyalist. William Kirkland had a son, also named William Kirkland (d. 1806). He was the father of Dr. Joseph Kirkland (1769?-1817), who was the father of Dr. William L. Kirkland Sr. (1797–1828) and the grandfather of William L. Kirkland Jr. (1828–1864). Leonard et al., *Kirkland Source Book of Records*, 1:20, 191–192, 2:405. See also "Historic Camden"; Mary Miller Withers Kirkland to Kate Withers, October 14, 1862; "Papers of the Kirkland, Withers, Snowden, and Trotter Families," 178; Lynah, "Tory Played Hide & Seek"; Brown, *The South Carolina Regulators*, 130.

48. Depositions by Mingo Van Dross, Apr. 9, 1901, and Dec. 11, 1908, pension file for Mingo (Emma) Van Dross.

49. "Trans-Atlantic Slave Trade Database."

50. "Trans-Atlantic Slave Trade Database"; Rebecca Shumway, *The Fante and the Trans-Atlantic Slave Trade* (Rochester, NY: University of Rochester Press, 2011), 22–23, 48, 50–52; Svend E. Green-Pedersen, "The Scope and Structure of the Danish Slave Trade," *Scandanavian Economic History Review* 19 (1971): 192–193.

51. Lambert, *House of Commons Sessional Papers*, 68:37–38; Linda M. Heywood, "Slavery and Its Transformation in the Kingdom of Kongo: 1491–1800," *Journal of African History* 50, no. 1 (2009): 16–19; Linda M. Heywood and John K. Thornton, *Central Africans, Atlantic Creoles, and the Foundation of the Americas, 1585–1660* (Cambridge: Cambridge University Press, 2007), 21–69, 360.

52. Elizabeth Donnan, ed., *Documents Illustrative of the History of the Slave Trade to America, Volume III, New England and the Middle Colonies* (Washington, DC: Carnegie Institute of Washington, 1932), 81; Michael E. Stevens, ed., *Journal of the House of Representatives, 1791* (Columbia: University of South Carolina Press, 1985), 28–29.

578 NOTES

53. "Trans-Atlantic Slave Trade Database"; Calbraith Bourn Perry, *Charles D'wWolf of Guadaloupe, His Ancestors and Descendants: Being a Complete Genealogy of the "Rhode Island D'wolfs," the Descendants of Simon De Wolf, with Their Common Descent from Balthasar De Wolf of Lyme, Conn. (1668): With a Biographical Introduction and Appendices of the Nova Scotian De Wolfs and Other Allied Families* (Salem, MA: Higginson, 1902), 29; George Locke Howe, *Mount Hope: A New England Chronicle* (New York: Viking Press, 1959), 122–123.

54. "Trans-Atlantic Slave Trade Database"; A. E. Rooks, *The* Black Joke: *The True Story of One Ship's Battle Against the Slave Trade* (New York: Scribner, 2022), 19, 21, 76; Sian Rees, *Sweet Water and Bitter: The Ships That Stopped the Slave Trade* (New York: Vintage, 2010), 4, 58, 133, 160, 184, 308.

55. Dusinberre, *Them Dark Days*, 48–79.

56. Virginia Glenn Crane, "Two Women, White and Brown, in the South Carolina Court of Equity, 1842–1845," *South Carolina Historical Magazine* 96, no. 3 (1995): 199.

57. "Nicholas Cruger and Ann Sarah his Wife v. Thomas Heyward . . . and Nathaniel Heyward" (Jan. 1802), in Henry William DeSaussure, *Reports of Cases Argued and Determined in the Court of Chancery of the State of South-Carolina, from the Revolution to December, 1813, Inclusive* (Philadelphia: R. H. Small, 1854), 2:92–114; Crane, "Two Women," 199–200, 204, 207; Michael P. Johnson, "Planters and Patriarchy—Charleston, 1800–1860," *Journal of Southern History* 46, no. 1 (1980): 49; Heyward, "The Heyward Family of South Carolina," 154.

58. Stephanie Jones-Rogers, *They Were Her Property: White Women as Slave Owners in the American South* (New Haven, CT: Yale University Press, 2019), 31, 33–34, 37, 45, 48, 52–53; Crane, "Two Women," 202–204; Marilyn McAdams Sibley, "James Hamilton, Jr., vs. Sam Houston: Repercussions of the Nullification Controversy," *Southwestern Historical Quarterly* 89, no. 2 (1985): 169; Heyward, "The Heyward Family of South Carolina (Continued)," 207; Heyward, "The Heyward Family of South Carolina," 148, 155.

59. Heyward, "The Heyward Family of South Carolina (Continued)," 207; Heyward, "The Heyward Family of South Carolina," 148, 155.

60. Hannah Shubrick to William Hayward, Bill of Sale, Jan. 10, 1817, "South Carolina, Charleston District, Bill of Sales of Negro Slaves, 1774–1872," South Carolina Department of Archives and History, Columbia; William Heyward to Hannah Shubrick Heyward, Mortgage, Jan. 10, 1817, "South Carolina, Secretary of State, Slave Mortgage Records, 1734–1780," South Carolina Department of Archives and History; Jones-Rogers, *They Were Her Property*, 31–33; Daina Ramey Berry, *The Price for Their Pound of Flesh: The Value of the Enslaved, from Womb to Grave, in the Building of a Nation* (Boston: Beacon Press, 2017), 11, 13, 27; Walter Johnson, *Soul by Soul Life Inside the Antebellum Slave Market* (Cambridge, MA: Harvard University, 1999), 25–26; Thomas D. Morris, *Southern Slavery and the Law, 1619–1860* (Chapel Hill: University of North Carolina, 1996), 88–89, 102; Richard Holcombe Kilbourne, *Debt, Investment, Slaves: Credit Relations in East Feliciana Parish, Louisiana, 1825–1885* (Tuscaloosa: University of Alabama

Press, 1995), 45–46, 48–50, 55; Frederic Bancroft, *Slave Trading in the Old South* (New York: Ungar, 1959), 67–68, 211.

61. Hannah Shubrick to William Heyward, Bill of Sale, Jan. 10, 1817; William Heyward to Hannah Shubrick Heyward, Mortgage, Jan. 10, 1817; Sarah Graves to William Heyward, Apr. 27, 1818, "South Carolina, Charleston District, Bill of Sales of Negro Slaves, 1774–1872," South Carolina Department of Archives and History; Sarah Barnwell, Jan. 17, 1872, Freedman's Bank Records; deposition C by Cuffie Bolze, Nov. 15, 1901, deposition by Peggy Brown, Nov. 14, 1901, and deposition B by Neptune Nicholas, Nov. 15, 1901, pension file for Edward (Peggy) Brown. Peggy Brown also reported different maiden names: Moultrie and Simmons.

62. Neighbor's affidavit by I. I. Coster [*sic*], Oct. 18, 1887, pension file for Andrew (Maria) Wyatt; deposition by Fannie Simmons, Apr. 11, 1914, pension file for Moses (Fannie) Simmons, RG 15, NARA; deposition by Elsie Jones, Apr. 30, 1895, pension file for Pool (Julia) Sellers.

63. John Huger Dawson to William Heyward, Bill of Sale, Mar. 1, 1822, "South Carolina, Charleston District, Bill of Sales of Negro Slaves, 1774–1872," South Carolina Department of Archives and History; William Heyward to John Huger Dawson, Mortgage, Mar. 18, 1822, "South Carolina, Secretary of State, Slave Mortgage Records, 1734–1780," South Carolina Department of Archives and History.

64. John Huger Dawson to William Heyward, Bill of Sale, Mar. 1, 1822, "South Carolina, Charleston District, Bill of Sales of Negro Slaves, 1774–1872"; William Heyward to John Huger Dawson, Mortgage, Mar. 18, 1822; March Chisolm, Oct. 10, 1868, Freedman's Bank Records; general affidavit by Lucius Robinson and Edward Brown, Aug. 5, 1893, pension file for July (Venus) Osborne, RG 15, NARA; Neptin Nickles to Sir, Aug. 24, 1899, Department of the Interior Bureau of Pensions by Neptune Nicholas and Moses Simmons, Apr. 13, 1899, deposition by Moses Simmons, Dec. 7, 1904, and general affidavit by Charles Nicholas, Feb. 7, 1907, in pension file for March (Molcy) Chisolm, RG 15, NARA; questionaire responses by Charles Nicholas, Jul. 21, 1903, and general affidavit by Charles Nicholas, Jul. 16, 1905, in pension file for Charles (Ella) Nicholas, RG 15, NARA.

65. John Huger Dawson to William Heyward, Bill of Sale, Mar. 1, 1822; March Chisolm, Oct. 10, 1868, Freedman's Bank Records; general affidavit by Charles Nicholas, Feb. 7, 1907, pension file for Charles (Ella) Nicholas; deposition by Moses Simmons, Dec. 7, 1904, pension file for Moses (Fannie) Simmons; Neptin Nickles to Sir, Aug. 24, 1899, and Department of the Interior Bureau of Pensions by Neptune Nicholas and Moses Simmons, Apr. 13, 1899, pension file for March (Molcy) Chisolm; general affidavit by Luscius Robinson and Edward Brown, Aug. 5, 1893, pension file for July (Venus) Osborne.

66. C. C. Keith, Admix. of Dr. Mathew Irvine, to William Heyward and Henry N. Cruger, Trustees for Catharine De Nully Hassell, Bill of Sale, Feb. 23, 1833,

"South Carolina, Charleston District, Bill of Sales of Negro Slaves, 1774–1872," South Carolina Department of Archives and History.

67. Phoebe Frazier testified to having different maiden names at different times: Burns, Grinnell, and Legree. See "Widow's Declaration of Pension or Increase of Pension" by Tyra Polite, Jun. 20, 1890, general affidavit by Tyra Polite, Sep. 27, 1890, declarations by Andrew Wyatt and Joan Lagree, Aug. 1, 1891, physician's affidavit by Tooman Lagare, Sep. 27, 1890, and "Declaration for Widow's Pension, Act of June 27, 1890" by Tyra Polite, Oct. 29, 1890, pension file for Prince (Tyra) Polite, RG 15, NARA; Tera Hunter, *Bound in Wedlock: Slave and Free Black Marriage* (Cambridge, MA: Belknap Press of Harvard University Press, 2017), 6, 281.

68. C. C. Keith, Admix. of Dr. Mathew Irvine, to William Heyward and Henry N. Cruger, Trustees for Catharine De Nully Hassell, Bill of Sale, Feb. 23, 1833; "Declaration for Widow's Pension, Act of June 27, 1890" by Tyra Polite, Oct. 29, 1890, general affidavit by Tyra Polite, Sep. 27, 1890, declarations by Andrew Wyatt and Joan Lagree, Aug. 1, 1891, physician's affidavit by Tooman Lagare, Sep. 27, 1890, "Record Proof of Marriage of Widow to Soldier, Act of June 27, 1890" by Renty Polite, Jan. 5, 1891, "Widow's Declaration of Pension or Increase of Pension" by Lyra Polite, Jun. 20, 1890, pension file for Prince (Tyra) Polite; Heyward, "The Heyward Family of South Carolina (Continued)," 207.

69. Mrs. Smith could have been the aforementioned Anne Rebecca Skirving Smith, her aunt, Ann Stock Smith, or Eliza Middleton Huger Smith, whose husband, William Mason Smith, owned Smithfield Plantation, which is adjacent to Cypress Plantation to the northwest. He likely referred to Anne Smith, because William Elliott's correspondence is replete with references to the Heyward family, particularly Nathaniel Heyward's children and grandchildren, but no references to William Mason Smith's family. The Elliotts and Heywards were both intermarried with the Cuthbert family and they moved in the same social circles in coastal South Carolina, Georgia, and New York. Colonel William Skirving Will, Jun. 7, 1810, in *Elliott and Gonzales Family Papers, 1701–1866, Beaufort and Colleton Districts, South Carolina* (Frederick, MD: University Publications of America, 1990); Beverly Robinson Scafidel, "The Letters of William Elliott," Ph.D. diss., University of South Carolina, 1978, 84, 181, 183–185, 189, 191, 193, 195n2; deposition by Moses Simmons, Apr. 8, 1901, pension file for Moses (Fannie) Simmons; Beverly Robinson Scafidel, "The Letters of William Elliott," Ph.D. diss., University of South Carolina, 1978, 84, 181, 183–85, 189, 191, 193, 195n2; Morris, *Southern Slavery and the Law*, 96–97.

70. Moses Simmons, Aug. 21, 1868, Freedman's Bank Records; Joshua Simmonds, Aug. 14, 1869, Freedman's Bank Records; "Widow's Declaration for Pension or Increase of Pension" by Margaret Simmons, Apr. 13, 1890, declaration for widow's pension by Margaret Simmons, Aug. 20, 1890, general affidavit by Margaret Simmons, Aug. 8, 1894, deposition by Margaret Simmons, Apr. 15, 1901, deposition by Margaret Simmons, Apr. 15, 1901, deposition A by Margaret Simmons, Jul. 23, 1901, pension file for Joshua (Margaret) Simmons, RG 15,

NARA; deposition A by Moses Simmons, Apr. 8, 1901, deposition B by Jane Barnwell, Apr. 14, 1911, pension file for Moses (Fannie) Simmons; deposition by Moses Simmons, Apr. 11, 1905, pension file for Neptune (Betsey) Nicholas.

71. Deposition A by Stephen Simmons, Apr. 10, 1901, pension file for Stephen (Jane) Simmons, RG 15, NARA.

72. William Heyward to William C. Heyward, Conveyance, Feb. 16, 1836, Deed Book, Colleton County Register of Deeds, Walterboro, SC, Book 28, 588; Nathaniel Heyward to William C. Heyward, Conveyance, Apr. 2, 1836, Deed Book, Colleton County Register of Deeds, Walterboro, SC, Book 34, 208; deposition by Sina Young, Apr. 24, 1875, affidavit by Sina Young Jun. 26, 1873, affidavits by Venus Lyons, Elsie Jones, and Lina Richards, Jun. 30, 1873, exhibit by Sina Young, Dec. 13, 1876, pension file for William (Sina) Young; depositions by Cuffie Bolze, Oct. 18, 1898, and Apr. 8, 1901, "Act of May 11, 1912, Declaration for Pension" by Cuffie Bolze, May 20, 1912, and "Act of February 6, 1907, Declaration for Pension" by Cuffie Bolze, Apr. 7, 1908, pension file for Cuffie (Sophia) Bolze; deposition by Friday Hamilton, Feb. 19, 1902, general affidavit by Cuffie Bolze and Samuel McPherson, Mar. 25, 1901, deposition by Peggy Brown, Nov. 14, 1901, deposition by Cuffie Bolze, Nov. 15, 1901, deposition by Friday Hamilton, Nov. 19, 1901, pension file for Edward (Peggy) Brown; affidavit by Primus Barnwell, Jan. 27, 1920, pension file for William (Relia) Middleton, RG 15, NARA; depositions by Cuffy Bolze, Jack Barnwell, and Annie Barnwell, Aug. 9, 1907, pension file for Charles (Ella) Nicholas; deposition by Cuffey Bolze, Oct. 20, 1896, pension file for Jackson (Jane) Grant; Suzanne Cameron Linder et al., *Historical Atlas of the Rice Plantations of the ACE River Basin—1860* (Columbia: South Carolina Department of Archives and History, 1995), 159.

73. Agnes Leland Baldwin, "Nemours," Agnes L. Baldwin Research Papers, 1966–2004, South Carolina Historical Society; South Carolina Department of Transportation, Brockington and Associates Inc., Eric D. Poplin, South Carolina Department of Transportation, and TRC Solutions Inc., "Crossing the Combahee: Mitigation of the Combahee Ferry Historic District: Beaufort and Colleton Counties South Carolina," Tidewater Atlantic Research, Inc., Brockington and Associates, 2017, 56–58.

74. "Obituary," *Charleston Mercury*, Jun. 20, 1828; "Kirkland Family" (pages in document 23, 34–35, 47–48, 55), "Extracts from letter of Joshua Nicholls★ to Thos. J. Kirkland★ written at Washington, DC Oct 15th 1899," and "Kirklands of Kershaw County," in Papers of the Kirkland, Withers, Snowden, and Trotter Families, 90, 112, 114, 221–222, 226–227, 231, 248, 280; Leonard et al., *Kirkland Source Book of Records*, 1:251–252.

75. "Obituary," *Charleston Mercury*, Jun. 20, 1828; "Kirkland Family" (pages in document 2, 55), "Kirkland-Withers-Snowden-Trotter Families Genealogy" (pages in document 10, 20–21, 40–41, 48, n.p.), and "Mary Anna Lynah m-1...," Papers of the Kirkland, Withers, Snowden, and Trotter Families, 69, 122, 218, 33, 34, 77; "Moses Kirkland" in "Vertical File 30–04"; "Rose Hill" in "Combahee River Plantations," private collection, Colleton County, SC, 5.

76. *Itinerant Observations in America. Reprinted from the London Magazine 1745–6* (Savannah: J. H. Estill, 1878), 13; Dubisch, "Low Country Fevers," 641, 643; Wood, *Black Majority*, 63–91; Philip D. Curtin, "'The White Man's Grave': Image and Reality, 1780–1850," *Journal of British Studies* 1, no. 1 (1961): 95, 106; Childs, "Malaria and Colonization," 204.

77. Philip D. Curtin, "Disease Exchange Across the Tropical Atlantic," *History and Philosophy of the Life Sciences* 15, no. 3 (1993): 345; Dubisch, "Low Country Fevers," 641, 643–644; Merrens and Terry, "Dying in Paradise," 534, 540–541, 547; Wood, *Black Majority*, 74–75, 87.

78. Sheldon Watts, *Epidemics and History: Disease* (New Haven, CT: Yale University Press, 1997), 291; Dubisch, "Low Country Fevers," 641–645; Merrens and Terry, "Dying in Paradise," 541–542, 545; Wood, *Black Majority*, 75, 83; Curtin, "'The White Man's Grave,'" 95; Lawrence Fay Brewster, *Summer Migrations and Resorts of South Carolina Low-Country Planters* (Durham, NC: Duke University Press, 1947), 113; Childs, "Malaria and Colonization," 191.

79. "Kirkland Family" (including Will of Joseph Kirkland, Jan. 6, 1817, pages in document 23–24, 26) and "Kirklands of Kershaw County," in Papers of the Kirkland, Withers, Snowden, and Trotter Families, 90–91, 93, 280; "Probate Court" in Vertical File 30–04; Leonard et al., *Kirkland Source Book of Records*, 1:252; "Rose Hill" in "Combahee River Plantations," 5; Linder et al., *Historical Atlas of the Rice Plantations of the ACE Basin—1860*, 511.

80. Sarah Bond I'on Marriage Settlement, Mar. 1798, "Marriage Settlements Vols. 3 (1796–1801) and 4 (1801–1805)," South Carolina Department of Archives and History; Thomas Rawlins to Charles T. Lowndes and Others, Deed, Jun. 1, 1835, "Miscellaneous Records, 1771–1868," Secretary of State, South Carolina, South Carolina Department of Archives and History.

81. Thomas Rawlins to Charles T. Lowndes and Others, Deed, Jun. 1, 1835; November Osborne, Aug. 21, 1869, and Nat Osborne, Aug. 21, 1869, Freedman's Bank Records.

82. Sarah Osborne's testimony that Rev. Comer performed her marriage likely reflects a mispronounciation (due to her age and Gullah dialect) of the minister's real name, Coleman. See deposition by Sarah Osborne, Oct. 21, 1901, and inability affidavit, Aug. 2, 1893, pension file for November (Sarah) Osborne.

83. Baldwin, "Nemours," 17–18, 23–24; Barbara Doyle, Mary Edna Sullivan, and Tracey Todd, *Beyond the Fields: Slavery at Middleton Place* (Columbia: University of South Carolina Press, 2008), 77; Linder et al., *Historical Atlas*, 372–373.

84. Agnes Leland Baldwin, "Newport Plantation," 19, 24, Agnes L. Baldwin Research Papers, 1966–2004, South Carolina Historical Society; Allecia Hopton Middleton, *Life in Carolina and New England During the Nineteenth Century: As Illustrated by Reminiscences and Letters of the Middleton Family of Charleston, South Carolina, and of the Dewolf Family of Bristol, Rhode Island* (Bristol, RI: Privately printed, 1929), 65–66, 152–153; Harrison, *Best Companions*, 3, 3n4, 4; Linder et al., *Historical Atlas*, 371; Loring, *Auldbrass*, 109–110; Cheves, "Middleton of South Carolina," 242–243, 244n4.

85. Harrison, *Best Companions*, 3–4, 5, 8–11, 448n1; Loring, *Auldbrass*, 111–112.

86. Williams Middleton to Martha Ann Matthews, Mortgage, Mar. 6, 1836, "South Carolina, Secretary of State, Slave Mortgage Records, 1734–1780," South Carolina Department of Archives and History; depositions by Wally Garrett, Apr. 5 and Oct. 18, 1902, in pension file for Wally (Bella) Garrett, RG 15, NARA; deposition by Daphney Wright, Apr. 8, 1902, pension file for Frank (Daphne) Wright, RG 15, NARA; E. D. Gallion to Hon. William Lochren, Jun. 27, 1895, pension file for Simon (Rachel) Washington, RG 15, NARA.

87. Williams Middleton to Martha Ann Matthews, mortgage, Mar. 6, 1836, "South Carolina, Secretary of State, Slave Mortgage Records, 1734–1780," South Carolina Department of Archives and History.

88. Williams Middleton to Martha Ann Matthews, Mortgage, March 6, 1836; Harrison, *Best Companions*, xiii–xiv.

89. Deposition by Diana Burnett, Dec. 6, 1901, deposition by Wally Garrett, Jan. 18, 1902, deposition by Henry Green, Jan. 18, 1902, deposition by Silas Prior, Jan. 27, 1902, "Statement of the Case," 1, pension file for Balaam (Diana) Burnett RG 15, NARA; deposition by Sally Sheppard, Dec. 30, 1901, deposition by Solomon Salter, Dec. 30, 1901, deposition by July Haywood, Dec. 30, 1901, deposition by Celia Haywood, Dec. 30, 1901, deposition by July Haywood, Jun. 12, 1895, deposition by Hamilton White, Jun. 13, 1895, deposition by Jake Aiken, Jun. 13, 1895, pension file for James (Sallie) Sheppard, RG 15, NARA.

90. Henry Middleton to Henry Augustus Middleton, Mortgage, Apr. 24, 1837, "South Carolina, Secretary of State, Slave Mortgage Records, 1734–1780," South Carolina Department of Archives and History; Cheves, "Middleton of South Carolina," 241–244, 246, 252, 258.

91. Henry Middleton to Henry Augustus Middleton, Mortgage, Apr. 24, 1837; Edward Brown, May 16, 1873, Fabry Bowers, Jun. 17, 1873, Frank Wright, Aug. 6, 1869, Freedman's Bank Records; Bancroft, *Slave Trading in the Old South*, 67–89, 119–120.

92. James Cuthbert Estate Inventory, 1838, "South Carolina Probate Records, Files and Loose Papers, 1732–1964," South Carolina Department of Archives and History; Jackson Grant, Feb. 16, 1872, Frank Hamilton, Feb. 16, 1872, Freedman's Bank Records; general affidavit by Friday Hamilton and Captain Brown, Apr. 8, 1895, pension file for Joe (Martha) Morrison, RG 15, NARA; deposition by Captain Brown, May 4, 1897, deposition by Dr. H. E. Bissell, May 8, 1897, pension file for Frank (Captain Brown) Hamilton, RG 15, NARA; "Kirkland-Withers-Snowden-Trotter Family Genealogy" (pages in document 19–48), in Papers of the Kirkland, Withers, Snowden, and Trotter Families, 220–231 (though the notes in the aforementioned documents are incorrect, as Mary Anna Lynah first married Dr. William Lennox Kirkland, then Henry F. Faber, and then Joshua Nicholls); "Rose Hill" in Combahee River Plantations," 6; Linder et al., *Historical Atlas*, 511, 512.

93. Henry F. Faber, Will, Apr. 2, 1839, "South Carolina Probate Records, Bound Volumes, 1671–1977," South Carolina Department of Archives and History; "Rose Hill" in "Combahee River Plantations," 6.

94. General affidavit by Isaac DeCosta, Dec. 13, 1887, general affidavit by Andrew Wyatt, Dec. 27, 1887, pension file for Aaron (Sallie) Ancrum, RG 15, NARA.

95. Deposition by Mary A. (Anne) Lewis, Aug. 26, 1891, pension file for Andrew (Maria) Wyatt; general affidavit by John A. Savage, Feb. 13, 1892, general affidavit by Mary Anne Lewis, Feb. 13, 1892, pension file for Isaac (Silvia) DeCosta, RG 15, NARA; neighbor's affidavit by Mary Anne Lewis, Jul. 9, 1892, pension file for Jack (Rebecca or Hercules) Wineglass, RG 15, NARA.

96. William Savage, Will, 1833, Jones Family Papers 1723–1936, Georgia Historical Society, Savannah; Mary Clay and Mary Nuttall to Henry Middleton Parker, Conveyance, 1839, Superior Court (Bryan County) Georgia, "Deeds and Mortgages, 1796–1922," Georgia Department of Archives and History, Atlanta.

97. William B. Nuttall and Mary W. Savage, Marriage Settlement, Jun. 19, 1832, Jones Family Papers 1723–1936, Georgia Historical Society.

98. "Notice," *Charleston Daily Courier*, Jan. 1, 1839, Jan. 3, 1839, Jan. 4, 1839, Jan. 5, 1839, Jan. 7, 1839, Jan. 15, 1839, Jan. 16, 1839, Jan. 17, 1839, Jan. 18, 1839, Jan. 24, 1839, Jan. 29, 1839, Feb. 1, 1839; Henry Middleton Parker to Mary Ann Faber, Bill of Sale, 1843, "South Carolina, Charleston District, Bill of Sales of Negro Slaves, 1774–1872," South Carolina Department of Archives and History; Mary Ann Lewis, Aug. 11, 1870, Freedman's Bank Records; John Savage, Nov. 27, 1886, deposition by John A. Savage, Mar. 14, 1890, pension file for Andrew (Diana) Harris, RG 15, NARA. John A. Savage did not have a Freedman's Bank account. But Mary Ann Lewis listed him (residing at W. Kurken's place) and Maria Wineglass (Jack Wineglass's wife) as her siblings; Mary Ann Lewis, Aug. 11, 1870, Freedman's Bank Records. Deposition by John A. Savage, Aug. 25, 1891, pension file for Andrew (Maria) Wyatt; deposition by Jacob Jackson, Feb. 25, 1890, pension file for William (Elsey) Jones, RG 15, NARA; Mary Louis in US Census, 1900, Microfilm Publication T623 (NARA).

99. James Lowndes Estate Inventory, 1839, "South Carolina Probate Records, Files and Loose Papers, 1732–1964," South Carolina Department of Archives and History; Thomas Wentworth Higginson, *Army Life in a Black Regiment and Other Writings* (Boston: Houghton, Mifflin, 1900), 238–239; LeRhonda S. Manigault-Bryant, *Talking to the Dead: Religion, Music, and Lived Memory Among Gullah/Geechee Women* (Durham, NC: Duke University Press, 2014), 117–119; email communication with Henry Lowndes, Aug. 13, 14, 17, and 18, 2022, and in person on Sep. 9, 2022.

100. James Lowndes Estate Inventory, 1839, "South Carolina Probate Records, Files and Loose Papers, 1732–1964," South Carolina Department of Archives and History, Columbia.

101. James Lowndes Estate Inventory, 1839.

102. James Lowndes Estate Inventory, 1839; Binah Mack, Dec. 28, 1872, Freedman's Bank Records, 1865–1874.

103. James Lowndes Estate Inventory, 1839.

CHAPTER 3

1. Atthow Pattison Will, Jan. 18, 1791, "Register of Wills of Orphans' Court," Dorchester County Court House, Cambridge, MD; Frank Sanborn, "Harriet Tubman," *The Commonwealth Boston*, Jul. 17, 1863; Ednah Dow Cheney, "Moses," *Freedmen's Record*, Mar. 1865, 34; Anne Fitzhugh Miller, "Harriet Tubman," *American Review*, Aug. 1912, 420.

2. Nell Irvin Painter, *Sojourner Truth: A Life, a Symbol* (New York: Norton, 1996), 12; Carleton Mabee and Susan Mabee Newhouse, *Sojourner Truth—Slave, Prophet, Legend* (New York: New York University Press, 1993), 3.

3. Alice Lucas Brickler to Earl Conrad, Apr. 23, 1940, Harriet Tubman/Earl Conrad Research Materials, New York Public Library (microfilm from Scholarly Resources, Wilmington, DE); Jeffrey R. Brackett, *The Negro in Maryland: A Study of the Institution of Slavery* (Baltimore: Johns Hopkins University, 1889), 149–157.

4. Sarah H. Bradford, *Scenes in the Life of Harriet Tubman* (1869; repr., North Stratford, NH: Ayer, 1971), 72–73; Sarah Bradford, *Harriet Tubman: The Moses of Her People* (1886; repr., New York: J. J. Little, 1901), 107–108.

5. Abroad marriages were exceedingly rare on the seven lower Combahee rice plantations destroyed in the Combahee River Raid. The only example I have found documented was on John Parker's plantation. Parker wrote in his will: "In a sale of my negroes if they cannot be dis-posed of to one person which would be very desirable my Will is that those connected by birth or mar-riage be not separated. I trust that Mr. Lowndes will take Billy on account of his wife & family." John Parker Will, 1849, 1845, "South Carolina Probate Records, Files and Loose Papers, 1732–1964," South Carolina Department of Archives and History, Columbia; Tera Hunter, *Bound in Wedlock: Slave and Free Black Marriage* (Cambridge, MA: Belknap Press of Harvard University Press, 2017), 13, 19–20, 34.

6. Sarah H. Bradford, *Scenes in the Life of Harriet Tubman* (Auburn, NY: W. J. Moses, 1869; repr., North Stratford, NH: Ayer, 1971), 72–73; Bradford, *Harriet Tubman*, 107–108.

7. Still, *The Underground Railroad*, 148; Painter, *Sojourner Truth*, 18–19, 34–36; Mabee and Newhouse, *Sojourner Truth*, 6–7.

8. Bradford, *Scenes in the Life of Harriet Tubman*, 73; Bradford, *Harriet Tubman*, 107–108.

9. Benjamin Drew et al., *A North-Side View of Slavery: The Refugee, or, the Narratives of Fugitive Slaves in Canada: Related by Themselves, with an Account of the History and Condition of the Colored Population of Upper Canada* (Boston: John P. Jewett, 1856), 30.

10. Emma P. Telford, *Harriet: The Modern Moses of Heroism and Visions* (Auburn, NY: Cayuga County Museum, 1905).

11. Cheney, "Moses," 34; Bradford, *Scenes in the Life of Harriet Tubman*, 73; Bradford, *Harriet Tubman*, 17.

12. Bradford, *Scenes in the Life of Harriet Tubman*, 73–74; Bradford, *Harriet Tubman*, 108–109; Allan Kulikoff, *Tobacco and Slaves: The Development of Southern Cultures in the Chesapeake, 1680–1800* (Chapel Hill: University of North Carolina Press, 1986), 101.

13. Bradford, *Scenes in the Life of Harriet Tubman*, 73–74; Bradford, *Harriet Tubman*, 108.

14. Cheney, "Moses," 35; Bradford, *Harriet Tubman*, 18–19.

15. Cheney, "Moses," 34–35; Bradford, *Scenes in the Life of Harriet Tubman*, 74–75; Bradford, *Harriet Tubman*, 22–23, 109; Samuel Hopkins Adams, *Grandfather Stories* (New York: Random House, 1955), 273–274.

16. Cheney, "Moses," 34–35; Still, *The Underground Railroad*, 297; John W. Blassingame, *Slave Testimony: Two Centuries of Letters, Speeches, Interviews and Autobiographies* (Baton Rouge: Louisiana State University Press, 1977), 458; Adams, *Grandfather Stories*, 273; Kate Clifford Larson, *Bound for the Promised Land: Harriet Tubman, Portrait of an American Hero* (New York: Ballantine Books, 2004), 36–39.

17. Bradford, *Scenes in the Life of Harriet Tubman*, 15; Bradford, *Harriet Tubman*, 22–23; Larson, *Bound for the Promised Land,* 36–39.

18. Cheney, "Moses," 35.

19. Cheney, "Moses," 35; Bradford, *Scenes in the Life of Harriet Tubman*, 75; Bradford, *Harriet Tubman*, 110; Phillip Hesser and Charlie Ewers, *A Guide to Harriet Tubman's Eastern Shore: The Old Home Is Not There* (Charleston, SC: History Press, 2021), 62.

20. Cheney, "Moses," 34; Bradford, *Scenes in the Life of Harriet Tubman*, 75; Bradford, *Harriet Tubman*, 110–111. For another example of an enslaved woman who performed men's labor against her will, see Drew et al., *A North-Side View of Slavery*, 44.

21. Cheney, "Moses," 34–35; Blassingame, *Slave Testimony*, 457–458; Hesser and Ewers, *A Guide to Harriet Tubman's Eastern Shore.*

22. Cheney, "Moses," 35; Bradford, *Scenes in the Life of Harriet Tubman*, 76; Bradford, *Harriet Tubman*, 111.

23. Bradford, *Scenes in the Life of Harriet Tubman*, 107; Bradford, *Harriet Tubman*, 128.

24. Cheney, "Moses," 34, 37; Ednah Dow Littlehale Cheney, *Reminiscences of Ednah Dow Cheney (Born Littlehale)* (Boston: Lee & Shepard, 1902), 82; Blassingame, *Slave Testimony*, 457, 461.

25. Edward E. Baptist, *The Half Has Never Been Told: Slavery and the Making of American Capitalism* (New York: Basic Books, 2014), 101, 294.

26. Drew et al., *A North-Side View of Slavery*, 30, 41; Bradford, *Scenes in the Life of Harriet Tubman*, 15–16; Bradford, *Harriet Tubman*, 26.

27. Drew et al., *A North-Side View of Slavery*, 29, 41; Baptist, *The Half Has Never Been Told*, 255; Painter, *Sojourner Truth*, 12–13, 39, 155; Mabee and Newhouse, *Sojourner Truth*, 3–5; Blassingame, *Slave Testimony*, 414.

28. Bradford, *Scenes in the Life of Harriet Tubman*, 14–15; Bradford, *Harriet Tubman*, 23–24; James A. McGowan, *Station Master on the Underground Railroad: The Life and Letters of Thomas Garrett* (Jefferson, NC: McFarland, 2009), 70.

CHAPTER 4

1. Deposition by Elsie Jones, Apr. 30, 1895, pension file for Pool (Julia) Sellers, RG 15, NARA; general affidavit by William Izzard, Feb. 3, 1893, pension file for Farbry (Aminda) Bowers, RG 15, NARA.

2. Frances Anne Kemble, *Journal of a Residence on a Georgian Plantation in 1838–1839*, ed. John A. Scott (1863; repr., Athens: University of Georgia Press, 1984), 65–66, 88, 157, 160, 175; S. Max Edelson, *Plantation Enterprise in Colonial South Carolina* (Cambridge, MA: Harvard University Press, 2006), 77, 83–87, 157, 421; Leslie Ann Schwalm, *"A Hard Fight for We": Women's Transition from Slavery to Freedom in South Carolina* (Urbana: University of Illinois Press, 1997), 14–15; William Dusinberre, *Them Dark Days: Slavery in the American Rice Swamps* (Oxford: Oxford University Press, 1996), 71, 108, 424; Lawrence S. Rowland, Alexander Moore, and George C. Rogers, *The History of Beaufort County, South Carolina, Volume I, 1514–1861* (Columbia: University of South Carolina Press, 1996), 351–353; Duncan Clinch Heyward, *Seed from Madagascar* (1937; Columbia: University of South Carolina Press, 1993), 30, 38, 40, 179.

3. "Declaration for Widow's Pension and Increase" by Sina Young, Feb. 19, 1869, deposition by Peter James, May 25, 1869, deposition by Elizabeth Small, May 25, 1869, depositions by Sina Young, Feb. 19 and Jun. 26, 1873, depositions by Bina Mack, Jun. 27 and 29, 1873, exhibit B by Sina Young, Dec. 13, 1876, depositions by Venus Lyons, Elsey Jones, and Lina Richards, Jun. 30, 1873, exhibit by Sina Young, Gibby Mike, Chanty Mike, and Elsie Jones, Apr. 24, 1875, exhibit by Sina Young, Dec. 13, 1876, pension file for William (Sina) Young, RG 15, NARA; "Incidental Matter," Dec. 1879, deposition (exhibit) G of Daphney Drayton, Nov. 8, 1884, general affidavit by Elsy Jones, Jan. 6, 1891, pension file for Robert (Phoebe) Frazier, RG 15, NARA; general affidavit by Sina Green, Jul. 17, 1887, general affidavit by Flora Young, Sep. 1, 1887, neighbor's affidavit by William Jones, Sep. 2, 1887, neighbor's affidavit by Annie Holmes, Sep. 2, 1887, general affidavit by Sina Green, Sep. 3, 1887, pension file for William (Sina) Young; general affidavit by Bella Garrett, Mar. 8, 1889, neighbor's affidavit by Carolina Watson, Mar. 11, 1889, general affidavit by James Sheppard, Mar. 11, 1889, deposition by Wally Garrett, Apr. 5, 1902, pension file for Wally (Bella) Garrett, RG 15, NARA; general affidavit by Jonas Green, Dec. 18, 1896, pension file for Smart (Lucretia) Washington, RG 15, NARA; Department of the Interior, Bureau of Pensions Questionnaire, Apr. 26, 1898, and Sep. 6, 1900, "Declaration for Widow's Pension," Feb. 5 and Oct. 20, 1901, deposition by Mingo Van Dross, Nov. 14, 1901, deposition by Peggy Brown, Nov. 14, 1901, deposition by Cuffee Bolze, Nov. 15, 1901, pension file for Edward (Peggy) Brown, RG 15, NARA; deposition A of Diana Burnett, Dec. 6, 1901, L. M. Kelley, Acting Commissioner of Bureau of Pensions, to Secretary of the Interior, Jul. 3, 1902, pension file for Balaam (Diana) Burnett, RG 15, NARA; deposition by Solomon Salter, Apr. 6, 1902, pension file for Solomon Salter, RG 15, NARA; deposition by Wally Watson, Apr. 7, 1902, pension file for

Wally (Mary) Watson, RG 15, NARA; deposition by Daphney Wright, Apr. 8, 1902, pension file for Frank (Daphne) Wright, RG 15, NARA; deposition by Jane Barnwell, Apr. 14, 1911, pension file for Moses (Fannie) Simmons, RG 15, NARA; Douglas R. Egerton, *He Shall Go Out Free: The Lives of Denmark Vesey* (Madison, WI: Madison House, 1999), 112–113.

4. General affidavit by Bella Garrett, Mar. 8, 1889, deposition by Wally Garrett, Oct. 13, 1901, and Apr. 5, 1902, general affidavit by Uriah Washington, Apr. 3, 1912, general affidavit by J. Polite, Apr. 3, 1912, deposition by Bella Garrett, Oct. 10, 1912, deposition by Mexico Washington, Oct. 10, 1912, deposition by Affie Green, Oct. 11, 1912, deposition by Richard Smith, Oct. 11, 1912, deposition by Jack Aiken, Oct. 12, 1912, pension file for Wally (Bella) Garrett; deposition by Moriah Bartley, Apr. 15, 1901, pension file for Anthony (Moriah) Bartley, RG 15, NARA; deposition by Daphne Snipe, Apr. 16, 1901, pension file for Ned (Daphney) Snipe, RG 15, NARA.

5. "Claims for Widow's Pension, with Minor Children," Jul. 25, 1864, "Declaration for Widow's Army Pension," Jul. 27, 1865, "Widow's Claim for Pension," Oct. 13, 1868, depositions by Quash Simmons and Harry Robinson, Nov. 11, 1868, pension file for June (Eliza) Singleton, RG 15, NARA; "Widow's Claim for Pension," Nov. 10, 1868, pension file for Hardtime (Flora) White, RG 15, NARA; general affidavit by John A. Savage, Nov. 27, 1886, general affidavit by W. M. Jones, Nov. 27, 1888, deposition by Diana Harris, Mar. 14, 1890, deposition B by John A. Savage, Mar. 14, 1890, pension file for Andrew (Diane) Harris, RG 15, NARA; "Declaration for Widow's Pension" by Margaret Simmons, Aug. 20, 1890, pension file for Joshua (Margaret) Simmons, RG 15, NARA.

6. This figure is calculated from my database of 108 men and women enslaved on the Combahee before the Combahee River Raid whose occupations could be identified, primarily from the US Civil War pension files, but also from slave lists and planters' letters where available. Of this subset, sixty-four performed skilled occupations (blacksmiths, bricklayers, carpenters, cattle minders, coachmen, coopers, hoemen, hostlers, house slaves, plasterers, sheep herders, plowmen, and wheelrights); forty-four performed field labor. Charles Lucas file, "Compiled Military Service Records of Volunteer Union Soldiers Who Served with the United States Colored Troops," RG 94, NARA; "Army of the United States. Certificate of Disability for Discharge," Jun. 2, 1865, pension file for Aaron (Sallie) Ancrum, RG 15, NARA; letter from War Department, Adjutant General's Office, Mar. 2, 1888, general affidavit by Andrew Wyatt, Mar. 27, 1889, pension file for Stepheny (Flora) Grant, RG 15, NARA; "Declaration for an Original Invalid Pension," Aug. 21, 1889, pension file for Edward (Peggy) Brown; depositions by John A. Savage and William Jones, Mar. 14, 1890, depositions by Edward Snipe and Jack Wineglass, Mar. 20, 1890, pension file for Andrew (Diana) Harris; "Declaration for Pension," Jun. 26, 1890, pension

file for Farbry (Aminda) Bowers; "War Department, Record and Pension Division," Jan. 16, 1891, "Department of the Interior, Bureau of Pensions," May 25, 1898, pension file for Moses (Fannie) Simmons; military service record for James Simmons, Jun. 11, 1891, pension file for James Simmons, RG 15, NARA; depositions by Andrew Wyatt and Silva De Coster, Aug. 25, 1891, pension file for Andrew (Marie) Wyatt, RG 15, NARA; deposition by Elsie Jones, Apr. 30, 1895, pension file for Pool (Julia) Sellers; "Department of the Interior, Bureau of Pensions," Jan. 24, 1896, pension file for William (Elsie) Jones, RG 15, NARA; "Department of the Interior, Bureau of Pensions," Apr. 11, 1896, pension file for James (Jone) Shields, RG 15, NARA; War Department, Record and Pension Office, description of Friday Barrington, Oct. 10, 1898, pension file for Friday Barrington, RG 15, NARA; deposition A by Jackson Grant, Oct. 16, 1898, deposition by William Hamilton, Oct. 31, 1898, pension file for Stepheny (Flora) Grant; "Department of the Interior, Bureau of Pensions," Mar. 31, 1899, pension file for Edward (Mary) Brown, RG 15, NARA; deposition by Stephen Simmons, Apr. 10, 1901, pension file for Stephen (Jane) Simmons; deposition by Nat Osborne, Jun. 28, 1902, pension file for Nat (Victoria) Osborne, RG 15, NARA; James M. Clifton, ed., *Life and Labor on Argyle Island: Letters and Documents of a Savannah River Rice Plantation, 1833–1867* (Savannah, GA: Beehive Press, 1978), xii; Eliza Cope Harrison, ed., *Best Companions: Letters of Eliza Middleton Fisher and Her Mother, Mary Hering Middleton, from Charleston, Philadelphia, and Newport, 1839–1846* (Columbia: University of South Carolina Press, 2001), 256; Heyward, *Seed from Madagascar*, 164.

7. Frank Hamilton file, "Compiled Military Service Records of Volunteer Union Soldiers Who Served with the United States Colored Troops," RG 94, NARA.

8. Heyward, *Seed from Madagascar*, 30–33.

9. In the pension files, the occupation "laborer" or "farm laborer" denotes field hands. See General Affidavit by Richard Smith, Feb. 19, 1894, "Military Service," Richard Smith, Sep. 5, 1891, "Record and Pension Office, War Department," Richard Smith, Oct. 28, 1893, "War Department, The Adjutant General's Office," Richard Smith, n.d., pension file for Richard (Mary) Smith, RG 15, NARA; "War Department, Adjutant General's Office," Charles Lucas, Mar. 6, 1888, deposition by Wally Garrett, Oct. 18, 1902, "Record and Pension Office, War Department," Wally Garrett, n.d., pension file for Wally (Bella) Garrett; claimant's affidavit by James Sheppard, "Department of the Interior, Bureau of Pensions," Jun. 30, 1898, "Department of the Interior, Bureau of Pensions," James Sheppard, Aug. 15, 1894, pension file for James (Sally) Sheppard; Simon Washington, Dec. 7, 1899, pension file for Simon (Rachel) Washington; "Act of May 11, 1912, Declaration for Pension," Cuffie Bolze, May 20, 1912, "Act of February 6, 1907, Declaration for Pension," Cuffie Bolze, Apr. 7, 1908, "Military Service," Cuffie Bolze, Feb. 7, 1891, pension file for Cuffie (Sophia)

Bolze; "Declaration for an Invalid Pension," Robert Frazier, Aug. 28, 1867, pension file for Robert (Phoebe) Frazier; "Department of the Interior, Bureau of Pensions," William Middleton, Jul. 19, 1904, "Military Service," William Middleton, Mar. 13, 1901, pension file for William Middleton; "Department of the Interior, Bureau of Pensions," Charles Nicholas, Jul. 18, 1903, pension file for Charles (Ella) Nicholas; "Record and Pension Office, War Department," Neptune Nicholas, Mar. 24, 1900, pension file for Neptune (Betsey) Nicholas; "Record and Pension Office, War Department," William Young, Sep. 3, 1901, pension file for William (Sina, Flora) Young; deposition D by Edward Snipe and deposition E by Jack Wineglass, Mar. 20, 1890, deposition A by Diana Harris, Mar. 14, 1890, pension file for Andres (Diana) Harris; "Record and Pension Office, War Department," Ned Snipe, n.d., pension file for Ned (Daphne) Snipe; "Declaration for an Original Invalid Pension," Jack Wineglass, May 15, 1890, and May 13, 1890, "Army of the United States Certificate of Disability for Discharge," Jack Wineglass, Sep. 15, 1863, pension file for Jack (Rebecca, Hercules) Wineglass; deposition by Moriah Bartley, Apr. 15, 1901, "Record and Pension Office, War Department, Anthony Bartley, n.d., general affidavit by Moriah Bartley, May 20, 1898, pension file for Anthony (Moriah) Bartley; "Record and Pension Office, War Department," Friday Hamilton, Jun. 11, 1900, pension file for Friday Hamilton; "Act of May 11, 1912, Declaration for Pension," Mingo Van Dross, May 25, 1912, "Act of February 6, 1907, Declaration for Pension," Mingo Van Dross, Nov. 17, 1908, pension file for Mingo (Emma) Van Dross; "Department of the Interior, Bureau of Pensions" by Lucy Smith, Jul. 28, 1908, pension file for Richard (Lucy, Fanny) Smith; deposition A by Andrew Wyatt and deposition B by Silva De Coster, Aug. 25, 1891, "Army of the United States Certificate of Disability for Discharge," Andrew Wyatt, Sept. 30, 1863, pension file for Andrew (Maria) Wyatt.

10. Henry Middleton Estate Record, 1847, "South Carolina Probate Records, Bound Volumes, 1671–1977," South Carolina Department of Archives and History, Columbia; Harrison, *Best Companions*, 2–3, 9–10, 106–107, 109, 122, 131, 193, 441, 443, 450–451; Barbara Doyle, Mary Edna Sullivan, and Tracey Todd, *Beyond the Fields: Slavery at Middleton Place* (Columbia: University of South Carolina Press, 2008), 53.

11. Allecia Hopton Middleton, *Life in Carolina and New England During the Nineteenth Century: As Illustrated by Reminiscences and Letters of the Middleton Family of Charleston, South Carolina, and of the Dewolf Family of Bristol, Rhode Island* (Bristol, RI: Privately printed, 1929), 152–153; Harrison, *Best Companions*, 2, 23, 315, 480, 489, 494.

12. Harrison, *Best Companions*, 2, 11, 305–306; Middleton, *Life in Carolina*, 67–69, 152–153.

13. Harrison, *Best Companions*, 2, 11, 23–24, 157, 311, 315, 376, 430, 443, 488–490, 494, 497; Middleton, *Life in Carolina*, 67–68, 152–153.

14. Harrison, *Best Companions*, xxiv, 6, 11, 34, 81, 85, 89, 100, 107–111, 130, 192, 353, 375, 378.

15. William Elliott, *Carolina Sports, by Land and Water: Including Incidents of Devil-Fishing, Wild-Cat, Deer and Bear Hunting, Etc. 1846* (New York: Derby & Jackson, 1859), 84, 88, 91, 92, 94, 96, 97–98, 100, 102–103, 106, 108, 110, 116–117, 120, 127, 131–132, 170; Harrison, *Best Companions*, 301, 378; Heyward, *Seed from Madagascar*, 31–33, 117–127.

16. Harrison, *Best Companions*, 430.

17. Harrison, *Best Companions*, 14, 18, 19, 24, 266, 296–297.

18. Eliza Middleton Fisher to Mary Helen Middleton, Mar. 19, 1842, Fisher Family Letters, Historical Society of Pennsylvania, Philadelphia; Harrison, *Best Companions*, 168, 251–252, 256, 259–260.

19. Harrison, *Best Companions*, 4–13, 168, 412, 420, 425, 436–439.

20. US House of Representatives, *Historical Statistics of the United States, Colonial Times to 1970*, No. 93–78 (Washington, DC: Bureau of the Census, 1975), 163; Harrison, *Best Companions*, 296–297.

21. Harrison, *Best Companions*, 233, 266, 270–272, 296–297.

22. Harrison, *Best Companions*, 89, 100, 130, 353, 359.

23. Harrison, *Best Companions*; Steven Hahn, "'Extravagant Expectations' of Freedom: Rumour, Political Struggle, and the Christmas Insurrection Scare of 1865 in the American South," *Past and Present* 157, no. 1 (1997): 138–141; Allan Kulikoff, *Tobacco and Slaves: The Development of Southern Cultures in the Chesapeake, 1680–1800* (Chapel Hill: University of North Carolina Press, 1986), 78–177; Charles Joyner, *Down by the Riverside: A South Carolina Slave Community* (Urbana: University of Illinois Press, 1984); Eugene D. Genovese, *Roll, Jordan, Roll: The World the Slaves Made* (New York: Vintage, 1976).

24. Henry Middleton Parker to Mary A. Faber, Bill of Sale, Jan. 1, 1843, "South Carolina, Charleston District, Bill of Sales of Negro Slaves, 1774–1872," South Carolina Department of Archives and History; Mary A. Faber to Henry Middleton Parker, Mortgage, Jan. 1, 1843, "South Carolina, Secretary of State, Slave Mortgage Records, 1734–1780," South Carolina Department of Archives and History; Mary Ann Lewis, Aug. 11, 1870, Freedman's Bank Records; general affidavit by Daphney Snipe, Oct. 6, 1894, pension file for Ned (Daphney) Snipe. Daphne Snipe did not have a Freedman's Bank account; see Anthony Bartley, n.d., Freedman's Bank Records. John A. Savage did not have a Freedman's Bank account; see Mary Ann Lewis, Aug. 11, 1870, Freedman's Bank Records; Mary Ann Lewis in the US Census, 1900.

25. For the planters, Henry Middleton Parker's sister, Emma Parker, married Mary Anna Lynah Kirkland Faber Nicholls's brother, Colonel James Lynah. For the enslaved, future historians may be able to reconnect the lineages of the Savage gangs purchased by Gabriel Manigault and William L. Kirkland Jr., which originated in William Savage's estate. Mary Ann Faber to Henry Middleton Parker, Mortgage, Jan. 1, 1843, "South Carolina, Secretary of State, Slave Mortgage

Records, 1734–1780," South Carolina Department of Archives and History; Henry Middleton Parker to Mary Anna Faber, Bill of Sale, Jan. 1, 1853, "South Carolina, Charleston District, Bill of Sales of Negro Slaves, 1774–1872," South Carolina Department of Archives and History; "Descendants of Dr. James Lynah," Nichols Family History and Genealogy Files, 30–34, South Carolina Historical Society, Charleston; "Trans-Atlantic Slave Trade Database," www. slavevoyages.org (David Eltis and Martin Halbert, original principal investigators); Dusinberre, *Them Dark Days,* 75, 84, 87–94; Mary Anna Faber to Henry Middleton Parker, Mortgage, Jan. 1, 1843, "South Carolina, Secretary of State, Slave Mortgage Records, 1734–1780," South Carolina Department of Archives and History; William Dusinberre, *Them Dark Days: Slavery in the American Rice Swamps* (Oxford: Oxford University Press, 1996), 75, 84, 87–89; Richard Holcombe Kilbourne, *Debt, Investment, Slaves: Credit Relations in East Feliciana Parish, Louisiana, 1825–1885* (Tuscaloosa: University of Alabama Press, 1995), 56.

26. Thomas Lowndes Estate Inventory, Dec. 13, 1844, "South Carolina Probate Records, Bound Volumes, 1671–1977," South Carolina Department of Archives and History; Charles T. Lowndes, St. Bartholomew Parish, Slave Schedule, US Census, 1860; Charles T. Lowndes, St. Bartholomew Parish, Agricultural Schedule, US Census, 1860.

27. The Bluff was one of Thomas Rhett Smith's plantations. Located between the Ashepoo and Chehaw Rivers, it was separated from another of Smith's plantations, Middle Place, by a swamp. According to Beverly Scafidel, William Elliott acquired the right to use Bluff Plantation in 1850 with the understanding that his children would inherit it. Beverly Robinson Scafidel, "The Letters of William Elliott," Ph.D. diss., University of South Carolina, 1978, 59, 117–118n1, 191, 193, 220, 509, 565–566; Thomas Rhett Smith DS to William Lenox Kirkland, January 4, 1823," African American and African Diaspora Collection, 1729–1966, Clements Library, University of Michigan, Ann Arbor; depositions by Mingo Van Dross, Apr. 9, 1901 and Dec. 14, 1908, pension file for Mingo (Emma) Van Dross, RG 15, NARA.

28. Henry Middleton, Will, 1846, "South Carolina Probate Records, Bound Volumes, 1671–1977, Wills," South Carolina Department of Archives and History; Harrison, *Best Companions,* 499–500; Ian Webster, "Inflation Calculator," https://www.in2013dollars.com.

29. Henry Middleton, Will, 1846; Henry Middleton Estate Inventory, 1847, "South Carolina Probate Records, Bound Volumes, 1671–1977," South Carolina Department of Archives and History; Jack Aiken, Aug. 10, 1869, Freedman's Bank Records; Smart Washington, Aug. 24, 1869, Freedman's Bank Records; general affidavit by Jack Furgerson, Jun. 20, 1889, general affidavit by Richard Gary, Mar. 22, 1915, deposition A by Ellen J. Harris, Sep. 1, 1915, deposition E by Tom Washington, Sep. 31, 1915, pension file for Jack (Jack Jr.) Aiken, RG 15, NARA; claimant's affidavit by Jack Aiken, Jan. 29, 1893, general affidavit by William Green, Feb. 13, 1893, pension file for Farbry (Aminda) Bowers;

general affidavit by Fabry Bowers and William Drayton, Feb. 16, 1894, deposition by Mary Brown, Jul. 18, 1902, general affidavit by Carolina Nelson, Jan. 14, 1907, pension file for Edward (Mary) Brown; general affidavits by Christianna Wilson, Feb. 23 and May 24, 1897, general affidavit by Joseph Brown, May 20, 1897; general affidavit by Elaine Frasier, Jun. 4, 1897, general affidavit by Christiana Wilson, Apr. 8, 1902, deposition A by Christiana Wilson, Mar. 27, 1902; deposition A by Christina Brown, Mar. 29, 1902, depositions by Anthony Alston and Clarinda Johnson, Apr. 1, 1902, deposition B by Joseph Brown, Apr. 2, 1902, depositions by George Frasier, Annette Lewis, and James Miller, Apr. 14, 1902, letter to the Hon. Commissioner Pensioner from Wayne W. Cordell, Apr. 16, 1902, pension file for Simon (Clarinda, Christiana Brown Wilson) Brown; deposition by Phoebe Gray, Apr. 8, 1902, pension file for Jeffrey (Phoebe) Gray, RG 15, NARA; Doyle, Sullivan, and Todd, *Beyond the Fields*, 50–54; Webster, "Inflation Calculator."

30. Henry Middleton Estate Record, Jan. 8, 1847, "South Carolina Probate Records, Bound Volumes, 1671–1977," South Carolina Department of Archives and History; Clifton, *Life and Labor on Argyle Island*, xxxii; Elizabeth Hyde Botume, *First Days Amongst the Contrabands* (Boston: Lee and Shepard, 1893), 61; Smart Washington, Aug. 24, 1869, Freedman's Bank Records; certificate of disability for discharge, May 13, 1865, depositions by Lucretia Washington, Jonas Green, Julia Scott, and Christiana Washington, Aug. 24, 1897, deposition D by Solomon Washington, Aug. 28, 1897, pension file for Smart (Lucretia) Washington; Doyle, Sullivan, and Todd, *Beyond the Fields*, 52–53; Rusty Fleetwood, *Tidecraft: The Boats of South Carolina, Georgia, and Northeastern Florida, 1550–1950* (Tybee Island, GA: WBG Marine Press, 1995), 311.

31. Kemble, *Journal of a Residence*, 79–81, 84; Anne C. Bailey, *The Weeping Time: Memory and the Largest Slave Auction in American History* (New York: Cambridge University Press, 2017), 3–7, 47–50, 52–55, 69–70, 95–96; Heyward, *Seed from Madagascar*, 5, 48–49, 191, 221. On the accuracy of Frances Kemble's diary, see Dusinberre, *Them Dark Days*, 225, 274, 421; Jennifer Berry Hawes, "How a Grad Student Uncovered the Largest Known Slave Auction in the U. S.," ProPublica, Jun. 16, 2023. For a comparison of enslaved drivers on Sea Island cotton plantations, see Rowland, Moore, and Rogers, *The History of Beaufort County, Vol. 1*, 352–353."

32. Clifton, *Life and Labor on Argyle Island*, xxxv; Kemble, *Journal of a Residence*, 79–81, 84, 157, 160, 176, 188, 215–216, 356.

33. Kemble, *Journal of a Residence*, 80, 176; Federal Writers' Project, *Slave Narrative Project: A Folk History of Slavery in the United States, from Interviews with Former Slaves, Volume 14, South Carolina, Part 2, Eddington–Hunter* (Washington, DC: Library of Congress, 1936), 323; Genevieve Chandler, Kincaid Mills, Genieve C. Peterkin, and Aaron McCollough, eds., *Coming Through: Voices of a South Carolina Gullah Community from WPA Oral Histories* (Columbia: University of South Carolina Press, 2008), 106; Dusinberre, *Them Dark Days*, 274.

34. Kemble, *Journal of a Residence*, 49–50; Baptist, *The Half Has Never Been Told*, 57; Dusinberre, *Them Dark Days*, 274; Rowland, Moore, and Rogers, *The History of Beaufort County*, 352; Clifton, *Life and Labor on Argyle Island*, xxxi.

35. Clifton, *Life and Labor on Argyle Island*, xxxv; Kemble, *Journal of a Residence*, 79, 110, 60; Chandler et al., *Coming Through*, 29, 40–41, 51–52, 95; Higginson, *Army Life in a Black Regiment*, 296; Dusinberre, *Them Dark Days*, 199, 420.

36. Clifton, *Life and Labor on Argyle Island*, xxxv; Kemble, *Journal of a Residence*, 48, 160; Thomas Wentworth Higginson, *Army Life in a Black Regiment and Other Writings* (Boston: Houghton, Mifflin, 1900), 296; Chandler et al., *Coming Through*, 47, 95, 97–99.

37. General affidavits by Fabry Bowers and William Drayton, Feb. 16, 1894, general affidavit by Carolina Watson, Jan. 14, 1907, pension file for Edward (Mary) Brown; deposition D by March Lawrence, Jun. 12, 1895, pension file for James (Sallie) Sheppard, RG 15, NARA; deposition I by March Lawrence, Jul. 12, 1895, pension file for Simon (Rachel) Washington.

38. General affidavit by William Green, Jun. 10, 1915, general affidavit by Ellen J. Harris, Apr. 21, 1915, deposition by Tom Washington, Sep. 3, 1915, deposition by Sam P. Gary, Sep. 4, 1915, deposition by William Green, Sep. 1, 1915, deposition by Ellen J. Harris, Sep. 1, 1915, depositions by Sarah Evans and Caesar Evans, Sep. 3, 1915, deposition by Charles Nicholas, Oct. 18, 1898, deposition by William Hamilton, Oct. 22, 1898, "Affidavit of Claimant" by Jonas Green, general affidavits by Sam Gary, Mar. 22 and Jun. 8, 1915; general affidavits by Caesar Evans, Nov. 13, 1914, and May 13, 1915; general affidavit by William Green, Oct. 31, 1914, pension file for Jack (Jack Jr.) Aiken, RG 15, NARA.

39. General affidavit by Fabry Bowers, Apr. 5, 1889, general affidavit by Solomon Solter, Oct. 5, 1887, deposition by S. White, May 11, 1897, deposition by William Izzard, May 11, 1897, deposition by Farbry Bowers, May 17, 1897, deposition by Phoebe Gray, Apr. 8, 1902, general affidavit by William Izzard, Dec. 8, 1894, "Widow's Claim for Pension Under Act of June 27th, 1890," deposition by Edward Brown, Feb. 2, 1891, general affidavit by Edward Brown, Apr. 29, 1891, general affidavit by Farbry Bowers, Jan. 10, 1893, pension file for Jeffrey (Phoebe) Gray.

40. Henry Middleton, Will, 1846, "South Carolina Probate Records, Bound Volumes, 1671–1977, Wills," South Carolina Department of Archives and History; John Middleton and five others, Prince William Parish, slave schedules, agricultural census, 1860 US Census; Agnes Leland Baldwin, "Newport Plantation," 24, Agnes L. Baldwin Research Papers, 1966–2004, South Carolina Historical Society, Charleston; Jessica Stevens Loring, *Auldbrass: The Plantation Complex Designed by Frank Lloyd Wright, a Documented History of Its South Carolina Lands* (Greenville, SC: Southern Historical Press, 1992), 112–113; Langdon Cheves, "Middleton of South Carolina." *South Carolina Historical and Genealogical Magazine* 1, no. 228 (1900): 246–247.

41. Deposition T by Mingo Van Dross, Nov. 14, 1901, deposition L by Friday Hamilton, Feb. 19, 1902, pension file for Edward (Peggy) Brown.

42. E. D. Gallion to William Lochren, Commissioner of Pensions, Jun. 28, 1895, pension file for Richard (Lucy, Fannie) Smith, RG 15, NARA; questionnaire, Sep. 6, 1900, "Act of June 27, 1890: Declaration for Widow's Pension," Feb. 5, 1901, deposition A by Peggy Brown, Nov. 14, 1901, deposition B by Neptune Nicholas, Nov. 15, 1901, deposition T by Mingo Van Dross, Nov. 14, 1901, deposition by Neptune Nicholas, Nov. 15, 1901, deposition by Friday Hamilton, Nov. 19, 1901, deposition I by Cuffie Bolze, Nov. 15, 1901, deposition H by Stephen Burlesque, Feb. 11, 1902, deposition E by Nepton Nicholas, Feb. 12, 1902, deposition L by Friday Hamilton, Feb. 19, 1902, deposition C by Cuffie Bolze, Nov. 15, 1901, deposition D by Friday Hamilton, Nov. 19, 1901, "Act of Jun 27, 1890: Declaration for Widow's Pension," Oct. 20, 1902, pension file for Edward (Peggy) Brown; depositions by Peggy Brown and Cuffy Bowles, Feb. 11, 1902, deposition by Cuffy Bolze, Feb. 17, 1902, Commissioner to Auditor for the War Department, Sep. 24, 1910, general affidavit by Sina Young, n.d., general affidavit by Peter James, Jun. 3, 1869, exhibit by Gibby and Chanty Mike, Apr. 24, 1875, exhibit by Bina Mack and Hager Hamilton, Apr. 24, 1875, "Declaration for Widow's Pension and Increase" by Sina Young, Feb. 19, 1869, neighbor's affidavit by Annie Holmes, Sep. 1, 1887, neighbor's affidavit by William Jones, Sep. 2, 1887, general affidavit by Sina Young, Jun. 26, 1873, general affidavit by Bina Mack, Jun. 29, 1873, general affidavit by John G. Stokes, Jun. 30, 1873, exhibit by Elsie Jones, Apr. 24, 1875, exhibit B by Sina Young and exhibit C by Jonas Green, Dec. 13, 1876, general affidavit by Sina Green, Sep. 3, 1887, general affidavit by Selam White, Aug. 6, 1901, pension file for William (Sina) Young.

43. Dr. James Heyward to William C. Heyward, Bill of Sale, Feb. 28, 1848, "South Carolina, Charleston District, Bill of Sales of Negro Slaves, 1774–1872," South Carolina Department of Archives and History; deposition by Harriet Eilliott and Friday Barrington, Nov. 29, 1884, deposition K by Friday Barrington, Nov. 22, 1884, "Widow's Pension: Incidental Matter," 1882, pension file for Robert (Phoebe) Frazier; general affidavit by Andrew Wyatt and Joan Legare, Aug. 1, 1891, pension file for Prince (Tyra) Polite, RG 15, NARA; E. D. Gallion to William Lochren, Commissioner of Pensions, Jun. 28, 1895, pension file for Richard (Lucy, Fannie) Smith.

44. Phoebe Frazier testified to having different maiden names at different times: Burns, Grinnell, and Legree. Questionnaire by Friday Barrington, Oct. 14, 1902, pension file for Friday Barrington, RG 15, NARA; deposition A by Neptune Nicholas, Apr. 8, 1901, depositions by Betsey Nicholas, Jack Barnwell, and Moses Simmons, Apr. 11, 1905, pension file for Neptune (Betsey) Nicholas, RG 15, NARA; deposition A by Moses Simmons, Apr. 8, 1901, pension file for Moses (Fannie) Simmons; deposition A by Jackson Grant, Oct. 16, 1896, depositions by Cuffy Bolze and Neptune Nichols, Oct.

20, 1896, deposition by Lucius Robinson, Oct. 24, 1896, deposition D by Andrew Nicholas, Oct. 20, 1896, deposition H by Friday Hamilton, Oct. 24, 1896, deposition A by Jackson Grant, Apr. 10, 1901, pension file for Jackson (Jane) Grant; general affidavit by Neptune Nicholas, Jun. 11, 1900, deposition A by Friday Hamilton, Apr. 17, 1901, pension file for Friday Hamilton, RG 15, NARA; depositions by Peter Green, William Jones, Daphny Drayton, and Edward Elliott, n.d., general affidavit by Elsy Jones, Jan. 6, 1891, exhibit A by Phoebe Frazer, Nov. 7, 1884, addendum to exhibit A by Phoebe Frazer, Dec. 11, 1903; "Widow's Claim for Pension," Mar. 8, 1878, depositions by William Jones and Daphney Drayton, Nov. 8, 1884, deposition K by Friday Barrington, Nov. 22, 1884, "Declaration for Widow's Pension," Apr. 4, 1908, "Widow's Pension: Incidental Matter," n.d., "Declaration for Widow's Pension: Act of June 27, 1890," Aug. 12 and Sep. 20, 1890, pension file for Robert (Phoebe) Frazier.

45. James Ladson and John Stock to John Parker, Deed, 1832, Charleston County and South Carolina Miscellaneous Land Records, 1719–1873, Charleston County Courthouse, D10: 460–463; John Parker, Will, 1845–1849, "South Carolina Probate Records, Bound Volumes, 1671–1977," South Carolina Department of Archives and History; John Parker Estate Inventory, 1849, "South Carolina Probate Records, Bound Volumes, 1671–1977," South Carolina Department of Archives and History; Agnes Leland Baldwin, "Paul Dalton," Agnes L. Baldwin Research Papers, 1966–2004, South Carolina Historical Society, Charleston, folders 1, 10, 15, 18, 83; Suzanne Cameron Linder et al., *Historical Atlas of the Rice Plantations of the ACE River Basin—1860* (Columbia: South Carolina Department of Archives and History, 1995), 445.

46. John Parker, Will, 1845–1849, "South Carolina Probate Records, Bound Volumes, 1671–1977, Wills," South Carolina Department of Archives and History; John Parker, Estate Record, 1849, "South Carolina Probate Records, Bound Volumes, 1671–1977," South Carolina Department of Archives and History; general affidavit by Mary Ann Lewis, Sep. 4, 1889, deposition B by Silva De Coster, Aug. 25, 1891, pension file for Andrew (Marie) Wyatt; general affidavits by Sylvia De Causter and Mary Ann Lewis, Feb. 15, 1892, inability affidavit, Feb. 15, 1892, pension file for Isaac (Silvia) De Costa, RG 15, NARA.

47. "Rose Hill" in "Combahee River Plantations," private collection, 6, 10; Linder et al., *Historical Atlas*, 511–512.

48. Mary Anna Faber and Joshua Nicholls, Marriage Settlement, 1848, South Carolina Court of Equity (Charleston District), "Bills of Complaint, 1800–1863; Indexes, 1721–1868," South Carolina Department of Archives and History; "Rose Hill" in "Combahee River Plantations," 6, 10, private collection, Colleton County, SC; Mary Anna/Joshua Nicholls, St. Bartholomew Parish, agricultural census, 1850 US Census; Mary Anna/Joshua Nicholls, St. Michael and St. Philip Parish, agricultural census, 1850 US Census.

49. Mary Anna Faber and Joshua Nicholls, Marriage Settlement, 1848; deposition by Daphney Snipe, Apr. 16, 1901, pension file for Ned (Daphney) Snipe.
50. "Declaration for an Original Pension of a Mother," pension file for Stepheny (Flora) Grant.
51. "Declaration for an Original Pension of a Mother," Jun. 22, 1874, and Nov. 4, 1886, "Declaration for the Original Pension of a Father or Mother," Aug. 26, 1887, general affidavit by John A. Savage, Mar. 13, 1889, general affidavit by Flora Grant, Nov. 19, 1888, general affidavit by R. N. Rutledge, Oct. 19, 1888, general testimony by Flora Grant, Reuben N. Rutledge, and John A. Savage, Oct. 19, 1888, general affidavit by John Savage, Mar. 13, 1889, general affidavit by Andrew Wyatt, Mar. 27, 1889, general testimony by R. N. Rutledge, Apr. 26, 1889, general affidavit by John A. Savage, Oct. 19, 1889, pension file for Stepheny (Flora) Grant; Fleetwood, *Tidecraft*, 311–313.
52. Judith A. Carney, *Black Rice: The African Origins of Rice Cultivation in the Americas* (Cambridge, MA: Harvard University Press, 2001), 133–135; Leigh Ann Pruneau, "All the Time Is Work Time: Gender and the Task System on Antebellum Lowcountry Rice Plantations (South Carolina, Georgia, Slavery)," Ph.D. diss, University of Arizona, 1997, 44, 46, 50, 59, 67, 79–81, 83–84, 88, 105, 125, 128, 177, 208, 268, 271, 274, 314; Dusinberre, *Them Dark Days*, 7, 51, 62, 70–74, 136, 142, 296, 351, 406, 427, 475; Fleetwood, *Tidecraft*; Heyward, *Seed from Madagascar*, 30.
53. "Threshing" and "Pounding," Plantation Book of William Lowndes, 1802 to 1822, 48, William Lowndes Papers, Library of Congress; Carney, *Black Rice*, 17, 19, 27, 31, 53, 111–113; Schwalm, *"A Hard Fight for We,"* 14–15.
54. "Threshing" and "Pounding," Plantation Book of William Lowndes, 1802 to 1822, 48; Richard Dwight Porcher and William Robert Judd, *The Market Preparation of Carolina Rice: An Illustrated History of Innovations in the Lowcountry Rice Kingdom* (Columbia: University of South Carolina Press, 2014), 160, 172; Carney, *Black Rice*, 125–126, 131, 139–141; Pruneau, "All the Time Is Work Time," 68; Dusinberre, *Them Dark Days*, 9–71; Heyward, *Seed from Madagascar*, 22–23, 41.

CHAPTER 5

1. Henry "Box" Brown, *Narrative of the Life of Henry Box Brown, Written by Himself* (Chapel Hill: University of North Carolina Press, 2008), 8, 76, 79–81.
2. Benjamin Drew et al., *A North-Side View of Slavery: The Refugee, or, the Narratives of Fugitive Slaves in Canada: Related by Themselves, with an Account of the History and Condition of the Colored Population of Upper Canada* (Boston: John P. Jewett, 1856), 28–29; William Still, *The Underground Railroad: A Record of Facts, Authentic Narratives, Letters, &c., Narrating the Hardships, Hair-Breadth Escapes and Death Struggles of the Slaves in Their Efforts for Freedom, as Related by Themselves and Others, or Witnessed by the Author; Together with Sketches of Some of the Largest Stockholders, and Most Liberal Aiders and Advisers, of the Road* (Philadelphia: People's Publishing, 1878), 98, 132.

3. Drew et al., *A North-Side View of Slavery*, 29; Still, *The Underground Railroad*, 72, 143, 227.

4. Still, *The Underground Railroad*, 137, 296, 300–301.

5. Still, *The Underground Railroad*, 145, 164–165.

6. Ednah Dow Cheney, "Moses," *Freedmen's Record*, Jan. 1865, 35; Sarah Bradford, *Scenes in the Life of Harriet Tubman* (Auburn, NY: W. J. Moses, 1869; repr., North Stratford, NH: Ayer, 2004), 16–17; Sarah Bradford, *Harriet Tubman: The Moses of Her People* (1886; repr., New York: J. J. Little, 1901), 26–27.

7. Bradford, *Scenes in the Life of Harriet Tubman*, 16–17; Bradford, *Harriet Tubman*, 26–27.

8. Drew et al., *A North-Side View of Slavery*, 24; Cheney, "Moses," 36; Bradford, *Scenes in the Life of Harriet Tubman*, 21, 27, 58; Bradford, *Harriet Tubman*, 29, 64; Ednah Dow Cheney, *Reminiscences of Ednah Dow Cheney (Born Littlehale)* (Boston: Lee & Shepard, 1902), 81; Samuel Hopkins Adams, *Grandfather Stories* (New York: Random House, 1975), 271, 275.

9. Senator John Heinz History Center, "From Slavery to Freedom," permanent exhibit and online exhibit; personal communication with exhibit curator Samuel W. Black; Chesapeake Bay Program, "Field Guide," https://www.chesapeakebay.net/discover/field-guide/critters?fieldGuideType=Mammals#entry-30886.

10. Drew et al., *A North-Side View of Slavery*, 24; Cheney, "Moses," 34–36; Bradford, *Scenes in the Life of Harriet Tubman*, 21, 76; Bradford, *Harriet Tubman*, 61; Cheney, *Reminiscences*, 81; John W. Blassingame, *Slave Testimony: Two Centuries of Letters, Speeches, Interviews and Autobiographies* (Baton Rouge: Louisiana State University Press, 1977), 458; Adams, *Grandfather Stories*, 275.

11. Cheney, "Moses, " 35.

12. Cheney, "Moses, " 36; Bradford, *Scenes in the Life of Harriet Tubman*, 21, 27, 58; Bradford, *Harriet Tubman*, 29; Adams, *Grandfather Stories*, 272.

13. Bradford, *Scenes in the Life of Harriet Tubman*, 30–31, 76; Bradford, *Harriet Tubman*, 44–45, 53–54, 111; James A. McGowan, *Station Master on the Underground Railroad: The Life and Letters of Thomas Garrett* (Jefferson, NC: McFarland, 2009), 2, 32, 35, 52–55, 201–203.

14. Still, *The Underground Railroad*, 716–717; McGowan, *Station Master*, 55–57, 201–204.

15. Still, *The Underground Railroad*, 718; McGowan, *Station Master*, 57–60, 204–205, 208.

16. McGowan, *Station Master*, 60–65, 164, 190, 207.

17. Still, *The Underground Railroad*, 719; McGowan, *Station Master*, 1, 33, 82, 91, 116, 127–128, 186, 209.

18. Cheney, "Moses," 35; Bradford, *Harriet Tubman*, 30–31; Bradford, *Scenes in the Life of Harriet Tubman*, 19; Blassingame, *Slave Testimony*, 458–459; Adams, *Grandfather Stories*, 274.

19. Andrew K. Diemer, *Vigilance: The Life of William Still, Father of the Underground Railroad* (New York: Knopf, 2022), 7–8, 43–45, 49–50, 52, 64, 75, 87; R. J. M. Blackett, *The Captive's Quest for Freedom: Fugitive Slaves, the 1850 Fugitive Slave Law, and the Politics of Slavery* (New York: Cambridge University Press, 2018), 46.

20. Diemer, *Vigilance*, 4–6, 11–15, 22, 26, 69; McGowan, *Station Master*, 137.

21. Diemer, *Vigilance*, 6, 11–15, 26, 267.

22. Still, *The Underground Railroad*, 132; Diemer, *Vigilance*, 89–90; William C. Kashatus, *William Still: The Underground Railroad and the Angel at Philadelphia* (Notre Dame: University of Notre Dame Press, 2021), 7–8, 54, 77, 97, 126, 157, 160, 173, 210, 221–278; Larry Gara, "William Still and the Underground Railroad," *Pennsylvania History: A Journal of Mid-Atlantic Studies* 28, no. 1 (1961): 33–37.

23. Still, *The Underground Railroad*, 39–45; Diemer, *Vigilance*, 68–70, 267; Kashatus, *William Still*, 2; McGowan, *Station Master*, 16–18, 70.

24. McGowan, *Station Master*, 13–17.

25. Still, *The Underground Railroad*, 99–100, 103–104, 164–165; Deborah G. White, *Ar'n't I a Woman?: Female Slaves in the Plantation South*, rev. ed. (New York: W. W. Norton, 1999), 70–75.

26. Still, *The Underground Railroad*, 281–284; Brown, *Narrative*, 2–3, 44–47, 49, 85–87, 124, 32–33, 42, 46, 59–61, 82, 201.

27. Still, *The Underground Railroad*, 282–284.

28. Still, *The Underground Railroad*, 302–303.

29. Still, *The Underground Railroad*, 136–137.

30. Still, *The Underground Railroad*, 143.

31. Still, *The Underground Railroad*, 163–164, 290.

32. Cheney, "Moses," 36; Still, *The Underground Railroad*, 297; Blassingame, *Slave Testimony*, 425; Brown, *Narrative*, 8, 51; Wilbur Henry Siebert, *The Underground Railroad from Slavery to Freedom* (1898; repr., New York: Arno Press, 1968), 28.

33. McGowan, *Station Master*, 168–169, 172.

34. Bradford, Scenes in the *Life of Harriet Tubman*, 20; Bradford, *Harriet Tubman*, 61; Drew et al., *A North-Side View of Slavery*, 35; Cheney, "Moses," 35.

35. Drew et al., *A North-Side View of Slavery*, 30; Bradford, Scenes in the *Life of Harriet Tubman*, 76–77; Still, *The Underground Railroad*, 136; Bradford, *Harriet Tubman*, 61; Diemer, *Vigilance*, 103.

36. Drew et al., *A North-Side View of Slavery*, 3; Manisha Sinha, *The Slave's Cause: A History of Abolition* (New Haven, CT: Yale University Press, 2016), 500–501.

37. Historian Catherine Clinton designated Harriet Tubman an "abductor," because Tubman took freedom seekers all the way to freedom, not just from one depot on the Underground Railroad to another; see her *Harriet Tubman: The Road to Freedom* (Boston: Little, Brown, 2004), 67, 69, 73, 77. See also Drew et al., *A North-Side View of Slavery*, 3; Sinha, *The Slave's Cause*, 500–501; McGowan, *Station Master*, 14, 71.

38. Cheney, "Moses," 35; Bradford, *Scenes in the Life of Harriet Tubman*, 77; Bradford, *Harriet Tubman*, 39, 47; McGowan, *Station Master*, 72, 166, 177.

39. McGowan, *Station Master*, 105.

40. Cheney, "Moses," 36; McGowan, *Station Master*, 72, 166, 177.

41. Cheney, "Moses," 35–36; Bradford, *Scenes in the Life of Harriet Tubman*, 78; Bradford, *Harriet Tubman*, 111–112; Cheney, *Reminiscences*, 81; Chesapeake Bay Program, "Field Guide"; McGowan, *Station Master*, 166; Adams, *Grandfather Stories*, 169, 171.

42. Bradford, *Scenes in the Life of Harriet Tubman*, 50–51; Still, *The Underground Railroad*, 296; Bradford, *Harriet Tubman*, 23; McGowan, *Station Master*, 166; Adams, *Grandfather Stories*, 277–278.

43. Drew et al., *A North-Side View of Slavery*; Bradford, *Scenes in the Life of Harriet Tubman*, 27; Bradford, *Harriet Tubman*, 37; Cheney, "Moses," 35–36; Blassingame, *Slave Testimony*, 459–462; Adams, *Grandfather Stories*, 274–275.

44. Bradford, *Scenes in the Life of Harriet Tubman*, 76–77; Bradford, *Harriet Tubman*, 111–112.

45. Cheney, "Moses," 35; Cheney, *Reminiscences*, 81.

46. Cheney, "Moses," 35; Cheney, *Reminiscences*, 81.

47. Brown, *Narrative*, 8, 76, 79–81.

48. For another example of sale of an enslaved spouse being equivalent to divorce, see "Accrued Pension," general affidavit by Annie Plowden, Aug. 6, 1894, Assistant Chief of Law Division J. O. C. Roberts to Chief of the Eastern Division, Oct. 15, 1894, pension file of Walter (Annie) Plowden, RG 15, NARA; Elizabeth Donnan, *Documents Illustrative of the History of the Slave Trade to America, Volume II, The Eighteenth Century* (Washington, DC: Carnegie Institute of Washington, 1931), 419; Tera Hunter, *Bound in Wedlock: Slave and Free Black Marriage* (Cambridge, MA: Belknap Press of Harvard University Press, 2017), 38; Sylviane A. Diouf, *Servants of Allah: African Muslims Enslaved in the Americas* (New York: New York University Press, 2013), 234.

49. Cheney, "Moses," 35; Bradford, *Scenes in the Life of Harriet Tubman*, 77; Bradford, *Harriet Tubman*, 61.

50. Reverend Sam Green was ultimately jailed for possessing a copy of Harriet Beecher Stowe's *Uncle Tom's Cabin*. See Bradford, *Scenes in the Life of Harriet Tubman*, 30; Bradford, *Harriet Tubman*, 42.

51. Bradford, *Scenes in the Life of Harriet Tubman*, 60–61; Bradford, *Harriet Tubman*, 64–68.

52. Drew et al., *A North-Side View of Slavery*, 81; Still, *The Underground Railroad*, 247, 298–299; Bradford, *Scenes in the Life of Harriet Tubman*, 59; Bradford, *Harriet Tubman*, 65; Blassingame, *Slave Testimony*, 415–416.

53. Cheney, "Moses," 82; Blassingame, *Slave Testimony*, 462; Diemer, *Vigilance*, 156; McGowan, *Station Master*, 120.

54. Cheney, "Moses," 36; Still, *The Underground Railroad*, 72–73; McGowan, *Station Master*, 107–109, 79–81.

55. Still, *The Underground Railroad*, 74, 448; McGowan, *Station Master*, 108–109, 112–113, 142.

56. McGowan, *Station Master*, 106–107.

57. Bradford, *Scenes in the Life of Harriet Tubman*, 48; Bradford, *Harriet Tubman*, 82–83.

58. Still, *The Underground Railroad*, 51–52, 248–249, 639, 716; McGowan, *Station Master*, 182, 202.

59. Cheney, "Moses," 35; Still, *The Underground Railroad*, 395–396; Bradford, *Scenes in the Life of Harriet Tubman*, 52–53, 80–81; Bradford, *Harriet Tubman*, 115–116; Blassingame, *Slave Testimony*, 460; McGowan, *Station Master*, 110–114, 193; Adams, *Grandfather Stories*, 271.

CHAPTER 6

1. Duncan Clinch Heyward, Seed from Madagascar (1937; Columbia: University of South Carolina Press, 1993), 31, 35–36.

2. Heyward, *Seed from Madagascar*, 37–38.

3. Heyward, *Seed from Madagascar*, 38–39.

4. Daina Ramey Berry, "*Swing the Sickle for the Harvest Is Ripe*": Gender and Slavery in Antebellum Georgia (Urbana: University of Illinois Press, 2007), 23; Heyward, *Seed from Madagascar*, 39.

5. Charles Ball, *Slavery in the United States: A Narrative of the Life and Adventures of Charles Ball, a Black Man* (New York: John S. Taylor, 1837), 137; William Dusinberre, *Them Dark Days: Slavery in the American Rice Swamps* (Oxford: Oxford University Press, 1996), 53–54, 74–75, 240–241, 274, 412; Jill Dubisch, "Low Country Fevers: Cultural Adaptations to Malaria in Antebellum South Carolina," *Social Science and Medicine* 21, no. 6 (1985): 641–645; Peter H. Wood, *Black Majority: Negroes in Colonial South Carolina from 1670 Through the Stono Rebellion* (New York: Knopf, 1974), 70–75, 83.

6. James M. Clifton, ed., *Life and Labor on Argyle Island: Letters and Documents of a Savannah River Rice Plantation, 1833–1867* (Savannah, GA: Beehive Press, 1978), 85–86, 97, 127, 311; depositions by Andrew Wyatt, Silvia De Caster, Charlotte Savage, John A. Savage, and Diana Harris, Aug. 25, 1891, and by Mary A. Lewis, Aug. 26, 1891, pension file for Andrew (Marie) Wyatt, RG 15, NARA.

7. Frederick Law Olmsted, *A Journey in the Seaboard States: With Remarks on Their Economy* (New York: Knickerbocker Press, 1856), 2:46–47; Tony Horwitz, *Spying on the South: An Odyssey Across the American Divide* (New York: Penguin, 2020), 158, 222, 352; Dusinberre, *Them Dark Days*, 54, 74, 135; Wood, *Black Majority*, 91.

8. Claimant's affidavit by Diana Harris, Nov. 27, 1886, general affidavit by John A. Savage, Nov. 27, 1886, deposition by Diana Days Harris, Apr. 27, 1889, additional evidence by Diana Days Harris, n.d., pension file for Andrew (Diana) Harris, RG 15, NARA; deposition A by Diana Harris, Aug. 25, 1891, depositions by

Andrew Wyatt, Silvia De Caster, Charlotte Savage, John A. Savage, and Diana Harris, Aug. 25, 1891, deposition by Mary A. Lewis, Aug. 26, 1891, pension file for Andrew (Marie) Wyatt; attachment to additional evidence by Diana Days Harris, n.d., testimony by Diana Days Harris, Apr. 27, 1889, claimant's affidavit by Diana Days Harris, general affidavit by William Jones and John A. Savage, Nov. 27, 1886, pension file for Andrew (Diana) Harris.

9. General affidavit by W. M. Jones, Nov. 27, 1886, deposition by John A. Savage, Mar. 14, 1890, deposition A by Diana Harris, Aug. 25, 1891, pension file for Andrew (Marie) Wyatt; deposition A by Andrew Wyatt, Aug. 25, 1891, deposition B by Silvia De Caster, Aug. 25, 1891, deposition C by Charlotte Savage, Aug. 25, 1891, deposition by Mary A. Lewis, Aug. 26, 1891, pension file for Andrew (Marie) Wyatt; Dusinberre, *Them Dark Days*, 199, 240–241.

10. General affidavit by Lucius Robinson and Edward Brown, Aug. 5, 1893, pension file for July (Venus) Osborne, RG 15, NARA; attachment to additional evidence by Diana Days Harris, n.d., testimony by Diana Days Harris, Apr. 27, 1889, claimant's affidavit by Diana Days Harris, general affidavit by William Jones and John A. Savage, Nov. 27, 1886, pension file for Andrew (Diana) Harris; depositions by Andrew Wyatt, Silvia De Caster, Charlotte Savage, John A. Savage, and Diana Harris, Aug. 25, 1891, deposition by Mary A. Lewis, Aug. 26, 1891, pension file for Andrew (Marie) Wyatt; Frances Anne Kemble, *Journal of a Residence on a Georgian Plantation in 1838–1839* (1863; repr., Athens: University of Georgia Press, 1984), 130; Dusinberre, *Them Dark Days*, 49–51, 53, 55–56, 58, 61, 74, 80–81, 103, 121, 188, 237–238, 240–241, 245, 412–413, 415–416.

11. Frances Anne Kemble, *Journal of a Residence on a Georgian Plantation in 1838–1839* (1863; repr., Athens: University of Georgia Press, 1984), 130; Dusinberre, *Them Dark Days*, 49–51, 53, 55–56, 58, 61, 74, 80–81, 103, 121, 188, 237–238, 240–241, 245, 412–413, 415–416.

12. Clifton, *Life and Labor on Argyle Island*, xxvii–xxix; Kemble, *Journal of a Residence*, 55; Sheldon Watts, *Epidemics and History: Disease* (New Haven, CT: Yale University Press, 1997), 213–214, 222, 291, 642, 644; Dusinberre, *Them Dark Days*, 180, 187–189, 192–193, 274; Philip D. Curtin, "Disease Exchange Across the Tropical Atlantic," *History and Philosophy of the Life Sciences* 15, no. 3 (1993): 329, 344–346; Dubisch, "Low Country Fevers," 550, 641–645; H. Roy Merrens and George D. Terry, "Dying in Paradise: Malaria, Mortality, and the Perceptual Environment in Colonial South Carolina," *Journal of Southern History* 50, no. 4 (1984): 534, 540–542, 545, 547; Wood, *Black Majority*, 70–75, 83, 87–90; G. M. Edington, "Pathology of Malaria in West Africa," *British Medical Journal* 1, no. 5542 (1967): 717; Philip D. Curtin, "'The White Man's Grave:' Image and Reality, 1780–1850," *Journal of British Studies* 1, no. 1 (1961): 95–96; John Duffy, "Eighteenth-Century Carolina Health Conditions," *Journal of Southern History* 18, no. 3 (1952): 290–293, 298, 301; Lawrence Fay Brewster, *Summer Migrations and Resorts of South Carolina Low-Country Planters* (Durham, NC: Duke University Press, 1947), 113; St. Julien Ravenel Childs, "Malaria and

Colonization in the Carolina Low Country," *Johns Hopkins University Studies in Historical and Political Science* 58, no. 1 (1940): 186–189, 191, 208.

13. Clifton, *Life and Labor on Argyle Island*, xix; Beverly Robinson Scafidel, "The Letters of William Elliott," Ph.D. diss., University of South Carolina, 1978, 485–486; Eliza Cope Harrison, ed., *Best Companions: Letters of Eliza Middleton Fisher and Her Mother, Mary Hering Middleton, from Charleston, Philadelphia, and Newport, 1839–1846* (Columbia: University of South Carolina Press, 2001), 220; Brewster, *Summer Migrations and Resorts*, 95.

14. Harrison, *Best Companions*, 12, 24, 52, 256, 274, 448, 495–496, 500; Brewster, *Summer Migrations and Resorts*, 30–31, 116–117; Carl Bridenbaugh, "Charlestonians at Newport, 1767–1775," *South Carolina Historical and Genealogical Magazine* 41, no. 2 (1940): 43–44.

15. Harrison, *Best Companions*, 12, 52, 141, 274–275, 325, 394, 398–400, 441, 452, 458; Brewster, *Summer Migrations and Resorts*, 30–31, 33, 95; Allecia Hopton Middleton, *Life in Carolina and New England During the Nineteenth Century: As Illustrated by Reminiscences and Letters of the Middleton Family of Charleston, South Carolina, and of the Dewolf Family of Bristol, Rhode Island* (Bristol, RI: Privately printed, 1929), 155.

16. Moses Simmons, Aug. 21, 1868, Freedman's Bank Records; depositions by Moriah Bartley, Apr. 15, 1901, depositions by Phyllis Pinckney, Jackson Grant, Moses Simmons, and Cuffie Bolze, Oct. 20, 1898, deposition by William Hamilton, Oct. 21, 1898, general affidavit by Moriah Bartley, May 20, 1898, pension file for Anthony (Moriah) Bartley, RG 15, NARA; deposition D by Moses Simmons, Jul. 25, 1901, pension file for Moses (Fannie) Simmons, RG 15, NARA.

17. James Cuthbert to Thomas Rhett Smith Elliott, Conveyance, May 12, 1849, "Miscellaneous Records," Charleston Library Society; James Cuthbert to Thomas Rhett Smith Elliott, Mortgage, 1849, "South Carolina, Secretary of State, Slave Mortgage Records, 1734–1780," South Carolina Department of Archives and History, Columbia; Captain Brown, Feb. 16, 1872, Freedman's Bank Records; Frank Hamilton, Feb. 16, 1872, Freedman's Bank Records; Jackson Grant, Feb. 16, 1872, Freedman's Bank Records; Scafidel, "The Letters of William Elliott," xii.

18. Depostion by Jackson Grant, Oct. 16, 1896, deposition by Lucius Robinson, Oct. 24, 1896, depositions by Cuffy Bolze, Neptune Nichols, and Andrew Nicholas, Oct. 20, 1896, depositions by Walley Garrett and Solomon Salter, Oct. 22, 1896, deposition by Friday Hamilton, Oct. 24, 1896, deposition by William Hamilton, Oct. 31, 1896, deposition by Jackson Grant, Apr. 10, 1901, pension file for Jackson (Jane) Grant, RG 15, NARA; deposition by Jackson Grant, Jun. 15, 1895, pension file for Richard (Lucy, Fannie) Smith, RG 15, NARA.

19. Additional evidence by Friday Hamilton and Joe Morrison, Apr. 9, 1895, pension file for Frank (Captain Brown) Hamilton, RG 15, NARA; deposition by Dorcus Grant, May 3, 1897, pension file for Jack (Rebecca, Hercules) Wineglass, RG 15, NARA; deposition A by Jackson Grant, Apr. 10, 1901, pension file for

Jackson (Jane) Grant; deposition by Cuffee Bolze, Aug. 9, 1907, pension file for Charles (Ella) Nicholas, RG 15, NARA; "Case of Relia Middleton," deposition by Relia Middleton, Jan. 30, 1920, pension file for William (Relia) Middleton, RG 15, NARA.

20. Peter A. Coclanis, *The Shadow of a Dream: Economic Life and Death in the South Carolina Low Country, 1670–1920* (New York: Oxford University Press, 1989), 142.

21. Charleston Equity Court to William L. Kirkland, Partition, 1853, "Bills of Complaint, 1800–1863; Indexes, 1721–1868," Charleston County court records; Agnes Leland Baldwin, "Paul and Dalton Plantation," folder 1, 18, Agnes L. Baldwin Research Papers, 1966–2004, South Carolina Historical Society, Charleston; Suzanne Cameron Linder et al., *Historical Atlas of the Rice Plantations of the ACE River Basin—1860* (Columbia: South Carolina Department of Archives and History, 1995), 513.

22. Charleston Equity Court to William L. Kirkland, Partition, 1853; ""Rose Hill," in "Combahee River Plantations," 4, 10; Carolina Grant, Freedman's Bank Records, 1865–1874; Aug. 4, 1869, Freedman's Bank Record; Friday Hamilton, Freedman's Bank Record; Treasury Department, Second Auditor's Office, Aug. 19, 1889, "Declaration for an Original Pension of a Mother," Nov. 4, 1886, "Declaration for an Original Pension of a Father or Mother," Aug. 26, 1887, general affidavits by R. N. Rutledge and John Savage, Oct. 19, 1888, pension file for Stepney (Carolina and Flora) Grant, RG 15, NARA; deposition by Friday Hamilton, Apr. 17, 1901, pension file for Friday Hamilton, RG 15, NARA.

23. Widow's claim for pension by Binah Mack, Jun. 10, 1867, deposition by Moses James, Apr. 7, 1868, deposition by Sancho Van Dross, May 2, 1868, pension file for Harry (Bina) Mack, RG 15, NARA; "An Entire Gang of Ninety-Six (96) Negroes," *Charleston Mercury*, Mar. 10, 1853, and *Charleston Daily Courier,* Mar. 4, 1853; Binah Mack, Freedman's Bank Records, 928,587; Edward Rutledge Lowndes Estate to Arthur Middleton Parker, Bill of Sale, Mar. 10, 1853, "South Carolina, Charleston District, Estate Inventories, 1732–1844," South Carolina Department of Archives and History; Jeffery Strickland, "'Our Domestic Trials with Freedmen and Others': A White South Carolinian's Diary of African-American 'Exhibitions of Freedom,' 1865–80," *Prospects* 30 (2009): 121, 133.

24. Joshua and Mary Anna Nicholls and William L. Kirkland engaged in multiple transactions to acquire more enslaved laborers, capital, and equipment to produce more rice. Joshua Nicholls and William L. Kirkland Jr. to William C. Heyward, Bill of Sale, Jan. 14, 1852; William L. Kirkland to I. M. Lason & Bro., Memorandum of Agreement, Aug. 29, 1854; William L. Kirkland to Thomas R. S. Elliott, Mortgage, Feb. 5, 1857, Papers of the Kirkland, Withers, Snowden, and Trotter Families, South Caroliniana Library, Columbia, SC, 157–158, 164,

171–172; Scafidel, "The Letters of William Elliott," 85, 99; "Rose Hill" in "Combahee River Plantations," 7, 11.

25. "Trans-Atlantic Slave Trade Database," www.slavevoyages.org (David Eltis and Martin Halbert, original principal investigators); Warren S. Howard, *American Slavers and the Federal Law, 1837–1862* (Berkeley: University of California Press, 1963), 145–147, 196, 198, 219–220, 250, 262, 300–301n15, 306–307n3.

26. Joshua and Mary Ann Nicholls to William L. Kirkland, Deed Exchange, Mar. 30, 1859, Papers of the Kirkland, Withers, Snowden, and Trotter Families, 175–181; Baldwin, "Paul and Dalton Plantation," folder 1, 15; "Rose Hill" in "Combahee River Plantations," 7; Linder al., *Historical Atlas*, 445, 513. The deed with which William L. Kirkland purchased 94 acres of swamp and 14 acres from Dr. Francis S. Parker and Sarah S. Parker has not been found; "Rose Hill" in "Combahee River Plantations," 4, 7, 10; Linder et al., *Historical Atlas*, 445, 513.

27. Joshua and Mary Anna Nicholls to William L. Kirkland, Deed Exchange, 1859; claimant's affidavit by Diana Harris Nov. 27, 1886, "Widow's Declaration for Pension or Increase of Pension," Sep. 14, 1886, general affidavits by W. M. Jones and John Savage, Nov. 27, 1886, depositions by Diana Harris and John A. Savage, Mar. 14, 1890, pension file for Andrew (Diana) Harris; Linder et al., *Historical Atlas*, 513.

28. Joshua and Mary Anna Nicholls to William L. Kirkland, Deed Exchange, 1859; Department of the Interior, Bureau of Pensions, Jan. 2, 1915, "Act of May 11, 1912, Declaration for Pension," May 20, 1912, "Act of February 6, 1907, Declaration for Pension," Nov. 17, 1908, [untitled] by William Elliott, depositions by Mingo Van Dross, Aug. 16, 1911, and Apr. 9, 1901, affidavit by Mingo Van Dross, Dec. 11, 1908, pension file for Mingo (Emma) Van Dross, RG 15, NARA.

29. "Carolina Judge: The Life of Thomas Jefferson Withers" (page in document n.p., n.p., n.p., 3), Papers of the Kirkland, Withers, Snowden, and Trotter Families; Randolph W. Kirkland, "Reminiscences of Childhood Mary Miller Withers Kirkland," Kirkland Family History and Genealogy Research Files, 4; "Rose Hill" in "Combahee River Plantations," 4.

30. Mary Miller Kirkland, "Reminiscences of My Childhood," 4, Withers Family Papers, 1823–1923, South Carolina Historical Society, Charleston.

31. Kirkland, "Reminiscences," 5–6.

32. "Carolina Judge: The Life of Thomas Jefferson Withers" (pages in document n.p., n.p.), Papers of the Kirkland, Withers, Snowden, and Trotter Families, 5, 7; Mary Withers Kirkland, "Reminiscences of Childhood," Withers Family Papers, 1823–1923, South Carolina Historical Society, Charleston, 5–6.

33. Joshua Nicholls, Mary Ann Nicholls, and William L. Kirkland Indenture 1859, Papers of the Kirkland, Withers, Snowden, and Trotter Families; "Carolina Judge" (pages in document n.p., n.p.), 5, 7; Kirkland, "Reminiscences of Childhood," 5–6; Kirkland, "Reminiscences," 6–7; Linder et al., *Historical Atlas*, 513.

34. 1860 US Census, St. Bartholomew Parish: Joshua Nicholls, Slave Schedule, William Kirkland, Slave Schedule, William L. Kirkland Jr., Slave Schedule, Joshua Nicholls, Slave Schedule, William L. Kirkland Jr., Agricultural Schedule, Joshua Nicholls, Agricultural Schedule (Kirkland is listed as W. C. Kirkland); "Rose Hill" in "Combahee River Plantations," 3, 8, 10.

35. Arthur M. Parker to James L. Parker, bill of sale, Dec. 20, 1859, "South Carolina, Charleston District, Bill of Sales of Negro Slaves, 1774–1872"; Charleston County, Register of Deeds, Deed Book Z-13, 86, South Carolina Department of Archives and History, Columbia; Colleton County, Register of Deeds, Deed Book D, 158–159; Linder et al., *Historical Atlas*, 264, 445.

36. Francis S. Parker and Arthur M. Parker to James L. Paul, bill of sale, Dec. 20, 1859, "South Carolina, Charleston District, Bill of Sales of Negro Slaves, 1774–1872"; James L. Paul, Slave Schedule, 1860, St. Bartholomew's Parish; Andrew Wiatt, United States Census, 1870; deposition by Andrew Wyatt, Aug. 25, 1891, pension file for Andrew (Marie) Wyatt.

37. Francis S. Parker and Arthur M. Parker to James L. Paul, Bill of Sale, Dec. 20, 1859, "South Carolina, Charleston District, Bill of Sales of Negro Slaves, 1774–1872"; Kemble, *Journal of a Residence*, 77.

38. Joseph Blake to Walter Blake, Conveyance, 1860, "South Carolina, Charleston District, Bill of Sales of Negro Slaves, 1774–1872," South Carolina Department of Archives and History; Agnes Leland Baldwin, "Bonny Hall," 24, Agnes L. Baldwin Research Papers, 1966–2004, South Carolina Historical Society, Charleston; Linder et al., *Historical Atlas*, 365.

39. Joseph Blake to Walter Blake, Conveyance, 1860; Walter Blake Undated Slave List, Pringle Family Papers, 1745–1897, South Carolina Historical Society, Charleston (sincere thanks to Darius Brown for sharing this document with me from his family research); "List of Negroes on Plantations Bonny Hall Pleasant Hill New Ground Packers Blakefield True Blue Cypress Gang & Their Increase Newington Gang Property of Jos Blake," Pringle Family Papers, 1745–1897; exhibit by Wally Graham, Dec. 14, 1876, pension file for William (Sina) Young; deposition by Hamilton Brown, Feb. 15, 1896, depositions by Diana Middleton and Henry Green, Feb. 17, 1896, pension file for Jack (Hammond Brown) Morton, RG 15, NARA; Langdon Cheves, "Blake of South Carolina," *South Carolina Historical and Genealogical Magazine* 1 (1990): 161–162.

40. 1860 US Census: Walter Blake, Slave Schedule, Agricultural Schedule, St. Peter's Parish; Walter Blake, Slave Schedule, Henderson, NC; Walter Blake Agt., Slave Schedule, St. William's Parish; Walter Blake Agt., Agricultural Schedule, Prince William's Parish.

41. Clifton, *Life and Labor on Argyle Island*, xxxv; Harrison, *Best Companions*, 295n1; D. E. Huger Smith, Alice R. Huger Smith, and Arney R. Childs, eds., *Mason Smith Family Letters, 1860–1868* (Columbia: University of South Carolina Press, 1950), 7.

CHAPTER 7

1. James A. McGowan, *Station Master on the Underground Railroad: The Life and Letters of Thomas Garrett* (Jefferson, NC: McFarland, 2009), 98, 106, 168.

2. Sarah Bradford, *Scenes in the Life of Harriet Tubman* (Auburn, NY: W. J. Moses, 1869; repr., North Stratford, NH: Ayer, 2004), 51–53, 80–81; Sarah Bradford, *Harriet Tubman: The Moses of Her People* (1886; repr., New York: J. J. Little, 1901), 76, 78; McGowan, *Station Master on the Underground Railroad: The Life and Letters of Thomas Garrett,* 14, 98, 104, 111–112, 164–166, 169, 171, 175–177, 181, 192.

3. Henry Mayer, *All on Fire: William Lloyd Garrison and the Abolition of Slavery* (New York: St. Martin's Press, 1998), xii, xv, xvii, 40, 445.

4. Frederick Douglass, *The Frederick Douglass Papers: Series One: Speeches, Debates and Interviews*, ed. John W. Blassingame, ed. (New Haven, CT: Yale University Press, 1979), 4:503–509; Manisha Sinha, *The Slave's Cause: A History of Abolition* (New Haven, CT: Yale University Press, 2016), 590.

5. Mayer, *All on Fire*, 131, 139, 145, 156, 170, 194.

6. Washington Irving, *The Complete Works of Washington Irving in One Volume: With a Memoir of the Author* (Paris: Baudry's European Library, 1834), 30; Sinha, *The Slave's Cause*, 590; Mayer, *All on Fire*, xiii, xvi–xviii, 40, 53–54, 67, 70, 101, 112, 115, 125, 128, 445, 468.

7. David W. Blight, *Frederick Douglass: Prophet of Freedom* (New York: Simon & Schuster, 2018), 98–100, 119–120; Sinha, *The Slave's Cause*, 590; Mayer, *All on Fire*, xiii, 101, 468.

8. Louisa May Alcott, *The Journals of Louisa May Alcott*, ed. Joel Myerson and Daniel Shealy (Boston: Little, Brown, 1989), 15.

9. Sinha, *The Slave's Cause*, 121–122, 131–144, 223, 510–511, 515, 541, 548; Mayer, *All on Fire*, 372.

10. Douglass, *The Frederick Douglass Papers: Series One*, 1:30; Blight, *Frederick Douglass,* 102, 108, 119, 127, 173, 191, 200, 292, 306; Mayer, *All on Fire*, 372.

11. Blight, *Frederick Douglass*, 215, 313; Sinha, *The Slave's Cause*, 495–496.

12. Thomas Wentworth Higginson, *Letters and Journals of Thomas Wentworth Higginson, 1846–1906*, ed. Mary Thacher Higginson (1921; repr., Boston: Houghton Mifflin, 1969), 77–79; Blight, *Frederick Douglass*, 104, 215; Sinha, *The Slave's Cause*, 416, 470–471, 473, 485; Mayer, *All on Fire*, 143, 222, 236, 250, 257, 261–262, 267, 313–315, 317–321, 326, 338–339, 341, 472, 551.

13. Mayer, *All on Fire*, 110, 115–117.

14. Virginia Elwood-Akers, *Caroline Severance* (New York: iUniverse, 2010), 22–23, 27–28, 34–35, 42–43, 51–53, 56.

15. Elwood-Akers, *Caroline Severance*, 62–63.

16. Robert Gould Shaw, *Blue-Eyed Child of Fortune: The Civil War Letters of Colonel Robert Gould Shaw*, ed. Russell Duncan (Athens: University of Georgia Press, 1992), 2–4, 6–7, 9–10, 13–15, 17, 21, 23.

17. Douglass, *The Frederick Douglass Papers: Series One*, 2:275–277; Blight, *Frederick Douglass*, 234, 240–242, 246, 279; Mayer, *All on Fire*, 405–413, 432, 441–443.

18. Sinha, *The Slave's Cause*, 545–546; Tony Horwitz, *Midnight Rising: John Brown and the Raid That Sparked the Civil War* (New York: Henry Holt, 2011), 15, 39, 41, 44; Mayer, *All on Fire*, 440, 479.

19. Higginson, *Letters and Journals*, 77; Blight, *Frederick Douglass*, 293–295; Sinha, *The Slave's Cause*, 545–546, 548; Horwitz, *Midnight Rising*, 45, 52–59.

20. Kenneth Walter Cameron, Franklin Benjamin Sanborn, and Benjamin Smith Lyman, *Young Reporter of Concord: A Checklist of F. B. Sanborn's Letters to Benjamin Smith Lyman, 1853–1867, with Extracts Emphasizing Life and Literary Events in the World of Emerson, Thoreau and Alcott* (Hartford, CT: Transcendental Books, 1978), 11–12; Benjamin Blakely Hicock, "The Political and Literary Careers of F. B. Sanborn," Ph.D. diss., Michigan State College of Agriculture and Applied Science, 1953, 126, 133, 194–196.

21. Cameron, Sanborn, and Lyman, *Young Reporter of Concord*, 9–11.

22. James Montgomery to Franklin Sanborn, Jan. 14, 1861, George L. Stearns Collection, Kansas Historical Society.

23. Higginson, *Letters and Journals*, 137–143; Eliza Cope Harrison, ed., *Best Companions: Letters of Eliza Middleton Fisher and Her Mother, Mary Hering Middleton, from Charleston, Philadelphia, and Newport, 1839–1846* (Columbia: University of South Carolina Press, 2001), 12, 12nn45–46, 70–71, 71n3, 95, 118, 123–124, 145, 154, 187; Blight, *Frederick Douglass*, 295–296; Sinha, *The Slave's Cause*, 550, 556.

24. Horwitz, *Midnight Rising*, 88–90.

25. Blight, *Frederick Douglass*, 282; Sinha, *The Slave's Cause*, 550–551; Horwitz, *Midnight Rising*, 113; Mayer, *All on Fire*, 477, 479–480.

26. Frederick Douglass, "Editorial Correspondence," *The North Star*, February 11, 1848; Frederick Douglass, *Life and Times of Frederick Douglass, Written by Himself. His Early Life as a Slave, His Escape from Bondage, and His Complete History to the Present Time, Including His Connection with the Anti-Slavery Movement* (Hartford, CT: Park, 1882), 278, 385; Blight, *Frederick Douglass*, 280–281, 288, 297; Horwitz, *Midnight Rising*, 30–31, 74, 122, 186, 337; Mayer, *All on Fire*, 477.

27. Douglass, *Life and Times*, 278; Blight, *Frederick Douglass*, 282, 303; Horwitz, *Midnight Rising*, 113–116, 234.

28. Bradford, *Scenes in the Life of Harriet Tubman*, 82; Bradford, *Harriet Tubman*, 96, 118–119; Kate Clifford Larson, *Bound for the Promised Land: Harriet Tubman, Portrait of an American Hero* (New York: Ballantine Books, 2009), 170–175; Richard Warch and Jonathan F. Fanton, *John Brown* (Englewood Cliffs, NJ: Prentice-Hall, 1973), 39–40; Horwitz, *Midnight Rising*, 82.

29. Horwitz, *Midnight Rising*, 66, 71–72, 84; Ralph Volney Harlow, "Gerrit Smith and the John Brown Raid," *American Historical Review* 38, no. 1 (1932): 42.

30. Bradford, *Scenes in the Life of Harriet Tubman*, 5–6, 82; Bradford, *Harriet Tubman*, 118–119, 155–156; Sinha, *The Slave's Cause*, 551; Horwitz, *Midnight Rising*, 238.

31. Douglass, *Life and Times*, 279; Blight, *Frederick Douglass*, 331–314; Horwitz, *Midnight Rising*, 71, 115.

32. Frederick Douglass, *John Brown: An Address by Frederick Douglass, at the Fourteenth Anniversary of Storer College, Harper's Ferry, West Virginia, May 30, 1881*

(Dover, NH: Morning Star, 1881), 9; Blight, *Frederick Douglass*, 280; Sinha, *The Slave's Cause*, 551; Horwitz, *Midnight Rising*, 509.

33. William Wells Brown, *The Rising Son; or, the Antecedents and Advancement of the Colored Race* (New York: Negro Universities Press, 1970), 537.

34. Higginson, *Letters and Journals*, 81.

35. J. M. W. Yerrington, "'Independence Day': Anti-Slavery Celebration at Framingham," *The Liberator*, Jul. 13, 1860, 1–2; Mayer, *All on Fire*, 347, 443–445.

36. Yerrington, "'Independence Day'"; Higginson, *Letters and Journals*, 81–82; Mayer, *All on Fire*, 347, 443–445.

37. Yerrington, "'Independence Day.'"

38. Sinha, *The Slave's Cause*, 554; Horwitz, *Midnight Rising*, 133, 136–911, 202–203, 206–207, 256.

39. Ednah Dow Cheney, "Moses," *Freedmen's Record*, Jan. 1865, 35; McGowan, *Station Master*, 168–169, 176, 183, 193.

40. Cheney, "Moses," 35; John W. Blassingame, *Slave Testimony: Two Centuries of Letters, Speeches, Interviews and Autobiographies* (Baton Rouge: Louisiana State University Press, 1977), 459.

41. Horwitz, *Midnight Rising*, 207, 213; Mayer, *All on Fire*, 504.

42. Bradford, *Scenes in the Life of Harriet Tubman*, 82–83; Bradford, *Harriet Tubman*, 118–119.

43. Blassingame, *Slave Testimony*, 463.

44. Mary Potter Thacher Higginson, *Thomas Wentworth Higginson; the Story of His Life* (Boston : Houghton Mifflin, 1914), 196–200.

45. Wendell Phillips, "The Burial of John Brown, the Funeral, Speeches of Mr. McKim and Mr. Phillips, " *New York Daily Tribune*, Dec. 17, 1859.

46. "Speech of William Lloyd Garrison, at the Annual Meeting of the Massachusetts Anti-Slavery Society," *The Liberator*, Feb. 17, 1860; Mayer, *All on Fire*, 505.

47. Bradford, *Scenes in the Life of Harriet Tubman*, 88, 92; Bradford, *Harriet Tubman*, 119–120.

48. Bradford, *Scenes in the Life of Harriet Tubman*, 90, 93–94; Bradford, *Harriet Tubman*, 119–120, 124–126; Scott Christianson, *Freeing Charles: The Struggle to Free a Slave on the Eve of the Civil War* (Urbana: University of Illinois Press, 2010), 7–9, 11–12, 17–18, 22, 42–43, 88–89, 199–200; Arthur James Weise, *History of the City of Troy: From the Expulsion of the Mohegan Indians to the Present Centennial Year of the Independence of the United States of America, 1876* (Troy, NY: W. H. Young, 1876), 224–225.

49. Bradford, *Scenes in the Life of Harriet Tubman*, 94–95; Bradford, *Harriet Tubman*, 166–167; Christianson, *Freeing Charles*, 107; Weise, *History of the City of Troy*, 225.

50. Bradford, *Scenes in the Life of Harriet Tubman*, 96–97; Bradford, *Harriet Tubman*, 127; Christianson, *Freeing Charles*, 86–87, 91, 107, 109, 111; Weise, *History of the City of Troy*, 225.

51. Bradford, *Scenes in the Life of Harriet Tubman*, 97; Bradford, *Harriet Tubman*, 120, 126; Christianson, *Freeing Charles*, 107.

52. Bradford, *Scenes in the Life of Harriet Tubman*, 97; Bradford, *Harriet Tubman*, 122–123, 126–127; Blassingame, *Slave Testimony*, 463; Christianson, *Freeing Charles*, 463; Samuel Hopkins Adams, *Grandfather Stories* (New York: Random

House, 1975), 275–276; Hildegarde Hoyt Swift, *The Railroad to Freedom: A Story of the Civil War* (New York: Harcourt, 1932), 231; Weise, *History of the City of Troy*, 225–226.

53. Bradford, *Scenes in the Life of Harriet Tubman*, 98–99; Bradford, *Harriet Tubman*, 123, 127; Christianson, *Freeing Charles*, 115–118, 120–211; Weise, *History of the City of Troy*, 226–227.

54. Cheney, "Moses," 37; Bradford, *Scenes in the Life of Harriet Tubman*, 88–91; Bradford, *Harriet Tubman*, 122–123; Adams, *Grandfather Stories*, 275–276.

55. "A Fugitive Slave Case in Troy," *Troy Daily Whig*, April 28, 1860; Cheney, "Moses," 37; Christianson, *Freeing Charles*, 222–225.

                                   CHAPTER 8

1. *Official Records of the Union and Confederate Navies in the War of the Rebellion*, ser. 1, vol. XII (Washington, DC: GPO, 1900), 300–302; Michael Coker, *The Battle of Port Royal* (Charleston, SC: History Press, 2009), 10; Kevin John Weddle, *Lincoln's Tragic Admiral: The Life of Samuel Francis Du Pont* (Charlottesville: University of Virginia Press, 2005), 127.

2. Augustus Alonzo Hoit to Rebecca Guptill Hoit, Nov. 7, 1861, Augustus Alonzo Hoit Papers, 1861–1865, South Caroliniana Library, University of South Carolina, Columbia; J. Smith DuShane to Adela McMillan, Nov. 22, 1861, J. Smith DuShane Letters, 1860–1862, Southern Historical Collection, University of North Carolina, Chapel Hill; *Official Records of the Union and Confederate Navies*, ser. 1, vol. XII, 262–265, 300–302; A Citizen of Alexandria, *Life of Luther C. Ladd: The First Martyr That Fell a Sacrifice to His Country in the City of Baltimore on the 19th of April, 1861, While Bravely Defending the Flag of the Nation, Exclaiming with His Dying Breath, "All Hail to the Stars and Stripes!"; Also an Account of the Brilliant Naval Engagement of Port Royal* (Concord, NH: P. B. Cogswell, 1862), 33; Weddle, *Lincoln's Tragic Admiral*, 131.

3. Augustus Alonzo Hoit to Rebecca Guptill Hoit, Nov. 7, 1861; J. Smith DuShane to Adela McMillan, Nov. 22, 1861; *The War of the Rebellion: A Compilation of the Official Records of the Union and Confederate Armies*, ser. 1, vol. VI (Washington, DC: GPO, 1880–1901), 186; *Official Records of the Union and Confederate Navies*, ser. 1, vol. XII, 262–265; Kate Clifford Larson, *Harriet Tubman Underground National Monument: Historic Resource Study* (Washington, DC: National Park Service, 2019), 264; Kate Clifford Larson, *Bound for the Promised Land: Harriet Tubman: Portrait of an American Hero* (New York: One World/Ballantine, 2009), 194; Weddle, *Lincoln's Tragic Admiral*, 131; Sarah Bradford, *Scenes in the Life of Harriet Tubman* (1869; repr., North Stratford, NH: Ayer, 2004), 84; Rowland, Moore, and Rogers, *The History of Beaufort County, Volume I*, 451–454; Charles Dana Gibson and E. Kay Gibson, *Assault and Logistics: Union Army Coastal and River Operations, 1861–1866*, vol. 2 (Camden, ME: Ensign Press, 1995), 15; George M. Blackburn, *With the Wandering Regiment: The Diary of Captain Ralph Ely of the Eighth Michigan Infantry* (Mount Pleasant: Central Michigan

University Press, 1965), 3; Willie Lee Rose, *Rehearsal for Reconstruction: The Port Royal Experiment* (Indianapolis: Bobbs-Merrill, 1964), 104–106.

4. Charles Nordhoff, "Two Weeks at Port Royal," *Harper's New Monthly Magazine*, Jun. 1863, 111; A Citizen of Alexandria, *Life of Luther C. Ladd*, 40; *Official Records of the Union and Confederate Navies*, ser. 1, vol. XII, 262–295, 298–299, 301, 304, 307; Blackburn, *With the Wandering Regiment*, 4; Elizabeth Hyde Botume, *First Days Amongst the Contrabands* (Boston: Lee and Shepard, 1893), 29; Coker, *The Battle of Port Royal*, 67. Daniel Ammen, *The Navy in the Civil War: The Atlantic Coast* (London: Sampson Low, Marston, 1898), 16, 18.

5. High tide at Ribaut Island was at 11:54 a.m. on November 7, 1861. See https://tidesandcurrents.noaa.gov/noaatidepredictions.html?id=8668918&units=standard&bdate=18611101&edate=18611129&timezone=LST/LDT&clock=12hour&datum=MLLW&interval=hilo&action=dailychart; Augustus Alonzo Hoit to Rebecca Guptill Hoit, Nov. 7, 1861; J. Smith DuShane to "My Dear Sister," Nov. 25, 1861, J. Smith Dushane Papers, 1860–1862"; A Citizen of Alexandria, *Life of Luther C. Ladd*; NOAA, "What Are Spring and Neap Tides?," https://oceanservice.noaa.gov/facts/springtide.html; *Official Records of the Union and Confederate Navies*, ser. 1, vol. XII, 262–265, 305, 335, 323.

6. A Citizen of Alexandria, *Life of Luther C. Ladd*, 35; *Official Records of the Union and Confederate Navies*, ser. 1, vol. XII, 262–265, 302.

7. Augustus Alonzo Hoit to Rebecca Guptill Hoit, Nov. 7, 1861; A Citizen of Alexandria, *Life of Luther C. Ladd*, 35; *Official Records of the Union and Confederate Navies*, ser. 1, vol. XII, 262–265, 302; Blackburn, *With the Wandering Regiment*, 4; Douglas Southall Freeman, *R. E. Lee, a Biography* (New York: Scribner, 1934–1935), 1:610; Ammen, *The Navy in the Civil War*, 22–25; Charles Cowley, *The Romance of History in "the Black County," and the Romance of War in the Career of Gen. Robert Smalls, "the Hero of the Planter"* (Lowell, MA: 1882), 7.

8. Augustus Alonzo Hoit to Rebecca Guptill Hoit, Nov. 7, 1861; *Official Records of the Union and Confederate Navies*, ser. 1, vol. XII, 262–265; Coker, *The Battle of Port Royal*, 75, 96; Ammen, *The Navy in the Civil War*, 22–25.

9. A Citizen of Alexandria, *Life of Luther C. Ladd*, 38–39; *Official Records of the Union and Confederate Navies*, ser. 1, vol. XII, 262–265; Ammen, *The Navy in the Civil War*, 22–25.

10. J. Smith DuShane to "My Dear Sister," Nov. 25, 1861; A Citizen of Alexandria, *Life of Luther C. Ladd*, 37, 39; *Official Records of the Union and Confederate Navies*, ser. 1, vol. XII, 262–302. 307.

11. J. Smith DuShane to Adela McMillan, Nov. 22, 1861; A Citizen of Alexandria, *Life of Luther C. Ladd*; *Official Records of the Union and Confederate Navies*, ser. 1, vol. XII, 295; Military Historical Society of Massachusetts, *Operations on the Atlantic Coast, 1861–1865, Virginia 1862, 1864, Vicksburg* (Boston: Military Historical Society, 1912), 113.

12. J. Smith DuShane to "My Dear Sister," Nov. 25, 1861; Egbert L. Viele, "The Port Royal Expedition," *Magazine of American History* 14, no. 4 (1885): 329–331; Weddle, *Lincoln's Tragic Admiral*, 140–141; Daniel Ammen, "Du Pont and the

Port Royal Experiment," in *Battle and Leaders of the Civil War*, ed. Robert Underwood Johnson and Clarence Buel (1888; repr., New York: Appleton-Century-Crofts, 1956), 691.

13. H. David Stone, *Vital Rails: The Charleston & Savannah Railroad and the Civil War in Coastal South Carolina* (Columbia: University of South Carolina Press, 2008), 70; Weddle, *Lincoln's Tragic Admiral*, 14; Rose, *Rehearsal for Reconstruction*, 22; Freeman, *R. E. Lee*, 608.

14. "The War on the Seacoast—Our Casualties on New Year's Day," *Charleston Mercury*, Jan. 9, 1862; Coker, *The Battle of Port Royal*, 10–11; Stone, *Vital Rails*, 18, 24–25, 51–52, 70–71, 80; Stephen R. Wise, *Gate of Hell: Campaign for Charleston Harbor*, 1863 (Columbia: University of South Carolina Press, 1994) 10; Rose, *Rehearsal for Reconstruction*, 23; Freeman, *R. E. Lee*, 608–609.

15. Charleston and Savannah Railroad, "Report of the President of the Charleston & Savannah Railroad, 1863," Southern Historical Collection, University of North Carolina, Chapel Hill, 9, 22–25; Ulrich Bonnell Phillips, *A History of Transportation in the Eastern Cotton Belt to 1860* (New York: Columbia University Press, 1908), 363–364.

16. *Official Records of the Union and Confederate Armies*, ser. 1, vol. VI, 312; Stone, *Vital Rails*, 70, 80, 89; Freeman, *R. E. Lee*, 610–611, 613–615, 628.

17. P. J. Staudenraus, "Occupied Beaufort, 1863: A War Correspondent's View," *South Carolina Historical Magazine* 64, no. 3 (1963): 142; Nordhoff, "Two Weeks at Port Royal," 111; Augustus Alonzo Hoit to Rebecca Guptill Hoit, Nov. 7, 1861; *The War of the Rebellion: A Compilation of the Official Records of the Union and Confederate Armies*, ser. 1, vol. VI (Washington, DC: GPO, 1880–1901), 186–187; Botume, *First Days Amongst the Contrabands*, 31; Blackburn, *With the Wandering Regiment*, 4; Stone, *Vital Rails*, 70–71; Weddle, *Lincoln's Tragic Admiral*, 128, 40–41; Wise, *Gate of Hell*, 10; Ammen, *The Navy in the Civil War*, 16, 18.

18. *Official Records of the Union and Confederate Armies*, ser. 1, vol. VI, 186, 257; Blackburn, *With the Wandering Regiment*, 3; John S. Barnes, "The Battle of Port Royal, SC, from the Journal of John Sanford Barnes," ed. John D. Hays, *New-York Historical Society Quarterly* 45, no. 4 (1961): 365; Weddle, *Lincoln's Tragic Admiral*, 137; Edward A. Miller, *Lincoln's Abolitionist General: The Biography of David Hunter* (Columbia: University of South Carolina Press, 1997), 93, 96; Rose, *Rehearsal for Reconstruction*, 144; Charles Dana Gibson and E. Kay Gibson, *Assault and Logistics: Union Army Coastal and River Operations, 1861–1866*, vol. 2 (Camden, ME: Ensign Press, 1995), 14; Bern Anderson, *By Sea and by River: The Naval History of the Civil War* (New York: Knopf, 1962), 38–40; Richard S. West, *Mr. Lincoln's Navy* (New York: Longmans Green, 1957), 73; Ammen, *The Navy in the Civil War*, 13.

19. Coker, *The Battle of Port Royal*, 10–11; Miller, *Lincoln's Abolitionist General*, 1–3, 45–46, 77, 87.

20. General David Hunter to Senator Lyman Trumbull, Dec. 9, 1861, in *The Papers of Lyman Trumbull, 1843–1894* (Washington, DC: Library of Congress, 1918),

microfilm reel 12; Miller, *Lincoln's Abolitionist General*, 77–79, 82, 87, 114; Rose, *Rehearsal for Reconstruction*, 16–17.

21. "Notes by A. R. Chisolm on the Life of General G. T. Beauregard," January 2, 1893, 11, Alexander Robert Chisolm Papers: Military Records and Memoirs, New-York Historical Society; *The War of the Rebellion: Official Records*, ser. 1, vol. VI, 312; *Official Records of the Union and Confederate Navies*, ser. 1, vol. XII, 299–300, 53; Stone, *Vital Rails*, 72, 136; William N. Still, *Iron Afloat: The Story of the Confederate Armorclads* (Columbia: University of South Carolina Press, 1985), 7.

22. Stone, *Vital Rails*, 80, 111–112.

23. *Official Records of the Union and Confederate Armies*, ser. 1, vol. VI, 367, 391–393; Stone, *Vital Rails*, 70, 80.

24. *Official Records of the Union and Confederate Navies*, ser. 1, vol. XII, 300–307; Botume, *First Days Amongst the Contrabands*, 27–28; Military Historical Society of Massachusetts, *Operations on the Atlantic Coast*, 113; James M. Guthrie, *Camp-Fires of the Afro-American; or, the Colored Man as a Patriot, Soldier, Sailor, and Hero, in the Cause of Free America: Displayed in Colonial Struggles, in the Revoluntion, the War of 1812, and in Later Wars, Particularly the Great Civil War, 1861–5, and the Spanish American War, 1898: Concluding with an Account of the War with the Filipinos, 1899* (Philadelphia: Afro-American Publishing Co., 1899), 305.

25. Staudenraus, "Occupied Beaufort, 1863," 137, 139–140, 143; Charlotte L. Forten, *The Journal of Charlotte L. Forten: A Young Black Woman's Reaction to the White World of the Civil War Era*, ed. Ray Allen Billington (New York: Dryden Press, 1953), 144, 163; Charlotte Forten Grimké, *The Journals of Charlotte Forten Grimké*, ed. Brenda Stevenson (New York: Oxford University Press, 1988), 412–414, 443–445; Botume, *First Days Amongst the Contrabands*, 16; Federal Writers' Project, *Slave Narratives: A Folk History of Slavery in the United States, from Interviews with Former Slaves* (Washington, DC: Library of Congress, 1941), vol. 14, pt. 2, 279, 283–284, vol. 14, pt. 3, 202, 271, vol. 14, pt. 4, 48; Genevieve Chandler, Kincaid Mills, Genevieve C. Peterkin, and Aaron McCollough, eds., *Coming Through: Voices of a South Carolina Gullah Community from WPA Oral Histories* (Columbia: University of South Carolina Press, 2008), 14, 29, 38, 46, 63–64, 66, 76, 78, 82, 84, 98, 103, 107, 352; Rose, *Rehearsal for Reconstruction*, xv, 11, 15–17, 104, 167.

26. US Census, 1860, Index (AIS), 448–449; Laura M. Towne, *Letters and Diary of Laura M. Towne: Written from the Sea Islands of South Carolina, 1862–1884*, ed. Rupert Holland (Cambridge, MA: Riverside Press, 1912), 95; Rose, *Rehearsal for Reconstruction*, 104; Military Historical Society of Massachusetts, *Operations on the Atlantic Coast*, 114; Botume, *First Days Amongst the Contrabands*, 29.

27. There are even instances of slaveholders invoking Haiti as a place to where "Yankees" would sell slaves, though slaves were emancipated in Haiti in 1803 as a result of the Haitian Revolution. Henry W. Ravenel, *The Private Journal of Henry William Ravenel, 1859–1867,* ed. Arney Robinson Childs (Columbia:

University of South Carolina, 1947), 97, 102, 106, 142, 147; New England Freedmen's Aid Society, *First Annual Report of the Education Commission with Extracts from Letters of Teachers and Superintendents* (Boston: David Clapp, 1863), 22–23; Charles Nordhoff, *The Freedmen of South-Carolina: Some of Their Appearance, Character, Condition and Peculiar Customs* (New York: C. T. Evans, 1863), 12; Edward L. Pierce, "The Freedmen at Port Royal," *Atlantic Monthly*, Dec. 1863, 296; Susan Walker, "Journal of Miss Susan Walker: March 3d to June 6th, 1862," ed. Henry Noble Sherwood, *Quarterly Publication of the Historical and Philosophical Society of Ohio* 7, no. 1 (1912): 22; Towne, *Letters and Diary*, 27, 29; Forten, *Journal*, 144; Charlotte Forten, "Life on the Sea Islands: A Young Black Woman Describes Her Experiences Teaching Freedmen During the Civil War, Part I," *Atlantic Monthly*, May 1864, 593; Botume, *First Days Amongst the Contrabands*, 13; Higginson, *Army Life in a Black Regiment and Other Writings* (1900; repr., New York: Penguin Books, 1997), 13; Rose, *Rehearsal for Reconstruction*, 12, 17, 104, 105.

28. Ravenel, *Private Journal*, 106; Walker, "Journal," 37; Forten, *Journal*, 148, 160; Grimké, *Journals*, 419–420, 438–440; Forten, "Life on the Sea Islands, Part II," *Atlantic Monthly*, Jun. 1864, 667; Charles C. Coffin, *Four Years of Fighting* (Boston: Ticknor and Fields, 1866), 227–228; Higginson, *Army Life in a Black Regiment*, 9; Federal Writers' Project, *Slave Narratives*, vol. 14, pt. 3, 202–203; Rose, *Rehearsal for Reconstruction*, xvi, 12, 105; Ammen, *The Navy in the Civil War*, 37.

29. There are many examples of enslaved people who were forced to go with slaveholders onto the mainland and who returned to US-occupied territory on the Sea Islands. See Forten, "Life on the Sea Islands, Part II," 667–668.

30. Walker, "Journal," 37; Edward L. Pierce, "The Freedmen of South Carolina: Official Report Port Royal June 2 1862 Edward L. Pierce," *New-York Daily Tribune*, Jun. 17, 1862; Towne, *Letters and Diary*, 94–95; Forten, "Life on the Sea Islands, Part II," 667; Botume, *First Days Amongst the Contrabands*, 14, 58, 140; Susie King Taylor, *Reminiscences of My Life in Camp with the 33rd U.S. Colored Troops, Late 1st South Carolina Volunteers: A Black Woman's Civil War Memoirs* (Boston: Author, 1902), 40.

31. Ravenel, *Private Journal*, 93–94; Towne, *Letters and Diary*, 73; Botume, *First Days Amongst the Contrabands*, 11, 15, 28; Higginson, *Army Life in a Black Regiment*, 9–10; Rose, *Rehearsal for Reconstruction*, xvi; Ammen, *The Navy in the Civil War*, 35.

32. Samuel Francis Dupont, *Samuel Francis Dupont: A Selection from His Civil War Letters*, ed. John D. Hayes, vol. 1, *The Mission: 1860–1862* (Ithaca, NY: Eleuthurian Mills Historical Library, 1969), 231, 237–238; Elizabeth Ware Pearson, ed., *Letters from Port Royal Written at the Time of the Civil War* (1906; Project Gutenberg, 2008), 186; Walker, "Journal," 14, 34; Towne, *Letters and Diary*, 27–28; Forten, "Life on the Sea Islands, Part II," 670; Botume, *First Days Amongst the Contrabands*, 11, 34; Rose, *Rehearsal for Reconstruction*, 17; Ammen, *The Navy in the Civil War*, 34, 38.

33. Ravenel, *Private Journal*, 96–97, 102–103, 142, 147; Commodore Du Pont to Henry Winter Davis, Dec. 9, 1861, Du Pont MSS; Towne, Walker, "Journal," 37; Pearson, *Letters from Port Royal*, 119–120, 151, 185–186; Towne, *Letters and Diary*, 27–29, 85, 109; Botume, *First Days Amongst the Contrabands*, 138–139; Rose, *Rehearsal for Reconstruction*, xvi; Military Historical Society of Massachusetts, *Operations on the Atlantic Coast*, 114; Ammen, *The Navy in the Civil War*, 37.

34. "Account of Union Occupation of Port Royal," *New York Tribune*, Nov. 20, 1861; Walker, "Journal," 14, 15, 20; Pearson, *Letters from Port Royal*, 6–8, 10; New England Freedmen's Aid Society, First Annual Report, 23; Staudenraus, "Occupied Beaufort, 1863," 136–144; Forten, "Life on the Sea Islands, Part I," 590; *Official Records of the Union and Confederate Navies*, ser. 1, vol. XII, 337, 353; Botume, *First Days Amongst the Contrabands*, 28, 34, 39; Rose, *Rehearsal for Reconstruction*, xvi, 16; Military Historical Society of Massachusetts, *Operations on the Atlantic Coast*, 114; Hazard Stevens, *Life of Isaac Ingalls Stevens* (Boston: Houghton Mifflin, 1901), 354–355; Ammen, *The Navy in the Civil War*, 30–34, 39.

35. Charles Francis Adams Jr., Charles Francis Adams Sr., and Henry Brooks Adams, *A Cycle of Adams Letters, 1861–1865*, ed. Worthington Chauncy Ford (Boston: Houghton Mifflin, 1920), 127; Pierce, "The Freedmen at Port Royal," 297; Rose, *Rehearsal for Reconstruction*, 152; Albert Bushnell Hart, *Salmon Portland Chase: American Statesman* (Boston: Houghton, Mifflin, 1899), 259.

36. Pierce, "The Contrabands at Fortress Monroe," 627; Adam Goodheart, "The Shrug That Made History," *New York Times Magazine*, Apr. 3, 2011, 40.

37. Pierce, "The Contrabands at Fortress Monroe," 627; *The War of the Rebellion: A Compilation of Official Records of the Union and Confederate Armies*, ser. 2, vol. I (Washington, DC: GPO, 1921), 752; Goodheart, "The Shrug That Made History," 40; Chandra Manning, *Troubled Refuge: Struggling for Freedom in the Civil War* (New York: Alfred A. Knopf, 2016), 172.

38. Pierce, "The Contrabands at Fortress Monroe," 627; *The War of the Rebellion: A Compilation of Official Records of the Union and Confederate Armies*, ser. 2, vol. I, 650, 752.

39. *The War of the Rebellion: A Compilation*, ser. 2, vol. I, 754; Manning, *Troubled Refuge*, 172.

40. *Official Records of the Union and Confederate Armies*, ser 2., vol. I, 752; Manning, *Troubled Refuge*, 172; Pierce, "The Contrabands at Fortress Monroe," 628; Goodheart, "The Shrug That Made History," 42; Hart, *Salmon Portland Chase*, 256–257; Rose, *Rehearsal for Reconstruction*, 14.

41. Pierce, "The Contrabands at Fortress Monroe," 628; *Official Records of the Union and Confederate Armies*, ser. 1, vol. II, 53, 649–650; *Official Records of the Union and Confederate Armies*, ser. 2, vol. 1, 773, 777; Manning, *Troubled Refuge*, 173–176; James Oakes, *Freedom National: The Destruction of Slavery in the United States, 1861–1865* (New York: W. W. Norton, 2012), 143, 144, 192–194, 196, 202–203; Rose, *Rehearsal for Reconstruction*, 13, 22.

42. The term "contraband" simultaneously connoted both the property claims of slaveholders and the uncertainty of enslaved Blacks who fled to Union lines after the war. Towne hypothesized that the soldiers reassured escaped slaves that they were free. Some superintendents threatened them with reenslavement if

they did not work as free men. Other soldiers told Blacks that they were free and need not work. See Towne, *Letters and Diary*, 18, 25; Walker, "Journal," 30; Forten, *Journal*, 139; Grimké, *Journals*, 406–408; Seth Rogers, "War-Time Letters of Seth Rogers, M.D., Surgeon of the First South Carolina Afterwards the Thirty-Third USCT 1862–1863," Florida History Online, https://www.unf.edu/floridahistoryonline/Projects/Rogers/letters.html, 17–18, 41–42; Educational Commission, *First Annual Report of the Education Commission with Extracts from Letters of Teachers and Superintendents* (Boston: David Clapp, 1863), 27; Kate Masur, "'A Rare Phenomenon of Philological Vegetation': The Word 'Contraband' and the Meanings of Emancipation in the United States," *Journal of American History* 93, no. 4 (2007): 1056, 57; Rose, *Rehearsal for Reconstruction*, 15.

43. Mary Boykin Miller Chesnut, *Mary Chesnut's Civil War*, ed. C. Vann Woodward (New Haven, CT: Yale University Press, 1981), 228.

44. Chesnut, *Mary Chesnut's Civil War*, 228–229; W. Eric Emerson, *Sons of Privilege: The Charleston Light Dragoons in the Civil War* (Columbia: University of South Carolina Press, 2005), 38.

45. Chesnut, *Mary Chesnut's Civil War*, 229–230.

46. Chesnut, *Mary Chesnut's Civil War*, 229–230.

47. Rogers, "War-Time Letters," 24; Botume, *First Days Amongst the Contrabands*, 178.

48. Jack Frowers, "Story of a Black Refugee," *New York Semi-Weekly Tribune*, Jun. 24, 1864; 390; Botume, *First Days Amongst the Contrabands*, 178–180.

49. Benjamin Guterman, "Doing 'Good Brave Work': Harriet Tubman's Testimony at Beaufort, South Carolina," *Prologue Quarterly of the National Archives* 32, no. 3 (2000): 158, 161; Rose, *Rehearsal for Reconstruction*, 24.

50. Edward L. Pierce, "Light on the Slavery Question: The Negroes in South Carolina," *New-York Daily Tribune*, Feb. 19, 1862; *The War of the Rebellion: A Compilation*, ser. 1, vol. VI, 218, 222–223; Botume, *First Days Amongst the Contrabands*, 16–18; Kevin Dougherty, *The Port Royal Experiment: A Case Study in Development* (Jackson: University Press of Mississippi, 2014), 39, 87, 89–90. Rose, *Rehearsal for Reconstruction*, 20.

51. "John M. Forbes to Edward Atkinson," *Boston Advertiser*, 1862; "To the Editors of the Boston Daily Advertiser," *Boston Advertiser*, Jun. 10, 1862; Edward L. Pierce, "The Freedmen of South Carolina: Official Report Port Royal June 2 1862; Edward L. Pierce," *New-York Daily Tribune*, Jun. 17, 1862; Adams, Adams, and Adams, *A Cycle of Adams Letters*, 127; Dougherty, *The Port Royal Experiment*, 19; Rose, *Rehearsal for Reconstruction*, xviii.

52. "Harriet Tubman," *The Liberator*, Feb. 21, 1862; Catherine Clinton, *Harriet Tubman: The Road to Freedom* (Boston: Little, Brown, 2004), 152; Larson, *Bound for the Promised Land*, 196; Jean McMahon Humez, *Harriet Tubman: The Life and the Life Stories* (Madison: University of Wisconsin Press, 2003), 51; Earl Conrad, *General Harriett Tubman* (1943; Baltimore: Black Classic Press, 2019), 158.

53. "Harriet Tubman," *The Liberator*, Feb. 12, 1862; Bradford, *Harriet Tubman*, 6, 93–94; Botume, *First Days Amongst the Contrabands*, 179; Catherine Clinton, *Harriet Tubman*, 152; Larson, *Bound for the Promised Land*, 198, 203, 204; Humez,

Harriet Tubman, 49; Conrad, *General Harriett Tubman*, 158; Wilbur Henry Siebert, *The Underground Railroad from Slavery to Freedom* (New York: Arno Press, 1968), 189; Rose, *Rehearsal for Reconstruction*, 17.

54. Frank E. Howe to John A. Andrew, Jan. 10, 1862, and Frank Howe to John A. Andrew, Jan. 21, 1862, John A. Andrew Papers, 1772–1895, Massachusetts Historical Society, Boston; Charles P. Wood, "A History Concerning the Pension Claim of Harriet Tubman," in *Record Group 233: Records of the U.S. House of Representatives, 1789–2015* (Washington, DC: National Archives, 1868), 1; Emma P. Telford, *Harriet: The Modern Moses of Heroism and Visions* (Auburn, NY: Cayuga County Museum, 1905), 15; "Harriet Tubman Is Dead," *Auburn Citizen*, Mar. 12, 1913; Larson, *Bound for the Promised Land*, 196; Clinton, *Harriet Tubman*, 153; Humez, *Harriet Tubman*, 302; Conrad, *General Harriett Tubman*, 158.

55. Erik Heyl, *Early American Steamers* (Buffalo, NY: n.p., 1953), 31, 39–40, 45–46; Frank O. Braynard, "Baltic—a Famous American Ship," *Steamboat Bill of Facts*, Jun. 1953, 25, 26.

56. Telford, "Harriet," 15; Larson, *Harriet Tubman Underground National Monument*, 268; Larson, *Bound for the Promised Land*, 195, 204; Humez, *Harriet Tubman*, 52.

57. Franklin Benjamin Sanborn and Benjamin Smith Lyman, *Young Reporter of Concord: A Checklist of F. B. Sanborn's Letters to Benjamin Smith Lyman, 1853–1867, with Extracts Emphasizing Life and Literary Events in the World of Emerson, Thoreau and Alcott*, ed. Kenneth Walter Cameron (Hartford, CT: Transcendental Books, 1978), 33, 35; Bradford, *Scenes in the Life of Harriet Tubman*, 68–69, 84–85; Bradford, *Harriet Tubman*, 162; Telford, "Harriet," 15; Larson, *Bound for the Promised Land*, 177, 195; Humez, *Harriet Tubman*, 52, 244; Guterman, "Doing 'Good Brave Work,'" 157; Miller, *Lincoln's Abolitionist General*, 96–97.

58. Ednah Dow Cheney, "Moses," *Freedmen's Record*, Jan. 1865, 34; Ednah Dow Cheney, *Reminiscences of Ednah Dow Cheney (Born Littlehale)* (Boston: Lee & Shepard, 1902), 82; John W. Blassingame, *Slave Testimony: Two Centuries of Letters, Speeches, Interviews and Autobiographies* (Baton Rouge: Louisiana State University Press, 1977), 463; Larson, *Bound for the Promised Land*, 177; Clinton, *Harriet Tubman*, 152; Humez, *Harriet Tubman*, 50; *The War of the Rebellion: A Compilation*, ser. 1, vol. VI, 222; Guterman, "Doing 'Good Brave Work,'" 157; Conrad, *General Harriett Tubman*, 92.

CHAPTER 9

1. "Port Royal and Beaufort," *Chicago Tribune*, Nov. 23, 1861; Elizabeth Ware Pearson, *Letters from Port Royal Written at the Time of the Civil War* (1906; repr., Project Gutenberg, 2008), 10, 17–19, 21, 30–31, 49, 71–72, 76–77, 208; Philip J. Staudenraus, "Occupied Beaufort, 1863: A War Correspondent's View," *South Carolina Historical Magazine* 64, no. 3 (1963): 136–137, 139; Thomas Wentworth Higginson, *Army Life in a Black Regiment and Other Writings* (Boston: Houghton, Mifflin, 1900), 9–10, 362–363.

2. Pearson, *Letters from Port Royal*, 5–6, 35, 72.

3. John Greenleaf Whittier and Charles T. Brooks, "The Negro Boatmen's Song," in *Songs for the Time*, ed. John G. Whittier (Boston: Oliver Ditson, 1861); Charlotte Forten, *The Journal of Charlotte L. Forten: A Young Black Woman's Reaction to the White World of the Civil War Era*, ed. Ray Allen Billington (New York: Dryden Press, 1953), 128, 169; Charlotte Forten Grimké, *The Journals of Charlotte Forten Grimké*, ed. Brenda Stevenson (New York: Oxford University Press, 1988), 455–457; Charlotte Forten, "Life on the Sea Islands, Part II," *Atlantic Monthly*, Jun. 1864, 666.

4. Staudenraus, "Occupied Beaufort, 1863," 137; Pearson, *Letters from Port Royal*, 5–7; Augusta M. French, *Slavery in South Carolina and the Ex-Slaves or the Port Royal Mission* (New York: W. M. French, 1862), 38; Willie Lee Rose, *Rehearsal for Reconstruction: The Port Royal Experiment* (Indianapolis: Bobbs-Merrill, 1964), 26–28, 40–41, 44.

5. J [pseud.], *Free South*, Jan. 17, 1863, 3.

6. J. Smith DuShane to Adela McMillan, Nov. 25, 1861, J. Smith DuShane Letters, 1860–1862, Southern Historical Collection, University of North Carolina, Chapel Hill; entry for May 11, 1862, James Seymour Severance journal, Severance Family Collection, private collection of Michael Emett, Billings, MO; French, *Slavery in South Carolina*, 38; J [pseud.], *Free South*, Jan. 17, 1863, 3; "The Celebration of the Emancipation of Slaves," *Free South*, Jan. 17, 1863, 3.

7. Forten, *Journal*, 181; J [pseud.], *Free South*, Jan. 17, 1863, 3; Orville Vernon Burton and Wilbur Cross, *Penn Center: A History Preserved* (Athens: University of Georgia Press, 2014), 13.

8. J.M.W., "From Gen. Hunter's Department," *New York Times*, Apr. 19, 1862, 2.

9. Pearson, *Letters from Port Royal*, 72, 150; J.M.W., "From Gen. Hunter's Department," 2; Staudenraus, "Occupied Beaufort," 134–144.

10. Forten, *Journal*, 181; Grimké, *Journals*, 473–475.

11. Edward L. Pierce, *The Negroes at Port Royal: Report of E. L. Pierce, Government Agent, to the Hon. Salmon P. Chase, Secretary of the Treasury* (Boston: R. F. Wallcut, 1862), 7; Laura M. Towne, *Letters and Diary Written from the Sea Islands of South Carolina, 1862–1884*, ed. Rupert Holland (Cambridge, MA: Riverside Press, 1912), xi–xii; Henry William Ravenel, *The Private Journal of Henry William Ravenel 1859–1867*, ed. Arney Robinson Childs (Columbia: University of South Carolina Press), 1947, 102; Michael Edward Scott Emett, "'Or This Whole Affair Is a Failure': A Special Treasury Agent's Observations of the Port Royal Experiment, Port Royal, South Carolina, April to May, 1862," M.A. thesis, Marshall University, 2016, 40–41, 62, 99, 133; Kevin Dougherty, *The Port Royal Experiment: A Case Study in Development* (Jackson: University Press of Mississippi, 2014), 58, 105; Rose, *Rehearsal for Reconstruction*, 19–20, 32.

12. *The War of the Rebellion: A Compilation of the Official Records of the Union and Confederate Armies*, ser. 1, vol. VI (Washington, DC: GPO, 1880–1901) 218; Pearson, *Letters from Port Royal*, xi; Towne, *Letters and Diary*, xi–xii;

Elizabeth Hyde Botume, *First Days Amongst the Contrabands* (Boston: Lee and Shepard, 1893), 16–18.

13. Edward L. Pierce, "The Contrabands at Fortress Monroe, " *Atlantic Monthly,* Nov. 1861, 635; Pierce, *The Negroes at Port Royal,* 6, 9, 53.

14. Pierce, *The Negroes at Port Royal,* 1; Edward L. Pierce, "The Freedmen at Port Royal," *Atlantic Monthly,* Sep. 1863, 296; Frank Moore, ed., *The Rebellion Record: A Diary of American Events, with Documents, Narratives, Illustrative Events, Poetry, Etc., Supplement. Vol. I* (New York: D. Van Nostrand, 1866), 304, 306; Dougherty, The Port Royal Experiment, 57, 136, 165; Rose, Rehearsal for Reconstruction, 28–30, 79.

15. Pierce, "The Freedmen at Port Royal," 3; Moore, *The Rebellion Record, Supplement, Vol. I,* 314; Rose, *Rehearsal for Reconstruction,* 30–31, 44.

16. Charles Francis Adams Jr., Charles Francis Adams Sr., and Henry Brooks Adams, *A Cycle of Adams Letters, 1861–1865,* ed. Worthington Chauncy Ford (Boston: Houghton Mifflin, 1920), 130; Pierce, "The Freedmen at Port Royal," 3, 291–292; Pierce, "The Contrabands at Fortress Monroe," 639; Pierce, *The Negroes at Port Royal,* 25; Pearson, *Letters from Port Royal,* 1–2; Moore, *The Rebellion Record,* 303; New England Freedmen's Aid Society, *First Annual Report of the Educational Commission for Freedmen May, 1863* (Boston: Prentiss & Deland, 1863), 30; Forten, *Journal,* 22; New England Freedmen's Aid Society, *Second Annual Report of the New England Freedmen's Aid Society (Educational Commission)* (Boston: Office of the Society, 1864), 58; Rose, *Rehearsal for Reconstruction,* 31.

17. Stephen Colwell, "A Plea for Freedmen," n.d., Stephen Colwell Collection, Historical Society of Pennsylvania; Pierce, "The Freedmen of South Carolina," 1–2; Pearson, *Letters from Port Royal,* 12; New England Freedmen's Aid Society, *First Annual Report,* 3, 8; *The War of the Rebellion: A Compilation,* ser. 1, vol. VI, 227; Botume, *First Days Amongst the Contrabands,* 18–19.

18. Pearson, *Letters from Port Royal,* 2, 4; Pierce, "The Freedmen at Port Royal," 279; New England Freedmen's Aid Society, *First Annual Report,* 10; Nancy Hoffman, *Woman's "True" Profession: Voices from the History of Teaching* (Old Westbury, NY: Feminist Press, 1981), 99; Rose, *Rehearsal for Reconstruction,* 49.

19. "John M. Forbes to Edward Atkinson," *Boston Advertiser,* 1862; "To the Editors of the Boston Daily Advertiser," *Boston Advertiser,* Jun. 10, 1862; Edward L. Pierce, "The Freedmen of South Carolina: Official Report Port Royal June 2 1862 Edward L. Pierce," *New-York Daily Tribune,* Jun. 17, 1862; Adams, Adams, and Adams, *A Cycle of Adams Letters,* 127; Dougherty, *The Port Royal Experiment,* 19; Rose, *Rehearsal for Reconstruction,* xviii, 32–34; Pierce, *The Negroes at Port Royal,* 24–25; Emett, "'Or This Whole Affair Is a Failure,'" 42.

20. Pierce, "The Freedmen at Port Royal," 307; Pearson, *Letters from Port Royal,* 114; Pennsylvania Freedmen's Relief Association, *Report of the Proceedings of a Meeting at Concert Hall, Philadelphia on Tuesday Evening, November 3, 1863, to Take into Consideration the Condition of the Freed People of the South* (Philadelphia:

Merrihew & Thompson, 1863), 9–11; New England Freedmen's Aid Society, *Second Annual Report*, 68; Moore, *The Rebellion Record*, 310.

21. Towne, *Letters and Diary*, 7, 18; Emett, "'Or This Whole Affair Is a Failure,'" 77; Dougherty, *The Port Royal Experiment*, 20, 26, 29–31, 58, 106, 139–140; Rose, *Rehearsal for Reconstruction*, 25, 33, 60–61, 67, 80, 143; Guion Griffis Johnson, *A Social History of the Sea Islands* (Chapel Hill: University of North Carolina Press, 1930), 160–161.

22. Towne, *Letters and Diary*, 7; Dougherty, *The Port Royal Experiment*, 31; Rose, *Rehearsal for Reconstruction*, 48, 142, 145, 146.

23. Susan Walker, "Journal of Miss Susan Walker: March 3d to June 6th, 1862," ed. Henry Noble Sherwood, *Quarterly Publication of the Historical and Philosophical Society of Ohio* 7, no. 1 (1912): 22; New England Freedmen's Aid Society, *First Annual Report*, 23.

24. Walker, "Journal," 40, 30, 32–33, 43; Towne, *Letters and Diary*, 55, 60; New England Freedmen's Aid Society, *First Annual Report*, 25, 27; Rose, *Rehearsal for Reconstruction*, 43–44.

25. Botume, *First Days Amongst the Contrabands*, 30–33; Walker, "Journal," 11; Pearson, *Letters from Port Royal*, xiii; Rose, *Rehearsals for Reconstruction*, 44, 48, 60–61.

26. Edward Atkinson is an example of a New England cotton manufacturer who thought plantation slavery had kept cotton prices high. He advocated opening up cotton culture to be produced on smallholdings of white or even freed Black farmers. Edward Philbrick wanted to see the monopoly for up-land cotton broken as well as lands throughout the South opened to small-holders. Others doubted that a "revolution in cotton production" breaking the southern planters' cotton monopoly would change the status of Blacks from forced laborers to free laborers. Edward S. Philbrick to the editors, *Evening Post* (Boston), Feb. 24, 1864; Walker, "Journal," 11; Pearson, *Letters from Port Royal*, xiii, 1; Adams, Adams, and Adams, *A Cycle of Adams Letters*, 129–132; New England Freedmen's Aid Society, *Second Annual Report*, 57; Pierce, "The Freedmen at Port Royal," 297–298; Botume, *First Days Amongst the Contrabands*, 30–33; Dougherty, *The Port Royal Experiment*, 28, 30, 32, 40, 53, 55; Virginia Elwood-Akers, *Caroline Severance* (New York: iUniverse, 2010), 68; Akiko Ochiai, *Harvesting Freedom: African American Agrarianism in Civil War Era South Carolina* (Westport, CT: Praeger, 2004), 61; Rose, *Rehearsal for Reconstruction*, xvi, 45, 47–48, 69–70.

27. Ochiai, *Harvesting Freedom*, 66–67; Dougherty, *The Port Royal Experiment*, 55, 109–110; William H. Pease, "William Channing Gannett; a Social Biography," Ph.D. diss., University of Rochester, 1955, 57–58; Rose, *Rehearsal for Reconstruction*, 67.

28. Pearson, *Letters from Port Royal*, 108–109, 112, 176; Educational Commission, *Extracts from Letters Received by the Educational Commission of Boston, from Teachers Employed at Port Royal and Its Vicinity* (Boston: Educational Commission, 1862), 2; New England Freedmen's Aid Society, *First Annual Report*, 28; Pease, "William Channing Gannett," 56–60.

29. New England Freedmen's Aid Society, *First Annual Report*, 12; Rose, *Rehearsal for Reconstruction*, 83–84.

30. Pierce, "The Freedmen of South Carolina," 8, 9; Pearson, *Letters from Port Royal*, 13; Towne, *Letters and Diary*, 7, 8, 9, 16–18, 21, 25; New England Freedmen's Aid Society, *First Annual Report*, 13; Moore, *The Rebellion Record*, 309–310; Emett, "'Or This Whole Affair Is a Failure,'" 2, 63–64; Ochiai, *Harvesting Freedom*, 65, 70–72; Rose, *Rehearsal for Reconstruction*, 82–83.

31. Pearson, *Letters from Port Royal*, 53–57, 93, 169, 243, 308–309; Towne, *Letters and Diary*, 13, 60–61; New England Freedmen's Aid Society, First Annual Report, 23–24; New England Freedmen's Aid Society, Second Annual Report, 66; Ochiai, Harvesting Freedom, 66.

32. Forten, *Journal*, 148; Grimké, *Journals*, 419–420; Pennsylvania Freedmen's Relief Association, Report of the Proceedings of a Meeting at Concert Hall, 20; New England Freedmen's Aid Society, Second Annual Report, 12.

33. Pennsylvania Freedmen's Relief Association, Report of the Proceedings of a Meeting at Concert Hall, 20; New England Freedmen's Aid Society, Second Annual Report, 12; Forten, Journal, 148.

34. Rose, *Rehearsal for Reconstruction*, 152–154.

35. Pearson, *Letters from Port Royal*, 3; Towne, *Letters and Diary*, 3; Forten, *Journal*, 126; Grimké, Journals, 388–389; Botume, *First Days Amongst the Contrabands*, 24–25; Rose, *Rehearsal for Reconstruction*, 44.

36. Towne, *Letters and Diary*, x–xi; Burton and Cross, *Penn Center*, 12–13; Dougherty, *The Port Royal Experiment*, 19, 44, 46; Calvin B. Knerr, Life of Hering: The Conversation, *Life and Times of Constantine Hering, Founder of the Allentown Academy of Homoeopathic Medicine, Hahnemann Hospital, Hahnemann College, American Institute of Homoeopathy, Author of the Leading Works in Homoeopathic Literature, Homoeopathic Practitioner* (Philadelphia: Magee Press, 1940), 61, 310–319.

37. J.S.S., Port Royal, Apr. 27, 1862 [journal entry], Severance Family Collection, private collection of Michael Emett, Billings, MO; Towne, *Letters and Diary*, xi.

38. Pearson, *Letters from Port Royal*, xii, 9; Towne, *Letters and Diary*, 10–11, 63, 67, 69, 82; Forten, *Journal*, 181–182; Taylor, *Reminiscences of My Life in Camp*, 35.

39. Towne, *Letters and Diary*, 67, 69, 82; Moore, *The Rebellion Record*, 303.

40. Pearson, *Letters from Port Royal*, 115–116; Towne, *Letters and Diary*, xiv, 26.

41. Pearson, *Letters from Port Royal*, 158; Towne, *Letters and Diary*, 190, 94, 213.

42. Towne, *Letters and Diary*, xiv–xv, 21, 37, 39–41, 58, 77, 87–89, 92, 122, 124, 130, 144, 178, 207–208.

43. Towne, *Letters and Diary*, 70; Burton and Cross, *Penn Center*, 15–16.

44. The War of the Rebellion: A Compilation, ser. 1, vol. VI, 202; Benjamin Guterman, "Doing 'Good Brave Work': Harriet Tubman's Testimony at Beaufort, South Carolina," *Prologue Quarterly of the National Archives*, 32, no. 3 (2000): 158.

45. Testimony by Bernard K. Lee; The War of the Rebellion: A Compilation, ser. 1, vol. VI, 202.

46. Pierce, "The Freedmen of South Carolina," 2; Pearson, *Letters from Port Royal*, 36, 53–58; New England Freedmen's Aid Society, *First Annual Report*, 25, 28, 30, 37; Forten, *Journal*, 148; Grimké, *Journals*, 419–420; Charlotte Forten, "Life on the Sea Islands: A Young Black Woman Describes Her Experiences Teaching Freedmen During the Civil War, Part I," *Atlantic Monthly*, May 1864, 5; *The War of the Rebellion: A Compilation*, ser. 1, vol. VI, 186–187, 205; Guterman, "Doing 'Good Brave Work,'" 157–158.

47. "Miscellaneous Lists, Beaufort (Contraband Department)."

48. "Miscellaneous Lists, Beaufort (Contraband Department), Records of the Field Offices for the State of South Carolina, Bureau of Refugees, Freedmen, and Abandoned Lands, 1865–1872," Microfilm Series M1910, Roll 62, NARA; "Contraband Negroes Employed in and Around the Camp of the 8th Regt Mich Vols," United States Union Provost Marshal Files of Two or More Civilians, 1861–1866, Microfilm Series M416, Roll 5, NARA; "Contraband Negroes Employed in and Around the Camp of the 50th Regt PA Vols," United States Union Provost Marshal Files of Two or More Civilians, 1861–1866, Microfilm Series M416, Roll 5, NARA; "Contraband Negroes Employed in and Around the Camp of the 100th Regt PA Vols," United States Union Provost Marshal Files of Two or More Civilians, 1861–1866, Microfilm Series M416, Roll 5, NARA; "Contraband Negroes Employed in Captain Rockwell's Co., 1st Conn Battery," United States Union Provost Marshal Files of Two or More Civilians, 1861–1866, Microfilm Series M416, Roll 5, NARA; "Contrabands Variously Employed," United States Union Provost Marshal Files of Two or More Civilians, 1861–1866, Microfilm Series M416, Roll 5, NARA; "List of Negroes Registered at the Office of the Provost Marshal," United States Union Provost Marshal Files of Two or More Civilians, 1861–1866, Microfilm Series M416, Roll 5, NARA/Miscellaneous Lists, Beaufort (Contraband Department), Records of the Field Offices for the State of South Carolina, Bureau of Refugees, Freedmen, and Abandoned Lands, 1865–1872, Microfilm Series M1910, Roll 62, NARA; "Contraband Negroes Employed in and Around Provost Marshal's Office," United States Union Provost Marshal Files of Two or More Civilians, 1861–1866, Microfilm Series M416, Roll 5, NARA; "Contraband Negroes Employed in and Around the Camp of 2nd Battalion, 1st Regt Mass Cavalry," United States Union Provost Marshal Files of Two or More Civilians, 1861–1866, Microfilm Series M416, Roll 5, NARA.

49. "Miscellaneous Lists, Beaufort (Contraband Department)."

50. Higginson, *Army Life in a Black Regiment*, 183.

51. Higginson, *Army Life in a Black Regiment*, 183; Susie King Taylor, *Reminiscences of My Life in Camp with the 33rd U.S. Colored Troops, Late 1st South Carolina Volunteers: A Black Woman's Civil War Memoirs* (Boston: Author, 1902), xi–xii, 5–10, 15, 21, 34–35.

52. "Miscellaneous Lists, Beaufort (Contraband Department)"; Langdon Cheves, "Blake of South Carolina," *South Carolina Historical and Genealogical Magazine* I (1900): 153–166.

53. "Exhibit F, Case of Sina Young," Dec. 14, 1876, pension file for William (Sina) Young, RG 15, NARA.

54. "List of Negroes Lost from the Estate of Jos. Blake," Pringle Family Collection, South Carolina Historical Society. Sincere thanks to Darius Brown for sharing this document with me from his personal family research.

55. "Miscellaneous Lists, Beaufort (Contraband Department)."

56. "Miscellaneous Lists, Beaufort (Contraband Department)"; "Negroes Ran Off in March 62," Papers of Kirkland, Withers, Snowden, and Trotter Families, 1790–1959, South Caroliniana Library, University of South Carolina, Columbia, 47.

57. Sarah Bradford, Scenes in the Life of Harriet Tubman (1869; repr., North Stratford, NH: Ayer, 2004), 37–38, 42, 64; Sarah Bradford, *Harriet Tubman: The Moses of Her People* (1886; repr., New York: J. J. Little, 1901), 95; Charles Wood, "A History Concerning the Pension Claim of Harriet Tubman," RG 233, NARA, 1, 6–7; Larson, *Bound for the Promised Land*, 205.

58. Lt. George Garrison to William Lloyd Garrison II, Feb. 10, 1864, Garrison Family Papers, Box 28, Folder 790, Sophia Smith Collection, Smith College, Northampton, MA; Henry Mayer, *All on Fire: William Lloyd Garrison and the Abolition of Slavery* (New York: St. Martin's Press, 1998), 508.

59. Lt. George Garrison to William Lloyd Garrison II, Feb. 10, 1864; Elwood-Akers, *Caroline Severance*, 72–73.

60. Lt. George Garrison to William Lloyd Garrison II, Feb. 10, 1864.

61. Taylor, *Reminiscences of My Life in Camp*, 67; P. K. Rose, "The Civil War: Black American Contributions to Union Intelligence," *Studies In Intelligence* 42, no. 5 (1999): 73–80. The US Navy also relied on freedom seekers to gather intelligance behind enemy lines. See Barbara Tomblin, *Bluejackets and Contrabands: African Americans and the Union Navy* (Lexington: University Press of Kentucky, 2009), 88, 99, 103, 109–110, 113, 120, 126, 131, 161, 167, 173, 229, 254, 261.

62. "MI Corps Hall of Fame Justification, Historical Figures Category, Harriet Tubman," "Nomination for Military Intelligence Hall of Fame Mrs. Harriet Tubman (Deceased)," "Memorandum for Military Intelligence Hall of Fame Board, US Army Intelligence Center & Fort Huachuca, ATTN: ATZS-HIS, Ft. Huachuca, AZ 85613–6000," and "Harriet Tubman Career Biography," all collection of Ernestine Wyatt; Rose, "The Civil War: Black American Contributions," 73. The U.S. Navy also relied on freedom seekers to gather intelligence behind enemy lines. See Barbara Tomblin, *Bluejackets and Contrabands: African Americans and the Union Navy* (Lexington: University Press of Kentucky, 2009), 88, 99, 103, 109–110, 113, 120, 126, 131, 161, 167, 173, 229, 254, 261.

63. Bradford, *Scenes in the Life of Harriet Tubman*, 39; Bradford, *Harriet Tubman*, 98–99.

CHAPTER 10

1. Willie Lee Rose, *Rehearsal for Reconstruction: The Port Royal Experiment* (Indianapolis: Bobbs-Merrill, 1964), 64–66, 80–81.

2. Michael Edward Scott Emett, "'Or This Whole Affair Is a Failure': A Special Treasury Agent's Observations of the Port Royal Experiment, Port Royal, South Carolina, April to May, 1862" (M.A. thesis, Marshall University, 2016), 56; Edward A. Miller, *Lincoln's Abolitionist General: The Biography of David Hunter* (Columbia: University of South Carolina Press, 1997), 98; Stephen R. Wise, *Gate of Hell: Campaign for Charleston Harbor, 1863* (Columbia: University of South Carolina Press, 1994), 21; E. Kay Gibson, *Dictionary of Transports and Combatant Vessels, Steam and Sail, Employed by the Union Army, 1861–1868* (Camden, Me: Ensign Press, 1985), 222.

3. Rufus Saxton, "Gilmore," Rufus Saxton Letters, 1862–1864, Rubenstein Library, Duke Library, Durham, NC; Miller, *Lincoln's Abolitionist General*, 98;

4. Saxton, "Gilmore"; Miller, *Lincoln's Abolitionist General*, 96, 98.

5. *The War of the Rebellion: A Compilation of the Official Records of the Union and Confederate Armies*, ser. 1, vol. XIV (Washington, DC: GPO, 1880–1901), 333, 341; *The War of the Rebellion: A Compilation of the Official Records of the Union and Confederate Armies*, ser. 3, vol. II (Washington, DC: GPO, 1880–1901), 42; James Oakes, *Freedom National: The Destruction of Slavery in the United States, 1861–1865* (New York: W. W. Norton, 2012), 213–214; Miller, *Lincoln's Abolitionist General*, 98; Military Historical Society of Massachusetts, *Operations on the Atlantic Coast 1861–1865: Virginia 1862, 1864 Vicksburg, Vol. IX* (Boston: Military Historical Society, 1912), 131.

6. Entry for May 1, 1862, James Seymour Severance journal, Severance Family Collection, private collection of Michael Emett, Billings, MO.

7. Louisa May Alcott, *The Selected Letters of Louisa May Alcott*, ed. Madeleine B. Stern, Joel Myerson, and Daniel Shealy (Boston: Little, Brown, 1987), 77; Michael Edward Scott Emett, "'Or This Whole Affair Is a Failure': A Special Treasury Agent's Observations of the Port Royal Experiment, Port Royal, South Carolina, April to May, 1862," M.A. thesis, Marshall University, 2016, 45, 59, 61; Virginia Elwood-Akers, *Caroline Severance* (New York: iUniverse, 2010), 68.

8. Mark Sibley Severance Journal, Severance Family Collection; entries for Apr. 18, Apr. 19, and Apr. 22, 1892, James Seymour Severance journal; *The War of the Rebellion: A Compilation*, ser. 3, vol. II, 42–43; Emett, "'Or This Whole Affair Is a Failure,'" 46, 61, 63–65; Elwood-Akers, *Caroline Severance*, 69, 71–72.

9. Entry for May 1, 1862, James Seymour Severance journal; Emett, "'Or This Whole Affair Is a Failure,'" 84.

10. Entry for May 1, 1862, James Seymour Severance journal; Emett, "'Or This Whole Affair Is a Failure,'" 84.

11. Edward L. Pierce, *The Negroes at Port Royal: Report of E. L. Pierce, Government Agent, to the Hon. Salmon P. Chase, Secretary of the Treasury* (Boston: R. F. Wallcut, 1862), 11, 12, 27; Elizabeth Ware Pearson, *Letters from Port Royal Written at the*

Time of the Civil War (1906; repr., Project Gutenberg, 2008), 8n12, 19n21; Laura M. Towne, *Letters and Diary Written from the Sea Islands of South Carolina, 1862–1884*, ed. Rupert Holland (Cambridge, MA: Riverside Press, 1912), 10–11n1; Frank Moore, ed., *The Rebellion Record, Supplement, Vol. I* (New York: D. Van Nostrand, 1869), 312–313.

12. Entres for Apr. 19, May 1, and May 11, 1862, James Seymour Severance journal; Emett, "'Or This Whole Affair Is a Failure,'" 67, 69, 74.

13. Entry for May 1, 1862, James Seymour Severance journal; Emett, "'Or This Whole Affair Is a Failure,'" 84–85.

14. Entry for May 1, 1862, James Seymour Severance journal; Emett, "'Or This Whole Affair Is a Failure,'" 85.

15. *The War of the Rebellion: A Compilation*, ser. 3, vol. II, 29–30; Oakes, *Freedom National*, 213–214; Miller, *Lincoln's Abolitionist General*, 99, 110–111; Rose, *Rehearsal for Reconstruction*, 144–145.

16. General David Hunter to Senator Lyman Trumbull, Dec. 9, 1861, Papers of Lyman Trumbull, 1843–1894, Library of Congress; Susan Walker, "Journal of Miss Susan Walker: March 3d to June 6th, 1862," ed. Henry Noble Sherwood, *Quarterly Publication of the Historical and Philosophical Society of Ohio* 7, no. 1 (1912), 40; Pearson, *Letters from Port Royal*, 42, 51–52, 54; William B. Howard, entry for May 12, 1862, "Diary of William B. Howard—48 New York Infantry Regiment," New York State Military Museum and Veterans Research Center, Saratoga Springs; *The War of the Rebellion: A Compilation*, ser. 1, vol. XIV, 341; *The War of the Rebellion: A Compilation*, ser. 3, vol. II, 57; Thomas Wentworth Higginson, *Army Life in a Black Regiment and Other Writings* (Boston: Houghton, Mifflin, 1900), 211; Miller, *Lincoln's Abolitionist General*, 1–3, 45–46, 67, 77–79, 82, 87, 98–101, 114, 127; Rose, *Rehearsal for Reconstruction*, 146; Military Historical Society of Massachusetts, *Operations on the Atlantic Coast*, 131.

17. Susan Walker, "Journal of Miss Susan Walker: March 3d to June 6th, 1862," ed. Henry Noble Sherwood, *Quarterly Publication of the Historical and Philosophical Society of Ohio* 8, no. 1 (1912): 38; Towne, *Letters and Diary*, 42, 108; *The War of the Rebellion: A Compilation*, ser. 3, vol. II, 55–57; Miller, *Lincoln's Abolitionist General*, 100; Rose, *Rehearsal for Reconstruction*, 146.

18. Walker, "Journal," 38–39; Pearson, *Letters from Port Royal*, 41; *The War of the Rebellion: A Compilation*, ser. 3, vol. II, 52–55, 57–58.

19. Walker, "Journal," 38, 39; Towne, *Letters and Diary*, 42, 107; Rose, *Rehearsal for Reconstruction*, 146

20. Towne, *Letters and Diary*, 107.

21. Walker, "Journal," 39–40; Towne, *Letters and Diary*, 41, 53; *The War of the Rebellion: A Compilation*, ser. 3, vol. II, 52–53, 57, 60; Miller, *Lincoln's Abolitionist General*, 100; Rose, *Rehearsal for Reconstruction*, 142, 145–146.

22. Walker, "Journal," 6, 22; Towne, *Letters and Diary*, 37, 94, 107; Forten, *Journal*, 24; *The War of the Rebellion: A Compilation*, ser. 3, vol. II, 56; Higginson, *Army Life in a Black Regiment*, 211–212; Rose, *Rehearsal for Reconstruction*, 142, 145–146.

23. Walker, "Journal," 39; Pearson, *Letters from Port Royal*, 97; Towne, *Letters and Diary*, 37, 46, 49, 53–54, 94; *War of the Rebellion: A Compilation*, ser. 3, vol. II, 53; Rose, Rehearsal for Reconstruction, 145–147.

24. Pearson, *Letters from Port Royal*, 179; Miller, *Lincoln's Abolitionist General*, 100–101.

25. *The War of the Rebellion: A Compilation*, ser. 3, vol. II, 55–57; Rose, *Rehearsal for Reconstruction*, 147.

26. Edward Pierce wrote letters to General Hunter asking to allow the drivers to remain on the plantations so that they could supervise the workers who were left. In most cases, the request was granted. Pierce, *The Negroes at Port Royal*, 10; New England Freedmen's Aid Society, *First Annual Report of the Education Commission with Extracts from Letters of Teachers and Superintendents* (Boston: David Clapp, 1863), 25, 37; *The War of the Rebellion: A Compilation*, ser. 3, vol. II, 52–53, 55–56; Rose, *Rehearsal for Reconstruction*, 147.

27. Pierce, "The Freedmen at Port Royal," 311.

28. Charles Francis Adams Jr., Charles Francis Adams Sr., and Henry Brooks Adams, *A Cycle of Adams Letters, 1861–1865*, ed. Worthington Chauncy Ford (Boston: Houghton Mifflin, 1920), 174; Pierce, "The Freedmen at Port Royal," 311; Pearson, *Letters from Port Royal*, 62n46, 99; Higginson, *Army Life in a Black Regiment*, 397; Miller, *Lincoln's Abolitionist General*, 110; Rose, *Rehearsal for Reconstruction*, 156–157.

29. Higginson, *Army Life in a Black Regiment*, 397, 399.

30. Pearson, *Letters from Port Royal*, 62–63; Miller, *Lincoln's Abolitionist General*, 110.

31. Oakes, *Freedom National*, 214; Miller, *Lincoln's Abolitionist General*, 111; Albert Bushnell Hart, *Salmon Portland Chase: American Statesman* (Boston: Houghton, Mifflin, 1899), 257.

32. Gideon Welles to Flag Ship Wabash, Dec. 11, 1861, [not signed] to USS Steamer Mohican, Apr. 13, 1862, A. C. Rhind to USS Crusader, Apr. 30, 1862, P. Drayton to USS Pawnee, May 30, 1862, Gideon Welles to Flag Ship Wabash, Jun. 11, 1862, C. B. Marchand to US Steamer James Adger, Aug. 2, 1862, USS Pawnee to P. Drayton, May 30, 1862, "Letters Received by the Secretary of the Navy from Commanding Officers of Squadrons, 1841–1886," RG 45, NARA; Barbara Tomblin, *Bluejackets and Contrabands: African Americans and the Union Navy* (Lexington: University Press of Kentucky, 2009), 169–172; Charles Cowley, *The Romance of History in "the Black County," and the Romance of War in the Career of Gen. Robert Smalls, "the Hero of the Planter"* (Lowell, MA: n.p., 1882), 7

33. March Haynes, [Confederate] Reference Card, "Declaration of Recruit," "Compiled Military Service Records of Volunteer Union Soldiers Who Served with the United States Colored Troops" (henceforth "Compiled Military Service Records"), RG 94, NARA; *The War of the Rebellion: A Compilation*, ser. 1, vol. XIV, 341; Oakes, *Freedom National*, 224–225, 239; Charles J. Elmore, *General David Hunter's Proclamation: The Quest for African-American Freedom Before and During the Civil War* (Washington, PA: Eastern National,

2002), 51; Clarence L. Mohr, "Before Sherman: Georgia Blacks and the Union War Effort, 1861–1864," *Journal of Southern History* 45, no. 3 (1979): 349; Hart, *Salmon Portland Chase*, 256–257; Military Historical Society of Massachusetts, *Operations on the Atlantic Coast*, 131–132; Emanuel King Love, *History of the First African Baptist Church, from Its Organization, January 10th, 1788, to July 1st, 1888: Including the Centennial Celebration, Addresses, Sermons, Etc.* (Savannah: Morning News Print, 1888), 177; Frederic Denison, *Shot and Shell: The Third Rhode Island Heavy Artillery Regiment in the Rebellion, 1861–1865* (Providence: Third R.I.H. Vet. Art. Association, 1879), 261.

34. March Haines, "Declaration of Recruit," Compiled Military Service Records. An officer from the Massachusetts 54th Regiment reports that a pilot delivered a boatload of contrabands in "Extracts from the Journal of an Officer in the 54th Regt., Mass Vols.," *The Commonwealth Boston*, Jun. 26 1863. Elmore, *General David Hunter's Proclamation*, 51; Denison, *Shot and Shell*, 260–261.

35. "The Escape of the Planter," *Post and Courier*, May 13, 1862; "The Steamer 'Planter' and Her Captor," *Harper's Weekly*, Jun. 14, 1862; *The War of the Rebellion: A Compilation*, ser. 1, vol. XIV, 13, 14; *Official Records of the Union and Confederate Navies in the War of the Rebellion*, ser. 1, vol. XII (Washington, DC: GPO, 1900), 822, 825–826; Cate Lineberry, *Be Free or Die: The Amazing Story of Robert Smalls' Escape from Slavery to Union Hero* (New York: St. Martin's, 2017), 1; Kevin J. Dougherty, *Ships of the Civil War 1861–1865: An Illustrated Guide to the Fighting Vessels of the Union and the Confederacy* (London: Amber Books, 2013), 96–97; Edward A. Miller, *Gullah Statesman : Robert Smalls from Slavery to Congress, 1839–1915* (Columbia: University of South Carolina Press, 2008), 1; Cowley, *The Romance of History*, 9–10.

36. "The Escape of the Planter"; "The Steamer 'Planter' and Her Captor"; The War of the Rebellion: A Compilation, ser. 1, vol. XIV, 13; *Official Records of the Union and Confederate Navies in the War of the Rebellion*, ser. 1, vol. XII (Washington, DC: GPO, 1900), 822, 825–826; Cate Lineberry, *Be Free or Die: The Amazing Story of Robert Smalls' Escape from Slavery to Union Hero* (New York: St. Martin's, 2017), 1; Kevin J. Dougherty, *Ships of the Civil War 1861–1865: An Illustrated Guide to the Fighting Vessels of the Union and the Confederacy* (London: Amber Books, 2013), 96–97; Edward A. Miller, *Gullah Statesman: Robert Smalls from Slavery to Congress, 1839–1915* (Columbia: University of South Carolina Press, 2008), 1; Andrew Billingsley, *Yearning to Breathe Free: Robert Smalls of South Carolina and His Families* (Charleston: University of South Carolina Press, 2007), 43, 54–55; Cowley, *The Romance of History*, 9–10.

37. "The Escape of the Planter"; entry for May 17, 1862, James Seymour Severance journal; *The War of the Rebellion: A Compilation*, ser. 1, vol. XIV, 14–15; Lineberry, *Be Free or Die*, 1, 11–13; Billingsley, *Yearning to Breathe Free*, 55–56; Cowley, *The Romance of History*, 10.

38. "The Escape of the Planter"; "The Steamer 'Planter' and Her Captor"; entry for May 17, 1862, James Seymour Severance journal; *The War of the Rebellion: A Compilation*, ser. 1, vol. XIV, 14–15; *Official Records of the Union and Confederate Navies*, ser. 1, vol. XII, 822; Lineberry, *Be Free or Die*, 20, 22–24; Dougherty,

Ships of the Civil War, 96–97; Billingsley, *Yearning to Breathe Free*, 54, 56, 58; Cowley, *The Romance of History*, 9–10.

39. Entry for May 17, 1862, James Seymour Severance journal; *The War of the Rebellion: A Compilation*, ser. 1, vol. XIV, 14–15; *Official Records of the Union and Confederate Navies*, ser. 1, vol. XII, 822, 825; *Official Records of the Union and Confederate Navies in the War of the Rebellion*, ser. 2, vol. I (Washington, DC: GPO, 1900), 180; Lineberry, *Be Free or Die*, 5; Wise et al., *The History of Beaufort County, Volume II*, 97; Dougherty, *Ships of the Civil War*, 96–97; Billingsley, *Yearning to Breathe Free*, 52. Colonel Thomas Wentworth Higginson remembered the *Planter* drawing four feet of water. See Higginson, *Army Life in a Black Regiment*, 88.

40. "The Steamer 'Planter' and Her Captor"; *The War of the Rebellion: A Compilation*, ser. 1, vol. XIV, 13–15, 506; *Official Records of the Union and Confederate Navies*, ser. 1, vol. XII, 821, 826; Lineberry, *Be Free or Die*, 11.

41. *The War of the Rebellion: A Compilation*, ser. 1, vol. XIV, 506; *Official Records of the Union and Confederate Navies*, ser. 1, vol. XII, 807, 821; Lineberry, *Be Free or Die*, 5–6, 10–11, 27–28, 7825; Billingsley, *Yearning to Breathe Free*, 52, 53, 5858; Cowley, *The Romance of History*, 10.

42. Entry for May 17, 1862, James Seymour Severance journal; *The War of the Rebellion: A Compilation*, ser. 1, vol. XIV, 13–15, 506; *Official Records of the Union and Confederate Navies*, ser. 1, vol. XII, 807, 821–822, 824–825; *The War of the Rebellion: A Compilation of the Official Records of the Union and Confederate Armies*, ser. 1, vol. I (Washington, DC: GPO, 1880–1901), 180, 807, 821–822, 824–826; Lineberry, *Be Free or Die*, 26–28, 73; Billingsley, *Yearning to Breathe Free*, 52, 53, 58.

43. *Official Records of the Union and Confederate Navies*, ser. 1, vol. XII, 803–804, 807, 821–822; *Official Records of the Union and Confederate Navies in the War of the Rebellion*, ser. 1, vol. XIII (Washington, DC: GPO, 1900), 92, 113–114; Lineberry, *Be Free or Die*, 72–73, 78–79; Cowley, *The Romance of History*, 10.

44. *Official Records of the Union and Confederate Navies*, ser. 1, vol. XII, 821; Emily Schmall, "Stripping Confederate Ties, the US Navy Renames Two Vessels," *New York Times*, March 31, 2023.

45. Gideon Welles to Flag Ship Wabash, May 31, 1862, Letters Received by the Secretary of the Navy from Commanding Officers of Squadrons, 1841–1886; *The War of the Rebellion: A Compilation*, ser. 1, vol. XIV, 506, 509, 983, 985; *Official Records of the Union and Confederate Navies*, ser. 1, vol. XII, 807, 821, 823–825; *Official Records of the Union and Confederate Navies*, ser. 1, vol. XIII, 5, 51–56, 85; *Official Records of the Union and Confederate Navies in the War of the Rebellion*, ser. 1, vol. XIV (Washington, DC: GPO, 1900), 72; Wise, *Gate of Hell*, 9, 14.

46. Entry for May 17, 1862, James Seymour Severance journal; *Official Records of the Union and Confederate Navies*, ser. 1, vol. XII, 807, 821, 823–825; *Official Records of the Union and Confederate Navies*, ser. 1, vol. XIII, 53–54; Lineberry, *Be Free or Die*, 88–91; Billingsley, *Yearning to Breathe Free*, 61, 65.

47. "The Steamer 'Planter' and Her Captor"; "The Running of the Steamer Planter," *Charleston Mercury*, Sep. 30, 1862; *The War of the Rebellion: A Compilation*, ser. 1, vol. XIV, 506; *Official Records of the Union and Confederate Navies*, ser. 1, vol. XII, 825–826; Lineberry, *Be Free or Die*, 81–83, 86–89; Billingsley, *Yearning to Breathe Free*, 62.

48. *Official Records of the Union and Confederate Navies*, ser. 1, vol. XII, 787; Cowley, *The Romance of History*, 9.

49. *Official Records of the Union and Confederate Navies*, ser. 1, vol. XII, 787.

50. "Unnamed Steamers Off Shore," Charleston Mercury, May 30, 1862; Charles Wood, "A History Concerning the Pension Claim of Harriet Tubman," RG 233, NARA, 1, 7; Committee on Invalid Pensions, "Report," Jan. 19, 1899, pension file for Nelson (Harriet) Davis, RG 15, NARA; "Harriet Tubman Request for Payment," private collection (Harriet Tubman Home, Auburn, NY).

51. Deposition by London Blake, Aug. 30, 1901, deposition by Ben Green, Sep. 3, 1902, deposition by Penda Blake, Oct. 18, 1894, deposition by Stephen Polite, Oct. 24, 1894, pension file for Peter (Penda) Blake, RG 15, NARA.

52. *The War of the Rebellion: A Compilation*, ser. 1, vol. XIV, 577–578; *Official Records of the Union and Confederate Navies*, ser. 1, vol. XIII, 22–23.

53. *Official Records of the Union and Confederate Navies*, ser. 1, vol. XIII, 21–23, 92, 113–114, 230.

54. *The War of the Rebellion: A Compilation*, ser. 1, vol. XIV, 113, 347–348; *Official Records of the Union and Confederate Navies*, ser. 1, vol. XIII, 93.

55. *Official Records of the Union and Confederate Navies*, ser. 1, vol. XIII, 23, 93, 114, 122–123, 203–204; *The War of the Rebellion: A Compilation*, ser. 1, vol. XIV, 577–578.

56. *Official Records of the Union and Confederate Navies*, ser. 1, vol. XIII, 121, 123.

57. *Official Records of the Union and Confederate Navies*, ser. 1, vol. XIII, 121–122, 124, 230. The spring tide occurred at Minim Creek on June 25, 1862, at 6:35 a.m. and 6:58 p.m.: https://tidesandcurrents.noaa.gov/noaatidepred ictions.html?id=8662796&units=standard&bdate=18620601&edate=18620 630&timezone=LST/LDT&clock=12hour&datum=MLLW&interval= hilo&action=dailychart.

58. *Official Records of the Union and Confederate Navies*, ser. 1, vol. XIII, 122–123, 230; *The War of the Rebellion: A Compilation*, ser. 1, vol. XIV, 573–574.

59. *Official Records of the Union and Confederate Navies*, ser. 1, vol. XIII, 122–124, 203–204, 230; *The War of the Rebellion: A Compilation*, ser. 1, vol. XIV, 573–574, 578, 744.

60. "Slave Schedules" and "Agricultural Schedules," Arthur Blake, St. James Santee, US Census, 1860; "From South Carolina," *Chicago Tribune*, Jun. 20, 1863.

61. Bella Garrett and her cousin Affie Green both testified that someone named Blake (Garrett gave the first name as David and Green said it was Daniel) married Bella to her first husband, Charles Lucas, in April 1866, before Lucas mustered out of the US Army. See "Widow's Declaration for Pension," Mar. 9, 1889, deposition E by Affie Green, Oct. 11, 1912, pension file for Wally

(Bella) Garrett, RG 15, NARA; deposition A by Mary White, May 12, 1892, deposition by Mary White, Jul. 21, 1902, pension file for Parris (Mary) White; "Declaration for Widow's Pension," Nov. 19, 1892, general affidavit, Feb. 15, 1893, pension file for Benjamin (Cornelia) Pryor, RG 15, NARA; "Declaration for an Original Pension of a Father or Mother," Dec. 22, 1892, general affidavit by Philip Johnson and Peter Blake, Mar. 1, 1898, pension file for William (Wamey, Sarah) Brown, RG 15, NARA; deposition G by Mary White, Oct. 19, 1894, questionnaire by Corbner Blake, May 4, 1898, pension file for Corbner (Hannah) Blake/Francis, RG 15, NARA; deposition A by Sally Burnett, Dec. 4, 1901, deposition H by Silas Prior, Jan. 27, 1902, pension file for Balaam (Diana, Sally) Burnett, RG 15, NARA.

62. Deposition A by Mary White, May 12, 1892, deposition D by William McNeil, May 12, 1892, deposition E by Mary White, May 12, 1892, general affidavits by Jonas Green, May 8, 1893, Wadley Waring, Jan. 16, 1884, Mary White, Jul. 21, 1902, pension file for Parris (Mary) White.

63. Arthur Blake, n.d., in Comptroller General, State Auditor, Claims of Property Loss Due to the Enemy, 1862–1864, South Carolina Department of Archives and History, Columbia; deposition A by Penda Blake, Oct. 18, 1894, depositions by Catherine Young and Mary White, Oct. 19, 1894, deposition E by R. F. Greaves alias Renty Cruel, Oct. 22, 1894, deposition by Stephen Polite, Oct. 24, 1894, depositions by Renty Greaves, Sam Singleton Oct. 24, 1894, and Joe Singleton, Oct. 19, 1894, pension file for Peter (Penda) Blake; Donald Robert Shaffer, *After the Glory: The Struggles of Black Civil War Veterans* (Lawrence: University Press of Kansas, 2004), 126.

64. Deposition I by Mary White, Oct. 19, 1894, pension file for Peter (Penda) Blake; deposition B by Mary White, May 12, 1892, [affidavit] by Mary White, Dec. 6, 1883, pension file for Parris (Mary) White; *The War of the Rebellion: A Compilation*, 124–127; Stephen R. Wise, Lawrence Sanders Rowland, Gerhard Spieler, and Alexander Moore, *The History of Beaufort County, South Carolina, Volume II, Rebellion, Reconstruction, and Redemption, 1861–1893* (Columbia: University of South Carolina Press, 2015), 20–24.

65. "List of Negroes on Plantations Bonny Hall Pleasant Hill New Ground Parkers Blakefield True Blue Cypress Gang and Their Increase Newington Gang Property of Jos Blake," Pringle Family Papers, 1745–1897, South Carolina Historical Society, Charleston; deposition A by Mary White, May 12, 1892, deposition C by Scipio Murry, May 12, 1892, general affidavit by Jonas Green, May 8, 1893, [affidavit] by Mary White, Dec. 6, 1883, deposition B by Stephen Polite (alias Blake), Oct. 24, 1894, deposition I by Mary White, Oct. 19, 1894, pension file for Parris (Mary) White.

66. James Shoolbred Estate Record, Nov. 27, 1847, and John Gibbes Shoolbred Estate Inventory, 1860, Inventories of Estates and Miscellaneous Records, Records of the Secretary of the Province, South Carolina Department of Archives and History, Columbia; Mott Blake, Dec. 19, 1865–Dec. 2, 1869, Freedman's Bank Records, 1865–1874; Suzanne Cameron Linder et al., *Historical Atlas of the Rice Plantations of Georgetown County and the Santee*

River (Columbia: South Carolina Department of Archives and History, 2001), 745.

67. Arthur Blake, n.d., in Comptroller General, State Auditor, Claims of Property Loss Due to the Enemy, 1862–1864, South Carolina Department of Archives and History, Columbia; Declaration for Pension, Jul. 5, 1909, circulars from Department of the Interior, Bureau of Pensions, Nov. 15, 1899, May 20, 1912, Mar. 24, 1902, pension file for Motte (Emma) Blake, RG 15, NARA; Linder et al., *Historical Atlas*, 606–607, 614.

68. *Official Records of the Union and Confederate Navies*, ser. 1, vol. XIII, 123–124, 203–204, 230; *The War of the Rebellion: A Compilation*, ser. 1, vol. XIV, 375.

CHAPTER 11

1. Susie King Taylor, *Reminiscences of My Life in Camp with the 33rd U.S. Colored Troops, Late 1st South Carolina Volunteers: A Black Woman's Civil War Memoirs* (Boston: Author, 1902), 5–6.

2. Joseph Sturge, *A Visit to the United States in 1841* (London: Hamilton, Adams, 1842), 10; Charlotte L. Forten, *The Journal of Charlotte L. Forten: A Young Black Woman's Reaction to the White World of the Civil War Era*, ed. Ray Allen Billington (New York: Dryden Press, 1953), 6–7, 15; Charlotte Forten Grimké, *The Journals of Charlotte Forten Grimké*, ed. Brenda Stevenson (New York: Oxford University, 1989), 55; Thomas Wentworth Higginson, *The Complete Civil War Journal and Selected Letters of Thomas Wentworth Higginson*, ed. Christopher Looby (Chicago: University of Chicago Press, 2000), 76; "Dr. Grimke's Obituary, July 23, 1914," Francis Grimké Papers, Moorland-Spingarn Research Center, Howard University; Kerri K. Greenidge, *The Grimkes: The Legacy of Slavery in an American Family* (New York: Liveright, 2023), 5, 40, 42; Orville Vernon Burton and Wilbur Cross, *Penn Center: A History Preserved* (Athens: University of Georgia Press, 2014); Julie Winch, *A Gentleman of Color: The Life of James Forten* (New York: Oxford University Press, 2002), 11–12, 14, 17–23, 25, 28–30, 64–65, 71–93, 113, 143.

3. Forten, *Journal*, 6, 7, 10, 12–13; Grimké, *Journals*, 8; Greenidge, *The Grimkes*, 5, 41, 103; Burton and Cross, *Penn Center*, 29; Winch, *A Gentleman of Color*, 112, 14, 17, 202, 36, 38, 60, 305; Henry Mayer, *All on Fire: William Lloyd Garrison and the Abolition of Slavery* (New York: St. Martin's Press, 1998), 173.

4. Forten, *Journal*, 6, 7, 10–13, 173; Grimké, *Journals*, 3–5, 9, 11, 13–15; Greenidge, *The Grimkes*, 127; Burton and Cross, *Penn Center*, 29; Winch, *A Gentleman of Color*, 114, 152–153, 232, 241, 245–246, 256–257; Mayer, *All on Fire*, 116.

5. Forten, *Journal*, 7–8, 10–13; Grimké, *Journals*, 6, 8; Greenidge, *The Grimkes*, 43, 104, 127–128; Burton and Cross, *Penn Center*, 29; Winch, *A Gentleman of Color*, 65, 241–242, 244–245, 248–249, 254, 258, 320, 342, 347–348; Mayer, *All on Fire*, 110, 241, 246.

6. Forten, *Journal*, 1, 2, 15–20, 115; Grimké, *Journals*, 5, 17, 23–24, 27, 32, 35–36, 40, 363; Greenidge, *The Grimkes*, 132, 140, 142; Burton and Cross, *Penn Center*, 29; Winch, *A Gentleman of Color*, 348, 357–358.

7. Forten, *Journal*, 25, 128–129, 131, 133; Grimké, *Journals*, 37; Greenidge, *The Grimkes*, 146–147; Burton and Cross, *Penn Center*, 20–21.

8. Forten, *Journal*, 4, 117; Grimké, *Journals*, 3, 10, 298, 369, 549n5, 580n4.

9. Forten, *Journal*, 4, 63; Grimké, *Journals*, 140.

10. Forten, *Journal*, 121, 31, 39–40, 131, 139–140; Burton and Cross, *Penn Center*, 12; Higginson, *The Complete Civil War Journal and Selected Letters*, 319; Willie Lee Rose, Rehearsal for *Reconstruction: The Port Royal Experiment* (Indianapolis: Bobbs-Merrill, 1964), 161.

11. Forten, *Journal*, 136; Grimké, *Journals*, 403.

12. Elizabeth Ware Pearson, *Letters from Port Royal Written at the Time of the Civil War* (1906; repr., Project Gutenberg, 2008), 208–209; New England Freedmen's Aid Society, *First Annual Report of the Education Commission with Extracts from Letters of Teachers and Superintendents* (Boston: David Clapp, 1863), 33–35; Port Royal Relief Committee, *Extracts from Letters Received by the Port Royal Relief Committee of Philadelphia from Teachers and Superintendents at the Sea Islands, S. C.* (Philadelphia: The Committee, 1863), 1; Edward L. Pierce, "The Freedmen at Port Royal," *Atlantic Monthly*, Sep. 1863, 303; New England Freedmen's Aid Society, *Second Annual Report of the New England Freedmen's Aid Society (Educational Commission)* (Boston: Office of the Society, 1864) 13, 33; William Channing Gannett and Edward Everett Hale, "The Education of the Freedmen," *North American Review* 101, no. 209 (Oct. 1865): 533; Rose, *Rehearsal for Reconstruction*, 80, 85, 88; Rose, *Rehearsal for Reconstruction*, 80, 85, 88.

13. Pierce, "The Freedmen at Port Royal," 302; New England Freedmen's Aid Society, *First Annual Report*, 8; New England Freedmen's Aid Society, *Second Annual Report*, 13, 33; Gannett and Hale, "The Education of the Freedmen," 533.

14. Pierce, "The Freedmen at Port Royal," 308; Charlotte Forten, "Life on the Sea Islands: A Young Black Woman Describes Her Experiences Teaching Freedmen During the Civil War, Part I," *Atlantic Monthly*, May 1864, 666.

15. Pierce, "The Freedmen at Port Royal," 308; Charlotte Forten, "Life on the Sea Islands, Part II," *Atlantic Monthly*, Jun. 1864, 666.

16. Edward L. Pierce, *The Negroes at Port Royal: Report of E. L. Pierce, Government Agent, to the Hon. Salmon P. Chase, Secretary of the Treasury* (Boston: R. F. Wallcut, 1862), 10–11; Educational Commission, *Extracts from Letters Received by the Educational Commission of Boston, from Teachers Employed at Port Royal and Its Vicinity* (Boston: Educational Commission, 1862), 1–4; Laura M. Towne, *Letters and Diary Written from the Sea Islands of South Carolina, 1862–1884*, ed. Rupert Holland (Cambridge, MA: Riverside Press, 1912), 27; New England Freedmen's Aid Society, *First Annual Report*, 21–22, 28–29; Pierce, "The Freedmen at Port Royal," 297–298, 304–305.

17. Botume, *First Days Amongst the Contrabands*, 21, 87, 96.

18. Pearson, *Letters from Port Royal*, 149; Towne, *Letters and Diary*, 135, 44, 85; Pierce, "The Freedmen at Port Royal," 303; Forten, *Journal*, 29, 126–127, 131–132, 197.

19. Port Royal Relief Committee, *Extracts from Letters Received*, 3; New England Freedmen's Aid Society, *First Annual Report*, 34; Port Royal Relief Committee, First Annual Report, 7; Forten, "Life on the Sea Islands, Part I," 589; Botume, *First Days Amongst the Contrabands*, 63, 102.

20. New England Freedmen's Aid Society, *First Annual Report*, 34–35; Forten, "Life on the Sea Islands, Part I," 591.

21. Port Royal Relief Committee, *Extracts from Letters Received*, 3; Forten, "Life on the Sea Islands, Part I," 591; Botume, *First Days Amongst the Contrabands*, 50, 94–95, 98.

22. New England Freedmen's Aid Society, *First Annual Report*, 25; Botume, *First Days Amongst the Contrabands*, 55, 57, 86, 88, 97, 249.

23. Botume, *First Days Amongst the Contrabands*, 62, 85, 92, 138, 140–141, 151, 201, 219, 221, 249.

24. Botume, *First Days Amongst the Contrabands*, 92.

25. Pearson, *Letters from Port Royal*, 83; Frances Gage, "From Hilton: Hilton Head, Oct. 18, 1862," *Daily Ohio State Journal*, Nov. 4, 1862, 2; Grimké, *Journals*, 133–135; New England Freedmen's Aid Society, *First Annual Report*, 22–23, 33; Educational Commission, *Extracts from Letters Received*, 4; Port Royal Relief Committee, *Extracts from Letters Received*, 2; Educational Commission for Freedmen, *Third Series of Extracts from Letters Received by the Educational Commission for Freedmen, from Teachers and Superintendents at Port Royal and Its Vicinity* (Boston: Educational Commission for Freedmen, 1863), 1; Forten, "Life on the Sea Islands, Part I," 593; Botume, *First Days Amongst the Contrabands*, 92, 96, 138, 143, 146, 147, 151.

26. Pierce, "The Freedmen at Port Royal," 303; Forten, *Journal*, 132–133; Grimké, *Journals*, 395–398; Burton and Cross, Penn Center, 20.

27. New England Freedmen's Aid Society, *First Annual Report*, 25, 32–33, 37; Pierce, "The Freedmen at Port Royal," 297.

28. Susan Walker, "Journal of Miss Susan Walker: March 3d to June 6th, 1862," ed. Henry Noble Sherwood, *Quarterly Publication of the Historical and Philosophical Society of Ohio* 7, no. 1 (1912): 32; New England Freedmen's Aid Society, *First Annual Report*, 25, 33; Port Royal Relief Committee, *Extracts from Letters Received*, 1; Port Royal Relief Committee, First Annual Report, 8; New England Freedmen's Aid Society, Second Annual Report, 68.

29. Friends' Association of Philadelphia and Its Vicinity, for the Relief of Colored Freedmen. Executive Board, *Report of the Executive Board of the Friends' Association of Philadelphia and Its Vicinity, for the Relief of Colored Freedmen* (Philadelphia: C. Sherman, Son & Co., 1864), 13–14.

30. Mayer, *All on Fire*, 551–552.

31. Pearson, *Letters from Port Royal*, 63–64, 89; Towne, *Letters and Diary*, 93; Pierce, "The Freedmen at Port Royal," 291, 300, 301.

32. Charles Francis Adams Jr., Charles Francis Adams Sr., and Henry Brooks Adams, *A Cycle of Adams Letters, 1861–1865*, ed. Worthington Chauncy Ford

(Boston: Houghton Mifflin, 1920), 171; Walker, "Journal," 37; Pierce, "The Freedmen at Port Royal," 291, 300; Pearson, *Letters from Port Royal*, 96–97.

33. Pearson, *Letters from Port Royal*, 63–64.

34. Pierce, "The Freedmen at Port Royal," 311; *The War of the Rebellion: A Compilation of the Official Records of the Union and Confederate Armies*, ser. I, vol. XIV (Washington, DC: GPO, 1880–1901), 377–378.

35. Pearson, *Letters from Port Royal*, 96–97, 100, 102–103, 173–174, 190, 192; Pierce, "The Freedmen at Port Royal," 312.

36. Pearson, *Letters from Port Royal*, 188–190, 283–284.

37. Pearson, *Letters from Port Royal*, 106.

38. Thomas Wentworth Higginson, *Army Life in a Black Regiment and Other Writings* (Boston: Houghton, Mifflin, 1900), 1, 2, 400–401; James Montgomery, "Letters of Dr. Seth Rogers, 1862, 1863," *Massachusetts Historical Society Proceedings* 42 (1910): 337; John David Smith, ed., *Black Soldiers in Blue: African American Troops in the Civil War Era* (Chapel Hill: University of North Carolina Press, 2002), 8, 20, 79–81; James G. Hollandsworth, *Louisiana Native Guards: The Black Military Experience During the Civil War* (Baton Rouge: Lousiana State University Press, 1995), 1–5, 7–8, 16–18, 21.

39. Pierce, "The Freedmen at Port Royal," 313; Higginson, *Army Life in a Black Regiment*, 303–304; David W. Blight, *Frederick Douglass: Prophet of Freedom* (New York: Simon & Schuster, 2018), 391–392, 394.

40. Higginson, *Army Life in a Black Regiment*, 6; Blight, *Frederick Douglass*, 391.

41. Adams, Adams, and Adams, *Cycle of Adams Letters*, 171; Kelly D. Mezurek, *For Their Own Cause: The 27th United States Colored Troops* (Kent, OH: Kent State University Press, 2016), 56–57; Dora L. Costa and Matthew E. Kahn, *Heroes and Cowards: The Social Face of War* (Princeton, NJ: Princeton University Press, 2008), 63; Smith, *Black Soldiers in Blue*, 8; Jacob Metzer, "The Records of the U.S. Colored Troops as a Historical Source: An Exploratory Examination," *Historical Methods* 14, no. 3 (1981): 123–125.

42. William Henry Ravenel, *Private Journal of Henry William Ravenel, 1859–1867*, ed. Arney Robinson Childs (Columbia: University of South Carolina Press, 1947), 176; Pierce, "The Freedmen at Port Royal," 312–313; Higginson, *Army Life in a Black Regiment*, 3–5, 114, 191, 194–195, 206, 331; Mezurek, *For Their Own Cause*, 55; Edward A. Miller, *Lincoln's Abolitionist General: The Biography of David Hunter* (Columbia: University of South Carolina Press, 1997), 131–132.

43. "Trans-Atlantic Slave Trade Database," www.slavevoyages.org (David Eltis and Martin Halbert, original principal investigators); Jim Jordan, "Charles Augustus Lafayette Lamar and the Movement to Reopen the African Slave Trade," *Georgia Historical Quarterly* 93 (2009): 227–249, 272–290; Rose, *Rehearsal for Reconstruction*, 97–100.

44. Pearson, *Letters from Port Royal*, 203; Towne, *Letters and Diary*, 20, 22, 143–145, 176–177; Pierce, "The Freedmen at Port Royal," 301; Forten, *Journal*, 160; Rose, *Rehearsal for Reconstruction*, 99.

45. Towne, *Letters and Diary*, 144–146; Forten, *Journal*, 143; Grimké, *Journals*, 411–412; Rose, *Rehearsal for Reconstruction*, 99.

46. Pearson, *Letters from Port Royal*, 26; Towne, *Letters and Diary*, 20; Educational Commission, *Extracts from Letters Received*, 3; New England Freedmen's Aid Society, *First Annual Report*, 25; Charlotte Forten, "Life on the Sea Islands, Part II," *Atlantic Monthly*, Jun. 1864, 672; William Watts Hart Davis, *History of the 104th Pennsylvania Regiment, from August 22nd, 1861, to September 30th, 1864* (Philadelphia: Jas. B. Rogers, 1866), 211; William Francis Allen, Charles Pickard Ware, and Lucy McKim Garrison, *Slave Songs of the United States* (New York: Peter Smith, 1929), xiii.

47. Towne, *Letters and Diary*, 80; Pearson, *Letters from Port Royal*, 34–35.

48. Pearson, *Letters from Port Royal*, 34–35; Towne, *Letters and Diary*, 80.

49. Pearson, *Letters from Port Royal*, 27n26; Educational Commission, *Extracts from Letters Received*, 3; Towne, *Letters and Diary*, 20, 23; Forten, *Journal*, 166, 185, 186; Grimké, *Journals*, 480–483; New England Freedmen's Aid Society, *First Annual Report*, 25; Forten, "Life on the Sea Islands, Part I," 593; Higginson, *Army Life in a Black Regiment*, 22–24, 232, 247, 270; Allen, Ware, and Garrison, *Slave Songs of the United States*, xiii; LeRhonda S. Manigault-Bryant, *Talking to the Dead: Religion, Music, and Lived Memory Among Gullah/Geechee Women* (Durham, NC: Duke University Press, 2014), 41, 159, 161–162, 164–165; Michael A. Gomez, *Exchanging Our Country Marks: The Transformation of African Identities in the Colonial and Antebellum South* (Chapel Hill: University of North Carolina Press, 1998), 15–16, 118, 149, 152; Art Rosenbaum and Johann S. Buis, *Shout Because You're Free: The African American Ring Shout Tradition in Coastal Georgia* (Athens: University of Georgia Press, 1998), 2, 4; Lydia Parrish, *Slave Songs of the Georgia Sea Islands* (Athens: University of Georgia Press, 1992), 54, 58; Margaret Washington Creel, *"A Peculiar People": Slave Religion and Community-Culture Among the Gullahs* (New York: New York University Press, 1989), 70; Sterling Stuckey, *Slave Culture: Nationalist Theory and the Foundations of Black America* (New York: Oxford University Press, 1987), 12, 16, 88, 156, 332; Davis, *History of the 104th Pennsylvania*, 210–211.

50. M. E. Peirce, "Paper," 17, Peirce Family Papers, 1850–1915, Massachusetts Historical Society, Boston; Catherine Porter Noyes to Ellen M. Balch, Dec. 26, 1864, Catherine Porter Noyes Correspondence, 1863–1864, University of Pennsylvania Kislak Center for Special Collections, Philadelphia; Pearson, *Letters from Port Royal*, 25–30; Botume, *First Days Amongst the Contrabands*, 256; Towne, *Letters and Diary*, 20, 22, 23; Higginson, *Army Life in a Black Regiment*, 13–14, 18, 23–24, 32, 47, 149, 270; Manigault-Bryant, *Talking to the Dead*, 162, 164; Rosenbaum and Buis, *Shout Because You're Free*, 4, 29, 32, 48; Margaret Washington Creel, "Community Regulation and Cultural Specialization in Gullah Folk Religion," in *African-American Christianity: Essays in History*, ed. Paul E. Johnson (Berkeley: University of California Press, 1994), 70; Stuckey, *Slave Culture*, 330; Allen, Ware, and Garrison, *Slave Songs*, xiii–xiv; Charles

Stearns, *The Black Man of the South, and the Rebels; or, the Characteristics of the Former, and the Recent Outrages of the Latter* (New York: American News Co., 1872), 371–372.

51. Sir Charles Lyell, *A Second Visit to the United States of North America* (New York: Harper & Bros., 1849), 1:269–270; Peirce, "Paper," 17; Pearson, *Letters from Port Royal*, 292–293; Walker, "Journal," 16; Educational Commission, *Extracts from Letters Received*, 3; New England Freedmen's Aid Society, *First Annual Report*, 25; Catherine Porter Noyes to Ellen M. Balch, Dec. 26, 1864; Towne, *Letters and Diary*, 20, 23; Forten, "Life on the Sea Islands, Part I," 593; Higginson, *Army Life in a Black Regiment*, 23; Manigault-Bryant, *Talking to the Dead*, 159, 161; Erskine Clarke, *Wrestlin' Jacob: A Portrait of Religion in Antebellum Georgia and the Carolina Low Country* (Tuscaloosa: University of Alabama Press, 2000), 45; Rosenbaum and Buis, *Shout Because You're Free,*, 2, 4, 29, 33, 48; Creel, "Community Regulation," 70; Parrish, *Slave Songs of the Georgia Sea Islands*, 54; Stuckey, *Slave Culture*, 11–12, 16, 40, 90, 92–93, 95–96, 331–332; Allen, Ware, and Garrison, *Slave Songs*, xiii–xiv; Davis, *History of the 104th Pennsylvania*; Elsie Clews Parsons, *Folklore of the Sea Islands, South Carolina* (New York: American Folk Lore Society, 1923), 206; Stearns, *The Black Man of the South*, 371–372.

52. Walker, "Journal," 16; Pearson, *Letters from Port Royal*, 34; Towne, *Letters and Diary*, 20, 23; New England Freedmen's Aid Society, *First Annual Report*, 25; Catherine Porter Noyes to Ellen M. Balch, Dec. 26, 1864; Manigault-Bryant, *Talking to the Dead*, 159; Parrish, *Slave Songs of the Georgia Sea Islands*, xvi, 56, 91; Stuckey, *Slave Culture*, 16–17, 40, 61–62, 93; Allen, Ware, and Garrison, *Slave Songs*, xiii–xiv; Stearns, *The Black Man of the South*, 371–372.

53. Northern observers disparaged other of Sea Island Blacks' religious practices, particularly sitting up all night keeping watch with dead, as "heathenish" too. Some ascribed Native American and Muslim origins to the ring shout. Thus, according to the commentators, shouters could have been possessed by West African or Native American gods, Muslim spirits, ancestors, and the Christian Trinity in the same night. Towne, *Letters and Diary*, 20, 22–23, 67; Higginson, *Army Life in a Black Regiment*, 23, 270; Parrish, *Slave Songs of the Georgia Sea Islands*, xvi; Melissa L. Cooper, *Making Gullah: A History of Sapelo Islanders, Race, and the American Imagination* (Chapel Hill: University of North Carolina Press, 2017), 91; Jeffry R. Halverson, "West African Islam in Colonial and Antebellum South Carolina," *Journal of Muslim Minority Affairs* 36, no. 3 (2016): 421–422; Manigault-Bryant, *Talking to the Dead*, 41, 85, 159, 163; Lorenzo Dow Turner, *Africanisms in the Gullah Dialect* (Columbia: University of South Carolina Press, 2002), 202; Clarke, *Wrestlin' Jacob*, vii–xiv, 44–46; Gomez, *Exchanging Our Country Marks*, 16, 118, 134–135, 149, 152; Rosenbaum and Buis, *Shout Because You're Free*, 4–5, 20–23, 25, 84, 127, 168, 170; Creel, "Community Regulation," 70–71; Creel, *"A Peculiar People,"* 299; Stuckey, *Slave Culture*, 79–80, 88–90, 92–94, 96,

106, 330–332; Rose, *Rehearsal for Reconstruction*, 91; Parsons, *Folklore of the Sea Islands*, 206; Davis, *History of the 104th Pennsylvania*, 211.

54. Forten, *Journal*, 122n20, 186; Forten, "Life on the Sea Islands, Part I," 594.

55. Frances Anne Kemble, *Journal of a Residence on a Georgian Plantation in 1838–1839*, ed. John A. Scott (Athens: University of Georgia Press, 1984), 147–149; Sarah Bradford, *Scenes in the Life of Harriet Tubman* (1869; repr., North Stratford, NH: Ayer, 2004), 42–43; Sarah Bradford, *Harriet Tubman: The Moses of Her People* (1886; repr., New York: J. J. Little, 1901), 103; Botume, *First Days Amongst the Contrabands*, 222–223; Cooper, *Making Gullah*, 89–90, 99; Mary A. Waring, "Mortuary Customs and Beliefs of South Carolina Negroes," *Journal of American Folklore* 7, no. 27 (1894): 318.

56. Frederick Law Olmsted, *A Journey in the Seaboard Slave States: With Remarks on Their Economy* (New York: Dix & Edwards, 1856), 2:79–80; Botume, *First Days Amongst the Contrabands*, 222.

57. Virginia Geraty defines "shum" as "see, saw, seeing, him/her/it/them." Virginia Mixson Geraty, *Gulluh fuh Oonuh = Gullah for You: A Guide to the Gullah Language* (Orangeburg, SC: Sandlapper, 2006), 14, 90; Kemble, *Journal*, 148; Bradford, *Scenes in the Life of Harriet Tubman*, 43–44; Bradford, *Harriet Tubman: The Moses of Her People*, 104.

58. Bradford, *Scenes in the Life of Harriet Tubman*, 44; Bradford, *Harriet Tubman*, 104–105.

59. Forten, *Journal*, 161; Grimké, *Journals*, 440–552; Records of the Office of the Judge Advocate (Army), "Civil War Court Martial File Ll5566, US v. Private John E. Webster," 25, Vo. G 47 Regiment Penn Vols, RG 153, NARA; Kate Clifford Larson, *Bound for the Promised Land: Harriet Tubman: Portrait of an American Hero* (New York: One World/Ballantine, 2009), 208.

60. Forten, *Journal*, 122, 131, 177–178, 202; Grimké, *Journals*, 381–383, 394–395, 468–470; James A. McGowan, *Station Master on the Underground Railroad: The Life and Letters of Thomas Garrett* (Jefferson, NC: McFarland, 2009), 117; Charles L. Blockson, *Hippocrene Guide to the Underground Railroad* (New York: Hippocrene Books, 1994), 26–27.

61. Forten, *Journal*, 162; Grimké, *Journals*, 442–443.

62. Forten, *Journal*, 162; Grimké, *Journals*, 442–443; "Civil War Court Martial File Ll5566, US v. Private John E. Webster," 15–16; Bradford, *Scenes in the Life of Harriet Tubman*, 37–38, 68; Bradford, *Harriet Tubman*, 97, 162; Samuel Hopkins Adams, *Grandfather Stories* (New York: Random House, 1955), 273; Cindy R. Lobel, *Urban Appetites: Food and Culture in Nineteenth-Century New York* (Chicago: University of Chicago Press, 2014), 108, 112, 194; Larson, *Bound for the Promised Land*, 208; Catherine Clinton, *Harriet Tubman: The Road to Freedom* (Boston: Little, Brown, 2004), 156–157; Earl Conrad, *General Harriett Tubman* (1943; Baltimore: Black Classic Press, 2019), 164.

63. Forten, *Journal*, 162; Grimké, *Journals*, 442–443; Botume, *First Days Amongst the Contrabands*, 170; Bradford, *Harriet Tubman*, 98; Bradford, *Scenes in the Life of Harriet Tubman*, 37.

CHAPTER 12

1. "Interesting from Port Royal. A Jubilee Among the Negroes on the First—the President's Emancipation Proclamation—How the Soldiers Enjoyed the Day—Cultivation of the Plantations, &C.," *New York Times*, Jan. 9, 1863; Elizabeth Ware Pearson, *Letters from Port Royal Written at the Time of the Civil War* (1906; repr., Project Gutenberg, 2008), 129, 155; Charlotte L. Forten, *The Journal of Charlotte L. Forten: A Young Black Woman's Reaction to the White World of the Civil War Era*, ed. Ray Allen Billington (New York: Dryden Press, 1953), 153, 240; Charlotte Forten Grimké, *The Journals of Charlotte Forten Grimké*, edited by Brenda Stevenson (New York: Oxford University Press, 1988), 427–428; Seth Rogers, "War-Time Letters of Seth Rogers, M.D., Surgeon of the First South Carolina Afterwards the Thirty-Third USCT 1862–1863," 3, Florida History Online, https://history.doma ins.unf.edu/floridahistoryonline/projects-proj-b-p-html/projects-rogers-index-html; Thomas Wentworth Higginson, *Army Life in a Black Regiment and Other Writings* (Boston: Houghton, Mifflin, 1900), 32, 53–54.

2. "Interesting from Port Royal"; "Emancipation Day in South Carolina," *Frank Leslie's Illustrated Newspaper*, Jan. 24, 1863; Pearson, *Letters from Port Royal*, 128, 130; Forten, *Journal*, 153; Grimké, *Journals*, 427–428; Higginson, Army Life in a Black Regiment, 53–54.

3. "Emancipation Day in South Carolina"; Pearson, *Letters from Port Royal*; Forten, *Journal*, 154; Higginson, *Army Life in a Black Regiment*, 10, 45, 54; Susie King Taylor, *Reminiscences of My Life in Camp with the 33rd U.S. Colored Troops, Late 1st South Carolina Volunteers: A Black Woman's Civil War Memoirs* (Boston: Author, 1902), 15; Esther Hill Hawks, *A Woman Doctor's Civil War: Esther Hill Hawks' Diary*, ed. Gerald Schwartz (Columbia: University of South Carolina Press, 1984), 41; J. Brent Morris, "'We Are Verily Guilty Concerning Our Brother': The Abolitionist Transformation of Planter William Henry Brisbane," *South Carolina Historical Magazine* 111, nos. 3–4 (2010): 148–149.

4. "Emancipation Day in South Carolina"; Pearson, *Letters from Port Royal*, 129; Forten, *Journal*, 154; Grimké, Journals, 429–430; Rogers, "War-Time Letters," 3; Higginson, *Army Life in a Black Regiment*, 54; Morris, "'We Are Verily Guilty,'" 119; Hawks, *A Woman Doctor's Civil War*, 41.

5. "Interesting from Port Royal"; Wm. H. Brisbane, *Speech of the Rev. Wm. H. Brisbane, Lately a Slaveholder in South Carolina; Containing an Account of the Change in His Views on the Subject of Slavery. Delivered before the Ladies' Anti-Slavery Society of Cincinnati, Feb. 12, 1840* (Hartford, CT: S. S. Cowles, 1840), 3–5; "Emancipation Day in South Carolina"; Pearson, *Letters from Port Royal*, 129; Rogers, "War-Time Letters," 3; Higginson, *Army Life in a Black Regiment*, 54; Morris, "'We Are Verily Guilty,'" 119; Hawks, *A Woman Doctor's Civil War*, 41; Forten, *Journal*, 154.

6. Brisbane, *Speech*, 5–8; Forten, *Journal*, 178; Grimké, *Journals*, 469–470; Morris, "'We Are Verily Guilty,'" 125–130, 148.

7. Morris, "'We Are Verily Guilty,'" 135, 145, 147.

8. This newspaper article presents a racist depiction of the event. "Emancipation Day in South Carolina"; Pearson, *Letters from Port Royal*, 129–130; Forten, *Journal*, 154; Higginson, *Army Life in a Black Regiment*, 54; Taylor, *Reminiscences of My Life in Camp*, 18; Morris, "'We Are Verily Guilty,'" 148–149.

9. "Interesting from Port Royal"; "Emancipation Day in South Carolina"; Pearson, *Letters from Port Royal*, 130; Forten, *Journal*, 154; Grimké, *Journals*, 429–430; Rogers, "War-Time Letters," 3; "Tiffany & Co.," n.d., James Seymour Severance Diary, 1865, Severance Family Collection, collection of Michael S. Emett, Billings, MO; Higginson, *Army Life in a Black Regiment*, 54–55.

10. "Interesting from Port Royal"; "Emancipation Day in South Carolina"; Pearson, *Letters from Port Royal*, 130; Forten, *Journal*, 154, 156; Grimké, *Journals*, 429–430, 432–433; Rogers, "War-Time Letters," 3, 4; Higginson, *Army Life in a Black Regiment*, 54–56, 76; Taylor, *Reminiscences of My Life in Camp*, 18, 48; Hawks, *A Woman Doctor's Civil War*, 42; Alan Axelrod, *Generals South, Generals North: The Commanders of the Civil War Reconsidered* (Guilford, CT: Lyons Press, 2011), 3, 6, 10; Willie Lee Rose, *Rehearsal for Reconstruction: The Port Royal Experiment* (Indianapolis: Bobbs-Merrill, 1964), 161.

11. "Interesting from Port Royal"; Pearson, *Letters from Port Royal*, 124, 132; Forten, *Journal*, 155; Grimké, *Journals*, 430–432; Rogers, "War-Time Letters," 2–3; Higginson, *Army Life in a Black Regiment*, 49–51; Hawks, *A Woman Doctor's Civil War*, 41.

12. "Interesting from Port Royal"; Forten, *Journal*, 156–157; Grimké, *Journals*, 432–435; Hawks, *A Woman Doctor's Civil War*, 42.

13. "Interesting from Port Royal"; Hawks, *A Woman Doctor's Civil War*, 41.

14. August A. Hoit to Brigadier General Lorenzo Thomas, Oct. 7, 1863, Brigadier General Rufus Saxton to Brigadier General Lorenzo Thomas, n.d., file for Augustus A. Hoit, Compiled Military Service Records; affidavit by James Montgomery, Jun. 12, 1871, Folder 6, James Montgomery Collection, Kansas State Historical Society, Topeka.

15. August A. Hoit to Brigadier General Lorenzo Thomas, Oct. 7, 1863, Brigadier General Rufus Saxton to Brigadier General Lorenzo Thomas, n.d., file for Augustus A. Hoit, Compiled Military Service Records; Colonel James Montgomery, Brigadier General Rufus Saxton, Major General David Hunter, and Secretary Edwin M. Stanton to Brigadier General Lorenzo Thomas, May 26, 1863, file for Homer H. Moore, Compiled Military Service Records; affidavit by James Montgomery, Jun. 12, 1871, James Montgomery Collection.

16. Augustus A. Hoit, Compiled Military Service Records; C. W. Foster to War Department A.G.O., Oct. 11, 1863, "Field and Staff Muster Roll," "Regimental Descriptive Book," "Individual Muster-In Roll," "Field and Staff Muster-Out Roll," "Copy," from M. French, J. D. Strong, Thos. Crowther, H. V. Emmons, n.d., Colonel James Montgomery, Brigadier General Rufus Saxton, and Major General David Hunter to Brigadier General Lorenzo Thomas, May 26, 1863, file for Homer H. Moore, Compiled Military Service Records; affidavit by James Montgomery, Jun. 12, 1871, and by John Francis, Dec. 19, 1905, James Montgomery Collection.

17. Rogers, "War-Time Letters," 11; Thomas Wentworth Higginson, "Up the St. Mary's," *Atlantic Monthly*, Apr. 1865, 423, 428; *The War of the Rebellion: A Compilation of the Official Records of the Union and Confederate Armies*, ser. I, vol. XIV (Washington, DC: GPO, 1880–1901), 195; Higginson, *Army Life in a Black Regiment*, 88; Mary Potter Thacher Higginson, *Thomas Wentworth Higginson: The Story of His Life* (Boston: Houghton Mifflin, 1914), 222.

18. "Three Boston Ferryboats Contracted by West Street Foundry 1854," *Boston Evening Transcript*, Mar. 3, 1854; Higginson, "Up the St. Mary's," 423, 425, 431; Thomas Wentworth Higginson, "Up the St. John's," *Atlantic Monthly*, Sep. 1865, 312; Higginson, *Army Life in a Black Regiment*, 88, 137, 232, 233; "Peoples Ferry Company v. Governor, Steamer," 1866, Records of District Courts of the United States 1685–2009, Case Files 1790–1917, RG 21, NARA; Rogers, "War-Time Letters"; Taylor, *Reminiscences of My Life in Camp*, 26–27; E. Kay Gibson, *Dictionary of Transports and Combatant Vessels, Steam and Sail, Employed by the Union Army, 1861–1868* (Camden, ME: Ensign Press, 1985), 177; Leon Reussille, *Steam Vessels Built in Old Monmouth, 1841–1894* (Brick Township, NJ: Farley, 1975), 26; William M. Lytle, *Merchant Steam Vessels of the United States, 1807–1868* (Mystic, CT: Steamship Historical Society of America, 1953), 99.

19. Higginson, "Up the St. Mary's," 435, 436; *The War of the Rebellion: A Compilation*, ser. I, vol. XIV, 195, 197; Higginson, *Army Life in a Black Regiment*, 125–126; Higginson, *Thomas Wentworth Higginson*, 222.

20. Forten, *Journal*, 165; Grimké, *Journals*, 446–448; Rogers, "War-Time Letters," 17; *The War of the Rebellion: A Compilation*, ser. I, vol. XIV, 195–197; Higginson, "Up the St. Mary's," 428, 432–433, 436; Higginson, *Thomas Wentworth Higginson*, 222.

21. Higginson, "Up the St. John's," 316; *The War of the Rebellion: A Compilation*, ser. I, vol. XIV, 197; Higginson, *Army Life in a Black Regiment*, 118, 119, 148–149.

22. Forten, *Journal*, 163–165; Grimké, *Journals*, 443–448; Higginson, *Thomas Wentworth Higginson*, 222.

23. Forten, *Journal*, 163–165; Grimké, *Journals*, 443–448; Rogers, "War-Time Letters," 18; Higginson, *Thomas Wentworth Higginson*, 222.

24. "Inv. 116915, War Department, Record and Pension Division," n.d., deposition by Edward Bennett, Jan. 22, 1901, pension file for Edward (Catherine) Bennett, RG 15, NARA.

25. "Declaration for Invalid Pension" and "Act of February 6, 1907," Aug. 28, 1894, "Invalid Pension," Jun. 8, 1901, Nov. 1, 1899, May 1, 1897, "Department of the Interior Bureau of Pensions," Dec. 20, 1874, "Widow's Pension," Jun. 5, 1924, Jun. 17, 1910, deposition by Edward Bennett, Jan. 22, 1901, deposition by Jacob Campbell, Feb. 12, 1901, depositions by Henry Smith, Feb. 14, 1901, Apr. 9, 1909, "Declaration for Widow's Pension," Jul. 9, 1918, pension file for Edward (Catherine) Bennett; affidavit by James Montgomery, Jun. 6, 1871, 1–2, Folder 6, James Montgomery Collection.

26. Deposition by Jacob Campbell, Feb. 12, 1901, pension file for Friday Barrington, RG 15, NARA. Campbell's file presents conflicting information about Jacob Campbell's enlistment. Untitled document on page 30 states that Campbell enlisted in 1862; all other documents in his pension file show that he enlisted on Jun. 1, 1863. Campbell testified for Edward Bennett that he, Bennett, and Barrington were with Colonel Montgomery before the 2nd South Carolina was organized. Deposition B by Alfred Fripp, Nov. 2, 1895, pension file for Corbner (Hannah) Blake/Francis, RG 15, NARA; depositions by Jacob Campbell, Feb. 12, 1901, and Henry Smith, Feb. 14, 1901, pension file for Edward (Catherine) Bennett.

27. William Lee Apthorp, "Montgomery's Raids in Florida, Georgia, and South Carolina" (1864), 3, Apthorp Family Papers, 1741–1964, Box 2, Folder 2.6, HistoryMiami Museum, Miami, FL; "Special Order No. 5," n.d., file for James Montgomery, 39, Compiled Military Service Records; Federal Writers' Project, *Slave Narratives: A Folk History of Slavery in the United States, from Interviews with Former Slaves* (Washington, DC: Library of Congress, 1941), vol. 3, 311–313.

28. Chaz G. Halpine to Colonel Morgan, Feb. 7, 1863, James Montgomery Collection, Folder 4, 10; "I Certify on Honor That . . . ," Jul. 7, 1864, file for David/Daniel Taylor, Records of the Adjutant General's Office, 1762–1984, RG 95, NARA; Federal Writers' Project, *Slave Narratives*, vol. 3, 313; Tom Hambright, "Forgotten Soldiers," *Florida Keys Sea Heritage Journal* 23, no. 4 (2013): 1, 3.

29. "Original Invalid Claim," n.d., "Renewal and Invalid Pension Increase," Sep. 24, 1894, Jan. 13, 1896, "Increase Invalid Pension," Oct. 10, 1905, May 1, 1906, May 18, 1902, "Reissue Act of February 6, 1907," Mar. 5, 1907, "War Department, Adjutant General's Office," Feb. 8, 1887, "Act of April 19, 1908, Widow's Pension," Oct. 6, 1909, "Declaration for an Invalid Pension," May 3, 1868, deposition by William Riley, Jun. 28, 1902, pension file for William (Nancy) Riley, RG 15, NARA.

30. Rogers, "War-Time Letters," 26–27; Thomas Wentworth Higginson, *Letters and Journals of Thomas Wentworth Higginson, 1846–1906*, ed. Mary Thacher Higginson (1921; repr., Boston: Houghton Mifflin, 1969), 186; John David Smith, ed., *Black Soldiers in Blue: African American Troops in the Civil War Era* (Chapel Hill: University of North Carolina, 2002), 317.

31. Forten, *Journal*, 180; Grimké, *Journals*, 472–473; Rogers, "War-Time Letters," 27– 29; [Affidavit] by John Francis, Dec. 19, 1905, Clarinda Montgomery to State Historical Society, Oct. 13, 1889, James Montgomery Collection, Folder 6, 24; James Brewer Stewart, *Joshua R. Giddings and the Tactics of Radical Politics* (Cleveland, OH: Case Western Reserve University Press, 1970), 10, 16, 24; Hans Louis Trefousse, *Benjamin Franklin Wade, Radical Republican from Ohio* (New York: Twayne, 1963), 24.

32. Stewart, *Joshua R. Giddings*, 41, 43–44, 56, 66, 70–71, 75–78, 86–87, 97, 126, 132, 146, 152, 198–200, 224–225, 240–241; Trefousse, *Benjamin Franklin Wade*, 27, 86–87.

33. *Appeal of the Independent Democrats in Congress to the People of the United State: Shall Slavery Be Permitted in Nebraska?* (n.p.: Towers, 1854), 7; Stewart, *Joshua R. Giddings*, 224–225, 255; Trefousse, *Benjamin Franklin Wade*, 85–86.

34. Trefousse, *Benjamin Franklin Wade*, 18, 25–26, 37–38, 41–42, 45–47, 51, 55, 58, 64, 67–68, 71, 84, 86–88, 90, 99, 100, 120, 156, 179, 180, 183, 218, 273–274, 325.

35. Higginson, *Letters and Journals*, 186; Rogers, "War-Time Letters," 27–28; Smith, *Black Soldiers in Blue*, 317.

36. Lydia Maria Childs to Colonel James Montgomery, Dec. 10 and Dec. 26, 1861, James Montgomery Collection, Folder 3, 2–5.

37. Rogers, "War-Time Letters," 26–28; Higginson, *Letters and Journals*, 186.

38. Higginson, *Letters and Journals*, 26–28, 186; affidavit by James Montgomery, Jun. 12, 1871, file for James Montgomery, Compiled Military Service Records.

39. "Company Muster-In Roll," May 22, 1863, "Individual Muster-Out Roll," "Field and Staff Muster-Out Roll," file for William Lee Apthorp, Compiled Military Service Records; Higginson, *Letters and Journals*, 188.

40. "Regimental Descriptive Roll," "Company Muster-In Roll," "Individual Muster-Out Roll," "Field and Staff Muster-Out Roll," Augustus A. Hoit to Brigadier General Lorenzo Thomas, Oct. 7, 1863, Brigadier General Rufus Saxton to General Lorenzo Thomas, Oct. 28, 1863, Augustus A. Hoit to Colonel M. S. Littlefield, Jun. 15, 1864, file for Augustus A. Hoit, Compiled Military Service Records.

41. Higginson, "Up the St. John's," 311, 314; Apthorp, "Montgomery's Raids in Florida, Georgia, and South Carolina," 3; *The War of the Rebellion: A Compilation*, ser. 1, vol. XIV, 226, 423, 838.

42. Forten, *Journal*, 172n1, 240; Rogers, "War-Time Letters," 23, 29; Higginson, *Army Life in a Black Regiment*, 133, 145; Higginson, *Thomas Wentworth Higginson*, 225; *The War of the Rebellion: A Compilation*, ser. 1, vol. XIV, 423, 485.

43. Forten, *Journal*, 169, 240; Grimké, *Journals*, 453; Rogers, "War-Time Letters," 23, 29; *The War of the Rebellion: A Compilation*, ser. 1, vol. XIV, 423, 485; Higginson, *Army Life in a Black Regiment*, 135, 145–146, 159, 177; Ash, *Firebrand of Liberty*, 73.

44. Pearson, *Letters from Port Royal*, 167; Higginson, "Up the St. John's," 311–312, 315; *The War of the Rebellion: A Compilation*, ser. 1, vol. XIV, 227, 838, 845; Higginson, *Army Life in a Black Regiment*, 134–137, 140, 145–146; Taylor, *Reminiscences of My Life in Camp*, 26–27; Higginson, *Thomas Wentworth Higginson*, 225.

45. Rogers, "War-Time Letters," 44; Higginson, "Up the St. John's," 311, 315, 320; Higginson, *Army Life in a Black Regiment*, 160–162, 167; *The War of the Rebellion: A Compilation*, ser. 1, vol. XIV, 228, 838, 845; Ash, *Firebrand of Liberty*, 141, 148.

46. Higginson, "Up the St. John's," 320, 324; *The War of the Rebellion: A Compilation*, ser. 1, vol. XIV, 233, 423; Higginson, *Army Life in a Black Regiment*, 172; Higginson, *Letters and Journals*, 188, 225; Ash, *Firebrand of Liberty*, 155, 157.

47. Forten, *Journal*, 169, 176; Grimké, *Journals*, 453, 466–468; Rogers, "War-Time Letters," 48; Higginson, "Up the St. John's," 314, 318, 319, 323–324; *The War of the Rebellion: A Compilation*, ser. 1, vol. XIV, 226, 423, 837–838; *Official Records of the Union and Confederate Navies in the War of the Rebellion*, ser. 1, vol. XIII (Washington, DC: GPO, 1900), 777; Higginson, *Army Life in a Black Regiment*, 143, 156–157, 172–174, 398; Higginson, *Letters and Journals*, 188–191; Ash, *Firebrand of Liberty*, 152, 154, 159–162.

48. Forten, *Journal*, 175–176; Grimké, *Journals*, 465–468; Rogers, "War-Time Letters," 47–48, 50; Higginson, "Up the St. John's," 311, 315, 324–325; *The War of the Rebellion: A Compilation*, ser. 1, vol. XIV, 226, 228, 233, 838; Higginson, *Army Life in a Black Regiment*, 133, 145–146, 172, 173, 175–176; Higginson, *Letters and Journals*, 190.

49. Forten, *Journal*, 176, 180; Grimké, *Journals*, 466–468, 472–473; Rogers, "War-Time Letters," 48; Higginson, "Up the St. John's," 324–325; *The War of the Rebellion: A Compilation*, ser. 1, vol. XIV, 226; Higginson, *Army Life in a Black Regiment*, 173–175; Higginson, *Letters and Journals*, 190–191.

50. Forten, *Journal*, 180; Grimké, *Journals*, 472–473; Rogers, "War-Time Letters," 49; Higginson, "Up the St. John's," 324; *The War of the Rebellion: A Compilation*, ser. 1, vol. XIV, 233; Higginson, *Army Life in a Black Regiment*, 174–175; Ash, *Firebrand of Liberty*, 177.

51. Fellow white soldiers who fought alongside the 1st South Carolina Volunteers came, often reluctantly, to admire their valor. For descriptions of white soldiers' change of heart, see Pierce, "The Freedmen at Port Royal," 301, 313–314; *The War of the Rebellion: A Compilation*, ser. 1, vol. XIV, 190; Higginson, *Army Life in a Black Regiment*, 359.

52. *The War of the Rebellion: A Compilation*, ser. 1, vol. XIV, 435–436; Edward A. Miller, *Lincoln's Abolitionist General: The Biography of David Hunter* (Columbia: University of South Carolina Press, 1997), 138.

53. "Declaration for Invalid Pension," Jun. 24, 1908, "Declaration for Pension," Jun. 4, 1910, depositions by Nellie Fields and Phoebe Washington, Jul. 29, 1914, deposition by Jonas Fields, Jun. 25, 1902, pension file for Jonas (Nellie) Fields, RG 15, NARA.

54. "Department of the Interior, Bureau of Pensions," Sep. 5, 1900, "No. 125396 War Department, Record and Pension Office," n.d., "Act of June 27, 1890, Invalid Pension," n.d., "No. 1252396, Act of June 27, 1890," n.d., file for Hector Fields, Compiled Military Service Records.

55. "No. 600219, Act of June 27, 1890," n.d., "Department of the Interior, Bureau of Pensions," Jul. 10, 1913, "Act of May 11, 1912 Cert. No. 519805," Jul. 1, 1912, "Department of the Interior, Pension Office," Aug. 3, 1887, "Act of April 19, 1908, Widow's Pension, Jun. 20, 1913, "Act of June 27, 1890, Invalid Pension,"

Jul. 5, 1890, "Act of February 6, 1907," Mar. 24, 1911, pension file for William (Emelyne) Fields, RG 15, NARA.

56. General affidavit by ?, Nov. 30, 1897, "Act of June 27, 1890," "Original Pension of Minor Children," Mar. 12, 1891, "Data Taken from the Records of the Veteran's Administrator," Mar. 18, 1937, pension file for John (Diana) Green, RG 15, NARA.

57. Deposition by William Williams, Sep. 22, 1896, depositions by Samuel Gilliard, Sep. 21, 1896, and Jul. 17, 1902, "Act of April 19, 1908, Amended by Act of September 8, 1918," Oct. 6, 1917, "Act of May 1, 1920, Widow's Pension," Aug. 27, 1921, "War of 1861, Act of July 14, 1862," n.d., "Increase Invalid Pension," Aug. 9, 1905, Mar. 26, 1910, and Feb. 26, 1902, "Invalid Pension, Reissue to Allow Additional Disability," Mar. 28, 1904, "Neighbor's Affidavit, Act of June 27, 1890" by Isaac Jackson, Oct. 31, 1891, "Claimant's Affidavit" by Samuel Gilliard, Nov. 23, 1883, and Oct. 3, 1891, [deposition] by Samuel Gilliard, Nov. 15, 1884, "Invalid Pension," Apr. 27, 1889, and Oct. 3, 1891, pension file for Samuel (Martha) Gilliard, RG 15, NARA; deposition by Samuel Gilliard, Dec. 27, 1887, pension file for William (Mollie) Green, RG 15, NARA; depositions by Sharper Rivers, Jan. 8, 1894, and Jul. 25, 1902, "Declaration for Pension," May 20, 1912, general affidavit by Sharper Rivers, Jan. 10, 1887, pension file for Sharper (Lydia) Rivers, RG 15, NARA.

58. Edward Bennett's testimony for Friday Barrington's pension claim contradicts Barrington's. On Jan. 23, 1901, Edward Bennett testified that he "would go with Col. Montgomery about the country getting up men. I was with him while he went up on the Combahee on the John Adams, where we took a lot of slaves back to Beaufort. The claimant, Friday Barrington, was in that lot & I have always said that I made him a soldier because I was one of the party who took him from Combahee." Bennett does not give a date when he supposedly went up the Combahee River and took Friday Barrington off the plantation. He names Colonel Montgomery, not General Stevens, as the commanding officer and identifies the *John Adams* as the US Army vessel that transported the soldiers. It would seem that he is talking about the Combahee River Raid. I deduce, however, that he is mistaken in his identification of Friday Barrington as the man he took off the Combahee and made a soldier (1) because Barrington testified on three separate occasions in the pension files for Edward Bennett and Jacob Campbell and in his own pension file that he was with Montgomery before the 2nd South Carolina's organization, (2) because Jacob Campbell also testified for Friday Barrington that he and Friday were with Colonel Montgomery before the 2nd South Carolina Volunteers was organized, and (3) because Campbell and Corporal Alfred Fripp were Barrington's tentmates and both enlisted in the 2nd South Carolina Volunteers before the Combahee River Raid. See "Declaration for Invalid Pension, Act of June 27, 1890," Sep. 14, 1898, "War Department, Record and Pension Office," n.d., depositions by Friday Barrington, Jan. 25 and Feb. 8, 1901, deposition

by Edward Bennett, Jan. 23, 1901, "Department of the Interior, Bureau of Pensions," Oct. 14, 1902, pension file for Friday Barrington; deposition by Edward Bennett, Feb. 8, 1901, pension file for Edward (Catherine) Bennett; deposition B by Alfred Frip, Nov. 3, 1895, pension file for Corbner (Hannah) Francis/Blake; deposition by Jacob Campbell, Apr. 9, 1901, pension file for Jacob (Elvira) Campbell, RG 15, NARA.

59. William Watts Hart Davis, *History of the 104th Pennsylvania Regiment, from August 22nd, 1861, to September 30th, 1864* (Philadelphia: Jas. B. Rogers, 1866), 204, 206–207.

60. Davis, *History of the 104th*, 207–208.

61. "Company Muster Roll," Jul.–Aug. and Sep.–Oct. 1863, Mar.–Apr. 1864, Captain James M. Carver to Brigadier General Lorenzo Thomas, Oct. 18, 1864, file for James M. Carver, Compiled Military Service Records; "Company Muster-In Roll," n.d., "Company Muster Roll," May–Jun., Jun. 1–30, Jul.–Aug. 1863, "Company Muster-Out Roll," n.d., file for Levi H. Markley, Compiled Military Service Records; Davis, *History of the 104th*, 204, 343, 360–362.

62. Kevin John Weddle, *Lincoln's Tragic Admiral: The Life of Samuel Francis Du Pont* (Charlottesville: University of Virginia Press, 2005), 155; Stephen R. Wise, *Gate of Hell: Campaign for Charleston Harbor, 1863* (Columbia: University of South Carolina Press, 1994), 7–8, 23–27.

63. Gabriel E. Manigault, "Autobiography of Gabriel E. Manigault," Manigault Family Papers, 1825–1897, Chatham County, Georgia, Also Charleston District, South Carolina, Southern Historical Collection, University of North Carolina at Chapel Hill; also microfilm version from University Publications of America, 1990, 306; Weddle, *Lincoln's Tragic Admiral*, 154–155; Wise, *Gate of Hell*, 21, 27–28; William N. Still, *Iron Afloat: The Story of the Confederate Armorclads* (Columbia: University of South Carolina Press, 1988), 33–35.

64. Frederic Denison to John L. Denison, Apr. 15, 1863, https://sparedcreative21.art.blog/2020/03/30/1863-frederic-denison-to-john-l-denison/; *Official Records of the Union and Confederate Navies*, ser. 1, vol. XIII, 533; "Autobiography of Gabriel E. Manigault" (microfilm version, 306).

65. *Official Records of the Union and Confederate Navies*, ser. 1, vol. XIII, 503; Wise, *Gate of Hell*, 26–27.

66. A. B. Mulligan, *"My Dear Mother & Sisters": Civil War Letters of Capt. A. B. Mulligan, Co. B, 5th South Carolina Cavalry—Butler's Division—Hampton's Corps, 1861–1865* (Spartanburg, SC: Reprint Company, 1992), 55, 67, 73; *Official Records of the Union and Confederate Navies*, ser. 1, vol. XIII, 503, 812–813; Weddle, *Lincoln's Tragic Admiral*, 177, 181–182, 189, 197; Wise, Gate of Hell, 2, 7, 22–27, 29; Still, *Iron Afloat*, 125.

67. *Official Records of the Union and Confederate Navies*, ser. 1, vol. XIII, 571; Weddle, *Tragic Admiral*, 189, 198.

68. *The War of the Rebellion: A Compilation*, ser. I, vol. XIV (Washington, DC: GPO, 1880–1901), 241, 247; *Official Records of the Union and Confederate Navies in the War of Rebellion*, ser. 1, vol. III, 5, 6, 35; Weddle, *Lincoln's Tragic Admiral*, 171, 87;

Miller, *Lincoln's Abolitionist General*, 140; Wise, *Gate of Hell*, 29–30; Still, *Iron Afloat*, 125.

69. *Official Records of the Union and Confederate Navies*, ser. 1, vol. XIII, 571; *The War of the Rebellion: A Compilation, ser. 1,* vol. XIV, 245–246; *Official Records of the Union and Confederate Navies in the War of Rebellion, ser. 1*, vol. XIV, 61; Weddle, *Lincoln's Tragic Admiral*, 189, 198.

70. Mulligan, "*My Dear Mother & Sisters,*" 67; *The War of the Rebellion: A Compilation*, ser. 1, vol. XIV, 241, 246–247, 257, 259; *Official Records of the Union and Confederate Navies*, ser. 1, vol. XIV, 5–6, 46; Weddle, *Lincoln's Tragic Admiral*, 189, 191, 195.

71. Mulligan, "*My Dear Mother & Sisters,*" 67; *The War of the Rebellion: A Compilation*, ser. 1, vol. XIV, 240–244, 264–266, 442; *Official Records of the Union and Confederate Navies*, ser. 1, vol. XIV, 3–6; "Autobiography of Gabriel E. Manigault" (microfilm version, 306); Kevin J. Dougherty, *Ships of the Civil War 1861–1865: An Illustrated Guide to the Fighting Vessels of the Union and the Confederacy* (London: Amber Books, 2013), 40–43, 48–49, 110–111; Weddle, *Lincoln's Tragic Admiral*, 106, 154–155, 160, 171, 179, 187–188, 191–192; Miller, *Lincoln's Abolitionist General*, 140; Wise, *Gate of Hell*, 21, 27–28; Still, *Iron Afloat*, 33–35, 125, 230.

72. Mulligan, "*My Dear Mother & Sisters,*" 67; Frederic Denison to John L. Denison, Apr. 15, 1863; *War of the Rebellion: A Compilation*, ser. 1, vol. XIV, 241, 245–247, 261; *Official Records of the Union and Confederate Navies*, ser. 1, vol. XIV, 3, 6–7, 31, 33, 46–47; Andrew Billingsley, *Yearning to Breathe Free: Robert Smalls of South Carolina and His Families* (Columbia: University of South Carolina Press, 2010), 75, 78–80; Weddle, *Lincoln's Tragic Admiral,* 172, 193, 195; Wise, *Gate of Hell*, 31; Still, *Iron Afloat*, 125.

73. Mulligan, "*My Dear Mother & Sisters,*" 67, 73; *The War of the Rebellion: A Compilation*, ser. 1, vol. XIV, 240–413, 46, 49, 57, 59–61, 437; *Official Records of the Union and Confederate Navies*, ser. 1, vol. XIV, 3–7, 41–43, 65–67, 75–78, 107–110; Frederic Denison to John L. Denison, Apr. 25, 1863, private collection; Dougherty, *Ships of the Civil War*, 54–55; Weddle, *Lincoln's Tragic Admiral*, 188–189, 195–196, 200; Wise, *Gate of Hell*, 8, 22, 30–31; Still, *Iron Afloat*, 125.

74. *War of the Rebellion: A Compilation*, ser. 1, vol. XIV, 437; *Official Records of the Union and Confederate Navies*, ser. 1, vol. XIV, 3, 30–33; Miller, *Lincoln's Abolitionist General*, 140.

75. *Official Records of the Union and Confederate Navies*, ser. 1, vol. XIV, 33–35; Weddle, *Lincoln's Tragic Admiral*, 206.

76. Mulligan, "*My Dear Mother & Sisters,*" 17, 73, 77; *Official Records of the Union and Confederate Navies*, ser. 1, vol. XIV, 3, 7, 31, 61–62, 71–72; Weddle, *Lincoln's Tragic Admiral*, 165, 167, 180, 199, 1203; Wise, *Gate of Hell*, 27–28.

77. *Official Records of the Union and Confederate Navies*, ser. 1, vol. XIV, 32–33.

78. Miller, *Lincoln's Abolitionist General*, 145; Wise, *Gate of Hell*, 32.

79. *The War of the Rebellion: A Compilation*, ser. 1, vol. XIV, 437; *Official Records of the Union and Confederate Navies*, ser. 1, vol. XIV, 31, 62–64; Weddle, *Lincoln's Tragic Admiral*, 2, 160, 188, 199, 203–205, 207; Wise, *Gate of Hell*, 25, 32, 35–36.

CHAPTER 13

1. *The War of the Rebellion: A Compilation of the Official Records of the Union and Confederate Armies*, ser. 1, vol. VI (Washington, DC: GPO, 1880–1901), 199, 324.

2. Samuel Prioleau Ravenel to Alexander Chisolm, Bill of Sale, Feb. 15, 1856, "South Carolina, Secretary of State, Slave Mortgage Records, 1734–1780," South Carolina Department of Archives and History, Columbia; "Notes on the Life of Gen'l G. T. Beauregard," 1, Alexander Robert Chisolm Papers, 1861–1912: Military Records and Memoirs, New-York Historical Society; *The War of the Rebellion: A Compilation*, ser. 1, vol. VI, 45–68; *The War of the Rebellion: A Compilation of the Official Records of the Union and Confederate Armies*, ser. 1, vol. XIV (Washington, DC: GPO, 1880–1901), 726; Marshall Clement Sanford, *The Progression of Coosaw Plantation into the 20thCentury* (n.p.: n.p., 1982), 4.

3. "The Raid on Combahee," *The Mercury*, June 19, 1863; States, *Official Records of the Union and Confederate Armies: Series 1, Volume Vi*, 323–24; Higginson, *Army Life in a Black Regiment*, 232; Heyward, *Seed from Madagascar*, 130; R. Douglas Hurt, *Agriculture and the Confederacy: Policy, Productivity, and Power in the Civil War South* (Chapel Hill: University of North Carolina, 2015), 34.

4. *The War of the Rebellion: A Compilation*, ser. 1, vol. VI, 339.

5. Smith, Childs, and Smith, *Mason Smith Family Letters, 1860–1868*, 70; W. Eric Emerson, *Sons of Privilege: The Charleston Light Dragoons in the Civil War* (Columbia: University of South Carolina Press, 2005), xiii–xiv, 1, 5–11, 14–17, 19–20, 24, 29, 31, 35–36, 38, 53–54, 60–61, 115, 121, 128, 132.

6. Gabriel E. Manigault, "Autobiography of Gabriel Manigault, 1887–1894," 307, South Caroliniana Library, University of South Carolina, Columbia; Emerson, *Sons of Privilege: The Charleston Light Dragoons in the Civil War*, 6, 35.

7. Gabriel E. Manigault, "Autobiography of Gabriel Manigault, 1887–1894," 307–309, South Caroliniana Library, University of South Carolina, Columbia; Daniel Elliott Huger Smith, Arney Robinson Childs, and Alice Ravenel Huger Smith, eds., *Mason Smith Family Letters, 1860–1868* (Columbia: University of South Carolina Press, 1950), 308–310; W. Eric Emerson, *Sons of Privilege: The Charleston Light Dragoons in the Civil War* (Columbia: University of South Carolina Press, 2005), 23–26, 35–36.

8. *The War of the Rebellion: A Compilation*, ser. 1, vol. XIV, 344.

9. "The Raid on Combahee"; *The War of the Rebellion: A Compilation*, ser. 1, vol. VI, 344.

10. *The War of the Rebellion: A Compilation*, ser. 1, vol. VI, 391–393.

11. *The War of the Rebellion: A Compilation*, ser. 1, vol. VI, 391–393, 395.

12. *The War of the Rebellion: A Compilation*, ser. 1, vol. VI, 91.

13. *The War of the Rebellion: A Compilation*, ser. 1, vol. VI, 91.

14. *The War of the Rebellion: A Compilation*, ser. 1, vol. VI, 92; Heyward, *Seed from Madagascar*, 30; George M. Blackburn, *With the Wandering Regiment: The Diary of Captain Ralph Ely of the Eighth Michigan Infantry* (Mount Pleasant: Central Michigan University, 1965), 30.

15. Blackburn, *With the Wandering Regiment*, 30.

16. Emerson, *Sons of Privilege: The Charleston Light Dragoons in the Civil War*, 45.

17. "The Enemy Raid on the Banks of the Combahee," *The Mercury*, 6/4/1863; Warren Ripley, *The Battles of Chapman's Fort May 26, 1864* (Green Pond, SC: Privately Printed, 1978), 12, 15, 21.

18. *The War of the Rebellion: A Compilation*, ser. 1, vol. XIV, 95–96; *The War of the Rebellion: A Compilation*, ser. 1, vol. XIV, 38; *Official Records of the Union and Confederate Navies*, ser. 1, vol. XIII, 96–98; Ripley, *The Battles of Chapman's Fort*, 22–28.

19. *The War of the Rebellion: A Compilation*, ser. 1, vol. XIV, 38; A. B. Mulligan, *"My Dear Mother & Sisters": Civil War Letters of Capt. A. B. Mulligan, Co. B, 5th South Carolina Cavalry—Butler's Division—Hampton's Corps, 1861–1865* (Spartanburg, SC: Reprint Company, 1992), 27, 31; *Official Records of the Union and Confederate Navies in the War of the Rebellion*, ser. 1, vol. XIII (Washington, DC: GPO, 1900), 95–98; Ripley, *The Battles of Chapman's Fort*, 21–28.

20. *The War of the Rebellion: A Compilation*, ser. 1, vol. XIV, 38; *Official Records of the Union and Confederate Navies in the War of the Rebellion*, ser. 1, vol. XIII (Washington, DC: GPO, 1900), 96–98; Ripley, *The Battles of Chapman's Fort*, 21–28; A. B. Mulligan, *"My Dear Mother & Sisters": Civil War Letters of Capt. A. B. Mulligan, Co. B, 5th South Carolina Cavalry—Butler's Division—Hampton's Corps, 1861–1865* (Spartanburg, SC: Reprint Company, 1992), 27.

21. *Official Records of the Union and Confederate Navies in the War of the Rebellion*, ser. 1, vol. XIII, 95–96.

22. *Official Records of the Union and Confederate Navies*, ser. 1, vol. XIII, 399. Robert H. Gudmestad, *Steamboats and the Rise of the Cotton Kingdom* (Baton Rouge: Louisiana State University Press, 2011), 13–14.

23. *Official Records of the Union and Confederate Navies*, ser. 1, vol. XIII, 113; Ripley, *The Battles of Chapman's Fort*, 28.

24. *Official Records of the Union and Confederate Navies*, ser. 1, vol. XIII, 185–186, 192, 199–200; E. D. Gallien to William Lochren, 6/27/1895, Simon (Rachel) US Civil War Pension File; Ripley, *The Battles of Chapman's Fort*, 30–32.

25. *Official Records of the Union and Confederate Navies*, ser. 1, vol. XIII, 199–200; Ripley, *The Battles of Chapman's Fort*, 32–34; "E. B. Hale," *Dictionary of American Fighting Ships*, Naval History and Heritage Command, https://www.history.navy.mil/research/histories/ship-histories/danfs/e/e-b-hale-screw-steamer.html.

26. *Official Records of the Union and Confederate Navies*, ser. 1, vol. XIII, 199–200; Ripley, *The Battles of Chapman's Fort*, 32–34.

27. *Official Records of the Union and Confederate Navies*, ser. 1, vol. XIII, 199–200; Ripley, *The Battles of Chapman's Fort*, 32–34.

28. *Official Records of the Union and Confederate Navies*, ser. 1, vol. XIII, 199–200.

29. *The War of the Rebellion: A Compilation*, ser. 1, vol. VI, 337–338; *The War of the Rebellion: A Compilation*, ser. 1, vol. XIV, 291–293; Margaret Belser Hollis and Allen H. Stokes, ed., *Twilight on the South Carolina Rice Fields: Letters of the Heyward Family, 1861–1871* (Columbia: University of South Carolina Press, 2010), 30; Jeff W. Grigg, *The Combahee River Raid: Harriet Tubman & Lowcountry Liberation* (Charleston, SC: The History Press, 2014), 69; Emerson, *Sons of Privilege*, 55.

30. H. David Stone, *Vital Rails: The Charleston & Savannah Railroad and the Civil War in Coastal South Carolina* (Columbia: University of South Carolina Press, 2008), 104, 136–137; Emerson, *Sons of Privilege: The Charleston Light Dragoons in the Civil War*, 54.

31. Lewis F. Knudsen Jr., *A History of the 5th South Carolina Cavalry, 1861–1865* (Wilmington, NC: Broadfoot Publishing, 2016), 53–56; Emerson, *Sons of Privilege: The Charleston Light Dragoons in the Civil War*, 44–45.

32. 1860 Agricultural Census, Marlboro, SC, William P. Emanuel, 1860 Slave Schedule, Marlboro, SC, William P. Emanuel; *The War of the Rebellion: A Compilation*, ser. 1, vol. XIV, 298–306; Emerson, *Sons of Privilege: The Charleston Light Dragoons in the Civil War*, 53.

33. W. P. Emanuel to Thomas Jordan, Jan. 21, 1863, W. P. Emanuel to Thomas Jordan, Sep. 21, 1863, Major W. P. Emanuel CSA Pension File, "Register of Appointments, Confederate States of America," S.O. no. 23–1, all "War Department Collection of Confederate Records, 1825–1927," RG 109.

34. "Our Correspondence from Hilton Head," New York Tribune 5/11/1863; "A Raid on the Combahee," *The Mercury*, Jun. 18, 1863; *The War of the Rebellion: A Compilation*, ser. 1, vol. XIV, 307; Grigg, *The Combahee River Raid*, 69.

35. Francis Izard, Jun. 1, 1863, US, "Union Provost Marshal's File of Papers Relating to Individual Civilians, 1861–1867," in *Record Group 109* (Washington, DC: National Archives, 1861–1867).

36. Francis Izard, Jun. 1, 1863, US, "Union Provost Marshal's File of Papers Relating to Individual Civilians, 1861–1867," in *Record Group 109* (Washington, DC: National Archives, 1861–1867).

37. Francis Izard, Jun. 1, 1863, US, "Union Provost Marshal's File of Papers Relating to Individual Civilians, 1861–1867," in *Record Group 109* (Washington, DC: National Archives, 1861–1867).

38. "The Raid on Combahee," *The Mercury* 6/19/1863; David Stephen Heidler, Jeanne T. Heidler, and David J. Coles, *Encyclopedia of the American Civil War. Volume I A-C: A Political Social and Military History* (Santa Barbara, CA: ABC-CLIO, 2000), 407–408.

39. "The Expedition Up the Combahee," *The New South*, June 6 1863; "The Raid on Combahee," *The Mercury,* Jun. 19, 1863; *The War of the Rebellion: A Compilation*, ser. 1, vol. XIV, 299–304, 307–308; Denison, *Shot and Shell*, 155.

40. US Senate, Committee on Claims, Subcommittee on S. 2810, "Elizabeth R. Nicholls and Joanna L. Nicholls, Hearing Hrg-1914-Cls-0001, Jun. 6, 8, 1914," 15.

41. US Senate, Committee on Claims, Subcommittee on S. 2810, "Elizabeth R. Nicholls and Joanna L. Nicholls, Hearing Hrg-1914-Cls-0001, Jun. 6, 8, 1914," 12, 15, 19.

42. Mary Anna Faber to Joshua Nicholls Marriage Settlement 1848, Bills of Complaint, 1800–1863, South Carolina Court of Equity (Columbia: Department of Archives and History); US Senate, Committee on Claims, Subcommittee on S. 2810, "Elizabeth R. Nicholls and Joanna L. Nicholls, Hearing Hrg-1914-Cls-0001, Jun. 6, 8, 1914," 8, 11, 16.

43. "The Raid on Combahee," *The Mercury*, Jun. 19, 1863.

44. "The Raid on Combahee," *The Mercury* 6/19/1863; An Eventful Life Ended: Harriet A. Weed Dies Among Her Father's Treasures," *The New York Times* (November 2; E. Kay Gibson, *Dictionary of Transports and Combatant Vessels, Steam and Sail, Employed by the Union Army, 1861–1868: An Annotated Compilation...* (Camden, Me: Ensign Press, 1985), 144.

45. "The Raid on Combahee," *The Mercury* 6/19/1863; Charles Dana Gibson and E. Kay Gibson, *Assault and Logistics: Union Army Coastal and River Operations, 1861–1866, Volume 2* (Camden, Me: Ensign Press, 1995), 25.

46. Heyward, *Seed from Madagascar*, 105–106.

47. Heyward, *Seed from Madagascar*, 105–106.

48. "From South Carolina."

49. "The Raid on Combahee."

50. "The Raid on Combahee"; "From South Carolina"; "A Raid Among the Rice Plantations," *Harper's Weekly*, Jul. 4, 1863.

51. Bradford, *Scenes in the Life of Harriet Tubman*, 39; Sarah Bradford, *Harriet Tubman: The Moses of Her People* (New York: J. J. Little, 1901), 99; Kate Clifford Larson, *Bound for the Promised Land: Harriet Tubman: Portrait of an American Hero* (New York: One World/Ballantine, 2009), 211; Jean McMahon Humez, *Harriet Tubman: The Life and the Life Stories* (Madison, WI: University of Wisconsin Press, 2003), 244–245; Conrad, *General Harriett Tubman*, 171.

52. "The Combahee Expedition," *Philadelphia North American and United States Gazette*, June 8 1863; Charles Wood, "A History Concerning the Pension Claim of Harriet Tubman," 2, RG 233, NARA; Bradford, *Scenes in the Life of Harriet Tubman*, 65–66; Bradford, *Harriet Tubman*, 99; Earl Conrad, "The Charles P. Wood Manuscripts of Harriet Tubman," *Negro History Bulletin* 13, no. 4 (1950): 92; Conrad, *General Harriett Tubman*, 179; Denison, *Shot and Shell*, 155.

53. P. K. Rose, "The Civil War: Black American Contributions to Union Intelligence," *Studies in Intelligence* 42, no. 5 (1999): 74–75, 78–79.

54. Wood, "A History Concerning the Pension Claim of Harriet Tubman," 1–2. Wood, "A History Concerning the Pension Claim of Harriet Tubman," 1; Bradford, *Scenes in the Life of Harriet Tubman*, 70–71; Conrad, "The Charles P. Wood Manuscripts of Harriet Tubman," 93; Grigg, *The Combahee River Raid*, 71; Jean McMahon Humez, *Harriet Tubman*; Larson, *Bound for the Promised Land*, 210; Catherine Clinton, *Harriet Tubman: The Road to Freedom* (Boston, MA: Little Brown, 2004), 164; Humez, *The Life and the Life Stories* (Madison, WI: University of Wisconsin Press, 2003), 368 n.29; Conrad, *General Harriett Tubman*, 165–166.

55. Walter Plowden in US Census, 1870, 1880; Walter Plowden, enumeration district sheet, NARA microfilm publication T9 (Washington, DC: NARA, n.d.); "Health Department, District of Columbia," Aug. 5, 1893," Declaration for an Original Invalid Pension" by Walter D. Plowden, Nov. 1, 1890, deposition A by James A. Hunt, Oct. 1, 1895, "Department of the Interior, Bureau of Pensions," Jul. 24, 1896, "Construction of the Act of July 25, 1866," Oct. 17, 1896, "Department of the Interior, Bureau of Pensions," Jul. 16, 1896 in Pension file for Walter (Annie) Plowden, RG 15, NARA.

56. Deposition A by James A. Hunt, Oct. 1, 1895, n.d., [deposition] by Walter Plowden, Jul. 17, 1876, Nero Crawford and Isaac S. Hawkins, Feb. 26, 1880, H. Jones M.D. to [no name], Mar. 17, 1880, "Act of June 27, 1890, Invalid Pension," Oct. 20, 1890, "Act of June 27, 1890, Declaration for Widow's Pension," Jun. 17, 1893, "Act of June 27, 1890, Widow's Pension," Oct. 27, 1896, "Act of June 27, 1890, Widow's Pension," Apr. 29, 1910, "No. 792984, Act of June 27, 1890," n.d., "No. 893306, Act of July 14, 1862, and March 3, 1873," Walter (Annie) Plowden, RG 15, NARA.

57. "Walter Plowden, Report [To Accompany bill H. R. No. 1323]," Walter (Annie) Plowden, RG 15, NARA.

58. "Walter Plowden, Report [To Accompany bill H. R. No. 1323]," Walter (Annie) Plowden, RG 15, NARA.

59. "Declaration for an Original Invalid Pension" by Walter D. Plowden, Nov. 1, 1890, Walter (Annie) Plowden, RG 15, NARA.

60. [Deposition] by Isaac Hawkins, Feb. 26, 1880, Walter (Annie) Plowden, RG 15, NARA.

61. Records of the Office of the Judge Advocate (Army), "Civil War Court Martial File L15566, US v. Private John E. Webster," Vo. G 47 Regiment Penn Vols, 4–5, 14–18, 22, 31, 33–34–36, 45–46, NARA.

62. Records of the Office of the Judge Advocate (Army), "Civil War Court Martial File L15566, US v. Private John E. Webster," Vo. G 47 Regiment Penn Vols, 25–26, 36, RG 153, NARA.

63. Mott Blake in US Census, 1870, Saint James Santee Parish, Charleston, SC, NARA; Mott Blake in US Census, 1880; Mott Blake in US Census, 1900; Mott Blake in US Census, 1910; Mott Blake, St. James Santee, Charleston, South Carolina, ED 81, NARA 1,375,466; "No. 927064, Act of June 27, 1890," n.d., "Declaration for Increase of Pension and New Disability Under Acts of June 27, 1890, May 9, 1900, and Order of March 14, 1904" by Mott Blake, Mar. 2, 1896, "Military Service, Name of Soldier," n.d., "Act of April 19, 1908, Widow's Pension," Mar. 16, 1916, general davit by Samuel Fiall, Jun. 23, 1902, pension file for Mott (Emma) Blake, RG 15, NARA.

64. Isaac Hayward, Mar. 2, 1870 in "Registers of Signatures of Depositors in Branches of the Freedman's Savings and Trust Company, 1865–1874," Records of the Office of the Comptroller of the Currency, RG 101, NARA.

65. "Exhibit F, Case of Sina Green," Dec. 14, 1876, in pension file for William (Sina) Young, RG 15, NARA.

66. Isaac Hayward, Mar. 2, 1870 in "Registers of Signatures of Depositors in Branches of the Freedman's Savings and Trust Company, 1865–1874," Records of the Office of the Comptroller of the Currency, RG 101, NARA. There are variant spellings of Hayward's name in the records. There is one man named "Isaac Hayward," one named "Isaac Haywood," and seven named "Isaac Heyward" in the 1870 census, for example. An "Isaac Heyward" testified in Marshall Newton's pension application and appears in the 1880 census living on St. Helena Island (Newton supposedly served in 34th Regiment, Company H). An "Isaac Hayward" enlisted in 128th Regiment USCT, Company D on April 11, 1865, and was discharged on September 21, 1865. He had been enslaved on William Ball's plantation on the Cooper River, possibly on Limerick Plantation, where his first wife died in bondage. He labored as a field hand up until enlistment. The two "Isaac Haywards" are not the same. Their physical descriptions don't match—the soldier in the 128th had a dark complexion, black hair and eyes; he would not have appeared to be biracial and does not seem to have had children. Isaac Hayward from Coosaw had at least seven children. Curiously, several witnesses, including the surgeon at the general hospital in Hilton Head who examined him before discharging him, testified that this Isaac Haywood from Charleston had ambiguous genitalia. This Isaac

Haywood lived in Charleston for many years after the end of the Civil War and died there in October 1902. I don't think he is Harriet Tubman's Isaac Hayward. [Deposition] by Moses Deas, Aug. 5, 1903, P. H. Martin, Oct. 24, 1903, deposition by Elias Ball, Aug. 18, 1904, Martin Deas, Aug. 6, 1904, P. H. Martin, Isabella Edwards, Aug. 8, 1904, Humphrey Moultrie, J. H. Brown, Aug. 15, 1908, Jordan Barnett, Aug. 19, 1904, claimant's affidavit by Lucy Heyward, Dec. 8, 1903, Isaac Haywood, May 2, 1891, "Accrued Pension, Act of March 2, 1895," Aug. 8, 1904, "Act of June 27, 1890, Invalid Pension," Nov. 11, 1891, "War Department, Record and Pension Division," May 9, 1891," Record and Pension Office, War Department," n.d., "Army of the United States Certificate of Disability for Discharge" for Isaac Haywood, Sep. 21, 1865, "Department of the Interior, Bureau of Pensions," Feb. 6, 1892, "Act of June 27, 1890, As Amended by Act of May 27, 1900, Widow's Pension," n.d., "Declaration for Widow's Pension, Act of June 27, 1890" by Lucy Hayward, Nov. 29, 1902, pension file for Mott (Emma) Blake, RG 15, NARA.

67. Seth Rogers, "War-Time Letters of Seth Rogers, M.D., Surgeon of the First South Carolina Afterwards the Thirty-Third USCT 1862–1863," 54, *Florida History Online*, https://history.domains.unf.edu/floridahistoryonline/proje cts-proj-b-p-html/projects-rogers-index-html/.

68. Peter Burns in US Census, 1870; Peter Burns, Jan. 11, 1872, Freedman's Bank Records, 1865–1874, NARA; Jack Burns Freedman's Bank Account, Jun. 2, 1869. Peter Burns' Freedman's Bank Account states that he was 17 years old with 5 children. The age is surely an error made by the recorder. Peter Burn's aplication lists his children as: "Lizzie, Martha, Jack, Thomas, and Paul." Jack Burns Freedman's Bank Account identifies Peter Burns as his father, Moses and Maurice as his siblings, and Thomas, Paul, Lizzie, and Martha as his half-siblings. This is Tubman's Peter Burns. There are two men named Peter Burns in the 1870 census, one in Beaufort and one in Sumter/Williamsburg. Peter Burns in Beaufort was seventy-eight years of age in 1870 and appears with his wife, Susan.

69. "No. 11996, Navy Widow, Act of June 27, 1890," n.d., "No. 23939, Navy Invalid, Act of June 27, 1890," "O. W. and N. Div. Naval Service," Mar. 30, 1893, "O. W. and N. Div. Naval Service," Feb. 26, 1892, "Form No. 137, Indorsement 23939,: Apr. 20, 1892, 1st Indorsement, War Department, Quartermaster General's Office, Mar. 18, 1892, "Act of June 27, 1890, Declaration for Invalid Pension" by Captain Turner alias Captain Blake, Oct. 11, 1890, Captain Turner alias (Millie) Blake, RG 15, NARA. Though his pension file was filed to the US Navy and forms within the file describe the vessel on which he served as the USS John Adams, a US Navy vessel, the USS John Adams did not join the South Atlantic Blockading Squadron until the summer of 1863). Captain Turner alias Blake surely served on the US Army John Adams, according to a letter from the US Army Quartermaster. For more information about Captain Blake and his probable connections to the Blake family's plantations on the Upper Combahee River, see Darius Brown's book about his family history, *At the Feet of the Elders: A Journey into the Lowcountry Family History* (forthcoming by Shortwood Press). George Chisolm (St. Helena

Township) in US Census, 1870; George Chisolm in entry for Susan Chisolm (Beaufort, SC) in US Census; George Chisolm (Orangeburg, SC) in US Census, 1870; George Chisolm (Johns Island, Charleston) in US Census, 1870; George Chisolm in entry for Will Hummock, US Census, 1870; Solomon Gregory (St. Paul's Parish, Colleton), in US Census, 1870; Bradford, *Scenes in the Life of Harriet Tubman*, 38–39; Bradford, *Harriet Tubman*, 98–99; Rogers, "War-Time Letters," 46, 48; Esther Hill Hawks, *A Woman Doctor's Civil War: Esther Hill Hawks' Diary*, ed. Gerald Schwartz (Columbia, SC: University of South Carolina Press, 1984), 46; Charles Dana Gibson and E. Kay Gibson, *Assault and Logistics: Union Army Coastal and River Operations, 1861–1866, Volume 2* (Camden, Me: Ensign Press, 1995), 26. Searches for names with differently configured spellings of the other scouts' and spies' names (e.g., Gabriel Cahern, Cohen, Cohern, Cahen, and Coven; Sandy Sellus, Salter, and Salters) turned up nothing.

70. "The Expedition Up the Combahee," *The New South*, June 6 1863; "The Combahee Expedition," *Philadelphia North American and United States Gazette*, June 8, 1863; Denison, *Shot and Shell*, 155–157; Heyward, *Seed from Madagascar*, 130.

71. "A Raid Among the Rice Plantations," *Harper's Weekly*, Jul. 4, 1863; Records of the Office of the Judge Advocate (Army), "Civil War Court Martial File L15566, US v. Private John E. Webster," Vo. G 47 Regiment Penn Vols, 28, RG 153, NARA; Jeff W. Grigg, *The Combahee River Raid: Harriet Tubman & Lowcountry Liberation* (Charleston, SC: The History Press, 2014), 71.

72. "A Raid Among the Rice Plantations."

73. "A Raid on the Combahee," *The Mercury*, Jun. 18, 1863; "A Raid Among the Rice Plantations," *Harper's Weekly*, Jul. 4, 1863; Surgeon Robinson, "The Siege of Charleston—Portion of the Obstructions in the Harbor, Washed Ashore in an Island," *Harper's Weekly*, Oct. 3, 1863; William T. Robinson, 104th Regiment Pennsylvania Infantry, Company Field & Staff, "Organization Index to Pension Files of Veterans Who Served Between 1861 and 1900, 1949–1949," RG 15, NARA; William Lee Apthorp, "Montgomery's Raids in Florida, Georgia, and South Carolina," in *Apthorp Family Papers, 1741–1964* (Miami, FL: HistoryMiami Museum, 1864), 15; Grigg, *The Combahee River Raid*, 74; Denison, *Shot and Shell*, 155–157.

74. C. R. Brayton to My Dear Father, May 21, 1863, Charlie to My Dear Father Aug. 16, 1863, Folders 1 and 2, Charles Ray Brayton Papers, 1853–1908, Rhode Island Historical Society, Providence; "From South Carolina."

75. "The Expedition Up the Combahee," *The New South*, June 6 1863; "The Combahee Expedition," *Philadelphia North American and United States Gazette*, June 8 1863; "Interesting from Hilton Head," *New York Herald*, Jun. 9, 1863; "From South Carolina—the New Federal Commander—Col. Montgomery's Late Raid," *Chicago Tribune*, Jun. 20, 1863; William Lee Apthorp, "Montgomery's Raids in Florida, Georgia, and South Carolina," in *Apthorp Family Papers, 1741–1964* (Miami, Florida: HistoryMiami Museum, 1864), 15; Jeff W. Grigg, *The Combahee River Raid: Harriet Tubman & Lowcountry Liberation* (Charleston, SC: The History Press, 2014), 69–70; Humez, Jean McMahon. Harriet Tubman: the Life and the Life Stories (Madison, Wis: University of Wisconsin Press, 2003),

245; Denison, *Shot and Shell*, 155–157; Astronomical Applications Department of the U. S. Naval Observatory, https://aa.usno.navy.mil/calculated/moon/phases?date=1863-06-01&nump=50&format=p&submit=Get+Data.

76. Fergus J. Wood, "Tidal Dynamics. Volume I: Theory and Analysis of Tidal Forces," *Journal of Coastal Research*, spec. issue no. 30 (2001): xli-xlii; Fergus J. Wood. Tidal Dynamics: Coastal Flooding, and Cycles of Gravitational Force (Dordrecht: D. Reidel Pub. Co., 1986), 501–502.

77. "The Expedition Up the Combahee," *The New South*, June 6, 1863; "The Combahee Expedition," *Philadelphia North American and United States Gazette*, June 8, 1863; "Interesting from Hilton Head," *New York Herald*, Jun. 9, 1863; "From South Carolina—the New Federal Commander—Col. Montgomery's Late Raid," *Chicago Tribune*, Jun. 20, 1863; William Lee Apthorp, "Montgomery's Raids in Florida, Georgia, and South Carolina," in *Apthorp Family Papers, 1741–1964* (Miami, FL: HistoryMiami Museum, 1864), 15; Robert H. Gudmestad, *Steamboats and the Rise of the Cotton Kingdom* (Baton Rouge: Louisiana State University, 2011), 120; Charles Dana Gibson and E. Kay Gibson, *Assault and Logistics: Union Army Coastal and River Operations, 1861–1866* (Camden, ME: Ensign Press, 1995), 2: 291; Denison, *Shot and Shell, 155–157*; NOAA Tide Predictions, 8667624 Brickyard Point, Coosaw River (from 1863/06/01 12:00AM to 1863/06/02 11:59PM): https://tidesandcurrents.noaa.gov/noaatidepredictions.html?id=8667624&units=standard&bdate=18630601&edate=18630602&timezone=LST&clock=12hour&datum=MLLW&interval=hilo&action=dailychart.

78. "The Expedition up the Combahee"; "A Raid on the Combahee," *The Mercury*, Jun. 18, 1863; "From South Carolina—the New Federal Commander—Col. Montgomery's Late Raid," Chicago Tribune, Jun. 20, 1863; Jeff W. Grigg, The Combahee River Raid: Harriet Tubman & Lowcountry Liberation (Charleston, SC: The History Press, 2014), 69–70; Humez, Jean McMahon. Harriet Tubman: the Life and the Life Stories (Madison: University of Wisconsin Press), 2003, 245–246; Denison, Shot and Shell, 155–157; William Watts Hart Davis, History of the 104th Pennsylvania Regiment, from August 22nd, 1861, to September 30th, 1864 (Philadelphia: Jas. B. Rogers, 1866), 209; NOAA Tide Predictions, 8667259 Field's Point, SC: https://tidesandcurrents.noaa.gov/noaatidepredictions.html?id=8667259&units=standard&bdate=18630601&edate=18630602&timezone=LST&clock=12hour&datum=MLLW&interval=hilo&action=dailychart.

79. "The Expedition up the Combahee"; "From South Carolina"; William Lee Apthorp, "Montgomery's Raids in Florida, Georgia, and South Carolina"; Gudmestad, *Steamboats*, 161; Denison, *Shot and Shell*, 155–157.

80. "The Expedition up the Combahee"; "From South Carolina"; Apthorp, "Montgomery's Raids in Florida, Georgia, and South Carolina," 15; "Miscellaneous Items, " *Douglass Monthly*, August 1863; Jeff W. Grigg, *The Combahee River Raid: Harriet Tubman & Lowcountry Liberation* (Charleston, SC: The History Press, 2014), 71, 73.

81. "The Enemy Raid on the Banks of the Combahee," *The Mercury*, 6/4/1863; "The Expedition up the Combahee"; "The Combahee Expedition," *Philadelphia North American and United States Gazette*, June 8 1863"; "From

South Carolina"; Apthorp, "Montgomery's Raids in Florida, Georgia, and South Carolina," 15; Denison, *Shot and Shell*, 155–157; Thomas N. Thompson, Compiled Military Service Records of Volunteer Union Soldiers who Served with the United States Colored Troops, Record Group 94, National Archives, Washington, DC; Jeff W. Grigg, *The Combahee River Raid: Harriet Tubman & Lowcountry Liberation* (Charleston, SC: The History Press, 2014), 71.

82. "The Expedition up the Combahee"; "From South Carolina"; Apthorp, "Montgomery's Raids in Florida, Georgia, and South Carolina," 15, 19–20; Denison, *Shot and Shell*; James M. Carver, Compiled Military Service Records of Volunteer Union Soldiers who Served with the United States Colored Troops, Record Group, 94, National Archives, Washington, DC.

83. "From South Carolina"; "A Raid among the Rice Plantations." *Harper's Weekly*, July 4 1863; Apthorp, "Montgomery's Raids in Florida, Georgia, and South Carolina," 19; *The War of the Rebellion: A Compilation*, ser. 1, vol. XIV, 293–295, 298–306; William E. Hewitt, Compiled Military Service Records of Volunteer Union Soldiers who Served with the United States Colored Troops, Record Group 109, National Archives, Washington, DC; Jeff W. Grigg, *The Combahee River Raid: Harriet Tubman & Lowcountry Liberation* (Charleston, SC: The History Press, 2014), 72, 74.

84. "The Enemy's Raid on the Banks of the Combahee"; "The Expedition up the Combahee;" "From South Carolina;" "A Raid on the Combahee"; "Combahee Rice Plantations: Rose Hill Plantation," private collection, Green Pond, SC.

85. Apthorp, "Montgomery's Raids—In Florida, Georgia and South Carolina," Apthorp Family Papers, 1741–1946, Folder 2.6, 15–16; Gudmestad, *Steamboats*, 13, 68, 100; William H. Ewen, *Days of the Steamboats* (2nd ed. Mystic, CT: Mystic Seaport Museum, 1988), 9.

86. "A Raid on the Combahee"; "The Enemy's Raid on the Banks of the Combahee"; Records of the Office of the Judge Advocate (Army), "Civil War Court Martial File L15566, US v. Private John E. Webster," Vo. G 47 Regiment Penn Vols, 28, RG 153, NARA, 28; John M. Adams, Compiled Military Service Records of Volunteer Union Soldiers who Served with the United States Colored Troops, National Archives, Washington, DC; Apthorp, "Montgomery's Raids in Florida, Georgia, and South Carolina," 15–16; Jeff W. Grigg, *The Combahee River Raid: Harriet Tubman & Lowcountry Liberation* (Charleston, SC: The History Press, 2014), 73.

87. "The Expedition Up the Combahee"; "The Combahee Expedition"; "Interesting from Hilton Head"; "From South Carolina"; "A Raid among the Rice Plantations"; "Miscellaneous Items." *Douglass' Monthly*, August 1863"; Apthorp, "Montgomery's Raids in Florida, Georgia, and South Carolina," 16–17; Davis, *History of the 104th Pennsylvania Regiment*, 209–210; Grigg, Jeff W. *The Combahee River Raid: Harriet Tubman & Lowcountry Liberation*. Charleston, SC: The History Press, 2014), 73–74, 77, 79; Denison, *Shot and Shell*, 155–157.

88. "The Raid on Combahee," *The Mercury*, Jun. 19, 1863; Apthorp, "Montgomery's Raids in Florida, Georgia, and South Carolina," 16; Denison, *Shot and Shell*, 155–157.

89. "The Raid on Combahee."

CHAPTER 14

1. Thomas Wentworth Higginson, *Army Life in a Black Regiment and Other Writings* (Boston: Houghton, Mifflin and Company, 1900), 237.

2. Christopher Looby, *The Complete Civil War Journal and Selected Letters of Thomas Wentworth Higginson* (Chicago: University of Chicago Press, 2000), 166; Higginson, *Army Life in a Black Regiment*, 237; Leslie Ann Schwalm, '*A Hard Fight for We': Women's Transition from Slavery to Freedom in South Carolina* (Urbana: University of Illinois, 1997), 95.

3. "The Raid on Combahee," *The Mercury*, June 19, 1863; Looby, *The Complete Civil War Journal*, 166. Thomas Wentworth Higginson, *Army Life in a Black Regiment and Other Writings* (Boston: Houghton, Mifflin, 1900), 237.

4. Riley Hale, "Common Misconceptions About Identifying a Cottonmouth," WRDW, Augusta, GA, May 18, 2018, https://www.wrdw.com/content/news/Common-misconceptions-about-identifying-a-cottonmouth-483078321.html; South Carolina Wild Life, "Venomous Snakes of South Carolina," South Carolina Department of Natural Resources, n.d., dnr.sc.gov/education/pdf/VenomousSnakesSC.pdf.

5. William Elliott, *Carolina Sports, by Land and Water: Including Incidents of Devil-Fishing, Wild-Cat, Deer and Bear Hunting, Etc. 1846* (New York: Derby & Jackson, 1859), 212; Smithsonian's National Zoo and Conservation Biology Institute, "Reptile Discovery Center: American Alligator," n.d., https://nationalzoo.si.edu/animals/american-alligator; Charles Q. Choi, "Mystery of Alligator Movement Solved," Live Science, Mar. 13, 2008, https://www.livescience.com/4851-mystery-alligator-movement-solved.html#:~:text=By%20moving%20the%20lungs%20around,also%20helped%20the%20reptiles%20roll; "A Day in the Life of a Gator," Experience Kissimmee Florida, n.d. https://www.experiencekissimmee.com/article/day-life-gator-kissimmee.

6. Duncan Clinch Heyward, *Seed from Madagascar* (Columbia: University of South Carolina Press, 1993), 30, 38.

7. "The Raid on Combahee"; *The Mercury*, Jun. 19, 1863; "From South Carolina—the New Federal Commander—Col. Montgomery's Late Raid," *Chicago Tribune*, Jun. 20, 1863; "A Raid Among the Rice Plantations," *Harper's Weekly*, Jul. 4, 1863; Sarah Bradford, *Harriet Tubman: The Moses of Her People* (1886; New York: J. J. Little, 1901), 100; Sarah Bradford, *Scenes in the Life of Harriet Tubman* (1869; repr., North Stratford, NH: Ayer, 2004), 40; Heyward, *Seed from Madagascar*, 37–39.

8. Ewen, *Days of the Steamboats*, 9–10.

9. Looby, *The Complete Civil War Journal*, 166; Higginson, Army Life in a Black Regiment, 237; Rudolph C. Troike, "Creole/L→/R in African American English/Gullah: Historical Fact and Fiction," American Speech 90, no. 1 (2015): 7, 38, 43–64; Lorenzo Dow Turner, Africanisms in the Gullah Dialect (Columbia: University of South Carolina Press, 2002), xliv, 27–28, 242–243; Schwalm, *A Hard Fight for We*, 95. [Looby 2000, 166; Higginson 1900, 237; Schwalm 1997, 95] (Many West African languages including Bambara, Twi, Yoruba, and Kru, have only the [l] or [r] sounds. Thus, the two sounds

alternate, particularly in the speech of African-born or first-generation speakers of English-based Creole-speakers in the Caribbean and Africa, in addition to what is today called Gullah Geechee. See John A. Holm, *Pidgins and Creoles: Vol. 1, Theory and Structure* (Cambridge: Cambridge University Press), 135–36.

10. "The Enemy Raid on the Banks of the Combahee," *The Mercury*, 6/4/1863; "The Expedition up the Combahee" *The New South*, June 6, 1863; "Interesting from Hilton Head," *New York Herald*, June 9, 1863; "A Raid among the Rice Plantations," *Harper's Weekly*, July 4, 1863; "Miscellaneous Items," *Douglass Monthly*, August 1863; Looby, *The Complete Civil War Journal*, 166; William Watts Hart Davis, *History of the 104th Pennsylvania Regiment, from August 22nd, 1861, to September 30th, 1864* (Philadelphia: Jas. B. Rogers, 1866), 209–210; Higginson, *Army Life in a Black Regiment*, 237–238; Schwalm, *A Hard Fight for We*, 95.

11. Looby, *The Complete Civil War Journal*, 166; Higginson, *Army Life in a Black Regiment*, 238; Schwalm, *A Hard Fight for We*, 95.

12. *The War of the Rebellion: A Compilation of the Official Records of the Union and Confederate Armies*, ser. 1, vol. XIV (Washington, DC: GPO, 1880–1901), 297.

13. "From South Carolina: Destruction of the Blckade-RunnerHuntress off Charleston—The Mntauk about Going to Work—An Attempt to be Made to Cut Out the Nashville—Gen. Saxton's Official Account of His Efforts in Raising Colored Trops—The Culture of Cotton Abandoned on the Islands—Arrival of the First Reinforcements—Arrival of Transports and Men-of-War, etc. etc.," *Chicago Tribune*, June 20, 1863; *The War of the Rebellion: A Compilation*, ser. 1, vol. XIV, 299, 305.

14. "The Expedition up the Combahee," *New South*, Jun. 6, 1863; "A Raid Among the Rice Plantations"; "Miscellaneous Items," *Douglass' Monthly*, Aug. 1863; Bradford, *Scenes in the Life of Harriet Tubman*, 40; Botume, *First Days Amongst the Contrabands*, 6; Bradford, *Harriet Tubman*, 100; Ewen, *Days of the Steamboats*, 9–10.

15. Apthorp, "Montgomery's Raids in Florida, Georgia, and South Carolina," 17; Higginson, *Army Life in a Black Regiment*, 238; Thomas Wentworth Higginson, *The Complete Civil War Journal and Selected Letters of Thomas Wentworth Higginson*, ed. Christopher Looby (Chicago: University of Chicago Press, 2000), 147; Salikoko Mufwene, "Gullah Morphology and Syntax," in *Handbook of Varieties of English*, ed. Walt Wolfram, Bernd Kortmann, and Edgar Schneider (Berlin: Mouton de Gruyter, 2004), 363; Turner, *Africanisms in the Gullah Dialect*, 227–229.

16. Looby, *The Complete Civil War Journal*, 167; Higginson, *Army Life in a Black Regiment*, 238–239.

17. "The Raid on Combahee," *The Mercury*, June 19, 1863.

18. "The Raid on Combahee"; "From South Carolina"; "A Raid among the Rice Plantations"; "Miscellaneous Items"; Frederic Denison, *Shot and Shell: The Third Rhode Island Heavy Artillery Regiment in the Rebellion, 1861–1865* (Providence: The Third R. I. H. Vet. Art. Association, 1879), 155–157; Davis, *History of the 104th Pennsylvania Regiment, from August 22nd, 1861, to September 30th, 1864*, 209–210.

19. "The Enemy's Raid on the Banks of the Combahee," *The Mercury*, Jun. 4, 1864; "The Raid on Combahee"; "Miscellaneous Items."

20. "The Raid on Combahee"; "From South Carolina"; Apthorp, "Montgomery's Raids in Florida, Georgia, and South Carolina," 16–17; "Jeff W. Grigg, *The Combahee River Raid: Harriet Tubman & Lowcountry Liberation* (Charleston, SC: The History Press, 2014), 74; Robert H. Gudmestad, *Steamboats and the Rise of the Cotton Kingdom* (Baton Rouge: Louisiana State University Press, 2011), 23.

21. John Savage, 1870 Census, Colleton County, SC, https://www.familysearch.org/ark:/61903/1:1:M8RD-F3G; "Deposition B" by John A. Savage 3/14/1890, Andrew (Maria) Wyatt US Civil War Pension File; W. Eric Emerson, *Sons of Privilege: The Charleston Light Dragoons in the Civil War* (Columbia: University of South Carolina Press, 2005), 55.

22. W. Eric Emerson, *Sons of Privilege: The Charleston Light Dragoons in the Civil War* (Columbia: University of South Carolina Press, 2005), 27.

23. Deposition by Margaret Moody, Mar. 14, 1890, pension file for Andrew (Diana) Harris.

24. Depositions by Edward Snipe, Jack Wineglass, and Jackson Grant, Mar. 20, 1890, and by Martha Singleton, Diane Harris, and William Jones, Mar. 14, 1890, pension file for Andrew (Diana) Harris; (Andrew (Diana) Harris US Civil War Pension File, 9, 10, 23, 25, 42, 46, 48, 67) deposition by Sarah Osborne, Nov. 21, 1901, pension file for November (Sarah) Osborne, RG 15, NARA.

25. "The Enemy Raid on the Banks of the Combahee," The Mercury, 6/4/1863; "The Expedition up the Combahee," The New South, Jun. 6, 1863; "The Combahee Expedition," Philadelphia North American and United States Gazette, Jun. 8, 1863; "Interesting from Hilton Head," New York Herald, June 9, 1893; "The Raid on Combahee," *The Mercury*, June 19, 1863; "From South Carolina"; "A Raid Among the Rice Plantations"; Apthorp, "Montgomery's Raids in Florida, Georgia, and South Carolina," 17; Higginson, *Army Life in a Black Regiment*, 238; William Watts Hart Davis, *History of the 104th Pennsylvania Regiment, from August 22nd, 1861, to September 30th, 1864* (Philadelphia: Jas. B. Rogers, 1866), 209–210; Grigg, *The Combahee River Raid*, 73–74.

26. "The Expedition up the Combahee"; "Interesting from Hilton Head"; "From South Carolina"; Apthorp, "Montgomery's Raids in Florida, Georgia, and South Carolina," 17–18, 209–210; Grigg, *The Combahee River Raid*, 79.

27. "The Expedition up the Combahee," *The New South*, June 6, 1863; "From South Carolina"; "The Enemy Raid on the Banks of the Combahee"; "COLONEL MONTGOMERY'S RAID"; "A Raid among the Rice Plantations." *Harper's Weekly*, July 4, 1863. "Miscellaneous Items," *Douglass Monthly*, August 1863; Apthorp, "Montgomery's Raids in Florida, Georgia, and South Carolina," 18; Grigg, *The Combahee River Raid*, 74; Denison, *Shot and Shell*, 155.

28. The Enemy's Raid on the Banks of the Combahee"; "The Expedition up the Combahee"; "Interesting from Hilton Head"; "From South Carolina"; "Miscellaneous Items," *Douglass Monthly*, August 1863; Apthorp, "Montgomery's Raids in Florida, Georgia, and South Carolina," 16; Denison, *Shot and Shell*, 155.

29. Timothy O'Sullivan, "Building a Pontoon Bridge at Beaufort, SC, March 1862," Civil War Photograph Collection, Library of Congress, Washington, DC; Timothy O'Sullivan, "Pontoon Bridge Opened for Steamers" (1862?), Prints and Photographs Division, Library of Congress, Washington, DC: Library of Congress; "Notes on the Life of Gen'l G.T. Beauregard," 2, Alexander Robert Chisholm Papers, 1861–1912: Military Records and Memoirs, New-York Historical Society; James Chatham Duane, *Manual for Engineer Troops* (New York: D. Van Nostrand, 1864), 17–18, 22–23, 32–33, 155–157.

30. "The Enemy Raid on the Banks of the Combahee," *The Mercury*, 6/4/1863; "The Expedition up the Combahee"; "The Combahee Expedition," *Philadelphia North American and United States Gazette,* June 8 1863; "Interesting from Hilton Head." *New York Herald*, June 9, 1863; "From South Carolina"; "Miscellaneous Items, " *Douglass Monthly*, August 1863; United States, ed. *Official Records of the Union and Confederate Armies: Series 1, Volume Xiv, vol. Series 1, Volume XIV* (Washington, DC: Govt. Print. Off., 1880), 307–308; Apthorp, "Montgomery's Raids in Florida, Georgia, and South Carolina," 17–18; Grigg, *The Combahee River Raid*, 75; Denison, *Shot and Shell*, 155–157.

31. "A Raid among the Rice Plantations." *Harper's Weekly*, July 4, 1863;" Apthorp, "Montgomery's Raids—In Florida, Georgia and South Carolina," Apthorp Family Papers, 1741–1946, Folder 2.6, 18; Grigg, *The Combahee River Raid*, 75; Shuler Kristrina A Eric C Poplin Edward G Salo Suzanne Johnson Eric D Sipes Jason Ellerbee Emily Jateff and Brockington and Associates Inc. 2005. Intensive Cultural Resources Survey of US Highway 17 Widening Project: Gardens Corner to Jacksonboro: Beaufort and Colleton Counties South Carolina: Draft Report: Pin Number: 29997; F.a. No. Br-Br88(039); File No. 715.101b: July 2005. Atlanta: Brockington & Associates, 64–67, 115–116, 136, 185–186, 188; Denison, *Shot and Shell*, 155–157.

32. *The War of the Rebellion: A Compilation*, ser. 1, vol. XIV, 307–308; Grigg, *The Combahee River Raid*, 76.

33. *The War of the Rebellion: A Compilation*, ser. 1, vol. XIV, 307–308; Grigg, *The Combahee River Raid*, 76; H. David Stone, *Vital Rails: The Charleston & Savannah Railroad and the Civil War in Coastal South Carolina* (Columbia: University of South Carolina Press, 2008), 73.

34. "A Raid Among the Rice Plantations"; "Miscellaneous Items"; *The War of the Rebellion: A Compilation*, ser. 1, vol. XIV, 307–308; Grigg, *The Combahee River Raid*, 76–77.

35. "Miscellaneous Items," Douglass Monthly, August 1863; Apthorp, "Montgomery's Raids—In Florida, Georgia and South Carolina," Apthorp Family Papers, 1741–1946, Folder 2.6, 17–18; *The War of the Rebellion: A Compilation*, ser. 1, vol. XIV, 307–308; Jeff W. Grigg, *The Combahee River Raid: Harriet Tubman and Lowcountry Liberation* (Charleston, SC: History Press, 2014), 76.

36. *The War of the Rebellion: A Compilation*, ser. 1, vol. XIV, 292, 298–306; Wesley D. Wall, War Department Collection of Confederate Records; Series: Carded Records Showing Military Service of Soldiers Who Fought in Confederate

Organizations, Record Group 109, National Archives, Washington, DC; Grigg, *The Combahee River Raid*, 69, 75; Emerson, *Sons of Privilege*, 54.

37. *The War of the Rebellion: A Compilation*, ser. 1, vol. XIV, 307–308; Grigg, *The Combahee River Raid*, 75.

38. *The War of the Rebellion: A Compilation*, ser. 1, vol. XIV, 307–308; Grigg, *The Combahee River Raid*, 75. On June 2, 1863, the full moon took place at 10:52am. See NOAA Tide Predictions, 8666659 Combahee River at US Highway 17, SC (from 1863/06/01 12:00AM to 1863/06/02 11:59PM): https://tidesand-currents.noaa.gov/noaatidepredictions.html?id=8666659&units=standard&b date=18630601&edate=18630602&timezone=LST&clock=12hour&datum= MLLW&interval=hilo&action=dailychart.

39. "The Enemy Raid on the Banks of the Combahee"; *The War of the Rebellion: A Compilation*, ser. 1, vol. XIV, 293–295, 298–306.

40. "The Enemy Raid on the Banks of the Combahee"; "The Expedition up the Combahee"; "From South Carolina"; "Miscellaneous Items"; Apthorp, "Montgomery's Raids—In Florida, Georgia and South Carolina," Apthorp Family Papers, 1741–1946, Folder 2.6, 18; *The War of the Rebellion: A Compilation*, ser. 1, vol. XIV, 300; Denison, *Shot and Shell*, 155–157.

41. "From South Carolina"; *The War of the Rebellion: A Compilation*, ser. 1, vol. XIV, 298–306.

42. *The War of the Rebellion: A Compilation*, ser. 1, vol. XIV, 307–308; Grigg, *The Combahee River Raid*, 77–80.

43. *The War of the Rebellion: A Compilation*, ser. 1, vol. XIV, 298–306.

44. "From South Carolina"; "COLONEL MONTGOMERY'S RAID"; Peter Lindsay Breeden, "Company Muster Roll," March and April 1863, War Department Collection of Confederate Records; Series: Carded Records Showing Military Service of Soldiers Who Fought in Confederate Organizations, Record Group 109, National Archives, Washington, DC); *The War of the Rebellion: A Compilation*, ser. 1, vol. XIV, 298–306; Davis, *History of the 104th Pennsylvania Regiment, from August 22nd, 1861, to September 30th, 1864*, 209–210.

45. *The War of the Rebellion: A Compilation*, ser. 1, vol. XIV, 293–295; H. Godbold, War Department Collection of Confederate Records; Series: Carded Records Showing Military Service of Soldiers Who Fought in Confederate Organizations, Record Group 109, National Archives, Washington, DC; A. E. Gilchrist, War Department Collection of Confederate Records; Series: Carded Records Showing Military Service of Soldiers Who Fought in Confederate Organizations, Record Group 109, National Archives, Washington, DC; Grigg, *The Combahee River Raid*, 76.

46. *The War of the Rebellion: A Compilation*, ser. 1, vol. XIV, 293–295; Thomas Haynes Bomar, War Department Collection of Confederate Records; Series: Carded Records Showing Military Service of Soldiers Who Fought in Confederate Organizations, Record Group 109, National Archives, Washington, DC).

47. "The Enemy Raid on the Banks of the Combahee"; "Miscellaneous Items"; *The War of the Rebellion: A Compilation*, ser. 1, vol. XIV, 307–308; Grigg, *The Combahee River Raid*, 75–77; Denison, *Shot and Shell*, 155–157.

48. *The War of the Rebellion: A Compilation*, ser. 1, vol. XIV, 307–308; Grigg, *The Combahee River Raid*, 77.

49. Deposition A by Peggy Brown, Nov. 14, 1901, pension file for Edward (Peggy) Brown, RG 15, NARA; deposition by Margaret Simmons, Apr. 15, 1901, pension file for Joshua (Margaret) Simmons; Department by the Interior, Bureau of Pensions questionnaire, May 13, 1895, pension file for Cuffee (Sophia) Bolze, RG 15, NARA; letter by P Barnwell, Mar. 27, 1926, pension file for William (Relia) Middleton, RG 15, NARA; deposition by Jack Barnwell, Sep. 9, 1901, pension file for Charles (Ella) Nicholas, RG 15, NARA; general affidavit by Jack Barnwell and deposition by Nicholas, Apr. 11, 1905, pension file for Neptune (Betsey) Nicholas; [depositions] by Sina Young, 2/19/1873 and 6/26/1873, pension file for William (Sina) Young, RG 15, NARA.

50. Deposition by Elsie Jones, Apr. 30, 1895, pension file for Pool (Julia) Sellers, RG 15, NARA; birth affidavits by Hager Miller, Jan. 2, 1894, and Ellen Harris, Jan. 4, 1894, pension file for Edward (Mary) Brown, RG 15, NARA: [depositions] by Sina Young, Jun. 26, 1873, and Venus Lyons, Elsie Jones, and Lina Richard, Jun. 30, 1873, pension file for William (Sina) Young; deposition by Samuel M. Sanders, Sep. 26, 1901, pension file for William (Harriet, Nancy) Hamilton, RG 15, NARA; depositions by Elsey Jones and Mary Ann Lewis, Feb. 24, 1890, pension file for William (Elsey) Jones, RG 15, NARA.

51. *The War of the Rebellion: A Compilation*, ser. 1, vol. XIV, 298–306; Denison, *Shot and Shell*, 155–157; Grigg, *The Combahee River Raid*, 75.

52. Deposition by Mrs. Sally White, 5/1/1895, pension file for Pool (Julia) Sellers, RG 15, NARA.

53. Deposition by Sally White, May 1, 1895, pension file for Pool (Julia) Sellers; deposition by William Jones, Jun. 19, 1895, pension file for James (Sallie) Sheppard, RG 15, NARA; deposition by Monday Lighthouse, Oct. 5, 1910, pension file for Simon (Rachel) Washington, RG 15, NARA.

54. Frank Sanborn, "Harriet Tubman," *The Commonwealth Boston*, Jul. 17, 1863; Harriet M. Buss, *My Work Among the Freedmen: The Civil War and Reconstruction Letters of Harriet M. Buss*, ed. Jonathan W. White and Lydia J. Davis (Charlottesville: University of Virginia Press, 2021), 20–21; Bradford, *Scenes in the Life of Harriet Tubman*, 40; Bradford, *Harriet Tubman*, 100–101; Telford, "Harriet," 9, 16–18; Miller, "Harriet Tubman," 422; Harkless Bowley to Earl Conrad, Aug. 8, 1839, "Conrad/Tubman Collection," ed. Scholarly Resources (Wilmington, DE, 1939–1940); Grigg, *The Combahee River Raid*, 75; Humez, *Harriet Tubman*, 245–247.

55. "The Expedition up the Combahee," *The New South*, Jun. 6, 1863; "Interesting from Hilton Head," *New York Herald*, Jun. 9, 1863; "Miscellaneous Items," *Douglass' Monthly*, Aug. 1863; Emma P. Telford, *Harriet: The Modern Moses of Heroism and Visions* (Auburn, NY: Cayuga County Museum, 1905), 17–18; Harkess Bowley to Earl Conrad, Denison, 8/6/1939, Harriet Tubman Earl Conrad, "Conrad/Tubman Collection," ed. Scholarly Resources (Wilmington, DE, 1939–1940); Denison, *Shot and Shell*, 155–157; Jean McMahon Humez, *Harriet Tubman: The Life and the Life Stories* (Madison: University of Wisconsin Press, 2003), 245–247.

56. "The Expedition up the Combahee;" *The War of the Rebellion: A Compilation*, ser. 1, vol. XIV, 298–306; Grigg, *The Combahee River Raid*, 75; Denison, *Shot and Shell*, 155–157.

57. *The War of the Rebellion: A Compilation*, ser. 1, vol. XIV, 298–306; Earl J. Hess, Animal Histories of the Civil War Era (Baton Rouge: Louisiana State University Press, 2022), 186–187, 191, 195, 203; Grigg, *The Combahee River Raid*, 75.

58. "Interesting from Hilton Head"; "From South Carolina"; "A Raid Among the Rice Plantations"; "Miscellaneous Items"; *The War of the Rebellion: A Compilation*, ser. 1, vol. XIV, 308; Bradford, *Scenes in the Life of Harriet Tubman*, 41; Bradford, *Harriet Tubman*, 101; Denison, *Shot and Shell*, 155–157; Harkess Bowley to Earl Conrad, Denison, 8/6/1939, Harriet Tubman Earl Conrad, "Conrad/Tubman Collection," ed. Scholarly Resources (Wilmington, DE, 1939–1940); Grigg, *The Combahee River Raid*, 75; Humez, *Harriet Tubman: The Life and the Life Stories*, 245–247.

59. "Interesting from Hilton Head"; Bradford, *Scenes in the Life of Harriet Tubman*, 41–42; Bradford, *Harriet Tubman*, 101–102; Telford, "Harriet: The Modern Moses of Heroism and Visions," 9, Cayuga County Museum, Auburn, NY, 18–19; Harkess Bowley to Earl Conrad, Denison, 8/6/1939, Harriet Tubman Earl Conrad, "Conrad/Tubman Collection," ed. Scholarly Resources (Wilmington, DE, 1939–1940); Humez, *Harriet Tubman*, 245–247; Earl Rivers, "The Hand That Holds the Bread: Progress and Protest in the Gilded Age; Songs from the Civil War to the Colombian Exposition." N.p., 1978. Television (lp and program notes, 21–22).

60. "Charles Heyward Plantation Book, 1858–1865," South Caroliniana Library, University of South Carolina, Columbia, 23; Agnes L. Baldwin, "Nemours," "Laurel Springs, Myrtle Grove, White Hall, Grove," and "Myrtle Grove," Agnes L. Baldwin Research Papers, 1966–2004, South Carolina Historical Society, Charleston; Denison, *Shot and Shell*, 155–156. "From South Carolina"; Deposition A by Simon Chisolm alias Blake, Oct. 16, 1900, "Act of June 27, 1890, Invalid Pension," Nov. 13, 1899, and Dec. 21, 1905, "Act of June 27, 1890, Increase Invalid Pension," Sep. 24, 1907, "Act of June 27, 1890, Increase Invalid Pension," Sep. 24, 1907, Sep. 14, 1908, Jun. 29, 1910, "Reissue Act of May 11, 1912," Apr. 2, 1913, "Act of Lay 1, 1920, Widow's Pension," Mar. 8. 1921, "Where Born?," n.d., pension file for Simon (Rina) Chisolm alias Blake, RG 15, NARA; Leslie A. Schwalm, *A Hard Fight for We: Women's Transition from Slavery to Freedom in South Carolina* (Urbana: University of Illinois Press, 1997), 111–112.

61. "The Enemy's Raid on the Banks of the Combahee"; "The Expedition up the Combahee"; "The Combahee Expedition," *Philadelphia North American and United States Gazette*, June 8, 1863; "Interesting from Hilton Head." *New York Herald*, June 9, 1863; "COLONEL MONTGOMERY'S RAID"; "A Raid Among the Rice Plantations"; "Miscellaneous Items"; Apthorp, "Montgomery's Raids in Florida, Georgia, and South Carolina," 16; *The War of the Rebellion: A Compilation*, ser. 1, vol. XIV, 295–296; Grigg, *The Combahee River Raid*, 76; Denison, *Shot and Shell*, 156; Davis, *History of the 104th*, 209–210. "The Combahee Expedition," *Philadelphia North American and United States Gazette*, June 8, 1863; "Interesting from Hilton Head." *New York Herald*, June 9, 1863; "COLONEL MONTGOMERY'S RAID."

62. "The Expedition up the Combahee"; "The Combahee Expedition"; "From South Carolina"; "Miscellaneous Items"; *The War of the Rebellion: A Compilation*, ser. 1, vol. XIV, 298–306; Apthorp, "Montgomery's Raids in Florida, Georgia, and South Carolina," 18, 20; Denison, *Shot and Shell*, 155–157.

63. Apthorp, "Montgomery's Raids—In Florida, Georgia and South Carolina," Apthorp Family Papers, 1741–1946, Folder 2.6, 18; *The War of the Rebellion: A Compilation*, ser. 1, vol. XIV, 298–306.

64. "The Enemy Raid on the Banks of the Combahee"; *The War of the Rebellion: A Compilation*, ser. 1, vol. XIV, 298–306; Grigg, *The Combahee River Raid*, 78.

65. "The Expedition up the Combahee"; "A Raid Among the Rice Plantations"; "Miscellaneous Items"; Apthorp, "Montgomery's Raids—In Florida, Georgia and South Carolina," Apthorp Family Papers, 1741–1946, Folder 2.6, 17–18; Grigg, *The Combahee River Raid*, 77–78, 80. *The War of the Rebellion: A Compilation*, ser. 1, vol. XIV, 293–295, 298–306.

66. "The Expedition up the Combahee"; "Miscellaneous Items"; *The War of the Rebellion: A Compilation*, ser. 1, vol. XIV, 293–294, 301; Denison, *Shot and Shell*, 155–157; Grigg, *The Combahee River Raid*, 79.

67. *The War of the Rebellion: A Compilation*, ser. 1, vol. XIV, 293–295; Grigg, *The Combahee River Raid*, 59.

68. *The War of the Rebellion: A Compilation*, ser. 1, vol. XIV, 298–306; Apthorp, "Montgomery's Raids in Florida, Georgia, and South Carolina," 18.

69. Apthorp, "Montgomery's Raids in Florida, Georgia, and South Carolina," 19; *The War of the Rebellion: A Compilation*, ser. 1, vol. XIV, 293–295; Grigg, *The Combahee River Raid*, 74, 76, 78–79.

70. "The Combahee Expedition"; "From South Carolina"; "A Raid among the Rice Plantations"; "Miscellaneous Item"; The War of the Rebellion: A Compilation, ser. 1, vol. XIV, 294, 296, 298–306; Davis, History of the 104th Pennsylvania Regiment, 209–210.

71. "The Expedition up the Combahee"; "The Combahee Expedition"; "From South Carolina"; "A Raid among the Rice Plantations." *Harper's Weekly*, July 4 1863. "Interesting from Hilton Head"; Apthorp, "Montgomery's Raids in Florida, Georgia, and South Carolina," 19: *The War of the Rebellion: A Compilation*, ser. 1, vol. XIV, 295–306; Grigg, *The Combahee River Raid*, 79.

72. "The Combahee Expedition"; "From South Carolina"; "A Raid among the Rice Plantations"; Apthorp, "Montgomery's Raids in Florida, Georgia, and South Carolina," 19; *The War of the Rebellion: A Compilation*, ser. 1, vol. XIV, 298–306; Grigg, *The Combahee River Raid*, 79–80.

73. "The Expedition up the Combahee"; "The Combahee Expedition"; "From South Carolina"; *The War of the Rebellion: A Compilation*, ser. 1, vol. XIV, 298–306; Apthorp, "Montgomery's Raids in Florida, Georgia, and South Carolina," 17; Grigg, *The Combahee River Raid*, 79–80.

74. "The Expedition up the Combahee"; "The Combahee Expedition"; "Interesting from Hilton Head"; "From South Carolina"; "A Raid among the Rice Plantations"; "Miscellaneous Items"; Apthorp, "Montgomery's Raids in Florida, Georgia, and South Carolina," 18–19; *The War of the Rebellion: A Compilation*, ser. 1, vol. XIV, 295–296; Grigg, *The Combahee River Raid*, 79.

75. Apthorp, "Montgomery's Raids in Florida, Georgia, and South Carolina," 21;
    Allen Edens, War Department Collection of Confederate Records; Series:
    Carded Records Showing Military Service of Soldiers Who Fought in
    Confederate Organizations, Record Group 109, National Archives, Washington,
    DC; *The War of the Rebellion: A Compilation*, ser. 1, vol. XIV, 293–295; Grigg, The
    Combahee River Raid, 79. Field's Point Spring Tide ebb tide was June 2, 1863
    at 9:05pm. NOAA Tide Predictions, 8667624 Brickyard Point, Coosaw River
    (from 1863/06/01 12:00AM to 1863/06/02 11:59PM): https://tidesandcurrents.
    noaa.gov/noaatidepredictions.html?id=8667624&units=standard&bdate=1863
    0601&edate=18630602&timezone=LST&clock=12hour&datum=MLLW&int
    erval=hilo&action=dailychart; NOAA Tide Predictions, 8667259 Field's Point,
    SC: https://tidesandcurrents.noaa.gov/noaatidepredictions.html?id=8667259&
    units=standard&bdate=18630601&edate=18630602&timezone=LST&clock=1
    2hour&datum=MLLW&interval=hilo&action=dailychart.
76. Apthorp, "Montgomery's Raids in Florida, Georgia, and South Carolina," 20;
    The War of the Rebellion: A Compilation, ser. 1, vol. XIV, 293–294, 300.
77. "Interesting from Hilton Head"; Apthorp, "Montgomery's Raids in Florida,
    Georgia, and South Carolina," 16, 20.
78. *The War of the Rebellion: A Compilation*, ser. 1, vol. XIV, 290–291.
79. *The War of the Rebellion: A Compilation*, ser. 1, vol. XIV, 290–291, 963;
    W. L. Trenholm, War Department Collection of Confederate Records; Series:
    Carded Records Showing Military Service of Soldiers Who Fought in Confederate
    Organizations, Record Group 109, National Archives, Washington, DC.
80. Higginson, *Army Life in a Black Regiment*, 238.

CHAPTER 15

1. "The Expedition up the Combahee," *New South*, Jun. 6, 1863; "The
   Combahee Expedition," *Philadelphia North American and United States Gazette*,
   June 8, 1863; "Interesting from Hilton Head," *New York Herald*, Jun. 9, 1863;
   "Col. Montgomery's Raid—the Rescued Black Chattel—a Black 'She'
   Moses—Her Wonderful Sagacity—the Black Regiments—Col. Higginson's
   Mistakes—Arrival of the 54th Massachusetts, & C., & C.," *Wisconsin State
   Journal*, Jun. 20, 1863. ["From South Carolina," *Chicago Tribune*, 6/20/1863)
2. "The Expedition up the Combahee."
3. "The Expedition up the Combahee"; "Miscellaneous Items," *Douglass'
   Monthly*, Aug. 1863.
4. "Expedition Up the Combahee," *The New South*, 6/6/1863; "Col. Montgomery's
   Raid"; William Watts Hart Davis, *History of the 104th Pennsylvania Regiment,
   from August 22nd, 1861, to September 30th, 1864* (Philadelphia: Jas. B. Rogers,
   1866), 209–210; Earl Conrad, *General Harriett Tubman* (Baltimore: Black Classic
   Press, 2019), 169–170.
5. Clara Barton, Diary 6/3/1863, "Clara Barton Papers, 1805–1958: Diaries and
   Journals; 1863, April 2–July 23, Library of Congress, MSS 11973, Box 1; Clara

Barton to Ira Moore Barton, Jul. 3, 1863, Clara Barton Papers 1832–1912, American Antiquarian Society.

6. Clara Barton, Diary 6/3/1863, "Clara Barton Papers, 1805–1958: Diaries and Journals; 1863, April 2–July 23, Library of Congress, MSS 11973, Box 1; "Col. Montgomery's Raid"; Clara to Ira Moore Barton, Jul. 3, 1863, Clara Barton Papers, 1832–1912, American Antiquarian Society, Worcester, MA.

7. "Clara Barton to Ira Moore Barton" 7/3/1863, Clara Barton Papers 1832–1912, American Antiquarian Society.

8. Clara Barton, Diary 6/3/1863, "Clara Barton Papers, 1805–1958: Diaries and Journals; 1863, April 2–July 23, Library of Congress, MSS 11973, Box 1; Elizabeth Brown Pryor, *Clara Barton: Professional Angel* (Philadelphia: University of Pennsylvania Press, 2011), 121; Stephen B. Oates, *Woman of Valor: Clara Barton and the Civil War* (New York: Free Press, 1994), 154–155, 159.

9. Clara Barton, Diary 6/3/1863, "Clara Barton Papers, 1805–1958: Diaries and Journals; 1863, April 2–July 23, Library of Congress, MSS 11973, Box 1; "The Expedition up the Combahee"; "The Combahee Expedition," *Philadelphia North American and United States Gazette*, Jun. 8, 1863; *The War of the Rebellion: A Compilation of the Official Records of the Union and Confederate Armies*, ser. 1, vol. XIV (Washington, DC: GPO, 1880–1901), 463, 963.

10. "The Expedition up the Combahee"; "The Combahee Expedition"; "Extracts from the Journal of an Officer in the 54th Regt., Mass Vols.," *The Commonwealth Boston*, Jun. 26, 1863; Frank Sanborn, "Harriet Tubman," *The Commonwealth Boston*, Jul. 17, 1863; "Miscellaneous Items."

11. "Col. Montgomery's Raid"; "From South Carolina—the New Federal Commander—Col. Montgomery's Late Raid," *Chicago Tribune*, Jun. 20, 1863; "A Raid Among the Rice Plantations," *Harper's Weekly*, Jul. 4, 1863. In her 1905 interview with Emma Telford, Tubman remembered liberating 800 or 900 people in the Combahee River Raid. See Emma P. Telford, "Harriet: The Modern Moses of Heroism and Visions", ed. Cayuga County Museum (Auburn, NY: Cayuga County Museum, 1905), 19. William Lee Apthorp, "Montgomery's Raids in Florida, Georgia, and South Carolina," 20, Apthorp Family Papers, 1741–1964, Folder 2.6, HistoryMiami Museum, Miami, FL; Davis, *History of the 104th*, 209, 299.

12. "The Combahee Expedition"; "Miscellaneous Items," *Douglass Monthly*, August 1863; Frederic Denison, *Shot and Shell: The Third Rhode Island Heavy Artillery Regiment in the Rebellion, 1861–1865* (Providence, RI: Third R.I.H. Vet. Art. Association, 1879), 155.

13. "The Combahee Expedition"; "Extracts from the Journal of an Officer in the 54th Regt., Mass Vols."

14. "From South Carolina—the New Federal Commander—Col. Montgomery's Late Raid"; Apthorp, "Montgomery's Raids in Florida, Georgia, and South Carolina," 20; Davis, *History of the 104th*, 209–210.

15. "From South Carolina"; Davis, *History of the 104th*, 299; CPI Inflation Calculator, "Value of $1,000,000 from 1863 to 2022," https://in2013dollars.com.

16. "Interesting from Hilton Head"; "Extracts from the Journal of an Officer"; Denison, *Shot and Shell*, 155–157.

17. Apthorp, "Apthorp Family Collection," in Folder 2.6, 1–2.

18. Apthorp, "Montgomery's Raids in Florida, Georgia, and South Carolina," 1–2, 20.

19. Davis, *History of the 104th Pennsylvania Regiment, from August 22nd, 1861, to September 30th, 1864*, 209–210.

20. Thomas Wentworth Higginson, *The Complete Civil War Journal and Selected Letters of Thomas Wentworth Higginson*, ed. Christopher Looby (Chicago: University of Chicago Press, 2000), 282; Davis, *History of the 104th*, 209–210; "Nomination for Military Intelligence Hall of Fame Mrs. Harriet Tubman (Deceased)," collection of Ernestine Wyatt, 7.

21. "Col. Montgomery's Raid"; Earl Conrad, *General Harriett Tubman* (Baltimore: Black Classic Press, 2019, 1943); Kate Clifford Larson, *Harriet Tubman Underground National Monument: Historic Resource Study* (Washington, DC: National Park Service/US Department of the Interior, 2019), 169.

22. ["Col. Montgomery's Raid—The Rescued Black Chattel—A Black "she" Moses—Her Wonderful Sagacity—The Black Regiments—Col. Higginson's Mistakes—Arrival of the 54th Massachusetts, & c., & c.," Wisconsin State Journal, 6/20/1863; Sanborn, "Harriet Tubman"; Benjamin Blakely Hickok, "The Political and Literary Careers of F. B. Sanborn" (Michigan State University, 1953), v, xii, 199, 208, 27, 36, 42.

23. Sanborn, "Harriet Tubman."

24. Franklin Benjamin Sanborn and Benjamin Smith Lyman, *Young Reporter of Concord: A Checklist of F. B. Sanborn's Letters to Benjamin Smith Lyman, 1853–1867, with Extracts Emphasizing Life and Literary Events in the World of Emerson, Thoreau and Alcott*, ed. Kenneth Walter Cameron (Hartford, CT: Transcendental Books, 1978), 17, 25.

25. "From South Carolina"; "A Raid among the Rice Plantations." *Harper's Weekly*, July 4, 1863"; Catherine Clinton, *Harriet Tubman: The Road to Freedom* (Boston, MA: Little Brown, 2004), 171, 173; Conrad, *General Harriett Tubman*, 176–177; Sanborn, "Harriet Tubman."

26. Conrad, *General Harriett Tubman*, 167–168, 170–171.

27. *Kate Clifford Larson, Bound for the Promised Land: Harriet Tubman: Portrait of an American Hero* (New York: One World/Ballantine, 2009), 210; Jean McMahon Humez, *Harriet Tubman: The Life and the Life Stories* (Madison: University of Wisconsin Press, 2003), 58; Benjamin Guterman, "Doing 'Good Brave Work': Harriet Tubman's Testimony at Beaufort, South Carolina," *Prologue Quarterly of the National Archives* 32, no. 3 (2000): 157.

28. Adam Goodheart, "'To Have a Revolver'," *New York Times*, 6/8/2011.

29. Charles Wood, "A History Concerning the Pension Claim of Harriet Tubman," 2, 3, 7, RG 233, NARA; Sarah Bradford, *Scenes in the Life of Harriet Tubman* (1869; repr., North Stratford, NH: Ayer, 2004), 64–66; Sarah Bradford, *Harriet Tubman: The Moses of Her People* (New York: J. J. Little & Company, 1901 (reprint of 1886), 160, 164; Emma P. Telford, *Harriet: The Modern Moses of Heroism and Visions* (Auburn, NY: Cayuga County Museum, 1905), 16; Benjamin Guterman, "Doing 'Good Brave Work': Harriet Tubman's

Testimony at Beaufort, South Carolina," *Prologue Quarterly of the National Archives* 32, no. 3 (2000): 165 n. 11; Earl Conrad, "The Charles P. Wood Manuscripts of Harriet Tubman," *Negro History Bulletin* 13, no. 4 (1950): 94.

30. Earl Conrad, "The Charles P. Wood Manuscripts of Harriet Tubman," *Negro History Bulletin* 13, no. 4 (1950): 90, 92–95; Wood, "A History Concerning the Pension Claim of Harriet Tubman," 6; "Nomination for Military Intelligence Hall of Fame Mrs. Harriet Tubman (Deceased)," 6; Larson, *Bound for the Promised Land: Harriet Tubman: Portrait of an American Hero*, 251.

31. "Col. Montgomery's Raid"; Lt. George Garrison to William Lloyd Garrison II, Feb. 10, 1864, Garrison Family Papers, Box 28, Folder 790, Sophia Smith Collection, Smith College, Northampton, MA; Bradford, *Scenes in the Life of Harriet Tubman*, 38–89; Sarah Bradford, *Harriet Tubman: The Moses of Her People* (1886; New York: J. J. Little, 1901), 93, 98, 102; Telford, *Harriet*, 16; Larson, *Bound for the Promised Land*, 206–207; Humez, *Harriet Tubman*, 244; Allen, *Intelligence in the Civil War*, 26–28; Alice Brickley to Earl Conrad, 7/28/1939, Harriet Tubman Earl Conrad, "Conrad/Tubman Collection," ed. Scholarly Resources (Wilmington, DE 1939–1940); Samuel Hopkins Adams, *Grandfather Stories* (New York: Random House, 1955), 271, 79.

32. Lewis Douglass to Helen Amelia Loguen, Jun. 18, 1863, Frederick Douglass and Douglass Family Papers, Series II, JWJ MSS 240, Box 3, Folder 63, Walter O. Evans Collection, Beinecke Rare Book Library, Yale University, New Haven, CT; "Col. Montgomery's Raid"; Sanborn, "Harriet Tubman"; "Nomination for Military Intelligence Hall of Fame Mrs. Harriet Tubman (Deceased)," 4, 12; Allen, *Intelligence in the Civil War*, 23.

33. *The War of the Rebellion: A Compilation*, ser. I, vol. XIV, 306.

34. "The Combahee Expedition"; Denison, *Shot and Shell*, 155; Bradford, *Scenes in the Life of Harriet Tubman*, 39; Conrad, *General Harriett Tubman*, 171.

35. "The Combahee Raid," *Charleston Daily Courier*, 6/5/1863; "Report of the President of the Charleston & Savannah Railroad, 1863," 3, 14, Southern Historical Collection, University of North Carolina, Chapel Hill; Jeff W. Grigg, *The Combahee River Raid: Harriet Tubman and Lowcountry Liberation* (Charleston, SC: History Press, 2014), 96.

CHAPTER 16

1. "The Raid on Combahee," *The Mercury*, Jun. 19, 1863.

2. "The Raid on Combahee."

3. "The Raid on Combahee."

4. "The Raid on Combahee."

5. "Company Muster Roll," October 13 to 31, 1861, Jan. & Fed. 1862, March & April, 1862, Sept. & Oct., 1862, Nov. & Dec. 1862, Jan. 1 to Aug. 31, 1864, service record for Thomas Haynes War Department Collection of Confederate Records, RG 109, NARA; *The War of the Rebellion: A Compilation of the Official Records of the Union and Confederate Armies*, ser. 1, vol. XIV (Washington, DC: GPO, 1880–1901), 291, 293, 862; military service record for Robert J. Jeffords, War Department Collection of Confederate Records, RG 109, NARA.

6. "The Raid on Combahee"; *The War of the Rebellion: A Compilation*, ser. 1, vol. XIV, 291, 294–295, 306.

7. "The Expedition up the Combahee," *New South*, Jun. 6, 1863; *The War of the Rebellion: A Compilation*, ser. 1, vol. XIV, 290, 291, 295, 304, 307.

8. *The War of the Rebellion: A Compilation*, ser. 1, vol. XIV, 304–307.

9. "The Raid on Combahee"; *The War of the Rebellion: A Compilation*, ser. 1, vol. XIV, 296, 305–306; *Official Records of the Union and Confederate Armies: Series I, Volume Liii*, vol. LIII, Series 1 (Washington, DC: Govt. Print. Off.), 300.

10. "Field and Staff Muster Roll," July & August, 1863 and Sept. 1 and Dec. 31, 1863, and Major William P. Emanuel to Brigadier General Thomas Jordan, Aug. 31, 1863, military service record for William P. Emanuel, War Department Collection of Confederate Records, RG 109, NARA; Company Muster Roll, Jan. & Feb. 1863, May & Jun. 1863, Jan. & Feb. 1864, Sergeant Major W. Allen Benton to Lieutenant Peter Lindsay Breeden, Jan. 12, 1864, military service record for Peter Lindsay Breeden, War Department Collection of Confederate Records, RG 109, NARA; Company Muster Roll, Jul./Aug. 1863 and Sergeant Major W. Allen Benton to Lieutenant W. E. Hewitt, Jan. 12, 1864, military service record for William E. Hewitt, War Department Collection of Confederate Records, RG 109, NARA; *The War of the Rebellion: A Compilation*, ser. 1, vol. XIV, 304, 306.

11. *The War of the Rebellion: A Compilation*, ser. 1, vol. XIV, 299–301, 304, 463; *The War of the Rebellion: A Compilation of the Official Records of the Union and Confederate Armies*, ser. 1, vol. LIII (Washington, DC: GPO, 1880–1901), 300;

12. "The Raid on Combahee"; Virgil, *The Aeneid*, trans. H. Rushton Fairclough (Cambridge, MA: Harvard University Press, 1916), 294.

13. Walter Blake to Maria Hough Blake, May 3, 1863, Walter Blake Papers, 1821–1874, ALSS 13, South Caroliniana Library, University of South Carolina, Columbia.

14. Walter Blake to Maria Hough Blake, May 3, 1863, Walter Blake Papers, 1821–1874, ALSS 13, South Caroliniana Library, University of South Carolina, Columbia.

15. The *Charleston Daily Courier* cited $6 million, the largest amount of damages from the Combahee River Raid. See, "The Combahee Raid," *Charleston Daily Courier*, 6/5/1863. Walter Blake to Maria Hough Blake, May 3, 1863, Walter Blake Papers, 1821–1874, ALSS 13, South Caroliniana Library, University of South Carolina, Columbia; Walter Blake, Company Muster Roll, May and June 1863, "War Department Collection of Confederate Records; Series: Carded Records Showing Military Service of Soldiers Who Fought in Confederate Organizations"; Earl J. Hess, ed. Animal Histories of the Civil War Era (Baton Rouge: Louisiana State University, 2022), 195.

16. Louis D. DeSaussure to my dear Kirkland, Jun. 4, 1863, Papers of the Kirkland, Withers, Snowden, and Trotter Families 1790–1959, South Caroliniana Library, University of South Carolina, Columbia, 48.

17. Thomas Taylor to William L. Kirkland Jr., June 9, 1863, ibid., 49. Papers of the Kirkland Withers Snowden Families, 1790–1959, South Caroliniana, Columbia, SC, 49.

18. Dago was shot to death in October 1864 while Nicholls hired him out against his will in Charleston. See Thomas Taylor to William L. Kirkland Jr., Jun. 9, 1863, and Louis D. DeSaussure to William L. Kirkland Jr., Jun. 11, 1863, Papers of the Kirkland, Withers, Snowden, and Trotter Families, 18, 48–49; W. Eric Emerson, *Sons of Privilege: The Charleston Light Dragoons in the Civil War* (Columbia: University of South Carolina Press, 2005), 139. Williams Middleton accused Captain T. A. Allen and his men of plundering what was left of Newport Plantation (including chickens, hogs, blankets, and homespun left behind by the freedom seekers) a few days after the raid. See Captain Thomas Pinckney to Colonel John Lay, Jun. 18, 1863, Brigadier General Thomas Jordan, Jun. 26, 1863, Williams Middleton to General Thomas Jordan, Jun. 15, 1863, file for William Middleton, Confederate Papers Relating to Citizens or Business Firms, 1861–65, microfilm publication M346, NARA.

19. I. S. K. Bennett, "Rose Hill Plantation on the Combahee," *Charleston Mercury,* Jun. 11, 1863.

20. Susan Middleton to Harriott Middleton, Jun. 5, 1863, collection of Jessica Loring, Beaufort County, SC; Langdon Cheves, "Middleton of South Carolina," *South Carolina Historical and Genealogical Magazine* 1, no. 228 (1900): 248–249, 258–259.

21. Susan Middleton to Harriott Middleton, Jun. 5, 1863, collection of Jessica Loring; Oliver Hering Middleton Jr. to Susan Matilda Chisholm Middleton, Jun. 9, 1863, Blake Family Papers, 1794–1915, South Carolina Historical Society, Charleston.

22. According to Governor Henry Middleton's will, Newport Plantation was to be divided between his sons, Henry Middleton, also known as Harry, and Arthur Middleton. Arthur Middleton died in 1853; thus, his heir, son Henry Bentivoglio Van Ness Middleton, should have inherited his father's share. See Will of Henry Middleton, Agnes L. Baldwin Research Papers, 1966–1982, South Carolina Historical Society, Oliver Hering Middleton Jr. to Susan Matilda Chisholm Middleton, Jun. 9, 1863, Blake Family Papers, 1794–1915, South Carolina Historical Society, Charleston; Middleton Family Genealogy Materials, Middleton Family Papers 1789–1974, South Caroliniana Library, University of South Carolina, Columbia.

23. Will of Henry Middleton; Susan Middleton to Harriott Middleton, Jun. 5, 1863, and Williams Middleton to Edward Middleton, Jun. 16, 1863, collection of Jessica Loring; "June 7, 1863—List of Negroes Brought Down from the Combahee River After the Yankee Raid at Newport, Owned by the Estate of Governor Henry Middleton," in Barbara Doyle, Mary Edna Sullivan, and Tracey Todd, *Beyond the Fields: Slavery at Middleton Place* (Columbia: University of South Carolina Press, 2008), 59; Cheves, "Middleton of South Carolina," 246, 247, 251.

24. Daniel Elliott Huger Smith, Amey Robinson Childs, and Alice Ravenel Huger Smith, eds., *Mason Smith Family Letters, 1860–1868* (Columbia: University of South Carolina Press, 1950), 44, 280.

25. Smith, Childs, and Smith, *Mason Smith Family Letters*, 45, 47, 280.

26. Smith, Childs, and Smith, *Mason Smith Family Letters*, 44, 50.

27. Smith, Childs, and Smith, *Mason Smith Family Letters*, 44.

28. Smith, Childs, and Smith, *Mason Smith Family Letters*, 44, 45.

29. William Mason Smith Estate Inventory 1/15/1852; Smith, Childs, and Smith, *Mason Smith Family Letters*, 60; Nat Nicks Freedmen's Bank Account, May 7, 1872; general affidavit by Ansel Gilliard and Josiah Greene, Oct. 21, 1892, pension file for March (Molcy) Chisolm, RG 15, NARA; Katie Richard, "Colleton, 1911–1939, Marriage Book," South Carolina County Marriage Records, 1907–2000, (Columbia: South Carolina Department of Archives and History).

30. Deposition by Sally Burnett, Dec. 4, 1901, pension file for Balaam (Diana, Sally) Burnett, RG 15, NARA; Margaret Belser Hollis and Allen H. Stokes, eds., Twilight on the South Carolina Rice Fields: Letters of the Heyward Family, 1861–1871 (Columbia: University of South Carolina Press, 2010), xii–xiii, 29–30; Duncan Clinch Heyward, *Seed from Madagascar* (Columbia: University of South Carolina Press, 1993), 130–131.

31. Hollis and Stokes, *Twilight on the South Carolina Rice Fields*, 29–30.

32. Hollis and Stokes, *Twilight on the South Carolina Rice Fields*, 30.

33. Hollis and Stokes, *Twilight on the South Carolina Rice Fields*, 30.

34. "Valuable Rice Lands on the Combahee" *The Charleston Mercury*, 6/6/1863, 6/8/1863, 6/9/1863, 6/10/1863, 6/12/1863, 6/13/1863, 6/15/1863, 6/16/1863, 6/17/1863; Hollis and Stokes, *Twilight on the South Carolina Rice Fields*, 42–43

35. Hollis and Stokes, *Twilight on the South Carolina Rice Fields*, 42–43.

36. "Losses from the War. State of South Carolina Office of State Auditor," *Charleston Mercury*, Jun. 18, 1863.

37. "Losses from the War. State of South Carolina Office of State Auditor."

38. "Losses from the War. State of South Carolina Office of State Auditor."

39. Claim by William C. Heyward, Jul. 1863, "Claims of Property Loss, 1862–1864," South Carolina Department of Archives and History, Columbia.

40. Claim by William C. Heyward, Jul. 1863.

41. Claim by William C. Heyward, July 1863; deposition by William Hamilton, Oct. 31, 1896, pension file for Jackson (Jane) Grant, RG 15, NARA; deposition by William Hamilton, Oct. 22, 1898, pension file for William (Elsey) Jones, RG 15, NARA.

42. Auditor, "Claims of Property Loss, 1862–1864."; "Widow's Pension (With Original Increase)," 3/29/1873, affidavits of Peter James, Sina Young 2/19/1873, 6/26/1873, Bina Mack 6/27/1863, Venus Lyons, Elsy Jones, and Lina Richard 6/30/1873, Elizabeth Small 5/25/1869, William (Sina) Young, "U. S. Civil War Pension File," in *National Archives, Record Group 15* (Washington, DC: National Archives and Record Administration); "Exhibit" by Sina Young, Elsie Jones, 4/24/1875, "Exhibit B" 12/13/1876, "Exhibit F" 12/14/1876, ibid.; "Declaration for Widow's Pension, Act of June 27, 1890" 8/20/1890, "Certificate of Marriage," "Neighbors Affidavit" by Mary Nesbit and John A. Savage 7/30/1891, by Charles Nicholas and Balaam Burnett 3/28/1892, July (Venus) Osbourne, ibid.; "General Affidavit" by Lucius Robinson and Edward Brown 8/5/1893, ibid.; "Declaration of Widow's Pension" 12/3/1913, "Certificate of Death" William Middleton, "General Affidavit" by P. Barnwell 7/17/1919, William (Relia) Middleton, ibid. (Washington, DC).

43. [Depositions] by Bina Mack, 6/27/1873, Venus Lyons, Elsy Jones, and Lina Richard, 6/30/1873, "exhibit F" by Wally Graham, 12/14/1876, William (Sina) Young US Civil War Pension File, RG 15, NARA; [Deposition] by William Drayton, 3/16/1892, "Widow's Declaration for Pension or Increase of Pension," Annie Holmes, 3/16/1892, 2/22/1890, "Secondary Proof of Marriage" by Annie Holmes, 2/22/1890, "Transcript of Record of Marriage, Birth or Death," Selem S. White, 7/7/1893, March Jackson, 3/28/1892, "Affidavit of Marriage," James Shields, 3/8/1893, [Deposition] by Annie Holmes, 6/17/1892, "Affidavit to Origin of Disability," S. S. White, 6/29/1892, Scipio (Annie Holmes) McNeal US Civil War Pension File.

44. "Affidavit of Claimant" by Jonas Green, Apr. 15, 1890, pension file for Jack (Jack Jr.) Aiken, RG 15, NARA; general affidavit by Selam White, Mar. 8, 1893, general affidavit by Solomon Washington, Sep. 19, 1895, deposition by Solomon Washington, Aug. 28, 1897, deposition I by Solomon Washington and deposition F by Jonas Green, Aug. 24, 1897, deposition A by Lucretia Washington, Aug. 24, 1897, deposition B by James Henry Bruce, Sep. 9, 1897, pension file for Smart (Lucretia) Washington, RG 15, NARA.

45. Claim by William C. Heyward, July 1863; "Case of Relia Middleton" by Cuffee Bolles, Feb. 2, 1920, "Case of Relia Middleton" by Primus Barnwell, Jan. 27, 1920, pension file for William (Relia) Middleton, RG 15, NARA; deposition by Jane Barnwell, Nov. 11, 1909, "Case of Fannie Smith," pension file for Richard (Lucy, Fannie) Smith, RG 15, NARA; deposition by Cuffie Bolze, Nov. 15, 1901, pension file for Edward (Peggy) Brown, RG 15, NARA: deposition O by Edward Brown, Jun. 14, 1895, pension file for Simon (Rachel) Washington, RG 15, NARA.

46. Claim by William C. Heyward, July 1863; Depositions by Betsy Nicholas, Cuffee Bolze, Elsie Singleton, Moses Simmons, Charles Nicholas, Apr. 11, 1905, pension file for Neptune (Betsey) Nicholas, RG 15, NARA; depositions by Margaret Simmons, Apr. 11, 1905, and Jul. 23, 1901, deposition D by Moses Simmons, Jul. 25, 1901, pension file for Joshua (Margaret) Simmons, RG 15, NARA; deposition by Fanny Simmons, Apr. 14, 1914, deposition B by Jane Barnwell, Apr. 14, 1914, deposition A by Moses Simmons, Apr. 8, 1901, and Oct. 18, 1898, "Board of Review, Department of the Interior, Bureau of Pensions," Feb. 11, 1919, "Declaration of an Original Invalid Pension," May 15, 1890, pension file for Moses (Fannie) Simmons, RG 15, NARA; deposition by Harriet Hamilton, Sep. 24, 1904, deposition by Bolton Pinckney, Sep. 25, 1901, deposition by William Hamilton, Sep. 21, 190[?], "Department of the Interior, Bureau of Pensions," Oct. 11, 1901, pension file for William (Harriet, Nancy) Hamilton, RG 15, NARA.

47. Claim by William C. Heyward, Jul. 1863.

48. Claim by Joshua Nicholls, Sep. 17, 1863, "Claims of Property Loss, 1862–1864," South Carolina Department of Archives and History, Columbia.

49. Claim by Joshua Nicholls, Sep. 17, 1863.

50. [Deposition] by Sancho Van Dross, 2/19/1869, Harry (Bina) Mack US Civil War Pension File.

51. "The Raid on Combahee"; "Claims of Property Loss, 1862–1864," South Carolina Department of Archives and History, Columbia; affidavits by Sancho Van Dross, Feb. 19, 1869, and Mar. 2, 1861, pension file for Harry (Bina) Mack, RG 15, NARA: affidavit by Mingo Van Dross, Oct. 11, 1908, deposition by Mingo Van Dross, pension file for Mingo (Emma) Van Dross, RG 15, NARA; general affidavits by Sylvia De Causter and John A. Savage, Feb. 26, 1892, general affidavit by Elizabeth Hyde Botume, May 29, 1890, general affidavits by November Osborne and Andrew Wyatt, June 7, 1890, pension file for Isaac (Silvia) De Causter, RG 15, NARA; deposition A by Andrew Wyatt, deposition B by Silvia De Coster, deposition C by Charlotte Savage, and deposition D by Edward Brown, Aug. 25, 1891, "For Officer's or Comrade's Testimony," Jun. 11, 1889, neighbor's affidavit by Isaac De Coster, Oct. 18, 1887, neighbor's affidavit by November Osborne, Sep. 4, 1889, pension file for Andrew (Marie) Wyatt, RG 15, NARA; general affidavit by William Drayton, Nov. 4, 1893, pension file for Nat (Victoria) Osborne, RG 15, NARA; "Alfred O. Halsey Map 1949," Preservation Society of Charleston, http://www.halseymap.com/flash/mayors-detail.asp?polID=31.

52. Depositions by Captain Brown and Daniel Jenkins, May 4, 1897, Jackson Grant, May 6, 1897, additional evidence by Friday Hamilton and Joe Morrison, Apr. 9, 1895, pension file for Frank (Captain Brown) Hamilton, RG 15, NARA; certification by C. M. Grace, Sep. 14, 1904, general affidavit by Friday Hamilton, Jul. 28, 1904, affidavit by Friday Hamilton, Aug. 11, 1904, pension file for Friday Hamilton, RG 15, NARA.

53. "The Raid on the Combahee," *The Mercury*, 6/19/1863.

54. [Deposition] by C. M. Grace, 9/6/1904, Friday Hamilton, 8/3/1904, Friday Hamilton US Civil War Pension File.

55. Dr William L. Kirkland Estate Inventory 1824, Charleston District, South Carolina Estate Inventories, 1732–1844, Inventory Book G (1824–34), 319–320, 330–332, "South Carolina Probate Records, Files and Loose Papers, 1732–1964 (Columbia: South Carolina Department of Archives and Histories); "The Raid on the Combahee," *The Mercury*, 6/19/1863; Suzanne Cameron Linder et al., *Historical Atlas of the Rice Plantations of the Ace River Basin—1860* (Columbia: South Carolina Department of Archives and History, 1995), 511.

56. Claim by Joshua Nicholls, Sep. 17, 1863.

57. Compensation affidavit by William Lennox Kirkland Jr., Nov. 5, 1863, "Claims of Property Loss, 1862–1864," South Carolina Department of Archives and History, Columbia; Mary Miller Kirkland, "Reminiscences of My Childhood," 7, Withers Family Papers, 1823–1923, South Carolina Historical Society, Charleston.

58. "1863 List of Negroes Carried Off on 2nd June by Yankees from Combahee," Papers of the Kirkland, Withers, Snowden, and Trotter Families, 47; compensation affidavit by William Lennox Kirkland Jr., Nov. 5, 1863.

59. General affidavit by Flora Grant, Oct. 19, 1888, general affidavit by Andrew Wyatt, Mar. 27, 1889, general testimony by R. M. Rutledge, Apr. 26, 1889, pension file for Stepney (Carolina and Flora) Grant, RG 15, NARA; compensation affidavit by William Lennox Kirkland Jr., Nov. 5, 1863.

60. Compensation affidavit by William Lennox Kirkland Jr., Nov. 5, 1863.

61. Compensation affidavit by William Lennox Kirkland Jr., Nov. 5, 1863; deposition by Moriah Bartley, Apr. 15, 1901, deposition B by Phillis Pinckney and deposition D by Moses Simmons, Oct. 20, 1898, deposition G by William Hamilton, Oct. 21, 1898, general affidavit by Moriah Bartley, May 20, 1898, pension file for Anthony (Moriah) Bartley, RG 15, NARA; "Army Certificate of Disability for Discharge," Dec. 2, 1863, "Record Proof of Marriages, Births, and Deaths," Sep. 27, 1890, pension file for Prince (Tyra) Polite, RG 15, NARA; depositions by Jackson Grant, Oct. 16, 1896, and Apr. 10, 1901, Commissioner to Mrs. Jane Grant, Jan. 13, 1913, "Declaration for Children Under Sixteen Years of Age," Nov. 21, 1912, affidavit by Jane Grant, Feb. 15, 1913, "Note," n.d., pension file for Jackson (Jane) Grant; general affidavit by Daphne Snipe, Oct. 6, 1894, general affidavit by George Singleton Sep. 6, 1894, pension file for Ned (Daphne) Snipe, RG 15; Marcus Rediker, The Slave Ship: A Human History (New York: Penguin, 2007), 305; Sidney Mintz and Richard Price, The Birth of African-American Culture: An Anthropological Perspective (Boston: Beacon Press, 1992), 43, 44.

62. Compensation affidavit by William Lennox Kirkland Jr., Nov. 5, 1863.

63. Compensation affidavit by William Lennox Kirkland Jr., Nov. 5, 1863; depositions by Phyllis Pinckney and Charles Brooks, May 4, 1897, deposition by Scipio Jenkins May 19, 1897, depositions by Rebecca Wineglass and Jackson Grant, May 3, 1897, general affidavit by Sam Savage, Nov. 29, 1892, "Declaration for Soldier's Children Who Are Permanently Helpless" by Phyllis Pinckney, Jul. 9, 1892, pension file for Jack (Rebecca, Hercules) Wineglass, RG 15, NARA; deposition B by Phyllis Pinckney, Oct. 20, 1898, pension file for Anthony (Moriah) Bartley.

64. Compensation affidavit by William Lennox Kirkland Jr., Nov. 5, 1863; depositions by Charlotte Savage and Diana Harris, Aug. 25, 1898, pension file for Andrew (Marie) Wyatt; "Respectfully Returned to the Commissioner of Pensions," Mar. 18, 1889, general affidavit by William Jones, Nov. 27, 1886, deposition by Diana Harris, Mar. 14, 1890, deposition by Pleasant Rutledge, Jul. 28, 1902, deposition B by John A. Savage and deposition C by William Jones, Mar. 14, 1890, pension file for Andrew (Diana) Harris; deposition by William Hamilton, Oct. 22, 1898, general affidavit by J. P. Rivers, Nov. 25, 1889, claimant's affidavit by William Jones, Jan. 8, 1890, pension file for William (Elsey) Jones.

65. ["Col. Montgomery's Raid—The Rescued Black Chattel—A Black "she" Moses—Her Wonderful Sagacity—The Black Regiments—Col. Higginson's Mistakes—Arrival of the 54th Massachusetts, & c., & c.," Wisconsin State Journal, 6/20/1863]

66. Reverend Arthur Waddell ministered to the Black congregants worshipping at Beaufort Baptist for the remainder of the war. At the end of the Civil War, the white members of Beaufort Baptist Church subsequently sold Tabernacle Baptist Church to the Black members. Tabernacle is the current site of monuments to Robert Smalls and Harriet Tubman. I acknowledge

there is some controversy about where the Combahee refugees were taken and where Harriet Tubman addressed them after the raid. It stems primarily from the scant documentation about the event, which does not identify the location. I also acknowledge that the federal government occupied many homes, churches, and other buildings in downtown Beaufort, including the Baptist Church of Beaufort, which was used as a hospital during the war. Based on the pension files of the 150 men who joined the 2nd South Carolina Volunteers before the raid, Beaufort area slaveholders—including but not limited to the Fuller family, which had enslaved no fewer than six of the regiment's men (three of whom we met in Chapter 12)—had held a large portion of the Beaufort recruits in bondage. It seems less likely that Colonel Montgomery would take 756 formerly enslaved people there—people who were scared, skittish, and suspicious, and who had just been delivered from bondage. It is possible, however, that after the Combahee refugees' needs were assessed, those who needed medical treatment were taken to Baptist Church of Beaufort. "From Beaufort South Carolina Baptist Church to Abraham Lincoln, January 1, 1863," Abraham Lincoln Papers, Library of Congress, Washington, DC; "Thanksgiving Day in Beaufort," *The Free South*, Aug. 8, 1863; Stephen R. Wise, Lawrence Sanders Rowland, Gerhard Spieler, and Alexander Moore, *The History of Beaufort County, South Carolina: Volume 2: Rebellion, Reconstruction, and Redemption, 1861–1893* (Columbia: University of South Carolina Press, 2015), 8, 65, 79, 159; Andrew Billingsley, *Yearning to Breathe Free: Robert Smalls of South Carolina and His Families* (Columbia: University of South Carolina Press, 2007), 8, 16, 19–21, 112; Alexia Jones Helsley, *A Guide to Historic Beaufort, South Carolina* (Charleston: History Press, 2006), 38; Maddox Annette Milliken, *A Lamp Unto the Lowcountry: The Baptist Church of Beaufort 1804–2004* (Brentwood, Tennessee and Nashville, Tennessee: Baptist History and Heritage Society, 2004), 125; "Tabernacle Baptist Church Dates to 1811," *Beaufort Gazette*, March 12, 2002.

67. "Col. Montgomery's Raid—the Rescued Black Chattel—a Black 'She' Moses—Her Wonderful Sagacity—the Black Regiments—Col. Higginson's Mistakes—Arrival of the 54th Massachusetts, & C., & C.," *Wisconsin State Journal*, Jun. 20, 1863; "Interesting from Port Royal. A Jubilee Among the Negroes on the First—the President's Emancipation Proclamation—How the Soldiers Enjoyed the Day—Cultivation of the Plantations, &C.," *New York Times*, Jan. 9, 1863.

68. "Col. Montgomery's Raid"; Sanborn, "Harriet Tubman." Susie King Taylor was with the First South Carolina Volunteers at Camp Saxton; see her *Reminiscences of My Life in Camp with the 33rd U.S. Colored Troops, Late 1st South Carolina Volunteers: A Black Woman's Civil War Memoirs* (Boston: Author, 1902), 25–26; Charlotte L. Forten, *The Journal of Charlotte L. Forten: A Young Black Woman's Reaction to the White World of the Civil War Era*, ed. Ray Allen Billington (New York: Dryden Press, 1953), 187–188.

69. Gullah translation by Ron Daise; Author, Performer, Cultural Interpreter.

70. "Interesting from Hilton Head," *New York Herald*, Jun. 9, 1863; deposition by Peggy Brown, Nov. 19, 1901, deposition by Neptune Nicholas, Feb. 12, 1901, "Act of June 27, 1890, Declaration for Widow's Pension," Oct. 20, 1902, pension file for Edward (Peggy) Brown; depositions by Jackson Grant, Oct. 16 and 20, 1896, Apr. 10, 1901, pension file for Jackson (Jane) Grant; depositions by William Jones and Martha Singleton, Mar. 14, 1890, pension file for Andrew (Diana) Harris; deposition by Sarah Osborne, Oct. 21, 1901, pension file for November (Sarah) Osborne; deposition by Elsey Jones, Apr. 30, 1895, deposition by Sally White, May 1, 1895, pension file for Pool (Julia) Sellers, RG 15, NARA; deposition by Margaret Simmons, n.d., pension file for Joshua (Margaret) Simmons; deposition by Cuffie Bolze, pension file for Cuffee (Sophia) Bolze, RG 15, NARA; [affidavit] by Abram Brown, n.d.,pension file for Abraham Brown, RG 15, NARA; deposition by Friday Hamilton, Apr. 18, 1901, pension file for Friday Hamilton; deposition by Neptune Nicholas, Apr. 8, 1901, "Supplementary Declaration of Claimant, Act of June 27, 1890" by Neptune Nicholas, Aug. 21 and Sep. 19, 1898, May 15, 1900, pension file for Neptune (Betsey) Nicholas; deposition by Moses Simmons, Apr. 8, 1901, "Proof of Disability," Oct. 9, 1901, pension file for Moses (Fannie) Simmons; deposition by Stephen Simmons, Apr. 10, 1901, pension file for Stephen (Jane) Simmons; deposition by Mingo Van Dross, pension file for Mingo (Emma) Van Dross; "Military Service," n.d., pension file for July (Sebley) Haywood, RG 15, NARA; "Act of June 27, 1890, Declaration for Invalid Pension" by Thomas Means, Oct. 26, 1896, "No. 1127560," n.d., pension file for Thomas (Annie) Means, RG 15, NARA; "Supplementary Declaration of Claimant, Act of June 27, 1890 and Amendments Thereto" by Neptune Nicholas, n.d., pension file for Neptune (Betsey) Nicholas; "Widow's Declaration for Pension or Increase of Pension" by Flora Robinson, Oct. 18, 1883, pension file for Harry (Flora) Robinson, RG 15, NARA; deposition by Mingo Van Dross, Jun. 15, 1895, pension file for Simon (Rachel) Washington, RG 15, NARA; claimant's affidavit by Wally Watson, Sep. 15, 1891, pension file for Wally (Mary) Watson, RG 15, NARA; "Declaration for Widow's Pension, Act of June 27, 1890" by Daphney Wright, Aug. 22, 1890, "Military Service," n.d., pension file for Frank (Daphne) Wright, RG 15, NARA.

71. Deposition by Moses Simmons, Apr. 8, 1901, pension file for Moses (Fannie) Simmons; deposition A by Simon Washington, Jun. 11, 1895, pension file for Simon (Rachel) Washington; depositions by Wally Garrett, Apr. 5 and Oct. 18, 1902, pension file for Wally (Bella) Garrett, RG 15, NARA; deposition by Jackson Grant, Oct. 18, 1896, pension file for Jackson (Jane) Grant; deposition by Solomon Salter, Apr. 6, 1902, pension file for Solomon Salter, RG 15, NARA; deposition by James Sheppard, Jun. 12, 1895, pension file for James (Sallie) Sheppard, RG 15, NARA; deposition by Neptune Nicholas, Apr. 8, 1901, pension file for Neptune (Betsey) Nicholas; deposition by Selam White, Jun. 12, 1902, pension file for Selem (Sallie) White, RG 15, NARA; Bob Luke and John David Smith, *Soldiering for Freedom: How the Union Army Recruited,*

Trained, and Deployed the U.S. Colored Troops (Baltimore: Johns Hopkins University Press, 2014), 20, 29, 68–69. Thomas J. Morgan, Reminiscences of Service with the Colored Troops in the Army of the Cumberland (Providence: Soldiers and Sailors Historical Society of Rhode Island, 1885), 11–15]

72. General affidavit by Rev. Samuel Chisolm and Ralph Brown, 8/22/1910, Deposition A by Soloman Cunningham, 2/11/1892, Deposition B by Selim S. White and Deposition C by William Jones, 2/17/1892, "Department of the Interior Bureau of Pensions, 4/5/1892 and n.d., "Declaration for an Invalid Pension," Solomon Cunningham, 1/27/1869, Solomon Lavinia) Cunningham US Civil War Pension File.

73. Deposition by Andrew Wyatt, Aug. 25, 1891, pension file for Andrew (Marie) Wyatt; deposition by William Hamilton, Apr. 12, 1901, pension file for William (Harriet, Nancy) Hamilton; deposition by Nat Osborne, Oct. 28, 1902, pension file for Nat (Victoria) Osborne; deposition by James Shields, Apr. 10, 1902, pension file for James (Jone) Shields, RG 15, NARA; deposition by Wally Watson, Apr. 7, 1902, pension file for Wally (Mary) Watson; Luis F. Emilio, *History of the Fifty Fourth Regiment of Massachusetts Volunteer Infantry* (Boston, 1891), 19–20.

74. Deposition B by Selim S. White, 2/17/1892, Solomon (Lavinia) Cunningham US Civil War Pension File; Deposition A by Stephen Gatson US Civil War Pension File; Deposition by William Hamilton, 4/12/1901, William (Harriet, Nancy) Hamilton US Civil War Pension File; Deposition A by James Sheppard, 6/12/1895, James (Sallie) Sheppard US Civil War Pension File; Thomas Wentworth Higginson, *Army Life in a Black Regiment and Other Writings* (Boston: Houghton, Mifflin, 1900), 352–353; Esther Hill Hawks and Gerald Schwartz, *A Woman Doctor's Civil War: Esther Hill Hawks' Diary*, 1st ed., Women's Diaries and Letters of the Nineteenth-Century South Series (Columbia: University of South Carolina, 1984), 19.

75. "Regimental Descriptive Book (List of Commissioned Officers)," "Individual Muster Roll," "Field and Staff Muster Roll," Colonel James Montgomery to Brigadier General Q. A. Gillmore, Jun. 28, 1863, military service record for Arthur Greenleaf, War Department Collection of Confederate Records, RG 109, NARA; "Company Descriptive Book," "Company Muster In Roll," "Hospital Muster Roll," "Co. Muster Out Roll," "Field and Staff Muster Out Roll," "Regimental Special Order No. 5" by Col. James Montgomery, Jun. 10, 1863, military service record for George Garvin, War Department Collection of Confederate Records, RG 109, NARA; Colonel James Montgomery to Brigadier General Quincy A. Gilmore, 6/28/1863, Arthur W. Greenleaf, Compiled Military Service Records of Volunteer Union Soldiers Who Served with the United States Colored Troops, RG 94, National Archives and Records Administration.

76. "A Typical Negro," *Harper's Weekly*, Jul. 4, 1863.

77. "A Typical Negro."

78. Vincent Colyer, *Report of the Services Rendered by the Freed People to the United States Army North Carolina, in the Spring of 1862, After the Battle of Newbern* (New York: V. Colyer, 1862); "The Realities of Slavery," *New-York Daily Tribune*, Dec. 3, 1863; "Company Descriptive Book," "Company Muster In Roll," "Company Muster Roll," military service record for Furney Bryant, War Department Collection of Confederate Records, RG 109, NARA; David Silkenat, "'A Typical Negro': Gordon, Peter, Vincent Colyer, and the Story Behind Slavery's Most Famous Photograph," *American Nineteenth Century History* 15, no. 2 (2014): 169–186.

79. Silkenat, "'A Typical Negro,'" 169–186; Margaret Abruzzo, *Polemical Pain: Slavery, Cruelty, and the Rise of Humanitarianism* (Baltimore: Johns Hopkins University Press, 2011), 200–206; Louis P. Masur, "'Pictures Have Now Become a Necessity': The Use of Images in American History Textbooks," *Journal of American History* 84, no. 4 (1998): 1417–1419.

80. "War Department, Adjutant General's Office," Mar. 18, 1889, "Bureau of Pensions," Jul. 16, 1887, "Widow's Declaration for Pension or Increase Pension" by Diana Harris, Sep. 14, 1886, "Widow's Pension," n.d., "Army of the United States, Certificate of Disability for Discharge," Nov. 18, 1863, depositions by Edward Snipe, Jack Wineglass, Jackson Grant, Diana Harris, and William Jones, Mar. 20, 1890, pension file for Andrew (Diana) Harris; "Proof of Disability" by Friday Hamilton, Nov. 4, 1897, "Widow's Pension," n.d., "Department of the Interior, Bureau of Pensions," Jul. 3, 1890, "Act of June 27, 1890" by Margaret Simmons, Nov. 16, 1891, pension file for Joshua (Margaret) Simmons; "No. 908608," "Invalid Pension," Aug. 27, 1890, "Declaration for Invalid Pension," Aug. 30, 1890, "Soldier's Application," Aug. 20, 1890, claimant's affidavit, Jun. 24, 1894, general affidavits by Anthony Bartley and Andrew Nicholas, May 24, 1894, "Military Service," Apr. 1891, "War Department, Record and Pension Division," Aug. 24, 1891, "Widow's Pension," Jun. 10, 1895, pension file for Ned (Daphne) Snipe; "No. 778745," "Widow's Pension," n.d., "Act of June 27, 1890, Invalid Pension," May 14, 1891, "Declaration for Invalid Pension," Jul. 15 and Aug. 20, 1890, "Soldier's Application," Aug. 20, 1890, "Supplementary Declaration of Claimant," May 17 and Dec. 4, 1897, Sep. 22, 1899, Oct. 9, 1901, Nov. 5, 1902, deposition, Apr. 8, 1901, "Declaration for an Original Invalid Pension," Aug. 15, 1890, "War Department Record and Pension Division," Sep. 16, 1891, "Department of the Interior, Bureau of Pensions," pension file for Moses (Fannie) Simmons; "Affidavit to Origin of Disability" by William Drayton and Andrew Nicholas, Apr. 11, 1894, pension file for Balaam (Diana, Sally) Burnett; general affidavits by Andrew Nicholas and Lucius Robinson, Nov. 5, 1894, "Department of the Interior, Bureau of Pensions," May 13, 1895, "Record and Pension Office, War Department," May 14, 1895, pension file for Cuffie (Sophia) Bolze; deposition by Andrew Nicholas, Jun. 15, 1895, pension file for Simon (Rachel) Washington; "No. 775975," "Where Born? Colleton County, SC," "Act of May 11, 1912," May 27, 1912, "Declaration of Pension" by

Mingo Vandross, May 20, 1912, and Nov. 17, 1908, "Act of February 6, 1907," Nov. 19, 1908, Aug. 17, 1911, and Feb. 24, 1911, "Invalid Pension," n.d., "Supplementary Declaration of the Claimant," Oct. 26, 1900, Apr. 15, 1899, Feb. 17 and Apr. 23, 1897, "History of Claim," May 17, 1890, "Declaration of Invalid Pension," Aug. 21, 1890, May 23, 1895, "Soldier's Application," Aug. 21, 1890, "Original Invalid Claim," n.d., "Declaration for an Original Invalid Pension," May 13, 1890, "Department of the Interior, Bureau of Pensions," Jan. 13, 1891, "Record and Pension Office War Department," Jan. 29, 1896, pension file for Mingo (Emma) Van Dross; "Adjutant General's Office," Dec. 5, 1897, "War 1861, Act July 4, 1862," n.d., "Declaration for an Invalid Person," Aug. 28, 1867, "Declaration for Widow's Pension," Apr. 4, 1908, Aug. 12, 1890, and Sep. 20, 1890, "Widow's Pension," n.d., pension file for Robert (Phoebe) Frazier; "Widow's Pension," n.d., "Adjutant General's Office," Apr. 12, 1869, Jno. G. Stokes to Hon. J. H. Baker, Jul. 1, 1873, [affidavit] of Sina Young, Jun. 23, 1873, [affidavit] of Sina Young, Jun. 26, 1873, [affidavit] of Venus Lyons, Elsy Jones, and Lina Richards, Jun. 30, 1873, "Record and Pension Office," Sep. 3, 1901, "Widow's Declaration for Pension or Increase of Pension," n.d., "Declaration for Pension or Increase of Pension of Children Under Sixteen years of Age," Apr. 26, 1887, "Original Pension for Minor Children," n.d., pension file for William (Sina) Young; "No. 970256," deposition by Moriah Bartley, Apr. 15, 1901, "Invalid Pension," n.d., "Declaration for Invalid Pension," n.d., "Soldier's Application," Aug. 25, 1890, "Military Service," Jun. 2, 1891, "War Department, Record and Pension Division," Jun. 3, 1891, "War Department, Record and Pension Division," n.d., "Declaration for Widow's Pension," Apr. 13, 1903, "Widow's Pension" n.d., "Act of June 27, 1890, Declaration for Widow's Pension," Feb. 21, 1898, general affidavit by Moriah Bartley, May 20, 1898, Jackson Grant, Feb. 21, 1898, pension file for Anthony (Moriah) Bartley, RG 15, NARA; "No. 908501," "Declaration for Widow's Pension," Jan. 15, 1909, "Widow's Pension," n.d., "Invalid Pension," n.d., "History of Claim," deposition by Neptune Nicholas, Apr. 18, 1901, "Declaration for Invalid Person," n.d., "Soldier's Application," Aug. 20, 1890, "Supplementary Declaration of Claimant," Aug. 21, 1896, Sep. 21, 1898, May 17, 1900, and Nov. 21, 1902, claimant's affidavit by Neptune Nicholas, n.d., "Record and Pension Office, War Department," n.d., "Military Service," n.d., pension file for Neptune (Betsey) Nicholas; "Declaration for Invalid Pension," Nov. 25, 1890, "Original Pension of Minor Children," n.d. "Declaration for Children Under Sixteen Years of Age," Feb. 7, 1910, "Declaration for Pension" by William Hamilton, Feb. 12, 1907, deposition by William Hamilton, Apr. 12, 1901, pension file for William (Harriet, Nancy) Hamilton; "Military Service," n.d., "War Department, Record and Pension Division," n.d., "Record and Pension Office, War Department," n.d., claimant's affidavit by March Lawrence, Sep. 9, 1891, "Invalid Pension," n.d., "Declaration for Invalid Pension" by March Lawrence, Mar. 19, 1891, Aug. 30, 1897, and Aug. 4, 1899, "No. 1009717," pension file for March (Rebecca) Lawrence; "No. 593886," "No. 725255," "Born in Colleton

County, South Carolina," "Act of May 11, 1912," n.d., "Act of February 6, 1907," n.d., "Invalid Pension," n.d., "Supplementary Declaration of Claimant," Oct. 8, 1901, and Apr. 20, 1900, "History of Claim," n.d., "Declaration for Invalid Pension," Jul. 15, 1890, deposition by Friday Hamilton, Apr. 17, 1901, "Department of Interior, Bureau of Pensions," Dec. 17, 1889, "War Department, Record and Pension Division," n.d., "Proof of Disability" by Neptune Nicholas, Mar. 32, 1895, "Supplementary Declaration of Claimant," Jul. 30, 1898, "Declaration for an Original Invalid Pension," Aug. 21, 1889, "Declaration for Pension," May 28, 1912, and Oct. 30, 1922, "Record and Pension Office, War Department," n.d., "Department of the Interior, Bureau of Pensions," Apr. 1, 1915, pension file for Friday Hamilton; depositions by Jackson Grant, Oct. 16, 1896, and Apr. 10, 1901, deposition D by Andrew Nicholas, Oct. 29, 1896, "No. 779201," "Act of February 6, 1907," "Declaration for Pension, Act of February 6, 1907," Jun. 26, 1909, "Invalid Pension," n.d., "Supplementary Declaration of Claimant," Nov. 23, 1900, Sep. 21, 1898, and Jun. 15, 1896, "Declaration for Invalid Pension," Jul. 15 and Aug. 20, 1890, "Declaration for an Original Invalid Pension," May 20, 1890, "War Department, Record and Pension Department," n.d., "Department of the Interior, Bureau of Pensions," Apr. 22, 1901, and Jul. 8, 1912, "Record and Pension Office, War Department," n.d., "Proof of Disability" by Jackson Grant, Aug. 21, 1895, pension file for Jackson (Jane) Grant; deposition by Jackson Grant, Oct. 20, 1898, "Widow's Pension," n.d., "No. 724884," general affidavit by James Sheppard, Nov. 28, 1892, "Affidavit to the Origin of Disability" by Edward Brown, Oct. 26, 1889, Selam White, Oct. 28, 1889, "Department of the Interior of Pensions," Dec. 21, 1889, "Declaration for an Original Invalid Pension," Aug. 19, 1885, "Disability Affidavit," Jan. 23, 1889, "Invalid Pension," "Declaration for Invalid Pension," pension file for William (Elsey) Jones; "Original Pension of Minor Children," n.d., pension file for Jack (Jack Jr.) Aiken, RG 15, NARA: "No. 725,142," "Original Invalid Claim," "Declaration for an Original Invalid Pension" by Edward Brown, Aug. 21, 1889, "Declaration for an Original Invalid Pension" by Edward Brown, May 17, 1895, [affidavit] by Edward Brown, Dec. 31, 1889, "Department of the Interior, Bureau of Pension," Dec. 19, 1889, "War Department, Record and Pension Division," Dec. 21, 1888, "Record and Pension Office, War Department," n.d., deposition C by Cuffy Bowls Feb. 11, 1902, deposition C by Neptune Nicholas Feb. 12, 1902, deposition I by Friday Hamilton Feb. 19, 1902, deposition W Jackson Grant, Nov. 27, 1901, "Invalid Pension," n.d., "Declaration for Invalid Pension, Act of June 27, 1890," Aug. 29, 1890, "Soldier's Application," Aug. 20, 1890, "Declaration for Invalid Pensions, Under Act of June 27, 1890," Nov. 15, 1890, "Act of June 27, 1890, Declaration for Invalid Pension" n.d., "Supplementary Declaration of Claimant," Feb. 20, 1900, general affidavit by Jackson Grant, Nov. 3, 1899, "Widow's Pension," n.d., "Act of June 27, 1890, Declaration for Widow's Pension" by Peggy Brown, Oct. 20, 1902, deposition by Peggy Brown, Nov. 14, 1902, pension file for Edward (Peggy) Brown; deposition by Daniel Jenkins, May 4, 1897, pension file for Frank (Captain Brown) Hamilton; "Increase Invalid Pension," n.d., "Invalid Pension," n.d., "Department of the Interior, Bureau of Pensions," Mar. 23, 1923, and Feb. 13, 1926, "Declaration for Invalid Pension, Act of June 27, 1890," Aug. 20, 1890, "Supplementary Declaration of Claimants, Act of June 27, 1890 and Amendments Thereto," Jun. 21, 1904, "War Department, Record and Pension Department," n.d., "Department of the Interior, Bureau of Pensions," Jun. 21, 1904, "Military Service," n.d., "War and Record Division," n.d., "Widow's Pension," n.d., "Where Born? Colleton Co., SC," n.d., "No. 931365," pension file for William (Relia) Middleton; "Widow's Pension," n.d., "Declaration for Widow's Pension" by Lucy Smith, May 29, 1900, "Department of the Interior, Bureau of Pensions," Jul. 28, 1908, "War Department, Record and Pension Department," n.d., pension file for Richard (Lucy, Fannie) Smith; "No. 921760," "Invalid Pension," n.d., "Declaration for Invalid Pension," Aug. 20, 1890, "Soldier's Application," Aug. 20, 1890, "Declaration for Invalid Pensions, Under Act of June 27, 1890," May 20, 1891, "Act of June 27, 1890, Declaration for Invalid Pension," Jul. 11, 1891, and Nov. 4, 1903, "Supplementary Declaration of Claimants, Act of June 27, 1890," Jan. 2 and Jul. 9, 1900, "Supplementary Declaration of Claimants, Act of June 27, 1890 and Amendments Thereto," Jun. 1, 1903, "Act of June 27, 1890, Amended by Act of May 9, 1900, and Order of March 14, 1904," May 17, 1904, "Original Invalid Claim," n.d., "Widow's Pension," n.d., "Acts of June 27, 1890 and May 9, 1900, Declaration for Widow's Pension," Sep. 29, 1905, general affidavit by Charles Nicholas, Feb. 14, 1895, "Military Service," n.d., "War Department, Record and Pension Division," May 2, Aug. 22, and Oct. 20, 1891, pension file for Charles (Ella) Nicholas.

81. Deposition by Solomon Salter, Apr. 6, 1902, "Invalid Pension," n.d., "History of Claim," n.d., "Act of June 27, 1890, Invalid Pension," n.d., "Declaration for Invalid Pension, Act of June 27, 1890" by Solomon Salter, Mar. 1, 1892, "Record and Pension Office, War Department," n.d., "War Department, Record and Pension Office," Jun. 2, 1892, pension file for Solomon Salter; deposition by Wally Garrett, Jan. 18, 1902, "Statement of the Case," n.d., "Certificate of Service," Jan. 8, 1892, "No. 589,978," "No. 780,516," "Increase Invalid Pension," n.d., "Renewal Invalid Pension," n.d., "Soldier's Application," Jul. 18, 1890, "Act of June 27, 1890, Declaration for Invalid Pension" by Baylaam Burnett, Jul. 18, 1890, "Declaration for Restoration to the Pension Roll" by Baylaam Burnett, Sep. 4, 1895, "Restoration, Declaration for Invalid Pension" by Balaam Burnett, Mar. 30, 1896, "Soldier's Application for Increase or for Increase and New Disability," Nov. 13, 1899, "Declaration for an Original Invalid Pension" by Baylaam Burnet, May 26, 1890, "Invalid Claim for Pension," n.d., "Invalid, No. 780516," n.d., "Department of the Interior, Bureau of Pensions," Jan. 6, 1891, "Record and Pension Office, War Department," Jan. 26, 1901, "Widow's Pension," n.d., "Act of June 27, 1890, Declaration for Widow's Pension" by Sally Burnett, Mar. 26, 1891, pension file for Balaam (Diana, Sally) Burnett; "No. 693773," "Widow's Pension," n.d., "Increase Invalid Pension," n.d.,

"Invalid Pension," n.d., claimant's affidavit by Jim Sheppard, Dec. 31, 1891, "Original Invalid Claim," n.d., deposition by William Jones, Jun. 19, 1895, pension file for James (Sallie) Sheppard; deposition by Selam White, Jun. 12, 1902, "Invalid Pension," n.d., pension file for Selem (Sallie) White; "Commissioner to Sir," Dec. 4, 1907, "No. 913,912," "Act of February 6, 1907," [affidavit] by Farbry Bowers, Mar. 5, 1908, "Increase Invalid Pension," n.d., "Application for Increase or for Increase and New Disability," n.d., "Act of June 27, 1890, Invalid Pension," n.d., "Act of June 27, 1890, Declaration of Invalid Pension," by Farbry Bowers, Nov. 17, 1890, "Supplementary Declaration of Invalid Pension, Act of June 27, 1890," Aug. 7, 1895, "Oath of Identity," Feb. 13, 1893, "Original Invalid Claim," n.d., "Record and Pension Office, War Department," n.d., pension file for Farbry (Aminda) Bowers, RG 15, NARA; "No. 1965671," "Widow's Pension" n.d., "Widow's Declaration for Pension" by Bella Garrett, Mar. 9, 1889, general affidavit by Bella Garrett, Mar. 8, 1889, "Original Pension of Minor Children," n.d., "War Department, Adjutant General's Office," Mar. 6, 1888, "Department of the Interior, Bureau of Pensions," Jan. 17, 1888, "Act of February 6, 1907," n.d., "Act of February 6, 1907, Declaration of Pension" by Wally Garrett, May 17, 1907, "Increase Invalid Pension," n.d., "Invalid Increase," n.d., "Declaration of Pension" by Wally Garrett, Oct. 16, 1891, claimant's affidavit by Wally Garrett, Nov. 30, 1891, deposition by Wally Garrett, Oct. 18, 1902, "Record and Pension File, War Department," n.d., "Military Service," n.d., "War Department, Record and Pension Office," Nov. 21, 1891, "Act of April 19, 1908, Widow's Pension," n.d., affidavit by Bella Garrett, May 23, 1912, pension file for Wally (Bella) Garrett; "Military Service," n.d., "War Department, Record and Pension Division," Jul. 22, 1891, "Record and Pension Office, War Department," n.d., claimant's affidavit by March Lawrence, Sep. 9, 1891, "Act of June 27, 1890, Invalid Pension," n.d., "Declaration for Invalid Pension, Act of June 27, 1890" by March Lawrence, Mar. 18, 1891, and Aug. 30, 1897, "No. 1009717," pension file for March (Rebecca) Lawrence, RG 15, NARA; "Act of June 27, 1890, Declaration of Original Pension of Minor Children," n.d., pension file for Jack (Jack Jr.) Aiken; "Act of June 27, 1890, War of the Rebellion, Dependent Father's Pension," n.d., "Father's No. 467426," n.d., "Department of the Interior, Bureau of Pensions," Jan. 26, 1891, pension file for John (Tom and Bella Drayton) Jones, RG 15, NARA.

82. "No. 698606," n.d., "Department of the Interior, Bureau of Pension," Jan. 14, 1895, E. D. Gallien to Honorable William Lochren [?], Jun. 27, 1895, [affidavit] by Simon Washington, Mar. 5, 1908, "Department of the Interior, Bureau of Pensions," Jan. 24, 1903, "Record and Pension Office, War Department," Dec. 8, 1889, deposition by Tom Washington, Sep. 3, 1915, pension file for Jack (Jack Jr.) Aiken; Simon Washington, Aug. 9, 1869, United States, Freedman's Bank Records, 1865–1874; "War Department, Record and Pension Division," n.d., "Army of the United States, Certificate of Disability for Discharge," Sep. 30, 1863, "Invalid Pension," n.d., "Widow's Pension," n.d., "Act of June 27, 1890, Original Pension of Minor Children," n.d., pension file for Jack (Rebecca

or Hercules) Wineglass; "Adjutant General's Office, Washington DC," Mar. 8, 1869, pension file for Harry (Bina) Mack; deposition by Mexico Washington, Jun. 13, 1895, pension file for Simon (Rachel) Washington; "Where Born? Colleton Co. S.C.," n.d., "No. 820038," depositions by Cuffie Bolze, Oct. 18, 1898, and Apr. 8, 1901, "Act of May 11, 1912," n.d., "Act of February 6, 1907," n.d., "Act of February 6, 1907, Declaration of Pension," Apr. 7, 1908, Mar. 23, 1906, and Mar. 4, 1892, "Increase Invalid Pension," n.d., "Act of June 27, 1890, Invalid Pension," n.d., "Declaration for an Original Invalid Pension, Under Act of Congress Approved June 27, 1890," Jul. 7, 1890, "Invalid Pension," n.d., "Declaration for an Original Invalid Pension," May 9, 1891, "War Department, Record and Pension Division," n.d., Feb. 9, 1891, "Military Service," n.d., "Sir: In reply to your request" [handwritten affidavit] by Neptune Nicholas, Feb. 24, 1897, "Widow's Pension," n.d., pension file for Cuffee (Sina) Bolze.

83. Deposition by Stephen Simmons, Apr. 10, 1901, pension file for Stephen (Jane) Simmons; "Where Born? Combahee," Jun. 16, 1912, "Department of the Interior, Bureau of Pensions," Apr. 15, 1915, depositions by Nat Ausborn, May 20, 1897, and Jun. 28, 1902, general affidavit by William Drayton, Nov. 14, 1893, pension file for Nat (Victoria) Osborne; deposition by Solomon Washington, Aug. 28, 1897, pension file for Smart (Lucretia) Washington; "Declaration for an Original Pension of a Mother" by Flora Grant, Nov. 4, 1886, "Declaration for an Original Pension of a Father or Mother" by Flora Grant, Aug. 26, 1887, "Adjutant General's Office," Feb. 25, 1875, "War Department, Adjutant General's Office," Mar. 2, 1888, "Department of Interior, Bureau of Pensions," Jan. 24, 1888, pension file for Stepney (Carolina and Flora) Grant; "No. 1009862," n.d., "Increase Invalid Pension Ctf. 939284," n.d., "History of Claim," n.d., "Supplemental Declaration for Invalid Pension, Act of June 27, 1890" by James Shields, Aug. 22, 1900, "Act of June 27, 1890, Invalid Pension," n.d., "Declaration for Invalid Pension, Act of June 27, 1890" by James Shields, Apr. 10, 1895, claimant's affidavit by James Shields, Sep. 9, 1891, general affidavit by James Shields, Sep. 11, 1896, "Record and Pension Office, War Department," n.d., "Military Service," "Widow's Pension," pension file for James (Jone) Shields; "Invalid Pension," n.d., "Declaration for Original Invalid Pension" by Edward Brown, Dec. 1, 1889, "Invalid Claim for Pension," "Original Invalid Pension," n.d., "Declaration for an Invalid Pension," Jan. 28, 1869, "Declaration of a Survivor for Service or Dependent Pension" by Edward Brown, Jul. 12, 1890, "Service or Dependent Pension," n.d., "Widow's Pension," n.d., "No. 514833," n.d., "Adjutant General's Office," Mar. 10, 1869, "Record and Pension Office, War Department," Mar. 31, 1899, pension file for Edward (Mary) Brown; "Department of the Interior, Pension Office," Feb. 25, 1869, "Supplemental Soldier's Declaration for a Pension," Jun. 18, 1892, "Invalid Pension," n.d., "Soldier's Declaration for a Pension, Under Act of 51st Congress, Approved June 27, 1890" by William Drayton, Sep. 24, 1891, "War of 1861, Act July 14, 1862," n.d., "Declaration for an Invalid Pension" by William Drayton, Jan. 28, 1869, "Affidavits Proving Disability and Incapacity to Labor"

by Edward Brown, Oct. 3, 1891, and by John Green, Oct. 8, 1891, pension file for William Drayton, RG 15, NARA; Comptroller General, State Auditor, "Claims of Property Loss, 1862–1864"; general affidavit by Reuben Rutledge, Dec. 16, 1887, pension file for Aaron (Sallie) Ancrum, RG 15, NARA.

84. "A Raid Among the Rice Plantations," *Harper's Weekly*, Jul. 4, 1863; Seth Rogers, "War-Time Letters of Seth Rogers, M.D., Surgeon of the First South Carolina Afterwards the Thirty-Third Usct 1862–1863," *Florida History Online*, no. https://history.domains.unf.edu/floridahistoryonline/projects-proj-b-p-html/projects-rogers-index-html/: 56; William Lee Apthorp, "Montgomery's Raids in Florida, Georgia, and South Carolina," 20, Apthorp Family Papers, 1741–1964, Folder 2.6, HistoryMiami Museum, Miami, FL; deposition by Cuffie Bolze, Apr. 8, 1901, pension file for Cuffee (Sophia) Bolze; Deposition by Sammuel Gilliard, 7/17/1902, [Deposition] by Samuel Gilliard, 1/29/1870, Samuel (Martha) Gilliard US Civil War Pension File; deposition by Neptune Nicholas, Oct. 26, 1896, deposition F by Wally Garrett, Oct. 22, 1896, pension file for Jackson (Jane) Grant; deposition by Neptune Nicholas, Apr. 8, 1901, pension file for Neptune (Betsey) Nicholas; "Department of the Interior, Bureau of Pensions," n.d., pension file for Nat (Victoria) Osborne; [affidavit] by Barcus Robinson, Jan. 13, 1870, pension file for Bacchies (Delia) Robinson, RG 15, NARA; depositions by James Sheppard and March Lawrence, Jun. 12, 1895, deposition H by Neptune Nicholas, deposition I by Edward Brown, deposition J by Lucius Robinson, Jun. 14, 1895, pension file for James (Sallie) Sheppard; deposition by Moses Simmons, Apr. 8, 1901, pension file for Moses (Fannie) Simmons; deposition by Mingo Van Dross, Apr. 9, 1901, pension file for Mingo (Emma) Van Dross; deposition by March Lawrence, Jul. 12, 1895, Neptune Nicholas, Edward Brown, Lucius Robinson, Jun. 14, 1895, Mingo Van Dross, Jun. 15, 1895, pension file for Simon (Rachel) Washington; Cornish Dudley Taylor Herman Hattaway and Frank and Virginia Williams Collection of Lincolniana (Mississippi State University Libraries), The Sable Arm: Black Troops in the Union Army 1861–1865 (Lawrence: University Press of Kansas, 1987), 86.

CHAPTER 17

1. Frank Sanborn, "Harriet Tubman," *The Commonwealth Boston*, Jul. 17, 1863.

2. "The New Costume for Ladies," *New-York Tribune*, Jun. 12, 1851; M. A. Griffin, "The New Costume," *The Liberator*, Jul. 11, 1851; Dexter C. Bloomer, *Life and Writings of Amelia Bloomer* (New York: Schocken Books, 1975, 1895), 78; "The New Style," *The Liberator*, Jul. 11, 1851; Gayle V. Fischer, "'Pantalets' and 'Turkish Trowsers': Designing Freedom in the Mid-Nineteenth-Century United States," *Feminist Studies* 23, no. 1 (1997): 113, 124–125, 135; Amy Kesselman, "The 'Freedom Suit': Feminism and Dress Reform in the United States, 1848–1875," *Gender and Society* 5, no. 4 (1991): 495–498.

3. Griffin, "The New Costume"; "The New Style"; "World's Temperance Convention," *The Liberator*, May 27, 1853; Virginia Elwood-Akers, *Caroline*

Severance (New York: iUniverse, 2010), 29, 71; Kesselman, "The 'Freedom Suit,'" 495, 497–498, 502, 506.

4. Sanborn, "Harriet Tubman"; Sarah Bradford, *Harriet Tubman: The Moses of Her People* (1886; New York: J. J. Little, 1901), 100; Alice Brickler to Earl Conrad, Jul. 28, 1939, Earl Conrad/ Harriet Tubman Collection, Schomburg Center for Research in Black Culture, New York Public Library (microform ed., Scholarly Resources); Dexter C. Bloomer, *Life and Writings of Amelia Bloomer* (1896; repr., New York: Schocken Books, 1975), 65–68, 70, 73–74, 78; "Harriet Tubman Is Dead," *Auburn Citizen*, Mar. 12, 1913.

5. Charles Wood, "A History Concerning the Pension Claim of Harriet Tubman," 3, RG 233, NARA; Earl Conrad, "The Charles P. Wood Manuscripts of Harriet Tubman," *Negro History Bulletin* 13, no. 4 (1950): 93.

6. Sanborn, "Harriet Tubman."

7. Deposition by Cuffee Bolze, Apr. 8, 1901, pension file for Cuffie (Sophia) Bolze, RG 15, NARA.

8. Russell Duncan, ed. *Blue-Eyed Child of Fortune: The Civil War Letters of Colonel Robert Gould Shaw* (Athens: University of Georgia, 1992), 2–5, 9–12, 16–17, 21–25.

9. Robert Gould Shaw, *Blue-Eyed Child of Fortune: The Civil War Letters of Colonel Robert Gould Shaw*, ed. Russell Duncan (Athens: University of Georgia Press, 1992), 40–42, 337.

10. Shaw, *Blue-Eyed Child of Fortune*, 42, 338–339, 43, 56–57; John David Smith, ed., *Black Soldiers in Blue: African American Troops in the Civil War Era* (Chapel Hill: University of North Carolina Press, 2002), 310, 318, 322, 324–325.

11. William Lee Apthorp, "Montgomery's Raids in Florida, Georgia, and South Carolina," 23, Apthorp Family Papers, 1741–1964, in Folder 2.6, 23, HistoryMiami Museum, Miami, FL; Shaw, *Blue-Eyed Child of Fortune*, 342, 348, 355; Smith, *Black Soldiers in Blue*, 322.

12. Deposition by Jack Wineglass, Mar. 20, 1890, pension file for Andrew (Diana) Harris, RG 15, NARA; Shaw, *Blue-Eyed Child of Fortune*, 345.

13. "The Destruction of Darien," *Charleston Mercury*, Jun. 18 1863; Shaw, *Blue-Eyed Child of Fortune*, 342.

14. "The Destruction of Darien."

15. "The Destruction of Darien"; "From South Carolina—the New Federal Commander—Col. Montgomery's Late Raid," *Chicago Tribune*, Jun. 20, 1863; "Miscellaneous Items," *Douglass' Monthly*, Aug. 1863; Apthorp, "Montgomery's Raids in Florida, Georgia, and South Carolina," 24; Shaw, *Blue-Eyed Child of Fortune*, 44, 342.

16. Shaw, *Blue-Eyed Child of Fortune*, 342–343, 348–349, 351; Smith, *Black Soldiers in Blue*, 310, 318, 322–325.

17. Thomas Wentworth Higginson, *Letters and Journals of Thomas Wentworth Higginson, 1846–1906*, ed. Mary Thacher Higginson (Boston: Houghton, Mifflin, 1921), 207–208; Smith, *Black Soldiers in Blue: African American Troops in the Civil War Era*, 310, 318.

18. Shaw, *Blue-Eyed Child of Fortune*, 42, 338–339, 342–346; Smith, *Black Soldiers in Blue*, 310, 322, 324.

19. Shaw, *Blue-Eyed Child of Fortune*, 42, 338–339, 342–346; Edward A. Miller, Lincoln's Abolitionist General: The Biography of David Hunter (Columbia: University of South Carolina Press), 19; Stephen R. Wise, *Gate of Hell: Campaign for Charleston Harbor, 1863* (Columbia: University of South Carolina Press, 1994), 24.

20. "From South Carolina"; "The Destruction of Darien"; "Miscellaneous Items"; Apthorp, "Montgomery's Raids in Florida, Georgia, and South Carolina," 21–24; deposition by Cuffie Bolze, Apr. 8, 1901, pension file for Cuffie (Sophia) Bolze; deposition by Jackson Grant, May 20, 1890, pension file for Andrew (Diana) Harris; [deposition] by Edward Brown, Dec. 31, 1899, general affidavit by Edward Brown, Apr. 16, 1890, pension file for Edward (Peggy) Brown, RG 15, NARA. As noted in the text, military actions can be defined in different ways. Though they participated in the action at Darien, Privates Jackson Grant and James Shields testified Morris Island was their first battle. See deposition by Jackson Grant, Apr. 10, 1902, pension file for Jackson (Jane) Grant, RG 15, NARA, and deposition by James Shields, Apr. 10, 1902, pension file for James (Jone) Shields, RG 15, NARA; depositions by Jack Wineglass and Jackson Grant, Mar. 20, 1890, pension file for Andrew (Diana) Harris; Stephen V. Ash, Firebrand of Liberty: The Story of Two Black Regiments That Changed the Course of the Civil War (New York: W. W. Norton, 2008), 207–208.

21. "Gillmore," Rufus Saxton Papers, 1862–1864, Rubenstein Library, Duke University, Durham, NC; Shaw, *Blue-Eyed Child of Fortune*, 49, 351–352, 357, 382 n. 3; Ash, *Firebrand of Liberty*, 208; Smith, *Black Soldiers in Blue*, 325.

22. Francis Jackson Meriam to Governor John A. Andrew, Jun. 13, 1863, John A. Andrew Papers, 1772–1895, Massachusetts Historical Society, Boston., Box 11, Folder 15–20.

23. Wood, "A History Concerning the Pension Claim of Harriet Tubman," 2; Bradford, *Harriet Tubman*, 163; Sarah H. Bradford, *Scenes in the Life of Harriet Tubman* (1869; repr., North Stratford, NH: Ayer, 1971), 69; Shaw, *Blue-Eyed Child of Fortune*, 348, 350, 354, 357; Smith, *Black Soldiers in Blue*, 324; Conrad, "The Charles P. Wood Manuscripts of Harriet Tubman," 93.

24. Higginson, *Letters and Journals*, 207, 209.

25. Charlotte L. Forten, *The Journal of Charlotte L. Forten: A Young Black Woman's Reaction to the White World of the Civil War*, ed. Ray Allen Billington (New York: Dryden, 1953), 193; Shaw, *Blue-Eyed Child of Fortune*, 353; ORA Series 1, Volume XXVIII, Part 2, 15–16, 31, 62; Ash, *Firebrand of Liberty*, 207; Smith, *Black Soldiers in Blue*, 318.

26. Carl W. Marino, "General Alfred Howe Terry: Soldier from Connecticut," Ph.D. diss., New York University, 1968, 220–221, 228.

27. "Daily Journal of Observations and Incidents Among the Federal Batteries on Morris Island, Before the Rebel Forts 'Sumter' and 'Wagner,' August 16, 1863," 1, Folder 5, Charles Ray Brayton Papers, 1853–1908, Rhode Island

Historical Society, Providence, RI; *The War of the Rebellion: A Compilation of the Official Records of the Union and Confederate Armies*, ser. 1, vol. XXVIII, pt. 1 (Washington, DC: GPO, 1880–1901), 72, 368, 370; neighbor's affidavit by William Washington, Apr. 30, 1888, [affidavit] by Wally Ford and June Young, Jul. 6, 1879, "Widow's Claim for Pension" by Phoebe Frazier, Mar. 8, 1878, and Mar. 9, 1897, pension file for Robert (Phoebe) Frazier, RG 15, NARA; Stephen R Wise, *Gate of Hell: Campaign for Charleston Harbor, 1863* (Univ. of South Carolina Press, 1994), 68, 72; Marino, "General Alfred Howe Terry," 230.

28. Stephen R Wise, *Gate of Hell: Campaign for Charleston Harbor, 1863* (Univ. of South Carolina Press, 1994), 71, 75–76; Marino, "General Alfred Howe Terry," 230–231.

29. "Daily Journal of Observations and Incidents Among the Federal Batteries on Morris Island, Before the Rebel Forts 'Sumter' and 'Wagner,' August 16, 1863," 1, 3, Folder 5, Charles Ray Brayton Papers, 1853–1908, Rhode Island Historical Society, Providence, RI; Shaw, *Blue-Eyed Child of Fortune*, 49–52, 380–382 n.3, 10; *The War of the Rebellion: A Compilation of the Official Records of the Union and Confederate Armies*, ser. 1, vol. XXVIII, pt. 1 (Washington, DC: GPO, 1880–1901), 72–73, 210–211, 345–349, 362–365, 367–371, 374; neighbor's affidavit by William Washington, Apr. 30, 1888, [affidavit] by Wally Ford and June Young, Jul. 6, 1879, "Widow's Claim for Pension" by Phoebe Frazier, Mar. 8, 1878, and Mar. 9, 1897, pension file for Robert (Phoebe) Frazier, RG 15, NARA; Marino, "General Alfred Howe Terry," 231–232.

30. "Proceedings of a General Court Martial Convened at Morris Island," Records of the US Army Department of the South, South Caroliniana Library, University of South Carolina, Columbia, court martial page numbers 40, 64, 71–72, 75, 78, 90.

31. "Daily Journal of Observations and Incidents," 3, 5; *The War of the Rebellion: A Compilation*, ser. 1, vol. XXVIII, pt. 1, 73; Shaw, *Blue-Eyed Child of Fortune*, 381; Marino, "General Alfred Howe Terry," 231–234.

32. Charles Ray Brayton to William D. Brayton, July 16, 1863, Charles Ray Brayton Papers; Folder 1, 1.

33. Charles Ray Brayton to William D. Brayton, July 16, 1863; *The War of the Rebellion: A Compilation*, ser. 1, vol. XXVIII, pt. 1, 75, 345–346, 372; Marino, "General Alfred Howe Terry," 225–226.

34. Wise, *Gate of Hell*, 92–93, 97, 99–100, 117–118.

35. Robert W. Taylor, *Harriet Tubman, the Heroine in Ebony* (Boston: [s.n.], 1901), 13; "Harriet Tubman Is Dead"; Hildegard Hoyt Swift to Earl Conrad, Sep. 8, 1939, Earl Conrad/Harriet Tubman Collection, Box 2, 42, File a-4a; Smith, *Black Soldiers in Blue*, 325; Wise, *Gate of Hell*, 98–100.

36. Shaw, *Blue-Eyed Child of Fortune*, 52; Wise, *Gate of Hell*, 101–102.

37. "Daily Journal of Observations and Incidents Among the Federal Batteries on Morris Island, Before the Rebel Forts 'Sumter' and 'Wagner,' August 16, 1863," 2, Folder 5, Charles Ray Brayton Papers, 1853–1908, Rhode Island Historical Society, Providence; Laura M. Towne, *Letters and Diary Written from*

the Sea Islands of South Carolina, 1862–1884 (Cambridge, MA: Riverside Press, 1912); Shaw, *Blue-Eyed Child of Fortune*; Edward Zwick, *Glory* (Culver City, CA Columbia TriStar Home Video, 1997); Wise, *Gate of Hell*, 102–105; Marino, "General Alfred Howe Terry," 239 n. 179.

38. "The Court Not Pursuant to . . . ," Dec. 8, 1863, "The Court Met Pursuant to Adjournment . . . ," Dec. 29 and 30, 1863, Jan. 1, 1864, "Major B. R. Corwin," n.d., "Proceedings of a General Court Martial Convened at Morris Island," 8–9, 14, 24, 29–30, 32, 36, 54, 64, Records of the US Army Department of the South, South Caroliniana Library, University of South Carolina, Columbia; file for Daniel D. Hanson, Compiled Military Service Records.

39. Forten, *Journal*, 193–194; Elizabeth Ware Pearson, *Letters from Port Royal Written at the Time of the Civil War, 1906* (n.p.: Project Gutenberg, 2008), 196; Bradford, *Harriet Tubman: The Moses of Her People*, 102; Bradford, Scenes in the Life of Harriet Tubman, 42; John W. Blassingame, *Slave Testimony: Two Centuries of Letters, Speeches, Interviews and Autobiographies* (Baton Rouge: Louisiana State University Press, 1977), 463; Earl Conrad, *General Harriett Tubman* (Baltimore: Black Classic Press, 2019), 180–181; Albert Bushnell Hart, *Slavery and Abolition, 1831–1841, the American Nation: A History, Vol. 16* (New York: Harper & Brothers, 1906), 209.

40. Bradford, *Harriet Tubman*, 97; Bradford, *Scenes in the Life of Harriet Tubman*, 37; Forten, *Journal*, 194, 96; Towne, *Letters and Diary*, 114–116; Esther Hill Hawks, *A Woman Doctor's Civil War: Esther Hill Hawks' Diary*, ed. Gerald Schwartz (Columbia: Univeristy of South Carolina Press, 1984), 88.

41. Deposition D by Edward Brown, Aug. 25, 1891, pension file for Andrew (Maria) Wyatt, RG 15, NARA.

42. Deposition by Moses Simmons, Apr. 11, 1905, pension file for Neptune (Betsey) Nicholas, RG 15, NARA.

43. Deposition by Catherine Bennett, Aug. 7, 1924, "Declaration for Invalid Pension, Act of June 27, 1890," Aug. 28, 1894, "Act of June 27, 1890, Declaration for Invalid Pension," Sep. 17, 1896, "Declaration for Invalid Pension, Act March 6, 1896," Jul. 15, 1897, "Act of June 27, 1890, Declaration for Invalid Pension," Jun. 7, 1899, "Declaration of Invalid Pension, Act of June 27, 1890," Aug. 10, 1900, "General Affidavit," Sep. 1, 1897, pension file for Edward (Catherine) Bennett, RG 15, NARA; "Act June 27, 1890, Increase Invalid Pension," Mar. 10, 1905, "Declaration for Increase of Pension," Nov. 12, 1904, "Act June 27, 1890, Increase Invalid Pension," Oct. 9, 1902, "Supplementary Declaration of Claimant," Oct. 8, 1901, "Act June 27, 1890, Increase Invalid Pension," May 22, 1901, "Supplementary Declaration of Claimant," Apr. 20, 1900, deposition by Friday Hamilton, Apr. 17, 1901, Jackson Grant to Sir, Jul. 7, 1901, pension file for Friday Hamilton, RG 15, NARA; J. D. Luke to Honorable Commissioner of Pensions, Sep. 1, 1891, depositions by Andrew Wyatt and Edward Brown, Aug. 25, 1891, "For Officer's or Comrade's Testimony" by William Drayton, Apr. 2, 1892, claimant's affidavit by Andrew Wyatt, Sep. 3, 1890, "Declaration

for Invalid Pension," Jun. 26, 1869, Jul. 24, 189[?], "Act of June 27, 1890," Aug. 14, 1890, "Act of June 27, 1890, Invalid Pension," Aug. 4, 1890, "Declaration for an Original Invalid Pension," Nov. 30, 1889, "For Officer's or Comrade's Testimony" by Jackson Green and Alex Johnson, Sep. 5, 1892, pension file for; Samuel Grimball, RG 15, NARA; general affidavit by Henry Green, Aug. 9, 1887, general affidavits by Daniel Simmons and John Green, Dec. 17, 1888, deposition by Julia Proctor, Jul. 28, 1902, "Original Invalid Pension," n.d., "Department of the Interior," Jul. 1, 1890, pension file for John (Julia) Proctor; "Declaration for Original Invalid Pension" by Andrew Waity, Apr. 7, 1887, pension file for Andrew (Maria) Wyatt.

44. Annie Simmons testified that her maiden name was Castle and she and Scipio married on Newport Plantation before the Civil War. His death date was incorrectly reported as October 1864 on Morris Island. It is not confirmed by official military records. See "Widow's Declaration for Pension or Increase of Pension" by Annie Holmes, Mar. 16, 1892, and Feb. 22, 1890, "Origin of Disability," n.d., "Affidavit of Marriage" by James Shields, Mar. 8, 1893, pension file for Scipio (Annie) McNeal.

45. "Proceedings of a General Court Martial Convened at Morris Island," "The Court Pursuant to . . . , " Dec. 8, 1863, Records of the US Army Department of the South, South Caroliniana Library, University of South Carolina, Charleston; *The War of the Rebellion: A Compilation*, ser. 1, vol. XXVIII, pt. 1, 76–78, 210, 346–348, 365, 369, 372, 374; Smith, *Black Soldiers in Blue*, 138, 325; Wise, *Gate of Hell*, 114; Marino, "General Alfred Howe Terry," 235–239.

46. South, "Proceedings of a General Court Martial Convened at Morris Island," 13–18, 38–40, 43, 64, 67, 71–72, 75, 77–78.

47. Marino, "General Alfred Howe Terry," 239–241.

48. File for William C. Heyward, Compiled Military Service Records; File for Joshua Nicholls, Compiled Military Service Records; Joshua Nicholls to William Lennox Kirkland Jr., July 24, 1863, Papers of the Kirkland, Withers, Snowden, and Trotter Families, 1790–1959, South Caroliniana Library, University of South Carolina, Columbia (page 51); W. Eric Emerson, *Sons of Privilege: The Charleston Light Dragoons in the Civil War* (Columbia: Univ of South Carolina, 2005), 38; Wise, *Gate of Hell*, 123.

49. Joshua Nicholls to William Lenox Kirkland Jr., July 24, 1863, Papers of the Kirkland, Withers, Snowden, and Trotter Families (pages 51 & 52); *The War of the Rebellion: A Compilation*, ser. 1, vol. XXVIII, pt. 1, 60, 71, 78; Marino, "General Alfred Howe Terry," 257.

50. Charles Ray Brayton to William D. Brayton, Aug. 1, 1863, Charles Ray Brayton Papers.

51. Lewis Douglass to Helen Amelia Loguen, August 15, 1863, Walter O. Evans Collection of Frederick Douglass and Douglass Family Papers, Series II, JWJ MSS 240, Box 3, Folder 63, Beinecke Rare Book Room, Yale University; *The War of the Rebellion: A Compilation*, ser. 1, vol. XXVIII, pt. 1, 83; Shaw, *Blue-Eyed Child of Fortune*, 342.

52. Charles R. Brayton to William D. Brayton, Aug. 1, 1863, and Aug. 16, 1863, Charles R. Brayton Papers; "Daily Journal of Observations and Incidents."

53. Private Journal of Charles R. Brayton, Assistant Chief of Artillery, Morris Island, SC, Aug. 16, 1863, and Charles Ray Brayton to William D. Brayton, Aug. 16, 1863, Charles R. Brayton Papers; "Daily Journal of Observations and Incidents," 3–4; *The War of the Rebellion: A Compilation*, ser. 1, vol. XXVIII, pt. 1, 83–84.

54. Private Journal of Charles R. Brayton, Aug. 16, 1863; "Daily Journal of Observations and Incidents," 3, 7–8; *The War of the Rebellion: A Compilation*, ser. 1, vol. XXVIII, pt. 1, 84; Marino, "General Alfred Howe Terry," 242.

55. "Daily Journal of Observations and Incidents," 7–8.

56. "Declaration for Invalid Pension," May 15, 1867, pension file for Aaron (Sallie) Ancrum, RG 15, NARA; Wise, *Gate of Hell*, 148–50, 169, 171.

57. General affidavit by Isaac De Costa, Dec. 13, 1887, [affidavits] by Solomon Cunningham and John Proctor, Jan. 27, 1869, "Declaration for an Invalid Pension" by Aaron Ancrum, May 15, 1867, "Affidavit for the Origin of Disability" by Robert Boutelle, May 21, 1885, "Affidavit for the Origin of Disability" by William Jones, Mar. 15, 1885, pension file for Aaron (Sallie) Ancrum; "Original Pension Claim No. 913381," May 13, 1891, "Act of June 27, 1890, Declaration for Invalid Pension," Oct. 9, 1890, "Declaration for an Original Invalid Pension," Feb. 7, 1891, "Origin of Disability" by William Hamilton and Simon Payas, Nov. 10, 1897, pension file for Jacob (Elvira) Campbell, RG 15, NARA; general affidavit by Edward Brown, Apr. 16, 1890, pension file for Edward (Peggy) Brown; Wise, *Gate of Hell*, 140–141.

58. "Declaration for an Original Pension of a Mother" by Flora Grant, Nov. 4, 1886, and Jun. 22, 1874, "Declaration for an Original Pension for a Father or Mother" by Flora Grant, Aug. 26, 1887, "Adjutant General's Office," Feb. 25, 1875, "War Department," Oct. 31, 1874, pension file for Stephany (Carolina and Flora) Grant, RG 15, NARA.

59. Williams Middleton to Susan Pringle Smith Middleton, Aug. 24–24, 1863, Williams Middleton Papers 1874–1888, South Caroliniana Library, University of South Carolina, Columbia, 10 July 1862 to 27 Aug 1863; Wise, *Gate of Hell: Campaign for Charleston Harbor, 1863*, 170–71.

60. Williams Middleton to Susan Pringle Smith Middleton, Aug. 24–24, 1863; *The War of the Rebellion: A Compilation*, ser. 1, vol. XXVIII, pt. 1, 60, 71, 84–85; Wise, *Gate of Hell*, 144–145, 171, 180.

61. Charles Ray Brayton to William D. Drayton, Aug. 1, 1863; [affidavit] by Barcus Robinson, Jan. 13, 1870, general affidavit by Israel Ferguson, Jun. 15, 1897, "Department of the Interior," Jul. 11, 1871, pension file for Bacchies (Delia) Robinson; *The War of the Rebellion: A Compilation*, ser. 1, vol. XXVIII, pt. 1, 85–86; Wise, *Gate of Hell*, 179.

62. Colonel James Montgomery to Clarinda Montgomery, Aug. 25, 1863, James Montgomery Collection, Kansas State Historical Society, Topeka.

63. Deposition by Moses Simmons, Apr. 8, 1901, general affidavit by Moses Simmons, Jun. 7, 1893, "Proof of Disability" by Cuffee Bolds, "Proof of

Disability" by Charles Nicholas, Jun. 26, 1895, "Proof of Disability" by Cuffy Bowls and "Proof of Disability" by Neptune Nicholas, Oct. 9, 1901, "Original Pension Claim No. 778745,'" Feb. 5, 1891, Charles Nicholas (his mark) to Sir, Sep. 19, 1899, pension file for Moses (Fannie) Simmons, RG 15, NARA.

64. Colonel James Montgomery to Clarinda Montgomery, Aug. 25, 1863; *The War of the Rebellion: A Compilation*, ser. 1, vol. XXVIII, pt. 1, 85; Wise, *Gate of Hell*, 187–188.

65. Lewis Douglass to Helen Amelia Loguen, Aug. 27, 1863, Box 3, Folder 62, Walter O. Evans Collection of Frederick Douglass and Douglass Family Papers, Series II; Colonel James Montgomery to Clarinda Montgomery, Aug. 29, 1863, James Montgomery Collection; Thomas Wentworth Higginson, *Army Life in a Black Regiment and Other Writings* (Boston: Houghton, Mifflin and Company, 1900), 322.

66. Colonel James Montgomery to Clarinda Montgomery, Aug. 29, 1863; *The War of the Rebellion: A Compilation*, ser. 1, vol. XXVIII, pt. 1, 85–87; Marino, "General Alfred Howe Terry," 244.

67. Lewis Douglass to Helen Amelia Loguen, Aug. 27, 1863; *The War of the Rebellion: A Compilation*, ser. 1, vol. XXVIII, pt. 1, 85.

68. Colonel James Montgomery to Clarinda Montgomery, Aug. 27 and Sep. 18, 1863, James Montgomery Collection; *The War of the Rebellion: A Compilation*, ser. 1, vol. XXVIII, pt. 1, 86.

69. Colonel James Montgomery to Clarinda Montgomery, Aug. 30 and Sep. 18, 1863, "No. 3," "I owe Mr. Mills . . ., " Sep. 3, 1863, "I will send 400 dollars . . .," Sep. 4, 1863, James Montgomery Collection; *The War of the Rebellion: A Compilation*, ser. 1, vol. XXVIII, pt. 1, 86.

70. Charles Ray Brayton to William D. Brayton, Aug. 16 and Aug. 31, 1863, Charles R. Brayton Papers; "Daily Journal of Observations and Incidents"; James Montgomery to Clarinda Montgomery, Aug. 31, 1863, James Montgomery Collection; Wise, *Gate of Hell*, 205.

71. James Montgomery to Clarinda Montgomery, Aug. 31, 1863; Wise, *Gate of Hell*, 189, 211.

72. *The War of the Rebellion: A Compilation*, ser. 1, vol. XXVIII, pt. 1, 88–92; Marino, "General Alfred Howe Terry," 245.

73. "Holtzlander No. 113148," n.d., "Declaration of a Widow for Original Pension When No Child Under Sixteen Years of Age Survives," Jun. 22, 1874, "Widow's Claim for Pension" by Beck Snipe, Sep. 2, 1870, [deposition] of John A. Savage and James Osborne, Sep. 2, 1870, "Declaration for a Widow's Army Pension," Jul. 27, 1865, pension file for Tony (Beck) Snipe; *The War of the Rebellion: A Compilation*, ser. 1, vol. XXVIII, pt. 1, 88–89; Marino, "General Alfred Howe Terry," 245.

74. *The War of the Rebellion: A Compilation*, ser. 1, vol. XXVIII, pt. 1, 209–210; Wise, *Gate of Hell*, 195; Marino, "General Alfred Howe Terry," 244–247.

75. Charles Ray Brayton to William D. Brayton, Sep. 9, 1863, Charles Ray Brayton Papers; *The War of the Rebellion: A Compilation*, ser. 1, vol. XXVIII, pt. 1, 91, 210; Wise, *Gate of Hell*, 203–205, 240–241.

76. Deposition by Neptune Nicholas, Apr. 8, 1901, "Supplemental Declaration of Claimant," Sep. 13, 1895, Aug. 21, 1896, Sep. 19, 1898, May 17, 1900, Nov. 21, 1902, "Declaration for the Increase of an Invalid Pension," Jul. 6, 1901, general affidavit by April Singleton, Jul. 21, 1897, general affidavit by Friday Hamilton, Jul. 5, 1897, general affidavit by Dr. H. E. Bissell, Feb. 26, 1894, "Surgeon's Certificate," Dec. 11, 1895, Aug. 19, 1897, Apr. 19, 1899, Dec. 5, 1900, Jan. 29, 1902, pension file for Neptune (Betsey) Nicholas; "Origin of Disability," Farbry Bowers, Feb. 19, 1889, general affidavit by Farbry Bowers, Apr. 5, 1889, Jan. 10, 1893, deposition by Farbry Bowers May 17, 1897, by S. White May 11, 1897, pension file for Jeffrey (Phoebe) Gray, RG 15, NARA; "Examining Surgeon's Certificate," Nov. 30, 1868, "'A' Declaration for Original Pension 'A,'" Mar. 9, 18[??], "Physician's Affidavit" by H. E. Bissell, May 26, 1886, H. E. Bissell to Dear Sir, Dec. 16, 1887, E. D. Gallion Sp. Ex. to Dear Sir, Feb. 22, 1896, general affidavit by James Shields, Aug. 24, 1887, [affidavits] by William Drayton and Thomas Means, Sep. 8, 1868, "Department of the Interior" by Sampson Drayton and James Shields, Dec. 9, 1887, deposition by H. E. Bissell, Feb. 15, 1896, depositions by James Shields, Richard Smith, Sunday Briscoe, Henry Green, and Wally Watson, Feb. 17, 1896, "Original (for a Board)," Aug. 19, 1885, "Affidavit to Origin of Disability" by Joseph R. Scott, Jan. 14, 1889, "Department of the Interior, Bureau of Pensions," Mar. 11, 1886, "Affidavit New Disabilities," n.d., "Affidavit of Origin of Disability" by Joseph Scott, Jan. 1, 1889 and "Affidavit of Origin of Disability" by Jacob E. Jones, Oct. 1, 1887, pension file for Abraham (Amy) Grant, RG 15, NARA; claimant's affidavit by Abraham Grant, Sep. 28, 1885, depositions by Joseph Scott and James Simmons, Apr. 29, 1890, pension file for Jack (Hammond Brown) Morton, RG 15, NARA.

77. "Claim for Widow's Pension, with Minor Children" by Bina Mack, n.d., "Widow's Claim for Pension" by Bina Mack, Jun. 10, 1867, "Adjutant General's Office," Jul. 24, 1867, "No. 148,886," "Department of the Interior," Jul. 19, 1867, [affidavits] by John Proctor and Friday Hamilton, Sep. 15, 1868, [affidavits] by William Drayton and Mexico Washington, Jun. 20, 1868, additional evidence by Bina Mack, Sep. 15, 1868, pension file for Harry (Bina) Mack, RG 15, NARA.

78. Charles Ray Brayton to William D. Brayton, Sep. 9, 1863.

79. Charles Ray Brayton to William D. Brayton, Sep. 9, 1863; Marino, "General Alfred Howe Terry," 250–252, 260.

80. The War of the Rebellion: A Compilation, ser. 1, vol. XXVIII, pt. 1, 209; Wise, Gate of Hell, 210–212, 214; Marino, "General Alfred Howe Terry," 250, 258–259.

81. "Proceedings of a General Court Martial Convened at Morris Island," 8, 13–15, 18–19, 27–28; William B. Howard, "Diary of William B. Howard— 48 New York Infantry Regiment," New York State Military Museum and Veterans Research Center, Saratoga Springs, Jun. 28, 1863; "Assistant Adjutant Genera to Sir," Jan. 8, 1869, "Department of the Interior, Pension Office," Dec. 26, 1868, pension file for Hardtime (Flora) White, RG 15, NARA; "War Department, Record and Pension Office," pension file for Hector Fields, RG 15, NARA; Smith, Black Soldiers in Blue, 306, 318.

82. "J. D. Luke to Hon. Commissioner of Pensions," Sep. 1, 1891, depositions by Andrew Wyatt and Edward Brown, Aug. 25, 1891, "No. 145536," n.d., "No. 145536, Act of July 14, 1862," n.d., "Original Invalid Claim," n.d., claimant's affidavit, Nov. 2, 1889, Sep. 3 and Oct. 25, 1890, "War Department Adjutant General's Office," Mar. 12, 1887, neighbor's affidavit by November Osborne, Sep. 4, 1889, "Original Invalid Claim," n.d., pension file for Andrew (Maria) Wyatt; "Declaration for an Invalid Pension" by Andrew Wyatt, Jun. 26, 1869, "Declaration for Invalid Pension, Act of June 27, 1890," Jul. 24, 1890, "Army of the United States Certificate of Disability for Discharge," Sep. 30, 1863, pension file for July (Venus) Osbourne, RG 15, NARA; deposition by Friday Hamilton, Oct. 24, 1896, pension file for Friday Hamilton; Frederic Denison, Shot and Shell: The Third Rhode Island Heavy Artillery Regiment in the Rebellion, 1861–1865 (Providence: Third R.I.H. Vet. Art. Association, 1879), 155.

83. "Declaration for an Original Invalid Pension" by Jack Wineglass, May 15 and May 13, 1890, "No. 776799," "Proof of Disability" by Jackson Grant, May 4, 1896, "Army of the United States Certificate of Disability for Discharge," Sep. 30, 1863, Jackson Grant to Sir, Jan. 4, 1898, "Invalid Pension 776799," n.d., "Declaration for an Invalid Pension," Aug. 20 and Jul. 15, 1890, "Invalid Pension Cert. No. 937.100," n.d., "The Soldier Died February 19, 1891," n.d., general affidavit by Friday Hamilton, Mar. 14, 1896, "Original Pension of Minor Children, No. 555228," "Supplement to Widow's Pension No. 555228 Org. 555475," pension file for Jack (Rebecca, Hercules) Wineglass, RG 15, NARA.

84. Deposition A by James Sheppard, deposition B by July Haywood, and deposition C by Wally Garrett, Jun. 12, 1895, deposition H by Neptune Nicholas and deposition I by Edward Brown, Jun. 14, 1895, deposition K by Mingo Van Dross and deposition L by Jack Grant, Jun. 15, 1895, claimant's affidavit by James Sheppard, Jun. 30, 1898, "[no name] to Sir," May 5, 1894, general affidavit by William Jones, Aug. 14, 1893, pension file for James (Sallie) Sheppard, RG 15, NARA.

85. "Widow's Pension Original with Increase," n.d., "No. 172481, Act of July 14, 1862," [affidavit] by Sina Young, Feb. 19, 1873, [affidavits] by Venus Lyons, Elsy Jones, and Lina Richards, Jun. 30, 1873, "Assistant Adjutant General to Commissioner of Pensions," May 22, 1872, James Clement to Dear Sir, Dec. 18, 1876, exhibit B by Sina Young, Dec. 13, 1876, exhibit F by Wally Graham, Dec. 14, 1876, exhibit J by William Jones, Dec. 16, 1876, "Widow's Declaration for Pension or Increase of Pension" by Sina Young, Dec. 12, 1889, "Widow's Pension Cert. No. 163733," n.d., general affidavit by Jack Aiken, May 16, 1901, general affidavit by Selem White, Aug. 6, 1901, neighbor's affidavit by William Jones, Sep. 2, 1887, pension file for William (Sina) Young, RG 15, NARA; deposition A by Jackson Grant, Apr. 10, 1901, pension file for Jackson (Jane) Grant; deposition by William Jones, Jun. 19, 1895, pension file for James (Sallie) Sheppard; deposition by Mingo Van Dross, Apr. 9, 1901, pension file for Mingo (Emma) Van Dross, RG 15, NARA; deposition by Friday Hamilton, Apr. 17, 1901, pension file for Friday Hamilton; deposition by Cuffie Bolze, Apr. 8, 1901, pension file for Cuffee (Sophia) Bolze.

86. "Origin of Disability" by William Hamilton, Nov. 10, 1897, pension file for Jacob (Elvira) Campbell, RG 15, NARA; [affidavit] by Friday Barrington, Sep. 2, 1897, pension file for Edward (Catherine) Bennett.

87. "Affidavit of Claimant," n.d., claimant's affidavit by James Simmons, Oct. 5, 1891, pension file for James Simmons, RG 15, NARA; general affidavit by William Bennett, Sep. 1, 1892, [affidavit] by Friday Barrington, Sep. 2, 1892, pension file for Edward (Catherine) Bennett; general affidavit by July Haywood, Feb. 19, 1894, pension file for James (Sallie) Sheppard; general affidavit by Jacob Campbell, Oct. 28, 1897, "Origin of Disability" by William Hamilton and Simon Payas, Nov. 10, 1897, pension file for Jacob (Elvira) Campbell; deposition by Jackson Grant, May 6, 1897, pension file for Frank (Captain Brown) Hamilton; deposition H by Chas. Nicholas, Oct. 18, 1898, deposition F by Selem S. White to Sir, Feb. 15, 1896, Charles Nicholas (his mark) to Sir, Jan. 28, 1896, general affidavit by Charles Nicholas, Nov. 22, 1892, "Affidavit to Origin of Disability" by Edward Brown, Oct. 26, 1889, "Affidavit to Origin of Disability" by Celim White, Oct. 28, 1889, "Declaration for an Original Invalid Pension," Aug. 19, 1889, pension file for William (Elsey) Jones.

88. "Widow's Declaration for Pension or Increase of Pension" by Diana Harris, Sep. 14, 1886, "Widow's Pension," n.d., "Army of the United States Certificate of Disability for Discharge," Dec. 2, 1863, "Proof of Disability" by William Jones, Dec. 18, 1886, "To All Whom It May Concern," Dec. 2, 1863, deposition C by William Jones, Mar. 14, 1890, pension file for Andrew (Diana) Harris.

89. General affidavit by Robin Washington, Mar. 16, 1891, general affidavit by Allen Frasier, Jan. 16, 1891, "Proof of Disability" by Mingo White, Mar. 16, 1891, pension file for John (Tom and Bella Drayton) Jones; deposition by Mingo Van Dross, Apr. 9, 1901, pension file for Mingo (Emma) Van Dross; deposition A by Stephen Simmons, Apr. 10, 1901, pension file for Stephen (Jane) Simmons.

90. Charles T. Lowndes, "Petition with Attached Sheriffs Letter, Order, and Copy of the Tax Execution, Asking to be Refunded Part of His Taxes Collected Under Execution for Property and Slaves Abandoned or Seized by the Enemy in Colleton District," Petitions to the General Assembly, 1864, no. 14, South Carolina Department of Archives and History, Columbia.

91. Charles T. Lowndes, "Petition."

CHAPTER 18

1. Lt. George Garrison to William Lloyd Garrison II, Feb. 10, 1864, Garrison Family Papers, Box 28, Folder 790, Sophia Smith Collection, Smith College, Northampton, MA; *The War of the Rebellion: A Compilation of the Official Records of the Union and Confederate Armies,* ser. 1, vol. XXXV, pt. 1 (Washington, DC: GPO, 1880–1901), 461; Carl W. Marino, "General Alfred Howe Terry: Soldier from Connecticut," Ph.D. diss., New York University, 1968, 261, 269.

2. *The War of the Rebellion: A Compilation*, ser. 1, vol. XXXV, pt. 1, 286, 288–290, 474; Samuel P. Ryan to John C. Black, Commissioner of Pensions, Apr. 15, 1885, pension file for Samuel (Martha) Gilliard, RG 15, NARA; John David Smith, ed., *Black Soldiers in Blue: African American Troops in the Civil War Era* (Chapel Hill: University of North Carolina Press, 2002), 136, 138; William H. Nulty, *Confederate Florida: The Road to Olustee* (Tuscaloosa: University of Alabama Press, 1994), 125–126; Stephen R. Wise, *Gate of Hell: Campaign for Charleston Harbor, 1863* (Columbia: University of South Carolina Press, 1994), 214; Marino, "General Alfred Howe Terry," 266, 269.

3. *The War of the Rebellion: A Compilation*, ser. 1, vol. XXXV, pt. 1, 289, 303–306, 318; Smith, *Black Soldiers in Blue*, 136, 138–139, 140–141, 146; Nulty, *Confederate Florida*, 137, 142–143, 152–153.

4. *The War of the Rebellion: A Compilation*, ser. 1, vol. XXXV, pt. 1, 288–289, 299, 303; Smith, *Black Soldiers in Blue*, 136, 139; Nulty, *Confederate Florida*, 124, 133–134.

5. *The War of the Rebellion: A Compilation*, ser. 1, vol. XXXV, pt. 1, 298, 303–304, 306; [affidavit] by Harriet Davis, May 28, 1892, and Nov. 10, 1894, general affidavit by Maggie Lucas, Jun. 3, 1892, "Department of the Interior" by Edgar J. Fryman, Jan. 25, 1895, "Declaration for Widow's Pension" by Harriet Davis, Jul. 14, 1890, general affidavit by Dorsey Brainard, Oct. 16, 1894, general affidavit by Anna E. Thompson, Jun. 19, 1894, general affidavit by Joshua Diggs, May 28, 1892, "Department of the Interior" by Joseph Hooper and Eazur W. Jolly, Jan. 26, 1895, "Department of the Interior" by Dorsey Brainard, Jan. 25, 1895, "Department of the Interior, Bureau of Pensions," Jan. 25, 1895, "Record and Pension Office, War Department," Jan. 26, 1895, "War Department, Record and Pension Division," Jan. 13, 1891, general affidavit by Charles H. Peterson, Jan. 7, 1895, general affidavit by Edgar J. Fryman, Nov. 9, 1894, neighbor's affidavit by Thornton Newton and Maggie Lucas, Jun. 15, 1893, [deposition] by Harriet Davis, Nov. 10, 1894, pension file for Nelson (Harriet) Davis, RG 15, NARA; Smith, *Black Soldiers in Blue*, 139–141; Nulty, *Confederate Florida*, 139–140, 145; Conrad, "The Charles P. Wood Manuscripts of Harriet Tubman," 93.

6. *The War of the Rebellion: A Compilation*, ser. 1, vol. XXXV, pt. 1, 289–290, 297, 299–300, 305–306, 315; James M. Carver to Commissioner of Pensions, Feb. 16, 1885, James M. Carver to Dear Sir, Apr. 11, 1885, pension file for Samuel (Martha) Gilliard; Smith, *Black Soldiers in Blue*, 141–143; Nulty, *Confederate Florida*, 158–159, 162–169.

7. *The War of the Rebellion: A Compilation*, ser. 1, vol. XXXV, pt. 1, 289, 300, 317–318; *The War of the Rebellion: A Compilation*, ser. 1, vol. XXXV, pt. 2, 29; Smith, *Black Soldiers in Blue*, 143–144; Nulty, *Confederate Florida*, 128, 141–142, 161, 210.

8. *Official Records of the Union and Confederate Navies in the War of the Rebellion*, ser. 1, vol. XIII (Washington, DC: GPO, 1900), 476, 794; *Official Records of the Union and Confederate Navies in the War of the Rebellion*, ser. 1, vol. XV (Washington, DC: GPO, 1900), 284–285, 311, 426–428; *The War of the Rebellion: A Compilation of the Official Records of the Union and Confederate Armies*, ser. 1, vol. XXIV (Washington, DC: GPO, 1880–1901), 195–197; *The War of the Rebellion: A*

Compilation, ser. 1, vol. XXXV, pt. 1, 392; W. Craig Gaines, *Encyclopedia of Civil War Shipwrecks* (Baton Rouge: Louisiana State University Press, 2008), 40–41; E. Kay Gibson, *Dictionary of Transports and Combatant Vessels, Steam and Sail, Employed by the Union Army, 1861–1868* (Camden, ME: Ensign Press, 1985), 144; Daniel Ammen, *The Navy in the Civil War: The Atlantic Coast* (London: Sampson Low, Marston, 1898), 148.

9. "Proceedings of a General Court Martial Convened at Morris Island," Records of the US Army Department of the South, South Caroliniana Library, University of South Carolina, Columbia, 95; "Civil War Court Martial File Ll5566, US v. Private John E. Webster," Records of the Office of the Judge Advocate (Army), Vo. G 47 Regiment Penn Vols, 11, 18, 32, 45–48, RG 153, NARA.

10. "Proceedings of a General Court Martial Convened at Morris Island," 14, 28, 101.

11. "The Court Met Pursuant to Adjournment," Jan. 11, 1864, "Mr. President and Gentlemen of the Court," "This Direct Is Given to the Record," May 24, 1864, "Proceedings of a General Court Martial Convened at Morris Island."

12. "Notes by Mary Miller Withers Kirkland" and "Carolina Judge: The Life of Thomas Jefferson Withers" (typescript, n.d.), 56, Papers of the Kirkland, Withers, Snowden, and Trotter Families, South Caroliniana Library, University of South Carolina, Columbia (page nos. 56, 200); Charlotte L. Forten, *The Journal of Charlotte L. Forten: A Young Black Woman's Reaction to the White World of the Civil War Era*, ed. Ray Allen Billington (New York: Dryden Press, 1953), 197, 203; A. B. Mulligan, *"My Dear Mother & Sisters": Civil War Letters of Capt. A. B. Mulligan, Co. B, 5th South Carolina Cavalry—Butler's Division—Hampton's Corps, 1861–1865* (Spartanburg, SC: Reprint Company, 1992), 179–181; Kerri K. Greenidge, Grimkes: The Legacy of Slavery in an American Family (New York: Liveright Publishing Corporation), 153; W. Eric Emerson, *Sons of Privilege: The Charleston Light Dragoons in the Civil War* (Columbia: University of South Carolina Press, 2005), 62–63, 140.

13. *The War of the Rebellion: A Compilation of the Official Records of the Union and Confederate Armies*, ser. 1, vol. XXXVI, pt. 1 (Washington, DC: GPO, 1880–1901), 14, 80–81; Lewis F. Knudsen, *A History of the 5th South Carolina Cavalry, 1861–1865* (Wilmington, NC: Broadfoot, 2016), 157–158.

14. *The War of the Rebellion: A Compilation*, ser. 1, vol. XXXVI, pt. 1, 80–81; Emerson, *Sons of Privilege*, 69–72; Knudsen, *A History of the 5th South Carolina Cavalry*, 155, 157; Gary W. Gallagher and Caroline E. Janney, *Cold Harbor to the Crater: The End of the Overland Campaign* (Chapel Hill: University of North Carolina Press, 2015), 49–50.

15. *The War of the Rebellion: A Compilation*, ser. 1, vol. XXXVI, pt. 1, 80–81; Emerson, *Sons of Privilege*, 25, 69–72; Gallagher and Janney, *Cold Harbor to the Crater*, 50.

16. Mary Boykin Miller Chesnut, *Mary Chesnut's Civil War*, ed. C. Vann Woodward (New Haven, CT: Yale University Press, 1981), 766; Emerson, *Sons of Privilege*, 72–75, 94.

17. Chesnut, *Mary Chesnut's Civil War*, 766; Emerson, *Sons of Privilege*, 50, 74–75, 78; Knudsen, *A History of the 5th South Carolina Cavalry*, 155, 157–159, 161–162;

Gallagher and Janney, *Cold Harbor to the Crater*, 50, 52; Edward Laight Wells, *A Sketch of the Charleston Light Dragoons* (Charleston, SC: Lucas, Richardson, 1888), 3, 45–46.

18. "Notes by Mary Miller Withers Kirkland"; "Combahee River Plantations: Rose Hill," 10, private collection, Colleton County, SC; *The War of the Rebellion: A Compilation*, ser. 1, vol. XXXVI, pt. 1, 80–81; Emerson, *Sons of Privilege*, 62–63; Knudsen, *A History of the 5th South Carolina Cavalry*, 157–159, 166; Gallagher and Janney, *Cold Harbor to the Crater*, 49–52.

19. William Randolph Withers to Thomas Jefferson Withers, May 29, 1864; Turner McFarland to Katherine Boykin Withers, Jun. 16, 1864, William Randolph Withers to Mary Miller Withers Kirkland, Jun. 19, 1864, William Randolph Withers to Thomas Jefferson Withers, n.d. (page nos. 1–3, 7–9, 62, 201), all in Papers of the Kirkland, Withers, Snowden, and Trotter Families; Columbia: "Combahee River Plantations: Rose Hill," in *Private Collection* (Colleton County, SC), 8, 12; Emerson, *Sons of Privilege*, Knudsen, *A History of the 5th South Carolina Cavalry*, 158, 165.

20. "Account Sales for 34 1/4 Bushels Whole Rice," May 30, 1864, Carlos Lytz to Thomas Jefferson Withers, May 30, 1864, Turner McFarland to Thomas Jefferson Withers, May 31, 1864, Turner McFarland to Katherine Boykin Withers Kirkland, Jun. 16, 1864, Papers of the Kirkland, Withers, Snowden, and Trotter Families (page nos. 1–3, 64–66).

21. Carlos Tracy to Thomas Jefferson Withers, Jun. 6, 1864, Turner McFarland to Katherine Boykin Withers, Jun. 16, 1864, Papers of the Kirkland, Withers, Snowden, and Trotter Families (page nos. 1–3, 253–255).

22. Carlos Tracy to Thomas Jefferson Withers, Jun. 6, 1864, Jun. 13 and Jun. 17, 1864, Papers of the Kirkland, Withers, Snowden, and Trotter Families (page nos. 4, 201, 253–255, 262).

23. William Randolph Withers to Mary Miller Withers Kirkland, Jun. 16, 1864, Turner McFarland to Katherine Boykin Withers, Jun. 16, 1864, "Carolina Judge: The Life of Thomas Jefferson Withers," Joshua Nicholls to Judge Withers, Jun. 19, 1864, Joshua Nicholls to Mary Miller Withers Kirkland, Jun. 20, 1864, Papers of the Kirkland, Withers, Snowden, and Trotter Families (page nos. 1–3, 5–9, 201, 252); Mary Miller Kirkland, "Reminiscences of My Childhood," 2, Withers Family Papers, 1823–1923, South Carolina Historical Society, Charleston; "Combahee River Plantations: Rose Hill," 10.

24. William Randolph to Mary Miller Withers Kirkland, 6/19/1864, "Notes by Mary Miller Withers Kirkland," n.d., 7–9, 56, 201, Papers of the Kirkland, Withers, Snowden, and Trotter Families.

25. Emerson, *Sons of Privilege*, 53, 81, 93–94, 132.

26. Eliza C. Middleton Huger Smith to Mary Miller Withers Kirkland, n.d.; Eliza C. Middleton Huger Smith to Mary Miller Withers Kirkland, Jul. 10, 1864, 7–13, Papers of the Kirkland, Withers, Snowden, and Trotter Families; Emerson, *Sons of Privilege*, 53, 81, 93–94, 132.

27. Deposition A by Jackson Grant, Oct. 16, 1896, pension file for Jackson (Jane) Grant, RG 15, NARA; Emerson, *Sons of Privilege*, 53, 93–94, 132.

28. "General Orders," *Free South*, Jan. 17, 1863; depositions by Moriah Bartley, Apr. 15, 1901, and Oct. 20, 1898, deposition C by Jackson Grant, deposition D by Moses Simmons, deposition F by Cuffie Bolze, Oct. 20, 1898, deposition G by William Hamilton, Oct. 21, 1898, marriage certificate, Jun. 17, 1864, "Declaration for Widow's Pension" by Moriah Bartley, Apr. 13, 1903, general affidavit by Jackson Grant and Friday Hamilton, Feb. 21, 1898, Commissioner to Sir, Jun. 10, 1898, pension file for Anthony (Moriah) Bartley, RG 15, NARA; Smith, *Black Soldiers in Blue: African American Troops in the Civil War Era*, 318.

29. E. H. Jennings to Sir, Apr. 14, 1905, depositions by Betsey Nicholas, Jack Barnwell, Cuffy Bolze, John Mackey, Elsie Bowers, Moses Simmons, Fannie Simmons, Apr. 11, 1905, "Letter to the Law Division," Apr. 28, 1905, "Department of the Interior, Bureau of Pensions," pension file for Neptune (Betsey) Nicholas, RG 15, NARA.

30. General affidavits by Anthony Bartley and Andrew Nicholas, May 24, 1894, pension file for Ned (Daphne) Snipe, RG 15, NARA; deposition by Moriah Bartley, Apr. 15, 1901, deposition A by Moriah Bartley, Oct. 20, 1898, deposition C by Jackson Grant, Oct. 20, 1898, deposition D by Moses Simmons, Oct. 20, 1898, deposition by William Hamilton, Oct. 20, 1898, pension file for Anthony (Moriah) Bartley.

31. Deposition by Moriah Bartley, Apr. 15, 1901, Oct. 20, 1898, certificate of marriage, Jun. 17, 1864, pension file for Anthony (Moriah) Bartley.

32. [Deposition] by Friday Hamilton, Mar. 14, 1910, deposition by Lucy Smith, Nov. 10, 1909, deposition C by Cuffy Bowles, Nov. 12, 1909, deposition D by Mingo Van Dross, Nov. 13, 1909, Chief, Law Division to Chief of the Southern Division, Jan. 16, 1909, depositions by Neptune Nicholas and Lucy Smith, Jun. 14, 1895, deposition C by Edward Brown, Jun. 14, 1895, deposition F by Jackson Grant and deposition H by Andrew Nicholas, Jun. 15, 1895, "Department of the Interior, Bureau of Pensions," Jul. 28, 1908, general affidavit by Hattie Rivers, Jul. 14, 1913, pension file for Richard (Lucy, Fanny) Smith, RG 15, NARA.

33. Deposition F by Jack Grant, Jun. 15, 1895, E. C. Tieman, Acting Commissioner to R. M. Sefton, Sep. 16, 1913, pension file for Richard (Lucy, Fannie) Smith, RG 15, NARA; "Application for Accrued Pension, (Widows)," May 5, 1894, deposition by Daphne Snipe, Apr. 16, 1901, general affidavits by Anthony Bartley and Andrew Nicholas, May 24 and May 29, 1894, "Department of the Interior, Bureau of Pensions," Jun. 7, 1894, "Act of June 27, 1890, Declaration for Widow's Pension," May 5, 1894, pension file for Ned (Daphne) Snipe; deposition by Joe Morrison, May 6, 1897, additional evidence by Friday Hamilton and Joe Morrison, Apr. 9, 1895, pension file for Frank (Captain Brown) Hamilton, RG 15, NARA; "3–202 Board of Review," Mar. 25, 1911, deposition by Moses Simmons, Apr. 8, 1901, pension file for Moses (Fannie) Simmons, RG 15, NARA; general affidavits by Charles Nicholas, Nov. 11 and 26, 1892, and by Pool Sellars, Jan. 25, 1893, pension file for Harry (Flora) Robinson, RG 15, NARA; Tera Hunter, *Bound in Wedlock: Slave and Free Black Marriage* (Cambridge, MA: Belknap Press of Harvard University Press, 2017), 6, 121–123, 127–129, 135, 153–154, 163, 349n17.

34. Deposition A by Diana Burnett, Dec. 6, 1901, deposition C by Wally Garrett, Jan. 18, 1902, deposition D by James Shields, Jan. 18, 1902, deposition F by Henry Green, Jan. 18, 1902, L. M. Kelley, Acting Commissioner to the Secretary of the Interior, Jul. 3, 1902, "Department of the Interior, Bureau of Pensions," Sep. 4, 1897, pension file for Balaam (Diana) Burnett, RG 15, NARA.

35. Sarah Bradford, *Scenes in the Life of Harriet Tubman* (1869; repr., North Stratford, NH: Ayer, 2004), 38; Sarah Bradford, *Harriet Tubman: The Moses of Her People* (1886; New York: J. J. Little, 1901), 98; Emma P. Telford, *Harriet: The Modern Moses of Heroism and Visions* (Auburn, NY: Cayuga County Museum, 1905), 16; Esther Hill Hawks, *A Woman Doctor's Civil War: Esther Hill Hawks' Diary*, ed. Gerald Schwartz (Columbia: University of South Carolina Press, 1984), 65, 78–79; Kate Clifford Larson, *Bound for the Promised Land: Harriet Tubman: Portrait of an American Hero* (New York: One World/Ballantine, 2009), 224; Jean McMahon Humez, *Harriet Tubman: The Life and the Life Stories* (Madison: University of Wisconsin Press, 2003), 63, 248; Earl Conrad, *General Harriett Tubman* (Baltimore: Black Classic Press, 2019, 1943), 163.

36. Bradford, *Harriet Tubman*, 98; Bradford, *Scenes in the Life of Harriet Tubman*, 38; Hawks, *A Woman Doctor's Civil War*, 65, 78–79; Kate Clifford Larson, *Bound for the Promised Land: Harriet Tubman: Portrait of an American Hero* (New York: One World/Ballantine, 2009), 224.

37. "War Department, Record and Pension Office," n.d. "Act of June 27, 1890, Invalid Pension, file for Hector Fields, Compiled Military Service Records.

38. Depositions by Cuffie Bolze, Jack Barnwell, Mingo Vanderhorst, Aug. 9, 1907, pension file for Charles (Ella) Nicholas, RG 15, NARA; deposition A by Lucy Smith, Nov. 10, 1909, deposition by Neptune Nicholas, Jun. 14, 1895, pension file for Richard (Lucy, Fannie) Smith.

39. Deposition A by Peggy Brown, Nov. 14, 1901, pension file for Edward (Peggy) Brown, RG 15, NARA; deposition by Daphne Snipe, Apr. 16, 1901, pension file for Ned (Daphne) Snipe; P. Barnwell to [no name], Mar. 27, 1920, Relia Middleton to Bureau of Pensions, Mar. 22, 1919, deposition by Relia Middleton, Jan. 30, 1920, pension file for William (Relia) Middleton, RG 15, NARA.

40. Ednah Dow Cheney, "Moses," *Freedmen's Record*, Jan. 1865, 38; Charles Wood, "A History Concerning the Pension Claim of Harriet Tubman," 6, 9, RG 233, NARA; Larson, *Bound for the Promised Land*, 225; Clinton, *Harriet Tubman*, 158; Humez, *Harriet Tubman*, 55, 303.

41. Catherine Porter Noyes to Nelly Balch, Oct. 26, 1864, Papers of Catherine Porter Noyes, 1863–1869, Schlesinger Library, Harvard University; "Field and Staff Muster Roll," Sept. & Oct., 1864, "Field and Staff Muster-out Roll," Feb. 28, 1866, Surgeon Daniel D. Hanson to [no name], 10/15/1863, L. B. Hiatt to [no name], 8/18/1864, Surgeon H. Ruckmaster to [no name], 8/22/1864, Colonel James Montgomery to Captain W. P. M. Burger, 8/24/1864, file for James Montgomery, Compiled Military Service Records; Elizabeth Hyde Botume, *First Days Amongst the Contrabands* (Boston: Lee and Shepard, 1893), 22–23.

42. Catherine Porter Noyes to Nelly Balch, Oct. 26, 1864; Botume, *First Days Amongst the Contrabands*, 22, 25, 26, 31; Forten, *Journal*, 126.

43. Botume, *First Days Amongst the Contrabands*, 31–32, 67, 79, 210.

44. Botume, *First Days Amongst the Contrabands*, 31, 34–35, 62–63, 67–68; Nancy Hoffman, *Woman's "True" Profession: Voices from the History of Teaching* (Old Westbury, NY: Feminist Press, 1981), 100–101, 104.

45. Catherine Porter Noyes to Nelly Balch, Nov. 3, 1869; Botume, *First Days Amongst the Contrabands*, 35–39, 126; Jingle Davis, *Following the Tabby Trail: Where Coastal History Is Captured in Unique Oyster-Shell Structures* (Athens: University of Georgia Press, 2022), 1; Brooker Colin, *The Shell Builders: Tabby Architecture of Beaufort, South Carolina, and the Sea Islands* (Columbia: University of South Carolina Press, 2020), 1:114; "Santa Elena Charlesfort: South Carolina Begins Here," last updated Dec. 15, 1999, https://web.archive.org/web/20120123143722/http://www.cas.sc.edu/sciaa/staff/depratterc/newweb.htm.

46. Catherine Porter Noyes to Nelly Balch, Nov. 3, 1869; Botume, *First Days Amongst the Contrabands*, 35, 37–38, 134; Florida Wildflower Foundation, "Spanish Bayonet," https://www.flawildflowers.org/flower-friday-yucca-aloifolia/.

47. Botume, *First Days Amongst the Contrabands*, 41–42, 129.

48. Laura M. Towne, *Letters and Diary Written from the Sea Islands of South Carolina, 1862–1884*, ed. Rupert Holland (Cambridge, MA: Riverside Press, 1912), xiv–xv, 6–7, 26; Botume, *First Days Amongst the Contrabands*, 45, 57, 103, 274, 277, 283; Forten, *Journal*, 21–22.

49. Pearson, *Letters from Port Royal*, 21–22, 25, 29, 90, 156–157, 160, 216, 260; Botume, *First Days Amongst the Contrabands*, 45, 274, 277, 283.

50. Ambrose E. Gonzales, *The Black Border: Gullah Stories of the Carolina Coast* (Columbia, SC: State Company, 1922), 10.

51. William E. Gonzales, "Golden Days of Southern Sport," 14, William E. Gonzales Papers 1922–1937, South Caroliniana Library, University of South Carolina, Columbia.

52. Margaret Wade-Lewis, *Lorenzo Dow Turner: Father of Gullah Studies* (Columbia: University of South Carolina Press, 2007), xvi, 72–92, 94; Lorenzo Dow Turner, *Africanisms in the Gullah Dialect* (Columbia: University of South Carolina Press, 2002), xxi.

53. Pearson, *Letters from Port Royal*, 209; Botume, *First Days Amongst the Contrabands*, 45–49, 61, 143; Troike, Rudolph C. "CREOLE/L→/R IN AFRICAN AMERICAN English/Gullah: HISTORICAL FACT AND FICTION." *American speech* 90.1 (2015): 19–23.

54. Botume, *First Days Amongst the Contrabands*, 48, 57, 62, 98, 104–105, 119, 137, 139, 157, 159, 221–222, 244–245; Pearson, *Letters from Port Royal*, 24, 34–35, 46, 112; William Francis Allen, Charles Pickard Ware, and Lucy McKim Garrison, *Slave Songs of the United States* (New York: Peter Smith, 1929), xxiv–xxviii.

55. Botume, *First Days Amongst the Contrabands*, 48, 119; Thomas Wentworth Higginson, *Army Life in a Black Regiment and Other Writings* (Boston: Houghton, Mifflin, 1900), 332.

56. Botume, *First Days Amongst the Contrabands*, 12–16, 128–129.

57. Botume, *First Days Amongst the Contrabands*, 16.

58. Botume, *First Days Amongst the Contrabands*, 50–51, 55, 151; Leslie Ann Schwalm, *"A Hard Fight for We": Women's Transition from Slavery to Freedom in South Carolina* (Urbana: University of Illinois Press, 1997), 98.

59. Botume, *First Days Amongst the Contrabands*, 50–55, 57, 117, 151; Schwalm, *"A Hard Fight for We,"* 98, 150, 151; Earl Conrad, *General Harriett Tubman* (Baltimore: Black Classic Press, 2019), 176.

60. Botume, *First Days Amongst the Contrabands*, 52, 55.

61. Botume, *First Days Amongst the Contrabands*, 52–54.

62. Botume, *First Days Amongst the Contrabands*, 54.

63. Botume, *First Days Amongst the Contrabands*, 64–65, 69–70; Benjamin Franklin Bronson, Joshua Lincoln, and Executive Committee New England Freedmen's Aid Commission, *First Annual Report of the Executive Committee of the New England's Aid Commission, November, 1864* (Boston, 1864), 14.

64. Botume, *First Days Amongst the Contrabands*, 66–67, 81, 174.

65. "Army of the United States Certificate of Disability for Discharge," Mar. 28, 1864, pension file for November (Sarah) Osborne, RG 15, NARA.

66. "Army of the United States Certificate of Disability for Discharge," Feb. 22, 1864, pension file for Frank (Daphne) Wright, RG 15, NARA; Botume, *First Days Amongst the Contrabands*, 55, 66–67, 81, 174.

67. "Widow's Pension," Feb. 15, 1892, "Army of the United States Certificate of Disability for Discharge," Feb. 15, 1892, "War Department Record and Pension Division," Feb. 15, 1892, general affidavit by Sylvia DeCauster, Feb. 15, 1892, general affidavits by November Osborne and Andrew Wyatt, Jun. 7, 1890, "Widow's Claim for Pension," Apr. 29, 1890, "Declaration for Widow's Pension, Act of June 27, 1890," Jul. 12, 1890, "Widow's Pension," pension file for Isaac (Silvia) DeCauster, RG 15, NARA.

68. Sarah Barnwell, Jan. 17, 1872, United States, Freedman's Bank Records, 1865–1874; general affidavit by P. Barnwell, Jul. 17, 1919, Chief Board of Review to the Chief Special Examination Division, Aug. 15, 1919, Chief Board of Special Examination to Chief Board of Review, Feb. 25, 1920, "Case of Relia Middleton No. 1132522" by Guffee Bolls, Feb. 2, 1920, pension file for William (Relia) Middleton; Botume, *First Days Amongst the Contrabands*, 93–94.

69. Botume, *First Days Amongst the Contrabands*, 94.

70. *The War of the Rebellion: A Compilation of the Official Records of the Union and Confederate Armies,* ser. 1, vol. XLIV (Washington, DC: GPO, 1880–1901), 7–9, 12–13; Botume, *First Days Amongst the Contrabands*, 50–55, 57, 117, 151; Jacqueline Jones, *Saving Savannah: The City and the Civil War* (New York: Alfred A. Knopf, 2008), 197, 199; Frederic Denison, *Shot and Shell: The Third Rhode Island Heavy Artillery Regiment in the Rebellion, 1861–1865* (Providence: Third R.I.H. Vet. Art. Association, 1879), 291.

71. *The War of the Rebellion: A Compilation,* ser. 1, vol. XLIV, 8–9; Jones, *Saving Savannah*, 201, 205; Noah Andre Trudeau, *Southern Storm: Sherman's March to the Sea* (New York: HarperCollins, 2009), 370, 421, 532.

72. *The War of the Rebellion: A Compilation*, ser. 1, vol. XLIV, 8–10; Jones, *Saving Savannah*, 205.

73. Trudeau, *Southern Storm*, 408, 21–48; Denison, *Shot and Shell*, 292.

74. *The War of the Rebellion: A Compilation*, ser. 1, vol. XLIV, 7, 11, 12; Botume, *First Days Amongst the Contrabands*, 168; Trudeau, *Southern Storm*, 206–207, 479–498, 502, 508; Jones, *Saving Savannah*, 197; Frederic Denison, *Shot and Shell*, 291–292.

75. Pearson, *Letters from Port Royal*, 295–296, 308; Towne, *Letters and Diary*, 156–157; Botume, *First Days Amongst the Contrabands*, 79–81, 133, 149; Denison, *Shot and Shell*, 291.

76. Pearson, *Letters from Port Royal*, 296; Botume, *First Days Amongst the Contrabands*, 78–89, 133–136, 138–140, 149–150; Towne, *Letters and Diary*, 156–157.

77. Towne, *Letters and Diary*, 148, 156–157; Botume, *First Days Amongst the Contrabands*, 120–121.

78. Pearson, *Letters from Port Royal*, 294–296, 306, 309; Towne, *Letters and Diary*, 149, 151, 154, 158; Botume, *First Days Amongst the Contrabands*, 83, 120–121, 150.

79. *The War of the Rebellion: A Compilation of the Official Records of the Union and Confederate Armies*, ser. 1, vol. XLVII, pt. 2, sec. 1 (Washington, DC: GPO, 1880–1901), 136–37; Robert N. Rosen, *Confederate Charleston: An Illustrated History of the City and the People During the Civil War* (Columbia: University of South Carolina Press, 1994), 132, 137; Denison, *Shot and Shell*, 287–288.

80. *The War of the Rebellion: A Compilation of the Official Records of the Union and Confederate Armies*, ser. 1, vol. XLVII, pt. 1 (Washington, DC: GPO, 1880–1901), 18.

81. William Tecumseh Sherman, *General Sherman's Official Account of His Great March Through Georgia and the Carolinas: From His Departure from Chattanooga to the Surrender of General Joseph E. Johnston and the Confederate Forces Under His Command. To Which Is Added, General Sherman's Evidence Before the Congressional Committee on the Conduct of the War; the Animadversions of Secretary Stanton and General Halleck: With a Defence of His Proceedings, Etc* (New York: Bunce & Huntington, 1865), 89; *The War of the Rebellion: A Compilation*, ser. 1, vol. XLVII, pt. 1, 18, 260, 289, 307, 347, 372, 769, 819–820, 1005, 1068, 1070, 1120–1121; *The War of the Rebellion: A Compilation*, ser. 1, vol. XLVII, pt. 2, sec. 1, 122, 129, 137, 151, 156, 203, 212, 312, 325, 402, 412, 423, 484; deposition A by Fannie Simmons, Apr. 14, 1911, deposition B by Jane Barnwell, Apr. 14, 1911, deposition C by Cuffee Bolze, Apr. 14, 1911, pension file for Moses (Fannie) Simmons; Denison, *Shot and Shell*, 287–288.

82. John M. Reynolds to Commissioner of Pensions, n.d., pension file for Parris (Penda) White, RG 15, NARA; Denison, *Shot and Shell*, 288, 290, 292, 297–298.

83. *The War of the Rebellion: A Compilation*, ser. 1, vol. XLVII, pt. 2, sec. 1, 165, 301, 339, 340; "Department of the Interior, Bureau of Pensions," Jan. 14, 1895, deposition by Sunday Briscoe, Oct. 5, 1910, deposition by Daphne Wright, Jun. 11, 1895, Special Examiner to Commissioner of Pensions, Jun. 27, 1895, deposition by Wally Garrett, Jun. 12, 1895, deposition by March Lawrence, Jul 12, 1895, deposition N by Neptune Nicholas, Jun. 14, 1895, "Increase Invalid Pension,"

Jan. 21, 1909, Mar. 6, 1907, "Act of June 27, 1890, Invalid Pension," Sep. 29, 1904, Aug. 6, 1903, "Act of February 6, 1907," "Original Invalid Claim," pension file for Simon (Rachel) Washington, RG 15, NARA; Denison, *Shot and Shell*, 298.

84. "Marching On!—the Fifty-Fifth Massachusetts Colored Regiment Singing John Brown's March in the Streets of Charleston, February 21, 1865," *Harper's Weekly*, Mar. 18, 1865, 165; Denison, *Shot and Shell*, 298–299.

85. Emerson, *Sons of Privilege*, 98–99.

86. Wood, "A History Concerning the Pension Claim of Harriet Tubman," 3; Bradford, *Harriet Tubman*, 163; Bradford, *Scenes in the Life of Harriet Tubman*, 69.

87. Julia Wilbur Pocket Diary, Jan. 5, Jan. 6, Jan. 12, Feb. 23, Feb. 25, Mar. 2, Mar. 5, Mar. 9, 1865, Julia Wilbur Papers, Quaker & Special Collections, 1843–1908, Haverford College, Haverford, PA; David W. Blight, Frederick Douglass: Prophet of Freedom (New York: Simon & Schuster, 2018), 457–459; Paula Whitacre, *A Civil Life in an Uncivil Time: Julia Wilbur's Struggle for Purpose* (Lincoln: University of Nebraska Press, 2017), 84, 85, 96.

88. New England Freedmen's Aid Society, *First Annual Report of the Education Commission with Extracts from Letters of Teachers and Superintendents* (Boston: David Clapp, 1863), 6.

89. "From Camp William Penn," *Christian Recorder*, Apr. 15, 1865; William Wells Brown, *The Rising Son; or, the Antecedents and Advancement of the Colored Race* (New York: Negro Universities Press, 1970), 538; James Elton Johnson, "A History of Camp William Penn and Its Black Troops in the Civil War, 1863–1865," Ph.D. diss., University of Pennsylvania, 1999, vi, 21, 48, 50, 59.

90. Wood, "A History Concerning the Pension Claim of Harriet Tubman," 3, 5; Larson, *Bound for the Promised Land*, 227; Johnson, "A History of Camp William Penn," 59.

91. "Army of the United States Certificate of Disability for Discharge," May 23, 1865, pension file for Benjamin (Cornelia) Pryor, RG 15, NARA; "Army of the United States Certificate of Disability for Discharge," May 23, 1865, pension file for Pool (Julia) Sellers, RG 15, NARA.

92. "Widow's Pension," "Army of the United States Certificate of Disability for Discharge," Jun. 2, 1865, "Physician's Affidavit—Proof of Physical Disability, Act of June 27, 1890," Nov. 19, 1890, "War Department, Record and Pension Division," Mar. 10, 1891, pension file for Smart (Lucretia) Washington, RG 15, NARA; Botume, *First Days Amongst the Contrabands*, 60, 116.

93. Wood, "A History Concerning the Pension Claim of Harriet Tubman," 3.

94. Wood, "A History Concerning the Pension Claim of Harriet Tubman," 4; Larson, *Bound for the Promised Land*, 227; Clinton, *Harriet Tubman*, 186–187; Humez, *Harriet Tubman*, 65; Earl Conrad, "The Charles P. Wood Manuscripts of Harriet Tubman," *Negro History Bulletin* 13, no. 4 (1950): 93; Conrad, *General Harriett Tubman*, 186–187.

95. Wood, "A History Concerning the Pension Claim of Harriet Tubman," 5, 8; Bradford, *Harriet Tubman*, 159; Bradford, *Scenes in the Life of Harriet Tubman*, 65; general affidavit by Charles Thornton, Sep. 12, 1894, pension file for Nelson (Harriet) Davis, RG 15, NARA; Earl Conrad, "The Charles P. Wood Manuscripts of Harriet Tubman," *Negro History Bulletin* 13, no. 4 (1950): 95;

Larson, *Bound for the Promised Land*, 227, 277–278; Clinton, *Harriet Tubman*, 187; Humez, *Harriet Tubman*, 68; Edward A. Miller, *Lincoln's Abolitionist General: The Biography of David Hunter* (Columbia: University of South Carolina Press, 1997), 242–244, 249–255; Earl Conrad, "The Charles P. Wood Manuscripts of Harriet Tubman," *Negro History Bulletin* 13, no. 4 (1950): 93–94; Conrad, *General Harriett Tubman*, 187.

96. David W. Blight, *Frederick Douglass: Prophet of Freedom* (New York: Simon & Schuster, 2018), 109; Nell Irvin Painter, *Sojourner Truth: A Life, a Symbol* (New York: W. W. Norton, 1997), 210–211.

97. "Widow's Declaration for Pension or Increase of Pension" by Mary Brown, Nov. 17, 1898, deposition by Mary Brown, Jul. 18, 1902, general affidavit by William Drayton, Jan. 4, 1894, general affidavit by Fabry Bowers, Jan. 2, 1894, pension file for Edward (Mary) Brown, RG 15, NARA.

98. "Ex A" by Phoebe Frazier, Nov. 7, 1884, deposition C by Wally Ford and deposition D by Peter Green, Nov. 7, 1884, deposition F by William Jones and deposition G by Daphne Drayton, Nov. 8, 1884, pension file for Robert (Phoebe) Frazier, RG 15, NARA; general affidavit by Stephen Tolbert, Mar. 18, 1897, "Declaration for Restoration to the Pension Roll" by Jack Aiken, Mar. 17, 1897, deposition D by Chas. Nicholas and deposition B by Edward Brown, Oct. 18, 1897, claimant's affidavit by Jack Aikens, Jun. 3, 1889, general affidavit by William Izzard, Jun. 20, 1889, "Affidavits Proving Disability and Incapacity to Labor" by Moses Washington and Daniel Grant, Apr. 23, 1891, pension file for Jack (Jack Jr.) Aiken, RG 15, NARA.

CHAPTER 19

1. Edward L. Pierce, "The Freedmen at Port Royal," *Atlantic Monthly*, Sep. 1864, 310; *Savannah Republican*, Feb. 5, 1865; William Channing Garrett and Edward Everett Hale, "The Education of the Freedmen," *North American Review*, Oct. 1865, 540; Akiko Ochiai, *Harvesting Freedom: African American Agrarianism in Civil War Era South Carolina* (Westport, Connecticut: Praeger, 2004), 112–113, 138; Steven Hahn, *A Nation Under Our Feet: Black Political Struggles in the Rural South, from Slavery to the Great Migration* (Cambridge, MA: Belknap Press of Harvard University Press, 2003), 144–146; Steven Hahn, "'Extravagant Expectations' of Freedom: Rumour, Political Struggle, and the Christmas Insurrection Scare of 1865 in the American South," *Past & Present* 157, no. 1 (1997): 130; Eric Foner, *Reconstruction: America's Unfinished Revolution, 1863–1877* (New York: Harper & Row, 1988), 53–70.

2. *The War of the Rebellion: A Compilation of the Official* Records of the Union and Confederate Armies, ser. 1, vol. XLVII, pt. 1 (Washington, DC: GPO, 1880–1901), 1005–1006; Elizabeth Hyde Botume, *First Days Amongst the Contrabands* (Boston: Lee and Shepard, 1893), 196; Akiko Ochiai, *Harvesting Freedom: African American Agrarianism in Civil War Era South Carolina* (Westport, CT: Praeger, 2004), 137–139, 196–197, 202.

3. Botume, *First Days Amongst the Contrabands*, 196; Ochiai, *Harvesting Freedom*, 139–141, 168, 207–208.

4. Daniel Elliott Huger Smith, Arney Robinson Childs, and Alice Ravenel Huger Smith, eds., *Mason Smith Family Letters, 1860–1868* (Columbia: University of South Carolina Press, 1950), xx, 230–231; Botume, *First Days Amongst the Contrabands*, 196–197; Ochiai, *Harvesting Freedom*, 138.

5. Smith, Childs, and Smith, *Mason Smith Family Letters, 1860–1868*, 234, 283.

6. Francis B. Percival, "Headquarters, Assistant Commissions, Bureau Refugees, Freedmen and Abandoned Lands, South Carolina," Feb. 6, 1866, Francis B. Percival Papers, 1741–1923, South Caroliniana Library, University of South Carolina, Columbia; Smith, Childs, and Smith, *Mason Smith Family Letters*, 237–239, 254; Leslie Ann Schwalm, *"A Hard Fight for We": Women's Transition from Slavery to Freedom in South Carolina* (Urbana: University of Illinois Press, 1997), 195.

7. Smith, Childs, and Smith, *Mason Smith Family Letters*, 263–265; Mr. C.T. Lowndes, Dear Sir from unknown, Jan. 21, 1870, Lowndes Family History and Genealogy Research Files (30–4 Lowndes), South Carolina Historical Society, Charleston.

8. Williams Middleton Contract with Freed people, Beaufort District, March 26, 1866, U.S. Records of the Field Offices for the State of South Carolina, Bureau of Refugees, Freedmen, and Abandoned Lands, 1865–1872 (Washington: NARA), RG 105; Schwalm, *A Hard Fight for We*, 195, 198–199, 214.

9. Depositions by Penda Blake, Oct. 18, 1894, Jul. 11, 1902, deposition B by Penda Blake, Aug. 28, 1902, deposition by Stephen Polite aka Blake, Oct. 24, 1894, Chief of Law Division to Chief of S.E. Division, Aug. 14, 1902, Special Examiner to Honorable Commissioner of Pensions, n.d., deposition E by London Blake, Aug. 30, 1901, deposition I by J. H. Dais, Aug. 27, 1902, deposition K by Mary White, Aug. 29, 1902, deposition Q by Stephen Polite, Oct. 21, 1902, pension file for Peter (Penda) Blake, RG 15, NARA; deposition G by Lamer Wilson and deposition F by Pender Blake, May 13, 1892, pesnsion file for Parris (Mary) White, RG 15, NARA.

10. Thomas Wentworth Higginson, *Army Life in a Black Regiment* and Other Writings (Boston: Houghton, Mifflin, 1900), 364–365, 385.

11. "Abstract of Title," Plantation Bonny Hall, Bonny Hall Property Records, South Carolina Historical Society, Charleston; "Department of the Interior, Bureau of Pensions," deposition B by Mexico Washington, Oct. 10, 1912, deposition E by Affie Green, deposition F by Richard Smith, and deposition G by Susan Blake, Oct. 11, 1912, general affidavit by Wally Garrett, Jul. 27, 1892, "Declaration for Widow's Pension, Act of April 18, 1911," Oct. 11, 1911, pension file for Wally (Bella) Garrett, RG 15, NARA; deposition by Dr. Henry E. Bissell, Jul. 15, 1896, deposition by James Shields, Jul. 17, 1896, pension file for Jack (Hammond Brown) Morton, RG 15, NARA; David Weston Hiott, "Dr. Henry E. Bissell," *From the Desk of David W. Hiott* (Walterboro, SC: Colleton Genealogy Society); Langdon Cheves, "Blake of South Carolina," *South Carolina Historical and Genealogical Magazine* 1 (1900): 162; Brian Kelly, "Black Laborers, the Republican Party, and the Crisis of Reconstruction in Lowcountry South Carolina," *International Review of Social History* 51, no. 3 (2006): 391.

12. Deposition by Ferby Bowers, May 17, 1897, pension file for Jeffrey (Phoebe) Gray, RG 15, NARA; deposition A by Simon Washington, Jun. 11, 1895, pension file for Simon (Rachel) Washington, RG 15, NARA.

13. Botume, *First Days Amongst the Contrabands*, 198, 200; Stephen R. Wise, Lawrence Sanders Rowland, Gerhard Spieler, and Alexander Moore, *The History of Beaufort County, South Carolina: Volume 2: Rebellion, Reconstruction, and Redemption, 1861–1893* (Columbia: University of South Carolina, 2015); Donald Robert Shaffer, *After the Glory: The Struggles of Black Civil War Veterans* (Lawrence: University of Kansas Press, 2004), 59, 121; Ochiai, *Harvesting Freedom*, 89, 111–113; Schwalm, *A Hard Fight for We*, 157.

14. Ochiai, *Harvesting Freedom*, 89.

15. Wise et al., *The History of Beaufort County, South Carolina, Volume 2*, 254, 64.

16. Sarah Bradford, *Harriet Tubman: The Moses of Her People* (1886; New York: J. J. Little, 1901), 9, 78, 107–108, 116–117; Bradford, *Harriet Tubman*, 73.

17. Jack Burns, Sep. 27, 1866, Jonas Green, Sep. 27, 1866, Sep. 28, 1866, Oct. 20, 1866, Hector Francis, Sep. 29, 1866, Feb. 13, 1867, Jan. 20, 1872, Internal Revenue Service, Direct Tax Commission for the District of South Carolina, Heads of Family Land Certificates, South Carolina Department of Archives and History, Columbia (henceforth "Heads of Family Land Certificates").

18. Special Agent to Honorable I. H. Baker, Commissioner of Pensions, Apr. 30, 1875, exhibits by Sina Young, Gibby Mike and Chanty Mike, Bina Mack and Hager Hamilton, and Elsie Jones, Apr. 24, 1875, exhibit by Jonas Green, Apr. 26, 1875, James H. Clements, Special Agent, to Commissioner of Pensions, Dec. 18, 1876, exhibit A by James Jenkins, Dec. 13, 1876, exhibit B by Sina Young, exhibit by Jonas Green, Dec. 13, 1876, exhibit G by Wally Graham, Dec. 14, 1876, exhibit G by Flora Young, Dec. 15, 1876, exhibit I by William Jones, Dec. 16, 1876, pension file for William (Sina) Young, RG 15, NARA; Elizabeth Ann Regosin and Donald Robert Shaffer, *Voices of Emancipation: Understanding Slavery, the Civil War, and Reconstruction Through the U.S. Pension Bureau Files* (New York: New York University Press, 2008), 2; Shaffer, *After the Glory*, 59.

19. William Fields, Oct. 12, 1866, Parris Dawson, Oct. 11, 1866, Samuel Gilliard, Oct. 13, 1866, William Green, Oct. 15, 1866, Jan. 19, 1867, July Green, Jul. 19, 1867, Heads of Family Land Certificates.

20. Dembo Frazer, Oct. 1, 1866, Jackson Grant, Oct. 20, 1866, Aaron Ancrum, Dec. 4, 1866, William Jones, Dec. 6, 1866, Jan. 21, 1867, Aug. 17, 1869, Heads of Family Land Certificates.

21. Dembo Frazier, Oct. 1, 1866, Aaron Ancrum, Dec. 4, 1866, William Jones, Dec, 6, 1866, Jan. 21, 1867, Aug. 17, 1869, Nat Osborne, Dec. 10, 1866, November Osborne, Dec. 18, 1866, Solomon Washington, Dec. 24, 1866, Smart Washington, Feb. 27, 1867, Heads of Family Land Certificates; "Widow's Pension," "Army of the United States Certificate of Disability for Discharge," Jun. 2, 1865, "Physician's Affidavit-Proof of Physical Disability—Act of June 27, 1890," Nov. 19, 1890, "War Department—Record and Pension Division," May 10, 1891, pension file for Smart (Lucretia) Washington; Botume, *First Days Amongst the Contrabands*, 60, 116.

22. Deposition by Solomon W. Washington, Aug. 28, 1897, pension file for Smart (Lucretia) Washington; Botume, *First Days Amongst the Contrabands*, 60, 157.

23. Depositions by Solomon Washington, Sep. 9 and Aug. 28, 1897, depositions by Lucretia Washington, Jonas Green, Julia Scott, Aug. 24, 1897, pension file for Smart (Lucretia) Washington; Botume, *First Days Amongst the Contrabands*, 60–62.

24. Botume, *First Days Amongst the Contrabands*, 198. 239, 241.

25. Botume, *First Days Amongst the Contrabands*, 241–243.

26. Mary Anna Faber and Joshua Nicholls Marriage Settlement, 1848, South Carolina. Court of Equity (Charleston District), Bills of Complaint, 1800–1863, South Carolina Department of Archives and History, Columbia; John W. Burbridge, "Letters of Testamentary," Apr. 16, 1863, Francis B. Percival Papers, 1741–1923; Benjamin Stokes Commissioner in Equity to John D. Warren, Deed of Realty, Nov. 9, 1868, Deed Book B, 486, Colleton County Register of Deeds, Walterboro, SC; Joshua Nicholls, Trustee, to John D. Warren, Dec. 11, 1867, Deed Book, Colleton County Register of Deeds; Botume, *First Days Amongst the Contrabands*, 241–243; "Combahee River Plantations: Rose Hill," in *Private Collection* (Colleton County, SC), 3, 8–9; "Combahee River Plantations: Rose Hill," in *Private Collection* (Colleton County, SC), 5.

27. Wally Graham, Aug. 17 and Apr. 7, 1868, Jonas Green, Oct. 20, 1868, William Jones, Aug. 17, 1869, Heads of Family Land Certificates; Botume, *First Days Amongst the Contrabands*, 277–279.

28. Wally Graham, Aug. 17 and Apr. 7, 1868, Jonas Green, Oct. 20, 1868, William Jones, Aug. 17, 1869, Heads of Family Land Certificates; US Direct Tax Commission to Mary Ann Lewis, Jul. 13, 1871, Deed Book 5, 499, Beaufort County Register of Deeds; Nelson R. Scovel to Bina Mack, Aug. 2, 1873, Deed Book 7, 359, Beaufort County Register of Deeds; Mary Nehemias to Margaret Moody, Oct. 18, 1876, Deed Book 10, 371, Beaufort County Register of Deeds; Botume, *First Days Amongst the Contrabands*, 277–279.

29. [Depositions] by Schancho Van Dross, Feb. 19, 1869, May 2, 1868, "Department of the Interior, Pension Office," Jul. 19, 1867, [deposition] by John Proctor, Sep. 15, 1868, pension file for Harry (Bina) Mack, RG 15, NARA; Shaffer, *After the Glory*, 41–42.

30. Herton Fields in Blake, Colleton, SC. R.M. Sims to Hector and Peggy Fields, Feb. 19, 1879, Deed Book P, 712, Colleton County Register of Deeds; State of South Carolina to Benjamin Prior, Dec. 1, 1879, Deed Book 11, 74, Colleton County Register of Deeds; Hector Fields (d. July 1879), Mortality Schedules, Census Year 1879, Census Place: Blake, Colleton, South Carolina, U.S. Census Bureau (1850–1885), Archive Roll 1, page 1; James B. Heyward, "The Heyward Family of South Carolina (Continued)," *South Carolina Historical Magazine* 59, no. 4 (1958): 207–208, 213.

31. William Manigault to Rappel Smith, Hector Hawk and others (includes Cuffee Bowles) Conveyance of Realty, Feb. 16, 1876, Colleton County Register of Deeds, Book F, 59; [deposition] by Charles Witsell, Sep. 17, 1872, pension file for Aaron (Sallie) Ancrum, RG 15, NARA; David Weston Hiott,

"Maria Barnwell Gough Smith" and Dr. Charles A. Witsell" in *From the Desk of David W. Hiott* (Walterboro: Colleton Genealogy Society).

32. "No. 310,257," general affidavits by Lucius Robinson, Venus Osborne, Annie Barnwell, Amy Barnwell, William Washington, Flora Robinson, Aug. 5, 1893, pension file for Harry (Flora) Robinson, RG 15, NARA.

33. "No. 310,257," general affidavits by Lucius Robinson, Venus Osborne, Annie Barnwell, Amy Barnwell, William Washington, Flora Robinson, Aug. 5, 1893, pension file for Harry (Flora) Robinson, RG 15, NARA.

34. Neptune Nicholas and Others to April Singleton Conveyance, Jan. 2, 1880, Colleton County Register of Deeds, Book 4, 85; deposition F by Neptune Nicholas, Feb. 12, 1902, pension file for Edward (Peggy) Brown, RG 15, NARA.

35. Neptune Nicholas and Others to April Singleton Conveyance, Jan. 2, 1880, Colleton County Register of Deeds, Book 4, 85; deposition F by Neptune Nicholas, Feb. 12, 1902, pension file for Edward (Peggy) Brown, RG 15, NARA; Case of Relia Middleton No. 1132532, 1/30/1920, 2/2/1902, William (Relia) Middleton US Civil War Pension File; Interview with Ernestine "Tina" Martin Wyatt, Upper Marlboro, MD, Feb. 20, 2023; "Escape to Freedom: The Molly Graham Story," Walterboro Live, 7/11/2019; Renee Givens, "South Carolina Bridge Dedicated to Molly Graham, African American Naturopathic Herb Doctor," Black Southern Belle, 7/4/2019. April Singleton and Neptune Nicholas to R. B. Grant Lease, Feb. 5m 1883, Colleton County Register of Deeds, Book 1, 107; Neptune Nicholas and April Singleton (acting as trustees for 29 Others) Elizabeth M. Grant Title of Real Estate, Dec. 30, 1885, Colleton County Register of Deeds, Book 3, 132; Maria Barnwell Gough Smith" and Dr. Charles A. Witsell" in *From the Desk of David W. Hiott* (Walterboro: Colleton Genealogy Society).

36. April Singleton to Neptune Nicholas, Jan. 6, 1886, Deed Book 3, 166, April Singleton to Moses Simmons, Jan. 6, 1886, Deed Book 3, 185, April Singleton to Lucius Robinson, Jan. 6, 1886, Deed Book 3, 187, April Singleton to Peter James, Jan. 6, 1886, Deed Book 3, 189, April Singleton to Joshua Simmons, Jan. 6, 1886, Deed Book 3, 190, April Singleton to Jack Barnwell, Jan. 6, 1886, Deed Book 4, 88, April Singleton to July Osborne, Jan. 6, 1886, Deed Book 3, 201, April Singleton to Edward Brown, Jan. 6, 1886, Deed Book 3, 162, Colleton County Register of Deeds.

37. Deposition by E. H. Botume, May 29, 1890, general affidavit by Elizabeth Hyde Botume, Feb. 23, 1892, pension file for Isaac De Causter, RG 15, NARA; "Declaration for Widow's Pension, Act of June 27, 1890," May 26, 1893, pension file for November (Sarah) Osborne, RG 15, NARA.

38. Catherine Noyes to Nelly [Balch], Nov. 3, 1869, Papers of Catherine Porter Noyes, 1863–1869, Schlesinger Library, Harvard University; Joseph Deas to Pleasant Rutledge, Sep. 6, 1889, Deed Book 16, 410, Ellen Crofut to Sina Green, Jan. 2, 1891, Deed Book 18, 135, Beaufort County Register of Deeds; Botume, *First Days Amongst the Contrabands*, 259–266, 278.

39. George W. Ford to Andrew Wyatt, Feb. 8, 1892, Deed Book 18, 147, Edward Brown to Julia Proctor, Jan. 10, 1893, Deed Book 18, 322, Eliza M. Fuller and

Phoebe Fuller to James Sheppard, Nov. 5, 1896, Deed Book 24, 379, Ben Josselon to Jack Aiken, Nov. [?], 1897, Deed Book 29, 364, Phoebe Fuller to Eliza M. Fuller to James Shields, Dec. 11, 1897, Deed Book 21, 531, Beaufort County Register of Deeds; neighbor's affidavit by William Fields, Mar. 31, 1891, neighbor's affidavits by Martha Frazer, Sylvia Decoster, and Charles Simmons, n.d., "For Comrade's or Officer's Testimony" by Isaac DeCosta, Jun. 11, 1889, pension file for Andrew (Maria) Wyatt, RG 15, NARA; deposition A by Sallie Sheppard, depositions by Solomon Salter and James Scott, Dec. 30, 1901, [affidavits] by Sally Sheppard, Solomon Salter, July Heywood, May 7, 1900, pension file for James (Sallie) Sheppard, RG 15, NARA.

40. Eliza M. Fuller and Phoebe Fuller to James Sheppard, Nov. 5, 1896, Deed Book 24, 379, Beaufort County Register of Deeds; "State of South Carolina Return for Taxation for the Fiscal Year Commencing November 1st, 1894," Sep. 16, 1895, general affidavit by Margaret Simmons, Sep. 16, 1895, general affidavits by L. M. Garvin and Cumsey Hamilton, Nov. 16, 1892, pension file for Joshua (Margaret) Simmons, RG 15, NARA; depositions by Sallie Sheppard, Solomon Salter, and James Scott, Dec. 30, 1901, [affidavits] by Sally Sheppard, Solomon Salter, and July Heywood, May 7, 1900, pension file for James (Sallie)Sheppard.

41. General affidavits by Sina Young, Oct. 5, 1901, Jack Aiken, May 16, 1901, James Harris, May 30, 1901, Anthony Carter, Oct. 3, 1901, B. H. Houston, Oct. 5, 1901, pension file for William (Sina) Young; Reva B. Siegel, "Home as Work: The First Woman's Rights Claims Concerning Wives' Household Labor, 1850–1880," *Yale Law Journal* 103, no. 5 (1994): 1083.

42. Phoebe Fuller and Eliza M. Fuller to James Shields, Dec. 11, 1897, Deed Book 21, 531, Moses Simmons to Fannie Simmons, Mar. 3, 1904, Colleton County Register of Deeds; "State of South Carolina Return for Taxation for the Fiscal Year Commencing November 1st, 1894," Sep.16, 1895, general affidavit by Margaret Simmons, Sep. 16, 1895, general affidavit by L. M. Garvin and Cumsey Hamilton, Nov. 16, 1892, pension file for Joshua (Margaret) Simmons; depositions by Eliza McQuire, Luvenia Mobly, and Kittie Miles, May 25, 1909, "Accrued Pension, Act of March 2, 1895," Oct. 26, 1908, claimant's affidavit by Eliza McQuire, May 28, 1908, pension file for Fulton (Eliza) McGuire, RG 15, NARA; claimant's affidavit by Jane Shield, Jan. 14, 1905, claimant's affidavit by Jone Shield, Feb. 20, 1905, general affidavits by Carolina Fields and James Washington, Jan. 14, 1905, general affidavit by Farbry Bowers, Feb. 20, 1905, pension file for James (Jone) Shields, RG 15, NARA.

43. "No. 796,289," "Act of April 18, 1908 Widow's Pension," Jul. 25, 1908, [no name] to Law Division to the Chief of the Bureau of Review, Apr. 28, 1905, "Department of the Interior, Bureau of Pensions," Apr. 20, 1905, "Act of June 27, 1890 as Amended by Act of May 9, 1900 Widow's Pension," Apr. 18, 1905, Oct. 22, 1904, "Act of June 27, 1890 as Amended by Act of May 9, 1900 Declaration for Widow's Pension" by Betsy Nicholas, Oct. 22, 1904, pension file for Neptune (Betsy) Nicholas, RG 15, NARA; "No. 1093873," "Department of the Interior, Bureau of Pensions," Feb. 11, 1919, "Act of April 19, 1908 as Amended by Act of September 8, 1916 Widow's Pension," Jan. 24,

`9`9, "Declaration for Widow's Pension Act of April 19, 1908 as Amended Act of September 8, 1916," by Fanny Simmons, Feb. 5, 1917, "Accrued Pension, Act of March 2, 1895," May 24, 1891, "Declaration of a Widow for Accrued Pension" by Fannie Simmons, Aug. 4, 1910, pension file for Moses (Fannie) Simmons, RG 15, NARA; "No. 996957," "Act of February 6, 1907," Jun. 29, 1909, "3–1089," pension file for Jackson (Jane) Grant, RG 15, NARA.

44. Chief of Law Division to Chief of Southern Division, Apr. 23, 1902, Chief of Law Division S. A. Cuddy to Chief of S.E. Division, Mar. 27, 1902, Special Examiner Jus. T. Clements to the Hon. Commissioner of Pensions, Mar. 20, 1902, deposition by Peggy Brown, Feb. 11, 1902, depositions by Ned Brown and Cuffy Bolze, Feb. 11, 1902, deposition by Cuffy Bolze, Feb. 17, 1902, Special Examiner R. K. Doe to Hon. Commissioner of Pensions, Jan. 15, 1902, deposition by Peggy Brown, Nov. 14, 1901, deposition by Neptune Nicholas, Nov. 15, 1901, deposition by R. H. Wichman, Dec. 17, 1901, pension file for Edward (Peggy) Brown; David Weston Hiott, "Capt. Alexander Castner Shaffer," *From the Desk of David W. Hiott* (Walterboro, SC: Colleton Genealogy Society). (Alexander Casner Shaffer, E. T. Shaffer, "Service in the South: Life and Letters of Alexander C. Shaffer, 1838–1910," South Caroliniana)

45. Deposition by Peggy Brown, Feb. 11, 1902, deposition by Ned Brown, Feb. 11, 1902, deposition by Cuffy Bolze, Feb. 17, 1902, deposition by Peggy Brown, Nov. 14, 1901, deposition by Neptune Nicholas, Nov. 15, 1901, deposition by R. H. Wichman, Dec. 17, 1901, pension file for Edward (Peggy) Brown; Mingo Vanderhorst, Mar. 21, 1909, Deed Book 33, 83, Friday Hamilton, Oct. 27, 1909, Deed Book 33, 384, Annie Barnwell, Oct. 16, 1919, Cuffy Bowles, Mar. 15, 1936, Annie Barnwell, Mar. 1932, Colleton County Register of Deeds.

46. I. S. McGrath to FDR, Oct. 9, 1934, I. S. McGrath to US Department of the Interior Bureau of Pensions, Jan. 18, 1935, I. S. McGrath to E. W. Morgan, Acting Commissioner of Pensions, Apr. 3, 1929, "Tax Receipt No. 8191," 1928, "Application for Reimbursement" by I. S. McGraw, Feb. 7, 1929, "In Reference Finance . . . , " depositions by Ella Nicholas and Cuffy Bolze, Aug. 9, 1907, general affidavits by Ella Nicholas, May 19 and Jul. 23, 1906, general affidavits by Cuffy Bolze, Jan. 11 and Nov. 20, 1906, pension file for Charles (Ella) Nicholas, RG 15, NARA.

47. Law Clerk to Chief of the Widow Division, Feb. 8, 1922, "Accrued Pension," general affidavit by Isaac Brown, Jan. 31, 1922, pension file for Cuffie (Sophia) Bolze, RG 15, NARA.

48. Fred Hamilton to Department of the Interior, Bureau of Pensions, Sep. 23, 1923, Director Dependents Claim Service to Irene Hamilton, Mar. 13, 1937, [affidavit] of Arizona Hamilton, Nov. 25, 1922, Irene Hamilton to Gentlemen, Mar. 2, 1937, E. L. Bailey to Irene Hamilton, Mar. 13, 1937, [affidavit] by Arizona Hamilton, Nov. 25, 1922, [affidavit] by Friday Hamilton, Jan. 15, 1898, pension file for Friday Hamilton, RG 15, NARA; Friday Hamilton, Walterboro, US Census 1870; Friday Hamilton, Walterboro, US Census 1880, NARA microfilm publication T9, FHL microfilm; Friday Hamilton, Walterboro, US Census 1900; George A. Hamilton and Harry Hamilton, US Census, 1900; Special Schedule—Surviving

Soldiers, Sailors, and Marines, and Widows, Etc., United States Census of Union Veterans and Widows of the Civil War, 1890, NARA microfilm publication M123; interview with Claire Hamilton, Dec. 4, 2022, White Plains, NY.

49. Exhibit by Sina Young, 4/24/1875, by Jonas Green, 4/26/1875, Gibby Mike, Bina Mack, 4/24/1875, James H. Clement, 12/18/1876, exhibit D Rev. James B. Middleton, exhibit E Rachel Haynes, 12/14/1876; [Depositions] by Venus Lyons, Elsie Jones, and Lina Richard, Jun. 30, 1873, pension file for William (Sina) Young.

50. Special Agent to Honorable I. H. Baker, Commissioner of Pensions, Apr. 30, 1875, pension file for William (Sina) Young; exhibits by Sina Young, Jonas Green, Gibby and Chanty Mike, Bina Mack and Hagar Hamilton, Elsie Jones, Apr. 24, 1875, [depositions] by Sina Young and Bina Mack, Jun. 27, 1873, [depositions] by Venus Lyons, Elsie Jones, and Lina Richards, Jun. 30, 1873, P. E. Ezekiel, Postmaster, to Commissioners of Pensions, Jun. 18, 1874, J. H. Clements, Special Agent, to Hon. J. A. Bently, Commissioner of Pensions, Dec. 18, 1876, exhibit B by Sina Young and exhibit C by Jonas Green, Dec. 13, 1876, "SSD No. 163,733," exhibit F by Wally Graham, Dec. 14, 1876, exhibit G by Flora Young, Dec. 15, 1872, exhibit H by William Black, Dec. 15, 1872, "Widow's Declaration for Pension or Increase of Pension," Dec. 12, 1889, James H. Tonkiey [?] to D. C. Cox, May 25, 1874, "Declaration for a Widow's Restoration of Pension," May 16, 1901, general affidavit by Selam White, Aug. 6, 1901, "Declaration for Pension or for Increase of a Pension of Children Under Sixteen Years of Age," Apr. 26, 1887, "Original Pension of Minor Child," Aug. 15, 1889, pension file for William (Sina) Young.

51. Special Examiner V. M. Johnson to the Commissioner of Pensions, May 22, 1897, deposition by Captain Brown, May 4, 1897, deposition by Jackson Grant, May 6, 1897, claimant's affidavit by Captain Brown, May 20, 1895, Jul. 27, 1896, general affidavit by Daniel Jenkins, Aug. 11, 1891, "Physician's Affidavit" by Dr. H. E. Bissell, Sep. 10, 1895, general affidavits by Moses Simmons and Jackson Grant, Feb. 4, 1895, general affidavits by Jackson Grant and January Harvey, Sep. 30, 1893, general affidavits by Jackson Grant and Cuffee Bolze, May 4, 1896, "Bureau of Pensions," Feb. 3, 1893, pension file for Frank (Captain Brown) Hamilton, RG 15, NARA.

52. Deposition by Margaret Simmons, Apr. 15, 1901, general affidavit by Friday Hamilton, Aug. 4, 1897, general affidavits by Jackson Grant and Andrew Nicholas, Feb. 18, 1895, "Widow's Declaration for Pension or Increase of Pension," general affidavits by Moses Simmons, Jackson Grant, Neptune Nicholas, and Margaret Simmons, Nov. 4, 1901, general affidavits by Jackson Grant and Andrew Nicholas, Sep. 16, 1895, "Department of the Interior, Bureau of Pensions," Jul. 3, 1890, general affidavit by Margaret Simmons, Aug. 8, 1894, deposition by Moses Simmons, Jul. 25, 1901, pension file for Joshua (Margaret) Simmons; [affidavit] by Jackson Grant, Aug. 19, 1901, general affidavits by Jackson Grant and Friday Hamilton, Feb. 21, 1898, pension file for Anthony (Moriah) Bartley, RG 15, NARA.

53. Ex A Phoebe Frazier, 11/7/1884, deposition C by Wally Ford, 11/7/1884, deposition G Dapheny Drayton, deposition H Edward E. Elliott, Harriet

Elliott, 11/11/1884, Friday Barrington, 11/22/1884, [deposition] by Friday Barrington, 12/1879, Nov. 11, 1884, pension file for Robert (Phoebe) Frazier.

54. "Claim for Invalid Pension," Apr. 14, 1869, Willam Harper to Sir, Nov. 22, 1884, deposition by Phoebe Frazier, Nov. 7, 1884, deposition by Daphney Drayton, Nov. 8, 1884, depositions by Edward F. Elliott and Harriet Elliott, Nov. 11, 1884, deposition by Friday Barrington, Nov. 22, 1884, "Ex. A" by Phoebe Frazier, Dec. 11, 1893, [affidavit] by Phoebe Frazier, Dec. 18, 1879, "No. 236,919," "Widow's Claim for Pension" by Mrs. Phoebe Frazer, Mar. 8, 1878, "Incidental Matter" [Phoebe Frazier], n.d., pension file for Robert (Phoebe) Frazier; Shaffer, *After the Glory*, 122, 168.

55. Sarah H. Bradford, *Scenes in the Life of Harriet Tubman* (Auburn, NY: W. J. Moses Printers, 1869), 1–2.

56. Bradford, *Scenes in the Life of Harriet Tubman* (1869), 1–2.

57. Bradford, *Scenes in the Life of Harriet Tubman* (1869), 4–8, 64–68.

58. Bradford, *Scenes in the Life of Harriet Tubman* (1869), 1, 3, 5.

59. Wood, "A History Concerning the Pension Claim of Harriet Tubman," 1; Bradford, *Harriet Tubman*, 6, 93–94, 156, 158–59, 162; Bradford, *Scenes in the Life of Harriet Tubman* (1869), vi, 5, 64, 66, 68–69, 84–85. Tubman's family inherited her sharpshooter's rifle, which she carried during the Civil War, and the pistols she carried on the Underground Railroad. Her nephew Elijah Stewart kept the rifle in his dining room until it was stolen in a home burglary in the 1930s, according to his granddaughter Joan Butler. While the rifle was no longer in the possession of the Tubman family, a gun specialist in Gettysburg examined the woodcut and identified the weapon pictured in it as a specially made (as opposed to US Army issue) sharpshooter's rifle. Family members in Tallahassee inherited and retained ownership of Tubman's pistols. Interview with Joan Butler, Nov. 18, 2021, private collection of Dr. Kate Larson.

60. Bradford, *Scenes in the Life of Harriet Tubman* (1869), 7.

61. Bradford, *Scenes in the Life of Harriet Tubman* (1869), 7.

62. Bradford, *Scenes in the Life of Harriet Tubman* (1869), 7.

63. [Depositions] by Harriet Davis, May 28, 1892, Nov. 10, 1894, "Record of Death," Jul. 14, 1890, [affidavits] by Charles C. Hemingway, Jul. 15, 1890, and Eazur W. Jolly, Nov. 22, 1892, general affidavit by Maggie Lucas, Jun. 3, 1892, [affidavit] by Joseph Henry Hooper, Nov. 22, 1892, "55th Congress, 3rd Session, House of Representatives, Report No. 1774," Jan. 19, 1899, "Declaration for Widow's Pension, Act of June 27, 1890" by Harriet Davis, Jul. 14, 1890, general affidavit by Dorsey Brainart, Oct. 14, 1894, general affidavit by William H. Stewart, Oct. 13, 1894, general affidavit by Anna E. Thompson, Jun. 19, 1894, "Department of the Interior, Bureau of Pensions," Aug. 15, 1894, Earl Conrad to W. C. Black, Chief Clerk Veterans Administration, Aug. 4, 1939, neighbor's affidavit by Thornton Newton and Maggie Lucas, Jun. 15, 1893, general affidavit by Joshua Diggs, May 28, 1892, general affidavit by Charles Thornton, Sep. 12, 1894, "No. 449,952," general affidavit by Harriet Davis, Nov. 28, 1892, general affidavit by Charles H. Peterson, Jan. 7, 1895, general affidavit by Edgar

J. Fryman, Nov. 9, 1894, "War Department, Record and Pension Division." Jan. 13, 1891, pension file for Nelson (Harriet) Davis, RG 15, NARA.

64. Hector Fields, "3–356 Act of June 27, 1890, Invalid Pension," Jan. 7, 1901, Compiled Military Service Records; E. A. Crofut, Oversized Ledger II, 53, Waterhouse-Crofut Family Papers, South Carolina Historical Society, Charleston.

65. Depositions by Andrew Wyatt, Silvia DeCaster, and Charlotte Savage, and general affidavit by Andrew Wyatt, Sep. 4, 1889, claimant's affidavit by Andrew Wyatt, Sep. 3, 1890, "For Officer's or Comrade's Testimony" by Isaac DeCoster, Jun. 11, 1889, neighbor's affidavit by Isaac Coster, Oct. 18, 1885, "For Officer's or Comrade's Testimony" by Edward Brown, Nov. 8, 1889, "For Officer's or Comrade's Testimony" by Jacob Vandross, Jul. 17, 1889, neighbor's affidavits by Jacob Vandross, Martha Frazier, and Sylvia DeCoster, n.d., neighbor's affidavit by Diana Singleton, Nov. 2, 1889, neighbor's affidavit by Robert Middleton n.d., neighbor's affidavit by Charles Simmons, Jul. 17, 1889, neighbor's affidavit by November Osborne, Sep. 4, 1889, "Declaration for Original Invalid Pension," Apr. 7, 1887, "Declaration of a Survivor for Service or Dependent Pension," Jul. 2, 1890, pension file for Andrew (Silvia) Wyatt, RG 15, NARA.

66. General affidavits by Andrew Nicholas and Anthony Bartley, May 28 and 29, 1894, pension file for Ned (Daphne) Snipe, RG 15, NARA.

67. "Act of June 27, 1890, Declaration for Widow's Pension," by Lucretia Washington, 3/30/1891, "General Affidavits," by Solomon Washington, 9/19/1895, Mary Williams, 2/6/1886, Jonas Green, 12/18/1896, M. W. Williams, 12/22/1886, Jubber Scott, 3/16/1897, "Physician's Affidavit Proof of Physical Disability—Act of June 27, 1890," Deposition A by Lucretia Washington, 10/21/1897, A. B. Parker to Hon. Commissioner of Pensions, 8/30/1897, "Deposition A" by Lucretia Washington, 8/24/1897, "Deposition D" by Solomon Washington, 8/24/1897, "Deposition F" by Jonas Green, "Deposition H" by Julia Scott, "Deposition I" by Christiana Washington, 8/24/1897, "Deposition G" by Monday W. Williams, 8/25/1897, pension file for Smart (Lucretia) Washington; Botume, *First Days Amongst the Contrabands*, 244.

68. E. D. Gallion, Special Examiner to William Lochren, Commissioner of Pensions, Jun. 28, 1895, deposition by Richard Smith, Jun. 12, 1895, deposition by George A. Bissell, Jun. 24, 1895, pension file for Richard (Bella) Smith, RG 15, NARA; E. D. Gallion, Special Examiner to William Lochren, Commissioner of Pensions, Jun. 28, 1895, pension file for Richard (Lucy, Fannie) Smith.

69. E. D. Gallion, Special Examiner to D. I. Murphy, Commissioner of Pensions, Oct. 31, 1896, deposition by Walley Garrett, Oct. 22, 1896, deposition by Friday Hamilton, Oct. 24, 1896, deposition by Dr. H. E. Bissell, Oct. 29, 1896, pension file for Jackson (Jane) Grant.

70. General affidavit by John A. Savage, Feb. 15, 1892, pension file for Isaac (Silvia) De Causter; V. M. Johnson, Special Examiner to the Commissioner of Pensions, May 22, 1897, neighbor's affidavit by John A. Savage, Aug. 12, 1891, pension file for Frank (Captain Brown) Hamilton.

71. Kristina Kathryn Dunn, "The Union Forever: The Development of Beaufort National Cemetery," MA thesis, University of South Carolina, 2005, 1, 2, 5–6, 11, 13.

72. [Affidavit] by Harriet Davis, Nov. 10, 1894, general affidavit by Anna E. Thompson, Jun. 19, 1894, general affidavit by Harriet Davis, Feb. 1, 1892, neighbor's affidavit by William H. Stewart, Jul. 21, 1892, Earl Conrad to W. C. Black, Chief Clerk Veterans Administration, Aug. 4, 1939, "Department of the Interior, Bureau of Pensions," Jan. 26, 1895, general affidavit by Horace C. Cook, Sep. 3, 1894, pension file for Nelson (Harriet) Davis.

73. Dunn, "The Union Forever," 1, 2, 5–6, 11, 13; J. E. McTeer, *Beaufort, Now and Then* (Beaufort, SC: Beaufort Book Co., 1971), 98–99.

74. "55th Congress, 3rd Session, House of Representatives, Report No. 1774," Jan. 19, 1899, pension file for Nelson (Harriet) Davis.

75. "55th Congress, 3rd Session, House of Representatives, Report No. 1774," Jan. 19, 1899, [affidavit] by Harriet Davis, Nov. 10, 1894, general affidavit by Anna E. Thompson, Jun. 19, 1894, general affidavit by Harriet Davis, Feb. 1, 1892, neighbor's affidavit by William H. Stewart, Jul. 21, 1892, Earl Conrad to W. C. Black, Chief Clerk Veterans Administration, Aug. 4, 1939, "Department of the Interior, Bureau of Pensions," Jan. 26, 1895, general affidavit by Horace C. Cook, Sep. 3, 1894, Earl Conrad to W. C. Black, Chief Clerk Veterans Administration, Aug. 14, 1939, pension file for Nelson (Harriet) Davis.

76. J. M. Johnson, Special Examiner, to Commissioner of Pensions, May 19, 1897, deposition by Rebecca Wineglass, May 3, 1897, deposition by Jackson Grant, May 3, 1897, Department of the Interior, Bureau of Pensions, Jun. 23, 1897, "Declaration for Widow's Pension, Act of June 27, 1890," Jul. 9, 1902, Apr. 22, 1905, neighbor's affidavit by Jackson Grant, Nov. 29, 1892, general affidavit by Jonas Green, Oct. 30, 1897, general affidavit by Adam Taylor, Nov. 20, 1895, general affidavit by Samuel Grant and Nellie Grant, Feb. 28, 1895, "Affidavit That Pensioner Has Not Remarried" by Sam Savage and Jackson Grant, Nov. 29, 1892, "Original Pension of Minor Children," n.d., "Widow's Pension," n.d., "Declaration for a Soldier's Children Who Are Permanently Helpless," Jul. 9, 1892, pension file for Jack (Rebecca, Hercules) Wineglass, RG 15, NARA.

77. Special Examiner to the Commissioner of Pensions, May 19, 1897, deposition by Phillis Pinckney, May 4, 1897, deposition by Rebecca Wineglass, May 3, 1897, "Department of the Interior, Bureau of Pensions," Jun. 23, 1897, "Widow's Pension," Jun. 16, 1897, "Declaration for Soldier's Children Who Are Permanently Helpless," Jul. 9, 1892, pension file for Jack (Rebecca, Hercules) Wineglass.

78. "Department of the Interior, Bureau of Pensions," Jul. 8, general affidavit by Jackson Grant, Oct. 30, 1897, "Original Pension of Minor Children," "Widow's Pension," "Declaration for Soldier's Children Who Are Permanently Helpless," Jul. 9, 1892, pension file for Jack (Rebecca, Hercules) Wineglass. According to his daughter, Jack Wineglass was reportedly principal party in a strike for wages on the rice plantation where she lived and was arrested and jailed. This was certainly the Combahee River Strike. See depositions by Phillis Pinckney and Charles Brooks, May 4, 1897, deposition by Scipio Jenkins, May 19, 1897, pension file for Jack (Rebecca, Hercules) Wineglass. There is also reference to it in Balaam Burnett's file. See deposition by John Gadsden, Dec. 5, 1901,

pension file for Balaam (Diana, Sally) Burnett, RG 15, NARA; Wise et al., *The History of Beaufort County, Volume 2*, 550–552; Kelly, "Black Laborers," 384, 386–387, 389, 391, 399, 404, 406–408; Foner, *Reconstruction*, 573.

79. Brimmer, *Claiming Union Widowhood*, 1, 3, 7, 10–11, 14–15, 17, 127, 129–130, 132, 134, 147–48, 162; Hunter, *Bound in Wedlock*, 275.

80. Deposition A by Diana Burnett, Dec. 6, 1901, deposition C by Wally Garrett, deposition D by James Shields, Jan. 18, 1902, deposition F by Henry Green, Jan. 18, 1902, deposition H by Silas Prior, Jan. 27, 1902, "Statement of Case," "The Evidence," "Declaration for Widow's Pension, Act of June 27, 1890, as Amended by Act of May 9, 1900" by Diana Burnett, Jun. 29, 1901, pension file for Balaam (Diana, Sally) Burnett.

81. Chief of Law Division to Chief of S. E. Division, Oct. 22, 1901, deposition A by Sally Burnett, Dec. 4, 1901, deposition F by Daniel Mack, Dec. 4, 1901, deposition L by John Gadsden, Dec. 5, 1901, general affidavits by Daniel Mack and Sam Singleton, May 23, 1901, pension file for Balaam (Diana, Sally) Burnett.

82. Chief of Law Division to Chief of S. E. Division, Oct. 22, 1901, deposition by Diana Burnett, Dec. 6, 1901, deposition by James Shields, Jan. 18, 1902, deposition by Sam Chisholm, Jan. 17, 1902, deposition by Sally Burnett, Dec. 4, 1901, deposition by Ben Jones, Jan. 27, 1902, L. M. Kelley to Secretary of the Interior, Jul. 3, 1902, pension file for Balaam (Diana, Sally) Burnett.

83. Chief of Law Division to Chief of S. E. Division, Oct. 22, 1901, deposition by Diana Burnett, Dec. 6, 1901, deposition by Sally Burnett, Dec. 4, 1901, deposition by E. B. Webb, Dec. 24, 1901, deposition by Daniel Mack, Dec. 4, 1901, deposition by John Gadsen, Dec. 5, 1901, L. M. Kelley to Secretary of the Interior, Jul. 3, 1902, general affidavits by Daniel Mack, Ben Jones, and Lucius Gadsen, May 23, 1901, pension file for Balaam (Diana, Sally) Burnett.

84. Deposition by Moriah Bartley, Apr. 15, 1901, Special Examiner to the Honorable Commissioner of Pensions, Jul. 13, 1901, deposition by Moriah Bartley, Apr. 16, 1901, deposition by Mingo Van Dross, Apr. 17, 1901, deposition by Morris Nowell, Jul. 12, 1901, depositions by Maria Nowell, Fortune Hamilton, and Clarissa Bartley, Jul. 12, 1901, "Widow's Pension," "Act of June 27, 1890 Declaration for Widow's Pension," Feb. 21, 1898, pension file for Anthony (Moriah) Bartley.

85. Moriah Bartley to Commissioner of Pensions and Board of Review, Aug. 19, 1901, [affidavits] by Moriah Bartley, Jackson Grant, and Charles Givens, Aug. 19, 1901, pension file for Anthony (Moriah) Bartley; [affidavit] by William Elliott, Jul. 30, 1910, pension file for Mingo (Emma) Van Dross, RG 15, NARA.

86. [Affidavits] by Moriah Bartley and Cumsey Bartley, Aug. 19, 1901, pension file for Anthony (Moriah) Bartley.

87. "Department of the Interior, Bureau of Pensions," 8/6/1901, Anthony (Moriah) Bartley US Civil War Pension File.

88. Deposition by Eliza McGuire, May 25, 1909, depositions by Davis McGee and Elizabeth Shaw, Jun. 21, 1909, deposition by James A. Roberts, May 26, 1909, depositions by Margaret Shavers, Janus Shavers, and Winnie Gabriel, Jun. 22, 1909, marriage license [?], Jun. 21, 1909, deposition by V. J. Dean, Jun. 12, 1909,

general affidavits by Henry Shavers and Dennis McGee, Jan. 2, 1908, general affidavit by Robert Pearce, Oct. 2, 1908, general affidavit by Lavenia Mobly, Sep. 23, 1908, "Declaration for Widow's Pension, Act of April 19, 1908," Sep. 8, 1908, pension file for Fulton (Eliza) McGuire.

89. Depositions by Frank Shavers, Margaret Shavers, Janus Shavers, and Winnie Gabriel, Jun. 22, 1909, depositions by Henry Shavers and Davis McGee, Jun. 21, 1909, deposition by James A. Roberts, May 26, 1909, depositions by Oren B. Armstrong and Eliza McGuire, Jun. 24, 1909, J. A. Davis, Special Examiner, to Honorable Commissioner of Pensions, Jun. 29, 1909, pension file for Fulton (Eliza) McGuire.

90. "One Mary E. Basquie," n.d., depositions by Frank Shavers, Janus Shavers, and Winnie Gabriel, Jun. 22, 1909, deposition by Henry Shavers, Jun. 21, 1909, deposition by V. J. Dean, Jun. 12, 1909, Letter to Honorable Commissioner of Pensions, Jun. 25, 1909, deposition by Mary E. Basquire, Jul. 13, 1909, [affidavit] by Dr. G. W. Wood, Aug. 19, 190[?], general affidavits by John Boyce and O. B. Armstrong, Jul. 12, 1907, letter by Chief, Law Divison, n.d., ibid.; "Declaration for Widow's Pension, Act of April 19, 1908," Sep. 8, 1908, deposition by William B. Barnett, May 21, 1909, deposition by Harriet H. Love, Jun. 12, 1909, deposition by Sarah A. Watkins, Jun. 19, 1909, d deposition by Eleanora Baquie, Jul. 13, 1909, pension file for Fulton (Eliza) McGuire.

91. Molcey Chisholm to Mr. Roosevelt, President of US, Mar. 14, 1907, [affidavit] by Moses Simmons, Dec. 7, 1904, "Original Pension of Minor Children," n.d., "Department of the Interior, Bureau of Pensions," Apr. 13, 1899, general affidavit by Ansel Gillard, Oct. 21, 1892, general affidavits by Moses Simmons and James Wineglass, Nov. 3, 1891, pension file for March (Molcy) Chisolm, RG 15, NARA.

92. Deposition by Fannie Simmons, Apr. 14, 1911, pension file for Moses (Fannie) Simmons; [affidavit] by Friday Hamilton, Mar. 10, 1910, deposition by Lucy Smith, Nov. 10, 1909, depositions by Fannie Simmons and Jane Barnwell, Nov. 11, 1909, depositions by Cuffy Bowles and Bella Smith, Nov. 12, 1909, deposition by Mingo Van Dross, Nov. 13, 1909, T. W. Cuddy, Chief, Law Division to Chief of the Southern Division, Jan. 16, 1909, depositions by Neptune Nicholas, Lucy Smith, and Edward Brown, Jun. 14, 1895, depositions by Fannie Green, William H. Higgins, Jackson Grant, and Anthony Bartlet, Jun. 15, 1895, deposition by Andrew Nichols, Jun. 15, 1895, "Acts of June 27, 1890 and May 9, 1900 Declaration for Widow's Pension," Oct. 17, 1905, "Lawful Widowhood, South Carolina and Georgia," Nov. 26, 1909, "Department of the Interior, Bureau of Pensions," Jul. 28, 1908, general affidavit by Lucy Smith, May 15, 1906, pension file for Richard (Lucy, Fannie) Smith.

93. Deposition by Fannie Simmons, Apr. 14, 1911, pension file for Moses (Fannie) Simmons; T. W. Cuddy, Chief, Law Division to Chief of the Southern Division, Jan. 16, 1909, N. D. Avis to the Commissioner of Pensions, Mar. 20, 1909, deposition by Nellie Ann Brown, Mar. 8, 1909, "Lawful Widowhood, South Carolina and Georgia," Nov. 26, 1909, pension file for Richard (Lucy, Fannie) Smith.

94. E. D. Gallien, Special Examiner to Hon. William Lochren, Commissioner of Pensions, Jun. 28, 1895, deposition by Lucy Smith, Jun. 14, 1895, Commissioner to the Auditor for the War Department, Feb. 20, 1911, "Lawful Widowhood,

South Carolina and Georgia," Nov. 26, 1909, pension file for Richard (Lucy, Fannie) Smith; Shaffer, *After the Glory*, 108.

95. Jonas Green, Beaufort County, US Census 1880; deposition by Mexico Washington, Oct. 10, 1912, deposition by Jack Aiken, Oct. 12, 1912, "Accrued Pension" by Bella Garrett, May 23, 1912, "Act of April 19, 1908 Widow's Pension," May 23, 1912, pension file for Wally (Bella) Garrett, RG 15, NARA; deposition by Ellen J. Harris, Sep. 1, 1915, deposition by Sarah Evans, Sep. 3, 1915, deposition by Charles Nicholas, Oct. 18, 1898, deposition by William Hamilton, Oct. 22, 1898, "No. 622,659 Pension Certificate of Jack Aiken," general affidavit by Caesar Evans, Nov. 13, 1914, general affidavit by M. A. Dessassure, Jun. 8, 1915, pension file for Jack (Jack Jr.) Aiken, RG 15, NARA; death certificate for Ellen Harris, South Carolina Deaths, 1915–1965, South Carolina Department of Archives and History, Columbia.

96. US House of Representatives, *Congressional Record*, Apr. 17, 1874, Feb. 1, 1875, Mar. 3, 1875, Jan. 17, 1876, Jan. 22, 1876, Jan. 7, 1891; "Charge of Receiving an Illegal Pension Fee Dismissed," *Washington Evening Star*, 3/17/1882; "Lawyer Hewlett's Cows," *Washington Critic*, 7/28/1886; "A Requisition from Gov. Lee, The Colored Lawyer Hewlett and Walter Plowden Surrendered to the Virginia Authorities on a Charge of Larceny," *Washington Evening Star*, 7/28/1886; Adverse Reports on War Claims," *Logansport Journal*, 2/28/1880.

97. Claim by John Hammond Moore, 1, 6, 40–41, South Carolina and the Southern Claims Commission, 1871–1888, South Caroliniana Library, University of South Carolina, Columbia, 1990.

98. *Claim of the Heirs of Joshua Nicholls: Hearings Before the United States House Committee on War Claims, Sixty-Third Congress, Second Session, on Feb. 28, 1914* (Washington, DC: GPO, 1914), 3–5, 9, 15–16; "Combahee River Plantations: Rose Hill," in *Private Collection* (Colleton County, SC), 10, 12.

99. *Claim of the Heirs of Joshua Nicholls*, 7, 9–10, 19–21, 24.

100. *Claim of the Heirs of Joshua Nicholls*, 4.

101. P. Barnwell to Dear Sir, Mar. 24, 1926, pension file for William (Relia) Middleton, RG 15, NARA.

102. P. Barnwell to Dear Sir, Mar. 24, 1926, pension file for William (Relia) Middleton.

103. Interview with Ernestine "Tina" Martin Wyatt, Upper Marlboro, MD, Feb. 20, 2023.

104. *The War of the Rebellion: A Compilation of the Official Records of the Union and Confederate Armies*, ser. 1, vol. XXV, pt. 2 (Washington, DC: GPO, 1880–1901), 862; "Nomination for Military Intelligence Hall of Fame Mrs. Harriet Tubman (Deceased)," 4, 15–17, collection of Tina Wyatt.

AFTERWORD

1. Melissa L. Cooper, *Making Gullah: A History of Sapelo Islanders, Race, and the American Imagination* (Chapel Hill: University of North Carolina Press, 2017).

Index

For the benefit of digital users, indexed terms that span two pages (e.g., 52–53) may, on occasion, appear on only one of those pages.

AAS (American Anti-Slavery Society), 134
Abigail (enslaved person), 76–77
Abram (enslaved person), 78
Act Prohibiting the Importation of Slaves (1808), 32, 124–25
Adam (enslaved person), 129–30
Adams, Charles Francis, 167, 182
Adams, Charles Francis, Jr., 236, 240
Adams, Henry, 167
Adams, John M., 270, 314
Adams, John Quincy, 167
Adams, Samuel Hopkins, 94–95
Adams, William, 100–1
Aiken, Jack, 46–47, 70–71, 78, 81, 379–80, 395–96, 432–33, 474, 491, 514–15, 517
Aiken, Jack, Jr., 514–15
Alberti family, 258
Alcott, Louisa May, 204–5
Alcott family, 204–5
Allen, Richard, 135
Allen, T. J., 333–34, 367, 368
Allen, William, 242, 243–44
Alto (enslaved person), 76–77
Amby, Lizzie, 111
Amby, Nat, 100, 111
American Anti-Slavery Society, 138–39, 228–29
American Colonization Society, 134
Ancrum, Aaron, 48–49, 69–70, 422–23, 482, 487, 488–89
Ancrum, Eliza, 69
Andrew (steamship), 220–21
Andrew, John Albion, 174–75, 218, 239–40, 248, 404, 407, 408–9
Anne (C. Barton's cousin), 348–49

Anthony, Kit, 100
Anthony, Leah, 100
Anthony, Susan B., 402
Anti-Slavery Convention (1837), 137–38
Appomattox Courthouse, 471
Apthorp, William Lee, 260, 265, 310, 313–14, 323, 324–25, 326–299, 336–37, 342, 344, 351, 353–54, 357, 405–6
Archie (enslaved person), 166
Army Life in a Black Regiment (Higginson), 239
Arthur, Blake, 223
Ash, Stephen, 267–68
Atlantic (steamship), 174, 189, 218
Atlantic (warship), 156
Austin, George, 25
Averill, Horatio, 150

Bailey, Joe, 144
Baker, Frank, 167, 169, 200
Baker, R. L., 313
Baker, Tom, 510
Ball, Charles, 116
Ball, Elias, 25–26
Baltic (steamship), 174–75, 218
Bannecker, Benjamin, 135
Barnes, Joseph K., 473
Barnett, Thomas, 60, 61
Barnwell, Annie, 493, 494
Barnwell, Jack (father), 37, 40–41, 82, 118, 333, 380, 488, 490, 492
Barnwell, Jack (son), 83, 118, 462
Barnwell, Jane Lee, 380–81
Barnwell, Joseph, 380, 462
Barnwell, Moses, 380, 462

Barnwell, Primus, 37, 40–41, 82–83, 118,
    380, 462, 517
Barnwell, Relia. *See* Middleton, Relia
    Barnwell
Barnwell, Rhina, 462
Barnwell, Robert, 288, 359
Barnwell, Sarah, 82, 83, 118, 380, 462
Barnwell, William, 380
Barnwell family, 462
Barrington, Friday
    in Combahee River Raid, 349–50,
        378, 433, 517
    enslavement of, 125
    escape from slavery, 383
    family of, 386–87, 498
    later years of, 494–95
    origins of, 83–84, 270–71
    pension testimony of, 498–99
    return to Cypress Plantation, 308–9,
        324
Barrington, Joan, 270–71
Barrington, Phoebe, 270–71
Barrington, Tooman, 270–71
Bartley, Anthony, 69, 70–71, 75, 85, 86–87,
        120–21, 126, 386, 387, 395, 447–49,
        497–98, 503, 510, 513, 514
Bartley, Cumsey, 510–11
Bartley, Moriah Haywood, 120–21, 126,
        386–87, 447–49, 451, 497–98, 503
    loss of pension benefits, 510–11, 514
Bartley, Moriah Heywood, 69
Bartley, Tecumseh, 386
Barton, Clara, 348–50
Barton, David, 348–49
Basquire, Mary, 511–12
Basquire, Rudoplh (Adolphus Beckwith;
    Rudolph Beckwith), 511–12
Battle of Olustee, 438–40
Battle of Port Royal, 155–59, 161, 162,
        163, 164–65, 166, 170–73
Beaufort, S.C., 177–80, 190, 192–99
Beauregard, P. T. G., 273–74, 283–84, 290,
        295–96, 364–65, 412, 428–29
Beckham, Fontaine, 146–47
Beckwith, Eliza. *See* McGuire, Elizabeth
    Gabriel Basquiat Lewis
Becky (student), 235
Beecher, Henry Ward, 135
Bell, James A., xxvii–xxviii
Bella (enslaved person), 166, 417, 447–48

Belton, Mary, 473–74
Ben (enslaved person), 197
Benham, Michael, 303
Bennett, Edward, 259–60, 270–71, 378,
        417–18, 433
Bennett, I. S. K., 368–69
Bess (enslaved person), 78
Bess, Aunt (enslaved person), 165
Beuregard, P. G. T., 254
Bibb (steamship), 274
Billingsley, Andrew, 389
Billington, Ray Allen, 228
Billy (enslaved person), 198, 289–90
Binah (enslaved person), 197
Bissell, George, 504–5
Bissell, Henry E., 479
Bissell, John Bennett, 479, 487, 504–5,
        508–9
Black, Robert, 488
"Black Dispataches," 200, 359, 365, 518
Black Joke (slave ship), 26
Blake, Ann Izard, 74
Blake, Arthur, 220–22, 224, 225, 305–6,
        467–68, 478
Blake, Benjamin, 16
Blake, Bungy or Berkley, 224–25, 305–6
Blake, Clarinda, 224–25, 305–6
Blake, Daniel, 72, 74, 78, 366–67
Blake, David, 222, 508
Blake, Elias, 305–6
Blake, Emma Rutledge, 74
Blake, Fibbie, 305–6
Blake, James, 305–6
Blake, Joseph, 223, 285, 479
    slave transactions, 130–31, 197
Blake, London, 218–19
Blake, Maria Hough, 366
Blake, Mary, 305–6
Blake, Mott, 224–25, 302, 305–6
Blake, Nancy, 305–6
Blake, Nitsey, 305–6
Blake, Otto. *See* Blake, Arthur
Blake, Penda Singleton, 221–24, 478
Blake, Peter, 218–19, 222, 223–24, 302,
        467–68, 478
Blake, Pompey, 223
Blake, Robert, 16
Blake, Robert, Jr., 17–18
Blake, Sarah, 305–6
Blake, Sheppard, 305–6

Blake, Simon (Chisholm), 338–39
Blake, Susan, 479
Blake, Walter, 69, 72, 74, 221–23, 224, 283, 285, 286–87, 289–90, 304, 306, 335, 338–39, 366, 368, 371, 374–76, 379, 395–96, 479
    slave transactions, 78, 130–31, 196–98
Blake, William, 74, 130–31, 196, 479
Blake family, 15, 16, 23–24, 138–39
"Bleeding Kansas," 139–40, 161–62
Blockson, Charles, 247
"Bloodhound Act." See Fugitive Slave Act (1850)
Bloomer, Amelia Jenks, 401–2
"Bloomer Delegation," 402
Bluett, Thomas, 7
Boineau, Stephen, 376
Bolze, Amelia, 37, 82, 83
Bolze, Cuffie
    and P. Bolze, 492–93
    death of, 494
    enslavement of, 27, 82–83
    escape from slavery, 333, 378–79, 380, 462, 488, 517
    family of, 37, 40–41, 118
    land purchase of, 488–89
    and F. Lee, 467
    in military, 396, 403–4, 424–25
    and Ella McG. Nicholas, 494
    pension testimony of, 121, 447–48, 449, 450–51, 513
    return to plantation, 487
Bolze, Cuffie (grandfather), 37, 40–41, 83
Bolze, Manuel, 23–24, 26, 27, 31–32, 40–41, 82–83
    family of, 37
Bolze, Primus, 37, 40–41
Bolze, Sarah, 40–41
Bolze, Sina (grandmother), 37, 40–41, 68–69, 83
Bomar, Thomas Haynes, 332, 341–43, 362–63
Bonny Hall Plantation, 15, 69–70, 72, 74, 130–31, 197, 221–23, 283, 304, 306, 334–35, 336, 367, 368, 395–96, 429, 434–35, 479, 504–5, 508
Boston (steamship), 251
Boston, Mass., 137–38
Boston Education Commission for Freedmen. See Education Commission for Freedmen (Boston, Mass.)

Botume, Elizabeth Hyde
    and Gullah Geechee dialect, 454–55, 456–57, 465–66
    on land speculation, 485–86
    pension testimony, 490
    and Port Royal Experiment, 451–54, 458–62, 471–72, 491
    on treatment of slaves, 171
    and Washington family, 483–84
Boutelle, Charles O., 274
Bowers, Charlotte, 47
Bowers, Farbry, 47, 67–68, 81–82, 395–96, 429, 479
    as carpenter at Middleton Place, 69–70, 71
Bowers, Sharper, 47
Bowley, Araminta, 92–93
Bowley, James Alfred, 92–93
Bowley, John, 103, 151
Bowley, Kessiah Jolly, 92–93, 104–5, 151
Boyd, William, 91–92
Boykin, Elizabeth Tunstall, 127
Bradford, Sarah
    as biographer of HT, xix, 4, 499–501
    on "Black Dispatches," 359
    on Combahee River Raid, 322
    on Creole dialect, xxi, 3
    on employment of HT, 357–58
    family of, 94–95
    on HT in refugee camps, 198
    on HT's brothers, 93
    on HT's condition as Brodess' property, 64
    on HT's spirituality, 106
    and misplaced documents, 358
    on Miss Susan's baby, 60
    on night burial, 244–45
Bradstreet, Lionel, 9
Bragg, Gen., 362–63
Bransom (enslaved person), 38
Brayton, Charles R.
    and Battle of Battery Wagner, 413–15, 428–29
    and Combahee River Raid, 310–11, 327, 335
    firing from John Adams, 328, 331, 339–40, 412
    and Fort Sumter, 420–22, 427, 428–29, 430
    Montgomery's report on, 351
    opinion of U.S. Navy, 428–29

Breeden, Peter Lindsay, 331–32, 339–42, 343–44, 363, 364–65, 369–70
Brickler, Alice, 402
Brinkley, William, 110–11
Brisbane, William Henry, 252–54, 480
Briscoe, Sunday, 468
Brodess, Edward
  asked for HT's freedom, 63
  birth of, 55
  death of, 65
  enslavement of Rit and her children, 64–65, 104
  family of, 61
  hires out HT, 58–60
  marriage to E. A. Keene, 58
  move to Bucktown, 57–58
  paid annual wage by HT, 61, 62
  reaches age of majority, 57
  sale of slaves, 92–93, 94
  and A. Thompson, 55–56, 57
Brodess, Eliza Ann Keene, 58, 65–66, 91, 92–93, 94, 104, 107–10, 147
Brodess, Joseph, 55
Brooks, Noah, 163
Brown, Bess, 47
Brown, Caesar, 47
Brown, Captain, 47–48, 70–71, 121, 124, 126–27, 382–83, 497, 505
Brown, Chloe, 47
Brown, Edward
  enslavement of, 47
  escape from slavery of, 380–81
  family of, 83
  land transactions of, 488–89, 490, 492–93
  marriages of, 68–69, 473–74
  in military, 395, 396–97, 408, 417, 431–32
  pension testimony of, 38, 81–82, 423, 449
  as Prime Hand, 69–71, 78, 81, 125
  return to plantation, 487
  and Smiths' marriage, 449
  with wife in military camp, 451
Brown, Emma, 382–83
Brown, Henry "Box," 4, 91, 100–1, 102–3, 108, 133, 135, 518–19
Brown, Honor, 47
Brown, Jane, 382–83

Brown, John
  appearance of, 307
  F. Douglass on, 501
  C. Forten's teachings on, 235
  and F. Sanborn, 356
  J. Giddings on, 263
  and Harper's Ferry Raid, 140–50
  and HT, 355–56, 519
  and J. Montgomery, 264, 301
  and F. Sanborn, 355
  and Secret Six, 9, 401–2
  supporters of, 138
Brown, John (escaped slave), 92
Brown, John, Jr., 143–44
Brown, London, 223
Brown, Mary, 151
Brown, Nancy, 91, 108
Brown, Ned (grandson), 492–93
Brown, Nellie Ann, 513–14
Brown, Oliver, 140
Brown, Peggy Simmons Moultrie, 37, 40–41, 68–69, 82–83, 333, 380, 451, 462
  loss of land, 492–93
Brown, Titus. See Burns, Titus
Brown, Tyra. See Polite, Tyra
Brown, William H., 174–75
Brown, William Wells, 470
Brunson. Lt., 333–34, 336, 341
Bryan, John, xxx
Bryant, Furney, 394–95
Buckra (term), 80, 245
Bull, William, 41, 45
Burnett, Balaam, 46–47, 222, 374, 395–96, 449, 508, 509–10, 511
Burnett, Diana Simmons, 508, 511
  loss of pension benefits, 509–10
Burnett, Jeremiah, 509–10
Burnett, Rose Middleton, 395–96, 449, 508, 509
Burnett, Sally Ladsden Frasier Dash, 374
Burns, Jack, 225, 481
Burns, Lizzie (daughter), 225
Burns, Lizzie (mother), 225
Burns, Martha, 225
Burns, Maurice, 225
Burns, Moses, 225
Burns, Peter, 307–8, 481
Burns, Peter (father), 225
Burns, Peter (son), 224–25

Burns, Phoebe. *See* Frazier, Phoebe Burns

Burns, Thomas, 225

Burns, Titus, 68–69, 83

Burnside, Ambrose, 299–300

Burris, Samuel D., 95–96, 105

Butcher, William, 91–92

Butler, Benjamin F., 168–69, 200, 239, 357

Butler, Matthew C., 443

Butler, Perce Mease, 79

Caesar (enslaved person), 78

Caldwell, James, 239–40

Calhoun, John C., 136–37

Campbell, Jacob, 260, 270–71, 423, 433–34

Campbell, Nannie, 223

Campbell, William, 29–30

Capers, William, 166, 232

Capps, Rusty, 518

Carolina Sports (Elliott), 119

Carver, James E., 309–10, 342, 369, 429

Carver, James M., 271–72, 312, 314

Cassell, Hettie, 78, 81–82

Cassell, Josiah, 81–82

Cassell, Phoebe. *See* Gray, Phoebe Cassell

Catey (enslaved person), 37

Catharina (enslaved person), 75, 86–87

Catton, Charles, 57

Cesar (enslaved person), 241

Chandler, Genevieve Wilcox, 80

Charles (enslaved person), 197, 366–67

Charles, Nelson. *See* Davis, Nelson

Charles II, King of England, 15

Charley (enslaved person), 366–67

Chase, John, 91–92

Chase, Salmon P., 167, 181–82, 204–5, 206, 210–11, 237

Cheever, George B., 253–54

Cheney, Ednah Dow, 138, 175

Chesapeake Bay, 4–5

Chesnut, James, Jr., 127

Chesnut, Mary Boykin, 127–29, 170–71, 443

Child, Lydia Marie, 137–39, 238

Chisholm, Alexander Robert, 283–84, 306–7, 327–28

Chisholm, March, 38, 82, 372–73, 512–13

Chisholm, Molcy, 372–73, 512–13, 515

Chisholm, Quarko, 69

Chisholm, Sam, 509

Chisholm, Sarah Constance, 283–84

Chisholm, Simon. *See* Blake, Simon

Chloe (enslaved person), 47, 78, 81

Chrisholm, George, 302, 307–8

Christy, Edward Pearce, 337

Civil War pension system. *See* pension system

Clark, Charles, 32–33

Clay, Mary, 49–50

Cleveland, Charles H., 518

Clinch, Mary Lamont, 373–74

Clinch, Sophia Gibbs Couper, 373–74

Clinton, Catherine, xxxii

Coburn, Reverend, 69

Coffin, Charles Carleton, 164–65

Cohen, Gabriel, 225, 302

Coleman, Reverend, 44–45, 87

Colleton, John, 18–19

Collins, Charles, 32–33

Combahee Ferry, 41, 286, 288–90, 296–97, 304, 325, 327, 328, 329, 330, 333–34, 335, 336, 338–40, 341, 344, 359, 363, 364–65, 366, 467

pontoon bridge, 289, 296–97, 327–28, 331, 332, 334–35, 336, 338–41, 344, 350, 351, 360, 363, 365, 366, 371–72, 375, 412, 463–64

Combahee Refugee Camp, 457–62. *See also* Old Fort Plantation

The Combahee River Raid (Grigg), xxii–xxiii

Comte du Nord (slave ship), 31–32

Confiscation Acts (1861-1862), 212

Conklin, Dick. *See* Kirkland, Dick

Connelly, J. H., 507

Conrad, Earl, xxii, 143–44, 357, 402, 414, 416, 518

Cook, James, 59–60, 93–94

Coomba (enslaved person), 197

Cooper, Anna Julia, 1

Cooper, Samuel, 362–63

Coosaw River, 171–72, 180, 190, 284, 288, 289, 306–7, 311–12, 313–14, 342, 343–44

Cornish, Aaron, 59, 100

Corwin, B. Ryder, 314, 412, 418–19, 431, 440–41, 492

Cosmopolitan (steamship), 260–61

Creole dialect, xxi, 3. *See also* Gullah Geechee culture and dialect

Crofut, E. A., 502–3
Crokatt, James, 18
Cruel, Renty. *See* Greaves, Renty
Cruger, Henry N., 38–39, 82
Cruger, Nicholas, 34
CSS Louisa, 220
CSS Merrimack (later *Virginia*), 272–73
Cuddy, T. A., 513–14
Cugoano, Ottobah, 4, 135
Cunningham, Solomon, 391–92
Cuthbert, James, 47–48
    slave transactions, 121–22, 124
Cuthbert, Sarah, 261
Cypress Plantation, 15, 27, 38, 40–41, 67,
    68–69, 84, 120–21, 130–31, 197, 304,
    308–9, 324, 328–29, 331–32, 333–34,
    338, 339, 340, 341, 364, 366–67, 370,
    371, 376, 377–79, 387–88, 417, 424–
    25, 432–33, 446–47, 449, 477, 490,
    496, 513, 522–23, 525

Dago (enslaved person), 368
Dahlgren, John A., 278, 412, 413–14, 419,
    427–28, 430, 437–38, 464, 467
Dall, Caroline, 138
Daniel (enslaved preacher), 69
Daniel (son of L. K. Simmons), 380–81
Daphne (enslaved person), 241
Daphne (enslaved person, likely mother
    of Peggy Simmons Brown), 37
Darling, Thomas, 511
Dash, Lewis, 374, 508–9
Dash, Sally Ladsden Fraser, 508–10
Davies, Henry E., Jr., 442–43
Davis, Jefferson, 159, 288
Davis, Nelson, xxii, 439, 499, 502
Davis, William Watts, 271
Davy (enslaved person), 338–39
Dawson, John Huger, 37, 82
Dawson, Parris, 482
DeCauster, Cornelia, 382
DeCauster, Isaac, 37, 48–49, 85, 86–87,
    126–27, 382–83, 461, 485, 490, 505
DeCauster, Kate, 49, 382, 490
DeCauster, May, 382
DeCauster, Pompey, 382, 490
DeCauster, Silvia Jackson Gaylord, 49,
    75–76, 84–85, 116–17, 129–30, 382,
    485, 490–91, 503
de la Conseillere, Benjamin, 18

Dellum, James, 92
Dellum, John P., 92
Denton, Vachell, 6
Dependent and Disability Pension Act
    (1890), 498–99, 502, 512–13
DeSaussure, Louis D., 367, 368
DeWolf, James, 32–33
Diallo, Ayuba Suleyman (Job ben
    Solomon), 5–8, 108
Dick (enslaved person), 196, 197, 289–90
Dick (student), 234–35
Dickey, William, 515–16
Dinah (enslaved person), 38, 131, 197
Doar, David, 23
Dolly (enslaved person), 338–39
Douglass, Charles, 239–40
Douglass, Frederick, 322
    as abolitionist, 518–19
    and John Brown, 142–43, 145, 146, 501
    on burning of Darien, 406–7
    Douglass' Monthly, 322
    family of, 359
    and W. L. Garrison, 134, 137
    lectures of, 135–36, 139, 469–70
    letters concerning HT, 499–500, 501
    The Life and Times of Frederick Douglass,
    142–43
    literacy of, 4
    Narrative of the Life of Frederick Douglass,
    an American Slave, 135
    racist treatment of, 473
    as recruiter, 239–40
Douglass, Lewis Henry, 239–40, 359,
    420–21, 425–26, 468–69, 499, 517–18
Douglass' Monthly, 322, 350–51
"Dover Eight," 111–12
Drayton, Daphney, 498
Drayton, Thomas F., 156, 158–59, 162, 170
Drayton, William, 81, 382, 396–97, 506,
    515–16
DuBois, Theodore B., 220
Du Pont (Confederate officer), 267–68
Du Pont, Samuel Francis, 156, 157, 166–
    67, 292, 293, 294–95
    Anaconda strategy of, 161
    criticism of U.S. Navy, 212–13
    dismissal of, 349
    and Fort Sumter, 426–27
    and S. F. Frizelle, 220–21
    and G. A. Prentiss, 219–20

and siege attempt on Charleston,
273–78
and R. Smalls, 216–17
Durant, Henry K., 403, 452, 499–500

E. B. Hale (steamship), 291–92, 293–95,
304, 313–14
Edens, Lt., 343–44
Edmundson, Mary, 133
Education Commission for Freedmen
(Boston, Mass.), 233, 235
Elliott, Edward, 498
Elliott, Thomas, 110–11, 144
Elliott, Thomas Rhett Smith
slave transactions, 121, 124, 126–27, 456,
510–11
Elliott, William, (son of T. S. R. Elliot),
510–11
Elliott, William, IV (son-in-law of T. R.
Smith and father of T. R. S. Elliott),
13–14, 76–77, 121–22, 126–27, 319,
456
author of *Carolina Sports, by Land and
Water: Including Incidents of Devil-
Fishing, Wild-Cat, Deer and Bear
Hunting Etc. 1846,* 119
Elliott family, 76–77
Elwell, John J., 348–49
Ely, Ralph, 288–89, 304, 359
Emancipation Proclamation, 212, 236,
251–55, 258, 390
Emanuel, William P., 290, 295–96, 313,
321–22, 330–33, 340, 341–44, 350,
362–65
Ennals, Marie, 147
Ennals, Stephen, 147
Ennells, Noah, 91–92
Ephraim (teaching assistant), 232
Equiano, Olaudah, 4, 135
Etowah (ship), 214
Eve (enslaved person), 338–39

Faber, Henry F., 85, 299
will of, 48–49
Faber, Joseph W., 48
Faber, Mary Anna Lynah Kirkland.
See Nicholls, Mary Anna Lynah
Kirkland Faber
Farmer, Charles H., 510–11
Ferguson, Peter, 509

"fever district", 293, 354, 365. *See also*
malaria; sickly season
Fields, Anson, xxix–xxx
Fields, Elizabeth, 69
Fields, Hector, xxix–xxx, 269–70, 314,
339, 450, 488, 502–3
Fields, Hector (son), 488
Fields, Jonas (brother of Hector and
great-great-great-uncle of author),
xxix, 269, 270, 488
Fields, Jonas (cousin of author's
grandfather), xxix–xxx
Fields, Judy, xxix–xxx
Fields, Margaret, xxix–
Fields, Peggy, 488
Fields, William "Billy," 270, 482
First Confiscation Act (1861), 169, 212
Fisher, Eliza Middleton, 73–74, 77–78,
141–42
Fisher, Joshua Francis, 72–73
Fletchall, Thomas, 29
Flora (enslaved person), 197
Flora (steamship), 251
Flowers, Jack, 171–72
Forbes, Hugh, 144, 145
Forten, Charlotte L.
on Battery Wagner, 416
on boatmen's hymns, 178
early life, 227–28
and Emancipation Proclamation
celebrations, 251–52, 254–55
and 1st South Carolina Volunteers, 258
and E. Hawks, 248
on language, 241
nursing work of, 416
and Port Royal Experiment, 166–67,
188, 229–30, 231, 233, 235, 257–58,
390, 441–42
and praise houses, 242–43, 244, 246
and C. L. Redmond, 239–40
on Shaw and his men, 411
on stories of HT, 246–49
Forten, James, 135–36, 227–29
Foster, Captain, 306–7
Foster, John G., 464
Fox, Gustavus, 166, 273
Francis, John, 236
Frank (enslaved person), 38
Fraser, Sam, 508–9
Frasier, W. E., 503–4

Frazier, Dembo, 482
Frazier, Lauretta, 474
Frazier, Phoebe Burns, 39, 68–69, 83–84, 125, 378, 386–87, 474, 498–99, 502
Frazier, Robert, 27, 68–69, 70–71, 84, 395, 411, 474, 498
Freedmen's Aid Society, 189–90, 192
Freedmen's Relief Association, 183
French, Austa Malinda Winchell, 178, 209, 242–43
French, Edwin, 506
French, Mansfield, 178, 182, 253–54, 271, 379
Fripp, Charles E., 489
Fripp, Edgar, 270
Fripp, Mr., 342–43
Frizelle, Seymour F., 220–21
Fugitive Slave Act (1850), 97–98, 104–6, 136, 139–40, 228
Fugitive Slave Law (1839; Ohio), 237
Fuller, C. E., 195
Fuller, Hector, 270
Fuller, Mintee, 270
Fuller, Thomas, 171–72, 270, 482
Furness, William Henry, 189–90

Gabriel, Winnie, 511–12
Gage, Frances, 186, 227
Gage, Thomas, 29–30
Gaillard, Bella, 380–81
Gaillard, Samuel, 482
Gannett, William Channing, 186, 191, 238, 465
Garibaldi, Giuseppe, 144
Garnett, Henry Highland, 4, 102–3, 469–70, 518–19
Garrett, Bella Jones Lucas, 395–96, 479, 514–15
Garrett, Daphne. See Wright, Daphne Garrett Washington
Garrett, Lucinda, 27, 46
Garrett, Ofney, 27, 46
Garrett, Rose, 46–47
Garrett, Thomas, 95–98, 99–100, 101, 103, 105–6, 110–11, 133–34, 247
Garrett, Wally, 27, 46–47, 69, 70–71, 121–22, 391–92, 395–96, 449, 468, 504–5, 508, 514–15
Garrett family, 46

Garrison, George, 198–200, 236, 359, 403, 437–38, 499, 517–18
Garrison, Helen Eliza Benson, 138–39, 198–99
Garrison, Lucy McKim, 242, 243–44
Garrison, William Lloyd, 134–40
    on John Brown, 149
    burning of Constitution, 145–46
    family of, 198–99, 236, 499
    and J. Forten, 228–29
    and HT, 146, 199, 200, 205–6, 359
    and introduction of HT and Gov. Andrew, 174
    and J. Montgomery, 263–64
    and PASS, 97–98
    and Shaw family, 404
    on "the shout," 243–44
    See also The Liberator
Garvin, George, 393
Gatson, Stephen, 393
Gaylord, Samson, 84–85, 129–30, 382
Gaylord, Silvia Jackson, 382
General Huth (slave ship), 31
General McClellan (steamship). See McClellan (steamship)
George (enslaved person), 370
George III, King, 29, 30
Georgie, Miss, 80
Gettes, Emmanuel, xxix–xxx
Gibson, Mary, 91–92
Giddings, Joshua, 237–38
Gignilliat, Jane Elizabeth, 19–20
Gilchrist, Archer E., 332, 341–42, 363
Gillard, Beck, 270
Gillard, Dan, 270
Gillard, Samuel, 270
Gilliard, Ansel, 372–73
Gilliard, Bella, 372–73
Gilliard, Harry, 372–73
Gilliard, Isiah, 372–73
Gilliard, Nat, 372–73
Gilliard, Nelly, 372–73
Gilliard, Polly Smith, 372–73
Gilliard, Richmond, 372–73
Gillison, Clara, xxx
Gillmore, Quincy Adams
    and Battery Wagner, 412–14, 417–18, 419
    and Battle of Olustee, 437–38, 440
    and Charleston, S.C., 430–31, 467

and Fort Sumter, 423, 425, 426, 427–28
and HT, 199, 301, 409–10, 450
military career of, 213, 278, 357, 393,
    407–8
on J. Montgomery, 411
and W. Plowden, 303, 357–58
and Tybee Island, 203–4
Glanding, Charles Wesley, 95–97
Godbold, H., 332, 341–42, 343, 363
Godfrey, Caleb, 24–25
Godin, Benjamin, 18
Godon, S. W., 292
Gonzalez, Ambrose Elliott, 455–56
"Gordon" (subject of engravings), 394–
    95, 397
Grace, C. M., 383–84
Gradual Abolition Act (1780;
    Pennsylvania), 96
Graham, John, 488–89
Graham, Molly, 488–89
Graham, Stephen, xxx
Graham, Wally, 131, 196–97, 204, 222–23,
    289, 306, 335, 349–50, 379, 485–86
    and William C. Heyward, 482
Grandfather Stories (Hopkins), 499
Grant, Abraham, 429
Grant, Anne, 47–48, 121
Grant, Carolina, 69–70, 86–88, 123, 126,
    386
Grant, Dorcas Lee, 387, 447
Grant, Elizabeth M., 490
Grant, Flora, 86–88, 123, 126, 386, 423
Grant, Jackson
    and Bartleys' marriage, 448
    death of, 492
    and deaths of comrades, 497–98
    enslavement of, 69–70, 120–22, 124,
        126, 326
    escape from slavery, 382–83, 387
    family of, 47–48
    marriage, 449, 513
    military service of, 391–92, 395
    pension claim, 504–5, 517
    pension testimony, 408, 432–34, 447,
        507, 510–11
    purchase of land, 482
    return to plantation, 487
    and Smiths' marriage, 449
    and Wineglass's marriage, 507
Grant, Jackson (grandfather), 121–22

Grant, Joseph, 91–92
Grant, Phillis, 386
Grant, R. B., 490
Grant, Sam, 47–48, 121–22, 126
Grant, Samuel, 124
Grant, Sarah, 47–48, 121, 124, 126
Grant, Stephany (Stepheny; Stepney),
    69–70, 86–87, 123, 126, 386, 396–97,
    423
Grant, Ulysses S., 442, 471
Graves, Sarah, 37
Gray, Jeffrey, 70–71, 81–82, 429, 479
Gray, Phoebe Cassell, 78, 81–82, 479
Great Skedaddle, 163–64, 210, 285
Greaves, Renty, 223
Green, Ben, 218–19
Green, Caesar, 513
Green, Dorcas, 131, 196–97
Green, Harriet "Rit" (mother of HT),
    9–10, 53–56, 57–58, 61, 63–64, 92–
    93, 104, 112
Green, John, 270
Green, Jonas
    death of, 492
    enslavement of, 131
    escape from slavery, 196–97, 204, 222–
        23, 289, 335, 349–50, 379–80
    family of, 514–15
    and S. B. Y. Green, 482, 496–97
    land purchase, 481–82, 485–86, 491
    pension testimony, 78–79, 81
    and S. Washington, 471–72
    and work for government, 224
Green, Joshua, 492
Green, July, 482
Green, Kitty, 108–9
Green, Lear, 100–1, 102–3
Green, Samuel (Reverend), 110–11, 112
Green, Samuel, Jr., 108–9
Green, Sina Bolze Young
    birth, 40–41
    enslavement of, xxvii–xxviii, 27, 37,
        40–41
    escape from slavery, 378–80
    family of, 82–83, 118, 462, 514–15
    and Jonas Green, 482
    landholdings of, 485, 491, 492, 493
    marriage of, 68–69
    pension claim, 496–97
    pension testimony of, 333, 432–33

Green, William, 81, 482
Greenleaf, Arthur W., 393
Gregory, Solomon, 302, 307–8
Griffith, Alexander, 98–99
Grigg, Jeff, xxii–xxiii
Grimball, Samuel, 417–18
Grimké, Charlotte Forten. *See* Forten, Charlotte L.
Guerard, Benjamin, 41–42
Gullah Geechee culture and dialect, xxvii–xxviii, 27, 51, 80, 244–46, 454–57, 466, 495
Guterman, Benjamin, xxii

Habersham, Robert, 49–50, 75–76
Hagar (enslaved person), 122
Hale (steamship), 220, 221
Hale, Edward Everett, 186
Hall, Albert Bushnell, 416
Hall, Charles, 144
Hall, Prince, 4
Hall, Romulus (George Weems), 112
Hamilton, Amy. *See* Hamilton, Emily
Hamilton, Arizona, 494–95, 517
Hamilton, Binah. *See* Mack, Binah Hamilton
Hamilton, Cilla, 47–48, 121, 126–27, 382–83
Hamilton, Elizabeth Matthews Heyward, 34–36
Hamilton, Emily, 123, 126, 380–81, 382–83
Hamilton, Florence, 380–81
Hamilton, Frank, 47–48, 69–70, 121, 122, 124, 126–27, 382–83, 433–34, 449, 497, 505
Hamilton, Frederick Ulysses, 494–95, 517
Hamilton, Friday
    and Bartleys' marriage, 448
    enslavement of, 47–48, 70–71, 83, 123, 126
    escape from slavery, 382–83
    family of, 383–84, 495
    on J. Grant, 121–22
    land purchase, 493, 494–95
    migration, 494
    military service of, 395, 417–18
    pension testimony of, 430, 504–5
    and J. Simmons, 497–98
Hamilton, George, 123, 126, 382–84

Hamilton, Hagar (grandmother), 47–48, 52, 121, 123–24, 129, 318, 320, 323–24, 347, 379, 430
Hamilton, Harry, 123–24, 129
Hamilton, Irene, 494–95, 517
Hamilton, James, 34–35, 38–39
Hamilton, Martha, 447–48
Hamilton, Minus
    death of, 486
    dialect of, 457
    enslavement of, 51–52, 123–24
    escape from slavery, 310, 317, 318, 320, 321–22, 323–24, 345, 347, 379, 382, 383, 406
    family of, 430
Hamilton, Samuel, 380–81
Hamilton, Sibby, 52, 123–24, 129
Hamilton, Sylla, 124
Hamilton, Tenah Jenkins, 121, 122, 126–27, 382–83, 386–87, 449, 497
Hamilton, William, 386–88, 395, 433–34, 447
Hamilton, William (father), 27
Hamilton, William (grandson), 380–81
Hamilton, William (son), 27, 69–70, 81, 120–22, 380–78
Hampton, Wade, 285, 444, 469
Hanna, Read, 510, 511
Hannah (enslaved person), 38
Hansbrough, Blucher W., 150
Hansbrough, Peter, 150
Hanson, Daniel D., 415, 431–32, 434
Hanson, Paul P., 471–72
Hardenbergh, Charles, 55, 65
Hardenbergh, Johannes, 55
Hare (slave ship), 24–25, 75–76
Harney, William S., 141–42
Harper's Ferry Raid, 140–45, 146–50
Harriet A. Weed (steamer), xix
    in Combahee River Raid, 322–23, 326–27, 341, 342, 343
    destruction of, 440
    "The Raid on Combahee," 299–301, 309, 310–15
Harriet Tubman (Johnson; painting), 500–1
Harriet Tubman, the Moses of Her People (Bradford), 500–1
Harrington, Samuel, 92
Harris, Abram, 112

Harris, Andrew, 50–51, 69–70, 75, 117, 118, 126, 325, 326, 387–88, 395, 405–6, 434, 471, 487
Harris, Diana Days, 69, 70–71, 116–18, 126, 131, 222, 325, 326, 387–88, 434, 487, 503
Harris, Ellen, 514–15, 517
Harris, Hagar, 117
Harris, Hannah, 117
Harris, Hercules, 117
Harris, Rachel, 117
Harris, Samuel, 117, 118, 126, 326, 387–88
Hassell, Catherine De Nully, 38–39, 82
Hauseman, Henry, 259
Hawkins, Chester, 95–96
Hawkins, Emeline, 95–97
Hawkins, Isaac, 304
Hawkins, Samuel, 95–96, 98–99, 112, 247
Hawkins, Samuel, Jr., 95–96
Hawks, Esther Hill, 227, 416, 450
Hawks, John, 248
Hawks, John Milton, 393
Hawley, J. R., 438
Haynes, March, 213, 218–19, 348, 357
Hayward, Adam, 283–84, 306
Hayward, Adeline, 306
Hayward, Cecilia, 306–7
Hayward, Celia, 306
Hayward, Cinda, 306
Hayward, Cipper, 306–7
Hayward, Emma, 306
Hayward, Harriet, 306–7
Hayward, Henrietta, 306
Hayward, Isaac, 218–19, 283–84, 302, 306–7, 311
    and William C. Heyward, 306
Hayward, Jane, 306–7
Hayward, January, 306
Hayward, Joe, 283–84, 306
Hayward, John, 120–21
Hayward, Kit, 283–84, 306
Hayward, Lucy, 306–7
Hayward, Mary, 306–7
Hayward, Oliver, 283–84
Hayward, Overt, 306
Hayward, Rosa, 306
Hayward, Samuel, 378
Hayward, Sarah, 306–7
Hayward, Tom, 306
Hayward, William C., 478

Haywood, Celia Cassell, 78
Haywood, Sandy, 393
Henderson, C. G., 492–93
Henderson, Edward P., 492–93, 509
Hendricks, Lt., 332
Hendrix, Lt., 363
Henry, John Campbell, 91–92
Henry, William, 150
Henry Parker Middleton, 126
Hercules (enslaved person), 76–77
Hering, Constantine, 189–90
Hessel, Andrew, 432
Hettie (teacher), 232
Hewitt, William E., 313, 321–22, 330, 342–43, 363, 364–65
Heyward, Barnwell, xxx
Heyward, Benjamin, 20
Heyward, Blake, xxx
Heyward, Catherine Maria Clinch, 371–76, 378
Heyward, Charles, 300, 308–9, 338–40, 373–74, 375–76, 475, 508–9
Heyward, Daniel (great-grandson), 19–20, 34, 35–36, 478
Heyward, Daniel (great-great-grandson), 34
Heyward, Daniel (immigrant to Carolina Colony), 15, 19–20, 32–33, 121–22
Heyward, Dolly, 27
Heyward, Duncan Clinch, 21, 22, 67–68, 70, 308–9
Heyward, Edward Barnwell, 373–74, 475, 476
Heyward, Hannah Shubrick, 35–36
    slave transactions, 36–37, 43–44, 82
Heyward, Henrietta, 21–22
Heyward, Horris, 27
Heyward, Isaac, 344
Heyward, James, 21–22, 39, 83, 120–21, 125, 126, 270–71, 386–87
Heyward, Jane (relative of Isaac), 306–7
Heyward, Mary Miles, 19–20, 34, 35–36
Heyward, Nathaniel, xxx, 20, 21–22, 34, 35–36, 40–41, 89, 290, 300, 373–74, 375, 475, 488
Heyward, Nathaniel Barnwell (grandson), 290, 488–89
Heyward, Samuel, 302
Heyward, Sarah Cruger, 34–36, 38–39, 119, 374–75

Heyward, Tattie. *See* Heyward, Catherine Maria Clinch
Heyward, Thomas, Jr., 20, 21–22, 34
Heyward, Thomas, Sr., 34
Heyward, Thomas Savage, 376
Heyward, W. H., 345
Heyward, William, 35–36, 119
  slave transactions, 82, 83, 125
Heyward, William, Jr., 35–37, 38–39, 40–41, 43–44
Heyward, William Cruger
  and Battery Wagner, 419
  claims for compensation, 377–81, 396, 435
  and Combahee River Raid, 317, 324, 328–30, 331, 332–34, 338, 345
  death of, 478
  family of, 36, 40–41, 119, 386–87, 488
  and W. Graham, 482
  military service of, 155, 158–59
  neighbors of, 131–32, 488–89
  plantation restored to heirs, 477
  "The Raid on Combahee," 283, 284, 290, 298, 300, 304, 306, 308–9
  rice harvest value, 384
  slaves of, 38, 39–41, 83, 84, 120–21, 462, 496
  slave transactions, 83, 125, 270–71
Heyward, William Henry, 488
Heyward family, 15, 19–22, 23–24, 35–36, 40, 51, 286, 369–70
Higgins, Billy, 40
Higgins, Venus Proctor, 38
Higgins, William, 68–69
Higginson, Hugh, 337
Higginson, Thomas Wentworth
  and 1st South Carolina Volunteers, 236, 239–41, 256–59, 354, 453–54
  and C. Barton, 348–49
  and "Bloomer Delegation," 402
  and John Brown, 148–49, 174
  on buring of Darien, 407
  and Camp Saxton, 251, 252
  and Combahee River Raid, 317, 318, 320, 321, 323–24, 345
  and Corwin's court-martial, 440–41
  and Emancipation Proclamation celebrations, 253–54
  on C. Forten, 227–28, 230
  and Gullah Geechee dialect, 457

  and HT, 145–46
  on laundresses, 195
  as member of "Secret Six," 140, 141–42, 144
  and J. Montgomery, 261, 264, 354, 410, 425–26, 431
  refugee camp named after, 482
  sermons of, 135, 136–37
  and St. Johns River expedition, 264–69
  as supporter of women's rights, 137–38
  on veteran landowners, 478–79
historical records, xxii–xxiv, xxx–xxxi, xxxii
Hitchcock, Ethan Allen, 516
Hodgson, Adam, 22–23
Hogg, William, 102
Hoit, Augustus Alonzo, 265, 312, 328, 335, 339–40
Holden, Oliver B., 412
Hollis, James, 110–11
Holmes, Annie Cassell McNeal Lawrence, 379
Honor (enslaved person), 78
Hopkins, Samuel M., Jr., 499
Horwitz, Tony, 142
Howard, Dick, 223
Howard, Oliver Otis, 462–63
Howard, William B., 431
Howe, Frank, 174
Howe, Julia Ward, 141–42, 235
Howe, Samuel Gridley, 141–42
Huger, Cleland Kinloch, Jr., 371
Huger, William Elliott, 476–77
Hughes, Denard, 110–11, 144
Hunn, John, 95–96, 97, 105, 112, 247
Hunn, Lizzie, 244, 246–48
Hunter, David, 161–62
  and C. Barton, 348–49
  Blacks' mistrust of, 255
  and P. Burns, 307
  and capture of Fort Pulaski, 203–4
  and Combahee River Raid, 350, 354, 357–58
  evacuation of refugees, 190–91
  and 54th Massachusetts regiment, 404–5
  and HT, 175, 248, 301
  "Hunter's Regiment," 208–14, 237–39, 242–43, 269

and A. Lincoln, 269
ousting of, 407–10
and W. Plowden, 303, 515
and 2nd South Carolina Volunteers, 255–56
and W. Seward, 472–513
and siege of Charleston, 273, 277–78
and St. Johns River expedition, 268
and 10th Army Corps, 260–61
and transport of refugees, 225
Hunter, Tera, 39, 449
Huron (gunboat), 216
Hutchinson, Jesse, Jr., 337
Hutchinson, Thomas Leger, 381

"I Have Come to Tell You Something About Slavery" (Douglass), 135–36
Incidents in the Life of a Slave Girl (Jacobs), 469–70
I'on, Jacob Bond, 43–44
Irvine, Matthew, 38–39
Irving, Washington, 134–35
Izard, Allen S., 476–77
Izard, Francis, 296–98, 301, 341, 474
Izzard, Alan, xxx
Izzard, Thomas, 81–82
Izzard, Tom, 46–47
Izzard, William, 67, 81–82, 474, 517

Jackson, Dorcas, 126
Jackson, Jacob, 50–51, 75, 86–87, 126
Jackson, Robin, 223
Jackson, Simon, 86–87
Jacob (enslaved person), 338–39, 380–81
Jacobs, Harriet, 469–70
James (enslaved person), 338–39
James, Peter, 378–79
Janie (wife of Jack Aiken), 81
Janus (enslaved person), 198, 289–90, 383
J. C. Smith (ship), 304
Jeffords, Robert J., 292–93, 441–44
and Hutchinson Island, 290–92
protested troops on lower Combahee River during sickly season, 362–63
Jemmy (Stono leader), 519
Jenkins, Daniel, 121, 126–27, 382–83, 386–87, 395
Jenkins, David, 70–71
Jenkins, Jack, 225
Jenkins, Miriam, 225

Jenkins, Tenah. *See* Hamilton, Tenah Jenkins
Joe (enslaved person), 248–49
Joe (enslaved person/freedom seeker), 196
John (enslaved person), 366–67
John Adams (gunboat), xix, 256–58, 266, 268, 371–72, 413, 434–35
in Combahee River Raid, 322, 326–28, 329, 330, 332, 335, 336, 337–38, 339–42, 343–44
"The Raid on Combahee," 299, 309, 310–11, 312–14
in St. John's expedition, 266, 268
in St. Mary's expedition, 256–58
Johnson, Andrew, 476
Johnson, Ann, 92
Johnson, Ben, 508–9
Johnson, Robert, 17–18
Johnson, Walter, 36
Johnson, William H., 500–1
Johnson, Winnebar, 108–9
Joiner, Tyra. *See* Polite, Tyra
Jolly, Linah Ross, 56, 64–65, 92–93, 94
Jones, Bella, 69, 222
Jones, Elsie Higgins, 37, 67, 68–70, 333, 387, 485, 496
Jones, George Noble, 50
Jones, John, 395–96
Jones, William, 50–51, 69–71, 83, 326, 334, 387–88, 395, 432–35, 482, 485–86, 496, 498
Jordan, Thomas, 296, 364–65
Joseph Whitney (steamship), 203
Josh (captured man), 238
Josiah (enslaved person), 78

Kane, Dempsey P., 64–65
Kane, Jane, 109
Kansas, 139–41
Kansas-Nebraska Act (1854), 136–37, 139–40, 237
Kate (enslaved person), 75, 86–87
Keach, Andrew O., 467
Keith, C. C., 38–39, 82
Keitt, Lawrence M., 345, 350
Kelley, Esther, 95
Kelley, L. M., 509–10
Kelly, Margaret, 69
Kelton, Patty, 223

Kemble, Frances (Fanny), 79, 244–45
Keokuk (ironclad), 274–75, 276
Kiah, Emily, 110–11
Kiah, Mary, 111
Kiah, William, 110–11
Kilpatrick, Judson, 462–63
Kinloch, Christie Anne, 68–69
Kirkland, Dick, 197–98
Kirkland, Joseph, 41–42
Kirkland, Marianne Kennan Guerard, 41–42
 will of, 43
Kirkland, Mary Anna Lynah. *See*
  Nicholls, Mary Anna Lynah
  Kirkland Faber
Kirkland, Mary Miller Withers, 125–26,
  127–29, 441–42, 444, 445–47
 gifts to, 384–85
Kirkland, Moses, Jr., 30
Kirkland, Moses, Sr., 29–31, 41–42
Kirkland, William Lennox, Jr., 334, 510–11
 and Battle of Port Royal, 170
 claims for compensation, 384–88, 435
 and Combahee River Raid, 325, 326,
  345, 367–71, 374–75, 376, 505
 exchange of property with mother,
  125–27, 382
 family of, 85–86, 443
 Hickory Hill plantation, 39
 inheritance, 43, 123
 injury and death of, 444–46, 447
 land transactions, 484–85
 marriage, 125–26, 127, 128
 marriages of slaves, 69
 military service of, 419–20, 441–42
 "The Raid on Combahee," 283, 285,
  286, 289–90, 298–99, 300, 304, 315
 slaves of, 47–48, 49, 50–51, 118, 197–98,
  486
 slave transactions, 76–77, 83, 120–22,
  124, 125–27, 382, 456
 and "William Savage Negroes," 50–51
Kirkland, William Lennox, Sr., 41–42,
  84–85
 will of, 43
Kirkland family, 15, 28, 29, 41–43, 76–77,
  87–88, 116–17, 300, 369–70, 444–45,
  447

Ladson, James, 84–85
Lampriere, Sarah, 43–44

Landers, Jean, 416
Langford, Fanny, 484
Larson, Kate Clifford, xxii, 60–61, 143–
  44, 518
Launch Plantation, 313, 342–43, 369, 370,
  446
Laurens, Henry, 25–26, 75–76
Lawrence, March, 81, 379, 395–96
Lay, John F., 313, 351, 359–60, 364–65, 368
Leah (enslaved person), 165
Old Leah, 459–60
LeCompte, Bill, 91–92
Lee, Bernard K., 192–93
Lee, Dorcas, 122
Lee, Francis D., 162
Lee, Lucy. *See* Smith, Lucy Lee
Lee, Robert E., 159, 160–61, 162–63, 217,
  284–85, 286–87, 365, 442–43, 462–63,
  471, 518
Lee, Siras, 83
Legare, Joan, 39, 83, 125, 378, 386–87
Legare, Tooman, 39, 83, 125, 378
Leightley, Private, 336, 341
Leverton, Hannah, 95
Lewis, James, 49
Lewis, Mary Ann, 49, 50–51, 75–76, 85,
  86–87, 116–17, 126, 387, 486, 503
Lewis, Noah, 511–12
The Liberator, 134–35, 137, 149, 173, 228–
  29, 402
The Life and Times of Frederick Douglass
  (Douglass), 142–43
Lighthouse, Monday, 334
Lincoln, Abraham
 allowing Blacks in military, 224,
  239–40
 cabinet of, 472
 and colonization, 134
 designates Beaufort National
  Cemetery, 506
 and F. Douglass, 501
 and Emancipation Proclamation, 212,
  236, 253, 255
 and General Orders No. 11, 210–11,
  212
 and D. Hunter, 269
 "Lincoln's gunboats," 322, 335–36
 and E. L. Pierce, 206, 207–8
 second inauguration, 469–70
Loguen, Jermain W., 143–44

London (enslaved person), 244–45
Longbrow Plantation, 15, 75–76, 84–85, 87, 125–26, 128–29, 171, 299–300, 301, 314, 335, 340, 365–66, 368–69, 379, 381–83, 386, 419, 479, 484–85, 488–89
"Losses from the War," 374–75
Lougen, Helen Amelia, 359, 420–21, 426
Louisa (mother of Hagar Nicholas), 380–81
Louisa (schooner), 225
Loundes, July, 123–24
Louverture, Toussaint, 235
Lowcountry Creoles. *See* Gullah Geechee culture and dialect
Lowcountry dialect. *See* Gullah Geechee culture and dialect
Lowndes, Charles, 16–19, 84–85, 89, 323
Lowndes, Charles (son of Charles Lowndes), 17–18
Lowndes, Charles Tidyman, 76, 131–32, 331, 340, 345, 369–71, 372, 374–76, 382, 435, 444–45, 477
    "The Raid on Combahee", 283, 285, 298, 314
    slave transactions, 44, 326
Lowndes, Edward Rutledge, 52, 123–24, 129, 320
Lowndes, James, 51, 89, 123–24, 296, 330, 350
    slave transactions, 51–52
Lowndes, James (nephew), 51
Lowndes, Rawlins, 17–18, 20, 44, 283, 285, 286–87, 444–45
Lowndes, Ruth Rawlins, 16
Lowndes, Sabina Elliott Huger, 131–32, 369–70
Lowndes, Sarah Bond I'on, 43–44
Lowndes, Thomas, 16, 44–45, 46, 87, 89, 326
    slave transactions, 43–44, 76
Lowndes, William, 16, 17–18, 89
Lowndes family, 15, 23–24, 28, 44–45, 51, 369–70
Lowry, William, 371
Lucas, Charles, 69–70, 222, 395–96, 479
Lucas, Mr., 477
Lyman, Benjamin, 140–41
Lynah, Edward (father), 41–42, 484–85
Lynah, Edward T. (son), 86–87, 123

Lyon, John, 394–95
Lyons, Frank, 38, 82, 378–79, 496
Lyons, Venus Proctor Higgins, 68–69, 333, 378–79, 496

Macbeth, Charles, 467–68
MacFarland, Turner, 444–45
MacFarland family, 445–46
Mack, Bina Hamilton, 47–48, 68–69, 121, 123–24, 129, 320, 333, 379, 382–83, 430
    land purchase, 486
Mack, Hagar, 129, 320, 379, 430, 486
Mack, Harry, 320, 379, 430, 486, 497
malaria, 42–43, 116–17, 192, 293, 319, 365, 503, 504–5. *See also* "fever district"; sickly season
Mallory, Charles, 168, 169
Mallory, Shepard, 167, 169, 200
Manigault, A. M. M., 295
Manigault, Gabriel, 21, 80
Manigault, Pierre, 21
Manokey, Aaron, 61–62
Manokey, Eliza, 61–62
Manokey, Jerry, 61–62
Manokey, John, 61–62
Manokey, Matilda, 61–62
Manokey, Moses, 61–62
Manokey, Polly, 61–62
Marchand, John B., 216
Marcy, Henry O., 450
Maria (sister of Silvia J. G. De Costa), 84–85
Markley, Levi H., 260, 271–72, 309–10, 431–32, 471–72
Marsh, Marvin Manville, 452–53
Marshall, Captain, 26
Martin (enslaved person), 37
Mary (enslaved person), 78
Mason, James, 142–43
Massachusetts Anti-Slavery Society, 145–46, 149
Massey, Henrietta, 102
Massey, James, 92, 102
Mathew (enslaved person), 338–39
Mathilda/Matilda (enslaved person), 283–84, 306
Matthews, Elizabeth, 34
Matthews, Martha Ann, 46
Maum Katie (enslaved person), 241

McBride, William. *See* McNeil, William
McClellan (steamship), 195, 203–4
McCormick, A. H., 440
McGrath, I. S., 494
McGuire, Elizabeth Gabriel Basquire
    Lewis, 492
    marriages of, 511–12
McGuire, Fulton, 440–41, 492, 511, 512
McKim, James Miller, 97–98, 133, 134,
    242
McLush, Mr., 498
McLush, Mrs., 498–99
McNeal, Annie Cassell, 418
McNeal, Scipio, 379, 418
McNeil, William, 222–23
Means, Edward, 126
Mercury (gunboat), 158
Meriam, Francis Jackson, 408–9
Middleton, Arthur, 15–16, 17–18, 20, 45,
    46, 77–78, 82
Middleton, Arthur, Jr., 41, 73
Middleton, Catharine, 77–78
Middleton, Diana, 131
Middleton, Edward, 15–16, 73, 77–78
Middleton, Edwardina (Edda) de
    Normann, 73
Middleton, Eliza. *See* Smith, Eliza C.
    Middleton Huger
Middleton, Harriott, 370
Middleton, Henry (governor), 45–46,
    71–72, 73, 81–82, 120, 131–32, 296–
    97, 370, 471–72, 474
    slave transactions, 45, 46, 47, 77–78
Middleton, Henry (grandfather of
    governor), 15–16, 20, 45
Middleton, Henry (son of governor),
    77–78
Middleton, Henry Augustus (cousin of
    governor), 47
Middleton, Henry Parker, 126
Middleton, John Izard, 27, 45, 46, 77–78,
    369–70
Middleton, John L., 82
Middleton, Juno, 380
Middleton, Liddy, 380
Middleton, Mary Helen Hering, 71,
    77–78
Middleton, Mary Izard, 45, 46
Middleton, Oliver Hering, Jr., 285,
    369–70, 446

Middleton, Oliver Hering, Sr., 77–78, 82,
    285, 313, 321–22, 341–43, 369, 446
Middleton, Paolina (Paula) Bentivoglio, 73
Middleton, Relia Barnwell, 37, 40–41, 83,
    118, 122, 380, 451, 462, 494, 517
Middleton, Susan Matilda Chisholm, 369,
    370
Middleton, Thomas, 130–31, 224–25
Middleton, William, 27, 70–71, 74, 81, 122,
    333, 366–67, 369–70, 379, 380, 395–
    96, 423–24, 451, 477, 515–16, 517
    slave transactions, 46
Middleton family, 15–16, 23–24, 27, 51,
    72, 73–74, 119, 286, 369–70, 447
Middleton Place, 15, 45, 46, 47, 69–70,
    71–72, 73–74, 77–78, 81–82, 370, 468
Miles, Samuel, 102
Militia Act (1862), 212
Miller, Elijah, 481
Miller, Elizabeth Smith, 401–2
Mintus, Tony, 39
Missouri Compromise (1820), 136–37,
    139–40, 237
Mitchel, Ormsby MacKnight, 273, 292, 303
Mitchell, Sam, 164–65
Mitchell, William. *See* Butcher, William
Modesty (HT's grandmother), 9, 53,
    55–56
Molly (enslaved person), 129–30, 338–39
Monitor, 272–73
Monroe (enslaved person), 446
Montagu, John, 6–7
Montauk (ironclad), 273
Montgomery, Clarinda, 236
Montgomery, James
    allows soldiers to bring wives to
        Florida, 450–51
    and F. Barrington, 270–71, 378, 433
    and Battle of Battery Wagner, 415
    and Battle of Olustee, 438–40
    and B. R. Corwin's court-martial,
        440–41, 492
    and John Brown, 148–49
    burning of Darien, 404–8
    burning of plantations, xxiii
    called insurrectionist, 361
    and Combahee River Raid, xix, 325,
        326, 327, 331–32, 333–34, 335, 336–
        37, 340, 342, 343–44, 347, 348–54,
        375, 379, 434

and B. R. Corwin, 431
draft of Combahee men, 391–93, 395,
    397
and Fort Sumter/Battery Wagner,
    424–28
and free states, 141, 142, 161–62
and HT, xxi, 219, 356–58, 359–60, 403,
    409–10, 470–71, 499
letters concerning HT, 499–500
J. Nicholls on, 365–66
orders freed slave couples to marry,
    447–49, 513
others' opinions of, 410–11
"The Raid on Combahee," 296, 299–
    300, 301, 303, 309–11, 312, 313
resigns commission, 451–52
return from Combahee River Raid,
    389–90
and Salkehatchie railroad, 360, 363
and 2nd South Carolina Volunteers,
    255–56, 259–62, 263–65, 266–68,
    269, 434–35, 437, 438
and R. G. Shaw, 403–4
Moody, Margaret, 326–299, 368–69, 486
Moore, Francis, 7
Moore, Henry, 302–3, 497–98
Moore, Homer H., 256, 448–49, 473–74,
    513
Moore, N. G., xxvii–xxviii
Moore, William, 92
Morgan, E. W., 494
Morgan, Joseph S., 260–61
Morgan, Thomas Jefferson, 391–92, 393
Morrison, Joe, 47–48
Morton, Henny Middleton, 131
Morton, Jack, 429, 479
Moultrie, Flora, 69
Moultrie, Peggy Simmons, 83
Moultrie, William Lennox, 41–42
Muir, John, 100
Mullany, J. R. M., 217
Mulligan, A. B., 291
Murray, Ellen, 192, 229
Murry, Scipio, 224
Myrtle Grove Plantation, 338–39

Nahant (ship), 276
Nalle, Agnes, 150
Nalle, Anne, 150
Nalle, Charles, 149–52

Nalle, Fanny, 150
Nalle, Harriet, 150
Nalle, Henry, 150
Nalle, Kitty, 150
Nalle, Lucy (daughter of Charles), 150
Nalle, Lucy (mother of Charles), 150
Nalle, Maria, 150
Nancy (enslaved person), 406
Nancy (slave ship), 32–33
Nantucket (ship), 276
Nantucket, Mass., 135–36
Narrative of the Life of Frederick Douglass,
    an American Slave, 135
National Women's Rights Conventions,
    137–38
Ndiaye, Lamine, 6, 7
NEAS (New England Anti-Slavery
    Society), 134
Ned (enslaved person), 78
Nelli (mother of Richard Smith), 513–14
Nelly (enslaved person), 338–39
Nester (enslaved person), 129–30
New England Freedmen's Aid Society,
    451–52, 470
New Ironsides (ironclad), 273, 274–76
Newport Plantation, 15, 27, 41, 45, 46–47,
    68–69, 71, 73, 74, 77–79, 81–82,
    333–34, 336, 366–67, 370, 379, 382,
    395–97, 418, 423–24, 429, 432–33,
    474, 477, 479, 514–15
Newton, H. H., 313, 321–22, 330, 339–40
Nicholas, Andrew, 121–22, 380–81, 395,
    449, 503, 507–8
Nicholas, Betsey Singleton Simmons, 333,
    447–48, 493
Nicholas, Charles, 38, 70–71, 81, 122, 333,
    380–81, 395, 424–25, 429, 433–34,
    449, 450–51, 459, 487, 488–89, 490,
    494, 517
Nicholas, Dorcas, 449
Nicholas, Ella McGrath, 494
Nicholas, Hagar, 333, 380–81, 450–51, 459,
    494
Nicholas, Neptune, 27, 38, 70–71, 83, 121–
    22, 333, 380–81, 391, 395, 397, 417,
    432, 447–48, 449, 468, 487, 488–90,
    492–93, 494
Nicholas, Rose, 380–81
Nicholas, Tobias, 27
Nicholas I, Tsar, 71–72

Nicholls, Elizabeth, 516
Nicholls, Ellen Rose Lynah, 484–85, 516
Nicholls, Joanna, 516
Nicholls, Joshua
  claims for compensation, 381–84, 435
  and Combahee River Raid, 317, 318,
    319–20, 321–22, 324–25, 326–27,
    328–29, 335, 345, 374–75
  continued support of Confederacy, 487
  and death of stepson, 446
  family of, 298
  losses in Combahee Raid, 376
  marriages, 85–86, 484–85
  on military commanders, 362, 363, 364,
    365–66
  military service of, 419–20
  petition U.S. Congress for
    compensation, 516
  "The Raid on Combahee," 283, 290,
    298–99, 300–1, 308–9, 314–15
  slaves of, 85, 87, 120–21, 126, 368
  slave transactions, 120–21
  and stepson's will, 484–85
  in Walterboro, S.C., 119
  and wife's marriage settlement, 86–87,
    120–21, 123, 299, 484–85
  and wife's will, 484–85
Nicholls, Mary Anna Lynah Kirkland
  Faber, 171, 516
  exchange of plantations with son, 123,
    125–26, 382, 386
  husband's background, 298–99
  inheritance of, 43
  land transactions, 484–85
  Longbrow Plantation, 128–29
  marriages, 41–42, 48–49, 85–86
  slaves of, 75–76, 85, 86–87, 386
  slave transactions, 120–21, 123, 125–27,
    382, 386
  and T. R. S. Elliott, 124
  will of, 484–85
Nicholls, Richard, 298
Nicholls, Simon, 298
Nicholls family, 87–88, 300
  Longbrow plantation, 15
Nicholls/Kirkland family, 123–24
  slaves of, 120–21
Nichols, John W., 518
Nickles, J. F., 215–16
Noble, James, 100–1

North, Richard L., 381
North Santee (steam tug), 225
North Star (newspaper), 501
Norwell, Maria, 510
Noyes, Catherine Porter, 451–52, 453–54,
  491
Nutall, Mary, 49–50
Nutall, William B., 50

Oakland Plantation, 15, 44–45, 76, 87,
  131–32, 283, 314, 324, 326, 331, 340–
  41, 369–71, 382, 412, 435, 444–45,
  446–47, 461, 477, 490, 497–98, 525
O'Brien, John F., 295
Ogee, Chance, 380–81
Oglethorpe, James, 6–7
Old Fort Plantation
  Primus and Sarah Barnwell at, 462
  Elizabeth Hyde Botume at, 453, 454,
    471–72
  Camp Saxton, 251
  Combahee Refugee Camp, 457–62
  Isaac and Silvia DeCauster at, 461–62
  freedom seekers at, 349–50, 351
  Hunter's Regiment at, 210
  Old Leah at, 459–60
  November and Sarah Osborne, 461
  school at, 233–34, 452, 454, 471–72
  Smart and Mary Washington at, 471–
    72, 483–84
  "We's Combee," 459
Old Heads (term), 37
Olmstead, Frederick Law, 117, 245
Oriental (ship), 189–90, 203
Osborne, Flora, 44
Osborne, July, 38, 378–79, 431–32, 471,
  488, 490
Osborne, Nat, 69–70, 76, 382, 396–97,
  461, 483, 494
Osborne, November, 44–45, 76, 87, 326,
  382, 396–97, 461–62, 471, 483, 490,
  494
Osborne, Rebecca, 461
Osborne, Sarah Small, 76, 326, 387, 461,
  490, 494
Osborne, William, 461
O'Sullivan, Timothy, 327–28
Oswald, Richard, 25
Ottawa (gunboat), 157–58, 216
Otwell, Thomas, 110–11

Palmetto Plantation, 15, 75–76, 84–85, 129. *See also* Paul's Place

Park, William, 206–7

Parker, Arthur Middleton, 84–85, 320
 slave transactions, 123–24, 129–30

Parker, Eliza Savage Heywood, 49–50, 75–76

Parker, Francis Simmons, 84–85, 123
 slave transactions, 123–24, 125–26, 129–30

Parker, Henry Middleton, 49–50, 75, 84–85
 slave transactions, 86–87

Parker, Isaac, 26

Parker, John, 84–85, 320
 slave transactions, 129–30

Parker, Sarah S., 125–26

Parker, Theodore, 141–42

Parker family, 123–24

Parris (enslaved person), 197

Parrott, E. G., 216

Passaic (ironclad), 273, 274–75, 276

PASS (Pennsylvania Anti-Slavery Society) Vigilance Committee, 97–98, 99–100, 105

Patapsco (ironclad), 273, 276

Pattison, Atthow, 9, 53–55, 63–64, 97, 104

Pattison, Elizabeth, 55

Pattison family, 8–9

Paul (teaching assistant), 232

Paul, James L., 129–30, 283, 286–87, 313–14, 318, 320, 322, 335, 345, 370–71, 382, 387, 417–18, 491

Paul, William, 121–22, 379–80, 503

Paul "Cypress" (enslaved person), 131

Paul family, 15

Paul's Place, 15, 37, 68–69, 116–17, 283, 313–14, 318, 320, 322, 335, 380, 382, 387–88, 417–18, 503, 525. *See also* Palmetto Plantation

Pawnee (gunboat), 216, 259, 413

Payne, Sereno, 506

Peck, Solomon, 232, 389

Pemberton, John C., 286

Pembina (gunboat), 157–58, 216

Penda, Blake, 223

Pennington, Peter, 144

Penn Normal School, 192

Pennsylvania Anti-Slavery Society (PASS) Vigilance Committee, 97–98, 99–100, 105

Pennsylvania Gazette, 29

Pennsylvania Society for the Abolition of Slavery, 95–96

Penny, James, 31–32

pension system, xxiv–xxix, 495–99, 502, 505–6

Peter (enslaved person), 366–67, 394–95

Peter (teaching assistant), 232

Peter, Blake, 223

Philadephia Port Royal Relief Association, 229

Philbrick, Edward, 212, 465–66

Philbrick, Edward S., 235, 237

Phillips, Wendell, 149, 151, 499–500

Phoebe (enslaved person, mother of November Osborne), 44

Phoenix, Maria. *See* Wyatt, Maria Phoenix

Pierce, Edward L., 169, 181–82, 183–85, 187–89, 191, 193–94, 204–8, 210–11, 231–32, 237, 238, 416

Pike, Stephen, 6

Pinckney, Gabriel, 217–18

Pinckney, Phyllis Wineglass, 387, 507–8

Pinckney, Pierre, 260

Pinckney, Thomas, 368, 443

Pinkerton, Allan, 301–2

Pipkin, Mr., 340–42, 369–70

Pipkins, Charles, 101–2

Pipkins, Emma, 101–2

Pipkins, Jefferson, 101–2

Pipkins, Patrick, 101–2

Pipkins, Susan, 101–2

Pittman, James, 92, 102

Planter (steamship), 213–16, 217, 237, 256, 257

Plowden, Annie, 303

Plowden, Walter D., 302–6, 410, 440–41, 515

Pocahontas (gunboat), 157–58

Polite, Emma, 270

Polite, Prince, 39, 82, 83, 125, 386–87

Polite, Stephen, 223, 478

Polite, Tyra Brown, 39, 82, 83, 125, 386–87

Polk, Ezekiel, 29

Pomeroy, Samuel, 469–70

Pompey (enslaved person), 47–48, 121, 124, 126–27, 382–83

Pope, Daniel, 164, 165, 166, 220

Port Royal Experiment, 169, 173, 180–89, 203, 205–7, 208, 451–54, 458–62, 471–72, 491. *See also* Combahee Refugee Camp
Port Royal Relief Committee, 183, 233
Powell, Daphne Jackson. *See* Snipe, Daphne Jackson Powell
Predeaux, Henry, 110–11
Predo, Henry, 92
Prentiss, George A., 219–20, 221, 225
Prime Hands (term), 67
Primus (captured man), 238
Prince (contraband pilot), 221
Prince (enslaved person), 366–67
Prior, Benjamin, 471
Priscilla (enslaved person), 25–26, 38, 450
Priscilla (wife of Jack Aiken), 81
Proctor, John, 417–18, 430
Proctor, Julia, 491
Pryor, Benjamin, 222
Pryor, Cornelia, 222
Pussy (enslaved person), 47–48, 121, 124, 126–27, 382–83

Quasheba (enslaved person), 75, 86–87

"Raid of South Carolina Volunteers (Col. Montgomery) Among the Rice Plantations on the Comabhee, SC" (Robinson), 309
Randall, John Bond, 43–44
Randolph, John P., 509
Rawlins, Henry, 16
Rebecca (wife of J. Aiken), 81
Redmond, Charles Lenox, 239–40
Relyea, C. J., 214
"Resistance to Blood-Houndism" (Douglass), 139
Reynolds, William H., 180, 184–85
Rhoads, George, 92
rice culture, 115–16
Ricesmith, Tom. *See* Smith, Thomas Rhett
Richard, Katie, 372–73
Richard, Lina, 68–69, 333, 379, 496
Riley, Billy (father of William), 261
Riley, Nannie, 261
Riley, William (son of Billy), 261
Rina (enslaved person), 166
Ripley, James W., 170

Ripley, Roswell S., 214, 217, 283, 284–85, 287–88, 421
Rivers, Prince, 254
Rivers, Sharper, 270
The Road to Freedom (Swift), 414
Robinson (surgeon), 394
Robinson, Bacchies, 424
Robinson, Flora, 433, 449, 488–89
Robinson, Harry, 432–33, 449, 488
Robinson, Lucius, 38, 121–22, 333, 490
Robinson, William T., 309–10, 351
Rogers, Christopher Raymond Perry, 156–57
Rogers, Seth, 224–25, 236, 238, 258–59, 261, 265–66, 268
Roosevelt, Franklin, 494
Roosevelt, Theodore, 512–13
Rose (enslaved person), 197
Rose, Willie Lee, 173
Rose Hill Plantation (Heyward family), 21–22, 129, 300, 338–39, 373–74, 375–76
Rose Hill Plantation (Kirkland/Nicholls family), 15, 47–48, 69, 75–77, 86, 116–17, 118, 120–21, 122, 123, 125–26, 128–29, 171, 289–90, 299–300, 304, 324, 325–26, 334, 367–69, 378, 382, 384–85, 386–88, 423, 444–45, 446–47, 448, 449, 484–85, 486, 490, 497, 507
Rosengarten, Theodore, 22–23
Ross, Angerine, 109–10
Ross, Araminta. *See* Tubman, Harriet
Ross, Ben (father of HT), 56, 57–58, 61–63, 92–93, 109, 110–11, 112
Ross, Ben (nephew of HT), 109–10
Ross, Ben, Jr., 92–94, 108–9
Ross, Harriet (niece of HT), 109–10
Ross, Harriet Ann Parker, 103, 109–10
Ross, Henry (brother of HT), 64–65, 92–94, 103, 108–10, 144
Ross, Isaac, 109–10
Ross, John Henry, 109–10
Ross, John Isaac, 109
Ross, Linah. *See* Jolly, Linah Ross
Ross, Mariah Ritty, 56, 64–65, 92–93, 94
Ross, Mary Manokey, 109–10, 112
Ross, Moses, 92–93, 104–5, 109–10
Ross, Rachel, 92–93, 109–10, 112, 147

Ross, Robert, 92–93, 108–10
Ross, Soph, 56, 64–65, 92–93, 94
Ross, William (nephew of HT), 109–10
Ross, William Henry, 109
Ruggles, David, 135
Russell (enslaved person), 197
Russell, William H., 178
Rutledge, Benjamin Huger, 295–96, 442–43
Rutledge, Pleasant, 387–88, 491
Rutledge, Reuben, 396–97

Sally (enslaved person), 197
Salter, Solomon, 81–82, 121–22, 391–92, 395–96
Salters, Sandy, 302
Sam (enslaved person), 196
Sams, Berners Bainbridge, xxix–xxx
Sams, Sarah F. Verdier, xxix–xxx, 269
Samuel (enslaved person). See Jones, Elsie Higgins
Sanborn, Franklin, 9, 140–42, 146, 149, 204–5, 335–36, 350–51, 355–56, 401, 517–18
Sancho (captured man), 238
Sanders, John D., 336, 341
Sanders, Mr., 492–93
Santee Raid, 219–25
Sarah (sister of Richard Smith), 513–14
Sary (enslaved person), 338–39
Saucey (enslaved person), 366–67
Savage, Cathy, 325
Savage, Charlotte, 69, 116–17, 325, 387–88, 503
Savage, John A., 50–51, 69, 75–76, 86–88, 116–17, 118, 126, 131, 325, 387, 503, 505
Savage, Mary (grandmother), 50
Savage, Mary (mother), 50
Savage, Mary W., 50
Savage, Nelly, 325
Savage, Primus, 325
Savage, Sandy, 325
Savage, Thomas, 50. See also "Thomas Savage Negroes"
Savage, William, 85, 117, 325
    slave transactions, 49–51, 75, 76, 86–87, 126
    See also "William Savage Negroes"
Saxton, Rufus
    and Battle of Port Royal, 172–73, 179

and P. Burns, 307
and Department of the South, 271
and Emancipation Proclamation celebration, 258, 390
and HT, 219, 302, 305, 307–8, 357–58, 403, 409–10, 499
as inspector of settlements and plantations, 475–77, 479–80, 484
in Jacksonville, Fla., 265–66, 267–68
and marriages of soldiers, 447–49
and W. Plowden, 303, 515
and Port Royal Experiment, 188–89, 192–93, 220–21, 451–52, 453–54, 460
and 2nd South Carolina Volunteers, 237–39, 255–56
and St. John's Raid, 268–69
Saxton, Willard, 451–52
Scott, George, 357
Scott, Winfield, 168
Second Confiscation Act (1862), 212. See also First Confiscation Act (1861)
"Secret Six," 9, 140, 141–43, 144, 146
Sellers, Molly, 27
Sellers, Pool, 27, 333, 334, 471, 485
Selters, Sandy, 225
Seneca (gunboat), 157–58
Seneca Falls Women's Convention, 137–38
Sentinel (ship), 310–12, 326–27
Sequestration Act (1861), 374–75
Severance, Caroline Seymour, 199, 203, 204–5, 402, 437
Severance, James Seymour, 137–38, 204, 205, 206–7, 215, 264
Severance, Mark Sibley, 205, 402
Severance, Theodoric "T. C.," 199, 204–6, 207–8
Severance family, 137–39
Seward, Frances, 481
Seward, William H., 133, 299, 358, 472, 481, 499–500, 506
Seymour, Truman, 414–15, 438, 439–40
Shadrach (enslaved person), 244–45
Shaffer, Alexander Castner, 448–49, 492–93
Shapard, Harriet, 101
Sharpe, Granville, 227–28
Shavers, Frank, 511–12
Shaw, Francis, 138–39, 404

Shaw, Robert Gould, 359, 403–5, 407–8, 410, 411, 412–13, 414–15, 425–26
Shaw, Sarah Blake Sturgis, 138–39, 404
Shaw family, 138–39
Sheppard, Betsey, 46–47
Sheppard, James, 46–47, 81, 334, 391–92, 393, 395–96, 432, 433–34, 491
Sheppard, Sally, 46–47, 491
Sherman, Thomas W., 159, 161, 163, 172–73, 180–82, 193, 265, 303, 357–58
Sherman, William Tecumseh, xxiii, 38–39, 188–89, 327–28, 460–61, 462–65, 467–68, 469, 475–76, 481, 482, 486–87, 513
Shields, James, 69–70, 396–97, 418, 429, 491, 492
Shields, Jone Colonel, 492
Shoolbred, James, 224–25
Shoolbred, John Gibbes, 224–25
Shoolbred, Mary Middleton, 224–25
Sibby (enslaved person), 283–84, 306–7
sickly season, 118, 177, 277–78, 287–88, 290, 293, 298, 299, 354, 362–63, 364, 365, 383–85, 446, 460. See also "fever district"; malaria
Silas (enslaved person), 197
Simmons (father of Isaac Simmons), 39–40
Simmons, Beauregard, 380–81
Simmons, Charles, 302
Simmons, Christie Ann Kinloch, xxvii–xxviii, 40, 449
Simmons, Daniel, 417–18
Simmons, Diana, 222
Simmons, Fannie Lee Green, xxviii–xxix, 55, 467, 492, 513
Simmons, George, 513–14
Simmons, Isaac, 39–40
Simmons, James, 40, 69–70, 120–21, 380–81, 386–87, 433–34, 491, 494
Simmons, Joshua, 40, 69, 120–21, 333, 380–81, 386–87, 395, 487, 488–89, 490, 493, 497–98, 508
Simmons, July, 40
Simmons, Lucretia Kinlaw, 380–81
Simmons, Margaret Kelly, 40, 333, 380–81, 491, 493, 508
Simmons, Moses
    and Bartleys' marriage, 448
    death of, 492

and death of comrades, 497–98, 512–13
enslavement of, 69–70
escape from slavery, 380–81, 386–87
family of, 39–40
land purchase, 490
land transactions, 488, 492
marriages of, xxvii–xxix, 68–69, 449
military service of, 391–92, 395, 397, 424–25
pension testimony of, 38, 120–21, 417
return to plantation, 487
and Smiths' marriage, 449
Simmons, Sarah, 222
Simmons, Shiloh, 447–48
Simmons, Stephen, 40, 69–70, 396–97, 434–35, 487
Simmons, Wamey, 222
Simon (enslaved person), 75
Simons, Elizabeth, 19–20
Singleton, April, 488–90, 492–93, 494, 517
Singleton, Joe, 223
Singleton, June, 69
Singleton, Martha, 326, 387–88
Singleton, Sam, 223
Slave Trade Act (1794), 32
Slocum, Henry Warner, 462–63
Small, Elizabeth, 378–79
Small, London, 44–45
Small, Nellie, xxix–xxx
Small, Sarah, 44–45, 87
Smalls, Robert, 213–14, 215–17, 218–19, 276, 306, 344, 348, 357, 359
Smith, Abram D., 480
Smith, Andrew, 372–73
Smith, Anne Rebecca Skirving, 39–40
Smith, Daniel Elliott, 371
Smith, Eliza C. Middleton Huger, 119, 446–47, 476–78
Smith, Emanuel, 372–73
Smith, Fannie Pitts, 513–14
Smith, Gerrit, 141–42, 143–44, 401–2, 499–500
Smith, Henry, 260
Smith, Isaac, 513–14
Smith, Isabella Johannes Middleton, 371
Smith, John, 298
Smith, Lucy Lee, 83, 125, 380–81, 449, 450–51, 513, 514
Smith, Marianna Barnwell Gough, 488–89

Smith, Martha, 298
Smith, Polly, 372–73
Smith, Richard, 70–71, 504
Smith, Richard, Jr., 121–22, 380, 387, 395, 449, 450–51, 494, 513–14
Smith, Robert Tilghman, 371
Smith, Thomas Rhett, 40, 76–77, 119, 456
Smith, Tom Wright. *See* Smith, Thomas Rhett
Smith, William, 298
Smith, William Mason, II, 370–74
Smith, William Mason, Jr., 476
Smith family, 76–77, 452–53
Smithfield Plantation, 371–73, 374, 446–47, 476, 477
Snipe, Betsey (or Beck) Brown, 428
Snipe, Daphne Jackson Powell, 69, 75, 86–87, 126, 387, 449, 450–51, 503
Snipe, Ned, 70–71, 126, 326, 387, 395, 449, 503–4
Snipe, Tony, 70–71, 428
Soule, Silas, 148–49
South Carolina, 483
Stanly, Caroline, 100
Stanly, Daniel, 100
Stanton, Edwin, 183, 208, 256, 267, 350, 358, 401–2, 469
Stearns, George Luther, 141–42
Stevens, Hazard, 193–94
Stevens, Isaac Ingalls, 218, 223, 224, 289, 357–58
Stewart, John T., 61, 62
Stewart, William. *See* Ross, Henry
Stewart's Canal, 62–63
Still, Charity. *See* Still, Sidney
Still, Levin, 98–99
Still, Levin, Jr., 98–99
Still, Peter, 98–99
Still, Sidney, 98–99
Still, William, 97–99, 101–2, 104, 105, 110–11, 112–13, 133, 134
Stock, John, 84–85
Stokes, Benjamin, 484–85
Stowe, Harriet Beecher, 112, 500
Stribben, Mr., 478
Strong, George C., 414–15
Stuart, J. E. B., 441–42
Stuart, John, 29–30
Stuckey, Sterling, 243
Sturge, Joseph, 227–28

Susan, Miss, 60
Susannah (enslaved person), 164, 165
Susquehanna (warship), 156, 158
Sutton, Robert, 254, 258
Swift, Hildegard Hoyt, 414
Swinton, Charles H., 479
Sylvia (enslaved person), 338–39

Tacky (leader of Jamaican rebellion), 519
Tappan, Arthur, 228–29
Tappan, Lewis, 228–29
Tattnall, Josiah, 156–58
Taylor, David (son), 260
Taylor, David or Daniel (father), 260–61
Taylor, Mr., 478
Taylor, Susie King, 195–96, 251–52, 266, 390
Taylor, Thomas, 367–68
Taylor, W. H., 287
Telford, Emma, 450
Terry, Alfred H., 199, 411, 413, 419, 425–26, 428, 430–31, 437–38
Thirteenth Amendment, 134–35, 469–70
Thomas (teaching assistant), 232
Thomas, L. (general), 255–56
"Thomas Savage Negroes," 50
Thompson, Anthony, 56, 57, 61–62, 93, 94, 104
Thompson, Anthony C., 61, 94–95
Thompson, Henry, 140
Thompson, John, 144
Thompson, Mary Pattison Brodess, 53–54, 55–56, 57, 63–65
Thompson, Thomas N., 312, 313, 314, 342–43
Thoreau, Henry David, 135
Thorpe, David, 206–7
Tilly (enslaved person), 109–10
Tim (enslaved person), 198, 289–90
Titus (enslaved person/freedom seeker), 196, 197
Tolsey, Mr., 6–7
Tom (enslaved person), 197, 289–90
Tomlinson, Reuben, 236
Tomson (enslaved person), 325
Toomer, Mr., 76–77
Towne, Laura, 184–85, 189–90, 191–92, 203, 205, 208–10, 227, 229, 230, 235, 241, 244, 348–49, 416, 452, 465
Townsend, James, 167, 169, 200

Townsend, Martin I., 151
Tracy, Carlos, 445–46
Trenholm, W. L., 345, 364
Trezevant, Ann, 34
Trowbridge, Charles T., 208, 211–12, 238
Troy, N.Y., 149–52
Trumbull, Lyman, 162
Truth, Sojourner, 4, 55, 57, 65, 135, 137–
    38, 239–40, 473, 518–19
Truxtun, W. T., 291–93, 294
Tubman, Harriet, 60–61
    African ancestry of, 8, 9–10
    in Beaufort, 198–99, 244–46
    begins taking others out of Maryland,
        103–7
    birth of, 4, 57
    brings parents to St. Catharine's,
        112–13
    changes name, 63
    directs others to freedom, 110–12
    early life in slavery, 53–54, 57–58
    escapes from slavery, 92–96, 97–98
    fears of stolen family, 64–65
    hired out to others, 58–60
    hires herself out to others, 61–62
    hires lawyer to look into her status,
        63–64
    intelligence gathering, 248–49, 305–6,
        307–8, 358–60, 518
    as landowner, 481
    need for funds, 401, 470, 472, 499–500
    pension claims, 502, 506–7, 515, 517–18
    recollections of Combahee River
        Raid, xix–xx, xxi, 301–2, 305, 322,
        335–37, 356–57, 416–17
    speeches of, 390, 470–71
    as subject of publications, 354–57, 358
    support of other abolitionists, 133–34
    temporal lobe epilepsy of, 60–61
    threat of sale, 91–92
Tubman, John, 63, 103, 107–9, 502
Turner, Elizabeth N., 95–97
Turner, Lorenzo Dow, 27, 455–57
Turner, Nat, 134, 519
"A Typical Negro" (engravings), 394

Unadilla (gunboat), 216
"Uncle Sam's Farm," 337
Uncle Tom's Cabin (Stowe), 112, 500
Underground Railroad (term), 99–100

USS Albatross, 219–20
USS Augusta, 216
USS Ben De Ford (steamship), 220, 223,
    256
USS Bienville, 217
USS Dale, 291–92
USS New Ironsides, 420–21
USS Onward, 215
USS Wabash, 216
USS Wabash (warship), 156–58, 259

Vanderbilt (warship), 156
Van Dross, Abigail, 126–27, 382
Van Dross, Hercules, 382
Van Dross, Mingo (Mingo Vanderhorst),
    30–31, 70–71, 76–77, 83, 126–27,
    382, 395, 434–35, 449, 456, 487, 493,
    510–11, 514
Van Dross, Robert, 382
Van Dross, Sancho (Sanko), 23–25, 26,
    30–31, 76–77, 123–24, 126–27, 382,
    456, 486
Van Wagenen, Elizabeth, 55, 65
Van Wagenen, Isabella. See Truth,
    Sojourner
Van Wagenen, James, 55, 65
Van Wagenen, Michael, 65
Van Wagenen, Nancy, 65
Van Wagenen, Peter, 55
Venus (enslaved person), 38
Verdier, James Robert, xxix–, 269
Vernon, Samuel, 24–25
Vernon, William, 24–25
Vesey, Denmark, 35, 68–69, 519
Vesey Insurrection Plot, 35
Villeponteaux, Peter, 89
Virginia. See CSS Merrimack
A Voice from the South (Cooper), 1

Wade, Benjamin F., 237–38
Walker, David, 135
Walker, Susan, 185, 209, 237, 242–43
Walker, William Stephen, 285–86, 295,
    297, 330, 331, 332–33, 344–45, 362–
    63, 365
Wall, Wesley D., 330–4, 331
Walters, Robert P., Jr., 518
Wanderer (slave ship), 124–25, 241
Ware, Charles Pickard, 187, 237, 238–39,
    242

Ware, Harriet, 242, 243–44
Warren, John D., 478, 484–85, 487
Washington, Daphne Garrett, 468
Washington, George, 20, 146–47
Washington, Lewis, 146–47
Washington, Lucretia Davis, 503–4
Washington, Mary, 78–79, 483–84, 503–4
Washington, Mexico, 396–97, 479, 514–15
Washington, Nancy, 81
Washington, Penda. *See* Blake, Penda;
    Blake, Penda Singleton
Washington, Phoebe Fields, xxix–xxx,
    269, 270
Washington, Rachel Grant, 27, 468
Washington, Simon, 27, 81–82, 391–92,
    396, 468, 487
Washington, Smart, 78–79, 81, 196–97,
    379–80, 396–97, 471–72, 483–84,
    503–4
Washington, Solomon, 78–79, 379–80,
    396–97, 483–84, 494
Washington, T. A., 283
Washington, Thomas, 468
Washington, Tom, 81
Washington family, 483–84
Watson, Carolina, 81
Webster, John E., 248, 305, 440–41
Weed, Harriet, 299. *See also Harriet A.
    Weed* (steamer)
Weed, Thurlow, 299
Weehawken (ironclad), 273, 274–75
Weems, George. *See* Hall, Romulus
Welles, Gideon, 212–13, 216, 273, 274,
    277–78
Wells, Edward Laight, 131–32, 443–44
Western World (ship), 220–21
"What to the Slave Is the Fourth of
    July?" (Douglass), 139
White, Alonzo J., 123–24
White, Dick, 47
White, Hardtime, 69, 431
White, Lucy, 47
White, Major, 302–3
White, Mary, 335
White, Mary Fields, 222–24, 289
White, Mingo, 434–35
White, Parris, 222–24, 289, 335, 467–68
White, Peter, 496
White, Rachel. *See* Washington, Rachel
    Grant

White, Salem, 395–96
White, Sally Middleton Green, 334
White, Selam, 47, 81–82, 432–33
Whittier, John Greenleaf, 135, 178, 229
Wichman, Albert, 489, 490, 492–93
Wigham, Eliza, 133
Wilbur, Julia, 469–70
William (enslaved person), 78, 338–39
William (slave ship), 7
Williams, Mary Baker, 45
"William Savage Negroes," 50–51
Willis (enslaved person), 366–67
Wilson, Hugh, 270
Wineglass, Hercules, 507–8
Wineglass, Jack, 326, 386–87, 396, 405,
    431–32, 507–8
Wineglass, Maria Savage, 75, 86–87, 126,
    387, 507–8
Wineglass, Rebecca Grant
    loss of pension benefits, 507–8,
    510–11
Winsor, Nelly, 186, 209–10, 227
Wise, John, 467
Withers, Betsey Boykin, 170
Withers, Kate, 444–45
Withers, Mary Miller. *See* Kirkland, Mary
    Miller Withers
Withers, Randolph, 441–42, 444–45, 446
Withers, Thomas Jefferson, 127, 170,
    445–46
Withers family, 444–45
Witsell, Charles, 488–89
Women's Rights Meeting, 138
Wood, Charles P., xxii, 358, 472, 499–500
Wood, William, 98
Woolford, James, 110–11
Woolford, Lavinia, 110–11
Worcester, Mass., 137–38
Wording, William E., 480
Wright, Daphne Garrett Washington, 27,
    46, 396, 461
Wright, Dick, 47
Wright, Frank, 47, 396, 461, 471
Wright, Lucy, 47
Wright, Mauro, 47
Wyatt, Andrew, 37, 39, 48–49, 84–85, 87,
    116–17, 129–30, 382, 387–88, 392,
    417–18, 423, 431–32, 471, 491, 503
Wyatt, Ernestine, 518
Wyatt, Fatima, 129–30

Wyatt, Maria Phoenix, 75–76, 129–30, 382
Wyatt, Sambo, 129–30
Wyatt, Tanebar, 129–30

Yaa Asantewaa, 8
Yerrington, James, 348, 389, 390
York (enslaved person), 78
Young, Binah, 378–79

Young, Catherine, 223
Young, Flora, 333, 378–79, 432–33
Young, Sina Bolze. *See* Green, Sina Bolze Young
Young, William, 68–69, 70–71, 83, 333, 378–79, 395, 432–33, 482, 496–97
Youngblood, Moses, xxx

Zahler (enslaved person), 370